Human Action

HUMAN ACTION

A Treatise on Economics

By LUDWIG VON MISES

THIRD REVISED EDITION

Contemporary Books, Inc.
Chicago

Printed in the United States of America

Third revised edition published by Henry Regnery Company in 1966, by arrangement with Yale University Press.

Permission has been granted by the publishers to use quotations from the following works: George Santayana, *Persons and Places* (Charles Scribner's Sons); William James, *The Varieties of Religious Experience* (Longmans, Green & Co.); Harley Lutz, *Guideposts to a Free Economy* (McGraw-Hill Book Company); Committee on Postwar Tax Policy, *A Tax Program for a Solvent America* (The Ronald Press Company).

Published by Contemporary Books, Inc.
180 North Michigan Avenue, Chicago, Illinois 60601
Library of Congress Catalog Card Number: 78-24781
International Standard Book Number: 0-8092-9743-4

FOREWORD TO THE THIRD EDITION

IT GIVES me great satisfaction to see this book, handsomely printed by a distinguished publishing house, appear in its third revised edition.

Two terminological remarks may be in order.

First, I employ the term "liberal" in the sense attached to it everywhere in the nineteenth century and still today in the countries of continental Europe. This usage is imperative because there is simply no other term available to signify the great political and intellectual movement that substituted free enterprise and the market economy for the precapitalistic methods of production; constitutional representative government for the absolutism of kings or oligarchies; and freedom of all individuals from slavery, serfdom, and other forms of bondage.

Secondly, in the last decades the meaning of the term "psychology" has been more and more restricted to the field of experimental psychology, a discipline that resorts to the research methods of the natural sciences. On the other hand, it has become usual to dismiss those studies that previously had been called psychological as "literary psychology" and as an unscientific way of reasoning. Whenever reference is made to "psychology" in economic studies, one has in mind precisely this literary psychology, and therefore it seems advisable to introduce a special term for it. I suggested in my book *Theory and History* (New Haven, 1957, pp. 264–274) the term "thymology," and I used this term also in my recently published essay *The Ultimate Foundation of Economic Science* (Princeton, 1962). However, my suggestion was not meant to be retroactive and to alter the use of the term "psychology" in books previously published, and so I continue in this new edition to use the term "psychology" in the same way I used it in the first edition.

Two translations of the first edition of *Human Action* have come out: an Italian translation by Mr. Tullio Bagiotti, Professor at the Università Bocconi in Milano, under the title *L'Azione Umana, Trattato di economia,* published by the Unione Tipografico-Editrice Torinese in 1959; and a Spanish-language translation by Mr. Joaquin Reig Albiol under the title *La Acción Humana* (*Tratado de Economia*), published in two volumes by Fundación Ignacio Villalonga in Valencia (Spain) in 1960.

I feel indebted to many good friends for help and advice in the preparation of this book.

First of all I want to remember two deceased scholars, Paul Mantoux and William E. Rappard, who by giving me the opportunity of teaching at the famous Graduate Institute of International Studies in Geneva, Switzerland, provided me with the time and the incentive to start work upon a long-projected plan.

I want to express my thanks for very valuable and helpful suggestions to Mr. Arthur Goddard, Mr. Percy Greaves, Doctor Henry Hazlitt, Professor Israel M. Kirzner, Mr. Leonard E. Read, Mr. Joaquin Reig Albiol and Doctor George Reisman.

But most of all I want to thank my wife for her steady encouragement and help.

LUDWIG VON MISES

New York
March, 1966

CONTENTS

Part Two Action Within the Framework of Society

Chapter VIII. Human Society

Chapter IX. The Role of Ideas

Chapter X. Exchange Within Society

Part Three Economic Calculation

Chapter XI. Valuation Without Calculation

Chapter XVI. Prices

Chapter XVII. Indirect Exchange

Chapter XVIII. Action in the Passing of Time

Chapter XIX. Interest

Chapter XX. Interest, Credit Expansion, and the Trade Cycle

Chapter XXI. Work and Wages

Chapter XXII. The Nonhuman Original Factors of Production

Chapter XXIII. The Data of the Market

Chapter XXIV. Harmony and Conflict of Interests

Part Five Social Cooperation Without a Market

Chapter XXV. The Imaginary Construction of a Socialist Society

Chapter XXVI. The Impossibility of Economic Calculation Under Socialism

Part Six The Hampered Market Economy

Chapter XXVII. The Government and the Market

Chapter XXVIII. Interference by Taxation

Chapter XXIX. Restriction of Production

Chapter XXX. Interference with the Structure of Prices

CHAPTER XXXI. Currency and Credit Manipulation

Chapter XXXII. Confiscation and Redistribution

Chapter XXXIII. Syndicalism and Corporativism

Chapter XXXIV. The Economics of War

Chapter XXXV. The Welfare Principle Versus the Market Principle

Chapter XXXVI. The Crisis of Interventionism

Part Seven The Place of Economics in Society

Chapter XXXVII. The Nondescript Character of Economics

Chapter XXXVIII. The Place of Economics in Learning

Chapter XXXIX. Economics and the Essential Problems of Human Existence

INTRODUCTION

1. Economics and Praxeology

ECONOMICS is the youngest of all sciences. In the last two hundred years, it is true, many new sciences have emerged from the disciplines familiar to the ancient Greeks. However, what happened here was merely that parts of knowledge which had already found their place in the complex of the old system of learning now became autonomous. The field of study was more nicely subdivided and treated with new methods; hitherto unnoticed provinces were discovered in it, and people began to see things from aspects different from those of their precursors. The field itself was not expanded. But economics opened to human science a domain previously inaccessible and never thought of. The discovery of a regularity in the sequence and interdependence of market phenomena went beyond the limits of the traditional system of learning. It conveyed knowledge which could be regarded neither as logic, mathematics, psychology, physics, nor biology.

Philosophers had long since been eager to ascertain the ends which God or Nature was trying to realize in the course of human history. They searched for the law of mankind's destiny and evolution. But even those thinkers whose inquiry was free from any theological tendency failed utterly in these endeavors because they were committed to a faulty method. They dealt with humanity as a whole or with other holistic concepts like nation, race, or church. They set up quite arbitrarily the ends to which the behavior of such wholes is bound to lead. But they could not satisfactorily answer the question regarding what factors compelled the various acting individuals to behave in such a way that the goal aimed at by the whole's inexorable evolution was attained. They had recourse to desperate shifts: miraculous interference of the Deity either by revelation or by the delegation of God-sent prophets and consecrated leaders, preestablished harmony, predestination, or the operation of a mystic and fabulous "world soul" or "national soul." Others spoke of a "cunning of nature" which implanted in man impulses driving him unwittingly along precisely the path Nature wanted him to take.

Other philosophers were more realistic. They did not try to guess the designs of Nature or God. They looked at human things from the viewpoint of government. They were intent upon establishing rules of political action, a technique, as it were, of government and statesmanship. Speculative minds drew ambitious plans for a thorough reform and reconstruction of society. The more modest were satisfied with a collection and systematization of the data of historical experience. But all were fully convinced that there was in the course of social events no such regularity and invariance of phenomena as had already been found in the operation of human reasoning and in the sequence of natural phenomena. They did not search for the laws of social cooperation because they thought that man could organize society as he pleased. If social conditions did not fulfill the wishes of the reformers, if their utopias proved unrealizable, the fault was seen in the moral failure of man. Social problems were considered ethical problems. What was needed in order to construct the ideal society, they thought, were good princes and virtuous citizens. With righteous men any utopia might be realized.

The discovery of the inescapable interdependence of market phenomena overthrew this opinion. Bewildered, people had to face a new view of society. They learned with stupefaction that there is another aspect from which human action might be viewed than that of good and bad, of fair and unfair, of just and unjust. In the course of social events there prevails a regularity of phenomena to which man must adjust his actions if he wishes to succeed. It is futile to approach social facts with the attitude of a censor who approves or disapproves from the point of view of quite arbitrary standards and subjective judgments of value. One must study the laws of human action and social cooperation as the physicist studies the laws of nature. Human action and social cooperation seen as the object of a science of given relations, no longer as a normative discipline of things that ought to be—this was a revolution of tremendous consequences for knowledge and philosophy as well as for social action.

For more than a hundred years, however, the effects of this radical change in the methods of reasoning were greatly restricted because people believed that they referred only to a narrow segment of the total field of human action, namely, to market phenomena. The classical economists met in the pursuit of their investigations an obstacle which they failed to remove, the apparent antinomy of value. Their theory of value was defective, and forced them to restrict the scope of their science. Until the late nineteenth century political economy remained a science of the "economic" aspects of human action, a theory of wealth and selfishness. It dealt with human action only to the extent that it is actuated by what was—very unsatisfactorily—described as the profit motive, and it asserted that there is in addition other human action whose treatment is the task of other disciplines. The transformation of thought which the classical economists had initiated was brought to its consummation only by modern subjectivist economics, which converted the theory of market prices into a general theory of human choice.

For a long time men failed to realize that the transition from the classical theory of value to the subjective theory of value was much more than the substitution of a more satisfactory theory of market exchange for a less satisfactory one. The general theory of choice and preference goes far beyond the horizon which encompassed the scope of economic problems as circumscribed by the economists from Cantillon, Hume, and Adam Smith down to John Stuart Mill. It is much more than merely a theory of the "economic side" of human endeavors and of man's striving for commodities and an improvement in his material well-being. It is the science of every kind of human action. Choosing determines all human decisions. In making his choice man chooses not only between various material things and services. All human values are offered for option. All ends and all means, both material and ideal issues, the sublime and the base, the noble and the ignoble, are ranged in a single row and subjected to a decision which picks out one thing and sets aside another. Nothing that men aim at or want to avoid remains outside of this arrangement into a unique scale of gradation and preference. The modern theory of value widens the scientific horizon and enlarges the field of economic studies. Out of the political economy of the classical school emerges the general theory of human action, *praxeology*.[1] The economic or catallactic problems[2] are embedded in a more general science, and can no longer be severed from this connection. No treatment of economic problems proper can avoid starting from acts of choice; economics becomes a part, although the hitherto best elaborated part, of a more universal science, praxeology.

1. The term *praxeology* was first used in 1890 by Espinas. Cf. his article "Les Origines de la technologie," *Revue Philosophique*, XVth year, XXX, 114–115, and his book published in Paris in 1897, with the same title.

2. The term *Catallactics or the Science of Exchanges* was first used by Whately. Cf. his book *Introductory Lectures on Political Economy* (London, 1831), p. 6.

2. The Epistemological Problem of a General Theory of Human Action

In the new science everything seemed to be problematic. It was a stranger in the traditional system of knowledge; people were perplexed and did not know how to classify it and to assign it its proper place. But on the other hand they were convinced that the inclusion of economics in the catalogue of knowledge did not require a rearrangement or expansion of the total scheme. They considered their catalogue system complete. If economics did not fit into it, the fault could only rest with the unsatisfactory treatment that the economists applied to their problems.

It is a complete misunderstanding of the meaning of the debates concerning the essence, scope, and logical character of economics to dismiss them as the scholastic quibbling of pedantic professors. It is a widespread misconception that while pedants squandered useless talk about the most appropriate method of procedure, economics itself, indifferent to these idle disputes, went quietly on its way. In the *Methodenstreit* between the Austrian economists and the Prussian Historical School, the self-styled "intellectual bodyguard of the House of Hohenzollern," and in the discussions between the school of John Bates Clark and American Institutionalism much more was at stake than the question of what kind of procedure was the most fruitful one. The real issue was the epistemological foundations of the science of human action and its logical legitimacy. Starting from an epistemological system to which praxeological thinking was strange and from a logic which acknowledged as scientific—besides logic and mathematics—only the empirical natural sciences and history, many authors tried to deny the value and usefulness of economic theory. Historicism aimed at replacing it by economic history; positivism recommended the substitution of an illusory social science which should adopt the logical structure and pattern of Newtonian mechanics. Both these schools agreed in a radical rejection of all the achievements of economic thought. It was impossible for the economists to keep silent in the face of all these attacks.

The radicalism of this wholesale condemnation of economics was very soon surpassed by a still more universal nihilism. From time immemorial men in thinking, speaking, and acting had taken the uniformity and immutability of the logical structure of the human mind as an unquestionable fact. All scientific inquiry was based on this assumption. In the discussions about the epistemological character of economics, writers, for the first time in human history, denied this proposition too. Marxism asserts that a man's thinking is determined by his class affiliation. Every social class has a logic of its own. The product of thought cannot be anything else than an "ideological disguise" of the selfish class interests of the thinker. It is the task of a "sociology of knowledge" to unmask philosophies and scientific theories and to expose their "ideological" emptiness. Economics is a "bourgeois" makeshift, the economists are "sycophants" of capital. Only the classless society of the socialist utopia will substitute truth for "ideological" lies.

This polylogism was later taught in various other forms also. Historicism asserts that the logical structure of human thought and action is liable to change in the course of historical evolution. Racial polylogism assigns to each race a logic of its own. Finally there is irrationalism, contending that reason as such is not fit to elucidate the irrational forces that determine human behavior.

Such doctrines go far beyond the limits of economics. They question not only economics and praxeology but all other human knowledge and human reasoning in general. They refer to mathematics and physics as well as to economics. It seems therefore that the task of refuting them does not fall to any single branch of knowledge but to epistemology and philosophy. This furnishes apparent justification for the attitude of those economists who quietly continue their studies without bothering about epistemological problems and the objections raised by polylogism and irrationalism. The physicist does not mind if someone stigmatizes his theories as bourgeois, Western or Jewish; in the same way the economist should ignore detraction and slander. He should let the dogs bark and pay no heed to their yelping. It is seemly for him to remember Spinoza's dictum: Sane sicut lux se ipsam et tenebras manifestat, sic veritas norma sui et falsi est.

However, the situation is not quite the same with regard to economics as it is with mathematics and the natural sciences. Polylogism and irrationalism attack praxeology and economics. Although they formulate their statements in a general way to refer to all branches of knowledge, it is the sciences of human action that they really have in view. They say that it is an illusion to believe that scientific research can achieve results valid for people of all eras, races, and social classes, and they take pleasure in disparaging certain physical and biological theories as bourgeois or Western. But if the solution of practical problems requires the application of these stigmatized doctrines, they forget their criticism. The technology of Soviet Russia utilizes without scruple all the results of bourgeois physics, chemistry, and biology just as if they were valid for all classes. The Nazi engineers and physicians did not disdain to utilize the theories, discoveries, and inventions of people of "inferior" races and nations. The behavior of people of all races, nations, religions, linguistic groups, and social classes clearly proves that they do not endorse the doctrines of polylogism and irrationalism as far as logic, mathematics, and the natural sciences are concerned.

But it is quite different with praxeology and economics. The main motive for the development of the doctrines of polylogism, historicism, and irrationalism was to provide a justification for disregarding the teachings of economics in the determination of economic policies. The socialists, racists, nationalists, and étatists failed in their endeavors to refute the theories of the economists and to demonstrate the correctness of their own spurious doctrines. It was precisely this frustration that prompted them to negate the logical and epistemological principles upon which all human reasoning both in mundane activities and in scientific research is founded.

It is not permissible to dispose of these objections merely on the ground of the political motives which inspired them. No scientist is entitled to assume beforehand that a disapprobation of his theories must be unfounded because his critics are imbued by passion and party bias. He is bound to reply to every censure without any regard to its underlying motives or its background. It is no less impermissible to keep silent in the face of the often asserted opinion that the theorems of economics are valid only under hypothetical assumptions never realized in life and that they are therefore useless for the mental grasp of reality. It is strange that some schools seem to approve of this opinion and nonetheless quietly proceed to draw their curves and to formulate their equations. They do not bother about the meaning of their reasoning and about its reference to the world of real life and action.

This is, of course, an untenable attitude. The first task of every scientific inquiry is the exhaustive description and definition of all conditions and assumptions under which its various statements claim validity. It is a mistake to set up physics as a model and pattern for economic research. But those committed to this fallacy should have learned one thing at least: that no physicist ever believed that the clarification of some of the assumptions and conditions of physical theorems is outside the scope of physical research. The main question that economics is bound to answer is what the relation of its statements is to the reality of human action whose mental grasp is the objective of economic studies.

It therefore devolves upon economics to deal thoroughly with the assertion that its teachings are valid only for the capitalistic system of the shortlived and already vanished liberal period of Western civilization. It is incumbent upon no branch of learning other than economics to examine all the objections raised from various points of view against the usefulness of the statements of economic theory for the elucidation of the problems of human action. The system of economic thought must be built up in such a way that it is proof against any criticism on the part of irrationalism, historicism, panphysicalism, behaviorism, and all varieties of polylogism. It is an intolerable state of affairs that while new arguments are daily advanced to demonstrate the absurdity and futility of the endeavors of economics, the economists pretend to ignore all this.

It is no longer enough to deal with the economic problems within the traditional framework. It is necessary to build the theory of catallactics upon the solid foundation of a general theory of human action, praxeology. This procedure will not only secure it against many fallacious criticisms but clarify many problems hitherto not even adequately seen, still less satisfactorily solved. There is, especially, the fundamental problem of economic calculation.

3. Economic Theory and the Practice of Human Action

It is customary for many people to blame economics for being backward. Now it is quite obvious that our economic theory is not perfect. There is no such thing as perfection in human knowledge, nor for that matter in any other human achievement. Omniscience is denied to man. The most elaborate theory that seems to satisfy completely our thirst for knowledge may one day be amended or supplanted by a new theory. Science does not give us absolute and final certainty. It only gives us assurance within the limits of our mental abilities and the prevailing state of scientific thought. A scientific system is but one station in an endlessly progressing search for knowledge. It is necessarily affected by the insufficiency inherent in every human effort. But to acknowledge these facts does not mean that present-day economics is backward. It merely means that economics is a living thing—and to live implies both imperfection and change.

The reproach of an alleged backwardness is raised against economics from two different points of view.

There are on the one hand some naturalists and physicists who censure economics for not being a natural science and not applying the methods and procedures of the laboratory. It is one of the tasks of this treatise to explode the fallacy of such ideas. In these introductory remarks it may be enough to say a few words about their psychological background. It is common with narrow-minded people to reflect upon every respect in which other people differ from themselves. The camel in the fable takes exception to all other animals for not having a hump, and the Ruritanian criticizes the Laputanian for not being a Ruritanian. The research worker in the laboratory considers it as the sole worthy home of inquiry, and differential equations as the only sound method of expressing the results of scientific thought. He is simply incapable of seeing the epistemological problems of human action. For him economics cannot be anything but a kind of mechanics.

Then there are people who assert that something must be wrong with the social sciences because social conditions are unsatisfactory. The natural sciences have achieved amazing results in the last two or three hundred years, and the practical utilization of these results has succeeded in improving the general standard of living to an unprecedented extent. But, say these critics, the social sciences have utterly failed in the task of rendering social conditions more satisfactory. They have not stamped out misery and starvation, economic crises and unemployment, war and tyranny. They are sterile and have contributed nothing to the promotion of happiness and human welfare.

These grumblers do not realize that the tremendous progress of technological methods of production and the resulting increase in wealth and welfare were feasible only through the pursuit of those liberal policies which were the practical application of the teachings of economics. It was the ideas of the classical economists that removed the checks imposed by age-old laws, customs, and prejudices upon technological improvement and freed the genius of reformers and innovators from the straitjackets of the guilds, government tutelage, and social pressure of various kinds. It was they that reduced the prestige of conquerors and expropriators and demonstrated the social benefits derived from business activity. None of the great modern inventions would have been put to use if the mentality of the precapitalistic era had not been thoroughly demolished by the economists. What is commonly called the "industrial revolution" was an offspring of the ideological revolution brought about by the doctrines of the economists. The economists exploded the old tenets: that it is unfair and unjust to outdo a competitor by producing better and cheaper goods; that it is iniquitous to deviate from the traditional methods of production; that machines are an evil because they bring about unemployment; that it is one of the tasks of civil government to prevent efficient businessmen from getting rich and to protect the less efficient against the competition of the more efficient; that to restrict the freedom of entrepreneurs by government compulsion or by coercion on the part of other social powers is an appropriate means to promote a nation's well-being. British political economy and French Physiocracy were the pacemakers of modern capitalism. It is they that made possible the progress of the applied natural sciences that has heaped benefits upon the masses.

What is wrong with our age is precisely the widespread ignorance of the role which these policies of economic freedom played in the technological evolution of the last two hundred years. People fell prey to the fallacy that the improvement of the methods of production was contemporaneous with the policy of laissez faire only by accident. Deluded by Marxian myths, they consider modern industrialism an outcome of the operation of mysterious "productive forces" that do not depend in any way on ideological factors. Classical economics, they believe, was not a factor in the rise of capitalism, but rather its product, its "ideological superstructure," i.e., a doctrine designed to defend the unfair claims of the capitalistic exploiters. Hence the abolition of capitalism and the substitution of socialist totalitarianism for a market economy and free enterprise would not impair the further progress of technology. It would, on the contrary, promote technological improvement by removing the obstacles which the selfish interests of the capitalists place in its way.

The characteristic feature of this age of destructive wars and social disintegration is the revolt against economics. Thomas Carlyle branded economics a "dismal science," and Karl Marx stigmatized the economists as "the sycophants of the bourgeoisie." Quacks—praising their patent medicines and short cuts to an earthly paradise—take pleasure in scorning economics as "orthodox" and "reactionary." Demagogues pride themselves on what they call their victories over economics. The "practical" man boasts of his contempt for economics and his ignorance of the teachings of "armchair" economists. The economic policies of the last decades have been the outcome of a mentality that scoffs at any variety of sound economic theory and glorifies the spurious doctrines of its detractors. What is called "orthodox" economics is in most countries barred from the universities and is virtually unknown to the leading statesmen, politicians, and writers.

The blame for the unsatisfactory state of economic affairs can certainly not be placed upon a science which both rulers and masses despise and ignore.

It must be emphasized that the destiny of modern civilization as developed by the white peoples in the last two hundred years is inseparably linked with the fate of economic science. This civilization was able to spring into existence because the peoples were dominated by ideas which were the application of the teachings of economics to the problems of economic policy. It will and must perish if the nations continue to pursue the course which they entered upon under the spell of doctrines rejecting economic thinking.

It is true that economics is a theoretical science and as such abstains from any judgment of value. It is not its task to tell people what ends they should aim at. It is a science of the means to be applied for the attainment of ends chosen, not, to be sure, a science of the choosing of ends. Ultimate decisions, the valuations and the choosing of ends, are beyond the scope of any science. Science never tells a man how he should act; it merely shows how a man must act if he wants to attain definite ends.

It seems to many people that this is very little indeed and that a science limited to the investigation of the *is* and unable to express a judgment of value about the highest and ultimate ends is of no importance for life and action. This too is a mistake. However, the exposure of this mistake is not a task of these introductory remarks. It is one of the ends of the treatise itself.

4. Résumé

It was necessary to make these preliminary remarks in order to explain why this treatise places economic problems within the broad frame of a general theory of human action. At the present stage both of economic thinking and of political discussions concerning the fundamental issues of social organization, it is no longer feasible to isolate the treatment of catallactic problems proper. These problems are only a segment of a general science of human action and must be dealt with as such.

Part One

Human Action

I. ACTING MAN

1. Purposeful Action and Animal Reaction

HUMAN action is purposeful behavior. Or we may say: Action is will put into operation and transformed into an agency, is aiming at ends and goals, is the ego's meaningful response to stimuli and to the conditions of its environment, is a person's conscious adjustment to the state of the universe that determines his life. Such paraphrases may clarify the definition given and prevent possible misinterpretations. But the definition itself is adequate and does not need complement or commentary.

Conscious or purposeful behavior is in sharp contrast to unconscious behavior, i.e., the reflexes and the involuntary responses of the body's cells and nerves to stimuli. People are sometimes prepared to believe that the boundaries between conscious behavior and the involuntary reaction of the forces operating within man's body are more or less indefinite. This is correct only as far as it is sometimes not easy to establish whether concrete behavior is to be considered voluntary or involuntary. But the distinction between consciousness and unconsciousness is nonetheless sharp and can be clearly determined.

The unconscious behavior of the bodily organs and cells is for the acting *ego* no less a datum than any other fact of the external world. Acting man must take into account all that goes on within his own body as well as other data, e.g., the weather or the attitudes of his neighbors. There is, of course, a margin within which purposeful behavior has the power to neutralize the working of bodily factors. It is feasible within certain limits to get the body under control. Man can sometimes succeed through the power of his will in overcoming sickness, in compensating for the innate or acquired insufficiency of his physical constitution, or in suppressing reflexes. As far as this is possible, the field of purposeful action is extended. If a man abstains from controlling the involuntary reaction of cells and nerve centers, although he would be in a position to do so, his behavior is from our point of view purposeful.

The field of our science is human action, not the psychological events which result in an action. It is precisely this which distinguishes the general theory of human action, praxeology, from psychology. The theme of psychology is the internal events that result or can result in a definite action. The theme of praxeology is action as such. This also settles the relation of praxeology to the psychoanalytical concept of the subconscious. Psychoanalysis too is psychology and does not investigate action but the forces and factors that impel a man toward a definite action. The psychoanalytical subconscious is a psychological and not a praxeological category. Whether an action stems from clear deliberation, or from forgotten memories and suppressed desires which from submerged regions, as it were, direct the will, does not influence the nature of the action. The murderer whom a subconscious urge (the *Id*) drives toward his crime and the neurotic whose aberrant behavior seems to be simply meaningless to an untrained observer both act; they like anybody else are aiming at certain ends. It is the merit of psychoanalysis that it has demonstrated that even the behavior of neurotics and psychopaths is meaningful, that they too act and aim at ends, although we who consider ourselves normal and sane call the reasoning determining their choice of ends nonsensical and the means they choose for the attainment of these ends contrary to purpose.

The term "unconscious" as used by praxeology and the terms "subconscious" and "unconscious" as applied by psychoanalysis belong to two different systems of thought and research. Praxeology no less than other branches of knowledge owes much to psychoanalysis. The more necessary is it then to become aware of the line which separates praxeology from psychoanalysis.

Action is not simply giving preference. Man also shows preference in situations in which things and events are unavoidable or are believed to be so. Thus a man may prefer sunshine to rain and may wish that the sun would dispel the clouds. He who only wishes and hopes does not interfere actively with the course of events and with the shaping of his own destiny. But acting man chooses, determines, and tries to reach an end. Of two things both of which he cannot have together he selects one and gives up the other. Action therefore always involves both taking and renunciation.

To express wishes and hopes and to announce planned action may be forms of action in so far as they aim in themselves at the realization of a certain purpose. But they must not be confused with the actions to which they refer. They are not identical with the actions they announce, recommend, or reject. Action is a real thing.

What counts is a man's total behavior, and not his talk about planned but not realized acts. On the other hand action must be clearly distinguished from the application of labor. Action means the employment of means for the attainment of ends. As a rule one of the means employed is the acting man's labor. But this is not always the case. Under special conditions a word is all that is needed. He who gives orders or interdictions may act without any expenditure of labor. To talk or not to talk, to smile or to remain serious, may be action. To consume and to enjoy are no less action than to abstain from accessible consumption and enjoyment.

Praxeology consequently does not distinguish between "active" or energetic and "passive" or indolent man. The vigorous man industriously striving for the improvement of his condition acts neither more nor less than the lethargic man who sluggishly takes things as they come. For to do nothing and to be idle are also action, they too determine the course of events. Wherever the conditions for human interference are present, man acts no matter whether he interferes or refrains from interfering. He who endures what he could change acts no less than he who interferes in order to attain another result. A man who abstains from influencing the operation of physiological and instinctive factors which he could influence also acts. Action is not only doing but no less omitting to do what possibly could be done.

We may say that action is the manifestation of a man's will. But this would not add anything to our knowledge. For the term *will* means nothing else than man's faculty to choose between different states of affairs, to prefer one, to set aside the other, and to behave according to the decision made in aiming at the chosen state and forsaking the other.

2. The Prerequisites of Human Action

We call contentment or satisfaction that state of a human being which does not and cannot result in any action. Acting man is eager to substitute a more satisfactory state of affairs for a less satisfactory. His mind imagines conditions which suit him better, and his action aims at bringing about this desired state. The incentive that impels a man to act is always some uneasiness.[1] A man perfectly content with the state of his affairs would have no incentive to change things. He would have neither wishes nor desires; he would be perfectly

1. Cf. Locke, *An Essay Concerning Human Understanding*, ed. Fraser (Oxford, 1894), I, 331–333; Leibniz, *Nouveaux essais sur l'entendement humain*, ed. Flammarion, p. 119.

happy. He would not act; he would simply live free from care.

But to make a man act, uneasiness and the image of a more satisfactory state alone are not sufficient. A third condition is required: the expectation that purposeful behavior has the power to remove or at least to alleviate the felt uneasiness. In the absence of this condition no action is feasible. Man must yield to the inevitable. He must submit to destiny.

These are the general conditions of human action. Man is the being that lives under these conditions. He is not only *homo sapiens,* but no less *homo agens*. Beings of human descent who either from birth or from acquired defects are unchangeably unfit for any action (in the strict sense of the term and not merely in the legal sense) are practically not human. Although the statutes and biology consider them to be men, they lack the essential feature of humanity. The newborn child too is not an acting being. It has not yet gone the whole way from conception to the full development of its human qualities. But at the end of this evolution it becomes an acting being.

On Happiness

In colloquial speech we call a man "happy" who has succeeded in attaining his ends. A more adequate description of his state would be that he is happier than he was before. There is however no valid objection to a usage that defines human action as the striving for happiness.

But we must avoid current misunderstandings. The ultimate goal of human action is always the satisfaction of the acting man's desire. There is no standard of greater or lesser satisfaction other than individual judgments of value, different for various people and for the same people at various times. What makes a man feel uneasy and less uneasy is established by him from the standard of his own will and judgment, from his personal and subjective valuation. Nobody is in a position to decree what should make a fellow man happier.

To establish this fact does not refer in any way to the antitheses of egoism and altruism, of materialism and idealism, of individualism and collectivism, of atheism and religion. There are people whose only aim is to improve the condition of their own ego. There are other people with whom awareness of the troubles of their fellow men causes as much uneasiness as or even more uneasiness than their own wants. There are people who desire nothing else than the satisfaction of their appetites for sexual intercourse, food, drinks, fine homes, and other material things. But other men care more for the satisfactions commonly called "higher" and "ideal." There are individuals eager to adjust their actions to the requirements of social cooperation; there are, on the other hand, refractory people who defy the rules of social life. There are people for whom the ultimate goal of the earthly pilgrimage is the preparation for a life of bliss. There are other people who do not believe in the teachings of any religion and do not allow their actions to be influenced by them.

Praxeology is indifferent to the ultimate goals of action. Its findings are valid for all kinds of action irrespective of the ends aimed at. It is a science of means, not of ends. It applies the term happiness in a purely formal sense. In the praxeological terminology the proposition: man's unique aim is to attain happiness, is tautological. It does not imply any statement about the state of affairs from which man expects happiness.

The idea that the incentive of human activity is always some uneasiness and its aim always to remove such uneasiness as far as possible, that is, to make the acting men feel happier, is the essence of the teachings of Eudaemonism and Hedonism. Epicurean ἀταραξία is that state of perfect happiness and contentment at which all human activity aims without ever wholly attaining it. In the face of the grandeur of this cognition it is of little avail only that many representatives of this philosophy failed to recognize the purely formal character of the notions *pain* and *pleasure* and gave them a material and carnal meaning. The theological, mystical, and other schools of a heteronomous ethic did not shake the core of Epicureanism because they could not raise any other objection than its neglect of the "higher" and "nobler" pleasures. It is true that the writings of many earlier champions of Eudaemonism, Hedonism, and Utilitarianism are in some points open to misinterpretation. But the language of modern philosophers and still more that of the modern economists is so precise and straightforward that no misinterpretation can possibly occur.

On Instincts and Impulses

One does not further the comprehension of the fundamental problem of human action by the methods of instinct-sociology. This school classifies the various concrete goals of human action and assigns to each class a special instinct as its motive. Man appears as a being driven by various innate instincts and dispositions. It is assumed that this explanation demolishes once for all the odious teachings of economics and utilitarian ethics. However, Feuerbach has already justly observed that every instinct is an instinct to happiness.[2] The method of instinct-psychology and instinct-sociology consists in an arbitrary classification of the immediate goals of action and in a hypostasis of each. Whereas praxeology says that the goal of an action is to remove

2. Cf. Feuerbach, *Sämmtliche Werke,* ed. Bolin and Jodl (Stuttgart, 1907), X, 231.

a certain uneasiness, instinct-psychology says it is the satisfaction of an instinctive urge.

Many champions of the instinct school are convinced that they have proved that action is not determined by reason, but stems from the profound depths of innate forces, impulses, instincts, and dispositions which are not open to any rational elucidation. They are certain they have succeeded in exposing the shallowness of rationalism and disparage economics as "a tissue of false conclusions drawn from false psychological assumptions."[3] Yet rationalism, praxeology, and economics do not deal with the ultimate springs and goals of action, but with the means applied for the attainment of an end sought. However unfathomable the depths may be from which an impulse or instinct emerges, the means which man chooses for its satisfaction are determined by a rational consideration of expense and success.[4]

He who acts under an emotional impulse also acts. What distinguishes an emotional action from other actions is the valuation of input and output. Emotions disarrange valuations. Inflamed with passion, man sees the goal as more desirable and the price he has to pay for it as less burdensome than he would in cool deliberation. Men have never doubted that even in the state of emotion means and ends are pondered and that it is possible to influence the outcome of this deliberation by rendering more costly the yielding to the passionate impulse. To punish criminal offenses committed in a state of emotional excitement or intoxication more mildly than other offenses is tantamount to encouraging such excesses. The threat of severe retaliation does not fail to deter even people driven by seemingly irresistible passion.

We interpret animal behavior on the assumption that the animal yields to the impulse which prevails at the moment. As we observe that the animal feeds, cohabits, and attacks other animals or men, we speak of its instincts of nourishment, of reproduction, and of aggression. We assume that such instincts are innate and peremptorily ask for satisfaction.

But it is different with man. Man is not a being who cannot help yielding to the impulse that most urgently asks for satisfaction. Man is a being capable of subduing his instincts, emotions, and impulses; he can rationalize his behavior. He renounces the satisfaction of a burning impulse in order to satisfy other desires. He is not a puppet of his appetites. A man does not ravish every female that stirs his senses; he does not devour every piece of food that entices him; he does not knock down every fellow he would like to kill. He arranges

3. Cf. William McDougall, *An Introduction to Social Psychology* (14th ed. Boston, 1921), p. 11.

4. Cf. Mises, *Epistemological Problems of Economics,* trans. by G. Reisman (New York, 1960), pp. 52 ff.

his wishes and desires into a scale, he chooses; in short, he acts. What distinguishes man from beasts is precisely that he adjusts his behavior deliberatively. Man is the being that has inhibitions, that can master his impulses and desires, that has the power to suppress instinctive desires and impulses.

It may happen that an impulse emerges with such vehemence that no disadvantage which its satisfaction may cause appears great enough to prevent the individual from satisfying it. In this case too there is choosing. Man decides in favor of yielding to the desire concerned.[5]

3. Human Action as an Ultimate Given

Since time immemorial men have been eager to know the prime mover, the cause of all being and of all change, the ultimate substance from which everything stems and which is the cause of itself. Science is more modest. It is aware of the limits of the human mind and of the human search for knowledge. It aims at tracing back every phenomenon to its cause. But it realizes that these endeavors must necessarily strike against insurmountable walls. There are phenomena which cannot be analyzed and traced back to other phenomena. They are the ultimate given. The progress of scientific research may succeed in demonstrating that something previously considered as an ultimate given can be reduced to components. But there will always be some irreducible and unanalyzable phenomena, some ultimate given.

Monism teaches that there is but one ultimate substance, dualism that there are two, pluralism that there are many. There is no point in quarreling about these problems. Such metaphysical disputes are interminable. The present state of our knowledge does not provide the means to solve them with an answer which every reasonable man must consider satisfactory.

Materialist monism contends that human thoughts and volitions are the product of the operation of bodily organs, the cells of the brain and the nerves. Human thought, will, and action are solely brought about by material processes which one day will be completely explained by the methods of physical and chemical inquiry. This too is a metaphysical hypothesis, although its supporters consider it as an unshakable and undeniable scientific truth.

Various doctrines have been advanced to explain the relation be-

5. In such cases a great role is played by the circumstance that the two satisfactions concerned—that expected from yielding to the impulse and that expected from the avoidance of its undesirable consequences—are not simultaneous. Cf. below, pp. 479–490.

tween mind and body. They are mere surmises without any reference to observed facts. All that can be said with certainty is that there are relations between mental and physiological processes. With regard to the nature and operation of this connection we know little if anything.

Concrete value judgments and definite human actions are not open to further analysis. We may fairly assume or believe that they are absolutely dependent upon and conditioned by their causes. But as long as we do not know how external facts—physical and physiological—produce in a human mind definite thoughts and volitions resulting in concrete acts, we have to face an insurmountable *methodological dualism.* In the present state of our knowledge the fundamental statements of positivism, monism and panphysicalism are mere metaphysical postulates devoid of any scientific foundation and both meaningless and useless for scientific research. Reason and experience show us two separate realms: the external world of physical, chemical, and physiological phenomena and the internal world of thought, feeling, valuation, and purposeful action. No bridge connects—as far as we can see today—these two spheres. Identical external events result sometimes in different human responses, and different external events produce sometimes the same human response. We do not know why.

In the face of this state of affairs we cannot help withholding judgment on the essential statements of monism and materialism. We may or may not believe that the natural sciences will succeed one day in explaining the production of definite ideas, judgments of value, and actions in the same way in which they explain the production of a chemical compound as the necessary and unavoidable outcome of a certain combination of elements. In the meantime we are bound to acquiesce in a methodological dualism.

Human action is one of the agencies bringing about change. It is an element of cosmic activity and becoming. Therefore it is a legitimate object of scientific investigation. As—at least under present conditions—it cannot be traced back to its causes, it must be considered as an ultimate given and must be studied as such.

It is true that the changes brought about by human action are but trifling when compared with the effects of the operation of the great cosmic forces. From the point of view of eternity and the infinite universe man is an infinitesimal speck. But for man human action and its vicissitudes are the real thing. Action is the essence of his nature and existence, his means of preserving his life and raising himself above the level of animals and plants. However perishable and evanescent all human efforts may be, for man and for human science they are of primary importance.

4. Rationality and Irrationality; Subjectivism and Objectivity of Praxeological Research

Human action is necessarily always rational. The term "rational action" is therefore pleonastic and must be rejected as such. When applied to the ultimate ends of action, the terms rational and irrational are inappropriate and meaningless. The ultimate end of action is always the satisfaction of some desires of the acting man. Since nobody is in a position to substitute his own value judgments for those of the acting individual, it is vain to pass judgment on other people's aims and volitions. No man is qualified to declare what would make another man happier or less discontented. The critic either tells us what he believes he would aim at if he were in the place of his fellow; or, in dictatorial arrogance blithely disposing of his fellow's will and aspirations, declares what condition of this other man would better suit himself, the critic.

It is usual to call an action irrational if it aims, at the expense of "material" and tangible advantages, at the attainment of "ideal" or "higher" satisfactions. In this sense people say, for instance—sometimes with approval, sometimes with disapproval—that a man who sacrifices life, health, or wealth to the attainment of "higher" goods—like fidelity to his religious, philosophical, and political convictions or the freedom and flowering of his nation—is motivated by irrational considerations. However, the striving after these higher ends is neither more nor less rational or irrational than that after other human ends. It is a mistake to assume that the desire to procure the bare necessities of life and health is more rational, natural, or justified than the striving after other goods or amenities. It is true that the appetite for food and warmth is common to men and other mammals and that as a rule a man who lacks food and shelter concentrates his efforts upon the satisfaction of these urgent needs and does not care much for other things. The impulse to live, to preserve one's own life, and to take advantage of every opportunity of strengthening one's vital forces is a primal feature of life, present in every living being. However, to yield to this impulse is not—for man—an inevitable necessity.

While all other animals are unconditionally driven by the impulse to preserve their own lives and by the impulse of proliferation, man has the power to master even these impulses. He can control both his sexual desires and his will to live. He can give up his life when the conditions under which alone he could preserve it seem intolerable. Man is capable of dying for a cause or of committing suicide. To live is for man the outcome of a choice, of a judgment of value.

It is the same with the desire to live in affluence. The very existence of ascetics and of men who renounce material gains for the sake of clinging to their convictions and of preserving their dignity and self-respect is evidence that the striving after more tangible amenities is not inevitable but rather the result of a choice. Of course, the immense majority prefer life to death and wealth to poverty.

It is arbitrary to consider only the satisfaction of the body's physiological needs as "natural" and therefore "rational" and everything else as "artificial" and therefore "irrational." It is the characteristic feature of human nature that man seeks not only food, shelter, and cohabitation like all other animals, but that he aims also at other kinds of satisfaction. Man has specifically human desires and needs which we may call "higher" than those which he has in common with the other mammals.[6]

When applied to the means chosen for the attainment of ends, the terms rational and irrational imply a judgment about the expediency and adequacy of the procedure employed. The critic approves or disapproves of the method from the point of view of whether or not it is best suited to attain the end in question. It is a fact that human reason is not infallible and that man very often errs in selecting and applying means. An action unsuited to the end sought falls short of expectation. It is contrary to purpose, but it is rational, i.e., the outcome of a reasonable—although faulty—deliberation and an attempt—although an ineffectual attempt—to attain a definite goal. The doctors who a hundred years ago employed certain methods for the treatment of cancer which our contemporary doctors reject were—from the point of view of present-day pathology—badly instructed and therefore inefficient. But they did not act irrationally; they did their best. It is probable that in a hundred years more doctors will have more efficient methods at hand for the treatment of this disease. They will be more efficient but not more rational than our physicians.

The opposite of action is not *irrational behavior,* but a reactive response to stimuli on the part of the bodily organs and instincts which cannot be controlled by the volition of the person concerned. To the same stimulus man can under certain conditions respond both by reactive response and by action. If a man absorbs a poison, the organs

6. On the errors involved in the iron law of wages see below, pp. 603 f.; on the misunderstanding of the Malthusian theory see below, pp. 667–672.

react by setting up their forces of antidotal defense; in addition, action may interfere by applying counterpoison.

With regard to the problem involved in the antithesis, rational and irrational, there is no difference between the natural sciences and the social sciences. Science always is and must be rational. It is the endeavor to attain a mental grasp of the phenomena of the universe by a systematic arrangement of the whole body of available knowledge. However, as has been pointed out above, the analysis of objects into their constituent elements must sooner or later necessarily reach a point beyond which it cannot go. The human mind is not even capable of conceiving a kind of knowledge not limited by an ultimate given inaccessible to further analysis and reduction. The scientific method that carries the mind up to this point is entirely rational. The ultimate given may be called an irrational fact.

It is fashionable nowadays to find fault with the social sciences for being purely rational. The most popular objection raised against economics is that it neglects the irrationality of life and reality and tries to press into dry rational schemes and bloodless abstractions the infinite variety of phenomena. No censure could be more absurd. Like every branch of knowledge economics goes as far as it can be carried by rational methods. Then it stops by establishing the fact that it is faced with an ultimate given, i.e., a phenomenon which cannot—at least in the present state of our knowledge—be further analyzed.[7]

The teachings of praxeology and economics are valid for every human action without regard to its underlying motives, causes, and goals. The ultimate judgments of value and the ultimate ends of human action are given for any kind of scientific inquiry; they are not open to any further analysis. Praxeology deals with the ways and means chosen for the attainment of such ultimate ends. Its object is means, not ends.

In this sense we speak of the subjectivism of the general science of human action. It takes the ultimate ends chosen by acting man as data, it is entirely neutral with regard to them, and it refrains from passing any value judgments. The only standard which it applies is whether or not the means chosen are fit for the attainment of the ends aimed at. If Eudaemonism says happiness, if Utilitarianism and economics say utility, we must interpret these terms in a subjectivistic way as that which acting man aims at because it is desirable in his eyes. It is in this formalism that the progress of the modern meaning of Eudaemonism, Hedonism, and Utilitarianism consists as opposed to

7. We shall see later (pp. 49–58) how the empirical social sciences deal with the ultimate given.

the older material meaning and the progress of the modern subjectivistic theory of value as opposed to the objectivistic theory of value as expounded by classical political economy. At the same time it is in this subjectivism that the objectivity of our science lies. Because it is subjectivistic and takes the value judgments of acting man as ultimate data not open to any further critical examination, it is itself above all strife of parties and factions, it is indifferent to the conflicts of all schools of dogmatism and ethical doctrines, it is free from valuations and preconceived ideas and judgments, it is universally valid and absolutely and plainly human.

5. Causality as a Requirement of Action

Man is in a position to act because he has the ability to discover causal relations which determine change and becoming in the universe. Acting requires and presupposes the category of causality. Only a man who sees the world in the light of causality is fitted to act. In this sense we may say that causality is a category of action. The category *means and ends* presupposes the category *cause and effect*. In a world without causality and regularity of phenomena there would be no field for human reasoning and human action. Such a world would be a chaos in which man would be at a loss to find any orientation and guidance. Man is not even capable of imagining the conditions of such a chaotic universe.

Where man does not see any causal relation, he cannot act. This statement is not reversible. Even when he knows the causal relation involved, man cannot act if he is not in a position to influence the cause.

The archetype of causality research was: where and how must I interfere in order to divert the course of events from the way it would go in the absence of my interference in a direction which better suits my wishes? In this sense man raises the question: who or what is at the bottom of things? He searches for the regularity and the "law," because he wants to interfere. Only later was this search more extensively interpreted by metaphysics as a search after the ultimate cause of being and existence. Centuries were needed to bring these exaggerated and extravagant ideas back again to the more modest question of where one must interfere or should one be able to interfere in order to attain this or that end.

The treatment accorded to the problem of causality in the last decades has been, due to a confusion brought about by some eminent physicists, rather unsatisfactory. We may hope that this unpleasant chapter in the history of philosophy will be a warning to future philosophers.

There are changes whose causes are, at least for the present time, unknown to us. Sometimes we succeed in acquiring a partial knowledge so that we are able to say: in 70 per cent of all cases *A* results in *B*, in the remaining cases in *C*, or even in *D*, *E*, *F*, and so on. In order to substitute for this fragmentary information more precise information it would be necessary to break up *A* into its elements. As long as this is not achieved, we must acquiesce in what is called a statistical law. But this does not affect the praxeological meaning of causality. Total or partial ignorance in some areas does not demolish the category of causality.

The philosophical, epistemological, and metaphysical problems of causality and of imperfect induction are beyond the scope of praxeology. We must simply establish the fact that in order to act, man must know the causal relationship between events, processes, or states of affairs. And only as far as he knows this relationship, can his action attain the ends sought. We are fully aware that in asserting this we are moving in a circle. For the evidence that we have correctly perceived a causal relation is provided only by the fact that action guided by this knowledge results in the expected outcome. But we cannot avoid this vicious circular evidence precisely because causality is a category of action. And because it is such a category, praxeology cannot help bestowing some attention on this fundamental problem of philosophy.

6. The Alter Ego

If we are prepared to take the term causality in its broadest sense, teleology can be called a variety of causal inquiry. Final causes are first of all causes. The cause of an event is seen as an action or quasi-action aiming at some end.

Both primitive man and the infant, in a naïve anthropomorphic attitude, consider it quite plausible that every change and event is the outcome of the action of a being acting in the same way as they themselves do. They believe that animals, plants, mountains, rivers, and fountains, even stones and celestial bodies, are, like themselves, feeling, willing, and acting beings. Only at a later stage of cultural development does man renounce these animistic ideas and substitute the mechanistic world view for them. Mechanicalism proves to be so satisfactory a principle of conduct that people finally believe it capable of solving all the problems of thought and scientific research. Materialism and panphysicalism proclaim mechanicalism as the essence of all knowledge and the experimental and mathematical methods of the natural sciences as the sole scientific mode of thinking. All changes are to be comprehended as motions subject to the laws of mechanics.

The champions of mechanicalism do not bother about the still unsolved problems of the logical and epistemological basis of the principles of causality and imperfect induction. In their eyes these principles are sound because they work. The fact that experiments in the laboratory bring about the results predicted by the theories and that machines in the factories run in the way predicted by technology proves, they say, the soundness of the methods and findings of modern natural science. Granted that science cannot give us truth—and who knows what truth really means?—at any rate it is certain that it works in leading us to success.

But it is precisely when we accept this pragmatic point of view that the emptiness of the panphysicalist dogma becomes manifest. Science, as has been pointed out above, has not succeeded in solving the problems of the mind-body relations. The panphysicalists certainly cannot contend that the procedures they recommend have ever worked in the field of interhuman relations and of the social sciences. But it is beyond doubt that the principle according to which an *Ego* deals with every human being as if the other were a thinking and acting being like himself has evidenced its usefulness both in mundane life and in scientific research. It cannot be denied that it works.

It is beyond doubt that the practice of considering fellow men as beings who think and act as I, the Ego, do has turned out well; on the other hand the prospect seems hopeless of getting a similar pragmatic verification for the postulate requiring them to be treated in the same manner as the objects of the natural sciences. The epistemological problems raised by the comprehension of other people's behavior are no less intricate than those of causality and incomplete induction. It may be admitted that it is impossible to provide conclusive evidence for the propositions that my logic is the logic of all other people and by all means absolutely the only human logic and that the categories of my action are the categories of all other people's action and by all means absolutely the categories of all human action. However, the pragmatist must remember that these propositions work both in practice and in science, and the positivist must not overlook the fact that in addressing his fellow men he presupposes—tacitly and implicitly—the intersubjective validity of logic and thereby the reality of the realm of the alter Ego's thought and action, of his eminent human character.[8]

8. Cf. Alfred Schütz, *Der sinnhafte Aufbau der sozialen Welt* (Vienna, 1932), p. 18.

Thinking and acting are the specific human features of man. They are peculiar to all human beings. They are, beyond membership in the zoological species homo sapiens, the characteristic mark of man as man. It is not the scope of praxeology to investigate the relation of thinking and acting. For praxeology it is enough to establish the fact that there is only one logic that is intelligible to the human mind, and that there is only one mode of action which is human and comprehensible to the human mind. Whether there are or can be somewhere other beings—superhuman or subhuman—who think and act in a different way, is beyond the reach of the human mind. We must restrict our endeavors to the study of human action.

This human action which is inextricably linked with human thought is conditioned by logical necessity. It is impossible for the human mind to conceive logical relations at variance with the logical structure of our mind. It is impossible for the human mind to conceive a mode of action whose categories would differ from the categories which determine our own actions.

There are for man only two principles available for a mental grasp of reality, namely, those of teleology and causality. What cannot be brought under either of these categories is absolutely hidden to the human mind. An event not open to an interpretation by one of these two principles is for man inconceivable and mysterious. Change can be conceived as the outcome either of the operation of mechanistic causality or of purposeful behavior; for the human mind there is no third way available.[9] It is true, as has already been mentioned, that teleology can be viewed as a variety of causality. But the establishment of this fact does not annul the essential differences between the two categories.

The panmechanistic world view is committed to a methodological monism; it acknowledges only mechanistic causality because it attributes to it alone any cognitive value or at least a higher cognitive value than to teleology. This is a metaphysical superstition. Both principles of cognition—causality and teleology—are, owing to the limitations of human reason, imperfect and do not convey ultimate knowledge. Causality leads to a *regressus in infinitum* which reason can never exhaust. Teleology is found wanting as soon as the question is raised of what moves the prime mover. Either method stops short at an ultimate given which cannot be analyzed and interpreted. Reasoning and scientific inquiry can never bring full ease of mind, apodictic certainty, and perfect cognition of all things. He who seeks

9. Cf. Karel Engliš, *Begründung der Teleologie als Form des empirischen Erkennens* (Brünn, 1930), pp. 15 ff.

this must apply to faith and try to quiet his conscience by embracing a creed or a metaphysical doctrine.

If we do not transcend the realm of reason and experience, we cannot help acknowledging that our fellow men act. We are not free to disregard this fact for the sake of a fashionable prepossession and an arbitrary opinion. Daily experience proves not only that the sole suitable method for studying the conditions of our nonhuman environment is provided by the category of causality; it proves no less convincingly that our fellow men are acting beings as we ourselves are. For the comprehension of action there is but one scheme of interpretation and analysis available, namely, that provided by the cognition and analysis of our own purposeful behavior.

The problem of the study and analysis of other people's action is in no way connected with the problem of the existence of a *soul* or of an *immortal soul.* As far as the objections of empiricism, behaviorism, and positivism are directed against any variety of the soul-theory, they are of no avail for our problem. The question we have to deal with is whether it is possible to grasp human action intellectually if one refuses to comprehend it as meaningful and purposeful behavior aiming at the attainment of definite ends. Behaviorism and positivism want to apply the methods of the empirical natural sciences to the reality of human action. They interpret it as a response to stimuli. But these stimuli themselves are not open to description by the methods of the natural sciences. Every attempt to describe them must refer to the meaning which acting men attach to them. We may call the offering of a commodity for sale a "stimulus." But what is essential in such an offer and distinguishes it from other offers cannot be described without entering into the meaning which the acting parties attribute to the situation. No dialectical artifice can spirit away the fact that man is driven by the aim to attain certain ends. It is this purposeful behavior—viz., action—that is the subject matter of our science. We cannot approach our subject if we disregard the meaning which acting man attaches to the situation, i.e., the given state of affairs, and to his own behavior with regard to this situation.

It is not appropriate for the physicist to search for final causes because there is no indication that the events which are the subject matter of physics are to be interpreted as the outcome of actions of a being, aiming at ends in a human way. Nor is it appropriate for the praxeologist to disregard the operation of the acting being's volition and intention; they are undoubtedly given facts. If he were to disregard it, he would cease to study human action. Very often —but not always—the events concerned can be investigated both from the point of view of praxeology and from that of the natural sciences. But he who deals with the discharging of a firearm from the physical and chemical point of view is not a praxeologist. He neglects the very problems which the science of purposeful human behavior aims to clarify.

On the Serviceableness of Instincts

The proof of the fact that only two avenues of approach are available for human research, causality or teleology, is provided by the problems raised in reference to the serviceableness of instincts. There are types of behavior which on the one hand cannot be thoroughly interpreted with the causal methods of the natural sciences, but on the other hand cannot be considered as purposeful human action. In order to grasp such behavior we are forced to resort to a makeshift. We assign to it the character of a quasi-action; we speak of serviceable instincts.

We observe two things: first the inherent tendency of a living organism to respond to a stimulus according to a regular pattern, and second the favorable effects of this kind of behavior for the strengthening or preservation of the organism's vital forces. If we were in a position to interpret such behavior as the outcome of purposeful aiming at certain ends, we would call it action and deal with it according to the teleological methods of praxeology. But as we found no trace of a conscious mind behind this behavior, we suppose that an unknown factor—we call it *instinct*—was instrumental. We say that the instinct directs quasi-purposeful animal behavior and unconscious but nonetheless serviceable responses of human muscles and nerves. Yet, the mere fact that we hypostatize the unexplained element of this behavior as a force and call it instinct does not enlarge our knowledge. We must never forget that this word instinct is nothing but a landmark to indicate a point beyond which we are unable, up to the present at least, to carry our scientific scrutiny.

Biology has succeeded in discovering a "natural," i.e., mechanistic, explanation for many processes which in earlier days were attributed to the operation of instincts. Nonetheless many others have remained which cannot be interpreted as mechanical or chemical responses to mechanical or chemical stimuli. Animals display attitudes which cannot be comprehended otherwise than through the assumption that a directing factor was operative.

The aim of behaviorism to study human action from without with the methods of animal psychology is illusory. As far as animal behavior goes beyond mere physiological processes like breathing and metabolism, it can only be investigated with the aid of the meaning-concepts developed by praxeology. The behaviorist approaches the object of his investigations with the human notions of purpose and success. He unwittingly applies to the subject matter of his studies the human concepts of serviceableness and perniciousness. He deceives himself in excluding all verbal reference to consciousness and aiming at ends. In fact his mind searches everywhere for ends and measures every attitude with the yardstick of a garbled notion of serviceableness. The science of human behavior—as far as it is not physiology—cannot abandon reference to meaning and purpose. It cannot learn anything from animal psychology and the observation of the unconscious reactions of newborn infants. It is, on the contrary, animal psychology and infant psychology which cannot renounce the aid afforded by the science of human action. Without praxeological categories we would be at a loss to conceive and to understand the behavior both of animals and of infants.

The observation of the instinctive behavior of animals fills man with astonishment and raises questions which nobody can answer satisfactorily. Yet the fact that animals and even plants react in a quasi-purposeful way is neither more nor less miraculous than that man thinks and acts, that in the inorganic universe those functional correspondences prevail which physics describes, and that in the organic universe biological processes occur. All this is miraculous in the sense that it is an ultimate given for our searching mind.

Such an ultimate given is also what we call animal instinct. Like the concepts of motion, force, life, and consciousness, the concept of instinct too is merely a term to signify an ultimate given. To be sure, it neither "explains" anything nor indicates a cause or an ultimate cause.[10]

The Absolute End

In order to avoid any possible misinterpretation of the praxeological categories it seems expedient to emphasize a truism.

Praxeology, like the historical sciences of human action, deals with purposeful *human* action. If it mentions *ends,* what it has in view is the ends at which acting men aim. If it speaks of *meaning,* it refers to the meaning which acting men attach to their actions.

Praxeology and history are manifestations of the human mind and as such are conditioned by the intellectual abilities of mortal men. Praxeology and history do not pretend to know anything about the intentions of an absolute and objective mind, about an objective meaning inherent in the course of events and of historical evolution, and about the plans which God or Nature or Weltgeist or Manifest

10. "La vie est une cause première qui nous échappe comme toutes les causes premières et dont la science expérimentale n'a pas à se préoccuper." Claude Bernard, *La Science expérimentale* (Paris, 1878), p. 137.

Destiny is trying to realize in directing the universe and human affairs. They have nothing in common with what is called philosophy of history. They do not, like the works of Hegel, Comte, Marx, and a host of other writers, claim to reveal information about the true, objective, and absolute meaning of life and history.[11]

Vegetative Man

Some philosophies advise men to seek as the ultimate end of conduct the complete renunciation of any action. They look upon life as an absolute evil full of pain, suffering, and anguish, and apodictically deny that any purposeful human effort can render it tolerable. Happiness can be attained only by complete extinction of consciousness, volition, and life. The only way toward bliss and salvation is to become perfectly passive, indifferent, and inert like the plants. The sovereign good is the abandonment of thinking and acting.

Such is the essence of the teachings of various Indian philosophies, especially of Buddhism, and of Schopenhauer. Praxeology does not comment upon them. It is neutral with regard to all judgments of value and the choice of ultimate ends. Its task is not to approve or to disapprove, but to describe what is.

The subject matter of praxeology is human action. It deals with acting man, not with man transformed into a plant and reduced to a merely vegetative existence.

11. On the philosophy of history, cf. Mises, *Theory and History* (New Haven, 1957), pp. 159 ff.

II. THE EPISTEMOLOGICAL PROBLEMS OF THE SCIENCES OF HUMAN ACTION

1. Praxeology and History

THERE are two main branches of the sciences of human action: praxeology and history.

History is the collection and systematic arrangement of all the data of experience concerning human action. It deals with the concrete content of human action. It studies all human endeavors in their infinite multiplicity and variety and all individual actions with all their accidental, special, and particular implications. It scrutinizes the ideas guiding acting men and the outcome of the actions performed. It embraces every aspect of human activities. It is on the one hand general history and on the other hand the history of various narrower fields. There is the history of political and military action, of ideas and philosophy, of economic activities, of technology, of literature, art, and science, of religion, of mores and customs, and of many other realms of human life. There is ethnology and anthropology, as far as they are not a part of biology, and there is psychology as far as it is neither physiology nor epistemology nor philosophy. There is linguistics as far as it is neither logic nor the physiology of speech.[1]

The subject matter of all historical sciences is the past. They cannot teach us anything which would be valid for all human actions, that is, for the future too. The study of history makes a man wise

1. Economic history, descriptive economics, and economic statistics are, of course, history. The term *sociology* is used in two different meanings. Descriptive sociology deals with those historical phenomena of human action which are not viewed in descriptive economics; it overlaps to some extent the field claimed by ethnology and anthropology. General sociology, on the other hand, approaches historical experience from a more nearly universal point of view than that of the other branches of history. History proper, for instance, deals with an individual town or with towns in a definite period or with an individual people or with a certain geographical area. Max Weber in his main treatise (*Wirtschaft und Gesellschaft* [Tübingen, 1922], pp. 513–600) deals with the town in general, i.e., with the whole historical experience concerning towns without any limitation to historical periods, geographical areas, or individual peoples, nations, races, and civilizations.

and judicious. But it does not by itself provide any knowledge and skill which could be utilized for handling concrete tasks.

The natural sciences too deal with past events. Every experience is an experience of something passed away; there is no experience of future happenings. But the experience to which the natural sciences owe all their success is the experience of the experiment in which the individual elements of change can be observed in isolation. The facts amassed in this way can be used for induction, a peculiar procedure of inference which has given pragmatic evidence of its expediency, although its satisfactory epistemological characterization is still an unsolved problem.

The experience with which the sciences of human action have to deal is always an experience of complex phenomena. No laboratory experiments can be performed with regard to human action. We are never in a position to observe the change in one element only, all other conditions of the event remaining unchanged. Historical experience as an experience of complex phenomena does not provide us with facts in the sense in which the natural sciences employ this term to signify isolated events tested in experiments. The information conveyed by historical experience cannot be used as building material for the construction of theories and the prediction of future events. Every historical experience is open to various interpretations, and is in fact interpreted in different ways.

The postulates of positivism and kindred schools of metaphysics are therefore illusory. It is impossible to reform the sciences of human action according to the pattern of physics and the other natural sciences. There is no means to establish an a posteriori theory of human conduct and social events. History can neither prove nor disprove any general statement in the manner in which the natural sciences accept or reject a hypothesis on the ground of laboratory experiments. Neither experimental verification nor experimental falsification of a general proposition is possible in its field.

Complex phenomena in the production of which various causal chains are interlaced cannot test any theory. Such phenomena, on the contrary, become intelligible only through an interpretation in terms of theories previously developed from other sources. In the case of natural phenomena the interpretation of an event must not be at variance with the theories satisfactorily verified by experiments. In the case of historical events there is no such restriction. Commentators would be free to resort to quite arbitrary explanations. Where there is something to explain, the human mind has never been at a loss to invent ad hoc some imaginary theories, lacking any logical justification.

In the field of human history a limitation similar to that which the experimentally tested theories enjoin upon the attempts to interpret and elucidate individual physical, chemical, and physiological events is provided by praxeology. Praxeology is a theoretical and systematic, not a historical, science. Its scope is human action as such, irrespective of all environmental, accidental, and individual circumstances of the concrete acts. Its cognition is purely formal and general without reference to the material content and the particular features of the actual case. It aims at knowledge valid for all instances in which the conditions exactly correspond to those implied in its assumptions and inferences. Its statements and propositions are not derived from experience. They are, like those of logic and mathematics, a priori. They are not subject to verification or falsification on the ground of experience and facts. They are both logically and temporally antecedent to any comprehension of historical facts. They are a necessary requirement of any intellectual grasp of historical events. Without them we should not be able to see in the course of events anything else than kaleidoscopic change and chaotic muddle.

2. The Formal and Aprioristic Character of Praxeology

A fashionable tendency in contemporary philosophy is to deny the existence of any a priori knowledge. All human knowledge, it is contended, is derived from experience. This attitude can easily be understood as an excessive reaction against the extravagances of theology and a spurious philosophy of history and of nature. Metaphysicians were eager to discover by intuition moral precepts, the meaning of historical evolution, the properties of soul and matter, and the laws governing physical, chemical, and physiological events. Their volatile speculations manifested a blithe disregard for matter-of-fact knowledge. They were convinced that, without reference to experience, reason could explain all things and answer all questions.

The modern natural sciences owe their success to the method of observation and experiment. There is no doubt that empiricism and pragmatism are right as far as they merely describe the procedures of the natural sciences. But it is no less certain that they are entirely wrong in their endeavors to reject any kind of a priori knowledge and to characterize logic, mathematics, and praxeology either as empirical and experimental disciplines or as mere tautologies.

With regard to praxeology the errors of the philosophers are due to their complete ignorance of economics[2] and very often to their shockingly insufficient knowledge of history. In the eyes of the philosopher the treatment of philosophical issues is a sublime and noble vocation which must not be put upon the low level of other gainful employments. The professor resents the fact that he derives an income from philosophizing; he is offended by the thought that he earns money like the artisan and the farm hand. Monetary matters are mean things, and the philosopher investigating the eminent problems of truth and absolute eternal values should not soil his mind by paying attention to problems of economics.

The problem of whether there are or whether there are not a priori elements of thought—i.e., necessary and ineluctable intellectual conditions of thinking, anterior to any actual instance of conception and experience—must not be confused with the genetic problem of how man acquired his characteristically human mental ability. Man is descended from nonhuman ancestors who lacked this ability. These ancestors were endowed with some potentiality which in the course of ages of evolution converted them into reasonable beings. This transformation was achieved by the influence of a changing cosmic environment operating upon succeeding generations. Hence the empiricist concludes that the fundamental principles of reasoning are an outcome of experience and represent an adaptation of man to the conditions of his environment.

This idea leads, when consistently followed, to the further conclusion that there were between our prehuman ancestors and homo sapiens various intermediate stages. There were beings which, although not yet equipped with the human faculty of reason, were endowed with some rudimentary elements of ratiocination. Theirs was not yet a logical mind, but a prelogical (or rather imperfectly logical) mind. Their desultory and defective logical functions evolved step by step from the prelogical state toward the logical state. Reason, intellect, and logic are historical phenomena. There is a history of logic as there is a history of technology. Nothing suggests that logic as we know it is the last and final stage of intellectual evolution. Human logic is a historical phase between prehuman nonlogic on the one

2. Hardly any philosopher had a more universal familiarity with various branches of contemporary knowledge than Bergson. Yet a casual remark in his last great book clearly proves that Bergson was completely ignorant of the fundamental theorem of the modern theory of value and exchange. Speaking of exchange he remarks "l'on ne peut le pratiquer sans s'être demandé si les deux objets échangés sont bien de même valeur, c'est-à-dire échangeables contre un même troisième." (*Les Deux Sources de la morale et de la religion* [Paris, 1932], p. 68.)

hand and superhuman logic on the other hand. Reason and mind, the human beings' most efficacious equipment in their struggle for survival, are embedded in the continuous flow of zoological events. They are neither eternal nor unchangeable. They are transitory.

Furthermore, there is no doubt that every human being repeats in his personal evolution not only the physiological metamorphosis from a simple cell into a highly complicated mammal organism but no less the spiritual metamorphosis from a purely vegetative and animal existence into a reasonable mind. This transformation is not completed in the prenatal life of the embryo, but only later when the newborn child step by step awakens to human consciousness. Thus every man in his early youth, starting from the depths of darkness, proceeds through various states of the mind's logical structure.

Then there is the case of the animals. We are fully aware of the unbridgeable gulf separating our reason from the reactive processes of their brains and nerves. But at the same time we divine that forces are desperately struggling in them toward the light of comprehension. They are like prisoners anxious to break out from the doom of eternal darkness and inescapable automatism. We feel with them because we ourselves are in a similar position: pressing in vain against the limitation of our intellectual apparatus, striving unavailingly after unattainable perfect cognition.

But the problem of the a priori is of a different character. It does not deal with the problem of how consciousness and reason have emerged. It refers to the essential and necessary character of the logical structure of the human mind.

The fundamental logical relations are not subject to proof or disproof. Every attempt to prove them must presuppose their validity. It is impossible to explain them to a being who would not possess them on his own account. Efforts to define them according to the rules of definition must fail. They are primary propositions antecedent to any nominal or real definition. They are ultimate unanalyzable categories. The human mind is utterly incapable of imagining logical categories at variance with them. No matter how they may appear to superhuman beings, they are for man inescapable and absolutely necessary. They are the indispensable prerequisite of perception, apperception, and experience.

They are no less an indispensable prerequisite of memory. There is a tendency in the natural sciences to describe memory as an instance of a more general phenomenon. Every living organism conserves the effects of earlier stimulation, and the present state of inorganic matter is shaped by the effects of all the influences to which it was exposed in the past. The present state of the universe is the product of its past. We may, therefore, in a loose metaphorical sense, say that the geological structure of our globe conserves the memory of all earlier cosmic changes, and that a man's body is the sedimentation of his ancestors' and his own destinies and vicissitudes. But memory is something entirely different from the fact of the structural unity and continuity of cosmic evolution. It is a phenomenon of consciousness and as such conditioned by the logical a priori. Psychologists have been puzzled by the fact that man does not remember anything from the time of his existence as an embryo and as a suckling. Freud tried to explain this absence of recollection as brought about by suppression of undesired reminiscences. The truth is that there is nothing to be remembered of unconscious states. Animal automatism and unconscious response to physiological stimulations are neither for embryos and sucklings nor for adults material for remembrance. Only conscious states can be remembered.

The human mind is not a tabula rasa on which the external events write their own history. It is equipped with a set of tools for grasping reality. Man acquired these tools, i.e., the logical structure of his mind, in the course of his evolution from an amoeba to his present state. But these tools are logically prior to any experience.

Man is not only an animal totally subject to the stimuli unavoidably determining the circumstances of his life. He is also an acting being. And the category of action is logically antecedent to any concrete act.

The fact that man does not have the creative power to imagine categories at variance with the fundamental logical relations and with the principles of causality and teleology enjoins upon us what may be called *methodological apriorism.*

Everybody in his daily behavior again and again bears witness to the immutability and universality of the categories of thought and action. He who addresses fellow men, who wants to inform and convince them, who asks questions and answers other people's questions, can proceed in this way only because he can appeal to something common to all men—namely, the logical structure of human reason. The idea that *A* could at the same time be *non-A* or that to prefer *A* to *B* could at the same time be to prefer *B* to *A* is simply inconceivable and absurd to a human mind. We are not in the position to comprehend any kind of prelogical or metalogical thinking. We cannot think of a world without causality and teleology.

It does not matter for man whether or not beyond the sphere accessible to the human mind there are other spheres in which there is something categorially different from human thinking and acting. No knowledge from such spheres penetrates to the human mind. It is idle to ask whether things-in-themselves are different from what they appear to us, and whether there are worlds which we cannot divine and ideas which we cannot comprehend. These are problems beyond the scope of human cognition. Human knowledge is conditioned by the structure of the human mind. If it chooses human action as the subject matter of its inquiries, it cannot mean anything else than the categories of action which are proper to the human mind and are its projection into the external world of becoming and change. All the theorems of praxeology refer only to these categories of action and are valid only in the orbit of their operation. They do not pretend to convey any information about never dreamed of and unimaginable worlds and relations.

Thus praxeology is human in a double sense. It is human because it claims for its theorems, within the sphere precisely defined in the underlying assumptions, universal validity for all human action. It is human moreover because it deals only with human action and does not aspire to know anything about nonhuman—whether subhuman or superhuman—action.

The Alleged Logical Heterogeneity of Primitive Man

It is a general fallacy to believe that the writings of Lucien Lévy-Bruhl give support to the doctrine that the logical structure of mind of primitive man was and is categorially different from that of civilized man. On the contrary, what Lévy-Bruhl, on the basis of a careful scrutiny of the entire ethnological material available, reports about the mental functions of primitive man proves clearly that the fundamental logical relations and the categories of thought and action play in the intellectual activities of savages the same role they play in our own life. The content of primitive man's thoughts differs from the content of our thoughts, but the formal and logical structure is common to both.

It is true that Lévy-Bruhl himself maintains that the mentality of primitive peoples is essentially "mystic and prelogical" in character; primitive man's collective representations are regulated by the "law of participation" and are consequently indifferent to the law of contradiction. However, Lévy-Bruhl's distinction between prelogical and logical thinking refers to the content and not to the form and categorial structure of thinking. For he declares that also among peoples like ourselves ideas and relations between ideas governed by the "law of participation" exist, more or less independently, more or less impaired, but yet ineradicable, side by side, with those subject to the law of reasoning. "The prelogical and the mystic are co-existent with the logical."[3]

Lévy-Bruhl relegates the essential teachings of Christianity to the realm of the prelogical mind.[4] Now, many objections can possibly be raised and have been raised against the Christian doctrines and their interpretation by theology. But nobody ever ventured to contend that the Christian fathers and philosophers—among them St. Augustine and St. Thomas—had minds whose logical structure was categorially different from that of our contemporaries. The dispute between a man who believes in miracles and another who does not refers to the content of thought, not to its logical form. A man who tries to demonstrate the possibility and reality of miracles may err. But to unmask his error is—as the brilliant essays of Hume and Mill show—certainly no less logically intricate than to explode any philosophical or economic fallacy.

Explorers and missionaries report that in Africa and Polynesia primitive man stops short at his earliest perception of things and never reasons if he can in any way avoid it.[5] European and American educators sometimes report the same of their students. With regard to the Mossi on the Niger Lévy-Bruhl quotes a missionary's observation: "Conversation with them turns only upon women, food, and (in the rainy season) the crops."[6] What other subjects did many contemporaries and neighbors of Newton, Kant, and Lévy-Bruhl prefer?

The conclusion to be drawn from Lévy-Bruhl's studies is best expressed in his own words: "The primitive mind, like our own, is anxious to find the reasons for what happens, but it does not seek these in the same direction as we do."[7]

A peasant eager to get a rich crop may—according to the content of his ideas—choose various methods. He may perform some magical rites, he may embark upon a pilgrimage, he may offer a candle to the image of his patron saint, or he may employ more and better fertilizer. But whatever he does, it is always action, i.e., the employment of means for the attainment of ends. Magic is in a broader sense a variety of technology. Exorcism is a deliberate purposeful action based on a world view which most of our contemporaries condemn as superstitious and therefore as inappropriate. But the concept of action does not imply that the action is guided by a correct theory and a technology promising success and that it attains the end aimed at. It only implies that the performer of the action believes that the means applied will produce the desired effect.

3. Lévy-Bruhl, *How Natives Think*, trans. by L. A. Clare (New York, 1932), p. 386.

4. *Ibid.*, p. 377.

5. Lévy-Bruhl, *Primitive Mentality*, trans. by L. A. Clare (New York, 1923), pp. 27–29.

6. *Ibid.*, p. 27.

7. *Ibid.*, p. 437.

No facts provided by ethnology or history contradict the assertion that the logical structure of mind is uniform with all men of all races, ages, and countries.[8]

3. The A Priori and Reality

Aprioristic reasoning is purely conceptual and deductive. It cannot produce anything else but tautologies and analytic judgments. All its implications are logically derived from the premises and were already contained in them. Hence, according to a popular objection, it cannot add anything to our knowledge.

All geometrical theorems are already implied in the axioms. The concept of a rectangular triangle already implies the theorem of Pythagoras. This theorem is a tautology, its deduction results in an analytic judgment. Nonetheless nobody would contend that geometry in general and the theorem of Pythagoras in particular do not enlarge our knowledge. Cognition from purely deductive reasoning is also creative and opens for our mind access to previously barred spheres. The significant task of aprioristic reasoning is on the one hand to bring into relief all that is implied in the categories, concepts, and premises and, on the other hand, to show what they do not imply. It is its vocation to render manifest and obvious what was hidden and unknown before.[9]

In the concept of money all the theorems of monetary theory are already implied. The quantity theory does not add to our knowledge anything which is not virtually contained in the concept of money. It transforms, develops, and unfolds; it only analyzes and is therefore tautological like the theorem of Pythagoras in relation to the concept of the rectangular triangle. However, nobody would deny the cognitive value of the quantity theory. To a mind not enlightened by economic reasoning it remains unknown. A long line of abortive attempts to solve the problems concerned shows that it was certainly not easy to attain the present state of knowledge.

It is not a deficiency of the system of aprioristic science that it does not convey to us full cognition of reality. Its concepts and theorems are mental tools opening the approach to a complete grasp of reality; they are, to be sure, not in themselves already the totality of factual knowledge about all things. Theory and the comprehension

8. Cf. the brilliant statements of Ernst Cassirer, *Philosophie der symbolischen Formen* (Berlin, 1925), II, 78.

9. Science, says Meyerson, is "l'acte per lequel nous ramenons à l'identique ce qui nous a, tout d'abord, paru n'être pas tel." (*De l'Explication dans les sciences* [Paris, 1927], p. 154). Cf. also Morris R. Cohen, *A Preface to Logic* (New York, 1944), pp. 11–14.

of living and changing reality are not in opposition to one another. Without theory, the general aprioristic science of human action, there is no comprehension of the reality of human action.

The relation between reason and experience has long been one of the fundamental philosophical problems. Like all other problems of the critique of knowledge, philosophers have approached it only with reference to the natural sciences. They have ignored the sciences of human action. Their contributions have been useless for praxeology.

It is customary in the treatment of the epistemological problems of economics to adopt one of the solutions suggested for the natural sciences. Some authors recommend Poincaré's conventionalism.[10] They regard the premises of economic reasoning as a matter of linguistic or postulational convention.[11] Others prefer to acquiesce in ideas advanced by Einstein. Einstein raises the question: "How can mathematics, a product of human reason that does not depend on any experience, so exquisitely fit the objects of reality? Is human reason able to discover, unaided by experience through pure reasoning the features of real things?" And his answer is: "As far as the theorems of mathematics refer to reality, they are not certain, and as far as they are certain, they do not refer to reality."[12]

However, the sciences of human action differ radically from the natural sciences. All authors eager to construct an epistemological system of the sciences of human action according to the pattern of the natural sciences err lamentably.

The real thing which is the subject matter of praxeology, human action, stems from the same source as human reasoning. Action and reason are congeneric and homogeneous; they may even be called two different aspects of the same thing. That reason has the power to make clear through pure ratiocination the essential features of action is a consequence of the fact that action is an offshoot of reason. The theorems attained by correct praxeological reasoning are not only perfectly certain and incontestable, like the correct mathematical theorems. They refer, moreover, with the full rigidity of their apodictic certainty and incontestability to the reality of action as it appears in life and history. Praxeology conveys exact and precise knowledge of real things.

The starting point of praxeology is not a choice of axioms and a decision about methods of procedure, but reflection about the essence of action. There is no action in which the praxeological categories

10. Henri Poincaré, *La Science et l'hypothèse* (Paris, 1918), p. 69.

11. Felix Kaufmann, *Methodology of the Social Sciences* (London, 1944), pp. 46–47.

12. Albert Einstein, *Geometrie und Erfahrung* (Berlin, 1923), p. 3.

do not appear fully and perfectly. There is no mode of action thinkable in which means and ends or costs and proceeds cannot be clearly distinguished and precisely separated. There is nothing which only approximately or incompletely fits the economic category of an exchange. There are only exchange and nonexchange; and with regard to any exchange all the general theorems concerning exchanges are valid in their full rigidity and with all their implications. There are no transitions from exchange to nonexchange or from direct exchange to indirect exchange. No experience can ever be had which would contradict these statements.

Such an experience would be impossible in the first place for the reason that all experience concerning human action is conditioned by the praxeological categories and becomes possible only through their application. If we had not in our mind the schemes provided by praxeological reasoning, we should never be in a position to discern and to grasp any action. We would perceive motions, but neither buying nor selling, nor prices, wage rates, interest rates, and so on. It is only through the utilization of the praxeological scheme that we become able to have an experience concerning an act of buying and selling, but then independently of the fact of whether or not our senses concomitantly perceive any motions of men and of nonhuman elements of the external world. Unaided by praxeological knowledge we would never learn anything about media of exchange. If we approach coins without such preexisting knowledge, we would see in them only round plates of metal, nothing more. Experience concerning money requires familiarity with the praxeological category *medium of exchange.*

Experience concerning human action differs from that concerning natural phenomena in that it requires and presupposes praxeological knowledge. This is why the methods of the natural sciences are inappropriate for the study of praxeology, economics, and history.

In asserting the a priori character of praxeology we are not drafting a plan for a future new science different from the traditional sciences of human action. We do not maintain that the theoretical science of human action should be aprioristic, but that it is and always has been so. Every attempt to reflect upon the problems raised by human action is necessarily bound to aprioristic reasoning. It does not make any difference in this regard whether the men discussing a problem are theorists aiming at pure knowledge only or statesmen, politicians, and regular citizens eager to comprehend occurring changes and to discover what kind of public policy or private conduct would best suit their own interests. People may begin arguing about the significance of any concrete experience, but the debate inevitably turns away from the accidental and environmental features of the event concerned to an analysis of fundamental principles, and imperceptibly abandons any reference to the factual happenings which evoked the argument. The history of the natural sciences is a record of theories and hypotheses discarded because they were disproved by experience. Remember for instance the fallacies of older mechanics disproved by Galileo or the fate of the phlogiston theory. No such case is recorded by the history of economics. The champions of logically incompatible theories claim the same events as the proof that their point of view has been tested by experience. The truth is that the experience of a complex phenomenon—and there is no other experience in the realm of human action—can always be interpreted on the ground of various antithetic theories. Whether the interpretation is considered satisfactory or unsatisfactory depends on the appreciation of the theories in question established beforehand on the ground of aprioristic reasoning.[13]

History cannot teach us any general rule, principle, or law. There is no means to abstract from a historical experience a posteriori any theories or theorems concerning human conduct and policies. The data of history would be nothing but a clumsy accumulation of disconnected occurrences, a heap of confusion, if they could not be clarified, arranged, and interpreted by systematic praxeological knowledge.

4. The Principle of Methodological Individualism

Praxeology deals with the actions of individual men. It is only in the further course of its inquiries that cognition of human cooperation is attained and social action is treated as a special case of the more universal category of human action as such.

This methodological individualism has been vehemently attacked by various metaphysical schools and disparaged as a nominalistic fallacy. The notion of an individual, say the critics, is an empty abstraction. Real man is necessarily always a member of a social whole. It is even impossible to imagine the existence of a man separated from the rest of mankind and not connected with society. Man as man is the product of a social evolution. His most eminent feature, reason, could only emerge within the framework of social mutuality. There is no thinking which does not depend on the concepts and notions of

13. Cf. E. P. Cheyney, *Law in History and Other Essays* (New York, 1927), p. 27.

language. But speech is manifestly a social phenomenon. Man is always the member of a collective. As the whole is both logically and temporally prior to its parts or members, the study of the individual is posterior to the study of society. The only adequate method for the scientific treatment of human problems is the method of universalism or collectivism.

Now the controversy whether the whole or its parts are logically prior is vain. Logically the notions of a whole and its parts are correlative. As logical concepts they are both apart from time.

No less inappropriate with regard to our problem is the reference to the antagonism of realism and nominalism, both these terms being understood in the meaning which medieval scholasticism attached to them. It is uncontested that in the sphere of human action social entities have real existence. Nobody ventures to deny that nations, states, municipalities, parties, religious communities, are real factors determining the course of human events. Methodological individualism, far from contesting the significance of such collective wholes, considers it as one of its main tasks to describe and to analyze their becoming and their disappearing, their changing structures, and their operation. And it chooses the only method fitted to solve this problem satisfactorily.

First we must realize that all actions are performed by individuals. A collective operates always through the intermediary of one or several individuals whose actions are related to the collective as the secondary source. It is the meaning which the acting individuals and all those who are touched by their action attribute to an action, that determines its character. It is the meaning that marks one action as the action of an individual and another action as the action of the state or of the municipality. The hangman, not the state, executes a criminal. It is the meaning of those concerned that discerns in the hangman's action an action of the state. A group of armed men occupies a place. It is the meaning of those concerned which imputes this occupation not to the officers and soldiers on the spot, but to their nation. If we scrutinize the meaning of the various actions performed by individuals we must necessarily learn everything about the actions of collective wholes. For a social collective has no existence and reality outside of the individual members' actions. The life of a collective is lived in the actions of the individuals constituting its body. There is no social collective conceivable which is not operative in the actions of some individuals. The reality of a social integer consists in its directing and releasing definite actions on the part of individuals. Thus the way to a cognition of collective wholes is through an analysis of the individuals' actions.

As a thinking and acting being man emerges from his prehuman existence already as a social being. The evolution of reason, language, and cooperation is the outcome of the same process; they were inseparably and necessarily linked together. But this process took place in individuals. It consisted in changes in the behavior of individuals. There is no other substance in which it occurred than the individuals. There is no substratum of society other than the actions of individuals.

That there are nations, states, and churches, that there is social cooperation under the division of labor, becomes discernible only in the actions of certain individuals. Nobody ever perceived a nation without perceiving its members. In this sense one may say that a social collective comes into being through the actions of individuals. That does not mean that the individual is temporally antecedent. It merely means that definite actions of individuals constitute the collective.

There is no need to argue whether a collective is the sum resulting from the addition of its elements or more, whether it is a being sui generis, and whether it is reasonable or not to speak of its will, plans, aims, and actions and to attribute to it a distinct "soul." Such pedantic talk is idle. A collective whole is a particular aspect of the actions of various individuals and as such a real thing determining the course of events.

It is illusory to believe that it is possible to visualize collective wholes. They are never visible; their cognition is always the outcome of the understanding of the meaning which acting men attribute to their acts. We can see a crowd, i.e., a multitude of people. Whether this crowd is a mere gathering or a mass (in the sense in which this term is used in contemporary psychology) or an organized body or any other kind of social entity is a question which can only be answered by understanding the meaning which they themselves attach to their presence. And this meaning is always the meaning of individuals. Not our senses, but understanding, a mental process, makes us recognize social entities.

Those who want to start the study of human action from the collective units encounter an insurmountable obstacle in the fact that an individual at the same time can belong and—with the exception of the most primitive tribesmen—really belongs to various collective entities. The problems raised by the multiplicity of coexisting social units and their mutual antagonisms can be solved only by methodological individualism.[14]

14. See below, pp. 145–153, the critique of the collectivist theory of society.

I and We

The *Ego* is the unity of the acting being. It is unquestionably given and cannot be dissolved or conjured away by any reasoning or quibbling.

The *We* is always the result of a summing up which puts together two or more *Egos.* If somebody says *I,* no further questioning is necessary in order to establish the meaning. The same is valid with regard to the *Thou* and, provided the person in view is precisely indicated, with regard to the *He.* But if a man says *We,* further information is needed to denote who the Egos are who are comprised in this *We.* It is always single individuals who say *We;* even if they say it in chorus, it yet remains an utterance of single individuals.

The *We* cannot act otherwise than each of them acting on his own behalf. They can either all act together in accord, or one of them may act for them all. In the latter case the cooperation of the others consists in their bringing about the situation which makes one man's action effective for them too. Only in this sense does the officer of a social entity act for the whole; the individual members of the collective body either cause or allow a single man's action to concern them too.

The endeavors of psychology to dissolve the *Ego* and to unmask it as an illusion are idle. The praxeological *Ego* is beyond any doubts. No matter what a man was and what he may become later, in the very act of choosing and acting he is an *Ego.*

From the pluralis logicus (and from the merely ceremonial pluralis majestaticus) we must distinguish the pluralis gloriosus. If a Canadian who never tried skating says, "We are the world's foremost ice hockey players," or if an Italian boor proudly contends, "We are the world's most eminent painters," nobody is fooled. But with reference to political and economic problems the pluralis gloriosus evolves into the pluralis imperialis and as such plays a significant role in paving the way for the acceptance of doctrines determining international economic policies.

5. The Principle of Methodological Singularism

No less than from the action of an individual praxeology begins its investigations from the individual action. It does not deal in vague terms with human action in general, but with concrete action which a definite man has performed at a definite date and at a definite place. But, of course, it does not concern itself with the accidental and environmental features of this action and with what distinguishes it from all other actions, but only with what is necessary and universal in its performance.

The philosophy of universalism has from time immemorial blocked access to a satisfactory grasp of praxeological problems, and contemporary universalists are utterly incapable of finding an approach to them. Universalism, collectivism, and conceptual realism see only wholes and universals. They speculate about mankind, nations, states, classes, about virtue and vice, right and wrong, about entire classes of wants and of commodities. They ask, for instance: Why is the value of "gold" higher than that of "iron"? Thus they never find solutions, but antinomies and paradoxes only. The best-known instance is the value-paradox which frustrated even the work of the classical economists.

Praxeology asks: What happens in acting? What does it mean to say that an individual then and there, today and here, at any time and at any place, acts? What results if he chooses one thing and rejects another?

The act of choosing is always a decision among various opportunities open to the choosing individual. Man never chooses between virtue and vice, but only between two modes of action which we call from an adopted point of view virtuous or vicious. A man never chooses between "gold" and "iron" in general, but always only between a definite quantity of gold and a definite quantity of iron. Every single action is strictly limited in its immediate consequences. If we want to reach correct conclusions, we must first of all look at these limitations.

Human life is an unceasing sequence of single actions. But the single action is by no means isolated. It is a link in a chain of actions which together form an action on a higher level aiming at a more distant end. Every action has two aspects. It is on the one hand a partial action in the framework of a further-stretching action, the performance of a fraction of the aims set by a more far-reaching action. It is on the other hand itself a whole with regard to the actions aimed at by the performance of its own parts.

It depends upon the scope of the project on which acting man is intent at the instant whether the more far-reaching action or a partial action directed to a more immediate end only is thrown into relief. There is no need for praxeology to raise questions of the type of those raised by *Gestaltpsychologie*. The road to the performance of great things must always lead through the performance of partial tasks. A cathedral is something other than a heap of stones joined together. But the only procedure for constructing a cathedral is to lay one stone upon another. For the architect the whole project is the main thing. For the mason it is the single wall, and for the bricklayer the single stones. What counts for praxeology is the fact that the only method to achieve greater tasks is to build from the foundations step by step, part by part.

6. The Individual and Changing Features of Human Action

The content of human action, i.e., the ends aimed at and the means chosen and applied for the attainment of these ends, is determined by the personal qualities of every acting man. Individual man is the product of a long line of zoological evolution which has shaped his physiological inheritance. He is born the offspring and the heir of his ancestors, and the precipitate and sediment of all that his forefathers experienced are his biological patrimony. When he is born, he does not enter the world in general as such, but a definite environment. The innate and inherited biological qualities and all that life has worked upon him make a man what he is at any instant of his pilgrimage. They are his fate and destiny. His will is not "free" in the metaphysical sense of this term. It is determined by his background and all the influences to which he himself and his ancestors were exposed.

Inheritance and environment direct a man's actions. They suggest to him both the ends and the means. He lives not simply as man *in abstracto;* he lives as a son of his family, his race, his people, and his age; as a citizen of his country; as a member of a definite social group; as a practitioner of a certain vocation; as a follower of definite religious, metaphysical, philosophical, and political ideas; as a partisan in many feuds and controversies. He does not himself create his ideas and standards of value; he borrows them from other people. His ideology is what his environment enjoins upon him. Only very few men have the gift of thinking new and original ideas and of changing the traditional body of creeds and doctrines.

Common man does not speculate about the great problems. With regard to them he relies upon other people's authority, he behaves as "every decent fellow must behave," he is like a sheep in the herd. It is precisely this intellectual inertia that characterizes a man as a common man. Yet the common man does choose. He chooses to adopt traditional patterns or patterns adopted by other people because he is convinced that this procedure is best fitted to achieve his own welfare. And he is ready to change his ideology and consequently his mode of action whenever he becomes convinced that this would better serve his own interests.

Most of a man's daily behavior is simple routine. He performs certain acts without paying special attention to them. He does many things because he was trained in his childhood to do them, because other people behave in the same way, and because it is customary in his environment. He acquires habits, he develops automatic reactions. But he indulges in these habits only because he welcomes their effects. As soon as he discovers that the pursuit of the habitual way may hinder the attainment of ends considered as more desirable, he changes his attitude. A man brought up in an area in which the water is clean acquires the habit of heedlessly drinking, washing, and bathing. When he moves to a place in which the water is polluted by morbific germs, he will devote the most careful attention to procedures about which he never bothered before. He will watch himself permanently in order not to hurt himself by indulging unthinkingly in his traditional routine and his automatic reactions. The fact that an action is in the regular course of affairs performed spontaneously, as it were, does not mean that it is not due to a conscious volition and to a deliberate choice. Indulgence in a routine which possibly could be changed is action.

Praxeology is not concerned with the changing content of acting, but with its pure form and its categorial structure. The study of the accidental and environmental features of human action is the task of history.

7. The Scope and the Specific Method of History

The study of all the data of experience concerning human action is the scope of history. The historian collects and critically sifts all available documents. On the ground of this evidence he approaches his genuine task.

It has been asserted that the task of history is to show how events actually happened, without imposing presuppositions and values (*wertfrei,* i.e., neutral with regard to all value judgments). The historian's report should be a faithful image of the past, an intellectual photograph, as it were, giving a complete and unbiased description of all facts. It should reproduce before our intellectual eye the past with all its features.

Now, a real reproduction of the past would require a duplication not humanly possible. History is not an intellectual reproduction, but a condensed representation of the past in conceptual terms. The historian does not simply let the events speak for themselves. He arranges them from the aspect of the ideas underlying the formation of the general notions he uses in their presentation. He does not report facts as they happened, but only *relevant* facts. He does not approach the documents without presuppositions, but equipped with the whole apparatus of his age's scientific knowledge, that is, with all the teachings of contemporary logic, mathematics, praxeology, and natural science.

It is obvious that the historian must not be biased by any prejudices and party tenets. Those writers who consider historical events as an arsenal of weapons for the conduct of their party feuds are not historians but propagandists and apologists. They are not eager to acquire knowledge but to justify the program of their parties. They are fighting for the dogmas of a metaphysical, religious, national, political or social doctrine. They usurp the name of history for their writings as a blind in order to deceive the credulous. A historian must first of all aim at cognition. He must free himself from any partiality. He must in this sense be neutral with regard to any value judgments.

This postulate of *Wertfreiheit* can easily be satisfied in the field of the aprioristic science—logic, mathematics, and praxeology—and in the field of the experimental natural sciences. It is logically not difficult to draw a sharp line between a scientific, unbiased treatment of these disciplines and a treatment distorted by superstition, preconceived ideas, and passion. It is much more difficult to comply with the requirement of valuational neutrality in history. For the subject matter of history, the concrete accidental and environmental content of human action, is value judgments and their projection into the reality of change. At every step of his activities the historian is concerned with value judgments. The value judgments of the men whose actions he reports are the substratum of his investigations.

It has been asserted that the historian himself cannot avoid judgments of value. No historian—not even the naïve chronicler or newspaper reporter—registers all facts as they happen. He must discriminate, he must select some events which he deems worthy of being registered and pass over in silence other events. This choice, it is said, implies in itself a value judgment. It is necessarily conditioned by the historian's world view and thus not impartial but an outcome of preconceived ideas. History can never be anything else than distortion of facts; it can never be really scientific, that is neutral with regard to values and intent only upon discovering truth.

There is, of course, no doubt that the discretion which the selection of facts places in the hands of the historian can be abused. It can and does happen that the historian's choice is guided by party bias. However, the problems involved are much more intricate than this popular doctrine would have us believe. Their solution must be sought on the ground of a much more thorough scrutiny of the methods of history.

In dealing with a historical problem the historian makes use of all the knowledge provided by logic, mathematics, the natural sciences, and especially by praxeology. However, the mental tools of these nonhistorical disciplines do not suffice for his task. They are indispensable auxiliaries for him, but in themselves they do not make it possible to answer those questions he has to deal with.

The course of history is determined by the actions of individuals and by the effects of these actions. The actions are determined by the value judgments of the acting individuals, i.e., the ends which they were eager to attain, and by the means which they applied for the attainment of these ends. The choice of the means is an outcome of the whole body of technological knowledge of the acting individuals. It is in many instances possible to appreciate the effects of the means applied from the point of view of praxeology or of the natural sciences. But there remain a great many things for the elucidation of which no such help is available.

The specific task of history for which it uses a specific method is the study of these value judgments and of the effects of the actions as far as they cannot be analyzed by the teachings of all other branches of knowledge. The historian's genuine problem is always to interpret things as they happened. But he cannot solve this problem on the ground of the theorems provided by all other sciences alone. There always remains at the bottom of each of his problems something which resists analysis at the hand of these teachings of other sciences. It is these individual and unique characteristics of each event which are studied by the *understanding*.

The uniqueness or individuality which remains at the bottom of every historical fact, when all the means for its interpretation provided by logic, mathematics, praxeology, and the natural sciences have been exhausted, is an ultimate datum. But whereas the natural sciences cannot say anything about their ultimate data than that they are such, history can try to make its ultimate data intelligible. Although it is impossible to reduce them to their causes—they would not be ultimate data if such a reduction were possible—the historian can understand them because he is himself a human being. In the philosophy of Bergson this understanding is called an intuition, viz., "la sympathie par laquelle on se transporte a l'intérieur d'un objet pour coïncider avec ce qu'il a d'unique et par conséquent d'inexprimable."[15] German epistemology calls this act *das spezifische Verstehen der*

15. Henri Bergson, *La Pensée et le mouvant* (4th ed. Paris, 1934), p. 205.

Geisteswissenschaften or simply *Verstehen.* It is the method which all historians and all other people always apply in commenting upon human events of the past and in forecasting future events. The discovery and the delimitation of understanding was one of the most important contributions of modern epistemology. It is, to be sure, neither a project for a new science which does not yet exist and is to be founded nor the recommendation of a new method of procedure for any of the already existing sciences.

The understanding must not be confused with approval, be it only conditional and circumstantial. The historian, the ethnologist, and the psychologist sometimes register actions which are for their feelings simply repulsive and disgusting; they understand them only as actions, i.e., in establishing the underlying aims and the technological and praxeological methods applied for their execution. To understand an individual case does not mean to justify or to excuse it.

Neither must understanding be confused with the act of aesthetic enjoyment of a phenomenon. Empathy (*Einfühlung*) and understanding are two radically different attitudes. It is a different thing, on the one hand, to understand a work of art historically, to determine its place, its meaning, and its importance in the flux of events, and, on the other hand, to appreciate it emotionally as a work of art. One can look at a cathedral with the eyes of a historian. But one can look at the same cathedral either as an enthusiastic admirer or as an unaffected and indifferent sightseer. The same individuals are capable of both modes of reaction, of the aesthetic appreciation and of the scientific grasp of understanding.

The understanding establishes the fact that an individual or a group of individuals have engaged in a definite action emanating from definite value judgments and choices and aiming at definite ends, and that they have applied for the attainment of these ends definite means suggested by definite technological, therapeutical, and praxeological doctrines. It furthermore tries to appreciate the effects and the intensity of the effects brought about by an action; it tries to assign to every action its relevance, i.e., its bearing upon the course of events.

The scope of understanding is the mental grasp of phenomena which cannot be totally elucidated by logic, mathematics, praxeology, and the natural sciences to the extent that they cannot be cleared up by all these sciences. It must never contradict the teachings of these other branches of knowledge.[16] The real corporeal existence of the

16. Cf. Ch. V. Langlois and Ch. Seignobos, *Introduction to the Study of History,* trans. by G. G. Berry (London, 1925), pp. 205–208.

devil is attested by innumerable historical documents which are rather reliable in all other regards. Many tribunals in due process of law have on the basis of the testimony of witnesses and the confessions of defendants established the fact that the devil had carnal intercourse with witches. However, no appeal to understanding could justify a historian's attempt to maintain that the devil really existed and interfered with human events otherwise than in the visions of an excited human brain.

While this is generally admitted with regard to the natural sciences, there are some historians who adopt another attitude with regard to economic theory. They try to oppose to the theorems of economics an appeal to documents allegedly proving things incompatible with these theorems. They do not realize that complex phenomena can neither prove nor disprove any theorem and therefore cannot bear witness against any statement of a theory. Economic history is possible only because there is an economic theory capable of throwing light upon economic actions. If there were no economic theory, reports concerning economic facts would be nothing more than a collection of unconnected data open to any arbitrary interpretation.

8. Conception and Understanding

The task of the sciences of human action is the comprehension of the meaning and relevance of human action. They apply for this purpose two different epistemological procedures: conception and understanding. Conception is the mental tool of praxeology; understanding is the specific mental tool of history.

The cognition of praxeology is conceptual cognition. It refers to what is necessary in human action. It is cognition of universals and categories.

The cognition of history refers to what is unique and individual in each event or class of events. It analyzes first each object of its studies with the aid of the mental tools provided by all other sciences. Having achieved this preliminary work, it faces its own specific problem: the elucidation of the unique and individual features of the case by means of the understanding.

As was mentioned above, it has been asserted that history can never be scientific because historical understanding depends on the historian's subjective value judgments. Understanding, it is maintained, is only a euphemistic term for arbitrariness. The writings of historians are always one-sided and partial; they do not report the facts; they distort them.

It is, of course, a fact that we have historical books written from various points of view. There are histories of the Reformation written from the Catholic point of view and others written from the Protestant point of view. There are "proletarian" histories and "bourgeois" histories, Tory historians and Whig historians; every nation, party, and linguistic group has its own historians and its own ideas about history.

But the problem which these differences of interpretation offer must not be confused with the intentional distortion of facts by propagandists and apologists parading as historians. Those facts which can be established in an unquestionable way on the ground of the source material available must be established as the preliminary work of the historian. This is not a field for understanding. It is a task to be accomplished by the employment of the tools provided by all nonhistorical sciences. The phenomena are gathered by cautious critical observation of the records available. As far as the theories of the nonhistorical sciences on which the historian grounds his critical examination of the sources are reasonably reliable and certain, there cannot be any arbitrary disagreement with regard to the establishment of the phenomena as such. What a historian asserts is either correct or contrary to fact, is either proved or disproved by the documents available, or vague because the sources do not provide us with sufficient information. The experts may disagree, but only on the ground of a reasonable interpretation of the evidence available. The discussion does not allow any arbitrary statements.

However, the historians very often do not agree with regard to the teachings of the nonhistorical sciences. Then, of course, disagreement with regard to the critical examination of the records and to the conclusions to be drawn from them can ensue. An unbridgeable conflict arises. But its cause is not an arbitrariness with regard to the concrete historical phenomenon. It stems from an undecided issue referring to the nonhistorical sciences.

An ancient Chinese historian could report that the emperor's sin brought about a catastrophic drought and that rain fell again when the ruler had atoned for his sin. No modern historian would accept such a report. The underlying meteorological doctrine is contrary to uncontested fundamentals of contemporary natural science. But no such unanimity exists in regard to many theological, biological, and economic issues. Accordingly historians disagree.

A supporter of the racial doctrine of Nordic-Aryanism will disregard as fabulous and simply unbelievable any report concerning intellectual and moral achievements of "inferior" races. He will treat such reports in the same way in which all modern historians deal with the above-mentioned Chinese report. No agreement with regard to any phenomenon of the history of Christianity can be attained between people for whom the gospels are Holy Writ and people in whose eyes they are human documents. Catholic and Protestant historians disagree about many questions of fact because they start from different theological ideas. A Mercantilist or Neo-Mercantilist must necessarily be at variance with an economist. An account of German monetary history in the years 1914 to 1923 is conditioned by the author's monetary doctrines. The facts of the French Revolution are presented in a quite different manner by those who believe in the sacred rights of the anointed king and those who hold other views.

The historians disagree on such issues not in their capacity as historians, but in their application of the nonhistorical sciences to the subject matter of history. They disagree as agnostic doctors disagree in regard to the miracles of Lourdes with the members of the medical committee for the collection of evidence concerning these miracles. Only those who believe that facts write their own story into the tabula rasa of the human mind blame the historians for such differences of opinion. They fail to realize that history can never be studied without presuppositions, and that dissension with regard to the presuppositions, i.e., the whole content of the nonhistorical branches of knowledge, must determine the establishment of historical facts.

These presuppositions also determine the historian's decision concerning the choice of facts to be mentioned and those to be omitted as irrelevant. In searching for the causes of a cow's not giving milk a modern veterinarian will disregard entirely all reports concerning a witch's evil eye; his view would have been different three hundred years ago. In the same way the historian selects from the indefinite multitude of events that preceded the fact he is dealing with those which could have contributed to its emergence—or have delayed it—and neglects those which, according to his grasp of the nonhistorical sciences, could not have influenced it.

Changes in the teachings of the nonhistorical sciences consequently must involve a rewriting of history. Every generation must treat anew the same historical problems because they appear to it in a different light. The theological world view of older times led to a treatment of history other than the theorems of modern natural science. Subjective economics produces historical works very different from those based on mercantilist doctrines. As far as divergences in the books of historians stem from these disagreements, they are not an outcome of alleged vagueness and precariousness in historical studies. They are, on the contrary, the result of the lack of unanimity in the realm of those other sciences which are popularly called certain and exact.

To avoid any possible misunderstanding it is expedient to emphasize some further points. The divergences referred to above must not be confused:

1. With purposeful ill-intentioned distortion of facts.

2. With attempts to justify or to condemn any actions from a legal or moral point of view.

3. With the merely incidental insertion of remarks expressing value judgments in a strictly objective representation of the state of affairs. A treatise on bacteriology does not lose its objectivity if the author, accepting the human viewpoint, considers the preservation of human life as an ultimate end and, applying this standard, labels effective methods of fighting germs good and fruitless methods bad. A germ writing such a book would reverse these judgments, but the material content of its book would not differ from that of the human bacteriologist. In the same way a European historian dealing with the Mongol invasions of the thirteenth century may speak of "favorable" and "unfavorable" events because he takes the standpoint of the European defenders of Western civilization. But this approval of one party's standard of value need not necessarily interfere with the material content of his study. It may—from the viewpoint of contemporary knowledge—be absolutely objective. A Mongolian historian could endorse it completely but for such casual remarks.

4. With a representation of one party's action in diplomatic or military antagonisms. The clash of conflicting groups can be dealt with from the point of view of the ideas, motives, and aims which impelled either side's acts. For a full comprehension of what happened it is necessary to take account of what was done on both sides. The outcome was the result of the interaction of both parties. But in order to understand their actions the historian must try to see things as they appeared to the acting men at the critical time, not only as we see them now from the point of view of our present-day knowledge. A history of Lincoln's policy in the weeks and months preceding the outbreak of the Civil War is of course incomplete. But no historical study is complete. Regardless of whether the historian sympathizes with the Unionists or with the Confederates or whether he is

absolutely neutral, he can deal in an objective way with Lincoln's policy in the spring of 1861. Such an investigation is an indispensable preliminary to answering the broader question of how the Civil War broke out.

Now finally, having settled these problems, it is possible to attack the genuine question: Is there any subjective element in historical understanding, and, if so, in what manner does it determine the result of historical studies?

As far as the task of understanding is to establish the facts that people were motivated by definite value judgments and aimed at definite means, there cannot be any disagreement among true historians, i.e., people intent upon cognition of past events. There may be uncertainty because of the insufficient information provided by the sources available. But this has nothing to do with understanding. It refers to the preliminary work to be achieved by the historian.

But understanding has a second task to fulfill. It must appraise the effects and the intensity of the effects brought about by an action; it must deal with the relevance of each motive and each action.

Here we are faced with one of the main differences between physics and chemistry on the one hand and the sciences of human action on the other. In the realm of physical and chemical events there exist (or, at least, it is generally assumed that there exist) constant relations between magnitudes, and man is capable of discovering these constants with a reasonable degree of precision by means of laboratory experiments. No such constant relations exist in the field of human action outside of physical and chemical technology and therapeutics. For some time economists believed that they had discovered such a constant relation in the effects of changes in the quantity of money upon commodity prices. It was asserted that a rise or fall in the quantity of money in circulation must result in proportional changes of commodity prices. Modern economics has clearly and irrefutably exposed the fallaciousness of this statement.[17] Those economists who want to substitute "quantitative economics" for what they call "qualitative economics" are utterly mistaken. There are, in the field of economics, no constant relations, and consequently no measurement is possible. If a statistician determines that a rise of 10 per cent in the supply of potatoes in Atlantis at a definite time was followed by a fall of 8 per cent in the price, he does not establish anything about what happened or may happen with a change in the supply of potatoes in another country or at another time. He has not "measured"

17. See below, pp. 412–414.

the "elasticity of demand" of potatoes. He has established a unique and individual historical fact. No intelligent man can doubt that the behavior of men with regard to potatoes and every other commodity is variable. Different individuals value the same things in a different way, and valuations change with the same individuals with changing conditions.[18]

Outside of the field of economic history nobody ever ventured to maintain that constant relations prevail in human history. It is a fact that in the armed conflicts fought in the past between Europeans and backward peoples of other races, one European soldier was usually a match for several native fighters. But nobody was ever foolish enough to "measure" the magnitude of European superiority.

The impracticability of measurement is not due to the lack of technical methods for the establishment of measure. It is due to the absence of constant relations. If it were only caused by technical insufficiency, at least an approximate estimation would be possible in some cases. But the main fact is that there are no constant relations. Economics is not, as ignorant positivists repeat again and again, backward because it is not "quantitative." It is not quantitative and does not measure because there are no constants. Statistical figures referring to economic events are historical data. They tell us what happened in a nonrepeatable historical case. Physical events can be interpreted on the ground of our knowledge concerning constant relations established by experiments. Historical events are not open to such an interpretation.

The historian can enumerate all the factors which cooperated in bringing about a known effect and all the factors which worked against them and may have resulted in delaying and mitigating the final outcome. But he cannot coordinate, except by understanding, the various causative factors in a quantitative way to the effects produced. He cannot, except by understanding, assign to each of n factors its role in producing the effect P. Understanding is in the realm of history the equivalent, as it were, of quantitative analysis and measurement.

Technology can tell us how thick a steel plate must be in order not to be pierced by a bullet fired at a distance of 300 yards from a Winchester rifle. It can thus answer the question why a man who took shelter behind a steel plate of a known thickness was hurt or not hurt by a shot fired. History is at a loss to explain with the same assurance why there was a rise in the price of milk of 10 per cent or

18. Cf. below, p. 351.

why President Roosevelt defeated Governor Dewey in the election of 1944 or why France was from 1870 to 1940 under a republican constitution. Such problems do not allow any treatment other than that of understanding.

To every historical factor understanding tries to assign its relevance. In the exercise of understanding there is no room for arbitrariness and capriciousness. The freedom of the historian is limited by his endeavor to provide a satisfactory explanation of reality. His guiding star must be the search for truth. But there necessarily enters into understanding an element of subjectivity. The understanding of the historian is always tinged with the marks of his personality. It reflects the mind of its author.

The a priori sciences—logic, mathematics, and praxeology—aim at a knowledge unconditionally valid for all beings endowed with the logical structure of the human mind. The natural sciences aim at a cognition valid for all those beings which are not only endowed with the faculty of human reason but with human senses. The uniformity of human logic and sensation bestows upon these branches of knowledge the character of universal validity. Such at least is the principle guiding the study of the physicists. Only in recent years have they begun to see the limits of their endeavors and, abandoning the excessive pretensions of older physicists, discovered the "uncertainty principle." They realize today that there are unobservables whose unobservability is a matter of epistemological principle.[19]

Historical understanding can never produce results which must be accepted by all men. Two historians who fully agree with regard to the teachings of the nonhistorical sciences and with regard to the establishment of the facts as far as they can be established without recourse to the understanding of relevance, may disagree in their understanding of the relevance of these facts. They may fully agree in establishing that the factors *a, b,* and *c* worked together in producing the effect *P*; nonetheless they can widely disagree with regard to the relevance of the respective contributions of *a, b,* and *c* to the final outcome. As far as understanding aims at assigning its relevance to each factor, it is open to the influence of subjective judgments. Of course, these are not judgments of value, they do not express preferences of the historian. They are judgments of relevance.[20]

19. Cf. A. Eddington, *The Philosophy of Physical Science* (New York, 1939), pp. 28–48.

20. As this is not a dissertation on general epistemology, but the indispensable foundation of a treatise of economics, there is no need to stress the analogies between the understanding of historical relevance and the tasks to be accomplished by a diagnosing physician. The epistemology of biology is outside of the scope of our inquiries.

Historians may disagree for various reasons. They may hold different views with regard to the teachings of the nonhistorical sciences; they may base their reasoning on a more or less complete familiarity with the records; they may differ in the understanding of the motives and aims of the acting men and of the means applied by them. All these differences are open to a settlement by "objective" reasoning; it is possible to reach a universal agreement with regard to them. But as far as historians disagree with regard to judgments of relevance it is impossible to find a solution which all sane men must accept.

The intellectual methods of science do not differ in kind from those applied by the common man in his daily mundane reasoning. The scientist uses the same tools which the layman uses; he merely uses them more skillfully and cautiously. Understanding is not a privilege of the historians. It is everybody's business. In observing the conditions of his environment everybody is a historian. Everybody uses understanding in dealing with the uncertainty of future events to which he must adjust his own actions. The distinctive reasoning of the speculator is an understanding of the relevance of the various factors determining future events. And—let us emphasize it even at this early point of our investigations—action necessarily always aims at future and therefore uncertain conditions and thus is always speculation. Acting man looks, as it were, with the eyes of a historian into the future.

Natural History and Human History

Cosmogony, geology, and the history of biological changes are historical disciplines as they deal with unique events of the past. However, they operate exclusively with the epistemological methods of the natural sciences and have no need for understanding. They must sometimes take recourse to only approximate estimates of magnitudes. But such estimates are not judgments of relevance. They are a less perfect method of determining quantitative relations than is "exact" measurement. They must not be confused with the state of affairs in the field of human action which is characterized by the absence of constant relations.

If we speak of history, what we have in mind is only the history of human action, whose specific mental tool is understanding.

The assertion that modern natural science owes all its achievements to the experimental method is sometimes assailed by referring to astronomy. Now, modern astronomy is essentially an application of the physical laws, experimentally discovered on the earth, to the celestial bodies. In earlier days astronomy was mainly based on the assumption that the movements of the celestial bodies would not change their course. Copernicus and Kepler simply tried to guess in what kind of curve the earth moves around the sun. As the circle was considered the "most perfect" curve, Copernicus chose it for his theory. Later, by similar guesswork, Kepler substituted the ellipse for the circle. Only since Newton's discoveries has astronomy become a natural science in the strict sense.

9. On Ideal Types

History deals with unique and unrepeatable events, with the irreversible flux of human affairs. A historical event cannot be described without reference to the persons involved and to the place and date of its occurrence. As far as a happening can be narrated without such a reference, it is not a historical event but a fact of the natural sciences. The report that Professor X on February 20, 1945, performed a certain experiment in his laboratory is an account of a historical event. The physicist believes that he is right in abstracting from the person of the experimenter and the date and place of the experiment. He relates only those circumstances which, in his opinion, are relevant for the production of the result achieved and, when repeated, will produce the same result again. He transforms the historical event into a *fact* of the empirical natural sciences. He disregards the active interference of the experimenter and tries to imagine him as an indifferent observer and relater of unadulterated reality. It is not the task of praxeology to deal with the epistemological issues of this philosophy.

Although unique and unrepeatable, historical events have one common feature: they are human action. History comprehends them as human actions; it conceives their meaning by the instrumentality of praxeological cognition and understands their meaning in looking at their individual and unique features. What counts for history is always the meaning of the men concerned: the meaning that they attach to the state of affairs they want to alter, the meaning they attach to their actions, and the meaning they attach to the effects produced by the actions.

The aspect from which history arranges and assorts the infinite multiplicity of events is their meaning. The only principle which it applies for the systemization of its objects—men, ideas, institutions, social entities, and artifacts—is meaning affinity. According to meaning affinity it arranges the elements into ideal types.

Ideal types are specific notions employed in historical research and in the representation of its results. They are concepts of understanding. As such they are entirely different from praxeological categories and concepts and from the concepts of the natural sciences. An ideal type is not a class concept, because its description does not indicate the marks whose presence definitely and unambiguously determines class membership. An ideal type cannot be defined; it must be characterized by an enumeration of those features whose presence by and large decides whether in a concrete instance we are or are not faced with a specimen belonging to the ideal type in question. It is peculiar to the ideal type that not all its characteristics need to be present in any one example. Whether or not the absence of some characteristics prevents the inclusion of a concrete specimen in the ideal type in question, depends on a relevance judgment by understanding. The ideal type itself is an outcome of an understanding of the motives, ideas, and aims of the acting individuals and of the means they apply.

An ideal type has nothing at all to do with statistical means and averages. Most of the characteristics concerned are not open to a numerical determination, and for this reason alone they could not enter into a calculation of averages. But the main reason is to be seen in something else. Statistical averages denote the behavior of the members of a class or a type, already constituted by means of a definition or characterization referring to other marks, with regard to features not referred to in the definition or characterization. The membership of the class or type must be known before the statistician can start investigating special features and use the result of this investigation for the establishment of an average. We can establish the average age of the United States Senators or we can reckon averages concerning the behavior of an age class of the population with regard to a special problem. But it is logically impossible to make the membership of a class or type depend upon an average.

No historical problem can be treated without the aid of ideal types. Even when the historian deals with an individual person or with a single event, he cannot avoid referring to ideal types. If he speaks of Napoleon, he must refer to such ideal types as commander, dictator, revolutionary leader; and if he deals with the French Revolution he must refer to ideal types such as revolution, disintegration of an established regime, anarchy. It may be that the reference to an ideal type consists merely in rejecting its applicability to the case in question. But all historical events are described and interpreted by means of ideal types. The layman too, in dealing with events of the past or of the future, must always make use of ideal types and unwittingly always does so.

Whether or not the employment of a definite ideal type is expedient and conducive to an adequate grasp of phenomena can only be decided by understanding. It is not the ideal type that determines the mode of understanding; it is the mode of understanding that requires the construction and use of corresponding ideal types.

The ideal types are constructed with the use of ideas and concepts developed by all nonhistorical branches of knowledge. Every cognition of history is, of course, conditioned by the findings of the other sciences, depends upon them, and must never contradict them. But historical knowledge has another subject matter and another method than these other sciences, and they in turn have no use for understanding. Thus the ideal types must not be confused with concepts of the nonhistorical sciences. This is valid also with regard to the praxeological categories and concepts. They provide, to be sure, the indispensable mental tools for the study of history. However, they do not refer to the understanding of the unique and individual events which are the subject matter of history. An ideal type can therefore never be a simple adoption of a praxeological concept.

It happens in many instances that a term used by praxeology to signify a praxeological concept serves to signify an ideal type for the historian. Then the historian uses *one* word for the expression of two different things. He applies the term sometimes to signify its praxeological connotation, but more often to signify an ideal type. In the latter case the historian attaches to the word a meaning different from its praxeological meaning; he transforms it by transferring it to a different field of inquiry. The economic concept "entrepreneur" belongs to a stratum other than the ideal type "entrepreneur" as used by economic history and descriptive economics. (On a third stratum lies the legal term "entrepreneur.") The economic term "entrepreneur" is a precisely defined concept which in the framework of a theory of market economy signifies a clearly integrated function.[21] The historical ideal type "entrepreneur" does not include the same members. Nobody in using it thinks of shoeshine boys, cab drivers who own their cars, small businessmen, and small farmers. What economics establishes with regard to entrepreneurs is rigidly valid for all members of the class without any regard to temporal and geographical conditions and to the various branches of business. What economic history establishes for its ideal types can differ according to the particular circumstances of various ages, countries, branches of business, and many other conditions. History has little use for a general ideal type of entrepreneur. It is more concerned with such types as: the American entrepreneur of the time of Jefferson, Ger-

21. See below, pp. 251–255.

man heavy industries in the age of William II, New England textile manufacturing in the last decades preceding the first World War, the Protestant *haute finance* of Paris, self-made entrepreneurs, and so on.

Whether the use of a definite ideal type is to be recommended or not depends entirely on the mode of understanding. It is quite common nowadays to employ two ideal types: Left-Wing Parties (Progressives) and Right-Wing Parties (Fascists). The former includes the Western democracies, some Latin American dictatorships, and Russian Bolshevism; the latter Italian Fascism and German Nazism. This typification is the outcome of a definite mode of understanding. Another mode would contrast Democracy and Dictatorship. Then Russian Bolshevism, Italian Fascism, and German Nazism belong to the ideal type of dictatorial government, and the Western systems to the ideal type of democratic government.

It was a fundamental mistake of the Historical School of *Wirtschaftliche Staatswissenschaften* in Germany and of Institutionalism in America to interpret economics as the characterization of the behavior of an ideal type, the *homo oeconomicus*. According to this doctrine traditional or orthodox economics does not deal with the behavior of man as he really is and acts, but with a fictitious or hypothetical image. It pictures a being driven exclusively by "economic" motives, i.e., solely by the intention of making the greatest possible material or monetary profit. Such a being, say these critics, does not have and never did have a counterpart in reality; it is a phantom of a spurious armchair philosophy. No man is exclusively motivated by the desire to become as rich as possible; many are not at all influenced by this mean craving. It is vain to refer to such an illusory homunculus in dealing with life and history.

Even if this really were the meaning of classical economics, the homo oeconomicus would certainly not be an ideal type. The ideal type is not an embodiment of one side or aspect of man's various aims and desires. It is always the representation of complex phenomena of reality, either of men, of institutions, or of ideologies.

The classical economists sought to explain the formation of prices. They were fully aware of the fact that prices are not a product of the activities of a special group of people, but the result of an interplay of all members of the market society. This was the meaning of their statement that demand and supply determine the formation of prices. However, the classical economists failed in their endeavors to provide a satisfactory theory of value. They were at a loss to find a solution for the apparent paradox of value. They were puzzled by the alleged paradox that "gold" is more highly valued than "iron," although the latter is more "useful" than the former. Thus they could not construct a general theory of value and could not trace back the phenomena of market exchange and of production to their ultimate sources, the behavior of the consumers. This shortcoming forced them to abandon their ambitious plan to develop a general theory of human action. They had to satisfy themselves with a theory explaining only the activities of the businessman without going back to the choices of everybody as the ultimate determinants. They dealt only with the actions of businessmen eager to buy in the cheapest market and to sell in the dearest. The consumer was left outside the field of their theorizing. Later the epigones of classical economics explained and justified this insufficiency as an intentional and methodologically necessary procedure. It was, they asserted, the deliberate design of economists to restrict their investigations to only one aspect of human endeavor—namely, to the "economic" aspect. It was their intention to use the fictitious image of a man driven solely by "economic" motives and to neglect all others although they were fully aware of the fact that real men are driven by many other, "noneconomic" motives. To deal with these other motives, one group of these interpreters maintained, is not the task of economics but of other branches of knowledge. Another group admitted that the treatment of these "noneconomic" motives and their influence on the formation of prices was a task of economics also, but they believed that it must be left to later generations. It will be shown at a later stage of our investigations that this distinction between "economic" and "noneconomic motives of human action is untenable.[22] At this point it is only important to realize that this doctrine of the "economic" side of human action utterly misrepresents the teachings of the classical economists. They never intended to do what this doctrine ascribes to them. They wanted to conceive the real formation of prices—not fictitious prices as they would be determined if men were acting under the sway of hypothetical conditions different from those really influencing them. The prices they try to explain and do explain—although without tracing them back to the choices of the consumers—are real market prices. The demand and supply of which they speak are real factors determined by all motives instigating men to buy or to sell. What was wrong with their theory was that they did not trace demand back to the choices of the consumers; they lacked a satisfactory theory of demand. But it was not their idea that demand as they used this concept in their dissertations was exclusively

22. See below, pp 232–234 and 239–244.

determined by "economic" motives as distinguished from "noneconomic" motives. As they restricted their theorizing to the actions of businessmen, they did not deal with the motives of the ultimate consumers. Nonetheless their theory of prices was intended as an explanation of real prices irrespective of the motives and ideas instigating the consumers.

Modern subjective economics starts with the solution of the apparent paradox of value. It neither limits its theorems to the actions of businessmen alone nor deals with a fictitious homo oeconomicus. It treats the inexorable categories of everybody's action. Its theorems concerning commodity prices, wage rates, and interest rates refer to all these phenomena without any regard to the motives causing people to buy or to sell or to abstain from buying or selling. It is time to discard entirely any reference to the abortive attempt to justify the shortcoming of older economists through the appeal to the homo oeconomicus phantom.

10. The Procedure of Economics

The scope of praxeology is the explication of the category of human action. All that is needed for the deduction of all praxeological theorems is knowledge of the essence of human action. It is a knowledge that is our own because we are men; no being of human descent that pathological conditions have not reduced to a merely vegetative existence lacks it. No special experience is needed in order to comprehend these theorems, and no experience, however rich, could disclose them to a being who did not know a priori what human action is. The only way to a cognition of these theorems is logical analysis of our inherent knowledge of the category of action. We must bethink ourselves and reflect upon the structure of human action. Like logic and mathematics, praxeological knowledge is in us; it does not come from without.

All the concepts and theorems of praxeology are implied in the category of human action. The first task is to extract and to deduce them, to expound their implications and to define the universal conditions of acting as such. Having shown what conditions are required by any action, one must go further and define—of course, in a categorial and formal sense—the less general conditions required for special modes of acting. It would be possible to deal with this second task by delineating all thinkable conditions and deducing from them all inferences logically permissible. Such an all-comprehensive system would provide a theory referring not only to human action as it is under the conditions and circumstances given in the real world in which man lives and acts. It would deal no less with hypothetical acting such as would take place under the unrealizable conditions of imaginary worlds.

But the end of science is to know reality. It is not mental gymnastics or a logical pastime. Therefore praxeology restricts its inquiries to the study of acting under those conditions and presuppositions which are given in reality. It studies acting under unrealized and unrealizable conditions only from two points of view. It deals with states of affairs which, although not real in the present and past world, could possibly become real at some future date. And it examines unreal and unrealizable conditions if such an inquiry is needed for a satisfactory grasp of what is going on under the conditions present in reality.

However, this reference to experience does not impair the aprioristic character of praxeology and economics. Experience merely directs our curiosity toward certain problems and diverts it from other problems. It tells us what we should explore, but it does not tell us how we could proceed in our search for knowledge. Moreover, it is not experience but thinking alone which teaches us that, and in what instances, it is necessary to investigate unrealizable hypothetical conditions in order to conceive what is going on in the real world.

The disutility of labor is not of a categorial and aprioristic character. We can without contradiction think of a world in which labor does not cause uneasiness, and we can depict the state of affairs prevailing in such a world.[23] But the real world is conditioned by the disutility of labor. Only theorems based on the assumption that labor is a source of uneasiness are applicable for the comprehension of what is going on in this world.

Experience teaches that there is disutility of labor. But it does not teach it directly. There is no phenomenon that introduces itself as disutility of labor. There are only data of experience which are interpreted, on the ground of aprioristic knowledge, to mean that men consider leisure—i.e., the absence of labor—other things being equal, as a more desirable condition than the expenditure of labor. We see that men renounce advantages which they could get by working more—that is, that they are ready to make sacrifices for the attainment of leisure. We infer from this fact that leisure is valued as a good and that labor is regarded as a burden. But for previous praxeological insight, we would never be in a position to reach this conclusion.

A theory of indirect exchange and all further theories built upon it—as the theory of circulation credit—are applicable only to the interpretation of events within a world in which indirect exchange

23. See below, pp. 131–133.

is practiced. In a world of barter trade only it would be mere intellectual play. It is unlikely that the economists of such a world, if economic science could have emerged at all in it, would have given any thought to the problems of indirect exchange, money, and all the rest. In our actual world, however, such studies are an essential part of economic theory.

The fact that praxeology, in fixing its eye on the comprehension of reality, concentrates upon the investigation of those problems which are useful for this purpose, does not alter the aprioristic character of its reasoning. But it marks the way in which economics, up to now the only elaborated part of praxeology, presents the results of its endeavors.

Economics does not follow the procedure of logic and mathematics. It does not present an integrated system of pure aprioristic ratiocination severed from any reference to reality. In introducing assumptions into its reasoning, it satisfies itself that the treatment of the assumptions concerned can render useful services for the comprehension of reality. It does not strictly separate in its treatises and monographs pure science from the application of its theorems to the solution of concrete historical and political problems. It adopts for the organized presentation of its results a form in which aprioristic theory and the interpretation of historical phenomena are intertwined.

It is obvious that this mode of procedure is enjoined upon economics by the very nature and essence of its subject matter. It has given proof of its expediency. However, one must not overlook the fact that the manipulation of this singular and logically somewhat strange procedure requires caution and subtlety, and that uncritical and superficial minds have again and again been led astray by careless confusion of the two epistemologically different methods implied.

There are no such things as a historical method of economics or a discipline of institutional economics. There is economics and there is economic history. The two must never be confused. All theorems of economics are necessarily valid in every instance in which all the assumptions presupposed are given. Of course, they have no practical significance in situations where these conditions are not present. The theorems referring to indirect exchange are not applicable to conditions where there is no indirect exchange. But this does not impair their validity.[24]

The issue has been obfuscated by the endeavors of governments

24. Cf. F. H. Knight, *The Ethics of Competition and Other Essays* (New York, 1935), p. 139.

and powerful pressure groups to disparage economics and to defame the economists. Despots and democratic majorities are drunk with power. They must reluctantly admit that they are subject to the laws of nature. But they reject the very notion of economic law. Are they not the supreme legislators? Don't they have the power to crush every opponent? No war lord is prone to acknowledge any limits other than those imposed on him by a superior armed force. Servile scribblers are always ready to foster such complacency by expounding the appropriate doctrines. They call their garbled presumptions "historical economics." In fact, economic history is a long record of government policies that failed because they were designed with a bold disregard for the laws of economics.

It is impossible to understand the history of economic thought if one does not pay attention to the fact that economics as such is a challenge to the conceit of those in power. An economist can never be a favorite of autocrats and demagogues. With them he is always the mischief-maker, and the more they are inwardly convinced that his objections are well founded, the more they hate him.

In the face of all this frenzied agitation it is expedient to establish the fact that the starting point of all praxeological and economic reasoning, the category of human action, is proof against any criticisms and objections. No appeal to any historical or empirical considerations whatever can discover any fault in the proposition that men purposefully aim at certain chosen ends. No talk about irrationality, the unfathomable depths of the human soul, the spontaneity of the phenomena of life, automatisms, reflexes, and tropisms, can invalidate the statement that man makes use of his reason for the realization of wishes and desires. From the unshakable foundation of the category of human action praxeology and economics proceed step by step by means of discursive reasoning. Precisely defining assumptions and conditions, they construct a system of concepts and draw all the inferences implied by logically unassailable ratiocination. With regard to the results thus obtained only two attitudes are possible: either one can unmask logical errors in the chain of the deductions which produced these results, or one must acknowledge their correctness and validity.

It is vain to object that life and reality are not logical. Life and reality are neither logical nor illogical; they are simply given. But logic is the only tool available to man for the comprehension of both. It is vain to object that life and history are inscrutable and ineffable and that human reason can never penetrate to their inner core. The critics contradict themselves in uttering words about the ineffable and expounding theories—of course, spurious theories—about the unfathomable. There are many things beyond the reach of the human mind. But as far as man is able to attain any knowledge, however limited, he can use only one avenue of approach, that opened by reason.

No less illusory are the endeavors to play off understanding against the theorems of economics. The domain of historical understanding is exclusively the elucidation of those problems which cannot be entirely elucidated by the nonhistorical sciences. Understanding must never contradict the theories developed by the nonhistorical sciences. Understanding can never do anything but, on the one hand, establish the fact that people were motivated by certain ideas, aimed at certain ends, and applied certain means for the attainment of these ends, and, on the other hand, assign to the various historical factors their relevance so far as this cannot be achieved by the nonhistorical sciences. Understanding does not entitle the modern historian to assert that exorcism ever was an appropriate means to cure sick cows. Neither does it permit him to maintain that an economic law was not valid in ancient Rome or in the empire of the Incas.

Man is not infallible. He searches for truth—that is, for the most adequate comprehension of reality as far as the structure of his mind and reason makes it accessible to him. Man can never become omniscient. He can never be absolutely certain that his inquiries were not misled and that what he considers as certain truth is not error. All that man can do is to submit all his theories again and again to the most critical reexamination. This means for the economist to trace back all theorems to their unquestionable and certain ultimate basis, the category of human action, and to test by the most careful scrutiny all assumptions and inferences leading from this basis to the theorem under examination. It cannot be contended that this procedure is a guarantee against error. But it is undoubtedly the most effective method of avoiding error.

Praxeology—and consequently economics too—is a deductive system. It draws its strength from the starting point of its deductions, from the category of action. No economic theorem can be considered sound that is not solidly fastened upon this foundation by an irrefutable chain of reasoning. A statement proclaimed without such a connection is arbitrary and floats in midair. It is impossible to deal with a special segment of economics if one does not encase it in a complete system of action.

The empirical sciences start from singular events and proceed from the unique and individual to the more universal. Their treatment is subject to specialization. They can deal with segments without paying attention to the whole field. The economist must never be a specialist. In dealing with any problem he must always fix his glance upon the whole system.

Historians often sin in this respect. They are ready to invent theorems ad hoc. They sometimes fail to recognize that it is impossible to abstract any causal relations from the study of complex phenomena. Their pretension to investigate reality without any reference to what they disparage as preconceived ideas is vain. In fact they unwittingly apply popular doctrines long since unmasked as fallacious and contradictory.

11. The Limitations on Praxeological Concepts

The praxeological categories and concepts are devised for the comprehension of human action. They become self-contradictory and nonsensical if one tries to apply them in dealing with conditions different from those of human life. The naïve anthropomorphism of primitive religions is unpalatable to the philosophic mind. However, the endeavors of philosophers to define, by the use of praxeological concepts, the attributes of an absolute being, free from all the limitations and frailties of human existence, are no less questionable.

Scholastic philosophers and theologians and likewise Theists and Deists of the Age of Reason conceived an absolute and perfect being, unchangeable, omnipotent, and omniscient, and yet planning and acting, aiming at ends and employing means for the attainment of these ends. But action can only be imputed to a discontented being, and repeated action only to a being who lacks the power to remove his uneasiness once and for all at one stroke. An acting being is discontented and therefore not almighty. If he were contented, he would not act, and if he were almighty, he would have long since radically removed his discontent. For an all-powerful being there is no pressure to choose between various states of uneasiness; he is not under the necessity of acquiescing in the lesser evil. Omnipotence would mean the power to achieve everything and to enjoy full satisfaction without being restrained by any limitations. But this is incompatible with the very concept of action. For an almighty being the categories of ends and means do not exist. He is above all human comprehension, concepts, and understanding. For the almighty being every "means" renders unlimited services, he can apply every "means" for the attainment of any ends, he can achieve every end without the employment of any means. It is beyond the faculties of the human mind to think the concept of almightiness consistently to its ultimate logical consequences. The paradoxes are insoluble. Has the almighty being the power to achieve something which is immune to his later interference? If he has this power, then there are limits to his might and he is no longer almighty; if he lacks this power, he is by virtue of this fact alone not almighty.

Are omnipotence and omniscience compatible? Omniscience presupposes that all future happenings are already unalterably determined. If there is omniscience, omnipotence is inconceivable. Impotence to change anything in the predetermined course of events would restrict the power of any agent.

Action is a display of potency and control that are limited. It is a manifestation of man who is restrained by the circumscribed powers of his mind, the physiological nature of his body, the vicissitudes of his environment, and the scarcity of the external factors on which his welfare depends. It is vain to refer to the imperfections and weaknesses of human life if one aims at depicting something absolutely perfect. The very idea of absolute perfection is in every way self-contradictory. The state of absolute perfection must be conceived as complete, final, and not exposed to any change. Change could only impair its perfection and transform it into a less perfect state; the mere possibility that a change can occur is incompatible with the concept of absolute perfection. But the absence of change—i.e., perfect immutability, rigidity and immobility—is tantamount to the absence of life. Life and perfection are incompatible, but so are death and perfection.

The living is not perfect because it is liable to change; the dead is not perfect because it does not live.

The language of living and acting men can form comparatives and superlatives in comparing degrees. But absoluteness is not a degree; it is a limiting notion. The absolute is indeterminable, unthinkable and ineffable. It is a chimerical conception. There are no such things as perfect happiness, perfect men, eternal bliss. Every attempt to describe the conditions of a land of Cockaigne, or the life of the Angels, results in paradoxes. Where there are conditions, there are limitations and not perfection; there are endeavors to conquer obstacles, there are frustration and discontent.

After the philosophers had abandoned the search for the absolute, the utopians took it up. They weave dreams about the perfect state. They do not realize that the state, the social apparatus of compulsion and coercion, is an institution to cope with human imperfection and that its essential function is to inflict punishment upon minorities in order to protect majorities against the detrimental consequences of certain actions. With "perfect" men there would not be any need for compulsion and coercion. But utopians do not pay heed to human nature and the inalterable conditions of human life. Godwin thought that man might become immortal after the abolition of private property.[25] Charles Fourier babbled about the ocean containing lemonade instead of salt water.[26] Marx's economic system blithely ignored the fact of the scarcity of material factors of production. Trotsky revealed that in the proletarian paradise "the average human type will rise to the heights of an Aristotle, a Goethe, or a Marx. And above this ridge new peaks will rise."[27]

Nowadays the most popular chimeras are stabilization and security. We will test these catchwords later.

25. William Godwin, *An Enquiry Concerning Political Justice and Its Influence on General Virtue and Happiness* (Dublin, 1793), II, 393–403.

26. Charles Fourier, *Théorie des quatre mouvements* (Oeuvres complètes, 3d ed. Paris, 1846), I, 43.

27. Leon Trotsky, *Literature and Revolution,* trans. by R. Strunsky (London, 1925), p. 256.

III. ECONOMICS AND THE REVOLT AGAINST REASON

1. The Revolt Against Reason

IT is true that some philosophers were ready to overrate the power of human reason. They believed that man can discover by ratiocination the final causes of cosmic events, the inherent ends the prime mover aims at in creating the universe and determining the course of its evolution. They expatiated on the "Absolute" as if it were their pocket watch. They did not shrink from announcing eternal absolute values and from establishing moral codes unconditionally binding on all men.

Then there was the long line of utopian authors. They drafted schemes for an earthly paradise in which pure reason alone should rule. They failed to realize that what they called absolute reason and manifest truth was the fancy of their own minds. They blithely arrogated to themselves infallibility and often advocated intolerance, the violent oppression of all dissenters and heretics. They aimed at dictatorship either for themselves or for men who would accurately put their plans into execution. There was, in their opinion, no other salvation for suffering mankind.

There was Hegel. He was a profound thinker and his writings are a treasury of stimulating ideas. But he was laboring under the delusion that *Geist,* the Absolute, revealed itself through his words. There was nothing in the universe that was hidden to Hegel. It was a pity that his language was so ambiguous that it could be interpreted in various ways. The right-wing Hegelians interpreted it as an endorsement of the Prussian system of autocratic government and of the dogmas of the Prussian Church. The left-wing Hegelians read out of it atheism, intransigent revolutionary radicalism, and anarchistic doctrines.

There was Auguste Comte. He knew precisely what the future had in store for mankind. And, of course, he considered himself as the supreme legislator. For example, he regarded certain astronomical studies as useless and wanted to prohibit them. He planned to substitute a new religion for Christianity, and selected a lady who in this new church was destined to replace the Virgin. Comte can be exculpated, as he was insane in the full sense which pathology attaches to this term. But what about his followers?

Many more facts of this kind could be mentioned. But they are no argument against reason, rationalism, and rationality. These dreams have nothing at all to do with the question of whether or not reason is the right and only instrument available for man in his endeavors to attain as much knowledge as is accessible to him. The honest and conscientious truth-seekers have never pretended that reason and scientific research can answer all questions. They were fully aware of the limitations imposed upon the human mind. They cannot be taxed with responsibility for the crudities of the philosophy of Haeckel and the simplism of the various materialist schools.

The rationalist philosophers themselves were always intent upon showing the boundaries both of aprioristic theory and of empirical research.[1] The first representative of British political economy, David Hume, the Utilitarians, and the American Pragmatists are certainly not guilty of having exaggerated the power of man to attain truth. It would be more justifiable to blame the philosophy of the last two hundred years for too much agnosticism and skepticism than for overconfidence in what could be achieved by the human mind.

The revolt against reason, the characteristic mental attitude of our age, was not caused by a lack of modesty, caution, and self-examination on the part of the philosophers. Neither was it due to failures in the evolution of modern natural science. The amazing achievements of technology and therapeutics speak a language which nobody can ignore. It is hopeless to attack modern science, whether from the angle of intuitionism and mysticism, or from any other point of view. The revolt against reason was directed against another target. It did not aim at the natural sciences, but at economics. The attack against the natural sciences was only the logically necessary outcome of the attack against economics. It was impermissible to dethrone reason in one field only and not to question it in other branches of knowledge also.

The great upheaval was born out of the historical situation existing in the middle of the nineteenth century. The economists had entirely demolished the fantastic delusions of the socialist utopians. The deficiencies of the classical system prevented them from comprehending why every socialist plan must be unrealizable; but they knew enough to demonstrate the futility of all socialist schemes produced up to their time. The communist ideas were done for. The socialists

1. Cf., for instance, Louis Rougier, *Les Paralogismes du rationalisme* (Paris, 1920).

were absolutely unable to raise any objection to the devastating criticism of their schemes and to advance any argument in their favor. It seemed as if socialism was dead forever.

Only one way could lead the socialists out of this impasse. They could attack logic and reason and substitute mystical intuition for ratiocination. It was the historical role of Karl Marx to propose this solution. On the basis of Hegel's dialectic mysticism, he blithely arrogated to himself the ability to predict the future. Hegel pretended to know that Geist, in creating the universe, wanted to bring about the Prussian monarchy of Frederick William III. But Marx was better informed about Geist's plans. He knew that the final cause of historical evolution was the establishment of the socialist millennium. Socialism is bound to come "with the inexorability of a law of nature." And as, according to Hegel, every later stage of history is a higher and better stage, there cannot be any doubt that socialism, the final and ultimate stage of mankind's evolution, will be perfect from any point of view. It is consequently useless to discuss the details of the operation of a socialist commonwealth. History, in due time, will arrange everything for the best. It does not need the advice of mortal men.

There was still the main obstacle to overcome: the devastating criticism of the economists. Marx had a solution at hand. Human reason, he asserted, is constitutionally unfitted to find truth. The logical structure of mind is different with various social classes. There is no such thing as a universally valid logic. What mind produces can never be anything but "ideology," that is, in the Marxian terminology, a set of ideas disguising the selfish interests of the thinker's own social class. Hence, the "bourgeois" mind of the economists is utterly incapable of producing more than an apology for capitalism. The teachings of "bourgeois" science, an offshoot of "bourgeois" logic, are of no avail for the proletarians, the rising class destined to abolish all classes and to convert the earth into a Garden of Eden.

But, of course, the logic of the proletarians is not merely a class logic. "The ideas of proletarian logic are not party ideas, but emanations of logic pure and simple."[2] Moreover, by virtue of a special privilege, the logic of certain elect bourgeois is not tainted with the original sin of being bourgeois. Karl Marx, the son of a well-to-do lawyer, married to the daughter of a Prussian noble, and his collaborator Frederick Engels, a wealthy textile manufacturer, never doubted that they themselves were above the law and, notwithstanding their bourgeois background, were endowed with the power to discover absolute truth.

2. Cf. Joseph Dietzgen, *Briefe über Logik, speziell demokratisch-proletarische Logik* (2d ed. Stuttgart, 1903), p. 112.

It is the task of history to describe the historical conditions which made such a crude doctrine popular. Economics has another task. It must analyze both Marxian polylogism and the other brands of polylogism formed after its pattern, and expose their fallacies and contradictions.

2. The Logical Aspect of Polylogism

Marxian polylogism asserts that the logical structure of the mind is different with the members of various social classes. Racial polylogism differs from Marxian polylogism only in so far as it ascribes to each race a peculiar logical structure of mind and maintains that all members of a definite race, no matter what their class affiliation may be, are endowed with this peculiar logical structure.

There is no need to enter here into a critique of the concepts *social class* and *race* as applied by these doctrines. It is not necessary to ask the Marxians when and how a proletarian who succeeds in joining the ranks of the bourgeoisie changes his proletarian mind into a bourgeois mind. It is superfluous to ask the racists to explain what kind of logic is peculiar to people who are not of pure racial stock. There are much more serious objections to be raised.

Neither the Marxians nor the racists nor the supporters of any other brand of polylogism ever went further than to declare that the logical structure of mind is different with various classes, races, or nations. They never ventured to demonstrate precisely in what the logic of the proletarians differs from the logic of the bourgeois, or in what the logic of the Aryans differs from the logic of the non-Aryans, or the logic of the Germans from the logic of the French or the British. In the eyes of the Marxians the Ricardian theory of comparative cost is spurious because Ricardo was a bourgeois. The German racists condemn the same theory because Ricardo was a Jew, and the German nationalists because he was an Englishman. Some German professors advanced all these three arguments together against the validity of Ricardo's teachings. However, it is not enough to reject a theory wholesale by unmasking the background of its author. What is wanted is first to expound a system of logic different from that applied by the criticized author. Then it would be necessary to examine the contested theory point by point and to show where in its reasoning inferences are made which—although correct from the point of view of its author's logic—are invalid from the point of view of the proletarian, Aryan, or German logic. And finally, it should be explained what kind of conclusions the replacement of the author's vicious inferences by the correct inferences of the critic's own logic must lead to. As everybody knows, this never has been and never can be attempted by anybody.

Then there is the fact that there is disagreement concerning essential problems among people belonging to the same class, race, or nation. Unfortunately there are, say the Nazis, Germans who do not think in a correct German way. But if a German does not always necessarily think as he should, but may think in the manner of a man equipped with a non-German logic, who is to decide which German's ideas are truly German and which un-German? Says the late Professor Franz Oppenheimer: "The individual errs often in looking after his interests; a class never errs in the long run."[3] This would suggest the infallibility of a majority vote. However, the Nazis rejected decision by majority vote as manifestly un-German. The Marxians pay lip service to the democratic principle of majority vote.[4] But whenever it comes to a test they favor minority rule, provided it is the rule of their own party. Let us remember how Lenin dispersed by force the Constituent Assembly elected, under the auspices of his own government, by adult franchise, because only about one-fifth of its members were Bolshevik.

A consistent supporter of polylogism would have to maintain that ideas are correct because their author is a member of the right class, nation, or race. But consistency is not one of their virtues. Thus the Marxians are prepared to assign the epithet "proletarian thinker" to everybody whose doctrines they approve. All the others they disparage either as foes of their class or as social traitors. Hitler was even frank enough to admit that the only method available for him to sift the true Germans from the mongrels and the aliens was to enunciate a genuinely German program and to see who were ready to support it.[5] A dark-haired man whose bodily features by no means fitted the prototype of the fair-haired Aryan master race, arrogated to himself the gift of discovering the only doctrine adequate to the German mind and of expelling from the ranks of the Germans all those who did not accept this doctrine whatever their bodily characteristics might be. No further proof is needed of the insincerity of the whole doctrine.

3. The Praxeological Aspect of Polylogism

An ideology in the Marxian sense of this term is a doctrine which,

3. Cf. Franz Oppenheimer, *System der Soziologie* (Jena, 1926), II, 559.

4. It must be emphasized that the case for democracy is not based on the assumption that majorities are always right, still less that they are infallible. Cf. below, pp. 149–151.

5. Cf. his speech on the Party Convention in Nuremberg, September 3, 1933 (*Frankfurter Zeitung*, September 4, 1933, p. 2).

although erroneous from the point of view of the correct logic of the proletarians, is beneficial to the selfish interests of the class which has developed it. An ideology is objectively vicious, but it furthers the interests of the thinker's class precisely on account of its viciousness. Many Marxians believe that they have proved this tenet by stressing the point that people do not thirst for knowledge only for its own sake. The aim of the scientist is to pave the way for successful action. Theories are always developed with a view to practical application. There are no such things as pure science and the disinterested search for truth.

For the sake of argument we may admit that every effort to attain truth is motivated by considerations of its practical utilization for the attainment of some end. But this does not answer the question why an "ideological"—i.e., a false—theory should render better service than a correct one. The fact that the practical application of a theory results in the outcome predicted on the basis of this theory is universally considered a confirmation of its correctness. It is paradoxical to assert that a vicious theory is from any point of view more useful than a correct one.

Men use firearms. In order to improve these weapons they developed the science of ballistics. But, of course, precisely because they were eager to hunt game and to kill one another, a correct ballistics. A merely "ideological" ballistics would not have been of any use.

For the Marxians the view that scientists labor for knowledge alone is nothing but an "arrogant pretense" of the scientists. Thus they declare that Maxwell was led to his theory of electromagnetic waves by the craving of business for wireless telegraphs.[6] It is of no relevance for the problem of ideology whether this is true or not. The question is whether the alleged fact that nineteenth-century industrialism considered telegraphy without wires "the philosopher's stone and the elixir of youth"[7] impelled Maxwell to formulate a correct theory or an ideological superstructure of the selfish class interests of the bourgeoisie. There is no doubt that bacteriological research was instigated not only by the desire to fight contagious diseases, but also by the desire of the producers of wine and of cheese to improve their methods of production. But the result obtained was certainly not "ideological" in the Marxian sense.

What induced Marx to invent his ideology-doctrine was the wish to sap the prestige of economics. He was fully aware of his impotence to refute the objections raised by the economists to the practicability

6. Cf. Lancelot Hogben, *Science for the Citizen* (New York, 1938), pp. 726–728.

7. *Ibid.*, p. 726.

of the socialist schemes. In fact he was so fascinated by the theoretical system of British classical economics that he firmly believed in its impregnability. He either never learned about the doubts that the classical theory of value raised in the minds of judicious scholars, or, if he ever heard of them, he did not comprehend their weight. His own economic ideas are hardly more than a garbled version of Ricardianism. When Jevons and Menger inaugurated a new era of economic thought, his career as an author of economic writings had already come to an end; the first volume of *Das Kapital* had already been published several years previously. Marx's only reaction to the marginal theory of value was that he postponed the publication of the later volumes of his main treatise. They were made accessible to the public only after his death.

In developing the ideology-doctrine Marx exclusively aims at economics and the social philosophy of Utilitarianism. His only intention was to destroy the reputation of economic teachings which he was unable to refute by means of logic and ratiocination. He gave to his doctrine the form of a universal law valid for the whole historical age of social classes because a statement which is applicable only to one individual historical event could not be considered as a law. For the same reasons he did not restrict its validity to economic thought only, but included every branch of knowledge.

The service which bourgeois economics rendered to the bourgeoisie was in Marx's eyes twofold. It aided them first in their fight against feudalism and royal despotism and then later again in their fight against the rising proletarian class. It provided a rational and moral justification for capitalist exploitation. It was, if we want to use a notion developed after Marx's death, a rationalization of the claims of the capitalists.[8] The capitalists, in their subconsciousness ashamed of the mean greed motivating their own conduct and anxious to avoid social disapproval, encouraged their sycophants, the economists, to proclaim doctrines which could rehabilitate them in public opinion.

Now, recourse to the notion of rationalization provides a psychological description of the incentives which impelled a man or a group of men to formulate a theorem or a whole theory. But it does not predicate anything about the validity or invalidity of the theory

8. Although the term rationalization is new, the thing itself was known long ago. Cf., for instance, the words of Benjamin Franklin: "So convenient a thing it is to be a *reasonable creature,* since it enables one to find or make a reason for every thing one has a mind to do." (*Autobiography,* ed. New York, 1944, p. 41.)

advanced. If it is proved that the theory concerned is untenable, the notion of rationalization is a psychological interpretation of the causes which made their authors liable to error. But if we are not in a position to find any fault in the theory advanced, no appeal to the concept of rationalization can possibly explode its validity. If it were true that the economists had in their subconsciousness no design other than that of justifying the unfair claims of the capitalists, their theories could nevertheless be quite correct. There is no means to expose a faulty theory other than to refute it by discursive reasoning and to substitute a better theory for it. In dealing with the theorem of Pythagoras or with the theory of comparative cost, we are not interested in the psychological factors that impelled Pythagoras and Ricardo to construct these theorems, although these things may be important for the historian and the biographer. For science the only relevant question is whether or not these theorems can stand the test of rational examination. The social or racial background of their authors is beside the point.

It is a fact that people in the pursuit of their selfish interests try to use doctrines more or less universally accepted by public opinion. Moreover, they are eager to invent and to propagate doctrines which they could possibly use for furthering their own interests. But this does not explain why such doctrines, favoring the interests of a minority and contrary to the interests of the rest of the people, are endorsed by public opinion. No matter whether such "ideological" doctrines are the product of a "false consciousness," forcing a man to think unwittingly in a manner that serves the interests of his class, or whether they are the product of a purposeful distortion of truth, they must encounter the ideologies of other classes and try to supplant them. Then a rivalry between antagonistic ideologies emerges. The Marxians explain victory and defeat in such conflicts as an outcome of the interference of historical providence. Geist, the mythical prime mover, operates according to a definite plan. He leads mankind through various preliminary stages to the final bliss of socialism. Every stage is the product of a certain state of technology; all its other characteristics are the necessary ideological superstructure of this technological state. Geist causes man to bring about in due time the technological ideas adequate to the stage in which he lives, and to realize them. All the rest is an outgrowth of the state of technology. The hand-mill made feudal society; the steam-mill made capitalism.[9]

9. "Le moulin à bras vous donnera la société avec le souzerain; le moulin à vapeur, la société avec le capitaliste industriel." Marx, *Misère de la philosophie* (Paris and Brussels, 1847), p. 100.

Human will and reason play only an ancillary role in these changes. The inexorable law of historical development forces men—independently of their wills—to think and to behave according to the patterns corresponding to the material basis of their age. Men fool themselves in believing that they are free to choose between various ideas and between what they call truth and error. They themselves do not think; it is historical providence that manifests itself in their thoughts.

This is a purely mystical doctrine. The only proof given in its support is the recourse of Hegelian dialectics. Capitalistic private property is the first negation of individual private property. It begets, with the inexorability of a law of nature, its own negation, namely common ownership of the means of production.[10] However, a mystical doctrine based on intuition does not lose its mysticism by referring to another no less mystical doctrine. This makeshift by no means answers the question why a thinker must necessarily develop an ideology in accordance with the interests of his class. For the sake of argument we may admit that man's thoughts must result in doctrines beneficial to his interests. But are a man's interests necessarily identical with those of his whole class? Marx himself had to admit that the organization of the proletarians into a class, and consequently into a political party, is continually being upset again by the competition between the workers themselves.[11] It is an undeniable fact that there prevails an irreconcilable conflict of interests between those workers who are employed at union wage rates and those who remain unemployed because the enforcement of union rates prevents the demand for and the supply of labor from finding the appropriate price for meeting. It is no less true that the interests of the workers of the comparatively overpopulated countries and those of the comparatively underpopulated countries are antagonistic with regard to migration barriers. The statement that the interests of all proletarians uniformly require the substitution of socialism for capitalism is an arbitrary postulate of Marx and the other socialists. It cannot be proved by the mere assertion that the socialist idea is the emanation of proletarian thought and therefore certainly beneficial to the interests of the proletariat as such.

A popular interpretation of the vicissitudes of British foreign trade policies, based on the ideas of Sismondi, Frederick List, Marx, and the German Historical School, runs this way: In the second part of the eighteenth century and in the greater part of the nineteenth century the class interests of the British bourgeoisie required a free

10. Marx, *Das Kapital* (7th ed. Hamburg, 1914), I, 728–729.
11. *The Communist Manifesto,* I.

trade policy. Therefore British political economy elaborated a free trade doctrine, and the British manufacturers organized a popular movement which finally succeeded in abolishing protective tariffs. Then later conditions changed. The British bourgeoisie could no longer stand the competition of foreign manufacturing and badly needed protective tariffs. Consequently the economists substituted a theory of protection for the antiquated free trade ideology, and Great Britain returned to protectionism.

The first error in this interpretation is that it considers the "bourgeoisie" as a homogeneous class composed of members whose interests are identical. A businessman is always under the necessity of adjusting the conduct of his business to the institutional conditions of his country. In the long run he is, in his capacity as entrepreneur and capitalist, neither favored nor injured by tariffs or the absence of tariffs. He will turn to the production of those commodities which under the given state of affairs he can most profitably produce. What may hurt or further his short-run interests are only *changes* in the institutional setting. But such changes do not affect the various branches of business and the various enterprises in the same way and to the same extent. A measure that benefits one branch or enterprise may be detrimental to other branches or enterprises. What counts for a businessman is only a limited number of customs items. And with regard to these items the interests of various branches and firms are mostly antagonistic.

The interests of every branch or firm can be favored by all kinds of privileges granted to it by the government. But if privileges are granted to the same extent also to the other branches and firms, every businessman loses—not only in his capacity as consumer, but also in his capacity as buyer of raw materials, half-finished products, machines and other equipment—on the one hand as much as he profits on the other. Selfish group interests may impel a man to ask for protection for his own branch or firm. They can never motivate him to ask for universal protection for all branches or firms if he is not sure to be protected to a greater extent than the other industries or enterprises.

Neither were the British manufacturers from the point of view of their class concerns more interested in the abolition of the Corn Laws than other British citizens. The landowners were opposed to the repeal of these laws because a lowering of the prices for agricultural products reduced the rent of land. A special class interest of the manufacturers can only be construed on the basis of the long since discarded iron law of wages and the no less untenable doctrine that profits are an outcome of the exploitation of the workers.

Within a world organized on the basis of the division of labor, every change must in one way or another affect the short-run interests of many groups. It is therefore always easy to expose every doctrine supporting an alteration of existing conditions as an "ideological" disguise of the selfish interests of a special group of people. The main occupation of many present-day authors is such unmasking. Marx did not invent this procedure. It was known long before him. Its most curious manifestation was the attempts of some eighteenth-century writers to explain religious creeds as a fraudulent deception on the part of the priests eager to gain power and wealth both for themselves and for their allies, the exploiters. The Marxians endorsed this statement in labeling religion "opium for the masses."[12] It never occurred to the supporters of such teachings that where there are selfish interests pro there must necessarily be selfish interests contra too. It is by no means a satisfactory explanation of any event that it favored a special class. The question to be answered is why the rest of the population whose interests it injured did not succeed in frustrating the endeavors of those favored by it.

Every firm and every branch of business is in the short run interested in increased sales of its products. In the long run, however, there prevails a tendency toward an equalization of returns in the various branches of production. If demand for the products of a branch increases and raises profits, more capital flows into it and the competition of the new enterprises cuts down the profits. Returns are by no means higher in the sale of socially detrimental articles than in the sale of socially beneficial articles. If a certain branch of business is outlawed and those engaged in it risk prosecution, penalties, and imprisonment, gross profits must be high enough to compensate for the risks involved. But this does not interfere with the height of net returns.

The rich, the owners of the already operating plants, have no particular class interest in the maintenance of free competition. They are opposed to confiscation and expropriation of their fortunes, but their vested interests are rather in favor of measures preventing newcomers from challenging their position. Those fighting for free enterprise and free competition do not defend the interests of those rich

12. The meaning that contemporary Marxism attaches to this phrase, viz., that the religious drug has been purposely administered to the people, may have been the meaning of Marx too. But it was not implied in the passage in which—in 1843—Marx coined this phrase. Cf. R. P. Casey, *Religion in Russia* (New York, 1946), pp. 67–69.

today. They want a free hand left to unknown men who will be the entrepreneurs of tomorrow and whose ingenuity will make the life of coming generations more agreeable. They want the way left open to further economic improvements. They are the spokesmen of material progress.

The nineteenth-century success of free trade ideas was effected by the theories of classical economics. The prestige of these ideas was so great that those whose selfish class interests they hurt could not hinder their endorsements by public opinion and their realization by legislative measures. It is ideas that make history, and not history that makes ideas.

It is useless to argue with mystics and seers. They base their assertions on intuition and are not prepared to submit them to rational examination. The Marxians pretend that what their inner voice proclaims is history's self-revelation. If other people do not hear this voice, it is only a proof that they are not chosen. It is insolence that those groping in darkness dare to contradict the inspired ones. Decency should impel them to creep into a corner and keep silent.

However, science cannot abstain from thinking although it is obvious that it will never succeed in convincing those who dispute the supremacy of reason. Science must emphasize that the appeal to intuition cannot settle the question which of several antagonistic doctrines is the right one and which are wrong. It is an undeniable fact that Marxism is not the only doctrine advanced in our time. There are other "ideologies" besides Marxism. The Marxians assert that the application of these other doctrines would hurt the interests of the many. But the supporters of these doctrines say precisely the same with regard to Marxism.

Of course, the Marxians consider a doctrine vicious if its author's background is not proletarian. But who is proletarian? Doctor Marx, the manufacturer and "exploiter" Engels, and Lenin, the scion of the Russian gentry, were certainly not of proletarian background. But Hitler and Mussolini were genuine proletarians and spent their youth in poverty. The conflict of the Bolsheviks and the Mensheviks or that between Stalin and Trotsky cannot be presented as class conflicts. They were conflicts between various sects of fanatics who called one another traitors.

The essence of Marxian philosophy is this: We are right because we are the spokesmen of the rising proletarian class. Discursive reasoning cannot invalidate our teachings, for they are inspired by the supreme power that determines the destiny of mankind. Our adversaries are wrong because they lack the intuition that guides our minds. It is, of course, not their fault that on account of their class affiliation they are not equipped with the genuine proletarian logic and are blinded by ideologies. The unfathomable decrees of history that have elected us have doomed them. The future is ours.

4. Racial Polylogism

Marxian polylogism is an abortive makeshift to salvage the untenable doctrines of socialism. Its attempt to substitute intuition for ratiocination appeals to popular superstitions. But it is precisely this attitude that places Marxian polylogism and its offshoot, the so-called "sociology of knowledge," in irreconcilable antagonism to science and reason.

It is different with the polylogism of the racists. This brand of polylogism is in agreement with fashionable, although mistaken, tendencies in present-day empiricism. It is an established fact that mankind is divided into various races. The races differ in bodily features. Materialist philosophers assert that thoughts are a secretion of the brain as bile is a secretion of the gall-bladder. It would be inconsistent for them to reject beforehand the hypothesis that the thought-secretion of the various races may differ in essential qualities. The fact that anatomy has not succeeded up to now in discovering anatomical differences in the brain cells of various races cannot invalidate the doctrine that the logical structure of mind is different with different races. It does not exclude the assumption that later research may discover such anatomical peculiarities.

Some ethnologists tell us that it is a mistake to speak of higher and lower civilizations and of an alleged backwardness of alien races. The civilizations of various races are different from the Western civilization of the peoples of Caucasian stock, but they are not inferior. Every race has its peculiar mentality. It is faulty to apply to the civilization of any of them yardsticks abstracted from the achievements of other races. Westerners call the civilization of China an arrested civilization and that of the inhabitants of New Guinea primitive barbarism. But the Chinese and the natives of New Guinea despise our civilization no less than we despise theirs. Such estimates are judgments of value and hence arbitrary. Those other races have a different structure of mind. Their civilizations are adequate to their mind as our civilization is adequate to our mind. We are incapable of comprehending that what we call backwardness does not appear such to them. It is, from the point of view of their logic, a better method of coming to a satisfactory arrangement with given natural conditions of life than is our progressivism.

These ethnologists are right in emphasizing that it is not the task of a historian—and the ethnologist too is a historian—to express value judgments. But they are utterly mistaken in contending that these other races have been guided in their activities by motives other than those which have actuated the white race. The Asiatics and the Africans no less than the peoples of European descent have been eager to struggle successfully for survival and to use reason as the foremost weapon in these endeavors. They have sought to get rid of the beasts of prey and of disease, to prevent famines and to raise the productivity of labor. There can be no doubt that in the pursuit of these aims they have been less successful than the whites. The proof is that they are eager to profit from all achievements of the West. Those ethnologists would be right, if Mongols or Africans, tormented by a painful disease, were to renounce the aid of a European doctor because their mentality or their world view led them to believe that it is better to suffer than to be relieved of pain. Mahatma Gandhi disavowed his whole philosophy when he entered a modern hospital to be treated for appendicitis.

The North American Indians lacked the ingenuity to invent the wheel. The inhabitants of the Alps were not keen enough to construct skis which would have rendered their hard life much more agreeable. Such shortcomings were not due to a mentality different from those of the races which had long since used wheels and skis; they were failures, even when judged from the point of view of the Indians and the Alpine mountaineers.

However, these considerations refer only to the motives determining concrete actions, not to the only relevant problem of whether or not there exists between various races a difference in the logical structure of mind. It is precisely this that the racists assert.[13]

We may refer to what has been said in the preceding chapters about the fundamental issues of the logical structure of mind and the categorial principles of thought and action. Some additional observations will suffice to give the finishing stroke to racial polylogism and to any other brand of polylogism.

The categories of human thought and action are neither arbitrary products of the human mind nor conventions. They are not outside of the universe and of the course of cosmic events. They are biological facts and have a definite function in life and reality. They are instruments in man's struggle for existence and in his endeavors to adjust himself as much as possible to the real state of the universe and to remove uneasiness as much as it is in his power to do so. They are

13. Cf. L. G. Tirala, *Rasse, Geist und Seele* (Munich, 1935), pp. 190 ff.

therefore appropriate to the structure of the external world and reflect properties of the world and of reality. They work, and are in this sense true and valid.

It is consequently incorrect to assert that aprioristic insight and pure reasoning do not convey any information about reality and the structure of the universe. The fundamental logical relations and the categories of thought and action are the ultimate source of all human knowledge. They are adequate to the structure of reality, they reveal this structure to the human mind and, in this sense, they are for man basic ontological facts.[14] We do not know what a superhuman intellect may think and comprehend. For man every cognition is conditioned by the logical structure of his mind and implied in this structure. It is precisely the satisfactory results of the empirical sciences and their practical application that evidence this truth. Within the orbit in which human action is able to attain ends aimed at there is no room left for agnosticism.

If there had been races which had developed a different logical structure of the mind, they would have failed in the use of reason as an aid in the struggle for existence. The only means for survival that could have protected them against extermination would have been their instinctive reactions. Natural selection would have eliminated those specimens of such races that tried to employ reasoning for the direction of their behavior. Those individuals alone would have survived that relied upon instincts only. This means that only those would have had a chance to survive that did not rise above the mental level of animals.

The scholars of the West have amassed an enormous amount of material concerning the high civilizations of China and India and the primitive civilizations of the Asiatic, American, Australian, and African aborigines. It is safe to say that all that is worth knowing about the ideas of these races is known. But never has any supporter of polylogism tried to use these data for a description of the allegedly different logic of these peoples and civilizations.

5. Polylogism and Understanding

Some supporters of the tenets of Marxism and racism interpret the epistemological teachings of their parties in a peculiar way. They are ready to admit that the logical structure of mind is uniform for all races, nations, and classes. Marxism or racism, they assert, never intended to deny this undeniable fact. What they really wanted to say

14. Cf. Morris R. Cohen, *Reason and Nature* (New York, 1931), pp. 202–205; *A Preface to Logic* (New York, 1944), pp. 42–44, 54–56, 92, 180–187.

was that historical understanding, aesthetic empathy, and value judgments are conditioned by a man's background. It is obvious that this interpretation cannot be supported on the basis of the writings of the champions of polylogism. However, it must be analyzed as a doctrine of its own.

There is no need to emphasize again that a man's value judgments and his choice of ends reflect his inborn bodily features and all the vicissitudes of his life.[15] But it is a far cry from the acknowledgment of this fact to the belief that racial inheritance or class affiliation ultimately determines judgments of value and the choice of ends. The fundamental discrepancies in world view and patterns of behavior do not correspond to differences in race, nationality, or class affiliation.

There is hardly any greater divergence in value judgments than that between ascetics and those eager to enjoy life lightheartedly. An unbridgeable gulf separates devout monks and nuns from the rest of mankind. But there have been people dedicated to the monkish ideals among all races, nations, classes, and castes. Some of them were sons and daughters of kings and wealthy noblemen, others were beggars. St. Francis, Santa Clara, and their ardent followers were natives of Italy, whose other inhabitants cannot be described as weary of temporal things. Puritanism was Anglo-Saxon, but so was the lasciviousness of the British under the Tudors, the Stuarts, and the Hanoverians. The nineteenth century's outstanding champion of asceticism was Count Leo Tolstoy, a wealthy member of the profligate Russian aristocracy. Tolstoy saw the pith of the philosophy he attacked embodied in Beethoven's Kreutzer Sonata, a masterpiece of the son of extremely poor parents.

It is the same with aesthetic values. All races and nations have had both classic and romantic art. With all their ardent propaganda the Marxians have not succeeded in bringing about a specifically proletarian art or literature. The "proletarian" writers, painters, and musicians have not created new styles and have not established new aesthetic values. What characterizes them is solely their tendency to call everything they detest "bourgeois" and everything they like "proletarian."

Historical understanding both of the historian and of the acting man always reflects the personality of its author.[16] But if the historian and the politician are imbued with the desire for truth, they will never let themselves be deluded by party bias, provided they are

15. Cf. above, pp. 46–47.
16. Cf. above, pp. 57–58.

efficient and not inept. It is immaterial whether a historian or a politician considers the interference of a certain factor beneficial or detrimental. He cannot derive any advantage from underrating or overrating the relevance of one of the operating factors. Only clumsy would-be historians believe that they can serve their cause by distortion.

This is no less true of the statesman's understanding. What use could a champion of Protestantism derive from misunderstanding the tremendous power and prestige of Catholicism, or a liberal from misunderstanding the relevance of socialist ideas? In order to succeed a politician must see things as they are; whoever indulges in wishful thinking will certainly fail. Judgments of relevance differ from judgments of value in that they aim at the appraisal of a state of affairs not dependent on the author's arbitrariness. They are colored by their author's personality and can therefore never be unanimously agreed upon by all people. But here again we must raise the question: What advantage could a race or class derive from an "ideological" distortion of understanding?

As has already been pointed out, the serious discrepancies to be found in historical studies are an outcome of differences in the field of the nonhistorical sciences and not in various modes of understanding.

Today many historians and writers are imbued with the Marxian dogma that the realization of the socialist plans is both unavoidable and the supreme good, and that the labor movement is entrusted with the historical mission of accomplishing this task by a violent overthrow of the capitalistic system. Starting from this tenet, they take it as a matter of course that the parties of the "Left," the elect, in the pursuit of their policies, should resort to acts of violence and to murder. A revolution cannot be consummated by peaceful methods. It is not worthwhile to dwell upon such trifles as the butchering of the four daughters of the last Tsar, of Leon Trotsky, of tens of thousands of Russian bourgeois and so on. "You can't make an omelet without breaking eggs"; why explicitly mention the eggs broken? But, of course, it is different if one of those assailed ventures to defend himself or even to strike back. Few only mention the acts of sabotage, destruction, and violence committed by strikers. But all authors enlarge upon the attempts of the companies to protect their property and the lives of their employees and their customers against such onslaughts.

Such discrepancies are due neither to judgments of value nor to differences in understanding. They are the outcome of antagonistic theories of economic and historical evolution. If the coming of socialism is unavoidable and can be achieved only by revolutionary methods, murders committed by the "progressives" are minor incidents of no significance. But the self-defense and counterattacks of the "reactionaries" which can possibly delay the final victory of socialism are of the greatest importance. They are remarkable events, while the revolutionary acts are simply routine.

6. The Case for Reason

Judicious rationalists do not pretend that human reason can ever make man omniscient. They are fully aware of the fact that, however knowledge may increase, there will always remain things ultimately given and not liable to any further elucidation. But, they say, as far as man is able to attain cognition, he must rely upon reason. The ultimate given is the irrational. The knowable is, as far as it is known already, necessarily rational. There is neither an irrational mode of cognition nor a science of irrationality.

With regard to unsolved problems, various hypotheses are permissible provided they do not contradict logic and the uncontested data of experience. But these are hypotheses only.

We do not know what causes the inborn differences in human abilities. Science is at a loss to explain why Newton and Mozart were full of creative genius and why most people are not. But it is by all means an unsatisfactory answer to say that a genius owes his greatness to his ancestry or to his race. The question is precisely why such a man differs from his brothers and from the other members of his race.

It is a little bit less faulty to attribute the great achievements of the white race to racial superiority. Yet this is no more than vague hypothesis which is at variance with the fact that the early foundations of civilization were laid by peoples of other races. We cannot know whether or not at a later date other races will supplant Western civilization.

However, such a hypothesis must be appraised on its own merits. It must not be condemned beforehand because the racists base on it their postulate that there is an irreconcilable conflict between various racial groups and that the superior races must enslave the inferior ones. Ricardo's law of association has long since discarded this mistaken interpretation of the inequality of men.[17] It is nonsensical to fight the racial hypothesis by negating obvious facts. It is vain to deny that up to now certain races have contributed nothing or very

17. See below, pp. 158–163.

little to the development of civilization and can, in this sense, be called inferior.

If somebody were eager to distill at any cost a grain of truth out of the Marxian teachings, he could say that emotions influence a man's reasoning very much. Nobody ever ventured to deny this obvious fact, and Marxism cannot be credited with its discovery. But it is without any significance for epistemology. There are many sources both of success and of error. It is the task of psychology to enumerate and to classify them.

Envy is a widespread frailty. It is certain that many intellectuals envy the higher income of prosperous businessmen and that these feelings drive them toward socialism. They believe that the authorities of a socialist commonwealth would pay them higher salaries than those that they earn under capitalism. But to prove the existence of this envy does not relieve science of the duty of making the most careful examination of the socialist doctrines. Scientists are bound to deal with every doctrine as if its supporters were inspired by nothing else than the thirst for knowledge. The various brands of polylogism substitute for a purely theoretical examination of opposite doctrines the unmasking of the background and the motives of their authors. Such a procedure is incompatible with the first principles of ratiocination.

It is a poor makeshift to dispose of a theory by referring to its historical background, to the "spirit" of its time, to the material conditions of the country of its origin, and to any personal qualities of its authors. A theory is subject to the tribunal of reason only. The yardstick to be applied is always the yardstick of reason. A theory is either correct or incorrect. It may happen that the present state of our knowledge does not allow a decision with regard to its correctness or incorrectness. But a theory can never be valid for a bourgeois or an American if it is invalid for a proletarian or a Chinese.

If the Marxians and the racists were right, it would be impossible to explain why those in power are anxious to suppress dissenting theories and to persecute their supporters. The very fact that there are intolerant governments and political parties intent upon outlawing and exterminating dissenters, is a proof of the excellence of reason. It is not a conclusive proof of a doctrine's correctness that its adversaries use the police, the hangman, and violent mobs to fight it. But it is a proof of the fact that those taking recourse to violent oppression are in their subconsciousness convinced of the untenability of their own doctrines.

It is impossible to demonstrate the validity of the a priori foundations of logic and praxeology without referring to these foundations themselves. Reason is an ultimate given and cannot be analyzed or questioned by itself. The very existence of human reason is a nonrational fact. The only statement that can be predicated with regard to reason is that it is the mark that distinguishes man from animals and has brought about everything that is specifically human.

To those pretending that man would be happier if he were to renounce the use of reason and try to let himself be guided by intuition and instincts only, no other answer can be given than an analysis of the achievements of human society. In describing the genesis and working of social cooperation, economics provides all the information required for an ultimate decision between reason and unreason. If man reconsiders freeing himself from the supremacy of reason, he must know what he will have to forsake.

IV. A FIRST ANALYSIS OF THE CATEGORY OF ACTION

1. Ends and Means

THE result sought by an action is called its end, goal, or aim. One uses these terms in ordinary speech also to signify intermediate ends, goals, or aims; these are points which acting man wants to attain only because he believes that he will reach his ultimate end, goal, or aim in passing beyond them. Strictly speaking the end, goal, or aim of any action is always the relief from a felt uneasiness.

A means is what serves to the attainment of any end, goal, or aim. Means are not in the given universe; in this universe there exist only things. A thing becomes a means when human reason plans to employ it for the attainment of some end and human action really employs it for this purpose. Thinking man sees the serviceableness of things, i.e., their ability to minister to his ends, and acting man makes them means. It is of primary importance to realize that parts of the external world become means only through the operation of the human mind and its offshoot, human action. External objects are as such only phenomena of the physical universe and the subject matter of the natural sciences. It is human meaning and action which transform them into means. Praxeology does not deal with the external world, but with man's conduct with regard to it. Praxeological reality is not the physical universe, but man's conscious reaction to the given state of this universe. Economics is not about things and tangible material objects; it is about men, their meanings and actions. Goods, commodities, and wealth and all the other notions of conduct are not elements of nature; they are elements of human meaning and conduct. He who wants to deal with them must not look at the external world; he must search for them in the meaning of acting men.

Praxeology and economics do not deal with human meaning and action as they should be or would be if all men were inspired by an absolutely valid philosophy and equipped with a perfect knowledge of technology. For such notions as absolute validity and omniscience there is no room in the frame of a science whose subject matter is erring man. An end is everything which men aim at. A means is everything which acting men consider as such.

It is the task of scientific technology and therapeutics to explode errors in their respective fields. It is the task of economics to expose erroneous doctrines in the field of social action. But if men do not follow the advice of science, but cling to their fallacious prejudices, these errors are reality and must be dealt with as such. Economists consider foreign exchange control as inappropriate to attain the ends aimed at by those who take recourse to it. However, if public opinion does not abandon its delusions and governments consequently resort to foreign exchange control, the course of events is determined by this attitude. Present-day medicine considers the doctrine of the therapeutic effects of mandrake as a fable. But as long as people took this fable as truth, mandrake was an economic good and prices were paid for its acquisition. In dealing with prices economics does not ask what things are in the eyes of other people, but only what they are in the meaning of those intent upon getting them. For it deals with real prices, paid and received in real transactions, not with prices as they would be if men were different from what they really are.

Means are necessarily always limited, i.e., scarce with regard to the services for which man wants to use them. If this were not the case, there would not be any action with regard to them. Where man is not restrained by the insufficient quantity of things available, there is no need for any action.

It is customary to call the end the ultimate good and the means goods. In applying this terminology economists mainly used to think as technologists and not as praxeologists. They differentiated between *free goods* and *economic goods*. They called free goods those things which, being available in superfluous abundance, do not need to be economized. Such goods are, however, not the object of any action. They are general conditions of human welfare; they are parts of the natural environment in which man lives and acts. Only the economic goods are the substratum of action. They alone are dealt with in economics.

Economic goods which in themselves are fitted to satisfy human wants directly and whose serviceableness does not depend on the cooperation of other economic goods, are called consumers' goods or goods of the first order. Means which can satisfy wants only indirectly when complemented by cooperation of other goods are called producers' goods or factors of production or goods of a remoter or higher order. The services rendered by a producers' good consist in bringing about, by the cooperation of complementary producers' goods, a product. This product may be a consumers' good; it may be a producers' good which when combined with other producers' goods will finally bring about a consumers' good. It is possible to think of the producers' goods as arranged in orders according to their proximity to the consumers' good for whose production they can be used. Those producers' goods which are nearest to the production of a consumers' good are ranged in the second order, and accordingly those which are used for the production of goods of the second order in the third order and so on.

The purpose of such an arrangement of goods in orders is to provide a basis for the theory of value and prices of the factors of production. It will be shown later how the valuation and the prices of the goods of higher orders are dependent on the valuation and the prices of the goods of lower orders produced by their expenditure. The first and ultimate valuation of external things refers only to consumers' goods. All other things are valued according to the part they play in the production of consumers' goods.

It is therefore not necessary actually to arrange producers' goods in various orders from the second to the *n*th. It is no less superfluous to enter into pedantic discussions of whether a concrete good has to be called a good of the lowest order or should rather be attributed to one of the higher orders. Whether raw coffee beans or roast coffee beans or ground coffee or coffee prepared for drinking or only coffee prepared and mixed with cream and sugar are to to called a consumers' good ready for consumption is of no importance. It is immaterial which manner of speech we adopt. For with regard to the problem of valuation, all that we say about a consumers' good can be applied to any good of a higher order (except those of the highest order) if we consider it as a product.

An economic good does not necessarily have to be embodied in a tangible thing. Nonmaterial economic goods are called services.

2. The Scale of Value

Acting man chooses between various opportunities offered for choice. He prefers one alternative to others.

It is customary to say that acting man has a scale of wants or values in his mind when he arranges his actions. On the basis of such a scale he satisfies what is of higher value, i.e., his more urgent wants, and leaves unsatisfied what is of lower value, i.e., what is a less urgent want. There is no objection to such a presentation of the state of affairs. However, one must not forget that the scale of values or wants manifests itself only in the reality of action. These scales have no independent existence apart from the actual behavior of individuals. The only source from which our knowledge concerning these scales is derived is the observation of a man's actions. Every action is always in perfect agreement with the scale of values or wants because these scales are nothing but an instrument for the interpretation of a man's acting.

Ethical doctrines are intent upon establishing scales of value according to which man should act but does not necessarily always act. They claim for themselves the vocation of telling right from wrong and of advising man concerning what he should aim at as the supreme good. They are normative disciplines aiming at the cognition of what ought to be. They are not neutral with regard to facts; they judge them from the point of view of freely adopted standards.

This is not the attitude of praxeology and economics. They are fully aware of the fact that the ultimate ends of human action are not open to examination from any absolute standard. Ultimate ends are ultimately given, they are purely subjective, they differ with various people and with the same people at various moments in their lives. Praxeology and economics deal with the means for the attainment of ends chosen by the acting individuals. They do not express any opinion with regard to such problems as whether or not sybaritism is better than asceticism. They apply to the means only one yardstick, viz., whether or not they are suitable to attain the ends at which the acting individuals aim.

The notions of abnormality and perversity therefore have no place in economics. It does not say that a man is perverse because he prefers the disagreeable, the detrimental, and the painful to the agreeable, the beneficial, and the pleasant. It says only that he is different from other people; that he likes what others detest; that he considers useful what others want to avoid; that he takes pleasure in enduring pain which others avoid because it hurts them. The polar notions normal and perverse can be used anthropologically for the distinction between those who behave as most people do and outsiders and atypical exceptions; they can be applied biologically for the distinction between those whose behavior preserves the vital forces and those whose behavior is self-destructive; they can be applied in an ethical sense for the distinction between those who behave correctly and those who act otherwise than they should. However, in the frame of a theoretical science of human action, there is no room for such a distinction.

Any examination of ultimate ends turns out to be purely subjective and therefore arbitrary.

Value is the importance that acting man attaches to ultimate ends. Only to ultimate ends is primary and original value assigned. Means are valued derivatively according to their serviceableness in contributing to the attainment of ultimate ends. Their valuation is derived from the valuation of the respective ends. They are important for man only as far as they make it possible for him to attain some ends.

Value is not intrinsic, it is not in things. It is within us; it is the way in which man reacts to the conditions of his environment.

Neither is value in words and doctrines. It is reflected in human conduct. It is not what a man or groups of men say about value that counts, but how they act. The oratory of moralists and the pompousness of party programs are significant as such. But they influence the course of human events only as far as they really determine the actions of men.

3. The Scale of Needs

Notwithstanding all declarations to the contrary, the immense majority of men aim first of all at an improvement of the material conditions of well-being. They want more and better food, better homes and clothes, and a thousand other amenities. They strive after abundance and health. Taking these goals as given, applied physiology tries to determine what means are best suited to provide as much satisfaction as possible. It distinguishes, from this point of view, between man's "real" needs and imaginary and spurious appetites. It teaches people how they should act and what they should aim at as a means.

The importance of such doctrines is obvious. From his point of view the physiologist is right in distinguishing between sensible action and action contrary to purpose. He is right in contrasting judicious methods of nourishment from unwise methods. He may condemn certain modes of behavior as absurd and opposed to "real" needs. However, such judgments are beside the point for a science dealing with the reality of human action. Not what a man should do, but what he does, counts for praxeology and economics. Hygiene may be right or wrong in calling alcohol and nicotine poisons. But economics must explain the prices of tobacco and liquor as they are, not as they would be under different conditions.

There is no room left in the field of economics for a scale of needs different from the scale of values as reflected in man's actual behavior. Economics deals with real man, weak and subject to error as he is, not with ideal beings, omniscient and perfect as only gods could be.

4. Action as an Exchange

Action is an attempt to substitute a more satisfactory state of affairs for a less satisfactory one. We call such a willfully induced alteration an exchange. A less desirable condition is bartered for a more desirable. What gratifies less is abandoned in order to attain something that pleases more. That which is abandoned is called the price paid for the attainment of the end sought. The value of the price paid is called costs. Costs are equal to the value attached to the satisfaction which one must forego in order to attain the end aimed at.

The difference between the value of the price paid (the costs incurred) and that of the goal attained is called gain or profit or net yield. Profit in this primary sense is purely subjective, it is an increase in the acting man's happiness, it is a psychical phenomenon that can be neither measured nor weighed. There is a more and a less in the removal of uneasiness felt; but how much one satisfaction surpasses another one can only be felt; it cannot be established and determined in an objective way. A judgment of value does not measure, it arranges in a scale of degrees, it grades. It is expressive of an order of preference and sequence, but not expressive of measure and weight. Only the ordinal numbers can be applied to it, but not the cardinal numbers.

It is vain to speak of any calculation of values. Calculation is possible only with cardinal numbers. The difference between the valuation of two states of affairs is entirely psychical and personal. It is not open to any projection into the external world. It can be sensed only by the individual. It cannot be communicated or imparted to any fellow man. It is an intensive magnitude.

Physiology and psychology have developed various methods by means of which they pretend to have attained a substitute for the unfeasible measurement of intensive magnitudes. There is no need for economics to enter into an examination of these rather questionable makeshifts. Their supporters themselves realize that they are not applicable to value judgments. But even if they were, they would not have any bearing on economic problems. For economics deals with action as such, and not with the psychical facts that result in definite actions.

It happens again and again that an action does not attain the end sought. Sometimes the result, although inferior to the end aimed at, is still an improvement when compared with the previous state of affairs; then there is still a profit, although a smaller one than that expected. But it can happen that the action produces a state of affairs less desirable than the previous state it was intended to alter. Then the difference between the valuation of the result and the costs incurred is called loss.

V. TIME

1. Time as a Praxeological Factor

THE notion of change implies the notion of temporal sequence. A rigid, eternally immutable universe would be out of time, but it would be dead. The concepts of change and of time are inseparably linked together. Action aims at change and is therefore in the temporal order. Human reason is even incapable of conceiving the ideas of timeless existence and of timeless action.

He who acts distinguishes between the time before the action, the time absorbed by the action, and the time after the action has been finished. He cannot be neutral with regard to the lapse of time.

Logic and mathematics deal with an ideal system of thought. The relations and implications of their system are coexistent and interdependent. We may say as well that they are synchronous or that they are out of time. A perfect mind could grasp them all in one thought. Man's inability to accomplish this makes thinking itself an action, proceeding step by step from the less satisfactory state of insufficient cognition to the more satisfactory state of better insight. But the temporal order in which knowledge is acquired must not be confused with the logical simultaneity of all parts of an aprioristic deductive system. Within such a system the notions of anteriority and consequence are metaphorical only. They do not refer to the system, but to our action in grasping it. The system itself implies neither the category of time nor that of causality. There is functional correspondence between elements, but there is neither cause nor effect.

What distinguishes epistemologically the praxeological system from the logical system is precisely that it implies the categories both of time and of causality. The praxeological system too is aprioristic and deductive. As a system it is out of time. But change is one of its elements. The notions of sooner and later and of cause and effect are among its constituents. Anteriority and consequence are essential concepts of praxeological reasoning. So is the irreversibility of events. In the frame of the praxeological system any reference to functional correspondence is no less metaphorical and misleading than is the reference to anteriority and consequence in the frame of the logical system.[1]

2. Past, Present, and Future

It is acting that provides man with the notion of time and makes him aware of the flux of time. The idea of time is a praxeological category.

Action is always directed toward the future; it is essentially and necessarily always a planning and acting for a better future. Its aim is always to render future conditions more satisfactory than they would be without the interference of action. The uneasiness that impels a man to act is caused by a dissatisfaction with expected future conditions as they would probably develop if nothing were done to alter them. In any case action can influence only the future, never the present that with every infinitesimal fraction of a second sinks down into the past. Man becomes conscious of time when he plans to convert a less satisfactory present state into a more satisfactory future state.

For contemplative meditation time is merely duration, "la durée pure, dont l'écoulement est continu, et où l'on passe, par gradations insensibles, d'un état à l'autre: Continuité réellement vécue."[2] The "now" of the present is continually shifted to the past and is retained in the memory only. Reflecting about the past, say the philosophers, man becomes aware of time.[3] However, it is not recollection that conveys to man the categories of change and of time, but the will to improve the conditions of his life.

Time as we measure it by various mechanical devices is always past, and time as the philosophers use this concept is always either past or future. The present is, from these aspects, nothing but an ideal boundary line separating the past from the future. But from the praxeological aspect there is between the past and the future a real extended present. Action is as such in the real present because it utilizes the instant and thus embodies its reality.[4] Later retrospective

1. In a treatise on economics there is no need to enter into a discussion of the endeavors to construct mechanics as an axiomatic system in which the concept of function is substituted for that of cause and effect. It will be shown later that axiomatic mechanics cannot serve as a model for the treatment of the economic system. Cf. below, pp. 353–357.

2. Henri Bergson, *Matière et mémoire* (7th ed. Paris, 1911), p. 205.

3. Edmund Husserl, "Vorlesungen zur Phänomenologie des inneren Zeitbewusstseins," *Jahrbuch für Philosophie und Phänomenologische Forschung*, IX (1928), 391 ff.; A. Schütz, *loc. cit.*, pp. 45 ff.

4. "Ce que j'appelle mon présent, c'est mon attitude vis-à-vis de l'avenir immédiat, c'est mon action imminente." Bergson, *op. cit.*, p. 152.

reflection discerns in the instant passed away first of all the action and the conditions which it offered to action. That which can no longer be done or consumed because the opportunity for it has passed away, contrasts the past with the present. That which cannot yet be done or consumed, because the conditions for undertaking it or the time for its ripening have not yet come, contrasts the future with the past. The present offers to acting opportunities and tasks for which it was hitherto too early and for which it will be hereafter too late.

The present qua duration is the continuation of the conditions and opportunities given for acting. Every kind of action requires special conditions to which it must be adjusted with regard to the aims sought. The concept of the present is therefore different for various fields of action. It has no reference whatever to the various methods of measuring the passing of time by spatial movements. The present encloses as much of the time passed away as still is actual, i.e., of importance for acting. The present contrasts itself, according to the various actions one has in view, with the Middle Ages, with the nineteenth century, with the past year, month, or day, but no less with the hour, minute, or second just passed away. If a man says: Nowadays Zeus is no longer worshipped, he has a present in mind other than that the motorcar driver who thinks: *Now* it is still too early to turn.

As the future is uncertain it always remains undecided and vague how much of it we can consider as *now* and present. If a man had said in 1913: At present—now—in Europe freedom of thought is undisputed, he would have not foreseen that this present would very soon be a past.

3. The Economization of Time

Man is subject to the passing of time. He comes into existence, grows, becomes old, and passes away. His time is scarce. He must economize it as he economizes other scarce factors.

The economization of time has a peculiar character because of the uniqueness and irreversibility of the temporal order. The importance of these facts manifests itself in every part of the theory of action.

Only one fact must be stressed at this point. The economization of time is independent of the economization of economic goods and services. Even in the land of Cockaigne man would be forced to economize time, provided he were not immortal and not endowed with eternal youth and indestructible health and vigor. Although all his appetites could be satisfied immediately without any expenditure of labor, he would have to arrange his time schedule, as there are states of satisfaction which are incompatible and cannot be consummated at the same time. For this man, too, time would be scarce and subject to the aspect of *sooner* and *later*.

4. The Temporal Relation Between Actions

Two actions of an individual are never synchronous; their temporal relation is that of sooner and later. Actions of various individuals can be considered as synchronous only in the light of the physical methods for the measurement of time. Synchronism is a praxeological notion only with regard to the concerted efforts of various acting men.[5]

A man's individual actions succeed one another. They can never be effected at the same instant; they can only follow one another in more or less rapid succession. There are actions which serve several purposes at one blow. It would be misleading to refer to them as a coincidence of various actions.

People have often failed to recognize the meaning of the term "scale of value" and have disregarded the obstacles preventing the assumption of synchronism in the various actions of an individual. They have interpreted a man's various acts as the outcome of a scale of value, independent of these acts and preceding them, and of a previously devised plan whose realization they aim at. The scale of value and the plan to which duration and immutability for a certain period of time were attributed, were hypostasized into the cause and motive of the various individual actions. Synchronism which could not be asserted with regard to various acts was then easily discovered in the scale of value and in the plan. But this overlooks the fact that the scale of value is nothing but a constructed tool of thought. The scale of value manifests itself only in real acting; it can be discerned only from the observation of real acting. It is therefore impermissible to contrast it with real acting and to use it as a yardstick for the appraisal of real actions.

It is no less impermissible to differentiate between rational and allegedly irrational acting on the basis of a comparison of real acting with earlier drafts and plans for future actions. It may be very inter-

5. In order to avoid any possible misunderstanding it may be expedient to emphasize that this theorem has nothing at all to do with Einstein's theorem concerning the temporal relation of spatially distant events.

esting that yesterday goals were set for today's acting other than those really aimed at today. But yesterday's plans do not provide us with any more objective and nonarbitrary standard for the appraisal of today's real acting than any other ideas and norms.

The attempt has been made to attain the notion of a nonrational action by this reasoning: If *a* is preferred to *b* and *b* to *c,* logically *a* should be preferred to *c*. But if actually *c* is preferred to *a,* we are faced with a mode of acting to which we cannot ascribe consistency and rationality.[6] This reasoning disregards the fact that two acts of an individual can never be synchronous. If in one action *a* is preferred to *b* and in another action *b* to *c,* it is, however short the interval between the two actions may be, not permissible to construct a uniform scale of value in which *a* precedes *b* and *b* precedes *c*. Nor is it permissible to consider a later third action as coincident with the two previous actions. All that the example proves is that value judgments are not immutable and that therefore a scale of value, which is abstracted from various, necessarily nonsynchronous actions of an individual, may be self-contradictory.[7]

One must not confuse the logical concept of consistency (viz., absence of contradiction) and the praxeological concept of consistency (viz., constancy or clinging to the same principles). Logical consistency has its place only in thinking, constancy has its place only in acting.

Constancy and rationality are entirely different notions. If one's valuations have changed, unremitting faithfulness to the once espoused principles of action merely for the sake of constancy would not be rational but simply stubborn. Only in one respect can acting be constant: in preferring the more valuable to the less valuable. If the valuations change, acting must change also. Faithfulness, under changed conditions, to an old plan would be nonsensical. A logical system must be consistent and free of contradictions because it implies the coexistence of all its parts and theorems. In acting, which is necessarily in the temporal order, there cannot be any question of such consistency. Acting must be suited to purpose, and purposefulness requires adjustment to changing conditions.

Presence of mind is considered a virtue in acting man. A man has presence of mind if he has the ability to think and to adjust his acting

6. Cf. Felix Kaufmann, "On the Subject-Matter of Economic Science," *Economica,* XIII, 390.

7. Cf. P. H. Wicksteed, *The Common Sense of Political Economy,* ed. Robbins (London, 1933), I, 32 ff.; L. Robbins, *An Essay on the Nature and Significance of Economic Science* (2d ed. London, 1935), pp. 91 ff.

so quickly that the interval between the emergence of new conditions and the adaptation of his actions to them becomes as short as possible. If constancy is viewed as faithfulness to a plan once designed without regard to changes in conditions, then presence of mind and quick reaction are the very opposite of constancy.

When the speculator goes to the stock exchange, he may sketch a definite plan for his operations. Whether or not he clings to this plan, his actions are rational also in the sense which those eager to distinguish rational acting from irrational attribute to the term "rational." This speculator in the course of the day may embark upon transactions which an observer, not taking into account the changes occurring in market conditions, will not be able to interpret as the outcome of constant behavior. But the speculator is firm in his intention to make profits and to avoid losses. Accordingly he must adjust his conduct to the change in market conditions and in his own judgment concerning the future development of prices.[8]

However one twists things, one will never succeed in formulating the notion of "irrational" action whose "irrationality" is not founded upon an arbitrary judgment of value. Let us suppose that somebody has chosen to act inconstantly for no other purpose than for the sake of refuting the praxeological assertion that there is no irrational action. What happens here is that a man aims at a peculiar goal, viz., the refutation of a praxeological theorem, and that he accordingly acts differently from what he would have done otherwise. He has chosen an unsuitable means for the refutation of praxeology, that is all.

8. Plans too, of course, may be self-contradictory. Sometimes their contradictions may be the effect of mistaken judgment. But sometimes such contradictions may be intentional and serve a definite purpose. If, for instance, a publicized program of a government or a political party promises high prices to the producers and at the same time low prices to the consumers, the purpose of such an espousal of incompatible goals may be demagogic. Then the program, the publicized plan, is self-contradictory; but the plan of its authors who wanted to attain a definite end through the endorsement of incompatible aims and their public announcement is free of any contradiction.

VI. UNCERTAINTY

1. Uncertainty and Acting

THE uncertainty of the future is already implied in the very notion of action. That man acts and that the future is uncertain are by no means two independent matters. They are only two different modes of establishing one thing.

We may assume that the outcome of all events and changes is uniquely determined by eternal unchangeable laws governing becoming and development in the whole universe. We may consider the necessary connection and interdependence of all phenomena, i.e., their causal concatenation, as the fundamental and ultimate fact. We may entirely discard the notion of undetermined chance. But however that may be, or appear to the mind of a perfect intelligence, the fact remains that to acting man the future is hidden. If man knew the future, he would not have to choose and would not act. He would be like an automaton, reacting to stimuli without any will of his own.

Some philosophers are prepared to explode the notion of man's will as an illusion and self-deception because man must unwittingly behave according to the inevitable laws of causality. They may be right or wrong from the point of view of the prime mover or the cause of itself. However, from the human point of view action is the ultimate thing. We do not assert that man is "free" in choosing and acting. We merely establish the fact that he chooses and acts and that we are at a loss to use the methods of the natural sciences for answering the question why he acts this way and not otherwise.

Natural science does not render the future predictable. It makes it possible to foretell the results to be obtained by definite actions. But it leaves unpredictable two spheres: that of insufficiently known natural phenomena and that of human acts of choice. Our ignorance with regard to these two spheres taints all human actions with uncertainty. Apodictic certainty is only within the orbit of the deductive system of aprioristic theory. The most that can be attained with regard to reality is probability.

It is not the task of praxeology to investigate whether or not it is permissible to consider as certain some of the theorems of the empirical natural sciences. This problem is without practical importance for praxeological considerations. At any rate, the theorems of physics and chemistry have such a high degree of probability that we are entitled to call them certain for all practical purposes. We can practically forecast the working of a machine constructed according to the rules of scientific technology. But the construction of a machine is only a part in a broader program that aims at supplying the consumers with the machine's products. Whether this was or was not the most appropriate plan depends on the development of future conditions which at the time of the plan's execution cannot be forecast with certainty. Thus the degree of certainty with regard to the technological outcome of the machine's construction, whatever it may be, does not remove the uncertainty inherent in the whole action. Future needs and valuations, the reaction of men to changes in conditions, future scientific and technological knowledge, future ideologies and policies can never be foretold with more than a greater or smaller degree of probability. Every action refers to an unknown future. It is in this sense always a risky speculation.

The problems of truth and certainty concern the general theory of human knowledge. The problem of probability, on the other hand, is a primary concern of praxeology.

2. The Meaning of Probability

The treatment of probability has been confused by the mathematicians. From the beginning there was an ambiguity in dealing with the calculus of probability. When the Chevalier de Méré consulted Pascal on the problems involved in the games of dice, the great mathematician should have frankly told his friend the truth, namely, that mathematics cannot be of any use to the gambler in a game of pure chance. Instead he wrapped his answer in the symbolic language of mathematics. What could easily be explained in a few sentences of mundane speech was expressed in a terminology which is unfamiliar to the immense majority and therefore regarded with reverential awe. People suspected that the puzzling formulas contain some important revelations, hidden to the uninitiated; they got the impression that a scientific method of gambling exists and that the esoteric teachings of mathematics provide a key for winning. The heavenly mystic Pascal unintentionally became the patron saint of gambling. The textbooks of the calculus of probability gratuitously propagandize for the gambling casinos precisely because they are sealed books to the layman.

No less havoc was spread by the equivocations of the calculus of probability in the field of scientific research. The history of every branch of knowledge records instances of the misapplication of the calculus of probability which, as John Stuart Mill observed, made it "the real opprobrium of mathematics."[1]

The problem of probable inference is much bigger than those problems which constitute the field of the calculus of probability. Only preoccupation with the mathematical treatment could result in the prejudice that probability always means frequency.

A further error confused the problem of probability with the problem of inductive reasoning as applied by the natural sciences. The attempt to substitute a universal theory of probability for the category of causality characterizes an abortive mode of philosophizing, very fashionable only a few years ago.

A statement is probable if our knowledge concerning its content is deficient. We do not know everything which would be required for a definite decision between true and not true. But, on the other hand, we do know something about it; we are in a position to say more than simply *non liquet* or *ignoramus*.

There are two entirely different instances of probability; we may call them class probability (or frequency probability) and case probability (or the specific understanding of the sciences of human action). The field for the application of the former is the field of the natural sciences, entirely ruled by causality; the field for the application of the latter is the field of the sciences of human action, entirely ruled by teleology.

3. Class Probability

Class probability means: We know or assume to know, with regard to the problem concerned, everything about the behavior of a whole class of events or phenomena; but about the actual singular events or phenomena we know nothing but that they are elements of this class.

We know, for instance, that there are ninety tickets in a lottery and that five of them will be drawn. Thus we know all about the behavior of the whole class of tickets. But with regard to the singular tickets we do not know anything but that they are elements of this class of tickets.

We have a complete table of mortality for a definite period of the past in a definite area. If we assume that with regard to mortality no changes will occur, we may say that we know everything about the mortality of the whole population in question. But with regard to the

1. John Stuart Mill, *A System of Logic Ratiocinative and Inductive* (new impression, London, 1936), p. 353.

life expectancy of the individuals we do not know anything but that they are members of this class of people.

For this defective knowledge the calculus of probability provides a presentation in symbols of the mathematical terminology. It neither expands nor deepens nor complements our knowledge. It translates it into mathematical language. Its calculations repeat in algebraic formulas what we knew beforehand. They do not lead to results that would tell us anything about the actual singular events. And, of course, they do not add anything to our knowledge concerning the behavior of the whole class, as this knowledge was already perfect—or was considered perfect—at the very outset of our consideration of the matter.

It is a serious mistake to believe that the calculus of probability provides the gambler with any information which could remove or lessen the risk of gambling. It is, contrary to popular fallacies, quite useless for the gambler, as is any other mode of logical or mathematical reasoning. It is the characteristic mark of gambling that it deals with the unknown, with pure chance. The gambler's hopes for success are not based on substantial considerations. The nonsuperstitious gambler thinks: "There is a slight chance [or, in other words: 'it is not impossible'] that I may win; I am ready to put up the stake required. I know very well that in putting it up I am behaving like a fool. But the biggest fools have the most luck. Anyway!"

Cool reasoning must show the gambler that he does not improve his chances by buying two tickets instead of one of a lottery in which the total amount of the winnings is smaller than the proceeds from the sale of all tickets. If he were to buy all the tickets, he would certainly lose a part of his outlay. Yet every lottery customer is firmly convinced that it is better to buy more tickets than less. The habitués of the casinos and slot machines never stop. They do not give a thought to the fact that, because the ruling odds favor the banker over the player, the outcome will the more certainly result in a loss for them the longer they continue to play. The lure of gambling consists precisely in its unpredictability and its adventurous vicissitudes.

Let us assume that ten tickets, each bearing the name of a different man, are put into a box. One ticket will be drawn, and the man whose name it bears will be liable to pay 100 dollars. Then an insurer can promise to the loser full indemnification if he is in a position to insure each of the ten for a premium of ten dollars. He will collect 100 dollars and will have to pay the same amount to one of the ten. But if he were to insure one only of them at a rate fixed by the calculus, he would embark not upon an insurance business, but upon gambling. He would substitute himself for the insured. He would collect ten dollars and would get the chance either of keeping it or of losing that ten dollars and ninety dollars more.

If a man promises to pay at the death of another man a definite sum and charges for this promise the amount adequate to the life expectancy as determined by the calculus of probability, he is not an insurer but a gambler. Insurance, whether conducted according to business principles or according to the principle of mutuality, requires the insurance of a whole class or what can reasonably be considered as such. Its basic idea is pooling and distribution of risks, not the calculus of probability. The mathematical operation that it requires are the four elementary operations of arithmetic. The calculus of probability is mere by-play.

This is clearly evidenced by the fact that the elimination of hazardous risk by pooling can also be effected without any recourse to actuarial methods. Everybody practices it in his daily life. Every businessman includes in his normal cost accounting the compensation for losses which regularly occur in the conduct of affairs. "Regularly" means in this context: The amount of these losses is known as far as the whole class of the various items is concerned. The fruit dealer may know, for instance, that one of every fifty apples will rot in this stock; but he does not know to which individual apple this will happen. He deals with such losses as with any other item in the bill of costs.

The definition of the essence of class probability as given above is the only logically satisfactory one. It avoids the crude circularity implied in all definitions referring to the equiprobability of possible events. In stating that we know nothing about actual singular events except that they are elements of a class the behavior of which is fully known, this vicious circle is disposed of. Moreover, it is superfluous to add a further condition called the absence of any regularity in the sequence of the singular events.

The characteristic mark of insurance is that it deals with the whole class of events. As we pretend to know everything about the behavior of the whole class, there seems to be no specific risk involved in the conduct of the business.

Neither is there any specific risk in the business of the keeper of a gambling bank or in the enterprise of a lottery. From the point of view of the lottery enterprise the outcome is predictable, provided that all tickets have been sold. If some tickets remain unsold, the enterpriser is in the same position with regard to them as every buyer of a ticket is with regard to the tickets he bought.

4. Case Probability

Case probability means: We know, with regard to a particular event, some of the factors which determine its outcome; but there are other determining factors about which we know nothing.

Case probability has nothing in common with class probability but the incompleteness of our knowledge. In every other regard the two are entirely different.

There are, of course, many instances in which men try to forecast a particular future event on the basis of their knowledge about the behavior of the class. A doctor may determine the chances for the full recovery of his patient if he knows that 70 per cent of those afflicted with the same disease recover. If he expresses his judgment correctly, he will not say more than that the probability of recovery is 0.7, that is, that out of ten patients not more than three on the average die. All such predictions about external events, i.e., events in the field of the natural sciences, are of this character. They are in fact not forecasts about the issue of the case in question, but statements about the frequency of the various possible outcomes. They are based either on statistical information or simply on the rough estimate of the frequency derived from nonstatistical experience.

So far as such types of probable statements are concerned, we are not faced with case probability. In fact we do not know anything about the case in question except that it is an instance of a class the behavior of which we know or think we know.

A surgeon tells a patient who considers submitting himself to an operation that thirty out of every hundred undergoing such an operation die. If the patient asks whether this number of deaths is already full, he has misunderstood the sense of the doctor's statement. He has fallen prey to the error known as the "gambler's fallacy." Like the roulette player who concludes from a run of ten red in succession that the probability of the next turn being black is now greater than it was before the run, he confuses case probability with class probability.

All medical prognoses, when based only on general physiological knowledge, deal with class probability. A doctor who hears that a man he does not know has been seized by a definite illness will, on the basis of his general medical experience, say: His chances for recovery are 7 to 3. If the doctor himself treats the patient, he may have a different opinion. The patient is a young, vigorous man; he was in good health before he was taken with the illness. In such cases, the doctor may think, the mortality figures are lower; the chances for this patient are not 7:3, but 9:1. The logical approach remains the same, although it may be based not on a collection of statistical data, but simply on a more or less exact résumé of the doctor's own experience with previous cases. What the doctor knows is always only the behavior of classes. In our instance the class is the class of young, vigorous men seized by the illness in question.

Case probability is a particular feature of our dealing with problems of human action. Here any reference to frequency is inappropriate, as our statements always deal with unique events which as such —i.e., with regard to the problem in question—are not members of any class. We can form a class "American presidential elections." This class concept may prove useful or even necessary for various kinds of reasoning, as, for instance, for a treatment of the matter from the viewpoint of constitutional law. But if we are dealing with the election of 1944—either, before the election, with its future outcome or, after the election, with an analysis of the factors which determined the outcome—we are grappling with an individual, unique, and nonrepeatable case. The case is characterized by its unique merits, it is a class by itself. All the marks which make it permissible to subsume it under any class are irrelevant for the problem in question.

Two football teams, the Blues and the Yellows, will play tomorrow. In the past the Blues have always defeated the Yellows. This knowledge is not knowledge about a class of events. If we were to consider it as such, we would have to conclude that the Blues are always victorious and that the Yellows are always defeated. We would not be uncertain with regard to the outcome of the game. We would know for certain that the Blues will win again. The mere fact that we consider our forecast about tomorrow's game as only probable shows that we do not argue this way.

On the other hand, we believe that the fact that the Blues were victorious in the past is not immaterial with regard to the outcome of tomorrow's game. We consider it as a favorable prognosis for the repeated success of the Blues. If we were to argue correctly according to the reasoning appropriate to class probability, we would not attach any importance to this fact. If we were not to resist the erroneous conclusion of the "gambler's fallacy," we would, on the contrary, argue that tomorrow's game will result in the success of the Yellows.

If we risk some money on the chance of one team's victory, the lawyers would qualify our action as a bet. They would call it gambling if class probability were involved.

Everything that outside the field of class probability is commonly implied in the term probability refers to the peculiar mode of reasoning involved in dealing with historical uniqueness or individuality, the specific understanding of the historical sciences.

Understanding is always based on incomplete knowledge. We may believe we know the motives of the acting men, the ends they are aiming at, and the means they plan to apply for the attainment of these ends. We have a definite opinion with regard to the effects to be expected from the operation of these factors. But this knowledge is defective. We cannot exclude beforehand the possibility that we have erred in the appraisal of their influence or have failed to take into consideration some factors whose interference we did not foresee at all, or not in a correct way.

Gambling, engineering, and speculating are three different modes of dealing with the future.

The gambler knows nothing about the event on which the outcome of his gambling depends. All that he knows is the frequency of a favorable outcome of a series of such events, knowledge which is useless for his undertaking. He trusts to good luck, that is his only plan.

Life itself is exposed to many risks. At any moment it is endangered by disastrous accidents which cannot be controlled, or at least not sufficiently. Every man banks on good luck. He counts upon not being struck by lightning and not being bitten by a viper. There is an element of gambling in human life. Man can remove some of the chrematistic consequences of such disasters and accidents by taking out insurance policies. In doing so he banks upon the opposite chances. On the part of the insured the insurance is gambling. His premiums were spent in vain if the disaster does not occur.[2] With regard to noncontrollable natural events man is always in the position of a gambler.

The engineer, on the other hand, knows everything that is needed for a technologically satisfactory solution of his problem, the construction of a machine. As far as some fringes of uncertainty are left in his power to control, he tries to eliminate them by taking safety

2. In life insurance the insured's stake spent in vain consists only in the difference between the amount collected and the amount he could have accumulated by saving.

margins. The engineer knows only soluble problems and problems which cannot be solved under the present state of knowledge. He may sometimes discover from adverse experience that his knowledge was less complete than he had assumed and that he failed to recognize the indeterminateness of some issues which he thought he was able to control. Then he will try to render his knowledge more complete. Of course he can never eliminate altogether the element of gambling present in human life. But it is his principle to operate only within an orbit of certainty. He aims at full control of the elements of his action.

It is customary nowadays to speak of "social engineering." Like planning, this term is a synonym for dictatorship and totalitarian tyranny. The idea is to treat human beings in the same way in which the engineer treats the stuff out of which he builds bridges, roads, and machines. The social engineer's will is to be substituted for the will of the various people he plans to use for the construction of his utopia. Mankind is to be divided into two classes: the almighty dictator, on the one hand, and the underlings who are to be reduced to the status of mere pawns in his plans and cogs in his machinery, on the other. If this were feasible, then of course the social engineer would not have to bother about understanding other people's actions. He would be free to deal with them as technology deals with lumber and iron.

In the real world acting man is faced with the fact that there are fellow men acting on their own behalf as he himself acts. The necessity to adjust his actions to other people's actions makes him a speculator for whom success and failure depend on his greater or lesser ability to understand the future. Every action is speculation. There is in the course of human events no stability and consequently no safety.

5. Numerical Evaluation of Case Probability

Case probability is not open to any kind of numerical evaluation. What is commonly considered as such exhibits, when more closely scrutinized, a different character.

On the eve of the 1944 presidential election people could have said:

(a) I am ready to bet three dollars against one that Roosevelt will be elected.

(b) I guess that out of the total amount of electors 45 millions will exercise their franchise, 25 millions of whom will vote for Roosevelt.

(c) I estimate Roosevelt's chances as 9 to 1.

(d) I am certain that Roosevelt will be elected.

Statement (d) is obviously inexact. If asked under oath on the witness stand whether he is as certain about Roosevelt's future victory as about the fact that a block of ice will melt when exposed to a temperature of 150 degrees, our man would have answered no. He would have rectified his statement and would have declared: I am personally fully convinced that Roosevelt will carry on. That is my opinion. But, of course, this is not certainty, only the way I understand the conditions involved.

The case of statement (a) is similar. This man believed that he risked very little when laying such a wager. The relation 3:1 is the outcome of the interplay of two factors: the opinion that Roosevelt will be elected and the man's propensity for betting.

Statement (b) is an evaluation of the outcome of the impending event. Its figures refer not to a greater or smaller degree of probability, but to the expected result of the voting. Such a statement may be based on a systematic investigation like the Gallup poll or simply on estimates.

It is different with statement (c). This is a proposition about the expected outcome couched in arithmetical terms. It certainly does not mean that out of ten cases of the same type nine are favorable for Roosevelt and one unfavorable. It cannot have any reference to class probability. But what else can it mean?

It is a metaphorical expression. Most of the metaphors used in daily speech imaginatively identify an abstract object with another object that can be apprehended directly by the senses. Yet this is not a necessary feature of metaphorical language, but merely a consequence of the fact that the concrete is as a rule more familiar to us than the abstract. As metaphors aim at an explanation of something which is less well known by comparing it with something better known, they consist for the most part in identifying something abstract with a better-known concrete. The specific mark of our case is that it is an attempt to elucidate a complicated state of affairs by resorting to an analogy borrowed from a branch of higher mathematics, the calculus of probability. As it happens, this mathematical discipline is more popular than the analysis of the epistemological nature of understanding.

There is no use in applying the yardstick of logic to a critique of metaphorical language. Analogies and metaphors are always defective and logically unsatisfactory. It is usual to search for the underlying *tertium comparationis*. But even this is not permissible with regard to the metaphor we are dealing with. For the comparison is based on a conception which is in itself faulty in the very frame of the calculus of probability, namely the gambler's fallacy. In asserting that Roosevelt's chances are 9:1, the idea is that Roosevelt is in regard to the impending election in the position of a man who owns 90 per cent of all tickets of a lottery in regard to the first prize. It is implied that this ratio 9:1 tells us something substantial about the outcome of the unique case in which we are interested. There is no need to repeat that this is a mistaken idea.

No less impermissible is the recourse to the calculus of probability in dealing with hypotheses in the field of the natural sciences. Hypotheses are tentative explanations consciously based on logically insufficient arguments. With regard to them all that can be asserted is: The hypothesis does or does not contradict either logical principles or the facts as experimentally established and considered as true. In the first case it is untenable, in the second case it is—under the present state of our experimental knowledge—not untenable. (The intensity of personal conviction is purely subjective.) Neither frequency probability nor historical understanding enters into the matter.

The term hypothesis, applied to definite modes of understanding historical events, is a misnomer. If a historian asserts that in the fall of the Romanoff dynasty the fact that this house was of German background played a relevant role, he does not advance a hypothesis. The facts on which his understanding is founded are beyond question. There was a widespread animosity against Germans in Russia, and the ruling line of the Romanoffs, having for 200 years intermarried exclusively with scions of families of German descent, was viewed by many Russians as a germanized family, even by those who assumed that Tsar Paul was not the son of Peter III. But the question remains what the relevance of these facts was in the chain of events which brought about the dethronement of this dynasty. Such problems are not open to any elucidation other than that provided by understanding.

6. Betting, Gambling, and Playing Games

A bet is the engagement to risk money or other things against another man on the result of an event about the outcome of which we know only so much as can be known on the ground of understanding. Thus people may bet on the result of an impending election or a tennis match. Or they may bet on whose opinion concerning the content of a factual assertion is right and whose is wrong.

Gambling is the engagement to risk money or other things against another man on the result of an event about which we do not know anything more than is known on the ground of knowledge concerning the behavior of the whole class.

Sometimes betting and gambling are combined. The outcome of horse racing depends both on human action—on the part of the owner of the horse, the trainer, and the jockey—and on nonhuman factors—the qualities of the horse. Most of those risking money on the turf are simply gamblers. But the experts believe they know something by understanding the people involved; as far as this factor influences their decision they are betters. Furthermore they pretend to know the horses; they make a prognosis on the ground of their knowledge about the behavior of the classes of horses to which they assign the various competing horses. So far they are gamblers.

Later chapters of this book deal with the methods business applies in handling the problem of the uncertainty of the future. On this point of our reasoning only one more observation must be made.

Embarking upon games can be either an end or a means. It is an end for people who yearn for the stimulation and excitement with which the vicissitudes of a game provide them, or whose vanity is flattered by the display of their skill and superiority in playing a game which requires cunning and expertness. It is a means for professionals who want to make money by winning.

Playing a game can therefore be called an action. But it is not permissible to reverse this statement and to call every action a game or to deal with all actions as if they were games. The immediate aim in playing a game is to defeat the partner according to the rules of the game. This is a peculiar and special case of acting. Most actions do not aim at anybody's defeat or loss. They aim at an improvement in conditions. It can happen that this improvement is attained at some other men's expense. But this is certainly not always the case. It is, to put it mildly, certainly not the case within the regular operation of a social system based on the division of labor.

There is not the slightest analogy between playing games and the conduct of business within a market society. The card player wins money by outsmarting his antagonist. The businessman makes money by supplying customers with goods they want to acquire. There may exist an analogy between the strategy of a card player and that of a bluffer. There is no need to investigate this problem. He who interprets the conduct of business as trickery is on the wrong path.

The characteristic feature of games is the antagonism of two or more players or groups of players.[3] The characteristic feature of business

3. "Patience" or "Solitaire" is not a one-person game, but a pastime, a means of escaping boredom. It certainly does not represent a pattern for what is going on in a communistic society, as John von Neumann and Oscar Morgenstern (*Theory of Games and Economic Behavior* [Princeton, 1944], p. 86) assert.

within a society, i.e., within an order based on the division of labor, is concord in the endeavors of its members. As soon as they begin to antagonize one another, a tendency toward social disintegration emerges.

Within the frame of a market economy competition does not involve antagonism in the sense in which this term is applied to the hostile clash of incompatible interests. Competition, it is true, may sometimes or even often evoke in the competitors those passions of hatred and malice which usually accompany the intention of inflicting evil on other people. Psychologists are therefore prone to confuse combat and competition. But praxeology must beware of such artificial and misleading equivocations. From its point of view there exists a fundamental difference between catallactic competition and combat. Competitors aim at excellence and preeminence in accomplishments within a system of mutual cooperation. The function of competition is to assign to every member of a social system that position in which he can best serve the whole of society and all its members. It is a method of selecting the most able man for each performance. Where there is social cooperation, there some variety of selection must be applied. Only where the assignment of various individuals to various tasks is effected by the dictator's decisions alone and the individuals concerned do not aid the dictator by endeavors to represent their own virtues and abilities in the most favorable light, is there no competition.

We will have to deal at a later stage of our investigations with the function of competition.[4] At this point we must only emphasize that it is misleading to apply the terminology of mutual extermination to the problems of mutual cooperation as it works within a society. Military terms are inappropriate for the description of business operations. It is, e.g., a bad metaphor to speak of the conquest of a market. There is no conquest in the fact that one firm offers better or cheaper products than its competitors. Only in a metaphorical sense is there strategy in business operations.

7. Praxeological Prediction

Praxeological knowledge makes it possible to predict with apodictic certainty the outcome of various modes of action. But, of course, such prediction can never imply anything regarding quantitative matters. Quantitative problems are in the field of human action open

4. See below, pp. 273–277.

to no other elucidation than that by understanding.

We can predict, as will be shown later, that—other things being equal—a fall in the demand for *a* will result in a drop in the price of *a*. But we cannot predict the extent of this drop. This question can be answered only by understanding.

The fundamental deficiency implied in every quantitative approach to economic problems consists in the neglect of the fact that there are no constant relations between what are called economic dimensions. There is neither constancy nor continuity in the valuations and in the formation of exchange ratios between various commodities. Every new datum brings about a reshuffling of the whole price structure. Understanding, by trying to grasp what is going on in the minds of the men concerned, can approach the problem of forecasting future conditions. We may call its methods unsatisfactory and the positivists may arrogantly scorn it. But such arbitrary judgments must not and cannot obscure the fact that understanding is the only appropriate method of dealing with the uncertainty of future conditions.

VII. ACTION WITHIN THE WORLD

1. The Law of Marginal Utility

ACTION sorts and grades; originally it knows only ordinal numbers, not cardinal numbers. But the external world to which acting man must adjust his conduct is a world of quantitative determinateness. In this world there exist quantitative relations between cause and effect. If it were otherwise, if definite things could render unlimited services, such things would never be scarce and could not be dealt with as means.

Acting man values things as means for the removal of his uneasiness. From the point of view of the natural sciences the various events which result in satisfying human needs appear as very different. Acting man sees in these events only a more or a less of the same kind. In valuing very different states of satisfaction and the means for their attainment, man arranges all things in *one* scale and sees in them only their relevance for an increase in his own satisfaction. The satisfaction derived from food and that derived from the enjoyment of a work of art are, in acting man's judgment, a more urgent or a less urgent need; valuation and action place them in one scale of what is more intensively desired and what is less. For acting man there exists primarily nothing but various degrees of relevance and urgency with regard to his own well-being.

Quantity and quality are categories of the external world. Only indirectly do they acquire importance and meaning for action. Because every thing can only produce a limited effect, some things are considered scarce and treated as means. Because the effects which things are able to produce are different, acting man distinguishes various classes of things. Because means of the same quantity and quality are apt always to produce the same quantity of an effect of the same quality, action does not differentiate between concrete definite quantities of homogeneous means. But this does not imply that it attaches the same value to the various portions of a supply of homogeneous means. Each portion is valued separately. To each portion its own rank in the scale of value is assigned. But these orders of rank can be ad libitum interchanged among the various portions of the same magnitude.

If acting man has to decide between two or more means of different classes, he grades the individual portions of each of them. He assigns to each portion its special rank. In doing so he need not assign to the various portions of the same means orders of rank which immediately succeed one another.

The assignment of orders of rank through valuation is done only in acting and through acting. How great the portions are to which a single order of rank is assigned depends on the individual and unique conditions under which man acts in every case. Action does not deal with physical or metaphysical units which it values in an abstract academic way; it is always faced with alternatives between which it chooses. The choice must always be made between definite quantities of means. It is permissible to call the smallest quantity which can be the object of such a decision a unit. But one must guard oneself against the error of assuming that the valuation of the sum of such units is derived from the valuation of the units, or that it represents the sum of the valuations attached to these units.

A man owns five units of commodity *a* and three units of commodity *b*. He attaches to the units of *a* the rank-orders 1, 2, 4, 7, and 8, to the units of *b* the rank-orders 3, 5, and 6. This means: If he must choose between two units of *a* and two units of *b,* he will prefer to lose two units of *a* rather than two units of *b*. But if he must choose between three units of *a* and two units of *b,* he will prefer to lose two units of *b* rather than three units of *a*. What counts always and alone in valuing a compound of several units is the utility of this compound as a whole—i.e., the increment in well-being dependent upon it or, what is the same, the impairment of well-being which its loss must bring about. There are no arithmetical processes involved, neither adding nor multiplying; there is a valuation of the utility dependent upon the having of the portion, compound, or supply in question.

Utility means in this context simply: causal relevance for the removal of felt uneasiness. Acting man believes that the services a thing can render are apt to improve his own well-being, and calls this the utility of the thing concerned. For praxeology the term utility is tantamount to importance attached to a thing on account of the belief that it can remove uneasiness. The praxeological notion of utility (*subjective use-value* in the terminology of the earlier Austrian economists) must be sharply distinguished from the technological notion of utility (*objective use-value* in the terminology of the same economists). Use-value in the objective sense is the relation between a thing and the effect it has the capacity to bring about. It is to objective use-value that people refer in employing such terms as the "heating value" or "heating power" of coal. Subjective use-value is not always based on true objective use-value. There are things to which subjective use-value is attached because people erroneously believe that they have the power to bring about a desired effect. On the other hand there are things able to produce a desired effect to which no use-value is attached because people are ignorant of this fact.

Let us look at the state of economic thought which prevailed on the eve of the elaboration of the modern theory of value by Carl Menger, William Stanley Jevons, and Léon Walras. Whoever wants to construct an elementary theory of value and prices must first think of utility. Nothing indeed is more plausible than to assume that things are valued according to their utility. But then a difficulty appears which presented to the older economists a problem they failed to solve. They observed that things whose "utility" is greater are valued less than other things of smaller utility. *Iron* is less appreciated than *gold*. This fact seems to be incompatible with a theory of value and prices based on the concepts of utility and use-value. The economists believed that they had to abandon such a theory and tried to explain the phenomena of value and market exchange by other theories.

Only late did the economists discover that the apparent paradox was the outcome of a vicious formulation of the problem involved. The valuations and choices that result in the exchange ratios of the market do not decide between *gold* and *iron*. Acting man is not in a position in which he must choose between *all* the gold and *all* the iron. He chooses at a definite time and place under definite conditions between a strictly limited quantity of gold and a strictly limited quantity of iron. His decision in choosing between 100 ounces of gold and 100 tons of iron does not depend at all on the decision he would make if he were in the highly improbable situation of choosing between all the gold and all the iron. What counts alone for his actual choice is whether under existing conditions he considers the direct or indirect satisfaction which 100 ounces of gold could give him as greater or smaller than the direct or indirect satisfaction he could derive from 100 tons of iron. He does not express an academic or philosophical judgment concerning the "absolute" value of gold and of iron; he does not determine whether gold or iron is more important for mankind; he does not perorate as an author of books on the philosophy of history or on ethical principles. He simply chooses between two satisfactions both of which he cannot have together.

To prefer and to set aside and the choices and decisions in which they result are not acts of measurement. Action does not measure utility or value; it chooses between alternatives. There is no abstract problem of total utility or total value.[1] There is no ratiocinative operation which could lead from the valuation of a definite quantity or number of things to the determination of the value of a greater or smaller quantity or number. There is no means of calculating the total value of a supply if only the values of its parts are known. There is no means of establishing the value of a part of a supply if only the value of the total supply is known. There are in the sphere of values and valuations no arithmetical operations; there is no such thing as a calculation of values. The valuation of the total stock of two things can differ from the valuation of parts of these stocks. An isolated man owning seven cows and seven horses may value one horse higher than one cow and may, when faced with the alternative, prefer to give up one cow rather than one horse. But at the same time the same man, when faced with the alternative of choosing between his whole supply of horses and his whole supply of cows, may prefer to keep the cows and to give up the horses. The concepts of total utility and total value are meaningless if not applied to a situation in which people must choose between total supplies. The question whether *gold* as such and *iron* as such is more useful and valuable is reasonable only with regard to a situation in which mankind or an isolated part of mankind must choose between *all* the gold and *all* the iron available.

The judgment of value refers only to the supply with which the concrete act of choice is concerned. A supply is *ex definitione* always composed of homogeneous parts each of which is capable of rendering the same services as, and of being substituted for, any other part. It is therefore immaterial for the act of choosing which particular part forms its object. All parts—units—of the available stock are considered as equally useful and valuable if the problem of giving up *one* of them is raised. If the supply decreased by the loss of one unit, acting man must decide anew how to use the various units of the remaining stock. It is obvious that the smaller stock cannot render all the services the greater stock could. That employment of the various units which under this new disposition is no longer provided for, was in the eyes of acting man the least urgent employment among

1. It is important to note that this chapter does not deal with prices or market values, but with subjective use-value. Prices are a derivative of subjective use-value. Cf. below, Chapter XVI.

all those for which he had previously assigned the various units of the greater stock. The satisfaction which he derived from the use of one unit for this employment was the smallest among the satisfactions which the units of the greater stock had rendered to him. It is only the value of this marginal satisfaction on which he must decide if the question of renouncing one unit of the total stock comes up. When faced with the problem of the value to be attached to one unit of a homogeneous supply, man decides on the basis of the value of the least important use he makes of the units of the whole supply; he decides on the basis of marginal utility.

If a man is faced with the alternative of giving up either one unit of his supply of *a* or one unit of his supply of *b,* he does not compare the total value of his total stock of *a* with the total value of his stock of *b*. He compares the marginal values both of *a* and of *b*. Although he may value the total supply of *a* higher than the total supply of *b,* the marginal value of *b* may be higher than the marginal value of *a*.

The same reasoning holds good for the question of increasing the available supply of any commodity by the acquisition of an additional definite number of units.

For the description of these facts economics does not need to employ the terminology of psychology. Neither does it need to resort to psychological reasoning and arguments for proving them. If we say that the acts of choice do not depend on the value attached to a whole class of wants, but on that attached to the concrete wants in question irrespective of the class in which they may be reckoned, we do not add anything to our knowledge and do not trace it back to some better-known or more general knowledge. This mode of speaking in terms of classes of wants becomes intelligible only if we remember the role played in the history of economic thought by the alleged paradox of value. Carl Menger and Böhm-Bawerk had to make use of the term "class of wants" in order to refute the objections raised by those who considered *bread* as such more valuable than *silk* because the class "want of nourishment" is more important than the class "want of luxurious clothing."[2] Today the concept "class of wants" is entirely superfluous. It has no meaning for action and therefore none for the theory of value; it is, moreover, liable to bring about error and confusion. Construction of concepts and classification are mental tools; they acquire meaning and sense only in the con-

2. Cf. Carl Menger, *Grundsätze der Volkswirtschaftslehre* (Vienna, 1871), pp. 88 ff.; Böhm-Bawerk, *Kapital und Kapitalzins* (3d ed. Innsbruck, 1909), Pt. II, pp. 237 ff.

text of theories which utilize them.[3] It is nonsensical to arrange various wants into "classes of wants" in order to establish that such a classification is of no avail whatever for the theory of value.

The law of marginal utility and decreasing marginal value is independent of Gossen's law of the saturation of wants (first law of Gossen). In treating marginal utility we deal neither with sensuous enjoyment nor with saturation and satiety. We do not transcend the sphere of praxeological reasoning in establishing the following definition: We call that employment of a unit of a homogeneous supply which a man makes if his supply is n units, but would not make if, other things being equal, his supply were only $n-1$ units, the least urgent employment or the marginal employment, and the utility derived from it marginal utility. In order to attain this knowledge we do not need any physiological or psychological experience, knowledge, or reasoning. It follows necessarily from our assumptions that people act (choose) and that in the first case acting man has n units of a homogeneous supply and in the second case $n-1$ units. Under these conditions no other result is thinkable. Our statement is formal and aprioristic and does not depend on any experience.

There are only two alternatives. Either there are or there are not intermediate stages between the felt uneasiness which impels a man to act and the state in which there can no longer be any action (be it because the state of perfect satisfaction is reached or because man is incapable of any further improvement in his conditions). In the second case there could be only one action; as soon as this action is consummated, a state would be reached in which no further action is possible. This is manifestly incompatible with our assumption that there is action; this case no longer implies the general conditions presupposed in the category of action. Only the first case remains. But then there are various degrees in the asymptotic approach to the state in which there can no longer be any action. Thus the law of marginal utility is already implied in the category of action. It is nothing else than the reverse of the statement that what satisfies more is preferred to what gives smaller satisfaction. If the supply available increases from $n-1$ units to n units, the increment can be employed only for the removal of a want which is less urgent or less painful than the least urgent or least painful among all those wants which could be removed by means of the supply $n-1$.

3. Classes are not in the world. It is our mind that classifies the phenomena in order to organize our knowledge. The question of whether a certain mode of classifying phenomena is conducive to this end or not is different from the question of whether it is logically permissible or not.

The law of marginal utility does not refer to objective use-value, but to subjective use-value. It does not deal with the physical or chemical capacity of things to bring about a definite effect in general, but with their relevance for the well-being of a man as he himself sees it under the prevailing momentary state of his affairs. It does not deal primarily with the value of things, but with the value of the services a man expects to get from them.

If we were to believe that marginal utility is about things and their objective use-value, we would be forced to assume that marginal utility can as well increase as decrease with an increase in the quantity of units available. It can happen that the employment of a certain minimum quantity—*n* units—of a good *a* can provide a satisfaction which is deemed more valuable than the services expected from one unit of a good *b*. But if the supply of *a* available is smaller than *n, a* can only be employed for another service which is considered less valuable than that of *b*. Then an increase in the quantity of *a* from $n-1$ units to *n* units results in an increase of the value attached to one unit of *a*. The owner of 100 logs may build a cabin which protects him against rain better than a raincoat. But if fewer than 100 logs are available, he can only use them for a berth that protects him against the dampness of the soil. As the owner of 95 logs he would be prepared to forsake the raincoat in order to get 5 logs more. As the owner of 10 logs he would not abandon the raincoat even for 10 logs. A man whose savings amount to $100 may not be willing to carry out some work for a remuneration of $200. But if his savings were $2,000 and he were extremely anxious to acquire an indivisible good which cannot be bought for less than $2,100, he would be ready to perform this work for $100. All this is in perfect agreement with the rightly formulated law of marginal utility according to which value depends on the utility of the services expected. There is no question of any such thing as a law of increasing marginal utility.

The law of marginal utility must be confused neither with Bernoulli's doctrine *de mensura sortis* nor with the Weber-Fechner law. At the bottom of Bernoulli's contribution were the generally known and never disputed facts that people are eager to satisfy the more urgent wants before they satisfy the less urgent, and that a rich man is in a position to provide better for his wants than a poor man. But the inferences Bernoulli drew from these truisms are all wrong. He developed a mathematical theory that the increment in gratification diminishes with the increase in a man's total wealth. He statement that as a rule it is highly probable that for a man whose income is 5,000 ducats one ducat means not more than half a ducat for a man with an income of 2,500 ducats is merely fanciful. Let us set aside the objection that there is no means of drawing comparisons other than entirely arbitrary ones between the valuations of various people. Bernoulli's method is no less inadequate for the valuations of the same individual with various amounts of income. He did not see that all that can be said about the case in question is that with increasing income every new increment is used for the satisfaction of a want less urgently felt than the least urgently felt want already satisfied before this increment took place. He did not see that in valuing, choosing, and acting there is no measurement and no establishment of equivalence, but grading, i.e., preferring and putting aside.[4] Thus neither Bernoulli nor the mathematicians and economists who adopted his mode of reasoning could succeed in solving the paradox of value.

The mistakes inherent in the confusion of the Weber-Fechner law of psychophysics and the subjective theory of value have already been attacked by Max Weber. Max Weber, it is true, was not sufficiently familiar with economics and was too much under the sway of historicism to get a correct insight into the fundamentals of economic thought. But ingenious intuition provided him with a suggestion of a way toward the correct solution. The theory of marginal utility, he asserts, is "not psychologically substantiated, but rather—if an epistemological term is to be applied—pragmatically, i.e., on the employment of the categories: ends and means."[5]

If a man wants to remove a pathological condition by taking a definite quantity of a remedy, the intake of a multiple will not bring about a better effect. The surplus will have either no effect other than the appropriate dose, the optimum, or it will have detrimental effects. The same is true of all kinds of satisfactions, although the optimum is often reached only by the application of a large dose, and the point at which further increments produce detrimental effects is often far away. This is so because our world is a world of causality and of quantitative relations between cause and effect. He who wants to remove the uneasiness caused by living in a room with a temperature of 35 degrees will aim at heating the room to a temperature of 65 or 70 degrees. It has nothing to do with the Weber-Fechner law that he does not aim at a temperature of 180 or 300 degrees. Neither has it

4. Cf. Daniel Bernoulli, *Versuch einer neuen Theorie zur Bestimmung von Glücksfällen,* trans. by Pringsheim (Leipzig, 1896), pp. 27 ff.

5. Cf. Max Weber, *Gesammelte Aufsätze zur Wissenschaftslehre* (Tübingen, 1922), p. 372; also p. 149. The term "pragmatical" as used by Weber is of course liable to bring about confusion. It is inexpedient to employ it for anything other than the philosophy of Pragmatism. If Weber had known the term "praxeology," he probably would have preferred it.

anything to do with psychology. All that psychology can do for the explanation of this fact is to establish as an ultimate given that man as a rule prefers the preservation of life and health to death and sickness. What counts for praxeology is only the fact that acting man chooses between alternatives. That man is placed at crossroads, that he must and does choose, is—apart from other conditions—due to the fact that he lives in a quantitative world and not in a world without quantity, which is even unimaginable for the human mind.

The confusion of marginal utility and the Weber-Fechner law originated from the mistake of looking only at the means for the attainment of satisfaction and not at the satisfaction itself. If the satisfaction had been thought of, the absurd idea would not have been adopted of explaining the configuration of the desire for warmth by referring to the decreasing intensity of the sensation of successive increments in the intensity of the stimuli. That the average man does not want to raise the temperature of his bedroom to 120 degrees has no reference whatever to the intensity of the sensation for warmth. That a man does not heat his room to the same degree as other normal people do and as he himself would probably do, if he were not more intent upon buying a new suit or attending the performance of a Beethoven symphony, cannot be explained by the methods of the natural sciences. Objective and open to a treatment by the methods of the natural sciences are only the problems of objective use-value; the valuation of objective use-value on the part of acting man is another thing.

2. The Law of Returns

Quantitative definiteness in the effects brought about by an economic good means with regard to the goods of the first order (consumers' goods): a quantity a of cause brings about—either once and for all or piecemeal over a definite period of time—a quantity α of effect. With regard to the goods of the higher orders (producers' goods) it means: a quantity b of cause brings about a quantity β of effect, provided the complementary cause c contributes the quantity γ of effect; only the concerted effects β and γ bring about the quantity p of the good of the first order D. There are in this case three quantities: b and c of the two complementary goods B and C, and p of the product D.

With b remaining unchanged, we call that value of c which results in the highest value of $\frac{p}{c}$ the optimum. If several values of c result in this highest value of $\frac{p}{c}$, then we call that the optimum which results also in the highest value of p. If the two complementary goods are employed in the optimal ratio, they both render the highest output; their power to produce, their objective use-value, is fully utilized; no fraction of them is wasted. If we deviate from this optimal combination by increasing the quantity of C without changing the quantity of B, the return will as a rule increase further, but not in proportion to the increase in the quantity of C. If it is at all possible to increase the return from p to p_1 by increasing the quantity of *one* of the complementary factors only, namely by substituting cx for c, x being greater than 1, we have at any rate: $p_1 > p$ and $p_1 c < pcx$. For if it were possible to compensate any decrease in b by a corresponding increase in c in such a way that p remains unchanged, the physical power of production proper to B would be unlimited and B would not be considered as scarce and as an economic good. It would be of no importance for acting man whether the supply of B available were greater or smaller. Even an infinitesimal quantity of B would be sufficient for the production of any quantity of D, provided the supply of C is large enough. On the other hand, an increase in the quantity of B available could not increase the output of D if the supply of C does not increase. The total return of the process would be imputed to C; B could not be an economic good. A thing rendering such unlimited services is, for instance, the knowledge of the causal relation implied. The formula, the recipe that teaches us how to prepare coffee, provided it is known, renders unlimited services. It does not lose anything from its capacity to produce however often it is used; its productive power is inexhaustible; it is therefore not an economic good. Acting man is never faced with a situation in which he must choose between the use-value of a known formula and any other useful thing.

The law of returns asserts that for the combination of economic goods of the higher orders (factors of production) there exists an optimum. If one deviates from this optimum by increasing the input of only one of the factors, the physical output either does not increase at all or at least not in the ratio of the increased input. This law, as has been demonstrated above, is implied in the fact that the quantitative definiteness of the effects brought about by any economic good is a necessary condition of its being an economic good.

That there is such an optimum of combination is all that the law of returns, popularly called the law of diminishing returns, teaches. There are many other questions which it does not answer at all and which can only be solved a posteriori by experience.

If the effect brought about by one of the complementary factors is indivisible, the optimum is the only combination which results in the outcome aimed at. In order to dye a piece of wool to a definite shade, a definite quantity of dye is required. A greater or smaller quantity would frustrate the aim sought. He who has more coloring matter must leave the surplus unused. He who has a smaller quantity can dye only a part of the piece. The diminishing return results in this instance in the complete uselessness of the additional quantity which must not even be employed because it would thwart the design.

In other instances a certain minimum is required for the production of the minimum effect. Between this minimum effect and the optimal effect there is a margin in which increased doses result either in a proportional increase in effect or in a more than proportional increase in effect. In order to make a machine turn, a certain minimum of lubricant is needed. Whether an increase of lubricant above this minimum increases the machine's performance in proportion to the increase in the amount applied, or to a greater extent, can only be ascertained by technological experience.

The law of returns does not answer the following questions: (1) Whether or not the optimum dose is the only one that is capable of producing the effect sought. (2) Whether or not there is a rigid limit above which any increase in the amount of the variable factor is quite useless. (3) Whether the decrease in output brought about by progressive deviation from the optimum and the increase in output brought about by progressive approach to the optimum result in proportional or nonproportional changes in output per unit of the variable factor. All this must be discerned by experience. But the law of returns itself, i.e., the fact that there must exist such an optimum combination, is valid a priori.

The Malthusian law of population and the concepts of absolute overpopulation and underpopulation and optimum population derived from it are the application of the law of returns to a special problem. They deal with changes in the supply of human labor, other factors being equal. Because people, for political considerations, wanted to reject the Malthusian law, they fought with passion but with faulty arguments against the law of returns—which, incidentally, they knew only as the law of diminishing returns of the use of capital and labor on land. Today we no longer need to pay any attention to these idle remonstrances. The law of returns is not limited to the use of complementary factors of production on land. The endeavors to refute or to demonstrate its validity by historical and experimental investigations of agricultural production are as needless as they are vain. He who wants to reject the law would have to explain why people are ready to pay prices for land. If the law were not valid, a farmer would never consider expanding the size of his farm. He would be in a position to multiply indefinitely the return of any piece of soil by multiplying his input of capital and labor.

People have sometimes believed that, while the law of diminishing returns is valid in agricultural production, with regard to the processing industries a law of increasing returns prevails. It took a long time before they realized that the law of returns refers to all branches of production equally. It is faulty to contrast agriculture and the processing industries with regard to this law. What is called—in a very inexpedient, even misleading terminology—the law of increasing returns is nothing but a reversal of the law of diminishing returns, an unsatisfactory formulation of the law of returns. If one approaches the optimum combination by increasing the quantity of one factor only, the quantity of other factors remaining unchanged, then the returns per unit of the variable factor increase either in proportion to the increase or even to a greater extent. A machine may, when operated by 2 workers, produce *p;* when operated by 3 workers, 3 *p;* when operated by 4 workers, 6 *p;* when operated by 5 workers, 7 *p;* when operated by 6 workers, also not more than $7p$. Then the employment of 4 workers renders the optimum return per head of the worker, namely $\frac{6}{4}p$, while under the other combinations the returns per head are respectively $\frac{1}{2}p$, p, $\frac{7}{5}p$ and $\frac{7}{6}p$. If, instead of 2 workers, 3 or 4 workers are employed, then the returns increase more than in relation to the increase in the number of workers; they do not increase in the proportion 2:3:4, but in the proportion 1:3:6. We are faced with increasing returns per head of the worker. But this is nothing else than the reverse of the law of diminishing returns.

If a plant or enterprise deviates from the optimum combination of the factors employed, it is less efficient than a plant or enterprise for which the deviation from the optimum is smaller. Both in agriculture and in the processing industries many factors of production are not perfectly divisible. It is, especially in the processing industries, for the most part easier to attain the optimum combination by expanding the size of the plant or enterprise than by restricting it. If the smallest unit of one or of several factors is too large to allow for its optimal exploitation in a small or medium-size plant or enterprise, the only way to attain the optimum is by increasing the outfit's size. It is these facts that bring about the superiority of big-scale production. The full importance of this problem will be shown later in discussing the issues of cost accounting.

3. Human Labor as a Means

The employment of the physiological functions and manifestations of human life as a means is called labor. The display of the potentialities of human energy and vital processes which the man whose life they manifest does not use for the attainment of external ends different from the mere running of these processes and from the physiological role they play in the biological consummation of his own vital economy, is not labor; it is simply life. Man works in using his forces and abilities as a means for the removal of uneasiness and in substituting purposeful exploitation of his vital energy for the spontaneous and carefree discharge of his faculties and nerve tensions. Labor is a means, not an end in itself.

Every individual has only a limited quantity of energy to expend, and every unit of labor can only bring about a limited effect. Otherwise human labor would be available in abundance; it would not be scarce and it would not be considered as a means for the removal of uneasiness and economized as such.

In a world in which labor is economized only on account of its being available in a quantity insufficient to attain all ends for which it can be used as a means, the supply of labor available would be equal to the whole quantity of labor which all men together are able to expend. In such a world everybody would be eager to work until he had completely exhausted his momentary capacity to work. The time which is not required for recreation and restoration of the capacity to work, used up by previous working, would be entirely devoted to work. Every nonutilization of the full capacity to work would be deemed a loss. Through the performance of more work one would have increased one's well-being. That a part of the available potential remained unused would be appraised as a forfeiture of well-being not compensated by any corresponding increase in well-being. The very idea of laziness would be unknown. Nobody would think: I could possibly do this or that; but it is not worthwhile; it does not pay; I prefer my leisure. Everybody would consider his whole capacity to work as a supply of factors of production which he would be anxious to utilize completely. Even a chance of the smallest increase in well-being would be considered a sufficient incentive to work more if it happened that at the instant no more profitable use could be made of the quantity of labor concerned.

In our actual world things are different. The expenditure of labor is deemed painful. Not to work is considered a state of affairs more satisfactory than working. Leisure is, other things being equal, preferred to travail. People work only when they value the return of labor higher than the decrease in satisfaction brought about by the curtailment of leisure. To work involves disutility.

Psychology and physiology may try to explain this fact. There is no need for praxeology to investigate whether or not they can succeed in such endeavors. For praxeology it is a datum that men are eager to enjoy leisure and therefore look upon their own capacity to bring about effects with feelings different from those with which they look upon the capacity of material factors of production. Man in considering an expenditure of his own labor investigates not only whether there is no more desirable end for the employment of the quantity of labor in question, but no less whether it would not be more desirable to abstain from any further expenditure of labor. We can express this fact also in calling the attainment of leisure an end of purposeful activity, or an economic good of the first order. In employing this somewhat sophisticated terminology, we must view leisure as any other economic good from the aspect of marginal utility. We must conclude that the first unit of leisure satisfies a desire more urgently felt than the second one, the second one a more urgent desire than the third one, and so on. Reversing this proposition, we get the statement that the disutility of labor felt by the worker increases in a greater proportion than the amount of labor expended.

However, it is needless for praxeology to study the question of whether or not the disutility of labor increases in proportion to the increase in the quantity of labor performed or to a greater extent. (Whether this problem is of any importance for physiology and psychology, and whether or not these sciences can elucidate it, can be left undecided.) At any rate the worker knocks off work at the point at which he no longer considers the utility of continuing work as a sufficient compensation for the disutility of the additional expenditure of labor. In forming this judgment he contrasts, if we disregard the decrease in yield brought about by increasing fatigue, each portion of working time with the same quantity of product as the preceding portions. But the utility of the units of yield decreases with the progress of the labor performed and the increase in the total amount of yield produced. The products of the prior units of working time have provided for the satisfaction of more important needs than the products of the work performed later. The satisfaction of these less important needs may not be considered as a sufficient reward for the further continuation of work, although they are compared with the same quantities of physical output.

It is therefore irrelevant for the praxeological treatment of the matter whether the disutility of labor is proportional to the total expenditure of labor or whether it increases to a greater extent than the time spent in working. At any rate, the propensity to expend the still unused portions of the total potential for work decreases, other things being equal, with the increase in the portions already expended. Whether this decrease in the readiness to work more proceeds with a more rapid or a less rapid acceleration, is always a question of economic data, not a question of categorial principles.

The disutility attached to labor explains why in the course of human history, concomitantly with the progressive increase in the physical productivity of labor brought about by technological improvement and a more abundant supply of capital, by and large a tendency toward shortening the hours of work developed. Among the amenities which civilized man can enjoy in a more abundant way than his less civilized ancestors there is also the enjoyment of more leisure time. In this sense one can answer the question, often raised by philosophers and philanthropists, whether or not economic progress has made men happier. If the productivity of labor were lower than it is in the present capitalist world, man would be forced either to toil more or to forsake many amenities. In establishing this fact the economists do not assert that the only means to attain happiness is to enjoy more material comfort, to live in luxury, or to have more leisure. They simply acknowledge the truth that men are in a position to provide themselves better with what they consider they need.

The fundamental praxeological insight that men prefer what satisfies them more to what satisfies them less and that they value things on the basis of their utility does not need to be corrected or complemented by an additional statement concerning the disutility of labor. These propositions already imply the statement that labor is preferred to leisure only in so far as the yield of labor is more urgently desired than the enjoyment of leisure.

The unique position which the factor labor occupies in our world is due to its nonspecific character. All nature-given primary factors of production—i.e., all those natural things and forces that man can use for improving his state of well-being—have specific powers and virtues. There are ends for whose attainment they are more suitable, ends for which they are less suitable, and ends for which they are altogether unsuitable. But human labor is both suitable and indispensable for the performance of all thinkable processes and modes of production.

It is, of course, impermissible to deal with human labor as such in general. It is a fundamental mistake not to see that men and their abilities to work are different. The work a certain individual can perform is more suitable for some ends, less suitable for other ends, and altogether unsuitable for still other ends. It was one of the deficiencies of classical economics that it did not pay enough attention to this fact and did not take it into account in the construction of its theory of value, prices, and wage rates. Men do not economize labor in general, but the particular kinds of labor available. Wages are not paid for labor expended, but for the achievements of labor, which differ widely in quality and quantity. The production of each particular product requires the employment of workers able to perform the particular kind of labor concerned. It is absurd to justify the failure to consider this point by reference to the alleged fact that the main demand for and supply of labor concerns unskilled common labor which every healthy man is able to perform, and that skilled labor, the labor of people with particular inborn faculties and special training, is by and large an exception. There is no need to investigate whether conditions were such in a remote past or whether even for primitive tribesmen the inequality of inborn and acquired capacities for work was the main factor in economizing labor. In dealing with conditions of civilized peoples it is impermissible to disregard the differences in the quality of labor performed. Work which various people are able to perform is different because men are born unequal and because the skill and experience they acquire in the course of their lives differentiate their capacities still more.

In speaking of the nonspecific character of human labor we certainly do not assert that all human labor is of the same quality. What we want to establish is rather that the differences in the kind of labor required for the production of various commodities are greater than the differences in the inborn capacities of men. (In emphasizing this point we are not dealing with the creative performances of the genius; the work of the genius is outside the orbit of ordinary human action and is like a free gift of destiny which comes to mankind overnight.[6] We furthermore disregard the institutional barriers denying some groups of people access to certain occupations and the training they require.) The innate inequality of various individuals does not break up the zoological uniformity and homogeneity of the species man to such an extent as to divide the supply of labor into disconnected sections. Thus the potential supply of labor available for the per-

6. See below, pp. 139–140.

formance of each particular kind of work exceeds the actual demand for such labor. The supply of every kind of specialized labor could be increased by the withdrawal of workers from other branches and their training. The quantity of need satisfaction is in none of the branches of production permanently limited by a scarcity of people capable of performing special tasks. Only in the short run can there emerge a dearth of specialists. In the long run it can be removed by training people who display the innate abilities required.

Labor is the most scarce of all primary means of production because it is in this restricted sense nonspecific and because every variety of production requires the expenditure of labor. Thus the scarcity of the other primary means of production—i.e., the nonhuman means of production supplied by nature—becomes for acting man a scarcity of those primary material means of production whose utilization requires the smallest expenditure of labor.[7] It is the supply of labor available that determines to what an extent the factor nature in each of its varieties can be exploited for the satisfaction of needs.

If the supply of labor which men are able and ready to perform increases, production increases too. Labor cannot remain unemployed on account of its being useless for the further improvement of need satisfaction. Isolated self-sufficient man always has the opportunity of improving his condition by expending more labor. On the labor market of a market society there are buyers for every supply of labor offered. There can be abundance and superfluity only in segments of the labor market; it results in pushing labor to other segments and in an expansion of production in some other provinces of the economic system. On the other hand, an increase in the quantity of land available—other things being equal—could result in an increase in production only if the additional land is more fertile than the marginal land tilled before.[8] The same is valid with regard to accumulated material equipment for future production. The serviceableness of capital goods also depends on the supply of labor available. It would be wasteful to use the capacity of existing facilities if the labor required could be employed for the satisfaction of more urgent needs.

Complementary factors of production can only be used to the extent allowed by the availability of the most scarce among them. Let us assume that the production of 1 unit of *p* requires the expenditure

7. Of course, some natural resources are so scarce that they are entirely utilized.

8. Under free mobility of labor it would be wasteful to improve barren soil if the reclaimed area is not so fertile that it compensates for the total cost of the operation.

of 7 units of *a* and of 3 units of *b* and that neither *a* nor *b* can be used for any production other than that of *p*. If 49 *a* and 2,000 *b* are available, no more than 7 *p* can be produced. The available supply of *a* determines the extent of the use of *b*. Only *a* is considered an economic good; only for *a* are people ready to pay prices; the full price of *p* is allowed for 7 units of *a*. On the other hand *b* is not an economic good and no prices are allowed for it. There are quantities of *b* which remain unused.

We may try to imagine the conditions within a world in which all material factors of production are so fully employed that there is no opportunity to employ all men or to employ all men to the extent that they are ready to work. In such a world labor is abundant; an increase in the supply of labor cannot add any increment whatever to the total amount of production. If we assume that all men have the same capacity and application for work and if we disregard the disutility of labor, labor in such a world would not be an economic good. If this world were a socialist commonwealth, an increase in population figures would be deemed an increase in the number of idle consumers. If it were a market society, wage rates paid would not be enough to prevent starvation. Those seeking employment would be ready to go to work for any wages, however low, even if insufficient for the preservation of their lives. They would be happy to delay for a while death by starvation.

There is no need to dwell upon the paradoxes of this hypothesis and to discuss the problems of such a world. Our world is different. Labor is more scarce than material factors of production. We are not dealing at this point with the problem of optimum population. We are dealing only with the fact that there are material factors of production which remain unused because the labor required is needed for the satisfaction of more urgent needs. In our world there is no abundance, but a shortage of manpower, and there are unused material factors of production, i.e, land, mineral deposits, and even plants and equipment.

This state of affairs could be changed by such an increase in population figures that all material factors required for the production of the foodstuffs indispensable—in the strict meaning of the word—for the preservation of human life are fully exploited. But as long as this is not the case, it cannot be changed by any improvement in technological methods of production. The substitution of more efficient methods of production for less efficient ones does not render labor abundant, provided there are still material factors available whose utilization can increase human well-being. On the contrary, it increases output and thereby the quantity of consumers' goods. "Labor-saving" devices increase supply. They do not bring about "technological unemployment."[9]

Every product is the result of the employment both of labor and of material factors. Man economizes both labor and material factors.

Immediately Gratifying Labor and Mediately Gratifying Labor

As a rule labor gratifies the performer only mediately, namely, through the removal of uneasiness which the attainment of the end brings about. The worker gives up leisure and submits to the disutility of labor in order to enjoy either the product or what other people are ready to give him for it. The expenditure of labor is for him a means for the attainment of certain ends, a price paid and a cost incurred.

But there are instances in which the performance of labor gratifies the worker immediately. He derives immediate satisfaction from the expenditure of labor. The yield is twofold. It consists on the one hand in the attainment of the product and on the other hand in the satisfaction that the performance itself gives to the worker.

People have misinterpreted this fact grotesquely and have based on this misinterpretation fantastic plans for social reforms. One of the main dogmas of socialism is that labor has disutility only within the capitalistic system of production, while under socialism it will be pure delight. We may disregard the effusions of the poor lunatic Charles Fourier. But Marxian "scientific" socialism does not differ in this point from the utopians. Some of its foremost champions, Frederick Engels and Karl Kautsky, expressly declare that a chief effect of a socialist regime will be to transform labor from a pain into a pleasure.[10]

The fact is often ignored that those activities which bring about immediate gratification and are thus direct sources of pleasure and enjoyment, are essentially different from labor and working. Only a very superficial treatment of the facts concerned can fail to recognize these differences. Paddling a canoe as it is practiced on Sundays for amusement on the lakes of public parks can only from the point of view of hydromechanics be likened to the rowing of boatsmen and galley slaves. When judged as a means for the attainment of ends it is as different as is the humming of an aria by a rambler from the recital of the same aria by the singer in the opera. The carefree Sunday paddler and the singing rambler derive immediate gratification from their activities, but not mediate gratification. What they do is therefore not labor, not the employment of their physiological functions for the attainment of ends other than the mere exercise of these

9. See below, pp. 769–779.

10. Karl Kautsky, *Die soziale Revolution* (3d ed. Berlin, 1911), II, 16 ff. About Engels see below, p. 591.

functions. It is merely pleasure. It is an end in itself; it is done for its own sake and does not render any further service. As it is not labor, it is not permissible to call it immediately gratifying labor.[11]

Sometimes a superficial observer may believe that labor performed by other people gives rise to immediate gratification because he himself would like to engage in a kind of play which apparently imitates the kind of labor concerned. As children play school, soldiers, and railroad, so adults too would like to play this and that. They think that the railroad engineer must enjoy operating and steering his engine as much as they would if they were permitted to toy with it. On his hurried way to the office the bookkeeper envies the patrolman who, he thinks, is paid for leisurely strolling around his beat. But the patrolman envies the bookkeeper who, sitting on a comfortable chair in a well-heated room, makes money by some scribbling which cannot seriously be called labor. Yet the opinions of people who misinterpret other people's work and consider it a mere pastime need not be taken seriously.

There are, however, also instances of genuine immediately gratifying labor. There are some kinds of labor of which, under special conditions, small quantities provide immediate gratification. But these quantities are so insignificant that they do not play any role at all in the complex of human action and production for the satisfaction of wants. Our world is characterized by the phenomenon of the disutility of labor. People trade the disutility-bringing labor for the products of labor; labor is for them a source of mediate gratification.

As far as a special kind of labor gives a limited amount of pleasure and not pain, immediate gratification and not disutility of labor, no wages are allowed for its performance. On the contrary, the performer, the "worker," must buy the pleasure and pay for it. Hunting game was and is for many people regular disutility-creating labor. But there are people for whom it is pure pleasure. In Europe amateur hunters buy from the owner of the hunting-ground the right to shoot a definite number of game of a definite type. The purchase of this right is separated from the price to be paid for the bag. If the two purchases are linked together, the price by far exceeds the prices that can be obtained on the market for the bag. A chamois buck still roaming on precipitous rocks has therefore a higher cash value than later when killed, brought down to the valley, and ready for the utilization of the meat, the skin, and the horns, although strenuous climbing and some material must be expended for its killing. One could say that one of the services which a living buck is able to render is to provide the hunter with the pleasure of killing it.

11. Rowing seriously practiced as a sport and singing seriously practiced by an amateur are introversive labor. See below, pp. 587–588.

The Creative Genius

Far above the millions that come and pass away tower the pioneers, the men whose deeds and ideas cut out new paths for mankind. For the pioneering genius[12] to create is the essence of life. To live means for him to create.

The activities of these prodigious men cannot be fully subsumed under the praxeological concept of labor. They are not labor because they are for the genius not means, but ends in themselves. He lives in creating and inventing. For him there is not leisure, only intermissions of temporary sterility and frustration. His incentive is not the desire to bring about a result, but the act of producing it. The accomplishment gratifies him neither mediately nor immediately. It does not gratify him mediately because his fellow men at best are unconcerned about it, more often even greet it with taunts, sneers, and persecution. Many a genius could have used his gifts to render his life agreeable and joyful; he did not even consider such a possibility and chose the thorny path without hesitation. The genius wants to accomplish what he considers his mission, even if he knows that he moves toward his own disaster.

Neither does the genius derive immediate gratification from his creative activities. Creating is for him agony and torment, a ceaseless excruciating struggle against internal and external obstacles; it consumes and crushes him. The Austrian poet Grillparzer has depicted this in a touching poem "Farewell to Gastein."[13] We may assume that in writing it he thought not only of his own sorrows and tribulations but also of the greater sufferings of a much greater man, of Beethoven, whose fate resembled his own and whom he understood, through devoted affection and sympathetic appreciation, better than any other of his contemporaries. Nietzsche compared himself to the flame that insatiably consumes and destroys itself.[14] Such agonies are phenomena which have nothing in common with the connotations generally attached to the notions of work and labor, production and success, breadwinning and enjoyment of life.

The achievements of the creative innovator, his thoughts and theories, his poems, paintings, and compositions, cannot be classified praxeologically as products of *labor*. They are not the outcome of

12. Leaders (Führers) are not pioneers. They guide people along the tracks pioneers have laid. The pioneer clears a road through land hitherto inaccessible and may not care whether or not anybody wants to go the new way. The leader directs people toward the goal they want to reach.

13. It seems that there is no English translation of this poem. The book of Douglas Yates (*Franz Grillparzer, a Critical Biography,* Oxford, 1946), I, 57, gives a short English résumé of its content.

14. For a translation of Nietzsche's poem see M. A. Mügge, *Friedrich Nietzsche* (New York, 1911), p. 275.

the employment of labor which could have been devoted to the production of other amenities for the "production" of a masterpiece of philosophy, art, or literature. Thinkers, poets, and artists are sometimes unfit to accomplish any other work. At any rate, the time and toil which they devote to creative activities are not withheld from employment for other purposes. Conditions may sometimes doom to sterility a man who would have had the power to bring forth things unheard of; they may leave him no alternative other than to die from starvation or to use all his forces in the struggle for mere physical survival. But if the genius succeeds in achieving his goals, nobody but himself pays the "costs" incurred. Goethe was perhaps in some respects hampered by his functions at the court of Weimar. But certainly he would not have accomplished more in his official duties as minister of state, theatre manager, and administrator of mines if he had not written his plays, poems, and novels.

It is, furthermore, impossible to substitute other people's work for that of the creators. If Dante and Beethoven had not existed, one would not have been in a position to produce the *Divina Commedia* or the Ninth Symphony by assigning other men to these tasks. Neither society nor single individuals can substantially further the genius and his work. The highest intensity of the "demand" and the most peremptory order of the government are ineffectual. The genius does not deliver to order. Men cannot improve the natural and social conditions which bring about the creator and his creation. It is impossible to rear geniuses by eugenics, to train them by schooling, or to organize their activities. But, of course, one can organize society in such a way that no room is left for pioneers and their path-breaking.

The creative accomplishment of the genius is an ultimate fact for praxeology. It comes to pass in history as a free gift of destiny. It is by no means the result of production in the sense in which economics uses this term.

4. Production

Action, if successful, attains the end sought. It produces the product.

Production is not an act of creation; it does not bring about something that did not exist before. It is a transformation of given elements through arrangement and combination. The producer is not a creator. Man is creative only in thinking and in the realm of imagination. In the world of external phenomena he is only a transformer. All that he can accomplish is to combine the means available in such a way that according to the laws of nature the result aimed at is bound to emerge.

It was once customary to distinguish between the production of tangible goods and the rendering of personal services. The carpenter who made tables and chairs was called productive; but this epithet was denied to the doctor whose advice helped the ailing carpenter to recover his capacity to make tables and chairs. A differentiation was made between the doctor-carpenter nexus and the carpenter-tailor nexus. The doctor, it was asserted, does not himself produce; he makes a living from what other people produce, he is maintained by carpenters and tailors. At a still earlier date the French Physiocrats contended that all labor was sterile unless it extracted something from the soil. Only cultivation, fishing and hunting, and the working of mines and quarries were in their opinion productive. The processing industries did not add to the value of the material employed anything more than the value of the things consumed by the workers.

Present-day economists laugh at their predecessors for having made such untenable distinctions. However, they should rather cast the beam out of their own eyes. The way in which many contemporary writers deal with various problems—for instance, advertising and marketing—is manifestly a relapse into the crude errors which should have disappeared long ago.

Another widely held opinion finds a difference between the employment of labor and that of material factors of production. Nature, it is assserted, dispenses its gifts gratuitously; but labor must be paid for by submitting to its disutility. In toiling and overcoming the disutility of labor man adds something to the universe that did not exist before. In this sense labor was called creative. This too is erroneous. Man's capacity to work is given in the universe as are the original and inherent capacities of the land and the animal substances. Nor does the fact that a part of the potentiality of labor can remain unused differentiate it from the nonhuman factors of production; these too can remain unused. The readiness of individuals to overcome the disutility of labor is the outcome of the fact that they prefer the produce of labor to the satisfaction derived from more leisure.

Only the human mind that directs action and production is creative. The mind too appertains to the universe and to nature; it is a part of the given and existing world. To call the mind creative is not to indulge in any metaphysical speculations. We call it creative because we are at a loss to trace the changes brought about by human action farther back than to the point at which we are faced with the intervention of reason directing human activities. Production is not something physical, material, and external; it is a spiritual and intellectual phenomenon. Its essential requisites are not human labor and external natural forces and things, but the decision of the mind to use these factors as means for the attainment of ends. What produces the product are not toil and trouble in themselves, but the fact that the toiling is guided by reason. The human mind alone has the power to remove uneasiness.

The materialist metaphysics of the Marxians misconstrues these things entirely. The "productive forces" are not material. Production is a spiritual, intellectual, and ideological phenomenon. It is the method that man, directed by reason, employs for the best possible removal of uneasiness. What distinguishes our conditions from those of our ancestors who lived one thousand or twenty thousand years ago is not something material, but something spiritual. The material changes are the outcome of the spiritual changes.

Production is alteration of the given according to the designs of reason. These designs—the recipes, the formulas, the ideologies—are the primary thing; they transform the original factors—both human and nonhuman—into means. Man produces by dint of his reason; he chooses ends and employs means for their attainment. The popular saying according to which economics deals with the material conditions of human life is entirely mistaken. Human action is a manifestation of the mind. In this sense praxeology can be called a moral science (*Geisteswissenschaft*).

Of course, we do not know what mind *is,* just as we do not know what motion, life, electricity *are*. Mind is simply the word to signify the unknown factor that has enabled men to achieve all that they have accomplished: the theories and the poems, the cathedrals and the symphonies, the motorcars and the airplanes.

Part Two

Action Within the Framework of Society

VIII. HUMAN SOCIETY

1. Human Cooperation

SOCIETY is concerted action, cooperation.

Society is the outcome of conscious and purposeful behavior. This does not mean that individuals have concluded contracts by virtue of which they have founded human society. The actions which have brought about social cooperation and daily bring it about anew do not aim at anything else than cooperation and coadjuvancy with others for the attainment of definite singular ends. The total complex of the mutual relations created by such concerted actions is called society. It substitutes collaboration for the—at least conceivable—isolated life of individuals. Society is division of labor and combination of labor. In his capacity as an acting animal man becomes a social animal.

Individual man is born into a socially organized environment. In this sense alone we may accept the saying that society is—logically or historically—antecedent to the individual. In every other sense this dictum is either empty or nonsensical. The individual lives and acts within society. But society is nothing but the combination of individuals for cooperative effort. It exists nowhere else than in the actions of individual men. It is a delusion to search for it outside the actions of individuals. To speak of a society's autonomous and independent existence, of its life, its soul, and its actions is a metaphor which can easily lead to crass errors.

The questions whether society or the individual is to be considered as the ultimate end, and whether the interests of society should be subordinated to those of the individuals or the interests of the individuals to those of society are fruitless. Action is always action of individual men. The social or societal element is a certain orientation of the actions of individual men. The category *end* makes sense only when applied to action. Theology and the metaphysics of history may discuss the ends of society and the designs which God wants to realize with regard to society in the same way in which they discuss the purpose of all other parts of the created universe. For science, which is inseparable from reason, a tool manifestly unfit for the treatment of such problems, it would be hopeless to embark upon speculations concerning these matters.

Within the frame of social cooperation there can emerge between members of society feelings of sympathy and friendship and a sense of belonging together. These feelings are the source of man's most delightful and most sublime experiences. They are the most precious adornment of life; they lift the animal species man to the heights of a really human existence. However, they are not, as some have asserted, the agents that have brought about social relationships. They are fruits of social cooperation, they thrive only within its frame; they did not precede the establishment of social relations and are not the seed from which they spring.

The fundamental facts that brought about cooperation, society, and civilization and transformed the animal man into a human being are the facts that work performed under the division of labor is more productive than isolated work and that man's reason is capable of recognizing this truth. But for these facts men would have forever remained deadly foes of one another, irreconcilable rivals in their endeavors to secure a portion of the scarce supply of means of sustenance provided by nature. Each man would have been forced to view all other men as his enemies; his craving for the satisfaction of his own appetites would have brought him into an implacable conflict with all his neighbors. No sympathy could possibly develop under such a state of affairs.

Some sociologists have asserted that the original and elementary subjective fact in society is a "consciousness of kind."[1] Others maintain that there would be no social systems if there were no "sense of community or of belonging together."[2] One may agree, provided that these somewhat vague and ambiguous terms are correctly interpreted. We may call consciousness of kind, sense of community, or sense of belonging together the acknowledgment of the fact that all other human beings are potential collaborators in the struggle for survival because they are capable of recognizing the mutual benefits of cooperation, while the animals lack this faculty. However, we must not forget that the primary facts that bring about such consciousness or such a sense are the two mentioned above. In a hypothetical world in which the division of labor would not increase productivity, there would not be any society. There would not be any sentiments of benevolence and good will.

1. F. H. Giddings, *The Principles of Sociology* (New York, 1926), p. 17.
2. R. M. MacIver, *Society* (New York, 1937), pp. 6–7.

The principle of the division of labor is one of the great basic principles of cosmic becoming and evolutionary change. The biologists were right in borrowing the concept of the division of labor from social philosophy and in adapting it to their field of investigation. There is division of labor between the various parts of any living organism. There are, furthermore, organic entities composed of collaborating animal individuals; it is customary to call metaphorically such aggregations of the ants and bees "animal societies." But one must never forget that the characteristic feature of human society is purposeful cooperation; society is an outcome of human action, i.e., of a conscious aiming at the attainment of ends. No such element is present, as far as we can ascertain, in the processes which have resulted in the emergence of the structure-function systems of plant and animal bodies and in the operation of the societies of ants, bees, and hornets. Human society is an intellectual and spiritual phenomenon. It is the outcome of a purposeful utilization of a universal law determining cosmic becoming, viz., the higher productivity of the division of labor. As with every instance of action, the recognition of the laws of nature is put into the service of man's efforts to improve his conditions.

2. A Critique of the Holistic and Metaphysical View of Society

According to the doctrines of universalism, conceptual realism, holism, collectivism, and some representatives of Gestaltpsychologie, society is an entity living its own life, independent of and separate from the lives of the various individuals, acting on its own behalf and aiming at its own ends which are different from the ends sought by the individuals. Then, of course, an antagonism between the aims of society and those of its members can emerge. In order to safeguard the flowering and further development of society it becomes necessary to master the selfishness of the individuals and to compel them to sacrifice their egoistic designs to the benefit of society. At this point all these holistic doctrines are bound to abandon the secular methods of human science and logical reasoning and to shift to theological or metaphysical professions of faith. They must assume that Providence, through its prophets, apostles, and charismatic leaders, forces men who are constitutionally wicked, i.e., prone to pursue their own ends, to walk in the ways of righteousness which the Lord or *Weltgeist* or history wants them to walk.

This is the philosophy which has characterized from time immemorial the creeds of primitive tribes. It has been an element in all religious teachings. Man is bound to comply with the law issued by a superhuman power and to obey the authorities which this power has entrusted with the enforcement of the law. The order created by this law, human society, is consequently the work of the Deity and not of man. If the Lord had not interfered and had not given enlightenment to erring mankind, society would not have come into existence. It is true that social cooperation is a blessing for man; it is true that man could work his way up from barbarism and the moral and material distress of his primitive state only within the framework of society. However, if left alone he would never have seen the road to his own salvation. For adjustment to the requirements of social cooperation and subordination to the precepts of the moral law put heavy restraints upon him. From the point of view of his wretched intellect he would deem the abandonment of some expected advantage an evil and a privation. He would fail to recognize the incomparably greater, but later, advantages which renunciation of present and visible pleasures will procure. But for supernatural revelation he would never have learned what destiny wants him to do for his own good and that of his offspring.

The scientific theory as developed by the social philosophy of eighteenth-century rationalism and liberalism and by modern economics does not resort to any miraculous interference of superhuman powers. Every step by which an individual substitutes concerted action for isolated action results in an immediate and recognizable improvement in his conditions. The advantages derived from peaceful cooperation and division of labor are universal. They immediately benefit every generation, and not only later descendants. For what the individual must sacrifice for the sake of society he is amply compensated by greater advantages. His sacrifice is only apparent and temporary; he foregoes a smaller gain in order to reap a greater one later. No reasonable being can fail to see this obvious fact. When social cooperation is intensified by enlarging the field in which there is division of labor or when legal protection and the safeguarding of peace are strengthened, the incentive is the desire of all those concerned to improve their own conditions. In striving after his own—rightly understood—interests the individual works toward an intensification of social cooperation and peaceful intercourse. Society is a product of human action, i.e., the human urge to remove uneasiness as far as possible. In order to explain its becoming and its evolution it is not necessary to have recourse to a doctrine, certainly offensive to a truly religious mind, according to which the original creation was so defective that reiterated superhuman intervention is needed to prevent its failure.

The historical role of the theory of the division of labor as elaborated by British political economy from Hume to Ricardo consisted in the complete demolition of all metaphysical doctrines concerning the origin and the operation of social cooperation. It consummated the spiritual, moral and intellectual emancipation of mankind inaugurated by the philosophy of Epicureanism. It substituted an autonomous rational morality for the heteronomous and intuitionist ethics of older days. Law and legality, the moral code and social institutions are no longer revered as unfathomable decrees of Heaven. They are of human origin, and the only yardstick that must be applied to them is that of expediency with regard to human welfare. The utilitarian economist does not say: Fiat justitia, pereat mundus. He says: Fiat justitia, *ne* pereat mundus. He does not ask a man to renounce his well-being for the benefit of society. He advises him to recognize what his rightly understood interests are. In his eyes God's magnificence does not manifest itself in busy interference with sundry affairs of princes and politicians, but in endowing his creatures with reason and the urge toward the pursuit of happiness.[3]

The essential problem of all varieties of universalistic, collectivistic, and holistic social philosophy is: By what mark do I recognize the true law, the authentic apostle of God's word, and the legitimate authority. For many claim that Providence has sent them, and each of these prophets preaches another gospel. For the faithful believer there cannot be any doubt; he is fully confident that he has espoused the only true doctrine. But it is precisely the firmness of such beliefs that renders the antagonisms irreconcilable. Each party is prepared to make its own tenets prevail. But as logical argumentation cannot decide between various dissenting creeds, there is no means left for the settlement of such disputes other than armed conflict. The non-

3. Many economists, among them Adam Smith and Bastiat, believed in God. Hence they admired in the facts they had discovered the providential care of "the great Director of Nature." Atheist critics blame them for this attitude. However, these critics fail to realize that to sneer at the references to the "invisible hand" does not invalidate the essential teachings of the rationalist and utilitarian social philosophy. One must comprehend that the alternative is this: Either association is a human process because it best serves the aims of the individuals concerned and the individuals themselves have the ability to realize the advantages they derive from their adjustment to life in social cooperation. Or a superior being enjoins upon reluctant men subordination to the law and to the social authorities. It is of minor importance whether one calls this supreme being God, Weltgeist, Destiny, History, Wotan, or Material Productive Forces and what title one assigns to its apostles, the dictators.

rationalist, nonutilitarian, and nonliberal social doctrines must beget wars and civil wars until one of the adversaries is annihilated or subdued. The history of the world's great religions is a record of battles and wars, as is the history of the present-day counterfeit religions, socialism, statolatry, and nationalism.

Intolerance and propaganda by the executioner's or the soldier's sword are inherent in any system of heteronomous ethics. The laws of God or Destiny claim universal validity, and to the authorities which they declare legitimate all men by rights owe obedience. As long as the prestige of heteronomous codes of morality and of their philosophical corollary, conceptual realism, was intact, there could not be any question of tolerance or of lasting peace. When fighting ceased, it was only to gather new strength for further battling. The idea of tolerance with regard to other people's dissenting views could take root only when the liberal doctrines had broken the spell of universalism. In the light of the utilitarian philosophy, society and state no longer appear as institutions for the maintenance of a world order that for considerations hidden to the human mind pleases the Deity although it manifestly hurts the secular interests of many or even of the immense majority of those living today. Society and state are on the contrary the primary means for all people to attain the ends they aim at of their own accord. They are created by human effort and their maintenance and most suitable organization are tasks not essentially different from all other concerns of human action. The supporters of a heteronomous morality and of the collectivistic doctrine cannot hope to demonstrate by ratiocination the correctness of their specific variety of ethical principles and the superiority and exclusive legitimacy of their particular social ideal. They are forced to ask people to accept credulously their ideological system and to surrender to the authority they consider the right one; they are intent upon silencing dissenters or upon beating them into submission.

Of course, there will always be individuals and groups of individuals whose intellect is so narrow that they cannot grasp the benefits which social cooperation brings them. There are others whose moral strength and will power are so weak that they cannot resist the temptation to strive for an ephemeral advantage by actions detrimental to the smooth functioning of the social system. For the adjustment of the individual to the requirements of social cooperation demands sacrifices. These are, it is true, only temporary and apparent sacrifices as they are more than compensated for by the incomparably greater advantages which living within society provides. However, at the instant, in the very act of renouncing an expected enjoyment, they are painful, and it is not for everybody to realize their later benefits and to behave accordingly. Anarchism believes that education could make all people comprehend what their own interests require them to do; rightly instructed they would of their own accord always comply with the rules of conduct indispensable for the preservation of society. The anarchists contend that a social order in which nobody enjoys privileges at the expense of his fellow-citizens could exist without any compulsion and coercion for the prevention of action detrimental to society. Such an ideal society could do without state and government, i.e., without a police force, the social apparatus of coercion and compulsion.

The anarchists overlook the undeniable fact that some people are either too narrow-minded or too weak to adjust themselves spontaneously to the conditions of social life. Even if we admit that every sane adult is endowed with the faculty of realizing the good of social cooperation and of acting accordingly, there still remains the problem of the infants, the aged, and the insane. We may agree that he who acts antisocially should be considered mentally sick and in need of care. But as long as not all are cured, and as long as there are infants and the senile, some provision must be taken lest they jeopardize society. An anarchistic society would be exposed to the mercy of every individual. Society cannot exist if the majority is not ready to hinder, by the application or threat of violent action, minorities from destroying the social order. This power is vested in the state or government.

State or government is the social apparatus of compulsion and coercion. It has the monopoly of violent action. No individual is free to use violence or the threat of violence if the government has not accorded this right to him. The state is essentially an institution for the preservation of peaceful interhuman relations. However, for the preservation of peace it must be prepared to crush the onslaughts of peace-breakers.

Liberal social doctrine, based on the teachings of utilitarian ethics and economics, sees the problem of the relation between the government and those ruled from a different angle than universalism and collectivism. Liberalism realizes that the rulers, who are always a minority, cannot lastingly remain in office if not supported by the consent of the majority of those ruled. Whatever the system of government may be, the foundation upon which it is built and rests is always the opinion of those ruled that to obey and to be loyal to this government better serves their own interests than insurrection and the establishment of another regime. The majority has the power to do away with an unpopular government and uses this power whenever it becomes convinced that its own welfare requires it. In the long run there is no such thing as an unpopular government. Civil war and revolution are the means by which the discontented majorities overthrow rulers and methods of government which do not suit them. For the sake of domestic peace liberalism aims at democratic government. Democracy is therefore not a revolutionary institution. On the contrary, it is the very means of preventing revolutions and civil wars. It provides a method for the peaceful adjustment of government to the will of the majority. When the men in office and their policies no longer please the majority of the nation, they will—in the next election—be eliminated and replaced by other men espousing different policies.

The principle of majority rule or government by the people as recommended by liberalism does not aim at the supremacy of the mean, of the lowbred, of the domestic barbarians. The liberals too believe that a nation should be ruled by those best fitted for this task. But they believe that a man's ability to rule proves itself better by convincing his fellow-citizens than by using force upon them. There is, of course, no guarantee that the voters will entrust office to the most competent candidate. But no other system could offer such a guarantee. If the majority of the nation is committed to unsound principles and prefers unworthy office-seekers, there is no remedy other than to try to change their mind by expounding more reasonable principles and recommending better men. A minority will never win lasting success by other means.

Universalism and collectivism cannot accept this democratic solution of the problem of government. In their opinion the individual in complying with the ethical code does not directly further his earthly concerns but, on the contrary, foregoes the attainment of his own ends for the benefit of the designs of the Deity or of the collective whole. Moreover reason alone is not capable of conceiving the supremacy of the absolute values and the unconditional validity of the sacred law and of interpreting correctly the canons and commandments. Hence it is in their eyes a hopeless task to try to convince the majority through persuasion and to lead them to righteousness by amicable admonition. Those blessed by heavenly inspiration, to whom their *charisma* has conveyed illumination, have the duty to propagate the gospel to the docile and to resort to violence against the intractable. The charismatic leader is the Deity's vicar, the mandatory of the collective whole, the tool of history. He is infallible and always right. His orders are the supreme norm.

Universalism and collectivism are by necessity systems of theocratic government. The common characteristic of all their varieties is that they postulate the existence of a superhuman entity which the individuals are bound to obey. What differentiates them from one another is only the appellation they give to this entity and the content of the laws they proclaim in its name. The dictatorial rule of a minority cannot find any legitimation other than the appeal to an alleged mandate obtained from a superhuman absolute authority. It does not matter whether the autocrat bases his claims on the divine rights of anointed kings or on the historical mission of the vanguard of the proletariat or whether the supreme being is called *Geist* (Hegel) or *Humanité* (Auguste Comte). The terms society and state as they are used by the contemporary advocates of socialism, planning, and social control of all the activities of individuals signify a deity. The priests of this new creed ascribe to their idol all those attributes which the theologians ascribe to God—omnipotence, omniscience, infinite goodness, and so on.

If one assumes that there exists above and beyond the individual's actions an imperishable entity aiming at its own ends, different from those of mortal men, one has already constructed the concept of a superhuman being. Then one cannot evade the question whose ends take precedence whenever an antagonism arises, those of the state or society or those of the individual. The answer to this question is already implied in the very concept of state or society as conceived by collectivism and universalism. If one postulates the existence of an entity which ex definitione is higher, nobler, and better than the individuals, then there cannot be any doubt that the aims of this eminent being must tower above those of the wretched individuals. (It is true that some lovers of paradox—for instance, Max Stirner[4]—took pleasure in turning the matter upside down and for all that asserted the precedence of the individual.) If society or state is an entity endowed with volition and intention and all the other qualities attributed to it by the collectivist doctrine, then it is simply nonsensical to set the shabby individual's trivial aims against its lofty designs.

The quasi-theological character of all collectivist doctrines becomes manifest in their mutual conflicts. A collectivist doctrine does not assert the superiority of a collective whole in abstracto; it always proclaims the eminence of a definite collectivist idol, and either flatly denies the existence of other such idols or relegates them to a sub-

4. Cf. Max Stirner (Johann Kaspar Schmidt). *The Ego and His Own,* trans. by S. T. Byington (New York, 1907).

ordinate and ancillary position with regard to its own idol. The worshipers of the state proclaim the excellence of a definite state, i.e., their own; the nationalists, the excellence of their own nation. If dissenters challenge their particular program by heralding the superiority of another collectivist idol, they resort to no objection other than to declare again and again: We are right because an inner voice tells us that we are right and you are wrong. The conflicts of antagonistic collectivist creeds and sects cannot be decided by ratiocination; they must be decided by arms. The alternatives to the liberal and democratic principle of majority rule are the militarist principles of armed conflict and dictatorial oppression.

All varieties of collectivist creeds are united in their implacable hostility to the fundamental political institutions of the liberal system: majority rule, tolerance of dissenting views, freedom of thought, speech, and the press, equality of all men under the law. This collaboration of collectivist creeds in their attempts to destroy freedom has brought about the mistaken belief that the issue in present-day political antagonisms is individualism versus collectivism. In fact it is a struggle between individualism on the one hand and a multitude of collectivist sects on the other hand whose mutual hatred and hostility is no less ferocious than their abomination of the liberal system. It is not a uniform Marxian sect that attacks capitalism, but a host of Marxian groups. These groups—for instance, Stalinists, Trotskyists, Mensheviks, supporters of the Second International, and so on—fight one another with the utmost brutality and inhumanity. And then there are again many other non-Marxian sects which apply the same atrocious methods in their mutual struggles. A substitution of collectivism for liberalism would result in endless bloody fighting.

The customary terminology misrepresents these things entirely. The philosophy commonly called individualism is a philosophy of social cooperation and the progressive intensification of the social nexus. On the other hand the application of the basic ideas of collectivism cannot result in anything but social disintegration and the perpetuation of armed conflict. It is true that every variety of collectivism promises eternal peace starting with the day of its own decisive victory and the final overthrow and extermination of all other ideologies and their supporters. However, the realization of these plans is conditioned upon a radical transformation in mankind. Men must be divided into two classes: the omnipotent godlike dictator on the one hand and the masses which must surrender volition and reasoning in order to become mere chessmen in the plans of the dictator. The masses must be dehumanized in order to make one man their godlike master. Thinking and acting, the foremost characteristics of man as man, would become the privilege of *one* man only. There is no need to point out that such designs are unrealizable. The chiliastic empires of dictators are doomed to failure; they have never lasted longer than a few years. We have just witnessed the breakdown of several of such "millennial" orders. Those remaining will hardly fare better.

The modern revival of the idea of collectivism, the main cause of all the agonies and disasters of our day, has succeeded so thoroughly that it has brought into oblivion the essential ideas of liberal social philosophy. Today even many of those favoring democratic institutions ignore these ideas. The arguments they bring forward for the justification of freedom and democracy are tainted with collectivist errors; their doctrines are rather a distortion than an endorsement of true liberalism. In their eyes majorities are always right simply because they have the power to crush any opposition; majority rule is the dictatorial rule of the most numerous party, and the ruling majority is not bound to restrain itself in the exercise of its power and in the conduct of political affairs. As soon as a faction has succeeded in winning the support of the majority of citizens and thereby attained control of the government machine, it is free to deny to the minority all those democratic rights by means of which it itself has previously carried on its own struggle for supremacy.

This pseudo-liberalism is, of course, the very antithesis of the liberal doctrine. The liberals do not maintain that majorities are godlike and infallible; they do not contend that the mere fact that a policy is advocated by the many is a proof of its merits for the common weal. They do not recommend the dictatorship of the majority and the violent oppression of dissenting minorities. Liberalism aims at a political constitution which safeguards the smooth working of social cooperation and the progressive intensification of mutual social relations. Its main objective is the avoidance of violent conflicts, of wars and revolutions that must disintegrate the social collaboration of men and throw people back into the primitive conditions of barbarism where all tribes and political bodies endlessly fought one another. Because the division of labor requires undisturbed peace, liberalism aims at the establishment of a system of government that is likely to preserve peace, viz., democracy.

Praxeology and Liberalism

Liberalism, in its 19th century sense, is a political doctrine. It is not a theory, but an application of the theories developed by praxeology and especially by economics to definite problems of human action within society.

As a political doctrine liberalism is not neutral with regard to values and the ultimate ends sought by action. It assumes that all men or at least the majority of people are intent upon attaining certain goals. It gives them information about the means suitable to the realization of their plans. The champions of liberal doctrines are fully aware of the fact that their teachings are valid only for people who are committed to these valuational principles.

While praxeology, and therefore economics too, uses the terms happiness and removal of uneasiness in a purely formal sense, liberalism attaches to them a concrete meaning. It presupposes that people prefer life to death, health to sickness, nourishment to starvation, abundance to poverty. It teaches man how to act in accordance with these valuations.

It is customary to call these concerns materialistic and to charge liberalism with an alleged crude materialism and a neglect of the "higher" and "nobler" pursuits of mankind. Man does not live by bread alone, say the critics, and they disparage the meanness and despicable baseness of the utilitarian philosophy. However, these passionate diatribes are wrong because they badly distort the teachings of liberalism.

First: The liberals do not assert that men *ought* to strive after the goals mentioned above. What they maintain is that the immense majority prefer a life of health and abundance to misery, starvation, and death. The correctness of this statement cannot be challenged. It is proved by the fact that all antiliberal doctrines—the theocratic tenets of the various religious, statist, nationalist, and socialist parties—adopt the same attitude with regard to these issues. They all promise their followers a life of plenty. They have never ventured to tell people that the realization of their program will impair their material well-being. They insist—on the contrary—that while the realization of the plans of their rival parties will result in indigence for the majority, they themselves want to provide their supporters with abundance. The Christian parties are no less eager in promising the masses a higher standard of living than the nationalists and the socialists. Present-day churches often speak more about raising wage rates and farm incomes than about the dogmas of the Christian doctrine.

Secondly: The liberals do not disdain the intellectual and spiritual aspirations of man. On the contrary. They are prompted by a passionate ardor for intellectual and moral perfection, for wisdom and for aesthetic excellence. But their view of these high and noble things is far from the crude representations of their adversaries. They do not share the naïve opinion that any system of social organization can directly succeed in encouraging philosophical or scientific thinking, in producing masterpieces of art and literature and in rendering the masses more enlightened. They realize that all that society can achieve in these fields is to provide an environment which does not put insurmountable obstacles in the way of the genius and makes the common man free enough from material concerns to become interested in things other than mere breadwinning. In their opinion the foremost social means of making man more human is to fight poverty. Wisdom and science and the arts thrive better in a world of affluence than among needy peoples.

It is a distortion of facts to blame the age of liberalism for an alleged materialism. The nineteenth century was not only a century of unprecedented improvement in technical methods of production and in the material well-being of the masses. It did much more than extend the average length of human life. Its scientific and artistic accomplishments are imperishable. It was an age of immortal musicians, writers, poets, painters, and sculptors; it revolutionized philosophy, economics, mathematics, physics, chemistry, and biology. And, for the first time in history, it made the great works and the great thoughts accessible to the common man.

Liberalism and Religion

Liberalism is based upon a purely rational and scientific theory of social cooperation. The policies it recommends are the application of a system of knowledge which does not refer in any way to sentiments, intuitive creeds for which no logically sufficient proof can be provided, mystical experiences, and the personal awareness of superhuman phenomena. In this sense the often misunderstood and erroneously interpreted epithets atheistic and agnostic can be attributed to it. It would, however, be a serious mistake to conclude that the sciences of human action and the policy derived from their teachings, liberalism, are antitheistic and hostile to religion. They are radically opposed to all systems of theocracy. But they are entirely neutral with regard to religious beliefs which do not pretend to interfere with the conduct of social, political, and economic affairs.

Theocracy is a social system which lays claim to a superhuman title for its legitimation. The fundamental law of a theocratic regime is an insight not open to examination by reason and to demonstration by logical methods. Its ultimate standard is intuition providing the mind with subjective certainty about things which cannot be conceived by reason and ratiocination. If this intuition refers to one of the traditional systems of teaching concerning the existence of a Divine Creator and Ruler of the universe, we call it a religious belief. If it refers to another system we call it a metaphysical belief. Thus a system of theocratic government need not be founded on one of the great historical religions of the world. It may be the outcome of metaphysical tenets which reject all traditional churches and denominations and take pride in emphasizing their antitheistic and antimetaphysical character. In our time the most powerful theocratic parties are opposed to Christianity and to all other religions which evolved from Jewish monotheism. What characterizes them as theocratic is their craving to organize the earthly affairs of mankind according to the contents of a complex of ideas whose validity cannot be demonstrated by reasoning. They pretend that their leaders are blessed by a knowledge inaccessible to the rest of mankind and contrary to the ideas maintained by those to whom the charisma is denied. The charismatic leaders have been entrusted by a mystical higher power with the office of managing the affairs of erring mankind. They alone are enlightened; all other people are either blind and deaf or malefactors.

It is a fact that many varieties of the great historical religions were affected by theocratic tendencies. Their apostles were inspired by a craving for power and the oppression and annihilation of all dissenting groups. However, we must not confuse the two things, religion and theocracy.

William James calls religious "the feelings, acts and experiences of individual men in their solitude, so far as they apprehend themselves to stand in relation to whatever they may consider the divine."[5] He enumerates the following beliefs as the characteristics of the religious life: That the visible world is part of a more spiritual universe from which it draws its chief significance; that union or harmonious relation with that higher universe is our true end; that prayer or inner communion with the spirit thereof—be that spirit "God" or "law"—is a process wherein work is really done, and spiritual energy flows in and produces effects, psychological or material, within the phenomenal world. Religion, James goes on to say, also includes the following psychological characteristics: A new zest which *adds* itself like a gift to life, and takes the form either of lyrical enchantment or of appeal to earnestness and heroism, and furthermore an assurance of safety and a temper of peace, and, in relation to others, a preponderance of loving affection.[6]

This characterization of mankind's religious experience and feelings does not make any reference to the arrangement of social cooperation. Religion, as James sees it, is a purely personal and individual relation between man and a holy, mysterious, and awe-inspiring divine Reality. It enjoins upon man a certain mode of individual conduct. But it does not assert anything with regard to the problems of social organization.

5. W. James, *The Varieties of Religious Experience* (35th impression, New York, 1925), p. 31.

6. *Ibid.*, pp. 485–486.

St. Francis d'Assisi, the greatest religious genius of the West, did not concern himself with politics and economics. He wanted to teach his disciples how to live piously; he did not draft a plan for the organization of production and did not urge his followers to resort to violence against dissenters. He is not responsible for the interpretation of his teachings by the order he founded.

Liberalism puts no obstacles in the way of a man eager to adjust his personal conduct and his private affairs according to the mode in which he individually or his church or denomination interprets the teachings of the Gospels. But it is radically opposed to all endeavors to silence the rational discussion of problems of social welfare by an appeal to religious intuition and revelation. It does not enjoin divorce or the practice of birth control upon anybody. But it fights those who want to prevent other people from freely discussing the pros and cons of these matters.

In the liberal opinion the aim of the moral law is to impel individuals to adjust their conduct to the requirements of life in society, to abstain from all acts detrimental to the preservation of peaceful social cooperation and to the improvement of interhuman relations. Liberals welcome the support which religious teachings may give to those moral precepts of which they themselves approve, but they are opposed to all those norms which are bound to bring about social disintegration from whatever source they may stem.

It is a distortion of fact to say, as many champions of religious theocracy do, that liberalism fights religion. Where the principle of church interference with secular issues is in force, the various churches, denominations and sects are fighting one another. By separating church and state, liberalism establishes peace between the various religious factions and gives to each of them the opportunity to preach its gospel unmolested.

Liberalism is rationalistic. It maintains that it is possible to convince the immense majority that peaceful cooperation within the framework of society better serves their rightly understood interests than mutual battling and social disintegration. It has full confidence in man's reason. It may be that this optimism is unfounded and that the liberals have erred. But then there is no hope left for mankind's future.

3. The Division of Labor

The fundamental social phenomenon is the division of labor and its counterpart human cooperation.

Experience teaches man that cooperative action is more efficient and productive than isolated action of self-sufficient individuals. The natural conditions determining man's life and effort are such that the division of labor increases output per unit of labor expended. These natural facts are:

First: the innate inequality of men with regard to their ability to perform various kinds of labor. Second: the unequal distribution of the nature-given, nonhuman opportunities of production on the surface of the earth. One may as well consider these two facts as one and the same fact, namely, the manifoldness of nature which makes the universe a complex of infinite varieties. If the earth's surface were such that the physical conditions of production were the same at every point and if one man were as equal to all other men as is a circle to another with the same diameter in Euclidian geometry, men would not have embarked upon the division of labor.

There is still a third fact, viz., that there are undertakings whose accomplishment exceeds the forces of a single man and requires the joint effort of several. Some of them require an expenditure of labor which no single man can perform because his capacity to work is not great enough. Others again could be accomplished by individuals; but the time which they would have to devote to the work would be so long that the result would only be attained late and would not compensate for the labor expended. In both cases only joint effort makes it possible to attain the end sought.

If only this third condition were present, temporary cooperation between men would have certainly emerged. However, such transient alliances to cope with specific tasks which are beyond the strength of an individual would not have brought about lasting social cooperation. Undertakings which could be performed only in this way were not very numerous at the early stages of civilization. Moreover, all those concerned may not often agree that the performance in question is more useful and urgent than the accomplishment of other tasks which they could perform alone. The great human society enclosing all men in all of their activities did not originate from such occasional alliances. Society is much more than a passing alliance concluded for a definite purpose and ceasing as soon as its objective is realized, even if the partners are ready to renew it should an occasion present itself.

The increase in productivity brought about by the division of labor is obvious whenever the inequality of the participants is such that every individual or every piece of land is superior at least in one regard to the other individuals or pieces of land concerned. If A is fit to produce in 1 unit of time 6 p or 4 q and B only 2 p, but 8 q, they both, when working in isolation, will produce together $4\ p+6\ q$; when working under the division of labor, each of them producing only that commodity in whose production he is more efficient than his partner, they will produce 6 p + 8 q. But what will happen, if *A* is more efficient than *B* not only in the production of p but also in the production of q?

This is the problem which Ricardo raised and solved immediately.

4. The Ricardian Law of Association

Ricardo expounded the law of association in order to demonstrate what the consequences of the division of labor are when an individual or a group, more efficient in every regard, cooperates with an individual or a group less efficient in every regard. He investigated the effects of trade between two areas, unequally endowed by nature, under the assumption that the products, but not the workers and the accumulated factors of future production (capital goods), can freely move from each area into the other. The division of labor between two such areas will, as Ricardo's law shows, increase the productivity of labor and is therefore advantageous to all concerned, even if the physical conditions of production for any commodity are more favorable in one of these two areas than in the other. It is advantageous for the better endowed area to concentrate its efforts upon the production of those commodities for which its superiority is greater, and to leave to the less endowed area the production of other goods in which its own superiority is less. The paradox that it is more advantageous to leave more favorable domestic conditions of production unused and to procure the commodities they could produce from areas in which conditions for their production are less favorable, is the outcome of the immobility of labor and capital, to which the more favorable places of production are inaccessible.

Ricardo was fully aware of the fact that his law of comparative cost, which he expounded mainly in order to deal with a special problem of international trade, is a particular instance of the more universal law of association.

If *A* is in such a way more efficient than *B* that he needs for the production of 1 unit of the commodity p 3 hours compared with *B's* 5, and for the production of 1 unit of q 2 hours compared with *B's* 4, then both will gain if *A* confines himself to producing q and leaves *B* to produce p. If each of them gives 60 hours to producing p and 60 hours to producing q, the result of *A's* labor is 20 p + 30 q; of *B's*, 12 p + 15 q; and for both together, 32 p + 45 q. If, however, *A* confines himself to producing q alone, he produces 60 q in 120 hours, while *B*, if he confines himself to producing p, produces in the same time 24 p. The result of their activities is then 24 p + 60 q, which, as p has for *A* a substitution ratio of $\frac{3}{2}q$ and for *B* one of $\frac{5}{4}q$, signifies a larger output than $32\,p+45\,q$. Therefore it is manifest that the division of labor brings advantages to all who take part in it. Collaboration of the more talented, more able, and more industrious with the less talented, less able, and less industrious results in benefit for both. The gains derived from the division of labor are always mutual.

The law of association makes us comprehend the tendencies which resulted in the progressive intensification of human cooperation. We conceive what incentive induced people not to consider themselves simply as rivals in a struggle for the appropriation of the limited supply of means of subsistence made available by nature. We realize what has impelled them and permanently impels them to consort with one another for the sake of cooperation. Every step forward on the way to a more developed mode of the division of labor serves the interests of all participants. In order to comprehend why man did not remain solitary, searching like the animals for food and shelter for himself only and at most also for his consort and his helpless infants, we do not need to have recourse to a miraculous interference of the Deity or to the empty hypostasis of an innate urge toward association. Neither are we forced to assume that the isolated individuals or primitive hordes one day pledged themselves by a contract to establish social bonds. The factor that brought about primitive society and daily works toward its progressive intensification is human action that is animated by the insight into the higher productivity of labor achieved under the division of labor.

Neither history nor ethnology nor any other branch of knowledge can provide a description of the evolution which has led from the packs and flocks of mankind's nonhuman ancestors to the primitive, yet already highly differentiated, societal groups about which information is provided in excavations, in the most ancient documents of history, and in the reports of explorers and travelers who have met savage tribes. The task with which science is faced in respect of the origins of society can only consist in the demonstration of those factors which can and must result in association and its progressive intensification. Praxeology solves the problem. If and as far as labor under the division of labor is more productive than isolated labor, and if and as far as man is able to realize this fact, human action itself tends toward cooperation and association; man becomes a social being not in sacrificing his own concerns for the sake of a mythical Moloch, society, but in aiming at an improvement in his own welfare. Experience teaches that this condition—higher productivity achieved under the division of labor—is present because its cause—the inborn inequality of men and the inequality in the geographical distribution of the natural factors of production—is real. Thus we are in a position to comprehend the course of social evolution.

Current Errors Concerning the Law of Association

People cavil much about Ricardo's law of association, better known under the name *law of comparative cost.* The reason is obvious. This law is an offense to all those eager to justify protection and national economic isolation from any point of view other than the selfish interests of some producers or the issues of war-preparedness.

Ricardo's first aim in expounding this law was to refute an objection raised against freedom of international trade. The protectionist asks: What under free trade will be the fate of a country in which the conditions for any kind of production are less favorable than in all other countries? Now, in a world in which there is free mobility not only for products, but no less for capital goods and for labor, a country so little suited for production would cease to be used as the seat of any human industry. If people fare better without exploiting the—comparatively unsatisfactory—physical conditions of production offered by this country, they will not settle here and will leave it as uninhabited as the polar regions, the tundras and the deserts. But Ricardo deals with a world whose conditions are determined by settlement in earlier days, a world in which capital goods and labor are bound to the soil by definite institutions. In such a milieu free trade, i.e., the free mobility of commodities only, cannot bring about a state of affairs in which capital and labor are distributed on the surface of the earth according to the better or poorer physical opportunities afforded to the productivity of labor. Here the law of comparative cost comes into operation. Each country turns toward those branches of production for which its conditions offer comparatively, although not absolutely, the most favorable opportunities. For the inhabitants of a country it is more advantageous to abstain from the exploitation of some opportunities which—absolutely and technologically—are more propitious and to import commodities produced abroad under conditions which—absolutely and technologically—are less favorable than the unused domestic resources. The case is analogous to that of a surgeon who finds it convenient to employ for the cleaning of the operating-room and the instruments a man whom he excels in this performance also and to devote himself exclusively to surgery, in which his superiority is higher.

The theorem of comparative cost is in no way connected with the value theory of classical economics. It does not deal with value or with prices. It is an analytic judgment; the conclusion is implied in the two propositions that the technically movable factors of production differ with regard to their productivity in various places and are institutionally restricted in their mobility. The theorem, without prejudice to the correctness of its conclusions, can disregard problems of valuation because it is free to resort to a set of simple assumptions. These are: that only two products are to be produced; that these products are freely movable; that for the production of each of them two factors are required; that one of these factors (it may be either labor or capital goods) is identical in the production of both, while the other factor (a specific property of the soil) is different for each of the two processes; that the greater scarcity of the factor common to both processes determines the extent of the exploitation of the different factor. In the frame of these assumptions, which make it possible to establish substitution ratios between the expenditure of the common factor and the output, the theorem answers the question raised.

The law of comparative cost is as independent of the classical theory of value as is the law of returns, which its reasoning resembles. In both cases we can content ourselves with comparing only physical input and physical output. With the law of returns we compare the output of the same product. With the law of comparative costs we compare the output of two different products. Such a comparison is feasible because we assume that for the production of each of them, apart from one specific factor, only nonspecific factors of the same kind are required.

Some critics blame the law of comparative cost for this simplification of assumptions. They believe that the modern theory of value would require a reformulation of the law in conformity with the principles of subjective value. Only such a formulation could provide a satisfactory conclusive demonstration. However, they do not want to calculate in terms of money. They prefer to resort to those methods of utility analysis which they consider a means for making value calculations in terms of utility. It will be shown in the further progress of our investigation that these attempts to eliminate monetary terms from economic calculation are delusive. Their fundamental assumptions are untenable and contradictory and all formulas derived from them are vicious. No method of economic calculation is possible other than one based on money prices as determined by the market.[7]

The meaning of the simple assumptions underlying the law of comparative cost is not precisely the same for the modern economists as it was for the classical economists. Some adherents of the classical school considered them as the starting point of a theory of value in international trade. We know now that they were mistaken in this belief. Besides, we realize that with regard to the determination of

7. See below, pp. 201–209.

value and of prices there is no difference between domestic and foreign trade. What makes people distinguish between the home market and markets abroad is only a difference in the data, i.e., varying institutional conditions restricting the mobility of factors of production and of products.

If we do not want to deal with the law of comparative cost under the simplified assumptions applied by Ricardo, we must openly employ money calculation. We must not fall prey to the illusion that a comparison between the expenditure of factors of production of various kinds and of the output of products of various kinds can be achieved without the aid of money calculation. If we consider the case of the surgeon and his handyman we must say: If the surgeon can employ his limited working time for the performance of operations for which he is compensated at $50 per hour, it is to his interest to employ a handyman to keep his instruments in good order and to pay him $2 per hour, although this man needs 3 hours to accomplish what the surgeon could do in 1 hour. In comparing the conditions of two countries we must say: If conditions are such that in England the production of 1 unit of each of the two commodities *a* and *b* requires the expenditure of 1 working day of the same kind of labor, while in India with the same investment of capital for *a* 2 days and for *b* 3 days are required, and if capital goods and *a* and *b* are freely movable from England to India and vice versa, while there is no mobility of labor, wage rates in India in the production of *a* must tend to be 50 per cent, and in the production of *b* 33⅓ per cent, of the English rates. If the English rate is 6 shillings, the rates in India would be the equivalent of 3 shillings in the production of *a* and the equivalent of 2 shillings in the production of *b*. Such a discrepancy in the remuneration of labor of the same kind cannot last if there is mobility of labor on the domestic Indian labor market. Workers would shift from the production of *b* into the production of *a*; their migration would tend to lower the remuneration in the *a* industry and to raise it in the *b* industry. Finally Indian wage rates would be equal in both industries. The production of *a* would tend to expand and to supplant English competition. On the other hand the production of *b* would become unprofitable in India and would have to be discontinued, while it would expand in England. The same reasoning is valid if we assume that the difference in the conditions of production consists also or exclusively in the amount of capital investment needed.

It has been asserted that Ricardo's law was valid only for his age and is of no avail for our time which offers other conditions. Ricardo saw the difference between domestic trade and foreign trade in differences in the mobility of capital and labor. If one assumes that capital, labor, and products are movable, then there exists a difference between regional and interregional trade only as far as the cost of transportation comes into play. Then it is superfluous to develop a theory of international trade as distinguished from national trade. Capital and labor are distributed on the earth's surface according to the better or poorer conditions which the various regions offer to production. There are areas more densely populated and better equipped with capital, there are others less densely populated and poorer in capital supply. There prevails on the whole earth a tendency toward an equalization of wage rates for the same kind of labor.

Ricardo, however, starts from the assumption that there is mobility of capital and labor only within each country, and not between the various countries. He raises the question what the consequences of the free mobility of products must be under such conditions. (If there is no mobility of products either, then every country is economically isolated and autarkic, and there is no international trade at all.) The theory of comparative cost answers this question. Now, Ricardo's assumptions by and large held good for his age. Later, in the course of the nineteenth century, conditions changed. The immobility of capital and labor gave way; international transfer of capital and labor became more and more common. Then came a reaction. Today capital and labor are again restricted in their mobility. Reality again corresponds to the Ricardian assumptions.

However, the teachings of the classical theory of interregional trade are above any change in institutional conditions. They enable us to study the problems involved under any imaginable assumptions.

5. The Effects of the Division of Labor

The division of labor is the outcome of man's conscious reaction to the multiplicity of natural conditions. On the other hand it is itself a factor bringing about differentiation. It assigns to the various geographic areas specific functions in the complex of the processes of production. It makes some areas urban, others rural; it locates the various branches of manufacturing, mining, and agriculture in different places. Still more important, however, is the fact that it intensifies the innate inequality of men. Exercise and practice of specific tasks adjust individuals better to the requirements of their performance; men develop some of their inborn faculties and stunt the development of others. Vocational types emerge, people become specialists.

The division of labor splits the various processes of production into minute tasks, many of which can be performed by mechanical devices. It is this fact that made the use of machinery possible and brought about the amazing improvements in technical methods of production. Mechanization is the fruit of the division of labor, its most beneficial achievement, not its motive and fountain spring. Power-driven specialized machinery could be employed only in a social environment under the division of labor. Every step forward on the road toward the use of more specialized, more refined, and more productive machines requires a further specialization of tasks.

6. The Individual Within Society

If praxeology speaks of the solitary individual, acting on his own behalf only and independent of fellow men, it does so for the sake of a better comprehension of the problems of social cooperation. We do not assert that such isolated autarkic human beings have ever lived and that the social stage of man's history was preceded by an age of independent individuals roaming like animals in search of food. The biological humanization of man's nonhuman ancestors and the emergence of the primitive social bonds were effected in the same process. Man appeared on the scene of earthly events as a social being. The isolated asocial man is a fictitious construction.

Seen from the point of view of the individual, society is the great means for the attainment of all his ends. The preservation of society is an essential condition of any plans an individual may want to realize by any action whatever. Even the refractory delinquent who fails to adjust his conduct to the requirements of life within the societal system of cooperation does not want to miss any of the advantages derived from the division of labor. He does not consciously aim at the destruction of society. He wants to lay his hands on a greater portion of the jointly produced wealth than the social order assigns to him. He would feel miserable if antisocial behavior were to become universal and its inevitable outcome, the return to primitive indigence, resulted.

It is illusory to maintain that individuals in renouncing the alleged blessings of a fabulous state of nature and entering into society have foregone some advantages and have a fair claim to be indemnified for what they have lost. The idea that anybody would have fared better under an asocial state of mankind and is wronged by the very existence of society is absurd. Thanks to the higher productivity of social cooperation the human species has multiplied far beyond the margin of subsistence offered by the conditions prevailing in ages with a rudimentary degree of the division of labor. Each man enjoys a standard of living much higher than that of his savage ancestors. The natural condition of man is extreme poverty and insecurity. It is romantic nonsense to lament the passing of the happy days of primitive barbarism. In a state of savagery the complainants would either not have reached the age of manhood, or if they had, they would have lacked the opportunities and amenities provided by civilization. Jean Jacques Rousseau and Frederick Engels, if they had lived in the primitive state which they describe with nostalgic yearning, would not have enjoyed the leisure required for their studies and for the writing of their books.

One of the privileges which society affords to the individual is the privilege of living in spite of sickness or physical disability. Sick animals are doomed. Their weakness handicaps them in their attempts to find food and to repel aggression on the part of other animals. Deaf, nearsighted, or crippled savages must perish. But such defects do not deprive a man of the opportunity to adjust himself to life in society. The majority of our contemporaries are afflicted with some bodily deficiencies which biology considers pathological. Our civilization is to a great extent the achievement of such men. The eliminative forces of natural selection are greatly reduced under social conditions. Hence some people say that civilization tends to deteriorate the hereditary qualities of the members of society.

Such judgments are reasonable if one looks at mankind with the eyes of a breeder intent upon raising a race of men equipped with certain qualities. But society is not a stud-farm operated for the production of a definite type of men. There is no "natural" standard to establish what is desirable and what is undesirable in the biological evolution of man. Any standard chosen is arbitrary, purely subjective, in short a judgment of value. The terms racial improvement and racial degeneration are meaningless when not based on definite plans for the future of mankind.

It is true, civilized man is adjusted to life in society and not to that of a hunter in virgin forests.

The Fable of the Mystic Communion

The praxeological theory of society is assailed by the fable of the mystic communion.

Society, assert the supporters of this doctrine, is not the product of man's purposeful action; it is not cooperation and division of tasks. It stems from unfathomable depths, from an urge ingrained in man's essential nature. It is, says one group, engrossment by the Spirit which is Divine Reality and participation, by virtue of a *unio mystica,* in God's power and love. Another group sees society as a biological phenomenon; it is the work of the voice of the blood, the bond uniting the offspring of common ancestors with these ancestors and with one another, and the mystical harmony between the ploughman and the soil he tills.

That such psychical phenomena are really felt is true. There are people who experience the unio mystica and place this experience above everything else, and there are men who are convinced that they hear the voice of the blood and smell with heart and soul the unique scent of the cherished soil of their country. The mystical experience and the ecstatic rapture are facts which psychology must consider real, like any other psychical phenomenon. The error of the communion-doctrines does not consist in their assertion that such phenomena really occur, but in the belief that they are primary facts not dependent on any rational consideration.

The voice of the blood which brings the father close to his child was not heard by those savages who did not know the causal relation between cohabitation and pregnancy. Today, as this relation is known to everybody, a man who has full confidence in his wife's fidelity may perceive it. But if there are doubts concerning the wife's fidelity, the voice of the blood is of no use. Nobody ever ventured to assert that doubts concerning paternity could be resolved by the voice of the blood. A mother who has kept watch over her child since its birth can hear the voice of the blood. If she loses touch with the infant at an early date, she may later identify it by some bodily marks, for instance those moles and scars which once were popular with novel writers. But the blood is mute if such observations and the conclusions derived from them do not make it speak. The voice of the blood, contend the German racists, mysteriously unifies all members of the German people. But anthropology reveals the fact that the German nation is a mixture of the descendants of various races, subraces, and strains and not a homogeneous stock descended from a common ancestry. The recently germanized Slav who has only a short time since changed his paternal family name for a German-sounding name believes that he is substantially attached to all Germans. But he does not experience any such inner urge impelling him to join the ranks of his brothers or cousins who remained Czechs or Poles.

The voice of the blood is not an original and primordial phenomenon. It is prompted by rational considerations. Because a man believes that he is related to other people by a common ancestry, he develops those feelings and sentiments which are poetically described as the voice of the blood.

The same is true with regard to religious ecstasy and mysticism of the soil. The unio mystica of the devout mystic is conditioned by familiarity with the basic teachings of his religion. Only a man who has learned about the greatness and glory of God can experience direct communion with Him. Mysticism of the soil is connected with the development of definite geopolitical ideas. Thus it may happen that inhabitants of the plains or the seashore include in the image of the soil with which they claim to be fervently joined and united also mountain districts which are unfamiliar to them and to whose conditions they could not adapt themselves, only because this territory belongs to the political body of which they are members, or would like to be members. On the other hand they often fail to include in this image of the soil whose voice they claim to hear neighboring areas of a geographic structure very similar to that of their own country if these areas happen to belong to a foreign nation.

The various members of a nation or linguistic group and the clusters they form are not always united in friendship and good will. The history of every nation is a record of mutual dislike and even hatred between its subdivisions. Think of the English and the Scotch, the Yankees and the Southerners, the Prussians and the Bavarians. It was ideologies that overcame such animosities and inspired all members of a nation or linguistic group with those feelings of community and belonging together which present-day nationalists consider a natural and original phenomenon.

The mutual sexual attraction of male and female is inherent in man's animal nature and independent of any thinking and theorizing. It is permissible to call it original, vegetative, instinctive, or mysterious; there is no harm in asserting metaphorically that it makes one being out of two. We may call it a mystic communion of two bodies, a community. However, neither cohabitation, nor what precedes it and follows, generates social cooperation and societal modes of life. The animals too join together in mating, but they have not developed social relations. Family life is not merely a product of sexual intercourse. It is by no means natural and necessary that parents and children live together in the way in which they do in the family. The mating relation need not result in a family organization. The human family is an outcome of thinking, planning, and acting. It is this very fact which distinguishes it radically from those animal groups which we call *per analogiam* animal families.

The mystical experience of communion or community is not the source of societal relations, but their product.

The counterpart of the fable of the mystical communion is the fable of a natural and original repulsion between races or nations. It is asserted that an instinct teaches man to distinguish congeners from strangers and to detest the latter. Scions of noble races abominate any contact with members of lower races. To refute this statement one need only mention the fact of racial mixture. As there are in present-day Europe no pure stocks, we must conclude that between members of the various stocks which once settled in that continent there was sexual attraction and not repulsion. Millions of mulattoes and other half-breeds are living counterevidence to the assertion that there exists a natural repulsion between the various races.

Like the mystical sense of communion, racial hatred is not a natural phenomenon innate in man. It is the product of ideologies. But even if such a thing as a natural and inborn hatred between various races existed, it would not render social cooperation futile and would not invalidate Ricardo's theory of association. Social cooperation has nothing to do with personal love or with a general commandment to love one another. People do not cooperate under the division of labor because they love or should love one another. They cooperate because this best serves their own interests. Neither love nor charity nor any other sympathetic sentiments but rightly understood selfishness is what originally impelled man to adjust himself to the requirements of society, to respect the rights and freedoms of his fellow men and to substitute peaceful collaboration for enmity and conflict.

7. The Great Society

Not every interhuman relation is a social relation. When groups of men rush upon one another in a war of outright extermination, when men fight against men as mercilessly as they crush pernicious animals and plants, there is, between the fighting parties, reciprocal effect and mutual relation, but no society. Society is joint action and cooperation in which each participant sees the other partner's success as a means for the attainment of his own.

The struggles in which primitive hordes and tribes fought one another for watering places, hunting and fishing grounds, pastures and booty were pitiless wars of annihilation. They were total wars. So in the nineteenth century were the first encounters of Europeans with the aborigines of territories newly made accessible. But already in the primeval age, long before the time of which historical records convey information, another mode of procedure began to develop. People preserved even in warfare some rudiments of social relations previously established; in fighting against peoples with whom they never before had had any contact, they began to take into account the idea that between human beings, notwithstanding their immediate enmity, a later arrangement and cooperation is possible. Wars were waged to hurt the foe; but the hostile acts were no longer merciless and pitiless in the full sense of these terms. The belligerents began to respect certain limits which in a struggle against men—as differentiated from that against beasts—should not be transcended. Above the implacable hatred and the frenzy of destruction and annihilation a societal element began to prevail. The idea emerged that every human adversary should be considered as a potential partner in a future cooperation, and that this fact should not be neglected in the conduct of military operations. War was no longer considered the normal state of interhuman relations. People recognized that peaceful cooperation is the best means to carry on the struggle for biological survival. We may even say that as soon as people realized that it is more advantageous to enslave the defeated than to kill them, the warriors, while still fighting, gave thought to the aftermath, the peace. Enslavement was by and large a preliminary step toward cooperation.

The ascendancy of the idea that even in war not every act is to be considered permissible, that there are legitimate and illicit acts of warfare, that there are laws, i.e., societal relationships which are above all nations, even above those momentarily fighting one another, has finally established the Great Society embracing all men and all nations. The various regional societies were merged into one ecumenical society.

Belligerents who do not wage war savagely in the manner of beasts, but according to "human" and social rules of warfare, renounce the use of some methods of destruction in order to attain the same concessions on the part of their foes. As far as such rules are complied with, social relations exist between the fighting parties. The hostile acts themselves are not only asocial, but antisocial. It is inexpedient to define the term "social relationships" in such a way as to include actions which aim at other people's annihilation and at the frustration of their actions.[8] Where the only relations between men are those directed at mutual detriment, there is neither society nor societal relations.

Society is not merely interaction. There is interaction—reciprocal influence—between all parts of the universe: between the wolf and the sheep he devours; between the germ and the man it kills; between the falling stone and the thing upon which it falls. Society, on the other hand, always involves men acting in cooperation with other men in order to let all participants attain their own ends.

8. The Instinct of Aggression and Destruction

It has been asserted that man is a beast of prey whose inborn natural instincts impel him to fight, to kill, and to destroy. Civilization, in creating unnatural humanitarian laxity which alienates man from his animal origin, has tried to quell these impulses and appetites. It has made civilized man a decadent weakling who is ashamed of his animality and proudly calls his depravity true humaneness. In order to prevent further degeneration of the species man, it is imperative to free him from the pernicious effects of civilization. For civilization is merely a cunning invention of inferior men. These underlings are too weak to be a match for the vigorous heroes, they are too cowardly to endure the well-deserved punishment of complete annihilation, and they are too lazy and too insolent to serve the masters as slaves. Thus they have resorted to a tricky makeshift. They have reversed the eternal standards of value, absolutely fixed by the

8. Such is the terminology used by Leopold von Wiese (*Allgemeine Soziologie* [Munich, 1924], I, 10 ff.).

immutable laws of the universe; they have propagated a morality which calls their own inferiority virtue and the eminence of the noble heroes vice. This moral rebellion of the slaves must be undone by a transvaluation of all values. The ethics of the slaves, this shameful product of the resentment of weaklings, must be entirely discarded; the ethics of the strong or, properly speaking, the nullification of any ethical restriction must be substituted for it. Man must become a worthy scion of his ancestors, the noble beasts of days gone by.

It is usual to call such doctrines social or sociological Darwinism. We need not decide here whether this terminology is appropriate or not. At any rate it is a mistake to assign the epithets evolutionary and biological to teachings which blithely disparage the whole of mankind's history from the ages in which man began to lift himself above the purely animal existence of his nonhuman ancestors as a continuous progression toward degeneration and decay. Biology does not provide any standard for the appraisal of changes occurring within living beings other than whether or not these changes succeeded in adjusting the individuals to the conditions of their environment and thereby in improving their chances in the struggle for survival. It is a fact that civilization, when judged from this point of view, is to be considered a benefit and not an evil. It has enabled man to hold his own in the struggle against all other living beings, both the big beasts of prey and the even more pernicious microbes; it has multiplied man's means of sustenance; it has made the average man taller, more agile, and more versatile and it has stretched his average length of life; it has given man the uncontested mastery of the earth; it has multiplied population figures and raised the standard of living to a level never dreamed of by the crude cave dwellers of prehistoric ages. It is true that this evolution stunted the development of certain knacks and gifts which were once useful in the struggle for survival and have lost their usefulness under changed conditions. On the other hand it developed other talents and skills which are indispensable for life within the frame of society. However, a biological and evolutionary view must not cavil at such changes. For primitive man hard fists and pugnacity were as useful as the ability to be clever at arithmetic and to spell correctly are for modern man. It is quite arbitrary and certainly contrary to any biological standard to call only those characteristics which were useful to primitive man natural and adequate to human nature and to condemn the talents and skills badly needed by civilized man as marks of degeneration and biological deterioration. To advise man to return to the physical and intellectual features of his prehistoric ancestors is no more reasonable than to ask him to renounce his upright gait and to grow a tail again.

It is noteworthy that the men who were foremost in extolling the eminence of the savage impulses of our barbarian forefathers were so frail that their bodies would not have come up to the requirements of "living dangerously." Nietzsche even before his mental breakdown was so sickly that the only climate he could stand was that of the Engadin valley and of some Italian districts. He would not have been in a position to accomplish his work if civilized society had not protected his delicate nerves against the roughness of life. The apostles of violence wrote their books under the sheltering roof of "bourgeois security" which they derided and disparaged. They were free to publish their incendiary sermons because the liberalism which they scorned safeguarded freedom of the press. They would have been desperate if they had had to forego the blessings of the civilization scorned by their philosophy. And what a spectacle was that timid writer Georges Sorel, who went so far in his praise of brutality as to blame the modern system of education for weakening man's inborn tendencies toward violence![9]

One may admit that in primitive man the propensity for killing and destroying and the disposition for cruelty were innate. We may also assume that under the conditions of earlier ages the inclination for aggression and murder was favorable to the preservation of life. Man was once a brutal beast. (There is no need to investigate whether prehistoric man was a carnivore or a herbivore.) But one must not forget that he was physically a weak animal; he would not have been a match for the big beasts of prey if he had not been equipped with a peculiar weapon, reason. The fact that man is a reasonable being, that he therefore does not yield without inhibitions to every impulse, but arranges his conduct according to reasonable deliberation, must not be called unnatural from a zoological point of view. Rational conduct means that man, in face of the fact that he cannot satisfy all his impulses, desires, and appetites, foregoes the satisfaction of those which he considers less urgent. In order not to endanger the working of social cooperation man is forced to abstain from satisfying those desires whose satisfaction would hinder the establishment of societal institutions. There is no doubt that such a renunciation is painful. However, man has made his choice. He has renounced the satisfaction of some desires incompatible with social life and has given priority to the satisfaction of those desires which can be realized only or in a more plentiful way under a system of the division of labor. He has entered upon the way toward civilization, social cooperation, and wealth.

9. Georges Sorel, *Réflexions sur la violence* (3d ed., Paris, 1912), p. 269.

This decision is not irrevocable and final. The choice of the fathers does not impair the sons' freedom to choose. They can reverse the resolution. Every day they can proceed to the transvaluation of values and prefer barbarism to civilization, or, as some authors say, the soul to the intellect, myths to reason, and violence to peace. But they must choose. It is impossible to have things incompatible with one another.

Science, from the point of view of its valuational neutrality, does not blame the apostles of the gospel of violence for praising the frenzy of murder and the mad delights of sadism. Value judgments are subjective, and liberal society grants to everybody the right to express his sentiments freely. Civilization has not extirpated the original tendency toward aggression, bloodthirstiness, and cruelty which characterized primitive man. In many civilized men they are dormant and burst forth as soon as the restraints developed by civilization give way. Remember the unspeakable horrors of the Nazi concentration camps. The newspapers continually report abominable crimes manifesting the latent urges toward bestiality. The most popular novels and moving pictures are those dealing with bloodshed and violent acts. Bull fights and cock fights attract large crowds.

If an author says: the rabble thirst for blood and I with them, he may be no less right than in asserting that primitive man too took delight in killing. But he errs if he passes over the fact that the satisfaction of such sadistic desires impairs the existence of society or if he asserts that "true" civilization and the "good" society are an achievement of people blithely indulging in their passion for violence, murder, and cruelty, that the repression of the impulses toward brutality endangers mankind's evolution and that a substitution of barbarism for humanitarianism would save man from degeneration. The social division of labor and cooperation rests upon conciliatory settlement of disputes. Not war, as Heraclitus said, but peace is the source of all social relations. To man desires other than that for bloodshed are inborn. If he wants to satisfy these other desires, he must forego his urge to kill. He who wants to preserve life and health as well and as long as possible, must realize that respect for other people's lives and health better serves his aim than the opposite mode of conduct. One may regret that such is the state of affairs. But no such lamentations can alter the hard facts.

It is useless to censure this statement by referring to irrationality. All instinctive impulses defy examination by reason because reason deals only with the means for attaining ends sought and not with ultimate ends. But what distinguishes man from other animals is precisely that he does not yield without any will of his own to an instinctive urge. Man uses reason in order to choose between the incompatible satisfactions of conflicting desires.

One must not tell the masses: Indulge in your urge for murder; it is genuinely human and best serves your well-being. One must tell them: If you satisfy your thirst for blood, you must forego many other desires. You want to eat, to drink, to live in fine homes, to clothe yourselves, and a thousand other things which only society can provide. You cannot have everything, you must choose. The dangerous life and the frenzy of sadism may please you, but they are incompatible with the security and plenty which you do not want to miss either.

Praxeology as a science cannot encroach upon the individual's right to choose and to act. The final decisions rest with acting men, not with the theorists. Science's contribution to life and action does not consist in establishing value judgments, but in clarification of the conditions under which man must act and in elucidation of the effects of various modes of action. It puts at the disposal of acting man all the information he needs in order to make his choices in full awareness of their consequences. It prepares an estimate of cost and yield, as it were. It would fail in this task if it were to omit from this statement one of the items which could influence people's choices and decisions.

Current Misinterpretations of Modern Natural Science, Especially of Darwinism

Some present-day antiliberals, both of the right-wing and of the left-wing variety, base their teachings on misinterpretations of the achievements of modern biology.

1. Men are unequal. Eighteenth-century liberalism and likewise present-day egalitarianism start from the "self-evident truth" that "all men are created equal, and that they are endowed by their Creator with certain unalienable Rights." However, say the advocates of a biological philosophy of society, natural science has demonstrated in an irrefutable way that men are different. There is no room left in the framework of an experimental observation of natural phenomena for such a concept as natural rights. Nature is unfeeling and insensible with regard to any being's life and happiness. Nature is iron necessity and regularity. It is metaphysical nonsense to link together the "slippery" and vague notion of liberty and the unchangeable absolute laws of cosmic order. Thus the fundamental idea of liberalism is unmasked as a fallacy.

Now it is true that the liberal and democratic movement of the eighteenth and nineteenth centuries drew a great part of its strength from the doctrine of natural law and the innate imprescriptible rights of the individual. These ideas, first developed by ancient philosophy and Jewish theology, permeated Christian thinking. Some anti-Catholic sects made them the focal point of their political programs. A long line of eminent philosophers substantiated them. They became popular and were the most powerful moving force in the prodemocratic evolution. They are still supported today. Their advocates do not concern themselves with the incontestable fact that God or nature did not create men equal since many are born hale and hearty while others are crippled and deformed. With them all differences between men are due to education, opportunity, and social institutions.

But the teachings of utilitarian philosophy and classical economics have nothing at all to do with the doctrine of natural right. With them the only point that matters is social utility. They recommend popular government, private property, tolerance, and freedom not because they are natural and just, but because they are beneficial. The core of Ricardo's philosophy is the demonstration that social cooperation and division of labor between men who are in every regard superior and more efficient and men who are in every regard inferior and less efficient is beneficial to both groups. Bentham, the radical, shouted: "*Natural rights* is simple nonsense: natural and imprescriptible rights, rhetorical nonsense."[10] With him "the sole object of government ought to be the greatest happiness of the greatest possible number of the community."[11] Accordingly, in investigating what ought to be right he does not care about preconceived ideas concerning God's or nature's plans and intentions, forever hidden to mortal men; he is intent upon discovering what best serves the promotion of human welfare and happiness. Malthus showed that nature in limiting the means of subsistence does not accord to any living being a right of existence, and that by indulging heedlessly in the natural impulse of proliferation man would never have risen above the verge of starvation. He contended that human civilization and well-being could develop only to the extent that man learned to rein his sexual appetites by moral restraint. The Utilitarians do not combat arbitrary government and privileges because they are against natural law but because they are detrimental to prosperity. They recommend equality under the civil law not because men are equal but because such a policy is beneficial to the commonweal. In rejecting the illusory notions of natural law and human equality modern biology only repeated what the utilitarian champions of liberalism and democracy long before had taught in a much more persuasive way. It is obvious that no biological doctrine can ever invalidate what utilitarian philosophy says about the social utility of democratic government, private property, freedom, and equality under the law.

10. Bentham, *Anarchical Fallacies; being an Examination of the Declaration of Rights issued during the French Revolution*, in *Works* (ed. by Bowring), II, 501.

11. Bentham, *Principles of the Civil Code*, in *Works*, I, 301.

The present-day prevalence of doctrines approving social disintegration and violent conflict is not the result of an alleged adaptation of social philosophy to the findings of biology but of the almost universal rejection of utilitarian philosophy and economic theory. People have substituted an ideology of irreconcilable class conflict and international conflict for the "orthodox" ideology of the harmony of the rightly understood, i.e., long-run, interests of all individuals, social groups, and nations. Men are fighting one another because they are convinced that the extermination and liquidation of adversaries is the only means of promoting their own well-being.

2. *The social implications of Darwinism.* The theory of evolution as expounded by Darwin, says a school of social Darwinism, has clearly demonstrated that in nature there are no such things as peace and respect for the lives and welfare of others. In nature there is always struggle and merciless annihilation of the weak who do not succeed in defending themselves. Liberalism's plans for eternal peace—both in domestic and in foreign relations—are the outcome of an illusory rationalism contrary to the natural order.

However, the notion of the struggle for existence as Darwin borrowed it from Malthus and applied it in his theory, is to be understood in a metaphorical sense. Its meaning is that a living being actively resists the forces detrimental to its own life. This resistance, if it is to succeed, must be appropriate to the environmental conditions in which the being concerned has to hold its own. It need not always be a war of extermination such as in the relations between men and morbific microbes. Reason has demonstrated that, for man, the most adequate means of improving his condition is social cooperation and division of labor. They are man's foremost tool in his struggle for survival. But they can work only where there is peace. Wars, civil wars, and revolutions are detrimental to man's success in the struggle for existence because they disintegrate the apparatus of social cooperation.

3. *Reason and rational behavior called unnatural.* Christian theology deprecated the animal functions of man's body and depicted the "soul" as something outside of all biological phenomena. In an excessive reaction against this philosophy some moderns are prone to disparage everything in which man differs from other animals. In their eyes human reason is inferior to the animal instincts and impulses; it is unnatural and therefore bad. With them the terms rationalism and rational behavior have an opprobrious connotation. The perfect man, the real man, is a being who obeys his primordial instincts more than his reason.

The obvious truth is that reason, man's most characteristic feature, is also a biological phenomenon. It is neither more nor less natural than any other feature of the species homo sapiens, for instance, the upright gait or the hairless skin.

IX. THE ROLE OF IDEAS

1. Human Reason

REASON is man's particular and characteristic feature. There is no need for praxeology to raise the question whether reason is a suitable tool for the cognition of ultimate and absolute truth. It deals with reason only as far as it enables man to act.

All those objects which are the substratum of human sensation, perception, and observation also pass before the senses of animals. But man alone has the faculty of transforming sensuous stimuli into observation and experience. And man alone can arrange his various observations and experiences into a coherent system.

Action is preceded by thinking. Thinking is to deliberate beforehand over future action and to reflect afterwards upon past action. Thinking and acting are inseparable. Every action is always based on a definite idea about causal relations. He who thinks a causal relation thinks a theorem. Action without thinking, practice without theory are unimaginable. The reasoning may be faulty and the theory incorrect; but thinking and theorizing are not lacking in any action. On the other hand thinking is always thinking of a potential action. Even he who thinks of a pure theory assumes that the theory is correct, i.e., that action complying with its content would result in an effect to be expected from its teachings. It is of no relevance for logic whether such action is feasible or not.

It is always the individual who thinks. Society does not think any more than it eats or drinks. The evolution of human reasoning from the naïve thinking of primitive man to the more subtle thinking of modern science took place within society. However, thinking itself is always an achievement of individuals. There is joint action, but no joint thinking. There is only tradition which preserves thoughts and communicates them to others as a stimulus to their thinking. However, man has no means of appropriating the thoughts of his precursors other than to think them over again. Then, of course, he is in a position to proceed farther on the basis of his forerunners' thoughts. The foremost vehicle of tradition is the word. Thinking is linked up with language and vice versa. Concepts are embodied in terms. Language is a tool of thinking as it is a tool of social action.

The history of thought and ideas is a discourse carried on from generation to generation. The thinking of later ages grows out of the thinking of earlier ages. Without the aid of this stimulation intellectual progress would have been impossible. The continuity of human evolution, sowing for the offspring and harvesting on land cleared and tilled by the ancestors, manifests itself also in the history of science and ideas. We have inherited from our forefathers not only a stock of products of various orders of goods which is the source of our material wealth; we have no less inherited ideas and thoughts, theories and technologies to which our thinking owes its productivity.

But thinking is always a manifestation of individuals.

2. World View and Ideology

The theories directing action are often imperfect and unsatisfactory. They may be contradictory and unfit to be arranged into a comprehensive and coherent system.

If we look at all the theorems and theories guiding the conduct of certain individuals and groups as a coherent complex and try to arrange them as far as is feasible into a system, i.e., a comprehensive body of knowledge, we may speak of it as a world view. A world view is, as a theory, an interpretation of all things, and as a precept for action, an opinion concerning the best means for removing uneasiness as much as possible. A world view is thus, on the one hand, an explanation of all phenomena and, on the other hand, a technology, both these terms being taken in their broadest sense. Religion, metaphysics, and philosophy aim at providing a world view. They interpret the universe and they advise men how to act.

The concept of an ideology is narrower than that of a world view. In speaking of ideology we have in view only human action and social cooperation and disregard the problems of metaphysics, religious dogma, the natural sciences, and the technologies derived from them. Ideology is the totality of our doctrines concerning individual conduct and social relations. Both, world view and ideology, go beyond the limits imposed upon a purely neutral and academic study of things as they are. They are not only scientific theories, but also doctrines about the ought, i.e., about the ultimate ends which man should aim at in his earthly concerns.

Asceticism teaches that the only means open to man for removing pain and for attaining complete quietude, contentment, and happiness is to turn away from earthly concerns and to live without bothering about worldly things. There is no salvation other than to renounce striving after material well-being, to endure submissively the adversities of the earthly pilgrimage and to dedicate oneself exclusively to the preparation for eternal bliss. However, the number of those who consistently and unswervingly comply with the principles of asceticism is so small that it is not easy to instance more than a few names. It seems that the complete passivity advocated by asceticism is contrary to nature. The enticement of life triumphs. The ascetic principles have been adulterated. Even the most saintly hermits made concessions to life and earthly concerns which did not agree with their rigid principles. But as soon as a man takes into account any earthly concerns, and substitutes for purely vegetative ideals an acknowledgment of worldly things, however conditioned and incompatible with the rest of his professed doctrine, he bridges over the gulf which separated him from those who say yes to the striving after earthly ends. Then he has something in common with everyone else.

Human thoughts about things of which neither pure reasoning nor experience provides any knowledge may differ so radically that no agreement can be reached. In this sphere in which the free reverie of the mind is restricted neither by logical thinking nor by sensory experience man can give vent to his individuality and subjectivity. Nothing is more personal than the notions and images about the transcendent. Linguistic terms are unable to communicate what is said about the transcendent; one can never establish whether the hearer conceives them in the same way as the speaker. With regard to things beyond there can be no agreement. Religious wars are the most terrible wars because they are waged without any prospect of conciliation.

But where earthly things are involved, the natural affinity of all men and the identity of the biological conditions for the preservation of their lives come into play. The higher productivity of cooperation under division of labor makes society the foremost means of every individual for the attainment of his own ends whatever they may be. The maintenance and further intensification of social cooperation become a concern of everybody. Every world view and every ideology which is not entirely and unconditionally committed to the practice of asceticism and to a life in anchoritic reclusion must pay heed to the fact that society is the great means for the attainment of earthly ends. But then a common ground is won to clear the way for an agreement concerning minor social problems and the details of society's organization. However various ideologies may conflict with one another, they harmonize in one point, in the acknowledgment of life in society.

People fail sometimes to see this fact because in dealing with philosophies and ideologies they look more at what these doctrines assert with regard to transcendent and unknowable things and less at their statements about action in this world. Between various parts of an ideological system there is often an unbridgeable gulf. For acting man only those teachings are of real importance which result in precepts for action, not those doctrines which are purely academic and do not apply to conduct within the frame of social cooperation. We may disregard the philosophy of adamant and consistent asceticism because such a rigid asceticism must ultimately result in the extinction of its supporters. All other ideologies, in approving of the search for the necessities of life, are forced in some measure to take into account the fact that division of labor is more productive than isolated work. They thus admit the need for social cooperation.

Praxeology and economics are not qualified to deal with the transcendent and metaphysical aspects of any doctrine. But, on the other hand, no appeal to any religious or metaphysical dogmas and creeds can invalidate the theorems and theories concerning social cooperation as developed by logically correct praxeological reasoning. If a philosophy has admitted the necessity of societal links between men, it has placed itself, as far as problems of social action come into play, on ground from which there is no escape into personal convictions and professions of faith not liable to a thorough examination by rational methods.

This fundamental fact is often ignored. People believe that differences in world view create irreconcilable conflicts. The basic antagonisms between parties committed to different world views, it is contended, cannot be settled by compromise. They stem from the deepest recesses of the human soul and are expressive of a man's innate communion with supernatural and eternal forces. There can never be any cooperation between people divided by different world views.

However, if we pass in review the programs of all parties—both the cleverly elaborated and publicized programs and those to which the parties really cling when in power—we can easily discover the fallacy of this interpretation. All present-day political parties strive after the earthly well-being and prosperity of their supporters. They promise that they will render economic conditions more satisfactory to their followers. With regard to this issue there is no difference between the Roman Catholic Church and the various Protestant denominations as far as they intervene in political and social questions, between Christianity and the non-Christian religions, between the advocates of economic freedom and the various brands of Marxian materialism, between nationalists and internationalists, between racists and the friends of interracial peace. It is true that many of these parties believe that their own group cannot prosper except at the expense of other groups, and even go so far as to consider the complete annihilation of other groups or their enslavement as the necessary condition of their own group's prosperity. Yet, extermination or enslavement of others is for them not an ultimate end, but a means for the attainment of what they aim at as an ultimate end: their own group's flowering. If they were to learn that their own designs are guided by spurious theories and would not bring about the beneficial results expected, they would change their programs.

The pompous statements which people make about things unknowable and beyond the power of the human mind, their cosmologies, world views, religions, mysticisms, metaphysics, and conceptual phantasies differ widely from one another. But the practical essence of their ideologies, i.e., their teachings dealing with the ends to be aimed at in earthly life and with the means for the attainment of these ends, show much uniformity. There are, to be sure, differences and antagonisms both with regard to ends and means. Yet the differences with regard to ends are not irreconcilable; they do not hinder cooperation and amicable arrangements in the sphere of social action. As far as they concern means and ways only, they are of a purely technical character and as such open to examination by rational methods. When in the heat of party conflicts one of the factions declares: "Here we cannot go on in our negotiations with you because we are faced with a question touching upon our world view; on this point we must be adamant and must cling rigidly to our principles whatever may result," one need only scrutinize matters more carefully to realize that such declarations describe the antagonism as more pointed than it really is. In fact, for all parties committed to pursuit of the people's earthly welfare and thus approving social cooperation, questions of social organization and the conduct of social action are not problems of ultimate principles and of world views, but ideological issues. They are technical problems with regard to which some arrangement is always possible. No party would wittingly prefer social disintegration, anarchy, and a return to primitive barbarism to a solution which must be bought at the price of the sacrifice of some ideological points.

In party programs these technical issues are, of course, of primary importance. A party is committed to certain means, it recommends certain methods of political action and rejects utterly all other methods and policies as inappropriate. A party is a body which combines all those eager to employ the same means for common action. The principle which differentiates men and integrates parties is the choice of means. Thus for the party as such the means chosen are essential. A party is doomed if the futility of the means recommended becomes obvious. Party chiefs whose prestige and political career are bound up with the party's program may have ample reasons for withdrawing its principles from unrestricted discussion; they may attribute to them the character of ultimate ends which must not be questioned because they are based on a world view. But for the people as whose mandataries the party chiefs pretend to act, for the voters whom they want to enlist and for whose votes they canvass, things offer another aspect. They have no objection to scrutinizing every point of a party's program. They look upon such a program only as a recommendation of means for the attainment of their own ends, viz., earthly well-being.

What divides those parties which one calls today world view parties, i.e., parties committed to basic philosophical decisions about ultimate ends, is only seeming disagreement with regard to ultimate ends. Their antagonisms refer either to religious creeds or to problems of international relations or to the problem of ownership of the means of production or to problems of political organization. It can be shown that all these controversies concern means and not ultimate ends.

Let us begin with the problems of a nation's political organization. There are supporters of a democratic system of government, of hereditary monarchy, of the rule of a self-styled elite and of Caesarist dictatorship.[1] It is true that these programs are often recommended by reference to divine institutions, to the eternal laws of the universe, to the natural order, to the inevitable trend of historical evolution, and to other objects of transcendent knowledge. But such statements are merely incidental adornment. In appealing to the electorate, the parties advance other arguments. They are eager to show that the system they support will succeed better than those advocated by other parties in realizing those ends which the citizens aim at. They specify the beneficial results achieved in the past or in other countries; they disparage the other parties' programs by relating their failures.

1. Caesarism is today exemplified by the Bolshevik, Fascist, or Nazi type of dictatorship.

They resort both to pure reasoning and to an interpretation of historical experience in order to demonstrate the superiority of their own proposals and the futility of those of their adversaries. Their main argument is always: the political system we support will render you more prosperous and more content.

In the field of society's economic organization there are the liberals advocating private ownership of the means of production, the socialists advocating public ownership of the means of production, and the interventionists advocating a third system which, they contend, is as far from socialism as it is from capitalism. In the clash of these parties there is again much talk about basic philosophical issues. People speak of true liberty, equality, social justice, the rights of the individual, community, solidarity, and humanitarianism. But each party is intent upon proving by ratiocination and by referring to historical experience that only the system it recommends will make the citizens prosperous and satisfied. They tell the people that realization of their program will raise the standard of living to a higher level than realization of any other party's program. They insist upon the expediency of their plans and upon their utility. It is obvious that they do not differ from one another with regard to ends but only as to means. They all pretend to aim at the highest material welfare for the majority of citizens.

The nationalists stress the point that there is an irreconcilable conflict between the interests of various nations, but that, on the other hand, the rightly understood interests of all the citizens within the nation are harmonious. A nation can prosper only at the expense of other nations; the individual citizen can fare well only if his nation flourishes. The liberals have a different opinion. They believe that the interests of various nations harmonize no less than those of the various groups, classes, and strata of individuals within a nation. They believe that peaceful international cooperation is a more appropriate means than conflict for the attainment of the end which they and the nationalists are both aiming at: their own nation's welfare. They do not, as the nationalists charge, advocate peace and free trade in order to betray their own nation's interests to those of foreigners. On the contrary, they consider peace and free trade the best means to make their own nation wealthy. What separates the free traders from the nationalists are not ends, but the means recommended for attainment of the ends common to both.

Dissension with regard to religious creeds cannot be settled by rational methods. Religious conflicts are essentially implacable and irreconcilable. Yet as soon as a religious community enters the field of political action and tries to deal with problems of social organization, it is bound to take into account earthly concerns, however this may conflict with its dogmas and articles of faith. No religion in its exoteric activities ever ventured to tell people frankly: The realization of our plans for social organization will make you poor and impair your earthly well-being. Those consistently committed to a life of poverty withdrew from the political scene and fled into anchoritic seclusion. But churches and religious communities which have aimed at making converts and at influencing political and social activities of their followers have espoused the principles of secular conduct. In dealing with questions of man's earthly pilgrimage they hardly differ from any other political party. In canvassing, they emphasize, more than bliss in the beyond, the material advantages which they have in store for their brothers in faith.

Only a world view whose supporters renounce any earthly activity whatever could neglect to pay heed to the rational considerations which show that social cooperation is the great means for the attainment of all human ends. Because man is a social animal that can thrive only within society, all ideologies are forced to acknowledge the preeminent importance of social cooperation. They must aim at the most satisfactory organization of society and must approve of man's concern for an improvement of his material well-being. Thus they all place themselves upon a common ground. They are separated from one another not by world views and transcendent issues not subject to reasonable discussion, but by problems of means and ways. Such ideological antagonisms are open to a thorough scrutiny by the scientific methods of praxeology and economics.

The Fight Against Error

A critical examination of the philosophical systems constructed by mankind's great thinkers has very often revealed fissures and flaws in the impressive structure of those seemingly consistent and coherent bodies of comprehensive thought. Even the genius in drafting a world view sometimes fails to avoid contradictions and fallacious syllogisms.

The ideologies accepted by public opinion are still more infected by the shortcomings of the human mind. They are mostly an eclectic juxtaposition of ideas utterly incompatible with one another. They cannot stand a logical examination of their content. Their inconsistencies are irreparable and defy any attempt to combine their various parts into a system of ideas compatible with one another.

Some authors try to justify the contradictions of generally accepted ideologies by pointing out the alleged advantages of a compromise, however unsatisfactory from the logical point of view, for the smooth functioning of interhuman relations. They refer to the popular fallacy that life and reality are "not logical"; they contend that a contradictory system may prove its expediency or even its truth by working satisfactorily while a logically consistent system would result in disaster. There is no need to refute anew such popular errors. Logical thinking and real life are not two separate orbits. Logic is for man the only means to master the problems of reality. What is contradictory in theory, is no less contradictory in reality. No ideological inconsistency can provide a satisfactory, i.e., working, solution for the problems offered by the facts of the world. The only effect of contradictory ideologies is to conceal the real problems and thus to prevent people from finding in time an appropriate policy for solving them. Inconsistent ideologies may sometimes postpone the emergence of a manifest conflict. But they certainly aggravate the evils which they mask and render a final solution more difficult. They multiply the agonies, they intensify the hatreds, and make peaceful settlement impossible. It is a serious blunder to consider ideological contradictions harmless or even beneficial.

The main objective of praxeology and economics is to substitute consistent correct ideologies for the contradictory tenets of popular eclecticism. There is no other means of preventing social disintegration and of safeguarding the steady improvement of human conditions than those provided by reason. Men must try to think through all the problems involved up to the point beyond which a human mind cannot proceed farther. They must never acquiesce in any solutions conveyed by older generations, they must always question anew every theory and every theorem, they must never relax in their endeavors to brush away fallacies and to find the best possible cognition. They must fight error by unmasking spurious doctrines and by expounding truth.

The problems involved are purely intellectual and must be dealt with as such. It is disastrous to shift them to the moral sphere and to dispose of supporters of opposite ideologies by calling them villains. It is vain to insist that what we are aiming at is good and what our adversaries want is bad. The question to be solved is precisely what is to be considered as good and what as bad. The rigid dogmatism peculiar to religious groups and to Marxism results only in irreconcilable conflict. It condemns beforehand all dissenters as evildoers, it calls into question their good faith, it asks them to surrender unconditionally. No social cooperation is possible where such an attitude prevails.

No better is the propensity, very popular nowadays, to brand supporters of other ideologies as lunatics. Psychiatrists are vague in drawing a line between sanity and insanity. It would be preposterous for laymen to interfere with this fundamental issue of psychiatry. However, it is clear that if the mere fact that a man shares erroneous views and acts according to his errors qualifies him as mentally disabled, it would be very hard to discover an individual to which the epithet sane or normal could be attributed. Then we are bound to call the past generations lunatic because their ideas about the problems of the natural sciences and concomitantly their techniques differed from ours. Coming generations will call us lunatics for the same reason. Man is liable to error. If to err were the characteristic feature of mental disability, then everybody should be called mentally disabled.

Neither can the fact that a man is at variance with the opinions held by the majority of his contemporaries qualify him as a lunatic. Were Copernicus, Galileo and Lavoisier insane? It is the regular course of history that a man conceives new ideas, contrary to those of other people. Some of these ideas are later embodied in the system of knowledge accepted by public opinion as true. Is it permissible to apply the epithet "sane" only to boors who never had ideas of their own and to deny it to all innovators?

The procedure of some contemporary psychiatrists is really outrageous. They are utterly ignorant of the theories of praxeology and economics. Their familiarity with present-day ideologies is superficial and uncritical. Yet they blithely call the supporters of some ideologies paranoid persons.

There are men who are commonly stigmatized as *monetary cranks*. The monetary crank suggests a method for making everybody prosperous by monetary measures. His plans are illusory. However, they are the consistent application of a monetary ideology entirely approved by contemporary public opinion and espoused by the policies of almost all governments. The objections raised against these ideological errors by the economists are not taken into account by the governments, political parties, and the press.

It is generally believed by those unfamiliar with economic theory that credit expansion and an increase in the quantity of money in circulation are efficacious means for lowering the rate of interest permanently below the height it would attain on a nonmanipulated capital and loan market. This theory is utterly illusory.[2] But it guides the monetary and credit policy of almost every contemporary government. Now, on the basis of this vicious ideology, no valid objection can be raised against the plans advanced by Pierre Joseph Proudhon, Ernest Solvay, Clifford Hugh Douglas and a host of other would-be reformers. They are only more consistent than other people are. They want to reduce the rate of interest to zero and thus to abolish altogether the scarcity of "capital." He who wants to refute them must attack the theories underlying the monetary and credit policies of the great nations.

The psychiatrist may object that what characterizes a man as a lunatic is precisely the fact that he lacks moderation and goes to extremes. While normal man is judicious enough to restrain himself, the paranoid person goes beyond all bounds. This is quite an unsatis-

2. Cf. below, Chapter XX.

factory rejoinder. All the arguments advanced in favor of the thesis that the rate of interest can be reduced by credit expansion from 5 or 4 per cent to 3 or 2 per cent are equally valid for a reduction to zero. The "monetary cranks" are certainly right from the point of view of the monetary fallacies approved by popular opinion.

There are psychiatrists who call the Germans who espoused the principles of Nazism lunatics and want to cure them by therapeutic procedures. Here again we are faced with the same problem. The doctrines of Nazism are vicious, but they do not essentially disagree with the ideologies of socialism and nationalism as approved by other peoples' public opinion. What characterized the Nazis was only the consistent application of these ideologies to the special conditions of Germany. Like all other contemporary nations the Nazis desired government control of business and economic self-sufficiency, i.e., autarky, for their own nation. The distinctive mark of their policy was that they refused to acquiesce in the disadvantages which the acceptance of the same system by other nations would impose upon them. They were not prepared to be forever "imprisoned," as they said, within a comparatively overpopulated area in which physical conditions render the productivity of human effort lower than in other countries. They believed that their nation's great population figures, the strategically propitious geographic situation of their country, and the inborn vigor and gallantry of their armed forces provided them with a good chance to remedy by aggression the evils they deplored.

Now, whoever accepts the ideology of nationalism and socialism as true and as the standard of his own nation's policy, is not in a position to refute the conclusions drawn from them by the Nazis. The only way for a refutation of Nazism left for foreign nations which have espoused these two principles was to defeat the Nazis in war. And as long as the ideology of socialism and nationalism is supreme in the world's public opinion, the Germans or other peoples will try again to succeed by aggression and conquest, should the opportunity ever be offered to them. There is no hope of eradicating the aggression mentality if one does not explode entirely the ideological fallacies from which it stems. This is not a task for psychiatrists, but for economists.[3]

Man has only one tool to fight error: reason.

3. Might

Society is a product of human action. Human action is directed by ideologies. Thus society and any concrete order of social affairs are an outcome of ideologies; ideologies are not, as Marxism asserts, a product of a certain state of social affairs. To be sure, human thoughts and ideas are not the achievement of isolated individuals.

3. Cf. Mises, *Omnipotent Government* (New Haven, 1944), pp. 221–228, 129–131, 135–140.

Thinking too succeeds only through the cooperation of the thinkers. No individual would make headway in his reasoning if he were under the necessity of starting from the beginning. A man can advance in thinking only because his efforts are aided by those of older generations who have formed the tools of thinking, the concepts and terminologies, and have raised the problems.

Any given social order was thought out and designed before it could be realized. This temporal and logical precedence of the ideological factor does not imply the proposition that people draft a complete plan of a social system as the utopians do. What is and must be thought out in advance is not the concerting of individual actions into an integrated system of social organization, but the actions of individuals with regard to their fellow men and of already formed groups of individuals with regard to other groups. Before a man aids his fellow in cutting a tree, such cooperation must be thought out. Before an act of barter takes place, the idea of mutual exchange of goods and services must be conceived. It is not necessary that the individuals concerned become aware of the fact that such mutuality results in the establishment of social bonds and in the emergence of a social system. The individual does not plan and execute actions intended to construct society. His conduct and the corresponding conduct of others generate social bodies.

Any existing state of social affairs is the product of ideologies previously thought out. Within society new ideologies may emerge and may supersede older ideologies and thus transform the social system. However, society is always the creation of ideologies temporally and logically anterior. Action is always directed by ideas; it realizes what previous thinking has designed.

If we hypostatize or anthropomorphize the notion of ideology, we may say that ideologies have might over men. Might is the faculty or power of directing actions. As a rule one says only of a man or of groups of men that they are mighty. Then the definition of might is: might is the power to direct other people's actions. He who is mighty, owes his might to an ideology. Only ideologies can convey to a man the power to influence other people's choices and conduct. One can become a leader only if one is supported by an ideology which makes other people tractable and accommodating. Might is thus not a physical and tangible thing, but a moral and spiritual phenomenon. A king's might rests upon the recognition of the monarchical ideology on the part of his subjects.

He who uses his might to run the state, i.e., the social apparatus of coercion and compulsion, rules. Rule is the exercise of might in the political body. Rule is always based upon might, i.e., the power to direct other people's actions.

Of course, it is possible to establish a government upon the violent oppression of reluctant people. It is the characteristic mark of state and government that they apply violent coercion or the threat of it against those not prepared to yield voluntarily. Yet such violent oppression is no less founded upon ideological might. He who wants to apply violence needs the voluntary cooperation of some people. An individual entirely dependent on himself can never rule by means of physical violence only.[4] He needs the ideological support of a group in order to subdue other groups. The tyrant must have a retinue of partisans who obey his orders of their own accord. Their spontaneous obedience provides him with the apparatus he needs for the conquest of other people. Whether or not he succeeds in making his sway last depends on the numerical relation of the two groups, those who support him voluntarily and those whom he beats into submission. Though a tyrant may temporarily rule through a minority if this minority is armed and the majority is not, in the long run a minority cannot keep the majority in subservience. The oppressed will rise in rebellion and cast off the yoke of tyranny.

A durable system of government must rest upon an ideology acknowledged by the majority. The "real" factor, the "real forces" that are the foundation of government and convey to the rulers the power to use violence against renitent minority groups are essentially ideological, moral, and spiritual. Rulers who failed to recognize this first principle of government and, relying upon the alleged irresistibility of their armed troops, disdained the spirit and ideas have finally been overthrown by the assault of their adversaries. The interpretation of might as a "real" factor not dependent upon ideologies, quite common to many political and historical books, is erroneous. The term *Realpolitik* makes sense only if used to signify a policy taking account of generally accepted ideologies as contrasted with a policy based upon ideologies not sufficiently acknowledged and therefore unfit to support a durable system of government.

He who interprets might as physical or "real" power to carry on and considers violent action as the very foundation of government, sees conditions from the narrow point of view of subordinate officers in charge of sections of an army or police force. To these subordinates a definite task within the framework of the ruling ideology is assigned. Their chiefs commit to their care troops which are not

4. A gangster may overpower a weaker or unarmed fellow. However, this has nothing to do with life in society. It is an isolated antisocial occurrence.

only equipped, armed, and organized for combat, but no less imbued with the spirit which makes them obey the orders issued. The commanders of such subdivisions consider this moral factor a matter of course because they themselves are animated by the same spirit and cannot even imagine a different ideology. The power of an ideology consists precisely in the fact that people submit to it without any wavering and scruples.

However, things are different for the head of the government. He must aim at preservation of the morale of the armed forces and of the loyalty of the rest of the population. For these moral factors are the only "real" elements upon which continuance of his mastery rests. His power dwindles if the ideology that supports it loses force.

Minorities too can sometimes conquer by means of superior military skill and can thus establish minority rule. But such an order of things cannot endure. If the victorious conquerors do not succeed in subsequently converting the system of rule by violence into a system of rule by ideological consent on the part of those ruled, they will succumb in new struggles. All victorious minorities who have established a lasting system of government have made their sway durable by means of a belated ideological ascendancy. They have legitimized their own supremacy either by submitting to the ideologies of the defeated or by transforming them. Where neither of these two things took place, the oppressed many dispossessed the oppressing few either by open rebellion or through the silent but steadfast operation of ideological forces.[5]

Many of the great historical conquests were able to endure because the invaders entered into alliance with those classes of the defeated nation which were supported by the ruling ideology and were thus considered legitimate rulers. This was the system adopted by the Tartars in Russia, by the Turks in the Danube principalities and by and large in Hungary and Transylvania, and by the British and the Dutch in the Indies. A comparatively insignificant number of Britons could rule many hundred millions of Indians because the Indian princes and aristocratic landowners looked upon British rule as a means for the preservation of their privileges and supplied it with the support which the generally acknowledged ideology of India gave to their own supremacy. England's Indian empire was firm as long as public opinion approved of the traditional social order. The Pax Britannica safeguarded the princes' and the landlords' privileges and protected the masses against the agonies of wars between the principalities and of succession wars within them. In our day the

5. Cf. below, pp. 649–650.

infiltration of subversive ideas from abroad has ended British rule and threatens the preservation of the country's age-old social order.

Victorious minorities sometimes owe their success to their technological superiority. This does not alter the case. In the long run it is impossible to withhold the better arms from the members of the majority. Not the equipment of their armed forces, but ideological factors safeguarded the British in India.[6]

A country's public opinion may be ideologically divided in such a way that no group is strong enough to establish a durable government. Then anarchy emerges. Revolutions and civil strife become permanent.

Traditionalism as an Ideology

Traditionalism is an ideology which considers loyalty to valuations, customs, and methods of procedure handed down or allegedly handed down from ancestors both right and expedient. It is not an essential mark of traditionalism that these forefathers were the ancestors in the biological meaning of the term or can be fairly considered such; they were sometimes only the previous inhabitants of the country concerned or supporters of the same religious creed or only precursors in the exercise of some special task. Who is to be considered an ancestor and what is the content of the body of tradition handed down are determined by the concrete teachings of each variety of traditionalism. The ideology brings into prominence some of the ancestors and relegates others to oblivion; it sometimes calls ancestors people who had nothing to do with the alleged posterity. It often constructs a "traditional" doctrine which is of recent origin and is at variance with the ideologies really held by the ancestors.

Traditionalism tries to justify its tenets by citing the success they secured in the past. Whether this assertion conforms with the facts, is another question. Research could sometimes unmask errors in the historical statements of a traditional belief. However, this did not always explode the traditional doctrine. For the core of traditionalism is not real historical facts, but an opinion about them, however mistaken, and a will to believe things to which the authority of ancient origin is attributed.

4. Meliorism and the Idea of Progress

The notions of progress and retrogression make sense only within a teleological system of thought. In such a framework it is sensible to call approach toward the goal aimed at progress and a movement

6. We are dealing here with the preservation of European minority rule in non-European countries. About the prospects of an Asiatic aggression on the West cf. below, pp. 669–670.

in the opposite direction retrogression. Without reference to some agent's action and to a definite goal both these notions are empty and void of any meaning.

It was one of the shortcomings of nineteenth-century philosophies to have misinterpreted the meaning of cosmic change and to have smuggled into the theory of biological transformation the idea of progress. Looking backward from any given state of things to the states of the past one can fairly use the terms development and evolution in a neutral sense. Then evolution signifies the process which led from past conditions to the present. But one must guard against the fatal error of confusing change with improvement and evolution with evolution toward higher forms of life. Neither is it permissible to substitute a pseudoscientific anthropocentrism for the anthropocentrism of religion and the older metaphysical doctrines.

However, there is no need for praxeology to enter into a critique of this philosophy. Its task is to explode the errors implied in current ideologies.

Eighteenth-century social philosophy was convinced that mankind has now finally entered the age of reason. While in the past theological and metaphysical errors were dominant, henceforth reason will be supreme. People will free themselves more and more from the chains of tradition and superstition and will dedicate all their efforts to the continuous improvement of social institutions. Every new generation will contribute its part to this glorious task. With the progress of time society will more and more become the society of free men, aiming at the greatest happiness of the greatest number. Temporary setbacks are, of course, not impossible. But finally the good cause will triumph because it is the cause of reason. People called themselves happy in that they were citizens of an age of enlightenment which through the discovery of the laws of rational conduct paved the way toward a steady amelioration of human affairs. What they lamented was only the fact that they themselves were too old to witness all the beneficial effects of the new philosophy. "I would wish," said Bentham to Philarète Chasles, "to be granted the privilege to live the years which I have still to live, at the end of each of the centuries following my death; thus I could witness the effects of my writing."[7]

All these hopes were founded on the firm conviction, proper to the age, that the masses are both morally good and reasonable. The upper strata, the privileged aristocrats living on the fat of the land, were

7. Philarète Chasles, *Études sur les hommes et les moers du* XIX*e* *siècle* (Paris, 1849), p. 89.

thought depraved. The common people, especially the peasants and the workers, were glorified in a romantic mood as noble and unerring in their judgment. Thus the philosophers were confident that democracy, government by the people, would bring about social perfection.

This prejudice was the fateful error of the humanitarians, the philosophers, and the liberals. Men are not infallible; they err very often. It is not true that the masses are always right and know the means for attaining the ends aimed at. "Belief in the common man" is no better founded than was belief in the supernatural gifts of kings, priests, and noblemen. Democracy guarantees a system of government in accordance with the wishes and plans of the majority. But it cannot prevent majorities from falling victim to erroneous ideas and from adopting inappropriate policies which not only fail to realize the ends aimed at but result in disaster. Majorities too may err and destroy our civilization. The good cause will not triumph merely on account of its reasonableness and expediency. Only if men are such that they will finally espouse policies reasonable and likely to attain the ultimate ends aimed at, will civilization improve and society and state render men more satisfied, although not happy in a metaphysical sense. Whether or not this condition is given, only the unknown future can reveal.

There is no room within a system of praxeology for meliorism and optimistic fatalism. Man is free in the sense that he must daily choose anew between policies that lead to success and those that lead to disaster, social disintegration, and barbarism.

The term progress is nonsensical when applied to cosmic events or to a comprehensive world view. We have no information about the plans of the prime mover. But it is different with its use in the frame of an ideological doctrine. The immense majority strives after a greater and better supply of food, clothes, homes, and other material amenities. In calling a rise in the masses' standard of living progress and improvement, economists do not espouse a mean materialism. They simply establish the fact that people are motivated by the urge to improve the material conditions of their existence. They judge policies from the point of view of the aims men want to attain. He who disdains the fall in infant mortality and the gradual disappearance of famines and plagues may cast the first stone upon the materialism of the economists.

There is but one yardstick for the appraisal of human action: whether or not it is fit to attain the ends aimed at by acting men.

X. EXCHANGE WITHIN SOCIETY

1. Autistic Exchange and Interpersonal Exchange

ACTION always is essentially the exchange of one state of affairs for another state of affairs. If the action is performed by an individual without any reference to cooperation with other individuals, we may call it autistic exchange. An instance: the isolated hunter who kills an animal for his own consumption; he exchanges leisure and a cartridge for food.

Within society cooperation substitutes interpersonal or social exchange for autistic exchanges. Man gives to other men in order to receive from them. Mutuality emerges. Man serves in order to be served.

The exchange relation is the fundamental social relation. Interpersonal exchange of goods and services weaves the bond which unites men into society. The societal formula is: *do ut des*. Where there is no intentional mutuality, where an action is performed without any design of being benefited by a concomitant action of other men, there is no interpersonal exchange, but autistic exchange. It does not matter whether the autistic action is beneficial or detrimental to other people or whether it does not concern them at all. A genius may perform his task for himself, not for the crowd; however, he is an outstanding benefactor of mankind. The robber kills the victim for his own advantage; the murdered man is by no means a partner in this crime, he is merely its object; what is done, is done against him.

Hostile aggression was a practice common to man's nonhuman forebears. Conscious and purposeful cooperation is the outcome of a long evolutionary process. Ethnology and history have provided us with interesting information concerning the beginning and the primitive patterns of interpersonal exchange. Some consider the custom of mutual giving and returning of presents and stipulating a certain return present in advance as a precursory pattern of interpersonal exchange.[1] Others consider dumb barter as the primitive mode of trade. However, to make presents in the expectation of being rewarded

1. Gustav Cassel, *The Theory of Social Economy,* trans. by S. L. Banon, (new ed. London, 1932), p. 371.

by the receiver's return present or in order to acquire the favor of a man whose animosity could be disastrous, is already tantamount to interpersonal exchange. The same applies to dumb barter which is distinguished from other modes of bartering and trading only through the absence of oral discussion.

It is the essential characteristic of the categories of human action that they are apodictic and absolute and do not admit of any gradation. There is action or nonaction, there is exchange or nonexchange; everything which applies to action and exchange as such is given or not given in every individual instance according to whether there is or there is not action and exchange. In the same way the boundaries between autistic exchange and interpersonal exchange are sharply distinct. Making one-sided presents without the aim of being rewarded by any conduct on the part of the receiver or of third persons is autistic exchange. The donor acquires the satisfaction which the better condition of the receiver gives to him. The receiver gets the present as a God-sent gift. But if presents are given in order to influence some people's conduct, they are no longer one-sided, but a variety of interpersonal exchange between the donor and the man whose conduct they are designed to influence. Although the emergence of interpersonal exchange was the result of a long evolution, no gradual transition is conceivable between autistic and interpersonal exchange. There were no intermediary modes of exchange between them. The step which leads from autistic to interpersonal exchange was no less a jump into something entirely new and essentially different than was the step from automatic reaction of the cells and nerves to conscious and purposeful behavior, to action.

2. Contractual Bonds and Hegemonic Bonds

There are two different kinds of social cooperation: cooperation by virtue of contract and coordination, and cooperation by virtue of command and subordination or hegemony.

Where and as far as cooperation is based on contract, the logical relation between the cooperating individuals is symmetrical. They are all parties to interpersonal exchange contracts. John has the same relation to Tom as Tom has to John. Where and as far as cooperation is based on command and subordination, there is the man who commands and there are those who obey his orders. The logical relation between these two classes of men is asymmetrical. There is a director and there are people under his care. The director alone chooses and directs; the others—the wards—are mere pawns in his actions.

The power that calls into life and animates any social body is always ideological might, and the fact that makes an individual a member of any social compound is always his own conduct. This is no less valid with regard to a hegemonic societal bond. It is true, people are as a rule born into the most important hegemonic bonds, into the family and into the state, and this was also the case with the hegemonic bonds of older days, slavery and serfdom, which disappeared in the realm of Western civilization. But no physical violence and compulsion can possibly force a man against his will to remain in the status of the ward of a hegemonic order. What violence or the threat of violence brings about is a state of affairs in which subjection as a rule is considered more desirable than rebellion. Faced with the choice between the consequences of obedience and of disobedience, the ward prefers the former and thus integrates himself into the hegemonic bond. Every new command places this choice before him again. In yielding again and again he himself contributes his share to the continuous existence of the hegemonic societal body. Even as a ward in such a system he is an acting human being, i.e., a being not simply yielding to blind impulses, but using his reason in choosing between alternatives.

What differentiates the hegemonic bond from the contractual bond is the scope in which the choices of the individuals determine the course of events. As soon as a man has decided in favor of his subjection to a hegemonic system, he becomes, within the margin of this system's activities and for the time of his subjection, a pawn of the director's actions. Within the hegemonic societal body and as far as it directs its subordinates' conduct, only the director acts. The wards act only in choosing subordination; having once chosen subordination they no longer act for themselves, they are taken care of.

In the frame of a contractual society the individual members exchange definite quantities of goods and services of a definite quality. In choosing subjection in a hegemonic body a man neither gives nor receives anything that is definite. He integrates himself into a system in which he has to render indefinite services and will receive what the director is willing to assign to him. He is at the mercy of the director. The director alone is free to choose. Whether the director is an individual or an organized group of individuals, a directorate, and whether the director is a selfish maniacal tyrant or a benevolent paternal despot is of no relevance for the structure of the whole system.

The distinction between these two kinds of social cooperation is common to all theories of society. Ferguson described it as the contrast between warlike nations and commercial nations;[2] Saint Simon as the contrast between pugnacious nations and peaceful or industrial nations; Herbert Spencer as the contrast between societies of individual freedom and those of a militant structure;[3] Sombart as the contrast between heroes and peddlers.[4] The Marxians distinguish between the "gentile organization" of a fabulous state of primitive society and the eternal bliss of socialism on the one hand and the unspeakable degradation of capitalism on the other hand.[5] The Nazi philosophers distinguish the counterfeit system of bourgeois security from the heroic system of authoritarian *Führertum*. The valuation of both systems is different with the various sociologists. But they fully agree in the establishment of the contrast and no less in recognizing that no third principle is thinkable and feasible.

Western civilization as well as the civilization of the more advanced Eastern peoples are achievements of men who have cooperated according to the pattern of contractual coordination. These civilizations, it is true, have adopted in some respects bonds of hegemonic structure. The state as an apparatus of compulsion and coercion is by necessity a hegemonic organization. So is the family and its household community. However, the characteristic feature of these civilizations is the contractual structure proper to the cooperation of the individual families. There once prevailed almost complete autarky and economic isolation of the individual household units. When interfamilial exchange of goods and services was substituted for each family's economic self-sufficiency, it was, in all nations commonly considered civilized, a cooperation based on contract. Human civilization as it has been hitherto known to historical experience is preponderantly a product of contractual relations.

Any kind of human cooperation and social mutuality is essentially an order of peace and conciliatory settlement of disputes. In the domestic relations of any societal unit, be it a contractual or a hegemonic bond, there must be peace. Where there are violent conflicts and as far as there are such conflicts, there is neither cooperation nor societal bonds. Those political parties which in their eagerness to substitute the hegemonic system for the contractual system point

2. Cf. Adam Ferguson, *An Essay on the History of Civil Society* (new ed. Basel, 1789), p. 208.

3. Cf. Herbert Spencer, *The Principles of Sociology* (New York, 1914), III, 575–611.

4. Cf. Werner Sombart, *Haendler und Helden* (Munich, 1915).

5. Cf. Frederick Engels, *The Origin of the Family, Private Property and the State* (New York, 1942), p. 144.

at the rottenness of peace and of bourgeois security, extol the moral nobility of violence and bloodshed and praise war and revolution as the eminently natural methods of interhuman relations, contradict themselves. For their own utopias are designed as realms of peace. The Reich of the Nazis and the commonwealth of the Marxians are planned as societies of undisturbed peace. They are to be created by pacification, i.e., the violent subjection of all those not ready to yield without resistance. In a contractual world various states can quietly coexist. In a hegemonic world there can only be one Reich or commonwealth and only one dictator. Socialism must choose between a renunciation of the advantages of division of labor encompassing the whole earth and all peoples and the establishment of a world-embracing hegemonic order. It is this fact that made Russian Bolshevism, German Nazism, and Italian Fascism "dynamic," i.e., aggressive. Under contractual conditions empires are dissolved into a loose league of autonomous member nations. The hegemonic system is bound to strive after annexation of all independent states.

The contractual order of society is an order of right and law. It is a government under the rule of law (*Rechtsstaat*) as differentiated from the welfare state (*Wohlfahrtsstaat*) or paternal state. Right or law is the complex of rules determining the orbit in which individuals are free to act. No such orbit is left to wards of a hegemonic society. In the hegemonic state there is neither right nor law; there are only directives and regulations which the director may change daily and apply with what discrimination he pleases and which the wards must obey. The wards have one freedom only: to obey without asking questions.

3. Calculative Action

All the praxeological categories are eternal and unchangeable as they are uniquely determined by the logical structure of the human mind and by the natural conditions of man's existence. Both in acting and in theorizing about acting, man can neither free himself from these categories nor go beyond them. A kind of acting categorially different from that determined by these categories is neither possible nor conceivable for man. Man can never comprehend something which would be neither action nor nonaction. There is no history of acting; there is no evolution which would lead from nonaction to action; there are no transitory stages between action and nonaction. There is only acting and nonacting. And for every concrete action all that is rigorously valid which is categorially established with regard to action in general.

Every action can make use of ordinal numbers. For the application of cardinal numbers and for the arithmetical computation based on them special conditions are required. These conditions emerged in the historical evolution of the contractual society. Thus the way was opened for computation and calculation in the planning of future action and in establishing the effects achieved by past action. Cardinal numbers and their use in arithmetical operations are also eternal and immutable categories of the human mind. But their applicability to premeditation and the recording of action depends on certain conditions which were not given in the early state of human affairs, which appeared only later, and which could possibly disappear again.

It was cognition of what is going on within a world in which action is computable and calculable that led men to the elaboration of the sciences of praxeology and economics. Economics is essentially a theory of that scope of action in which calculation is applied or can be applied if certain conditions are realized. No other distinction is of greater significance, both for human life and for the study of human action, than that between calculable action and noncalculable action. Modern civilization is above all characterized by the fact that it has elaborated a method which makes the use of arithmetic possible in a broad field of activities. This is what people have in mind when attributing to it the—not very expedient and often misleading—epithet of rationality.

The mental grasp and analysis of the problems present in a calculating market system were the starting point of economic thinking which finally led to general praxeological cognition. However, it is not the consideration of this historical fact that makes it necessary to start exposition of a comprehensive system of economics by an analysis of the market economy and to place before this analysis an examination of the problem of economic calculation. Neither historical nor heuristic aspects enjoin such a procedure, but the requirements of logical and systematic rigor. The problems concerned are apparent and practical only within the sphere of the calculating market economy. It is only a hypothetical and figurative transfer which makes them utilizable for the scrutiny of other systems of society's economic organization which do not allow of any calculation. Economic calculation is the fundamental issue in the comprehension of all problems commonly called economic.

Part Three

Economic Calculation

XI. VALUATION WITHOUT CALCULATION

1. The Gradation of the Means

ACTING man transfers the valuation of ends he aims at to the means. Other things being equal, he assigns to the total amount of the various means the same value he attaches to the end which they are fit to bring about. For the moment we may disregard the time needed for production of the end and its influence upon the relation between the value of the ends and that of the means.

The gradation of the means is like that of the ends a process of preferring *a* to *b*. It is preferring and setting aside. It is manifestation of a judgment that *a* is more intensely desired than is *b*. It opens a field for application of ordinal numbers, but it is not open to application of cardinal numbers and arithmetical operations based on them. If somebody gives me the choice among three tickets entitling one to attend the operas *Aïda, Falstaff,* and *Traviata* and I take, if I can only take one of them, *Aïda,* and if I can take one more, *Falstaff* also, I have made a choice. That means: under given conditions I prefer *Aïda* and *Falstaff* to *Traviata;* if I could only choose one of them, I would prefer *Aïda* and renounce *Falstaff*. If I call the admission to *Aïda a,* that to *Falstaff b* and that to *Traviata c,* I can say: I prefer *a* to *b* and *b* to *c*.

The immediate goal of acting is frequently the acquisition of countable and measurable supplies of tangible things. Then acting man has to choose between countable quantities; he prefers, for example, 15 *r* to 7 *p;* but if he had to choose between 15 r and 8 *p,* he might prefer 8 *p*. We can express this state of affairs by declaring that he values 15 *r* less than 8 *p,* but higher than 7 *p*. This is tantamount to the statement that he prefers *a* to *b* and *b* to *c*. The substitution of 8 *p* for *a,* of 15 *r* for *b* and of 7 *p* for *c* changes neither the meaning of the statement nor the fact that it describes. It certainly does not render reckoning with cardinal numbers possible. It does not open a field for economic calculation and the mental operations based upon such calculation.

2. The Barter-Fiction of the Elementary Theory of Value and Prices

The elaboration of economic theory is heuristically dependent on the logical processes of reckoning to such an extent that the economists failed to realize the fundamental problem involved in the methods of economic calculation. They were prone to take economic calculation as a matter of course; they did not see that it is not an ultimate given, but a derivative requiring reduction to more elementary phenomena. They misconstrued economic calculation. They took it for a category of all human action and ignored the fact that it is only a category inherent in acting under special conditions. They were fully aware of the fact that interpersonal exchange, and consequently market exchange effected by the intermediary of a common medium of exchange—money, and therefore prices, are special features of a certain state of society's economic organization which did not exist in primitive civilizations and could possibly disappear in the further course of historical change.[1] But they did not comprehend that money prices are the only vehicle of economic calculation. Thus most of their studies are of little use. Even the writings of the most eminent economists are vitiated to some extent by the fallacies implied in their ideas about economic calculation.

The modern theory of value and prices shows how the choices of individuals, their preferring of some things and setting aside of other things, result, in the sphere of interpersonal exchange, in the emergence of market prices.[2] These masterful expositions are unsatisfactory in some minor points and disfigured by unsuitable expressions. But they are essentially irrefutable. As far as they need to be amended, it must be done by a consistent elaboration of the fundamental thoughts of their authors rather than by a refutation of their reasoning.

In order to trace back the phenomena of the market to the universal category of preferring *a* to *b*, the elementary theory of value and prices is bound to use some imaginary constructions. The use of imaginary constructions to which nothing corresponds in reality is an indispensable tool of thinking. No other method would have contributed anything to the interpretation of reality. But one of the most

1. The German Historical School expressed this by asserting that private ownership of the means of production, market exchange, and money are "historical categories."

2. Cf. especially Eugen von Böhm-Bawerk, *Kapital und Kapitalzins,* Pt. II, Bk. III.

important problems of science is to avoid the fallacies which ill-considered employment of such constructions can entail.

The elementary theory of value and prices employs, apart from other imaginary constructions to be dealt with later,[3] the construction of a market in which all transactions are performed in direct exchange. There is no money; goods and services are directly bartered against other goods and services. This imaginary construction is necessary. One must disregard the intermediary role played by money in order to realize that what is ultimately exchanged is always economic goods of the first order against other such goods. Money is nothing but a medium of interpersonal exchange. But one must carefully guard oneself against the delusions which this construction of a market with direct exchange can easily engender.

A serious blunder that owes its origin and its tenacity to a misinterpretation of this imaginary construction was the assumption that the medium of exchange is a neutral factor only. According to this opinion the only difference between direct and indirect exchange was that only in the latter was a medium of exchange used. The interpolation of money into the transaction, it was asserted, did not affect the main features of the business. One did not ignore the fact that in the course of history tremendous alterations in the purchasing power of money have occurred and that these fluctuations often convulsed the whole system of exchange. But it was believed that such events were exceptional facts caused by inappropriate policies. Only "bad" money, it was said, can bring about such disarrangements. In addition people misunderstood the causes and effects of these disturbances. They tacitly assumed that changes in purchasing power occur with regard to all goods and services at the same time and to the same extent. This is, of course, what the fable of money's neutrality implies. The whole theory of catallactics, it was held, can be elaborated under the assumption that there is direct exchange only. If this is once achieved, the only thing to be added is the "simple" insertion of money terms into the complex of theorems concerning direct exchange. However, this final completion of the catallactic system was considered of minor importance only. It was not believed that it could alter anything essential in the structure of economic teachings. The main task of economics was conceived as the study of direct exchange. What remained to be done besides this was at best only a scrutiny of the problems of "bad" money.

Complying with this opinion, economists neglected to lay due stress upon the problems of indirect exchange. Their treatment of

3. See below, pp. 236–256.

monetary problems was superficial; it was only loosely connected with the main body of their scrutiny of the market process. About the beginning of the twentieth century the problems of indirect exchange were by and large relegated to a subordinate place. There were treatises on catallactics which dealt only incidentally and cursorily with monetary matters, and there were books on currency and banking which did not even attempt to integrate their subject into the structure of a catallactic system. At the universities of the Anglo-Saxon countries there were separate chairs for economics and for currency and banking, and at most of the German universities monetary problems were almost entirely disregarded.[4] Only later economists realized that some of the most important and most intricate problems of catallactics are to be found in the field of indirect exchange and that an economic theory which does not pay full regard to them is lamentably defective. The coming into vogue of investigations concerning the relation between the "natural rate of interest" and the "money rate of interest," the ascendancy of the monetary theory of the trade cycle, and the entire demolition of the doctrine of the simultaneousness and evenness of the changes in the purchasing power of money were marks of the new tenor of economic thought. Of course, these new ideas were essentially a continuation of the work gloriously begun by David Hume, the British Currency School, John Stuart Mill and Cairnes.

Still more detrimental was a second error which emerged from the careless use of the imaginary construction of a market with direct exchange.

An inveterate fallacy asserted that things and services exchanged are of equal value. Value was considered as objective, as an intrinsic quality inherent in things and not merely as the expression of various people's eagerness to acquire them. People, it was assumed, first established the magnitude of value proper to goods and services by an act of measurement and then proceeded to barter them against quantities of goods and services of the same amount of value. This fallacy frustrated Aristotle's approach to economic problems and, for almost

4. Neglect of the problems of indirect exchange was certainly influenced by political prepossessions. People did not want to give up the thesis according to which economic depressions are an evil inherent in the capitalist mode of production and are in no way caused by attempts to lower the rate of interest by credit expansion. Fashionable teachers of economics deemed it "unscientific" to explain depressions as a phenomenon originating "only" out of events in the sphere of money and credit. There were even surveys of the history of business cycle theory which omitted any discussion of the monetary thesis. Cf., e.g., Eugen von Bergmann, *Geschichte der nationalökonomischen Krisentheorien* (Stuttgart, 1895).

two thousand years, the reasoning of all those for whom Aristotle's opinions were authoritative. It seriously vitiated the marvelous achievements of the classical economists and rendered the writings of their epigones, especially those of Marx and the Marxian school, entirely futile. The basis of modern economics is the cognition that it is precisely the disparity in the value attached to the objects exchanged that results in their being exchanged. People buy and sell only because they appraise the things given up less than those received. Thus the notion of a measurement of value is vain. An act of exchange is neither preceded nor accompanied by any process which could be called a measuring of value. An individual may attach the same value to two things; but then no exchange can result. But if there is a diversity in valuation, all that can be asserted with regard to it is that one *a* is valued higher, that it is preferred to one *b*. Values and valuations are intensive quantities and not extensive quantities. They are not susceptible to mental grasp by the application of cardinal numbers.

However, the spurious idea that values are measurable and are really measured in the conduct of economic transactions was so deeply rooted that even eminent economists fell victim to the fallacy implied. Even Friedrich von Wieser and Irving Fisher took it for granted that there must be something like measurement of value and that economics must be able to indicate and to explain the method by which such measurement is effected.[5] Most of the lesser economists simply maintained that money serves "as a measure of values."

Now, we must realize that valuing means to prefer *a* to *b*. There is —logically, epistemologically, psychologically, and praxeologically— only one pattern of preferring. It does not matter whether a lover prefers one girl to other girls, a man one friend to other people, an amateur one painting to other paintings, or a consumer a loaf of bread to a piece of candy. Preferring always means to love or to desire *a* more than *b*. Just as there is no standard and no measurement of sexual love, of friendship and sympathy, and of aesthetic enjoyment, so there is no measurement of the value of commodities. If a man exchanges two pounds of butter for a shirt, all that we can assert with regard to this transaction is that he—at the instant of the transaction and under the conditions which this instant offers to him— prefers one shirt to two pounds of butter. It is certain that every act

5. For a critical analysis and refutation of Fisher's argument, cf. Mises, *The Theory of Money and Credit,* trans. by H. E. Batson (London, 1934), pp. 42–44; for the same with regard to Wieser's argument, Mises, *Nationalökonomie* (Geneva, 1940), pp. 192–194.

of preferring is characterized by a definite psychic intensity of the feelings it implies. There are grades in the intensity of the desire to attain a definite goal and this intensity determines the psychic profit which the successful action brings to the acting individual. But psychic quantities can only be felt. They are entirely personal, and there is no semantic means to express their intensity and to convey information about them to other people.

There is no method available to construct a unit of value. Let us remember that two units of a homogeneous supply are necessarily valued differently. The value attached to the nth unit is lower than that attached to the $(n — 1)$ th unit.

In the market society there are money prices. Economic calculation is calculation in terms of money prices. The various quantities of goods and services enter into this calculation with the amount of money for which they are bought and sold on the market or for which they could prospectively be bought and sold. It is a fictitious assumption that an isolated self-sufficient individual or the general manager of a socialist system, i.e., a system in which there is no market for means of production, could calculate. There is no way which could lead one from the money computation of a market economy to any kind of computation in a nonmarket system.

The Theory of Value and Socialism

Socialists, Institutionalists and the Historical School have blamed economists for having employed the imaginary construction of an isolated individual's thinking and acting. This Robinson Crusoe pattern, it is asserted, is of no use for the study of the conditions of a market economy. The rebuke is somewhat justified. Imaginary constructions of an isolated individual and of a planned economy without market exchange become utilizable only through the implication of the fictitious assumption, self-contradictory in thought and contrary to reality, that economic calculation is possible also within a system without a market for the means of production.

It was certainly a serious blunder that economists did not become aware of this difference between the conditions of a market economy and a nonmarket economy. Yet the socialists had little reason for criticizing this fault. For it consisted precisely in the fact that the economists tacitly implied the assumption that a socialist order of society could also resort to economic calculation and that they thus asserted the possibility of the realization of the socialist plans.

The classical economists and their epigones could not, of course, recognize the problems involved. If it were true that the value of things is determined by the quantity of labor required for their production or reproduction, then there is no further problem of economic calculation. The supporters of the labor theory of value cannot be blamed for having misconstrued the problems of a socialist system. Their fateful failure was their untenable doctrine of value. That some of them were ready to consider the imaginary construction of a socialist economy as a useful and realizable pattern for a thorough reform of social organization did not contradict the essential content of their theoretical analysis. But it was different with subjective catallactics. It was unpardonable for the modern economists to have failed to recognize the problems involved.

Wieser was right when he once declared that many economists have unwittingly dealt with the value theory of communism and have on that account neglected to elaborate that of the present state of society.[6] It is tragic that he himself did not avoid this failure.

The illusion that a rational order of economic management is possible in a society based on public ownership of the means of production owed its origin to the value theory of the classical economists and its tenacity to the failure of many modern economists to think through consistently to its ultimate conclusions the fundamental theorem of the subjectivist theory. Thus the socialist utopias were generated and preserved by the shortcomings of those schools of thought which the Marxians reject as "an ideological disguise of the selfish class interest of the exploiting bourgeoisie." In truth it was the errors of these schools that made the socialist ideas thrive. This fact clearly demonstrates the emptiness of the Marxian teachings concerning "ideologies" and its modern offshoot, the sociology of knowledge.

3. The Problem of Economic Calculation

Acting man uses knowledge provided by the natural sciences for the elaboration of technology, the applied science of action possible in the field of external events. Technology shows what could be achieved if one wanted to achieve it, and how it could be achieved provided people were prepared to employ the means indicated. With the progress of the natural sciences technology progressed too; many would prefer to say that the desire to improve technological methods prompted the progress of the natural sciences. The quantification of the natural sciences made technology quantitative. Modern technology is essentially the applied art of quantitative prediction of the outcome of possible action. One calculates with a reasonable degree of precision the outcome of planned actions, and one calculates in order to arrange an action in such a way that a definite result emerges.

However, the mere information conveyed by technology would suffice for the performance of calculation only if all means of produc-

6. Cf. Friedrich von Wieser, *Der natürliche Wert* (Vienna, 1889), p. 60, n. 3.

tion—both material and human—could be perfectly substituted for one another according to definite ratios, or if they all were absolutely specific. In the former case all means of production would be fit, although according to different ratios, for the attainment of all ends whatever; things would be as if only one kind of means—one kind of economic goods of a higher order existed. In the latter case each means could be employed for the attainment of one end only; one would attach to each group of complementary factors of production the value attached to the respective good of the first order. (Here again we disregard provisionally the modifications brought about by the time factor.) Neither of these two conditions is present in the universe in which man acts. The means can only be substituted for one another within narrow limits; they are more or less specific means for the attainment of various ends. But, on the other hand, most means are not absolutely specific; most of them are fit for various purposes. The facts that there are different classes of means, that most of the means are better suited for the realization of some ends, less suited for the attainment of some other ends and absolutely useless for the production of a third group of ends, and that therefore the various means allow for various uses, set man the task of allocating them to those employments in which they can render the best service. Here computation in kind as applied by technology is of no avail. Technology operates with countable and measurable quantities of external things and effects; it knows causal relations between them, but it is foreign to their relevance to human wants and desires. Its field is that of objective use-value only. It judges all problems from the disinterested point of view of a neutral observer of physical, chemical, and biological events. For the notion of subjective use-value, for the specifically human angle, and for the dilemmas of acting man there is no room in the teachings of technology. It ignores the economic problem: to employ the available means in such a way that no want more urgently felt should remain unsatisfied because the means suitable for its attainment were employed—wasted—for the attainment of a want less urgently felt. For the solution of such problems technology and its methods of counting and measuring are unfit. Technology tells how a given end could be attained by the employment of various means which can be used together in various combinations, or how various available means could be employed for certain purposes. But it is at a loss to tell man which procedures he should choose out of the infinite variety of imaginable and possible modes of production. What acting man wants to know is how he must employ the available means for the best possible—the most economic—removal of felt uneasiness. But technology provides him with nothing more than statements about causal relations between external things. It tells, for example, $7\,a + 3\,b + 5\,c + \ldots x\,n$ are liable to bring about $8\,P$. But although it knows the value attached by acting man to the various goods of the first order, it cannot decide whether this formula or any other out of the infinite multitude of similarly constructed formulas best serves the attainment of the ends sought by acting man. The art of engineering can establish how a bridge must be built in order to span a river at a given point and to carry definite loads. But it cannot answer the question whether or not the construction of such a bridge would withdraw material factors of production and labor from an employment in which they could satisfy needs more urgently felt. It cannot tell whether or not the bridge should be built at all, where it should be built, what capacity for bearing burdens it should have, and which of the many possibilities for its construction should be chosen. Technological computation can establish relations between various classes of means only to the extent that they can be substituted for one another in the attempts to attain a definite goal. But action is bound to discover relations among all means, however dissimilar they may be, without any regard to the question whether or not they can replace one another in performing the same services.

Technology and the considerations derived from it would be of little use for acting man if it were impossible to introduce into their schemes the money prices of goods and services. The projects and designs of engineers would be purely academic if they could not compare input and output on a common basis. The lofty theorist in the seclusion of his laboratory does not bother about such trifling things; what he is searching for is causal relations between various elements of the universe. But the practical man, eager to improve human conditions by removing uneasiness as far as possible, must know whether, under given conditions, what he is planning is the best method, or even a method, to make people less uneasy. He must know whether what he wants to achieve will be an improvement when compared with the present state of affairs and with the advantages to be expected from the execution of other technically realizable projects which cannot be put into execution if the project he has in mind absorbs the available means. Such comparisons can only be made by the use of money prices.

Thus money becomes the vehicle of economic calculation. This is not a separate function of money. Money is the universally used medium of exchange, nothing else. Only because money is the common medium of exchange, because most goods and services can be sold and bought on the market against money, and only as far as this is the case, can men use money prices in reckoning. The exchange ratios between money and the various goods and services as established on the market of the past and as expected to be established on the market of the future are the mental tools of economic planning. Where there are no money prices, there are no such things as economic quantities. There are only various quantitative relations between various causes and effects in the external world. There is no means for man to find out what kind of action would best serve his endeavors to remove uneasiness as far as possible.

There is no need to dwell upon the primitive conditions of the household economy of self-sufficient farmers. These people performed only very simple processes of production. For them no calculation was needed, as they could directly compare input and output. If they wanted shirts, they grew hemp, they spun, wove, and sewed. They could, without any calculation, easily make up their minds whether or not the toil and trouble expended were compensated by the product. But for civilized mankind a return to such a life is out of the question.

4. Economic Calculation and the Market

The quantitative treatment of economic problems must not be confused with the quantitative methods applied in dealing with the problems of the external universe of physical and chemical events. The distinctive mark of economic calculation is that it is neither based upon nor related to anything which could be characterized as measurement.

A process of measurement consists in the establishment of the numerical relation of an object with regard to another object, viz., the unit of the measurement. The ultimate source of measurement is that of spatial dimensions. With the aid of the unit defined in reference to extension one measures energy and potentiality, the power of a thing to bring about changes in other things and relations, and the passing of time. A pointer-reading is directly indicative of a spatial relation and only indirectly of other quantities. The assumption underlying measurement is the immutability of the unit. The unit of length is the rock upon which all measurement is based. It is assumed that man cannot help considering it immutable.

The last decades have witnessed a revolution in the traditional epistemological setting of physics, chemistry, and mathematics. We are on the eve of innovations whose scope cannot be foreseen. It may be that the coming generations of physicists will have to face problems in some way similar to those with which praxeology must deal. Perhaps they will be forced to drop the idea that there is something unaffected by cosmic changes which the observer can use as a standard of measurement. But however that may come, the logical structure of the measurement of earthly entities in the macroscopic or molar field of physics will not alter. Measurement in the orbit of microscopic physics too is made with meter scales, micrometers, spectrographs—ultimately with the gross sense organs of man, the observer and experimenter, who himself is molar.[7] It cannot free itself from Euclidian geometry and from the notion of an unchangeable standard.

There are monetary units and there are measurable physical units of various economic goods and of many—but not of all—services bought and sold. But the exchange ratios which we have to deal with are permanently fluctuating. There is nothing constant and invariable in them. They defy any attempt to measure them. They are not facts in the sense in which a physicist calls the establishment of the weight of a quantity of copper a fact. They are historical events, expressive of what happened once at a definite instant and under definite circumstances. The same numerical exchange ratio may appear again, but it is by no means certain whether this will really happen and, if it happens, the question is open whether this identical result was the outcome of preservation of the same circumstances or of a return to them rather than the outcome of the interplay of a very different constellation of price-determining factors. Numbers applied by acting man in economic calculation do not refer to quantities measured but to exchange ratios as they are expected—on the basis of understanding—to be realized on the markets of the future to which alone all acting is directed and which alone counts for acting man.

We are not dealing at this point of our investigation with the problem of a "quantitative science of economics," but with the analysis of the mental processes performed by acting man in applying quantitative distinctions when planning conduct. As action is always directed toward influencing a future state of affairs, economic calculation always deals with the future. As far as it takes past events and exchange ratios of the past into consideration, it does so only for the sake of an arrangement of future action.

The task which acting man wants to achieve by economic calculation is to establish the outcome of acting by contrasting input and output. Economic calculation is either an estimate of the expected

7. Cf. A. Eddington, *The Philosophy of Physical Science*, pp. 70–79, 168–169.

outcome of future action or the establishment of the outcome of past action. But the latter does not serve merely historical and didactic aims. Its practical meaning is to show how much one is free to consume without impairing the future capacity to produce. It is with regard to this problem that the fundamental notions of economic calculation—capital and income, profit and loss, spending and saving, cost and yield—are developed. The practical employment of these notions and of all notions derived from them is inseparably linked with the operation of a market in which goods and services of all orders are exchanged against a universally used medium of exchange, viz., money. They would be merely academic, without any relevance for acting within a world with a different structure of action.

XII. THE SPHERE OF ECONOMIC CALCULATION

1. The Character of Monetary Entries

ECONOMIC calculation can comprehend everything that is exchanged against money.

The prices of goods and services are either historical data describing past events or anticipations of probable future events. Information about a past price conveys the knowledge that one or several acts of interpersonal exchange were effected according to this ratio. It does not convey directly any knowledge about future prices. We may often assume that the market conditions which determined the formation of prices in the recent past will not change at all or at least not change considerably in the immediate future so that prices too will remain unchanged or change only slightly. Such expectations are reasonable if the prices concerned were the result of the interaction of many people ready to buy or to sell provided the exchange ratios seemed propitious to them and if the market situation was not influenced by conditions which are considered as accidental, extraordinary, and not likely to return. However, the main task of economic calculation is not to deal with the problems of unchanging or only slightly changing market situations and prices, but to deal with change. The acting individual either anticipates changes which will occur without his own interference and wants to adjust his actions to this anticipated state of affairs; or he wants to embark upon a project which will change conditions even if no other factors produce a change. The prices of the past are for him merely starting points in his endeavors to anticipate future prices.

Historians and statisticians content themselves with prices of the past. Practical man looks at the prices of the future, be it only the immediate future of the next hour, day, or month. For him the prices of the past are merely a help in anticipating future prices. Not only in his preliminary calculation of the expected outcome of planned action, but no less in his attempts to establish the result of his past transactions, he is primarily concerned with future prices.

In balance sheets and in profit-and-loss statements the result of past action becomes visible as the difference between the money equivalent of funds owned (total assets minus total liabilities) at the beginning and at the end of the period reported, and as the difference between the money equivalent of costs incurred and gross proceeds earned. In such statements it is necessary to enter the estimated money equivalent of all assets and liabilities other than cash. These items should be appraised according to the prices at which they could probably be sold in the future or, as is especially the case with equipment for production processes, in reference to the prices to be expected in the sale of merchandise manufactured with their aid. However, old business customs and the provisions of commercial law and of the tax laws have brought about a deviation from sound principles of accounting which aim merely at the best attainable degree of correctness. These customs and laws are not so much concerned with correctness in balance sheets and profit-and-loss statements as with the pursuit of other aims. Commercial legislation aims at a method of accounting which could indirectly protect creditors against loss. It tends more or less to an appraisal of assets below their estimated market value in order to make the net profit and the total funds owned appear smaller than they really are. Thus a safety margin is created which reduces the danger that, to the prejudice of creditors, too much might be withdrawn from the firm as alleged profit and that an already insolvent firm might go on until it had exhausted the means available for the satisfaction of its creditors. Contrariwise tax laws often tend toward a method of computation which makes earnings appear higher than an unbiased method would. The idea is to raise effective tax rates without making this raise visible in the nominal tax rate schedules. We must therefore distinguish between economic calculation as it is practiced by businessmen planning future transactions and those computations of business facts which serve other purposes. The determination of taxes due and economic calculation are two different things. If a law imposing a tax upon the keeping of domestic servants prescribes that one male servant should be counted as two female servants, nobody would interpret such a provision as anything other than a method for determining the amount of tax due. Likewise if an inheritance tax law prescribes that securities should be appraised at the stock market quotation on the day of the decedent's death, we are merely provided with a way of determining the amount of the tax.

The duly kept accounts in a system of correct bookkeeping are accurate as to dollars and cents. They display an impressive precision, and the numerical exactitude of their items seems to remove all doubts. In fact, the most important figures they contain are speculative anticipations of future market constellations. It is a mistake to compare the items of any commercial account to the items used in purely technological reckoning, e.g., in the design for the construction of a machine. The engineer—as far as he attends to the technological side of his job—applies only numerical relations established by the methods of the experimental natural sciences; the businessman cannot avoid numerical terms which are the outcome of his understanding of future human conduct. The main thing in balance sheets and in profit-and-loss statements is the evaluation of assets and liabilities not embodied in cash. All such balances and statements are virtually interim balances and interim statements. They describe as well as possible the state of affairs at an arbitrarily chosen instant while life and action go on and do not stop. It is possible to wind up individual business units, but the whole system of social production never ceases. Nor are the assets and liabilities consisting in cash exempt from the indeterminacy inherent in all business accounting items. They depend on the future constellation of the market no less than any item of inventory or equipment. The numerical exactitude of business accounts and calculations must not prevent us from realizing the uncertainty and speculative character of their items and of all computations based on them.

Yet, these facts do not detract from the efficiency of economic calculation. Economic calculation is as efficient as it can be. No reform could add to its efficiency. It renders to acting man all the services which he can obtain from numerical computation. It is, of course, not a means of knowing future conditions with certainty, and it does not deprive action of its speculative character. But this can be considered a deficiency only by those who do not come to recognize the facts that life is not rigid, that all things are perpetually fluctuating, and that men have no certain knowledge about the future.

It is not the task of economic calculation to expand man's information about future conditions. Its task is to adjust his actions as well as possible to his present opinion concerning want-satisfaction in the future. For this purpose acting man needs a method of computation, and computation requires a common denominator to which all items entered are to be referable. The common denominator of economic calculation is money.

2. The Limits of Economic Calculation

Economic calculation cannot comprehend things which are not sold and bought against money.

There are things which are not for sale and for whose acquisition sacrifices other than money and money's worth must be expended. He who wants to train himself for great achievements must employ many means, some of which may require expenditure of money. But the essential things to be devoted to such an endeavor are not purchasable. Honor, virtue, glory, and likewise vigor, health, and life itself play a role in action both as means and as ends, but they do not enter into economic calculation.

There are things which cannot at all be evaluated in money, and there are other things which can be appraised in money only with regard to a fraction of the value assigned to them. The appraisal of an old building must disregard its artistic and historical eminence as far as these qualities are not a source of proceeds in money or goods vendible. What touches a man's heart only and does not induce other people to make sacrifices for its attainment remains outside the pale of economic calculation.

However, all this does not in the least impair the usefulness of economic calculation. Those things which do not enter into the items of accountancy and calculation are either ends or goods of the first order. No calculation is required to acknowledge them fully and to make due allowance for them. All that acting man needs in order to make his choice is to contrast them with the total amount of costs their acquisition or preservation requires. Let us assume that a town council has to decide between two water supply projects. One of them implies the demolition of a historical landmark, while the other at the cost of an increase in money expenditure spares this landmark. The fact that the feelings which recommend the conservation of the monument cannot be estimated in a sum of money does not in any way impede the councilmen's decision. The values that are not reflected in any monetary exchange ratio are, on the contrary, by this very fact lifted into a particular position which makes the decision rather easier. No complaint is less justified than the lamentation that the computation methods of the market do not comprehend things not vendible. Moral and aesthetic values do not suffer any damage on account of this fact.

Money, money prices, market transactions, and economic calculation based upon them are the main targets of criticism. Loquacious sermonizers disparage Western civilization as a mean system of mongering and peddling. Complacency, self-righteousness, and hypocrisy exult in scorning the "dollar-philosophy" of our age. Neurotic reformers, mentally unbalanced literati, and ambitious demagogues take pleasure in indicting "rationality" and in preaching the gospel of the "irrational." In the eyes of these babblers money and calculation are the source of the most serious evils. However, the fact that men have developed a method of ascertaining as far as possible the expediency of their actions and of removing uneasiness in the most practical and economic way does not prevent anybody from arranging his conduct according to the principle he considers to be right. The "materialism" of the stock exchange and of business accountancy does not hinder anybody from living up to the standards of Thomas à Kempis or from dying for a noble cause. The fact that the masses prefer detective stories to poetry and that it therefore pays better to write the former than the latter, is not caused by the use of money and monetary accounting. It is not the fault of money that there are gangsters, thieves, murderers, prostitutes, corruptible officials and judges. It is not true that honesty does not "pay." It pays for those who prefer fidelity to what they consider to be right to the advantages which they could derive from a different attitude.

Other critics of economic calculation fail to realize that it is a method available only to people acting in the economic system of the division of labor in a social order based upon private ownership of the means of production. It can only serve the considerations of individuals or groups of individuals operating in the institutional setting of this social order. It is consequently a calculation of private profits and not of "social welfare." This means that the prices of the market are the ultimate fact for economic calculation. It cannot be applied for considerations whose standard is not the demand of the consumers as manifested on the market but the hypothetical valuations of a dictatorial body managing all national or earthly affairs. He who seeks to judge actions from the point of view of a pretended "social value," i.e., from the point of view of the "whole society," and to criticize them by comparison with the events in an imaginary socialist system in which his own will is supreme, has no use for economic calculation. Economic calculation in terms of money prices is the calculation of entrepreneurs producing for the consumers of a market society. It is of no avail for other tasks.

He who wants to employ economic calculation must not look at affairs in the manner of a despotic mind. Prices can be used for calculation by the entrepreneurs, capitalists, landowners, and wage earners of a capitalist society. For matters beyond the pursuits of these categories it is inadequate. It is nonsensical to evaluate in money objects which are not negotiated on the market and to employ in calculations arbitrary items which do not refer to reality. The law determines the amount which ought to be paid as indemnification for having caused a man's death. But the statute enacted for the determination of the amends due does not mean that there is a price for human life. Where there is slavery, there are market prices of slaves. Where there is no slavery man, human life, and health are *res extra commercium*. In a society of free men the preservation of life and health are ends, not means. They do not enter into any process of accounting means.

It is possible to determine in terms of money prices the sum of the income or the wealth of a number of people. But it is nonsensical to reckon national income or national wealth. As soon as we embark upon considerations foreign to the reasoning of a man operating within the pale of a market society, we are no longer helped by monetary calculation methods. The attempts to determine in money the wealth of a nation or of the whole of mankind are as childish as the mystic efforts to solve the riddles of the universe by worrying about the dimensions of the pyramid of Cheops. If a business calculation values a supply of potatoes at $100, the idea is that it will be possible to sell it or to replace it against this sum. If a whole entrepreneurial unit is estimated $1,000,000, it means that one expects to sell it for this amount. But what is the meaning of the items in a statement of a nation's total wealth? What is the meaning of the computation's final result? What must be entered into it and what is to be left outside? Is it correct or not to enclose the "value" of the country's climate and the people's innate abilities and acquired skill? The businessman can convert his property into money, but a nation cannot.

The money equivalents as used in acting and in economic calculation are money prices, i.e., exchange ratios between money and other goods and services. The prices are not measured in money; they consist in money. Prices are either prices of the past or expected prices of the future. A price is necessarily a historical fact either of the past or of the future. There is nothing in prices which permits one to liken them to the measurement of physical and chemical phenomena.

3. The Changeability of Prices

Exchange ratios are subject to perpetual change because the conditions which produce them are perpetually changing. The value that an individual attaches both to money and to various goods and services is the outcome of a moment's choice. Every later instant may generate something new and bring about other considerations and valuations. Not that prices are fluctuating, but that they do not alter more quickly could fairly be deemed a problem requiring explanation.

Daily experience teaches people that the exchange ratios of the market are mutable. One would assume that their ideas about prices would take full account of this fact. Nevertheless all popular notions of production and consumption, marketing and prices are more or less contaminated by a vague and contradictory notion of price rigidity. The layman is prone to consider the preservation of yesterday's price structure both as normal and as fair, and to condemn changes in the exchange ratios as a violation of the rules of nature and of justice.

It would be a mistake to explain these popular beliefs as a precipitate of old opinions conceived in earlier ages of more stable conditions of production and marketing. It is questionable whether or not prices were less changeable in those older days. On the contrary, it could rather be asserted that the merger of local markets into larger national markets, the final emergence of a world embracing world market, and the evolution of commerce aiming at continuously supplying the consumers have made price changes less frequent and less sharp. In precapitalistic times there was more stability in technological methods of production, but there was much more irregularity in supplying the various local markets and in adjusting supply to their changing demands. But even if it were true that prices were somewhat more stable in a remote past, it would be of little avail for our age. The popular notions about money and money prices are not derived from ideas formed in the past. It would be wrong to interpret them as atavistic remnants. Under modern conditions every individual is daily faced with so many problems of buying and selling that we are right in assuming that his thinking about these matters is not simply a thoughtless reception of traditional ideas.

It is easy to understand why those whose short-run interests are hurt by a change in prices resent such changes, emphasize that the previous prices were not only fairer but also more normal, and maintain that price stability is in conformity with the laws of nature and of morality. But every change in prices furthers the short-run interests of other people. Those favored will certainly not be prompted by the urge to stress the fairness and normalcy of price rigidity.

Neither atavistic reminiscences nor the state of selfish group interests can explain the popularity of the idea of price stability. Its roots are to be seen in the fact that notions concerning social relations have been constructed according to the pattern of the natural sciences. The economists and sociologists who aimed at shaping the social sciences according to the pattern of physics or physiology only indulged in a way of thinking which popular fallacies had adopted long before.

Even the classical economists were slow to free themselves from this error. With them value was something objective, i.e., a phenomenon of the external world and a quality inherent in things and therefore measurable. They utterly failed to comprehend the purely human and voluntaristic character of value judgments. As far as we can see today, it was Samuel Bailey who first disclosed what is going on in preferring one thing to another.[1] But his book was overlooked as were the writings of other precursors of the subjective theory of value.

It is not only a task of economic science to discard the errors concerning measurability in the field of action. It is no less a task of economic policy. For the failures of present-day economic policies are to some extent due to the lamentable confusion brought about by the idea that there is something fixed and therefore measurable in interhuman relations.

4. Stabilization

An outgrowth of all these errors is the idea of stabilization.

Shortcomings in the governments' handling of monetary matters and the disastrous consequences of policies aimed at lowering the rate of interest and at encouraging business activities through credit expansion gave birth to the ideas which finally generated the slogan "stabilization." One can explain its emergence and its popular appeal, one can understand it as the fruit of the last hundred and fifty years' history of currency and banking, one can, as it were, plead extenuating circumstances for the error involved. But no such sympathetic appreciation can render its fallacies any more tenable.

Stability, the establishment of which the program of stabilization aims at, is an empty and contradictory notion. The urge toward action, i.e., improvement of the conditions of life, is inborn in man. Man himself changes from moment to moment and his valuations, volitions, and acts change with him. In the realm of action there is nothing perpetual but change. There is no fixed point in this ceaseless fluctuation other than the eternal aprioristic categories of action. It is vain to sever valuation and action from man's unsteadiness and the changeability of his conduct and to argue as if there were in the universe eternal values independent of human value judgments and suitable to serve as a yardstick for the appraisal of real action.[2]

All methods suggested for a measurement of the changes in the

1. Cf. Samuel Bailey, *A Critical Dissertation on the Nature, Measures and Causes of Values*. London, 1825. No. 7 in Series of Reprints of Scarce Tracts in Economics and Political Science, London School of Economics (London, 1931).

2. For the propensity of the mind to view rigidity and unchangeability as the essential thing and change and motion as the accidental, cf. Bergson, *La Pensée et le mouvant,* pp. 85 ff.

monetary unit's purchasing power are more or less unwittingly founded on the illusory image of an eternal and immutable being who determines by the application of an immutable standard the quantity of satisfaction which a unit of money conveys to him. It is a poor justification of this ill-thought idea that what is wanted is merely to measure changes in the purchasing power of money. The crux of the stability notion lies precisely in *this* concept of purchasing power. The layman, laboring under the ideas of physics, once considered money as a yardstick of prices. He believed that fluctuations of exchange ratios occur only in the relations between the various commodities and services and not also in the relation between money and the "totality" of goods and services. Later, people reversed the argument. It was no longer money to which constancy of value was attributed, but the "totality" of things vendible and purchasable. People began to devise methods for working up complexes of commodity units to be contrasted to the monetary unit. Eagerness to find indexes for the measurement of purchasing power silenced all scruples. Both the doubtfulness and the incomparability of the price records employed and the arbitrary character of the procedures used for the computation of averages were disregarded.

Irving Fisher, the eminent economist, who was the champion of the American stabilization movement, contrasts with the dollar a basket containing all the goods the housewife buys on the market for the current provision of her household. In the proportion in which the amount of money required for the purchase of the content of this basket changes, the purchasing power of the dollar has changed. The goal assigned to the policy of stabilization is the preservation of the immutability of this money expenditure.[3] This would be all right if the housewife and her imaginary basket were constant elements, if the basket were always to contain the same goods and the same quantity of each and if the role which this assortment of goods plays in the family's life were not to change. But we are living in a world in which none of these conditions is realized.

First of all there is the fact that the quality of the commodities produced and consumed changes continuously. It is a mistake to identify wheat with wheat, not to speak of shoes, hats, and other manufactures. The great price differences in the synchronous sales of commodities which mundane speech and statistics arrange in the same class clearly evidence this truism. An idiomatic expression asserts that two peas are alike; but buyers and sellers distinguish

3. Cf. Irving Fisher, *The Money Illusion* (New York, 1928), pp. 19–20.

various qualities and grades of peas. A comparison of prices paid at different places or at different dates for commodities which technology or statistics calls by the same name, is useless if it is not certain that their qualities—but for the place difference—are perfectly the same. Quality means in this connection: all those properties to which the buyers and would-be-buyers pay heed. The mere fact that the quality of all goods and services of the first order is subject to change explodes one of the fundamental assumptions of all index number methods. It is irrelevant that a limited amount of goods of the higher orders—especially metals and chemicals which can be uniquely determined by a formula—are liable to a precise description of their characteristic features. A measurement of purchasing power would have to rely upon the prices of the goods and services of the first order and, what is more, of *all* of them. To employ the prices of the producers' goods is not helpful because it could not avoid counting the various stages of the production of one and the same consumers' good several times and thus falsifying the result. A restriction to a group of selected goods would be quite arbitrary and therefore vicious.

But even apart from all these insurmountable obstacles the task would remain insoluble. For not only do the technological features of commodities change and new kinds of goods appear while many old ones disappear. Valuations change too, and they cause changes in demand and production. The assumptions of the measurement doctrine would require men whose wants and valuations are rigid. Only if people were to value the same things always in the same way, could we consider price changes as expressive of changes in the power of money to buy things.

As it is impossible to establish the total amount of money spent at a given fraction of time for consumers' goods, statisticians must rely upon the prices paid for individual commodities. This raises two further problems for which there is no apodictic solution. It becomes necessary to attach to the various commodities coefficients of importance. It would be manifestly wrong to let the prices of various commodities enter into the computation without taking into account the different roles they play in the total system of the individuals' households. But the establishment of such proper weighting is again arbitrary. Secondly, it becomes necessary to compute averages out of the data collected and adjusted. But there exist different methods for the computation of averages. There are the arithmetic, the geometric, the harmonic averages, there is the quasi-average known as the median. Each of them leads to different results. None of them can be recognized as the unique way to attain a logically unassailable answer. The decision in favor of one of these methods of computation is arbitrary.

If all human conditions were unchangeable, if all people were always to repeat the same actions because their uneasiness and their ideas about its removal were constant, or if we were in a position to assume that changes in these factors occurring with some individuals or groups are always outweighed by opposite changes with other individuals or groups and therefore do not affect total demand and total supply, we would live in a world of stability. But the idea that in such a world money's purchasing power could change is contradictory. As will be shown later, changes in the purchasing power of money must necessarily affect the prices of different commodities and services at different times and to different extents; they must consequently bring about changes in demand and supply, in production and consumption.[4] The idea implied in the inappropriate term *level of prices,* as if—other things being equal—all prices could rise or drop evenly, is untenable. Other things cannot remain equal if the purchasing power of money changes.

In the field of praxeology and economics no sense can be given to the notion of measurement. In the hypothetical state of rigid conditions there are no changes to be measured. In the actual world of change there are no fixed points, dimensions, or relations which could serve as a standard. The monetary unit's purchasing power never changes evenly with regard to all things vendible and purchasable. The notions of stability and stabilization are empty if they do not refer to a state of rigidity and its preservation. However, this state of rigidity cannot even be thought out consistently to its ultimate logical consequences; still less can it be realized.[5] Where there is action, there is change. Action is a lever of change.

The pretentious solemnity which statisticians and statistical bureaus display in computing indexes of purchasing power and cost of living is out of place. These index numbers are at best rather crude and inaccurate illustrations of changes which have occurred. In periods of slow alterations in the relation between the supply of and the demand for money they do not convey any information at all. In periods of inflation and consequently of sharp price changes they provide a rough image of events which every individual experiences in his daily life. A judicious housewife knows much more about price changes as far as they affect her own household than the statistical

4. See below, pp. 411–413.
5. See below, pp. 247–250.

averages can tell. She has little use for computations disregarding changes both in quality and in the amount of goods which she is able or permitted to buy at the prices entering into the computation. If she "measures" the changes for her personal appreciation by taking the prices of only two or three commodities as a yardstick, she is no less "scientific" and no more arbitrary than the sophisticated mathematicians in choosing their methods for the manipulation of the data of the market.

In practical life nobody lets himself be fooled by index numbers. Nobody agrees with the fiction that they are to be considered as measurements. Where quantities are measured, all further doubts and disagreements concerning their dimensions cease. These questions are settled. Nobody ventures to argue with the meteorologists about their measurements of temperature, humidity, atmospheric pressure, and other meteorological data. But on the other hand nobody acquiesces in an index number if he does not expect a personal advantage from its acknowledgment by public opinion. The establishment of index numbers does not settle disputes; it merely shifts them into a field in which the clash of antagonistic opinions and interests is irreconcilable.

Human action originates change. As far as there is human action there is no stability, but ceaseless alteration. The historical process is a sequence of changes. It is beyond the power of man to stop it and to bring about an age of stability in which all history comes to a standstill. It is man's nature to strive after improvement, to beget new ideas, and to rearrange the conditions of his life according to these ideas.

The prices of the market are historical facts expressive of a state of affairs that prevailed at a definite instant of the irreversible historical process. In the praxeological orbit the concept of measurement does not make any sense. In the imaginary—and, of course, unrealizable—state of rigidity and stability there are no changes to be measured. In the actual world of permanent change there are no fixed points, objects, qualities or relations with regard to which changes could be measured.

5. The Root of the Stabilization Idea

Economic calculation does not require monetary stability in the sense in which this term is used by the champions of the stabilization movement. The fact that rigidity in the monetary unit's purchasing power is unthinkable and unrealizable does not impair the methods of economic calculation. What economic calculation requires is a monetary system whose functioning is not sabotaged by government interference. The endeavors to expand the quantity of money in circulation either in order to increase the government's capacity to spend or in order to bring about a temporary lowering of the rate of interest disintegrate all currency matters and derange economic calculation. The first aim of monetary policy must be to prevent governments from embarking upon inflation and from creating conditions which encourage credit expansion on the part of banks. But this program is very different from the confused and self-contradictory program of stabilizing purchasing power.

For the sake of economic calculation all that is needed is to avoid great and abrupt fluctuations in the supply of money. Gold and, up to the middle of the nineteenth century, silver served very well all the purposes of economic calculation. Changes in the relation between the supply of and the demand for the precious metals and the resulting alterations in purchasing power went on so slowly that the entrepreneur's economic calculation could disregard them without going too far afield. Precision is unattainable in economic calculation quite apart from the shortcomings emanating from not paying due consideration to monetary changes.[6] The planning businessman cannot help employing data concerning the unknown future; he deals with future prices and future costs of production. Accounting and bookkeeping in their endeavors to establish the result of past action are in the same position as far as they rely upon the estimation of fixed equipment, inventories, and receivables. In spite of all these uncertainties economic calculation can achieve its tasks. For these uncertainties do not stem from deficiencies of the system of calculation. They are inherent in the essence of acting that always deals with the uncertain future.

The idea of rendering purchasing power stable did not originate from endeavors to make economic calculation more correct. Its source is the wish to create a sphere withdrawn from the ceaseless flux of human affairs, a realm which the historical process does not affect. Endowments which were designed to provide in perpetuity for an ecclesiastic body, for a charitable institution, or for a family were long established in land or in disbursement of agricultural prod-

6. No practical calculation can ever be precise. The formula underlying the process of calculation may be exact; the calculation itself depends on the approximate establishment of quantities and is therefore necessarily inaccurate. Economics is, as has been shown above (p. 39), an exact science of real things. But as soon as price data are introduced into the chain of thought, exactitude is abandoned and economic history is substituted for economic theory.

ucts in kind. Later annuities to be settled in money were added. Endowers and beneficiaries expected that an annuity determined in terms of a definite amount of precious metals would not be affected by changes in economic conditions. But these hopes were illusory. Later generations learned that the plans of their ancestors were not realized. Stimulated by this experience they began to investigate how the aims sought could be attained. Thus they embarked upon attempts to measure changes in purchasing power and to eliminate such changes.

The problem assumed much greater importance when governments initiated their policies of long-term irredeemable and perpetual loans. The state, this new deity of the dawning age of statolatry, this eternal and superhuman institution beyond the reach of earthly frailties, offered to the citizen an opportunity to put his wealth in safety and to enjoy a stable income secure against all vicissitudes. It opened a way to free the individual from the necessity of risking and acquiring his wealth and his income anew each day in the capitalist market. He who invested his funds in bonds issued by the government and its subdivisions was no longer subject to the inescapable laws of the market and to the sovereignty of the consumers. He was no longer under the necessity of investing his funds in such a way that they would best serve the wants and needs of the consumers. He was secure, he was safeguarded against the dangers of the competitive market in which losses are the penalty of inefficiency; the eternal state had taken him under its wing and guaranteed him the undisturbed enjoyment of his funds. Henceforth his income no longer stemmed from the process of supplying the wants of the consumers in the best possible way, but from the taxes levied by the state's apparatus of compulsion and coercion. He was no longer a servant of his fellow citizens, subject to their sovereignty; he was a partner of the government which ruled the people and exacted tribute from them. What the government paid as interest was less than the market offered. But this difference was far outweighed by the unquestionable solvency of the debtor, the state whose revenue did not depend on satisfying the public, but on insisting on the payment of taxes.

In spite of the unpleasant experiences with public debts in earlier days, people were ready to trust freely the modernized state of the nineteenth century. It was generally assumed that this new state would scrupulously meet its voluntarily contracted obligations. Capitalists and entrepreneurs were fully aware of the fact that in the market society there is no means of preserving acquired wealth other than by acquiring it anew each day in tough competition with everybody, with the already existing firms as well as with newcomers "operating on a shoe string." The entrepreneur, grown old and weary and no longer prepared to risk his hard-earned wealth by new attempts to meet the wants of consumers, and the heir of other people's profits, lazy and fully conscious of his own inefficiency, preferred investment in bonds of the public debt because they wanted to be free from the law of the market.

Now, the irredeemable perpetual public debt presupposes the stability of purchasing power. Although the state and its compulsion may be eternal, the interest paid on the public debt could be eternal only if based on a standard of unchanging value. In this form the investor who for security's sake shuns the market, entrepreneurship, and investment in free enterprise and prefers government bonds is faced again with the problem of the changeability of all human affairs. He discovers that in the frame of a market society there is no room left for wealth not dependent upon the market. His endeavors to find an inexhaustible source of income fail.

There are in this world no such things as stability and security and no human endeavors are powerful enough to bring them about. There is in the social system of the market society no other means of acquiring wealth and of preserving it than successful service to the consumers. The state is, of course, in a position to exact payments from its subjects and to borrow funds. However, even the most ruthless government in the long run is not able to defy the laws determining human life and action. If the government uses the sums borrowed for investment in those lines in which they best serve the wants of the consumers, and if it succeeds in these entrepreneurial activities in free and equal competition with all private entrepreneurs, it is in the same position as any other businessman; it can pay interest because it has made surpluses. But if the government invests funds unsuccessfully and no surplus results, or if it spends the money for current expenditure, the capital borrowed shrinks or disappears entirely, and no source is opened from which interest and principal could be paid. Then taxing the people is the only method available for complying with the articles of the credit contract. In asking taxes for such payments the government makes the citizens answerable for money squandered in the past. The taxes paid are not compensated by any present service rendered by the government's apparatus.

The government pays interest on capital which has been consumed and no longer exists. The treasury is burdened with the unfortunate results of past policies.

A good case can be made out for short-term government debts under special conditions. Of course, the popular justification of war loans is nonsensical. All the materials needed for the conduct of a war must be provided by restriction of civilian consumption, by using up a part of the capital available and by working harder. The whole burden of warring falls upon the living generation. The coming generations are only affected to the extent to which, on account of the war expenditure, they will inherit less from those now living than they would have if no war had been fought. Financing a war through loans does not shift the burden to the sons and grandsons.[7] It is merely a method of distributing the burden among the citizens. If the whole expenditure had to be provided by taxes, only those who have liquid funds could be approached. The rest of the people would not contribute adequately. Short-term loans can be instrumental in removing such inequalities, as they allow for a fair assessment on the owners of fixed capital.

The long-term public and semipublic credit is a foreign and disturbing element in the structure of a market society. Its establishment was a futile attempt to go beyond the limits of human action and to create an orbit of security and eternity removed from the transitoriness and instability of earthly affairs. What an arrogant presumption to borrow and to lend money for ever and ever, to make contracts for eternity, to stipulate for all times to come! In this respect it mattered little whether the loans were in a formal manner made irredeemable or not; intentionally and practically they were as a rule considered and dealt with as such. In the heyday of liberalism some Western nations really retired parts of their long-term debt by honest reimbursement. But for the most part new debts were only heaped upon old ones. The financial history of the last century shows a steady increase in the amount of public indebtedness. Nobody believes that the states will eternally drag the burden of these interest payments. It is obvious that sooner or later all these debts will be liquidated in some way or other, but certainly not by payment of interest and principal according to the terms of the contract. A host

7. Loans, in this context, mean funds borrowed from those who have money available for lending. We do not refer here to credit expansion of which the main vehicle in present-day America is borrowing from the commercial banks.

of sophisticated writers are already busy elaborating the moral palliation for the day of final settlement.[8]

The fact that economic calculation in terms of money is unequal to the tasks which are assigned to it in these illusory schemes for establishment of an unrealizable realm of calm removed from the inescapable limitations of human action and providing eternal security cannot be called a deficiency. There are no such things as eternal, absolute, and unchanging values. The search for a standard of such values is vain. Economic calculation is not imperfect because it does not correspond to the confused ideas of people yearning for a stable income not dependent on the productive processes of men.

8. The most popular of these doctrines is crystallized in the phrase: A public debt is no burden because we owe it to ourselves. If this were true, then the wholesale obliteration of the public debt would be an innocuous operation, a mere act of bookkeeping and accountancy. The fact is that the public debt embodies claims of people who have in the past entrusted funds to the government against all those who are daily producing new wealth. It burdens the producing strata for the benefit of another part of the people. It is possible to free the producers of new wealth from this burden by collecting the taxes required for the payments exclusively from the bondholders. But this means undisguised repudiation.

XIII. MONETARY CALCULATION AS A TOOL OF ACTION

1. Monetary Calculation as a Method of Thinking

MONETARY calculation is the guiding star of action under the social system of division of labor. It is the compass of the man embarking upon production. He calculates in order to distinguish the remunerative lines of production from the unprofitable ones, those of which the sovereign consumers are likely to approve from those of which they are likely to disapprove. Every single step of entrepreneurial activities is subject to scrutiny by monetary calculation. The premeditation of planned action becomes commercial precalculation of expected costs and expected proceeds. The retrospective establishment of the outcome of past action becomes accounting of profit and loss.

The system of economic calculation in monetary terms is conditioned by certain social institutions. It can operate only in an institutional setting of the division of labor and private ownership of the means of production in which goods and services of all orders are bought and sold against a generally used medium of exchange, i.e., money.

Monetary calculation is the method of calculating employed by people acting within the frame of society based on private control of the means of production. It is a device of acting individuals; it is a mode of computation designed for ascertaining private wealth and income and private profits and losses of individuals acting on their own behalf within a free enterprise society.[1] All its results refer to the actions of individuals only. When statisticians summarize these results, the outcome shows the sum of the autonomous actions of a plurality of self-directing individuals, but not the effect of the action of a collective body, of a whole, or of a totality. Monetary calculation is entirely inapplicable and useless for any consideration which does not look at things from the point of view of individuals. It involves calculating the individuals' profits, not imaginary "social" values and "social" welfare.

1. In partnerships and corporations it is always individuals who act, although not only one individual.

Monetary calculation is the main vehicle of planning and acting in the social setting of a society of free enterprise directed and controlled by the market and its prices. It developed in this frame and was gradually perfected with the improvement of the market mechanism and with the expansion of the scope of things which are negotiated on markets against money. It was economic calculation that assigned to measurement, number, and reckoning the role they play in our quantitative and computing civilization. The measurements of physics and chemistry make sense for practical action only because there is economic calculation. It is monetary calculation that made arithmetic a tool in the struggle for a better life. It provides a mode of using the achievements of laboratory experiments for the most efficacious removal of uneasiness.

Monetary calculation reaches its full perfection in capital accounting. It establishes the money prices of the available means and confronts this total with the changes brought about by action and by the operation of other factors. This confrontation shows what changes occurred in the state of the acting men's affairs and the magnitude of those changes; it makes success and failure, profit and loss ascertainable. The system of free enterprise has been dubbed capitalism in order to deprecate and to smear it. However, this term can be considered very pertinent. It refers to the most characteristic feature of the system, its main eminence, viz., the role the notion of capital plays in its conduct.

There are people to whom monetary calculation is repulsive. They do not want to be roused from their daydreams by the voice of critical reason. Reality sickens them, they long for a realm of unlimited opportunity. They are disgusted by the meanness of a social order in which everything is nicely reckoned in dollars and pennies. They call their grumbling the noble deportment worthy of the friends of the spirit, of beauty, and virtue as opposed to the ignoble baseness and villainy of Babbittry. However, the cult of beauty and virtue, wisdom and the search for truth are not hindered by the rationality of the calculating and computing mind. It is only romantic reverie that cannot thrive in a milieu of sober criticism. The cool-headed reckoner is the stern chastiser of the ecstatic visionary.

Our civilization is inseparably linked with our methods of economic calculation. It would perish if we were to abandon this most precious intellectual tool of acting. Goethe was right in calling bookkeeping by double entry "one of the finest inventions of the human mind."[2]

2. Cf. Goethe, *Wilhelm Meister's Apprenticeship,* Bk. I, chap. x.

2. Economic Calculation and the Science of Human Action

The evolution of capitalist economic calculation was the necessary condition for the establishment of a systematic and logically coherent science of human action. Praxeology and economics have a definite place in the evolution of human history and in the process of scientific research. They could only emerge when acting man had succeeded in creating methods of thinking that made it possible to calculate his actions. The science of human action was at the beginning merely a discipline dealing with those actions which can be tested by monetary calculation. It dealt exclusively with what we may call the orbit of economics in the narrower sense, that is, with those actions which within a market society are transacted by the intermediary of money. The first steps on the way to its elaboration were odd investigations concerning currency, moneylending, and the prices of various goods. The knowledge conveyed by Gresham's Law, the first crude formulations of the quantity theory of money—such as those of Bodin and Davanzati—and the Law of Gregory King mark the first dawn of the cognition that regularity of phenomena and inevitable necessity prevail in the field of action. The first comprehensive system of economic theory, that brilliant achievement of the classical economists, was essentially a theory of calculated action. It drew implicitly the borderline between what is to be considered economic and what extra-economic along the line which separates action calculated in monetary terms from other action. Starting from this basis, the economists were bound to widen step by step the field of their studies until they finally developed a system dealing with all human choices, a general theory of action.

Part Four

Catallactics or Economics of the Market Society

XIV. THE SCOPE AND METHOD OF CATALLACTICS

1. The Delimitation of Catallactic Problems

THERE have never been any doubts and uncertainties about the scope of economic science. Ever since people have been eager for a systematic study of economics or political economy, all have agreed that it is the task of this branch of knowledge to investigate the market phenomena, that is, the determination of the mutual exchange ratios of the goods and services negotiated on markets, their origin in human action and their effects upon later action. The intricacy of a precise definition of the scope of economics does not stem from uncertainty with regard to the orbit of the phenomena to be investigated. It is due to the fact that the attempts to elucidate the phenomena concerned must go beyond the range of the market and of market transactions. In order to conceive the market fully one is forced to study the action of hypothetical isolated individuals on one hand and to contrast the market system with an imaginary socialist commonwealth on the other hand. In studying interpersonal exchange one cannot avoid dealing with autistic exchange. But then it is no longer possible to define neatly the boundaries between the kind of action which is the proper field of economic science in the narrower sense, and other action. Economics widens its horizon and turns into a general science of all and every human action, into praxeology. The question emerges of how to distinguish precisely, within the broader field of general praxeology, a narrower orbit of specifically economic problems.

The abortive attempts to solve this problem of a precise delimitation of the scope of catallactics have chosen as a criterion either the motives causing action or the goals which action aims at. But the variety and manifoldness of the motives instigating a man's action are without relevance for a comprehensive study of acting. Every action is motivated by the urge to remove a felt uneasiness. It does not matter for the science of action how people qualify this uneasiness from a physiological, psychological, or ethical point of view. It is the task of economics to deal with all commodity prices as they are really asked and paid in market transactions. It must not restrict its investigations to the study of those prices which result or are likely to result from a conduct displaying attitudes to which psychology, ethics, or any other way of looking at human behavior would attach a definite label. The classification of actions according to their various motives may be momentous for psychology and may provide a yardstick for a moral evaluation; for economics it is inconsequential. Essentially the same is valid with regard to the endeavors to restrict the scope of economics to those actions which aim at supplying people with tangible material things of the external universe. Strictly speaking, people do not long for tangible goods as such, but for the services which these goods are fitted to render them. They want to attain the increment in well-being which these services are able to convey. But if this is so, it is not permissible to except from the orbit of "economic" action those actions which remove uneasiness directly without the interposition of any tangible and visible things. The advice of a doctor, the instruction of a teacher, the recital of an artist, and other personal services are no less an object of economic studies than the architect's plans for the construction of a building, the scientist's formula for the production of a chemical compound, and the author's contribution to the publishing of a book.

The subject matter of catallactics is all market phenomena with all their roots, ramifications, and consequences. It is a fact that people in dealing on the market are motivated not only by the desire to get food, shelter, and sexual enjoyment, but also by manifold "ideal" urges. Acting man is always concerned both with "material" and "ideal" things. He chooses between various alternatives, no matter whether they are to be classified as material or ideal. In the actual scales of value material and ideal things are jumbled together. Even if it were feasible to draw a sharp line between material and ideal concerns, one must realize that every concrete action either aims at the realization both of material and ideal ends or is the outcome of a choice between something material and something ideal.

Whether it is possible to separate neatly those actions which aim at the satisfaction of needs exclusively conditioned by man's physiological constitution from other "higher" needs can be left undecided. But we must not overlook the fact that in reality no food is valued solely for its nutritive power and no garment or house solely for the protection it affords against cold weather and rain. It cannot be denied that the demand for goods is widely influenced by metaphysical, religious, and ethical considerations, by aesthetic value judgments, by customs, habits, prejudices, tradition, changing fashions, and many other things. To an economist who would try to restrict his investigations to "material" aspects only, the subject matter of inquiry vanishes as soon as he wants to catch it.

All that can be contended is this: Economics is mainly concerned with the analysis of the determination of money prices of goods and services exchanged on the market. In order to accomplish this task it must start from a comprehensive theory of human action. Moreover, it must study not only the market phenomena, but no less the hypothetical conduct of an isolated man and of a socialist community. Finally, it must not restrict its investigations to those modes of action which in mundane speech are called "economic" actions, but must deal also with actions which are in a loose manner of speech called "noneconomic."

The scope of praxeology, the general theory of human action, can be precisely defined and circumscribed. The specifically economic problems, the problems of economic action in the narrower sense, can only by and large be disengaged from the comprehensive body of praxeological theory. Accidental facts of the history of science of conventions play a role in all attempts to provide a definition of the scope of "genuine" economics.

Not logical or epistemological rigor, but considerations of expediency and traditional convention make us declare that the field of catallactics or of economics in the narrower sense is the analysis of the market phenomena. This is tantamount to the statement: Catallactics is the analysis of those actions which are conducted on the basis of monetary calculation. Market exchange and monetary calculation are inseparably linked together. A market in which there is direct exchange only is merely an imaginary construction. On the other hand, money and monetary calculation are conditioned by the existence of the market.

It is certainly one of the tasks of economics to analyze the working of an imaginary socialist system of production. But access to this study too is possible only through the study of catallactics, the elucidation of a system in which there are money prices and economic calculation.

The Denial of Economics

There are doctrines flatly denying that there can be a science of economics. What is taught nowadays at most of the universities under the label of economics is practically a denial of it.

He who contests the existence of economics virtually denies that man's well-being is disturbed by any scarcity of external factors. Everybody, he implies, could enjoy the perfect satisfaction of all his wishes, provided a reform succeeds in overcoming certain obstacles brought about by inappropriate man-made institutions. Nature is open-handed, it lavishly loads mankind with presents. Conditions could be paradisiac for an indefinite number of people. Scarcity is an artificial product of established practices. The abolition of such practices would result in abundance.

In the doctrine of Karl Marx and his followers scarcity is a historical category only. It is the feature of the primeval history of mankind which will be forever liquidated by the abolition of private property. Once mankind has effected the leap from the realm of necessity into the realm of freedom[1] and thereby reached "the higher phase of communist society," there will be abundance and consequently it will be feasible to give "to each according to his needs."[2] There is in the vast flood of Marxian writings not the slightest allusion to the possibility that a communist society in its "higher phase" might have to face a scarcity of natural factors of production. The fact of the disutility of labor is spirited away by the assertion that to work, under communism of course, will no longer be pain but pleasure, "the primary necessity of life."[3] The unpleasant experiences of the Russian "experiment" are interpreted as caused by the capitalists' hostility, by the fact that socialism in one country only is not yet perfect and therefore has not yet been able to bring about the "higher phase," and, more recently, by the war.

Then there are the radical inflationists as represented, for example, by Proudhon and by Ernest Solvay. In their opinion scarcity is created by the artificial checks upon credit expansion and other methods of increasing the quantity of money in circulation, enjoined upon the gullible public by the selfish class interests of bankers and other exploiters. They recommend unlimited public spending as the panacea.

Such is the myth of potential plenty and abundance. Economics may leave it to the historians and psychologists to explain the popularity of this kind of wishful thinking and indulgence in daydreams. All that economics has to say about such idle talk is that economics deals with the problems man has to face on account of the fact that his life is conditioned by natural factors. It deals with action, i.e., with the conscious endeavors to remove as far as possible felt uneasiness. It has nothing to assert with regard to the state of affairs in an unrealizable and for human reason even inconceivable universe of unlimited opportunities. In such a world, it may be admitted, there will be no law of value, no scarcity, and no economic problems. These things will be

1. Cf. Engels, *Herrn Eugen Dührings Umwälzung der Wissenschaft* (7th ed. Stuttgart, 1910), p. 306.

2. Cf. Karl Marx, *Zur Kritik des sozialdemokratischen Parteiprogramms von Gotha,* ed. Kreibich (Reichenberg, 1920), p. 17.

3. Cf. *ibid.*

absent because there will be no choices to be made, no action, and no tasks to be solved by reason. Beings which would have thrived in such a world would never have developed reasoning and thinking. If ever such a world were to be given to the descendants of the human race, these blessed beings would see their power to think wither away and would cease to be human. For the primary task of reason is to cope consciously with the limitations imposed upon man by nature, is to fight against scarcity. Acting and thinking man is the product of a universe of scarcity in which whatever well-being can be attained is the prize of toil and trouble, of conduct popularly called economic.

2. The Method of Imaginary Constructions

The specific method of economics is the method of imaginary constructions.

This method is the method of praxeology. That it has been carefully elaborated and perfected in the field of economic studies in the narrower sense is due to the fact that economics, at least until now, has been the best-developed part of praxeology. Everyone who wants to express an opinion about the problems commonly called economic takes recourse to this method. The employment of these imaginary constructions is, to be sure, not a procedure peculiar to the scientific analysis of these problems. The layman in dealing with them resorts to the same method. But while the layman's constructions are more or less confused and muddled, economics is intent upon elaborating them with the utmost care, scrupulousness, and precision, and upon examining their conditions and assumptions critically.

An imaginary construction is a conceptual image of a sequence of events logically evolved from the elements of action employed in its formation. It is a product of deduction, ultimately derived from the fundamental category of action, the act of preferring and setting aside. In designing such an imaginary construction the economist is not concerned with the question of whether or not it depicts the conditions of reality which he wants to analyze. Nor does he bother about the question of whether or not such a system as his imaginary construction posits could be conceived as really existent and in operation. Even imaginary constructions which are inconceivable, self-contradictory, or unrealizable can render useful, even indispensable services in the comprehension of reality, provided the economist knows how to use them properly.

The method of imaginary constructions is justified by its success. Praxeology cannot, like the natural sciences, base its teachings upon laboratory experiments and sensory perception of external objects.

It had to develop methods entirely different from those of physics and biology. It would be a serious blunder to look for analogies to the imaginary constructions in the field of the natural sciences. The imaginary constructions of praxeology can never be confronted with any experience of things external and can never be appraised from the point of view of such experience. Their function is to serve man in a scrutiny which cannot rely upon his senses. In confronting the imaginary constructions with reality we cannot raise the question of whether they correspond to experience and depict adequately the empirical data. We must ask whether the assumptions of our construction are identical with the conditions of those actions which we want to conceive.

The main formula for designing of imaginary constructions is to abstract from the operation of some conditions present in actual action. Then we are in a position to grasp the hypothetical consequences of the absence of these conditions and to conceive the effects of their existence. Thus we conceive the category of action by constructing the image of a state in which there is no action, either because the individual is fully contented and does not feel any uneasiness or because he does not know any procedure from which an improvement in his well-being (state of satisfaction) could be expected. Thus we conceive the notion of originary interest from an imaginary construction in which no distinction is made between satisfactions in periods of time equal in length but unequal with regard to their distance from the instant of action.

The method of imaginary constructions is indispensable for praxeology; it is the only method of praxeological and economic inquiry. It is, to be sure, a method difficult to handle because it can easily result in fallacious syllogisms. It leads along a sharp edge; on both sides yawns the chasm of absurdity and nonsense. Only merciless self-criticism can prevent a man from falling headlong into these abysmal depths.

3. The Pure Market Economy

The imaginary construction of a pure or unhampered market economy assumes that there is division of labor and private ownership (control) of the means of production and that consequently there is market exchange of goods and services. It assumes that the operation of the market is not obstructed by institutional factors. It assumes that the government, the social apparatus of compulsion and coercion, is intent upon preserving the operation of the market system, abstains from hindering its functioning, and protects it against encroachments on the part of other people. The market is free; there is no interference of factors, foreign to the market, with prices, wage rates, and interest rates. Starting from these assumptions economics tries to elucidate the operation of a pure market economy. Only at a later stage, having exhausted everything which can be learned from the study of this imaginary construction, does it turn to the study of the various problems raised by interference with the market on the part of governments and other agencies employing coercion and compulsion.

It is amazing that this logically incontestable procedure, the only one that is fitted to solve the problems involved, has been passionately attacked. People have branded it as a prepossession in favor of a liberal economic policy, which they stigmatize as reactionary, economic royalism, Manchesterism, negativism, and so on. They deny that anything can be gained for the knowledge of reality from occupation with this imaginary construction. However, these turbulent critics contradict themselves as they take recourse to the same method in advancing their own assertions. In asking for minimum wage rates they depict the alleged unsatisfactory conditions of a free labor market and in asking for tariffs they describe the alleged disasters brought about by free trade. There is, of course, no other way available for the elucidation of a measure limiting the free play of the factors operating on an unhampered market than to study first the state of affairs prevailing under economic freedom.

It is true that economists have drawn from their investigations the conclusion that the goals which most people, practically even all people, are intent on attaining by toiling and working and by economic policy can best be realized where the free market system is not impeded by government decrees. But this is not a preconceived judgment stemming from an insufficient occupation with the operation of government interference with business. It is, on the contrary, the result of a careful unbiased scrutiny of all aspects of interventionism.

It is also true that the classical economists and their epigones used to call the system of the unhampered market economy "natural" and government meddling with market phenomena "artificial" and "disturbing." But this terminology also was the product of their careful scrutiny of the problems of interventionism. They were in conformity with the semantic practice of their age in calling an undesirable state of social affairs "contrary to nature."

Theism and Deism of the Age of Enlightenment viewed the regularity of natural phenomena as an emanation of the decrees of Providence. When the philosophers of the Enlightenment discovered that there prevails a regularity of phenomena also in human action and in social evolution, they were prepared to interpret it likewise as evidence of the paternal care of the Creator of the universe. This was the true meaning of the doctrine of the predetermined harmony as expounded by some economists.[4] The social philosophy of paternal despotism laid stress upon the divine mission of kings and autocrats predestined to rule the peoples. The liberal retorted that the operation of an unhampered market, on which the consumer—i.e., every citizen—is sovereign, brings about more satisfactory results than the decrees of anointed rulers. Observe the functioning of the market system, they said, and you will discover in it too the finger of God.

Along with the imaginary construction of a pure market economy the classical economists elaborated its logical counterpart, the imaginary construction of a socialist commonwealth. In the heuristic process which finally led to the discovery of the operation of a market economy this image of a socialist order even had logical priority. The question which preoccupied the economists was whether a tailor could be supplied with bread and shoes if there was no government decree compelling the baker and the shoemaker to provide for his needs. The first thought was that authoritarian interference is required to make every specialist serve his fellow citizens. The economists were taken aback when they discovered that no such compulsion is needed. In contrasting productivity and profitability, self-interest and public welfare, selfishness and altruism, the economists implicitly referred to the image of a socialist system. Their astonishment at the "automatic," as it were, steering of the market system was precisely due to the fact that they realized that an "anarchic" state of production results in supplying people better than the orders of a centralized omnipotent government. The idea of socialism—a system of the division of labor entirely controlled and managed by a planning authority—did not originate in the heads of utopian reformers. These utopians aimed rather at the autarkic coexistence of small self-sufficient bodies; take, for instance, Fourier's *phalanstère*. The radicalism of the reformers turned toward socialism when they took the image of an economy managed by a national government or a world authority, implied in the theories of the economists, as a model for their new order.

The Maximization of Profits

It is generally believed that economists, in dealing with the problems of a market economy, are quite unrealistic in assuming that all

4. The doctrine of the predetermined harmony in the operation of an unhampered market system must not be confused with the theorem of the harmony of the rightly understood interests within a market system, although there is something akin between them. Cf. below, pp. 673–682.

men are always eager to gain the highest attainable advantage. They construct, it is said, the image of a perfectly selfish and rationalistic being for whom nothing counts but profit. Such a homo oeconomicus may be a likeness of stock jobbers and speculators. But the immense majority are very different. Nothing for the cognition of reality can be learned from the study of the conduct of this delusive image.

It is not necessary to enter again into a refutation of all the confusion, error, and distortion inherent in this contention. The first two parts of this book have unmasked the fallacies implied. At this point it is enough to deal with the problem of the maximization of profits.

Praxeology in general and economics in its special field assume with regard to the springs of human action nothing other than that acting man wants to remove uneasiness. Under the particular conditions of dealing on the market, action means buying and selling. Everything that economics asserts about demand and supply refers to every instance of demand and supply and not only to demand and supply brought about by some special circumstances requiring a particular description or definition. To assert that a man, faced with the alternative of getting more or less for a commodity he wants to sell, *ceteris paribus* chooses the high price, does not require any further assumption. A higher price means for the seller a better satisfaction of his wants. The same applies mutatis mutandis to the buyer. The amount saved in buying the commodity concerned enables him to spend more for the satisfaction of other needs. To buy in the cheapest market and to sell in the dearest market is, other things being equal, not conduct which would presuppose any special assumptions concerning the actor's motives and morality. It is merely the necessary offshoot of any action under the conditions of market exchange.

In his capacity as a businessman a man is a servant of the consumers, bound to comply with their wishes. He cannot indulge in his own whims and fancies. But his customers' whims and fancies are for him ultimate law, provided these customers are ready to pay for them. He is under the necessity of adjusting his conduct to the demand of the consumers. If the consumers, without a taste for the beautiful, prefer things ugly and vulgar, he must, contrary to his own convictions, supply them with such things.[5] If consumers do not want to pay a higher price for domestic products than for those produced abroad, he must buy the foreign product, provided it is cheaper. An employer cannot grant favors at the expense of his customers. He cannot pay wage rates higher than those determined by the market if the buyers are not ready to pay proportionately higher prices for

5. A painter is a businessman if he is intent upon making paintings which could be sold at the highest price. A painter who does not compromise with the taste of the buying public and, disdaining all unpleasant consequences, lets himself be guided solely by his own ideals is an artist, a creative genius. Cf. above, pp. 139–140.

commodities produced in plants in which wage rates are higher than in other plants.

It is different with man in his capacity as spender of his income. He is free to do what he likes best. He can bestow alms. He can, motivated by various doctrines and prejudices, discriminate against goods of a certain origin or source and prefer the worse or more expensive product to the—technologically—better and cheaper one.

As a rule people in buying do not make gifts to the seller. But nonetheless that happens. The boundaries between buying goods and services needed and giving alms are sometimes difficult to discern. He who buys at a charity sale usually combines a purchase with a donation for a charitable purpose. He who gives a dime to a blind street musician certainly does not pay for the questionable performance; he simply gives alms.

Man in acting is a unity. The businessman who owns the whole firm may sometimes efface the boundaries between business and charity. If he wants to relieve a distressed friend, delicacy of feeling may prompt him to resort to a procedure which spares the latter the embarrassment of living on alms. He gives the friend a job in his office although he does not need his help or could hire an equivalent helper at a lower salary. Then the salary granted appears formally as a part of business outlays. In fact it is the spending of a fraction of the businessman's income. It is, from a correct point of view, consumption and not an expenditure designed to increase the firm's profits.[6]

Awkward mistakes are due to the tendency to look only upon things tangible, visible, and measurable, and to neglect everything else. What the consumer buys is not simply food or calories. He does not want to feed like a wolf, he wants to eat like a man. Food satisfies the appetite of many people the better, the more appetizingly and tastefully it is prepared, the finer the table is set, and the more agreeable the environment is in which the food is consumed. Such things are regarded as of no consequence by a consideration exclusively occupied with the chemical aspects of the process of digestion.[7] But the fact that they play an important role in the determination of food prices is perfectly compatible with the assertion that people prefer, ceteris paribus, to buy in the cheapest market. Whenever a buyer, in choosing between two things which chemists and technologists deem perfectly equal, prefers the more expensive, he has a reason. If he does not err, he

6. Such overlapping of the boundaries between business outlays and consumptive spending is often encouraged by institutional conditions. An expenditure debited to the account of trading expenses reduces net profits and thereby the amount of taxes due. If taxes absorb 50 per cent of profits, the charitable businessman spends only 50 per cent of the gift out of his own pocket. The rest burdens the Department of Internal Revenue.

7. To be sure, a consideration from the point of view of the physiology of nutrition will not regard such things as negligible.

pays for services which chemistry and technology cannot comprehend with their specific methods of investigation. If a man prefers an expensive place to a cheaper one because he likes to sip his cocktails in the neighborhood of a duke, we may remark on his ridiculous vanity. But we must not say that the man's conduct does not aim at an improvement of his own state of satisfaction.

What a man does is always aimed at an improvement of his own state of satisfaction. In this sense—and in no other—we are free to use the term selfishness and to emphasize that action is necessarily always selfish. Even an action directly aiming at the improvement of other people's conditions is selfish. The actor considers it as more satisfactory for himself to make other people eat than to eat himself. His uneasiness is caused by the awareness of the fact that other people are in want.

It is a fact that many people behave in another way and prefer to fill their own stomach and not that of their fellow citizens. But this has nothing to do with economics; it is a datum of historical experience. At any rate, economics refers to every kind of action, no matter whether motivated by the urge of a man to eat or to make other people eat.

If maximizing profits means that a man in all market transactions aims at increasing to the utmost the advantage derived, it is a pleonastic and periphrastic circumlocution. It only asserts what is implied in the very category of action. If it means anything else, it is the expression of an erroneous idea.

Some economists believe that it is the task of economics to establish how in the whole of society the greatest possible satisfaction of all people or of the greatest number could be attained. They do not realize that there is no method which would allow us to measure the state of satisfaction attained by various individuals. They misconstrue the character of judgments which are based on the comparison between various people's happiness. While expressing arbitrary value judgments, they believe themselves to be establishing facts. One may call it just to rob the rich in order to make presents to the poor. However, to call something fair or unfair is always a subjective value judgment and as such purely personal and not liable to any verification or falsification. Economics is not intent upon pronouncing value judgments. It aims at a cognition of the consequences of certain modes of acting.

It has been asserted that the physiological needs of all men are of the same kind and that this equality provides a standard for the measurement of the degree of their objective satisfaction. In expressing such opinions and in recommending the use of such criteria to guide the government's policy, one proposes to deal with men as the breeder deals with his cattle. But the reformers fail to realize that there is no universal principle of alimentation valid for all men. Which one of the various principles one chooses depends entirely on the aims one wants to attain. The cattle breeder does not feed his cows in order to make them happy, but in order to attain the ends which he has assigned to them in his own plans. He may prefer more milk or more meat or something else. What type of men do the man breeders want to rear—athletes or mathematicians? Warriors or factory hands? He who would make man the material of a purposeful system of breeding and feeding would arrogate to himself despotic powers and would use his fellow citizens as means for the attainment of his own ends, which differ from those they themselves are aiming at.

The value judgments of an individual differentiate between what makes him more satisfied and what less. The value judgments a man pronounces about another man's satisfaction do not assert anything about this other man's satisfaction. They only assert what condition of this other man better satisfies the man who pronounces the judgment. The reformers searching for the maximum of general satisfaction have told us merely what state of other people's affairs would best suit themselves.

4. The Autistic Economy

No other imaginary construction has caused more offense than that of an isolated economic actor entirely dependent on himself. However, economics cannot do without it. In order to study interpersonal exchange it must compare it with conditions under which it is absent. It constructs two varieties of the image of an autistic economy in which there is only autistic exchange: the economy of an isolated individual and the economy of a socialist society. In employing this imaginary construction the economists do not bother about the problem of whether or not such a system could really work.[8] They are fully aware of the fact that their imaginary construction is fictitious. Robinson Crusoe, who, for all that, may have existed, and the general manager of a perfectly isolated socialist commonwealth that never existed, would not have been in a position to plan and to act as people can only when taking recourse to economic calculation. However, in the frame of our imaginary construction we are free to pretend that they could calculate whenever such a fiction may be useful for the discussion of the specific problem to be dealt with.

The imaginary construction of an autistic economy is at the bottom of the popular distinction between productivity and profitability as it

8. We are dealing here with problems of theory, not of history. We can therefore abstain from refuting the objections raised against the concept of an isolated actor by referring to the historical role of the self-sufficient household economy.

developed as a yardstick of value judgments. Those resorting to this distinction consider the autistic economy, especially that of the socialist type, the most desirable and most perfect system of economic management. Every phenomenon of the market economy is judged with regard to whether or not it could be justified from the viewpoint of a socialist system. Only to acting that would be purposeful in the plans of such a system's manager are positive value and the epithet *productive* attached. All other activities performed in the market economy are called unproductive in spite of the fact that they may be profitable to those who perform them. Thus, for example, sales promotion, advertising, and banking are considered as activities profitable but nonproductive.

Economics, of course, has nothing to say about such arbitrary value judgments.

5. The State of Rest and the Evenly Rotating Economy

The only method of dealing with the problem of action is to conceive that action ultimately aims at bringing about a state of affairs in which there is no longer any action, whether because all uneasiness has been removed or because any further removal of felt uneasiness is out of the question. Action thus tends toward a state of rest, absence of action.

The theory of prices accordingly analyzes interpersonal exchange from this aspect. People keep on exchanging on the market until no further exchange is possible because no party expects any further improvement of its own conditions from a new act of exchange. The potential buyers consider the prices asked by the potential sellers unsatisfactory, and vice versa. No more transactions take place. A state of rest emerges. This state of rest, which we may call the *plain state of rest,* is not an imaginary construction. It comes to pass again and again. When the stock market closes, the brokers have carried out all orders which could be executed at the market price. Only those potential sellers and buyers who consider the market price too low or too high respectively have not sold or bought.[9] The same is valid with regard to all transactions. The whole market economy is a big exchange or market place, as it were. At any instant all those transactions take place which the parties are ready to enter into at the realizable price. New sales can be effected only when the valuations of at least one of the parties have changed.

9. For the sake of simplicity we disregard the price fluctuations in the course of the business day.

It has been asserted that the notion of the plain state of rest is unsatisfactory. It refers, people have said, only to the determination of prices of goods of which a definite supply is already available, and does not say anything about the effects brought about by these prices upon production. The objection is unfounded. The theorems implied in the notion of the plain state of rest are valid with regard to all transactions without exception. It is true, the buyers of factors of production will immediately embark upon producing and very soon reenter the market in order to sell their products and to buy what they want for their own consumption and for continuing production processes. But this does not invalidate the scheme. This scheme, to be sure, does not contend that the state of rest will last. The lull will certainly disappear as soon as the momentary conditions which brought it about change.

The notion of the plain state of rest is not an imaginary construction but the adequate description of what happens again and again on every market. In this regard it differs radically from the imaginary construction of the final state of rest.

In dealing with the plain state of rest we look only at what is going on right now. We restrict our attention to what has happened momentarily and disregard what will happen later, in the next instant or tomorrow or later. We are dealing only with prices really paid in sales, i.e., with the prices of the immediate past. We do not ask whether or not future prices will equal these prices.

But now we go a step further. We pay attention to factors which are bound to bring about a tendency toward price changes. We try to find out to what goal this tendency must lead before all its driving force is exhausted and a new state of rest emerges. The price corresponding to this future state of rest was called the *natural price* by older economists; nowadays the term *static price* is often used. In order to avoid misleading associations it is more expedient to call it the *final price* and accordingly to speak of the *final state of rest*. This final state of rest is an imaginary construction, not a description of reality. For the final state of rest will never be attained. New disturbing factors will emerge before it will be realized. What makes it necessary to take recourse to this imaginary construction is the fact that the market at every instant is moving toward a final state of rest. Every later new instant can create new facts altering this final state of rest. But the market is always disquieted by a striving after a definite final state of rest.

The market price is a real phenomenon; it is the exchange ratio which was actual in business transacted. The final price is a hypothetical price. The market prices are historical facts and we are therefore in a position to note them with numerical exactitude in dollars and cents. The final price can only be defined by defining the conditions required for its emergence. No definite numerical value in monetary terms or in quantities of other goods can be attributed to it. It will never appear on the market. The market price can never coincide with the final price coordinated to the instant in which this market structure is actual. But catallactics would fail lamentably in its task of analyzing the problems of price determination if it were to neglect dealing with the final price. For in the market situation from which the market price emerges there are already latent forces operating which will go on bringing about price changes until, provided no new data appear, the final price and the final state of rest are established. We would unduly restrict our study of price determination if we were to look only upon the momentary market prices and the plain state of rest and to disregard the fact that the market is already agitated by factors which must result in further price changes and a tendency toward a different state of rest.

The phenomenon with which we have to cope is the fact that changes in the factors which determine the formation of prices do not produce all their effects at once. A span of time must elapse before all their effects are exhausted. Between the appearance of a new datum and the perfect adjustment of the market to it some time must pass. (And, of course, while this period of time elapses, other new data appear.) In dealing with the effects of any change in the factors operating on the market, we must never forget that we are dealing with events taking place in succession, with a series of effects succeeding one another. We are not in a position to know in advance how much time will have to elapse. But we know for certain that some time must elapse, although this period may sometimes be so small that it hardly plays any role in practical life.

Economists often erred in neglecting the element of time. Take for instance the controversy concerning the effects of changes in the quantity of money. Some people were only concerned with its long-run effects, i.e., with the final prices and the final state of rest. Others saw only the short-run effects, i.e., the prices of the instant following the change in the data. Both were mistaken and their conclusions were consequently vitiated. Many more examples of the same blunder could be cited.

The imaginary construction of the final state of rest is marked by paying full regard to change in the temporal succession of events. In this respect it differs from the imaginary construction of the *evenly rotating economy* which is characterized by the elimination of change in the data and of the time element. (It is inexpedient and misleading to call this imaginary construction, as is usual, the static economy or the static equilibrium, and it is a bad mistake to confuse it with the imaginary construction of a stationary economy.[10]) The evenly rotating economy is a fictitious system in which the market prices of all goods and services coincide with the final prices. There are in its frame no price changes whatever; there is perfect price stability. The same market transactions are repeated again and again. The goods of the higher orders pass in the same quantities through the same stages of processing until ultimately the produced consumers' goods come into the hands of the consumers and are consumed. No changes in the market data occur. Today does not differ from yesterday and tomorrow will not differ from today. The system is in perpetual flux, but it remains always at the same spot. It revolves evenly round a fixed center, it rotates evenly. The plain state of rest is disarranged again and again, but it is instantly reestablished at the previous level. All factors, including those bringing about the recurring disarrangement of the plain state of rest, are constant. Therefore prices—commonly called static or equilibrium prices—remain constant too.

The essence of this imaginary construction is the elimination of the lapse of time and of the perpetual change in the market phenomena. The notion of any change with regard to supply and demand is incompatible with this construction. Only such changes as do not affect the configuration of the price-determining factors can be considered in its frame. It is not necessary to people the imaginary world of the evenly rotating economy with immortal, non-aging and nonproliferating men. We are free to assume that infants are born, grow old, and finally die, provided that total population figures and the number of people in every age group remain equal. Then the demand for commodities whose consumption is limited to certain age groups does not alter, although the individuals from whom it originates are not the same.

In reality there is never such a thing as an evenly rotating economic system. However, in order to analyze the problems of change in the data and of unevenly and irregularly varying movement, we must confront them with a fictitious state in which both are hypothetically eliminated. It is therefore preposterous to maintain that the construction of an evenly rotating economy does not elucidate conditions within a changing universe and to require the economists to

10. See below, pp. 250–251.

substitute a study of "dynamics" for their alleged exclusive occupation with "statics." This so-called static method is precisely the proper mental tool for the examination of change. There is no means of studying the complex phenomena of action other than first to abstract from change altogether, then to introduce an isolated factor provoking change, and ultimately to analyze its effects under the assumption that other things remain equal. It is furthermore absurd to believe that the services rendered by the construction of an evenly rotating economy are the more valuable the more the object of our studies, the realm of real action, corresponds to this construction in respect to absence of change. The static method, the employment of the imaginary construction of an evenly rotating economy, is the only adequate method of analyzing the changes concerned without regard to whether they are great or small, sudden or slow.

The objections hitherto raised against the use of the imaginary construction of an evenly rotating economy missed the mark entirely. Their authors did not grasp in what respect this construction is problematic and why it can easily engender error and confusion.

Action is change, and change is in the temporal sequence. But in the evenly rotating economy change and succession of events are eliminated. Action is to make choices and to cope with an uncertain future. But in the evenly rotating economy there is no choosing and the future is not uncertain as it does not differ from the present known state. Such a rigid system is not peopled with living men making choices and liable to error; it is a world of soulless unthinking automatons; it is not a human society, it is an ant hill.

These insoluble contradictions, however, do not affect the service which this imaginary construction renders for the only problems for whose treatment it is both appropriate and indispensable: the problem of the relation between the prices of products and those of the factors required for their production, and the implied problems of entrepreneurship and of profit and loss. In order to grasp the function of entrepreneurship and the meaning of profit and loss, we construct a system from which they are absent. This image is merely a tool for our thinking. It is not the description of a possible and realizable state of affairs. It is even out of the question to carry the imaginary construction of an evenly rotating system to its ultimate logical consequences. For it is impossible to eliminate the entrepreneur from the picture of a market economy. The various complementary factors of production cannot come together spontaneously. They need to be combined by the purposive efforts of men aiming at certain ends and motivated by the urge to improve their state of satisfaction. In eliminating the entrepreneur one eliminates the driving force of the whole market system.

Then there is a second deficiency. In the imaginary construction of an evenly rotating economy, indirect exchange and the use of money are tacitly implied. But what kind of money can that be? In a system without change in which there is no uncertainty whatever about the future, nobody needs to hold cash. Every individual knows precisely what amount of money he will need at any future date. He is therefore in a position to lend all the funds he receives in such a way that the loans fall due on the date he will need them. Let us assume that there is only gold money and only one central bank. With the successive progress toward the state of an evenly rotating economy all individuals and firms restrict step by step their holding of cash and the quantities of gold thus released flow into nonmonetary—industrial—employment. When the equilibrium of the evenly rotating economy is finally reached, there are no more cash holdings; no more gold is used for monetary purposes. The individuals and firms own claims against the central bank, the maturity of each part of which precisely corresponds to the amount they will need on the respective dates for the settlement of their obligations. The central bank does not need any reserves as the total sum of the daily payments of its customers exactly equals the total sum of withdrawals. All transactions can in fact be effected through transfer in the bank's books without any recourse to cash. Thus the "money" of this system is not a medium of exchange; it is not money at all; it is merely a *numéraire,* an ethereal and undetermined unit of accounting of that vague and indefinable character which the fancy of some economists and the errors of many laymen mistakenly have attributed to money. The interposition of these numerical expressions between seller and buyer does not affect the essence of the sales; it is neutral with regard to the people's economic activities. But the notion of a neutral money is unrealizable and inconceivable in itself.[11] If we were to use the inexpedient terminology employed in many contemporary economic writings, we would have to say: Money is necessarily a "dynamic factor"; there is no room left for money in a "static" system. But the very notion of a market economy without money is self-contradictory.

The imaginary construction of an evenly rotating system is a limiting notion. In its frame there is in fact no longer any action. Automatic reaction is substituted for the conscious striving of thinking man after the removal of uneasiness. We can employ this problem-

11. Cf. below, pp. 416–419.

atic imaginary construction only if we never forget what purposes it is designed to serve. We want first of all to analyze the tendency, prevailing in every action, toward the establishment of an evenly rotating economy; in doing so, we must always take into account that this tendency can never attain its goal in a universe not perfectly rigid and immutable, that is, in a universe which is living and not dead. Secondly, we need to comprehend in what respects the conditions of a living world in which there is action differ from those of a rigid world. This we can discover only by the *argumentum a contrario* provided by the image of a rigid economy. Thus we are led to the insight that dealing with the uncertain conditions of the unknown future—that is, speculation—is inherent in every action, and that profit and loss are necessary features of acting which cannot be conjured away by any wishful thinking. The procedures adopted by those economists who are fully aware of these fundamental cognitions may be called the *logical method* of economics as contrasted with the technique of the *mathematical method.*

The mathematical economists disregard dealing with the actions which, under the imaginary and unrealizable assumption that no further new data will emerge, are supposed to bring about the evenly rotating economy. They do not notice the individual speculator who aims not at the establishment of the evenly rotating economy but at profiting from an action which adjusts the conduct of affairs better to the attainment of the ends sought by acting, the best possible removal of uneasiness. They stress exclusively the imaginary state of equilibrium which the whole complex of all such actions would attain in the absence of any further change in the data. They describe this imaginary equilibrium by sets of simultaneous differential equations. They fail to recognize that the state of affairs they are dealing with is a state in which there is no longer any action but only a succession of events provoked by a mystical prime mover. They devote all their efforts to describing, in mathematical symbols, various "equilibria," that is, states of rest and the absence of action. They deal with equilibrium as if it were a real entity and not a limiting notion, a mere mental tool. What they are doing is vain playing with mathematical symbols, a pastime not suited to convey any knowledge.[12]

6. The Stationary Economy

The imaginary construction of a stationary economy has sometimes been confused with that of an evenly rotating economy. But in

12. For a further critical examination of mathematical economics see below, pp. 350–357.

fact these two constructions differ.

The stationary economy is an economy in which the wealth and income of the individuals remain unchanged. With this image changes are compatible which would be incompatible with the construction of the evenly rotating economy. Population figures may rise or drop provided that they are accompanied by a corresponding rise or drop in the sum of wealth and income. The demand for some commodities may change; but these changes must occur so slowly that the transfer of capital from those branches of production which are to be restricted in accordance with them into those to be expanded can be effected by not replacing equipment used up in the shrinking branches and instead investing in the expanding ones.

The imaginary construction of a stationary economy leads to two further imaginary constructions: the progressing (expanding) economy and the retrogressing (shrinking) economy. In the former the per capita quota of wealth and income of the individuals and the population figure tend toward a higher numerical value, in the latter toward a lower numerical value.

In the stationary economy the total sum of all profits and of all losses is zero. In the progressing economy the total amount of profits exceeds the total amount of losses. In the retrogressing economy the total amount of profits is smaller than the total amount of losses.

The precariousness of these three imaginary constructions is to be seen in the fact that they imply the possibility of the measurement of wealth and income. As such measurements cannot be made and are not even conceivable, it is out of the question to apply them for a rigorous classification of the conditions of reality. Whenever economic history ventures to classify economic evolution within a certain period according to the scheme stationary, progressing or retrogressing, it resorts in fact to historical understanding and does not "measure."

7. The Integration of Catallactic Functions

When men in dealing with the problems of their own actions, and when economic history, descriptive economics, and economic statistics in reporting other people's actions, employ the terms entrepreneur, capitalist, landowner, worker, and consumer, they speak of ideal types. When economics employs the same terms it speaks of catallactic categories. The entrepreneurs, capitalists, landowners, workers, and consumers of economic theory are not living men as one meets them in the reality of life and history. They are the embodiment of distinct functions in the market operations. The fact that both acting men and historical sciences apply in their reasoning the results of economics and that they construct their ideal types on the basis of and with reference to the categories of praxeological theory, does not modify the radical logical distinction between ideal type and economic category. The economic categories we are concerned with refer to purely integrated functions, the ideal types refer to historical events. Living and acting man by necessity combines various functions. He is never merely a consumer. He is in addition either an entrepreneur, landowner, capitalist, or worker, or a person supported by the intake earned by such people. Moreover, the functions of the entrepreneur, the landowner, the capitalist, and the worker are very often combined in the same persons. History is intent upon classifying men according to the ends they aim at and the means they employ for the attainment of these ends. Economics, exploring the structure of acting in the market society without any regard to the ends people aim at and the means they employ, is intent upon discerning categories and functions. These are two different tasks. The difference can best be demonstrated in discussing the catallactic concept of the entrepreneur.

In the imaginary construction of the evenly rotating economy there is no room left for entrepreneurial activity, because this construction eliminates any change of data that could affect prices. As soon as one abandons this assumption of rigidity of data, one finds that action must needs be affected by every change in the data. As action necessarily is directed toward influencing a future state of affairs, even if sometimes only the immediate future of the next instant, it is affected by every incorrectly anticipated change in the data occurring in the period of time between its beginning and the end of the period for which it aimed to provide (period of provision[13]). Thus the outcome of action is always uncertain. Action is always speculation. This is valid not only with regard to a market economy but no less for Robinson Crusoe, the imaginary isolated actor, and for the conditions of a socialist economy. In the imaginary construction of an evenly rotating system nobody is an entrepreneur and speculator. In any real and living economy every actor is always an entrepreneur and speculator; the people taken care of by the actors—the minor family members in the market society and the masses of a socialist society—are, although themselves not actors and therefore not speculators, affected by the outcome of the actors' speculations.

Economics, in speaking of entrepreneurs, has in view not men, but a definite function. This function is not the particular feature of a

13. Cf. below, p. 481.

special group or class of men; it is inherent in every action and burdens every actor. In embodying this function in an imaginary figure, we resort to a methodological makeshift. The term entrepreneur as used by catallactic theory means: acting man exclusively seen from the aspect of the uncertainty inherent in every action. In using this term one must never forget that every action is embedded in the flux of time and therefore involves a speculation. The capitalists, the landowners, and the laborers are by necessity speculators. So is the consumer in providing for anticipated future needs. There's many a slip 'twixt cup and lip.

Let us try to think the imaginary construction of a pure entrepreneur to its ultimate logical consequences. This entrepreneur does not own any capital. The capital required for his entrepreneurial activities is lent to him by the capitalists in the form of money loans. The law, it is true, considers him the proprietor of the various means of production purchased by expanding the sums borrowed. Nevertheless he remains propertyless as the amount of his assets is balanced by his liabilities. If he succeeds, the net profit is his. If he fails, the loss must fall upon the capitalists who have lent him the funds. Such an entrepreneur would, in fact, be an employee of the capitalists who speculates on their account and takes a 100 per cent share in the net profits without being concerned about the losses. But even if the entrepreneur is in a position to provide himself a part of the capital required and borrows only the rest, things are essentially not different. To the extent that the losses incurred cannot be borne out of the entrepreneur's own funds, they fall upon the lending capitalists, whatever the terms of the contract may be. A capitalist is always also virtually an entrepreneur and speculator. He always runs the chance of losing his funds. There is no such thing as a perfectly safe investment.

The self-sufficient landowner who tills his estate only to supply his own household is affected by all changes influencing the fertility of his farm or his personal needs. Within a market economy the result of a farmer's activities is affected by all changes regarding the importance of his piece of land for supplying the market. The farmer is clearly, even from the point of view of mundane terminology, an entrepreneur. No proprietor of any means of production, whether they are represented in tangible goods or in money, remains untouched by the uncertainty of the future. The employment of any tangible goods or money for production, i.e., the provision for later days, is in itself an entrepreneurial activity.

Things are essentially the same for the laborer. He is born the proprietor of certain abilities; his innate faculties are a means of production which is better fitted for some kinds of work, less fitted for others, and not at all fitted for still others.[14] If he has acquired the skill needed for the performance of certain kinds of labor, he is, with regard to the time and the material outlays absorbed by this training in the position of an investor. He has made an input in the expectation of being compensated by an adequate output. The laborer is an entrepreneur in so far as his wages are determined by the price the market allows for the kind of work he can perform. This price varies according to the change in conditions in the same way in which the price of every other factor of production varies.

In the context of economic theory the meaning of the terms concerned is this: Entrepreneur means acting man in regard to the changes occurring in the data of the market. Capitalist and landowner mean acting man in regard to the changes in value and price which, even with all the market data remaining equal, are brought about by the mere passing of time as a consequence of the different valuation of present goods and of future goods. Worker means man in regard to the employment of the factor of production human labor. Thus every function is nicely integrated: the entrepreneur earns profit or suffers loss; the owners of means of production (capital goods or land) earn originary interest; the workers earn wages. In this sense we elaborate the imaginary construction of *functional distribution* as different from the actual historical distribution.[15]

Economics, however, always did and still does use the term "entrepreneur" in a sense other than that attached to it in the imaginary construction of functional distribution. It also calls entrepreneurs those who are especially eager to profit from adjusting production to the

14. In what sense labor is to be seen as a nonspecific factor of production see above, pp. 133–135.

15. Let us emphasize again that everybody, laymen included, in dealing with the problems of income determination always takes recourse to this imaginary construction. The economists did not invent it; they only purged it of the deficiencies peculiar to the popular notion. For an epistemological treatment of functional distribution cf. John Bates Clark, *The Distribution of Wealth* (New York, 1908), p. 5, and Eugen von Böhm-Bawerk, *Gesammelte Schriften,* ed. F. X. Weiss (Vienna, 1924), p. 299. The term "distribution" must not deceive anybody; its employment in this context is to be explained by the role played in the history of economic thought by the imaginary construction of a socialist state (cf. above, p. 240). There is in the operation of a market economy nothing which could properly be called distribution. Goods are not first produced and then distributed, as would be the case in a socialist state. The word "distribution" as applied in the term "functional distribution" complies with the meaning attached to "distribution" 150 years ago. In present-day English usage "distribution" signifies dispersal of goods among consumers as effected by commerce.

expected changes in conditions, those who have more initiative, more venturesomeness, and a quicker eye than the crowd, the pushing and promoting pioneers of economic improvement. This notion is narrower than the concept of an entrepreneur as used in the construction of functional distribution; it does not include many instances which the latter includes. It is awkward that the same term should be used to signify two different notions. It would have been more expedient to employ another term for this second notion—for instance, the term "promoter."

It is to be admitted that the notion of the entrepreneur-promoter cannot be defined with praxeological rigor. (In this it is like the notion of money which also defies—different from the notion of a medium of exchange—a rigid praxeological definition.[16]) However, economics cannot do without the promoter concept. For it refers to a datum that is a general characteristic of human nature, that is present in all market transactions and marks them profoundly. This is the fact that various individuals do not react to a change in conditions with the same quickness and in the same way. The inequality of men, which is due to differences both in their inborn qualities and in the vicissitudes of their lives, manifests itself in this way too. There are in the market pacemakers and others who only imitate the procedures of their more agile fellow citizens. The phenomenon of leadership is no less real on the market than in any other branch of human activities. The driving force of the market, the element tending toward unceasing innovation and improvement, is provided by the restlessness of the promoter and his eagerness to make profits as large as possible.

There is, however, no danger that the equivocal use of this term may result in any ambiguity in the exposition of the catallactic system. Wherever any doubts are likely to appear, they can be dispelled by the employment of the term promoter instead of entrepreneur.

The Entrepreneurial Function in the Stationary Economy

The futures market can relieve a promoter of a part of his entrepreneurial function. As far as an entrepreneur has hedged himself through suitable forward transactions against losses he may possibly suffer, he ceases to be an entrepreneur and the entrepreneurial function devolves on the other party to the contract. The cotton spinner who, buying raw cotton for his mill, sells the same quantity forward has abandoned a part of his entrepreneurial function. He will neither profit nor lose from changes in the cotton price occurring in the period concerned. Of course, he does not entirely cease to serve in

16. Cf. below, p. 398.

the entrepreneurial function. Those changes in the price of yarn in general or in the price of the special counts and kinds he produces which are not brought about by a change in the price of raw cotton affect him nonetheless. Even if he spins only as a contractor for a remuneration agreed upon, he is still in an entrepreneurial function with regard to the funds invested in his outfit.

We may construct the image of an economy in which the conditions required for the establishment of futures markets are realized for all kinds of goods and services. In such an imaginary construction the entrepreneurial function is fully separated from all other functions. There emerges a class of pure entrepreneurs. The prices determined on the futures markets direct the whole apparatus of production. The dealers in futures alone make profits and suffer losses. All other people are insured, as it were, against the possible adverse effects of the uncertainty of the future. They enjoy security in this regard. The heads of the various business units are virtually employees, as it were, with a fixed income.

If we further assume that this economy is a stationary economy and that all futures transactions are concentrated in one corporation, it is obvious that the total amount of this corporation's losses precisely equals the total amount of its profits. We need only to nationalize this corporation in order to bring about a socialist state without profits and losses, a state of undisturbed security and stability. But this is so only because our definition of a stationary economy implies equality of the total sum of losses and that of profits. In a changing economy an excess either of profits or of losses must emerge.

It would be a waste of time to dwell longer upon such oversophisticated images which do not further the analysis of economic problems. The only reason for mentioning them is that they reflect ideas which are at the bottom of some criticisms made against the economic system of capitalism and of some delusive plans suggested for a socialist control of business. Now, it is true that a socialist scheme is logically compatible with the unrealizable imaginary constructions of an evenly rotating economy and of a stationary economy. The predilection with which mathematical economists almost exclusively deal with the conditions of these imaginary constructions and with the state of "equilibrium" implied in them, has made people oblivious of the fact that these are unreal, self-contradictory and imaginary expedients of thought and nothing else. They are certainly not suitable models for the construction of a living society of acting men.

XV. THE MARKET

1. The Characteristics of the Market Economy

THE market economy is the social system of the division of labor under private ownership of the means of production. Everybody acts on his own behalf; but everybody's actions aim at the satisfaction of other people's needs as well as at the satisfaction of his own. Everybody in acting serves his fellow citizens. Everybody, on the other hand, is served by his fellow citizens. Everybody is both a means and an end in himself, an ultimate end for himself and a means to other people in their endeavors to attain their own ends.

This system is steered by the market. The market directs the individual's activities into those channels in which he best serves the wants of his fellow men. There is in the operation of the market no compulsion and coercion. The state, the social apparatus of coercion and compulsion, does not interfere with the market and with the citizens' activities directed by the market. It employs its power to beat people into submission solely for the prevention of actions destructive to the preservation and the smooth operation of the market economy. It protects the individual's life, health, and property against violent or fraudulent aggression on the part of domestic gangsters and external foes. Thus the state creates and preserves the environment in which the market economy can safely operate. The Marxian slogan "anarchic production" pertinently characterizes this social structure as an economic system which is not directed by a dictator, a production tsar who assigns to each a task and compels him to obey this command. Each man is free; nobody is subject to a despot. Of his own accord the individual integrates himself into the cooperative system. The market directs him and reveals to him in what way he can best promote his own welfare as well as that of other people. The market is supreme. The market alone puts the whole social system in order and provides it with sense and meaning.

The market is not a place, a thing, or a collective entity. The market is a process, actuated by the interplay of the actions of the various individuals cooperating under the division of labor. The forces determining the—continually changing—state of the market are the value judgments of these individuals and their actions as directed by these value judgments. The state of the market at any instant is the price structure, i.e., the totality of the exchange ratios as established by the interaction of those eager to buy and those eager to sell. There is nothing inhuman or mystical with regard to the market. The market process is entirely a resultant of human actions. Every market phenomenon can be traced back to definite choices of the members of the market society.

The market process is the adjustment of the individual actions of the various members of the market society to the requirements of mutual cooperation. The market prices tell the producers what to produce, how to produce, and in what quantity. The market is the focal point to which the activities of the individuals converge. It is the center from which the activities of the individuals radiate.

The market economy must be strictly differentiated from the second thinkable—although not realizable—system of social cooperation under the division of labor: the system of social or governmental ownership of the means of production. This second system is commonly called socialism, communism, planned economy, or state capitalism. The market economy or capitalism, as it is usually called, and the socialist economy preclude one another. There is no mixture of the two systems possible or thinkable; there is no such thing as a mixed economy, a system that would be in part capitalistic and in part socialist. Production is directed by the market or by the decrees of a production tsar or a committee of production tsars.

If within a society based on private ownership by the means of production some of these means are publicly owned and operated—that is, owned and operated by the government or one of its agencies—this does not make for a mixed system which would combine socialism and capitalism. The fact that the state or municipalities own and operate some plants does not alter the characteristic features of the market economy. These publicly owned and operated enterprises are subject to the sovereignty of the market. They must fit themselves, as buyers of raw materials, equipment, and labor, and as sellers of goods and services, into the scheme of the market economy. They are subject to the laws of the market and thereby depend on the consumers who may or may not patronize them. They must strive for profits or, at least, to avoid losses. The government may cover losses of its plants or shops by drawing on public funds. But this neither eliminates nor mitigates the supremacy of the market; it merely shifts it to another sector. For the means for covering the losses must be raised by the imposition of taxes. But this taxation has its effects on the market and influences the economic structure according to the laws of the market. It is the operation of the market, and not the government collecting the taxes, that decides upon whom the incidence of the taxes falls and how they affect production and consumption. Thus the market, not a government bureau, determines the working of these publicly operated enterprises.

Nothing that is in any way connected with the operation of a market is in the praxeological or economic sense to be called socialism. The notion of socialism as conceived and defined by all socialists implies the absence of a market for factors of production and of prices of such factors. The "socialization" of individual plants, shops, and farms—that is, their transfer from private into public ownership—is a method of bringing about socialism by successive measures. It is a step on the way toward socialism, but not in itself socialism. (Marx and the orthodox Marxians flatly deny the possibility of such a gradual approach to socialism. According to their doctrine the evolution of capitalism will one day reach a point in which at one stroke capitalism is transformed into socialism.)

Government-operated enterprises and the Russian Soviet economy are, by the mere fact that they buy and sell on markets, connected with the capitalist system. They themselves bear witness to this connection by calculating in terms of money. They thus utilize the intellectual methods of the capitalist system that they fanatically condemn.

For monetary economic calculation is the intellectual basis of the market economy. The tasks set to acting within any system of the division of labor cannot be achieved without economic calculation. The market economy calculates in terms of money prices. That it is capable of such calculation was instrumental in its evolution and conditions its present-day operation. The market economy is real because it can calculate.

2. Capital Goods and Capital

There is an impulse inwrought in all living beings that directs them toward the assimilation of matter that preserves, renews, and strengthens their vital energy. The eminence of acting man is manifested in the fact that he consciously and purposefully aims at maintaining and enhancing his vitality. In the pursuit of this aim his ingenuity leads him to the construction of tools that first aid him in the appropriation of food, then, at a later stage, induce him to design methods of increasing the quantity of foodstuffs available, and, finally, enable him to provide for the satisfaction of the most urgently felt among those desires that are specifically human. As Böhm-Bawerk described it: Man chooses roundabout methods of production that require more time but compensate for this delay by generating more and better products.

At the outset of every step forward on the road to a more plentiful existence is saving—the provisionment of products that makes it possible to prolong the average period of time elapsing between the beginning of the production process and its turning out of a product ready for use and consumption. The products accumulated for this purpose are either intermediary stages in the technological process, i.e., tools and half-finished products, or goods ready for consumption that make it possible for man to substitute, without suffering want during the waiting period, a more time-absorbing process for another absorbing a shorter time. These goods are called capital goods. Thus, saving and the resulting accumulation of capital goods are at the beginning of every attempt to improve the material conditions of man; they are the foundation of human civilization. Without saving and capital accumulation there could not be any striving toward non-material ends.[1]

From the notion of capital goods one must clearly distinguish the concept of capital.[2] The concept of capital is the fundamental concept of economic calculation, the foremost mental tool of the conduct of affairs in the market economy. Its correlative is the concept of income.

The notions of capital and income as applied in accountancy and in the mundane reflections of which accountancy is merely a refinement, contrast the means and the ends. The calculating mind of the actor draws a boundary line between the consumer's goods which he plans to employ for the immediate satisfaction of his wants and the goods of all orders—including those of the first order[3]—which he plans to employ for providing by further acting, for the satisfaction of future wants. The differentiation of means and ends thus becomes a differentiation of acquisition and consumption, of business and

1. Capital goods have been defined also as produced factors of production and as such have been opposed to the nature given or original factors of production, i.e., natural resources (land) and human labor. This terminology must be used with great caution as it can be easily misinterpreted and lead to the erroneous concept of real capital criticized below.

2. But, of course, no harm can result if, following the customary terminology, one occasionally adopts for the sake of simplicity the terms "capital accumulation" (or "supply of capital," "capital shortage," etc.) for the terms "accumulation of capital goods," "supply of capital goods," etc.

3. For this man these goods are not goods of the first order, but goods of a higher order, factors of further production.

household, of trading funds and of household goods. The whole complex of goods destined for acquisition is evaluated in money terms, and this sum—the capital—is the starting point of economic calculation. The immediate end of acquisitive action is to increase or, at least, to preserve the capital. That amount which can be consumed within a definite period without lowering the capital is called income. If consumption exceeds the income available, the difference is called capital consumption. If the income available is greater than the amount consumed, the difference is called saving. Among the main tasks of economic calculation are those of establishing the magnitudes of income, saving, and capital consumption.

The reflection which led acting man to the notions implied in the concepts of capital and income are latent in every premeditation and planning of action. Even the most primitive husbandmen are dimly aware of the consequences of acts which to a modern accountant would appear as capital consumption. The hunter's reluctance to kill a pregnant hind and the uneasiness felt even by the most ruthless warriors in cutting fruit trees were manifestations of a mentality which was influenced by such considerations. These considerations were present in the age-old legal institution of usufruct and in analogous customs and practices. But only people who are in a position to resort to monetary calculation can evolve to full clarity the distinction between an economic substance and the advantages derived from it, and can apply it neatly to all classes, kinds, and orders of goods and services. They alone can establish such distinctions with regard to the perpetually changing conditions of highly developed processing industries and the complicated structure of the social cooperation of hundreds of thousands of specialized jobs and performances.

Looking backward from the cognition provided by modern accountancy to the conditions of the savage ancestors of the human race, we may say metaphorically that they too used "capital." A contemporary accountant could apply all the methods of his profession to their primitive tools of hunting and fishing, to their cattle breeding and their tilling of the soil, if he knew what prices to assign to the various items concerned. Some economists concluded therefrom that "capital" is a category of all human production, that it is present in every thinkable system of the conduct of production processes—i.e., no less in Robinson Crusoe's involuntary hermitage than in a socialist society—and that it does not depend upon the practice of monetary calculation.[4] This is, however, a confusion.

4. Cf. e.g., R. v. Strigl, *Kapital und Produktion* (Vienna, 1934), p. 3.

The concept of capital cannot be separated from the context of monetary calculation and from the social structure of a market economy in which alone monetary calculation is possible. It is a concept which makes no sense outside the conditions of a market economy. It plays a role exclusively in the plans and records of individuals acting on their own account in such a system of private ownership of the means of production, and it developed with the spread of economic calculation in monetary terms.[5]

Modern accountancy is the fruit of a long historical evolution. Today there is, among businessmen and accountants, unanimity with regard to the meaning of capital. Capital is the sum of the money equivalent of all assets minus the sum of the money equivalent of all liabilities as dedicated at a definite date to the conduct of the operations of a definite business unit. It does not matter in what these assets may consist, whether they are pieces of land, buildings, equipment, tools, goods of any kind and order, claims, receivables, cash, or whatever.

It is a historical fact that in the early days of accountancy the tradesmen, the pacemakers on the way toward monetary calculation, did not for the most part include the money equivalent of their buildings and land in the notion of capital. It is another historical fact that agriculturists were slow in applying the capital concept to their land. Even today in the most advanced countries only a part of the farmers are familiar with the practice of sound accountancy. Many farmers acquiesce in a system of bookkeeping that neglects to pay heed to the land and its contribution to production. Their book entries do not include the money equivalent of the land and are consequently indifferent to changes in this equivalent. Such accounts are defective because they fail to convey that information which is the sole aim sought by capital accounting. They do not indicate whether or not the operation of the farm has brought about a deterioration in the land's capacity to contribute to production, that is, in its objective use value. If an erosion of the soil has taken place, their books ignore it, and thus the calculated income (net yield) is greater than a more complete method of bookkeeping would have shown.

It is necessary to mention these historical facts because they influenced the endeavors of the economists to construct the notion of *real capital.*

The economists were and are still today confronted with the superstitious belief that the scarcity of factors of production could be brushed away, either entirely or at least to some extent, by increas-

5. Cf. Frank A. Fetter in *Encyclopaedia of the Social Sciences.* III, 190.

ing the amount of money in circulation and by credit expansion. In order to deal adequately with this fundamental problem of economic policy they considered it necessary to construct a notion of real capital and to oppose it to the notion of capital as applied by the businessman whose calculation refers to the whole complex of his acquisitive activities. At the time the economists embarked upon these endeavors the place of the money equivalent of land in the concept of capital was still questioned. Thus the economists thought it reasonable to disregard land in constructing their notion of real capital. They defined real capital as the totality of the produced factors of production available. Hairsplitting discussions were started as to whether inventories of consumers' goods held by business units are or are not real capital. But there was almost unanimity that cash is not real capital.

Now this concept of a totality of the produced factors of production is an empty concept. The money equivalent of the various factors of production owned by a business unit can be determined and summed up. But if we abstract from such an evaluation in money terms, the totality of the produced factors of production is merely an enumeration of physical quantities of thousands and thousands of various goods. Such an inventory is of no use to acting. It is a description of a part of the universe in terms of technology and topography and has no reference whatever to the problems raised by the endeavors to improve human well-being. We may acquiesce in the terminological usage of calling the produced factors of production *capital goods*. But this does not render the concept of real capital any more meaningful.

The worst outgrowth of the use of the mythical notion of real capital was that economists began to speculate about a spurious problem called the productivity of (real) capital. A factor of production is by definition a thing that is able to contribute to the success of a process of production. Its market price reflects entirely the value that people attach to this contribution. The services expected from the employment of a factor of production (i.e., its contribution to productivity) are in market transactions paid according to the full value people attach to them. These factors are considered valuable only on account of these services. These services are the only reason why prices are paid for them. Once these prices are paid, nothing remains that can bring about further payments on the part of anybody as a compensation for additional productive services of these factors of production. It was a blunder to explain interest as an income derived from the productivity of capital.[6]

6. Cf. below, pp. 526–534.

No less detrimental was a second confusion derived from the real capital concept. People began to mediate upon a concept of *social capital* as different from *private capital.* Starting from the imaginary construction of a socialist economy, they were intent upon defining a capital concept suitable to the economic activities of the general manager of such a system. They were right in assuming that this manager would be eager to know whether his conduct of affairs was successful (viz., from the point of view of his own valuations and the ends aimed at in accordance with these valuations) and how much he could expend for his wards' consumption without diminishing the available stock of factors of production and thus impairing the yield of further production. A socialist government would badly need the concepts of capital and income as a guide for its operations. However, in an economic system in which there is no private ownership of the means of production, no market, and no prices for such goods the concepts of capital and income are mere academic postulates devoid of any practical application. In a socialist economy there are capital goods, but no capital.

The notion of capital makes sense only in the market economy. It serves the deliberations and calculations of individuals or groups of individuals operating on their own account in such an economy. It is a device of capitalists, entrepreneurs, and farmers eager to make profits and to avoid losses. It is not a category of all acting. It is a category of acting within a market economy.

3. Capitalism

All civilizations have up to now been based on private ownership of the means of production. In the past civilization and private property have been linked together. Those who maintain that economics is an experimental science and nevertheless recommend public control of the means of production, lamentably contradict themselves. If historical experience could teach us anything, it would be that private property is inextricably linked with civilization. There is no experience to the effect that socialism could provide a standard of living as high as that provided by capitalism.[7]

The system of market economy has never been fully and purely tried. But there prevailed in the orbit of Western civilization since the Middle Ages by and large a general tendency toward the abolition of institutions hindering the operation of the market economy. With the successive progress of this tendency, population figures multiplied

7. For an examination of the Russian "experiment" see Mises, *Planned Chaos* (Irvington-on-Hudson, 1947), pp. 80–87 (reprinted in the new edition of Mises, *Socialism* [New Haven, 1951] pp. 527–592).

and the masses' standard of living was raised to an unprecedented and hitherto undreamed of level. The average American worker enjoys amenities for which Croesus, Crassus, the Medici, and Louis XIV would have envied him.

The problems raised by the socialist and interventionist critique of the market economy are purely economic and can be dealt with only in the way in which this book tries to deal with them: by a thorough analysis of human action and all thinkable systems of social cooperation. The psychological problem of why people scorn and disparage capitalism and call everything they dislike "capitalistic" and everything they praise "socialistic" concerns history and must be left to the historians. But there are several other issues which we must stress at this point.

The advocates of totalitarianism consider "capitalism" a ghastly evil, an awful illness that came upon mankind. In the eyes of Marx it was an inevitable stage of mankind's evolution, but for all that the worst of evils; fortunately salvation is imminent and will free man forever from this disaster. In the opinion of other people it would have been possible to avoid capitalism if only men had been more moral or more skillful in the choice of economic policies. All such lucubrations have one feature in common. They look upon capitalism as if it were an accidental phenomenon which could be eliminated without altering conditions that are essential in civilized man's acting and thinking. As they neglect to bother about the problem of economic calculation, they are not aware of the consequences which the abolition of the monetary calculus is bound to bring about. They do not realize that socialist men for whom arithmetic will be of no use in planning action, will differ entirely in their mentality and in their mode of thinking from our contemporaries. In dealing with socialism, we must not overlook this mental transformation, even if we were ready to pass over in silence the disastrous consequences which would result for man's material well-being.

The market economy is a man-made mode of acting under the division of labor. But this does not imply that it is something accidental or artificial and could be replaced by another mode. The market economy is the product of a long evolutionary process. It is the outcome of man's endeavors to adjust his action in the best possible way to the given conditions of his environment that he cannot alter. It is the strategy, as it were, by the application of which man has triumphantly progressed from savagery to civilization.

Some authors argue: Capitalism was the economic system which brought about the marvelous achievements of the last two hundred years; therefore it is done for because what was beneficial in the past cannot be so for our time and for the future. Such reasoning is in open contradiction to the principles of experimental cognition. There is no need at this point to raise again the question of whether or not the science of human action can adopt the methods of the experimental natural sciences. Even if it were permissible to answer this question in the affirmative, it would be absurd to argue as these *à rebours* experimentalists do. Experimental science argues that because *a* was valid in the past, it will be valid in the future too. It must never argue the other way round and assert that because *a* was valid in the past, it is not valid in the future.

It is customary to blame the economists for an alleged disregard of history. The economists, it is contended, consider the market economy as the ideal and eternal pattern of social cooperation. They concentrate their studies upon investigating the conditions of the market economy and neglect everything else. They do not bother about the fact that capitalism emerged only in the last two hundred years and that even today it is restricted to a comparatively small area of the earth's surface and to a minority of peoples. There were and are, say these critics, other civilizations with a different mentality and different modes of conducting economic affairs. Capitalism is, when seen *sub specie aeternitatis,* a passing phenomenon, an ephemeral stage of historical evolution, just the transition from precapitalistic ages to a postcapitalistic future.

All these criticisms are spurious. Economics is, of course, not a branch of history or of any other historical science. It is the theory of all human action, the general science of the immutable categories of action and of their operation under all thinkable special conditions under which man acts. It provides as such the indispensable mental tool for dealing with historical and ethnographic problems. A historian or an ethnographer who neglects in his work to take full advantage of the results of economics is doing a poor job. In fact he does not approach the subject matter of his research unaffected by what he disregards as theory. He is at every step of his gathering of allegedly unadulterated facts, in arranging these facts, and in his conclusions derived from them, guided by confused and garbled remnants of perfunctory economic doctrines constructed by botchers in the centuries preceding the elaboration of an economic science and long since entirely exploded.

The analysis of the problems of the market society, the only pattern of human action in which calculation can be applied in planning action, opens access to the analysis of all thinkable modes of action and of all economic problems with which historians and ethnographers are confronted. All noncapitalistic methods of economic management can be studied only under the hypothetical assumption that in them too cardinal numbers can be used in recording past action and planning future action. This is why economists place the study of the pure market economy in the center of their investigations.

It is not the economists who lack the "historical sense" and ignore the factor of evolution, but their critics. The economists have always been fully aware of the fact that the market economy is the product of a long historical process which began when the human race emerged from the ranks of the other primates. The champions of what is mistakenly called "historicism" are intent upon undoing the effects of evolutionary changes. In their eyes everything the existence of which they cannot trace back to a remote past or cannot discover in the customs of some primitive Polynesian tribes is artificial, even decadent. They consider the fact that an institution was unknown to savages as a proof of its uselessness and rottenness. Marx and Engels and the Prussian professors of the Historical School exulted when they learned that private property is "only" a historical phenomenon. For them this was the proof that their socialist plans were realizable.[8]

The creative genius is at variance with his fellow citizens. As the pioneer of things new and unheard of he is in conflict with their uncritical acceptance of traditional standards and values. In his eyes the routine of the regular citizen, the average or common man, is simply stupidity. For him "bourgeois" is a synonym of imbecility.[9]

8. The most amazing product of this widespread mode of thought is the book of a Prussian professor, Bernhard Laum (*Die geschlossene Wirtschaft* [Tübingen, 1933]). Laum assembles a vast collection of quotations from ethnographical writings showing that many primitive tribes considered economic autarky as natural, necessary, and morally good. He concludes from this that autarky is the natural and most expedient state of economic management and that the return to autarky which he advocates is "a biologically necessary process." (p. 491).

9. Guy de Maupassant analyzed Flaubert's alleged hatred of the bourgeois in *Etude sur Gustave Flaubert* (reprinted in *Oeuvres complètes de Gustave Flaubert* [Paris, 1885], Vol. VII). Flaubert, says Maupassant, "aimait le monde" (p. 67); that is, he liked to move in the circle of Paris society composed of aristocrats, wealthy bourgeois, and the élite of artists, writers, philosophers, scientists, statesmen, and entrepreneurs (promoters). He used the term bourgeois as synonymous with imbecility and defined it this way: "I call a bourgeois whoever has mean thoughts (*pense bassement*)." Hence it is obvious that in employing the term bourgeois Flaubert did not have in mind the *bourgeoisie* as a social class, but a kind of imbecility he most frequently found in this class. He was full of contempt for the common man (*"le bon peuple"*) as well. However, as he had more frequent contacts with the *"gens du monde"* than with workers, the stupidity of the former annoyed him more than that of the latter (p. 59). These observations of Maupassant held good not only for Flaubert, but for the "anti-bourgeois" sentiments of all artists. Incidentally, it must be emphasized that from a Marxian point of view Flaubert is a "bourgeois" writer and his novels are an "ideological superstructure" of the "capitalist or bourgeois mode of production."

The frustrated artists who take delight in aping the genius's mannerism in order to forget and to conceal their own impotence adopt this terminology. These Bohemians call everything they dislike "bourgeois." Since Marx has made the term "capitalist" equivalent to "bourgeois," they use both words synonymously. In the vocabularies of all languages the words "capitalistic" and "bourgeois" signify today all that is shameful, degrading, and infamous.[10] Contrariwise, people call all that they deem good and praiseworthy "socialist." The regular scheme of arguing is this: A man arbitrarily calls anything he dislikes "capitalistic," and then deduces from this appellation that the thing is bad.

This semantic confusion goes still further. Sismondi, the romantic eulogists of the Middle Ages, all socialist authors, the Prussian Historical School, and the American Institutionalists taught that capitalism is an unfair system of exploitation sacrificing the vital interests of the majority of people for the sole benefit of a small group of profiteers. No decent man can advocate this "mad" system. The economists who contend that capitalism is beneficial not only to a small group but to everyone are "sycophants of the bourgeoisie." They are either too dull to recognize the truth or bribed apologists of the selfish class interests of the exploiters.

Capitalism, in the terminology of these foes of liberty, democracy, and the market economy, means the economic policy advocated by big business and millionaires. Confronted with the fact that some—but certainly not all—wealthy entrepreneurs and capitalists nowadays favor measures restricting free trade and competition and resulting in monopoly, they say: Contemporary capitalism stands for protectionism, cartels, and the abolition of competition. It is true, they add, that at a definite period of the past British capitalism favored free trade both on the domestic market and in international relations. This was because at that time the class interests of the British bourgeoisie were best served by such a policy. Conditions, however, changed and today capitalism, i.e., the doctrine advocated by the exploiters, aims at another policy.

It has already been pointed out that this doctrine badly distorts both economic theory and historical facts.[11] There were and there will always be people whose selfish ambitions demand protection for vested interests and who hope to derive advantage from measures restricting competition. Entrepreneurs grown old and tired and the decadent heirs of people who succeeded in the past dislike the agile

10. The Nazis used "Jewish" as a synonym of both "capitalist" and "bourgeois."
11. Cf. above, pp. 80–84.

parvenus who challenge their wealth and their eminent social position. Whether or not their desire to make economic conditions rigid and to hinder improvements can be realized, depends on the climate of public opinion. The ideological structure of the nineteenth century, as fashioned by the prestige of the teachings of the liberal economists, rendered such wishes vain. When the technological improvements of the age of liberalism revolutionized the traditional methods of production, transportation, and marketing, those whose vested interests were hurt did not ask for protection because it would have been a hopeless venture. But today it is deemed a legitimate task of government to prevent an efficient man from competing with the less efficient. Public opinion sympathizes with the demands of powerful pressure groups to stop progress. The butter producers are with considerable success fighting against margarine and the musicians against recorded music. The labor unions are deadly foes of every new machine. It is not amazing that in such an environment less efficient businessmen aim at protection against more efficient competitors.

It would be correct to describe this state of affairs in this way: Today many or some groups of business are no longer liberal; they do not advocate a pure market economy and free enterprise, but, on the contrary, are asking for various measures of government interference with business. But it is entirely misleading to say that the meaning of the concept of capitalism has changed and that "mature capitalism"—as the American Institutionalists call it—or "late capitalism"—as the Marxians call it—is characterized by restrictive policies to protect the vested interests of wage earners, farmers, shopkeepers, artisans, and sometimes also of capitalists and entrepreneurs. The concept of capitalism is as an economic concept immutable; if it means anything, it means the market economy. One deprives oneself of the semantic tools to deal adequately with the problems of contemporary history and economic policies if one acquiesces in a different terminology. This faulty nomenclature becomes understandable only if we realize that the pseudo-economists and the politicians who apply it want to prevent people from knowing what the market economy really is. They want to make people believe that all the repulsive manifestations of restrictive government policies are produced by "capitalism."

4. The Sovereignty of the Consumers

The direction of all economic affairs is in the market society a task of the entrepreneurs. Theirs is the control of production. They are at the helm and steer the ship. A superficial observer would believe that they are supreme. But they are not. They are bound to obey unconditionally the captain's orders. The captain is the consumer. Neither the entrepreneurs nor the farmers nor the capitalists determine what has to be produced. The consumers do that. If a businessman does not strictly obey the orders of the public as they are conveyed to him by the structure of market prices, he suffers losses, he goes bankrupt, and is thus removed from his eminent position at the helm. Other men who did better in satisfying the demand of the consumers replace him.

The consumers patronize those shops in which they can buy what they want at the cheapest price. Their buying and their abstention from buying decides who should own and run the plants and the farms. They make poor people rich and rich people poor. They determine precisely what should be produced, in what quality, and in what quantities. They are merciless bosses, full of whims and fancies, changeable and unpredictable. For them nothing counts other than their own satisfaction. They do not care a whit for past merit and vested interests. If something is offered to them that they like better or that is cheaper, they desert their old purveyors. In their capacity as buyers and consumers they are hard-hearted and callous, without consideration for other people.

Only the sellers of goods and services of the first order are in direct contact with the consumers and directly depend on their orders. But they transmit the orders received from the public to all those producing goods and services of the higher orders. For the manufacturers of consumers' goods, the retailers, the service trades, and the professions are forced to acquire what they need for the conduct of their own business from those purveyors who offer them at the cheapest price. If they were not intent upon buying in the cheapest market and arranging their processing of the factors of production so as to fill the demands of the consumers in the best and cheapest way, they would be forced to go out of business. More efficient men who succeeded better in buying and processing the factors of production would supplant them. The consumer is in a position to give free rein to his caprices and fancies. The entrepreneurs, capitalists, and farmers have their hands tied; they are bound to comply in their operations with the orders of the buying public. Every deviation from the lines prescribed by the demand of the consumers debits their account. The slightest deviation, whether willfully brought about or caused by error, bad judgment, or inefficiency, restricts their profits or makes them disappear. A more serious deviation results in losses and thus impairs or entirely absorbs their wealth. Capitalists, entrepreneurs, and landowners can only preserve and increase their wealth by filling best the orders of the consumers. They are not free to spend money which the consumers are not prepared to refund to them in paying more for the products. In the conduct of their business affairs they must be unfeeling and stony-hearted because the consumers, their bosses, are themselves unfeeling and stony-hearted.

The consumers determine ultimately not only the prices of the consumers' goods, but no less the prices of all factors of production. They determine the income of every member of the market economy. The consumers, not the entrepreneurs, pay ultimately the wages earned by every worker, the glamorous movie star as well as the charwoman. With every penny spent the consumers determine the direction of all production processes and the details of the organization of all business activities. This state of affairs has been described by calling the market a democracy in which every penny gives a right to cast a ballot.[12] It would be more correct to say that a democratic constitution is a scheme to assign to the citizens in the conduct of government the same supremacy the market economy gives them in their capacity as consumers. However, the comparison is imperfect. In the political democracy only the votes cast for the majority candidate or the majority plan are effective in shaping the course of affairs. The votes polled by the minority do not directly influence policies. But on the market no vote is cast in vain. Every penny spent has the power to work upon the production processes. The publishers cater not only to the majority by publishing detective stories, but also to the minority reading lyrical poetry and philosophical tracts. The bakeries bake bread not only for healthy people, but also for the sick on special diets. The decision of a consumer is carried into effect with the full momentum he gives it through his readiness to spend a definite amount of money.

It is true, in the market the various consumers have not the same voting right. The rich cast more votes than the poorer citizens. But this inequality is itself the outcome of a previous voting process. To be rich, in a pure market economy, is the outcome of success in filling best the demands of the consumers. A wealthy man can preserve his wealth only by continuing to serve the consumers in the most efficient way.

Thus the owners of the material factors of production and the entrepreneurs are virtually mandataries or trustees of the consumers, revocably appointed by an election daily repeated.

There is in the operation of a market economy only one instance in which the proprietary class is not completely subject to the suprem-

12. Cf. Frank A. Fetter, *The Principles of Economics* (3d ed. New York, 1913), pp. 394, 410.

acy of the consumers. Monopoly prices are an infringement of the sway of the consumers.

The Metaphorical Employment of the Terminology of Political Rule

The orders given by businessmen in the conduct of their affairs can be heard and seen. Nobody can fail to become aware of them. Even messenger boys know that the boss runs things around the shop. But it requires a little more brains to notice the entrepreneur's dependence on the market. The orders given by the consumers are not tangible, they cannot be perceived by the senses. Many people lack the discernment to take cognizance of them. They fall victim to the delusion that entrepreneurs and capitalists are irresponsible autocrats whom nobody calls to account for their actions.[13]

The outgrowth of this mentality is the practice of applying to business the terminology of political rule and military action. Successful businessmen are called kings or dukes, their enterprises an empire, a kingdom, or a dukedom. If this idiom were only a harmless metaphor, there would be no need to criticize it. But it is the source of serious errors which play a sinister role in contemporary doctrines.

Government is an apparatus of compulsion and coercion. It has the power to obtain obedience by force. The political sovereign, be it an autocrat or the people as represented by its mandataries, has power to crush rebellions as long as his ideological might subsists.

The position which entrepreneurs and capitalists occupy in the market economy is of a different character. A "chocolate king" has no power over the consumers, his patrons. He provides them with chocolate of the best possible quality and at the cheapest price. He does not rule the consumers, he serves them. The consumers are not tied to him. They are free to stop patronizing his shops. He loses his "kingdom" if the consumers prefer to spend their pennies elsewhere. Nor does he "rule" his workers. He hires their services by paying them precisely that amount which the consumers are ready to restore to him in buying the product. Still less do the capitalists and entrepreneurs exercise political control. The civilized nations of Europe and America were long controlled by governments which did not considerably hinder the operation of the market economy. Today these countries too are dominated by parties which are hostile to capitalism and believe that every harm inflicted upon capitalists and entrepreneurs is extremely beneficial to the people.

In an unhampered market economy the capitalists and entrepre-

13. Beatrice Webb, Lady Passfield, herself the daughter of a wealthy businessman, may be quoted as an outstanding example of this mentality. Cf. *My Apprenticeship* (New York, 1926), p. 42.

neurs cannot expect an advantage from bribing officeholders and politicians. On the other hand, the officeholders and politicians are not in a position to blackmail businessmen and to extort graft from them. In an interventionist country powerful pressure groups are intent upon securing for their members privileges at the expense of weaker groups and individuals. Then the businessmen may deem it expedient to protect themselves against discriminatory acts on the part of the executive officers and the legislature by bribery; once used to such methods, they may try to employ them in order to secure privileges for themselves. At any rate the fact that businessmen bribe politicians and officeholders and are blackmailed by such people does not indicate that they are supreme and rule the countries. It is those ruled—and not the rulers—who bribe and are paying tribute.

The majority of businessmen are prevented from resorting to bribery either by their moral convictions or by fear. They venture to preserve the free enterprise system and to defend themselves against discrimination by legitimate democratic methods. They form trade associations and try to influence public opinion. The results of these endeavors have been rather poor, as is evidenced by the triumphant advance of anticapitalist policies. The best that they have been able to achieve is to delay for a while some especially obnoxious measures.

Demagogues misrepresent this state of affairs in the crassest way. They tell us that these associations of bankers and manufacturers are the true rulers of their countries and that the whole apparatus of what they call "plutodemocratic" government is dominated by them. A simple enumeration of the laws passed in the last decades by any country's legislature is enough to explode such legends.

5. Competition

In nature there prevail irreconcilable conflicts of interests. The means of subsistence are scarce. Proliferation tends to outrun subsistence. Only the fittest plants and animals survive. The antagonism between an animal starving to death and another that snatches the food away from it is implacable.

Social cooperation under the division of labor removes such antagonisms. It substitutes partnership and mutuality for hostility. The members of society are united in a common venture.

The term competition as applied to the conditions of animal life signifies the rivalry between animals which manifests itself in their search for food. We may call this phenomenon *biological competition*. Biological competition must not be confused with *social competition,* i.e., the striving of individuals to attain the most favorable position in the system of social cooperation. As there will always be positions which men value more highly than others, people will strive for them and try to outdo rivals. Social competition is consequently present in every conceivable mode of social organization. If we want to think of a state of affairs in which there is no social competition, we must construct the image of a socialist system in which the chief in his endeavors to assign to everybody his place and task in society is not aided by any ambition on the part of his subjects. The individuals are entirely indifferent and do not apply for special appointments. They behave like the stud horses which do not try to put themselves in a favorable light when the owner picks out the stallion to impregnate his best brood mare. But such people would no longer be acting men.

Catallactic competition is emulation between people who want to surpass one another. It is not a fight, although it is usual to apply to it in a metaphorical sense the terminology of war and internecine conflict, of attack and defense, of strategy and tactics. Those who fail are not annihilated; they are removed to a place in the social system that is more modest, but more adequate to their achievements than that which they had planned to attain.

In a totalitarian system, social competition manifests itself in the endeavors of people to court the favor of those in power. In the market economy, competition manifests itself in the fact that the sellers must outdo one another by offering better or cheaper goods and services, and that the buyers must outdo one another by offering higher prices. In dealing with this variety of social competition which may be called *catallactic competition,* we must guard ourselves against various popular fallacies.

The classical economists favored the abolition of all trade barriers preventing people from competing on the market. Such restrictive laws, they explained, result in shifting production from those places in which natural conditions of production are more favorable to places in which they are less favorable. They protect the less efficient man against his more efficient rival. They tend to perpetuate backward technological methods of production. In short they curtail production and thus lower the standard of living. In order to make all people more prosperous, the economists argued, competition should be free to everybody. In this sense they used the term *free competition.* There was nothing metaphysical in their employment of the term *free.* They advocated the nullification of privileges barring people from access to certain trades and markets. All the sophisticated lucubrations caviling at the metaphysical connotations of the adjective *free* as applied to competition are spurious; they have no reference whatever to the catallactic problem of competition.

As far as natural conditions come into play, competition can only be "free" with regard to those factors of production which are not scarce and therefore not objects of human action. In the catallactic field competition is always restricted by the inexorable scarcity of the economic goods and services. Even in the absence of institutional barriers erected to restrict the number of those competing, the state of affairs is never such as to enable everyone to compete in all sectors of the market. In each sector only comparatively small groups can engage in competition.

Catallactic competition, one of the characteristic features of the market economy, is a social phenomenon. It is not a right, guaranteed by the state and the laws, that would make it possible for every individual to choose ad libitum the place in the structure of the division of labor he likes best. To assign to everybody his proper place in society is the task of the consumers. Their buying and abstention from buying is instrumental in determining each individual's social position. Their supremacy is not impaired by any privileges granted to the individuals qua producers. Entrance into a definite branch of industry is virtually free to newcomers only as far as the consumers approve of this branch's expansion or as far as the newcomers succeed in supplanting those already occupied in it by filling better or more cheaply the demands of the consumers. Additional investment is reasonable only to the extent that it fills the most urgent among the not yet satisfied needs of the consumers. If the existing plants are sufficient, it would be wasteful to invest more capital in the same industry. The structure of market prices pushes the new investors into other branches.

It is necessary to emphasize this point because the failure to grasp it is at the root of many popular complaints about the impossibility of competition. Some sixty years ago people used to declare: You cannot compete with the railroad companies; it is impossible to challenge their position by starting competing lines; in the field of land transportation there is no longer competition. The truth was that at that time the already operating lines were by and large sufficient. For additional capital investment the prospects were more favorable in improving the serviceableness of the already operating lines and in other branches of business than in the construction of new railroads. However, this did not interfere with further technological progress in transportation technique. The bigness and the economic "power" of the railroad companies did not impede the emergence of the motor car and the airplane.

Today people assert the same with regard to various branches of big business: You cannot challenge their position, they are too big and too powerful. But competition does not mean that anybody can prosper by simply imitating what other people do. It means the opportunity to serve the consumers in a better or cheaper way without being restrained by privileges granted to those whose vested interests the innovation hurts. What a newcomer who wants to defy the vested interests of the old established firms needs most is brains and ideas. If his project is fit to fill the most urgent of the unsatisfied needs of the consumers or to purvey them at a cheaper price than their old purveyors, he will succeed in spite of the much talked of bigness and power of the old firms.

Catallactic competition must not be confused with prize fights and beauty contests. The purpose of such fights and contests is to discover who is the best boxer or the prettiest girl. The social function of catallactic competition is, to be sure, not to establish who is the smartest boy and to reward the winner by a title and medals. Its function is to safeguard the best satisfaction of the consumers attainable under the given state of the economic data.

Equality of opportunity is a factor neither in prize fights and beauty contests nor in any other field of competition, whether biological or social. The immense majority of people are by the physiological structure of their bodies deprived of a chance to attain the honors of a boxing champion or a beauty queen. Only very few people can compete on the labor market as opera singers and movie stars. The most favorable opportunity to compete in the field of scientific achievement is provided to the university professors. Yet, thousands and thousands of professors pass away without leaving any trace in the history of ideas and scientific progress, while many of the handicapped outsiders win glory through marvelous contributions.

It is usual to find fault with the fact that catallactic competition is not open to everybody in the same way. The start is much more difficult for a poor boy than for the son of a wealthy man. But the consumers are not concerned about the problem of whether or not the men who shall serve them start their careers under equal conditions. Their only interest is to secure the best possible satisfaction of their needs. As the system of hereditary property is more efficient in this regard, they prefer it to other less efficient systems. They look at the matter from the point of view of social expediency and social welfare, not from the point of view of an alleged, imaginary, and unrealizable "natural" right of every individual to compete with equal opportunity. The realization of such a right would require placing at a disadvantage those born with better intelligence and greater will power than the average man. It is obvious that this would be absurd.

The term competition is mainly employed as the antithesis of monopoly. In this mode of speech the term monopoly is applied in different meanings which must be clearly separated.

The first connotation of monopoly, very frequently implied in the popular use of the term, signifies a state of affairs in which the monopolist, whether an individual or a group of individuals, exclusively controls one of the vital conditions of human survival. Such a monopolist has the power to starve to death all those who do not obey his orders. He dictates and the others have no alternative but either to surrender or to die. With regard to such a monopoly there is no market or any kind of catallactic competition. The monopolist is the master and the rest are slaves entirely dependent on his good graces. There is no need to dwell upon this kind of monopoly. It has no reference whatever to a market economy. It is enough to cite one instance. A world-embracing socialist state would exercise such an absolute and total monopoly; it would have the power to crush its opponents by starving them to death.[14]

The second connotation of monopoly differs from the first in that it describes a state of affairs compatible with the conditions of a market economy. A monopolist in this sense is an individual or a group of individuals, fully combining for joint action, who has the exclusive control of the supply of a definite commodity. If we define the term monopoly in this way, the domain of monopoly appears very vast. The products of the processing industries are more or less different from one another. Each factory turns out products different from those of the other plants. Each hotel has a monopoly on the sale of its services on the site of its premises. The professional services rendered by a physician or a lawyer are never perfectly equal to those rendered by any other physician or lawyer. Except for certain raw materials, foodstuffs, and other staple goods, monopoly is everywhere on the market.

However, the mere phenomenon of monopoly is without any significance and relevance for the operation of the market and the determination of prices. It does not give the monopolist any advantage in selling his products. Under copyright law every rhymester enjoys a monopoly in the sale of his poetry. But this does not influence the market. It may happen that no price whatever can be realized for his stuff and that his books can only be sold at their waste paper value.

Monopoly in this second connotation of the term becomes a factor in the determination of prices only if the demand curve for the

14. Cf. Trotsky (1937) as quoted by Hayek, *The Road to Serfdom* (London, 1944), p. 89.

monopoly good concerned is shaped in a particular way. If conditions are such that the monopolist can secure higher net proceeds by selling a smaller quantity of his product at a higher price than by selling a greater quantity of his supply at a lower price, there emerges a *monopoly price* higher than the potential market price would have been in the absence of monopoly. Monopoly prices are an important market phenomenon, while monopoly as such is only important if it can result in the formation of monopoly prices.

It is customary to call prices which are not monopoly prices *competitive prices*. While it is questionable whether or not this terminology is expedient, it is generally accepted and it would be difficult to change it. But one must guard oneself against its misinterpretation. It would be a serious blunder to deduce from the antithesis between monopoly price and competitive price that the monopoly price is the outgrowth of the absence of competition. There is always catallactic competition on the market. Catallactic competition is no less a factor in the determination of monopoly prices than it is in the determination of competitive prices. The shape of the demand curve that makes the appearance of monopoly prices possible and directs the monopolists' conduct is determined by the competition of all other commodities competing for the buyers' dollars. The higher the monopolist fixes the price at which he is ready to sell, the more potential buyers turn their dollars toward other vendible goods. On the market every commodity competes with all other commodities.

There are people who maintain that the catallactic theory of prices is of no use for the study of reality because there has never been "free" competition or because, at least today, there is no longer any such thing. All these doctrines are wrong.[15] They misconstrue the phenomena and simply do not know what competition really is. It is a fact that the history of the last decades is a record of policies aiming at the restriction of competition. It is the manifest intention of these schemes to grant privileges to certain groups of producers by protecting them against the competition of more efficient competitors. In many instances these policies have brought about the conditions required for the emergence of monopoly prices. In many other instances this was not the case and the result was only a state of affairs preventing many capitalists, entrepreneurs, farmers, and workers from entering those branches of industry in which they would have rendered the most valuable services to their fellow citizens. Catallactic

15. For a refutation of the fashionable doctrines of imperfect and of monopolistic competition cf. F. A. Hayek, *Individualism and Economic Order* (Chicago, 1948), pp. 92–118.

competition has been seriously restricted, but the market economy is still in operation although sabotaged by government and labor union interference. The system of catallactic competition is still functioning although the productivity of labor has been seriously reduced.

It is the ultimate end of these anticompetition policies to substitute for capitalism a socialist system of planning in which there is no catallactic competition at all. While shedding crocodile tears about the decline of competition, the planners want to abolish this "mad" competitive system. They have attained their goal in some countries. But in the rest of the world they have only restricted competition in some branches of business by increasing the number of people competing in other branches.

The forces aiming at a restriction of competition play a great role in our day. It is an important task of the history of our age to deal with them. Economic theory has no need to refer to them in particular. The fact that there are trade barriers, privileges, cartels, government monopolies and labor unions is merely a datum of economic history. It does not require special theorems for its interpretation.

6. Freedom

Philosophers and lawyers have bestowed much pain upon attempts to define the concept of freedom or liberty. It can hardly be maintained that these endeavors have been successful.

The concept of freedom makes sense only as far as it refers to interhuman relations. There were authors who told stories about an original—natural—freedom which man was supposed to have enjoyed in a fabulous state of nature that preceded the establishment of social relations. Yet such mentally and economically self-sufficient individuals or families, roaming about the country, were only free as long as they did not run into a stronger fellow's way. In the pitiless biological competition the stronger was always right, and the weaker was left no choice except unconditional surrender. Primitive man was certainly not born free.

Only within the frame of a social system can a meaning be attached to the term *freedom*. As a praxeological term, freedom refers to the sphere within which an acting individual is in a position to choose between alternative modes of action. A man is free in so far as he is permitted to choose ends and the means to be used for the attainment of those ends. A man's freedom is most rigidly restricted by the laws of nature as well as by the laws of praxeology. He cannot attain ends which are incompatible with one another. If he chooses to indulge in gratifications that produce definite effects upon the functioning of his body or his mind, he must put up with these consequences. It would be inexpedient to say that man is not free because he cannot enjoy the pleasures of indulgence in certain drugs without being affected by their inevitable results, commonly considered as highly undesirable. While this is admitted by and large by all reasonable people, there is no such unanimity with regard to the appreciation of the laws of praxeology.

Man cannot have both the advantages derived from peaceful cooperation under the principle of the division of labor within society and the licence of embarking upon conduct that is bound to disintegrate society. He must choose between the observance of certain rules that make life within society possible and the poverty and insecurity of the "dangerous life" in a state of perpetual warfare among independent individuals. This is no less rigid a law determining the outcome of all human action than are the laws of physics.

Yet there is a far-reaching difference between the sequels resulting from a disregard of the laws of nature and those resulting from a disregard of the laws of praxeology. Of course, both categories of law take care of themselves without requiring any enforcement on the part of man. But the effects of a choice made by an individual are different. A man who absorbs poison harms himself alone. But a man who chooses to resort to robbery upsets the whole social order. While he alone enjoys the short-term gains derived from his action, the disastrous long-term effects harm all the people. His deed is a crime because it has detrimental effects on his fellow men. If society were not to prevent such conduct, it would soon become general and put an end to social cooperation and all the boons the latter confers upon everybody.

In order to establish and to preserve social cooperation and civilization, measures are needed to prevent asocial individuals from committing acts that are bound to undo all that man has accomplished in his progress from the Neanderthal level. In order to preserve the state of affairs in which there is protection of the individual against the unlimited tyranny of stronger and smarter fellows, an institution is needed that curbs all antisocial elements. Peace—the absence of perpetual fighting by everyone against everyone—can be attained only by the establishment of a system in which the power to resort to violent action is monopolized by a social apparatus of compulsion and coercion and the application of this power in any individual case is regulated by a set of rules—the man-made laws as distinguished both from the laws of nature and those of praxeology. The essential implement of a social system is the operation of such an apparatus commonly called government.

The concepts of freedom and bondage make sense only when referring to the way in which government operates. It would be highly inexpedient and misleading to say that a man is not free because, if he wants to stay alive, his power to choose between a drink of water and one of potassium cyanide is restricted by nature. It would be no less inconvenient to call a man unfree because the law imposes sanctions upon his desire to kill another man and because the police and the penal courts enforce them. As far as the government—the social apparatus of compulsion and oppression—confines the exercise of its violence and the threat of such violence to the suppression and prevention of antisocial action, there prevails what reasonably and meaningfully can be called liberty. What is restrained is merely conduct that is bound to disintegrate social cooperation and civilization, thus throwing all people back to conditions that existed at the time homo sapiens emerged from the purely animal existence of its nonhuman ancestors. Such coercion does not substantially restrict man's power to choose. Even if there were no government enforcing man-made laws, the individual could not have both the advantages derived from the existence of social cooperation on the one hand, and, on the other, the pleasures of freely indulging in the rapacious animal instincts of aggression.

In the market economy, the laissez-faire type of social organization, there is a sphere within which the individual is free to choose between various modes of acting without being restrained by the threat of being punished. If, however, the government does more than protect people against violent or fraudulent aggression on the part of antisocial individuals, it reduces the sphere of the individual's freedom to act beyond the degree to which it is restricted by praxeological law. Thus we may define freedom as that state of affairs in which the individual's discretion to choose is not constrained by governmental violence beyond the margin within which the praxeological law restricts it anyway.

This is what is meant if one defines freedom as the condition of an individual within the frame of the market economy. He is free in the sense that the laws and the government do not force him to renounce his autonomy and self-determination to a greater extent than the inevitable praxeological law does. What he foregoes is only the animal freedom of living without any regard to the existence of other specimens of his species. What the social apparatus of compulsion and coercion achieves is that individuals whom malice, shortsightedness or mental inferiority prevent from realizing that by indulging in acts that are destroying society they are hurting themselves and all other human beings are compelled to avoid such acts.

From this point of view one has to deal with the often-raised problem of whether conscription and the levy of taxes mean a restriction of freedom. If the principles of the market economy were acknowledged by all people all over the world, there would not be any reason to wage war and the individual states could live in undisturbed peace.[16] But as conditions are in our age, a free nation is continually threatened by the aggressive schemes of totalitarian autocracies. If it wants to preserve its freedom, it must be prepared to defend its independence. If the government of a free country forces every citizen to cooperate fully in its designs to repel the aggressors and every able-bodied man to join the armed forces, it does not impose upon the individual a duty that would step beyond the tasks the praxeological law dictates. In a world full of unswerving aggressors and enslavers, integral unconditional pacifism is tantamount to unconditional surrender to the most ruthless oppressors. He who wants to remain free, must fight unto death those who are intent upon depriving him of his freedom. As isolated attempts on the part of each individual to resist are doomed to failure, the only workable way is to organize resistance by the government. The essential task of government is defense of the social system not only against domestic gangsters but also against external foes. He who in our age opposes armaments and conscription is, perhaps unbeknown to himself, an abettor of those aiming at the enslavement of all.

The maintenance of a government apparatus of courts, police officers, prisons, and of armed forces requires considerable expenditure. To levy taxes for these purposes is fully compatible with the freedom the individual enjoys in a free market economy. To assert this does not, of course, amount to a justification of the confiscatory and discriminatory taxation methods practiced today by the self-styled progressive governments. There is need to stress this fact, because in our age of interventionism and the steady "progress" toward totalitarianism the governments employ the power to tax for the destruction of the market economy.

Every step a government takes beyond the fulfillment of its essential functions of protecting the smooth operation of the market economy against aggression, whether on the part of domestic or foreign disturbers, is a step forward on a road that directly leads into the totalitarian system where there is no freedom at all.

Liberty and freedom are the conditions of man within a contractual society. Social cooperation under a system of private ownership of the factors of production means that within the range of the market

16. See below, p. 685.

the individual is not bound to obey and to serve an overlord. As far as he gives and serves other people, he does so of his own accord in order to be rewarded and served by the receivers. He exchanges goods and services, he does not do compulsory labor and does not pay tribute. He is certainly not independent. He depends on the other members of society. But this dependence is mutual. The buyer depends on the seller and the seller on the buyer.

The main concern of many writers of the nineteenth and twentieth centuries was to misrepresent and to distort this obvious state of affairs. The workers, they said, are at the mercy of their employers. Now, it is true that the employer has the right to fire the employee. But if he makes use of this right in order to indulge in his whims, he hurts his own interests. It is to his own disadvantage if he discharges a better man in order to hire a less efficient one. The market does not directly prevent anybody from arbitrarily inflicting harm on his fellow citizens; it only puts a penalty upon such conduct. The shopkeeper is free to be rude to his customers provided he is ready to bear the consequences. The consumers are free to boycott a purveyor provided they are ready to pay the costs. What impels every man to the utmost exertion in the service of his fellow men and curbs innate tendencies toward arbitrariness and malice is, in the market, not compulsion and coercion on the part of gendarmes, hangmen, and penal courts; it is self-interest. The member of a contractual society is free because he serves others only in serving himself. What restrains him is only the inevitable natural phenomenon of scarcity. For the rest he is free in the range of the market.

There is no kind of freedom and liberty other than the kind which the market economy brings about. In a totalitarian hegemonic society the only freedom that is left to the individual, because it cannot be denied to him, is the freedom to commit suicide.

The state, the social apparatus of coercion and compulsion, is by necessity a hegemonic bond. If government were in a position to expand its power ad libitum, it could abolish the market economy and substitute for it all-round totalitarian socialism. In order to prevent this, it is necessary to curb the power of government. This is the task of all constitutions, bills of rights, and laws. This is the meaning of all struggles which men have fought for liberty.

The detractors of liberty are in this sense right in calling it a 'bourgeois" issue and in blaming the rights guaranteeing liberty for being negative. In the realm of state and government, liberty means restraint imposed upon the exercise of the police power.

There would be no need to dwell upon this obvious fact if the champions of the abolition of liberty had not purposely brought about a semantic confusion. They realized that it was hopeless for them to fight openly and sincerely for restraint and servitude. The notions liberty and freedom had such prestige that no propaganda could shake their popularity. Since time immemorial in the realm of Western civilization liberty has been considered as the most precious good. What gave to the West its eminence was precisely its concern about liberty, a social ideal foreign to the oriental peoples. The social philosophy of the Occident is essentially a philosophy of freedom. The main content of the history of Europe and the communities founded by European emigrants and their descendants in other parts of the world was the struggle for liberty. "Rugged" individualism is the signature of our civilization. No open attack upon the freedom of the individual had any prospect of success.

Thus the advocates of totalitarianism chose other tactics. They reversed the meaning of words. They call true or genuine liberty the condition of the individuals under a system in which they have no right other than to obey orders. In the United States, they call themselves true *liberals* because they strive after such a social order. They call democracy the Russian methods of dictatorial government. They call the labor union methods of violence and coercion "industrial democracy." They call freedom of the press a state of affairs in which only the government is free to publish books and newspapers. They define liberty as the opportunity to do the "right" things, and, of course, they arrogate to themselves the determination of what is right and what is not. In their eyes government omnipotence means full liberty. To free the police power from all restraints is the true meaning of their struggle for freedom.

The market economy, say these self-styled liberals, grants liberty only to a parasitic class of exploiters, the bourgeoisie. These scoundrels enjoy the freedom to enslave the masses. The wage earner is not free; he must toil for the sole benefit of his masters, the employers. The capitalists appropriate to themselves what according to the inalienable rights of man should belong to the worker. Under socialism the worker will enjoy freedom and human dignity because he will no longer have to slave for a capitalist. Socialism means the emancipation of the common man, means freedom for all. It means, moreover, riches for all.

These doctrines have been able to triumph because they did not encounter effective rational criticism. Some economists did a brilliant job in unmasking their crass fallacies and contradictions. But the public ignores the teachings of economics. The arguments advanced by average politicians and writers against socialism are either silly or irrelevant. It is useless to stand upon an alleged "natural" right of individuals to own property if other people assert that the foremost "natural" right is that of income equality. Such disputes can never be settled. It is beside the point to criticize nonessential, attendant features of the socialist program. One does not refute socialism by attacking the socialists' stand on religion, marriage, birth control, and art. Moreover, in dealing with such matters the critics of socialism were often in the wrong.

In spite of these serious shortcomings of the defenders of economic freedom it was impossible to fool all the people all the time about the essential features of socialism. The most fanatical planners were forced to admit that their projects involve the abolition of many freedoms people enjoy under capitalism and "plutodemocracy." Pressed hard, they resorted to a new subterfuge. The freedom to be abolished, they emphasize, is merely the spurious "economic" freedom of the capitalists that harms the common man. Outside the "economic sphere" freedom will not only be fully preserved, but considerably expanded. "Planning for Freedom" has lately become the most popular slogan of the champions of totalitarian government and the Russification of all nations.

The fallacy of this argument stems from the spurious distinction between two realms of human life and action, entirely separated from one another, viz., the "economic" sphere and the "noneconomic" sphere. With regard to this issue there is no need to add anything to what has been said in the preceding parts of this book. However, there is another point to be stressed.

Freedom, as people enjoyed it in the democratic countries of Western civilization in the years of the old liberalism's triumph, was not a product of constitutions, bills of rights, laws, and statutes. Those documents aimed only at safeguarding liberty and freedom, firmly established by the operation of the market economy, against encroachments on the part of officeholders. No government and no civil law can guarantee and bring about freedom otherwise than by supporting and defending the fundamental institutions of the market economy. Government means always coercion and compulsion and is by necessity the opposite of liberty. Government is a guarantor of liberty and is compatible with liberty only if its range is adequately restricted to the preservation of what is called economic freedom. Where there is no market economy, the best-intentioned provisions of constitutions and laws remain a dead letter.

The freedom of man under capitalism is an effect of competition.

The worker does not depend on the good graces of an employer. If his employer discharges him, he finds another employer.[17] The consumer is not at the mercy of the shopkeeper. He is free to patronize another shop if he likes. Nobody must kiss other people's hands or fear their disfavor. Interpersonal relations are businesslike. The exchange of goods and services is mutual; it is not a favor to sell or to buy, it is a transaction dictated by selfishness on either side.

It is true that in his capacity as a producer every man depends either directly—e.g., the entrepreneur—or indirectly—e. g., the hired worker—on the demands of the consumers. However, this dependence upon the supremacy of the consumers is not unlimited. If a man has a weighty reason for defying the sovereignty of the consumers, he can try it. There is in the range of the market a very substantial and effective right to resist oppression. Nobody is forced to go into the liquor industry or into a gun factory if his conscience objects. He may have to pay a price for his conviction; there are in this world no ends the attainment of which is gratuitous. But it is left to a man's own decision to choose between a material advantage and the call of what he believes to be his duty. In the market economy the individual alone is the supreme arbiter in matters of his satisfaction.[18]

Capitalist society has no means of compelling a man to change his occupation or his place of work other than to reward those complying with the wants of the consumers by higher pay. It is precisely this kind of pressure which many people consider as unbearable and hope to see abolished under socialism. They are too dull to realize that the only alternative is to convey to the authorities full power to determine in what branch and at what place a man should work.

17. See below, pp. 598–600.

18. In the political sphere resistance to oppression on the part of the established government is the *ultima ratio* of those oppressed. However illegal and unbearable the oppression, however lofty and noble the motives of the rebels, and however beneficial the consequences of their violent resistance, a revolution is always an illegal act, disintegrating the established order of state and government. It is an essential mark of civil government that it is in its territory the only agency which is in a position to resort to measures of violence or to declare legitimate whatever violence is practiced by other agencies. A revolution is an act of warfare between the citizens, it abolishes the very foundations of legality and is at best restrained by the questionable international customs concerning belligerency. If victorious, it can afterwards establish a new legal order and a new government. But it can never enact a legal "right to resist oppression." Such an impunity granted to people venturing armed resistance to the armed forces of the government is tantamount to anarchy and incompatible with any mode of government. The Constituent Assembly of the first French Revolution was foolish enough to decree such a right; but it was not so foolish as to take its own decree seriously.

In his capacity as consumer man is no less free. He alone decides what is more and what is less important for him. He chooses how to spend his money according to his own will.

The substitution of economic planning for the market economy removes all freedom and leaves to the individual merely the right to obey. The authority directing all economic matters controls all aspects of a man's life and activities. It is the only employer. All labor becomes compulsory labor because the employee must accept what the chief deigns to offer him. The economic tsar determines what and how much of each the consumer may consume. There is no sector of human life in which a decision is left to the individual's value judgments. The authority assigns a definite task to him, trains him for his job, and employs him at the place and in the manner it deems expedient.

As soon as the economic freedom which the market economy grants to its members is removed, all political liberties and bills of rights become humbug. Habeas corpus and trial by jury are a sham if, under the pretext of economic expediency, the authority has full power to relegate every citizen it dislikes to the arctic or to a desert and to assign him "hard labor" for life. Freedom of the press is a mere blind if the authority controls all printing offices and paper plants. And so are all the other rights of men.

A man is free as far as he shapes his life according to his own plans. A man whose fate is determined by the plans of a superior authority, in which the exclusive power to plan is vested, is not free in the sense in which this term "free" was used and understood by all people until the semantic revolution of our day brought about a confusion of tongues.

7. Inequality of Wealth and Income

The inequality of individuals with regard to wealth and income is an essential feature of the market economy.

The fact that freedom is incompatible with equality of wealth and income has been stressed by many authors. There is no need to enter into an examination of the emotional arguments advanced in these writings. Neither is it necessary to raise the question of whether the renunciation of liberty could in itself guarantee the establishment of equality of wealth and income and whether or not a society could subsist on the basis of such an equality. Our task is merely to describe the role inequality plays in the framework of the market society.

In the market society direct compulsion and coercion are practiced only for the sake of preventing acts detrimental to social cooperation.

For the rest individuals are not molested by the police power. The law-abiding citizen is free from the interference of jailers and hangmen. What pressure is needed to impel an individual to contribute his share to the cooperative effort of production is exercised by the price structure of the market. This pressure is indirect. It puts on each individual's contribution a premium graduated according to the value which the consumers attach to this contribution. In rewarding the individual's effort according to its value, it leaves to everybody the choice between a more or less complete utilization of his own faculties and abilities. This method cannot, of course, eliminate the disadvantages of inherent personal inferiority. But it provides an incentive to everybody to exert his faculties and abilities to the utmost.

The only alternative to this financial pressure as exercised by the market is direct pressure and compulsion as exercised by the police power. The authorities must be entrusted with the task of determining the quantity and quality of work that each individual is bound to perform. As individuals are unequal with regard to their abilities, this requires an examination of their personalities on the part of the authorities. The individual becomes an inmate of a penitentiary, as it were, to whom a definite task is assigned. If he fails to achieve what the authorities have ordered him to do, he is liable to punishment.

It is important to realize in what the difference consists between direct pressure exercised for the prevention of crime and that exercised for the extortion of a definite performance. In the former case all that is required from the individual is to avoid a certain mode of conduct, precisely determined by law. As a rule it is easy to establish whether or not this interdiction has been observed. In the second case the individual is liable to accomplish a definite task; the law forces him toward an indefinite action, the determination of which is left to the decision of the executive power. The individual is bound to obey whatever the administration orders him to do. Whether or not the command issued by the executive power was adequate to his forces and faculties and whether or not he has complied with it to the best of his abilities is extremely difficult to establish. Every citizen is with regard to all aspects of his personality and with regard to all manifestations of his conduct subject to the decisions of the authorities. In the market economy in a trial before a penal court the prosecutor is obliged to produce sufficient evidence that the defendant is guilty. But in matters of the performance of compulsory work it devolves upon the defendant to prove that the task assigned to him was beyond his abilities or that he has done all that can be expected of him. The administrators combine in their persons the offices of the legislator, the executor of the law, the public prosecutor, and the judge. The defendants are entirely at their mercy. This is what people have in mind when speaking of lack of freedom.

No system of the social division of labor can do without a method that makes individuals responsible for their contributions to the joint productive effort. If this responsibility is not brought about by the price structure of the market and the inequality of wealth and income it begets, it must be enforced by the methods of direct compulsion as practiced by the police.

8. Entrepreneurial Profit and Loss

Profit, in a broader sense, is the gain derived from action; it is the increase in satisfaction (decrease in uneasiness) brought about; it is the difference between the higher value attached to the result attained and the lower value attached to the sacrifices made for its attainment; it is, in other words, yield minus costs. To make profit is invariably the aim sought by any action. If an action fails to attain the ends sought, yield either does not exceed costs or lags behind costs. In the latter case the outcome means a loss, a decrease in satisfaction.

Profit and loss in this original sense are psychic phenomena and as such not open to measurement and a mode of expression which could convey to other people precise information concerning their intensity. A man can tell a fellow man that *a* suits him better than *b;* but he cannot communicate to another man, except in vague and indistinct terms, how much the satisfaction derived from *a* exceeds that derived from *b*.

In the market economy all those things that are bought and sold against money are marked with money prices. In the monetary calculus profit appears as a surplus of money received over money expended and loss as a surplus of money expended over money received. Profit and loss can be expressed in definite amounts of money. It is possible to ascertain in terms of money how much an individual has profited or lost. However, this is not a statement about this individual's psychic profit or loss. It is a statement about a social phenomenon, about the individual's contribution to the societal effort as it is appraised by the other members of society. It does not tell us anything about the individual's increase or decrease in satisfaction or happiness. It merely reflects his fellow men's evaluation of his contribution to social cooperation. This evaluation is ultimately determined by the efforts of every member of society to attain the highest possible psychic profit. It is the resultant of the composite effect of all these people's subjective and personal value judgments as manifested in their conduct on the market. But it must not be confused with these value judgments as such.

We cannot even think of a state of affairs in which people act without the intention of attaining psychic profit and in which their actions result neither in psychic profit nor in psychic loss.[19] In the imaginary construction of an evenly rotating economy there are neither money profits nor money losses. But every individual derives a psychic profit from his actions, or else he would not act at all. The farmer feeds and milks his cows and sells the milk because he values the things he can buy against the money thus earned more highly than the costs expended. The absence of money profits or losses in such an evenly rotating system is due to the fact that, if we disregard the differences brought about by the higher valuation of present goods as compared with future goods, the sum of the prices of all complementary factors needed for production precisely equals the price of the product.

In the changing world of reality differences between the sum of the prices of the complementary factors of production and the prices of the products emerge again and again. It is these differences that bring about money profits and money losses. As far as such changes affect the sellers of labor and those of the original nature-given factors of production and of the capitalists as moneylenders, we will deal with them later. At this point we are dealing with the promoters' entrepreneurial profit and loss. It is this problem that people have in mind when employing the terms profit and loss in mundane speech.

Like every acting man, the entrepreneur is always a speculator. He deals with the uncertain conditions of the future. His success or failure depends on the correctness of his anticipation of uncertain events. If he fails in his understanding of things to come, he is doomed. The only source from which an entrepreneur's profits stem is his ability to anticipate better than other people the future demand of the consumers. If everybody is correct in anticipating the future state of the market of a certain commodity, its price and the prices of the complementary factors of production concerned would already today be adjusted to this future state. Neither profit nor loss can emerge for those embarking upon this line of business.

The specific entrepreneurial function consists in determining the

19. If an action neither improves nor impairs the state of satisfaction, it still involves a psychic loss because of the uselessness of the expended psychic effort. The individual concerned would have been better off if he had inertly enjoyed life.

employment of the factors of production. The entrepreneur is the man who dedicates them to special purposes. In doing so he is driven solely by the selfish interest in making profits and in acquiring wealth. But he cannot evade the law of the market. He can succeed only by best serving the consumers. His profit depends on the approval of his conduct by the consumers.

One must not confuse entrepreneurial profit and loss with other factors affecting the entrepreneur's proceeds.

The entrepreneur's technological ability does not affect the specific entrepreneurial profit or loss. As far as his own technological activities contribute to the returns earned and increase his net income, we are confronted with a compensation for work rendered. It is wages paid to the entrepreneur for his labor. Neither does the fact that not every process of production succeeds technologically in bringing about the product expected, influence the specific entrepreneurial profit or loss. Such failures are either avoidable or unavoidable. In the first case they are due to the technologically inefficient conduct of affairs. Then the losses resulting are to be debited to the entrepreneur's personal insufficiency, i.e., either to his lack of technological ability or to his lack of the ability to hire adequate helpers. In the second case the failures are due to the fact that the present state of technological knowledge prevents us from fully controlling the conditions on which success depends. This deficiency may be caused either by incomplete knowledge concerning the conditions of success or by ignorance of methods for controlling fully some of the known conditions. The price of the factors of production takes into account this unsatisfactory state of our knowledge and technological power. The price of arable land, for instance, takes into full account the fact that there are bad harvests, as it is determined by the anticipated average yield. The fact that the bursting of bottles reduces the output of champagne does not affect entrepreneurial profit and loss. It is merely one of the factors determining the cost of production and the price of champagne.[20]

Accidents affecting the process of production, the means of production, or the products while they are still in the hands of the entrepreneur are an item in the bill of production costs. Experience, which conveys to the businessman all other technological knowledge, pro-

20. Cf. Mangoldt, *Die Lehre vom Unternehmergewinn* (Leipzig, 1855), p. 82. The fact that out of 100 liters of plain wine one cannot produce 100 liters of champagne, but a smaller quantity, has the same significance as the fact that 100 kilograms of sugar beet do not yield 100 kilograms of sugar but a smaller quantity.

vides him also with information about the average reduction in the quantity of physical output which such accidents are likely to bring about. By opening contingency reserves, he converts their effects into regular costs of production. With regard to contingencies the expected incidence of which is too rare and too irregular to be dealt with in this way by individual firms of normal size, concerted action on the part of sufficiently large groups of firms takes care of the matter. The individual firms cooperate under the principle of insurance against damage caused by fire, flood, or other similar contingencies. Then an insurance premium is substituted for an appropriation to a contingency reserve. At any rate, the risks incurred by accidents do not introduce uncertainty into the conduct of the technological processes.[21] If an entrepreneur neglects to deal with them duly, he gives proof of his technical insufficiency. The losses thus incurred are to be debited to bad techniques applied, not to his entrepreneurial function.

The elimination of those entrepreneurs who fail to give to their enterprises the adequate degree of technological efficiency or whose technological ignorance vitiates their cost calculation is effected on the market in the same way in which those deficient in the performance of the specific entrepreneurial functions are eliminated. It may happen that an entrepreneur is so successful in his specific entrepreneurial function that he can compensate losses caused by his technological failure. It may also happen that an entrepreneur can counterbalance losses due to failure in his entrepreneurial function by the advantages derived from his technological superiority or from the differential rent yielded by the higher productivity of the factors of production he employs. But one must not confuse the various functions which are combined in the conduct of a business unit. The technologically more efficient entrepreneur earns higher wage rates or quasi-wage rates than the less efficient in the same way in which the more efficient worker earns more than the less efficient. The more efficient machine and the more fertile soil produce higher physical returns per unit of costs expended; they yield a differential rent when compared with the less efficient machine and the less fertile soil. The higher wage rates and the higher rent are, ceteris paribus, the corollary of higher physical output. But the specific entrepreneurial profits and losses are not produced by the quantity of physical output. They depend on the adjustment of output to the most urgent wants of the consumers. What produces them is the extent to which

21. Cf. Knight, *Risk, Uncertainty and Profit* (Boston, 1921), pp. 211–213.

the entrepreneur has succeeded or failed in anticipating the future—necessarily uncertain—state of the market.

The entrepreneur is also jeopardized by political dangers. Government policies, revolutions, and wars can damage or annihilate his enterprise. Such events do not affect him alone; they affect the market economy as such and all individuals, although not all of them to the same extent. For the individual entrepreneur they are data which he cannot alter. If he is efficient, he will anticipate them in time. But it is not always possible for him to adjust his operations in such a way as to avoid damage. If the dangers expected concern only a part of the territory which is accessible to his entrepreneurial activities, he can avoid operating in the menaced areas and can prefer countries in which the danger is less imminent. But if he cannot emigrate, he must stay where he is. If all entrepreneurs were fully convinced that the total victory of Bolshevism was impending, they would nevertheless not abandon their entrepreneurial activities. The expectation of imminent expropriation will impel the capitalists to consume their funds. The entrepreneurs will be forced to adjust their plans to the market situation created by such capital consumption and the threatened nationalization of their shops and plants. But they will not stop operating. If some entrepreneurs go out of business, others will take their place—newcomers or old entrepreneurs expanding the size of their enterprises. In the market economy there will always be entrepreneurs. Policies hostile to capitalism may deprive the consumers of the greater part of the benefits they would have reaped from unhampered entrepreneurial activities. But they cannot eliminate the entrepreneurs as such if they do not entirely destroy the market economy.

The ultimate source from which entrepreneurial profit and loss are derived is the uncertainty of the future constellation of demand and supply.

If all entrepreneurs were to anticipate correctly the future state of the market, there would be neither profits nor losses. The prices of all the factors of production would already today be fully adjusted to tomorrow's prices of the products. In buying the factors of production the entrepreneur would have to expend (with due allowance for the difference between the prices of present goods and future goods) no less an amount than the buyers will pay him later for the product. An entrepreneur can make a profit only if he anticipates future conditions more correctly than other entrepreneurs. Then he buys the complementary factors of production at prices the sum of which, including allowance for the time difference, is smaller than the price at which he sells the product.

If we want to construct the image of changing economic conditions in which there are neither profits nor losses, we must resort to an unrealizable assumption: perfect foresight of all future events on the part of all individuals. If those primitive hunters and fishermen to whom it is customary to ascribe the first accumulation of produced factors of production had known in advance all the future vicissitudes of human affairs, and if they and all their descendants until the last day of judgment, equipped with the same omniscience, had appraised all factors of production accordingly, entrepreneurial profits and losses would never have emerged. Entrepreneurial profits and losses are created through the discrepancy between the expected prices and the prices later really fixed on the markets. It is possible to confiscate profits and to transfer them from the individuals to whom they have accrued to other people. But neither profits nor losses can ever disappear from a changing world not populated solely with omniscient people.

9. Entrepreneurial Profits and Losses in a Progressing Economy

In the imaginary construction of a stationary economy the total sum of all entrepreneurs' profits equals the total sum of all entrepreneurs' losses. What one entrepreneur profits is in the total economic system counterbalanced by another entrepreneur's loss. The surplus which all the consumers together expend for the acquisition of a certain commodity is counterbalanced by the reduction in their expenditure for the acquisition of other commodities.[22]

It is different in a progressing economy.

We call a progressing economy an economy in which the per capita quota of capital invested is increasing. In using this term we do not imply value judgments. We adopt neither the "materialistic" view that such a progression is good nor the "idealistic" view that it is bad or at least irrelevant from a "higher point of view." Of course, it is a well-known fact that the immense majority of people consider the consequences of progress in this sense as the most desirable state of affairs and yearn for conditions which can be realized only in a progressing economy.

In the stationary economy the entrepreneurs, in the pursuit of their

22. If we were to apply the faulty concept of a "national income" as used in popular speech, we would have to say that no part of national income goes into profits.

specific functions, cannot achieve anything other than to withdraw factors of production, provided that they are still convertible,[23] from one line of business in order to employ them in another line, or to direct the restoration of the equivalent of capital goods used up in the course of production processes toward the expansion of certain branches of industry at the expense of other branches. In the progressing economy the range of entrepreneurial activities includes, moreover, the determination of the employment of the additional capital goods accumulated by new savings. The injection of these additional capital goods is bound to increase the total sum of the income produced, i.e., of that supply of consumers' goods which can be consumed without diminishing the capital available and thereby without reducing the output of future production. The increase of income is effected either by an expansion of production without altering the technological methods of production or by an improvement in technological methods which would not have been feasible under the previous conditions of a less ample supply of capital goods.

It is out of this additional wealth that the surplus of the total sum of entrepreneurial profits over the total sum of entrepreneurial losses flows. But it can be easily demonstrated that this surplus can never exhaust the total increase in wealth brought about by economic progress. The laws of the market divide this additional wealth between the entrepreneurs and the suppliers of labor and those of certain material factors of production in such a way that the lion's share goes to the nonentrepreneurial groups.

First of all we must realize that entrepreneurial profits are not a lasting phenomenon but only temporary. There prevails an inherent tendency for profits and losses to disappear. The market is always moving toward the emergence of the final prices and the final state of rest. If new changes in the data were not to interrupt this movement and not to create the need for a new adjustment of production to the altered conditions, the prices of all complementary factors of production would—due allowance being made for time preference—finally equal the price of the product, and nothing would be left for profits or losses. In the long run every increase of productivity benefits exclusively the workers and some groups of the owners of land and of capital goods.

In the groups of the owners of capital goods there are benefited:

1. Those whose saving has increased the quantity of capital goods

23. The problem of the convertibility of capital goods is dealt with below, pp. 503–505.

available. They own this additional wealth, the outcome of their restraint in consuming.

2. The owners of those capital goods already previously existing which, thanks to the improvement in technological methods of production, are now better utilized than before. Such gains are, of course, temporary only. They are bound to disappear as they cause a tendency toward an intensified production of the capital goods concerned.

On the other hand, the increase in the quantity of capital goods available lowers the marginal productivity of these capital goods; it thus brings about a fall in the prices of the capital goods and thereby hurts the interests of all those capitalists who did not share at all or not sufficiently in the process of saving and the accumulation of the additional supply of capital goods.

In the group of the landowners all those are benefited for whom the new state of affairs results in a higher productivity of their farms, forests, fisheries, mines, and so on. On the other hand, all those are hurt whose property may become submarginal on account of the higher return yielded by the land owned by those benefited.

In the group of labor all derive a lasting gain from the increase in the marginal productivity of labor. But, on the other hand, in the short run some may suffer disadvantages. These are people who were specialized in the performance of work which becomes obsolete as a result of technological improvement and are fitted only for jobs in which—in spite of the general rise in wage rates—they earn less than before.

All these changes in the prices of the factors of production begin immediately with the initiation of the entrepreneurial actions designed to adjust the processes of production to the new state of affairs. In dealing with this problem as with the other problems of changes in the market data, we must guard ourselves against the popular fallacy of drawing a sharp line between short-run and long-run effects. What happens in the short run is precisely the first stages of the chain of successive transformations which tend to bring about the long-run effects. The long-run effect is in our case the disappearance of entrepreneurial profits and losses. The short-run effects are the preliminary stages of this process of elimination which finally, if not interrupted by a further change in the data, would result in the emergence of the evenly rotating economy.

It is necessary to comprehend that the very appearance of an excess in the total amount of entrepreneurial profits over the total amount of entrepreneurial losses depends upon the fact that this process of the elimination of entrepreneurial profit and loss begins at the same time as the entrepreneurs begin to adjust the complex of production activities to the changed data. There is never in the whole sequence of events an instant in which the advantages derived from the increase in the amount of capital available and from technical improvements benefit the entrepreneurs only. If the wealth and the income of the other strata were to remain unaffected, these people could buy the additional products only by restricting their purchases of other products accordingly. Then the profits of one group of entrepreneurs would exactly equal the losses incurred by other groups.

What happens is this: The entrepreneurs embarking upon the utilization of the newly accumulated capital goods and the improved technological methods of production are in need of complementary factors of production. Their demand for these factors is a new additional demand which must raise their prices. Only as far as this rise in prices and wage rates occurs, are the consumers in a position to buy the new products without curtailing the purchase of other goods. Only so far can a surplus of the total sum of all entrepreneurial profits over all entrepreneurial losses come into existence.

The vehicle of economic progress is the accumulation of additional capital goods by means of saving and improvement in technological methods of production the execution of which is almost always conditioned by the availability of such new capital. The agents of progress are the promoting entrepreneurs intent upon profiting by means of adjusting the conduct of affairs to the best possible satisfaction of the consumers. In the performance of their projects for the realization of progress they are bound to share the benefits derived from progress with the workers and also with a part of the capitalists and landowners and to increase the portion allotted to these people step by step until their own share melts away entirely.

From this it becomes evident that it is absurd to speak of a "rate of profit" or a "normal rate of profit" or an "average rate of profit." Profit is not related to or dependent on the amount of capital employed by the entrepreneur. Capital does not "beget" profit. Profit and loss are entirely determined by the success or failure of the entrepreneur to adjust production to the demand of the consumers. There is nothing "normal" in profits and there can never be an "equilibrium" with regard to them. Profit and loss are, on the contrary, always a phenomenon of a deviation from "normalcy," of changes unforeseen by the majority, and of a "disequilibrium." They have no place in an imaginary world of normalcy and equilibrium. In a changing economy there prevails always an inherent tendency for profits and losses to disappear. It is only the emergence of new changes which revives them again. Under stationary conditions the "average rate" of profits and losses is zero. An excess of the total amount of profits over that of losses is a proof of the fact that there is economic progress and an improvement in the standard of living of all strata of the population. The greater this excess is, the greater is the increment in general prosperity.

Many people are utterly unfit to deal with the phenomenon of entrepreneurial profit without indulging in envious resentment. In their eyes the source of profit is exploitation of the wage earners and the consumers, i.e., an unfair reduction in wage rates and a no less unfair increase in the prices of the products. By rights there should not be any profits at all.

Economics is indifferent with regard to such arbitrary value judgments. It is not interested in the problem of whether profits are to be approved or condemned from the point of view of an alleged natural law and of an alleged eternal and immutable code of morality about which personal intuition or divine revelation are supposed to convey precise information. Economics merely establishes the fact that entrepreneurial profits and losses are essential phenomena of the market economy. There cannot be a market economy without them. It is certainly possible for the police to confiscate all profits. But such a policy would by necessity convert the market economy into a senseless chaos. Man has, there is no doubt, the power to destroy many things, and he has made in the course of history ample use of this faculty. He could destroy the market economy too.

If those self-styled moralists were not blinded by their envy, they would not deal with profit without dealing simultaneously with its corollary, loss. They would not pass over in silence the fact that the preliminary conditions of economic improvement are an achievement of those whose saving accumulates the additional capital goods and of the inventors, and that the utilization of these conditions for the realization of economic improvement is effected by the entrepreneurs. The rest of the people do not contribute to progress, but they are benefited by the horn of plenty which other people's activities pour upon them.

What has been said about the progressing economy is *mutatis mutandis* to be applied to the conditions of a retrogressing economy, i.e., an economy in which the per capita quota of capital invested is decreasing. In such an economy there is an excess in the total sum of entrepreneurial losses over that of profits. People who cannot free themselves from the fallacy of thinking in concepts of collectives and whole groups might raise the question of how in such a retrogressing economy there could be any entrepreneurial activity at all. Why should anybody embark upon an enterprise if he knows in advance that mathematically his chances of earning profits are smaller than those of suffering losses? However, this mode of posing the problem is fallacious. Like everyone else, entrepreneurs do not act as members of a class, but as individuals. No entrepreneur bothers a whit about the fate of the totality of the entrepreneurs. It is irrelevant to the individual entrepreneur what happens to other people whom theories, according to a certain characteristic, assign to the same class they assign him. In the living, perpetually changing market society there are always profits to be earned by efficient entrepreneurs. The fact that in a retrogressing economy the total amount of losses exceeds the total amount of profits does not deter a man who has confidence in his own superior efficiency. A prospective entrepreneur does not consult the calculus of probability which is of no avail in the field of understanding. He trusts his own ability to understand future market conditions better than his less gifted fellow men.

The entrepreneurial function, the striving of entrepreneurs after profits, is the driving power in the market economy. Profit and loss are the devices by means of which the consumers exercise their supremacy on the market. The behavior of the consumers makes profits and losses appear and thereby shifts ownership of the means of production from the hands of the less efficient into those of the more efficient. It makes a man the more influential in the direction of business activities the better he succeeds in serving the consumers. In the absence of profit and loss the entrepreneurs would not know what the most urgent needs of the consumers are. If some entrepreneurs were to guess it, they would lack the means to adjust production accordingly.

Profit-seeking business is subject to the sovereignty of the consumers, while nonprofit institutions are sovereign unto themselves and not responsible to the public. Production for profit is necessarily production for use, as profits can only be earned by providing the consumers with those things they most urgently want to use.

The moralists' and sermonizers' critique of profits misses the point. It is not the fault of the entrepreneurs that the consumers—the people, the common man—prefer liquor to Bibles and detective stories to serious books, and that governments prefer guns to butter. The entrepreneur does not make greater profits in selling "bad" things than in selling "good" things. His profits are the greater the better he succeeds in providing the consumers with those things they ask for most intensely. People do not drink intoxicating beverages in order to make the "alcohol capital" happy, and they do not go to war in order to increase the profits of the "merchants of death." The existence of the armaments industries is a consequence of the warlike spirit, not its cause.

It is not the business of the entrepreneurs to make people substitute sound ideologies for unsound. It rests with the philosophers to change people's ideas and ideals. The entrepreneur serves the consumers as they are today, however wicked and ignorant.

We may admire those who abstain from making gains they could reap in producing deadly weapons or hard liquor. However, their laudable conduct is a mere gesture without any practical effects. Even if all entrepreneurs and capitalists were to follow their example, wars and dipsomania would not disappear. As was the case in the pre-capitalistic ages, governments would produce the weapons in their own arsenals and drinkers would distill their own liquor.

The Moral Condemnation of Profit

Profit is earned by the adjustment of the utilization of the human and material factors of production to changes in conditions. It is those benefited by this adjustment who, scrambling for the products concerned and offering and paying for them prices that exceed the costs expended by the seller, generate the profits. Entrepreneurial profit is not a "reward" granted by the customer to the supplier who served him better than the sluggish routinists; it is the result of the eagerness of the buyers to outbid others who are equally anxious to acquire a share of the limited supply.

The dividends of corporations are popularly called profits. Actually they are interest on the capital invested plus that part of profits that is not ploughed back into the enterprise. If the enterprise does not operate successfully, either no dividends are paid or the dividends contain only interest on the whole or a part of the capital.

Socialists and interventionists call profit and interest *unearned income,* the result of depriving the workers of a considerable part of the fruits of their effort. As they see it, the products come into existence through toiling as such and nothing else, and should by rights benefit the toilers alone.

Yet bare labor produces very little if not aided by the employment of the outcome of previous saving and accumulation of capital. The products are the outgrowth of a cooperation of labor with tools and other capital goods directed by provident entrepreneurial design. The savers, whose saving accumulated and maintains the capital, and the entrepreneurs, who channel the capital into those employments in which it best serves the consumers, are no less indispensable for the process of production than the toilers. It is nonsensical to impute the whole product to the purveyors of labor and to pass over in silence the contribution of the purveyors of capital and of entrepreneurial ideas. What brings forth usable goods is not physical effort as such, but physical effort aptly directed by the human mind toward a definite goal. The greater (with the advance of general well-being) the role of capital goods, and the more efficient their utilization in the cooperation of the factors of production, the more absurd becomes the romantic glorification of the mere performing of manual routine jobs. The marvelous economic improvements of the last two hundred years were an achievement of the capitalists who provided the capital goods required and of the elite of technologists and entrepreneurs. The masses of the manual workers were benefited by changes which they not only did not generate but which, more often than not, they tried to cut short.

Some Observations on the Underconsumption Bogey and on the Purchasing Power Argument

In speaking of underconsumption, people mean to describe a state of affairs in which a part of the goods produced cannot be consumed because the people who could consume them are by their poverty prevented from buying them. These goods remain unsold or can be swapped only at prices not covering the cost of production. Hence various disarrangements and disturbances arise, the total complex of which is called economic depression.

Now it happens again and again that entrepreneurs err in anticipating the future state of the market. Instead of producing those goods for which the demand of the consumers is most intense, they produce less urgently needed goods or things which cannot be sold at all. These inefficient entrepreneurs suffer losses while their more efficient competitors who anticipated the wishes of the consumers earn profits. The losses of the former group of entrepreneurs are not caused by a general abstention from buying on the part of the public; they are due to the fact that the public prefers to buy other goods.

If it were true, as the underconsumption myth implies, that the workers are too poor to buy the products because the entrepreneurs and the capitalists unfairly appropriate to themselves what by rights should go to the wage earners, the state of affairs would not be altered. The "exploiters" are not supposed to exploit from sheer wantonness. They want, it is insinuated, to increase at the expense of the "exploited" either their own consumption or their own investments. They do not withdraw their booty from the universe. They spend it either in buying luxuries for their own household or in buying producers' goods for the expansion of their enterprises. Of course, their demand is directed toward goods other than those the wage earners would have bought if the profits had been confiscated and distributed among them.

Entrepreneurial errors with regard to the state of the market of various classes of commodities as created by such "exploitation" are in no way different from any other entrepreneurial shortcomings. Entrepreneurial errors result in losses for the inefficient entrepreneurs which are counterbalanced by the profits of the efficient entrepreneurs. They make business bad for some groups of industries and good for other groups. They do not bring about a general depression of trade.

The underconsumption myth is baseless self-contradictory balderdash. Its reasoning crumbles away as soon as one begins to examine it. It is untenable even if one, for the sake of argument, accepts the "exploitation" doctrine as correct.

The purchasing power argument runs in a slightly different manner. It contends that a rise in wage rates is a prerequisite of the expansion of production. If wage rates do not rise, there is no use for business to increase the quantity and to improve the quality of the goods produced. For the additional products would find no buyers or only such buyers as restrict their purchases of other goods. What is needed first for the realization of economic progress is to make wage rates rise continually. Government or labor union pressure and compulsion aiming at the enforcement of higher wage rates are the main vehicles of progress.

As has been demonstrated above the emergence of an excess in the total sum of entrepreneurial profits over the total sum of entrepreneurial losses is inseparably bound up with the fact that a portion of the benefits derived from the increase in the quantity of capital goods available and from the improvement of technological procedures goes to the nonentrepreneurial groups. The rise in the prices of complementary factors of production, first among them wage rates, is neither a concession which the entrepreneurs willy-nilly must make to the rest of the people nor a clever device of the entrepreneurs in order to make profits. It is an unavoidable and necessary phenomenon in the chain of successive events which the endeavors of the entrepreneurs to make profits by adjusting the supply of the consumers' goods to the new state of affairs are bound to bring about. The same process which results in an excess of entrepreneurial profits over losses causes first —i.e., before such an excess appears—the emergence of a tendency toward a rise in wage rates and in the prices of many material factors of production. And it is again the same process that would in the further course of events make this excess of profits over losses disappear, provided that no further changes, increasing the amount of capital goods available, were to occur. The excess of profits over losses is not a consequence of the rise in the prices of the factors of production. The two phenomena—the rise in the prices of the factors of production and the excess of profits over losses—are both steps in the process of adjustment of production to the increase in the quantity of capital goods and to the technological changes which the entrepreneurial actions actuate. Only to the extent that the other strata of the population are enriched by this adjustment can an excess of profits over losses temporarily come into being.

The basic error of the purchasing power argument consists in misconstruing this causal relation. It turns things upside down when considering the rise in wage rates as the force bringing about economic improvement.

We will discuss at a later stage of this book the consequences of the attempts of the governments and of organized labor violence to enforce wage rates higher than those determined by a nonhampered market.[24] Here we must only add one more explanatory remark.

When speaking of profits and losses, prices and wage rates, what we have in mind is always real profits and losses, real prices and real wage rates. It is the arbitrary interchange of money terms and real terms that has led many people astray. This problem too will be dealt with exhaustively in later chapters. Let us incidentally only mention the fact that a rise in real wage rates is compatible with a drop in nominal wage rates.

10. Promoters, Managers, Technicians, and Bureaucrats

The entrepreneur hires the technicians, i.e., people who have the ability and the skill to perform definite kinds and quantities of work. The class of technicians includes the great inventors, the champions in the field of applied science, the constructors and designers as well as the performers of the most simple tasks. The entrepreneur joins their ranks as far as he himself takes part in the technical execution of his entrepreneurial plans. The technician contributes his own toil and trouble; but it is the entrepreneur qua entrepreneur who directs his labor toward definite goals. And the entrepreneur himself acts as a mandatary, as it were, of the consumers.

The entrepreneurs are not omnipresent. They cannot themselves attend to the manifold tasks which are incumbent upon them. Adjustment of production to the best possible supplying of the consumers with the goods they are asking for most urgently does not merely consist in determining the general plan for the utilization of resources. There is, of course, no doubt that this is the main function of the promoter and speculator. But besides the great adjustments, many small adjustments are necessary too. Each of them may seem trifling and of little bearing upon the total result. But the cumulative effect of shortcomings in many of these minor matters can be such as to frustrate entirely the success of a correct solution of the great problems. At any rate, it is certain that every failure to handle the smaller

24. Cf. below, pp. 769–779.

problems results in a squandering of scarce factors of production and consequently in impairing the best possible satisfaction of the consumers.

It is important to conceive in what respects the problem we have in mind differs from the technological tasks of the technicians. The execution of every project upon which the entrepreneur has embarked in making his decision with regard to the general plan of action requires a multiplicity of minute decisions. Each of these decisions must be effected in such a way as to prefer that solution of the problem which—without interfering with the designs of the general plan for the whole project—is the most economical one. It must avoid superfluous costs in the same way as does the general plan. The technician from his purely technological point of view either may not see any difference in the alternatives offered by various methods for the solution of such a detail or may give preference to one of these methods on account of its greater output in physical quantities. But the entrepreneur is actuated by the profit motive. This enjoins upon him the urge to prefer the most economical solution, i.e., that solution which avoids employing factors of production whose employment would impair the satisfaction of the more intensely felt wants of the consumers. He will prefer among the various methods with regard to which the technicians are neutral, the one the application of which requires the smallest cost. He may reject the technicians' suggestion to choose a more costly method securing a greater physical output if his calculation shows that the increase in output would not outweigh the increase in cost required. Not only in the great decisions and plans but no less in the daily decisions of small problems as they turn up in the current conduct of affairs, the entrepreneur must perform his task of adjusting production to the demand of the consumers as reflected in the prices of the market.

Economic calculation as practiced in the market economy, and especially the system of double-entry bookkeeping, make it possible to relieve the entrepreneur of involvement in too much detail. He can devote himself to his great tasks without being entangled in a multitude of trifles beyond any mortal man's range of sight. He can appoint assistants to whose solicitude he entrusts the care of subordinate entrepreneurial duties. And these assistants in their turn can be aided according to the same principle by assistants appointed for a smaller sphere of duties. In this way a whole managerial hierarchy can be built up.

A *manager* is a junior partner of the entrepreneur, as it were, no matter what the contractual and financial terms of his employment are. The only relevant thing is that his own financial interests force him to attend to the best of his abilities to the entrepreneurial functions which are assigned to him within a limited and precisely determined sphere of action.

It is the system of double-entry bookkeeping that makes the functioning of the managerial system possible. Thanks to it, the entrepreneur is in a position to separate the calculation of each part of his total enterprise in such a way that he can determine the role it plays within his whole enterprise. Thus he can look at each section as if it were a separate entity and can appraise it according to the share it contributes to the success of the total enterprise. Within this system of business calculation each section of a firm represents an integral entity, a hypothetical independent business, as it were. It is assumed that this section "owns" a definite part of the whole capital employed in the enterprise, that it buys from other sections and sells to them, that it has its own expenses and its own revenues, that its dealings result either in a profit or in a loss which is imputed to its own conduct of affairs as distinguished from the result of the other sections. Thus the entrepreneur can assign to each section's management a great deal of independence. The only directive he gives to a man whom he entrusts with the management of a circumscribed job is to make as much profit as possible. An examination of the accounts shows how successful or unsuccessful the managers were in executing this directive. Every manager and submanager is responsible for the working of his section or subsection. It is to his credit if the accounts show a profit, and it is to his disadvantage if they show a loss. His own interests impel him toward the utmost care and exertion in the conduct of his section's affairs. If he incurs losses, he will be replaced by a man whom the entrepreneur expects to be more successful, or the whole section will be discontinued. At any rate, the manager will lose his job. If he succeeds in making profits, his income will be increased, or at least he will not be in danger of losing it. Whether or not a manager is entitled to a share in the profit imputed to his section is not important with regard to the personal interest he takes in the results of his section's dealings. His welfare is at any rate closely connected with that of his section. His task is not like that of the technician, to perform a definite piece of work according to a definite precept. It is to adjust—within the limited scope left to his discretion—the operation of his section to the state of the market. Of course, just as an entrepreneur may combine in his person entrepreneurial functions and those of a technician, such a union of various functions can also occur with a manager.

The managerial function is always subservient to the entrepreneurial function. It can relieve the entrepreneur of a part of his minor duties; it can never evolve into a substitute for entrepreneurship. The fallacy to the contrary is due to the error confusing the category of entrepreneurship as it is defined in the imaginary construction of functional distribution with conditions in a living and operating market economy. The function of the entrepreneur cannot be separated from the direction of the employment of factors of production for the accomplishment of definite tasks. The entrepreneur controls the factors of production; it is this control that brings him either entrepreneurial profit or loss.

It is possible to reward the manager by paying for his services in proportion to the contribution of his section to the profit earned by the entrepreneur. But this is of no avail. As has been pointed out, the manager is under any circumstances interested in the success of that part of the business which is entrusted to his care. But the manager cannot be made answerable for the losses incurred. These losses are suffered by the owners of the capital employed. They cannot be shifted to the manager.

Society can freely leave the care for the best possible employment of capital goods to their owners. In embarking upon definite projects these owners expose their own property, wealth, and social position. They are even more interested in the success of their entrepreneurial activities than is society as a whole. For society as a whole the squandering of capital invested in a definite project means only the loss of a small part of its total funds; for the owner it means much more, for the most part the loss of his total fortune. But if a manager is given a completely free hand, things are different. He speculates in risking other people's money. He sees the prospects of an uncertain enterprise from another angle than that of the man who is answerable for the losses. It is precisely when he is rewarded by a share of the profits that he becomes foolhardy because he does not share in the losses too.

The illusion that management is the totality of entrepreneurial activities and that management is a perfect substitute for entrepreneurship is the outgrowth of a misinterpretation of the conditions of the corporations, the typical form of present-day business. It is asserted that the corporation is operated by the salaried managers, while the shareholders are merely passive spectators. All the powers are concentrated in the hands of hired employees. The shareholders are idle and useless; they harvest what the managers have sown.

This doctrine disregards entirely the role that the capital and money market, the stock and bond exchange, which a pertinent idiom simply calls the "market," plays in the direction of corporate business. The dealings of this market are branded by popular anti-capitalistic bias as a hazardous game, as mere gambling. In fact, the changes in the prices of common and preferred stock and of corporate bonds are the means applied by the capitalists for the supreme control of the flow of capital. The price structure as determined by the speculations on the capital and money markets and on the big commodity exchanges not only decides how much capital is available for the conduct of each corporation's business; it creates a state of affairs to which the managers must adjust their operations in detail.

The general direction of a corporation's conduct of business is exercised by the stockholders and their elected mandataries, the directors. The directors appoint and discharge the managers. In smaller companies and sometimes even in bigger ones the offices of the directors and the managers are often combined in the same persons. A successful corporation is ultimately never controlled by hired managers. The emergence of an omnipotent managerial class is not a phenomenon of the unhampered market economy. It was, on the contrary, an outgrowth of the interventionist policies consciously aiming at an elimination of the influence of the shareholders and at their virtual expropriation. In Germany, Italy, and Austria it was a preliminary step on the way toward the substitution of government control of business for free enterprise, as has been the case in Great Britain with regard to the Bank of England and the railroads. Similar tendencies are prevalent in the American public utilities. The marvelous achievements of corporate business were not a result of the activities of a salaried managerial oligarchy; they were accomplished by people who were connected with the corporation by means of the ownership of a considerable part or of the greater part of its stock and whom part of the public scorned as promoters and profiteers.

The entrepreneur determines alone, without any managerial interference, in what lines of business to employ capital and how much capital to employ. He determines the expansion and contraction of the size of the total business and its main sections. He determines the enterprise's financial structure. These are the essential decisions which are instrumental in the conduct of business. They always fall upon the entrepreneur, in corporations as well as in other types of a firm's legal structure. Any assistance given to the entrepreneur in this regard is of ancillary character only; he takes information about the past state of affairs from experts in the fields of law, statistics, and technology; but the final decision implying a judgment about the future state of the market rests with him alone. The execution of the details of his projects may then be entrusted to managers.

The social functions of the managerial elite are no less indispensable for the operation of the market economy than are the functions of the elite of inventors, technologists, engineers, designers, scientists, and experimenters. In the ranks of the managers many of the most eminent men serve the cause of economic progress. Successful managers are remunerated by high salaries and often by a share in the enterprise's gross profits. Many of them in the course of their careers become themselves capitalists and entrepreneurs. Nonetheless, the managerial function is different from the entrepreneurial function.

It is a serious mistake to identify entrepreneurship with management as in the popular antithesis of "management" and "labor." This confusion is, of course, intentional. It is designed to obscure the fact that the functions of entrepreneurship are entirely different from those of the managers attending to the minor details of the conduct of business. The structure of business, the allocation of capital to the various branches of production and firms, the size and the line of operation of each plant and shop are considered as given facts and it is implied that no further changes will be effected with regard to them. The only task is to go on in the old routine. In such a stationary world, of course, there is no need for innovators and promoters; the total amount of profits is counterbalanced by the total amount of losses. To explode the fallacies of this doctrine it is enough to compare the structure of American business in 1960 with that of 1940.

But even in a stationary world it would be nonsensical to give "labor," as a popular slogan demands, a share in management. The realization of such a postulate would result in syndicalism.[25]

There is furthermore a readiness to confuse the manager with a bureaucrat.

Bureaucratic management, as distinguished from *profit management,* is the method applied in the conduct of administrative affairs, the result of which has no cash value on the market. The successful performance of the duties entrusted to the care of a police department is of the greatest importance for the preservation of social cooperation and benefits each member of society. But it has no price on the market, it cannot be bought or sold; it can therefore not be confronted with the expenses incurred in the endeavors to secure it. It results in gains, but these gains are not reflected in profits liable to expression in terms of money. The methods of economic calculation, and especially those of double-entry bookkeeping, are not applicable

25. Cf. below, pp. 812–820.

to them. Success or failure of a police department's activities cannot be ascertained according to the arithmetical procedures of profit-seeking business. No accountant can establish whether or not a police department or one of its subdivisions has succeeded.

The amount of money to be expended in every branch of profit-seeking business is determined by the behavior of the consumers. If the automobile industry were to treble the capital employed, it would certainly improve the services it renders to the public. There would be more cars available. But this expansion of the industry would withhold capital from other branches of production in which it could fill more urgent wants of the consumers. This fact would render the expansion of the automobile industry unprofitable and increase profits in other branches of business. In their endeavors to strive after the highest profit obtainable, entrepreneurs are forced to allocate to each branch of business only as much capital as can be employed in it without impairing the satisfaction of more urgent wants of the consumers. Thus the entrepreneurial activities are automatically, as it were, directed by the consumers' wishes as they are reflected in the price structure of consumers' goods.

No such limitation is enjoined upon the allocation of funds for the performance of the tasks incumbent upon government activities. There is no doubt that the services rendered by the police department of the City of New York could be considerably improved by trebling the budgetary allocation. But the question is whether or not this improvement would be considerable enough to justify either the restriction of the services rendered by other departments—e.g., those of the department of sanitation—or the restriction of the private consumption of the taxpayers. This question cannot be answered by the accounts of the police department. These accounts provide information only about the expenses incurred. They cannot provide any information about the results obtained, as these results cannot be expressed in money equivalents. The citizens must directly determine the amount of services they want to get and are ready to pay for. They discharge this task by electing councilmen and officeholders who are prepared to comply with their intentions.

Thus the mayor and the chiefs of the city's various departments are restricted by the budget. They are not free to act upon what they themselves consider the most beneficial solution of the various problems the citizenry has to face. They are bound to spend the funds allocated for the purposes the budget has assigned them. They must not use them for other tasks. Auditing in the field of public administration is entirely different from that in the field of profit-seeking business. Its goal is to establish whether or not the funds allocated have been expended in strict compliance with the provisions of the budget.

In profit-seeking business the discretion of the managers and sub-managers is restricted by considerations of profit and loss. The profit motive is the only directive needed to make them subservient to the wishes of the consumers. There is no need to restrict their discretion by minute instructions and rules. If they are efficient, such meddling with details would at best be superfluous, if not pernicious in tying their hands. If they are inefficient, it would not render their activities more successful. It would only provide them with a lame excuse that the failure was caused by inappropriate rules. The only instruction required is self-understood and does not need to be especially mentioned: Seek profit.

Things are different in public administration, in the conduct of government affairs. In this field the discretion of the officeholders and their subaltern aids is not restricted by considerations of profit and loss. If their supreme boss—no matter whether he is the sovereign people or a sovereign despot—were to leave them a free hand, he would renounce his own supremacy in their favor. These officers would become irresponsible agents, and their power would supersede that of the people or the despot. They would do what pleased them, not what their bosses wanted them to do. To prevent this outcome and to make them subservient to the will of their bosses it is necessary to give them detailed instructions regulating their conduct of affairs in every respect. Then it becomes their duty to handle all affairs in strict compliance with these rules and regulations. Their freedom to adjust their acts to what seems to them the most appropriate solution of a concrete problem is limited by these norms. They are bureaucrats, i.e., men who in every instance must observe a set of inflexible regulations.

Bureaucratic conduct of affairs is conduct bound to comply with detailed rules and regulations fixed by the authority of a superior body. It is the only alternative to profit management. Profit management is inapplicable in the pursuit of affairs which have no cash value on the market and in the non-profit conduct of affairs which could also be operated on a profit basis. The former is the case of the administration of the social apparatus of coercion and compulsion; the latter is the case in the conduct of an institution on a non-profit basis, e.g., a school, a hospital, or a postal system. Whenever the operation of a system is not directed by the profit motive, it must be directed by bureaucratic rules.

Bureaucratic conduct of affairs is, as such, not an evil. It is the only appropriate method of handling governmental affairs, i.e., the social apparatus of compulsion and coercion. As government is necessary, bureaucratism is—in this field—no less necessary. Where economic calculation is unfeasible, bureaucratic methods are indispensable. A socialist government must apply them to all affairs.

No business, whatever its size or specific task, can ever become bureaucratic so long as it is entirely and solely operated on a profit basis. But as soon as it abandons profit seeking and substitutes for it what is called the service principle—i.e., the rendering of services without regard as to whether or not the prices to be obtained for them cover the expenses—it must substitute bureaucratic methods for those of entrepreneurial management.[26]

11. The Selective Process

The selective process of the market is actuated by the composite effort of all members of the market economy. Driven by the urge to remove his own uneasiness as much as possible, each individual is intent, on the one hand, upon attaining that position in which he can contribute most to the best satisfaction of everyone else and, on the other hand, upon taking best advantage of the services offered by everyone else. This means that he tries to sell on the dearest market and to buy on the cheapest market. The resultant of these endeavors is not only the price structure but no less the social structure, the assignment of definite tasks to the various individuals. The market makes people rich or poor, determines who shall run the big plants and who shall scrub the floors, fixes how many people shall work in the copper mines and how many in the symphony orchestras. None of these decisions is made once and for all; they are revocable every day. The selective process never stops. It goes on adjusting the social apparatus of production to the changes in demand and supply. It reviews again and again its previous decisions and forces everybody to submit to a new examination of his case. There is no security and no such thing as a right to preserve any position acquired in the past. Nobody is exempt from the law of the market, the consumers' sovereignty.

Ownership of the means of production is not a privilege, but a social liability. Capitalists and landowners are compelled to employ their property for the best possible satisfaction of the consumers. If they are slow and inept in the performance of their duties, they are penalized by losses. If they do not learn the lesson and do not

26. For a detailed treatment of the problems involved, cf. Mises, *Bureaucracy* (New Haven, 1944).

reform their conduct of affairs, they lose their wealth. No investment is safe forever. He who does not use his property in serving the consumers in the most efficient way is doomed to failure. There is no room left for people who would like to enjoy their fortunes in idleness and thoughtlessness. The proprietor must aim to invest his funds in such a way that principal and yield are at least not impaired.

In the ages of caste privileges and trade barriers there were revenues not dependent on the market. Princes and lords lived at the expense of the humble slaves and serfs who owed them tithes, statute labor, and tributes. Ownership of land could only be acquired either by conquest or by largesse on the part of a conqueror. It could be forfeited only by recantation on the part of the donor or by conquest on the part of another conqueror. Even later, when the lords and their liegemen began to sell their surpluses on the market, they could not be ousted by the competition of more efficient people. Competition was free only within very narrow limits. The acquisition of manorial estates was reserved to the nobility, that of urban real property to the citizens of the township, that of farm land to the peasants. Competition in the arts and crafts was restricted by the guilds. The consumers were not in a position to satisfy their wants in the cheapest way, as price control made underbidding impossible to the sellers. The buyers were at the mercy of their purveyors. If the privileged producers refused to resort to the employment of the most adequate raw materials and of the most efficient methods of processing, the consumers were forced to endure the consequences of such stubbornness and conservatism.

The landowner who lives in perfect self-sufficiency from the fruits of his own farming is independent of the market. But the modern farmer who buys equipment, fertilizers, seed, labor, and other factors of production and sells agricultural products is subject to the law of the market. His income depends on the consumers and he must adjust his operations to their wishes.

The selective function of the market works also with regard to labor. The worker is attracted by that kind of work in which he can expect to earn most. As is the case with material factors of production, the factor labor too is allocated to those employments in which it best serves the consumers. There prevails the tendency not to waste any quantity of labor for the satisfaction of less urgent demand if more urgent demand is still unsatisfied. Like all other strata of society, the worker is subject to the supremacy of the consumers. If he disobeys, he is penalized by a cut in earnings.

The selection of the market does not establish social orders, castes, or classes in the Marxian sense. Nor do the entrepreneurs and promoters form an integrated social class. Each individual is free to become a promoter if he relies upon his own ability to anticipate future market conditions better than his fellow citizens and if his attempts to act at his own peril and on his own responsibility are approved by the consumers. One enters the ranks of the promoters by spontaneously pushing forward and thus submitting to the trial to which the market subjects, without respect for persons, everybody who wants to become a promoter or to remain in this eminent position. Everybody has the opportunity to take his chance. A newcomer does not need to wait for an invitation or encouragement from anyone. He must leap forward on his own account and must himself know how to provide the means needed.

It has been contended again and again that under the conditions of "late" or "mature" capitalism it is no longer possible for penniless people to climb the ladder to wealth and entrepreneurial position. No attempt has ever been made to prove this thesis. Since it was first advanced, the composition of the entrepreneurial and capitalist groups has changed considerably. A great part of the former entrepreneurs and their heirs have been eliminated and other people, newcomers, have taken their places. It is, of course, true that in the last years institutions have been purposely developed which, if not abolished very soon, will make the functioning of the market in every regard impossible.

The point of view from which the consumers choose the captains of industry and business is exclusively their qualification to adjust production to the needs of the consumers. They do not bother about other features and merits. They want a shoe manufacturer to fabricate good and cheap shoes. They are not intent upon entrusting the conduct of the shoe trade to handsome amiable boys, to people of good drawing-room manners, of artistic gifts, of scholarly habits, or of any other virtues or talents. A proficient businessman may often be deficient in many accomplishments which contribute to the success of a man in other spheres of life.

It is quite common nowadays to deprecate the capitalists and entrepreneurs. A man is prone to sneer at those who are more prosperous than himself. These people, he contends, are richer only because they are less scrupulous than he. If he were not restrained by due consideration for the laws of morality and decency, he would be no less successful than they are. Thus men glory in the aureole of self-complacency and Pharisaic self-righteousness.

Now it is true that under the conditions brought about by interventionism many people can acquire wealth by graft and bribery. In many countries interventionism has so undermined the supremacy of the market that it is more advantageous for a businessman to rely upon the aid of those in political office than upon the best satisfaction of the needs of the consumers. But it is not this that the popular critics of other people's wealth have in mind. They contend that the methods by which wealth is acquired in a pure market society are objectionable from the ethical point of view.

Against such statements it is necessary to emphasize that, so far as the operation of the market is not sabotaged by the interference of governments and other factors of coercion, success in business is the proof of services rendered to the consumers. The poor man need not be inferior to the prosperous businessman in other regards; he may sometimes be outstanding in scientific, literary, and artistic achievements or in civic leadership. But in the social system of production he is inferior. The creative genius may be right in his disdain for commercial success; it may be true that he would have been prosperous in business if he had not preferred other things. But the clerks and workers who boast of their moral superiority deceive themselves and find consolation in this self-deception. They do not admit that they have been tried and found wanting by their fellow citizens, the consumers.

It is often asserted that the poor man's failure in the competition of the market is caused by his lack of education. Equality of opportunity, it is said, could be provided only by making education at every level accessible to all. There prevails today the tendency to reduce all differences among various peoples to their education and to deny the existence of inborn inequalities in intellect, will power, and character. It is not generally realized that education can never be more than indoctrination with theories and ideas already developed. Education, whatever benefits it may confer, is transmission of traditional doctrines and valuations; it is by necessity conservative. It produces imitation and routine, not improvement and progress. Innovators and creative geniuses cannot be reared in schools. They are precisely the men who defy what the school has taught them.

In order to succeed in business a man does not need a degree from a school of business administration. These schools train the subalterns for routine jobs. They certainly do not train entrepreneurs. An entrepreneur cannot be trained. A man becomes an entrepreneur in seizing an opportunity and filling the gap. No special education is required for such a display of keen judgment, foresight, and energy. The most successful businessmen were often uneducated when measured by the scholastic standards of the teaching profession. But they were equal to their social function of adjusting production to the most urgent demand. Because of these merits the consumers chose them for business leadership.

12. The Individual and the Market

It is customary to speak metaphorically of the automatic and anonymous forces actuating the "mechanism" of the market. In employing such metaphors people are ready to disregard the fact that the only factors directing the market and the determination of prices are purposive acts of men. There is no automatism; there are only men consciously and deliberately aiming at ends chosen. There are no mysterious mechanical forces; there is only the human will to remove uneasiness. There is no anonymity; there is I and you and Bill and Joe and all the rest. And each of us is both a producer and a consumer.

The market is a social body; it is the foremost social body. The market phenomena are social phenomena. They are the resultant of each individual's active contribution. But they are different from each such contribution. They appear to the individual as something given which he himself cannot alter. He does not always see that he himself is a part, although a small part, of the complex of elements determining each momentary state of the market. Because he fails to realize this fact, he feels himself free, in criticizing the market phenomena, to condemn with regard to his fellow men a mode of conduct which he considers as quite right with regard to himself. He blames the market for its callousness and disregard of persons and asks for social control of the market in order to "humanize" it. He asks on the one hand for measures to protect the consumer against the producers. But on the other hand he insists even more passionately upon the necessity of protecting himself as a producer against the consumers. The outcome of these contradictory demands is the modern methods of government interference whose most outstanding examples were the Sozialpolitik of imperial Germany and the American New Deal.

It is an old fallacy that it is a legitimate task of civil government to protect the less efficient producer against the competition of the more efficient. One asks for a "producers' policy" as distinct from a "consumers' policy." While flamboyantly repeating the truism that the only aim of production is to provide ample supplies for consumption, people emphasize with no less eloquence that the "industrious" producer should be protected against the "idle" consumer.

However, producers and consumers are identical. Production and consumption are different stages in acting. Catallactics embodies these differences in speaking of producers and consumers. But in reality they are the same people. It is, of course, possible to protect a less efficient producer against the competition of more efficient fellows. Such a privilege conveys to the privileged the benefits which the unhampered market provides only to those who succeed in best filling the wants of the consumers. But it necessarily impairs the satisfaction of the consumers. If only one producer or a small group is privileged, the beneficiaries enjoy an advantage at the expense of the rest of the people. But if all producers are privileged to the same extent, everybody loses in his capacity as consumer as much as he gains in his capacity as a producer. Moreover, all are injured because the supply of products drops if the most efficient men are prevented from employing their skill in that field in which they could render the best services to the consumers.

If a consumer believes that it is expedient or right to pay a higher price for domestic cereals than for cereals imported from abroad, or for manufactures processed in plants operated by small business or employing unionized workers than for those of another provenance, he is free to do so. He would only have to satisfy himself that the commodity offered for sale meets the conditions upon which he makes the allowance of a higher price depend. Laws which forbid counterfeiting of labels of origin and trademarks would succeed in attaining the ends aimed at by tariffs, labor legislation, and privileges granted to small business. But it is beyond doubt that the consumers are not prepared to act in this way. The fact that a commodity is marked as imported does not impair its salability if it is better or cheaper, or both. As a rule the buyers want to buy as cheaply as possible without regard for the origin of the article or some particular characteristics of the producers.

The psychological root of the producers' policy as practiced today in all parts of the world is to be seen in spurious economic doctrines. These doctrines flatly deny that the privileges granted to less efficient producers burden the consumer. Their advocates contend that such measures are prejudicial only to those against whom they discriminate. When, pressed further, they are forced to admit that the consumers are damaged too, they maintain that the losses of the consumers are more than compensated by an increase in their money income which the measures in question are bound to bring about.

Thus in the predominantly industrial countries of Europe the protectionists were first eager to declare that the tariff on agricultural products hurts exclusively the interests of the farmers of the predominantly agricultural countries and of the grain dealers. It is certain that these exporting interests are damaged too. But it is no less certain that the consumers of the country that adopts the tariff policy are losing with them. They must pay higher prices for their food. Of course, the protectionist retorts, that this is not a burden. For, he argues, the additional amount that the domestic consumer pays increases the farmers' income and their purchasing power; they will spend the whole surplus in buying more of the products manufactured by the nonagricultural strata of the population. This paralogism can easily be exploded by referring to the well-known anecdote of the man who asks an innkeeper for a gift of ten dollars; it will not cost him anything because the beggar promises to spend the whole amount in his inn. But for all that, the protectionist fallacy got hold of public opinion, and this alone explains the popularity of the measures inspired by it. Many people simply do not realize that the only effect of protection is to divert production from those places in which it could produce more per unit of capital and labor expended to places in which it produces less. It makes people poorer, not more prosperous.

The ultimate foundation of modern protectionism and of the striving for economic autarky of each country is to be found in this mistaken belief that they are the best means to make every citizen, or at least the immense majority of them, richer. The term riches means in this connection an increase in the individual's real income and an improvement in his standard of living. It is true that the policy of national economic insulation is a necessary corollary of the endeavors to interfere with domestic business, and that it is an outcome of warlike tendencies as well as one of the factors producing these tendencies. But the fact remains that it would never have been possible to sell the idea of protection to the voters if one had not been able to convince them that protection not only does not impair their standard of living but raises it considerably.

It is important to emphasize this fact because it utterly explodes a myth propagated by many popular books. According to these myths, contemporary man is no longer motivated by the desire to improve his material well-being and to raise his standard of living. The assertions of the economists to the contrary are mistaken. Modern man gives priority to "noneconomic" or "irrational" things and is ready to forego material betterment whenever its attainment stands in the way of those "ideal" concerns. It is a serious blunder, common mostly with economists and businessmen, to interpret the events of our time from an "economic" point of view and to criticize current ideologies with regard to the alleged economic fallacies implied. People long for other things more than for a good life.

It is hardly possible to misconstrue the history of our age more crassly. Our contemporaries are driven by a fanatical zeal to get more amenities and by an unrestrained appetite to enjoy life. A characteristic social phenomenon of our day is the pressure group, an alliance of people eager to promote their own material well-being by the employment of all means, legal or illegal, peaceful or violent. For the pressure group nothing matters but the increase of its members' real income. It is not concerned with any other aspects of life. It does not bother whether or not the realization of its program hurts the vital interests of other men, of their own nation or country, and of the whole of mankind. But, of course, every pressure group is anxious to justify its demands as beneficial to the general public welfare and to stigmatize its critics as abject scoundrels, idiots, and traitors. In the pursuit of its plans it displays a quasi-religious ardor.

Without exception all political parties promise their supporters a higher real income. There is no difference in this respect between nationalists and internationalists and between the supporters of a market economy and the advocates of either socialism or interventionism. If a party asks its supporters to make sacrifices for its cause, it always explains these sacrifices as the necessary temporary means for the attainment of the ultimate goal, the improvement of the material well-being of its members. Each party considers it as an insidious plot against its prestige and its survival if somebody ventures to question the capacity of its projects to make the group members more prosperous. Each party regards with a deadly hatred the economists embarking upon such a critique.

All varieties of the producers' policy are advocated on the ground of their alleged ability to raise the party members' standard of living. Protectionism and economic self-sufficiency, labor union pressure and compulsion, labor legislation, minimum wage rates, public spending, credit expansion, subsidies, and other makeshifts are always recommended by their advocates as the most suitable or the only means to increase the real income of the people for whose votes they canvass. Every contemporary statesman or politician invariably tells his voters: My program will make you as affluent as conditions may permit, while my adversaries' program will bring you want and misery.

It is true that some secluded intellectuals in their esoteric circles talk differently. They proclaim the priority of what they call eternal absolute values and feign in their declamations—not in their personal conduct—a disdain of things secular and transitory. But the public ignores such utterances. The main goal of present-day political action is to secure for the respective pressure group memberships the highest material well-being. The only way for a leader to succeed is to instill in people the conviction that his program best serves the attainment of this goal.

What is wrong with the producers' policies is their faulty economics.

If one is prepared to indulge in the fashionable tendency to explain human things by resorting to the terminology of psychopathology, one might be tempted to say that modern man in contrasting a producers' policy with a consumers' policy has fallen victim to a kind of schizophrenia. He fails to realize that he is an undivided and indivisible person, i.e., an individual, and as such no less a consumer than a producer. The unity of his consciousness is split into two parts; his mind is inwardly divided against himself. But it matters little whether or not we adopt this mode of describing the fact that the economic doctrine resulting in these policies is faulty. We are not concerned with the pathological source from which an error may stem, but with the error as such and with its logical roots. The unmasking of the error by means of ratiocination is the primary fact. If a statement were not exposed as logically erroneous, psychopathology would not be in a position to qualify the state of mind from which it stems as pathological. If a man imagines himself to be the king of Siam, the first thing which the psychiatrist has to establish is whether or not he really is what he believes himself to be. Only if this question is answered in the negative can the man be considered insane.

It is true that most of our contemporaries are committed to a fallacious interpretation of the producer-consumer nexus. In buying they behave as if they were connected with the market only as buyers, and vice versa in selling. As buyers they advocate stern measures to protect them against the sellers, and as sellers they advocate no less harsh measures against the buyers. But this antisocial conduct which shakes the very foundations of social cooperation is not an outgrowth of a pathological state of mind. It is the outcome of a narrow-mindedness which fails to conceive the operation of the market economy and to anticipate the ultimate effects of one's own actions.

It is permissible to contend that the immense majority of our contemporaries are mentally and intellectually not adjusted to life in the market society although they themselves and their fathers have unwittingly created this society by their actions. But this maladjustment consists in nothing else than in the failure to recognize erroneous doctrines as such.

13. Business Propaganda

The consumer is not omniscient. He does not know where he can obtain at the cheapest price what he is looking for. Very often he does not even know what kind of commodity or service is suitable to remove most efficaciously the particular uneasiness he wants to remove. At best he is familiar with the market conditions of the immediate past and arranges his plans on the basis of this information. To convey to him information about the actual state of the market is the task of business propaganda.

Business propaganda must be obtrusive and blatant. It is its aim to attract the attention of slow people, to rouse latent wishes, to entice men to substitute innovation for inert clinging to traditional routine. In order to succeed, advertising must be adjusted to the mentality of the people courted. It must suit their tastes and speak their idiom. Advertising is shrill, noisy, coarse, puffing, because the public does not react to dignified allusions. It is the bad taste of the public that forces the advertisers to display bad taste in their publicity campaigns. The art of advertising has evolved into a branch of applied psychology, a sister discipline of pedagogy.

Like all things designed to suit the taste of the masses, advertising is repellent to people of delicate feeling. This abhorrence influences the appraisal of business propaganda. Advertising and all other methods of business propaganda are condemned as one of the most outrageous outgrowths of unlimited competition. It should be forbidden. The consumers should be instructed by impartial experts; the public schools, the "nonpartisan" press, and cooperatives should perform this task.

The restriction of the right of businessmen to advertise their products would restrict the freedom of the consumers to spend their income according to their own wants and desires. It would make it impossible for them to learn as much as they can and want about the state of the market and the conditions which they may consider as relevant in choosing what to buy and what not to buy. They would no longer be in a position to decide on the basis of the opinion which they themselves have formed about the seller's appraisal of his products; they would be forced to act on the recommendation of other people. It is not unlikely that these mentors would save them some mistakes. But the individual consumers would be under the tutelage of guardians. If advertising is not restricted, the consumers are by and large in the position of a jury which learns about the case by hearing the witnesses and examining directly all other means of evidence. If advertising is restricted, they are in the position of a jury to whom an officer reports about the result of his own examination of evidence.

It is a widespread fallacy that skillful advertising can talk the consumers into buying everything that the advertiser wants them to buy. The consumer is, according to this legend, simply defenseless against "high-pressure" advertising. If this were true, success or failure in business would depend on the mode of advertising only. However, nobody believes that any kind of advertising would have succeeded in making the candlemakers hold the field against the electric bulb, the horsedrivers against the motorcars, the goose quill against the steel pen and later against the fountain pen. But whoever admits this implies that the quality of the commodity advertised is instrumental in bringing about the success of an advertising campaign. Then there is no reason to maintain that advertising is a method of cheating the gullible public.

It is certainly possible for an advertiser to induce a man to try an article which he would not have bought if he had known its qualities beforehand. But as long as advertising is free to all competing firms, the article which is better from the point of view of the consumers' appetites will finally outstrip the less appropriate article, whatever methods of advertising may be applied. The tricks and artifices of advertising are available to the seller of the better product no less than to the seller of the poorer product. But only the former enjoys the advantage derived from the better quality of his product.

The effects of advertising of commodities are determined by the fact that as a rule the buyer is in a position to form a correct opinion about the usefulness of an article bought. The housewife who has tried a particular brand of soap or canned food learns from experience whether it is good for her to buy and consume that product in the future too. Therefore advertising pays the advertiser only if the examination of the first sample bought does not result in the consumer's refusal to buy more of it. It is agreed among businessmen that it does not pay to advertise products other than good ones.

Entirely different are conditions in those fields in which experience cannot teach us anything. The statements of religious, metaphysical, and political propaganda can be neither verified nor falsified by experience. With regard to the life beyond and the absolute, any experience is denied to men living in this world. In political matters experience is always the experience of complex phenomena which is open to different interpretations; the only yardstick which can be applied to political doctrines is aprioristic reasoning. Thus political propaganda and business propaganda are essentially different things, although they often resort to the same technical methods.

There are many evils for which contemporary technology and therapeutics have no remedy. There are incurable diseases and there are irreparable personal defects. It is a sad fact that some people try to exploit their fellow men's plight by offering them patent medicines. Such quackeries do not make old people young and ugly girls pretty. They only raise hopes. It would not impair the operation of the market if the authorities were to prevent such advertising, the truth of which cannot be evidenced by the methods of the experimental natural sciences. But whoever is ready to grant to the government this power would be inconsistent if he objected to the demand to submit the statements of churches and sects to the same examination. Freedom is indivisible. As soon as one starts to restrict it, one enters upon a decline on which it is difficult to stop. If one assigns to the government the task of making truth prevail in the advertising of perfumes and tooth paste, one cannot contest it the right to look after truth in the more important matters of religion, philosophy, and social ideology.

The idea that business propaganda can force the consumers to submit to the will of the advertisers is spurious. Advertising can never succeed in supplanting better or cheaper goods by poorer goods.

The costs incurred by advertising are, from the point of view of the advertiser, a part of the total bill of production costs. A businessman expends money for advertising if and as far as he expects that the increase in sales resulting will increase the total net proceeds. In this regard there is no difference between the costs of advertising and all other costs of production. An attempt has been made to distinguish between production costs and sales costs. An increase in production costs, it has been said, increases supply, while an increase in sales costs (advertising costs included) increases demand.[27] This is a mistake. All costs of production are expended with the intention of increasing demand. If the manufacturer of candy employs a better raw material, he aims at an increase in demand in the same way as he does in making the wrappings more attractive and his stores more inviting and in spending more for advertisements. In increasing production costs per unit of the product the idea is always to increase demand. If a businessman wants to increase supply, he must increase the total cost of production, which often results in lowering production costs per unit.

27. Cf. Chamberlin, *The Theory of Monopolistic Competition* (Cambridge, Mass., 1935), pp. 123 ff.

14. The "Volkswirtschaft"

The market economy as such does not respect political frontiers. Its field is the world.

The term *Volkswirtschaft* was long applied by the German champions of government omnipotence. Only much later did the British and the French begin to speak of the "British economy" and *"l'économie francaise"* as distinct from the economies of other nations. But neither the English nor the French language produced an equivalent of the term Volkswirtschaft. With the modern trend toward national planning and national autarky, the doctrine involved in this German word became popular everywhere. Nonetheless, only the German language is able to express in one word all the ideas implied.

The Volkswirtschaft is a sovereign nation's total complex of economic activities directed and controlled by the government. It is socialism realized within the political frontiers of each nation. In employing this term people are fully aware of the fact that real conditions differ from the state of affairs which they deem the only adequate and desirable state. But they judge everything that happens in the market economy from the point of view of their ideal. They assume that there is an irreconcilable conflict between the interests of the Volkswirtschaft and those of the selfish individuals eager to seek profit. They do not hesitate to assign priority to the interests of the Volkswirtschaft over those of the individuals. The righteous citizen should always place the *volkswirtschaftliche* interests above his own selfish interests. He should act of his own accord as if he were an officer of the government executing its orders. *Gemeinnutz geht vor Eigennutz* (the welfare of the nation takes precedence over the selfishness of the individuals) was the fundamental principle of Nazi economic management. But as people are too dull and too vicious to comply with this rule, it is the task of government to enforce it. The German princes of the seventeenth and eighteenth century, foremost among them the Hohenzollern Electors of Brandenburg and Kings of Prussia, were fully equal to this task. In the nineteenth century, even in Germany the liberal ideologies imported from the West superseded the well-tried and natural policies of nationalism and socialism. However, Bismarck's and his successors' *Sozialpolitik* and finally Nazism restored them.

The interests of a Volkswirtschaft are seen as implacably opposed not only to those of the individuals, but no less to those of the Volkswirtschaft of any foreign nation. The most desirable state of a Volkswirtschaft is complete economic self-sufficiency. A nation which depends on any imports from abroad lacks economic independence; its sovereignty is only a sham. Therefore a nation which cannot produce at home all that it needs is bound to conquer all the territories required. To be really sovereign and independent a nation must have *Lebensraum,* i.e., a territory so large and rich in natural resources that it can live in autarky at a standard no lower than that of any other nation.

Thus the idea of the Volkswirtschaft is the most radical denial of all the principles of the market economy. It was this idea that guided, more or less, the economic policies of all nations in the last decades. It was the pursuit of this idea that brought about the terrific wars of our century and may kindle still more pernicious wars in the future.

From the early beginnings of human history the two opposite principles of the market economy and of the Volkswirtschaft fought each other. Government, i.e., a social apparatus of coercion and compulsion, is a necessary requisite of peaceful cooperation. The market economy cannot do without a police power safeguarding its smooth functioning by the threat or the application of violence against peacebreakers. But the indispensable administrators and their armed satellites are always tempted to use their arms for the establishment of their own totalitarian rule. For ambitious kings and generalissimos the very existence of a sphere of the individuals' lives not subject to regimentation is a challenge. Princes, governors, and generals are never spontaneously liberal. They become liberal only when forced to by the citizens.

The problems raised by the plans of the socialists and the interventionists will be dealt with in later parts of this book. Here we have only to answer the question of whether or not any of the essential features of the Volkswirtschaft are compatible with the market economy. For the champions of the idea of the Volkswirtschaft do not consider their scheme merely as a pattern for the establishment of a future social order. They declare emphatically that even under the system of the market economy, which, of course, in their eyes is a debased and vicious product of policies contrary to human nature, the Volkswirtschaften of the various nations are integrated units whose interests are irreconcilably opposed to those of all other nations' Volkswirtschaften. As they see it, what separates one Volkswirtschaft from all the others is not, as the economists would have us believe, merely political institutions. It is not the trade and migration barriers established by government interference with business and the differences in legislation and in the protection granted to the individuals by the courts and tribunals that bring about the distinction between domestic trade and foreign trade. This diversity, they say, is, on the contrary, the necessary outcome of the very nature of things, of an inextricable factor; it cannot be removed by any ideology and produces its effects whether the laws and the administrators and judges are prepared to take notice of it or not. Thus in their eyes the Volkswirtschaft appears as a nature-given reality, while the world-embracing ecumenic society of men, the world economy (*Weltwirtschaft*), is only an imaginary phantom of a spurious doctrine, a plan devised for the destruction of civilization.

The truth is that individuals in their acting, in their capacity as producers and consumers, as sellers and buyers, do not make any distinction as between the domestic market and the foreign market. They make a distinction as between local trade and trading with more distant places as far as the costs of transportation play a role. If government interference, such as tariffs, renders international transactions more expensive, they take this fact into account in the same way in which they pay regard to shipping costs. A tariff on caviar has no effect other than would a rise in the cost of transportation. A rigid prohibition of the importation of caviar produces a state of affairs no different from that which would prevail if caviar could not stand shipping without an essential deterioration in its quality.

There has never been in the history of the West such a thing as regional or national autarky. There was, as we may admit, a period in which the division of labor did not go beyond the members of a family household. There was autarky of families and tribes which did not practice interpersonal exchange. But as soon as interpersonal exchange emerged, it crossed the boundaries of the political communities. Barter between the inhabitants of regions more remote from one another, between the members of various tribes, villages, and political communities preceded the practice of barter between neighbors. What people wanted first to acquire by barter and trade were things they could not produce themselves out of their own resources. Salt, other minerals and metals the deposits of which are unequally distributed over the earth's surface, cereals which one could not grow on the domestic soil, and artifacts which only the inhabitants of some regions were able to manufacture, were the first objects of trade. Trade started as foreign trade. Only later did domestic exchange develop between neighbors. The first holes that opened the closed household economy to interpersonal exchange were made by the products of distant regions. No consumer cared on his own account whether the salt and the metals he bought were of "domestic" or of "foreign" provenance. If it had been otherwise, the governments would not have had any reason to interfere by means of tariffs and other barriers to foreign trade.

But even if a government succeeds in making the barriers separating its domestic market from foreign markets insurmountable and thus establishes perfect national autarky, it does not create a Volkswirtschaft. A market economy which is perfectly autarkic remains for all that a market economy; it forms a closed and isolated catallactic system. The fact that its citizens miss the advantages which they could derive from the international division of labor is simply a datum of their economic conditions. Only if such an isolated country goes outright socialist, does it convert its market economy into a Volkswirtschaft.

Fascinated by the propaganda of Neo-Mercantilism, people apply idioms which are in contrast to the principles they take as guides in their acting and to all the characteristics of the social order in which they are living. Long ago the British began to call plants and farms located in Great Britain, and even those located in the Dominions, in the East Indies, and in the colonies, "ours." But if a man did not just want to make a show of his patriotic zeal and to impress other people, he was not prepared to pay a higher price for the products of his "own" plants than for those of the "foreign" plants. Even if he had behaved in this way, the designation of the plants located within the political boundaries of his nation as "ours" would not be adequate. In what sense could a Londoner, before the nationalization, call coalmines located in England which he did not own "our" mines and those of the Ruhr "foreign" mines? Whether he bought "British" coal or "German" coal, he always had to pay the full market price. It is not "America" that buys champagne from "France." It is always an individual American who buys it from an individual Frenchman.

As far as there is still some room left for the actions of individuals, as far as there is private ownership and exchange of goods and services between individuals, there is no Volkswirtschaft. Only if full government control is substituted for the choices of individuals does the Volkswirtschaft emerge as a real entity.

XVI. PRICES

1. The Pricing Process

IN an occasional act of barter in which men who ordinarily do not resort to trading with other people exchange goods ordinarily not negotiated, the ratio of exchange is determined only within broad margins. Catallactics, the theory of exchange ratios and prices, cannot determine at what point within these margins the concrete ratio will be established. All that it can assert with regard to such exchanges is that they can be effected only if each party values what he receives more highly than what he gives away.

The recurrence of individual acts of exchange generates the market step by step with the evolution of the division of labor within a society based on private property. As it becomes a rule to produce for other people's consumption, the members of society must sell and buy. The multiplication of the acts of exchange and the increase in the number of people offering or asking for the same commodities narrow the margins between the valuations of the parties. Indirect exchange and its perfection through the use of money divide the transactions into two different parts: sale and purchase. What in the eyes of one party is a sale, is for the other party a purchase. The divisibility of money, unlimited for all practical purposes, makes it possible to determine the exchange ratios with nicety. The exchange ratios are now as a rule money prices. They are determined between extremely narrow margins: the valuations on the one hand of the marginal buyer and those of the marginal offerer who abstains from selling, and the valuations on the other hand of the marginal seller and those of the marginal potential buyer who abstains from buying.

The concatenation of the market is an outcome of the activities of entrepreneurs, promoters, speculators, and dealers in futures and in arbitrage. It has been asserted that catallactics is based on the assumption—contrary to reality—that all parties are provided with perfect knowledge concerning the market data and are therefore in a position to take best advantage of the most favorable opportunities for buying and selling. It is true that some economists really believed that such an assumption is implied in the theory of prices. These authors not only failed to realize in what respects a world peopled with men perfectly equal in knowledge and foresight would differ from the real world which all economists wanted to interpret in developing their theories; they also erred in being unaware of the fact that they themselves did not resort to such an assumption in their own treatment of prices.

In an economic system in which every actor is in a position to recognize correctly the market situation with the same degree of insight, the adjustment of prices to every change in the data would be achieved at one stroke. It is impossible to imagine such uniformity in the correct cognition and appraisal of changes in data except by the intercession of superhuman agencies. We would have to assume that every man is approached by an angel informing him of the change in data which has occurred and advising him how to adjust his own conduct in the most adequate way to this change. Certainly the market that catallactics deals with is filled with people who are to different degrees aware of the changes in data and who, even if they have the same information, appraise it differently. The operation of the market reflects the fact that changes in the data are first perceived only by a few people and that different men draw different conclusions in appraising their effects. The more enterprising and brighter individuals take the lead, others follow later. The shrewder individuals appreciate conditions more correctly than the less intelligent and therefore succeed better in their actions. Economists must never disregard in their reasoning the fact that the innate and acquired inequality of men differentiates their adjustment to the conditions of their environment.

The driving force of the market process is provided neither by the consumers nor by the owners of the means of production—land, capital goods, and labor—but by the promoting and speculating entrepreneurs. These are people intent upon profiting by taking advantage of differences in prices. Quicker of apprehension and farther-sighted than other men, they look around for sources of profit. They buy where and when they deem prices too low, and they sell where and when they deem prices too high. They approach the owners of the factors of production, and their competition sends the prices of these factors up to the limit corresponding to their anticipation of the future prices of the products. They approach the consumers, and their competition forces prices of consumers' goods down to the point at which the whole supply can be sold. Profit-seeking speculation is the driving force of the market as it is the driving force of production.

On the market agitation never stops. The imaginary construction of an evenly rotating economy has no counterpart in reality. There can never emerge a state of affairs in which the sum of the prices of the complementary factors of production, due allowance being made for time preference, equals the prices of the products and no further changes are to be expected. There are always profits to be earned by somebody. The speculators are always enticed by the expectation of profit.

The imaginary construction of the evenly rotating economy is a mental tool for comprehension of entrepreneurial profit and loss. It is, to be sure, not a design for comprehension of the pricing process. The final prices corresponding to this imaginary conception are by no means identical with the market prices. The activities of the entrepreneurs or of any other actors on the economic scene are not guided by consideration of any such things as equilibrium prices and the evenly rotating economy. The entrepreneurs take into account anticipated future prices, not final prices or equilibrium prices. They discover discrepancies between the height of the prices of the complementary factors of production and the anticipated future prices of the products, and they are intent upon taking advantage of such discrepancies. These endeavors of the entrepreneurs would finally result in the emergence of the evenly rotating economy if no further changes in the data were to appear.

The operation of the entrepreneurs brings about a tendency toward an equalization of prices for the same goods in all subdivisions of the market, due allowance being made for the cost of transportation and the time absorbed by it. Differences in prices which are not merely transitory and bound to be wiped out by entrepreneurial action are always the outcome of particular obstacles obstructing the inherent tendency toward equalization. Some check prevents profit-seeking business from interfering. An observer not sufficiently familiar with actual commercial conditions is often at a loss to recognize the institutional barrier hindering such equalization. But the merchants concerned always know what makes it impossible for them to take advantage of such differences.

Statisticians treat this problem too lightly. When they have discovered differences in the wholesale price of a commodity between two cities or countries, not entirely accounted for by the cost of transportation, tariffs, and excise duties, they acquiesce in asserting that the purchasing power of money and the "level" of prices are different.[1] On the basis of such statements people draft programs to remove these differences by monetary measures. However, the root cause of these differences cannot lie in monetary conditions. If prices in both countries are quoted in terms of the same kind of money, it is necessary to answer the question as to what prevents businessmen from embarking upon dealings which are bound to make price differences disappear. Things are essentially the same if the prices are expressed in terms of different kinds of money. For the mutual exchange ratio between various kinds of money tends toward a point at which there is no further margin left to profitable exploitation of differences in commodity prices. Whenever differences in commodity prices between various places persist, it is a task for economic history and descriptive economics to establish what institutional barriers hinder the execution of transactions which must result in the equalization of prices.

All the prices we know are past prices. They are facts of economic history. In speaking of present prices we imply that the prices of the immediate future will not differ from those of the immediate past. However, all that is asserted with regard to future prices is merely an outcome of the understanding of future events.

The experience of economic history never tells us more than that at a definite date and definite place two parties *A* and *B* traded a definite quantity of the commodity *a* against a definite number of units of the money *p*. In speaking of such acts of buying and selling as the market price of *a,* we are guided by a theoretical insight, deduced from an aprioristic starting point. This is the insight that, in the absence of particular factors making for price differences, the prices paid at the same time and the same place for equal quantities of the same commodity tend toward equalization, viz., a final price. But the actual market prices never reach this final state. The various market prices about which we can get information were determined under different conditions. It is impermissible to confuse averages computed from them with the final prices.

Only with regard to fungible commodities negotiated on organized stock or commodity exchanges is it permissible, in comparing prices, to assume that they refer to the same quality. Apart from such prices negotiated in exchanges and from prices of commodities the homogeneity of which can be precisely established by technological anal-

1. Sometimes the difference in price as established by price statistics is apparent only. The price quotations may refer to various qualities of the article concerned. Or they may, complying with the local usages of commerce, mean different things. They may, for instance, include or not include packing charges; they may refer to cash payment or to payment at a later date; and so on.

ysis, it is a serious blunder to disregard differences in the quality of the commodity in question. Even in the wholesale trade of raw textiles the diversity of the articles plays the main role. A comparison of prices of consumers' goods is mainly misleading on account of the difference in quality. The quantity traded in one transaction too is relevant in the determination of the price paid per unit. Shares of a corporation sold in one large lot bring a different price than those sold in several small lots.

It is necessary to emphasize these facts again and again because it is customary nowadays to play off the statistical elaboration of price data against the theory of prices. However, the statistics of prices is altogether questionable. Its foundations are precarious because circumstances for the most part do not permit the comparison of the various data, their linking together in series, and the computation of averages. Full of zeal to embark upon mathematical operations, the statisticians yield to the temptation of disregarding the incomparability of the data available. The information that a certain firm sold at a definite date a definite type of shoes for six dollars a pair relates a fact of economic history. A study of the behavior of shoe prices from 1923 to 1939 is conjectural, however sophisticated the methods applied may be.

Catallactics shows that entrepreneurial activities tend toward an abolition of price differences not caused by the costs of transportation and trade barriers. No experience has ever contradicted this theorem. The results obtained by an arbitrary identification of unequal things are irrelevant.

2. Valuation and Appraisement

The ultimate source of the determination of prices is the value judgments of the consumers. Prices are the outcome of the valuation preferring *a* to *b*. They are social phenomena as they are brought about by the interplay of the valuations of all individuals participating in the operation of the market. Each individual, in buying or not buying and in selling or not selling, contributes his share to the formation of the market prices. But the larger the market is, the smaller is the weight of each individual's contribution. Thus the structure of market prices appears to the individual as a datum to which he must adjust his own conduct.

The valuations which result in determination of definite prices are different. Each party attaches a higher value to the good he receives than to that he gives away. The exchange ratio, the price, is not the product of an equality of valuation, but, on the contrary, the product of a discrepancy in valuation.

Appraisement must be clearly distinguished from valuation. Appraisement in no way depends upon the subjective valuation of the man who appraises. He is not intent upon establishing the subjective use-value of the good concerned, but upon anticipating the prices which the market will determine. Valuation is a value judgment expressive of a difference in value. Appraisement is the anticipation of an expected fact. It aims at establishing what prices will be paid on the market for a particular commodity or what amount of money will be required for the purchase of a definite commodity.

Valuation and appraisement are, however, closely connected. The valuations of an autarkic husbandman directly compare the weight he attaches to different means for the removal of uneasiness. The valuations of a man buying and selling on the market must not disregard the structure of market prices; they depend upon appraisement. In order to know the meaning of a price one must know the purchasing power of the amount of money concerned. It is necessary by and large to be familiar with the prices of those goods which one would like to acquire and to form on the ground of such knowledge an opinion about their future prices. If an individual speaks of the costs incurred by the purchase of some goods already acquired or to be incurred by the purchase of goods he plans to acquire, he expresses these costs in terms of money. But this amount of money represents in his eyes the degree of satisfaction he could obtain by employing it for the acquisition of other goods. The valuation makes a detour, it goes via the appraisement of the structure of market prices; but it always aims finally at the comparison of alternative modes for the removal of felt uneasiness.

It is ultimately always the subjective value judgments of individuals that determine the formation of prices. Catallactics in conceiving the pricing process necessarily reverts to the fundamental category of action, the preference given to *a* over *b*. In view of popular errors it is expedient to emphasize that catallactics deals with the real prices as they are paid in definite transactions and not with imaginary prices. The concept of final prices is merely a mental tool for the grasp of a particular problem, the emergence of entrepreneurial profit and loss. The concept of a "just" or "fair" price is devoid of any scientific meaning; it is a disguise for wishes, a striving for a state of affairs different from reality. Market prices are entirely determined by the value judgments of men as they really act.

If one says that prices tend toward a point at which total demand is equal to total supply, one resorts to another mode of expressing the same concatenation of phenomena. Demand and supply are the outcome of the conduct of those buying and selling. If, other things being equal, supply increases, prices must drop. At the previous price all those ready to pay this price could buy the quantity they wanted to buy. If the supply increases, they must buy larger quantities or other people who did not buy before must become interested in buying. This can only be attained at a lower price.

It is possible to visualize this interaction by drawing two curves, the demand curve and the supply curve, whose intersection shows the price. It is no less possible to express it in mathematical symbols. But it is necessary to comprehend that such pictorial or mathematical modes of representation do not affect the essence of our interpretation and that they do not add a whit to our insight. Furthermore it is important to realize that we do not have any knowledge or experience concerning the shape of such curves. Always, what we know is only market prices—that is, not the curves but only a point which we interpret as the intersection of two hypothetical curves. The drawing of such curves may prove expedient in visualizing the problems for undergraduates. For the real tasks of catallactics they are mere byplay.

3. The Prices of the Goods of Higher Orders

The market process is coherent and indivisible. It is an indissoluble intertwinement of actions and reactions, of moves and countermoves. But the insufficiency of our mental abilities enjoins upon us the necessity of dividing it into parts and analyzing each of these parts separately. In resorting to such artificial cleavages we must never forget that the seemingly autonomous existence of these parts is an imaginary makeshift of our minds. They are only parts, that is, they cannot even be thought of as existing outside the structure of which they are parts.

The prices of the goods of higher orders are ultimately determined by the prices of the goods of the first or lowest order, that is, the consumers' goods. As a consequence of this dependence they are ultimately determined by the subjective valuations of all members of the market society. It is, however, important to realize that we are faced with a connection of prices, not with a connection of valuations. The prices of the complementary factors of production are conditioned by the prices of the consumers' goods. The factors of production are appraised with regard to the prices of the products, and from this appraisement their prices emerge. Not the valuations but the appraisements are transferred from the goods of the first order to those of higher orders. The prices of the consumers' goods engender the actions resulting in the determination of the prices of the factors of production. These prices are primarily connected only with the prices of the consumers' goods. With the valuations of the individuals they are only indirectly connected, viz., through the intermediary of the prices of the consumers' goods, the products of their joint employment.

The tasks incumbent upon the theory of the prices of factors of production are to be solved by the same methods which are employed for treatment of the prices of consumers' goods. We conceive the operation of the market of consumers' goods in a twofold way. We think on the one hand of a state of affairs which leads to acts of exchange; the situation is such that the uneasiness of various individuals can be removed to some extent because various people value the same goods in a different way. On the other hand we think of a situation in which no further acts of exchange can happen because no actor expects any further improvement of his satisfaction by further acts of exchange. We proceed in the same way in comprehending the formation of the prices of factors of production. The operation of this market is actuated and kept in motion by the exertion of the promoting entrepreneurs, eager to profit from differences in the market prices of the factors of production and the expected prices of the products. The operation of this market would stop if a situation were ever to emerge in which the sum of the prices of the complementary factors of production—but for interest—equaled the prices of the products and nobody believed that further price changes were to be expected. Thus we have described the process adequately and completely by pointing out, positively, what actuates it and, negatively, what would suspend its motion. The main importance is to be attached to the positive description. The negative description resulting in the imaginary constructions of the final price and the evenly rotating economy is merely auxiliary. For the task is not the treatment of imaginary concepts, which never appear in life and action, but the treatment of the market prices at which the goods of higher orders are really bought and sold.

This method we owe to Gossen, Carl Menger, and Böhm-Bawerk. Its main merit is that it implies the cognition that we are faced with a phenomenon of price determination inextricably linked with the market process. It distinguishes between two things: (*a*) the direct valuation of the factors of production which attaches the value of the product to the total complex of the complementary factors of production, and (*b*) the prices of the single factors of production which are formed on the market as the resultant of the concurring actions of competing highest bidders. Valuation as it can be practiced by an isolated actor (Robinson Crusoe or a socialist board of production management) can never result in a determination of such a thing as quotas of value. Valuation can only arrange goods in scales of preference. It can never attach to a good something that could be called a quantity or magnitude of value. It would be absurd to speak of a sum of valuations or values. It is permissible to declare that, due allowance being made for time preference, the value attached to a product is equal to the value of the total complex of complementary factors of production. But it would be nonsensical to assert that the value attached to a product is equal to the "sum" of the values attached to the various complementary factors of production. One cannot add up values or valuations. One can add up prices expressed in terms of money, but not scales of preference. One cannot divide values or single out quotas of them. A value judgment never consists in anything other than preferring *a* to *b*.

The process of value imputation does not result in derivation of the value of the single productive agents from the value of their joint product. It does not bring about results which could serve as elements of economic calculation. It is only the market that, in establishing prices for each factor of production, creates the conditions required for economic calculation. Economic calculation always deals with prices, never with values.

The market determines prices of factors of production in the same way in which it determines prices of consumers' goods. The market process is an interaction of men deliberately striving after the best possible removal of dissatisfaction. It is impossible to think away or to eliminate from the market process the men actuating its operation. One cannot deal with the market of consumers' goods and disregard the actions of the consumers. One cannot deal with the market of the goods of higher orders while disregarding the actions of the entrepreneurs and the fact that the use of money is essential in their transactions. There is nothing automatic or mechanical in the operation of the market. The entrepreneurs, eager to earn profits, appear as bidders at an auction, as it were, in which the owners of the factors of production put up for sale land, capital goods, and labor. The entrepreneurs are eager to outdo one another by bidding higher prices than their rivals. Their offers are limited on the one hand by their anticipation of future prices of the products and on the other hand by the necessity to snatch the factors of production away from the hands of other entrepreneurs competing with them.

The entrepreneur is the agency that prevents the persistence of a state of production unsuitable to fill the most urgent wants of the consumers in the cheapest way. All people are anxious for the best possible satisfaction of their wants and are in this sense striving after the highest profit they can reap. The mentality of the promoters, speculators, and entrepreneurs is not different from that of their fellow men. They are merely superior to the masses in mental power and energy. They are the leaders on the way toward material progress. They are the first to understand that there is a discrepancy between what is done and what could be done. They guess what the consumers would like to have and are intent upon providing them with these things. In the pursuit of such plans they bid higher prices for some factors of production and lower the prices of other factors of production by restricting their demand for them. In supplying the market with those consumers' goods in the sale of which the highest profits can be earned, they create a tendency toward a fall in their prices. In restricting the output of those consumers' goods the production of which does not offer chances for reaping profit, they bring about a tendency toward a rise in their prices. All these transformations go on ceaselessly and could stop only if the unrealizable conditions of the evenly rotating economy and of static equilibrium were to be attained.

In drafting their plans the entrepreneurs look first at the prices of the immediate past which are mistakenly called *present* prices. Of course, the entrepreneurs never make these prices enter into their calculations without paying regard to anticipated changes. The prices of the immediate past are for them only the starting point of deliberations leading to forecasts of future prices. The prices of the past do not influence the determination of future prices. It is, on the contrary, the anticipation of future prices of the products that determines the state of prices of the complementary factors of production. The determination of prices has, as far as the mutual exchange ratios between various commodities are concerned,[2] no direct causal relation whatever with the prices of the past. The allocation of the nonconvertible factors of production among the various branches of production[3] and the amount of capital goods available for future production are historical magnitudes; in this regard the past is instrumental in shaping the course of future production and in affecting the prices of the future. But directly the prices of the factors of production are deter-

2. It is different with regard to the mutual exchange ratios between money and the vendible commodities and services. Cf. below, pp. 410–411.

3. The problem of the nonconvertible capital goods is dealt with below, pp. 503–509.

mined exclusively by the anticipation of future prices of the products. The fact that yesterday people valued and appraised commodities in a different way is irrelevant. The consumers do not care about the investments made with regard to past market conditions and do not bother about the vested interests of entrepreneurs, capitalists, landowners, and workers, who may be hurt by changes in the structure of prices. Such sentiments play no role in the formation of prices. (It is precisely the fact that the market does not respect vested interests that makes the people concerned ask for government interference.) The prices of the past are for the entrepreneur, the shaper of future production, merely a mental tool. The entrepreneurs do not construct afresh every day a radically new structure of prices or allocate anew the factors of production to the various branches of industry. They merely transform what the past has transmitted in better adapting it to the altered conditions. How much of the previous conditions they preserve and how much they change depends on the extent to which the data have changed.

The economic process is a continuous interplay of production and consumption. Today's activities are linked with those of the past through the technological knowledge at hand, the amount and the quality of the capital goods available, and the distribution of the ownership of these goods among various individuals. They are linked with the future through the very essence of human action; action is always directed toward the improvement of future conditions. In order to see his way in the unknown and uncertain future man has within his reach only two aids: experience of past events and his faculty of understanding. Knowledge about past prices is a part of this experience and at the same time the starting point of understanding the future.

If the memory of all prices of the past were to fade away, the pricing process would become more troublesome, but not impossible as far as the mutual exchange ratios between various commodities are concerned. It would be harder for the entrepreneurs to adjust production to the demand of the public, but it could be done nonetheless. It would be necessary for them to assemble anew all the data they need as the basis of their operations. They would not avoid mistakes which they now evade on account of experience at their disposal. Price fluctuations would be more violent at the beginning, factors of production would be wasted, want-satisfaction would be impaired. But finally, having paid dearly, people would again have acquired the experience needed for a smooth working of the market process.

The essential fact is that it is the competition of profit-seeking entrepreneurs that does not tolerate the preservation of *false* prices of the factors of production. The activities of the entrepreneurs are the element that would bring about the unrealizable state of the evenly rotating economy if no further changes were to occur. In the world-embracing public sale called the market they are the bidders for the factors of production. In bidding, they are the mandataries of the consumers, as it were. Each entrepreneur represents a different aspect of the consumers' wants, either a different commodity or another way of producing the same commodity. The competition among the entrepreneurs is ultimately a competition among the various possibilities open to men to remove their uneasiness as far as possible by the acquisition of consumers' goods. The decisions of the consumers to buy one commodity and to postpone buying another determine the prices of factors of production required for manufacturing these commodities. The competition between the entrepreneurs reflects the prices of consumers' goods in the formation of the prices of the factors of production. It reflects in the external world the conflict which the inexorable scarcity of the factors of production brings about in the soul of each individual. It makes effective the subsumed decisions of the consumers as to what purpose the nonspecific factors should be used for and to what extent the specific factors of production should be used.

The pricing process is a social process. It is consummated by an interaction of all members of the society. All collaborate and cooperate, each in the particular role he has chosen for himself in the framework of the division of labor. Competing in cooperation and cooperating in competition all people are instrumental in bringing about the result, viz., the price structure of the market, the allocation of the factors of production to the various lines of want-satisfaction, and the determination of the share of each individual. These three events are not three different matters. They are only different aspects of one indivisible phenomenon which our analytical scrutiny separates into three parts. In the market process they are accomplished *uno actu*. Only people prepossessed by socialist leanings who cannot free themselves from longing glances at socialist methods speak of three different processes in dealing with the market phenomena: the determination of prices, the direction of productive efforts, and distribution.

A Limitation on the Pricing of Factors of Production

The process which makes the prices of the factors of production spring from the prices of products can achieve its results only if, of the complementary factors not replaceable by substitutes, not more than one is of absolutely specific character, that is, is not suitable for any other employment. If the production of a product requires two or more absolutely specific factors, only a cumulative price can be assigned to them. If all factors of production were absolutely specific, the pricing process would not achieve more than such cumulative prices. It would accomplish nothing more than statements like this: as combining 3 *a* and 5 *b* produces one unit of *p*, 3 *a* and 5 *b* together are equal to 1 *p* and the final price of 3 $a+5$ *b* is—due allowance being made for time preference—equal to the final price of 1 *p*. As entrepreneurs who want to use *a* and *b* for purposes other than the production of *p* do not bid for them, a more detailed price determination is impossible. Only if a demand emerges for *a* (or for *b*) on the part of entrepreneurs who want to employ *a* (or *b*) for other purposes, does competition between them and the entrepreneurs planning the production of *p* arise and a price for *a* (or for *b*) come into existence, the height of which determines also the price of *b* (or *a*).

A world in which all the factors of production are absolutely specific could manage its affairs with such cumulative prices. In such a world there would not exist the problem of how to allocate the means of production to various branches of want-satisfaction. In our real world things are different. There are many scarce means of production which can be employed for various tasks. There the economic problem is to employ these factors in such a way that no unit of them should be used for the satisfaction of a less urgent need if this employment prevents the satisfaction of a more urgent need. It is this that the market solves in determining the prices of the factors of production. The social service rendered by this solution is not in the least impaired by the fact that for factors which can be employed only cumulatively no other than cumulative prices are determined.

Factors of production which can be used in the same ratio of combination for the production of various commodities but do not allow of any other use, are to be considered as absolutely specific factors. They are absolutely specific with regard to the production of an intermediary product which can be utilized for various purposes. The price of this intermediary product can be assigned to them cumulatively only. Whether this intermediary product can be directly apperceived by the senses or whether it is merely the invisible and intangible outcome of their joint employment makes no difference.

4. Cost Accounting

In the calculation of the entrepreneur costs are the amount of money required for the procurement of the factors of production. The entrepreneur is intent upon embarking upon those business projects from which he expects the highest surplus of proceeds over costs and upon shunning projects from which he expects a lower amount of profit or even a loss. In doing this he adjusts his effort to the best possible satisfaction of the needs of the consumers. The fact that a project is not profitable because costs are higher than proceeds is the outcome of the fact that there is a more useful employment available for the factors of production required. There are other products in the purchase of which the consumers are prepared to allow for the prices of these factors of production. But the consumers are not prepared to pay these prices in buying the commodity the production of which is not profitable.

Cost accounting is affected by the fact that the two following conditions are not always present:

First, every increase in the quantity of factors expended for the production of a consumers' good increases its power to remove uneasiness.

Second, every increase in the quantity of a consumers' good requires a proportional increase in the expenditure of factors of production or even a more than proportional increase in their expenditure.

If both these conditions were always and without any exception fulfilled, every increment z expended for increasing the quantity m of a commodity g would be employed for the satisfaction of a need viewed as less urgent than the least urgent need already satisfied by the quantity m available previously. At the same time the increment z would require the employment of factors of production to be withdrawn from the satisfaction of other needs considered as more pressing than those needs whose satisfaction was foregone in order to produce the marginal unit of m. On the one hand the marginal value of the satisfaction derived from the increase in the quantity available of g would drop. On the other hand the costs required for the production of additional quantities of g would increase in marginal disutility; factors of production would be withheld from employments in which they could satisfy more urgent needs. Production must stop at the point at which the marginal utility of the increment no longer compensates for the marginal increase in the disutility of costs.

Now these two conditions are present very often, but not generally without exception. There exist many commodities of all orders of goods whose physical structure is not homogeneous and which are therefore not perfectly divisible.

It would, of course, be possible to conjure away the deviation from the first condition mentioned above by a sophisticated play on words. One could say: half a motorcar is not a motorcar. If one adds to half a motorcar a quarter of a motorcar, one does not increase the "quantity" available; only the perfection of the process of production which turns out a complete car produces a unit and an increase in the "quantity" available. However, such an interpretation misses the point. The problem we must face is that not every increase in expenditure increases proportionately the objective use-value, the physical power of a thing to render a definite service. The various increments in expenditure bring about different results. There are increments the expenditure of which remains useless if no further increments of a definite quantity are added.

On the other hand—and this is the deviation from the second condition—an increase in physical output does not always require a proportionate increase in expenditure or even any additional expenditure. It may happen that costs do not rise at all or that their rise increases output more than proportionately. For many means of production are not homogeneous either and not perfectly divisible. This is the phenomenon known to business as the superiority of big-scale production. The economists speak of the law of increasing returns or decreasing costs.

We consider—as case *A*—a state of affairs in which all factors of production are not perfectly divisible and in which full utilization of the productive services rendered by every further indivisible element of each factor requires full utilization of the further indivisible elements of every other of the complementary factors. Then in every aggregate of productive agents each of the assembled elements—every machine, every worker, every piece of raw material—can be fully utilized only if all the productive services of the other elements are fully employed too. Within these limits the production of a part of the maximum output attainable does not require a higher expenditure than the production of the highest possible output. We may also say that the minimum-size aggregate always produces the same quantity of products; it is impossible to produce a smaller quantity of products even if there is no use for a part of it.

We consider—as case *B*—a state of affairs in which one group of the productive agents (p) is for all practical purposes perfectly divisible. On the other hand the imperfectly divisible agents can be divided in such a way that full utilization of the services rendered by each further indivisible part of one agent requires full utilization of the further indivisible parts of the other imperfectly divisible complementary factors. Then increasing production of an aggregate of further indivisible factors from a partial to a more complete utilization of their productive capacity requires merely an increase in the quantity of p, the perfectly divisible factors. However, one must guard oneself against the fallacy that this necessarily implies a decrease in the average cost of production. It is true that within the aggregate of imperfectly divisible factors each of them is now better utilized, that therefore costs of production as far as they are caused by the cooperation of these factors remain unchanged, and that the quotas falling to a unit of output are decreasing. But on the other hand an increase in the employment of the perfectly divisible factors of production can be attained only by withdrawing them from other employments. The value of these other employments increases, other things being equal, with their shrinking; the price of these perfectly divisible factors tends to rise as more of them are used for the better utilization of the productive capacity of the aggregate of the not further divisible factors in question. One must not limit the consideration of our problem to the case in which the additional quantity of *p* is withdrawn from other enterprises producing the same product in a less efficient way and forces these enterprises to restrict their output. It is obvious that in this case—competition between a more and a less efficient enterprise producing the same article out of the same raw materials—the average cost of production is decreasing in the expanding plant. A more general scrutiny of the problem leads to a different result. If the units of *p* are withdrawn from other employments in which they would have been utilized for the production of other articles, there emerges a tendency toward an increase in the price of these units. This tendency may be compensated by accidental tendencies operating in the opposite direction; it may sometimes be so feeble that its effects are negligible. But it is always present and potentially influences the configuration of costs.

Finally we consider—as case *C*—a state of affairs in which various imperfectly divisible factors of production can be divided only in such a way that, given the conditions of the market, any size which can be chosen for their assemblage in a production aggregate does not allow for a combination in which full utilization of the productive capacity of one factor makes possible full utilization of the productive capacity of the other imperfectly divisible factors. This case *C* alone is of practical significance, while the cases *A* and *B* hardly play any role in real business. The characteristic feature of case *C* is that the configuration of production costs varies unevenly. If all imperfectly divisible factors are utilized to less than full capacity, an expansion of production results in a decrease of average costs of production unless a rise in the prices to be paid for the perfectly divisible factors counterbalances this outcome. But as soon as full utilization of the capacity of one of the imperfectly divisible factors is attained, further expansion of production causes a sudden sharp rise in costs. Then again a tendency toward a decrease in average production costs sets in and goes on working until full utilization of one of the imperfectly divisible factors is attained anew.

Other things being equal, the more production of a certain article increases, the more factors of production must be withdrawn from other employments in which they would have been used for the production of other articles. Hence—other things being equal—average production costs increase with the increase in the quantity produced. But this general law is by sections superseded by the phenomenon that not all factors of production are perfectly divisible and that, as far as they can be divided, they are not divisible in such a way that full utilization of one of them results in full utilization of the other imperfectly divisible factors.

The planning entrepreneur is always faced with the question: To what extent will the anticipated prices of the products exceed the anticipated costs? If the entrepreneur is still free with regard to the project in question, because he has not yet made any inconvertible investments for its realization, it is average costs that count for him. But if he has already a vested interest in the line of business concerned, he sees things from the angle of additional costs to be expended. He who already owns a not fully utilized production aggregate does not take into account average cost of production but marginal cost. Without regard to the amount already expended for inconvertible investments he is merely interested in the question whether or not the proceeds from the sale of an additional quantity of products will exceed the additional cost incurred by their production. Even if the whole amount invested in the inconvertible production facilities must be wiped off as a loss, he goes on producing provided he expects a reasonable[4] surplus of proceeds over current costs.

With regard to popular errors it is necessary to emphasize that if the conditions required for the appearance of monopoly prices are not present, an entrepreneur is not in a position to increase his net returns by restricting production beyond the amount conforming with consumers' demand. But this problem will be dealt with later in section 6.

That a factor of production is not perfectly divisible does not always mean that it can be constructed and employed in one size only. This, of course, may occur in some cases. But as a rule it is

4. Reasonable means in this connection that the anticipated returns on the convertible capital used for the continuation of production are at least not lower than the anticipated returns on its use for other projects.

possible to vary the dimensions of these factors. If out of the various dimensions which are possible for such a factor—e.g., a machine—one dimension is distinguished by the fact that the costs incurred by its production and operation are rendered lower per unit of the productive services than those for other dimensions, things are essentially identical. Then the superiority of the bigger plant does not consist in the fact that it utilizes a machine to full capacity while the smaller plant utilizes only a part of the capacity of a machine of the same size. It consists rather in the fact that the bigger plant employs a machine which operates with a better utilization of the factors of production required for its construction and operation than does the smaller machine employed by the smaller plant.

The role played in all branches of production by the fact that many factors of production are not perfectly divisible is very great. It is of paramount importance in the course of industrial affairs. But one must guard oneself against many misinterpretations of its significance.

One of these errors was the doctrine according to which in the processing industries there prevails a law of increasing returns, while in agriculture and mining a law of decreasing returns prevails. The fallacies implied have been exploded above.[5] As far as there is a difference in this regard between conditions in agriculture and those in the processing industries, differences in the data bring them about. The immobility of the soil and the fact that the performance of the various agricultural operations depends on the seasons make it impossible for farmers to take advantage of the capacity of many movable factors of production to the degree which conditions in manufacturing for the most part allow. The optimum size of a production outfit in agricultural production is as a rule much smaller than in the processing industries. It is obvious and does not need any further explanation why the concentration of farming cannot be pushed to anything near the degree obtaining in the processing industries.

However, the inequality in the distribution of natural resources over the earth's surface, which is one of the two factors making for the higher productivity of the division of labor, puts a limit to the progress of concentration in the processing industries also. The tendency toward a progressive specialization and the concentration of integrated industrial processes in only a few plants is counteracted by the geographical dispersion of natural resources. The fact that the production of raw materials and foodstuffs cannot be centralized and forces people to disperse over the various part of the earth's

5. Cf. above, p. 130.

surface enjoins also upon the processing industries a certain degree of decentralization. It makes it necessary to consider the problems of transportation as a particular factor of production costs. The costs of transportation must be weighed against the economies to be expected from more thoroughgoing specialization. While in some branches of the processing industries the utmost concentration is the most adequate method of reducing costs, in other branches a certain degree of decentralization is more advantageous. In the servicing trades the disadvantages of concentration become so great that they almost entirely overweigh the advantages derived.

Then a historical factor comes into play. In the past capital goods were immobilized on sites on which our contemporaries would not have set them. It is immaterial whether or not this immobilization was the most economical procedure to which the generations that brought it about could resort. In any event the present generation is faced with a *fait accompli*. It must adjust its operations to the fact and it must take it into account in dealing with problems of the location of the processing industries.[6]

Finally there are institutional factors. There are trade and migration barriers. There are differences in political organization and methods of government between various countries. Vast areas are administered in such a way that it is practically out of the question to choose them as a seat for any capital investment no matter how favorable their physical conditions may be.

Entrepreneurial cost accounting must deal with all these geographical, historical and institutional factors. But even apart from them there are purely technical factors limiting the optimum size of plants and firms. The greater plant or firm may require provisions and procedures which the smaller plant or firm can avoid. In many instances the outlays caused by such provisions and procedures may be overcompensated by the reduction in costs derived from better utilization of the capacity of some of the not perfectly divisible factors employed. In other instances this may not be the case.

Under capitalism the arithmetical operations required for cost accounting and the confrontation of costs and proceeds can easily be effected as there are methods of economic calculation available. However, cost accounting and calculation of the economic significance of business projects under consideration is not merely a mathematical problem which can be solved satisfactorily by all those familiar with

6. For a thoroughgoing treatment of the conservatism enjoined upon men by the limited convertibility of many capital goods, the historically determined element in production, see below, pp. 503–514.

the elementary rules of arithmetic. The main question is the determination of the money equivalents of the items which are to enter into the calculation. It is a mistake to assume, as many economists do, that these equivalents are given magnitudes, uniquely determined by the state of economic conditions. They are speculative anticipations of uncertain future conditions and as such depend on the entrepreneur's understanding of the future state of the market. The term *fixed* costs is also in this regard somewhat misleading.

Every action aims at the best possible supplying of future needs. To achieve these ends it must make the best possible use of the available factors of production. However, the historical process which brought about the present state of factors available is beside the point. What counts and influences the decisions concerning future action is solely the outcome of this historical process, the quantity and the quality of the factors available today. These factors are appraised only with regard to their ability to render productive services for the removal of future uneasiness. The amount of money spent in the past for their production and acquisition is immaterial.

It has already been pointed out that an entrepreneur who by the time he has to make a new decision has expended money for the realization of a definite project is in a different position from that of a man who starts afresh. The former owns a complex of inconvertible factors of production which he can employ for certain purposes. His decisions concerning further action will be influenced by this fact. But he appraises this complex not according to what he expended in the past for its acquisition. He appraises it exclusively from the point of view of its usefulness for future action. The fact that he has spent more or less for its acquisition is insignificant. This fact is only a factor in determining the amount of the entrepreneur's past losses or profits and the present state of his fortune. It is an element in the historical process that brought about the present state of the supply of factors of production and as such it is of importance for future action. But it does not count for the planning of future action and the calculation regarding such action. It is irrelevant that the entries in the firm's books differ from the actual price of such inconvertible factors of production.

Of course, such consummated losses or profits may motivate a firm to operate in a different way from which it would if it were not affected by them. Past losses may render a firm's financial position precarious, especially if they bring about indebtedness and burden it with payments of interest and installments on the principal. However, it is not correct to refer to such payments as a part of fixed costs. They have no relation whatever to the current operations. They are not caused by the process of production, but by the methods employed by the entrepreneur in the past for the procurement of the capital and capital goods needed. They are only accidental with reference to the going concern. But they may enforce upon the firm in question a conduct of affairs which it would not adopt if it were financially stronger. The urgent need for cash in order to meet payments due does not affect its cost accounting, but its appraisal of ready cash as compared with cash that can only be received at a later day. It may impel the firm to sell inventories at an inappropriate moment and to use its durable production equipment in a way that unduly neglects its conservation for later use.

It is immaterial for the problems of cost accounting whether a firm owns the capital invested in its enterprise or whether it has borrowed a greater or smaller part of it and is bound to comply with the terms of a loan contract rigidly fixing the rate of interest and the dates of maturity for interest and principal. The costs of production include only the interest on the capital which is still existent and working in the enterprise. It does not include interest on capital squandered in the past by bad investment or by inefficiency in the conduct of current business operations. The task incumbent upon the businessman is always to use the supply of capital goods *now* available in the best possible way for the satisfaction of future needs. In the pursuit of this aim he must not be misled by past errors and failures the consequences of which cannot be brushed away. A plant may have been constructed in the past which would not have been built if one had better forecast the present situation. It is vain to lament this historical fact. The main thing is to find out whether or not the plant can still render any service and, if this question is answered in the affirmative, how it can be best utilized. It is certainly sad for the individual entrepreneur that he did not avoid errors. The losses incurred impair his financial situation. They do not affect the costs to be taken into account in planning further action.

It is important to stress this point because it has been distorted in the current interpretation and justification of various measures. One does not "reduce costs" by alleviating some firms' and corporations' burden of debts. A policy of wiping out debts or the interest due on them totally or in part does not reduce costs. It transfers wealth from creditors to debtors; it shifts the incidence of losses incurred in the past from one group of people to another group, e.g., from the owners of common stock to those of preferred stock and corporate bonds. This argument of cost reduction is often advanced in favor of currency devaluation. It is no less fallacious in this case than all the other arguments brought forward for this purpose.

What are commonly called fixed costs are also costs incurred by the exploitation of the already available factors of production which are either rigidly inconvertible or can be adapted for other productive purposes only at a considerable loss. These factors are of a more durable character than the other factors of production required. But they are not permanent. They are used up in the process of production. With each unit of product turned out a part of the machine's power to produce is exhausted. The extent of this attrition can be precisely ascertained by technology and can be appraised accordingly in terms of money.

However, it is not only this money equivalent of the machine's wearing out which the entrepreneurial calculation has to consider. The businessman is not merely concerned with the duration of the machine's technological life. He must take into account the future state of the market. Although a machine may still be technologically perfectly utilizable, market conditions may render it obsolete and worthless. If the demand for its products drops considerably or disappears altogether or if more efficient methods for supplying the consumers with these products appear, the machine is economically merely scrap iron. In planning the conduct of his business the entrepreneur must pay full regard to the anticipated future state of the market. The amount of "fixed" costs which enter into his calculation depends on his understanding of future events. It is not to be fixed simply by technological reasoning.

The technologist may determine the optimum for a production aggregate's utilization. But this technological optimum may differ from that which the entrepreneur on the ground of his judgment concerning future market conditions enters into his economic calculation. Let us assume that a factory is equipped with machines which can be utilized for a period of ten years. Every year 10 per cent of their prime costs is laid aside for depreciation. In the third year market conditions place a dilemma before the entrepreneur. He can double his output for the year and sell it at a price which (apart from covering the increase in variable costs) exceeds the quota of depreciation for the current year and the present value of the last depreciation quota. But this doubling of production trebles the wearing out of the equipment and the surplus proceeds from the sale of the double quantity of products are not great enough to make good also for the present value of the depreciation quota of the ninth year. If the entrepreneur were to consider the annual depreciation quota as a rigid element for his calculation, he would have to deem the doubling of production as not profitable, as additional proceeds lag behind additional cost. He would abstain from expanding production beyond the technological optimum. But the entrepreneur calculates in a different way, although in his accountancy he may lay aside the same quota for depreciation every year. Whether or not the entrepreneur prefers a fraction of the present value of the ninth year's depreciation quota to the technological services which the machines could render him in the ninth year, depends on his opinion concerning the future state of the market.

Public opinion, governments and legislators, and the tax laws look upon a business outfit as a source of permanent revenue. They believe that the entrepreneur who makes due allowance for capital maintenance by annual depreciation quotas will always be in a position to reap a reasonable return from the capital invested in his durable producers' goods. Real conditions are different. A production aggregate such as a plant and its equipment is a factor of production whose usefulness depends on changing market conditions and the skill of the entrepreneur in employing it in accordance with the change in conditions.

There is in the field of economic calculation nothing that is certain in the sense in which this term is used with regard to technological facts. The essential elements of economic calculation are speculative anticipations of future conditions. Commercial usages and customs and commercial laws have established definite rules for accountancy and auditing. There is accuracy in the keeping of books. But they are accurate only with regard to these rules. The book values do not reflect precisely the real state of affairs. The market value of an aggregate of durable producers' goods may differ from the nominal figures the books show. The proof is that the Stock Exchange appraises them without any regard to these figures.

Cost accounting is therefore not an arithmetical process which can be established and examined by an indifferent umpire. It does not operate with uniquely determined magnitudes which can be found out in an objective way. Its essential items are the result of an understanding of future conditions, necessarily always colored by the entrepreneur's opinion about the future state of the market.

Attempts to establish cost accounts on an "impartial" basis are doomed to failure. Calculating costs is a mental tool of action, the purposive design to make the best of the available means for an improvement of future conditions. It is necessarily volitional, not factual. In the hands of an indifferent umpire it changes its character entirely. The umpire does not look forward to the future. He looks backward to the dead past and to rigid rules which are useless for real life and action. He does not anticipate changes. He is unwittingly guided by the prepossession that the evenly rotating economy is the normal and most desirable state of human affairs. Profits do not fit into his scheme. He has a confused idea about a "fair" rate of profit or a "fair" return on capital invested. However, there are no such things. In the evenly rotating economy there are no profits. In a changing economy profits are not determined with reference to any set of rules by which they could be classified as fair or unfair. Profits are never normal. Where there is normality, i.e., absence of change, no profits can emerge.

5. Logical Catallactics Versus Mathematical Catallactics

The problems of prices and costs have been treated also with mathematical methods. There have even been economists who held that the only appropriate method of dealing with economic problems is the mathematical method and who derided the logical economists as "literary" economists.

If this antagonism between the logical and the mathematical economists were merely a disagreement concerning the most adequate procedure to be applied in the study of economics, it would be superfluous to pay attention to it. The better method would prove its preeminence by bringing about better results. It may also be that different varieties of procedure are necessary for the solution of different problems and that for some of them one method is more useful than the other.

However, this is not a dispute about heuristic questions, but a controversy concerning the foundations of economics. The mathematical method must be rejected not only on account of its barrenness. It is an entirely vicious method, starting from false assumptions and leading to fallacious inferences. Its syllogisms are not only sterile; they divert the mind from the study of the real problems and distort the relations between the various phenomena.

The ideas and procedures of the mathematical economists are not uniform. There are three main currents of thought which must be dealt with separately.

The first variety is represented by the statisticians who aim at discovering economic laws from the study of economic experience. They aim to transform economics into a "quantitative" science. Their program is condensed in the motto of the Econometric Society: Science is measurement.

The fundamental error implied in this reasoning has been shown above.[7] Experience of economic history is always experience of complex phenomena. It can never convey knowledge of the kind the experimenter abstracts from a laboratory experiment. Statistics is a method for the presentation of historical facts concerning prices and other relevant data of human action. It is not economics and cannot produce economic theorems and theories. The statistics of prices is economic history. The insight that, *ceteris paribus,* an increase in demand must result in an increase in prices is not derived from experience. Nobody ever was or ever will be in a position to observe a change in one of the market data *ceteris paribus.* There is no such thing as quantitative economics. All economic quantities we know about are data of economic history. No reasonable man can contend that the relation between price and supply is in general, or in respect of certain commodities, constant. We know, on the contrary, that external phenomena affect different people in different ways, that the reactions of the same people to the same external events vary, and that it is not possible to assign individuals to classes of men reacting in the same way. This insight is a product of our aprioristic theory. It is true the empiricists reject this theory; they pretend that they aim to learn only from historical experience. However, they contradict their own principles as soon as they pass beyond the unadulterated recording of individual single prices and begin to construct series and to compute averages. A datum of experience and a statistical fact is only a price paid at a definite time and a definite place for a definite quantity of a certain commodity. The arrangement of various price data in groups and the computation of averages are guided by theoretical deliberations which are logically and temporally antecedent. The extent to which certain attending features and circumstantial contingencies of the price data concerned are taken or not taken into consideration depends on theoretical reasoning of the same kind. Nobody is so bold as to maintain that a rise of a per cent in the supply of any commodity must always—in every country and at any time—result in a fall of b per cent in its price. But as no quantitative economist ever ventured to define precisely on the ground of statistical experience the special conditions producing a definite deviation from the ratio $a : b$, the futility of his endeavors is manifest. Moreover, money is not a standard for the measurement of prices; it is a medium whose exchange ratio varies in the same way, although as a rule not with the same speed and to

7. Cf. above, pp. 31, 55–56.

the same extent, in which the mutual exchange ratios of the vendible commodities and services vary.

There is hardly any need to dwell longer upon the exposure of the claims of quantitative economics. In spite of all the high-sounding pronouncements of its advocates, nothing has been done for the realization of its program. The late Henry Schultz devoted his research to the measurement of elasticities of demand for various commodities. Professor Paul H. Douglas has praised the outcome of Schultz's studies as "a work as necessary to help make economics a more or less exact science as was the determination of atomic weights for the development of chemistry."[8] The truth is that Schultz never embarked upon a determination of the elasticity of demand for any commodity as such; the data he relied upon were limited to certain geographical areas and historical periods. His results for a definite commodity, for instance potatoes, do not refer to potatoes in general, but to potatoes in the United States in the years from 1875 to 1929.[9] They are, at best, rather questionable and unsatisfactory contributions to various chapters of economic history. They are certainly not steps toward the realization of the confused and contradictory program of quantitative economics. It must be emphasized that the two other varieties of mathematical economics are fully aware of the futility of quantitative economics. For they have never ventured to make any magnitudes as found by the econometricians enter into their formulas and equations and thus to adapt them for the solution of particular problems. There is in the field of human action no means for dealing with future events other than that provided by understanding.

The second field treated by mathematical economists is that of the relation of prices and costs. In dealing with these problems the mathematical economists disregard the operation of the market process and moreover pretend to abstract from the use of money inherent in all economic calculations. However, as they speak of prices and costs in general and confront prices and costs, they tacitly imply the existence and the use of money. Prices are always money prices, and costs cannot be taken into account in economic calculation if not expressed in terms of money. If one does not resort to terms of money, costs are expressed in complex quantities of diverse goods and services to be expended for the procurement of a product. On the other hand prices—if this term is applicable at all to exchange ratios determined by barter—are the enumeration of quantities of various goods against which the "seller" can exchange a definite supply. The goods

8. Cf. Paul H. Douglas in *Econometrica,* VII, 105.

9. Cf. Henry Schultz, *The Theory and Measurement of Demand* (University of Chicago Press, 1938), pp. 405–427.

which are referred to in such "prices" are not the same to which the "costs" refer. A comparison of such prices in kind and costs in kind is not feasible. That the seller values the goods he gives away less than those he receives in exchange for them, that the seller and the buyer disagree with regard to the subjective valuation of the two goods exchanged, and that an entrepreneur embarks upon a project only if he expects to receive for the product goods that he values higher than those expended in their production, all this we know already on the ground of praxeological comprehension. It is this aprioristic knowledge that enables us to anticipate the conduct of an entrepreneur who is in a position to resort to economic calculation. But the mathematical economist deludes himself when he pretends to treat these problems in a more general way by omitting any reference to terms of money. It is vain to investigate instances of nonperfect divisibility of factors of production without reference to economic calculation in terms of money. Such a scrutiny can never go beyond the knowledge already available; namely that every entrepreneur is intent upon producing those articles the sale of which will bring him proceeds that he values higher than the total complex of goods expended in their production. But if there is no indirect exchange and if no medium of exchange is in common use, he can succeed, provided he has correctly anticipated the future state of the market, only if he is endowed with a superhuman intellect. He would have to take in at a glance all exchange ratios determined at the market in such a way as to assign in his deliberations precisely the place due to every good according to these ratios.

It cannot be denied that all investigations concerning the relation of prices and costs presuppose both the use of money and the market process. But the mathematical economists shut their eyes to this obvious fact. They formulate equations and draw curves which are supposed to describe reality. In fact they describe only a hypothetical and unrealizable state of affairs, in no way similar to the catallactic problems in question. They substitute algebraic symbols for the determinate terms of money as used in economic calculation and believe that this procedure renders their reasoning more scientific. They strongly impress the gullible layman. In fact they only confuse and muddle things which are satisfactorily dealt with in textbooks of commercial arithmetic and accountancy.

Some of these mathematicians have gone so far as to declare that economic calculation could be established on the basis of units of utility. They call their methods utility analysis. Their error is shared by the third variety of mathematical economics.

The characteristic mark of this third group is that they are openly and consciously intent upon solving catallactic problems without any reference to the market process. Their ideal is to construct an economic theory according to the pattern of mechanics. They again and again resort to analogies with classical mechanics which in their opinion is the unique and absolute model of scientific inquiry. There is no need to explain again why this analogy is superficial and misleading and in what respects purposive human action radically differs from motion, the subject matter of mechanics. It is enough to stress one point, viz., the practical significance of the differential equations in both fields.

The deliberations which result in the formulation of an equation are necessarily of a nonmathematical character. The formulation of the equation is the consummation of our knowledge; it does not directly enlarge our knowledge. Yet, in mechanics the equation can render very important practical services. As there exist constant relations between various mechanical elements and as these relations can be ascertained by experiments, it becomes possible to use equations for the solution of definite technological problems. Our modern industrial civilization is mainly an accomplishment of this utilization of the differential equations of physics. No such constant relations exist, however, between economic elements. The equations formulated by mathematical economics remain a useless piece of mental gymnastics and would remain so even if they were to express much more than they really do.

A sound economic deliberation must never forget these two fundamental principles of the theory of value: First, valuing that results in action always means preferring and setting aside; it never means equivalence or indifference. Second, there is no means of comparing the valuations of different individuals or the valuations of the same individuals at different instants other than by establishing whether or not they arrange the alternatives in question in the same order of preference.

In the imaginary construction of the evenly rotating economy all factors of production are employed in such a way that each of them renders the most valuable service. No thinkable and possible change could improve the state of satisfaction; no factor is employed for the satisfaction of a need *a* if this employment prevents the satisfaction of a need *b* that is considered more valuable than the satisfaction of *a*. It is, of course, possible to describe this imaginary state of the allocation of resources in differential equations and to visualize it graphically in curves. But such devices do not assert anything about the market process. They merely mark out an imaginary situation in which the market process would cease to operate. The mathematical economists disregard the whole theoretical elucidation of the market process and evasively amuse themselves with an auxiliary notion employed in its context and devoid of any sense when used outside of this context.

In physics we are faced with changes occurring in various sense phenomena. We discover a regularity in the sequence of these changes and these observations lead us to the construction of a science of physics. We know nothing about the ultimate forces actuating these changes. They are for the searching mind ultimately given and defy any further analysis. What we know from observation is the regular concatenation of various observable entities and attributes. It is this mutual interdependence of data that the physicist describes in differential equations.

In praxeology the first fact we know is that men are purposively intent upon bringing about some changes. It is this knowledge that integrates the subject matter of praxeology and differentiates it from the subject matter of the natural sciences. We know the forces behind the changes, and this aprioristic knowledge leads us to a cognition of the praxeological processes. The physicist does not know what electricity "is." He knows only phenomena attributed to something called electricity. But the economist knows what actuates the market process. It is only thanks to this knowledge that he is in a position to distinguish market phenomena from other phenomena and to describe the market process.

Now, the mathematical economist does not contribute anything to the elucidation of the market process. He merely describes an auxiliary makeshift employed by the logical economists as a limiting notion, the definition of a state of affairs in which there is no longer any action and the market process has come to a standstill. That is all he can say. What the logical economist sets forth in words when defining the imaginary constructions of the final state of rest and the evenly rotating economy and what the mathematical economist himself must describe in words before he embarks upon his mathematical work, is translated into algebraic symbols. A superficial analogy is spun out too long, that is all.

Both the logical and the mathematical economists assert that human action ultimately aims at the establishment of such a state of equilibrium and would reach it if all further changes in data were to cease. But the logical economist knows much more than that. He shows how the activities of enterprising men, the promoters and speculators, eager to profit from discrepancies in the price structure, tend toward eradicating such discrepancies and thereby also toward blotting out the sources of entrepreneurial profit and loss. He shows how this process would finally result in the establishment of the evenly rotating economy. This is the task of economic theory. The mathematical description of various states of equilibrium is mere play. The problem is the analysis of the market process.

A comparison of both methods of economic analysis makes us understand the meaning of the often raised request to enlarge the scope of economic science by the construction of a dynamic theory instead of the mere occupation with static problems. With regard to logical economics this postulate is devoid of any sense. Logical economics is essentially a theory of processes and changes. It resorts to the imaginary constructions of changelessness merely for the elucidation of the phenomena of change. But it is different with mathematical economics. Its equations and formulas are limited to the description of states of equilibrium and nonacting. It cannot assert anything with regard to the formation of such states and their transformation into other states as long as it remains in the realm of mathematical procedures. As against mathematical economics the request for a dynamic theory is well substantiated. But there is no means for mathematical economics to comply with this request. The problems of process analysis, i.e., the only economic problems that matter, defy any mathematical approach. The introduction of time parameters into the equations is no solution. It does not even indicate the essential shortcomings of the mathematical method. The statements that every change involves time and that change is always in the temporal sequence are merely a way of expressing the fact that as far as there is rigidity and unchangeability there is no time. The main deficiency of mathematical economics is not the fact that it ignores the temporal sequence, but that it ignores the operation of the market process.

The mathematical method is at a loss to show how from a state of nonequilibrium those actions spring up which tend toward the establishment of equilibrium. It is, of course, possible to indicate the mathematical operations required for the transformation of the mathematical description of a definite state of nonequilibrium into the mathematical description of the state of equilibrium. But these mathematical operations by no means describe the market process actuated by the discrepancies in the price structure. The differential equations of mechanics are supposed to describe precisely the motions concerned at any instant of the time traveled through. The economic equations have no reference whatever to conditions as they really are in each instant of the time interval between the state of nonequilibrium and that of equilibrium. Only those entirely blinded by the prepossession that economics must be a pale replica of mechanics will underrate the weight of this objection. A very imperfect and superficial metaphor is not a substitute for the services rendered by logical economics.

In every chapter of catallactics the devastating consequences of the mathematical treatment of economics can be tested. It is enough to refer to two instances only. One is provided by the so-called equation of exchange, the mathematical economists' futile and misleading attempt to deal with changes in the purchasing power of money.[10] The second can be best expressed in referring to Professor Schumpeter's dictum according to which consumers in evaluating consumers' goods "*ipso facto* also evaluate the means of production which enter into the production of these goods."[11] It is hardly possible to construe the market process in a more erroneous way.

Economics is not about goods and services, it is about the actions of living men. Its goal is not to dwell upon imaginary constructions such as equilibrium. These constructions are only tools of reasoning. The sole task of economics is analysis of the actions of men, is the analysis of processes.

6. Monopoly Prices

Competitive prices are the outcome of a complete adjustment of the sellers to the demand of the consumers. Under the competitive price the whole supply available is sold, and the specific factors of production are employed to the extent permitted by the prices of the nonspecific complementary factors. No part of a supply available is permanently withheld from the market, and the marginal unit of specific factors of production employed does not yield any net proceed. The whole economic process is conducted for the benefit of the consumers. There is no conflict between the interests of the buyers and those of the sellers, between the interests of the producers and those of the consumers. The owners of the various commodities are not in a position to divert consumption and production from the lines enjoined by the valuations of the consumers, the state of supply of goods and services of all orders and the state of technological knowledge.

Every single seller would see his own proceeds increased if a fall

10. Cf. below, p. 399.

11. Cf. Joseph A. Schumpeter, *Capitalism, Socialism and Democracy* (New York, 1942), p. 175. For a critique of this statement, cf. Hayek, "The Use of Knowledge in Society," *Individualism and the Social Order* (Chicago, 1948), pp. 89 ff.

in the supply at the disposal of his competitors were to increase the price at which he himself could sell his own supply. But on a competitive market he is not in a position to bring about this outcome. Except for a privilege derived from government interference with business he must submit to the state of the market as it is.

The entrepreneur in his entrepreneurial capacity is always subject to the full supremacy of the consumers. It is different with the owners of vendible goods and factors of production and, of course, with the entrepreneurs in their capacity as owners of such goods and factors. Under certain conditions they fare better by restricting supply and selling it at a higher price per unit. The prices thus determined, the monopoly prices, are an infringement of the supremacy of the consumers and the democracy of the market.

The special conditions and circumstances required for the emergence of monopoly prices and their catallactic features are:

1. There must prevail a monopoly of supply. The whole supply of the monopolized commodity is controlled by a single seller or a group of sellers acting in concert. The monopolist—whether one individual or a group of individuals—is in a position to restrict the supply offered for sale or employed for production in order to raise the price per unit sold and need not fear that his plan will be frustrated by interference on the part of other sellers of the same commodity.

2. Either the monopolist is not in a position to discriminate among the buyers or he voluntarily abstains from such discrimination.[12]

3. The reaction of the buying public to the rise in prices beyond the potential competitive price, the fall in demand, is not such as to render the proceeds resulting from total sales at any price exceeding the competitive price smaller than total proceeds resulting from total sales at the competitive price. Hence it is superfluous to enter into sophisticated disquisitions concerning what must be considered the mark of the sameness of an article. It is not necessary to raise the question whether all neckties are to be called specimens of the *same* article or whether one should distinguish them with regard to fabric, color, and pattern. An academic delimitation of various articles is useless. The only point that counts is the way in which the buyers react to the rise in prices. For the theory of monopoly prices it is irrelevant to observe that every necktie manufacturer turns out different articles and to call each of them a monopolist. Catallactics does not deal with monopoly as such but with monopoly prices. A seller of neckties which are different from those offered for sale by other

12. Price discrimination is dealt with below, pp. 388–391.

people could attain monopoly prices only if the buyers did not react to any rise in prices in such a way as to make such a rise disadvantageous for him.

Monopoly is a prerequisite for the emergence of monopoly prices, but it is not the only prerequisite. There is a further condition required, namely a certain shape of the demand curve. The mere existence of monopoly does not mean anything in this regard. The publisher of a copyright book is a monopolist. But he may not be able to sell a single copy, no matter how low the price he asks. Not every price at which a monopolist sells a monopolized commodity is a monopoly price. Monopoly prices are only prices at which it is more advantageous for the monopolist to restrict the total amount to be sold than to expand his sales to the limit which a competitive market would allow. They are the outcome of a deliberate design tending toward a restriction of trade.

4. It is a fundamental mistake to assume that there is a third category of prices which are neither monopoly prices nor competitive prices. If we disregard the problem of price discrimination to be dealt with later, a definite price is either a competitive price or a monopoly price. The assertions to the contrary are due to the erroneous belief that competition is not free or perfect unless everybody is in a position to present himself as a seller of a definite commodity.

The available supply of every commodity is limited. If it were not scarce with regard to the demand of the public, the thing in question would not be considered an economic good, and no price would be paid for it. It is therefore misleading to apply the concept of monopoly in such a way as to make it cover the entire field of economic goods. Mere limitation of supply is the source of economic value and of all prices paid; as such it is not yet sufficient to generate monopoly prices.[13]

The term monopolistic or imperfect competition is applied today to cases in which there are some differences in the products of different producers and sellers. This means that almost all consumers' goods are included in the class of monopolized goods. However, the only question relevant in the study of the determination of prices is whether these differences can be used by the seller for a scheme of deliberate restriction of supply for the sake of increasing his total net proceeds. Only if this is possible and put into effect, can monopoly prices emerge as differentiated from competitive prices. It may be true that every seller has a clientele which prefers his brand to those

13. Cf. the refutation of the misleading extension of the concept of monopoly by Richard T. Ely, *Monopolies and Trusts* (New York, 1906), pp. 1–36.

of his competitors and would not stop buying it even if the price were higher. But the problem for the seller is whether the number of such people is great enough to overcompensate the reduction of total sales which the abstention from buying on the part of other people would bring about. Only if this is the case, can he consider the substitution of monopoly prices for competitive prices advantageous.

Considerable confusion stems from a misinterpretation of the term *control of supply*. Every producer of every product has his share in controlling the supply of the commodities offered for sale. If he had produced more *a*, he would have increased supply and brought about a tendency toward a lower price. But the question is why he did not produce more of *a*. Was he in restricting his production of *a* to the amount of *p* intent upon complying to the best of his abilities with the wishes of the consumers? Or was he intent upon defying the orders of the consumers for his own advantage? In the first case he did not produce more of *a*, because increasing the quantity of *a* beyond *p* would have withdrawn scarce factors of production from other branches in which they would have been employed for the satisfaction of more urgent needs of the consumers. He does not produce $p + r$, but merely *p*, because such an increase would have rendered his business unprofitable or less profitable, while there are still other more profitable employments available for capital investment. In the second case he did not produce *r*, because it was more advantageous for him to leave a part of the available supply of a monopolized specific factor of production *m* unused. If *m* were not monopolized by him, it would have been impossible for him to expect any advantage from restricting his production of *a*. His competitors would have filled the gap and he would not have been in a position to ask higher prices.

In dealing with monopoly prices we must always search for the monopolized factor *m*. If no such factor is in the case, no monopoly prices can emerge. The first requirement for monopoly prices is the existence of a monopolized good. If no quantity of such a good *m* is withheld, there is no opportunity for an entrepreneur to substitute monopoly prices for competitive prices.

Entrepreneurial profit has nothing at all to do with monopoly. If an entrepreneur is in a position to sell at monopoly prices, he owes this advantage to his monopoly with regard to a monopolized factor *m*. He earns the specific monopoly gain from his ownership of *m*, not from his specific entrepreneurial activities.

Let us assume that an accident cuts a city's electrical supply for several days and forces the residents to resort to candlelight only.

The price of candles rises to s; at this price the whole supply available is sold out. The stores selling candles reap a high profit in selling their whole supply at s. But it could happen that the storekeepers combine in order to withhold a part of their stock from the market and to sell the rest at a price $s + t$. While s would have been the competitive price, $s + t$ is a monopoly price. The surplus earned by the storekeepers at the price $s + t$ over the proceeds they would have earned when selling at s only is their specific monopoly gain.

It is immaterial in what way the storekeepers bring about the restriction of the supply offered for sale. The physical destruction of a part of the supply available is the classical case of monopolistic action. Only a short time ago it was practiced by the Brazilian government in burning large quantities of coffee. But the same effect can be attained by leaving a part of the supply unused.

While profits are incompatible with the imaginary construction of the evenly rotating economy, monopoly prices and specific monopoly gains are not.

5. If the available quantities of the good m are owned not by just one man, firm, corporation, or institution but by several owners who want to cooperate in the substitution of a monopoly price for the competitive price, an agreement among them (commonly called a cartel and branded in the American antitrust legislation as a conspiracy) is required to assign to each party the amount of m it is allowed to sell, viz., at the monopoly price. The essential part of any cartel agreement is the assignment of definite quotas to the partners. The art of cartel-making consists in skill in bringing about an agreement about the quotas. A cartel collapses as soon as the members are no longer prepared to cling to a quota agreement. Mere talk among the owners of m about the desirability of higher prices is of no avail.

As a rule the state of affairs that makes the emergence of monopoly prices possible is brought about by government policies, e.g., customs barriers. If the owners of m do not take advantage of the opportunity to combine for the achievement of monopoly prices offered to them, governments frequently take upon themselves the organization of what the American law calls "restraint of trade." The police power forces the owners of m—mostly land and mining and fishing facilities —to restrict output. The most eminent examples of this method are provided on the national level by the American farm policy and on the international level by the treaties euphemistically styled Intergovernmental Commodity Control Agreements. There has developed a new semantics to describe this branch of government interference with business. The restriction of output, and consequently of the consumption involved, is called "avoidance of surpluses" and the effect aimed at, a higher price for the unit sold, is called "stabilization." It is obvious that these quantities of *m* did not appear as "surpluses" in the eyes of those who would have consumed them. It is also obvious that these people would have preferred a lower price to the "stabilization" of a higher price.

6. The concept of competition does not include the requirement that there should be a multitude of competing units. Competing is always the competition of one man or firm against another man or firm, no matter how many others are striving after the same prize. Competition among the few is not a kind of competition praxeologically different from competition among the many. Nobody ever maintained that the competition for elective office is under a two-party system less competitive than under a system of many parties. The number of competitors plays a role in the analysis of monopoly prices only as far as it is one of the factors upon which the success of the endeavors to unite competitors into a cartel depends.

7. If it is possible for the seller to increase his net proceeds by restricting sales and increasing the price of the units sold, there are usually several monopoly prices that satisfy this condition. As a rule *one* of these monopoly prices yields the highest net proceeds. But it may also happen that various monopoly prices are equally advantageous to the monopolist. We may call this monopoly price or these monopoly prices most advantageous to the monopolist the optimum monopoly price or the optimum monopoly prices.

8. The monopolist does not know beforehand in what way the consumers will react to a rise in prices. He must resort to trial and error in his endeavors to find out whether the monopolized good can be sold to his advantage at any price exceeding the competitive price and, if this is so, which of various possible monopoly prices is the optimum monopoly price or one of the optimum monopoly prices. This is in practice much more difficult than the economist assumes when, in drawing demand curves, he ascribes perfect foresight to the monopolist. We must therefore list as a special condition required for the appearance of monopoly prices the monopolist's ability to discover such prices.

9. A special case is provided by the incomplete monopoly. The greater part of the total supply available is owned by the monopolist; the rest is owned by one or several men who are not prepared to cooperate with the monopolist in a scheme for restricting sales and bringing about monopoly prices. However, the reluctance of these outsiders does not prevent the establishment of monopoly prices if

the portion p_1 controlled by the monopolist is large enough when compared with the sum of the outsiders' portions p_2. Let us assume that the whole supply ($p = p_1 + p_2$) can be sold at the price c per unit and a supply of $p — z$ at the monopoly price d. If $d\ (p_1 — z)$ is higher than $c\ p_1$, it is to the advantage of the monopolist to embark upon a monopolistic restriction of his sales, no matter what the conduct of the outsiders may be. They may go on selling at the price c or they may raise their prices up to the maximum of d. The only point that counts is that the outsiders are not willing to put up with a reduction in the quantity which they themselves are selling. The whole reduction required must be borne by the owner of p_1. This influences his plans and will as a rule result in the emergence of a monopoly price which is different from that which would have been established under complete monopoly.[14]

10. Duopoly and oligopoly are not special varieties of monopoly prices, but merely a variety of the methods applied for the establishment of a monopoly price. Two or several men own the whole supply. They all are prepared to sell at monopoly prices and to restrict their total sales accordingly. But for some reason they do not want to act in concert. Each of them goes his own way without any formal or tacit agreement with his competitors. But each of them knows also that his rivals are intent upon a monopolistic restriction of their sales in order to reap higher prices per unit and specific monopoly gains. Each of them watches carefully the conduct of his rivals and tries to adjust his own plans to their actions. A succession of moves and countermoves, a mutual outwitting results, the outcome of which depends on the personal cunning of the adverse parties. The duopolists and oligopolists have two objectives in mind: to find out the monopoly price most advantageous to the sellers on the one hand and to shift as much as possible of the burden of restricting the amount of sales to their rivals. Precisely because they do not agree with regard to the quotas of the reduced amount of sales to be allotted to each party, they do not act in concert as the members of a cartel do.

One must not confuse duopoly and oligopoly with the incomplete monopoly or with competition aiming at the establishment of monopoly. In the case of incomplete monopoly only the monopolistic group is prepared to restrict its sales in order to make a monopoly price prevail; the other sellers decline to restrict their sales. But duopolists and oligopolists are ready to withhold a part of their supply from the market. In the case of price slashing one group *A* plans to attain full

14. It is obvious that an incomplete monopoly scheme is bound to collapse if the outsiders come into a position to expand their sales.

monopoly or incomplete monopoly by forcing all or most of its competitors, the *B's,* to go out of business. It cuts prices to a level which makes selling ruinous to its more vulnerable competitors. *A* may also incur losses by selling at this low rate; but it is in a position to undergo such losses for a longer time than the others and it is confident that it will make good for them later by ample monopoly gains. This process has nothing to do with monopoly prices. It is a scheme for the attainment of a monopoly position.

One may wonder whether duopoly and oligopoly are of practical significance. As a rule the parties concerned will come to at least a tacit understanding concerning their quotas of the reduced amount of sales.

11. The monopolized good by whose partial withholding from the market the monopoly prices are made to prevail can be either a good of the lowest order or a good of a higher order, a factor of production. It may consist in the control of the technological knowledge required for production, the "recipe." Such recipes are as a rule free goods as their ability to produce definite effects is unlimited. They can become economic goods only if they are monopolized and their use is restricted. Any price paid for the services rendered by a recipe is always a monopoly price. It is immaterial whether the restriction of a recipe's use is made possible by institutional conditions—such as patents and copyright laws—or by the fact that a formula is kept secret and other people fail to guess it.

The complementary factor of production the monopolization of which can result in the establishment of monopoly prices may also consist in a man's opportunity to make his cooperation in the production of a good known to consumers who attribute to this cooperation a special significance. This opportunity may be given either by the nature of the commodities or services in question or by institutional provisions such as protection of trademarks. The reasons why the consumers value the contribution of a man or a firm so highly are manifold. They may be: special confidence placed on the individual or firm concerned on account of previous experience;[15] merely baseless prejudice or error; snobbishness; magic or metaphysical prepossessions whose groundlessness is ridiculed by more reasonable people. A drug marked by a trademark may not differ in its chemical structure and its physiological efficacy from other compounds not marked with the same label. However, if the buyers attach a special significance to this label and are ready to pay higher prices for the

15. Cf. below, pp. 379–383, on good will.

product marked with it, the seller can, provided the configuration of demand is propitious, reap monopoly prices.

The monopoly which enables the monopolist to restrict the amount offered without counteraction on the part of other people can consist in the greater productivity of a factor which he has at his disposal as against the lower productivity of the corresponding factor at the disposal of his potential competitors. If the margin between the higher productivity of his supply of the monopolized factor and that of his potential competitors is broad enough for the emergence of a monopoly price, a situation results which we may call margin monopoly.[16]

Let us illustrate margin monopoly by referring to its most frequent instance in present-day conditions, the power of a protective tariff to generate a monopoly price under special circumstances. Atlantis puts a tariff t on the importation of each unit of the commodity p, the world market price of which is s. If domestic consumption of p in Atlantis at the price $s + t$ is a and domestic production of p is b, b being smaller than a, then the costs of the marginal dealer are $s + t$. The domestic plants are in a position to sell their total output at the price $s + t$. The tariff is effective and offers to domestic business the incentive to expand the production of p from b to a quantity slightly smaller than a. But if b is greater than a, things are different. If we assume that b is so large that even at the price s domestic consumption lags behind it and the surplus must be exported and sold abroad, the imposition of a tariff does not effect the price of p. Both the domestic and the world market price of p remain unchanged. However the tariff, in discriminating between domestic and foreign production of p, accords to the domestic plants a privilege which can be used for a monopolistic combine, provided certain further conditions are present. If it is possible to find within the margin between $s + t$ and s a monopoly price, it becomes lucrative for the domestic enterprises to form a cartel. The cartel sells in the home market of Atlantis at a monopoly price and disposes of the surplus abroad at the world market price. Of course, as the quantity of p offered at the world market increases as a consequence of the restriction of the quantity sold in Atlantis, the world market price drops from s to s_1. It is therefore a further requirement for the emergence of the domestic monopoly price that the total restriction in proceeds resulting from this fall in the world market price is not so great as to absorb the whole monopoly gain of the domestic cartel.

16. The use of this term "margin monopoly" is, like that of any other, optional. It would be vain to object that every other monopoly which results in monopoly prices could also be called a margin monopoly.

In the long run such a national cartel cannot preserve its monopolistic position if entrance into its branch of production is free to newcomers. The monopolized factor the services of which the cartel restricts (as far as the domestic market is concerned) for the sake of monopoly prices is a geographical condition which can easily be duplicated by every new investor who establishes a new plant within the borders of Atlantis. Under modern industrial conditions, the characteristic feature of which is steady technological progress, the latest plant will as a rule be more efficient than the older plants and produce at lower average costs. The incentive to prospective newcomers is therefore twofold. It consists not only in the monopoly gain of the cartel members, but also in the possibility of outstripping them by lower costs of production.

Here again institutions come to the aid of the old firms that form the cartel. The patents give them a legal monopoly which nobody may infringe. Of course, only some of their production processes may be protected by patents. But a competitor who is prevented from resorting to these processes and to the production of the articles concerned may be handicapped in such a serious way that he cannot consider entrance into the field of the cartelized industry.

The owner of a patent enjoys a legal monopoly which, other conditions being propitious, can be used for the attainment of monopoly prices. Beyond the field covered by the patent itself a patent may render auxiliary services in the establishment and preservation of margin monopoly where the primary institutional conditions for the emergence of such a monopoly prevail.

We may assume that some world cartels would exist even in the absence of any government interference which provides for other commodities the indispensable conditions required for the construction of a monopolistic combine. There are some commodities, e.g., diamonds and mercury, the supply of which is by nature limited to a few sources. The owners of these resources can easily be united for concerted action. But such cartels would play only a minor role in the setting of world production. Their economic significance would be rather small. The important place that cartels occupy in our time is an outcome of the interventionist policies adopted by the governments of all countries. The monopoly problem mankind has to face today is not an outgrowth of the operation of the market economy. It is a product of purposive action on the part of governments. It is not one of the evils inherent in capitalism as the demagogues trumpet. It is, on the contrary, the fruit of policies hostile to capitalism and intent upon sabotaging and destroying its operation.

The classical country of the cartels was Germany. In the last decades of the nineteenth century the German Reich embarked upon a vast scheme of *Sozialpolitik.* The idea was to raise the income and the standard of living of the wage earners by various measures of what is called prolabor legislation, by the much glorified Bismarck scheme of social security, and by labor-union pressure and compulsion for the attainment of higher wage rates. The advocates of this policy defied the warnings of the economists. There is no such thing as economic law, they announced.

In stark reality the Sozialpolitik raised costs of production within Germany. Every progress of the alleged prolabor legislation and every successful strike disarranged industrial conditions to the disadvantage of the German enterprises. It made it harder for them to outdo foreign competitors for whom the domestic events of Germany did not raise costs of production. If the Germans had been in a position to renounce the export of manufactures and to produce only for the domestic market, the tariff could have sheltered the German plants against the intensified competition of foreign business. They would have been in a position to sell at higher prices. What the wage earner would have profited from the achievements of the legislature and the unions, would have been absorbed by the higher prices he would have had to pay for the articles he bought. Real wage rates would have risen only to the extent the entrepreneurs could improve technological procedures and thereby increase the productivity of labor. The tariff would have rendered the Sozialpolitik harmless.

But Germany is, and was already at the time Bismarck inaugurated his prolabor policy, a predominantly industrial country. Its plants exported a considerable part of their total output. These exports enabled the Germans to import the foodstuffs and raw materials they could not grow in their own country, comparatively overpopulated and poorly endowed with natural resources as it was. This situation could not be remedied simply by a protective tariff. Only cartels could free Germany from the catastrophic consequences of its "progressive" prolabor policies. The cartels charged monopoly prices at home and sold abroad at cheaper prices. The cartels are the necessary accompaniment and upshot of a "progressive" labor policy as far as it affects industries dependent for their sales on foreign markets. The cartels do not, of course, safeguard for the wage earners the illusory social gains which the labor politicians and the union leaders promise them. There is no means of raising wage rates for all those eager to earn wages above the height determined by the productivity of each kind of labor. What the cartels achieved was merely to counterbalance the apparent gains in nominal wage rates by corresponding increases in domestic commodity prices. But the most disastrous effect of minimum wage rates, permanent mass unemployment, was at first avoided.

With all industries which cannot content themselves with the domestic market and are intent upon selling a part of their output abroad the function of the tariff, in this age of government interference with business, is to enable the establishment of domestic monopoly prices. Whatever the purpose and the effects of tariffs may have been in the past, as soon as an exporting country embarks upon measures designed to increase the revenues of the wage earners or the farmers above the potential market rates, it must foster schemes which result in domestic monopoly prices for the commodities concerned. A national government's might is limited to the territory subject to its sovereignty. It has the power to raise domestic costs of production. It does not have the power to force foreigners to pay correspondingly higher prices for the products. If exports are not to be discontinued, they must be subsidized. The subsidy can be paid openly by the treasury or its burden can be imposed upon the consumers by the cartel's monopoly prices.

The advocates of government interference with business ascribe to the "State" the power to benefit certain groups within the framework of the market by a mere *fiat*. In fact this power is the government's power to foster monopolistic combines. The monopoly gains are the funds out of which the "social gains" are financed. As far as these monopoly gains do not suffice, the various measures of interventionism immediately paralyze the operation of the market; mass unemployment, depression, and capital consumption appear. This explains the eagerness of all contemporary governments to foster monopoly in all those sectors of the market which are in some way or other connected with export trade.

If a government does not or cannot succeed in attaining its monopolistic aims indirectly, it resorts to other means. In the field of coal and potash the Imperial Government of Germany fostered compulsory cartels. The American New Deal was prevented by the opposition of business from organizing the nation's great industries on an obligatory cartel basis. It fared better in some vital branches of farming with measures designed to restrict output for the sake of monopoly prices. A long series of agreements concluded between the world's most prominent governments aimed at the establishment of world-market monopoly prices for various raw materials and foodstuffs.[17] It is the avowed purpose of the United Nations to continue these plans.

17. A collection of these agreements was published in 1943 by the International Labor Office under the title *Intergovernmental Commodity Control Agreements*.

12. It is necessary to view this promonopoly policy of the contemporary governments as a uniform phenomenon in order to discern the reasons which motivated it. From the catallactic point of view these monopolies are not uniform. The contractual cartels into which entrepreneurs enter in taking advantage of the incentive offered by protective tariffs are instances of margin monopoly. Where the government directly fosters monopoly prices we are faced with instances of license monopoly. The factor of production by the restriction of the use of which the monopoly price is brought about is the license[18] which the laws make a requisite for supplying the consumers.

Such licenses may be granted in different ways:

(*a*) An unlimited license is granted to practically every applicant. This amounts to a state of affairs under which no license at all is required.

(*b*) Licenses are granted only to selected applicants. Competition is restricted. However, monopoly prices can emerge only if the licensees act in concert and the configuration of demand is propitious.

(*c*) There is only one licensee. The licensee, e.g., the holder of a patent or a copyright, is a monopolist. If the configuration of the demand is propitious and if the licensee wants to reap monopoly gains, he can ask monopoly prices.

(*d*) The licenses granted are limited. They confer upon the licensee only the right to produce or to sell a definite quantity, in order to prevent him from disarranging the authority's scheme. The authority itself directs the establishment of monopoly prices.

Finally there are the instances in which a government establishes a monopoly for fiscal purposes. The monopoly gains go to the treasury. Many European governments have instituted tobacco monopolies. Others have monopolized salt, matches, telegraph and telephone service, broadcasting, and so on. Without exception every country has a government monopoly of the postal service.

13. Margin monopoly need not always owe its appearance to an institutional factor such as tariffs. It can also be produced by sufficient differences in the fertility or productivity of some factors of production.

It has already been said that it is a serious blunder to speak of a land monopoly and to refer to monopoly prices and monopoly gains in explaining the prices of agricultural products and the rent of land. As far as history is confronted with instances of monopoly prices for agricultural products, it was license monopoly fostered by govern-

18. The terms *license* and *licensee* are not employed here in the technical sense of patent legislation.

ment decree. However, the acknowledgement of these facts does not mean that differences in the fertility of the soil could never bring about monopoly prices. If the difference between the fertility of the poorest soil still tilled and the richest fallow fields available for an expansion of production were so great as to enable the owners of the already exploited soil to find an advantageous monopoly price within this margin, they could consider restricting production by concerted action in order to reap monopoly prices. But it is a fact that physical conditions in agriculture do not comply with these requirements. It is precisely on account of this fact that farmers longing for monopoly prices do not resort to spontaneous action but ask for the interference of governments.

In various branches of mining conditions are often more propitious for the emergence of monopoly prices based on margin monopoly.

14. It has been asserted again and again that the economies of big-scale production have generated a tendency toward monopoly prices in the processing industries. Such a monopoly would be called in our terminology a margin monopoly.

Before entering into a discussion of this topic one must clarify the role an increase or decrease in the unit's average cost of production plays in the considerations of a monopolist searching for the most advantageous monopoly price. We consider a case in which the owner of a monopolized complementary factor of production, e.g., a patent, at the same time manufactures the product *p*. If the average cost of production of one unit of *p*, without any regard to the patent, decreases with the increase in the quantity produced, the monopolist must weigh this against the gains expected from the restriction of output. If, on the other hand, cost of production per unit decreases with the restriction of total production, the incentive to embark upon monopolistic restraint is augmented. It is obvious that the mere fact that big-scale production tends as a rule to lower average costs of production is in itself not a factor driving toward the emergence of monopoly prices. It is rather a checking factor.

What those who blame the economies of big-scale production for the spread of monopoly prices are trying to say is that the higher efficiency of big-scale production makes it difficult or even impossible for small-scale plants to compete successfully. A big-scale plant could, they believe, resort to monopoly prices with impunity because small business is not in a position to challenge its monopoly. Now, it is certainly true that in many branches of the processing industries it would be foolish to enter the market with the high-cost products of small, inadequate plants. A modern cotton mill does not need to fear the competition of old-fashioned distaffs; its rivals are other more or less adequately equipped mills. But this does not mean that it enjoys the opportunity of selling at monopoly prices. There is competition between big businesses too. If monopoly prices prevail in the sale of the products of big-size business, the reasons are either patents or monopoly in the ownership of mines or other sources of raw material or cartels based on tariffs.

One must not confuse the notions of monopoly and of monopoly prices. Mere monopoly as such is catallactically of no importance if it does not result in monopoly prices. Monopoly prices are consequential only because they are the outcome of a conduct of business defying the supremacy of the consumers and substituting the private interests of the monopolist for those of the public. They are the only instance in the operation of a market economy in which the distinction between production for profit and production for use could to some extent be made if one were prepared to disregard the fact that monopoly gains have nothing at all to do with profits proper. They are not a part of what catallactics can call profits; they are an increase in the price earned from the sale of the services rendered by some factors of production, some of these factors being physical factors, some of them merely institutional. If the entrepreneurs and capitalists in the absence of a monopoly price constellation abstain from expanding production in a certain branch of industry because the opportunities offered to them in other branches are more attractive, they do not act in defiance of the wants of the consumers. On the contrary, they follow precisely the line indicated by the demand as expressed on the market.

The political bias which has obfuscated the discussion of the monopoly problem has neglected to pay attention to the essential issues involved. In dealing with every case of monopoly prices one must first of all raise the question of what obstacles restrain people from challenging the monopolists. In answering this question one discovers the role played in the emergence of monopoly prices by institutional factors. It was nonsense to speak of conspiracy with regard to the deals between American firms and German cartels. If an American wanted to manufacture an article protected by a patent owned by Germans, he was compelled by the American law to come to an arrangement with German business.

15. A special case is what may be called the failure monopoly.

In the past capitalists invested funds in a plant designed for the production of the article *p*. Later events proved the investment a failure. The prices which can be obtained in selling *p* are so low that the capital invested in the plant's inconvertible equipment does not yield a return. It is lost. However, these prices are high enough to yield a reasonable return for the variable capital to be employed for the current production of *p*. If the irrevocable loss of the capital invested in the inconvertible equipment is written off on the books and all corresponding alterations are made in the accounts, the reduced capital working in the conduct of the business is by and large so profitable that it would be a new mistake to stop production altogether. The plant works at full capacity producing the quantity *q* of *p* and selling the unit at the price *s*.

But conditions may be such that it is possible for the enterprise to reap a monopoly gain by restricting output to $q/2$ and selling the unit of *q* at the price 3 *s*. Then the capital invested in the inconvertible equipment no longer appears completely lost. It yields a modest return, namely, the monopoly gain.

This enterprise now sells at monopoly prices and reaps monopoly gains although the total capital invested yields little when compared with what the investors would have earned if they had invested in other lines of business. The enterprise withholds from the market the services which the unused production capacity of its durable equipment could render and fares better than it would by producing at full capacity. It defies the orders of the public. The public would have been in a better position if the investors had avoided the mistake of immobilizing a part of their capital in the production of *p*. They would, of course, not get any *p*. But they would instead obtain those articles which they miss now because the capital required for their production has been wasted in the construction of an aggregate for the production of *p*. However, as things are now after this irreparable fault has been committed, they want to get more of *p* and are ready to pay for it what is now its potential competitive market price, namely, *s*. They do not approve, as conditions are now, the action of the enterprise in withholding an amount of variable capital from employment for the production of *p*. This amount certainly does not remain unused. It goes into other lines of business and produces there something else, namely, *m*. But as conditions are now, the consumers would prefer an increase of the available quantity of *p* to an increase in the available quantity of *m*. The proof is that in the absence of a monopolistic restriction of the capacity for the production of *p*, as it is under given conditions, the profitability of a production of the quantity *q* selling at the price *s* would be such that it would pay better than an increase in the quantity of the article *m* produced.

There are two distinctive features of this case. First, the monopoly prices paid by the buyers are still lower than the total cost of production of p would be if full account is taken of the whole input of the investors. Second, the monopoly gains of the firm are so small that they do not make the total venture appear a good investment. It remains malinvestment. It is precisely this fact that constitutes the monopolistic position of the firm. No outsider wants to enter its field of entrepreneurial activity because the production of p results in losses.

Failure monopoly is by no means a merely academic construction. It is, for instance, actual today in the case of some railroad companies. But one must guard against the mistake of interpreting every instance of unused production capacity as a failure monopoly. Even in the absence of monopoly it may be more profitable to employ variable capital for other purposes instead of expanding a firm's production to the limit fixed by the capacity of its durable inconvertible equipment; then the output restriction complies precisely with the state of the competitive market and the wishes of the public.

16. Local monopolies are, as a rule, of institutional origin. But there are also local monopolies which originate out of conditions of the unhampered market. Often the institutional monopoly is designed to deal with a monopoly which came into existence or would be likely to come into existence without any authoritarian interference with the market.

A catallactic classification of local monopolies must distinguish three groups: margin monopoly, limited-space monopoly and license monopoly.

A *local margin monopoly* is characterized by the fact that the barrier preventing outsiders from competing on the local market and breaking the monopoly of the local sellers is the comparative height of transportation costs. No tariffs are needed to grant limited protection to a firm which owns all the adjacent natural resources required for the production of bricks against the competition of far distant tile works. The costs of transportation provide them with a margin in which, the configuration of demand being propitious, an advantageous monopoly price can be found.

So far local margin monopolies do not differ catallactically from other instances of margin monopoly. What distinguishes them and makes it necessary to deal with them in a special way is their relation to the rent of urban land on the one hand and their relation to city development on the other.

Let us assume that an area A offering favorable conditions for the aggregation of an increasing urban population is subject to monopoly prices for building materials. Consequently building costs are higher than they would be in the absence of such a monopoly. But there is no reason for those weighing the pros and cons of choosing the location of their homes and their workshops in *A* to pay higher prices for the purchase or the renting of such houses and workshops. These prices are determined on the one hand by the corresponding prices in other areas and on the other by the advantages which settling in *A* offers when compared with settling somewhere else. The higher expenditure required for construction does not affect these prices; its incidence falls upon the yield of land. The burden of the monopoly gains of the sellers of building materials falls on the owners of the urban soil. These gains absorb proceeds which in their absence would go to these owners. Even in the—not very likely—case that the demand for houses and workshops is such as to make it possible for the owners of the land to attain monopoly prices in selling and leasing, the monopoly prices of the building materials would affect only the proceeds of the landowners, not the prices to be paid by the buyers or tenants.

The fact that the burden of the monopoly gains reverts to the price of urban employment of the land does not mean that it does not check the growth of the city. It postpones the employment of the peripheral land for the expansion of the urban settlement. The instant at which it becomes advantageous for the owner of a piece of suburban land to withdraw it from agricultural or other nonurban employment and to use it for urban development appears at a later date.

Now arresting a city's development is a two-edged action. Its usefulness for the monopolist is ambiguous. He cannot know whether future conditions will be such as to attract more people to *A*, the only market for his products. One of the attractions a city offers to newcomers is its bigness, the multitude of its population. Industry and commerce tend toward centers. If the monopolist's action delays the growth of the urban community, it may direct the stream toward other places. An opportunity may be missed which never comes back. Greater proceeds in the future may be sacrificed to comparatively small short-run gains.

It is therefore at least questionable whether the owner of a local margin monopoly in the long run serves his own interests well by embarking upon selling at monopoly prices. It would often be more advantageous for him to discriminate between the various buyers. He could sell at higher prices for construction projects in the central parts of the city and at lower prices for such projects in peripheral districts. The range of local margin monopoly is more restricted than is generally assumed.

Limited-space monopoly is the outcome of the fact that physical conditions restrict the field of operation in such a way that only one or a few enterprises can enter it. Monopoly emerges when there is only one enterprise in the field or when the few operating enterprises combine for concerted action.

It is sometimes possible for two competing trolley companies to operate in the same streets of a city. There were instances in which two or even more companies shared in supplying the residents of an area with gas, electricity, and telephone service. But even in such exceptional cases there is hardly any real competition. Conditions suggest to the rivals that they combine at least tacitly. The narrowness of the space results, one way or another, in monopoly.

In practice limited-space monopoly is closely connected with license monopoly. It is practically impossible to enter the field without an understanding with the local authorities controlling the streets and their subsoil. Even in the absence of laws requiring a franchise for the establishment of public utility services, it would be necessary for the enterprises to come to an agreement with the municipal authorities. Whether or not such agreements are to be legally described as franchises is unimportant.

Monopoly, of course, need not result in monopoly prices. It depends on the special data of each case whether or not a monopolistic public utility company could resort to monopoly prices. But there are certainly cases in which it can. It may be that the company is ill-advised in choosing a monopoly-price policy and that it would better serve its long-run interests by lower prices. But there is no guarantee that a monopolist will find out what is most advantageous for him.

One must realize that limited-space monopoly may often result in monopoly prices. In this case we are confronted with a situation in which the market process does not accomplish its democratic function.[19]

Private enterprise is very unpopular with our contemporaries. Private ownership of the means of production is especially disliked in those fields in which limited-space monopoly emerges even if the company does not charge monopoly prices and even if its business yields only small profits or results in losses. A "public utility" company is in the eyes of the interventionist and socialist politicians a public enemy. The voters approve of any evil inflicted upon it by the authorities. It is generally assumed that these enterprises should be nationalized or municipalized. Monopoly gains, it is said, must

19. About the significance of this fact see below, pp. 680–682.

never go to private citizens. They should go to the public funds exclusively.

The outcome of the municipalization and nationalization policies of the last decades was almost without exception financial failure, poor service, and political corruption. Blinded by their anticapitalistic prejudices people condone poor service and corruption and for a long time did not bother about the financial failure. However, this failure is one of the factors which contributed to the emergence of the present-day crisis of interventionism.[20]

17. It is customary to characterize labor-union policies as monopolistic schemes aiming at the substitution of monopoly wage rates for competitive wage rates. However, as a rule labor unions do not aim at monopoly wage rates. A union is intent upon restricting competition on its own sector of the labor market in order to raise its wage rates. But restriction of competition and monopoly price policy must not be confused. The characteristic feature of monopoly prices is the fact that the sale of only a part p of the total supply P available nets higher proceeds than the sale of P. The monopolist earns a monopoly gain by withholding $P - p$ from the market. It is not the height of this gain that marks the monopoly price situation as such, but the purposive action of the monopolists in bringing it about. The monopolist is concerned with the employment of the whole stock available. He is equally interested in every fraction of this stock. If a part of it remains unsold, it is his loss. Nonetheless he chooses to have a part unused because under the prevailing configuration of demand it is more advantageous for him to proceed in this way. It is the peculiar state of the market that motivates his decision. The monopoly which is one of the two indispensable conditions of the emergence of monopoly prices may be—and is as a rule—the product of an institutional interference with the market data. But these external forces do not directly result in monopoly prices. Only if a second requirement is fulfilled is the opportunity for monopolistic action set.

It is different in the case of simple supply restriction. Here the authors of the restriction are not concerned with what may happen to the part of the supply they bar from access to the market. The fate of the people who own this part does not matter to them. They are looking only at that part of the supply which remains on the market. Monopolistic action is advantageous for the monopolist only if total net proceeds at a monopoly price exceed total net proceeds at the potential competitive price. Restrictive action on the other hand is

20. See below, pp. 855–857.

always advantageous for the privileged group and disadvantageous for those whom it excludes from the market. It always raises the price per unit and therefore the total net proceeds of the privileged group. The losses of the excluded group are not taken into account by the privileged group.

It may happen that the benefits which the privileged group derives from the restriction of competition are much more lucrative for them than any imaginable monopoly price policy could be. But this is another question. It does not blot out the catallactic differences between these two modes of action.

The labor unions aim at a monopolistic position on the labor market. But once they have attained it, their policies are restrictive and not monopoly price policies. They are intent upon restricting the supply of labor in their field without bothering about the fate of those excluded. They have succeeded in every comparatively underpopulated country in erecting immigration barriers. Thus they preserve their comparatively high wage rates. The excluded foreign workers are forced to stay in their countries in which the marginal productivity of labor, and consequently wage rates, are lower. The tendency toward an equalization of wage rates which prevails under free mobility of labor from country to country is paralyzed. On the domestic market the unions do not tolerate the competition of non-unionized workers and admit only a restricted number to union membership. Those not admitted must go into less remunerative jobs or must remain unemployed. The unions are not interested in the fate of these people.

Even if a union takes over the responsibility for its unemployed members and pays them, out of contributions of its employed members, unemployment doles not lower than the earnings of the employed members, its action is not a monopoly price policy. For the unemployed union members are not the only people whose earning power is adversely affected by the union's policy of substituting higher rates for the potential lower market rates. The interests of those excluded from membership are not taken into account.

The Mathematical Treatment of the Theory of Monopoly Prices

Mathematical economists have paid special attention to the theory of monopoly prices. It looks as if monopoly prices would be a chapter of catallactics for which mathematical treatment is more appropriate than it is for other chapters of catallactics. However, the services which mathematics can render in this field are rather poor too.

With regard to competitive prices mathematics cannot give more than a mathematical description of various states of equilibrium and of conditions in the imaginary construction of the evenly rotating economy. It cannot say anything about the actions which would finally establish these equilibria and this evenly rotating system if no further changes in the data were to occur.

In the theory of monopoly prices mathematics comes a little nearer to the reality of action. It shows how the monopolist could find out the optimum monopoly price provided he had at his disposal all the data required. But the monopolist does not know the shape of the curve of demand. What he knows is only points at which the curves of demand and supply intersected one another in the past. He is therefore not in a position to make use of the mathematical formulas in order to discover whether there is any monopoly price for his monopolized article and, if so, which of various monopoly prices is the optimum price. The mathematical and graphical disquisitions are therefore no less futile in this sector of action than in any other sector. But, at least, they schematize the deliberations of the monopolist and do not, as in the case of competitive prices, satisfy themselves in describing a merely auxiliary construction of theoretical analysis which does not play a role in real action.

Contemporary mathematical economists have confused the study of monopoly prices. They consider the monopolist not as the seller of a monopolized commodity, but as an entrepreneur and producer. However, it is necessary to distinguish the monopoly gain clearly from entrepreneurial profit. Monopoly gains can only be reaped by the seller of a commodity or a service. An entrepreneur can reap them only in his capacity as seller of a monopolized commodity, not in his entrepreneurial capacity. The advantages and disadvantages which may result from the fall or rise in cost of production per unit with increasing total production, diminish or increase the monopolist's total net proceeds and influence his conduct. But the catallactic treatment of monopoly prices must not forget that the specific monopoly gain stems, with due allowance made to the configuration of demand, only from the monopoly of a commodity or a right. It is this alone which affords to the monopolist the opportunity to restrict supply without fear that other people can frustrate his action by expanding the quantity they offer for sale. Attempts to define the conditions required for the emergence of monopoly prices by resorting to the configuration of production costs are vain.

It is misleading to describe the market situation resulting in competitive prices by declaring that the individual producer could sell at the market price also a greater quantity than what he really sells. This is true only when two special conditions are fulfilled: the producer concerned, *A*, is not the marginal producer, and expanding production does not require additional costs which cannot be recovered in selling the additional quantity of products. Then *A*'s expansion forces the marginal producer to discontinue production; the supply offered for sale remains unchanged.

The characteristic mark of the competitive price as distinguished from the monopoly price is that the former is the outcome of a situation under which the owners of goods and services of all orders are compelled to serve best the wishes of the consumers. On a competitive market there is no such thing as a price policy of the sellers. They have no alternative other than to sell as much as they can at the highest price offered to them. But the monopolist fares better by withholding from the market a part of the supply at his disposal in order to make specific monopoly gains.

7. Good Will

It must be emphasized again that the market is peopled by men who are not omniscient and have only a more or less defective knowledge of prevailing conditions.

The buyer must always rely upon the trustworthiness of the seller. Even in the purchase of producers' goods the buyer, although as a rule an expert in the field, depends to some extent on the reliability of the seller. This is still more the case on the market for consumers' goods. Here the seller for the most part excels the buyer in technological and commercial insight. The salesman's task is not simply to sell what the customer is asking for. He must often advise the customer how to choose the merchandise which can best satisfy his needs. The retailer is not only a vendor; he is also a friendly helper. The public does not heedlessly patronize every shop. If possible, a man prefers a store or a brand with which he himself or trustworthy friends have had good experience in the past.

Good will is the renown a business acquires on account of past achievements. It implies the expectation that the bearer of the good will in the future will live up to his earlier standards. Good will is not a phenomenon appearing only in business relations. It is present in all social relations. It determines a person's choice of his spouse and of his friends and his voting for a candidate in elections. Catallactics, of course, deals only with commercial good will.

It does not matter whether the good will is based on real achievements and merits or whether it is only a product of imagination and fallacious ideas. What counts in human action is not truth as it may appear to an omniscient being, but the opinions of people liable to error. There are some instances in which customers are prepared to pay a higher price for a special brand of a compound although the branded article does not differ in its physical and chemical structure from another cheaper product. Experts may deem such conduct unreasonable. But no man can acquire expertness in all fields which are relevant for his choices. He cannot entirely avoid substituting confidence in men for knowledge of the true state of affairs. The regular customer does not always select the article or the service, but the purveyor whom he trusts. He pays a premium to those whom he considers reliable.

The role which good will plays on the market does not impair or restrict competition. Everybody is free to acquire good will, and every bearer of good will can lose good will once acquired. Many reformers, impelled by their bias for paternal government, advocate authoritarian grade labeling as a substitute for trademarks. They would be right if rulers and bureaucrats were endowed with omniscience and perfect impartiality. But as officeholders are not free from human weakness, the realization of such plans would merely substitute the defects of government appointees for those of individual citizens. One does not make a man happier by preventing him from discriminating between a brand of cigarettes or canned food he prefers and another brand he likes less.

The acquisition of good will requires not only honesty and zeal in attending to the customers, but no less money expenditure. It takes time until a firm has acquired a steady clientele. In the interval it must often put up with losses against which it balances expected later profits.

From the point of view of the seller good will is, as it were, a necessary factor of production. It is appraised accordingly. It does not matter that as a rule the money equivalent of the good will does not appear in book entries and balance sheets. If a business is sold, a price is paid for the good will provided it is possible to transfer it to the acquirer.

It is consequently a problem of catallactics to investigate the nature of this peculiar thing called good will. In this scrutiny we must distinguish three different cases.

Case 1. The good will gives to the seller the opportunity to sell at monopoly prices or to discriminate among various classes of buyers. This does not differ from other instances of monopoly prices or price discrimination.

Case 2. The good will gives to the seller merely the opportunity to sell at prices corresponding to those which his competitors attain. If he had no good will, he would not sell at all or only by cutting prices. Good will is for him no less necessary than the business premises, the keeping of a well-assorted stock of merchandise and the hiring of skilled helpers. The costs incurred by the acquisition of good will play the same role as any other business expenses. They must be defrayed in the same way by an excess of total proceeds over total costs.

Case 3. The seller enjoys within a limited circle of staunch patrons such a brilliant reputation that he can sell to them at higher prices than those paid to his less renowned competitors. However, these prices are not monopoly prices. They are not the result of a deliberate policy aiming at a restriction in total sales for the sake of raising total net proceeds. It may be that the seller has no opportunity whatsoever to sell a larger quantity, as is the case for example, with a doctor who is busy to the limit of his powers although he charges more than his less popular colleagues. It may also be that the expansion of sales would require additional capital investment and that the seller either lacks this capital or believes that he has a more profitable employment for it. What prevents an expansion of output and of the quantity of merchandise or services offered for sale is not a purposive action on the part of the seller, but the state of the market.

As the misinterpretation of these facts has generated a whole mythology of "imperfect competition" and "monopolistic competition," it is necessary to enter into a more detailed scrutiny of the considerations of an entrepreneur who is weighing the pros and cons of an expansion of his business.

Expansion of a production aggregate, and no less increasing production from partial utilization of such an aggregate to full capacity production, requires additional capital investment which is reasonable only if there is no more profitable investment available.[21] It does not matter whether the entrepreneur is rich enough to invest his own funds or whether he would have to borrow the funds needed. Also that part of an entrepreneur's own capital which is not employed in his firm is not "idle." It is utilized somewhere in the framework of the economic system. In order to be employed for the expansion of the business concerned these funds must be withdrawn from their present employment.[22] The entrepreneur will only embark upon this change of investment if he expects from it an increase in his net returns. In addition there are other doubts which may check the propensity to expand a prospering enterprise even if the market situation seems to offer propitious chances. The entrepreneur may

21. Expenditure for additional advertising also means additional input of capital.

22. Cash holding, even if it exceeds the customary amount and is called "hoarding," is a variety of employing funds available. Under the prevailing state of the market the actor considers cash holding the most appropriate employment of a part of his assets.

mistrust his own ability to manage a bigger outfit successfully. He may also be frightened by the example provided by once prosperous enterprises for which expansion resulted in failure.

A businessman who, thanks to his splendid good will, is in a position to sell at higher prices than less renowned competitors, could, of course, renounce his advantage and reduce his prices to the level of his competitors. Like every seller of commodities or of labor he could abstain from taking fullest advantage of the state of the market and sell at a price at which demand exceeds supply. In doing so he would be making presents to some people. The donees would be those who could buy at this lowered price. Others, although ready to buy at the same price, would have to go away empty-handed because the supply was not sufficient.

The restriction of the quantity of every article produced and offered for sale is always the outcome of the decisions of entrepreneurs intent upon reaping the highest possible profit and avoiding losses. The characteristic mark of monopoly prices is not to be seen in the fact that the entrepreneurs did not produce more of the article concerned and thus did not bring about a fall in its price. Neither is it to be seen in the fact that complementary factors of production remain unused although their fuller employment would have lowered the price of the product. The only relevant question is whether or not the restriction of production is the outcome of the action of the—monopolistic—owner of a supply of goods and services who withholds a part of this supply in order to attain higher prices for the rest. The characteristic feature of monopoly prices is the monopolist's defiance of the wishes of the consumers. A competitive price for copper means that the final price of copper tends toward a point at which the deposits are exploited to the extent permitted by the prices of the required nonspecific complementary factors of production; the marginal mine does not yield mining rent. The consumers are getting as much copper as they themselves determine by the prices they allow for copper and all other commodities. A monopoly price of copper means that the deposits of copper are utilized only to a smaller degree because this is more advantageous to the owners; capital and labor which, if the supremacy of the consumers were not infringed, would have been employed for the production of additional copper, are employed for the production of other articles for which the demand of the consumers is less intense. The interests of the owners of the copper deposits take precedence over those of the consumers. The available resources of copper are not employed according to the wishes and plans of the public.

Profits are, of course, also the outcome of a discrepancy between the wishes of the consumers and the actions of the entrepreneurs. If all entrepreneurs had had in the past perfect foresight of the present state of the market, no profits and losses would have emerged. Their competition would have already adjusted in the past—due allowance being made for time preference—the prices of the complementary factors of production to the present prices of the products. But this statement cannot brush away the fundamental difference between profits and monopoly gains. The entrepreneur profits to the extent he has succeeded in serving the consumers better than other people have done. The monopolist reaps monopoly gains through impairing the satisfaction of the consumers.

8. Monopoly of Demand

Monopoly prices can emerge only from a monopoly of supply. A monopoly of demand does not bring about a market situation different from that under not monopolized demand. The monopolistic buyer—whether he is an individual or a group of individuals acting in concert—cannot reap a specific gain corresponding to the monopoly gains of monopolistic sellers. If he restricts demand, he will buy at a lower price. But then the quantity bought will drop too.

In the same way in which governments restrict competition in order to improve the position of privileged sellers, they can also restrict competition for the benefit of privileged buyers. Again and again governments have put an embargo on the export of certain commodities. Thus by excluding foreign buyers they have aimed at lowering the domestic price. But such a lower price is not a counterpart of monopoly prices.

What is commonly dealt with as monopoly of demand are certain phenomena of the determination of prices for specific complementary factors of production.

The production of one unit of the commodity *m* requires, besides the employment of various nonspecific factors, the employment of one unit of each of the two absolutely specific factors *a* and *b*. Neither *a* nor *b* can be replaced by any other factor; on the other hand *a* is of no use when not combined with *b* and vice versa. The available supply of *a* by far exceeds the available supply of *b*. It is therefore not possible for the owners of *a* to attain any price for *a*. The demand for *a* always lags behind the supply; *a* is not an economic good. If *a* is a mineral deposit the extraction of which requires the use of capital and labor, the ownership of the deposits does not yield a royalty. There is no mining rent.

But if the owners of *a* form a cartel, they can turn the tables. They can restrict the supply of *a* offered for sale to such a fraction that the supply of *b* exceeds the supply of *a*. Now *a* becomes an economic good for which prices are paid while the price of *b* dwindles to zero. If then the owners of *b* react by forming a cartel too, a price struggle develops between the two monopolistic combines about the outcome of which catallactics can make no statements. As has already been pointed out, the pricing process does not bring about a uniquely determined result in cases in which more than one of the factors of production required is of an absolutely specific character.

It does not matter whether or not the market situation is such that the factors *a* and *b* together could be sold at monopoly prices. It does not make any difference whether the price for a lot including one unit of both *a* and *b* is a monopoly price or a competitive price.

Thus what is sometimes viewed as a monopoly of demand turns out to be a monopoly of supply formed under particular conditions. The sellers of *a* and *b* are intent upon selling at monopoly prices without regard to the question whether or not the price of *m* can become a monopoly price. What alone matters for them is to obtain as great a share as possible of the joint price which the buyers are ready to pay for *a* and *b* together. The case does not indicate any feature which would make it permissible to apply to it the term *monopoly of demand.* This mode of expression becomes understandable, however, if one takes into account the accidental features marking the contest between the two groups. If the owners of *a* (or *b*) are at the same time the entrepreneurs conducting the processing of *m,* their cartel takes on the outward appearance of a monopoly of demand. But this personal union combining two separate catallactic functions does not alter the essential issue; what is at stake is the settlement of affairs between two groups of monopolistic sellers.

Our example fits, *mutatis mutandis,* the case in which *a* and *b* can also be employed for purposes other than the production of *m,* provided these other employments only yield smaller returns.

9. Consumption as Affected by Monopoly Prices

The individual consumer may react to monopoly prices in different ways.

1. Notwithstanding the rise in price, the individual consumer does not restrict his purchases of the monopolized article. He prefers to restrict the purchase of other goods. (If all consumers were to react in this way, the competitive price would have already risen to the height of the monopoly price.)

2. The consumer restricts his purchase of the monopolized article to such an extent that he does not spend for it more than he would have spent—for the purchase of a larger quantity—under the competitive price. (If all people were to react in this way, the seller would not get more under the monopoly price than he did under the competitive price; he would not derive any gain by deviating from the competitive price.)

3. The consumer restricts his purchase of the monopolized commodity to such an extent that he spends less for it than he would have spent under the competitive price; he buys with the money thus saved goods which he would not have bought otherwise. (If all people were to react in this way, the seller would harm his interests by substituting a higher price for the competitive price; no monopoly price could emerge. Only a benefactor who wanted to wean his fellow men from the consumption of pernicious drugs would in this case raise the price of the article concerned above the competitive level.)

4. The consumer spends more for the monopolized commodity than he would have spent under the competitive price and acquires only a smaller quantity of it.

However the consumer may react, his satisfaction appears to be impaired from the viewpoint of his own valuations. He is not so well served under monopoly prices as under competitive prices. The monopoly gain of the seller is borne by a monopoly deprivation of the buyer. Even if some consumers (as in case 3) acquire goods which they would not have bought in the absence of the monopoly price, their satisfaction is lower than it would have been under a different state of prices. Capital and labor which are withdrawn from the production of products which drops on account of the monopolistic restriction of the supply of one of the complementary factors required for their production, are employed for the production of other things which would otherwise not have been produced. But the consumers value these other things less.

Yet there is an exception to this general rule that monopoly prices benefit the seller and harm the buyer and infringe the supremacy of the consumers' interests. If on a competitive market one of the complementary factors, namely *f*, needed for the production of the consumers' good *g*, does not attain any price at all, although the production of *f* requires various expenditures and consumers are ready to pay for the consumers' good *g* a price which makes its production profitable on a competitive market, the monopoly price for *f* becomes a necessary requirement for the production of *g*. It is this idea that people advance in favor of patent and copyright legislation. If inventors and authors were not in a position to make money by inventing and writing, they would be prevented from devoting their time to these activities and from defraying the costs involved. The public would not derive any advantage from the absence of monopoly prices for *f*. It would, on the contrary, miss the satisfaction it could derive from the acquisition of *g*.[23]

Many people are alarmed by the reckless use of the deposits of minerals and oil which cannot be replaced. Our contemporaries, they say, squander an exhaustible stock without any regard for the coming generations. We are consuming our own birthright and that of the future. Now these complaints make little sense. We do not know whether later ages will still rely upon the same raw materials on which we depend today. It is true that the exhaustion of the oil deposits and even those of coal is progressing at a quick rate. But it is very likely that in a hundred or five hundred years people will resort to other methods of producing heat and power. Nobody knows whether we, in being less profligate with these deposits, would not deprive ourselves without any advantage to men of the twenty-first or of the twenty-fourth centuries. It is vain to provide for the needs of ages the technological abilities of which we cannot even dream.

But it is contradictory if the same people who lament the depletion of some natural resources are no less vehement in indicting monopolistic restraint in their present-day exploitation. The effect of monopoly prices of mercury is certainly a slowing down of the rate of depletion. In the eyes of those frightened by the aspect of a future scarcity of mercury this effect must appear highly desirable.

Economics in unmasking such contradictions does not aim at a "justification" of monopoly prices for oil, minerals, and ore. Economics has neither the task of justifying nor of condemning. It has merely to scrutinize the effects of all modes of human action. It does not enter the arena in which friends and foes of monopoly prices are intent upon pleading their causes.

Both sides in this heated controversy resort to fallacious arguments. The antimonopoly party is wrong in attributing to every monopoly the power to impair the situation of the buyers by restricting supply and bringing about monopoly prices. It is no less wrong in assuming that there prevails within a market economy, not hampered and sabotaged by government interference, a general tendency toward the formation of monopoly. It is a grotesque distortion of the true

23. See below, pp. 680–681.

state of affairs to speak of *monopoly capitalism* instead of *monopoly interventionism* and of *private cartels* instead of *government-made cartels*. Monopoly prices would be limited to some minerals which can be mined in only a few places and to the field of local limited-space monopolies if the governments were not intent upon fostering them.[24]

The promonopoly party is wrong in crediting to the cartels the economics of big-scale production. Monopolistic concentration of production on one hand, they say, as a rule reduces average costs of production and thus increases the amount of capital and labor available for additional production. However, no cartel is needed in order to eliminate the plants producing at higher costs. Competition on the free market achieves this effect in the absence of any monopoly and of any monopoly prices. It is, on the contrary, often the purpose of government-sponsored cartelization to preserve the existence of plants and farms which the free market would force to discontinue operations precisely because they are producing at too high costs of production. The free market would have eliminated, for example, the submarginal farms and preserved only those for which production pays under the prevailing market price. But the New Deal preferred a different arrangement. It forced all farmers to a proportional restriction of output. It raised by its monopolistic policy the price of agricultural products to such a height that production became reasonable again on submarginal soil.

No less erroneous are the conclusions derived from a confusion of the economies of product standardization and monopoly. If men asked only for one standard type of a definite commodity, production of some articles could be arranged in a more economical way and costs would be lowered accordingly. But if people were to behave in such a manner, standardization and the corresponding cost reduction would emerge also in the absence of monopoly. If, on the other hand, one *forces* the consumers to be content with one standard type only, one does not increase their satisfaction; one impairs it. A dictator may deem the conduct of the consumers rather foolish. Why should not women be dressed in uniforms like soldiers? Why should they be so crazy about individually fashioned clothes? He may be right from the point of view of his own value judgments. But the trouble is that valuation is personal, individual, and arbitrary. The democracy of the market consists in the fact that people themselves make their choices and that no dictator has the power to force them to submit to his value judgments.

24. See above, p. 366.

10. Price Discrimination on the Part of the Seller

Both competitive prices and monopoly prices are the same for all buyers. There prevails on the market a permanent tendency to eliminate all discrepancies in prices for the same commodity or service. Although the valuations of the buyers and the intensity of their demand as effective on the market are different, they pay the same prices. The wealthy man does not pay more for bread than the less wealthy man, although he would be ready to pay a higher price if he could not buy it cheaper. The enthusiast who would rather restrict his consumption of food than miss a performance of a Beethoven symphony pays no more for admission than a man for whom music is merely a pastime and who would not care for the concert if he could attend it only by renouncing his desire for some trifles. The difference between the price one must pay for a good and the highest amount one would be prepared to pay for it has sometimes been called consumers' surplus.[25]

But there can appear on the market conditions which make it possible for the seller to discriminate between the buyers. He can sell a commodity or a service at different prices to different buyers. He can obtain prices which may sometimes even rise to the point at which the whole consumers' surplus of a buyer disappears. Two conditions must coincide in order to make price discrimination advantageous to the seller.

The first condition is that those buying at a cheaper price are not in a position to resell the commodity or the service to people to whom the discriminating seller sells only at a higher price. If such reselling cannot be prevented, the first seller's intention would be thwarted. The second condition is that the public does not react in such a way that the total net proceeds of the seller lag behind the total net proceeds he would obtain under price uniformity. This second condition is always present under conditions which would make it advantageous to a seller to substitute monopoly prices for competitive prices. But it can also appear under a market situation which would not bring about monopoly gains. For price discrimination does not enjoin upon the seller the necessity of restricting the amount sold. He does not lose any buyer completely; he must merely take into account that some buyers may restrict the amount of their purchases. But as a rule he has the opportunity to sell the remainder of his supply to people who would not have bought at all or would

25. Cf. A. Marshall, *Principles of Economics* (8th ed. London, 1930), pp. 124–127.

have bought only smaller quantities if they had had to pay the uniform competitive price.

Consequently the configuration of production costs plays no role in the considerations of the discriminating seller. Production costs are not affected as the total amount produced and sold remains unaltered.

The most common case of price discrimination is that of physicians. A doctor who can perform 80 treatments in a week and charges $3 for each treatment is fully employed by attending to 30 patients and makes $240 a week. If he charges the 10 wealthiest patients, who together consume 50 treatments, $4 instead of $3, they will consume only 40 treatments. The doctor sells the remaining 10 treatments at $2 each to patients who would not have expended $3 for his professional services. Then his weekly proceeds rise to $270.

As price discrimination is practiced by the seller only if it is more advantageous to him than selling at a uniform price, it is obvious that it results in an alteration of consumption and the allocation of factors of production to various employments. The outcome of discrimination is always that the total amount expended for the acquisition of the good concerned increases. The buyers must provide for their excess expenditure by cutting down other purchases. As it is very unlikely that those benefited by price discrimination will spend their gains for the purchase of the same goods as those the other people no longer buy in the same quantity, changes in the market data and in production become unavoidable.

In the above example the 10 wealthiest patients are damaged; they pay $4 for a service for which they used to pay only $3. But it is not only the doctor who derives advantage from the discrimination; the patients whom he charges $2 are benefited too. It is true they must provide the doctor's fees by renouncing other satisfactions. However, they value these other satisfactions less than that conveyed to them by the doctor's treatment. Their degree of contentment attained is increased.

For a full comprehension of price discrimination it is well to remember that, under the division of labor, competition among those eager to acquire the same product does not necessarily impair the individual competitor's position. The competitors' interests are antagonistic only with regard to the services rendered by the complementary nature-given factors of production. This inescapable natural antagonism is superseded by the advantages derived from the division of labor. As far as average costs of production can be reduced by big-scale production, competition among those eager to acquire the same commodity brings about an improvement in the individual competitor's situation. The fact that not only a few people but a great number are eager to acquire the commodity *c* makes it possible to manufacture it in cost-saving processes; then even people with modest means can afford it. In the same way it can sometimes happen that price discrimination renders the satisfaction of a need possible which would have remained unsatisfied in its absence.

There live in a city *p* lovers of music, each of whom would be prepared to spend $2 for the recital of a virtuoso. But such a concert requires an expenditure greater than 2 *p* dollars and can therefore not be arranged. But if discrimination of admission fees is possible and among the *p* friends of music *n* are ready to spend $4, the recital becomes feasible, provided that the amount 2 $(n + p)$ dollars is sufficient. Then *n* people spend $4 each and $(p - n)$ people $2 each for the admission and forego the satisfaction of the least urgent need they would have satisfied if they had not preferred to attend the recital. Each person in the audience fares better than he would have if the unfeasibility of price discrimination had prevented the performance. It is to the interest of the organizers to enlarge the audience to the point at which the admission of additional customers involves higher costs than the fees they are ready to spend.

Things would be different if the recital could have been arranged even if no more than $2 was charged for admission. Then price discrimination would have impaired the satisfaction of those who are charged $4.

The most common practices in selling admission tickets for artistic performances and railroad tickets at different rates are not the outcome of price discrimination in the catallactic sense of the term. He who pays a higher rate gets something appreciated more than he who pays less. He gets a better seat, a more comfortable traveling opportunity, and so on. Genuine price discrimination is present in the case of physicians who, although attending to each patient with the same care, charge the wealthier clients more than the less wealthy. It is present in the case of railroads charging more for the shipping of goods the transportation of which adds more to their value than for others although the costs incurred by the railroad are the same. It is obvious that both the doctor and the railroad can practice discrimination only within the limits fixed by the opportunity given to the patient and the shipper to find another solution of their problems that is more to their own advantage. But this refers to one of the two conditions required for the emergence of price discrimination.

It would be idle to point out a state of affairs in which price discrimination could be practiced by all sellers of all kinds of commodities and services. It is more important to establish the fact that within a market economy not sabotaged by government interference the conditions required for price discrimination are so rare that it can fairly be called an exceptional phenomenon.

11. Price Discrimination on the Part of the Buyer

While monopoly prices and monopoly gains cannot be realized to the advantage of a monopolistic buyer, the case is different with price discrimination. There is only one condition required for the emergence of price discrimination on the part of a monopolistic buyer on a free market, namely, crass ignorance of the state of the market on the part of the sellers. As such ignorance is unlikely to last for any length of time, price discrimination can only be practiced if the government interferes.

The Swiss Government has established a government owned and operated trade monopoly for cereals. It buys cereals at world-market prices on foreign markets and at higher prices from domestic farmers. In domestic purchases it pays a higher price to farmers producing at higher costs on the rocky soil of the mountain districts and a lower price—although still higher than the world-market price—to the farmers tilling more fertile land.

12. The Connexity of Prices

If a definite process of production brings about the products *p* and *q* simultaneously, the entrepreneurial decisions and actions are directed by weighing the sum of the anticipated prices of *p* and *q*. The prices of *p* and *q* are particularly connected with one another as changes in the demand for *p* (or for *q*) generate changes in the supply of *q* (or of *p*). The mutual relation of the prices of *p* and *q* can be called connexity of production. The businessman calls *p* (or *q*) a by-product of *q* (or *p*).

The production of the consumers' good *z* requires the employment of the factors *p* and *q*, the production of *p* the employment of the factors *a* and *b*, and the production of *q* the employment of the factors *c* and *d*. Then changes in the supply of *p* (or of *q*) bring about changes in the demand for *q* (or for *p*). It does not matter whether the process of producing *z* out of *p* and *q* is accomplished by the same enterprises which produce *p* out of *a* and *b* and *q* out of *c* and *d*, or by entrepreneurs financially independent of one another, or by the consumers themselves as a preliminary step in their consuming. The prices of *p* and *q* are particularly connected with one another because *p* is useless or of a smaller utility without *q* and vice versa. The mutual relation of the prices of *p* and *q* can be called connexity of consumption.

If the services rendered by a commodity *b* can be substituted, even though in a not perfectly satisfactory way, for those rendered by another commodity *a,* a change in the price of one of them affects the price of the other too. The mutual relation of the prices of *a* and *b* can be called connexity of substitution.

Connexity of production, connexity of consumption, and connexity of substitution are particular connexities of the prices of a limited number of commodities. From these particular connexities one must distinguish the general connexity of the prices of all goods and services. This general connexity is the outcome of the fact that for every kind of want-satisfaction, besides various more or less specific factors, one scarce factor is required which, in spite of the differences in its qualitative power to produce, can, within the limits precisely defined above,[26] be called a nonspecific factor—namely, labor.

Within a hypothetical world in which all factors of production are absolutely specific, human action would operate in a multiplicity of fields of want-satisfaction independent of one another. What links together in our actual world the various fields of want-satisfaction is the existence of a great many nonspecific factors, suitable to be employed for the attainment of various ends and to be substituted in some degree for one another. The fact that *one* factor, labor, is on the one hand required for every kind of production and on the other hand is, within the limits defined, nonspecific, brings about the general connexity of all human activities. It integrates the pricing process into a whole in which all gears work on one another. It makes the market a concatenation of mutually interdependent phenomena.

It would be absurd to look upon a definite price as if it were an isolated object in itself. A price is expressive of the position which acting men attach to a thing under the present state of their efforts to remove uneasiness. It does not indicate a relationship to something unchanging, but merely the instantaneous position in a kaleidoscopically changing assemblage. In this collection of things considered valuable by the value judgments of acting men each particle's place is interrelated with those of all other particles. What is called a price is always a relationship within an integrated system which is the composite effect of human relations.

26. Cf. above, pp. 133–135.

13. Prices and Income

A market price is a real historical phenomenon, the quantitative ratio at which at a definite place and at a definite date two individuals exchanged definite quantities of two definite goods. It refers to the special conditions of the concrete act of exchange. It is ultimately determined by the value judgments of the individuals involved. It is not derived from the general price structure or from the structure of the prices of a special class of commodities or services. What is called the price structure is an abstract notion derived from a multiplicity of individual concrete prices. The market does not generate prices of land or motorcars in general nor wage rates in general, but prices for a certain piece of land and for a certain car and wage rates for a performance of a certain kind. It does not make any difference for the pricing process to what class the things exchanged are to be assigned from any point of view. However they may differ in other regards, in the very act of exchange they are nothing but commodities, i.e., things valued on account of their power to remove felt uneasiness.

The market does not create or determine incomes. It is not a process of income formation. If the owner of a piece of land and the worker husband the physical resources concerned, the land and the man will renew and preserve their power to render services; the agricultural and urban land for a practically indefinite period, the man for a number of years. If the market situation for these factors of production does not deteriorate, it will be possible in the future too to attain a price for their productive employment. Land and working power can be considered as sources of income if they are dealt with as such, that is, if their capacity to produce is not prematurely exhausted by reckless exploitation. It is provident restraint in the use of factors of production, not their natural and physical properties, which convert them into somewhat durable sources of income. There is in nature no such thing as a stream of income. Income is a category of action; it is the outcome of careful economizing of scarce factors. This is still more obvious in the case of capital goods. The produced factors of production are not permanent. Although some of them may have a life of many years, all of them eventually become useless through wear and tear, sometimes even by the mere passing of time. They become durable sources of income only if their owners treat them as such. Capital can be preserved as a source of income if the consumption of its products, market conditions remaining unchanged, is restricted in such a way as not to impair the replacement of the worn out parts.

Changes in the market data can frustrate every endeavor to perpetuate a source of income. Industrial equipment becomes obsolete if demand changes or if it is superseded by something better. Land becomes useless if more fertile soil is made accessible in sufficient quantities. Expertness and skill for the performance of special kinds of work lose their remunerativeness when new fashions or new methods of production narrow the opportunity for their employment. The success of any provision for the uncertain future depends on the correctness of the anticipations which guided it. No income can be made safe against changes not adequately foreseen.

Neither is the pricing process a form of distribution. As has been pointed out already, there is nothing in the market economy to which the notion of distribution could be applied.

14. Prices and Production

The pricing process of the unhampered market directs production into those channels in which it best serves the wishes of the consumers as manifested on the market. Only in the case of monopoly prices have the monopolists the power to divert production, within a limited range, from this line into other lines to their own benefit.

The prices determine which of the factors of production should be employed and which should be left unused. The specific factors of production are employed only if there is no more valuable employment available for the complementary nonspecific factors. There are technological recipes, land, and nonconvertible capital goods whose capacity to produce remains unused because their employment would mean a waste of the scarcest of all factors, labor. While under the conditions present in our world there cannot be in the long run unemployment of labor in a free labor market, unused capacity of land and of inconvertible industrial equipment is a regular phenomenon.

It is nonsense to lament the fact of unused capacity. The unused capacity of equipment made obsolete by technological improvement is a landmark of material progress. It would be a blessing if the establishment of durable peace would render munitions plants unused or if the discovery of an efficient method of preventing and curing tuberculosis would render obsolete sanatoria for the treatment of people affected by this evil. It would be sensible to deplore the lack of provision in the past which resulted in malinvestment of capital goods. Yet, men are not infallible. A certain amount of malinvestment is unavoidable. What has to be done is to shun policies that like credit expansion artificially foster malinvestment.

Modern technology could easily grow oranges and grapes in hothouses in the arctic and subarctic countries. Everybody would call such a venture lunacy. But it is essentially the same to preserve the growing of cereals in rocky mountain valleys by tariffs and other devices of protectionism while elsewhere there is plenty of fallow fertile land. The difference is merely one of degree.

The inhabitants of the Swiss Jura prefer to manufacture watches instead of growing wheat. Watchmaking is for them the cheapest way to acquire wheat. On the other hand the growing of wheat is the cheapest way for the Canadian farmer to acquire watches. The fact that the inhabitants of the Jura do not grow wheat and the Canadians do not manufacture watches is not more worthy of notice than the fact that tailors do not make their shoes and shoemakers do not make their clothes.

15. The Chimera of Nonmarket Prices

Prices are a market phenomenon. They are generated by the market process and are the pith of the market economy. There is no such thing as prices outside the market. Prices cannot be constructed synthetically, as it were. They are the resultant of a certain constellation of market data, of actions and reactions of the members of a market society. It is vain to meditate what prices would have been if some of their determinants had been different. Such fantastic designs are no more sensible than whimsical speculations about what the course of history would have been if Napoleon had been killed in the battle of Arcole or if Lincoln had ordered Major Anderson to withdraw from Fort Sumter.

It is no less vain to ponder on what prices ought to be. Everybody is pleased if the prices of things he wants to buy drop and the prices of the things he wants to sell rise. In expressing such wishes a man is sincere if he admits that his point of view is personal. It is another question whether, from his personal point of view, he would be well advised to prompt the government to use its power of coercion and oppression to interfere with the market's price structure. It will be shown in the sixth part of this book what the inescapable consequences of such a policy of interventionism must be.

But one deludes oneself or practices deception if one calls such wishes and arbitrary value judgments the voice of objective truth. In human action nothing counts but the various individuals' desires for the attainment of ends. With regard to the choice of these ends there is no question of truth; all that matters is value. Value judgments are necessarily always subjective, whether they are passed by one man only or by many men, by a blockhead, a professor, or a statesman.

Any price determined on a market is the necessary outgrowth of the interplay of the forces operating, that is, demand and supply. Whatever the market situation which generated this price may be, with regard to it the price is always adequate, genuine, and real. It cannot be higher if no bidder ready to offer a higher price turns up, and it cannot be lower if no seller ready to deliver at a lower price turns up. Only the appearance of such people ready to buy or to sell can alter prices.

Economics analyzes the market process which generates commodity prices, wage rates, and interest rates. It does not develop formulas which would enable anybody to compute a "correct" price different from that established on the market by the interaction of buyers and sellers.

At the bottom of many efforts to determine nonmarket prices is the confused and contradictory notion of real costs. If costs were a real thing, i.e., a quantity independent of personal value judgments and objectively discernible and measurable, it would be possible for a disinterested arbiter to determine their height and thus the correct price. There is no need to dwell any longer on the absurdity of this idea. Costs are a phenomenon of valuation. Costs are the value attached to the most valuable want-satisfaction which remains unsatisfied because the means required for its satisfaction are employed for that want-satisfaction the cost of which we are dealing with. The attainment of an excess of the value of the product over the costs, a profit, is the goal of every production effort. Profit is the pay-off of successful action. It cannot be defined without reference to valuation. It is a phenomenon of valuation and has no direct relation to physical and other phenomena of the external world.

Economic analysis cannot help reducing all items of cost to value judgments. The socialists and interventionists call entrepreneurial profit, interest on capital, and rent of land "unearned" because they consider that only the toil and trouble of the worker is real and worthy of being rewarded. However, reality does not reward toil and trouble. If toil and trouble is expended according to well-conceived plans, its outcome increases the means available for want-satisfaction. Whatever some people may consider as just and fair, the only relevant question is always the same. What alone matters is which system of social organization is better suited to attain those ends for which people are ready to expend toil and trouble. The question is: market economy, or socialism? There is no third solution. The notion of a market economy with nonmarket prices is absurd. The very idea of cost prices is unrealizable. Even if the cost price formula is applied only to entrepreneurial profits, it paralyzes the market. If commodities and services are to be sold below the price the market would have determined for them, supply always lags behind demand. Then the market can neither determine what should or should not be produced, nor to whom the commodities and services should go. Chaos results.

This refers also to monopoly prices. It is reasonable to abstain from all policies which could result in the emergence of monopoly prices. But whether monopoly prices are brought about by such promonopoly government policies or in spite of the absence of such policies, no alleged "fact finding" and no armchair speculation can discover another price at which demand and supply would become equal. The failure of all experiments to find a satisfactory solution for the limited-space monopoly of public utilities clearly proves this truth.

It is the very essence of prices that they are the offshoot of the actions of individuals and groups of individuals acting on their own behalf. The catallactic concept of exchange ratios and prices precludes anything that is the effect of actions of a central authority, of people resorting to violence and threats in the name of society or the state or of an armed pressure group. In declaring that it is not the business of the government to determine prices, we do not step beyond the borders of logical thinking. A government can no more determine prices than a goose can lay hen's eggs.

We can think of a social system in which there are no prices at all, and we can think of government decrees which aim at fixing prices at a height different from that which the market would determine. It is one of the tasks of economics to study the problems implied. However, precisely because we want to examine these problems it is necessary clearly to distinguish between prices and government decrees. Prices are by definition determined by peoples' buying and selling or abstention from buying and selling. They must not be confused with fiats issued by governments or other agencies enforcing their orders by an apparatus of coercion and compulsion.[27]

27. In order not to confuse the reader by the introduction of too many new terms, we shall keep to the widespread usage of calling such fiats *prices, interest rates, wage rates decreed and enforced by governments or other agencies of compulsion* (*e.g., labor unions*). But one must never lose sight of the fundamental difference between the market phenomena of prices, wages, and interest rates on the one hand, and the legal phenomena of maximum or minimum prices, wages, and interest rates, designed to nullify these market phenomena, on the other hand.

XVII. INDIRECT EXCHANGE

1. Media of Exchange and Money

INTERPERSONAL exchange is called indirect exchange if, between the commodities and services the reciprocal exchange of which is the ultimate end of exchanging, one or several media of exchange are interposed. The subject matter of the theory of indirect exchange is the study of the ratios of exchange between the media of exchange on the one hand and the goods and services of all orders on the other hand. The statements of the theory of indirect exchange refer to all instances of indirect exchange and to all things which are employed as media of exchange.

A medium of exchange which is commonly used as such is called money. The notion of money is vague, as its definition refers to the vague term "commonly used." There are borderline cases in which it cannot be decided whether a medium of exchange is or is not "commonly" used and should be called money. But this vagueness in the denotation of money in no way affects the exactitude and precision required by praxeological theory. For all that is to be predicated of money is valid for every medium of exchange. It is therefore immaterial whether one preserves the traditional term *theory of money* or substitutes for it another term. The theory of money was and is always the theory of indirect exchange and of the media of exchange.[1]

2. Observations on Some Widespread Errors

The fateful errors of popular monetary doctrines which have led astray the monetary policies of almost all governments would hardly have come into existence if many economists had not themselves committed blunders in dealing with monetary issues and did not stubbornly cling to them.

There is first of all the spurious idea of the supposed neutrality of money.[2] An outgrowth of this doctrine was the notion of the "level"

1. The theory of monetary calculation does not belong to the theory of indirect exchange. It is a part of the general theory of praxeology.

2. Cf. above, p. 202. Important contributions to the history and terminology of this doctrine are provided by Hayek, *Prices and Production* (rev. ed. London, 1935), pp. 1 ff., 129 ff.

of prices that rises or falls proportionately with the increase or decrease in the quantity of money in circulation. It was not realized that changes in the quantity of money can never affect the prices of all goods and services at the same time and to the same extent. Nor was it realized that changes in the purchasing power of the monetary unit are necessarily linked with changes in the mutual relations between those buying and selling. In order to prove the doctrine that the quantity of money and prices rise and fall proportionately, recourse was had in dealing with the theory of money to a procedure entirely different from that modern economics applies in dealing with all its other problems. Instead of starting from the actions of individuals, as catallactics must do without exception, formulas were constructed designed to comprehend the whole of the market economy. Elements of these formulas were: the total supply of money available in the *Volkswirtschaft;* the volume of trade—i.e., the money equivalent of all transfers of commodities and services as effected in the Volkswirtschaft; the average velocity of circulation of the monetary units; the level of prices. These formulas seemingly provided evidence of the correctness of the price level doctrine. In fact, however, this whole mode of reasoning is a typical case of arguing in a circle. For the equation of exchange already involves the level doctrines which it tries to prove. It is essentially nothing but a mathematical expression of the—untenable—doctrine that there is proportionality in the movements of the quantity of money and of prices.

In analyzing the equation of exchange one assumes that one of its elements—total supply of money, volume of trade, velocity of circulation—changes, without asking how such changes occur. It is not recognized that changes in these magnitudes do not emerge in the Volkswirtschaft as such, but in the individual actors' conditions, and that it is the interplay of the reactions of these actors that results in alterations of the price structure. The mathematical economists refuse to start from the various individuals' demand for and supply of money. They introduce instead the spurious notion of velocity of circulation fashioned according to the patterns of mechanics.

There is at this point of our reasoning no need to deal with the question of whether or not the mathematical economists are right in assuming that the services rendered by money consist wholly or essentially in its turnover, in its circulation. Even if this were true, it would still be faulty to explain the purchasing power—the price—of the monetary unit on the basis of its services. The services rendered by water, whisky, and coffee do not explain the prices paid for these things. What they explain is only why people, as far as they recognize these services, under certain further conditions demand definite quantities of these things. It is always demand that influences the price structure, not the objective value in use.

It is true that with regard to money the task of catallactics is broader than with regard to vendible goods. It is not the task of catallactics, but of psychology and physiology, to explain why people are intent on securing the services which the various vendible commodities can render. It *is* a task of catallactics, however, to deal with this question with regard to money. Catallactics alone can tell us what advantages a man expects from holding money. But it is not these expected advantages which determine the purchasing power of money. The eagerness to secure these advantages is only one of the factors in bringing about the demand for money. It is demand, a subjective element whose intensity is entirely determined by value judgments, and not any objective fact, any power to bring about a certain effect, that plays a role in the formation of the market's exchange ratios.

The deficiency of the equation of exchange and its basic elements is that they look at market phenomena from a holistic point of view. They are deluded by their prepossession with the Volkswirtschaft notion. But where there is, in the strict sense of the term, a Volkswirtschaft, there is neither a market nor prices and money. On a market there are only individuals or groups of individuals acting in concert. What motivate these actors are their own concerns, not those of the whole market economy. If there is any sense in such notions as volume of trade and velocity of circulation, then they refer to the resultant of the individuals' actions. It is not permissible to resort to these notions in order to explain the actions of the individuals. The first question that catallactics must raise with regard to changes in the total quantity of money available in the market system is how such changes affect the various individuals' conduct. Modern economics does not ask what "iron" or "bread" is worth, but what a definite piece of iron or of bread is worth to an acting individual at a definite date and a definite place. It cannot help proceeding in the same way with regard to money. The equation of exchange is incompatible with the fundamental principles of economic thought. It is a relapse to the thinking of ages in which people failed to comprehend praxeological phenomena because they were committed to holistic notions. It is sterile, as were the speculations of earlier ages concerning the value of "iron" and "bread" in general.

The theory of money is an essential part of the catallactic theory.

It must be dealt with in the same manner which is applied to all other catallactic problems.

3. Demand for Money and Supply of Money

In the marketability of the various commodities and services there prevail considerable differences. There are goods for which it is not difficult to find applicants ready to disburse the highest recompense which, under the given state of affairs, can possibly be obtained, or a recompense only slightly smaller. There are other goods for which it is very hard to find a customer quickly, even if the vendor is ready to be content with a compensation much smaller than he could reap if he could find another aspirant whose demand is more intense. It is these differences in the marketability of the various commodities and services which created indirect exchange. A man who at the instant cannot acquire what he wants to get for the conduct of his own household or business, or who does not yet know what kind of goods he will need in the uncertain future, comes nearer to his ultimate goal if he exchanges a less marketable good he wants to trade against a more marketable one. It may also happen that the physical properties of the merchandise he wants to give away (as, for instance, its perishability or the costs incurred by its storage or similar circumstances) impel him not to wait longer. Sometimes he may be prompted to hurry in giving away the good concerned because he is afraid of a deterioration of its market value. In all such cases he improves his own situation in acquiring a more marketable good, even if this good is not suitable to satisfy directly any of his own needs.

A medium of exchange is a good which people acquire neither for their own consumption nor for employment in their own production activities, but with the intention of exchanging it at a later date against those goods which they want to use either for consumption or for production.

Money is a medium of exchange. It is the most marketable good which people acquire because they want to offer it in later acts of interpersonal exchange. Money is the thing which serves as the generally accepted and commonly used medium of exchange. This is its only function. All the other functions which people ascribe to money are merely particular aspects of its primary and sole function, that of a medium of exchange.[3]

Media of exchange are economic goods. They are scarce; there is

3. Cf. Mises, *The Theory of Money and Credit,* trans. by H. E. Batson (London and New York, 1934), pp. 34–37.

a demand for them. There are on the market people who desire to acquire them and are ready to exchange goods and services against them. Media of exchange have value in exchange. People make sacrifices for their acquisition; they pay "prices" for them. The peculiarity of these prices lies merely in the fact that they cannot be expressed in terms of money. In reference to the vendible goods and services we speak of prices or of money prices. In reference to money we speak of its purchasing power with regard to various vendible goods.

There exists a demand for media of exchange because people want to keep a store of them. Every member of a market society wants to have a definite amount of money in his pocket or box, a cash holding or cash balance of a definite height. Sometimes he wants to keep a larger cash holding, sometimes a smaller; in exceptional cases he may even renounce any cash holding. At any rate, the immense majority of people aim not only to own various vendible goods; they want no less to hold money. Their cash holding is not merely a residuum, an unspent margin of their wealth. It is not an unintentional remainder left over after all intentional acts of buying and selling have been consummated. Its amount is determined by a deliberate demand for cash. And as with all other goods, it is the changes in the relation between demand for and supply of money that bring about changes in the exchange ratio between money and the vendible goods.

Every piece of money is owned by one of the members of the market economy. The transfer of money from the control of one actor into that of another is temporally immediate and continuous. There is no fraction of time in between in which the money is not a part of an individual's or a firm's cash holding, but just in "circulation."[4] It is unsound to distinguish between circulating and idle money. It is no less faulty to distinguish between circulating money and hoarded money. What is called hoarding is a height of cash holding which—according to the personal opinion of an observer—exceeds what is deemed normal and adequate. However, hoarding is cash holding. Hoarded money is still money and it serves in the hoards the same purposes which it serves in cash holdings called normal. He who hoards money believes that some special conditions make it expedient to accumulate a cash holding which exceeds the amount he himself would keep under different conditions, or other people keep, or an economist censuring his action considers appropriate. That he acts in this way influences the configuration of the

4. Money can be in the process of transportation, it can travel in trains, ships, or planes from one place to another. But it is in this case, too, always subject to somebody's control, is somebody's property.

demand for money in the same way in which every "normal" demand influences it.

Many economists avoid applying the terms demand and supply in the sense of demand for and supply of money for cash holding because they fear a confusion with the current terminology as used by the bankers. It is, in fact, customary to call demand for money the demand for short-term loans and supply of money the supply of such loans. Accordingly, one calls the market for short-term loans the money market. One says money is scarce if there prevails a tendency toward a rise in the rate of interest for short-term loans, and one says money is plentiful if the rate of interest for such loans is decreasing. These modes of speech are so firmly entrenched that it is out of the question to venture to discard them. But they have favored the spread of fateful errors. They made people confound the notions of money and of capital and believe that increasing the quantity of money could lower the rate of interest lastingly. But it is precisely the crassness of these errors which makes it unlikely that the terminology suggested could create any misunderstanding. It is hard to assume that economists could err with regard to such fundamental issues.

Others maintained that one should not speak of the demand for and supply of money because the aims of those demanding money differ from the aims of those demanding vendible commodities. Commodities, they say, are demanded ultimately for consumption, while money is demanded in order to be given away in further acts of exchange. This objection is no less invalid. The use which people make of a medium of exchange consists eventually in its being given away. But first of all they are eager to accumulate a certain amount of it in order to be ready for the moment in which a purchase may be accomplished. Precisely because people do not want to provide for their own needs right at the instant at which they give away the goods and services they themselves bring to the market, precisely because they want to wait or are forced to wait until propitious conditions for buying appear, they barter not directly but indirectly through the interposition of a medium of exchange. The fact that money is not worn out by the use one makes of it and that it can render its services practically for an unlimited length of time is an important factor in the configuration of its supply. But it does not alter the fact that the appraisement of money is to be explained in the same way as the appraisement of all other goods: by the demand on the part of those who are eager to acquire a definite quantity of it.

Economists have tried to enumerate the factors which within the whole economic system may increase or decrease the demand for money. Such factors are: the population figure; the extent to which the individual households provide for their own needs by autarkic production and the extent to which they produce for other people's needs, selling their products and buying for their own consumption on the market; the distribution of business activity and the settlement of payments over the various seasons of the year; institutions for the settlement of claims and counterclaims by mutual cancellation, such as clearinghouses. All these factors indeed influence the demand for money and the height of the various individuals' and firms' cash holding. But they influence them only indirectly by the role they play in the considerations of people concerning the determination of the amount of cash balances they deem appropriate. What decides the matter is always the value judgments of the men concerned. The various actors make up their minds about what they believe the adequate height of their cash holding should be. They carry out their resolution by renouncing the purchase of commodities, securities, and interest-bearing claims, and by selling such assets or conversely by increasing their purchases. With money, things are not different from what they are with regard to all other goods and services. The demand for money is determined by the conduct of people intent upon acquiring it for their cash holding.

Another objection raised against the notion of the demand for money was this: The marginal utility of the money unit decreases much more slowly than that of the other commodities; in fact its decrease is so slow that it can be practically ignored. With regard to money nobody ever says that his demand is satisfied, and nobody ever forsakes an opportunity to acquire more money provided the sacrifice required is not too great. It is therefore impermissible to consider the demand for money as limited. The very notion of an unlimited demand is, however, contradictory. This popular reasoning is entirely fallacious. It confounds the demand for money for cash holding with the desire for more wealth as expressed in terms of money. He who says that his thirst for more money can never be quenched, does not mean to say that his cash holding can never be too large. What he really means is that he can never be rich enough. If additional money flows into his hands, he will not use it for an increase of his cash balance or he will use only a part of it for this purpose. He will expend the surplus either for instantaneous consumption or for investment. Nobody ever keeps more money than he wants to have as cash holding.

The insight that the exchange ratio between money on the one hand and the vendible commodities and services on the other is determined, in the same way as the mutual exchange ratios between the various vendible goods, by demand and supply was the essence of the *quantity theory of money*. This theory is essentially an application of the general theory of supply and demand to the special instance of money. Its merit was the endeavor to explain the determination of money's purchasing power by resorting to the same reasoning which is employed for the explanation of all other exchange ratios. Its shortcoming was that it resorted to a holistic interpretation. It looked at the total supply of money in the Volkswirtschaft and not at the actions of the individual men and firms. An outgrowth of this erroneous point of view was the idea that there prevails a proportionality in the changes of the—total—quantity of money and of money prices. But the older critics failed in their attempts to explode the errors inherent in the quantity theory and to substitute a more satisfactory theory for it. They did not fight what was wrong in the quantity theory; they attacked, on the contrary, its nucleus of truth. They were intent upon denying that there is a causal relation between the movements of prices and those of the quantity of money. This denial led them into a labyrinth of errors, contradictions, and nonsense. Modern monetary theory takes up the thread of the traditional quantity theory as far as it starts from the cognition that changes in the purchasing power of money must be dealt with according to the principles applied to all other market phenomena and that there exists a connection between the changes in the demand for and supply of money on the one hand and those of purchasing power on the other. In this sense one may call the modern theory of money an improved variety of the quantity theory.

The Epistemological Import of Carl Menger's Theory of the Origin of Money

Carl Menger has not only provided an irrefutable praxeological theory of the origin of money. He has also recognized the import of his theory for the elucidation of fundamental principles of praxeology and its methods of research.[5]

There were authors who tried to explain the origin of money by decree or covenant. The authority, the state, or a compact between citizens has purposively and consciously established indirect exchange and money. The main deficiency of this doctrine is not to be seen in the assumption that people of an age unfamiliar with indirect

5. Cf. Carl Menger's books *Grundsätze der Volkswirtschaftslehre* (Vienna, 1871), pp. 250 ff.; *ibid.* (2d ed. Vienna, 1923), pp. 241 ff.; *Untersuchungen über die Methode der Sozialwissenschaften* (Leipzig, 1883), p. 171 ff.

exchange and money could design a plan of a new economic order, entirely different from the real conditions of their own age, and could comprehend the importance of such a plan. Neither is it to be seen in the fact that history does not afford a clue for the support of such statements. There are more substantial reasons for rejecting it.

If it is assumed that the conditions of the parties concerned are improved by every step that leads from direct exchange to indirect exchange and subsequently to giving preference for use as a medium of exchange to certain goods distinguished by their especially high marketability, it is difficult to conceive why one should, in dealing with the origin of indirect exchange, resort in addition to authoritarian decree or an explicit compact between citizens. A man who finds it hard to obtain in direct barter what he wants to acquire renders better his chances of acquiring it in later acts of exchange by the procurement of a more marketable good. Under these circumstances there was no need of government interference or of a compact between the citizens. The happy idea of proceeding in this way could strike the shrewdest individuals, and the less resourceful could imitate the former's method. It is certainly more plausible to take for granted that the immediate advantages conferred by indirect exchange were recognized by the acting parties than to assume that the whole image of a society trading by means of money was conceived by a genius and, if we adopt the covenant doctrine, made obvious to the rest of the people by persuasion.

If, however, we do not assume that individuals discovered the fact that they fare better through indirect exchange than through waiting for an opportunity for direct exchange, and, for the sake of argument, admit that the authorities or a compact introduced money, further questions are raised. We must ask what kind of measures were applied in order to induce people to adopt a procedure the utility of which they did not comprehend and which was technically more complicated than direct exchange. We may assume that compulsion was practiced. But then we must ask, further, at what time and by what occurrences indirect exchange and the use of money later ceased to be procedures troublesome or at least indifferent to the individuals concerned and became advantageous to them.

The praxeological method traces all phenomena back to the actions of individuals. If conditions of interpersonal exchange are such that indirect exchange facilitates the transactions, and if and as far as people realize these advantages, indirect exchange and money come into being. Historical experience shows that these conditions were and are present. How, in the absence of these conditions, people could have adopted indirect exchange and money and clung to these modes of exchanging is inconceivable.

The historical question concerning the origin of indirect exchange and money is after all of no concern to praxeology. The only relevant thing is that indirect exchange and money exist because the conditions for their existence were and are present. If this is so, praxeology does not need to resort to the hypothesis that authoritarian decree or a covenant invented these modes of exchanging. The étatists may if they like continue to ascribe the "invention" of money to the state, however unlikely this may be. What matters is that a man acquires a good not in order to consume it or to use it in production, but in order to give it away in a further act of exchange. Such conduct on the part of people makes a good a medium of exchange and, if such conduct becomes common with regard to a certain good, makes it money. All theorems of the catallactic theory of media of exchange and of money refer to the services which a good renders in its capacity as a medium of exchange. Even if it were true that the impulse for the introduction of indirect exchange and money was provided by the authorities or by an agreement between the members of society, the statement remains unshaken that only the conduct of exchanging people can create indirect exchange and money.

History may tell us where and when for the first time media of exchange came into use and how, subsequently, the range of goods employed for this purpose was more and more restricted. As the differentiation between the broader notion of a medium of exchange and the narrower notion of money is not sharp, but gradual, no agreement can be reached about the historical transition from simple media of exchange to money. Answering such a question is a matter of historical understanding. But, as has been mentioned, the distinction between direct exchange and indirect exchange is sharp and everything that catallactics establishes with regard to media of exchange refers categorially to all goods which are demanded and acquired as such media.

As far as the statement that indirect exchange and money were established by decree or by covenant is meant to be an account of historical events, it is the task of historians to expose its falsity. As far as it is advanced merely as a historical statement, it can in no way affect the catallactic theory of money and its explanation of the evolution of indirect exchange. But if it is designed as a statement about human action and social events, it is useless because it states nothing about action. It is not a statement about human action to declare that one day rulers or citizens assembled in convention were suddenly struck by the inspiration that it would be a good idea to exchange indirectly and through the intermediary of a commonly used medium of exchange. It is merely pushing back the problem involved.

It is necessary to comprehend that one does not contribute anything to the scientific conception of human actions and social phenomena if one declares that the state or a charismatic leader or an inspiration which descended upon all the people have created them. Neither do such statements refute the teachings of a theory showing how such phenomena can be acknowledged as "the unintentional outcome, the resultant not deliberately designed and aimed at by specifically individual endeavors of the members of a society."[6]

4. The Determination of the Purchasing Power of Money

As soon as an economic good is demanded not only by those who want to use it for consumption or production, but also by people who want to keep it as a medium of exchange and to give it away at need in a later act of exchange, the demand for it increases. A new employment for this good has emerged and creates an additional demand for it. As with every other economic good, such an additional demand brings about a rise in its value in exchange, i.e., in the quantity of other goods which are offered for its acquisition. The amount of other goods which can be obtained in giving away a medium of exchange, its "price" as expressed in terms of various goods and services, is in part determined by the demand of those who want to acquire it as a medium of exchange. If people stop using the good in question as a medium of exchange, this additional specific demand disappears and the "price" drops concomitantly.

Thus the demand for a medium of exchange is the composite of two partial demands: the demand displayed by the intention to use it in consumption and production and that displayed by the intention to use it as a medium of exchange.[7] With regard to modern metallic money one speaks of the industrial demand and of the monetary demand. The value in exchange (purchasing power) of a medium of exchange is the resultant of the cumulative effect of both partial demands.

Now the extent of that part of the demand for a medium of exchange which is displayed on account of its service as a medium of exchange depends on its value in exchange. This fact raises difficulties which many economists considered insoluble so that they abstained from following farther along this line of reasoning. It is illogical, they said, to explain the purchasing power of money by reference to the demand for money, and the demand for money by reference to its purchasing power.

The difficulty is, however, merely apparent. The purchasing power

6. Cf. Menger, *Untersuchungen,* l.c., p. 178.

7. The problems of money exclusively dedicated to the service of a medium of exchange and not fit to render any other services on account of which it would be demanded are dealt with below in section 9.

which we explain by referring to the extent of specific demand is not the same purchasing power the height of which determines this specific demand. The problem is to conceive the determination of the purchasing power of the immediate future, of the impending moment. For the solution of this problem we refer to the purchasing power of the immediate past, of the moment just passed. These are two distinct magnitudes. It is erroneous to object to our theorem, which may be called the regression theorem, that it moves in a vicious circle.[8]

But, say the critics, this is tantamount to merely pushing back the problem. For now one must still explain the determination of yesterday's purchasing power. If one explains this in the same way by referring to the purchasing power of the day before yesterday and so on, one slips into a *regressus in infinitum*. This reasoning, they assert, is certainly not a complete and logically satisfactory solution of the problem involved. What these critics fail to see is that the regression does not go back endlessly. It reaches a point at which the explanation is completed and no further question remains unanswered. If we trace the purchasing power of money back step by step, we finally arrive at the point at which the service of the good concerned as a medium of exchange begins. At this point yesterday's exchange value is exclusively determined by the nonmonetary—industrial—demand which is displayed only by those who want to use this good for other employments than that of a medium of exchange.

But, the critics continue, this means explaining that part of money's purchasing power which is due to its service as a medium of exchange by its employment for industrial purposes. The very problem, the explanation of the specific monetary component of its exchange value, remains unsolved. Here too the critics are mistaken. That component of money's value which is an outcome of the services it renders as a medium of exchange is entirely explained by reference to these specific monetary services and the demand they create. Two facts are not to be denied and are not denied by anybody. First, that the demand for a medium of exchange is determined by considerations

8. The present writer first developed this regression theorem of purchasing power in the first edition of his book *Theory of Money and Credit,* published in 1912 (pp. 97–123 of the English-language translation). His theorem has been criticized from various points of view. Some of the objections raised, especially those by B. M. Anderson in his thoughtful book *The Value of Money,* first published in 1917 (cf. pp. 100 ff. of the 1936 edition), deserve a very careful examination. The importance of the problems involved makes it necessary to weigh also the objections of H. Ellis (*German Monetary Theory 1905–1933* [Cambridge, 1934], pp. 77 ff.). In the text above, all objections raised are particularized and critically examined.

of its exchange value which is an outcome both of the monetary and the industrial services it renders. Second, that the exchange value of a good which has not yet been demanded for service as a medium of exchange is determined solely by a demand on the part of people eager to use it for industrial purposes, i.e., either for consumption or for production. Now, the regression theorem aims at interpreting the first emergence of a monetary demand for a good which previously had been demanded exclusively for industrial purposes as influenced by the exchange value that was ascribed to it at this moment on account of its nonmonetary services only. This certainly does not involve explaining the specific monetary exchange value of a medium of exchange on the ground of its industrial exchange value.

Finally it was objected to the regression theorem that its approach is historical, not theoretical. This objection is no less mistaken. To explain an event historically means to show how it was produced by forces and factors operating at a definite date and a definite place. These individual forces and factors are the ultimate elements of the interpretation. They are ultimate data and as such not open to any further analysis and reduction. To explain a phenomenon theoretically means to trace back its appearance to the operation of general rules which are already comprised in the theoretical system. The regression theorem complies with this requirement. It traces the specific exchange value of a medium of exchange back to its function as such a medium and to the theorems concerning the process of valuing and pricing as developed by the general catallactic theory. It deduces a more special case from the rules of a more universal theory. It shows how the special phenomenon necessarily emerges out of the operation of the rules generally valid for all phenomena. It does not say: This happened at that time and at that place. It says: This always happens when the conditions appear; whenever a good which has not been demanded previously for the employment as a medium of exchange begins to be demanded for this employment, the same effects must appear again; no good can be employed for the function of a medium of exchange which at the very beginning of its use for this purpose did not have exchange value on account of other employments. And all these statements implied in the regression theorem are enounced apodictically as implied in the apriorism of praxeology. It *must* happen this way. Nobody can ever succeed in constructing a hypothetical case in which things were to occur in a different way.

The purchasing power of money is determined by demand and supply, as is the case with the prices of all vendible goods and services. As action always aims at a more satisfactory arrangement of future conditions, he who considers acquiring or giving away money is, of course, first of all interested in its future purchasing power and the future structure of prices. But he cannot form a judgment about the future purchasing power of money otherwise than by looking at its configuration in the immediate past. It is this fact that radically distinguishes the determination of the purchasing power of money from the determination of the mutual exchange ratios between the various vendible goods and services. With regard to these latter the actors have nothing else to consider than their importance for future want-satisfaction. If a new commodity unheard of before is offered for sale, as was, for instance, the case with radio sets a few decades ago, the only question that matters for the individual is whether or not the satisfaction that the new gadget will provide is greater than that expected from those goods he would have to renounce in order to buy the new thing. Knowledge about past prices is for the buyer merely a means to reap a consumer's surplus. If he were not intent upon this goal, he could, if need be, arrange his purchases without any familiarity with the market prices of the immediate past, which are popularly called present prices. He could make value judgments without appraisement. As has been mentioned already, the obliteration of the memory of all prices of the past would not prevent the formation of new exchange ratios between the various vendible things. But if knowledge about money's purchasing power were to fade away, the process of developing indirect exchange and media of exchange would have to start anew. It would become necessary to begin again with employing some goods, more marketable than the rest, as media of exchange. The demand for these goods would increase and would add to the amount of exchange value derived from their industrial (nonmonetary) employment a specific component due to their new use as a medium of exchange. A value judgment is, with reference to money, only possible if it can be based on appraisement. The acceptance of a new kind of money presupposes that the thing in question already has previous exchange value on account of the services it can render directly to consumption or production. Neither a buyer nor a seller could judge the value of a monetary unit if he had no information about its exchange value—its purchasing power—in the immediate past.

The relation between the demand for money and the supply of money, which may be called the money relation, determines the height of purchasing power. Today's money relation, as it is shaped on the ground of yesterday's purchasing power, determines today's purchasing power. He who wants to increase his cash holding restricts his purchases and increases his sales and thus brings about a tendency toward falling prices. He who wants to reduce his cash holding increases his purchases—either for consumption or for production and investment—and restricts his sales; thus he brings about a tendency toward rising prices.

Changes in the supply of money must necessarily alter the disposition of vendible goods as owned by various individuals and firms. The quantity of money available in the whole market system cannot increase or decrease otherwise than by first increasing or decreasing the cash holdings of certain individual members. We may, if we like, assume that every member gets a share of the additional money right at the moment of its inflow into the system, or shares in the reduction of the quantity of money. But whether we assume this or not, the final result of our demonstration will remain the same. This result will be that changes in the structure of prices brought about by changes in the supply of money available in the economic system never affect the prices of the various commodities and services to the same extent and at the same date.

Let us assume that the government issues an additional quantity of paper money. The government plans either to buy commodities and services or to repay debts incurred or to pay interest on such debts. However this may be, the treasury enters the market with an additional demand for goods and services; it is now in a position to buy more goods than it could buy before. The prices of the commodities it buys rise. If the government had expended in its purchases money collected by taxation, the taxpayers would have restricted their purchases and, while the prices of goods bought by the government would have risen, those of other goods would have dropped. But this fall in the prices of the goods the taxpayers used to buy does not occur if the government increases the quantity of money at its disposal without reducing the quantity of money in the hands of the public. The prices of some commodities—viz., of those the government buys—rise immediately, while those of the other commodities remain unaltered for the time being. But the process goes on. Those selling the commodities asked for by the government are now themselves in a position to buy more than they used previously. The prices of the things these people are buying in larger quantities therefore rise too. Thus the boom spreads from one group of commodities and services to other groups until all prices and wage rates have risen. The rise in prices is thus not synchronous for the various commodities and services.

When eventually, in the further course of the increase in the quantity of money, all prices have risen, the rise does not affect the various commodities and services to the same extent. For the process has affected the material position of various individuals to different degrees. While the process is under way, some people enjoy the benefit of higher prices for the goods or services they sell, while the prices of the things they buy have not yet risen or have not risen to the same extent. On the other hand, there are people who are in the unhappy situation of selling commodities and services whose prices have not yet risen or not in the same degree as the prices of the goods they must buy for their daily consumption. For the former the progressive rise in prices is a boon, for the latter a calamity. Besides, the debtors are favored at the expense of the creditors. When the process once comes to an end, the wealth of various individuals has been affected in different ways and to different degrees. Some are enriched, some impoverished. Conditions are no longer what they were before. The new order of things results in changes in the intensity of demand for various goods. The mutual ratio of the money prices of the vendible goods and services is no longer the same as before. The price structure has changed apart from the fact that all prices in terms of money have risen. The final prices to the establishment of which the market tends after the effects of the increase in the quantity of money have been fully consummated are not equal to the previous final prices multiplied by the same multiplier.

The main fault of the old quantity theory as well as the mathematical economists' equation of exchange is that they have ignored this fundamental issue. Changes in the supply of money must bring about changes in other data too. The market system before and after the inflow or outflow of a quantity of money is not merely changed in that the cash holdings of the individuals and prices have increased or decreased. There have been effected also changes in the reciprocal exchange ratios between the various commodities and services which, if one wants to resort to metaphors, are more adequately described by the image of price revolution than by the misleading figure of an elevation or a sinking of the "price level."

We may at this point disregard the effects brought about by the influence on the content of all deferred payments as stipulated by contracts. We will deal later with them and with the operation of monetary events on consumption and production, investment in capital goods, and accumulation and consumption of capital. But even in setting aside all these things, we must never forget that changes in the quantity of money affect prices in an uneven way. It depends on the data of each particular case at what moment and to what extent the prices of the various commodities and services are affected. In the course of a monetary expansion (inflation) the first reaction is not only that the prices of some of them rise more quickly and more steeply than others. It may also occur that some fall at first as they are for the most part demanded by those groups whose interests are hurt.

Changes in the money relation are not only caused by governments issuing additional paper money. An increase in the production of the precious metals employed as money has the same effects although, of course, other classes of the population may be favored or hurt by it. Prices also rise in the same way if, without a corresponding reduction in the quantity of money available, the demand for money falls because of a general tendency toward a diminution of cash holdings. The money expended additionally by such a "dishoarding" brings about a tendency toward higher prices in the same way as that flowing from the gold mines or from the printing press. Conversely, prices drop when the supply of money falls (e.g., through a withdrawal of paper money) or the demand for money increases (e.g., through a tendency toward "hoarding," the keeping of greater cash balances). The process is always uneven and by steps, disproportionate and asymmetrical.

It could be and has been objected that the normal production of the gold mines brought to the market may well entail an increase in the quantity of money, but does not increase the income, still less the wealth, of the owners of the mines. These people earn only their "normal" income and thus their spending of it cannot disarrange market conditions and the prevailing tendencies toward the establishment of final prices and the equilibrium of the evenly rotating economy. For them, the annual output of the mines does not mean an increase in riches and does not impel them to offer higher prices. They will continue to live at the standard at which they used to live before. Their spending within these limits will not revolutionize the market. Thus the normal amount of gold production, although certainly increasing the quantity of money available, cannot put into motion the process of depreciation. It is neutral with regard to prices.

As against this reasoning one must first of all observe that within a progressing economy in which population figures are increasing and the division of labor and its corollary, industrial specialization, are perfected, there prevails a tendency toward an increase in the demand for money. Additional people appear on the scene and want to establish cash holdings. The extent of economic self-sufficiency, i.e., of production for the household's own needs, shrinks and people become more dependent upon the market; this will, by and large, impel them to increase their holding of cash. Thus the price-raising tendency emanating from what is called the "normal" gold production encounters a price-cutting tendency emanating from the increased demand for cash holding. However, these two opposite tendencies do not neutralize each other. Both processes take their own course, both result in a disarrangement of existing social conditions, making some people richer, some people poorer. Both affect the prices of various goods at different dates and to a different degree. It is true that the rise in the prices of some commodities caused by one of these processes can finally be compensated by the fall caused by the other process. It may happen that at the end some or many prices come back to their previous height. But this final result is not the outcome of an absence of movements provoked by changes in the money relation. It is rather the outcome of the joint effect of the coincidence of two processes independent of each other, each of which brings about alterations in the market data as well as in the material conditions of various individuals and groups of individuals. The new structure of prices may not differ very much from the previous one. But it is the resultant of two series of changes which have accomplished all inherent social transformations.

The fact that the owners of gold mines rely upon steady yearly proceeds from their gold production does not cancel the newly mined gold's impression upon prices. The owners of the mines take from the market, in exchange for the gold produced, the goods and services required for their mining and the goods needed for their consumption and their investments in other lines of production. If they had not produced this amount of gold, prices would not have been affected by it. It is beside the point that they have anticipated the future yield of the mines and capitalized it and that they have adjusted their standard of living to the expectation of steady proceeds from the mining operations. The effects which the newly mined gold exercises on their expenditure and on that of those people whose cash holdings it enters later step by step begin only at the instant this gold is available in the hands of the mine owners. If, in the expectation of future yields, they had expended money at an earlier date and the expected yield failed to appear, conditions would not differ from other cases in which consumption was financed by credit based on expectations not realized by later events.

Changes in the extent of the desired cash holding of various people neutralize one another only to the extent that they are regularly recurring and mutually connected by a causal reciprocity. Salaried people and wage earners are not paid daily, but at certain pay days for a period of one or several weeks. They do not plan to keep their cash holding within the period between pay days at the same level; the amount of cash in their pockets declines with the approach of the next pay day. On the other hand, the merchants who supply them with the necessities of life increase their cash holdings concomitantly. The two movements condition each other; there is a causal interdependence between them which harmonizes them both with regard to time and to quantitative amount. Neither the dealer nor his customer lets himself be influenced by these recurrent fluctuations. Their plans concerning cash holding as well as their business operations and their spending for consumption respectively have the whole period in view and take it into account as a whole.

It was this phenomenon that led economists to the image of a regular circulation of money and to the neglect of the changes in the individuals' cash holdings. However, we are faced with a concatenation which is limited to a narrow, neatly circumscribed field. Only as far as the increase in the cash holding of one group of people is temporally and quantitatively related to the decrease in the cash holding of another group and as far as these changes are self-liquidating within the course of a period which the members of both groups consider as a whole in planning their cash holding, can the neutralization take place. Beyond this field there is no question of such a neutralization.

5. The Problem of Hume and Mill and the Driving Force of Money

Is it possible to think of a state of affairs in which changes in the purchasing power of money occur at the same time and to the same extent with regard to all commodities and services and in proportion to the changes effected in either the demand for or the supply of money? In other words, is it possible to think of neutral money within the frame of an economic system which does not correspond to the imaginary construction of an evenly rotating economy? We may call this pertinent question the problem of Hume and Mill.

It is uncontested that neither Hume nor Mill succeeded in finding a positive answer to this question.[9] Is it possible to answer it categorically in the negative?

We imagine two systems of an evenly rotating economy *A* and *B*. The two systems are independent and in no way connected with one another. The two systems differ from one another only in the fact

9. Cf. Mises, *Theory of Money and Credit*, pp. 140–142.

that to each amount of money *m* in *A* there corresponds an amount *n m* in *B*, *n* being greater or smaller than 1; we assume that there are no deferred payments and that the money used in both systems serves only monetary purposes and does not allow of any nonmonetary use. Consequently the prices in the two systems are in the ratio 1 : *n*. Is it thinkable that conditions in *A* can be altered at one stroke in such a way as to make them entirely equivalent to conditions in *B?*

The answer to this question must obviously be in the negative. He who wants to answer it in the positive must assume that a *deus ex machina* approaches every individual at the same instant, increases or decreases his cash holding by multiplying it by *n,* and tells him that henceforth he must multiply by *n* all price data which he employs in his appraisements and calculations. This cannot happen without a miracle.

It has been pointed out already that in the imaginary construction of an evenly rotating economy the very notion of money vanishes into an unsubstantial calculation process, self-contradictory and devoid of any meaning.[10] It is impossible to assign any function to indirect exchange, media of exchange, and money within an imaginary construction the characteristic mark of which is unchangeability and rigidity of conditions.

Where there is no uncertainty concerning the future, there is no need for any cash holding. As money must necessarily be kept by people in their cash holdings, there cannot be any money. The use of media of exchange and the keeping of cash holdings are conditioned by the changeability of economic data. Money in itself is an element of change; its existence is incompatible with the idea of a regular flow of events in an evenly rotating economy.

Every change in the money relation alters—apart from its effects upon deferred payments—the conditions of the individual members of society. Some become richer, some poorer. It may happen that the effects of a change in the demand for and supply of money encounter the effects of opposite changes occurring by and large at the same time and to the same extent; it may happen that the resultant of the two opposite movements is such that no conspicuous changes in the price structure emerge. But even then the effects on the conditions of the various individuals are not absent. Each change in the money relation takes its own course and produces its own particular effects. If an inflationary movement and a deflationary one occur at the same time or if an inflation is temporally followed by a deflation in such a

10. Cf. above, p. 249.

way that prices finally are not very much changed, the social consequences of each of the two movements do not cancel each other. To the social consequences of an inflation those of a deflation are added. There is no reason to assume that all or even most of those favored by one movement will be hurt by the second one, or vice versa.

Money is neither an abstract *numéraire* nor a standard of value or prices. It is necessarily an economic good and as such it is valued and appraised on its own merits, i.e., the services which a man expects from holding cash. On the market there is always change and movement. Only because there are fluctuations is there money. Money is an element of change not because it "circulates," but because it is kept in cash holdings. Only because people expect changes about the kind and extent of which they have no certain knowledge whatsoever, do they keep money.

While money can be thought of only in a changing economy, it is in itself an element of further changes. Every change in the economic data sets it in motion and makes it the driving force of new changes. Every shift in the mutual relation of the exchange ratios between the various nonmonetary goods not only brings about changes in production and in what is popularly called distribution, but also provokes changes in the money relation and thus further changes. Nothing can happen in the orbit of vendible goods without affecting the orbit of money, and all that happens in the orbit of money affects the orbit of commodities.

The notion of a neutral money is no less contradictory than that of a money of stable purchasing power. Money without a driving force of its own would not, as people assume, be a perfect money; it would not be money at all.

It is a popular fallacy to believe that perfect money should be neutral and endowed with unchanging purchasing power, and that the goal of monetary policy should be to realize this perfect money. It is easy to understand this idea as a reaction against the still more popular postulates of the inflationists. But it is an excessive reaction, it is in itself confused and contradictory, and it has worked havoc because it was strengthened by an inveterate error inherent in the thought of many philosophers and economists.

These thinkers are misled by the widespread belief that a state of rest is more perfect than one of movement. Their idea of perfection implies that no more perfect state can be thought of and consequently that every change would impair it. The best that can be said of a motion is that it is directed toward the attainment of a state of perfection in which there is rest because every further movement would lead into a less perfect state. Motion is seen as the absence of equilibrium and full satisfaction, as a manifestation of trouble and want. As far as such thoughts merely establish the fact that action aims at the removal of uneasiness and ultimately at the attainment of full satisfaction, they are well founded. But one must not forget that rest and equilibrium are not only present in a state in which perfect contentment has made people perfectly happy, but no less in a state in which, although wanting in many regards, they do not see any means of improving their condition. The absence of action is not only the result of full satisfaction; it can no less be the corollary of the inability to render things more satisfactory. It can mean hopelessness as well as contentment.

With the real universe of action and unceasing change, with the economic system which cannot be rigid, neither neutrality of money nor stability of its purchasing power are compatible. A world of the kind which the necessary requirements of neutral and stable money presuppose would be a world without action.

It is therefore neither strange nor vicious that in the frame of such a changing world money is neither neutral nor stable in purchasing power. All plans to render money neutral and stable are contradictory. Money is an element of action and consequently of change. Changes in the money relation, i.e., in the relation of the demand for and the supply of money, affect the exchange ratio between money on the one hand and the vendible commodities on the other hand. These changes do not affect at the same time and to the same extent the prices of the various commodities and services. They consequently affect the wealth of the various members of society in a different way.

6. Cash-Induced and Goods-Induced Changes in Purchasing Power

Changes in the purchasing power of money, i.e., in the exchange ratio between money and the vendible goods and commodities, can originate either from the side of money or from the side of the vendible goods and commodities. The change in the data which provokes them can either occur in the demand for and supply of money or in the demand for and supply of the other goods and services. We may accordingly distinguish between cash-induced and goods-induced changes in purchasing power.

Goods-induced changes in purchasing power can be brought about by changes in the supply of commodities and services or in the demand for individual commodities and services. A general rise or fall in the demand for all goods and services or the greater part of them can be effected only from the side of money.

Let us now scrutinize the social and economic consequences of changes in the purchasing power of money under the following three assumptions: first, that the money in question can only be used as money—i.e., as a medium of exchange—and can serve no other purpose; second, that there is only exchange of present goods and no exchange of present goods against future goods; third, that we disregard the effects of changes in purchasing power on monetary calculation.

Under these assumptions all that cash-induced changes in purchasing power bring about are shifts in the disposition of wealth among different individuals. Some get richer, others poorer; some are better supplied, others less; what some people gain is paid for by the loss of others. It would, however, be impermissible to interpret this fact by saying that total satisfaction remained unchanged or that, while no changes have occurred in total supply, the state of total satisfaction or of the sum of happiness has been increased or decreased by changes in the distribution of wealth. The notions of total satisfaction or total happiness are empty. It is impossible to discover a standard for comparing the different degrees of satisfaction or happiness attained by various individuals.

Cash-induced changes in purchasing power indirectly generate further changes by favoring either the accumulation of additional capital or the consumption of capital available. Whether and in what direction such secondary effects are brought about depends on the specific data of each case. We shall deal with these important problems at a later point.[11]

Goods-induced changes in purchasing power are sometimes nothing else but consequences of a shift of demand from some goods to others. If they are brought about by an increase or a decrease in the supply of goods they are not merely transfers from some people to other people. They do not mean that Peter gains what Paul has lost. Some people may become richer although nobody is impoverished, and vice versa.

We may describe this fact in the following way: Let *A* and *B* be two independent systems which are in no way connected with each other. In both systems the same kind of money is used, a money which cannot be used for any nonmonetary purpose. Now we assume, as case 1, that *A* and *B* differ from each other only in so far as in *B* the

11. Cf. below, Chapter XX.

total supply of money is $n\ m$, m being the total supply of money in A, and that to every cash holding of c and to every claim in terms of money d in A there corresponds a cash holding of $n\ c$ and a claim of $n\ d$ in B. In every other respect A equals B. Then we assume, as case 2, that A and B differ from each other only in so far as in B the total supply of a certain commodity r is $n\ p$, p being the total supply of this commodity in A, and that to every stock v of this commodity r in A there corresponds a stock of $n\ v$ in B. In both cases n is greater than 1. If we ask every individual of A whether he is ready to make the slightest sacrifice in order to exchange his position for the corresponding place in B, the answer will be unanimously in the negative in case 1. But in case 2 all owners of r and all those who do not own any r, but are eager to acquire a quantity of it—i.e., at least one individual—will answer in the affirmative.

The services money renders are conditioned by the height of its purchasing power. Nobody wants to have in his cash holding a definite number of pieces of money or a definite weight of money; he wants to keep a cash holding of a definite amount of purchasing power. As the operation of the market tends to determine the final state of money's purchasing power at a height at which the supply of and the demand for money coincide, there can never be an excess or a deficiency of money. Each individual and all individuals together always enjoy fully the advantages which they can derive from indirect exchange and the use of money, no matter whether the total quantity of money is great or small. Changes in money's purchasing power generate changes in the disposition of wealth among the various members of society. From the point of view of people eager to be enriched by such changes, the supply of money may be called insufficient or excessive, and the appetite for such gains may result in policies designed to bring about cash-induced alterations in purchasing power. However, the services which money renders can be neither improved nor repaired by changing the supply of money. There may appear an excess or a deficiency of money in an individual's cash holding. But such a condition can be remedied by increasing or decreasing consumption or investment. (Of course, one must not fall prey to the popular confusion between the demand for money for cash holding and the appetite for more wealth.) The quantity of money available in the whole economy is always sufficient to secure for everybody all that money does and can do.

From the point of view of this insight one may call wasteful all expenditures incurred for increasing the quantity of money. The fact that things which could render some other useful services are employed as money and thus withheld from these other employments appears as a superfluous curtailment of limited opportunities for want-satisfaction. It was this idea that led Adam Smith and Ricardo to the opinion that it was very beneficial to reduce the cost of producing money by resorting to the use of paper printed currency. However, things appear in a different light to the students of monetary history. If one looks at the catastrophic consequences of the great paper money inflations, one must admit that the expensiveness of gold production is the minor evil. It would be futile to retort that these catastrophes were brought about by the improper use which the governments made of the powers that credit money and fiat money placed in their hands and that wiser governments would have adopted sounder policies. As money can never be neutral and stable in purchasing power, a government's plans concerning the determination of the quantity of money can never be impartial and fair to all members of society. Whatever a government does in the pursuit of aims to influence the height of purchasing power depends necessarily upon the rulers' personal value judgments. It always furthers the interests of some groups of people at the expense of other groups. It never serves what is called the commonweal or the public welfare. In the field of monetary policies too there is no such thing as a scientific ought.

The choice of the good to be employed as a medium of exchange and as money is never indifferent. It determines the course of the cash-induced changes in purchasing power. The question is only who should make the choice: the people buying and selling on the market, or the government? It was the market which in a selective process, going on for ages, finally assigned to the precious metals gold and silver the character of money. For two hundred years the governments have interfered with the market's choice of the money medium. Even the most bigoted étatists do not venture to assert that this interference has proved beneficial.

Inflation and Deflation; Inflationism and Deflationism

The notions of inflation and deflation are not praxeological concepts. They were not created by economists, but by the mundane speech of the public and of politicians. They implied the popular fallacy that there is such a thing as neutral money or money of stable purchasing power and that sound money should be neutral and stable in purchasing power. From this point of view the term inflation was applied to signify cash-induced changes resulting in a drop in purchasing power, and the term deflation to signify cash-induced changes resulting in a rise in purchasing power.

However, those applying these terms are not aware of the fact that purchasing power never remains unchanged and that consequently there is always either inflation or deflation. They ignore these necessarily perpetual fluctuations as far as they are only small and inconspicuous, and reserve the use of the terms to big changes in purchasing power. Since the question at what point a change in purchasing power begins to deserve being called big depends on personal relevance judgments, it becomes manifest that inflation and deflation are terms lacking the categorial precision required for praxeological, economic, and catallactic concepts. Their application is appropriate for history and politics. Catallactics is free to resort to them only when applying its theorems to the interpretation of events of economic history and of political programs. Moreover, it is very expedient even in rigid catallactic disquisitions to make use of these two terms whenever no misinterpretation can possibly result and pedantic heaviness of expression can be avoided. But it is necessary never to forget that all that catallactics says with regard to inflation and deflation—i.e., *big* cash-induced changes in purchasing power—is valid also with regard to small changes, although, of course, the consequences of smaller changes are less conspicuous than those of big changes.

The terms inflationism and deflationism, inflationist and deflationist, signify the political programs aiming at inflation and deflation in the sense of big cash-induced changes in purchasing power.

The semantic revolution which is one of the characteristic features of our day has also changed the traditional connotation of the terms inflation and deflation. What many people today call inflation or deflation is no longer the great increase or decrease in the supply of money, but its inexorable consequences, the general tendency toward a rise or a fall in commodity prices and wage rates. This innovation is by no means harmless. It plays an important role in fomenting the popular tendencies toward inflationism.

First of all there is no longer any term available to signify what inflation used to signify. It is impossible to fight a policy which you cannot name. Statesmen and writers no longer have the opportunity of resorting to a terminology accepted and understood by the public when they want to question the expediency of issuing huge amounts of additional money. They must enter into a detailed analysis and description of this policy with full particulars and minute accounts whenever they want to refer to it, and they must repeat this bothersome procedure in every sentence in which they deal with the subject. As this policy has no name, it becomes self-understood and a matter of fact. It goes on luxuriantly.

The second mischief is that those engaged in futile and hopeless attempts to fight the inevitable consequences of inflation—the rise in prices—are disguising their endeavors as a fight against inflation.

While merely fighting symptoms, they pretend to fight the root causes of the evil. Because they do not comprehend the causal relation between the increase in the quantity of money on the one hand and the rise in prices on the other, they practically make things worse. The best example was provided by the subsidies granted in the Second World War on the part of the governments of the United States, Canada, and Great Britain to farmers. Price ceilings reduce the supply of the commodities concerned because production involves a loss for the marginal producers. To prevent this outcome the governments granted subsidies to the farmers producing at the highest costs. These subsidies were financed out of additional increases in the quantity of money. If the consumers had had to pay higher prices for the products concerned, no further inflationary effects would have emerged. The consumers would have had to use for such surplus expenditure only money which had already been issued previously. Thus the confusion of inflation and its consequences in fact can directly bring about more inflation.

It is obvious that this new-fangled connotation of the terms inflation and deflation is utterly confusing and misleading and must be unconditionally rejected.

7. Monetary Calculation and Changes in Purchasing Power

Monetary calculation reckons with the prices of commodities and services as they were determined or would have been determined or presumably will be determined on the market. It is eager to detect price discrepancies and to draw conclusions from such a detection.

Cash-induced changes in purchasing power cannot be taken into account in such calculations. It is possible to put in the place of calculation based on a definite kind of money *a* a mode of calculating based on another kind of money *b*. Then the result of the calculation is made safe against adulteration on the part of changes effected in the purchasing power of *a;* but it can still be adulterated by changes effected in the purchasing power of *b*. There is no means of freeing any mode of economic calculation from the influence of changes in the purchasing power of the definite kind of money on which it is based.

All results of economic calculation and all conclusions derived from them are conditioned by the vicissitudes of cash-induced changes in purchasing power. In accordance with the rise or fall in purchasing power there emerge between items reflecting earlier prices and those reflecting later prices specific differences; the calculation shows profits or losses which are merely produced by cash-induced changes effected in the purchasing power of money. If we compare such profits or losses with the result of a calculation accomplished on the basis of a kind of money whose purchasing power had been subject to less vehement changes, we can call them imaginary or apparent only. But one must not forget that such statements are only possible as a result of the comparison of calculations carried out in different kinds of money. As there is no such thing as a money with stable purchasing power, such apparent profits and losses are present with every mode of economic calculation, no matter on what kind of money it may be based. It is impossible to distinguish precisely between genuine profits and losses and merely apparent profits and losses.

It is therefore possible to maintain that economic calculation is not perfect. However, nobody can suggest a method which could free economic calculation from these defects or design a monetary system which could remove this source of error entirely.

It is an undeniable fact that the free market has succeeded in developing a currency system which well served all the requirements both of indirect exchange and of economic calculation. The aims of monetary calculation are such that they cannot be frustrated by the inaccuracies which stem from slow and comparatively slight movements in purchasing power. Cash-induced changes in purchasing power of the extent to which they occurred in the last two centuries with metallic money, especially with gold money, cannot influence the result of the businessmen's economic calculations so considerably as to render such calculations useless. Historical experience shows that one could, for all practical purposes of the conduct of business, manage very well with these methods of calculation. Theoretical consideration shows that it is impossible to design, still less to realize, a better method. In view of these facts it is vain to call monetary calculation imperfect. Man has not the power to change the categories of human action. He must adjust his conduct to them.

Businessmen never deemed it necessary to free economic calculation in terms of gold from its dependence on the fluctuations in purchasing power. The proposals to improve the currency system by adopting a tabular standard based on index numbers or by adopting various methods of commodity standards were not advanced with regard to business transactions and to monetary calculation. Their aim was to provide a less fluctuating standard for long-run loan contracts. Businessmen did not even consider it expedient to modify their accounting methods in those regards in which it would have been easy to narrow down certain errors induced by fluctuations in purchasing power. It would, for instance, have been possible to discard the practice of writing off durable equipment by means of yearly its acquisition. In its place one could resort to the device of laying depreciation quotas, invariably fixed in a percentage of the cost of aside in renewal funds as much as seems necessary to provide the full costs of the replacement at the time when it is required. But business was not eager to adopt such a procedure.

All this is valid only with regard to money which is not subject to rapid, big cash-induced changes in purchasing power. But money with which such rapid and big changes occur loses its suitability to serve as a medium of exchange altogether.

8. The Anticipation of Expected Changes in Purchasing Power

The deliberations of the individuals which determine their conduct with regard to money are based on their knowledge concerning the prices of the immediate past. If they lacked this knowledge, they would not be in a position to decide what the appropriate height of their cash holdings should be and how much they should spend for the acquisition of various goods. A medium of exchange without a past is unthinkable. Nothing can enter into the function of a medium of exchange which was not already previously an economic good and to which people assigned exchange value already before it was demanded as such a medium.

But the purchasing power handed down from the immediate past is modified by today's demand for and supply of money. Human action is always providing for the future, be it sometimes only the future of the impending hour. He who buys, buys for future consumption and production. As far as he believes that the future will differ from the present and the past, he modifies his valuation and appraisement. This is no less true with regard to money than it is with regard to all vendible goods. In this sense we may say that today's exchange value of money is an anticipation of tomorrow's exchange value. The basis of all judgments concerning money is its purchasing power as it was in the immediate past. But as far as cash-induced changes in purchasing power are expected, a second factor enters the scene, the anticipation of these changes.

He who believes that the prices of the goods in which he takes an interest will rise, buys more of them than he would have bought in the absence of this belief; accordingly he restricts his cash holding. He who believes that prices will drop, restricts his purchases and thus enlarges his cash holding. As long as such speculative anticipations are limited to some commodities, they do not bring about a general tendency toward changes in cash holding. But it is different if people believe that they are on the eve of big cash-induced changes in purchasing power. When they expect that the money prices of all goods will rise or fall, they expand or restrict their purchases. These attitudes strengthen and accelerate the expected tendencies considerably. This goes on until the point is reached beyond which no further changes in the purchasing power of money are expected. Only then does this inclination to buy or to sell stop and do people begin again to increase or to decrease their cash holdings.

But if once public opinion is convinced that the increase in the quantity of money will continue and never come to an end, and that consequently the prices of all commodities and services will not cease to rise, everybody becomes eager to buy as much as possible and to restrict his cash holding to a minimum size. For under these circumstances the regular costs incurred by holding cash are increased by the losses caused by the progressive fall in purchasing power. The advantages of holding cash must be paid for by sacrifices which are deemed unreasonably burdensome. This phenomenon was, in the great European inflations of the 'twenties, called *flight into real goods (Flucht in die Sachwerte)* or *crack-up boom (Katastrophenhausse).* The mathematical economists are at a loss to comprehend the causal relation between the increase in the quantity of money and what they call "velocity of circulation."

The characteristic mark of this phenomenon is that the increase in the quantity of money causes a fall in the demand for money. The tendency toward a fall in purchasing power as generated by the increased supply of money is intensified by the general propensity to restrict cash holdings which it brings about. Eventually a point is reached where the prices at which people would be prepared to part with "real" goods discount to such an extent the expected progress in the fall of purchasing power that nobody has a sufficient amount of cash at hand to pay them. The monetary system breaks down; all transactions in the money concerned cease; a panic makes its purchasing power vanish altogether. People return either to barter or to the use of another kind of money.

The course of a progressing inflation is this: At the beginning the inflow of additional money makes the prices of some commodities and services rise; other prices rise later. The price rise affects the various commodities and services, as has been shown, at different dates and to a different extent.

This first stage of the inflationary process may last for many years. While it lasts, the prices of many goods and services are not yet adjusted to the altered money relation. There are still people in the country who have not yet become aware of the fact that they are confronted with a price revolution which will finally result in a considerable rise of all prices, although the extent of this rise will not be the same in the various commodities and services. These people still believe that prices one day will drop. Waiting for this day, they restrict their purchases and concomitantly increase their cash holdings. As long as such ideas are still held by public opinion, it is not yet too late for the government to abandon its inflationary policy.

But then finally the masses wake up. They become suddenly aware of the fact that inflation is a deliberate policy and will go on endlessly. A breakdown occurs. The crack-up boom appears. Everybody is anxious to swap his money against "real" goods, no matter whether he needs them or not, no matter how much money he has to pay for them. Within a very short time, within a few weeks or even days, the things which were used as money are no longer used as media of exchange. They become scrap paper. Nobody wants to give away anything against them.

It was this that happened with the *Continental currency* in America in 1781, with the French *mandats territoriaux* in 1796, and with the German *Mark* in 1923. It will happen again whenever the same conditions appear. If a thing has to be used as a medium of exchange, public opinion must not believe that the quantity of this thing will increase beyond all bounds. Inflation is a policy that cannot last.

9. The Specific Value of Money

As far as a good used as money is valued and appraised on account of the services it renders for nonmonetary purposes, no problems are raised which would require special treatment. The task of the theory of money consists merely in dealing with that component in the valuation of money which is conditioned by its function as a medium of exchange.

In the course of history various commodities have been employed as media of exchange. A long evolution eliminated the greater part of these commodities from the monetary function. Only two, the precious metals gold and silver, remained. In the second part of the nineteenth century more and more governments deliberately turned toward the demonetization of silver.

In all these cases what is employed as money is a commodity which is used also for nonmonetary purposes. Under the gold standard gold is money and money is gold. It is immaterial whether or not the laws assign legal tender quality only to gold coins minted by the government. What counts is that these coins really contain a fixed weight of gold and that every quantity of bullion can be transformed into coins. Under the gold standard the dollar and the pound sterling were merely names for a definite weight of gold, within very narrow margins precisely determined by the laws. We may call such a sort of money *commodity money.*

A second sort of money is *credit money.* Credit money evolved out of the use of money-substitutes. It was customary to use claims, payable on demand and absolutely secure, as substitutes for the sum of money to which they gave a claim. (We shall deal with the features and problems of money-substitutes in the next sections.) The market did not stop using such claims when one day their prompt redemption was suspended and thereby doubts about their safety and the solvency of the obligee were raised. As long as these claims had been daily maturing claims against a debtor of undisputed solvency and could be collected without notice and free of expense, their exchange value was equal to their face value; it was this perfect equivalence which assigned to them the character of money-substitutes. Now, as redemption was suspended, the maturity date postponed to an undetermined day, and consequently doubts about the solvency of the debtor or at least about his willingness to pay emerged, they lost a part of the value previously ascribed to them. They were now merely claims, which did not bear interest, against a questionable debtor and falling due on an undefined day. But as they were used as media of exchange, their exchange value did not drop to the level to which it would have dropped if they were merely claims.

One can fairly assume that such credit money could remain in use as a medium of exchange even if it were to lose its character as a claim against a bank or a treasury, and thus would become *fiat money.* Fiat money is a money consisting of mere tokens which can neither be employed for any industrial purposes nor convey a claim against anybody.

It is not a task of catallactics but of economic history to investigate whether there appeared in the past specimens of fiat money or whether all the sorts of money which were not commodity money were credit money. The only thing that catallactics has to establish is that the possibility of the existence of fiat money must be admitted.

The important thing to be remembered is that with every sort of money, demonetization—i.e., the abandonment of its use as a medium of exchange—must result in a serious fall of its exchange value. What this practically means has become manifest when in the last ninety years the use of silver as commodity money has been progressively restricted.

There are specimens of credit money and fiat money which are embodied in metallic coins. Such money is printed, as it were, on silver, nickel, or copper. If such a piece of fiat money is demonetized, it still retains exchange value as a piece of metal. But this is only a very small indemnification of the owner. It has no practical importance.

The keeping of cash holding requires sacrifices. To the extent that a man keeps money in his pockets or in his balance with a bank, he forsakes the instantaneous acquisition of goods he could consume or employ for production. In the market economy these sacrifices can be precisely determined by calculation. They are equal to the amount of originary interest he would have earned by investing the sum. The fact that a man takes this falling off into account is proof that he prefers the advantages of cash holding to the loss in interest yield.

It is possible to specify the advantages which people expect from keeping a definite amount of cash. But it is a delusion to assume that an analysis of these motives could provide us with a theory of the determination of purchasing power which could do without the notions of cash holding and demand for and supply of money.[12] The advantages and disadvantages derived from cash holding are not objective factors which could directly influence the size of cash holdings. They are put on the scales by each individual and weighed against one another. The result is a subjective judgment of value, colored by the individual's personality. Different people and the same people at different times value the same objective facts in a different way. Just as knowledge of a man's wealth and his physical condition does not tell us how much he would be prepared to spend for food of a certain nutritive power, so knowledge about data concerning a man's material situation does not enable us to make definite assertions with regard to the size of his cash holding.

10. The Import of the Money Relation

The money relation, i.e., the relation between demand for and supply of money, uniquely determines the price structure as far as the reciprocal exchange ratio between money and the vendible commodities and services is involved.

If the money relation remains unchanged, neither an inflationary (expansionist) nor a deflationary (contractionist) pressure on trade, business, production, consumption, and employment can emerge. The assertions to the contrary reflect the grievances of people reluctant to

12. Such an attempt was made by Greidanus, *The Value of Money* (London, 1932), pp. 197 ff.

adjust their activities to the demands of their fellow men as manifested on the market. However, it is not an account of an alleged scarcity of money that prices of agricultural products are too low to secure to the submarginal farmers proceeds of the amount they would like to earn. The cause of these farmers' distress is that other farmers are producing at lower costs.

An increase in the quantity of goods produced, other things being unchanged, must bring about an improvement in people's conditions. Its consequence is a fall in the money prices of the goods the production of which has been increased. But such a fall in money prices does not in the least impair the benefits derived from the additional wealth produced. One may consider as unfair the increase in the share of the additional wealth which goes to the creditors, although such criticisms are questionable as far as the rise in purchasing power has been correctly anticipated and adequately taken into account by a negative price premium.[13] But one must not say that a fall in prices caused by an increase in the production of the goods concerned is the proof of some disequilibrium which cannot be eliminated otherwise than by increasing the quantity of money. Of course, as a rule every increase in production of some or of all commodities requires a new allocation of factors of production to the various branches of business. If the quantity of money remains unchanged, the necessity of such a reallocation becomes visible in the price structure. Some lines of production become more profitable, while in others profits drop or losses appear. Thus the operation of the market tends to eliminate these much discussed disequilibria. It is possible by means of an increase in the quantity of money to delay or to interrupt this process of adjustment. It is impossible either to make it superfluous or less painful for those concerned.

If the government-made cash-induced changes in the purchasing power of money resulted only in shifts of wealth from some people to other people, it would not be permissible to condemn them from the point of view of catallactics' scientific neutrality. It is obviously fraudulent to justify them under the pretext of the commonweal or public welfare. But one could still consider them as political measures suitable to promote the interests of some groups of people at the expense of others without further detriment. However, there are still other things involved.

It is not necessary to point out the consequences to which a continued deflationary policy must lead. Nobody advocates such a

13. About the relations of the market rate of interest and changes in purchasing power, cf. below, Chapter XX.

policy. The favor of the masses and of the writers and politicians eager for applause goes to inflation. With regard to these endeavors we must emphasize three points. First: Inflationary or expansionist policy must result in overconsumption on the one hand and in malinvestment on the other. It thus squanders capital and impairs the future state of want-satisfaction.[14] Second: The inflationary process does not remove the necessity of adjusting production and reallocating resources. It merely postpones it and thereby makes it more troublesome. Third: Inflation cannot be employed as a permanent policy because it must, when continued, finally result in a breakdown of the monetary system.

A retailer or innkeeper can easily fall prey to the illusion that all that is needed to make him and his colleagues more prosperous is more spending on the part of the public. In his eyes the main thing is to impel people to spend more. But it is amazing that this belief could be presented to the world as a new social philosophy. Lord Keynes and his disciples make the lack of the propensity to consume responsible for what they deem unsatisfactory in economic conditions. What is needed, in their eyes, to make men more prosperous is not an increase in production, but an increase in spending. In order to make it possible for people to spend more, an "expansionist" policy is recommended.

This doctrine is as old as it is bad. Its analysis and refutation will be undertaken in the chapter dealing with the trade cycle.[15]

11. The Money-Substitutes

Claims to a definite amount of money, payable and redeemable on demand, against a debtor about whose solvency and willingness to pay there does not prevail the slightest doubt, render to the individual all the services money can render, provided that all parties with whom he could possibly transact business are perfectly familiar with these essential qualities of the claims concerned: daily maturity as well as undoubted solvency and willingness to pay on the part of the debtor. We may call such claims *money-substitutes,* as they can fully replace money in an individual's or a firm's cash holding. The technical and legal features of the money-substitutes do not concern catallactics. A money-substitute can be embodied either in a banknote or in a demand deposit with a bank subject to check ("checkbook money" or deposit currency), provided the bank is prepared to

14. Cf. below, pp. 564–565.
15. Cf. below, pp. 548–565.

exchange the note or the deposit daily free of charge against money proper. Token coins are also money-substitutes, provided the owner is in a position to exchange them at need, free of expense and without delay, against money. To achieve this it is not required that the government be bound by law to redeem them. What counts is the fact that these tokens can be really converted free of expense and without delay. If the total amount of token coins issued is kept within reasonable limits, no special provisions on the part of the government are necessary to keep their exchange value at par with their face value. The demand of the public for small change gives everybody the opportunity to exchange them easily against pieces of money. The main thing is that every owner of a money-substitute is perfectly certain that it can, at every instant and free of expense, be exchanged against money.

If the debtor—the government or a bank—keeps against the whole amount of money-substitutes a 100% reserve of money proper, we call the money-substitute a *money-certificate.* The individual money-certificate is—not necessarily in a legal sense, but always in the catallactic sense—a representative of a corresponding amount of money kept in the reserve. The issuing of money-certificates does not increase the quantity of things suitable to satisfy the demand for money for cash holding. Changes in the quantity of money-certificates therefore do not alter the supply of money and the money relation. They do not play any role in the determination of the purchasing power of money.

If the money reserve kept by the debtor against the money-substitutes issued is less than the total amount of such substitutes, we call that amount of substitutes which exceeds the reserve *fiduciary media.* As a rule it is not possible to ascertain whether a concrete specimen of money-substitutes is a money-certificate or a fiduciary medium. A part of the total amount of money-substitutes issued is usually covered by a money reserve held. Thus a part of the total amount of money-substitutes issued is money-certificates, the rest fiduciary media. But this fact can only be recognized by those familiar with the bank's balance sheets. The individual banknote, deposit, or token coin does not indicate its catallactic character.

The issue of money-certificates does not increase the funds which the bank can employ in the conduct of its lending business. A bank which does not issue fiduciary media can only grant *commodity credit,* i.e., it can only lend its own funds and the amount of money which its customers have entrusted to it. The issue of fiduciary media enlarges the bank's funds available for lending beyond these limits.

It can now not only grant commodity credit, but also *circulation credit,* i.e., credit granted out of the issue of fiduciary media.

While the quantity of money-certificates is indifferent, the quantity of fiduciary media is not. The fiduciary media affect the market phenomena in the same way as money does. Changes in their quantity influence the determination of money's purchasing power and of prices and—temporarily—also of the rate of interest.

Earlier economists applied a different terminology. Many were prepared to call the money-substitutes simply money, as they are fit to render the services money renders. However, this terminology is not expedient. The first purpose of a scientific terminology is to facilitate the analysis of the problems involved. The task of the catallactic theory of money—as differentiated from the legal theory and from the technical disciplines of bank management and accountancy —is the study of the problems of the determination of prices and interest rates. This task requires a sharp distinction between money-certificates and fiduciary media.

The term *credit expansion* has often been misinterpreted. It is important to realize that commodity credit cannot be expanded. The only vehicle of credit expansion is circulation credit. But the granting of circulation credit does not always mean credit expansion. If the amount of fiduciary media previously issued has consummated all its effects upon the market, if prices, wage rates, and interest rates have been adjusted to the total supply of money proper plus fiduciary media (supply of money in the broader sense), granting of circulation credit without a further increase in the quantity of fiduciary media is no longer credit expansion. Credit expansion is present only if credit is granted by the issue of an additional amount of fiduciary media, not if banks lend anew fiduciary media paid back to them by the old debtors.

12. The Limitation on the Issuance of Fiduciary Media

People deal with money-substitutes as if they were money because they are fully confident that it will be possible to exchange them at any time without delay and without cost against money. We may call those who share in this confidence and are therefore ready to deal with money-substitutes as if they were money, the *clients* of the issuing banker, bank, or authority. It does not matter whether or not this issuing establishment is operated according to the patterns of conduct customary in the banking business. Token coins issued by a country's treasury are money-substitutes too, although the treasury as a rule does not enter the amount issued into its accounts as a liability and does not consider this amount a part of the national debt. It is no less immaterial whether or not the owner of a money-substitute has an actionable claim to redemption. What counts is whether the money-substitute can really be exchanged against money without delay and cost.[16]

Issuing money-certificates is an expensive venture. The banknotes must be printed, the token coins minted; a complicated accounting system for the deposits must be organized; the reserves must be kept in safety; then there is the risk of being cheated by counterfeit banknotes and checks. Against all these expenses stands only the slight chance that some of the banknotes issued may be destroyed and the still slighter chance that some depositors may forget their deposits. Issuing money-certificates is a ruinous business if not connected with issuing fiduciary media. In the early history of banking there were banks whose only operation consisted in issuing money-certificates. But these banks were indemnified by their clients for the costs incurred. At any rate, catallactics is not interested in the purely technical problems of banks not issuing fiduciary media. The only interest that catallactics takes in money-certificates is the connection between issuing them and the issuing of fiduciary media.

While the quantity of money-certificates is catallactically unimportant, an increase or decrease in the quantity of fiduciary media affects the determination of money's purchasing power in the same way as do changes in the quantity of money. Hence the question of whether there are or are not limits to the increase in the quantity of fiduciary media has fundamental importance.

If the clientele of the bank includes all members of the market economy, the limit to the issue of fiduciary media is the same as that drawn to the increase in the quantity of money. A bank which is, in an isolated country or in the whole world, the only institution issuing fiduciary media and the clientele of which comprises all individuals and firms, is bound to comply in its conduct of affairs with two rules:

16. It is furthermore immaterial whether or not the laws assign to the money-substitutes legal tender quality. If these things are really dealt with by people as money-substitutes and are therefore money-substitutes and equal in purchasing power to the respective amount of money, the only effect of the legal tender quality is to prevent malicious people from resorting to chicanery for the mere sake of annoying their fellow men. If, however, the things concerned are not money-substitutes and are traded at a discount below their face value, the assignment of legal tender quality is tantamount to an authoritarian price ceiling, the fixing of a maximum price for gold and foreign exchange and of a minimum price for the things which are no longer money-substitutes but either credit money or fiat money. Then the effects appear which Gresham's Law describes.

First: It must avoid any action which could make the clients—i.e., the public—suspicious. As soon as the clients begin to lose confidence, they will ask for the redemption of the banknotes and withdraw their deposits. How far the bank can go on increasing its issues of fiduciary media without arousing distrust, depends on psychological factors.

Second: It must not increase the amount of fiduciary media at such a rate and with such speed that the clients get the conviction that the rise in prices will continue endlessly at an accelerated pace. For if the public believes that this is the case, they will reduce their cash holdings, flee into "real" values, and bring about the crack-up boom. It is impossible to imagine the approach of this catastrophe without assuming that its first manifestation consists in the evanescence of confidence. The public will certainly prefer exchanging the fiduciary media against money to fleeing into real values, i.e., to the indiscriminate buying of various commodities. Then the bank must go bankrupt. If the government interferes by freeing the bank from the obligation of redeeming its banknotes and of paying back the deposits in compliance with the terms of the contract, the fiduciary media become either credit money or fiat money. The suspension of specie payments entirely changes the state of affairs. There is no longer any question of fiduciary media, of money-certificates, and of money-substitutes. The government enters the scene with its government-made legal tender laws. The bank loses its independent existence; it becomes a tool of government policies, a subordinate office of the treasury.

The catallactically most important problems of the issuance of fiduciary media on the part of a single bank, or of banks acting in concert, the clientele of which comprehends all individuals, are not those of the limitations drawn to the amount of their issuance. We will deal with them in Chapter XX, devoted to the relations between the quantity of money and the rate of interest.

At this point of our investigations we have to scrutinize the problem of the coexistence of a multiplicity of independent banks. Independence means that every bank in issuing fiduciary media follows its own course and does not act in concert with other banks. Coexistence means that every bank has a clientele which does not include all members of the market system. For the sake of simplicity we will assume that no individual or firm is a client of more than one bank. It would not affect the result of our demonstration if we were to assume that there are also people who are clients of more than one bank and people who are not clients of any bank.

The question to be raised is not whether or not there are limits to the issuance of fiduciary media on the part of such independently coexisting banks. As there are even limits to the issuance of fiduciary media on the part of a unique bank the clientele of which comprises all people, it is obvious that there are such limits for a multiplicity of independently coexisting banks too. What we want to show is that for such a multiplicity of independently coexisting banks the limits are narrower than those drawn for a single bank with an unlimited clientele.

We assume that within a market system several independent banks have been established in the past. While previously only money was in use, these banks have introduced the use of money-substitutes a part of which are fiduciary media. Each bank has a clientele and has issued a certain quantity of fiduciary media which are kept as money-substitutes in the cash holdings of various clients. The total quantity of the fiduciary media as issued by the banks and absorbed by the cash holdings of their clients has altered the structure of prices and the monetary unit's purchasing power. But these effects have already been consummated and at present the market is no longer stirred by any movements generated from this past credit expansion.

But now, we assume further, one bank alone embarks upon an additional issue of fiduciary media while the other banks do not follow suit. The clients of the expanding bank—whether its old clients or new ones acquired on account of the expansion—receive additional credits, they expand their business activities, they appear on the market with an additional demand for goods and services, they bid up prices. Those people who are not clients of the expanding bank are not in a position to afford these higher prices; they are forced to restrict their purchases. Thus there prevails on the market a shifting of goods from the nonclients to the clients of the expanding bank. The clients buy more from the nonclients than they sell to them; they have more to pay to the nonclients than they receive from them. But money-substitutes issued by the expanding bank are not suitable for payments to nonclients, as these people do not assign to them the character of money-substitutes. In order to settle the payments due to nonclients, the clients must first exchange the money-substitutes issued by their own—viz., the expanding bank—against money. The expanding bank must redeem its banknotes and pay out its deposits. Its reserve—we suppose that only a part of the money-substitutes it had issued had the character of fiduciary media—dwindles. The instant approaches in which the bank will—after the exhaustion of its money reserve—no longer be in a position to redeem the money-substitutes still current. In order to avoid insolvency it must as soon as possible return to a policy of strengthening its money reserve. It must abandon its expansionist methods.

This reaction of the market to a credit expansion on the part of a bank with a limited clientele has been brilliantly described by the Currency School. The special case dealt with by the Currency School referred to the coincidence of credit expansion on the part of one country's privileged central bank or of all banks of one country and of a nonexpansionist policy on the part of the banks of other countries. Our demonstration covers the more general case of the coexistence of a multiplicity of banks with different clientele as well as the most general case of the existence of one bank with a limited clientele in a system in which the rest of the people do not patronize any bank and do not consider any claims as money-substitutes. It does not matter, of course, whether one assumes that the clients of a bank live neatly separated from those of the other banks in a definite district or country or whether they live side by side with those of the other banks. These are merely differences in the data not affecting the catallactic problems involved.

A bank can never issue more money-substitutes than its clients can keep in their cash holdings. The individual client can never keep a larger portion of his total cash holding in money-substitutes than that corresponding to the proportion which his turnover with other clients of his bank bears to his total turnover. For considerations of convenience he will, as a rule, remain far below this maximum proportion. Thus a limit is drawn to the issue of fiduciary media. We may admit that everybody is ready to accept in his current transactions indiscriminately banknotes issued by any bank and checks drawn upon any bank. But he deposits without delay with his own bank not only the checks but also the banknotes of banks of which he is not himself a client. In the further course his bank settles its accounts with the bank engaged. Thus the process described above comes into motion.

A lot of nonsense has been written about a perverse predilection of the public for banknotes issued by dubious banks. The truth is that, except for small groups of businessmen who were able to distinguish between good and bad banks, banknotes were always looked upon with distrust. It was the special charters which the governments granted to privileged banks that slowly made these suspicions disappear. The often advanced argument that small banknotes come into the hands of poor and ignorant people who cannot distinguish between good and bad notes cannot be taken seriously. The poorer the recipient of a banknote is and the less familiar he is with bank affairs, the more quickly will he spend the note and the more quickly will it return, by way of retail and wholesale trade, to the issuing bank or to people conversant with banking conditions.

It is very easy for a bank to increase the number of people who are ready to accept loans granted by credit expansion and paid out in an amount of money-substitutes. But it is very difficult for any bank to enlarge its clientele, that is, the number of people who are ready to consider these claims as money-substitutes and to keep them as such in their cash holdings. To enlarge this clientele is a troublesome and slow process, as is the acquisition of any kind of good will. On the other hand, a bank can lose its clientele very quickly. If it wants to preserve it, it must never permit any doubt about its ability and readiness to discharge all its liabilities in due compliance with the terms of the contract. A reserve must be kept large enough to redeem all banknotes which a holder may submit for redemption. Therefore no bank can content itself with issuing fiduciary media only; it must keep a reserve against the total amount of money-substitutes issued and thus combine issuing fiduciary media and money-certificates.

It was a serious blunder to believe that the reserve's task is to provide the means for the redemption of those banknotes the holders of which have lost confidence in the bank. The confidence which a bank and the money-substitutes it has issued enjoy is indivisible. It is either present with all its clients or it vanishes entirely. If some of the clients lose confidence, the rest of them lose it too. No bank issuing fiduciary media and granting circulation credit can fulfill the obligations which it has taken over in issuing money-substitutes if all clients are losing confidence and want to have their banknotes redeemed and their deposits paid back. This is an essential feature or weakness of the business of issuing fiduciary media and granting circulation credit. No system of reserve policy and no reserve requirements as enforced by the laws can remedy it. All that a reserve can do is to make it possible for the bank to withdraw from the market an excessive amount of fiduciary media issued. If the bank has issued more banknotes than its clients can use in doing business with other clients, it must redeem such an excess.

The laws which compelled the banks to keep a reserve in a definite ratio of the total amount of deposits and of banknotes issued were effective in so far as they restricted the increase in the amount of fiduciary media and of circulation credit. They were futile as far as they aimed at safeguarding, in the event of a loss of confidence, the prompt redemption of the banknotes and the prompt payment on deposits.

The Banking School failed entirely in dealing with these problems.

It was confused by a spurious idea according to which the requirements of business rigidly limit the maximum amount of convertible banknotes that a bank can issue. They did not see that the demand of the public for credit is a magnitude dependent on the banks' readiness to lend, and that banks which do not bother about their own solvency are in a position to expand circulation credit by lowering the rate of interest below the market rate. It is not true that the maximum amount which a bank can lend if it limits its lending to discounting short-term bills of exchange resulting from the sale and purchase of raw materials and half-manufactured goods, is a quantity uniquely determined by the state of business and independent of the bank's policies. This quantity expands or shrinks with the lowering or raising of the rate of discount. Lowering the rate of interest is tantamount to increasing the quantity of what is mistakenly considered as the fair and normal requirements of business.

The Currency School gave a quite correct explanation of the recurring crises as they upset English business conditions in the 'thirties and 'forties of the nineteenth century. There was credit expansion on the part of the Bank of England and the other British banks and bankers, while there was no credit expansion, or at least not to the same degree, in the countries with which Great Britain traded. The external drain occurred as the necessary consequence of this state of affairs. Everything that the Banking School advanced in order to refute this theory was vain. Unfortunately, the Currency School erred in two respects. It never realized that the remedy it suggested, namely strict legal limitation of the amount of banknotes issued beyond the specie reserve, was not the only one. It never gave a thought to the idea of free banking. The second fault of the Currency School was that it failed to recognize that deposits subject to check are money-substitutes and, as far as their amount exceeds the reserve kept, fiduciary media, and consequently no less a vehicle of credit expansion than are banknotes. It was the only merit of the Banking School that it recognized that what is called deposit currency is a money-substitute no less than banknotes. But except for this point, all the doctrines of the Banking School were spurious. It was guided by contradictory ideas concerning money's neutrality; it tried to refute the quantity theory of money by referring to a *deus ex machina,* the much talked about hoards, and it misconstrued entirely the problems of the rate of interest.

It must be emphasized that the problem of legal restrictions upon the issuance of fiduciary media could emerge only because governments had granted special privileges to one or several banks and had thus prevented the free evolution of banking. If the governments had never interfered for the benefit of special banks, if they had never released some banks from the obligation, incumbent upon all individuals and firms in the market economy, to settle their liabilities in full compliance with the terms of the contract, no bank problem would have come into being. The limits which are drawn to credit expansion would have worked effectively. Considerations of its own solvency would have forced every bank to cautious restraint in issuing fiduciary media. Those banks which would not have observed these indispensable rules would have gone bankrupt, and the public, warned through damage, would have become doubly suspicious and reserved.

The attitudes of the European governments with regard to banking were from the beginning insincere and mendacious. The pretended solicitude for the nation's welfare, for the public in general, and for the poor ignorant masses in particular was a mere blind. The governments wanted inflation and credit expansion, they wanted booms and easy money. Those Americans who twice succeeded in doing away with a central bank were aware of the dangers of such institutions; it was only too bad that they failed to see that the evils they fought were present in every kind of government interference with banking. Today even the most bigoted étatists cannot deny that all the alleged evils of free banking count little when compared with the disastrous effects of the tremendous inflations which the privileged and government-controlled banks have brought about.

It is a fable that governments interfered with banking in order to restrict the issue of fiduciary media and to prevent credit expansion. The idea that guided governments was, on the contrary, the lust for inflation and credit expansion. They privileged banks because they wanted to widen the limits that the unhampered market draws to credit expansion or because they were eager to open to the treasury a source of revenue. For the most part both of these considerations motivated the authorities. They were convinced that the fiduciary media are an efficient means of lowering the rate of interest, and asked the banks to expand credit for the benefit of both business and the treasury. Only when the undesired effects of credit expansion became visible, were laws enacted to restrict the issue of banknotes—and sometimes also of deposits—not covered by specie. The establishment of free banking was never seriously considered precisely because it would have been too efficient in restricting credit expansion. For rulers, writers, and the public were unanimous in the belief that business has a fair claim to a "normal" and "necessary" amount of circulation credit and that this amount could not be attained under free banking.[17]

Many governments never looked upon the issuance of fiduciary media from a point of view other than that of fiscal concerns. In their eyes the foremost task of the banks was to lend money to the treasury. The money-substitutes were favorably considered as pacemakers for government-issued paper money. The convertible banknote was merely a first step on the way to the nonredeemable banknote. With the progress of statolatry and the policy of interventionism these ideas have become general and are no longer questioned by anybody. No government is willing today to give any thought to the program of free banking because no government wants to renounce what it considers a handy source of revenue. What is called today financial war preparedness is merely the ability to procure by means of privileged and government-controlled banks all the money a warring nation may need. Radical inflationism, although not admitted explicitly, is an essential feature of the economic ideology of our age.

But even at the time liberalism enjoyed its highest prestige and governments were more eager to preserve peace and well-being than to foment war, death, destruction, and misery, people were biased in dealing with the problems of banking. Outside of the Anglo-Saxon countries public opinion was convinced that it is one of the main tasks of good government to lower the rate of interest and that credit expansion is the appropriate means for the attainment of this end.

Great Britain was free from these errors when in 1844 it reformed its bank laws. But the two shortcomings of the Currency School vitiated this famous act. On one hand, the system of government interference with banking was preserved. On the other hand, limits were placed only on the issuance of banknotes not covered by specie. The fiduciary media were suppressed only in the shape of banknotes. They could thrive as deposit currency.

In carrying the idea implied in the Currency Theory to its full logical conclusion, one could suggest that all banks be forced by law to keep against the total amount of money-substitutes (banknotes plus demand deposits) a 100 per cent money reserve. This is the core of Professor Irving Fisher's 100 per cent plan. But Professor Fisher combined his plan with his proposals concerning the adoption of an

17. The notion of "normal" credit expansion is absurd. Issuance of additional fiduciary media, no matter what its quantity may be, always sets in motion those changes in the price structure the description of which is the task of the theory of the trade cycle. Of course, if the additional amount issued is not large, neither are the inevitable effects of the expansion.

index-number standard. It has been pointed out already why such a scheme is illusory and tantamount to open approval of the government's power to manipulate purchasing power according to the appetites of powerful pressure groups. But even if the 100 per cent reserve plan were to be adopted on the basis of the unadulterated gold standard, it would not entirely remove the drawbacks inherent in every kind of government interference with banking. What is needed to prevent any further credit expansion is to place the banking business under the general rules of commercial and civil laws compelling every individual and firm to fulfill all obligations in full compliance with the terms of the contract. If banks are preserved as privileged establishments subject to special legislative provisions, the tool remains that governments can use for fiscal purposes. Then every restriction imposed upon the issuance of fiduciary media depends upon the government's and the parliament's good intentions. They may limit the issuance for periods which are called normal. The restriction will be withdrawn whenever a government deems that an emergency justifies resorting to extraordinary measures. If an administration and the party backing it want to increase expenditure without jeopardizing their popularity through the imposition of higher taxes, they will always be ready to call their impasse an emergency. Recourse to the printing press and to the obsequiousness of bank managers willing to oblige the authorities regulating their conduct of affairs is the foremost means of governments eager to spend money for purposes for which the taxpayers are not ready to pay higher taxes.

Free banking is the only method available for the prevention of the dangers inherent in credit expansion. It would, it is true, not hinder a slow credit expansion, kept within very narrow limits, on the part of cautious banks which provide the public with all information required about their financial status. But under free banking it would have been impossible for credit expansion with all its inevitable consequences to have developed into a regular—one is tempted to say normal—feature of the economic system. Only free banking would have rendered the market economy secure against crises and depressions.

Looking backward upon the history of the last two centuries, one cannot help realizing that the blunders committed by liberalism in handling the problems of banking were a deadly blow to the market economy. There was no reason whatever to abandon the principle of free enterprise in the field of banking. The majority of liberal politicians simply surrendered to the popular hostility against moneylending and interest taking. They failed to realize that the rate of interest is a market phenomenon which cannot be manipulated *ad libitum* by the authorities or by any other agency. They adopted the superstition that lowering the rate of interest is beneficial and that credit expansion is the right means of attaining such cheap money. Nothing harmed the cause of liberalism more than the almost regular return of feverish booms and of the dramatic breakdown of bull markets followed by lingering slumps. Public opinion has become convinced that such happenings are inevitable in the unhampered market economy. People did not conceive that what they lamented was the necessary outcome of policies directed toward a lowering of the rate of interest by means of credit expansion. They stubbornly kept to these policies and tried in vain to fight their undesired consequences by more and more government interference.

Observations on the Discussions Concerning Free Banking

The Banking School taught that an overissuance of banknotes is impossible if the bank limits its business to the granting of short-term loans.[18] When the loan is paid back at maturity, the banknotes return to the bank and thus disappear from the market. However, this happens only if the bank restricts the amount of credits granted. (But even then it would not undo the effects of its previous credit expansion. It would merely add to it the effects of a later credit contraction.) The regular course of affairs is that the bank replaces the bills expired and paid back by discounting new bills of exchange. Then to the amount of banknotes withdrawn from the market by the repayment of the earlier loan there corresponds an amount of newly issued banknotes.

The concatenation which sets a limit to credit expansion under a system of free banking works in a different way. It has no reference whatever to the process which this so-called Principle of Fullarton has in mind. It is brought about by the fact that credit expansion in itself does not expand a bank's clientele, viz., the number of people who assign to the demand-claims against this bank the character of money-substitutes. Since the overissuance of fiduciary media on the part of one bank, as has been shown above, increases the amount to be paid by the expanding bank's clients to other people, it increases concomitantly the demand for the redemption of its money-substitutes. It thus forces the expanding bank back to a restraint.

This fact was never questioned with regard to demand deposits subject to check. It is obvious that an expanding bank would very soon find itself in a difficult position in clearing with the other banks.

18. See above, pp. 437–438.

However, people sometimes maintained that things are different as far as banknotes are concerned.

In dealing with the problems of money-substitutes, catallactics maintains that the claims in question are dealt with by a number of people like money, that they are, like money, given away and received in transactions and kept in cash holdings. Everything that catallactics asserts with regard to money-substitutes presupposes this state of affairs. But it would be preposterous to believe that every banknote issued by any bank really becomes a money-substitute. What makes a banknote a money-substitute is the special kind of good will of the issuing bank. The slightest doubt concerning the bank's ability or willingness to redeem every banknote without any delay at any time and with no expense to the bearer impairs this special good will and deprives the banknotes of their character as a money-substitute. We may assume that everybody not only is prepared to get such questionable banknotes as a loan but also prefers to receive them as payment instead of waiting longer. But if any doubts exist concerning their prime character, people will hurry to get rid of them as soon as possible. They will keep in their cash holdings money and such money-substitutes as they consider perfectly safe and will dispose of the suspect banknotes. These banknotes will be traded at a discount, and this fact will carry them back to the issuing bank which alone is bound to redeem them at their full face value.

The issue can still better be clarified by reviewing banking conditions in continental Europe. Here the commercial banks were free from any limitation concerning the amount of deposits subject to check. They would have been in a position to grant circulation credit and thus expand credit by adopting the methods applied by the banks of the Anglo-Saxon countries. However, the public was not ready to treat such bank deposits as money-substitutes. As a rule a man who received a check cashed it immediately and thereby withdrew the amount from the bank. It was impossible for a commercial bank to lend, except for negligible sums, by crediting the debtor's account. As soon as the debtor wrote out a check, a withdrawal of the amount concerned from the bank resulted. Only big business treated deposits as money-substitutes. Although the Central Banks in most of these countries were not submitted to any legal restrictions with regard to their deposit business, they were prevented from using it as a vehicle of large-scale credit expansion because the clientele for deposit currency was too small. Banknotes were practically the sole instrument of circulation credit and credit expansion.

In the 'eighties of the nineteenth century the Austrian Government embarked upon a project of popularizing checkbook money by establishing a checking account department with the Post Office Savings Service. It succeeded to some degree. Balances with this department of the Post Office were treated as money-substitutes by a clientele which was broader than that of the checking account department of the country's Central Bank of Issue. The system was later preserved by the new states which in 1918 succeeded the Habsburg Empire. It has also been adopted by many other European nations, for instance Germany. It is important to realize that this kind of deposit currency was a purely governmental venture and that the circulation credit that the system granted was exclusively lent to the governments. It is characteristic that the name of the Austrian Post Office Savings Institution, and likewise of most of its foreign replicas, was not Savings *Bank,* but Savings *Office* (*Amt*). Apart from these demand deposits with the government post system in most of the non-Anglo-Saxon countries, banknotes—and, to a small extent, also deposits with the Government-controlled Central Bank of Issue—are the main vehicles of circulation credit. In speaking of credit expansion with regard to these countries, one refers almost entirely to banknotes.

In the United States many employers pay salaries and even wages by writing out checks. As far as the payees immediately cash the checks received and withdraw the whole amount from the bank, the method means merely that the onerous burden of manipulating coins and banknotes is shifted from the employer's cashier to the bank's cashier. It has no catallactic implications. If all citizens were to deal in this way with checks received, the deposits would not be money-substitutes and could not be used as instruments of circulation credit. It is solely the fact that a considerable part of the public looks upon deposits as money-substitutes that makes them what is popularly called checkbook money or deposit currency.

It is a mistake to associate with the notion of free banking the image of a state of affairs under which everybody is free to issue banknotes and to cheat the public *ad libitum.* People often refer to the dictum of an anonymous American quoted by Tooke: "Free trade in banking is free trade in swindling." However, freedom in the issuance of banknotes would have narrowed down the use of banknotes considerably if it had not entirely suppressed it. It was this idea which Cernuschi advanced in the hearings of the French Banking Inquiry on October 24, 1865: "I believe that what is called freedom of banking would result in a total suppression of banknotes in France. I want to give everybody the right to issue banknotes so that nobody should take any banknotes any longer."[19]

People may uphold the opinion that banknotes are more handy than coins and that considerations of convenience recommend their use. As far as this is the case, the public would be prepared to pay a premium for the avoidance of the inconveniences involved in carrying a heavy weight of coins in their pockets. Thus in earlier days banknotes issued

19. Cf. Cernuschi, *Contre le billet de banque* (Paris, 1866), p. 55.

by banks of unquestionable solvency stood at a slight premium as against metallic currency. Thus travelers' checks are rather popular although the bank issuing them charges a commission for their issuance. But all this has no reference whatever to the problem in question. It does not provide a justification for the policies urging the public to resort to the use of banknotes. Governments did not foster the use of banknotes in order to avoid inconvenience to ladies shopping. Their idea was to lower the rate of interest and to open a source of cheap credit to their treasuries. In their eyes the increase in the quantity of fiduciary media was a means of promoting welfare.

Banknotes are not indispensable. All the economic achievements of capitalism would have been accomplished if they had never existed. Besides, deposit currency can do all the things banknotes do. And government interference with the deposits of commercial banks cannot be justified by the hypocritical pretext that poor ignorant wage earners and farmers must be protected against wicked bankers.

But, some people may ask, what about a cartel of the commercial banks? Could not the banks collude for the sake of a boundless expansion of their issuance of fiduciary media? The objection is preposterous. As long as the public is not, by government interference, deprived of the right of withdrawing its deposits, no bank can risk its own good will by collusion with banks whose good will is not so high as its own. One must not forget that every bank issuing fiduciary media is in a rather precarious position. Its most valuable asset is its reputation. It must go bankrupt as soon as doubts arise concerning its perfect trustworthiness and solvency. It would be suicidal for a bank of good standing to link its name with that of other banks with a poorer good will. Under free banking a cartel of the banks would destroy the country's whole banking system. It would not serve the interests of any bank.

For the most part the banks of good repute are blamed for their conservatism and their reluctance to expand credit. In the eyes of people not deserving of credit such restraint appears as a vice. But it is the first and supreme rule for the conduct of banking operations under free banking.

It is extremely difficult for our contemporaries to conceive of the conditions of free banking because they take government interference with banking for granted and as necessary. However, one must remember that this government interference was based on the erroneous assumption that credit expansion is a proper means of lowering the rate of interest permanently and without harm to anybody but the callous capitalists. The governments interfered precisely because they knew that free banking keeps credit expansion within narrow limits.

Economists may be right in asserting that the present state of banking makes government interference with banking problems advisable.

But this present state of banking is not the outcome of the operation of the unhampered market economy. It is a product of the various governments' attempts to bring about the conditions required for large-scale credit expansion. If the governments had never interfered, the use of banknotes and of deposit currency would be limited to those strata of the population who know very well how to distinguish between solvent and insolvent banks. No large-scale credit expansion would have been possible. The governments alone are responsible for the spread of the superstitious awe with which the common man looks upon every bit of paper upon which the treasury or agencies which it controls have printed the magical words *legal tender*.

Government interference with the present state of banking affairs could be justified if its aim were to liquidate the unsatisfactory conditions by preventing or at least seriously restricting any further credit expansion. In fact, the chief objective of present-day government interference is to intensify further credit expansion. This policy is doomed to failure. Sooner or later it must result in a catastrophe.

13. The Size and Composition of Cash Holdings

The total amount of money and money-substitutes is kept by individuals and firms in their cash holdings. The share of each is determined by marginal utility. Each is eager to keep a certain portion of his total wealth in cash. He gets rid of an excess of cash by increased purchases and remedies a deficiency of cash by increased sales. The popular terminology confusing the demand for money for cash holding and the demand for wealth and vendible goods must not delude an economist.

What is valid with regard to individuals and firms is no less true with regard to every sum of the cash holdings of a number of individuals and firms. The point of view from which we treat a number of such individuals and firms as a totality and sum up their cash holdings is immaterial. The cash holdings of a city, a province, or a country is the sum of the cash holdings of all its residents.

Let us assume that the market economy uses only one kind of money and that money-substitutes are either unknown or used in the whole area by everybody without any difference. There are, for example, gold money and redeemable banknotes, issued by a world bank and treated by everybody as money-substitutes. On these assumptions measures hindering the exchange of commodities and services do not affect the state of monetary affairs and the size of cash holdings. Tariffs, embargoes, and migration barriers affect the tendencies toward an equalization of prices, wages, and interest rates. They do not react directly upon cash holdings.

If a government aims at increasing the amount of cash kept by its subjects, it must order them to deposit a certain amount with an office and to leave it there untouched. The necessity of procuring this amount would force everybody to sell more and to buy less; domestic prices would drop; exports would be increased and imports reduced; a quantity of cash would be imported. But if the government were simply to obstruct the importation of goods and the exportation of money, it would fail to attain its goal. If imports drop, other things being equal, exports drop concomitantly.

The role money plays in international trade is not different from that which it plays in domestic trade. Money is no less a medium of exchange in foreign trade than it is in domestic trade. Both in domestic trade and in international trade purchases and sales result in a more than passing change in the cash holdings of individuals and firms only if people are purposely intent upon increasing or restricting the size of their cash holdings. A surplus of money flows into a country only when its residents are more eager to increase their cash holdings than are the foreigners. An outflow of money occurs only if the residents are more eager to reduce their cash holdings than are the foreigners. A transfer of money from one country into another country which is not compensated by a transfer in the opposite direction is never the unintended result of international trade transactions. It is always the outcome of intended changes in the cash holdings of the residents. Just as wheat is exported only if a country's residents want to export a surplus of wheat, so money is exported only if the residents want to export a sum of money which they consider as a surplus.

If a country turns to the employment of money-substitutes which are not employed abroad, such a surplus emerges. The appearance of these money-substitutes is tantamount to an increase in the country's supply of money in the broader sense, i.e., supply of money plus fiduciary media; it brings about a surplus in the supply of money in the broader sense. The residents are eager to get rid of their share in the surplus by increasing their purchases either of domestic or of foreign goods. In the first case exports drop and in the second case imports increase. In both cases the surplus of money goes abroad. As, according to our assumption, money-substitutes cannot be exported, only money proper flows out. The result is that within the domestic supply of money in the broader sense (money + fiduciary media) the portion of money drops and the portion of fiduciary media increases. The domestic stock of money in the narrower sense is now smaller than it was previously.

Now, we assume further, the domestic money-substitutes cease to be money-substitutes. The bank which issued them no longer redeems them in money. These former money-substitutes are now claims against a bank which does not fulfill its obligations, a bank whose ability and willingness to pay its debts is questionable. Nobody knows whether and when they will ever be redeemed. But it may be that these claims are used by the public as credit money. As money-substitutes they had been considered as equivalents of the sum of money to which they gave a claim payable at any moment. As credit money they are now traded at a discount.

At this point the government may interfere. It decrees that these pieces of credit money are legal tender at their face value.[20] Every creditor is bound to accept them in payment at their face value. No trader is free to discriminate against them. The decree tries to force the public to treat things of different exchange value as if they had the same exchange value. It interferes with the structure of prices as determined by the market. It fixes minimum prices for the credit money and maximum prices for the commodity money (gold) and foreign exchange. The result is not what the government aimed at. The difference in exchange value between credit money and gold does not disappear. As it is forbidden to employ the coins according to their market price, people no longer employ them in buying and selling and in paying debts. They keep them or they export them. The commodity money disappears from the domestic market. Bad money, says Gresham's Law, drives good money out of the country. It would be more correct to say that the money which the government's decree has undervalued disappears from the market and the money which the decree has overvalued remains.

The outflow of commodity money is thus not the effect of an unfavorable balance of payments, but the effect of a government interference with the price structure.

14. Balances of Payments

The confrontation of the money equivalent of all incomings and outgoings of an individual or a group of individuals during any particular period of time is called the balance of payments. The credit side and the debit side are always equal. The balance is always in balance.

20. Very often the legal tender quality had been given to those banknotes at a time when they still were money-substitutes and as such equal to money in their exchange value. At that time the decree had no catallactic importance. Now it becomes important because the market no longer considers them money-substitutes.

If we want to know an individual's position in the frame of the market economy, we must look at his balance of payments. It tells us everything about the role he plays in the system of the social division of labor. It shows what he gives to his fellow men and what he receives or takes from them. It shows whether he is a self-supporting decent citizen or a thief or an almsman. It shows whether he consumes all his proceeds or whether he saves a part of them. There are many human things which are not reflected in the sheets of the ledger; there are virtues and achievements, vices and crimes that do not leave any traces in the accounts. But as far as a man is integrated into social life and activities, as far as he contributes to the joint effort of society and his contributions are appreciated by his fellow men, and as far as he consumes what is or could be sold and bought on the market, the information conveyed is complete.

If we combine the balances of payments of a definite number of individuals and leave out of account the items referring to transactions between the members of this group, we draw up the group's balance of payment. This balance tells us how the members of the group, considered as an integrated complex of people, are connected with the rest of the market society. Thus we can draw up the balance of payments of the members of the New York Bar, of the Belgian farmers, of the residents of Paris, or of those of the Swiss Canton of Bern. Statisticians are mostly interested in establishing the balance of payments of the residents of the various countries which are organized as independent nations.

While an individual's balance of payments conveys exhaustive information about his social position, a group's balance discloses much less. It says nothing about the mutual relations between the members of the group. The greater the group is and the less homogeneous its members are, the more defective is the information vouchsafed by the balance of payments. The balance of payments of Denmark tells more about the conditions of the Danes than the United States balance of payments about the conditions of the Americans. If one wants to describe a country's social and economic condition, one does not need to deal with every single inhabitant's personal balance of payments. But one must not form other groups than such as are composed of members who are by and large homogeneous in their social standing and their economic activities.

Reading balances of payments is thus very instructive. However, to guard against popular fallacies, one must know how to interpret them.

It is customary to list separately the monetary and the nonmonetary items of a country's balance of payments. One calls the balance favorable if there is a surplus of the imports of money and bullion over the exports of money and bullion. One calls the balance unfavorable if the exports of money and bullion exceed the imports. This terminology stems from inveterate Mercantilist errors unfortunately still surviving in spite of the devastating criticism of the economists. The imports and exports of money and bullion are viewed as the unintentional outcome of the configuration of the nonmonetary items of the balance of payments. This opinion is utterly fallacious. An excess in the exports of money and bullion is not the product of an unhappy concatenation of circumstances that befalls a nation like an act of God. It is the result of the fact that the residents of the country concerned are intent upon reducing the amount of money held and upon buying goods instead. This is why the balance of payments of the gold-producing countries is as a rule "unfavorable"; this is why the balance of payments of a country substituting fiduciary media for a part of its money stock is "unfavorable" as long as this process goes on.

No provident action on the part of a paternal authority is required lest a country lose its whole money stock by an unfavorable balance of payments. Things are in this regard not different between the personal balances of payments of individuals and those of groups. Neither are they different between the balances of payments of a city or a district and those of a sovereign nation. No government interference is needed to prevent the residents of New York from spending all their money in dealings with the other forty-nine states of the Union. As long as any American attaches any weights to the keeping of cash, he will spontaneously take charge of the matter. Thus he will contribute his share to the maintenance of an adequate supply of money in his country. But if no American were interested in keeping any cash holding, no government measure concerning foreign trade and the settlement of international payments could prevent an outflow of America's total monetary stock. A rigidly enforced embargo upon the exportation of money and bullion would be required.

15. Interlocal Exchange Rates

Let us first assume that there is only one kind of money. Then with regard to money's purchasing power at various places the same is valid as with regard to commodity prices. The final price of cotton in Liverpool cannot exceed the final price in Houston, Texas, by more than the cost of transportation. As soon as the price in Liverpool rises to a higher point, merchants will ship cotton to Liverpool and thus will bring about a tendency toward a return to the final price. In the absence of institutional obstacles, the price of an order for the payment of a definite amount of guilders in Amsterdam cannot rise in New York above the amount determined by the costs involved by reminting the coins, shipment, insurance, and the interest during the period required for all these manipulations. As soon as the difference rises above this point—the gold export point—it becomes profitable to ship gold from New York to Amsterdam. Such shipments force the guilder exchange rate in New York down below the gold export point. A difference between the configuration of interlocal exchange rates for commodities and those for money is brought about by the fact that as a rule commodities move only in one direction, namely, from the places of surplus production to those of surplus consumption. Cotton is shipped from Houston to Liverpool and not from Liverpool to Houston. Its price is lower in Houston than in Liverpool by the amount of shipping costs. But money is shipped now this way, now that.

The error of those who try to interpret the fluctuations of the interlocal exchange rates and the interlocal shipments of money as determined by the configuration of the nonmonetary items of the balance of payments is that they assign to money an exceptional position. They do not see that with regard to interlocal exchange rates there is no difference between money and commodities. If cotton trade between Houston and Liverpool is possible at all, the cotton prices at these two places cannot differ by more than the total amount of costs required for shipment. In the same way in which there is a flow of cotton from the southern parts of the United States to Europe, gold flows from the gold-producing countries like South Africa to Europe.

Let us disregard triangular trade and the case of the gold-producing countries and let us assume that the individuals and firms trading with one another on the basis of the gold standard do not have the intention of changing the size of their cash holdings. From their purchases and sales, claims are generated which necessitate interlocal payments. But according to our assumption these interlocal payments are equal in amount. The amount that the residents of *A* have to pay to the residents of *B* is equal to the amount that the residents of *B* have to pay to the residents of *A*. It is therefore possible to save the costs of shipping gold from *A* to *B* and from *B* to *A*. Claims and debts can be settled by a sort of interlocal clearing. It is merely a technical problem whether this evening up is effected by an interlocal clearinghouse organization or by the turnovers of a special market for foreign exchange. At any rate, the price which a resident of *A* (or of *B*) has to pay for a payment due in *B* (or in *A*) is kept within the margins determined by the shipment costs. It cannot rise above the par value by more than the shipment costs (gold export point) and cannot fall below the shipment costs (gold import point).

It may happen that—all our other assumptions remaining unaltered—there is a temporal discrepancy between the payments due from *A* to *B* and those from *B* to *A*. Then an interlocal shipment of gold can only be avoided by the interposition of a credit transaction. If the importer who today has to pay from *A* to *B* can buy at the market of foreign exchange claims against residents of *B* as fall due in ninety days, he can save the costs of shipping gold by borrowing the sum concerned in *B* for a period of ninety days. The dealers in foreign exchange will resort to this makeshift if the costs of borrowing in *B* do not exceed the costs of borrowing in *A* by more than double the costs of shipping gold. If the cost of shipping gold is ⅛ per cent, they will be ready to pay for a three months' loan in *B* up to 1 per cent (pro anno) more as interest than corresponds to the state of the money-market interest rate at which, in the absence of such requirements for interlocal payments, credit transactions between *A* and *B* would be effected.

It is permissible to express these facts by contending that the daily state of the balance of payments between *A* and *B* determines the point at which, within the margins drawn by the gold export point and the gold import point, the foreign exchange rates are fixed. But one must not forget to add that this happens only if the residents of *A* and of *B* do not intend to change the size of their cash holdings. Only because this is the case does it become possible to avoid the transfer of gold altogether and to keep foreign exchange rates within the limits drawn by the two gold points. If the residents of *A* want to reduce their cash holdings and those of *B* want to increase theirs, gold must be shipped from *A* to *B* and the rate for cable transfer *B* reaches in *A* the gold export point. Then gold is sent from *A* to *B* in the same way in which cotton is regularly sent from the United States to Europe. The rate of cable transfer *B* reaches the gold export point because the residents of *A* are selling gold to those of *B*, not because their balance of payments is unfavorable.

All this is valid with regard to any payments to be transacted between various places. It makes no difference whether the cities concerned belong to the same sovereign nation or to different sovereign nations. However, government interference has considerably changed the conditions. All governments have created institutions which make it possible for the residents of their countries to make interlocal domestic payments at par. The costs involved in shipment of currency from one place to another are borne either by the treasury or by the country's central bank system or by another government bank such as the postal savings banks of various European countries. Thus there is no longer any market for domestic interlocal exchange. The public is not charged more for an interlocal order to pay than for a local one or, if the charge is slightly different, it no longer has any reference to the fluctuations of the interlocal movements of currency within the country. It is this government interference which has sharpened the difference between domestic payment and payment abroad. Domestic payments are transacted at par, while with regard to foreign payments fluctuations occur within the limits drawn by the gold points.

If more than one kind of money is used as medium of exchange, the mutual exchange ratio between them is determined by their purchasing power. The final prices of the various commodities, as expressed in each of the two or several kinds of money, are in proportion to each other. The final exchange ratio between the various kinds of money reflects their purchasing power with regard to the commodities. If any discrepancy appears, opportunity for profitable transactions presents itself and the endeavors of businessmen eager to take advantage of this opportunity tend to make it disappear again. The purchasing-power parity theory of foreign exchange is merely the application of the general theorems concerning the determination of prices to the special case of the coexistence of various kinds of money.

It does not matter whether the various kinds of money coexist in the same territory or whether their use is limited to distinct areas. In any case the mutual exchange ratio between them tends to a final state at which it no longer makes any difference whether one buys and sells against this or that kind of money. As far as costs of interlocal transfer come into play, these costs must be added or deducted.

The changes in purchasing power do not occur at the same time with regard to all commodities and services. Let us consider again the practically very important instance of an inflation in one country only. The increase in the quantity of domestic credit money or fiat money affects at first only the prices of some commodities and services. The prices of the other commodities remain for some time still at their previous stand. The exchange ratio between the domestic currency and the foreign currencies is determined on the bourse, a market organized and managed according to the pattern and the commercial customs of the stock exchange. The dealers on this special market are quicker than the rest of the people in anticipating future changes. Consequently the price structure of the market for foreign exchange reflects the new money relation sooner than the prices of many commodities and services. As soon as the domestic inflation begins to affect the prices of some commodities, at any rate long before it has exhausted all its effects upon the greater part of the prices of commodities and services, the price of foreign exchange tends to rise to the point corresponding to the final state of domestic prices and wage rates.

This fact has been entirely misinterpreted. People failed to realize that the rise in foreign exchange rates merely anticipates the movement of domestic commodity prices. They explained the boom in foreign exchange as an outcome of an unfavorable balance of payments. The demand for foreign exchange, they maintained, has been increased by a deterioration of the balance of trade or of other items of the balance of payments, or simply by sinister machinations on the part of unpatriotic speculators. The higher prices to be paid for foreign exchange cause the domestic prices of imported goods to rise. The prices of the domestic products must follow suit because otherwise their low state would encourage business to withhold them from domestic consumption and to sell them abroad at a premium.

The fallacies involved in this popular doctrine can easily be shown. If the nominal income of the domestic public had not been increased by the inflation, they would be forced to restrict their consumption either of imported or of domestic products. In the first case imports would drop and in the second case exports would increase. Thus the balance of trade would again be brought back to what the Mercantilists call a favorable state.

Pressed hard, the Mercantilists cannot help admitting the cogency of this reasoning. But, they say, it applies only to normal trade conditions. It does not take into account the state of affairs in countries which are under the necessity of importing vital commodities such as food and essential raw materials. The importation of such goods cannot be curtailed below a certain minimum. They are imported no matter what prices must be paid for them. If the foreign exchange required for importing them cannot be procured by an adequate amount of exports, the balance of trade becomes unfavorable and the foreign exchange rates must rise more and more.

This is no less illusory than all other Mercantilist ideas. However urgent and vital an individual's or a group of individuals' demand for some goods may be, they can satisfy it on the market only by paying the market price. If an Austrian wants to buy Canadian wheat, he must pay the market price in Canadian dollars. He must procure these Canadian dollars by exporting goods either directly to Canada or to some other country. He does not increase the amount of Canadian dollars available by paying higher prices (in schillings, the Austrian domestic currency) for Canadian dollars. Moreover, he cannot afford to pay such higher prices (in schillings) for imported wheat if his income (in schillings) remains unchanged. Only if the Austrian Government embarks upon an inflationary policy and thus increases the number of schillings in the pockets of its citizens, are the Austrians in a position to continue to buy the quantities of Canadian wheat they used to buy without curtailing other expenditures. If there were no domestic inflation, any rise in the price of imported goods would result either in a drop in their consumption or in a restriction in the consumption of other goods. Thus the process of readjustment as described above would have come into motion.

If a man lacks the money to buy bread from his neighbor, the village baker, the cause is not to be seen in an alleged scarcity of money. The cause is that this man did not succeed in earning the amount of money needed either by selling goods or by rendering services for which people are prepared to pay. The same is true with regard to international trade. A country may be distressed on account of the fact that it is at a loss to sell abroad as many commodities as it would have to sell in order to buy all the food its citizens want. But this does not mean that foreign exchange is scarce. It means that the residents are poor. And domestic inflation is certainly not an appropriate means to remove this poverty.

Neither has speculation any reference to the determination of foreign exchange rates. The speculators merely anticipate the expected alterations. If they err, if their opinion that an inflation is in progress is wrong, the structure of prices and foreign exchange rates will not correspond to their anticipations and they will have to pay for their mistakes by losses.

The doctrine according to which foreign exchange rates are determined by the balance of payments is based upon an illicit generalization of a special case. If two places, *A* and *B*, use the same kind of money and if the residents do not want to make any changes in the size of their cash holdings, over a given period of time the amount of money paid from the residents of *A* to those of *B* equals the amount paid from the residents of *B* to those of *A* and all payments can be settled without shipping money from *A* to *B* or from *B* to *A*. Then the rate of cable transfer *B* in *A* cannot rise above a point slightly below the gold export point and cannot drop below a point slightly above the gold import point, and vice versa. Within this margin the daily state of the balance of payments determines the daily state of the foreign exchange rate. This is the case only because neither the residents of *A* nor those of *B* want to alter the amount of their cash holdings. If the residents of *A* want to decrease their cash holdings and those of *B* to increase theirs, money is shipped from *A* to *B* and the cable rate *B* reaches in *A* the gold export point. But money is not shipped because *A*'s balance of payments has become unfavorable. What is called by the Mercantilists an unfavorable balance of payments is the effect of a deliberate restriction of cash holdings on the part of the citizens of *A* and a deliberate increase in cash holdings on the part of the citizens of *B*. If no resident of *A* were ready to reduce his cash holding, such an outflow of money from *A* could never materialize.

The difference between the trade in money and that in the vendible commodities is this: As a rule commodities move on a one-way road, viz., from the places of surplus production to those of surplus consumption. Consequently the price of a certain commodity in the places of surplus production is as a rule lower by the amount of shipping costs than in the places of surplus consumption. Things are different with money if we do not take into account the conditions of the gold-mining countries and of those countries whose residents deliberately aim at altering the size of their cash holdings. Money moves now this way, now that. At one time a country exports money, at another time it imports money. Every exporting country very soon becomes an importing country precisely on account of its previous exports. For this reason alone it is possible to save the costs of shipping money by the interplay of the market for foreign exchange.

16. Interest Rates and the Money Relation

Money plays in credit transaction the same role it plays in all other business transactions. As a rule loans are granted in money, and interest and principal are paid in money. The payments resulting from such dealings influence the size of cash holding only temporarily. The recipients of loans, interest, and principal spend the sums received either for consumption or for investment. They increase their cash holdings only if definite considerations, independent of the inflow of the money received, motivate them to act in this way.

The final state of the market rate of interest is the same for all loans of the same character. Differences in the rate of interest are caused either by differences in the soundness and trustworthiness of the debtor or by differences in the terms of the contract.[21] Differences in interest rates which are not brought about by these differences in conditions tend to disappear. The applicants for credits approach the lenders who ask a lower rate of interest. The lenders are eager to cater to people who are ready to pay higher interest rates. Things on the money market are the same as on all other markets.

With regard to interlocal credit transactions the interlocal exchange rates are to be taken into account as well as differences in the monetary standard if there are any. Let us contemplate the case of two countries, *A* and *B*. *A* is under the gold standard, *B* under the silver standard. The lender who considers lending money from *A* to *B* must first sell gold against silver and later, at the termination of the loan, silver against gold. If at that later date the price of silver has dropped as against gold, the principal repaid by the debtor (in silver) will buy a smaller amount of gold than that expended by the creditor when he previously embarked upon the transaction. He will therefore only venture lending in *B* if the difference in the market rate of interest between *A* and *B* is large enough to cover an expected fall in the price of silver as against gold. The tendency toward an equalization of the market rate of interest for short-term loans which prevails if *A* and *B* are both under the same monetary standard is seriously impaired under a diversity of standards.

If *A* and *B* are both under the same standard, it is impossible for the banks of *A* to expand credit if those of *B* do not espouse the same policy. Credit expansion in *A* makes prices rise, and short-term interest rates temporarily drop in *A*, while prices and interest rates in *B* remain unchanged. Consequently exports from *A* drop and imports to *A* increase. In addition, the money lenders of *A* become eager to lend on the short-term loan market of *B*. The result is an external drain from *A* which makes the money reserves of *A*'s banks dwindle. If the banks of *A* do not abandon their expansionist policy, they will become insolvent.

This process has been entirely misinterpreted. People speak of an important and vital function which a country's central bank has to fulfill on behalf of the nation. It is, they say, the central bank's sacred duty to preserve the stability of foreign exchange rates and to protect the nation's gold reserve against attacks on the part of foreign speculators and their domestic abettors. The truth is that all that a central bank does lest its gold reserve evaporate is done for the sake of the preservation of its own solvency. It has jeopardized its financial position by embarking upon credit expansion and must now undo

21. For a more elaborate analysis, see below, pp. 539–548.

its previous action in order to avoid its disastrous consequences. Its expansionist policy has encountered the obstacles limiting the issuance of fiduciary media.

The use of the terminology of warfare is inappropriate in dealing with monetary matters, as it is in the treatment of all other catallactic problems. There is no such thing as a "war" between the central banks. No sinister forces are "attacking" a bank's position and threatening the stability of foreign exchange rates. No "defender" is needed to "protect" a nation's currency system. It is, moreover, not true that what prevent a nation's central bank or its private banks from lowering the domestic market rate of interest are considerations of the preservation of the gold standard and of foreign exchange stability and of frustrating the machinations of an international combine of capitalistic moneylenders. The market rate of interest cannot be lowered by a credit expansion except for a short time, and even then it brings about all those effects which the theory of the trade cycle describes.

When the Bank of England redeemed a banknote issued according to the terms of the contract, it did not render unselfishly a vital service to the British people. It simply did what every housewife does in paying the grocer's bill. The idea that there is some special merit in a central bank's fulfillment of its voluntarily assumed responsibilities could originate only because again and again governments granted to these banks the privilege of denying to their clients the payments to which they had a legal title. In fact, the central banks became more and more subordinate offices of the treasuries, mere tools for the performance of credit expansion and inflation. It does not make any difference practically whether they are or are not owned by the government and directly managed by government officials. In effect the banks granting circulation credit are in every country today only affiliates of the treasuries.

There is but one means of keeping a local and national currency permanently at par with gold and foreign exchange: unconditional redemption. The central bank has to buy at the parity rate any amount of gold and foreign exchange offered against domestic banknotes and deposit currency; on the other hand it has to sell, without discrimination, any amount of gold and foreign exchange asked for by people ready to pay the parity price in domestic banknotes, coins, or deposit currency. Such was the policy of central banks under the gold standard. Such was also the policy of those governments and central banks which had adopted the currency system commonly known under the name of the gold exchange standard. The only difference between the "orthodox" or classical gold standard as it existed in Great Britain from the early 'twenties of the nineteenth century until the outbreak of the first World War and in other countries on the one hand, and the gold exchange standard on the other, concerned the use of gold coins on the domestic market. Under the classical gold standard a part of the cash holdings of the citizens consisted in gold coins and the rest in money substitutes. Under the gold exchange standard the cash holdings consisted entirely in money-substitutes.

Pegging a certain rate of foreign exchange is tantamount to redemption at this rate.

A foreign exchange equalization account, too, can succeed in its operations only as far as it clings to the same methods.

The reasons why in the last decades European governments have preferred foreign exchange equalization accounts to the operation of central banks are obvious. Central bank legislation was an achievement of liberal governments or of governments which did not dare to challenge openly, at least in the conduct of financial policies, public opinion of the liberal countries. The operations of central banks were therefore adjusted to economic freedom. For that reason they were considered unsatisfactory in this age of rising totalitarianism. The main characteristics of the operation of a foreign exchange equalization account as distinguished from central bank policy are:

1. The authorities keep the transactions of the account secret. The laws have obliged the central banks to publicize their actual status at short intervals, as a rule every week. But the status of the foreign exchange equalization accounts is known only to the initiated. Officialdom renders a report to the public only after a lapse of time when the figures are of interest to historians alone and of no use whatever to the businessman.

2. This secrecy makes it possible to discriminate against people not in great favor with the authorities. In many continental countries of Europe it resulted in scandalous corruption. Other governments used the power to discriminate to the detriment of businessmen belonging to linguistic or religious minorities or supporting opposition parties.

3. A parity is no longer fixed by a law duly promulgated by parliament and therefore known to every citizen. The determination depends upon the arbitrariness of bureaucrats. From time to time the newspapers reported: The Ruritanian currency is weak. A more correct description would have been: The Ruritanian authorities have decided to raise the price of foreign exchange.[22]

A foreign exchange equalization account is not a magic wand for

22. See below, pp. 786–789.

remedying the evils of inflation. It cannot apply any means other than those available to "orthodox" central banks. And it must, like the central banks, fail in the endeavors to keep foreign exchange rates at par if there is domestic inflation and credit expansion.

It has been asserted that the "orthodox" methods of fighting an external drain by using the rate of discount no longer work because nations are no longer prepared to comply with "the rules of the game." Now, the gold standard is not a game, but a social institution. Its working does not depend on the preparedness of any people to observe some arbitrary rules. It is controlled by the operation of inexorable economic law.

The critics give point to their objection by citing the fact that in the interwar period a rise in the rate of discount failed to stop the external drain, i.e., the outflow of specie and the transfer of deposits into foreign countries. But this phenomenon was caused by the governments' anti-gold and pro-inflation policies. If a man expects that he will lose 40 per cent of his balance by an impending devaluation, he will try to transfer his deposit into another country and will not change his mind if the bank rate in the country planning a devaluation rises 1 or 2 per cent. Such a rise in the rate of discount is obviously not a compensation for a loss ten or twenty or even forty times greater. Of course, the gold standard cannot work if governments are eager to sabotage its operations.

17. Secondary Media of Exchange

The use of money does not remove the differences which exist between the various nonmonetary goods with regard to their marketability. In the money economy there is a very substantial difference between the marketability of money and that of the vendible goods. But there remain differences between the various specimens of this latter group. For some of them it is easier to find without delay a buyer ready to pay the highest price which, under the state of the market, can possibly be attained. With others it is more difficult. A first-class bond is more marketable than a house in a city's main street, and an old fur coat is more marketable than an autograph of an eighteenth-century statesman. One no longer compares the marketability of the various vendible goods with the perfect marketability of money. One merely compares the degree of marketability of the various commodities. One may speak of the secondary marketability of the vendible goods.

He who owns a stock of goods of a high degree of secondary marketability is in a position to restrict his cash holding. He can expect that when one day it is necessary for him to increase his cash holding he will be in a position to sell these goods of a high degree of secondary marketability without delay at the highest price attainable at the market. Thus the size of a man's or a firm's cash holding is influenced by whether or not he owns a stock of goods with a high degree of secondary marketability. The size of cash holding and the expense incurred in keeping it can be reduced if income-producing goods of a high degree of secondary marketability are available.

Consequently there emerges a specific demand for such goods on the part of people eager to keep them in order to reduce the costs of cash holding. The prices of these goods are partly determined by this specific demand; they would be lower in its absence. These goods are secondary media of exchange, as it were, and their exchange value is the resultant of two kinds of demand: the demand related to their services as secondary media of exchange, and the demand related to the other services they render.

The costs incurred by holding cash are equal to the amount of interest which the sum concerned would have borne when invested. The cost incurred by holding a stock of secondary media of exchange consists in the difference between the interest yield of the securities employed for this purpose and the higher yield of other securities which differ from the former only in regard to their lower marketability and are therefore not suited for the role of secondary media of exchange.

From time immemorial jewels have been used as secondary media of exchange. Today the secondary media of exchange commonly used are:

1. Claims against banks, bankers, and savings banks which—although not money-substitutes[23]—are daily maturing or can be withdrawn on short notice.

2. Bonds whose volume and popularity are so great that it is, as a rule, possible to sell moderate quantities of them without depressing the market.

3. Finally, sometimes even certain especially marketable stocks or even commodities.

Of course, the advantages to be expected from lowering the costs of holding cash must be confronted with certain hazards incurred. The sale of securities and still more that of commodities may only be feasible with a loss. This danger is not present with bank balances and the hazard of the bank's insolvency is usually negligible. Therefore interest-bearing claims against banks and bankers, which can be withdrawn at short notice, are the most popular secondary media of exchange.

23. For instance, demand deposits not subject to check.

One must not confuse secondary media of exchange with money-substitutes. Money-substitutes are in the settlement of payments given away and received like money. But the secondary media of exchange must first be exchanged against money or money-substitutes if one wants to use them—in a roundabout way—for paying or for increasing cash holdings.

Claims employed as secondary media of exchange have, because of this employment, a broader market and a higher price. The outcome of this is that they yield lower interest than claims of the same kind which are not fit to serve as secondary media of exchange. Government bonds and treasury bills which can be used as secondary media of exchange can be floated on conditions more favorable to the debtor than loans not suitable for this purpose. The debtors concerned are therefore eager to organize the market for their certificates of indebtedness in such a way as to make them attractive for those in search of secondary media of exchange. They are intent upon making it possible for every holder of such securities to sell them or to use them as collateral in borrowing under the most reasonable terms. In advertising their bond issues to the public they stress these opportunities as a special boon.

In the same way banks and bankers are intent upon attracting demand for secondary media of exchange. They offer convenient terms to their customers. They try to outdo one another by shortening the time allowed for notice. Sometimes they pay interest even for money maturing without notice. In this rivalry some banks have gone too far and endangered their solvency.

Political conditions of the last decades have given to bank balances which can be used as secondary media of exchange an increased importance. The governments of almost all countries are engaged in a campaign against the capitalists. They are intent upon expropriating them by means of taxation and monetary measures. The capitalists are eager to protect their property by keeping a part of their funds liquid in order to evade confiscatory measures in time. They keep balances with the banks of those countries in which the danger of confiscation or currency devaluation is for the moment less than in other countries. As soon as the prospects change, they transfer their balances into countries which temporarily seem to offer more security. It is these funds which people have in mind when speaking of "hot money."

The significance of hot money for the constellation of monetary affairs is the outcome of the one-reserve system. In order to make it easier for the central banks to embark upon credit expansion, the European governments aimed long ago at a concentration of their countries' gold reserves with the central banks. The other banks (the private banks, i.e., those not endowed with special privileges and not entitled to issue banknotes) restrict their cash holdings to the requirements of their daily transactions. They no longer keep a reserve against their daily maturing liabilities. They do not consider it necessary to balance the maturity dates of their liabilities and their assets in such a way as to be any day ready to comply unaided with their obligations to their creditors. They rely upon the central bank. When the creditors want to withdraw more than the "normal" amount, the private banks borrow the funds needed from the central bank. A private bank considers itself liquid if it owns a sufficient amount either of collateral against which the central bank will lend or of bills of exchange which the central bank will rediscount.[24]

When the inflow of hot money began, the private banks of the countries in which it was temporarily deposited saw nothing wrong in treating these funds in the usual way. They employed the additional funds entrusted to them in increasing their loans to business. They did not worry about the consequences, although they knew that these funds would be withdrawn as soon as any doubts about their country's fiscal or monetary policy emerged. The illiquidity of the status of these banks was manifest: on the one hand large sums which the customers had the right to withdraw at short notice, and on the other hand loans to business which could be recovered only at a later date. The only cautious method of dealing with hot money would have been to keep a reserve of gold and foreign exchange big enough to pay back the whole amount in case of a sudden withdrawal. Of course, this method would have required the banks to charge the customers a commission for keeping their funds safe.

The showdown came for the Swiss banks on the day in September, 1936, on which France devalued the French franc. The depositors of hot money became frightened; they feared that Switzerland might follow the French example. It was to be expected that they would all try to transfer their funds immediately to London or New York, or even to Paris, which for the immediate coming weeks seemed to offer a smaller hazard of currency depreciation. But the Swiss commercial banks were not in a position to pay back these funds without the aid of the National Bank. They had lent them to business—a great part to business in countries which, by foreign exchange control, had blocked their balances. The only way out would have been for them to borrow from the National Bank. Then they would have maintained their own solvency. But the depositors paid would have im-

24. All this refers to European conditions. American conditions differ only technically, but not economically.

mediately asked the National Bank for the redemption, in gold or foreign exchange, of the banknotes received. If the National Bank were not to comply with this request, it would thereby have actually abandoned the gold standard and devalued the Swiss franc. If, on the other hand, the Bank had redeemed the notes, it would have lost the greater part of its reserve. A panic would have resulted. The Swiss themselves would have tried to procure as much gold and foreign exchange as possible. The whole monetary system of the country would have collapsed.

The only alternative for the Swiss National Bank would have been not to assist the private banks at all. But this would have been equivalent to the insolvency of the country's most important credit institutions.

Thus for the Swiss Government no choice was left. It had only one means to prevent an economic catastrophe: to follow suit forthwith and to devalue the Swiss franc. The matter did not brook delay.

By and large, Great Britain, at the outbreak of the war in September, 1939, had to face similar conditions. The City of London was once the world's banking center. It has long since lost this function. But foreigners and citizens of the Dominions still kept, on the eve of the war, considerable short-term balances in the British banks. Besides, there were the large deposits due to the central banks in the "sterling area." If the British Government had not frozen all these balances by means of foreign exchange restrictions, the insolvency of the British banks would have become manifest. Foreign exchange control was a disguised moratorium for the banks. It relieved them from the plight of having to confess publicly their inability to fulfill their obligations.

18. The Inflationist View of History

A very popular doctrine maintains that progressive lowering of the monetary unit's purchasing power played a decisive role in historical evolution. It is asserted that mankind would not have reached its present state of well-being if the supply of money had not increased to a greater extent than the demand for money. The resulting fall in purchasing power, it is said, was a necessary condition of economic progress. The intensification of the division of labor and the continuous growth of capital accumulation, which have centupled the productivity of labor, could ensue only in a world of progressive price rises. Inflation creates prosperity and wealth; deflation distress and economic decay.[25] A survey of political literature and of the

25. Cf. the critical study of Marianne von Herzfeld, "Die Geschichte als Funktion der Geldbewegung," *Archiv fuer Sozialwissenschaft,* LVI, 654–686, and the writings quoted in this study.

ideas that guided for centuries the monetary and credit policies of the nations reveals that this opinion is almost generally accepted. In spite of all warnings on the part of economists it is still today the core of the layman's economic philosophy. It is no less the essence of the teachings of Lord Keynes and his disciples in both hemispheres.

The popularity of inflationism is in great part due to deep-rooted hatred of creditors. Inflation is considered just because it favors debtors at the expense of creditors. However, the inflationist view of history which we have to deal with in this section is only loosely related to this anticreditor argument. Its assertion that "expansionism" is the driving force of economic progress and that "restrictionism" is the worst of all evils is mainly based on other arguments.

It is obvious that the problems raised by the inflationist doctrine cannot be solved by a recourse to the teachings of historical experience. It is beyond doubt that the history of prices shows, by and large, a continuous, although sometimes for short periods interrupted, upward trend. It is of course impossible to establish this fact otherwise than by historical understanding. Catallactic precision cannot be applied to historical problems. The endeavors of some historians and statisticians to trace back the changes in the purchasing power of the precious metals for centuries, and to measure them, are futile. It has been shown already that all attempts to measure economic magnitudes are based on entirely fallacious assumptions and display ignorance of the fundamental principles both of economics and of history. But what history by means of its specific methods can tell us in this field is enough to justify the assertion that the purchasing power of money has for centuries shown a tendency to fall. With regard to this point all people agree.

But this is not the problem to be elucidated. The question is whether the fall in purchasing power was or was not an indispensable factor in the evolution which led from the poverty of ages gone by to the more satisfactory conditions of modern Western capitalism. This question must be answered without reference to the historical experience, which can be and always is interpreted in different ways, and to which supporters and adversaries of every theory and of every explanation of history refer as a proof of their mutually contradictory and incompatible statements. What is needed is a clarification of the effects of changes in purchasing power on the division of labor, the accumulation of capital, and technological improvement.

In dealing with this problem one cannot satisfy oneself with the refutation of the arguments advanced by the inflationists in support of their thesis. The absurdity of these arguments is so manifest that their refutation and exposure is easy indeed. From its very beginnings economics has shown again and again that assertions concerning the alleged blessings of an abundance of money and the alleged disasters of a scarcity of money are the outcome of crass errors in reasoning. The endeavors of the apostles of inflationism and expansionism to refute the correctness of the economists' teachings have failed utterly.

The only relevant question is this: Is it possible or not to lower the rate of interest lastingly by means of credit expansion? This problem will be treated exhaustively in the chapter dealing with the interconnection between the money relation and the rate of interest. There it will be shown what the consequences of booms created by credit expansion must be.

But we must ask ourselves at this point of our inquiries whether it is not possible that there are other reasons which could be advanced in favor of the inflationary interpretation of history. Is it not possible that the champions of inflationism have neglected to resort to some valid arguments which could support their stand? It is certainly necessary to approach the issue from every possible avenue.

Let us think of a world in which the quantity of money is rigid. At an early stage of history the inhabitants of this world have produced the whole quantity of the commodity employed for the monetary service which can possibly be produced. A further increase in the quantity of money is out of the question. Fiduciary media are unknown. All money-substitutes—the subsidiary coins included—are money-certificates.

On these assumptions the intensification of the division of labor, the evolution from the economic self-sufficiency of households, villages, districts, and countries to the world-embracing market system of the nineteenth century, the progressive accumulation of capital, and the improvement of technological methods of production would have resulted in a continuous trend toward falling prices. Would such a rise in the purchasing power of the monetary unit have stopped the evolution of capitalism?

The average businessman will answer this question in the affirmative. Living and acting in an environment in which a slow but continuous fall in the monetary unit's purchasing power is deemed normal, necessary, and beneficial, he simply cannot comprehend a different state of affairs. He associates the notions of rising prices and profits on the one hand and of falling prices and losses on the other. The fact that there are bear operations too and that great fortunes have been made by bears does not shake his dogmatism. These are, he says, merely speculative transactions of people eager to profit from the fall in the prices of goods already produced and available. Creative innovations, new investments, and the application of improved technological methods require the inducement brought about by the expectation of price rises. Economic progress is possible only in a world of rising prices.

This opinion is untenable. In a world of a rising purchasing power of the monetary unit everybody's mode of thinking would have adjusted itself to this state of affairs, just as in our actual world it has adjusted itself to a falling purchasing power of the monetary unit. Today everybody is prepared to consider a rise in his nominal or monetary income as an improvement of his material well-being. People's attention is directed more toward the rise in nominal wage rates and the money equivalent of wealth than to the increase in the supply of commodities. In a world of rising purchasing power for the monetary unit they would concern themselves more with the fall in living costs. This would bring into clearer relief the fact that economic progress consists primarily in making the amenities of life more easily accessible.

In the conduct of business, reflections concerning the secular trend of prices do not play any role whatever. Entrepreneurs and investors do not bother about secular trends. What guides their actions is their opinion about the movement of prices in the coming weeks, months, or at most years. They do not heed the general movement of all prices. What matters for them is the existence of discrepancies between the prices of the complementary factors of production and the anticipated prices of the products. No businessman embarks upon a definite production project because he believes that *the prices,* i.e., the prices of all goods and services, will rise. He engages himself if he believes that he can profit from a difference between the prices of goods of various orders. In a world with a secular tendency toward falling prices, such opportunities for earning profit will appear in the same way in which they appear in a world with a secular trend toward rising prices. The expectation of a *general* progressive upward movement of *all* prices does not bring about intensified production and improvement in well-being. It results in the "flight to real values," in the crack-up boom and the complete breakdown of the monetary system.

If the opinion that the prices of all commodities will drop becomes general, the short-term market rate of interest is lowered by the amount of the negative price premium.[26] Thus the entrepreneur employing borrowed funds is secured against the consequences of such a drop in prices to the same extent to which, under conditions

26. Cf. below, pp. 541–545.

of rising prices, the lender is secured through the price premium against the consequences of falling purchasing power.

A secular tendency toward a rise in the monetary unit's purchasing power would require rules of thumb on the part of businessmen and investors other than those developed under the secular tendency toward a fall in its purchasing power. But it would certainly not influence substantially the course of economic affairs. It would not remove the urge of people to improve their material well-being as far as possible by an appropriate arrangement of production. It would not deprive the economic system of the factors making for material improvement, namely, the striving of enterprising promoters after profit and the readiness of the public to buy those commodities which are apt to provide them the greatest satisfaction at the lowest costs.

Such observations are certainly not a plea for a policy of deflation. They imply merely a refutation of the ineradicable inflationist fables. They unmask the illusiveness of Lord Keyne's doctrine that the source of poverty and distress, of depression of trade, and of unemployment is to be seen in a "contractionist pressure." It is not true that "a deflationary pressure . . . would have . . . prevented the development of modern industry." It is not true that credit expansion brings about the "miracle . . . of turning a stone into bread."[27]

Economics recommends neither inflationary nor deflationary policy. It does not urge the governments to tamper with the market's choice of a medium of exchange. It establishes only the following truths:

1. By committing itself to an inflationary or deflationary policy a government does not promote the public welfare, the commonweal, or the interests of the whole nation. It merely favors one or several groups of the population at the expense of other groups.

2. It is impossible to know in advance which group will be favored by a definite inflationary or deflationary measure and to what extent. These effects depend on the whole complex of the market data involved. They also depend largely on the speed of the inflationary or deflationary movements and may be completely reversed with the progress of these movements.

3. At any rate, a monetary expansion results in misinvestment of capital and overconsumption. It leaves the nation as a whole poorer, not richer. These problems are dealt with in Chapter XX.

27. Quoted from: *International Clearing Union, Text of a Paper Containing Proposals by British Experts for an International Clearing Union, April 8, 1943* (published by British Information Services, an Agency of the British Government), p. 12.

4. Continued inflation must finally end in the crack-up boom, the complete breakdown of the currency system.

5. Deflationary policy is costly for the treasury and unpopular with the masses. But inflationary policy is a boon for the treasury and very popular with the ignorant. Practically, the danger of deflation is but slight and the danger of inflation tremendous.

19. The Gold Standard

Men have chosen the precious metals gold and silver for the money service on account of their mineralogical, physical, and chemical features. The use of money in a market economy is a praxeologically necessary fact. That gold—and not something else—is used as money is merely a historical fact and as such cannot be conceived by catallactics. In monetary history too, as in all other branches of history, one must resort to historical understanding. If one takes pleasure in calling the gold standard a "barbarous relic,"[28] one cannot object to the application of the same term to every historically determined institution. Then the fact that the British speak English—and not Danish, German, or French—is a barbarous relic too, and every Briton who opposes the substitution of Esperanto for English is no less dogmatic and orthodox than those who do not wax rapturous about the plans for a managed currency.

The demonetization of silver and the establishment of gold monometallism was the outcome of deliberate government interference with monetary matters. It is pointless to raise the question concerning what would have happened in the absence of these policies. But it must not be forgotten that it was not the intention of the governments to establish the gold standard. What the governments aimed at was the double standard. They wanted to substitute a rigid, government-decreed exchange ratio between gold and silver for the fluctuating market ratios between the independently coexistent gold and silver coins. The monetary doctrines underlying these endeavors misconstrued the market phenomena in that complete way in which only bureaucrats can misconstrue them. The attempts to create a double standard of both metals, gold and silver, failed lamentably. It was this failure which generated the gold standard. The emergence of the gold standard was the manifestation of a crushing defeat of the governments and their cherished doctrines.

In the seventeenth century the rates at which the English government tariffed the coins overvalued the guinea with regard to silver and thus made the silver coins disappear. Only those silver coins which

28. Lord Keynes in the speech delivered before the House of Lords, May 23, 1944.

were much worn by usage or in any other way defaced or reduced in weight remained in current use; it did not pay to export and to sell them on the bullion market. Thus England got the gold standard against the intention of its government. Only much later the laws made the *de facto* gold standard a *de jure* standard. The government abandoned further fruitless attempts to pump silver standard coins into the market and minted silver only as subsidiary coins with a limited legal tender power. These subsidiary coins were not money, but money-substitutes. Their exchange value depended not on their silver content, but on the fact that they could be exchanged at every instant, without delay and without cost, at their full face value against gold. They were *de facto* silver printed notes, claims against a definite amount of gold.

Later in the course of the nineteenth century the double standard resulted in a similar way in France and in the other countries of the Latin Monetary Union in the emergence of *de facto* gold monometallism. When the drop in the price of silver in the later 'seventies would automatically have effected the replacement of the *de facto* gold standard by the *de facto* silver standard, these governments suspended the coinage of silver in order to preserve the gold standard. In the United States the price structure on the bullion market had already, before the outbreak of the Civil War, transformed the legal bimetallism into *de facto* gold monometallism. After the greenback period there ensued a struggle between the friends of the gold standard on the one hand and those of silver on the other hand. The result was a victory for the gold standard. Once the economically most advanced nations had adopted the gold standard, all other nations followed suit. After the great inflationary adventures of the first World War most countries hastened to return to the gold standard or the gold exchange standard.

The gold standard was the world standard of the age of capitalism, increasing welfare, liberty, and democracy, both political and economic. In the eyes of the free traders its main eminence was precisely the fact that it was an international standard as required by international trade and the transactions of the international money and capital market.[29] It was the medium of exchange by means of which Western industrialism and Western capital had borne Western civilization into the remotest parts of the earth's surface, everywhere destroying the fetters of age-old prejudices and superstitions, sowing the seeds of new life and new well-being, freeing minds and souls, and creating riches unheard of before. It accompanied the triumphal

29. T. E. Gregory, *The Gold Standard and Its Future* (1d ed. London, 1934), pp. 22 ff.

unprecedented progress of Western liberalism ready to unite all nations into a community of free nations peacefully cooperating with one another.

It is easy to understand why people viewed the gold standard as the symbol of this greatest and most beneficial of all historical changes. All those intent upon sabotaging the evolution toward welfare, peace, freedom, and democracy loathed the gold standard, and not only on account of its economic significance. In their eyes the gold standard was the labarum, the symbol, of all those doctrines and policies they wanted to destroy. In the struggle against the gold standard much more was at stake than commodity prices and foreign exchange rates.

The nationalists are fighting the gold standard because they want to sever their countries from the world market and to establish national autarky as far as possible. Interventionist governments and pressure groups are fighting the gold standard because they consider it the most serious obstacle to their endeavors to manipulate prices and wage rates. But the most fanatical attacks against gold are made by those intent upon credit expansion. With them credit expansion is the panacea for all economic ills. It could lower or even entirely abolish interest rates, raise wages and prices for the benefit of all except the parasitic capitalists and the exploiting employers, free the state from the necessity of balancing its budget—in short, make all decent people prosperous and happy. Only the gold standard, that devilish contrivance of the wicked and stupid "orthodox" economists, prevents mankind from attaining everlasting prosperity.

The gold standard is certainly not a perfect or ideal standard. There is no such thing as perfection in human things. But nobody is in a position to tell us how something more satisfactory could be put in place of the gold standard. The purchasing power of gold is not stable. But the very notions of stability and unchangeability of purchasing power are absurd. In a living and changing world there cannot be any such thing as stability of purchasing power. In the imaginary construction of an evenly rotating economy there is no room left for a medium of exchange. It is an essential feature of money that its purchasing power is changing. In fact, the adversaries of the gold standard do not want to make money's purchasing power stable. They want rather to give to the governments the power to manipulate purchasing power without being hindered by an "external" factor, namely, the money relation of the gold standard.

The main objection raised against the gold standard is that it makes operative in the determination of prices a factor which no government can control—the vicissitudes of gold production. Thus an "external" or "automatic" force restrains a national government's power to make its subjects as prosperous as it would like to make them. The international capitalists dictate and the nation's sovereignty becomes a sham.

However, the futility of interventionist policies has nothing at all to do with monetary matters. It will be shown later why all isolated measures of government interference with market phenomena must fail to attain the ends sought. If the interventionist government wants to remedy the shortcomings of its first interferences by going further and further, it finally converts its country's economic system into socialism of the German pattern. Then it abolishes the domestic market altogether, and with it money and all monetary problems, even though it may retain some of the terms and labels of the market economy.[30] In both cases it is not the gold standard that frustrates the good intentions of the benevolent authority.

The significance of the fact that the gold standard makes the increase in the supply of gold depend upon the profitability of producing gold is, of course, that it limits the government's power to resort to inflation. The gold standard makes the determination of money's purchasing power independent of the changing ambitions and doctrines of political parties and pressure groups. This is not a defect of the gold standard; it is its main excellence. Every method of manipulating purchasing power is by necessity arbitrary. All methods recommended for the discovery of an allegedly objective and "scientific" yardstick for monetary manipulation are based on the illusion that changes in purchasing power can be "measured." The gold standard removes the determination of cash-induced changes in purchasing power from the political arena. Its general acceptance requires the acknowledgment of the truth that one cannot make all people richer by printing money. The abhorrence of the gold standard is inspired by the superstition that omnipotent governments can create wealth out of little scraps of paper.

It has been asserted that the gold standard too is a manipulated standard. The governments may influence the height of gold's purchasing power either by credit expansion, even if it is kept within the limits drawn by considerations of preserving the redeemability of the money-substitutes, or indirectly by furthering measures which induce people to restrict the size of their cash holdings. This is true. It cannot be denied that the rise in commodity prices which occurred between 1896 and 1914 was to a great extent provoked by such government policies. But the main thing is that the gold standard keeps all such endeavors toward lowering money's purchasing power within narrow limits. The inflationists are fighting the gold standard pre-

30. Cf. below, Chapters XXVII–XXXI.

cisely because they consider these limits a serious obstacle to the realization of their plans.

What the expansionists call the defects of the gold standard are indeed its very eminence and usefulness. It checks large-scale inflationary ventures on the part of governments. The gold standard did not fail. The governments were eager to destroy it, because they were committed to the fallacies that credit expansion is an appropriate means of lowering the rate of interest and of "improving" the balance of trade.

No government is, however, powerful enough to abolish the gold standard. Gold is the money of international trade and of the supernational economic community of mankind. It cannot be affected by measures of governments whose sovereignty is limited to definite countries. As long as a country is not economically self-sufficient in the strict sense of the term, as long as there are still some loopholes left in the walls by which national governments try to isolate their countries from the rest of the world, gold is still used as money. It does not matter that governments confiscate the gold coins and bullion they can seize and punish those holding gold as felons. The language of bilateral clearing agreements by means of which governments are intent upon eliminating gold from international trade, avoids any reference to gold. But the turnovers performed on the ground of those agreements are calculated on gold prices. He who buys or sells on a foreign market calculates the advantages and disadvantages of such transactions in gold. In spite of the fact that a country has severed its local currency from any link with gold, its domestic structure of prices remains closely connected with gold and the gold prices of the world market. If a government wants to sever its domestic price structure from that of the world market, it must resort to other measures, such as prohibitive import and export duties and embargoes. Nationalization of foreign trade, whether effected openly or directly by foreign exchange control, does not eliminate gold. The governments qua traders are trading by the use of gold as a medium of exchange.

The struggle against gold which is one of the main concerns of all contemporary governments must not be looked upon as an isolated phenomenon. It is but one item in the gigantic process of destruction which is the mark of our time. People fight the gold standard because they want to substitute national autarky for free trade, war for peace, totalitarian government omnipotence for liberty.

It may happen one day that technology will discover a method of enlarging the supply of gold at such a low cost that gold will become useless for the monetary service. Then people will have to replace the gold standard by another standard. It is futile to bother today about the way in which this problem will be solved. We do not know anything about the conditions under which the decision will have to be made.

International Monetary Cooperation

The international gold standard works without any action on the part of governments. It is effective real cooperation of all members of the world-embracing market economy. There is no need for any government to interfere in order to make the gold standard work as an international standard.

What governments call international monetary cooperation is concerted action for the sake of credit expansion. They have learned that credit expansion, when limited to one country only, results in an external drain. They believe that it is only the external drain that frustrates their plans of lowering the rate of interest and thus of creating an everlasting boom. If all governments were to cooperate in their expansionist policies, they think, they could remove this obstacle. What is required is an international bank issuing fiduciary media which are dealt with as money-substitutes by all people in all countries.

There is no need to stress again here the point that what makes it impossible to lower the rate of interest by means of credit expansion is not merely the external drain. This fundamental issue is dealt with exhaustively in other chapters and sections of this book.[31]

But there is another important question to be raised.

Let us assume that there exists an international bank issuing fiduciary media the clientele of which is the world's whole population. It does not matter whether these money-substitutes go directly into the cash holdings of the individuals and firms, or are only kept by the various nations' central banks as reserves against the issuance of national money-substitutes. The deciding point is that there is a uniform world currency. The national banknotes and checkbook money are redeemable in money-substitutes issued by the international bank. The necessity of keeping its national currency at par with the international currency limits the power of every nation's central banking system to expand credit. But the world bank is restrained only by those factors which limit credit expansion on the part of a single bank operating in an isolated economic system or in the whole world.

We may as well assume that the international bank is not a bank issuing money-substitutes a part of which are fiduciary media, but a world authority issuing international fiat money. Gold has been entirely demonetized. The only money in use is that created by the international authority. The international authority is free to increase the quantity of this money provided it does not go so far as to bring about the crack-up boom and the breakdown of the currency.

31. Cf. above, pp. 441–442, and below, pp. 550–586.

Then the ideal of the Keynesians is realized. There is an institution operating which can exercise an "expansionist pressure on world trade."

However, the champions of such plans have neglected a fundamental problem, namely, that of the distribution of the additional quantities of this credit money or of this paper money.

Let us assume that the international authority increases the amount of its issuance by a definite sum, all of which goes to one country, Ruritania. The final result of this inflationary action will be a rise in prices of commodities and services all over the world. But while this process is going on, the conditions of the citizens of various countries are affected in a different way. The Ruritanians are the first group blessed by the additional manna. They have more money in their pockets while the rest of the world's inhabitants have not yet got a share of the new money. They can bid higher prices, while the others cannot. Therefore the Ruritanians withdraw more goods from the world market than they did before. The non-Ruritanians are forced to restrict their consumption because they cannot compete with the higher prices paid by the Ruritanians. While the process of adjusting prices to the altered money relation is still in progress, the Ruritanians are in an advantageous position against the non-Ruritanians. When the process finally comes to an end, the Ruritanians have been enriched at the expense of the non-Ruritanians.

The main problem in such expansionist ventures is the proportion according to which the additional money is to be allotted to the various nations. Each nation will be eager to advocate a mode of distribution which will give it the greatest possible share in the additional currency. The industrially backward nations of the East will, for instance, probably recommend equal distribution per capita of population, a mode which would obviously favor them at the expense of the industrially advanced nations. Whatever mode may be adopted, all nations would be dissatisfied and would complain of unfair treatment. Serious conflicts would ensue and would disrupt the whole scheme.

It would be irrelevant to object that this problem did not play an important role in the negotiations which preceded the establishment of the International Monetary Fund and that it was easy to reach an agreement concerning the use of the Fund's resources. The Bretton Woods Conference was held under very particular circumstances. Most of the participating nations were at that time entirely dependent on the benevolence of the United States. They would have been doomed if the United States had stopped fighting for their freedom and aiding them materially by lend-lease. The government of the United States, on the other hand, looked upon the monetary agreement as a scheme for a disguised continuation of lend-lease after the cessation of hostilities. The United States was ready to give and the other participants—especially those of the European countries, most of them at that time still occupied by the German armies, and those of the Asiatic countries—were ready to take whatever was offered to them. The problems involved will become discernible once the delusive attitude of the United States toward financial and trade matters is replaced by a more realistic mentality.

The International Monetary Fund did not achieve what its sponsors had expected. At the annual meetings of the Fund there is a good deal of discussion, and occasionally pertinent observations and criticisms concerning the monetary and credit policies of governments and central banks are brought forward. The Fund itself engages in lending and borrowing transactions with various governments and central banks. It considers its main function to be that of assisting governments to maintain an unrealistic exchange rate for their overexpanded national currency. The methods it resorts to in these endeavors do not differ essentially from those always applied for this purpose. Monetary affairs in the world are going on as if no Bretton Woods Agreement and no International Monetary Fund existed.

The constellation of the world's political and economic affairs enabled the American government to keep its promise of letting foreign governments and central banks get an ounce of gold by paying thirty-five dollars. But the continuation and intensification of the American "expansionist" policy has considerably increased the withdrawal of gold and makes people worry about the future of monetary conditions. They are frightened by the spectre of a farther increase in the demand for gold that may exhaust the gold funds of the United States and force it to abandon its present methods of dealing with gold.

The characteristic feature of the public discussion of the problems involved is that it carefully avoids mentioning the facts that are causing the extension of the demand for gold. No reference is made to the policies of deficit spending and credit expansion. Instead, complaints are raised about something called "insufficient liquidity" and a shortage of "reserves." The remedy suggested is more liquidity, to be achieved by "creating" new additional "reserves." This means it is proposed to cure the effects of inflation by more inflation.

There is need to remember that the policies of the American government and the Bank of England of maintaining on the London gold market a price of 35 dollars for an ounce of gold is the only measure that today prevents the Western nations from embarking upon boundless inflation. These policies are not immediately affected by the size of the various nations' "reserves." The plans for new "reserves" seem therefore not to concern directly the problem of the relation of gold to the dollar. They concern it indirectly as they try to divert the public's attention from the real problem, inflation. For the rest, the official doctrine relies upon the long since discredited balance-of-payments interpretation of monetary troubles.

XVIII. ACTION IN THE PASSING OF TIME

1. Perspective in the Valuation of Time Periods

ACTING man distinguishes the time before satisfaction of a want is attained and the time for which the satisfaction continues.

Action always aims at the removal of future uneasiness, be it only the future of the impending instant. Between the setting in of action and the attainment of the end sought there always elapses a fraction of time, viz., the maturing time in which the seed sown by the action grows to maturity. The most obvious example is provided by agriculture. Between the tilling of the soil and the ripening of the fruit there passes a considerable period of time. Another example is the improvement of the quality of wine by aging. In some cases, however, the maturing time is so short that ordinary speech may assert that the success appears instantly.

As far as action requires the employment of labor, it is concerned with the working time. The performance of every kind of labor absorbs time. In some cases the working time is so short that people say the performance requires no time at all.

Only in rare cases does a simple, indivisible and nonrepeated act suffice to attain the end aimed at. As a rule what separates the actor from the goal of his endeavors is more than one step only. He must make many steps. And every further step to be added to those previously made raises anew the question whether or not he should continue marching toward the goal once chosen. Most goals are so far away that only determined persistence leads to them. Persevering action, unflinchingly directed to the end sought, is needed in order to succeed. The total expenditure of time required, i.e., working time plus maturing time, may be called the period of production. The period of production is long in some cases and short in other cases. It is sometimes so short that it can be entirely neglected in practice.

The increment in want-satisfaction which the attainment of the end brings about is temporally limited. The result produced extends services only over a period of time which we may call the duration of serviceableness. The duration of serviceableness is shorter with some products and longer with other goods which are commonly called durable goods. Hence acting man must always take into account the period of production and the duration of serviceableness of the product. In estimating the disutility of a project considered he is not only concerned with the expenditure of material factors and labor required, but also with the period of production. In estimating the utility of the expected product he is concerned with the duration of its serviceableness. Of course, the more durable a product is, the greater is the amount of services it renders. But if these services are not cumulatively available on the same date, but extended piecemeal over a certain period of time, the time element, as will be shown, plays a particular role in their evaluation. It makes a difference whether *n* units of service are rendered on the same date or whether they are stretched over a period of *n* days in such a way that only one unit is available daily.

It is important to realize that the period of production as well as the duration of serviceableness are categories of human action and not concepts constructed by philosophers, economists, and historians as mental tools for their interpretation of events. They are essential elements present in every act of reasoning that precedes and directs action. It is necessary to stress this point because Böhm-Bawerk, to whom economics owes the discovery of the role played by the period of production, failed to comprehend the difference.

Acting man does not look at his condition with the eyes of a historian. He is not concerned with how the present situation originated. His only concern is to make the best use of the means available today for the best possible removal of future uneasiness. The past does not count for him. He has at his disposal a definite quantity of material factors of production. He does not ask whether these factors are nature-given or the product of production processes accomplished in the past. It does not matter for him how great a quantity of nature-given, i.e., original material factors of production and labor, was expended in their production and how much time these processes of production have absorbed. He values the available means exclusively from the aspect of the services they can render him in his endeavors to make future conditions more satisfactory. The period of production and the duration of serviceableness are for him categories in planning future action, not concepts of academic retrospection and historical research. They play a role in so far as the actor has to choose between periods of production of different length and between the production of more durable and less durable goods.

Action is not concerned with the future in general, but always with a definite and limited fraction of the future. This fraction is limited, on the one side, by the instant in which the action must take place. Where its other end lies depends on the actor's decision and choice. There are people who are concerned with only the impending instant. There are other people whose provident care stretches far beyond the prospective length of their own life. We may call the fraction of future time for which the actor in a definite action wants to provide in some way and to some extent, the period of provision. In the same way in which acting man chooses among various kinds of want-satisfaction within the same fraction of future time, he chooses also between want-satisfaction in the nearer and in the remoter future. Every choice implies also a choice of a period of provision. In making up his mind how to employ the various means available for the removal of uneasiness, man also determines implicitly the period of provision. In the market economy the demand of the consumers also determines the length of the period of provision.

There are various methods available for a lengthening of the period of provision:

1. The accumulation of larger stocks of consumers' goods destined for later consumption.

2. The production of goods which are more durable.

3. The production of goods requiring a longer period of production.

4. The choice of methods of production consuming more time for the production of goods which could also be produced within a shorter period of production.

The first two methods do not require any further comment. The third and the fourth methods must be scrutinized more closely.

It is one of the fundamental data of human life and action that the shortest processes of production, i.e., those with the shortest period of production, do not remove felt uneasiness entirely. If all those goods which these shortest processes can provide are produced, unsatisfied wants remain and incentive to further action is still present. As acting man prefers those processes which, other things being equal, produce the products in the shortest time,[1] only such processes are left for further action which consume more time. People embark upon these more time-consuming processes because they value the increment in satisfaction expected more highly than the disadvantage of waiting longer for their fruits. Böhm-Bawerk speaks of the higher productivity of roundabout ways of production requiring more time. It is more appropriate to speak of the higher physical productiv-

1. Why man proceeds in this way, will be shown on the following pages.

ity of production processes requiring more time. The higher productivity of these processes does not always consist in the fact that they produce—with the same quantity of factors of production expended—a greater quantity of products. More often it consists in the fact that they produce products which could not be produced at all in shorter periods of production. These processes are not roundabout processes. They are the shortest and quickest way to the goal chosen. If one wants to catch more fish, there is no other method available than the substitution of fishing with the aid of nets and canoes for fishing without the aid of this equipment. There is no better, shorter, and cheaper method for the production of aspirin known than that adopted by the chemical plants. If one disregards error and ignorance, there cannot be any doubt about the highest productivity and expediency of the processes chosen. If people had not considered them the most direct processes, viz., those leading by the shortest way to the end sought, they would not have adopted them.

The lengthening of the period of provision through the mere accumulation of stocks of consumers' goods is the outcome of the desire to provide in advance for a longer period of time. The same is valid for the production of goods the durability of which is greater in proportion to the greater expenditure of factors of production required.[2] But if temporally remoter goals are aimed at, lengthening of the period of production is a necessary corollary of the venture. The end sought cannot be attained in a shorter period of production.

The postponement of an act of consumption means that the individual prefers the satisfaction which later consumption will provide to the satisfaction which immediate consumption could provide. The choice of a longer period of production means that the actor values the product of the process bearing fruit only at a later date more highly than the products which a process consuming less time could provide. In such deliberations and the resulting choices the period of production appears as waiting time. It was the great contribution of Jevons and Böhm-Bawerk to have shown the role played by taking account of waiting time.

If acting men were not to pay heed to the length of the waiting time, they would never say that a goal is temporally so distant that one cannot consider aiming at it. Faced with the alternative of choosing between two processes of production which render different output with the same input, they would always prefer that process which renders the greater quantity of the same products or better products

2. If the lengthening of durability were not at least proportionate to the increment in expenditure needed, it would be more advantageous to increase the quantity of units of a shorter durability.

in the same quantity, even if this result could be attained only by lengthening the period of production. Increments in input which result in a more than proportionate increase in the products' duration of serviceableness would unconditionally be deemed advantageous. The fact that men do not act in this way evidences that they value fractions of time of the same length in a different way according as they are nearer or remoter from the instant of the actor's decision. Other things being equal, satisfaction in a nearer period of the future is preferred to satisfaction in a more distant period; disutility is seen in waiting.

This fact is already implied in the statement stressed in the opening of this chapter that man distinguishes the time before satisfaction is attained and the time for the duration of which there is satisfaction. If any role at all is played by the time element in human life, there cannot be any question of equal valuation of nearer and remoter periods of the same length. Such an equal valuation would mean that people do not care whether success is attained sooner or later. It would be tantamount to a complete elimination of the time element from the process of valuation.

The mere fact that goods with a longer duration of serviceableness are valued more highly than those with a shorter duration does not yet in itself imply a consideration of time. A roof that can protect a house against the weather during a period of ten years is more valuable than a roof which renders this service only for a period of five years. The quantity of service rendered is different in both cases. But the question which we have to deal with is whether or not an actor in making his choices attaches to a service to be available in a later period of the future the same value he attaches to a service available at an earlier period.

2. Time Preference as an Essential Requisite of Action

The answer to this question is that acting man does not appraise time periods merely with regard to their dimension. His choices regarding the removal of future uneasiness are directed by the categories *sooner* and *later*. Time for man is not a homogeneous substance of which only length counts. It is not a *more* or a *less* in dimension. It is an irreversible flux the fractions of which appear in different perspective according to whether they are nearer to or remoter from the instant of valuation and decision. Satisfaction of a want in the nearer future is, other things being equal, preferred to that in the farther distant future. Present goods are more valuable than future goods.

Time preference is a categorial requisite of human action. No mode of action can be thought of in which satisfaction within a nearer period of the future is not—other things being equal—preferred to that in a later period. The very act of gratifying a desire implies that gratification at the present instant is preferred to that at a later instant. He who consumes a nonperishable good instead of postponing consumption for an indefinite later moment thereby reveals a higher valuation of present satisfaction as compared with later satisfaction. If he were not to prefer satisfaction in a nearer period of the future to that in a remoter period, he would never consume and so satisfy wants. He would always accumulate, he would never consume and enjoy. He would not consume today, but he would not consume tomorrow either, as the morrow would confront him with the same alternative.

Not only the first step toward want-satisfaction, but also any further step is guided by time preference. Once the desire *a* to which the scale of values assigns the rank 1 is satisfied, one must choose between the desire *b* to which the rank 2 is assigned and *c* that desire of tomorrow to which—in the absence of time preference—the rank 1 would have been assigned. If *b* is preferred to *c*, the choice clearly involves time preference. Purposive striving after want-satisfaction must needs be guided by a preference for satisfaction in the nearer future over that in a remoter future.

The conditions under which modern man of the capitalist West must act are different from those under which his primitive ancestors lived and acted. As a result of the providential care of our forebears we have at our disposal an ample stock of intermediate products (capital goods or produced factors of production) and of consumers' goods. Our activities are designed for a longer period of provision because we are the lucky heirs of a past which has lengthened, step by step, the period of provision and has bequeathed to us the means to expand the waiting period. In acting we are concerned with longer periods and are aiming at an even satisfaction in all parts of the period chosen as the period of provision. We are in a position to rely upon a continuing influx of consumers' goods and have at our disposal not only stocks of goods ready for consumption but also stocks of producers' goods out of which our continuous efforts again and again make new consumers' goods mature. In our dealing with this increasing "stream of income," says the superficial observer, there is no heed paid to any considerations related to a different valuation of present and of future goods. We synchronize, he asserts, and thus the time element loses any importance for the conduct of affairs. It is, therefore, pointless, he continues, in the interpretation of modern conditions to resort to time preference.

The fundamental error involved in this popular objection is caused, like so many other errors, by a lamentable misapprehension of the imaginary construction of the evenly rotating economy. In the frame of this imaginary construction no change occurs; there prevails an unvarying course of all affairs. In the evenly rotating economy consequently nothing is altered in the allocation of goods for the satisfaction of wants in nearer and in remoter periods of the future. No one plans any change because—according to our assumptions—the prevailing allocation best serves him and because he does not believe that any possible rearrangement could improve his condition. No one wants to increase his consumption in a nearer period of the future at the expense of his consumption in a more distant period or vice versa because the existing mode of allocation pleases him better than any other thinkable and feasible mode.

The praxeological distinction between capital and income is a category of thought based on a different valuation of want-satisfaction in various periods of the future. In the imaginary construction of the evenly rotating economy it is implied that the whole income but not more than the income is consumed and that therefore the capital remains unchanged. An equilibrium is reached in the allocation of goods for want-satisfaction in different periods of the future. It is permissible to describe this state of affairs by asserting that nobody wants to consume tomorrow's income today. We have precisely designed the imaginary construction of the evenly rotating economy in such a way as to make it fit just this condition. But it is necessary to realize that we can assert with the same apodictic assurance that, in the evenly rotating economy, nobody wants to have more of any commodity than he really has. These statements are true with regard to the evenly rotating economy because they are implied in our definition of this imaginary construction. They are nonsensical when asserted with regard to a changing economy which is the only real economy. As soon as a change in the data occurs, the individuals are faced anew with the necessity of choosing both between various modes of want-satisfaction in the same period and between want-satisfaction in different periods. An increment can be either employed for immediate consumption or invested for further production. No matter how the actors employ it, their choice must needs be the result of a weighing of the advantages expected from want-satisfaction in different periods of the future. In the world of reality, in the living and changing universe, each individual in each of his actions is forced to choose between satisfaction in various periods of time. Some people consume all that they earn, others consume a part of their capital, others save a part of their income.

Those contesting the universal validity of time preference fail to explain why a man does not always invest a sum of 100 dollars available today, although these 100 dollars would increase to 104 dollars within a year's time. It is obvious that this man in consuming this sum today is determined by a judgment of value which values 100 present dollars higher than 104 dollars available a year later. But even in case he chooses to invest these 100 dollars, the meaning is not that he prefers satisfaction in a later period to that of today. It means that he values 100 dollars today less than 104 dollars a year later. Every penny spent today is, precisely under the conditions of a capitalist economy in which institutions make it possible to invest even the smallest sums, a proof of the higher valuation of present satisfaction as compared with later satisfaction.

The theorem of time preference must be demonstrated in a double way. First for the case of plain saving in which people must choose between the immediate consumption of a quantity of goods and the later consumption of the same quantity. Second for the case of capitalist saving in which the choice is to be made between the immediate consumption of a quantity of goods and the later consumption either of a greater quantity or of goods which are fit to provide a satisfaction which—except for the difference in time—is valued more highly. The proof has been given for both cases. No other case is thinkable.

It is possible to search for a psychological understanding of the problem of time preference. Impatience and the pains caused by waiting are certainly psychological phenomena. One may approach their elucidation by referring to the temporal limitations of human life, to the individual's coming into existence, his growth and maturing, and his inevitable decay and passing away. There is in the course of a man's life a right moment for everything as well as a *too early* and a *too late*. However, the praxeological problem is in no way related to psychological issues. We must conceive, not merely understand. We must conceive that a man who does not prefer satisfaction within a nearer period of the future to that in a remoter period would never achieve consumption and enjoyment at all.

Neither must the praxeological problem be confused with the physiological. He who wants to live to see the later day, must first of all care for the preservation of his life in the intermediate period. Survival and appeasement of vital needs are thus requirements for the satisfaction of any wants in the remoter future. This makes us understand why in all those situations in which bare life in the strict sense of the term is at stake satisfaction in the nearer future is preferred to that in later periods. But we are dealing with action as such, not with the motives directing its course. In the same way in which as economists we do not ask why albumin, carbohydrates, and fat are demanded by man, we do not inquire why the satisfaction of vital needs appears imperative and does not brook any delay. We must conceive that consumption and enjoyment of any kind presuppose a preference for present satisfaction to later satisfaction. The knowledge provided by this insight far exceeds the orbit for which the physiological facts concerned provide explanation. It refers to every kind of want-satisfaction, not only to the satisfaction of the vital necessities of mere survival.

It is important to stress this point because the term "supply of subsistence, available for advances of subsistence," as used by Böhm-Bawerk, can easily be misinterpreted. It is certainly one of the tasks of this stock to provide the means for a satisfaction of the bare necessities of life and thus to secure survival. But besides it must be large enough to satisfy, beyond the requirements of necessary maintenance for the waiting time, all those wants and desires which—apart from mere survival—are considered more urgent than the harvesting of the physically more abundant fruits of production processes consuming more time.

Böhm-Bawerk declared that every lengthening of the period of production depends on the condition that "a sufficient quantity of present goods is available to make it possible to overbridge the lengthened average interval between the starting of preparatory work and the harvesting of its product."[3] The expression "sufficient quantity" needs elucidation. It does not mean a quantity sufficient for necessary sustenance. The quantity in question must be large enough to secure the satisfaction of all those wants the satisfaction of which during the waiting time is considered more urgent than the advantages which a still greater lengthening of the period of production would provide. If the quantity in question were smaller, a shortening of the period of production would appear advantageous; the increase in the quantity of products or the improvement of their quality to be expected from the preservation of the longer period of production would no longer be considered a sufficient remuneration for the restriction of consumption enjoined during the waiting time. Whether or not the supply of subsistence is sufficient, does not depend on any

3. Böhm-Bawerk, *Kleinere Abhandlungen über Kapital und Zins,* vol. II in *Gesammelte Schriften,* ed. F. X. Weiss (Vienna, 1926), p. 169.

physiological or other facts open to objective determination by the methods of technology and physiology. The metaphorical term "overbridge," suggesting a body of water the breadth of which poses to the bridge builder an objectively determined task, is misleading. The quantity in question is valued by men, and their subjective judgments decide whether or not it is sufficient.

Even in a hypothetical world in which nature provides every man with the means for the preservation of biological survival (in the strict sense of the term), in which the most important foodstuffs are not scarce and action is not concerned with the provision for bare life, the phenomenon of time preference would be present and direct all actions.[4]

Observations on the Evolution of the Time-Preference Theory

It seems plausible to assume that the mere fact that interest is graduated in reference to periods of time should have directed the attention of the economists, intent upon developing a theory of interest, upon the role played by time. However, the classical economists were prevented by their faulty theory of value and their misconstruction of the cost concept from recognizing the significance of the time element.

Economics owes the time-preference theory to William Stanley Jevons and its elaboration, most of all, to Eugen von Böhm-Bawerk. Böhm-Bawerk was the first to formulate correctly the problem to be solved, the first to unmask the fallacies implied in the productivity theories of interest, and the first to stress the role played by the period of production. But he did not entirely succeed in avoiding the pitfalls in the elucidation of the interest problem. His demonstration of the universal validity of time preference is inadequate because it is based on psychological considerations. However, psychology can never demonstrate the validity of a praxeological theorem. It may show that some people or many people let themselves be influenced by certain motives. It can never make evident that all human action is necessarily dominated by a definite categorial element which, without any exception, is operative in every instance of action.[5]

The second shortcoming of Böhm-Bawerk's reasoning was his misconstruction of the concept of the period of production. He was not fully aware of the fact that the period of production is a praxeological category and that the role it plays in action consists entirely in the choices acting man makes between periods of production of different

4. Time preference is not specifically human. It is an inherent feature of the behavior of all living things. The distinction of man consists in the very fact that with him time preference is not inexorable and the lengthening of the period of provision not merely instinctive as with certain animals that store food, but the result of a process of valuation.

5. For a detailed critical analysis of this part of Böhm-Bawerk's reasoning the reader is referred to Mises, *Nationalökonomie,* pp. 439–443.

length. The length of time expended in the past for the production of capital goods available today does not count at all. These capital goods are valued only with regard to their usefulness for future want-satisfaction. The "average period of production" is an empty concept. What determines action is the fact that in choosing among various ways which can remove future uneasiness the length of the waiting time in each case is a necessary element.

It was an outcome of these two errors that Böhm-Bawerk in the elaboration of his theory did not entirely avoid the productivity approach which he himself had so brilliantly refuted in his critical history of the doctrines of capital and interest.

These observations do not detract at all from the imperishable merits of Böhm-Bawerk's contributions. It was on the foundation laid by him that later economists—foremost among them Knut Wicksell, Frank Albert Fetter and Irving Fisher—were successful in perfecting the time-preference theory.

It is customary to express the essence of the time-preference theory by saying that there prevails a preference for present over future goods. In dealing with this mode of expression some economists have been puzzled by the fact that in some cases present uses are worth less than future uses. However, the problem raised by the apparent exceptions is caused merely by a misapprehension of the true state of affairs.

There are enjoyments which cannot be had at the same time. A man cannot on the same evening attend performances of *Carmen* and of *Hamlet*. In buying a ticket he must choose between the two performances. If tickets to both theaters for the same evening are presented to him as a gift, he must likewise choose. He may think with regard to the ticket which he refuses: "I don't care for it just now," or "If only it had been later."[6] However, this does not mean that he prefers future goods to present goods. He does not have to choose between future goods and present goods. He must choose between two enjoyments both of which he cannot have together. This is the dilemma in every instance of choosing. In the present state of his affairs he may prefer *Hamlet* to *Carmen*. The different conditions of a later date may possibly result in another decision.

The second seeming exception is presented by the case of perishable goods. They may be available in abundance in one season of the year and may be scarce in other seasons. However, the difference between ice in winter and ice in summer is not that between a present good and a future good. It is the difference between a good that loses its specific usefulness even if not consumed and another good which requires a different process of production. Ice available in winter can only be used in summer when subjected to a special process of conservation. It is, in respect to ice utilizable in summer, at best one of

6. Cf. F. A. Fetter, *Economic Principles* (New York, 1923), I, 239.

the complementary factors required for production. It is impossible to increase the quantity of ice available in summer simply by restricting the consumption of ice in winter. The two things are for all practical purposes different commodities.

The case of the miser does not contradict the universal validity of time preference. The miser too, in spending some of his means for a scanty livelihood, prefers some amount of satisfaction in the nearer future to that in the remoter future. Extreme instances in which the miser denies himself even the indispensable minimum of food represent a pathological withering away of vital energy, as is the case with the man who abstains from eating out of fear of morbific germs, the man who commits suicide rather than meet a dangerous situation, and the man who cannot sleep because he is afraid of undetermined accidents which could befall him while asleep.

3. Capital Goods

As soon as those present wants are sated the satisfaction of which is considered more urgent than any provision for the morrow, people begin to save a part of the available supply of consumers' goods for later use. This postponement of consumption makes it possible to direct action toward temporally remoter ends. It is now feasible to aim at goals which could not be thought of before on account of the length of the period of production required. It is furthermore feasible to choose methods of production in which the output of products is greater per unit of input than in other methods requiring a shorter period of production. The sine qua non of any lengthening of the processes of production adopted is saving, i.e., an excess of current production over current consumption. Saving is the first step on the way toward improvement of material well-being and toward every further progress on this way.

The postponement of consumption and the accumulation of stocks of consumers' goods destined for later consumption would be practiced even in the absence of the stimulus offered by the technological superiority of processes with a longer period of production. The higher productivity of such processes consuming more time strengthens considerably the propensity to save. The sacrifice made by restricting consumption in nearer periods of the future is henceforth not only counterbalanced by the expectation of consuming the saved goods in remoter periods; it also opens the way to a more ample supply in the remoter future and to the attainment of goods which could not be procured at all without this provisional sacrifice. If acting man, other conditions being equal, were not to prefer, without exception, consumption in the nearer future to that in the remoter future, he would always save, never consume. What restricts the amount of saving and investment is time preference.

People eager to embark upon processes with a longer period of production must first accumulate, by means of saving, that quantity of consumers' goods which is needed to satisfy, during the waiting time, all those wants the satisfaction of which they consider more urgent than the increment in well-being expected from the more time-consuming process. Accumulation of capital begins with the formation of stocks of consumers' goods the consumption of which is postponed for later days. If these surpluses are merely stored and kept for later consumption, they are simply wealth or, more precisely, a reserve for rainy days and emergencies. They remain outside the orbit of production. They become integrated—economically, not physically—into production activities only when employed as means of subsistence of workers engaged in more time-consuming processes. If expended in this way, they are physically consumed. But economically they do not disappear. They are replaced first by the intermediary products of a process with a longer period of production and then later by the consumers' goods which are the final product of these processes.

All these ventures and processes are intellectually controlled by capital accounting, the acme of economic calculation in monetary terms. Without the aid of monetary calculation men could not even learn whether—apart from the length of the period of production—a definite process promises a higher productivity than another. The expenditures required by various processes cannot be weighed against one another without the aid of monetary terms. Capital accounting starts with the market prices of the capital goods available for further production, the sum of which it calls capital. It records every expenditure from this fund and the price of all incoming items induced by such expenditures. It establishes finally the ultimate outcome of all these transformations in the composition of the capital and thereby the success or the failure of the whole process. It shows not only the final result; it mirrors also every one of its intermediary stages. It produces interim balances for every day such a balance may be required and statements of profit and loss for every part or stage of the process. It is the indispensable compass of production in the market economy.

In the market economy production is a continuous, never-ending pursuit split up into an immense variety of partial processes. Innumerable processes of production with different periods of production are in progress simultaneously. They complement one another and at the same time are in rivalry with one another in competing for scarce factors of production. Continuously either new capital is accumulated by saving or previously accumulated capital is eaten up by overconsumption. Production is distributed among numerous individual plants, farms, workshops, and enterprises each of which serves only limited purposes. The intermediary products or capital goods, the produced factors of further production, change hands in the course of events; they pass from one plant to another until finally the consumers' goods reach those who use and enjoy them. The social process of production never stops. At each instant numberless processes are in progress some of which are nearer to, some remoter from, the achievement of their special tasks.

Every single performance in this ceaseless pursuit of wealth production is based upon the saving and the preparatory work of earlier generations. We are the lucky heirs of our fathers and forefathers whose saving has accumulated the capital goods with the aid of which we are working today. We favorite children of the age of electricity still derive advantage from the original saving of the primitive fishermen who, in producing the first nets and canoes, devoted a part of their working time to provision for a remoter future. If the sons of these legendary fishermen had worn out these intermediary products—nets and canoes—without replacing them by new ones, they would have consumed capital and the process of saving and capital accumulation would have had to start afresh. We are better off than earlier generations because we are equipped with the capital goods they have accumulated for us.[7]

The businessman, the acting man, is entirely absorbed in one task only: to take best advantage of all the means available for the improvement of future conditions. He does not look at the present state of affairs with the aim of analyzing and comprehending it. In classifying the means for further production and appraising their importance he adopts superficial rules of thumb. He distinguishes three classes of factors of production: the nature-given material factors, the human factor—labor, and capital goods—the intermediary factors produced in the past. He does not analyze the nature of the capital goods. They are in his eyes means of increasing the productivity of labor. Quite naïvely he ascribes to them productive power of their own. He does not trace their instrumentality back to nature and labor. He does not ask how they came into existence. They

7. These considerations explode the objections raised against the time-preference theory by Frank H. Knight in his article, "Capital, Time and the Interest Rate," *Economica*, n.s., I, 257–286.

count only as far as they may contribute to the success of his efforts.

This mode of reasoning is all right for the businessman. But it was a serious mistake for the economists to agree with the businessman's superficial view. They erred in classifying "capital" as an independent factor of production along with the nature-given material resources and labor. The capital goods—the factors of further production produced in the past—are not an independent factor. They are the joint products of the cooperation of the two original factors—nature and labor—expended in the past. They have no productive power of their own.

Neither is it correct to call the capital goods labor and nature stored up. They are rather labor, nature, and time stored up. The difference between production without the aid of capital goods and that assisted by the employment of capital goods consists in time. Capital goods are intermediary stations on the way leading from the very beginning of production to its final goal, the turning out of consumers' goods. He who produces with the aid of capital goods enjoys one great advantage over the man who starts without capital goods; he is nearer in time to the ultimate goal of his endeavors.

There is no question of an alleged productivity of capital goods. The difference between the price of a capital good, e.g., a machine, and the sum of the prices of the complementary original factors of production required for its reproduction is entirely due to the time difference. He who employs the machine is nearer the goal of production. The period of production is shorter for him than for a competitor who must start from the beginning. In buying a machine he buys the original factors of production that were expended in producing it plus time, i.e., the time by which his period of production is shortened.

The value of time, i.e., time preference or the higher valuation of want-satisfaction in nearer periods of the future as against that in remoter periods, is an essential element in human action. It determines every choice and every action. There is no man for whom the difference between sooner and later does not count. The time element is instrumental in the formation of all prices of all commodities and services.

4. Period of Production, Waiting Time, and Period of Provision

If one were to measure the length of the period of production spent in the fabrication of the various goods available now, one would have to trace back their history to the point at which the first expenditure of original factors of production took place. One would have to establish when natural resources and labor were first employed for processes which—besides contributing to the production of other goods—also contributed ultimately to the production of the good in question. The solution of this problem would require the solubility of the problem of physical imputation. It would be necessary to establish in quantitative terms to what extent tools, raw materials, and labor which directly or indirectly were used in the production of the good concerned contributed to the result. One would have to go back in these inquiries to the very origins of capital accumulation by saving on the part of people who previously lived from hand to mouth. It is not only practical difficulties which prevent such historical studies. The very insolubility of the problem of physical imputation stops us at the first step of such ventures.

Neither acting man himself nor economic theory needs a measurement of the time expended in the past for the production of goods available today. They would have no use for such data even if they knew them. Acting man is faced with the problem of how to take best advantage of the available supply of goods. He makes his choices in employing each part of this supply in such a way as to satisfy the most urgent of the not yet satisfied wants. For the achievement of this task he must know the length of the waiting time which separates him from the attainment of the various goals among which he has to choose. As has been pointed out and must be emphasized again, there is no need for him to look backward to the history of the various capital goods available. Acting man counts waiting time and the period of production always from today on. In the same way in which there is no need to know whether more or less labor and material factors of production have been expended in the production of the products available now, there is no need to know whether their production has absorbed more or less time. Things are valued exclusively from the point of view of the services they can render for the satisfaction of future wants. The actual sacrifices made and the time absorbed in their production are beside the point. These things belong to the dead past.

It is necessary to realize that all economic categories are related to human action and have nothing at all to do directly with the physical properties of things. Economics is not about goods and services; it is about human choice and action. The praxeological concept of time is not the concept of physics or biology. It refers to the *sooner* or the *later* as operative in the actors' judgments of value. The distinction between capital goods and consumers' goods is not a rigid distinction based on the physical and physiological properties of the goods concerned. It depends on the position of the actors and the choices they have to make. The same goods can be looked upon as capital goods or as consumers' goods. A supply of goods ready for immediate enjoyment is capital goods from the point of view of a man who looks upon it as a means for his own sustenance and that of hired workers during a waiting time.

An increase in the quantity of capital goods available is a necessary condition for the adoption of processes in which the period of production and therefore waiting time are longer. If one wants to attain ends which are temporally farther away, one must resort to a longer period of production because it is impossible to attain the end sought in a shorter period of production. If one wants to resort to methods of production with which the quantity of output is higher per unit of input expended, one must lengthen the period of production. For the processes with which output is smaller per unit of input have been chosen only on account of the shorter period of production they require. But on the other hand, not every employment chosen for the utilization of capital goods accumulated by means of additional saving requires a process of production in which the period of production from today on to the maturing of the product is longer than with all processes already adopted previously. It may be that people, having satisfied their more urgent needs, now want goods which can be produced within a comparatively short period. The reason why these goods have not been produced previously was not that the period of production they require was deemed too long, but that there was a more urgent employment open for the factors required.

If one chooses to assert that every increase in the supply of capital goods available results in a lengthening of the period of production and of waiting time, one reasons in the following way: If *a* are the goods already previously produced and *b* the goods produced in the new processes started with the aid of the increase in capital goods, it is obvious that people had to wait longer for *a* and *b* than they had to wait for *a* alone. In order to produce *a* and *b* it was not only necessary to acquire the capital goods required for the production of *a*, but also those required for the production of *b*. If one had expended for an increase of immediate consumption the means of sustenance saved to make workers available for the production of *b*, one would have attained the satisfaction of some wants sooner.

The treatment of the capital problem customary with those economists who are opposed to the so-called "Austrian" view assumes that the technique employed in production is unalterably determined by the given state of technological knowledge. The "Austrian" economists, on the other hand, show that it is the supply of capital goods available at each moment that determines which of the many known technological methods of production will be employed.[8] The correctness of the "Austrian" point of view can easily be demonstrated by a scrutiny of the problem of relative scarcity of capital.

Let us look at the condition of a country suffering from such scarcity of capital. Take, for instance, the state of affairs in Rumania about 1860. What was lacking was certainly not technological knowledge. There was no secrecy concerning the technological methods practiced by the advanced nations of the West. They were described in innumerable books and taught at many schools. The elite of Rumanian youth had received full information about them at the technological universities of Austria, Switzerland, and France. Hundreds of foreign experts were ready to apply their knowledge and skill in Rumania. What was wanting were the capital goods needed for a transformation of the backward Rumanian apparatus of production, transportation, and communication according to Western patterns. If the aid granted to the Rumanians on the part of the advanced foreign nations had consisted merely in providing them with technological knowledge, they would have had to realize that it would take a very long time until they caught up with the West. The first thing for them to have done would have been to save in order to make workers and material factors of production available for the performance of more time-consuming processes. Only then could they successively produce the tools required for the construction of those plants which in the further course were to produce the equipment needed for the construction and operation of modern plants, farms, mines, railroads, telegraph lines, and buildings. Scores of decades would have passed until they had made up for the time lost. There would not have been any means of accelerating this process than by restricting current consumption as far as physiologically possible for the intermediary period.

However, things developed in a different way. The capitalist West lent to the backward countries the capital goods needed for an instantaneous transformation of a great part of their methods of production. It saved them time and made it possible for them to

8. Cf. F. A. Hayek, *The Pure Theory of Capital* (London, 1941), p. 48. It is awkward indeed to attach to certain lines of thought national labels. As Hayek remarks pertinently (p. 47, n. 1), the classical English economists since Ricardo, and particularly J. S. Mill (the latter probably partly under the influence of J. Rae) were in some regards more "Austrian" than their recent Anglo-Saxon successors.

multiply very soon the productivity of their labor. The effect for the Rumanians was that they could immediately enjoy the advantages derived from the modern technological procedures. It was as if they had started at a much earlier date to save and to accumulate capital goods.

Shortage of capital means that one is further away from the attainment of a goal sought than if one had started to aim at it at an earlier date. Because one neglected to do this in the past, the intermediary products are wanting, although the nature-given factors from which they are to be produced are available. Capital shortage is dearth of time. It is the effect of the fact that one was late in beginning the march toward the aim concerned. It is impossible to describe the advantages derived from capital goods available and the disadvantages resulting from the paucity of capital goods without resorting to the time element of *sooner* and *later*.[9]

To have capital goods at one's disposal is tantamount to being nearer to a goal aimed at. An increment in capital goods available makes it possible to attain temporally remoter ends without being forced to restrict consumption. A loss in capital goods, on the other hand, makes it necessary either to abstain from striving after certain goals which one could aim at before or to restrict consumption. To have capital goods means, other things being equal,[10] a temporal gain. As against those who lack capital goods, the capitalist, under the given state of technological knowledge, is in a position to reach a definite goal sooner without restricting consumption and without increasing the input of labor and nature-given material factors of production. His head start is in time. A rival endowed with a smaller supply of capital goods can catch up only by restricting his consumption.

The start which the peoples of the West have gained over the other peoples consists in the fact that they have long since created the political and institutional conditions required for a smooth and by and large uninterrupted progress of the process of larger-scale saving, capital accumulation, and investment. Thus, by the middle of the nineteenth century, they had already attained a state of well-being which far surpassed that of races and nations less successful in substituting the ideas of acquisitive capitalism for those of predatory militarism. Left alone and unaided by foreign capital these backward peoples would have needed much more time to improve their methods of production, transportation, and communication.

9. Cf. W. S. Jevons, *The Theory of Political Economy* (4th ed. London, 1924), pp. 224–229.

10. This implies also equality in the quantity of nature-given factors available.

It is impossible to understand the course of world affairs and the development of the relations between West and East in the last centuries, if one does not comprehend the importance of this large-scale transfer of capital. The West has given to the East not only technological and therapeutical knowledge, but also the capital goods needed for an immediate practical application of this knowledge. These nations of Eastern Europe, Asia, and Africa have been able, thanks to the foreign capital imported, to reap the fruits of modern industry at an earlier date. They were to some extent relieved from the necessity of restricting their consumption in order to accumulate a sufficient stock of capital goods. This was the true nature of the alleged exploitation of the backward nations on the part of Western capitalism about which their nationalists and the Marxians lament. It was a fecundation of the economically backward nations by the wealth of the more advanced nations.

The benefits derived were mutual. What impelled the capitalists of the West to embark upon foreign investment was the demand on the part of the domestic consumers. Consumers asked for goods which could not be produced at all at home and for a cheapening of goods which could be produced at home only with rising costs. If the consumers of the capitalist West had behaved in a different way or if the institutional obstacles to capital export had proved insurmountable, no capital export would have occurred. There would have been more longitudinal expansion of domestic production instead of lateral expansion abroad.

It is not the task of catallactics but of history to deal with the consequences of the internationalization of the capital market, its working, and its final disintegration brought about by the expropriation policies adopted by the receiving countries. Catallactics has only to scrutinize the effects of a richer or poorer supply of capital goods. We compare the conditions of two isolated market systems *A* and *B*. Both are equal in size and population figures, the state of technological knowledge, and in natural resources. They differ from one another only in the supply of capital goods, this supply being larger in *A* than in *B*. This enjoins that in *A* many processes of production are employed with which the output is greater per unit of input than with those employed in *B*. In *B* one cannot consider the adoption of these processes on account of the comparative scarcity of capital goods. Their adoption would require a restriction of consumption. In *B* many manipulations are performed by manual labor which in *A* are performed by labor-saving machines. In *A* goods are produced with a longer durability; in *B* one must abstain from producing them although the lengthening of durability is obtained by a less than proportionate increase in input. In *A* the productivity of labor and consequently wage rates and the standard of living of the wage earners are higher than in *B*.[11]

Prolongation of the Period of Provision Beyond the Expected Duration of the Actor's Life

The judgments of value which determine the choice between satisfaction in nearer and in remoter periods of the future are expressive of present valuation and not of future valuation. They weigh the significance attached today to satisfaction in the nearer future against the significance attached today to satisfaction in the remoter future.

The uneasiness which acting man wants to remove as far as possible is always present uneasiness, i.e., uneasiness felt in the very moment of action, and it always refers to future conditions. The actor is discontented today with the expected state of affairs in various periods of the future and tries to alter it through purposive conduct.

If action is primarily directed toward the improvement of other people's conditions and is therefore commonly called altruistic, the uneasiness the actor wants to remove is his own present dissatisfaction with the expected state of other people's affairs in various periods of the future. In taking care of other people he aims at alleviating his own dissatisfaction.

It is therefore not surprising that acting man often is intent upon prolonging the period of provision beyond the expected duration of his own life.

Some Applications of the Time-Preference Theory

Every part of economics is open to intentional misrepresentation and misinterpretation on the part of people eager to excuse or to justify fallacious doctrines underlying their party programs. To prevent such misuse as far as possible it seems expedient to add some explanatory remarks to the exposition of the time-preference theory.

There are schools of thought which flatly deny that men differ with regard to innate characteristics inherited from their ancestors.[12] In the opinion of these authors the only difference between the white men of Western civilization and Eskimos is that the latter are in arrears in their progress toward modern industrial civilization. This merely temporal difference of a few thousand years is insignificant when compared with the many hundreds of thousands of years which were absorbed

11. Cf. John Bates Clark, *Essentials of Economic Theory* (New York, 1907), pp. 133 ff.

12. About the Marxian attack against genetics, cf. T. D. Lysenko, *Heredity and Variability* (New York, 1945). A critical appraisal of the controversy is provided by J. R. Baker, *Science and the Planned State* (New York, 1945), pp. 71–76.

by man's evolution from the simian state of his apelike forebears to the conditions of present-day homo sapiens. It does not support the assumption that racial differences prevail between the various specimens of mankind.

Praxeology and economics are foreign to the issues raised by this controversy. But they must take precautionary measures lest they become implicated by partisan spirit in this clash of antagonistic ideas. If those fanatically rejecting the teachings of modern genetics were not entirely ignorant of economics, they would certainly try to turn the time-preference theory to their advantage. They would refer to the circumstance that the superiority of the Western nations consists merely in their having started earlier in endeavors to save and to accumulate capital goods. They would explain this temporal difference by accidental factors, the better opportunity offered by environment.

Against such possible misinterpretations one must emphasize the fact that the temporal head start gained by the Western nations was conditioned by ideological factors which cannot be reduced simply to the operation of environment. What is called human civilization has up to now been a progress from cooperation by virtue of hegemonic bonds to cooperation by virtue of contractual bonds. But while many races and peoples were arrested at an early stage of this movement, others kept on advancing. The eminence of the Western nations consisted in the fact that they succeeded better in checking the spirit of predatory militarism than the rest of mankind and that they thus brought forth the social institutions required for saving and investment on a broader scale. Even Marx did not contest the fact that private initiative and private ownership of the means of production were indispensable stages in the progress from primitive man's penury to the more satisfactory conditions of nineteenth-century Western Europe and North America. What the East Indies, China, Japan, and the Mohammedan countries lacked were institutions for safeguarding the individual's rights. The arbitrary administration of pashas, kadis, rajahs, mandarins, and daimios was not conducive to large-scale accumulation of capital. The legal guarantees effectively protecting the individual against expropriation and confiscation were the foundations upon which the unprecedented economic progress of the West came into flower. These laws were not an outgrowth of chance, historical accidents, and geographical environment. They were the product of reason.

We do not know what course the history of Asia and Africa would have taken if these peoples had been left alone. What happened was that some of these peoples were subject to European rule and others —like China and Japan—were forced by the display of naval power to open their frontiers. The achievements of Western industrialism came to them from abroad. They were ready to take advantage of the foreign capital lent to them and invested in their territories. But they were rather slow in the reception of the ideologies from which modern industrialism had sprung. Their assimilation to Western ways of life is superficial.

We are in the midst of a revolutionary process which will very soon do away with all varieties of colonialism. This revolution is not limited to those countries which were subject to the rule of the British, the French and the Dutch. Even nations which without any infringement of their political sovereignty had profited from foreign capital are intent upon throwing off what they call the yoke of foreign capitalists. They are expropriating the foreigners by various devices—discriminatory taxation, repudiation of debts, undisguised confiscation, foreign exchange restrictions. We are on the eve of the complete disintegration of the international capital market. The economic consequences of this event are obvious; its political repercussions are unpredictable.

In order to appreciate the political consequences of the disintegration of the international capital market it is necessary to remember what effects were brought about by the internationalization of the capital market. Under the conditions of the later nineteenth century it did not matter whether or not a nation was prepared and equipped with the required capital in order to utilize adequately the natural resources of its territory. There was practically free access for everybody to every area's natural wealth. In searching for the most advantageous opportunities for investment capitalists and promoters were not stopped by national borderlines. As far as investment for the best possible utilization of the known natural resources was concerned, the greater part of the earth's surface could be considered as integrated into a uniform world-embracing market system. It is true that this result was attained in some areas, like the British and the Dutch East Indies and Malaya, only by colonial regimes and that autochthonous governments of these territories would probably not have created the institutional setting indispensable for the importation of capital. But Eastern and Southern Europe and the Western Hemisphere had of their own accord joined the community of the international capital market.

The Marxians were intent upon indicting foreign loans and investments for the lust for war, conquest, and colonial expansion. In fact the internationalization of the capital market, together with free trade and the freedom of migration, was instrumental in removing the economic incentives to war and conquest. It no longer mattered for a man where the political boundaries of his country were drawn. The entrepreneur and the investor were not checked by them. Precisely those nations which in the age preceding the first World War were paramount in foreign lending and investment were committed to the ideas of peace-loving "decadent" liberalism. Of the foremost aggressor nations Russia, Italy, and Japan were not capital exporters; they themselves needed foreign capital for the development of their own natural resources. Germany's imperialist adventures were not supported by its big business and finance.[13]

The disappearance of the international capital market alters conditions entirely. It abolishes the freedom of access to natural resources. If one of the socialist governments of the economically backward nations lacks the capital needed for the utilization of its natural resources, there will be no means to remedy this situation. If this system had been adopted a hundred years ago, it would have been impossible to exploit the oil fields of Mexico, Venezuela, and Iran, to establish the rubber plantations in Malaya or to develop the banana production of Central America. It is illusory to assume that the advanced nations will acquiesce forever in such a state of affairs. They will resort to the only method which gives them access to badly needed raw materials; they will resort to conquest. War is the alternative to freedom of foreign investment as realized by the international capital market.

The inflow of foreign capital did not harm the receiving nations. It was European capital that accelerated considerably the marvelous economic evolution of the United States and the British Dominions. Thanks to foreign capital the countries of Latin America and Asia are today equipped with facilities for production and transportation which they would have had to forego for a very long time if they had not received this aid. Real wage rates and farm yields are higher today in those areas than they would have been in the absence of foreign capital. The mere fact that almost all nations are vehemently asking today for "foreign aid" explodes the fables of the Marxians and the nationalists.

However, the mere lust for imported capital goods does not resuscitate the international capital market. Investment and lending abroad are only possible if the receiving nations are unconditionally and sincerely committed to the principle of private property and do not plan to expropriate the foreign capitalists at a later date. It was such expropriations that destroyed the international capital market.

Intergovernmental loans are no substitute for the functioning of an international capital market. If they are granted on business terms, they presuppose no less than private loans the full acknowledgment of property rights. If they are granted, as is usually the case, as virtual subsidies without any regard for payment of principal and interest, they impose restrictions upon the debtor nation's sovereignty. In fact such "loans" are for the most part the price paid for military assistance in coming wars. Such military considerations already played an important role in the years in which the European powers prepared the great wars of our age. The outstanding example was provided by the huge sums which the French capitalists, pressed hard by the Govern-

13. Cf. Mises, *Omnipotent Government* (New Haven, 1944), p. 99 and the books quoted there.

ment of the Third Republic, lent to Imperial Russia. The Tsars used the capital borrowed for armaments, not for an improvement of the Russian apparatus of production.

5. The Convertibility of Capital Goods

Capital goods are intermediary steps on the way toward a definite goal. If in the course of the period of production the goal is changed, it is not always possible to use the intermediary products already available for the pursuit of the new goal. Some of the capital goods may become absolutely useless, and all expenditure made in their production appears now as waste. Other capital goods could be utilized for the new project but only after having been subjected to a process of adjustment; it would have been possible to spare the costs required by this alteration if one had from the start aimed at the new goal. A third group of capital goods can be employed for the new process without any alteration; but if it had been known at the time they were produced that they would be used in the new way, it would have been possible to manufacture at smaller cost other goods which could render the same service. Finally there are also capital goods which can be employed for the new project just as well as for the original one.

It would hardly be necessary to mention these obvious facts if it were not essential to refute popular misconceptions. There is no such thing as an abstract or ideal capital that exists apart from concrete capital goods. If we disregard the role cash holding plays in the composition of capital (we will deal with this problem in one of the later sections) we must realize that capital is always embodied in definite capital goods and is affected by everything that happens with regard to them. The value of an amount of capital is a derivative of the value of the capital goods in which it is embodied. The money equivalent of an amount of capital is the sum of the money equivalents of the aggregate of capital goods to which one refers in speaking of capital in the abstract. There is nothing which could be called "free" capital. Capital is always in the form of definite capital goods. These capital goods are better utilizable for some purposes, less utilizable for others, and absolutely useless for still other purposes. Every unit of capital is therefore in some way or other fixed capital, i.e., dedicated to definite processes of production. The businessman's distinction between fixed capital and circulating capital is a difference of degree, not of kind. Everything that is valid with regard to fixed capital is also valid, although to a smaller degree, with regard to circulating capital. All capital goods have a more or less specific character. Of course, with many of them it is rather unlikely that a change in wants and plans will make them entirely useless.

The more a definite process of production approaches its ultimate end, the closer becomes the tie between its intermediary products and the goal aimed at. Iron is less specific in character than iron tubes, and iron tubes less so than iron machine-parts. The conversion of a process of production becomes as a rule the more difficult, the farther it has been pursued and the nearer it has come to its termination, the turning out of consumers' goods.

In looking at the process of capital accumulation from its very beginnings one can easily recognize that there cannot be such a thing as free capital. There is only capital embodied in goods of a more specific character and in goods of a less specific character. When the wants or the opinions concerning the methods of want-satisfaction change, the value of the capital goods is altered accordingly. Additional capital goods can come into existence only through making consumption lag behind current production. The additional capital is already in the very moment of its coming into existence embodied in concrete capital goods. These goods had to be produced before they could—as an excess of production over consumption—become capital goods. The role which the intraposition of money plays in the sequence of these events will be dealt with later. Here we need only recognize that even the capitalist whose whole capital consists in money and in claims to money does not own free capital. His funds are tied up with money. They are affected by changes in money's purchasing power and—as far as they are invested in claims to definite sums of money—also by changes in the debtor's solvency.

It is expedient to substitute the notion of the convertibility of capital goods for the misleading distinction between fixed and free or circulating capital. The convertibility of capital goods is the opportunity offered to adjust their utilization to a change in the data of production. Convertibility is graduated. It is never perfect, i.e., present with regard to all possible changes in the data. In the case of absolutely specific factors it is entirely absent. As the conversion of capital goods from the employment originally planned to other employments becomes necessary through the emergence of unforeseen changes in the data, it is impossible to speak of convertibility in general without reference to changes in the data which have already occurred or are expected. A radical change in the data could make capital goods previously considered to be easily convertible either not convertible at all or convertible only with difficulty.

It is obvious that in practice the problem of convertibility plays a greater role with goods the serviceability of which consists in rendering a series of services over a period of time than with capital goods the serviceability of which is exhausted by rendering only one service in the process of production. The unused capacity of plants and transportation facilities and the scrapping of equipment which according to the plans underlying its production was designed for longer use are more momentous than the throwing away of fabrics and clothing out of fashion and of physically perishable goods. The problem of convertibility is peculiarly a problem of capital and capital goods only in so far as capital accounting makes it especially visible with regard to capital goods. Essentially it is a phenomenon present also in the case of consumers' goods which an individual has acquired for his own use and consumption. If the conditions which resulted in their acquisition change, the problem of convertibility becomes actual with them too.

Capitalists and entrepreneurs in their capacity as owners of capital are never perfectly free; they are never on the eve of the first decision and action which will bind them. They are always already engaged in some way or other. Their funds are not outside the social process of production, but invested in definite lines. If they own cash, this is, according to the state of the market, either a sound or an unsound "investment"; but it is always an investment. They have either let slip the right moment for the purchase of concrete factors of production which they must buy sooner or later, or the right moment to buy has not yet come. In the first case their holding of cash is unsound; they have missed an opportunity. In the second case their choice was correct.

Capitalists and entrepreneurs in expending money for the purchase of concrete factors of production value the goods exclusively from the point of view of the anticipated future state of the market. They pay prices adjusted to future conditions as they themselves appraise them today. Errors committed in the past in the production of capital goods available today do not burden the buyer; their incidence falls entirely on the seller. In this sense the entrepreneur who proceeds to buy against money capital goods for future production crosses out the past. His entrepreneurial ventures are not affected by changes which in the past occurred in the valuation and the prices of the factors of production he acquires. In this sense alone one may say that the owner of ready cash owns liquid funds and is free.

6. The Influence of the Past Upon Action

The more the accumulation of capital goods proceeds, the greater becomes the problem of convertibility. The primitive methods of farmers and handicraftsmen of earlier ages could more easily be adjusted to new tasks than modern capitalist methods. But it is precisely modern capitalism that is faced with rapid changes in conditions. Changes in technological knowledge and in the demand of the consumers as they occur daily in our time make obsolete many of the plans directing the course of production and raise the question whether or not one should pursue the path started on.

The spirit of sweeping innovation may get hold of men, may triumph over the inhibitions of sluggishness and indolence, may incite the slothful slaves of routine to a radical rescission of traditional valuations, and may peremptorily urge people to enter upon new paths leading to new goals. Doctrinaires may try to forget that we are in all our endeavors the heirs of our fathers, and that our civilization, the product of a long evolution, cannot be transformed at one stroke. But however strong the propensity for innovation may be, it is kept in bounds by a factor that forces men not to deviate too hastily from the course chosen by their forebears. All material wealth is a residuum of past activities and is embodied in concrete capital goods of limited convertibility. The capital goods accumulated direct the actions of the living into lines which they would not have chosen if their discretion had not been restricted by binding action accomplished in the past. The choice of ends and of the means for the attainment of these ends is influenced by the past. Capital goods are a conservative element. They force us to adjust our actions to conditions brought about by our own conduct in earlier days and by the thinking, choosing and acting of bygone generations.

We may picture to ourselves the image of how things would be if, equipped with our present knowledge of natural resources, geography, technology, and hygienics, we had arranged all processes of production and manufactured all capital goods accordingly. We would have located the centers of production in other places. We would have populated the earth's surface in a different way. Some areas which are today densely inhabited and full of plants and farms would be less occupied. We would have assembled more people and more shops and farms in other areas. All establishments would be equipped with the most efficient machines and tools. Each of them would be the size required for the most economical utilization of its capacity of production. In the world of our perfect planning there would be no technological backwardness, no unused capacity to produce, and no avoidable shipping of men or of goods. The productivity of human exertion would far surpass that prevailing in our actual, imperfect state.

The writings of the socialists are full of such utopian fancies.

Whether they call themselves Marxian or non-Marxian socialists, technocrats, or simply planners, they are all eager to show us how foolishly things are arranged in reality and how happily men could live if they were to invest the reformers with dictatorial powers. It is, they say, only the inadequacy of the capitalist mode of production that prevents mankind from enjoying all the amenities which could be produced under the contemporary state of technological knowledge.

The fundamental error involved in this rationalistic romanticism is the misconception of the character of the capital goods available and of their scarcity. The intermediary products available today were manufactured in the past by our ancestors and by ourselves. The plans which guided their production were an outgrowth of the then prevailing ideas concerning ends and technological procedures. If we consider aiming at different ends and choosing different methods of production, we are faced with an alternative. We must either leave unused a great part of the capital goods available and start afresh producing modern equipment, or we must adjust our production processes as far as possible to the specific character of the capital goods available. The choice rests, as it always does in the market economy, with the consumers. Their conduct in buying or not buying settles the issue. In choosing between old tenements and new ones equipped with all the gadgets of comfort, between railroad and motorcar, between gas and electric light, between cotton and rayon goods, between silk and nylon hosiery, they implicitly choose between a continued employment of previously accumulated capital goods and their scrapping. When an old building which could still be inhabited for years is not prematurely demolished and replaced by a modern house because the tenants are not prepared to pay higher rents and prefer to satisfy other wants instead of living in more comfortable homes, it is obvious how present consumption is influenced by conditions of the past.

The fact that not every technological improvement is instantly applied in the whole field is not more conspicuous than the fact that not everybody throws away his old car or his old clothes as soon as a better car is on the market or new patterns become fashionable. In all such things people are motivated by the scarcity of goods available.

A new machine, more efficient than those used previously, is constructed. Whether or not the plants equipped with the old, less efficient machines will discard them in spite of the fact that they are still utilizable and replace them by the new model depends on the degree of the new machine's superiority. Only if this superiority is great enough to compensate for the additional expenditure required, is the scrapping of the old equipment economically sound. Let p be the price of the new machine, q the price that can be realized by selling the old machine as scrap iron, a the cost of producing one unit of product by the old machine, b the cost of producing one unit of product by the new machine without taking into account the costs required for its purchase. Let us further assume that the eminence of the new machine consists merely in a better utilization of raw material and labor employed and not in manufacturing a greater quantity of products and that thus the annual output z remains unchanged. Then the replacement of the old machine by the new one is advantageous if the yield $z\ (a—b)$ is large enough to make good for the expenditure of $p - q$. We may disregard the writing off of depreciation in assuming that the annual quotas are not greater for the new machine than for the old one. The same considerations hold true also for the transfer of an already existing plant from a place in which conditions of production are less favorable to a location offering more favorable conditions.

Technological backwardness and economic inferiority are two different things and must not be confused. It can happen that a production aggregate which from a merely technological point of view appears outclassed is in a position to compete successfully with aggregates better equipped or located at more favorable sites. The degree of the superiority provided by the technologically more efficient equipment or by the more propitious location as compared with the surplus expenditure required for the transformation decides the issue. This relation depends on the convertibility of the capital goods concerned.

The distinction between technological perfection and economic expediency is not, as romantic engineers would have us believe, a feature of capitalism. It is true that only economic calculation as possible solely in a market economy gives the opportunity to establish all the computations required for the cognition of the relevant facts. A socialist management would not be in a position to ascertain the state of affairs by arithmetical methods. It would therefore not know whether or not what it plans and puts into operation is the most appropriate procedure to employ the means available for the satisfaction of what it considers to be the most urgent of the still unsatisfied wants of the people. But if it were in a position to calculate, it would not proceed in a way different from that of the calculating businessman. It would not squander scarce factors of production for the satisfaction of wants deemed less urgent if this would prevent the satisfaction of more urgent wants. It would not hurry to scrap still utilizable production facilities if the investment required would impair the expansion of the production of more urgently needed goods.

If one takes the problem of convertibility into proper account, one can easily explode many widespread fallacies. Take, for instance, the infant industries argument advanced in favor of protection. Its supporters assert that temporary protection is needed in order to develop processing industries in places in which natural conditions for their operation are more favorable or, at least, no less favorable than in the areas in which the already established competitors are located. These older industries have acquired an advantage by their early start. They are now fostered by a merely historical, accidental, and manifestly "irrational" factor. This advantage prevents the establishment of competing plants in areas the conditions of which give promise of becoming able to produce more cheaply than, or at least as cheaply as, the old ones. It may be admitted that protection for infant industries is temporarily expensive. But the sacrifices made will be more than repaid by the gains to be reaped later.

The truth is that the establishment of an infant industry is advantageous from the economic point of view only if the superiority of the new location is so momentous that it outweighs the disadvantages resulting from the abandonment of nonconvertible and nontransferable capital goods invested in the already established plants. If this is the case, the new plants will be able to compete successfully with the old ones without any aid given by the government. If it is not the case, the protection granted to them is wasteful, even if it is only temporary and enables the new industry to hold its own at a later period. The tariff amounts virtually to a subsidy which the consumers are forced to pay as a compensation for the employment of scarce factors of production for the replacement of still utilizable capital goods to be scrapped and the withholding of these scarce factors from other employments in which they could render services valued higher by the consumers. The consumers are deprived of the opportunity to satisfy certain wants because the capital goods required are directed toward the production of goods which were already available to them in the absence of tariffs.

There prevails a universal tendency for all industries to move to those locations in which the potentialities for production are most propitious. In the unhampered market economy this tendency is slowed down as much as due consideration to the inconvertibility of scarce capital goods requires. This historical element does not give a permanent superiority to the old industries. It only prevents the waste originating from investments which bring about unused capacity of still utilizable production facilities on the one hand and a restriction of capital goods available for the satisfaction of unsatisfied wants on the other hand. In the absence of tariffs the migration of industries is postponed until the capital goods invested in the old plants are worn out or become obsolete by technological improvements which are so momentous as to necessitate their replacement by new equipment. The industrial history of the United States provides numerous examples of the shifting, within the boundaries of the country, of centers of industrial production which was not fostered by any protective measures on the part of the authorities. The infant industries argument is no less spurious than all the other arguments advanced in favor of protection.

Another popular fallacy refers to the alleged suppression of useful patents. A patent is a legal monopoly granted for a limited number of years to the inventor of a new contrivance. At this point we are not concerned with the question whether or not it is a good policy to grant such exclusive privileges to inventors.[14] We have to deal only with the assertion that "big business" misuses the patent system to withhold from the public benefits it could derive from technological improvement.

In granting a patent to an inventor the authorities do not investigate the invention's economic significance. They are concerned merely with the priority of the idea and limit their examination to technological problems. They deal with the same impartial scrupulousness with an invention which revolutionizes a whole industry and with some trifling gadget, the uselessness of which is obvious. Thus patent protection is provided to a vast number of quite worthless inventions. Their authors are ready to overrate the importance of their contribution to the progress of technological knowledge and build exaggerated hopes upon the material gain it could bring them. Disappointed, they grumble about the absurdity of an economic system that deprives the people of the benefit of technological progress.

The conditions under which it is economical to substitute new improved equipment for still utilizable older tools have been pointed out above. If these conditions are absent, it does not pay, either for private enterprise in a market economy or for the socialist management of a totalitarian system, to adopt the new technological process immediately. The new machinery to be produced for new plants, the expansion of already existing plants and the replacement of old

14. Cf. above, pp. 385–386, and below, pp. 680–681.

equipment torn out will be effected according to the new design. But the still utilizable equipment will not be scrapped. The new process will be adopted only step by step. The plants equipped with the old devices are for some time still in a position to stand the competition of those equipped with the new ones. Those questioning the correctness of this statement should ask themselves whether they always throw away their vacuum cleaners or radio sets as soon as better models are offered for sale.

It does not make any difference in this regard whether the new invention is or is not protected by a patent. A firm that has acquired a license has already expended money for the new invention. If it nonetheless does not adopt the new method, the reason is that its adoption does not pay. It is of no avail that the government-created monopoly which the patent provides prevents competitors from applying it. What counts alone is the degree of superiority secured by the new invention as against old methods. Superiority means reduction in the cost of production per unit or such an improvement in the quality of the product that buyers are ready to pay adequately higher prices. The absence of a sufficient degree of superiority to make the cost of transformation profitable is proof of the fact that consumers are more intent upon acquiring other goods than upon enjoying the benefits of the new invention. It is the consumers with whom the ultimate decision rests.

Superficial observers sometimes fail to see these facts because they are deluded by the practice of many big enterprises of acquiring the rights granted by a patent in their field regardless of its usefulness. This practice stems from various considerations:

1. The economic significance of the innovation is not yet recognizable.

2. The innovation is obviously useless. But the firm believes that it could develop it in such a way as to make it useful.

3. The immediate application of the innovation does not pay. But the firm intends to apply it later when replacing its worn-out equipment.

4. The firm wants to encourage the inventor to continue his research in spite of the fact that up to now his endeavors have not resulted in a practically utilizable innovation.

5. The firm wants to placate litigious inventors in order to spare the money, time, and nervous strain which frivolous infringement suits bring about.

6. The firm resorts to hardly disguised bribery or yields to veiled blackmail when paying for quite useless patents to officers, engineers,

or other influential personnel of firms or institutions which are its customers or potential customers.

If an invention is so superior to the old processes that it makes the old equipment obsolete and peremptorily demands its immediate replacement by new machines, the transformation will be effected no matter whether the privilege conferred by the patent is in the hands of the owners of the old equipment or of an independent firm. The assertions to the contrary are based on the assumption that not only the inventor and his attorneys but also all people already active in the field of production concerned or prepared to enter into it if an opportunity is offered to them fail entirely to grasp the importance of the invention. The inventor sells his rights to the old firm for a trifle because no one else wants to acquire them. And this old firm is also too dull to see the advantage that it could derive from the application of the invention.

Now, it is true that a technological improvement cannot be adopted if people are blind to its usefulness. Under a socialist management the incompetence or stubbornness of the officers in charge of the department concerned would be enough to prevent the adoption of a more economical method of production. The same is the case with regard to inventions in fields dominated by the government. The most conspicuous examples are provided by the failure of eminent military experts to comprehend the significance of new devices. The great Napoleon did not recognize the help which steamboats could give to his plans to invade Great Britain; both Foch and the German general staff underestimated on the eve of the first World War the importance of aviation, and later the eminent pioneer of air power, General Billy Mitchell, had very unpleasant experiences. But things are entirely different in the orbit in which the market economy is not hampered by bureaucratic narrow-mindedness. There, a tendency to overrate rather than to underestimate the potentialities of an innovation prevails. The history of modern capitalism shows innumerable instances of abortive attempts to push innovations which proved futile. Many promoters have paid heavily for unfounded optimism. It would be more realistic to blame capitalism for its propensity to overvalue useless innovations than for its alleged suppression of useful innovations. It is a fact that large sums have been wasted for the purchase of quite useless patent rights and for fruitless ventures to apply them in practice.

It is absurd to speak of an alleged bias of modern big business against technological improvement. The great corporations spend huge sums in the search for new processes and new devices.

Those lamenting an alleged suppression of inventions on the part of free enterprise must not think that they have proved their case by referring to the fact that many patents are either never utilized at all or only used after a long delay. It is manifest that numerous patents, perhaps the far greater number of them, are quite useless. Those alleging suppression of useful innovations do not cite a single instance of such an innovation's being unused in the countries protecting it by a patent while it is used by the Soviets—no respecters of patent privileges.

The limited convertibility of capital goods plays an important role in human geography. The present distribution of human abodes and industrial centers over the earth's surface is to a certain degree determined by historical factors. The fact that definite sites were chosen in a distant past is still operative. There prevails, it is true, a universal tendency for people to move to those areas which offer the most propitious potentialities for production. However, this tendency is restrained not only by institutional factors, such as migration barriers. A historical factor also plays a momentous role. Capital goods of limited convertibility have been invested in areas which, from the point of view of our present knowledge, offer less favorable opportunities. Their immobilization counteracts the tendency to locate plants, farms, and dwelling places according to the state of our contemporary information about geography, geology, plant and animal physiology, climatology, and other branches of science. Against the advantages of moving toward sites offering better physical opportunities one must weigh the disadvantages of leaving unused capital goods of limited convertibility and transferability.

Thus the degree of convertibility of the supply of capital goods available affects all decisions concerning production and consumption. The smaller the degree of convertibility, the more realization of technological improvement is delayed. Yet it would be absurd to refer to this retarding effect as irrational and antiprogressive. To consider, in planning action, all the advantages and disadvantages expected and to weigh them against one another is a manifestation of rationality. Not the soberly calculating businessman, but the romantic technocrat is to blame for a delusive incomprehension of reality. What slows down technological improvement is not the imperfect convertibility of capital goods, but their scarcity. We are not rich enough to renounce the services which still utilizable capital goods could provide. The fact that a supply of capital goods is available does not check progress; it is, on the contrary, the indispensable condition of any improvement and progress. The heritage of the past embodied in our supply of capital goods is our wealth and the foremost means of further advancement in well-being. It is true we would be still better off if our ancestors and we ourselves in our past actions had succeeded in better anticipating the conditions under which we must act today. The cognizance of this fact explains many phenomena of our time. But it does not cast any blame upon the past nor does it show any imperfection inherent in the market economy.

7. Accumulation, Maintenance and Consumption of Capital

Capital goods are intermediary products which in the further course of production activities are transformed into consumers' goods. All capital goods, including those not called perishable, perish either in wearing out their serviceableness in the performance of production processes or in losing their serviceableness, even before this happens, through a change in the market data. There is no question of keeping a stock of capital goods intact. They are transient.

The notion of wealth constancy is an outgrowth of deliberate planning and acting. It refers to the concept of capital as applied in capital accounting, not to the capital goods as such. The idea of capital has no counterpart in the physical universe of tangible things. It is nowhere but in the minds of planning men. It is an element in economic calculation. Capital accounting serves one purpose only. It is designed to make us know how our arrangement of production and consumption acts upon our power to satisfy future wants. The question it answers is whether a certain course of conduct increases or decreases the productivity of our future exertion.

The intention of preserving the available supply of capital goods in full power or of increasing it could also direct the actions of men who did not have the mental tool of economic calculation. Primitive fishermen and hunters were certainly aware of the difference between maintaining their tools and devices in good shape and serviceableness and wearing them out without providing for adequate replacements. An old-fashioned peasant, committed to traditional routine and ignorant of accountancy, knows very well the significance of maintaining intact his live and dead stock. Under the simple conditions of a stationary or slowly progressing economy it is feasible to operate successfully even in the absence of capital accounting. There the maintenance of a by and large unchanged supply of capital goods can be effected either by current production of pieces destined to replace those worn out or by the accumulation of a fund of consumers' goods which makes it possible to devote effort at a later time toward the replacement of such capital goods without being forced to restrict consumption temporarily. But a changing industrial economy cannot do without economic calculation and its fundamental concepts of capital and income.

Conceptual realism has muddled the comprehension of the concept of capital. It has brought about a mythology of capital.[15] An existence has been attributed to "capital," independent of the capital goods in which it is embodied. Capital, it is said, reproduces itself and thus provides for its own maintenance. Capital, says the Marxian, hatches out profit. All this is nonsense.

Capital is a praxeological concept. It is a product of reasoning, and its place is in the human mind. It is a mode of looking at the problems of acting, a method of appraising them from the point of view of a definite plan. It determines the course of human action and is, in this sense only, a real factor. It is inescapably linked with capitalism, the market economy.

The capital concept is operative as far as men in their actions let themselves be guided by capital accounting. If the entrepreneur has employed factors of production in such a way that the money equivalent of the products at least equals the money equivalent of the factors expended, he is in a position to replace the capital goods expended by new capital goods the money equivalent of which equals the money equivalent of those expended. But the employment of the gross proceeds, their allotment to the maintenance of capital, consumption, and the accumulation of new capital is always the outcome of purposive action on the part of the entrepreneurs and capitalists. It is not "automatic"; it is by necessity the result of deliberate action. And it can be frustrated if the computation on which it is based was vitiated by negligence, error, or misjudgment of future conditions.

Additional capital can be accumulated only by saving, i.e., a surplus of production over consumption. Saving may consist in a restriction of consumption. But it can also be brought about, without a further restriction in consumption and without a change in the input of capital goods, by an increase in net production. Such an increase can appear in different ways:

1. Natural conditions have become more propitious. Harvests are more plentiful. People have access to more fertile soil and have discovered mines yielding higher returns per unit of input. Cataclysms and catastrophes which in repeated occurrence frustrated human

15. Cf. Hayek, "The Mythology of Capital," *The Quarterly Journal of Economics*, L (1936), 223 ff.

effort have become less frequent. Epidemics and cattle plagues have subsided.

2. People have succeeded in rendering some production processes more fruitful without investing more capital goods and without a further lengthening of the period of production.

3. Institutional disturbances of production activities have become less frequent. The losses caused by war, revolutions, strikes, sabotage, and other crimes have been reduced.

If the surpluses thus brought about are employed as additional investment, they further increase future net proceeds. Then it becomes possible to expand consumption without prejudice to the supply of capital goods available and the productivity of labor.

Capital is always accumulated by individuals or groups of individuals acting in concert, never by the Volkswirtschaft or the society.[16] It may happen that while some actors are accumulating additional capital, others are at the same time consuming capital previously accumulated. If these two processes are equal in amount, the sum of the capital funds available in the market system remains unaltered and it is as if no change in the total amount of capital goods available had occurred. The accumulation of additional capital on the part of some people merely removes the necessity of shortening the period of production of some processes. But no further adoption of processes with a longer period of production becomes feasible. If we look at affairs from this angle we may say that a transfer of capital took place. But one must guard oneself against confusing this notion of capital transfer with the conveyance of property from one individual or group of individuals to others.

The sale and purchase of capital goods and the loans granted to business are not as such capital transfer. They are transactions which are instrumental in conveying the concrete capital goods into the hands of those entrepreneurs who want to employ them for the performance of definite projects. They are only ancillary steps in the course of a long-range sequence of acts. Their composite effect decides the success or failure of the whole project. But neither profit nor loss directly brings about either capital accumulation or capital consumption. It is the way in which those in whose fortune profit or loss occurs arrange their consumption that alters the amount of capital available.

Capital transfer can be effected both without and with a conveyance in the ownership of capital goods. The former is the case when

16. The state and the municipalities, in the market economy, are also merely actors representing concerted action on the part of definite groups of individuals.

one man consumes capital while another man independently accumulates capital in the same amount. The latter is the case if the seller of capital goods consumes the proceeds while the buyer pays the price out of a nonconsumed—saved—surplus of net proceeds over consumption.

Capital consumption and the physical extinction of capital goods are two different things. All capital goods sooner or later enter into final products and cease to exist through use, consumption, wear and tear. What can be preserved by an appropriate arrangement of consumption is only the value of a capital fund, never the concrete capital goods. It may sometimes happen that acts of God or man-made destruction result in so great an extinction of capital goods that no possible restriction of consumption can bring about in a short time a replenishment of the capital funds to its previous level. But what brings about such a depletion is always the fact that the net proceeds of current production devoted to the maintenance of capital are not sufficiently large.

8. The Mobility of the Investor

The limited convertibility of the capital goods does not immovably bind their owner. The investor is free to alter the investment of his funds. If he is able to anticipate the future state of the market more correctly than other people, he can succeed in choosing only investments whose price will rise and in avoiding investments whose price will drop.

Entrepreneurial profit and loss emanate from the dedication of factors of production to definite projects. Stock exchange speculation and analogous transactions outside the securities market determine on whom the incidence of these profits and losses shall fall. A tendency prevails to make a sharp distinction between such purely speculative ventures and genuinely sound investment. The distinction is one of degree only. There is no such thing as a nonspeculative investment. In a changing economy action always involves speculation. Investments may be good or bad, but they are always speculative. A radical change in conditions may render bad even investments commonly considered perfectly safe.

Stock speculation cannot undo past action and cannot change anything with regard to the limited convertibility of capital goods already in existence. What it can do is to prevent additional investment in branches and enterprises in which, according to the opinion of the speculators, it would be misplaced. It points the specific way for a tendency, prevailing in the market economy, to expand profitable production ventures and to restrict the unprofitable. In this sense the stock exchange becomes simply "the market," the focal point of the market economy, the ultimate device to make the anticipated demand of the consumers supreme in the conduct of business.

The mobility of the investor manifests itself in the phenomenon misleadingly called capital flight. Individual investors can go away from investments which they consider unsafe provided that they are ready to take the loss already discounted by the market. Thus they can protect themselves against anticipated further losses and shift them to people who are less realistic in their appraisal of the future prices of the goods concerned. Capital flight does not withdraw inconvertible capital goods from the lines of their investment. It consists merely in a change of ownership.

It makes no difference in this regard whether the capitalist "flees" into another domestic investment or into a foreign investment. One of the main objectives of foreign exchange control is to prevent capital flight into foreign countries. However, foreign exchange control only succeeds in preventing the owners of domestic investments from restricting their losses by exchanging in time a domestic investment they consider unsafe for a foreign investment they consider safe.

If all or certain classes of domestic investment are threatened by partial or total expropriation, the market discounts the unfavorable consequences of this policy by an adequate change in their prices. When this happens, it is too late to resort to flight in order to avoid being victimized. Only those investors can come off with a small loss who are keen enough to forecast the disaster at a time when the majority is still unaware of its approach and its significance. Whatever the various capitalists and entrepreneurs may do, they can never make inconvertible capital goods mobile and transferable. While this, at least, is admitted by and large with regard to fixed capital, it is denied with regard to circulating capital. It is asserted that a businessman can export products and fail to reimport the proceeds. People do not see that an enterprise cannot continue its operations when deprived of its circulating capital. If a businessman exports his own funds employed for the current purchase of raw materials, labor, and other essential requirements, he must replace them by funds borrowed. The grain of truth in the fable of the mobility of circulating capital is the fact that it is possible for an investor to avoid losses menacing his circulating capital independently of the avoidance of such losses menacing his fixed capital. However, the process of capital flight is in both instances the same. It is a change in the person of the investor. The investment itself is not affected; the capital concerned does not emigrate.

Capital flight into a foreign country presupposes the propensity of foreigners to exchange their investments abroad against those in the country from which capital flees. A British capitalist cannot flee from his British investments if no foreigner buys them. It follows that capital flight can never result in the much talked about deterioration of the balance of payments. Neither can it make foreign exchange rates rise. If many capitalists—whether British or foreign—want to get rid of British securities, a drop in their prices will ensue. But it will not affect the exchange ratio between the sterling and foreign currencies.

The same is valid with regard to capital invested in ready cash. The owner of French francs who anticipates the consequences of the French Government's inflationary policy can either flee into "real goods" by the purchase of goods or into foreign exchange. But he must find people who are ready to take francs in exchange. He can flee only as long as there are still people left who appraise the future of the franc more optimistically than he himself does. What makes commodity prices and foreign exchange rates rise is not the conduct of those ready to give away francs, but the conduct of those refusing to take them except at a low rate of exchange.

Governments pretend that in resorting to foreign exchange restrictions to prevent capital flight they are motivated by consideration of the nation's vital interests. What they really bring about is contrary to the material interests of many citizens without any benefit to any citizen or to the phantom of the Volkswirtschaft. If there is inflation going on in France, it is certainly not to the advantage either of the nation as a whole or of any citizen that all the disastrous consequences should affect Frenchmen only. If some Frenchmen were to unload the burden of these losses on foreigners by selling them French banknotes or bonds redeemable in such banknotes, a part of these losses would fall upon foreigners. The manifest outcome of the prevention of such transactions is to make some Frenchmen poorer without making any Frenchmen richer. From the nationalist point of view this hardly seems desirable.

Popular opinion finds something objectionable in every possible aspect of stock market transactions. If prices are rising, the speculators are denounced as profiteers who appropriate to themselves what by rights belongs to other people. If prices drop, the speculators are denounced for squandering the nation's wealth. The profits of the speculators are vilified as robbery and theft at the expense of the rest of the nation. It is insinuated that they are the cause of the public's poverty. It is customary to draw a distinction between this dishonest bounty of the jobbers and the profits of the manufacturer who does not merely gamble but supplies the consumers. Even financial writers fail to realize that stock exchange transactions produce neither profits nor losses, but are only the consummation of profits and losses arising in trading and manufacturing. These profits and losses, the outgrowth of the buying public's approval or disapproval of the investments effected in the past, are made visible by the stock market. The turnover on the stock market does not affect the public. It is, on the contrary, the public's reaction to the mode in which investors arranged production activities that determines the price structure of the securities market. It is ultimately the consumers' attitude that makes some stocks rise, others drop. Those not saving and investing neither profit nor lose on account of fluctuations in stock exchange quotations. The trade on the securities market merely decides which investors shall earn profits and which shall suffer losses.[17]

9. Money and Capital; Saving and Investment

Capital is computed in terms of money and represents in such accounting a definite sum of money. But capital can also consist of amounts of money. As capital goods also are exchanged and as such exchanges are effected under the same conditions as the exchange of all other goods, here too indirect exchange and the use of money become peremptory. In the market economy no participant can forego the advantages which cash holding conveys. Not only in their capacity as consumers, but also in their capacity as capitalists and entrepreneurs, individuals are under the necessity of keeping cash holdings.

Those who have seen in this fact something puzzling and contradictory have been misled by a misconstruction of monetary calculation and capital accounting. They attempt to assign to capital accounting tasks which it can never achieve. Capital accounting is a mental tool of calculating and computing suitable for individuals and groups of individuals acting in the market economy. Only in the frame of monetary calculation can capital become computable. The sole task that capital accounting can perform is to show to the various individuals acting within a market economy whether the money equivalent of their funds devoted to acquisitive action has changed and to

17. The popular doctrine that the stock exchange "absorbs" capital and money is critically analyzed and entirely refuted by F. Machlup, *The Stock Market, Credit and Capital Formation*, trans. by V. Smith (London, 1940), pp. 6–153.

what extent. For all other purposes capital accounting is quite useless.

If one tries to ascertain a magnitude called the *volkswirtschaftliche* capital or the social capital as distinct both from the acquisitive capital of various individuals and from the meaningless concept of the sum of the various individuals' acquisitive capital funds, then, of course, one is troubled by a spurious problem. What is the role of money, one asks, in such a concept of social capital? One discovers a momentous difference between capital as seen from the individual's point of view and as seen from the standpoint of society. However, this whole reasoning is utterly fallacious. It is obviously contradictory to eliminate reference to money from the computation of a magnitude which cannot be computed otherwise than in terms of money. It is nonsensical to resort to monetary calculation in an attempt to ascertain a magnitude which is meaningless in an economic system in which there cannot be any money and no money prices for factors of production. As soon as our reasoning passes beyond the frame of a market society, it must renounce every reference to money and money prices. The concept of social capital can only be thought of as a collection of various goods. It is impossible to compare two collections of this type otherwise than by declaring that one of them is more serviceable in removing the uneasiness felt by the whole of society than the other. (Whether or not such a comprehensive judgment can be pronounced by any mortal man is another question.) No monetary expression can be applied to such collections. Monetary terms are void of any meaning in dealing with the capital problems of a social system in which there is no market for factors of production.

In recent years economists have paid special attention to the role cash holding plays in the process of saving and capital accumulation. Many fallacious conclusions have been advanced about this role.

If an individual employs a sum of money not for consumption but for the purchase of factors of production, saving is directly turned into capital accumulation. If the individual saver employs his additional savings for increasing his cash holding because this is in his eyes the most advantageous mode of using them, he brings about a tendency toward a fall in commodity prices and a rise in the monetary unit's purchasing power. If we assume that the supply of money in the market system does not change, this conduct on the part of the saver will not directly influence the accumulation of capital and its employment for an expansion of production.[18] The effect of our

18. Indirectly capital accumulation is affected by the changes in wealth and incomes which every instance of cash-induced change in the purchasing power of money brings about.

saver's saving, i.e., the surplus of goods produced over goods consumed, does not disappear on account of his hoarding. The prices of capital goods do not rise to the height they would have attained in the absence of such hoarding. But the fact that more capital goods are available is not affected by the striving of a number of people to increase their cash holdings. If nobody employs the goods—the nonconsumption of which brought about the additional saving—for an expansion of his consumptive spending, they remain as an increment in the amount of capital goods available, whatever their prices may be. Tho two processes—increased cash holding of some people and increased capital accumulation—take place side by side.

A drop in commodity prices, other things being equal, causes a drop in the money equivalent of the various individuals' capital. But this is not tantamount to a reduction in the supply of capital goods and does not require an adjustment of production activities to an alleged impoverishment. It merely alters the money items to be applied in monetary calculation.

Now let us assume that an increase in the quantity of credit money or of fiat money or credit expansion produces the additional money required for an expansion of the individuals' cash holdings. Then three processes take their course independently: a tendency toward a fall in commodity prices brought about by the increase in the amount of capital goods available and the resulting expansion of production activities, a tendency toward a fall in prices brought about by an increased demand of money for cash holding, and finally a tendency toward a rise in prices brought about by the increase in the supply of money (in the broader sense). The three processes are to some extent synchronous. Each of them brings about its particular effects which, according to the circumstances, may be intensified or weakened by the opposite effects originating from one of the other two. But the main thing is that the capital goods resulting from the additional saving are not destroyed by the coincident monetary changes—changes in the demand for and the supply of money (in the broader sense). Whenever an individual devotes a sum of money to saving instead of spending it for consumption, the process of saving agrees perfectly with the process of capital accumulation and investment. It does not matter whether the individual saver does or does not increase his cash holding. The act of saving always has its counterpart in a supply of goods produced and not consumed, of goods available for further production activities. A man's savings are always embodied in concrete capital goods.

The idea that hoarded money is a barren part of the total amount of wealth and that its increase causes shrinkage in that part of wealth that is devoted to production is correct only to the extent that the rise in the monetary unit's purchasing power results in the employment of additional factors of production for the mining of gold and in the transfer of gold from industrial to monetary employment. But this is brought about by the striving after increased cash holdings and not by saving. Saving, in the market economy, is possible only through abstention from the consumption of a part of income. The individual saver's employment of his savings for hoarding influences the determination of money's purchasing power, and may thus reduce the nominal amount of capital, i.e., its money equivalent; it does not render any part of the accumulated capital sterile.

XIX. INTEREST

1. The Phenomenon of Interest

It has been shown that time preference is a category inherent in every human action. Time preference manifests itself in the phenomenon of originary interest, i.e., the discount of future goods as against present goods.

Interest is not merely interest on capital. Interest is not the specific income derived from the utilization of capital goods. The correspondence between three factors of production—labor, capital, and land—and three classes of income—wages, profit, and rent—as taught by the classical economists is untenable. Rent is not the specific revenue from land. Rent is a general catallactic phenomenon; it plays in the yield of labor and capital goods the same role it plays in the yield of land. Furthermore there is no homogeneous source of income that could be called profit in the sense in which the classical economists applied this term. Profit (in the sense of entrepreneurial profit) and interest are no more characteristic of capital than they are of land.

The prices of consumers' goods are by the interplay of the forces operating on the market apportioned to the various complementary factors cooperating in their production. As the consumers' goods are present goods, while the factors of production are means for the production of future goods, and as present goods are valued higher than future goods of the same kind and quantity, the sum thus apportioned, even in the imaginary construction of the evenly rotating economy, falls behind the present price of the consumers' goods concerned. This difference is the originary interest. It is not specifically connected with any of the three classes of factors of production which the classical economists distinguished. Entrepreneurial profit and loss are produced by changes in the data and the resulting price changes which occur in the passing of the period of production.

Naïve reasoning does not see any problem in the current revenue derived from hunting, fishing, cattle breeding, forestry, and agriculture. Nature generates deer, fish, and cattle and makes them grow, causes the cows to give milk and the chickens to lay eggs, the trees to put on wood and to bear fruit, and the seeds to shoot into ears.

He who has a title to appropriate for himself this recurring wealth enjoys a steady income. Like a stream which continually carries new water, the "stream of income" flows continually and conveys again and again new wealth. The whole process appears as a natural phenomenon. But for the economist a problem is presented in the determination of prices for land, cattle, and all the rest. If future goods were not bought and sold at a discount as against present goods, the buyer of land would have to pay a price which equals the sum of all future net revenues and which would leave nothing for a current reiterated income.

The yearly recurring proceeds of the owners of land and cattle are not marked by any characteristic which would catallactically distinguish them from the proceeds stemming from produced factors of production which are used up sooner or later in the processes of production. The power of disposal over a piece of land is the control of this field's cooperation in the production of all the fruit which can ever be grown on it, and the power of disposal over a mine is the control of its cooperation in the extraction of all the minerals which can ever be brought to the surface from it. In the same way the ownership of a machine or a bale of cotton is the control of its cooperation in the manufacture of all goods which are produced with its cooperation. The fundamental fallacy implied in all the productivity and use approaches to the problem of interest was that they traced back the phenomenon of interest to these productive services rendered by the factors of production. However, the serviceableness of the factors of production determines the prices paid for them, not interest. These prices exhaust the whole difference between the productivity of a process aided by a definite factor's cooperation and that of a process lacking this cooperation. The difference between the sum of the prices of the complementary factors of production and the products which emerges even in the absence of changes in the market data concerned, is an outcome of the higher valuation of present goods as compared with future goods. As production goes on, the factors of production are transformed or ripen into present goods of a higher value. This increment is the source of specific proceeds flowing into the hands of the owners of the factors of production, of originary interest.

The owners of the material factors of production—as distinct from the pure entrepreneurs of the imaginary construction of an integration of catallactic functions—harvest two catallactically different items: the prices paid for the productive cooperation of the factors they control on the one hand and interest on the other hand. These two things must not be confused. It is not permissible to refer, in the explanation of interest, to the services rendered by the factors of production in the turning out of products.

Interest is a homogeneous phenomenon. There are no different sources of interest. Interest on durable goods and interest on consumption-credit are like other kinds of interest an outgrowth of the higher valuation of present goods as against future goods.

2. Originary Interest

Originary interest is the ratio of the value assigned to want-satisfaction in the immediate future and the value assigned to want-satisfaction in remote periods of the future. It manifests itself in the market economy in the discount of future goods as against present goods. It is a ratio of commodity prices, not a price in itself. There prevails a tendency toward the equalization of this ratio for all commodities. In the imaginary construction of the evenly rotating economy the rate of originary interest is the same for all commodities.

Originary interest is not "the price paid for the services of capital."[1] The higher productivity of more time-consuming roundabout methods of production which is referred to by Böhm-Bawerk and by some later economists in the explanation of interest, does not explain the phenomenon. It is, on the contrary, the phenomenon of originary interest that explains why less time-consuming methods of production are resorted to in spite of the fact that more time-consuming methods would render a higher output per unit of input. Moreover, the phenomenon of originary interest explains why pieces of usable land can be sold and bought at finite prices. If the future services which a piece of land can render were to be valued in the same way in which its present services are valued, no finite price would be high enough to impel its owner to sell it. Land could neither be bought nor sold against definite amounts of money, nor bartered against goods which can render only a finite number of services. Pieces of land would be bartered only against other pieces of land. A superstructure that can yield during a period of ten years an annual revenue of one hundred dollars would be priced (apart from the soil on which it is built) at the beginning of this period at one thousand dollars, at the beginning of the second year at nine hundred dollars, and so on.

Originary interest is not a price determined on the market by the

1. This is the popular definition of interest as, for instance, given by Ely, Adams, Lorenz, and Young, *Outlines of Economics* (3d ed. New York, 1920), p. 493.

interplay of the demand for and the supply of capital or capital goods. Its height does not depend on the extent of this demand and supply. It is rather the rate of originary interest that determines both the demand for and the supply of capital and capital goods. It determines how much of the available supply of goods is to be devoted to consumption in the immediate future and how much to provision for remoter periods of the future.

People do not save and accumulate capital because there is interest. Interest is neither the impetus to saving nor the reward or the compensation granted for abstaining from immediate consumption. It is the ratio in the mutual valuation of present goods as against future goods.

The loan market does not determine the rate of interest. It adjusts the rate of interest on loans to the rate of originary interest as manifested in the discount of future goods.

Originary interest is a category of human action. It is operative in any valuation of external things and can never disappear. If one day the state of affairs were to return which was actual at the close of the first millennium of the Christian era when some people believed that the ultimate end of all earthly things was impending, men would stop providing for future secular wants. The factors of production would in their eyes become useless and worthless. The discount of future goods as against present goods would not vanish. It would, on the contrary, increase beyond all measure. On the other hand, the fading away of originary interest would mean that people do not care at all for want-satisfaction in nearer periods of the future. It would mean that they prefer to an apple available today, tomorrow, in one year or in ten years, two apples available in a thousand or ten thousand years.

We cannot even think of a world in which originary interest would not exist as an inexorable element in every kind of action. Whether there is or is not division of labor and social cooperation and whether society is organized on the basis of private or of public control of the means of production, originary interest is always present. In a socialist commonwealth its role would not differ from that in the market economy.

Böhm-Bawerk has once for all unmasked the fallacies of the naïve productivity explanations of interest, i.e., of the idea that interest is the expression of the physical productivity of factors of production. However, Böhm-Bawerk has himself based his own theory to some extent on the productivity approach. In referring in his explanation to the technological superiority of more time-consuming, roundabout processes of production, he avoids the crudity of the naïve productivity fallacies. But in fact he returns, although in a subtler form, to the productivity approach. Those later economists who, neglecting the time-preference idea, have stressed exclusively the productivity idea contained in Böhm-Bawerk's theory cannot help concluding that originary interest must disappear if men were one day to reach a state of affairs in which no further lengthening of the period of production could bring about a further increase in productivity.[2] This is, however, utterly wrong. Originary interest cannot disappear as long as there is scarcity and therefore action.

As long as the world is not transformed into a land of Cockaigne, men are faced with scarcity and must act and economize; they are forced to choose between satisfaction in nearer and in remoter periods of the future because neither for the former nor for the latter can full contentment be attained. Then a change in the employment of factors of production which withdraws such factors from their employment for want-satisfaction in the nearer future and devotes them to want-satisfaction in the remoter future must necessarily impair the state of satisfaction in the nearer future and improve it in the remoter future. If we were to assume that this is not the case, we should become embroiled in insoluble contradictions. We may at best think of a state of affairs in which technological knowledge and skill have reached a point beyond which no further progress is possible for mortal men. No new processes increasing the output per unit of input can henceforth be invented. But if we suppose that some factors of production are scarce, we must not assume that all processes which—apart from the time they absorb—are the most productive ones are fully utilized, and that no process rendering a smaller output per unit of input is resorted to merely because of the fact that it produces its final result sooner than other, physically more productive processes. Scarcity of factors of production means that we are in a position to draft plans for the improvement of our well-being the realization of which is unfeasible because of the insufficient quantity of the means available. It is precisely the unfeasibility of such desirable improvements that constitutes the element of scarcity. The reasoning of the modern supporters of the productivity approach is misled by the connotations of Böhm-Bawerk's term *roundabout methods of production* and the idea of

2. Cf. Hayek, "The Mythology of Capital," *The Quarterly Journal of Economics,* L (1936), 223 ff. However Professor Hayek has since partly changed his point of view. (Cf. his article "Time-Preference and Productivity, a Reconsideration," *Economica,* XII [1945], 22–25.) But the idea criticized in the text is still widely held by economists.

technological improvement which it suggests. However, if there is scarcity, there must always be an unused technological opportunity to improve the state of well-being by a lengthening of the period of production in some branches of industry, regardless of whether or not the state of technological knowledge has changed. If the means are scarce, if the praxeological correlation of ends and means still exists, there are by logical necessity unsatisfied wants with regard both to nearer and to remoter periods of the future. There are always goods the procurement of which we must forego because the way that leads to their production is too long and would prevent us from satisfying more urgent needs. The fact that we do not provide more amply for the future is the outcome of a weighing of satisfaction in nearer periods of the future against satisfaction in remoter periods of the future. The ratio which is the outcome of this valuation is originary interest.

In such a world of perfect technological knowledge a promoter drafts a plan *A* according to which a hotel in picturesque, but not easily accessible, mountain districts and the roads leading to it should be built. In examining the practicability of this plan he discovers that the means available are not sufficient for its execution. Calculating the prospects of the profitability of the investment, he comes to the conclusion that the expected proceeds are not great enough to cover the costs of material and labor to be expended and interest on the capital to be invested. He renounces the execution of project *A* and embarks instead upon the realization of another plan, *B*. According to plan *B* the hotel is to be erected in a more easily accessible location which does not offer all the advantages of the picturesque landscape which plan *A* had selected, but in which it can be built either with lower costs of construction or finished in a shorter time. If no interest on the capital invested were to enter into the calculation, the illusion could arise that the state of the market data—supply of capital goods and the valuations of the public—allows for the execution of plan *A*. However, the realization of plan *A* would withdraw scarce factors of production from employments in which they could satisfy wants considered more urgent by the consumers. It would mean a manifest malinvestment, a squandering of the means available.

A lengthening of the period of production can increase the quantity of output per unit of input or produce goods which cannot be produced at all within a shorter period of production. But it is not true that the imputation of the value of this additional wealth to the capital goods required for the lengthening of the period of production generates interest. If one were to assume this, one would relapse into the crassest errors of the productivity approach, irrefutably exploded by Böhm-Bawerk. The contribution of the complementary factors of production to the result of the process is the reason for their being considered as valuable; it explains the prices paid for them and is fully taken into account in the determination of these prices. No residuum is left that is not accounted for and could explain interest.

It has been asserted that in the imaginary construction of the evenly rotating economy no interest would appear.[3] However, it can be shown that this assertion is incompatible with the assumptions on which the construction of the evenly rotating economy is based.

We begin with the distinction between two classes of saving: plain saving and capitalist saving. Plain saving is merely the piling up of consumers' goods for later consumption. Capitalist saving is the accumulation of goods which are designed for an improvement of production processes. The aim of plain saving is later consumption; it is merely postponement of consumption. Sooner or later the goods accumulated will be consumed and nothing will be left. The aim of capitalist saving is first an improvement in the productivity of effort. It accumulates capital goods which are employed for further production and are not merely reserves for later consumption. The boon derived from plain saving is later consumption of the stock not instantly consumed but accumulated for later use. The boon derived from capitalist saving is the increase of the quantity of goods produced or the production of goods which could not be produced at all without its aid. In constructing the image of an evenly rotating (static) economy, economists disregard the process of capital accumulation; the capital goods are given and remain, as, according to the underlying assumptions, no changes occur in the data. There is neither accumulation of new capital through saving, nor consumption of capital available through a surplus of consumption over income, i.e., current production minus the funds required for the maintenance of capital. It is now our task to demonstrate that these assumptions are incompatible with the idea that there is no interest.

There is no need to dwell, in this reasoning, upon plain saving. The objective of plain saving is to provide for a future in which the saver could possibly be less amply supplied than in the present. Yet, one of the fundamental assumptions characterizing the imaginary construction of the evenly rotating economy is that the future does not differ at all from the present, that the actors are fully aware of this fact

3. Cf. J. Schumpeter, *The Theory of Economic Development,* trans. by R. Opie (Cambridge, 1934), pp. 34–46, 54.

and act accordingly. Hence, in the frame of this construction, no room is left for the phenomenon of plain saving.

It is different with the fruit of capitalist saving, the accumulated stock of capital goods. There is in the evenly rotating economy neither saving and accumulation of additional capital goods nor eating up of already existing capital goods. Both phenomena would amount to a change in the data and would thus disturb the even rotation of such an imaginary system. Now, the magnitude of saving and capital accumulation in the past—i.e., in the period preceding the establishment of the evenly rotating economy—was adjusted to the height of the rate of interest. If—with the establishment of the conditions of the evenly rotating economy—the owners of the capital goods were no longer to receive any interest, the conditions which were operative in the allocation of the available stocks of goods to the satisfaction of wants in the various periods of the future would be upset. The altered state of affairs requires a new allocation. Also in the evenly rotating economy the difference in the valuation of want-satisfaction in various periods of the future cannot disappear. Also in the frame of this imaginary construction, people will assign a higher value to an apple available today as against an apple available in ten or a hundred years. If the capitalist no longer receives interest, the balance between satisfaction in nearer and remoter periods of the future is disarranged. The fact that a capitalist has maintained his capital at just 100,000 dollars was conditioned by the fact that 100,000 present dollars were equal to 105,000 dollars available twelve months later. These 5,000 dollars were in his eyes sufficient to outweigh the advantages to be expected from an instantaneous consumption of a part of this sum. If interest payments are eliminated, capital consumption ensues.

This is the essential deficiency of the static system as Schumpeter depicts it. It is not sufficient to assume that the capital equipment of such a system has been accumulated in the past, that it is now available to the extent of this previous accumulation and is henceforth unalterably maintained at this level. We must also assign in the frame of this imaginary system a role to the operation of forces which bring about such a maintenance. If one eliminates the capitalist's role as receiver of interest, one replaces it by the capitalist's role as consumer of capital. There is no longer any reason why the owner of capital goods should abstain from employing them for consumption. Under the assumptions implied in the imaginary construction of static conditions (the evenly rotating economy) there is no need to keep them in reserve for rainy days. But even if, inconsistently enough, we were to assume that a part of them is devoted to this purpose and therefore withheld from current consumption, at least that part of capital will be consumed which corresponds to the amount that capitalist saving exceeds plain saving.[4]

If there were no originary interest, capital goods would not be devoted to immediate consumption and capital would not be consumed. On the contrary, under such an unthinkable and unimaginable state of affairs there would be no consumption at all, but only saving, accumulation of capital, and investment. Not the impossible disappearance of originary interest, but the abolition of payment of interest to the owners of capital, would result in capital consumption. The capitalists would consume their capital goods and their capital precisely because there is originary interest and present want-satisfaction is preferred to later satisfaction.

Therefore there cannot be any question of abolishing interest by any institutions, laws, or devices of bank manipulation. He who wants to "abolish" interest will have to induce people to value an apple available in a hundred years no less than a present apple. What can be abolished by laws and decrees is merely the right of the capitalists to receive interest. But such decrees would bring about capital consumption and would very soon throw mankind back into the original state of natural poverty.

3. The Height of Interest Rates

In plain saving and in the capitalist saving of isolated economic actors the difference in the valuation of want-satisfaction in various periods of the future manifests itself in the extent to which people provide in a more ample way for nearer than for remoter periods of the future. Under the conditions of a market economy the rate of originary interest is, provided the assumptions involved in the imaginary construction of the evenly rotating economy are present, equal to the ratio of a definite amount of money available today and the amount available at a later date which is considered as its equivalent.

The rate of originary interest directs the investment activities of the entrepreneurs. It determines the length of waiting time and of the period of production in every branch of industry.

People often raise the question of which rate of interest, a "high" or a "low," stimulates saving and capital accumulation more and which less. The question makes no sense. The lower the discount attached to future goods is, the lower is the rate of originary interest. People

4. Cf. Robbins, "On a Certain Ambiguity in the Conception of Stationary Equilibrium," *The Economic Journal,* XL (1930), 211 ff.

do not save more because the rate of originary interest rises, and the rate of originary interest does not drop on account of an increase in the amount of saving. Changes in the originary rates of interest and in the amount of saving are—other things, especially the institutional conditions, being equal—two aspects of the same phenomenon. The disappearance of originary interest would be tantamount to the disappearance of consumption. The increase of originary interest beyond all measure would be tantamount to the disappearance of saving and any provision for the future.

The quantity of the available supply of capital goods influences neither the rate of originary interest nor the amount of further saving. Even the most plentiful supply of capital need not necessarily bring about either a lowering of the rate of originary interest or a drop in the propensity to save. The increase in capital accumulation and the per capita quota of capital invested which is a characteristic mark of economically advanced nations does not necessarily either lower the rate of originary interest or weaken the propensity of individuals to make additional savings. People are, in dealing with these problems, for the most part misled by comparing merely the market rates of interest as they are determined on the loan market. However, these gross rates are not merely expressive of the height of originary interest. They contain, as will be shown later, other elements besides, the effect of which accounts for the fact that the gross rates are as a rule higher in poorer countries than in richer ones.

It is generally asserted that, other things being equal, the better individuals are supplied for the immediate future, the better they provide for wants for the remoter future. Consequently, it is said, the amount of total saving and capital accumulation within an economic system depends on the arrangement of the population into groups of different income levels. In a society with approximate income equality there is, it is said, less saving than in a society in which there is more inequality. There is a grain of truth in such observations. However, they are statements about psychological facts and as such lack the universal validity and necessity inherent in praxeological statements. Moreover, the other things the equality of which they presuppose comprehend the various individuals' valuations, their subjective value judgment in weighing the pros and cons of immediate consumption and of postponement of consumption. There are certainly many individuals whose behavior they describe correctly, but there also are other individuals who act in a different way. The French peasants, although for the most part people of moderate wealth and income, were in the nineteenth century widely known for their parsimonious habits, while wealthy members of the aristocracy and heirs of huge fortunes amassed in commerce and industry were no less renowned for their profligacy.

It is therefore impossible to formulate any praxeological theorem concerning the relation of the amount of capital available in the whole nation or to individual people on the one hand and the amount of saving or capital consumption and the height of the originary rate of interest on the other hand. The allocation of scarce resources to want-satisfaction in various periods of the future is determined by value judgments and indirectly by all those factors which constitute the individuality of the acting man.

4. Originary Interest in the Changing Economy

So far we have dealt with the problem of originary interest under certain assumptions: that the turnover of goods is effected by the employment of neutral money; that saving, capital accumulation, and the determination of interest rates are not hampered by institutional obstacles; and that the whole economic process goes on in the frame of an evenly rotating economy. We shall drop the first two of these assumptions in the following chapter. Now we want to deal with originary interest in a changing economy.

He who wants to provide for the satisfaction of future needs must correctly anticipate these needs. If he fails in this understanding of the future, his provision will prove less satisfactory or totally futile. There is no such thing as an abstract saving that could provide for all classes of want-satisfaction and would be neutral with regard to changes occurring in conditions and valuations. Originary interest can therefore in the changing economy never appear in a pure unalloyed form. It is only in the imaginary construction of the evenly rotating economy that the mere passing of time matures originary interest; in the passage of time and with the progress of the process of production more and more value accrues, as it were, to the complementary factors of production; with the termination of the process of production the lapse of time has generated in the price of the product the full quota of originary interest. In the changing economy during the period of production there also arise synchronously other changes in valuations. Some goods are valued higher than previously, some lower. These alterations are the source from which entrepreneurial profits and losses stem. Only those entrepreneurs who in their planning have correctly anticipated the future state of the market are in a position to reap, in selling the products, an excess over the costs of production (inclusive of net originary interest) expended. An entrepreneur who has failed in his speculative understanding of the future can sell his products, if at all, only at prices which do not cover completely his expenditures plus originary interest on the capital invested.

Like entrepreneurial profit and loss, interest is not a price, but a magnitude which is to be disengaged by a particular mode of computation from the price of the products of successful business operations. The gross difference between the price at which a commodity is sold and the costs expended in its production (exclusive of interest on the capital invested) was called profit in the terminology of British classical economics.[5] Modern economics conceives this magnitude as a complex of catallactically disparate items. The excess of gross receipts over expenditures which the classical economists called profit includes the price for the entrepreneur's own labor employed in the process of production, interest on the capital invested, and finally entrepreneurial profit proper. If such an excess has not been reaped at all in the sale of the products, the entrepreneur not only fails to get profit proper, he receives neither an equivalent for the market value of the labor he has contributed nor interest on the capital invested.

The breaking down of gross profit (in the classical sense of the term) into managerial wages, interest, and entrepreneurial profit is not merely a device of economic theory. It developed, with progressing perfection in business practices of accountancy and calculation, in the field of commercial routine independently of the reasoning of the economists. The judicious and sensible businessman does not attach practical significance to the confused and garbled concept of profit as employed by the classical economists. His notion of costs of production includes the potential market price of his own services contributed, the interest paid on capital borrowed, and the potential interest he could earn, according to the conditions of the market, on his own capital invested in the enterprise by lending it to other people. Only the excess of proceeds over the costs so calculated is in his eyes entrepreneurial profit.[6]

The precipitation of entrepreneurial wages from the complex of all the other items included in the profit concept of classical economics presents no particular problem. It is more difficult to sunder entrepreneurial profit from originary interest. In the changing economy

5. Cf. R. Whately, *Elements of Logic* (9th ed. London, 1848), pp. 354 ff.; E. Cannan, *A History of the Theories of Production and Distribution in English Political Economy from 1776 to 1848* (3d ed. London, 1924), pp. 189 ff.

6. But, of course, the present-day intentional confusion of all economic concepts is conducive to obscuring this distinction. Thus, in the United States, in dealing with the dividends paid by corporations people speak of "profits."

interest stipulated in loan contracts is always a gross magnitude out of which the pure rate of originary interest must be computed by a particular process of computation and analytical repartition. It has been shown already that in every act of lending, even apart from the problem of changes in the monetary unit's purchasing power, there is an element of entrepreneurial venture. The granting of credit is necessarily always an entrepreneurial speculation which can possibly result in failure and the loss of a part or of the total amount lent. Every interest stipulated and paid in loans includes not only originary interest but also entrepreneurial profit.

This fact for a long time misled the attempts to construct a satisfactory theory of interest. It was only the elaboration of the imaginary construction of the evenly rotating economy that made it possible to distinguish precisely between originary interest and entrepreneurial profit and loss.

5. The Computation of Interest

Originary interest is the outgrowth of valuations unceasingly fluctuating and changing. It fluctuates and changes with them. The custom of computing interest pro anno is merely commercial usage and a convenient rule of reckoning. It does not affect the height of the interest rates as determined by the market.

The activities of the entrepreneurs tend toward the establishment of a uniform rate of originary interest in the whole market economy. If there turns up in one sector of the market a margin between the prices of present goods and those of future goods which deviates from the margin prevailing in other sectors, a trend toward equalization is brought about by the striving of businessmen to enter those sectors in which this margin is higher and to avoid those in which it is lower. The final rate of originary interest is the same in all parts of the market of the evenly rotating economy.

The valuations resulting in the emergence of originary interest prefer satisfaction in a nearer period of the future to satisfaction of the same kind and extent in a remoter period of the future. Nothing would justify the assumption that this discounting of satisfaction in remoter periods progresses continuously and evenly. If we were to assume this, we would imply that the period of provision is infinite. However, the mere fact that individuals differ in their provision for future needs and that even to the most provident actor provision beyond a definite period appears supererogatory, forbids us to think of the period of provision as infinite.

The usages of the loan market must not mislead us. It is customary to stipulate a uniform rate of interest for the whole duration of a loan contract[7] and to apply a uniform rate in computing compound interest. The real determination of interest rates is independent of these and other arithmetical devices of interest computation. If the rate of interest is unalterably fixed by contract for a period of time, intervening changes in the market rate of interest are reflected in corresponding changes in the prices paid for the principal, due allowance being made for the fact that the amount of principal to be paid back at the maturity of the loan is unalterably stipulated. It does not affect the result whether one calculates with an unchanging rate of interest and changing prices of the principal or with changing interest rates and an unchanging amount of the principal, or with changes in both magnitudes.

The terms of a loan contract are not independent of the stipulated duration of the loan. Not only because those components of the gross rate of market interest which made it deviate from the rate of originary interest are affected by differences in the duration of the loan, but also on account of factors which bring about changes in the rate of originary interest, loan contracts are valued and appraised differently according to the duration of the loan stipulated.

7. There are, of course, also deviations from this usage.

XX. INTEREST, CREDIT EXPANSION, AND THE TRADE CYCLE

1. The Problems

IN the market economy in which all acts of interpersonal exchange are performed by the intermediary of money, the category of originary interest manifests itself primarily in the interest on money loans.

It has been pointed out already that in the imaginary construction of the evenly rotating economy the rate of originary interest is uniform. There prevails in the whole system only one rate of interest. The rate of interest on loans coincides with the rate of originary interest as manifested in the ratio between prices of present and of future goods. We may call this rate the neutral rate of interest.

The evenly rotating economy presupposes neutral money. As money can never be neutral, special problems arise.

If the money relation—i.e., the ratio between the demand for and the supply of money for cash holding—changes, all prices of goods and services are affected. These changes, however, do not affect the prices of the various goods and services at the same time and to the same extent. The resulting modifications in the wealth and income of various individuals can also alter the data determining the height of originary interest. The final state of the rate of originary interest to the establishment of which the system tends after the appearance of changes in the money relation, is no longer that final state toward which it had tended before. Thus, the driving force of money has the power to bring about lasting changes in the final rate of originary interest and neutral interest.

Then there is a second, even more momentous, problem which, of course, may also be looked upon as another aspect of the same problem. Changes in the money relation may under certain circumstances first affect the loan market in which the demand for and the supply of loans influence the market rate of interest on loans, which we may call the gross money (or market) rate of interest. Can such changes in the gross money rate cause the net rate of interest included in it to deviate lastingly from the height which corresponds to the rate of originary interest, i.e., the difference between the valuation of present and future goods? Can events on the loan market partially or totally eliminate originary interest? No economist will hesitate to answer these questions in the negative. But then a further problem arises: How does the interplay of the market factors readjust the gross money rate to the height conditioned by the rate of originary interest?

These are great problems. These were the problems economists tried to solve in discussing banking, fiduciary media and circulation credit, credit expansion, gratuitousness or nongratuitousness of credit, the cyclical movements of trade, and all other problems of indirect exchange.

2. The Entrepreneurial Component in the Gross Market Rate of Interest

The market rates of interest on loans are not pure interest rates. Among the components contributing to their determination there are also elements which are not interest. The moneylender is always an entrepreneur. Every grant of credit is a speculative entrepreneurial venture, the success or failure of which is uncertain. The lender is always faced with the possibility that he may lose a part or the whole of the principal lent. His appraisal of this danger determines his conduct in bargaining with the prospective debtor about the terms of the contract.

There can never be perfect safety either in moneylending or in other classes of credit transactions and deferred payments. Debtors, guarantors, and warrantors may become insolvent; collateral and mortgages may become worthless. The creditor is always a virtual partner of the debtor or a virtual owner of the pledged and mortgaged property. He can be affected by changes in the market data concerning them. He has linked his fate with that of the debtor or with the changes occurring in the price of the collateral. Capital as such does not bear interest; it must be well employed and invested not only in order to yield interest, but also lest it disappear entirely. The dictum *pecunia pecuniam parere non potest* (money cannot beget money) is meaningful in this sense, which, of course, differs radically from the sense which ancient and medieval philosophers attached to it. Gross interest can be reaped only by creditors who have been successful in their lending. If they earn any net interest at all, it is included in a yield which contains more than merely net interest. Net interest is a magnitude which only analytical thinking can extract from the gross proceeds of the creditor.

The entrepreneurial component included in the creditor's gross proceeds is determined by all those factors which are operative in every entrepreneurial venture. It is, moreover, codetermined by the legal and institutional setting. The contracts which place the debtor and his fortune or the collateral as a buffer between the creditor and the disastrous consequences of malinvestment of the capital lent, are conditioned by laws and institutions. The creditor is less exposed to loss and failure than the debtor only in so far as this legal and institutional framework makes it possible for him to enforce his claims against refractory debtors. There is, however, no need for economics to enter into a detailed scrutiny of the legal aspects involved in bonds and debentures, preferred stock, mortgages, and other kinds of credit transactions.

The entrepreneurial component is present in all species of loans. It is customary to distinguish between consumption or personal loans on the one hand, and productive or business loans on the other. The characteristic mark of the former class is that it enables the borrower to spend expected future proceeds. In acquiring a claim to a share in these future proceeds, the lender becomes virtually an entrepreneur, as in acquiring a claim to a share in the future proceeds of a business. The particular uncertainty of the outcome of his lending consists in the uncertainty about these future proceeds.

It is furthermore customary to distinguish between private and public loans, i.e., loans to governments and subdivisions of governments. The particular uncertainty inherent in such loans concerns the life of secular power. Empires may crumble and governments may be overthrown by revolutionaries who are not prepared to assume responsibility for the debts contracted by their predecessors. That there is, besides, something basically vicious in all kinds of long-term government debts, has been pointed out already.[1]

Over all species of deferred payments hangs, like the sword of Damocles, the danger of government interference. Public opinion has always been biased against creditors. It identifies creditors with the idle rich and debtors with the industrious poor. It abhors the former as ruthless exploiters and pities the latter as innocent victims of oppression. It considers government action designed to curtail the claims of the creditors as measures extremely beneficial to the immense majority at the expense of a small minority of hardboiled usurers. It did not notice at all that nineteenth-century capitalist innovations have wholly changed the composition of the classes of creditors and debtors. In the days of Solon the Athenian, of ancient

1. Cf. above, pp. 226–228.

Rome's agrarian laws, and of the Middle Ages, the creditors were by and large the rich and the debtors the poor. But in this age of bonds and debentures, mortgage banks, saving banks, life insurance policies, and social security benefits, the masses of people with more moderate income are rather themselves creditors. On the other hand, the rich, in their capacity as owners of common stock, of plants, farms, and real estate, are more often debtors than creditors. In asking for the expropriation of creditors, the masses are unwittingly attacking their own particular interests.

With public opinion in this state, the creditor's unfavorable chance of being harmed by anticreditor measures is not balanced by a favorable chance of being privileged by antidebtor measures. This unbalance would bring about a unilateral tendency toward a rise of the entrepreneurial component contained in the gross rate of interest if the political danger were limited to the loan market, and would not in the same way affect today all kinds of private ownership of the means of production. As things are in our day, no kind of investment is safe against the political dangers of anticapitalistic measures. A capitalist cannot reduce the vulnerability of his wealth by preferring direct investment in business to lending his capital to business or to the government.

The political risks involved in moneylending do not affect the height of originary interest; they affect the entrepreneurial component included in the gross market rate. In the extreme case—i.e., in a situation in which the impending nullification of all contracts concerning deferred payments is expected—they would cause the entrepreneurial component to increase beyond all measure.[2]

3. The Price Premium as a Component of the Gross Market Rate of Interest

Money is neutral if the cash-induced changes in the monetary unit's purchasing power affect at the same time and to the same extent the prices of all commodities and services. With neutral money, a neutral rate of interest would be conceivable, provided there were no deferred payments. If there are deferred payments and if we disregard the entrepreneurial position of the creditor and the ensuing entrepreneurial component in the gross rate of interest, we must furthermore assume that the eventuality of future changes in purchas-

2. The difference between this case (case *b*) and the case of the expected end of all earthly things dealt with on p. 527 (case *a*) is this: in case *a* originary interest increases beyond all measure because future goods become entirely worthless; in case *b* originary interest does not change while the entrepreneurial component increases beyond all measure.

ing power is taken into account in stipulating the terms of the contract. The principal is to be multiplied periodically by the index number and thus to be increased or decreased in accordance with the changes that have come to pass in purchasing power. With the adjustment of the principal, the amount from which the rate of interest is to be calculated changes too. Thus, this rate is a neutral rate of interest.

With neutral money, neutralization of the rate of interest could also be attained by another stipulation, provided the parties are in a position to anticipate correctly the future changes in purchasing power. They could stipulate a gross rate of interest containing an allowance for such changes, a percentile addendum to, or subtrahendum from, the rate of originary interest. We may call this allowance the—positive or negative—price premium. In the case of a quickly progressing deflation, the negative price premium could not only swallow the whole rate of originary interest, but even reverse the gross rate into a minus quantity, an amount charged to the creditor's account. If the price premium is correctly calculated, neither the creditor's nor the debtor's position is affected by intervening changes in purchasing power. The rate of interest is neutral.

However, all these assumptions are not only imaginary, they cannot even hypothetically be thought of without contradiction. In the changing economy, the rate of interest can never be neutral. In the changing economy, there is no uniform rate of originary interest; there only prevails a tendency toward the establishment of such uniformity. Before the final state of originary interest is attained, new changes in the data emerge which divert anew the movement of interest rates toward a new final state. Where everything is unceasingly in flux, no neutral rate of interest can be established.

In the world of reality all prices are fluctuating and acting men are forced to take full account of these changes. Entrepreneurs embark upon business ventures and capitalists change their investments only because they anticipate such changes and want to profit from them. The market economy is essentially characterized as a social system in which there prevails an incessant urge toward improvement. The most provident and enterprising individuals are driven to earn profit by readjusting again and again the arrangement of production activities so as to fill in the best possible way the needs of the consumers, both those needs of which the consumers themselves are already aware and those latent needs of the satisfaction of which they have not yet thought themselves. These speculative ventures of the promoters revolutionize afresh each day the structure of prices and thereby also the height of the gross market rate of interest.

He who expects a rise in certain prices enters the loan market as a borrower and is ready to allow a higher gross rate of interest than he would allow if he were to expect a less momentous rise in prices or no rise at all. On the other hand, the lender, if he himself expects a rise in prices, grants loans only if the gross rate is higher than it would be under a state of the market in which less momentous or no upward changes in prices are anticipated. The borrower is not deterred by a higher rate if his project seems to offer such good chances that it can afford higher costs. The lender would abstain from lending and would himself enter the market as an entrepreneur and bidder for commodities and services if the gross rate of interest were not to compensate him for the profits he could reap this way. The expectation of rising prices thus has the tendency to make the gross rate of interest rise, while the expectation of dropping prices makes it drop. If the expected changes in the price structure concern only a limited group of commodities and services, and are counterbalanced by the expectation of an opposite change in the prices of other goods, as is the case in the absence of changes in the money relation, the two opposite trends by and large counterpoise each other. But if the money relation is sensibly altered and a general rise or fall in the prices of all commodities and services is expected, one tendency carries on. A positive or negative price premium emerges in all deals concerning deferred payments.[3]

The role of the price premium in the changing economy is different from that we ascribed to it in the hypothetical and unrealizable scheme developed above. It can never entirely remove, even as far as credit operations alone are concerned, the effects of changes in the money relation; it can never make interest rates neutral. It cannot alter the fact that money is essentially equipped with a driving force of its own. Even if all actors were to know correctly and completely the quantitative data concerning the changes in the supply of money (in the broader sense) in the whole economic system, the dates on which such changes were to occur and what individuals were to be first affected by them, they would not be in a position to know beforehand whether and to what extent the demand for money for cash holding would change and in what temporal sequence and to what extent the prices of the various commodities would change. The price premium could counterpoise the effects of changes in the money relation upon the substantial importance and the economic significance of credit contracts only if its appearance were to precede the occurrence of the price changes generated by the alteration in the money relation. It would have to be the result of a reasoning by virtue

3. Cf. Irving Fisher, *The Rate of Interest* (New York, 1907), pp. 77 ff.

of which the actors try to compute in advance the date and the extent of such price changes with regard to all commodities and services which directly or indirectly count for their own state of satisfaction. However, such computations cannot be established because their performance would require a perfect knowledge of future conditions and valuations.

The emergence of the price premium is not the product of an arithmetical operation which could provide reliable knowledge and eliminate the uncertainty concerning the future. It is the outcome of the promoters' understanding of the future and their calculations based on such an understanding. It comes into existence step by step as soon as first a few and then successively more and more actors become aware of the fact that the market is faced with cash-induced changes in the money relation and consequently with a trend oriented in a definite direction. Only when people begin to buy or to sell in order to take advantage of this trend, does the price premium come into existence.

It is necessary to realize that the price premium is the outgrowth of speculations anticipating changes in the money relation. What induces it, in the case of the expectation that an inflationary trend will keep on going, is already the first sign of that phenomenon which later, when it becomes general, is called "flight into real values" and finally produces the crack-up boom and the crash of the monetary system concerned. As in every case of the understanding of future developments, it is possible that the speculators may err, that the inflationary or deflationary movement will be stopped or slowed down, and that prices will differ from what they expected.

The increased propensity to buy or to sell, which generates the price premium, affects as a rule short-term loans sooner and to a greater extent than long-term loans. As far as this is the case, the price premium affects the market for short-term loans first, and only later, by virtue of the concatenation of all parts of the market, also the market for long-term loans. However, there are instances in which a price premium in long-term loans appears independently of what is going on with regard to short-term loans. This was especially the case in international lending in the days in which there was still a live international capital market. It happened occasionally that lenders were confident with regard to the short-term development of a foreign country's national currency; in short-term loans stipulated in this currency there was no price premium at all or only a slight one. But the appraisal of the long-term aspects of the currency concerned was less favorable, and consequently in long-term contracts a considerable price premium was taken into account. The result was that long-term loans stipulated in this currency could be floated only at a higher rate than the same debtor's loans stipulated in terms of gold or a foreign currency.

We have shown one reason why the price premium can at best practically deaden, but never eliminate entirely, the repercussions of cash-induced changes in the money relation upon the content of credit transactions. (A second reason will be dealt with in the next section.) The price premium always lags behind the changes in purchasing power because what generates it is not the change in the supply of money (in the broader sense), but the—necessarily later-occurring—effects of these changes upon the price structure. Only in the final state of a ceaseless inflation do things become different. The panic of the currency catastrophe, the crack-up boom, is not only characterized by a tendency for prices to rise beyond all measure, but also by a rise beyond all measure of the positive price premium. No gross rate of interest, however great, appears to a prospective lender high enough to compensate for the losses expected from the progressing drop in the monetary unit's purchasing power. He abstains from lending and prefers to buy himself "real" goods. The loan market comes to a standstill.

4. The Loan Market

The gross rates of interest as determined on the loan market are not uniform. The entrepreneurial component which they always include varies according to the peculiar characteristics of the specific deal. It is one of the most serious shortcomings of all historical and statistical studies devoted to the movement of interest rates that they neglect this factor. It is useless to arrange data concerning interest rates of the open market or the discount rates of the central banks in time series. The various data available for the construction of such time series are incommensurable. The same central bank's rate of discount meant something different in various periods of time. The institutional conditions affecting the activities of various nations' central banks, their private banks, and their organized loan markets are so different, that it is entirely misleading to compare the nominal interest rates without paying full regard to these diversities. We know a priori that, other things being equal, the lenders are intent upon preferring high interest rates to low ones, and the debtors upon preferring low rates to high ones. But these other things are never equal. There prevails upon the loan market a tendency toward the equalization of gross interest rates for loans for which the factors determining the height of the entrepreneurial component and the price premium are equal. This knowledge provides a mental tool for the interpretation of the facts concerning the history of interest rates. Without the aid of this knowledge, the vast historical and statistical material available would be merely an accumulation of meaningless figures. In arranging time series of the prices of certain primary commodities, empiricism has at least an apparent justification in the fact that the price data dealt with refer to the same physical object. It is a spurious excuse indeed as prices are not related to the unchanging physical properties of things, but to the changing values which acting men attach to them. But in the study of interest rates, even this lame excuse cannot be advanced. Gross interest rates as they appear in reality have nothing else in common than those characteristics which catallactic theory sees in them. They are complex phenomena and can never be used for the construction of an empirical or a posteriori theory of interest. They can neither verify nor falsify what economics teaches about the problems involved. They constitute, if carefully analyzed with all the knowledge economics conveys, invaluable documentation for economic history; they are of no avail for economic theory.

It is customary to distinguish the market for short-term loans (money market) from the market for long-term loans (capital market). A more penetrating analysis must even go further in classifying loans according to their duration. Besides, there are differences with regard to the legal characteristics which the terms of the contract assign to the lender's claim. In short, the loan market is not homogeneous. But the most conspicuous differences arise from the entrepreneurial component included in the gross rates of interest. It is this that people refer to when asserting that credit is based on trust or confidence.

The connexity between all sectors of the loan market and the gross rates of interest determined on them is brought about by the inherent tendency of the net rates of interest included in these gross rates toward the final state of originary interest. With regard to this tendency, catallactic theory is free to deal with the market rate of interest as if it were a uniform phenomenon, and to abstract from the entrepreneurial component which is necessarily always included in the gross rates and from the price premium which is occasionally included.

The prices of all commodities and services are at any instant moving toward a final state. If this final state were ever to be reached, it would show in the ratio between the prices of present goods and future goods the final state of originary interest. However, the changing economy never reaches the imaginary final state. New data emerge again and again and divert the trend of prices from the previous goal of their movement toward a different final state to which a different rate of originary interest may correspond. In the rate of originary interest there is no more permanence than in prices and wage rates.

Those people whose provident action is intent upon adjusting the employment of the factors of production to the changes occurring in the data—viz., the entrepreneurs and promotors—base their calculations upon the prices, wage rates, and interest rates as determined on the market. They discover discrepancies between the present prices of the complementary factors of production and the anticipated prices of the products minus the market rate of interest, and are eager to profit from them. The role which the rate of interest plays in these deliberations of the planning businessman is obvious. It shows him how far he can go in withholding factors of production from employment for want-satisfaction in nearer periods of the future and in dedicating them to want-satisfaction in remoter periods. It shows him what period of production conforms in every concrete case to the difference which the public makes in the ratio of valuation between present goods and future goods. It prevents him from embarking upon projects the execution of which would not agree with the limited amount of capital goods provided by the saving of the public.

It is in influencing this primordial function of the rate of interest that the driving force of money can become operative in a particular way. Cash-induced changes in the money relation can under certain circumstances affect the loan market before they affect the prices of commodities and of labor. The increase or decrease in the supply of money (in the broader sense) can increase or decrease the supply of money offered on the loan market and thereby lower or raise the gross market rate of interest although no change in the rate of originary interest has taken place. If this happens, the market rate deviates from the height which the state of originary interest and the supply of capital goods available for production would require. Then the market rate of interest fails to fulfill the function it plays in guiding entrepreneurial decisions. It frustrates the entrepreneur's calculation and diverts his actions from those lines in which they would in the best possible way satisfy the most urgent needs of the consumers.

Then there is a second important fact to realize. If, other things being equal, the supply of money (in the broader sense) increases or decreases and thus brings about a general tendency for prices to rise or to drop, a positive or negative price premium would have to appear and to raise or lower the gross rate of market interest. But if such changes in the money relation affect first the loan market, they bring about just the opposite changes in the configuration of the gross market rates of interest. While a positive or negative price premium would be required to adjust the market rates of interest to the changes in the money relation, gross interest rates are in fact dropping or rising. This is the second reason why the instrumentality of the price premium cannot entirely eliminate the repercussions of cash-induced changes in the money relation upon the content of contracts concerning deferred payments. Its operation begins too late, it lags behind the changes in purchasing power, as has been shown above. Now we see that under certain circumstances the forces that push in the opposite direction manifest themselves sooner on the market than an adequate price premium.

5. The Effects of Changes in the Money Relation Upon Originary Interest

Like every change in the market data, changes in the money relation can possibly influence the rate of originary interest. According to the advocates of the inflationist view of history, inflation by and large tends to increase the earnings of the entrepreneurs. They reason this way: Commodity prices rise sooner and to a steeper level than wage rates. On the one hand, wage earners and salaried people, classes who spend the greater part of their income for consumption and save little, are adversely affected and must accordingly restrict their expenditures. On the other hand, the proprietary strata of the population, whose propensity to save a considerable part of their income is much greater, are favored; they do not increase their consumption in proportion, but also increase their savings. Thus in the community as a whole there arises a tendency toward an intensified accumulation of new capital. Additional investment is the corollary of the restriction of consumption imposed upon that part of the population which consumes the much greater part of the annual produce of the economic system. This *forced saving* lowers the rate of originary interest. It accelerates the pace of economic progress and the improvement in technological methods.

It is true that such forced saving can originate from an inflationary movement and occasionally did originate in the past. In dealing with the effects of changes in the money relation upon the height of interest rates, one must not neglect the fact that such changes can under certain circumstances really alter the rate of originary interest. But several other facts must be taken into account, too.

First one must realize that forced saving can result from inflation, but need not necessarily. It depends on the particular data of each instance of inflation whether or not the rise in wage rates lags behind the rise in commodity prices. A tendency for real wage rates to drop is not an inescapable consequence of a decline in the monetary unit's purchasing power. It could happen that nominal wage rates rise more or sooner than commodity prices.[4]

Furthermore, it is necessary to remember that the greater propensity of the wealthier classes to save and to accumulate capital is merely a psychological and not a praxeological fact. It could happen that these people to whom the inflationary movement conveys additional proceeds do not save and invest their boon but employ it for an increase in their consumption. It is impossible to predict with the apodictic definiteness which characterizes all theorems of economics, in what way those profiting from the inflation will act. History can tell us what happened in the past. But it cannot assert that it must happen again in the future.

It would be a serious blunder to neglect the fact that inflation also generates forces which tend toward capital consumption. One of its consequences is that it falsifies economic calculation and accounting. It produces the phenomenon of illusory or apparent profits. If the annual depreciation quotas are determined in such a way as not to pay full regard to the fact that the replacement of worn-out equipment will require higher costs than the amount for which it was purchased in the past, they are obviously insufficient. If in selling inventories and products the whole difference between the price spent for their acquisition and the price realized in the sale is entered in the books as a surplus, the error is the same. If the rise in the prices of stocks and real estate is considered as a gain, the illusion is no less manifest. What makes people believe that inflation results in general prosperity is precisely such illusory gains. They feel lucky and become openhanded in spending and enjoying life. They embellish their homes, they build new mansions and patronize the entertainment business. In spending apparent gains, the fanciful result of false reckoning, they are consuming capital. It does not matter who these spenders are. They may be businessmen or stock jobbers. They may be wage earners whose demand for higher pay is satisfied by the easygoing employers who think that they are getting richer from

4. We are dealing here with conditions on an unhampered labor market. About the argument advanced by Lord Keynes, see below, pp. 777 and 792–793.

day to day. They may be people supported by taxes which usually absorb a great part of the apparent gains.

Finally, with the progress of inflation more and more people become aware of the fall in purchasing power. For those not personally engaged in business and not familiar with the conditions of the stock market, the main vehicle of saving is the accumulation of savings deposits, the purchase of bonds and life insurance. All such savings are prejudiced by inflation. Thus saving is discouraged and extravagance seems to be indicated. The ultimate reaction of the public, the "flight into real values," is a desperate attempt to salvage some debris from the ruinous breakdown. It is, viewed from the angle of capital preservation, not a remedy, but merely a poor emergency measure. It can, at best, rescue a fraction of the saver's funds.

The main thesis of the champions of inflationism and expansionism is thus rather weak. It may be admitted that in the past inflation sometimes, but not always, resulted in forced saving and an increase in capital available. However, this does not mean that it must produce the same effects in the future too. On the contrary, one must realize that under modern conditions the forces driving toward capital consumption are more likely to prevail under inflationary conditions than those driving toward capital accumulation. At any rate, the final effect of such changes upon saving, capital, and the originary rate of interest depends upon the particular data of each instance.

The same is valid, with the necessary changes, with regard to the analogous consequences and effects of a deflationist or restrictionist movement.

6. The Gross Market Rate of Interest as Affected by Inflation and Credit Expansion

Whatever the ultimate effects of an inflationary or deflationary movement upon the height of the rate of originary interest may be, there is no correspondence between them and the temporary alterations which a cash-induced change in the money relation can bring about in the gross market rate of interest. If the inflow of money and money-substitutes into the market system or the outflow from it affects the loan market first, it temporarily disarranges the congruity between the gross market rates of interest and the rate of originary interest. The market rate rises or drops on account of the decrease or increase in the amount of money offered for lending, with no correlation to changes in the originary rate of interest which in the later course of events can possibly occur from the changes in the money relation. The market rate deviates from the height determined by that of the originary rate of interest, and forces come into operation which tend to adjust it anew to the ratio which corresponds to that of originary interest. It may happen that in the period of time which this adjustment requires, the height of originary interest varies, and this change can also be caused by the inflationary or deflationary process which brought about the deviation. Then the final rate of originary interest determining the final market rate toward which the readjustment tends is not the same rate which prevailed on the eve of the disarrangement. Such an occurrence may affect the data of the process of adjustment, but it does not affect its essence.

The phenomenon to be dealt with is this: The rate of originary interest is determined by the discount of future goods as against present goods. It is essentially independent of the supply of money and money-substitutes, notwithstanding the fact that changes in the supply of money and money-substitutes can indirectly affect its height. But the gross market rate of interest can be affected by changes in the money relation. A readjustment must take place. What is the nature of the process which brings it about?

In this section we are concerned only with inflation and credit expansion. For the sake of simplicity we assume that the whole additional amount of money and money-substitutes flows into the loan market and reaches the rest of the market only via the loans granted. This corresponds precisely to the conditions of an expansion of circulation credit.[5] Our scrutiny thus amounts to an analysis of the process caused by credit expansion.

In dealing with this analysis, we must refer again to the price premium. It has been mentioned already that at the very beginning of a credit expansion no positive price premium arises. A price premium cannot appear until the additional supply of money (in the broader sense) has already begun to affect the prices of commodities and services. But as long as credit expansion goes on and additional quantities of fiduciary media are hurled on the loan market, there continues a pressure upon the gross market rate of interest. The gross market rate would have to rise on account of the positive price premium which, with the progress of the expansionist process, would have to rise continually. But as credit expansion goes on, the gross market rate continues to lag behind the height at which it would cover both originary interest plus the positive price premium.

It is necessary to stress this point because it explodes the customary methods according to which people distinguish between what they consider low and high rates of interest. It is usual to take into account

5. About the "long-wave" fluctuations, see below, p. 575.

merely the arithmetical height of the rates or the trend which appears in their movement. Public opinion has definite ideas about a "normal" rate, something between 3 and 5 per cent. When the market rate rises above this height or when the market rates—without regard to their arithmetical ratio—are rising above their previous height, people believe that they are right in speaking of high or rising interest rates. As against these errors, it is necessary to emphasize that under the conditions of a general rise in prices (drop in the monetary unit's purchasing power) the gross market rate of interest can be considered as unchanged with regard to conditions of a period of a by and large unchanging purchasing power only if it includes a by and large adequate positive price premium. In this sense, the German Reichsbank's discount rate of 90 per cent was, in the fall of 1923, a low rate—indeed a ridiculously low rate—as it considerably lagged behind the price premium and did not leave anything for the other components of the gross market rate of interest. Essentially the same phenomenon manifests itself in every instance of a prolonged credit expansion. Gross market rates of interest rise in the further course of every expansion, but they are nonetheless low as they do not correspond to the height required by the expected further general rise in prices.

In analyzing the process of credit expansion, let us assume that the economic system's process of adjustment to the market data and of movement toward the establishment of final prices and interest rates is disturbed by the appearance of a new datum, namely, an additional quantity of fiduciary media offered on the loan market. At the gross market rate which prevailed on the eve of this disturbance, all those who were ready to borrow money at this rate, due allowance being made for the entrepreneurial component in each case, could borrow as much as they wanted. Additional loans can be placed only at a lower gross market rate. It does not matter whether this drop in the gross market rate expresses itself in an arithmetical drop in the percentage stipulated in the loan contracts. It could happen that the nominal interest rates remain unchanged and that the expansion manifests itself in the fact that at these rates loans are negotiated which would not have been made before on account of the height of the entrepreneurial component to be included. Such an outcome too amounts to a drop in gross market rates and brings about the same consequences.

A drop in the gross market rate of interest affects the entrepreneur's calculation concerning the chances of the profitability of projects considered. Along with the prices of the material factors of production, wage rates, and the anticipated future prices of the products, interest rates are items that enter into the planning businessman's calculation. The result of this calculation shows the businessman whether or not a definite project will pay. It shows him what investments can be made under the given state of the ratio in the public's valuation of future goods as against present goods. It brings his actions into agreement with this valuation. It prevents him from embarking upon projects the realization of which would be disapproved by the public because of the length of the waiting time they require. It forces him to employ the available stock of capital goods in such a way as to satisfy best the most urgent wants of the consumers.

But now the drop in interest rates falsifies the businessman's calculation. Although the amount of capital goods available did not increase, the calculation employs figures which would be utilizable only if such an increase had taken place. The result of such calculations is therefore misleading. They make some projects appear profitable and realizable which a correct calculation, based on an interest rate not manipulated by credit expansion, would have shown as unrealizable. Entrepreneurs embark upon the execution of such projects. Business activities are stimulated. A boom begins.

The additional demand on the part of the expanding entrepreneurs tends to raise the prices of producers' goods and wage rates. With the rise in wage rates, the prices of consumers' goods rise too. Besides, the entrepreneurs are contributing a share to the rise in the prices of consumers' goods as they too, deluded by the illusory gains which their business accounts show, are ready to consume more. The general upswing in prices spreads optimism. If only the prices of producers' goods had risen and those of consumers' goods had not been affected, the entrepreneurs would have become embarrassed. They would have had doubts concerning the soundness of their plans, as the rise in costs of production would have upset their calculations. But they are reassured by the fact that the demand for consumers' goods is intensified and makes it possible to expand sales in spite of rising prices. Thus they are confident that production will pay, notwithstanding the higher costs it involves. They are resolved to go on.

Of course, in order to continue production on the enlarged scale brought about by the expansion of credit, all entrepreneurs, those who did expand their activities no less than those who produce only within the limits in which they produced previously, need additional funds as the costs of production are now higher. If the credit expansion consists merely in a single, not repeated injection of a definite amount of fiduciary media into the loan market and then ceases altogether, the boom must very soon stop. The entrepreneurs cannot procure the funds they need for the further conduct of their ventures. The gross market rate of interest rises because the increased demand for loans is not counterpoised by a corresponding increase in the quantity of money available for lending. Commodity prices drop because some entrepreneurs are selling inventories and others abstain from buying. The size of business activities shrinks again. The boom ends because the forces which brought it about are no longer in operation. The additional quantity of circulation credit has exhausted its operation upon prices and wage rates. Prices, wage rates, and the various individuals' cash holdings are adjusted to the new money relation; they move toward the final state which corresponds to this money relation, without being disturbed by further injections of additional fiduciary media. The rate of originary interest which is coordinated to this new structure of the market acts with full momentum upon the gross market rate of interest. The gross market rate is no longer subject to disturbing influences exercised by cash-induced changes in the supply of money (in the broader sense).

The main deficiency of all attempts to explain the boom—viz., the general tendency to expand production and of all prices to rise—without reference to changes in the supply of money or fiduciary media, is to be seen in the fact that they disregard this circumstance. A general rise in prices can only occur if there is either a drop in the supply of *all* commodities or an increase in the supply of money (in the broader sense). Let us, for the sake of argument, admit for the moment that the statements of these nonmonetary explanations of the boom and the trade cycle are correct. Prices advance and business activities expand although no increase in the supply of money has occurred. Then very soon a tendency toward a drop in prices must arise, the demand for loans must increase, the gross market rates of interest must rise, and the short-lived boom comes to an end. In fact, every nonmonetary trade-cycle doctrine tacitly assumes—or ought logically to assume—that credit expansion is an attendant phenomenon of the boom.[6] It cannot help admitting that in the absence of such a credit expansion no boom could emerge and that the increase in the supply of money (in the broader sense) is a necessary condition of the general upward movement of prices. Thus on close inspection the statements of the nonmonetary explanations of cyclical fluctuations shrink to the assertion that credit expansion, while an indispensable

6. Cf. G. v. Haberler, *Prosperity and Depression* (new ed. League of Nations' Report, Geneva, 1939), p. 7.

requisite of the boom, is in itself alone not sufficient to bring it about and that some further conditions are required for its appearance.

Yet, even in this restricted sense, the teachings of the nonmonetary doctrines are vain. It is evident that every expansion of credit must bring about the boom as described above. The boom-creating tendency of credit expansion can fail to come only if another factor simultaneously counterbalances its growth. If, for instance, while the banks expand credit, it is expected that the government will completely tax away the businessmen's "excess" profits or that it will stop the further progress of credit expansion as soon as "pump-priming" will have resulted in rising prices, no boom can develop. The entrepreneurs will abstain from expanding their ventures with the aid of the cheap credits offered by the banks because they cannot expect to increase their gains. It is necessary to mention this fact because it explains the failure of the New Deal's pump-priming measures and other events of the 'thirties.

The boom can last only as long as the credit expansion progresses at an ever-accelerated pace. The boom comes to an end as soon as additional quantities of fiduciary media are no longer thrown upon the loan market. But it could not last forever even if inflation and credit expansion were to go on endlessly. It would then encounter the barriers which prevent the boundless expansion of circulation credit. It would lead to the crack-up boom and the breakdown of the whole monetary system.

The essence of monetary theory is the cognition that cash-induced changes in the money relation affect the various prices, wage rates, and interest rates neither at the same time nor to the same extent. If this unevenness were absent, money would be neutral; changes in the money relation would not affect the structure of business, the size and direction of production in the various branches of industry, consumption, and the wealth and income of the various strata of the population. Then the gross market rate of interest too would not be affected—either temporarily or lastingly—by changes in the sphere of money and circulation credit. The fact that such changes can modify the rate of originary interest is caused by the changes which this unevenness brings about in the wealth and income of various individuals. The fact that, apart from these changes in the rate of originary interest, the gross market rate is temporarily affected is in itself a manifestation of this unevenness. If the additional quantity of money enters the economic system in such a way as to reach the loan market only at a date at which it has already made commodity prices and wage rates rise, these immediate temporary effects upon the gross market rate of interest will be either slight or entirely absent. The gross market rate of interest is the more violently affected, the sooner the inflowing additional supply of money or fiduciary media reaches the loan market.

When under the conditions of credit expansion the whole amount of the additional money substitutes is lent to business, production is expanded. The entrepreneurs embark either upon lateral expansion of production (viz., the expansion of production without lengthening the period of production in the individual industry) or upon longitudinal expansion (viz., the lengthening of the period of production). In either case, the additional plants require the investment of additional factors of production. But the amount of capital goods available for investment has not increased. Neither does credit expansion bring about a tendency toward a restriction of consumption. It is true, as has been pointed out above in dealing with forced saving, that in the further progress of the expansion a part of the population will be compelled to restrict its consumption. But it depends on the particular conditions of each instance of credit expansion whether this forced saving of some groups of the people will overcompensate the increase in consumption on the part of other groups and will thus result in a net increase in the total amount of saving in the whole market system. At any rate, the immediate consequence of credit expansion is a rise in consumption on the part of those wage earners whose wages have risen on account of the intensified demand for labor displayed by the expanding entrepreneurs. Let us for the sake of argument assume that the increased consumption of these wage earners favored by the inflation and the forced saving of other groups prejudiced by the inflation are equal in amount and that no change in the total amount of consumption has occurred. Then the situation is this: Production has been altered in such a way that the length of waiting time has been extended. But the demand for consumers' goods has not dropped so as to make the available supply last for a longer period. Of course, this fact results in a rise in the prices of consumers' goods and thus brings about the tendency toward forced saving. However, this rise in the prices of consumers' goods strengthens the tendency of business to expand. The entrepreneurs draw from the fact that demand and prices are rising the inference that it will pay to invest and to produce more. They go on and their intensified activities bring about a further rise in the prices of producers' goods, in wage rates, and thereby again in the prices of consumers' goods. Business booms as long as the banks are expanding credit more and more.

On the eve of the credit expansion all those production processes were in operation which, under the given state of the market data, were deemed profitable. The system was moving toward a state in which all those eager to earn wages would be employed and all nonconvertible factors of production would be employed to the extent that the demand of the consumers and the available supply of nonspecific material factors and of labor would permit. A further expansion of production is possible only if the amount of capital goods is increased by additional saving, i.e., by surpluses produced and not consumed. The characteristic mark of the credit-expansion boom is that such additional capital goods have not been made available. The capital goods required for the expansion of business activities must be withdrawn from other lines of production.

We may call p the total supply of capital goods available on the eve of the credit expansion, and g the total amount of consumers' goods which these p could, over a definite period of time, make available for consumption without prejudice to further production. Now the entrepreneurs, enticed by credit expansion, embark upon the production of an additional quantity of g_3 of goods of the same kind which they already used to produce, and of a quantity of g_4 of goods of a kind not produced by them before. For the production of g_3 a supply of p_3 of capital goods is needed, and for the production of g_4 a supply of p_4. But as, according to our assumptions, the amount of capital goods available has remained unaltered, the quantities p_3 and p_4 are lacking. It is precisely this fact that distinguishes the "artificial" boom created by credit expansion from a "normal" expansion of production which only the addition of p_3 and p_4 to p can bring about.

Let us call r that amount of capital goods which, out of the gross proceeds of production over a definite period of time, must be reinvested for the replacement of those parts of p used up in the process of production. If r is employed for such replacement, one will be in a position to turn out g again in the following period of time; if r is withheld from this employment, p will be reduced by r, and $p — r$ will turn out in the following period of time only $g — a$. We may further assume that the economic system affected by credit expansion is a progressing system. It produced "normally," as it were, in the period of time preceding the credit expansion a surplus of capital goods $p_1 + p_2$. If no credit expansion had intervened, p_1 would have been employed for the production of an additional quantity of g_1 of the kind of goods produced previously, and p_2 for the production of the supply of g_2 of a kind of goods not produced before. The total amount of capital goods which are at the entrepreneurs' disposal and with regard to which they are free to make plans is $r + p_1 + p_2$. However, deluded by the cheap money, they act as if $r + p_1 + p_2 + p_3 + p_4$ were available and as if they were in a position to produce not only $g + g_1 + g_2$, but beyond this also $g_3 + g_4$. They outbid one another in competing for a share of a supply of capital goods which is insufficient for the realization of their overambitious plans.

The ensuing boom in the prices of producers' goods may at the beginning outrun the rise in the prices of consumer's goods. It may thus bring about a tendency toward a fall in the originary rate of interest. But with further progress of the expansionist movement the rise in the prices of the consumers' goods will outstrip the rise in the prices of producers' goods. The rise in wages and salaries and the additional gains of the capitalists, entrepreneurs, and farmers, although a great part of them is merely apparent, intensify the demand for consumers' goods. There is no need to enter into a scrutiny of the assertion of the advocates of credit expansion that the boom can, by means of forced saving, really increase the total supply of consumers' goods. At any rate, it is certain that the intensified demand for consumers' goods affects the market at a time when the additional investments are not yet in a position to turn out their products. The gulf between the prices of present goods and those of future goods widens again. A tendency toward a rise in the rate of originary interest is substituted for the tendency toward the opposite which may have come into operation at the earlier stages of the expansion.

This tendency toward a rise in the rate of originary interest and the emergence of a positive price premium explain some characteristics of the boom. The banks are faced with an increased demand for loans and advances on the part of business. The entrepreneurs are prepared to borrow money at higher gross rates of interest. They go on borrowing in spite of the fact that banks charge more interest. Arithmetically, the gross rates of interest are rising above their height on the eve of the expansion. Nonetheless, they lag catallactically behind the height at which they would cover originary interest plus entrepreneurial component and price premium. The banks believe that they have done all that is needed to stop "unsound" speculation when they lend on more onerous terms. They think that those critics who blame them for fanning the flames of the boom-frenzy of the market are wrong. They fail to see that in injecting more and more fiduciary media into the market they are in fact kindling the boom. It is the continuous increase in the supply of the fiduciary media that produces, feeds, and accelerates the boom. The state of the gross market rates of interest is only an outgrowth of this increase. If one wants to know whether or not there is credit expansion, one must look at the state of the supply of fiduciary media, not at the arithmetical state of interest rates.

It is customary to describe the boom as overinvestment. However, additional investment is only possible to the extent that there is an additional supply of capital goods available. As, apart from forced saving, the boom itself does not result in a restriction but rather in an increase in consumption, it does not procure more capital goods for new investment. The essence of the credit-expansion boom is not overinvestment, but investment in wrong lines, i.e., malinvestment. The entrepreneurs employ the available supply of $r + p_1 + p_2$ as if they were in a position to employ a supply of $r + p_1 + p_2 + p_3 + p_4$. They embark upon an expansion of investment on a scale for which the capital goods available do not suffice. Their projects are unrealizable on account of the insufficient supply of capital goods. They must fail sooner or later. The unavoidable end of the credit expansion makes the faults committed visible. There are plants which cannot be utilized because the plants needed for the production of the complementary factors of production are lacking; plants the products of which cannot be sold because the consumers are more intent upon purchasing other goods which, however, are not produced in sufficient quantities; plants the construction of which cannot be continued and finished because it has become obvious that they will not pay.

The erroneous belief that the essential feature of the boom is overinvestment and not malinvestment is due to the habit of judging conditions merely according to what is perceptible and tangible. The observer notices only the malinvestments which are visible and fails to recognize that these establishments are malinvestments only because of the fact that other plants—those required for the production of the complementary factors of production and those required for the production of consumers' goods more urgently demanded by the public—are lacking. Technological conditions make it necessary to start an expansion of production by expanding first the size of the plants producing the goods of those orders which are farthest removed from the finished consumers' goods. In order to expand the production of shoes, clothes, motorcars, furniture, houses, one must begin with increasing the production of iron, steel, copper, and other such goods. In employing the supply of $r + p_1 + p_2$ which would suffice for the production of $a + g_1 + g_2$ as if it were $r + p_1 + p_2 + p_3 + p_4$ and would suffice for the production of $a + g_1 + g_2 + g_3 +$

g_4, one must first engage in increasing the output of those products and structures which for physical reasons are first required. The whole entrepreneurial class is, as it were, in the position of a master-builder whose task it is to erect a building out of a limited supply of building materials. If this man overestimates the quantity of the available supply, he drafts a plan for the execution of which the means at his disposal are not sufficient. He oversizes the groundwork and the foundations and only discovers later in the progress of the construction that he lacks the material needed for the completion of the structure. It is obvious that our master-builder's fault was not overinvestment, but an inappropriate employment of the means at his disposal.

It is no less erroneous to believe that the events which resulted in the crisis amounted to an undue conversion of "circulating" capital into "fixed" capital. The individual entrepreneur, when faced with the credit stringency of the crisis, is right in regretting that he has expended too much for an expansion of his plant and for the purchase of durable equipment; he would have been in a better situation if the funds used for these purposes were still at his disposal for the current conduct of business. However, raw materials, primary commodities, half-finished manufactures and foodstuffs are not lacking at the turning point at which the upswing turns into the depression. On the contrary, the crisis is precisely characterized by the fact that these goods are offered in such quantities as to make their prices drop sharply.

The foregoing statements explain why an expansion in the production facilities and the production of the heavy industries, and in the production of durable producers' goods, is the most conspicuous mark of the boom. The editors of the financial and commercial chronicles were right when—for more than a hundred years—they looked upon production figures of these industries as well as of the construction trades as an index of business fluctuations. They were only mistaken in referring to an alleged overinvestment.

Of course, the boom affects also the consumers' goods industries. They too invest more and expand their production capacity. However, the new plants and the new annexes added to the already existing plants are not always those for the products of which the demand of the public is most intense. They may well have agreed with the whole plan aiming at the production of $r + g_1 + g_2 + g_3 + g_4$. The failure of this oversized plan discloses their inappropriateness.

A sharp rise in commodity prices is not always an attending phenomenon of the boom. The increase of the quantity of fiduciary media certainly always has the potential effect of making prices rise.

But it may happen that at the same time forces operating in the opposite direction are strong enough to keep the rise in prices within narrow limits or even to remove it entirely. The historical period in which the smooth working of the market economy was again and again interrupted through expansionist ventures was an epoch of continuous economic progress. The steady advance in the accumulation of new capital made technological improvement possible. Output per unit of input was increased and business filled the markets with increasing quantities of cheap goods. If the synchronous increase in the supply of money (in the broader sense) had been less plentiful than it really was, a tendency toward a drop in the prices of all commodities would have taken effect. As an actual historical event credit expansion was always embedded in an environment in which powerful factors were counteracting its tendency to raise prices. As a rule the resultant of the clash of opposite forces was a preponderance of those producing a rise in prices. But there were some exceptional instances too in which the upward movement of prices was only slight. The most remarkable example was provided by the American boom of 1926–29.[7]

The essential features of a credit expansion are not affected by such a particular constellation of the market data. What induces an entrepreneur to embark upon definite projects is neither high prices nor low prices as such, but a discrepancy between the costs of production, inclusive of interest on the capital required, and the anticipated prices of the products. A lowering of the gross market rate of interest as brought about by credit expansion always has the effect of making some projects appear profitable which did not appear so before. It actuates business to employ $r + p_1 + p_2$ as if it were $r + p_1 + p_2 + p_3 + p_4$. It necessarily brings about a structure of investment and production activities which is at variance with the real supply of capital goods and must finally collapse. That sometimes the price changes involved are laid against a background of a general tendency toward a rise in purchasing power and do not convert this tendency into its manifest opposite but only into something which may by and large be called price stability, modifies merely some accessories of the process.

However conditions may be, it is certain that no manipulations of the banks can provide the economic system with capital goods. What is needed for a sound expansion of production is additional capital goods, not money or fiduciary media. The credit expansion boom is built on the sands of banknotes and deposits. It must collapse.

The breakdown appears as soon as the banks become frightened

7. Cf. M. N. Rothbard, *America's Great Depression* (Princeton, 1963).

by the accelerated pace of the boom and begin to abstain from further expansion of credit. The boom could continue only as long as the banks were ready to grant freely all those credits which business needed for the execution of its excessive projects, utterly disagreeing with the real state of the supply of factors of production and the valuations of the consumers. These illusory plans, suggested by the falsification of business calculation as brought about by the cheap money policy, can be pushed forward only if new credits can be obtained at gross market rates which are artificially lowered below the height they would reach at an unhampered loan market. It is this margin that gives them the deceptive appearance of profitability. The change in the banks' conduct does not create the crisis. It merely makes visible the havoc spread by the faults which business has committed in the boom period.

Neither could the boom last endlessly if the banks were to cling stubbornly to their expansionist policies. Any attempt to substitute additional fiduciary media for nonexisting capital goods (namely, the quantities p_3 and p_4) is doomed to failure. If the credit expansion is not stopped in time, the boom turns into the crack-up boom; the flight into real values begins, and the whole monetary system founders. However, as a rule, the banks in the past have not pushed things to extremes. They have become alarmed at a date when the final catastrophe was still far away.[8]

As soon as the afflux of additional fiduciary media comes to an end, the airy castle of the boom collapses. The entrepreneurs must restrict their activities because they lack the funds for their continuation on the exaggerated scale. Prices drop suddenly because these distressed firms try to obtain cash by throwing inventories on the market dirt cheap. Factories are closed, the continuation of construction projects in progress is halted, workers are discharged. As on the one hand many firms badly need money in order to avoid bankruptcy, and on the other hand no firm any longer enjoys confidence, the entrepreneurial component in the gross market rate of interest jumps to an excessive height.

8. One should not fall prey to the illusion that these changes in the credit policies of the banks were caused by the bankers' and the monetary authorities' insight into the unavoidable consequences of a continued credit expansion. What induced the turn in the banks' conduct was certain institutional conditions to be dealt with further below, on pp. 796–797. Among the champions of economics some private bankers were prominent; in particular, the elaboration of the early form of the theory of business fluctuations, the Currency Theory, was for the most part an achievement of British bankers. But the management of central banks and the conduct of the various governments' monetary policies was as a rule entrusted to men who did not find any fault with boundless credit expansion and took offense at every criticism of their expansionist ventures.

Accidental institutional and psychological circumstances generally turn the outbreak of the crisis into a panic. The description of these awful events can be left to the historians. It is not the task of catallactic theory to depict in detail the calamities of panicky days and weeks and to dwell upon their sometimes grotesque aspects. Economics is not interested in what is accidental and conditioned by the individual historical circumstances of each instance. Its aim is, on the contrary, to distinguish what is essential and necessary from what is merely adventitious. It is not interested in the psychological aspects of the panic, but only in the fact that a credit-expansion boom must unavoidably lead to a process which everyday speech calls the depression. It must realize that the depression is in fact the process of readjustment, of putting production activities anew in agreement with the given state of the market data: the available supply of factors of production, the valuations of the consumers, and particularly also the state of originary interest as manifested in the public's valuations.

These data, however, are no longer identical with those that prevailed on the eve of the expansionist process. A good many things have changed. Forced saving and, to an even greater extent, regular voluntary saving may have provided new capital goods which were not totally squandered through malinvestment and overconsumption as induced by the boom. Changes in the wealth and income of various individuals and groups of individuals have been brought about by the unevenness inherent in every inflationary movement. Apart from any causal relation to the credit expansion, population may have changed with regard to figures and the characteristics of the individuals comprising them; technological knowledge may have advanced, demand for certain goods may have been altered. The final state to the establishment of which the market tends is no longer the same toward which it tended before the disturbances created by the credit expansion.

Some of the investments made in the boom period appear, when appraised with the sober judgment of the readjustment period, no longer dimmed by the illusions of the upswing, as absolutely hopeless failures. They must simply be abandoned because the current means required for their further exploitation cannot be recovered in selling their products; this "circulating" capital is more urgently needed in other branches of want-satisfaction; the proof is that it can be employed in a more profitable way in other fields. Other malinvestments offer somewhat more favorable chances. It is, of course, true that one would not have embarked upon putting capital goods into them if one had correctly calculated. The inconvertible investments made on their behalf are certainly wasted. But as they are inconvertible, a *fait accompli,* they present further action with a new problem. If the proceeds which the sale of their products promises are expected to exceed the costs of current operation, it is profitable to carry on. Although the prices which the buying public is prepared to allow for their products are not high enough to make the whole of the inconvertible investment profitable, they are sufficient to make a fraction, however small, of the investment profitable. The rest of the investment must be considered as expenditure without any offset, as capital squandered and lost.

If one looks at this outcome from the point of view of the consumers, the result is, of course, the same. The consumers would be better off if the illusions created by the easy-money policy had not enticed the entrepreneurs to waste scarce capital goods by investing them for the satisfaction of less urgent needs and thereby withholding them from lines of production in which they would have satisfied more urgent needs. But as things are now, they cannot but put up with what is irrevocable. They must for the time being renounce certain amenities which they could have enjoyed if the boom had not engendered malinvestment. But, on the other hand, they can find partial compensation in the fact that some enjoyments are now available to them which would have been beyond their reach if the smooth course of economic activities had not been disturbed by the orgies of the boom. It is slight compensation only, as their demand for those other things which they do not get because of inappropriate employment of capital goods is more intense than their demand for these "substitutes," as it were. But it is the only choice left to them as conditions and data are now.

The final outcome of the credit expansion is general impoverishment. Some people may have increased their wealth; they did not let their reasoning be obfuscated by the mass hysteria, and took advantage in time of the opportunities offered by the mobility of the individual investor. Other individuals and groups of individuals may have been favored, without any initiative of their own, by the mere time lag between the rise in the prices of the goods they sell and those they buy. But the immense majority must foot the bill for the malinvestments and the overconsumption of the boom episode.

One must guard oneself against a misinterpretation of this term impoverishment. It does not necesarily mean impoverishment when compared with the conditions that prevailed on the eve of the credit expansion. Whether or not an impoverishment in this sense takes place depends on the particular data of each case; it cannot be predicated apodictically by catallactics. What catallactics has in mind when asserting that impoverishment is an unavoidable outgrowth of credit expansion is impoverishment as compared with the state of affairs which would have developed in the absence of credit expansion and the boom. The characteristic mark of economic history under capitalism is unceasing economic progress, a steady increase in the quantity of capital goods available, and a continuous trend toward an improvement in the general standard of living. The pace of this progress is so rapid that, in the course of a boom period, it may well outstrip the synchronous losses caused by malinvestment and overconsumption. Then the economic system as a whole is more prosperous at the end of the boom than it was at its very beginning; it appears impoverished only when compared with the potentialities which existed for a still better state of satisfaction.

The Alleged Absence of Depressions Under Totalitarian Management

Many socialist authors emphasize that the recurrence of economic crises and business depressions is a phenomenon inherent in the capitalist mode of production. On the other hand, they say, a socialist system is safe against this evil.

As has already become obvious and will be shown later again, the cyclical fluctuations of business are not an occurrence originating in the sphere of the unhampered market, but a product of government interference with business conditions designed to lower the rate of interest below the height at which the free market would have fixed it.[9] At this point we have only to deal with the alleged stability as secured by socialist planning.

It is essential to realize that what makes the economic crisis emerge is the democratic process of the market. The consumers disapprove of the employment of the factors of production as effected by the entrepreneurs. They manifest their disapprobation by their conduct in buying and abstention from buying. The entrepreneurs, misled by the illusions of the artificially lowered gross market rate of interest, have failed to invest in those lines in which the most urgent needs of the public would have been satisfied in the best possible way. As soon as the credit expansion comes to an end, these faults become manifest. The attitudes of the consumers force the businessmen to adjust their activities anew to the best possible want-satisfaction. It is this process of liquidation of the faults committed in the boom and of readjustment to the wishes of the consumers which is called the depression.

But in a socialist economy it is only the government's value judgments that count, and the people are deprived of any means of making their own value judgments prevail. A dictator does not bother about whether or not the masses approve of his decision concerning how

9. Cf. below, pp. 793–795.

much to devote for current consumption and how much for additional investment. If the dictator invests more and thus curtails the means available for current consumption, the people must eat less and hold their tongues. No crisis emerges because the subjects have no opportunity to utter their dissatisfaction. Where there is no business at all, business can be neither good nor bad. There may be starvation and famine, but no depression in the sense in which this term is used in dealing with the problems of a market economy. Where the individuals are not free to choose, they cannot protest against the methods applied by those directing the course of production activities.

7. The Gross Market Rate of Interest as Affected by Deflation and Credit Contraction

We assume that in the course of a deflationary process the whole amount by which the supply of money (in the broader sense) is reduced is taken from the loan market. Then the loan market and the gross market rate of interest are affected at the very beginning of the process, at a moment at which the prices of commodities and services are not yet altered by the change going on in the money relation. We may, for instance, posit that a government aiming at deflation floats a loan and destroys the paper money borrowed. Such a procedure has been, in the last two hundred years, adopted again and again. The idea was to raise, after a prolonged period of inflationary policy, the national monetary unit to its previous metallic parity. Of course, in most cases the deflationary projects were soon abandoned as their execution encountered increasing opposition and, moreover, heavily burdened the treasury. Or we may assume that the banks, frightened by their adverse experience in the crisis brought about by credit expansion, are intent upon increasing the reserves held against their liabilities and therefore restrict the amount of circulation credit. A third possibility would be that the crisis has resulted in the bankruptcy of banks which granted circulation credit and that the annihilation of the fiduciary media issued by these banks reduces the supply of credit on the loan market.

In all these cases a temporary tendency toward a rise in the gross market rate of interest ensues. Projects which would have appeared profitable before appear so no longer. A tendency develops toward a fall in the prices of factors of production and later toward a fall in the prices of consumers' goods also. Business becomes slack. The deadlock ceases only when prices and wage rates are by and large adjusted to the new money relation. Then the loan market too adapts itself to the new state of affairs, and the gross market rate of interest is no longer disarranged by a shortage of money offered for advances.

Thus a cash-induced rise in the gross market rate of interest produces a temporary stagnation of business. Deflation and credit contraction no less than inflation and credit expansion are elements disarranging the smooth course of economic activities. However, it is a blunder to look upon deflation and contraction as if they were simply counterparts of inflation and expansion.

Expansion produces first the illusory appearance of prosperity. It is extremely popular because it seems to make the majority, even everybody, more affluent. It has an enticing quality. A special moral effort is needed to stop it. On the other hand, contraction immediately produces conditions which everybody is ready to condemn as evil. Its unpopularity is even greater than the popularity of expansion. It creates violent opposition. Very soon the political forces fighting it become irresistible.

Fiat money inflation and cheap loans to the government convey additional funds to the treasury; deflation depletes the treasury's vaults. Credit expansion is a boon for the banks, contraction is a forfeiture. There is a temptation in inflation and expansion and a repellent in deflation and contraction.

But the dissimilarity between the two opposite modes of money and credit manipulation not only consists in the fact that while one of them is popular the other is universally loathed. Deflation and contraction are less likely to spread havoc than inflation and expansion not merely because they are only rarely resorted to. They are less disastrous also on account of their inherent effects. Expansion squanders scarce factors of production by malinvestment and overconsumption. If it once comes to an end, a tedious process of recovery is needed in order to wipe out the impoverishment it has left behind. But contraction produces neither malinvestment nor overconsumption. The temporary restriction in business activities that it engenders may by and large be offset by the drop in consumption on the part of the discharged wage earners and the owners of the material factors of production the sales of which drop. No protracted scars are left. When the contraction comes to an end, the process of readjustment does not need to make good for losses caused by capital consumption.

Deflation and credit restriction never played a noticeable role in economic history. The outstanding examples were provided by Great Britain's return, both after the wartime inflation of the Napoleonic wars and after that of the first World War, to the prewar gold parity of the sterling. In each case Parliament and Cabinet adopted the deflationist policy without having weighed the pros and cons of the two methods open for a return to the gold standard. In the second decade of the nineteenth century they could be exonerated, as at that time monetary theory had not yet clarified the problems involved. More than a hundred years later it was simply a display of inexcusable ignorance of economics as well as of monetary history.[10]

Ignorance manifests itself also in the confusion of deflation and contraction and of the process of readjustment into which every expansionist boom must lead. It depends on the institutional structure of the credit system which created the boom whether or not the crisis brings about a restriction in the amount of fiduciary media. Such a restriction may occur when the crisis results in the bankruptcy of banks granting circulation credit and the falling off is not counterpoised by a corresponding expansion on the part of the remaining banks. But it is not necessarily an attendant phenomenon of the depression; it is beyond doubt that it has not appeared in the last eighty years in Europe and that the extent to which it occurred in the United States under the Federal Reserve Act of 1913 has been grossly exaggerated. The dearth of credit which marks the crisis is caused not by contraction but by the abstention from further credit expansion. It hurts all enterprises—not only those which are doomed at any rate, but no less those whose business is sound and could flourish if appropriate credit were available. As the outstanding debts are not paid back, the banks lack the means to grant credits even to the most solid firms. The crisis becomes general and forces all branches of business and all firms to restrict the scope of their activities. But there is no means of avoiding these secondary consequences of the preceding boom.

As soon as the depression appears, there is a general lament over deflation and people clamor for a continuation of the expansionist policy. Now, it is true that even with no restrictions in the supply of money proper and fiduciary media available, the depression brings about a cash-induced tendency toward an increase in the purchasing power of the monetary unit. Every firm is intent upon increasing its cash holdings, and these endeavors affect the ratio between the supply of money (in the broader sense) and the demand for money (in the broader sense) for cash holding. This may be properly called deflation. But it is a serious blunder to believe that the fall in commodity prices is caused by this striving after greater cash holding. The causation is the other way around. Prices of the factors of production—both material and human—have reached an excessive height in the boom period. They must come down before business can become profitable again. The entrepreneurs enlarge their cash holding because they

10. See below, p. 784.

abstain from buying goods and hiring workers as long as the structure of prices and wages is not adjusted to the real state of the market data. Thus any attempt of the government or the labor unions to prevent or to delay this adjustment merely prolongs the stagnation.

Even economists often failed to comprehend this concatenation. They argued thus: The structure of prices as it developed in the boom was a product of the expansionist pressure. If the further increase in fiduciary media comes to an end, the upward movement of prices and wages must stop. But, if there were no deflation, no drop in prices and wage rates could result.

This reasoning would be correct if the inflationary pressure had not affected the loan market before it had exhausted its direct effects upon commodity prices. Let us assume that a government of an isolated country issues additional paper money in order to pay doles to the citizens of moderate income. The rise in commodity prices thus brought about would disarrange production; it would tend to shift production from the consumers' goods regularly bought by the nonsubsidized groups of the nation to those which the subsidized groups are demanding. If the policy of subsidizing some groups in this way is later abandoned, the prices of the goods demanded by those formerly subsidized will drop and the prices of the goods demanded by those formerly nonsubsidized will rise more sharply. But there will be no tendency of the monetary unit's purchasing power to return to the state of the pre-inflation period. The structure of prices will be lastingly affected by the inflationary venture if the government does not withdraw from the market the additional quantity of paper money it has injected in the shape of subsidies.

Conditions are different under a credit expansion which first affects the loan market. In this case the inflationary effects are multiplied by the consequences of capital malinvestment and overconsumption. Overbidding one another in the struggle for a greater share in the limited supply of capital goods and labor, the entrepreneurs push prices to a height at which they can remain only as long as the credit expansion goes on at an accelerated pace. A sharp drop in the prices of all commodities and services is unavoidable as soon as the further inflow of additional fiduciary media stops.

While the boom is in progress, there prevails a general tendency to buy as much as one can buy because a further rise in prices is anticipated. In the depression, on the other hand, people abstain from buying because they expect that prices will continue to drop. The recovery and the return to "normalcy" can only begin when prices and wage rates are so low that a sufficient number of people assume that they will not drop still more. Therefore the only means to shorten the period of bad business is to avoid any attempts to delay or to check the fall in prices and wage rates.

Only when the recovery begins to take shape does the change in the money relation, as effected by the increase in the quantity of fiduciary media, begin to manifest itself in the structure of prices.

The Difference Between Credit Expansion and Simple Inflation

In dealing with the consequences of credit expansion we assumed that the total amount of additional fiduciary media enters the market system via the loan market as advances to business. All that has been predicated with regard to the effects of credit expansion refers to this condition.

There are, however, instances in which the legal and technical methods of credit expansion are used for a procedure catallactically utterly different from genuine credit expansion. Political and institutional convenience sometimes makes it expedient for a government to take advantage of the facilities of banking as a substitute for issuing government fiat money. The treasury borrows from the bank, and the bank provides the funds needed by issuing additional banknotes or crediting the government on a deposit account. Legally the bank becomes the treasury's creditor. In fact the whole transaction amounts to fiat money inflation. The additional fiduciary media enter the market by way of the treasury as payment for various items of government expenditure. It is this additional government demand that incites business to expand its activities. The issuance of these newly created fiat money sums does not directly interfere with the gross market rate of interest, whatever the rate of interest may be which the government pays to the bank. They affect the loan market and the gross market rate of interest, apart from the emergence of a positive price premium, only if a part of them reaches the loan market at a time at which their effects upon commodity prices and wage rates have not yet been consummated.

Such were, for example, the conditions in the United States in the second World War. Apart from the credit expansion policy, which the Administration had already adopted before the outbreak of the war, the government borrowed heavily from the commercial banks. This was technically credit expansion; essentially it was a substitute for the issuance of greenbacks. Even more complicated techniques were resorted to in other countries. Thus, for instance, the German Reich in the first World War sold bonds to the public. The Reichsbank financed these purchases by lending the greater part of the funds needed to the buyers against the same bonds as collateral. Apart from the fraction which the buyer contributed from his own funds, the role that the Bank and the public played in the whole transaction was merely formal.

Virtually, the additional banknotes were inconvertible paper money.

It is important to pay heed to these facts in order not to confuse the consequences of credit expansion proper and those of government-made fiat money inflation.

8. The Monetary or Circulation Credit Theory of the Trade Cycle

The theory of the cyclical fluctuations of business as elaborated by the British Currency School was in two respects unsatisfactory.

First it failed to recognize that circulation credit can be granted not only by the issue of banknotes in excess of the banks' holding of cash reserves, but also by creating bank deposits subject to check in excess of such reserves (checkbook money, deposit currency). Consequently it did not realize that deposits payable on demand can also be used as a device of credit expansion. This error is of little weight, as it can be easily amended. It is enough to stress the point that all that refers to credit expansion is valid for all varieties of credit expansion no matter whether the additional fiduciary media are banknotes or deposits. However, the teachings of the Currency School inspired British legislation designed to prevent the return of credit-expansion booms and their necessary consequence, depressions, at a time when this fundamental defect was not yet widely enough recognized. Peel's Act of 1844 and its imitations in other countries did not attain the ends sought, and this failure shook the prestige of the Currency School. The Banking School triumphed undeservedly.

The second shortcoming of the Currency Theory was more momentous. It restricted its reasoning to the problem of the external drain. It dealt only with a particular case, viz., credit expansion in one country only while there is either no credit expansion or only credit expansion to a smaller extent in other areas. This was, by and large, sufficient to explain the British crises of the first part of the nineteenth century. But it touched only the surface of the problem. The essential question was not raised at all. Nothing was done to clarify the consequences of a general expansion of credit not confined to a number of banks with a restricted clientele. The reciprocal relations between the supply of money (in the broader sense) and the rate of interest were not analyzed. The multifarious projects to lower or to abolish interest altogether by means of a banking reform were haughtily derided as quackery, but not critically dissected and refuted. The naïve presumption of money's neutrality was tacitly ratified. Thus a free hand was left to all futile attempts to interpret crises and business fluctuations by means of the theory of direct exchange. Many decades passed before the spell was broken.

The hindrance that the monetary or circulation credit theory had to overcome was not merely theoretical error but also political bias. Public opinion is prone to see in interest nothing but a merely institutional obstacle to the expansion of production. It does not realize that the discount of future goods as against present goods is a necessary and eternal category of human action and cannot be abolished by bank manipulation. In the eyes of cranks and demagogues, interest is a product of the sinister machinations of rugged exploiters. The age-old disapprobation of interest has been fully revived by modern interventionism. It clings to the dogma that it is one of the foremost duties of good government to lower the rate of interest as far as possible or to abolish it altogether. All present-day governments are fanatically committed to an easy money policy. As has been mentioned already, the British Government has asserted that credit expansion has performed "the miracle . . . of turning a stone into bread ."[11] A Chairman of the Federal Reserve Bank of New York has declared that "final freedom from the domestic money market exists for every sovereign national state where there exists an institution which functions in the manner of a modern central bank, and whose currency is not convertible into gold or into some other commodity."[12] Many governments, universities, and institutes of economic research lavishly subsidize publications whose main purpose is to praise the blessings of unbridled credit expansion and to slander all opponents as ill-intentioned advocates of the selfish interests of usurers.

The wavelike movement affecting the economic system, the recurrence of periods of boom which are followed by periods of depression, is the unavoidable outcome of the attempts, repeated again and again, to lower the gross market rate of interest by means of credit expansion. There is no means of avoiding the final collapse of a boom brought about by credit expansion. The alternative is only whether the crisis should come sooner as the result of a voluntary abandonment of further credit expansion, or later as a final and total catastrophe of the currency system involved.

The only objection ever raised against the circulation credit theory is lame indeed. It has been asserted that the lowering of the gross market rate of interest below the height it would have reached on an unhampered loan market may appear not as the outcome of an intentional policy on the part of the banks or the monetary authorities but as the unintentional effect of their conservatism. Faced with a

11. See above, p. 470.

12. Beardsley Ruml, "Taxes for Revenue Are Obsolete," *American Affairs,* VIII (1946), 35–36.

situation which would, when left alone, result in a raise in the market rate, the banks refrain from altering the interest they charge on advances and thus willy-nilly tumble into expansion.[13] These assertions are unwarranted. But if we are prepared to admit their correctness for the sake of argument, they do not affect at all the essence of the monetary explanation of the trade cycle. It is of no concern what the particular conditions are that induce the banks to expand credit and to underbid the gross market rate of interest which the unhampered market would have determined. What counts is solely that the banks and the monetary authorities are guided by the idea that the height of interest rates as the free loan market determines it is an evil, that it is the objective of a good economic policy to lower it, and that credit expansion is an appropriate means of achieving this end without harm to anybody but parasitic moneylenders. It is this infatuation that causes them to embark upon ventures which must finally bring about the slump.

If one takes these facts into consideration one could be tempted to abstain from any discussion of the problems involved in the frame of the theory of the pure market economy and to relegate it to the analysis of interventionism, the interference of government with the market phenomena. It is beyond doubt that credit expansion is one of the primary issues of interventionism. Nevertheless the right place for the analysis of the problems involved is not in the theory of interventionism but in that of the pure market economy. For the problem we have to deal with is essentially the relation between the supply of money and the rate of interest, a problem of which the consequences of credit expansion are only a particular instance.

Everything that has been asserted with regard to credit expansion is equally valid with regard to the effects of any increase in the supply of money proper as far as this additional supply reaches the loan market at an early stage of its inflow into the market system. If the additional quantity of money increases the quantity of money offered for loans at a time when commodity prices and wage rates have not yet been completely adjusted to the change in the money relation, the effects are no different from those of a credit expansion. In analyzing the problem of credit expansion, catallactics completes the teachings of the theory of money and of interest. It implicitly demolishes the age-old errors concerning interest and explodes the fantastic plans to "abolish" interest by means of monetary or credit reform.

What differentiates credit expansion from an increase in the supply

13. Machlup (*The Stock Market, Credit and Capital Formation,* p. 248) calls this conduct of the banks "passive inflationism."

of money as it can appear in an economy employing only commodity money and no fiduciary media at all is conditioned by divergences in the quantity of the increase and in the temporal sequence of its effects on the various parts of the market. Even a rapid increase in the production of the precious metals can never have the range which credit expansion can attain. The gold standard was an efficacious check upon credit expansion, as it forced the banks not to exceed certain limits in their expansionist ventures.[14] The gold standard's own inflationary potentialities were kept within limits by the vicissitudes of gold mining. Moreover, only a part of the additional gold immediately increased the supply offered on the loan market. The greater part acted first upon commodity prices and wage rates and affected the loan market only at a later stage of the inflationary process.

However, the continuous increase in the quantity of commodity money exercised a steady expansionist pressure on the loan market. The gross market rate of interest was, in the course of the last centuries, continually subject to the impact of an inflow of additional money into the loan market. Of course, this pressure for the last hundred and fifty years in the Anglo-Saxon countries and for the last hundred years in the countries of the European continent, was far exceeded by the effects of the synchronous development of circulation credit as granted by the banks apart from their—from time to time reiterated—straightforward endeavors to lower the gross market rate of interest by an intensified expansion of credit. Thus three tendencies toward a lowering of the gross market rate of interest were operating at the same time and strengthening one another. One was the outgrowth of the steady increase in the quantity of commodity money, the second the outgrowth of a spontaneous development of fiduciary media in banking operations, the third the fruit of intentional anti-interest policies sponsored by the authorities and approved by public opinion. It is, of course, impossible to ascertain in a quantitative way the effect of their joint operation and the contribution of each of them; an answer to such a question can only be provided by historical understanding.

What catallactic reasoning can show us is merely that a slight although continuous pressure on the gross market rate of interest as originating from a continuous increase in the quantity of gold, and also from a slight increase in the quantity of fiduciary media, which is not overdone and intensified by purposeful easy money policy, can be counterpoised by the forces of readjustment and accomodation in-

14. Cf. above, p. 475.

herent in the market economy. The adaptability of business not purposely sabotaged by forces extraneous to the market is powerful enough to offset the effects which such slight disturbances of the loan market can possibly bring about.

Statisticians have tried to investigate long waves of business fluctuations with statistical methods. Such attempts are futile. The history of modern capitalism is a record of steady economic progress, again and again interrupted by feverish booms and their aftermath, depressions. It is generally possible to discern statistically these recurring oscillations from the general trend toward an increase in the amount of capital invested and the quantity of products turned out. It is impossible to discover any rhythmical fluctuation in the general trend itself.

9. The Market Economy as Affected by the Recurrence of the Trade Cycle

The popularity of inflation and credit expansion, the ultimate source of the repeated attempts to render people prosperous by credit expansion, and thus the cause of the cyclical fluctuations of business, manifests itself clearly in the customary terminology. The boom is called good business, prosperity, and upswing. Its unavoidable aftermath, the readjustment of conditions to the real data of the market, is called crisis, slump, bad business, depression. People rebel against the insight that the disturbing element is to be seen in the malinvestment and the overconsumption of the boom period and that such an artificially induced boom is doomed. They are looking for the philosophers' stone to make it last.

It has been pointed out already in what respect we are free to call an improvement in the quality and an increase in the quantity of products economic progress. If we apply this yardstick to the various phases of the cyclical fluctuations of business, we must call the boom retrogression and the depression progress. The boom squanders through malinvestment scarce factors of production and reduces the stock available through overconsumption; its alleged blessings are paid for by impoverishment. The depression, on the other hand, is the way back to a state of affairs in which all factors of production are employed for the best possible satisfaction of the most urgent needs of the consumers.

Desperate attempts have been made to find in the boom some positive contribution to economic progress. Stress has been laid upon the role forced saving plays in fostering capital accumulation. The argument is vain. It has been shown already that it is very questionable whether forced saving can ever achieve more than to counterbalance a part of the capital consumption generated by the boom. If those praising the allegedly beneficial effects of forced saving were consistent, they would advocate a fiscal system subsidizing the rich out of taxes collected from people with modest incomes. The forced saving achieved by this method would provide a net increase in the amount of capital available without simultaneously bringing about capital consumption of a much greater size.

Advocates of credit expansion have furthermore emphasized that some of the malinvestments made in the boom later become profitable. These investments, they say, were made too early, i.e., at a date when the state of the supply of capital goods and the valuations of the consumers did not yet allow their construction. However, the havoc caused was not too bad, as these projects would have been executed anyway at a later date. It may be admitted that this description is adequate with regard to some instances of malinvestment induced by a boom. But nobody would dare to assert that the statement is correct with regard to all projects whose execution has been encouraged by the illusions created by the easy money policy. However this may be, it cannot influence the consequences of the boom and cannot undo or deaden the ensuing depression. The effects of the malinvestment appear without regard to whether or not these malinvestments will appear as sound investments at a later time under changed conditions. When, in 1845, a railroad was constructed in England which would not have been constructed in the absence of credit expansion, conditions in the following years were not affected by the prospect that in 1870 or 1880 the capital goods required for its construction would be available. The gain which later resulted from the fact that the railroad concerned did not have to be built by a fresh expenditure of capital and labor, was in 1847 no compensation for the losses incurred by its premature construction.

The boom produces impoverishment. But still more disastrous are its moral ravages. It makes people despondent and dispirited. The more optimistic they were under the illusory prosperity of the boom, the greater is their despair and their feeling of frustration. The individual is always ready to ascribe his good luck to his own efficiency and to take it as a well-deserved reward for his talent, application, and probity. But reverses of fortune he always charges to other people, and most of all to the absurdity of social and political institutions. He does not blame the authorities for having fostered the boom. He reviles them for the inevitable collapse. In the opinion of the public, more inflation and more credit expansion are the only remedy against the evils which inflation and credit expansion have brought about.

Here, they say, are plants and farms whose capacity to produce is either not used at all or not to its full extent. Here are piles of unsalable commodities and hosts of unemployed workers. But here are also masses of people who would be lucky if they only could satisfy their wants more amply. All that is lacking is credit. Additional credit would enable the entrepreneurs to resume or to expand production. The unemployed would find jobs again and could buy the products. This reasoning seems plausible. Nonetheless it is utterly wrong.

If commodities cannot be sold and workers cannot find jobs, the reason can only be that the prices and wages asked are too high. He who wants to sell his inventories or his capacity to work must reduce his demand until he finds a buyer. Such is the law of the market. Such is the device by means of which the market directs every individual's activities into those lines in which they can best contribute to the satisfaction of the wants of the consumers. The malinvestments of the boom have misplaced inconvertible factors of production in some lines at the expense of other lines in which they were more urgently needed. There is disproportion in the allocation of nonconvertible factors to the various branches of industry. This disproportion can be remedied only by the accumulation of new capital and its employment in those branches in which it is most urgently required. This is a slow process. While it is in progress, it is impossible to utilize fully the productive capacity of some plants for which the complementary production facilities are lacking.

It is vain to object that there is also unused capacity of plants turning out goods whose specific character is low. The slack in the sale of these goods, it is said, cannot be explained by disproportionality in the capital equipment of various branches; they can be used and are needed for many different employments. This too is an error. If steel and iron works, copper mines, and sawmills cannot be operated to their full capacity, the reason can only be that there are not enough buyers on the market ready to purchase their whole output at prices which cover the costs of their current exploitation. As the variable costs can merely consist in prices of other products and in wages, and as the same is valid with regard to the prices of these other products, this always means that wage rates are too high to provide all those eager to work with jobs and to employ the inconvertible equipment to the full limits drawn by the requirement that nonspecific capital goods and labor should not be withdrawn from employments in which they fill more urgent needs.

Out of the collapse of the boom there is only one way back to a state of affairs in which progressive accumulation of capital safeguards a steady improvement of material well-being: new saving must accumulate the capital goods needed for a harmonious equipment of all branches of production with the capital required. One must provide the capital goods lacking in those branches which were unduly neglected in the boom. Wage rates must drop; people must restrict their consumption temporarily until the capital wasted by malinvestment is restored. Those who dislike these hardships of the readjustment period must abstain in time from credit expansion.

There is no use in interfering by means of a new credit expansion with the process of readjustment. This would at best only interrupt, disturb, and prolong the curative process of the depression, if not bring about a new boom with all its inevitable consequences.

The process of readjustment, even in the absence of any new credit expansion, is delayed by the psychological effects of disappointment and frustration. People are slow to free themselves from the self-deception of delusive prosperity. Businessmen try to continue unprofitable projects; they shut their eyes to an insight that hurts. The workers delay reducing their claims to the level required by the state of the market; they want, if possible, to avoid lowering their standard of living and changing their occupation and their dwelling place. People are the more discouraged the greater their optimism was in the days of the upswing. They have for the moment lost self-confidence and the spirit of enterprise to such an extent that they even fail to take advantage of good opportunities. But the worst is that people are incorrigible. After a few years they embark anew upon credit expansion, and the old story repeats itself.

The Role Played by Unemployed Factors of Production in the First Stages of a Boom

There are in the changing economy always unsold inventories (exceeding those quantities which for technical reasons must be kept in stock), unemployed workers, and unused capacity of inconvertible production facilities. The system is moving toward a state in which there will be neither unemployed workers nor surplus inventories.[15] But as the appearance of new data continually diverts the course toward a new goal, the conditions of the evenly rotating economy are never realized.

The presence of unused capacity of inconvertible investments is an

15. In the evenly rotating economy also there may be unused capacity of inconvertible equipment. Its nonutilization does not disturb the equilibrium any more than the fallowness of submarginal soil.

outgrowth of errors committed in the past. The assumptions made by the investors were, as later events proved, not correct; the market asks more intensively for other goods than for those which these plants can turn out. The piling up of excessive inventories and the catallactic unemployment of workers are speculative. The owner of the stock refuses to sell at the market price because he hopes to obtain a higher price at a later date. The unemployed worker refuses to change his occupation or his residence or to content himself with lower pay because he hopes to obtain at a later date a job with higher pay in the place of his residence and in the branch of business he likes best. Both hesitate to adjust their claims to the present situation of the market because they wait for a change in the data which will alter conditions to their advantage. Their hesitation is one of the reasons why the system has not yet adjusted itself to the conditions of the market.

The advocates of credit expansion argue that what is wanted is more fiduciary media. Then the plants will work at full capacity, the inventories will be sold at prices their owners consider satisfactory, and the unemployed will get jobs at wages they consider satisfactory. This very popular doctrine implies that the rise in prices, brought about by the additional fiduciary media, would at the same time and to the same extent affect all other commodities and services, while the owners of the excessive inventories and the unemployed workers would content themselves with those nominal prices and wages they are asking—in vain, of course—today. For if this were to happen, the real prices and the real wage rates obtained by these owners of unsold inventories and unemployed workers would drop—in proportion to the prices of other commodities and services—to the height to which they must drop in order to find buyers and employers.

The course of the boom is not substantially affected by the fact that at its eve there are unused capacity, unsold surplus inventories, and unemployed workers. Let us assume that there are unused facilities for the mining of copper, unsold piles of copper, and unemployed workers of copper mines. The price of copper is at a level at which mining does not pay for some mines; their workers are discharged; there are speculators who abstain from selling their stocks. What is needed in order to make these mines profitable again, to give jobs to the unemployed, and to sell the piles without forcing prices down below costs of production, is an increment *p* in the amount of capital goods available large enough to make possible such an increase in investment and in the size of production and consumption that an adequate rise in the demand for copper ensues. If, however, this increment *p* does not appear and the entrepreneurs, deceived by the credit expansion, nevertheless act as if *p* had really been available, conditions on the copper market, while the boom lasts, are as if *p* had really been added to the amount of capital goods available. But everything that has been predicated about the inevitable consequences of credit expansion fits this case too. The only difference is that, as far as copper is concerned, the inappropriate expansion of production need not be achieved by the withdrawal of capital and labor from employments in which they would better have filled the wants of the consumers. As far as copper is concerned, the new boom encounters a piece of malinvestment of capital and malemployment of labor already effected in a previous boom, which the process of readjustment has not yet absorbed.

Thus it becomes obvious how vain it is to justify a new credit expansion by referring to unused capacity, unsold—or, as people say incorrectly, "unsalable"—stocks, and unemployed workers. The beginning of a new credit expansion runs across remainders of preceding malinvestment and malemployment, not yet obliterated in the course of the readjustment process, and seemingly remedies the faults involved. In fact, however, this is merely an interruption of the process of readjustment and of the return to sound conditions.[16] The existence of unused capacity and unemployment is not a valid argument against the correctness of the circulation credit theory. The belief of the advocates of credit expansion and inflation that abstention from further credit expansion and inflation would perpetuate the depression is utterly false. The remedies these authors suggest would not make the boom last forever. They would merely upset the process of recovery.

The Fallacies of the Nonmonetary Explanations of the Trade Cycle

In dealing with the futile attempts to explain the cyclical fluctuations of business by a nonmonetary doctrine, one point must first of all be stressed which has hitherto been unduly neglected.

There were schools of thought for whom interest was merely a price paid for obtaining the disposition of a quantity of money or money substitutes. From this belief they quite logically drew the inference that abolishing the scarcity of money and money-substitutes would abolish interest altogether and result in the gratuitousness of credit. If, however, one does not endorse this view and comprehends the nature of originary interest, a problem presents itself the treatment of which one must not evade. An additional supply of credit, brought about by an increase in the quantity of money or fiduciary media, has certainly the power to lower the gross market rate of interest. If interest is not merely a monetary phenomenon and consequently cannot be lastingly lowered or brushed away by any increase, however large, in the supply of money and fiduciary media, it devolves upon economics to show how the height of the rate of interest conforming to the state of the market's nonmonetary data reestablishes itself. It must explain

16. Hayek (*Prices and Production* [2d ed. London, 1935], pp. 96 ff.) reaches the same conclusion by way of a somewhat different chain of reasoning.

what kind of process removes the cash-induced deviation of the market rate from that state which is consonant with the ratio in people's valuation of present and future goods. If economics were at a loss to achieve this, it would implicitly admit that interest is a monetary phenomenon and could even disappear completely in the course of changes in the money relation.

For the nonmonetary explanations of the trade cycle the experience that there are recurrent depressions is the primary thing. Their champions first do not see in their scheme of the sequence of economic events any clue which could suggest a satisfactory interpretation of these enigmatic disorders. They desperately search for a makeshift in order to patch it onto their teachings as an alleged cycle theory.

The case is different with the monetary or circulation credit theory. Modern monetary theory has finally cleared away all notions of an alleged neutrality of money. It has proved irrefutably that there are in the market economy factors operating about which a doctrine ignorant of the driving force of money has nothing to say. The catallactic system that involves the knowledge of money's non-neutrality and driving force presses the questions of how changes in the money relation affect the rate of interest first in the short run and later in the long run. The system would be defective if it could not answer these questions. It would be contradictory if it were to provide an answer which would not simultaneously explain the cyclical fluctuations of trade. Even if there had never been such things as fiduciary media and circulation credit, modern catallactics would have been forced to raise the problem concerning the relations between changes in the money relation and the rate of interest.

It has been mentioned already that every nonmonetary explanation of the cycle is bound to admit that an increase in the quantity of money or fiduciary media is an indispensable condition of the emergence of a boom. It is obvious that a general tendency of prices to rise which is not caused by a general drop in production and in the supply of commodities offered for sale, cannot appear if the supply of money (in the broader sense) has not increased. Now we can see that those fighting the monetary explanation are also forced to resort to the theory they slander for a second reason. For this theory alone answers the question of how an inflow of additional money and fiduciary media affects the loan market and the market rate of interest. Only those for whom interest is merely the outgrowth of an institutionally conditioned scarcity of money can dispense with an implicit acknowledgment of the circulation credit theory of the cycle. This explains why no critic has ever advanced any tenable objection against this theory.

The fanaticism with which the supporters of all these nonmonetary doctrines refuse to acknowledge their errors is, of course, a display of political bias. The Marxians have inaugurated the usage of interpreting the commercial crisis as an inherent evil of capitalism, as the necessary outgrowth of its "anarchy" of production.[17] The non-Marxian socialists and the interventionists are no less anxious to demonstrate that the market economy cannot avoid the return of depressions. They are the more eager to assail the monetary theory as currency and credit manipulation is today the main instrument by means of which the anticapitalist governments are intent upon establishing government omnipotence.[18]

The attempts to connect business depressions with cosmic influences, the most remarkable of which was William Stanley Jevons' sunspot theory, failed utterly. The market economy has succeeded in a fairly satisfactory way in adjusting production and marketing to all the natural conditions of human life and its environment. It is quite arbitrary to assume that there is just one natural fact—namely, allegedly rhythmic harvest variations—with which the market economy does not know how to cope. Why do entrepreneurs fail to recognize the fact of crop fluctuations and to adjust business activities in such a way as to discount their disastrous effects upon their plans?

Guided by the Marxian slogan "anarchy of production," the present-day nonmonetary cycle doctrines explain the cyclical fluctuations of trade in terms of a tendency, allegedly inherent in the capitalist economy, to develop disproportionality in the size of investments made in various branches of industry. Yet even these disproportionality doctrines do not contest the fact that every businessman is eager to avoid such mistakes, which must bring him serious financial losses. The essence of the activities of entrepreneurs and capitalists is precisely not to embark upon projects which they consider unprofitable. If one assumes that there prevails a tendency for businessmen to fail in these endeavors, one implies that all businessmen are short-sighted. They are too dull to avoid certain pitfalls, and thus blunder again and again in their conduct of affairs. The whole of society has to foot the bill for the shortcomings of the thick-headed speculators, promoters, and entrepreneurs.

Now it is obvious that men are fallible, and businessmen are certainly not free from this human weakness. But one should not forget that on the market a process of selection is in continual operation. There prevails an unceasing tendency to weed out the less efficient entrepreneurs, that is, those who fail in their endeavors to anticipate correctly the future demands of the consumers. If one group of entrepreneurs produces commodities in excess of the demand of the consumers and consequently cannot sell these goods at remunerative

17. About the fundamental fault of the Marxian and all other underconsumption theories, cf. above, p. 301.

18. About these currency and credit manipulations, cf. below, pp. 780–803.

prices and suffers losses, other groups who produce those things for which the public scrambles make all the greater profits. Some sectors of business are distressed while others thrive. No general depression of trade can emerge.

But the proponents of the doctrines we have to deal with argue differently. They assume that not only the whole entrepreneurial class but all of the people are struck with blindness. As the entrepreneurial class is not a closed social order to which access is denied to outsiders, as every enterprising man is virtually in a position to challenge those who already belong to the class of entrepreneurs, as the history of capitalism provides innumerable examples of penniless newcomers who brilliantly succeeded in embarking upon the production of those goods which according to their own judgment were fitted to satisfy the most urgent needs of consumers, the assumption that all entrepreneurs regularly fall prey to certain errors tacitly implies that all practical men lack intelligence. It implies that nobody who is engaged in business and nobody who considers engaging in business if some opportunity is offered to him by the shortcomings of those already engaged in it, is shrewd enough to understand the real state of the market. But on the other hand the theorists, who are not themselves active in the conduct of affairs and merely philosophize about other people's actions, consider themselves smart enough to discover the fallacies leading astray those doing business. These omniscient professors are never deluded by the errors which cloud the judgment of everyone else. They know precisely what is wrong with private enterprise. Their claims to be invested with dictatorial powers to control business are therefore fully justified.

The most amazing thing about these doctrines is that they furthermore imply that businessmen, in their littleness of mind, obstinately cling to their erroneous procedures in spite of the fact that the scholars have long since unmasked their faults. Although every textbook explodes them, the businessmen cannot help repeating them. There is manifestly no means to prevent the recurrence of economic depression other than to entrust—in accordance with Plato's utopian ideas—supreme power to the philosophers.

Let us examine briefly the two most popular varieties of these disproportionality doctrines.

There is first the durable goods doctrine. These goods retain their serviceableness for some time. As long as their life period lasts, the buyer who has acquired a piece abstains from replacing it by the purchase of a new one. Thus, once all people have made their purchases, the demand for new products dwindles. Business becomes bad. A revival is possible only when, after the lapse of some time, the old houses, cars, refrigerators, and the like are worn out, and their owners must buy new ones.

However, businessmen are as a rule more provident than this doctrine assumes. They are intent upon adjusting the size of their production to the anticipated size of consumers' demand. The bakers take account of the fact that every day a housewife needs a new loaf of bread, and the manufacturers of coffins take into account the fact that the total annual sale of coffins cannot exceed the number of people decreased during this period. The machine industry reckons with the average "life" of its products no less than do the tailors, the shoemakers, the manufacturers of motorcars, radio sets, and refrigerators, and the construction firms. There are, to be sure, always promoters who in a mood of deceptive optimism are prone to overexpand their enterprises. In the pursuit of such projects they snatch away factors of production from other plants of the same industry and from other branches of industry. Thus their overexpansion results in a relative restriction of output in other fields. One branch goes on expanding while others shrink until the unprofitability of the former and the profitability of the latter rearranges conditions. Both the preceding boom and the following slump concern only a part of business.

The second variety of these disproportionality doctrines is known as the acceleration principle. A temporary rise in the demand for a certain commodity results in increased production of the commodity concerned. If demand later drops again, the investments made for this expansion of production appear as malinvestments. This becomes especially pernicious in the field of durable producers' goods. If the demand for the consumers' good *a* increases by 10 per cent, business increases the equipment *p* required for its production by 10 per cent. The resulting rise in the demand for *p* is the more momentous in proportion to the previous demand for *p,* the longer the duration of serviceableness of a piece of *p* is and the smaller consequently the previous demand for the replacement of worn-out pieces of *p* was. If the life of a piece of *p* is 10 years, the annual demand for *p* for replacement was 10 per cent of the stock of *p* previously employed by the industry. The rise of 10 per cent in the demand for *a* doubles therefore the demand for *p* and results in a 100 per cent expansion in the equipment *r* needed for the production of *p*. If then the demand for *a* stops increasing, 50 per cent of the production capacity of *r* remains idle. If the annual increase in the demand for *a* drops from 10 per cent to 5 per cent, 25 per cent of the production capacity of *r* cannot be used.

The fundamental error of this doctrine is that it considers entrepreneurial activities as a blindly automatic response to the momentary state of demand. Whenever demand increases and renders a branch of business more profitable, production facilities are supposed instantly to expand in proportion. This view is untenable. Entrepreneurs often err. They pay heavily for their errors. But whoever acted in the way the acceleration principle describes would not be an entrepreneur, but a soulless automaton. Yet the real entrepreneur is a *speculator,*[19] a man eager to utilize his opinion about the future structure of the market for business operations promising profits. This specific anticipative understanding of the conditions of the uncertain future defies any rules and systematization. It can be neither taught nor learned. If it were different, everybody could embark upon entrepreneurship with the same prospect of success. What distinguishes the successful entrepreneur and promoter from other people is precisely the fact that he does not let himself be guided by what was and is, but arranges his affairs on the ground of his opinion about the future. He sees the past and the present as other people do; but he judges the future in a different way. In his actions he is directed by an opinion about the future which deviates from those held by the crowd. The impulse of his actions is that he appraises the factors of production and the future prices of the commodities which can be produced out of them in a different way from other people. If the present structure of prices renders very profitable the business of those who are today selling the articles concerned, their production will expand only to the extent that entrepreneurs believe that the favorable market constellation will last long enough to make new investments pay. If entrepreneurs do not expect this, even very high profits of the enterprises already operating will not bring about an expansion. It is exactly this reluctance of the capitalists and entrepreneurs to invest in lines which they consider unprofitable that is violently criticized by people who do not comprehend the operation of the market economy. Technocratically minded engineers complain that the supremacy of the profit motive prevents consumers from being amply supplied with all those goods with which technological knowledge could provide them. Demagogues cry out against the greed of capitalists intent upon preserving scarcity.

A satisfactory explanation of business fluctuations must not be built upon the fact that individual firms or groups of firms misjudge the future state of the market and therefore make bad investments. The objective of the trade cycle is the *general* upswing of business activities, the propensity to expand production in *all* branches of industry, and the following *general* depression. These phenomena cannot be brought about by the fact that increased profits in some branches of business result in their expansion and a corresponding overproportional investment in the industries manufacturing the equipment needed for such an expansion.

It is a very well known fact that the more the boom progresses, the harder it becomes to buy machines and other equipment. The plants producing these things are overloaded with orders. Their customers

19. It is noteworthy that the same term is employed to signify the premeditation and the ensuing actions of the promoters and entrepreneurs and the purely academic reasoning of theorists that does not directly result in any action.

must wait a long time until the machines ordered are delivered. This clearly shows that the producers' goods industries are not so quick in the expansion of their own production facilities as the acceleration principle assumes.

But even if, for the sake of argument, we were ready to admit that capitalists and entrepreneurs behave in the way the disproportionality doctrines describe, it remains inexplicable how they could go on in the absence of credit expansion. The striving after such additional investments raises the prices of the complementary factors of production and the rate of interest on the loan market. These effects would curb the expansionist tendencies very soon if there were no credit expansion.

The supporters of the disproportionality doctrines refer to certain occurrences in the field of farming as a confirmation of their assertion concerning the inherent lack of provision on the part of private business. However, it is impermissible to demonstrate characteristic features of free competitive enterprise as operating in the market economy by pointing to conditions in the sphere of medium-size and small farming. In many countries this sphere is institutionally removed from the supremacy of the market and the consumers. Government interference is eager to protect the farmer against the vicissitudes of the market. These farmers do not operate in a free market; they are privileged and pampered by various devices. The orbit of their production activities is a reservation, as it were, in which technological backwardness, narrow-minded obstinacy, and entrepreneurial inefficiency are artificially preserved at the expense of the nonagricultural strata of the people. If they blunder in their conduct of affairs, the government forces the consumers, the taxpayers, and the mortgagees to foot the bill.

It is true that there is such a thing as the *corn-hog cycle* and analogous happenings in the production of other farm products. But the recurrence of such cycles is due to the fact that the penalties which the market applies against inefficient and clumsy entrepreneurs do not affect a great part of the farmers. These farmers are not answerable for their actions because they are the pet children of governments and politicians. If it were not so, they would long since have gone bankrupt and their former farms would be operated by more intelligent people.

XXI. WORK AND WAGES

1. Introversive Labor and Extroversive Labor

A MAN may overcome the disutility of labor (forego the enjoyment of leisure) for various reasons.

1. He may work in order to make his mind and body strong, vigorous, and agile. The disutility of labor is not a price expended for the attainment of these goals; overcoming it is inseparable from the contentment sought. The most conspicuous examples are genuine sport, practiced without any design for reward and social success, and the search for truth and knowledge pursued for its own sake and not as a means of improving one's own efficiency and skill in the performance of other kinds of labor aiming at other ends.[1]

2. He may submit to the disutility of labor in order to serve God. He sacrifices leisure to please God and to be rewarded in the beyond by eternal bliss and in the earthly pilgrimage by the supreme delight which the certainty of having complied with all religious duties affords. (If, however, he serves God in order to attain worldly ends —his daily bread and success in his secular affairs—his conduct does not differ substantially from other endeavors to attain mundane advantages by expending labor. Whether the theory guiding his conduct is correct and whether his expectations will materialize are irrelevant to the catallactic qualification of his mode of acting.[2])

3. He may toil in order to avoid greater mischief. He submits to the disutility of labor in order to forget, to escape from depressing thoughts and to banish annoying moods; work for him is, as it were, a perfected refinement of play. This refined playing must not be confused with the simple games of children which are merely pleasure-producing. (However, there are also other children's games. Children too are sophisticated enough to indulge in refined play.)

1. Cognition does not aim at a goal beyond the act of knowing. What satisfies the thinker is thinking as such, not obtaining perfect knowledge, a goal inaccessible to man.

2. It is hardly necessary to remark that comparing the craving for knowledge and the conduct of a pious life with sport and play does not imply any disparagement of either.

4. He may work because he prefers the proceeds he can earn by working to the disutility of labor and the pleasures of leisure.

The labor of the classes 1, 2, and 3 is expended because the disutility of labor in itself—and not its product—satisfies. One toils and troubles not in order to reach a goal at the termination of the march, but for the very sake of marching. The mountain-climber does not want simply to reach the peak, he wants to reach it by climbing. He disdains the rack railway which would bring him to the summit more quickly and without trouble even though the fare is cheaper than the costs incurred by climbing (e.g., the guide's fee). The toil of climbing does not gratify him immediately; it involves disutility of labor. But it is precisely overcoming the disutility of labor that satisfies him. A less exerting ascent would please him not better, but less.

We may call the labor of classes 1, 2, and 3 introversive labor and distinguish it from the extroversive labor of class 4. In some cases introversive labor may bring about—as a by-product as it were—results for the attainment of which other people would submit to the disutility of labor. The devout may nurse sick people for a heavenly reward; the truth seeker, exclusively devoted to the search for knowledge, may discover a practically useful device. To this extent introversive labor may influence the supply on the market. But as a rule catallactics is concerned only with extroversive labor.

The psychological problems raised by introversive labor are catallactically irrelevant. Seen from the point of view of economics introversive labor is to be qualified as consumption. Its performance as a rule requires not only the personal efforts of the individuals concerned, but also the expenditure of material factors of production and the produce of other peoples' extroversive, not immediately gratifying labor that must be bought by the payment of wages. The practice of religion requires places of worship and their equipment; sport requires diverse utensils and apparatus, trainers and coaches. All these things belong in the orbit of consumption.

2. Joy and Tedium of Labor

Only extroversive, not immediately gratifying labor is a topic of catallactic disquisition. The characteristic mark of this kind of labor is that it is performed for the sake of an end which is beyond its performance and the disutility which it involves. People work because they want to reap the produce of labor. The labor itself causes disutility. But apart from this disutility which is irksome and would enjoin upon man the urge to economize labor even if his power to work were not limited and he were able to perform unlimited work, special emotional phenomena sometimes appear, feelings of joy or tedium, accompanying the execution of certain kinds of labor.

Both, the joy and the tedium of labor, are in a domain other than the disutility of labor. The joy of labor therefore can neither alleviate nor remove the disutility of labor. Neither must the joy of labor be confused with the immediate gratification provided by certain kinds of work. It is an attendant phenomenon which proceeds either from labor's mediate gratification, the produce or reward, or from some accessory circumstances.

People do not submit to the disutility of labor for the sake of the joy which accompanies the labor, but for the sake of its mediate gratification. In fact the joy of labor presupposes for the most part the disutility of the labor concerned.

The sources from which the joy of labor springs are:

1. The expectation of the labor's mediate gratification, the anticipation of the enjoyment of its success and yield. The toiler looks at his work as a means for the attainment of an end sought, and the progress of his work delights him as an approach toward his goal. His joy is a foretaste of the satisfaction conveyed by the mediate gratification. In the frame of social cooperation this joy manifests itself in the contentment of being capable of holding one's ground in the social organism and of rendering services which one's fellow men appreciate either in buying the product or in remunerating the labor expended. The worker rejoices because he gets self-respect and the consciousness of supporting himself and his family and not being dependent on other people's mercy.

2. In the pursuit of his work the worker enjoys the aesthetic appreciation of his skill and its product. This is not merely the contemplative pleasure of the man who views things performed by other people. It is the pride of a man who is in a position to say: I know how to make such things, this is my work.

3. Having completed a task the worker enjoys the feeling of having successfully overcome all the toil and trouble involved. He is happy in being rid of something difficult, unpleasant, and painful, in being relieved for a certain time of the disutility of labor. His is the feeling of "I have done it."

4. Some kinds of work satisfy particular wishes. There are, for example, occupations which meet erotic desires—either conscious or subconscious ones. These desires may be normal or perverse. Also fetishists, homosexuals, sadists and other perverts can sometimes find in their work an opportunity to satisfy their strange appetites. There are occupations which are especially attractive to such people. Cruelty

and blood-thirstiness luxuriantly thrive under various occupational cloaks.

The various kinds of work offer different conditions for the appearance of the joy of labor. These conditions may be by and large more homogeneous in classes 1 and 3 than in class 2. It is obvious that they are more rarely present for class 4.

The joy of labor can be entirely absent. Psychical factors may eliminate it altogether. On the other hand one can purposely aim at increasing the joy of labor.

Keen discerners of the human soul have always been intent upon enhancing the joy of labor. A great part of the achievements of the organizers and leaders of armies of mercenaries belonged to this field. Their task was easy as far as the profession of arms provides the satisfactions of class 4. However, these satisfactions do not depend on the arms-bearer's loyalty. They also come to the soldier who leaves his war-lord in the lurch and turns against him in the service of new leaders. Thus the particular task of the employers of mercenaries was to promote an esprit de corps and loyalty that could render their hirelings proof against temptations. There were also, of course, chiefs who did not bother about such impalpable matters. In the armies and navies of the eighteenth century the only means of securing obedience and preventing desertion were barbarous punishments.

Modern industrialism was not intent upon designedly increasing the joy of labor. It relied upon the material improvement that it brought to its employees in their capacity as wage earners as well as in their capacity as consumers and buyers of the products. In view of the fact that job-seekers thronged to the plants and everyone scrambled for the manufactures, there seemed to be no need to resort to special devices. The benefits which the masses derived from the capitalist system were so obvious that no entrepreneur considered it necessary to harangue the workers with procapitalist propaganda. Modern capitalism is essentially mass production for the needs of the masses. The buyers of the products are by and large the same people who as wage earners cooperate in their manufacturing. Rising sales provided dependable information to the employer about the improvement of the masses' standard of living. He did not bother about the feelings of his employees as workers. He was exclusively intent upon serving them as consumers. Even today, in face of the most persistent and fanatical anticapitalist propaganda, there is hardly any counter-propaganda.

This anticapitalist propaganda is a systematic scheme for the substitution of tedium for the joy of labor. The joy of labor of classes 1 and 2 depends to some extent on ideological factors. The worker rejoices in his place in society and his active cooperation in its productive effort. If one disparages this ideology and replaces it by another which represents the wage earner as the distressed victim of ruthless exploiters, one turns the joy of labor into a feeling of disgust and tedium.

No ideology, however impressively emphasized and taught, can affect the disutility of labor. It is impossible to remove or to alleviate it by persuasion or hypnotic suggestion. On the other hand it cannot be increased by words and doctrines. The disutility of labor is a phenomenon unconditionally given. The spontaneous and carefree discharge of one's own energies and vital functions in aimless freedom suits everybody better than the stern restraint of purposive effort. The disutility of labor also pains a man who with heart and soul and even with self-denial is devoted to his work. He too is eager to reduce the lump of labor if it can be done without prejudice to the mediate gratification expected, and he enjoys the joy of labor of class 3.

However, the joy of labor of classes 1 and 2 and sometimes even that of class 3 can be eliminated by ideological influences and be replaced by the tedium of labor. The worker begins to hate his work if he becomes convinced that what makes him submit to the disutility of labor is not his own higher valuation of the stipulated compensation, but merely an unfair social system. Deluded by the slogans of the socialist propagandists, he fails to realize that the disutility of labor is an inexorable fact of human conditions, something ultimately given that cannot be removed by devices or methods of social organization. He falls prey to the Marxian fallacy that in a socialist commonwealth work will arouse not pain but pleasure.[3]

The fact that the tedium of labor is substituted for the joy of labor affects the valuation neither of the disutility of labor nor of the produce of labor. Both the demand for labor and the supply of labor remain unchanged. For people do not work for the sake of labor's joy, but for the sake of the mediate gratification. What is altered is merely the worker's emotional attitude. His work, his position in the complex of the social division of labor, his relations to other members of society and to the whole of society appear to him in a new light. He pities himself as the defenseless victim of an absurd and unjust system. He becomes an ill-humored grumbler, an unbalanced personality, an easy prey to all sorts of quacks and cranks. To be joyful in the performance of one's tasks and in overcoming the disutility of labor makes people cheerful and strengthens their energies and vital forces. To feel tedium in working makes people morose and neurotic. A

3. Engels, *Herrn Eugen Dührings Umwälzung der Wissenschaft* (7th ed. Stuttgart, 1910), p 317. See above, p. 137.

commonwealth in which the tedium of labor prevails is an assemblage of rancorous, quarrelsome and wrathful malcontents.

However, with regard to the volitional springs for overcoming the disutility of labor, the role played by the joy and the tedium of labor is merely accidental and supererogatory. There cannot be any question of making people work for the mere sake of the joy of labor. The joy of labor is no substitute for the mediate gratification of labor. The only means of inducing a man to work more and better is to offer him a higher reward. It is vain to bait him with the joy of labor. When the dictators of Soviet Russia, Nazi Germany, and Fascist Italy tried to assign to the joy of labor a definite function in their system of production, they saw their expectations blighted.

Neither the joy nor the tedium of labor can influence the amount of labor offered on the market. As far as these feelings are present with the same intensity in all kinds of work, the case is obvious. But it is the same with regard to joy and tedium which are conditioned by the particular features of the work concerned or the particular character of the worker. Let us look, for example, at the joy of class 4. The eagerness of certain people to get jobs which offer an opportunity for the enjoyment of these particular satisfactions tends to lower wage rates in this field. But it is precisely this effect that makes other people, less responsive to these questionable pleasures, prefer other sectors of the labor market in which they can earn more. Thus an opposite tendency develops which neutralizes the first one.

The joy and the tedium of labor are psychological phenomena which influence neither the individual's subjective valuation of the disutility and the mediate gratification of labor nor the price paid for labor on the market.

3. Wages

Labor is a scarce factor of production. As such it is sold and bought on the market. The price paid for labor is included in the price allowed for the product or the services if the performer of the work is the seller of the product or the services. If bare labor is sold and bought as such, either by an entrepreneur engaged in production for sale or by a consumer eager to use the services rendered for his own consumption, the price paid is called wages.

For acting man his own labor is not merely a factor of production but also the source of disutility; he values it not only with regard to the mediate gratification expected but also with regard to the disutility it causes. But for him, as for everyone, other people's labor as offered for sale on the market is nothing but a factor of production. Man deals with other people's labor in the same way that he deals with all scarce material factors of production. He appraises it according to the principles he applies in the appraisal of all other goods. The height of wage rates is determined on the market in the same way in which the prices of all commodities are determined. In this sense we may say that labor is a commodity. The emotional associations which people, under the influence of Marxism, attach to this term do not matter. It suffices to observe incidentally that the employers deal with labor as they do with commodities because the conduct of the consumers forces them to proceed in this way.

It is not permissible to speak of labor and wages in general without resorting to certain restrictions. A uniform type of labor or a general rate of wages do not exist. Labor is very different in quality, and each kind of labor renders specific services. Each is appraised as a complementary factor for turning out definite consumers' goods and services. Between the appraisal of the performance of a surgeon and that of a stevedore there is no direct connection. But indirectly each sector of the labor market is connected with all other sectors. An increase in the demand for surgical services, however great, will not make stevedores flock into the practice of surgery. Yet the lines between the various sectors of the labor market are not sharply drawn. There prevails a continuous tendency for workers to shift from their branch to other similar occupations in which conditions seem to offer better opportunities. Thus finally every change in demand or supply in one sector affects all other sectors indirectly. All groups indirectly compete with one another. If more people enter the medical profession, men are withdrawn from kindred occupations who again are replaced by an inflow of people from other branches and so on. In this sense there exists a connexity between all occupational groups however different the requirements in each of them may be. There again we are faced with the fact that the disparity in the quality of work needed for the satisfaction of wants is greater than the diversity in men's inborn ability to perform work.[4]

Connexity exists not only between different types of labor and the prices paid for them but no less between labor and the material factors of production. Within certain limits labor can be substituted for material factors of production and vice versa. The extent that such substitutions are resorted to depends on the height of wage rates and the prices of material factors.

The determination of wage rates—like that of the prices of material factors of production—can be achieved only on the market. There is no such thing as nonmarket wage rates, just as there are no nonmarket prices. As far as there are wages, labor is dealt with like any

4. Cf. above, pp. 133–135.

material factor of production and sold and bought on the market. It is usual to call the sector of the market of producers' goods on which labor is hired the labor market. As with all other sectors of the market, the labor market is actuated by the entrepreneurs intent upon making profits. Each entrepreneur is eager to buy all the kinds of specific labor he needs for the realization of his plans at the cheapest price. But the wages he offers must be high enough to take the workers away from competing entrepreneurs. The upper limit of his bidding is determined by anticipation of the price he can obtain for the increment in salable goods he expects from the employment of the worker concerned. The lower limit is determined by the bids of competing entrepreneurs who themselves are guided by analogous considerations. It is this that economists have in mind in asserting that the height of wage rates for each kind of labor is determined by its marginal productivity. Another way to express the same truth is to say that wage rates are determined by the supply of labor and of material factors of production on the one hand and by the anticipated future prices of the consumers' goods.

This catallactic explanation of the determination of wage rates has been the target of passionate but entirely erroneous attacks. It has been asserted that there is a monopoly of the demand for labor. Most of the supporters of this doctrine think that they have sufficiently proved their case by referring to some incidental remarks of Adam Smith concerning "a sort of tacit but constant and uniform combination" among employers to keep wages down.[5] Others refer in vague terms to the existence of trade associations of various groups of businessmen. The emptiness of all this talk is evident. However, the fact that these garbled ideas are the main ideological foundation of labor unionism and the labor policy of all contemporary governments makes it necessary to analyze them with the utmost care.

The entrepreneurs are in the same position with regard to the sellers of labor as they are with regard to the sellers of the material factors of production. They are under the necessity of acquiring all factors of production at the cheapest price. But if in the pursuit of this endeavor some entrepreneurs, certain groups of entrepreneurs, or all entrepreneurs offer prices or wage rates which are too low, i.e., do not agree with the state of the unhampered market, they will succeed in acquiring what they want to acquire only if entrance into the ranks of entrepreneurship is blocked through institutional barriers. If the emergence of new entrepreneurs or the expansion of the activi-

5. Cf. Adam Smith, *An Inquiry into the Nature and Causes of the Wealth of Nations* (Basle, 1791), vol. I, Bk. I, chap. viii, p. 100. Adam Smith himself seems to have unconsciously given up the idea. Cf. W. H. Hutt, *The Theory of Collective Bargaining* (London, 1930), pp. 24–25.

ties of already operating entrepreneurs is not prevented, any drop in the prices of factors of production not consonant with the structure of the market must open new chances for the earning of profits. There will be people eager to take advantage of the margin between the prevailing wage rate and the marginal productivity of labor. Their demand for labor will bring wage rates back to the height conditioned by labor's marginal productivity. The tacit combination among the employers to which Adam Smith referred, even if it existed, could not lower wages below the competitive market rate unless access to entrepreneurship required not only brains and capital (the latter always available to enterprises promising the highest returns), but in addition also an institutional title, a patent, or a license, reserved to a class of privileged people.

It has been asserted that a job-seeker must sell his labor at any price, however low, as he depends exclusively on his capacity to work and has no other source of income. He cannot wait and is forced to content himself with any reward the employers are kind enough to offer him. This inherent weakness makes it easy for the concerted action of the masters to lower wage rates. They can, if need be, wait longer, as their demand for labor is not so urgent as the worker's demand for subsistence. The argument is defective. It takes it for granted that the employers pocket the difference between the marginal-productivity wage rate and the lower monopoly rate as an extra monopoly gain and do not pass it on to the consumers in the form of a reduction in prices. For if they were to reduce prices according to the drop in costs of production, they, in their capacity as entrepreneurs and sellers of the products, would derive no advantage from cutting wages. The whole gain would go to the consumers and thereby also to the wage-earners in their capacity as buyers; the entrepreneurs themselves would be benefited only as consumers. To retain the extra profit resulting from the "exploitation" of the workers' alleged poor bargaining power would require concerted action on the part of employers in their capacity as sellers of the products. It would require a universal monopoly of all kinds of production activities which can be created only by an institutional restriction of access to entrepreneurship.

The essential point of the matter is that the alleged monopolistic combination of the employers about which Adam Smith and a great part of public opinion speak would be a monopoly of demand. But we have already seen that such alleged monopolies of demand are in fact monopolies of supply of a particular character. The employers would be in a position enabling them to lower wage rates by concerted action only if they were to monopolize a factor indispensable for every kind of production and to restrict the employment of this factor in a monopolistic way. As there is no single material factor indispensable for every kind of production, they would have to monopolize all material factors of production. This condition would be present only in a socialist community, in which there is neither a market nor prices and wage rates.

Neither would it be possible for the proprietors of the material factors of production, the capitalists and the landowners, to combine in a universal cartel against the interests of the workers. The characteristic mark of production activities in the past and in the foreseeable future is that the scarcity of labor exceeds the scarcity of most of the primary, nature-given material factors of production. The comparatively greater scarcity of labor determines the extent to which the comparatively abundant primary natural factors can be utilized. There is unused soil, there are unused mineral deposits and so on because there is not enough labor available for their utilization. If the owners of the soil that is tilled today were to form a cartel in order to reap monopoly gains, their plans would be frustrated by the competition of the owners of the submarginal land. The owners of the produced factors of production in their turn could not combine in a comprehensive cartel without the cooperation of the owners of the primary factors.

Various other objections have been advanced against the doctrine of the monopolistic exploitation of labor by a tacit or avowed combine of the employers. It has been demonstrated that at no time and at no place in the unhampered market economy can the existence of such cartels be discovered. It has been shown that it is not true that the job-seekers cannot wait and are therefore under the necessity of accepting any wage rates, however low, offered to them by the employers. It is not true that every unemployed worker is faced with starvation; the workers too have reserves and can wait; the proof is that they really do wait. On the other hand waiting can be financially ruinous to the entrepreneurs and capitalists too. If they cannot employ their capital, they suffer losses. Thus all the disquisitions about an alleged "employers' advantage" and "workers' disadvantage" in bargaining are without substance.[6]

But these are secondary and accidental considerations. The central fact is that a monopoly of the demand for labor cannot and does not exist in an unhampered market economy. It could originate only as an outgrowth of institutional restrictions of access to entrepreneurship.

Yet one more point must be stressed. The doctrine of the monopo-

6. All these and many other points are carefully analyzed by Hutt, *op. cit.*, pp. 35–72.

listic manipulation of wage rates by the employers speaks of labor as if it were a homogeneous entity. It deals with such concepts as demand for "labor in general" and supply of "labor in general." But such notions have, as has been pointed out already, no counterpart in reality. What is sold and bought on the labor market is not "labor in general," but definite specific labor suitable to render definite services. Each entrepreneur is in search of workers who are fitted to accomplish those specific tasks which he needs for the execution of his plans. He must withdraw these specialists from the employments in which they happen to work at the moment. The only means he has to achieve this is to offer them higher pay. Every innovation which an entrepreneur plans—the production of a new article, the application of a new process of production, the choice of a new location for a specific branch or simply the expansion of production already in existence either in his own enterprise or in other enterprises—requires the employment of workers hitherto engaged somewhere else. The entrepreneurs are not merely faced with a shortage of "labor in general," but with a shortage of those specific types of labor they need for their plants. The competition among the entrepreneurs in bidding for the most suitable hands is no less keen than their competition in bidding for the required raw materials, tools, and machines and in their bidding for capital on the capital and loan market. The expansion of the activities of the individual firms as well as of the whole society is not only limited by the amount of capital goods available and of the supply of "labor in general." In each branch of production it is also limited by the available supply of specialists. This is, of course, only a temporary obstacle which vanishes in the long run when more workers, attracted by the higher pay of the specialists in comparatively undermanned branches, will have trained themselves for the special tasks concerned. But in the changing economy such a scarcity of specialists emerges anew daily and determines the conduct of employers in their search for workers.

Every employer must aim at buying the factors of production needed, inclusive of labor, at the cheapest price. An employer who paid more than agrees with the market price of the services his employees render him, would be soon removed from his entrepreneurial position. On the other hand an employer who tried to reduce wage rates below the height consonant with the marginal productivity of labor would not recruit the type of men that the most efficient utilization of his equipment requires. There prevails a tendency for wage rates to reach the point at which they are equal to the price of the marginal product of the kind of labor in question. If wage rates drop below this point, the gain derived from the employment of every additional worker will increase the demand for labor and thus make wage rates rise again. If wage rates rise above this point, the loss incurred from the employment of every worker will force the employers to discharge workers. The competition of the unemployed for jobs will create a tendency for wage rates to drop.

4. Catallactic Unemployment

If a job-seeker cannot obtain the position he prefers, he must look for another kind of job. If he cannot find an employer ready to pay him as much as he would like to earn, he must abate his pretensions. If he refuses, he will not get any job. He remains unemployed.

What causes unemployment is the fact that—contrary to the above-mentioned doctrine of the worker's inability to wait—those eager to earn wages can and do wait. A job-seeker who does not want to wait will always get a job in the unhampered market economy in which there is always unused capacity of natural resources and very often also unused capacity of produced factors of production. It is only necessary for him either to reduce the amount of pay he is asking for or to alter his occupation or his place of work.

There were and still are people who work only for some time and then live for another period from the savings they have accumulated by working. In countries in which the cultural state of the masses is low, it is often difficult to recruit workers who are ready to stay on the job. The average man there is so callous and inert that he knows of no other use for his earnings than to buy some leisure time. He works only in order to remain unemployed for some time.

It is different in the civilized countries. Here the worker looks upon unemployment as an evil. He would like to avoid it provided the sacrifice required is not too grievous. He chooses between employment and unemployment in the same way in which he proceeds in all other actions and choices: he weighs the pros and cons. If he chooses unemployment, this unemployment is a market phenomenon whose nature is not different from other market phenomena as they appear in a changing market economy. We may call this kind of unemployment market-generated or *catallactic unemployment.*

The various considerations which may induce a man to decide for unemployment can be classified in this way:

1. The individual believes that he will find at a later date a remunerative job in his dwelling place and in an occupation which he likes better and for which he has been trained. He seeks to avoid the expenditure and other disadvantages involved in shifting from one occupation to another and from one geographical point to another. There may be special conditions increasing these costs. A worker who

owns a homestead is more firmly linked with the place of his residence than people living in rented apartments. A married woman is less mobile than an unmarried girl. Then there are occupations which impair the worker's ability to resume his previous job at a later date. A watchmaker who works for some time as a lumberman may lose the dexterity required for his previous job. In all these cases the individual chooses temporary unemployment because he believes that this choice pays better in the long run.

2. There are occupations the demand for which is subject to considerable seasonal variations. In some months of the year the demand is very intense, in other months it dwindles or disappears altogether. The structure of wage rates discounts these seasonal fluctuations. The branches of industry subject to them can compete on the labor market only if the wages they pay in the good season are high enough to indemnify the wage earners for the disadvantages resulting from the seasonal irregularity in demand. Then many of the workers, having saved a part of their ample earnings in the good season, remain unemployed in the bad season.

3. The individual chooses temporary unemployment for considerations which in popular speech are called noneconomic or even irrational. He does not take jobs which are incompatible with his religious, moral, and political convictions. He shuns occupations the exercise of which would impair his social prestige. He lets himself be guided by traditional standards of what is proper for a gentleman and what is unworthy. He does not want to lose face or caste.

Unemployment in the unhampered market is always voluntary. In the eyes of the unemployed man, unemployment is the minor of two evils between which he has to choose. The structure of the market may sometimes cause wage rates to drop. But, on the unhampered market, there is always for each type of labor a rate at which all those eager to work can get a job. The final wage rate is that rate at which all job-seekers get jobs and all employers as many workers as they want to hire. Its height is determined by the marginal productivity of each type of work.

Wage rate fluctuations are the device by means of which the sovereignty of the consumers manifests itself on the labor market. They are the measure adopted for the allocation of labor to the various branches of production. They penalize disobedience by cutting wage rates in the comparatively overmanned branches and recompense obedience by raising wage rates in the comparatively undermanned branches. They thus submit the individual to a harsh social pressure. It is obvious that they indirectly limit the individual's freedom to choose his occupation. But this pressure is not rigid. It leaves to the individual a margin in the limits of which he can choose between what suits him better and what less. Within this orbit he is free to act of his own accord. This amount of freedom is the maximum of freedom that an individual can enjoy in the framework of the social division of labor, and this amount of pressure is the minimum of pressure that is indispensable for the preservation of the system of social cooperation. There is only one alternative left to the catallactic pressure exercised by the wages system: the assignment of occupations and jobs to each individual by the peremptory decrees of an authority, a central board planning all production activities. This is tantamount to the suppression of all freedom.

It is true that under the wages system the individual is not free to choose permanent unemployment. But no other imaginable social system could grant him a right to unlimited leisure. That man cannot avoid submitting to the disutility of labor is not an outgrowth of any social institution. It is an inescapable natural condition of human life and conduct.

It is not expedient to call catallactic unemployment in a metaphor borrowed from mechanics "frictional" unemployment. In the imaginary construction of the evenly rotating economy there is no unemployment because we have based this construction on such an assumption. Unemployment is a phenomenon of a changing economy. The fact that a worker discharged on account of changes occurring in the arrangement of production processes does not instantly take advantage of every opportunity to get another job but waits for a more propitious opportunity is not a consequence of the tardiness of the adjustment to the change in conditions, but is one of the factors slowing down the pace of this adjustment. It is not an automatic reaction to the changes which have occurred, independent of the will and the choices of the job-seekers concerned, but the effect of their intentional actions. It is speculative, not frictional.

Catallactic unemployment must not be confused with *institutional unemployment.* Institutional unemployment is not the outcome of the decisions of the individual job-seekers. It is the effect of interference with the market phenomena intent upon enforcing by coercion and compulsion wage rates higher than those the unhampered market would have determined. The treatment of institutional unemployment belongs to the analysis of the problems of interventionism.

5. Gross Wage Rates and Net Wage Rates

What the employer buys on the labor market and what he gets in exchange for the wages paid is always a definite performance which he appraises according to its market price. The customs and usages prevailing on the various sectors of the labor market do not influence the prices paid for definite quantities of specific performances. Gross wage rates always tend toward the point at which they are equal to the price for which the increment resulting from the employment of the marginal worker can be sold on the market, due allowance being made for the price of the required materials and to originary interest on the capital needed.

In weighing the pros and cons of the hiring of workers the employer does not ask himself what the worker gets as take-home wages. The only relevant question for him is: What is the total price I have to expend for securing the services of this worker? In speaking of the determination of wage rates catallactics always refers to the total price which the employer must spend for a definite quantity of work of a definite type, i.e., to gross wage rates. If laws or business customs force the employer to make other expenditures besides the wages he pays to the employee, the take-home wages are reduced accordingly. Such accessory expenditures do not affect the gross rate of wages. Their incidence falls upon the wage-earner. Their total amount reduces the height of take-home wages, i.e., of net wage rates.

It is necessary to realize the following consequences of this state of affairs:

1. It does not matter whether wages are time wages or piecework wages. Also where there are time wages, the employer takes only one thing into account; namely, the average performance he expects to obtain from each worker employed. His calculation discounts all the opportunities time work offers to shirkers and cheaters. He discharges workers who do not perform the minimum expected. On the other hand a worker eager to earn more must either shift to piecework or seek a job in which pay is higher because the minimum of achievement expected is greater.

Neither does it matter on an unhampered labor market whether time wages are paid daily, weekly, monthly, or as annual wages. It does not matter whether the time allowed for notice of discharge is longer or shorter, whether agreements are made for definite periods or for the worker's lifetime, whether the employee is entitled to retirement and a pension for himself, his widow, and his orphans, to paid or unpaid vacations, to certain assistance in case of illness or invalidism or to any other benefits and privileges. The question the employer faces is always the same: Does it or does it not pay for me to enter into such a contract? Don't I pay too much for what I am getting in return?

2. Consequently the incidence of all so-called social burdens and gains ultimately falls upon the worker's net wage rates. It is irrelevant whether or not the employer is entitled to deduct the contributions

to all kinds of social security from the wages he pays in cash to the employee. At any rate these contributions burden the employee, not the employer.

3. The same holds true with regard to taxes on wages. Here too it does not matter whether the employer has or has not the right to deduct them from take-home wages.

4. Neither is a shortening of the hours of work a free gift to the worker. If he does not compensate for the shorter hours of work by increasing his output accordingly, time wages will drop correspondingly. If the law decreeing a shortening of the hours of work prohibits such a reduction in wage rates, all the consequences of a government-decreed rise in wage rates appear. The same is valid with regard to all other so-called social gains, such as paid vacations and so on.

5. If the government grants to the employer a subsidy for the employment of certain classes of workers, their take-home wages are increased by the total amount of such a subsidy.

6. If the authorities grant to every employed worker whose own earnings lag behind a certain minimum standard an allowance raising his income to this minimum, the height of wage rates is not directly affected. Indirectly a drop in wage rates could possibly result as far as this system could induce people who did not work before to seek jobs and thus bring about an increase in the supply of labor.[7]

6. Wages and Subsistence

The life of primitive man was an unceasing struggle against the scantiness of the nature-given means for his sustenance. In this desperate effort to secure bare survival, many individuals and whole families, tribes, and races succumbed. Primitive man was always haunted by the specter of death from starvation. Civilization has freed us from these perils. Human life is menaced day and night by innumerable dangers; it can be destroyed at any instant by natural forces which are beyond control or at least cannot be controlled at the present stage of our knowledge and our potentialities. But the horror of starvation no longer terrifies people living in a capitalist society. He who is able to work earns much more than is needed for bare sustenance.

There are also, of course, disabled people who are incapable of

7. In the last years of the eighteenth century, amidst the distress produced by the protracted war with France and the inflationary methods of financing it, England resorted to this makeshift (the Speenhamland system). The real aim was to prevent agricultural workers from leaving their jobs and going into the factories where they could earn more. The Speenhamland system was thus a disguised subsidy for the landed gentry saving them the expense of higher wages.

work. Then there are invalids who can perform a small quantity of work, but whose disability prevents them from earning as much as normal workers do; sometimes the wage rates they could earn are so low that they could not maintain themselves. These people can keep body and soul together only if other people help them. The next of kin, friends, the charity of benefactors and endowments, and communal poor relief take care of the destitute. Alms-folk do not cooperate in the social process of production; as far as the provision of the means for the satisfaction of wants is concerned, they do not act; they live because other people look after them. The problems of poor relief are problems of the arrangement of consumption, not of the arrangement of production activities. They are as such beyond the frame of a theory of human action which refers only to the provision of the means required for consumption, not to the way in which these means are consumed. Catallactic theory deals with the methods adopted for the charitable support of the destitute only as far as they can possibly affect the supply of labor. It has sometimes happened that the policies applied in poor relief have encouraged unwillingness to work and the idleness of able-bodied adults.

In the capitalist society there prevails a tendency toward a steady increase in the per capita quota of capital invested. The accumulation of capital soars above the increase in population figures. Consequently the marginal productivity of labor, real wage rates, and the wage earners' standard of living tend to rise continually. But this improvement in well-being is not the manifestation of the operation of an inevitable law of human evolution; it is a tendency resulting from the interplay of forces which can freely produce their effects only under capitalism. It is possible and, if we take into account the direction of present-day policies, even not unlikely that capital consumption on the one hand and an increase or an insufficient drop in population figures on the other hand will reverse things. Then it could happen that men will again learn what starvation means and that the relation of the quantity of capital goods available and population figures will become so unfavorable as to make part of the workers earn less than a bare subsistence. The mere approach to such conditions would certainly cause irreconcilable dissensions within society, conflicts the violence of which must result in a complete disintegration of all societal bonds. The social division of labor cannot be preserved if part of the cooperating members of society are doomed to earn less than a bare subsistence.

The notion of a physiological minimum of subsistence to which the "iron law of wages" refers and which demagogues put forward again and again is of no use for a catallactic theory of the determination of wage rates. One of the foundations upon which social cooperation rests is the fact that labor performed according to the principle of the division of labor is so much more productive than the efforts of isolated individuals that able-bodied people are not troubled by the fear of starvation which daily threatened their forebears. Within a capitalist commonwealth the minimum of subsistence plays no catallactic role.

Furthermore, the notion of a physiological minimum of subsistence lacks that precision and scientific rigor which people have ascribed to it. Primitive man, adjusted to a more animal-like than human existence, could keep himself alive under conditions which are unbearable to his dainty scions pampered by capitalism. There is no such thing as a physiologically and biologically determined minimum of subsistence, valid for every specimen of the zoological species homo sapiens. No more tenable is the idea that a definite quantity of calories is needed to keep a man healthy and progenitive, and a further definite quantity to replace the energy expended in working. The appeal to such notions of cattle breeding and the vivisection of guinea pigs does not aid the economist in his endeavors to comprehend the problems of purposive human action. The "iron law of wages" and the essentially identical Marxian doctrine of the determination of "the value of labor power" by "the working time necessary for its production, consequently also for its reproduction,"[8] are the least tenable of all that has ever been taught in the field of catallactics.

Yet it was possible to attach some meaning to the ideas implied in the iron law of wages. If one sees in the wage earner merely a chattel and believes that he plays no other role in society, if one assumes that he aims at no other satisfaction than feeding and proliferation and does not know of any employment for his earnings other than the procurement of those animal satisfactions, one may consider the iron law as a theory of the determination of wage rates. In fact the classical economists, frustrated by their abortive value theory, could not think of any other solution of the problem involved. For Torrens and Ricardo the theorem that the natural price of labor is the price which enables the wage earners to subsist and to perpetuate their race, without any increase or diminution, was the logically inescapable inference from their untenable value theory. But when their epigones saw that they could no longer satisfy themselves with this manifestly preposterous law, they resorted to a modification of it which was tanta-

8. Cf. Marx, *Das Kapital* (7th ed. Hamburg, 1914), I, 133. In the *Communist Manifesto* (Section II) Marx and Engels formulate their doctrine in this way: "The average price of wage labor is the minimum wage, i.e., that quantum of means of subsistence which is absolutely required to keep the laborer in bare existence as laborer." It "merely suffices to prolong and reproduce a bare existence."

mount to a complete abandonment of any attempt to provide an economic explanation of the determination of wage rates. They tried to preserve the cherished notion of the minimum of subsistence by substituting the concept of a "social" minimum for the concept of a physiological minimum. They no longer spoke of the minimum required for the necessary subsistence of the laborer and for the preservation of an undiminished supply of labor. They spoke instead of the minimum required for the preservation of a standard of living sanctified by historical tradition and inherited customs and habits. While daily experience taught impressively that under capitalism real wage rates and the wage earners' standard of living were steadily rising, while it became from day to day more obvious that the traditional walls separating the various strata of the population could no longer be preserved because the social improvement in the conditions of the industrial workers demolished the vested ideas of social rank and dignity, these doctrinaires announced that old customs and social convention determine the height of wage rates. Only people blinded by preconceived prejudices and party bias could resort to such an explanation in an age in which industry supplies the consumption of the masses again and again with new commodities hitherto unknown and makes accessible to the average worker satisfactions of which no king could dream in the past.

It is not especially remarkable that the Prussian Historical School of the *wirtschaftliche Staatswissenschaften* viewed wage rates no less than commodity prices and interest rates as "historical categories" and that in dealing with wage rates it had recourse to the concept of "income adequate to the individual's hierarchical station in the social scale of ranks." It was the essence of the teachings of this school to deny the existence of economics and to substitute history for it. But it is amazing that Marx and the Marxians did not recognize that their endorsement of this spurious doctrine entirely disintegrated the body of the so-called Marxian system of economics. When the articles and dissertations published in England in the early 'sixties convinced Marx that it was no longer permissible to cling unswervingly to the wage theory of the classical economists, he modified his theory of the value of labor power. He declared that "the extent of the so-called natural wants and the manner in which they are satisfied, are in themselves a product of historical evolution" and "depend to a large extent on the degree of civilization attained by any given country and, among other factors, especially on the conditions and customs and pretensions concerning the standard of life under which the class of free laborers has been formed." Thus "a historical and moral element enter into the determination of the value of labor power." But when Marx adds that nonetheless "for a given country at any given time, the average quantity of *indispensable* necessaries of life is a given fact,"[9] he contradicts himself and misleads the reader. What he has in mind is no longer the "indispensable necessaries," but the things considered indispensable from a traditional point of view, the means necessary for the preservation of a standard of living adequate to the workers' station in the traditional social hierarchy. The recourse to such an explanation means virtually the renunciation of any economic or catallactic elucidation of the determination of wage rates. Wage rates are explained as a datum of history. They are no longer seen as a market phenomenon, but as a factor originating outside of the interplay of the forces operating on the market.

However, even those who believe that the height of wage rates as they are actually paid and received in reality are forced upon the market from without as a datum cannot avoid developing a theory which explains the determination of wage rates as the outcome of the valuations and decisions of the consumers. Without such a catallactic theory of wages, no economic analysis of the market can be complete and logically satisfactory. It is simply nonsensical to restrict the catallactic disquisitions to the problems of the determination of commodity prices and interest rates and to accept wage rates as a historical datum. An economic theory worthy of the name must be in a position to assert with regard to wage rates more than that they are determined by a "historical and moral element." The characteristic mark of economics is that it explains the exchange ratios manifested in market transactions as market phenomena the determination of which is subject to a regularity in the concatenation and sequence of events. It is precisely this that distinguishes economic conception from the historical understanding, theory from history.

We can well imagine a historical situation in which the height of wage rates is forced upon the market by the interference of external compulsion and coercion. Such institutional fixing of wage rates is one of the most important features of our age of interventionist policies. But with regard to such a state of affairs it is the task of economics to investigate what effects are brought about by the disparity between the two wage rates, the potential rate which the unhampered market would have produced by the interplay of the supply of and the demand for labor on the one hand, and on the other the rate which external compulsion and coercion impose upon the parties to the market transactions.

9. Cf. Marx, *Das Kapital,* p. 134. Italics are mine. The term used by Marx which in the text is translated as "necessaries of life" is *"Lebensmittel."* The *Muret-Sanders Dictionary* (16th ed.) translates this term "articles of food, provisions, victuals, grub."

It is true, wage earners are imbued with the idea that wages must be at least high enough to enable them to maintain a standard of living adequate to their station in the hierarchical gradation of society. Every single worker has his particular opinion about the claims he is entitled to raise on account of "status," "rank," "tradition," and "custom" in the same way as he has his particular opinion about his own efficiency and his own achievements. But such pretensions and self-complacent assumptions are without any relevance for the determination of wage rates. They limit neither the upward nor the downward movement of wage rates. The wage earner must sometimes satisfy himself with much less than what, according to his opinion, is adequate to his rank and efficiency. If he is offered more than he expected, he pockets the surplus without a qualm. The age of laissez faire for which the iron law and Marx's doctrine of the historically determined formation of wage rates claim validity witnessed a progressive, although sometimes temporarily interrupted, tendency for real wage rates to rise. The wage earners' standard of living rose to a height unprecedented in history and never thought of in earlier periods.

The labor unions pretend that nominal wage rates at least must always be raised in accordance with the changes occurring in the monetary unit's purchasing power in such a way as to secure to the wage earner the unabated enjoyment of the previous standard of living. They raise these claims also with regard to wartime conditions and the measures adopted for the financing of war expenditure. In their opinion even in wartime neither inflation nor the withholding of income taxes must affect the worker's take-home *real* wage rates. This doctrine tacitly implies the thesis of the *Communist Manifesto* that "the working men have no country" and have "nothing to lose but their chains"; consequently they are neutral in the wars waged by the bourgeois exploiters and do not care whether their nation conquers or is conquered. It is not the task of economics to scrutinize these statements. It only has to establish the fact that it does not matter what kind of justification is advanced in favor of the enforcement of wage rates higher than those the unhampered labor market would have determined. If as a result of such claims real wage rates are really raised above the height consonant with the marginal productivity of the various types of labor concerned, the unavoidable consequences must appear without any regard to the underlying philosophy.

In reviewing the whole history of mankind from the early beginnings of civilization up to our age, it makes sense to establish in general terms the fact that the productivity of human labor has been multiplied, for indeed the members of a civilized nation produce today much more than their ancestors did. But this concept of the productivity of labor in general is devoid of any praxeological or catallactic meaning and does not allow any expression in numerical terms. Still less is it permissible to refer to it in attempts to deal with the problems of the market.

Present-day labor-union doctrine operates with a concept of productivity of labor that is designedly constructed to provide an alleged ethical justification for syndicalistic ventures. It defines productivity either as the total market value in terms of money that is added to the products by the processing (either of one firm or by all the firms of a branch of industry), divided by the number of workers employed, or as output (of this firm or branch of industry) per man-hour of work. Comparing the magnitudes computed in this way for the beginning of a definite period of time and for its end, they call the amount by which the figure computed for the later date exceeds that for the earlier date "increase in productivity of labor," and they pretend that it by rights belongs entirely to the workers. They demand that this whole amount should be added to the wage rates which the workers received at the beginning of the period. Confronted with these claims of the unions, the employers for the most part do not contest the underlying doctrine and do not question the concept of productivity of labor involved. They accept it implicitly in pointing out that wage rates have already risen to the full extent of the increase in productivity, computed according to this method, or that they have already risen beyond this limit.

Now this procedure of computing the productivity of the work performed by the labor force of a firm or an industry is entirely fallacious. One thousand men working forty hours a week in a modern American shoe factory turn out every month *m* pairs of shoes. One thousand men working with the traditional old-fashioned tools in small artisan shops somewhere in the backward countries of Asia produce over the same period of time, even when working much longer than forty hours weekly, many fewer than *m* pairs. Between the United States and Asia the difference in productivity computed according to the methods of the union doctrine is enormous. It is certainly not due to any inherent virtues of the American worker. He is not more diligent, painstaking, skillful, or intelligent than the Asiatics. (We may even assume that many of those employed in a modern factory perform much simpler operations than those required from a man handling the old-fashioned tools.) The superiority of the American plant is entirely caused by the superiority of its equipment and the prudence of its entrepreneurial conduct. What prevents the businessmen of the backward countries from adopting the American methods of production is lack of capital accumulated, not any insufficiency on the part of their workers.

On the eve of the "Industrial Revolution," conditions in the West did not differ much from what they are today in the East. The radical change of conditions that bestowed on the masses of the West the present average standard of living (a high standard indeed when compared with precapitalistic or with Soviet conditions) was the effect of capital accumulation by saving and the wise investment of it by farsighted entrepreneurship. No technological improvement would have been possible if the additional capital goods required for the practical utilization of new inventions had not previously been made available by saving.

While the workers in their capacity as workers did not, and do not, contribute to the improvement of the apparatus of production, they are (in a market economy which is not sabotaged by government or union violence), both in their capacity as workers and in their capacity as consumers, the foremost beneficiaries of the ensuing betterment of conditions.

What initiates the chain of actions that results in an improvement of economic conditions is the accumulation of new capital through saving. These additional funds render the execution of projects possible which, for the lack of capital goods, could not have been executed previously. Embarking upon the realization of the new projects, the entrepreneurs compete on the market for the factors of production with all those already engaged in projects previously entered upon. In their attempts to secure the necessary quantity of raw materials and of manpower, they push up the prices of raw materials and wage rates. Thus the wage earners, already at the start of the process, reap a share of the benefits that the abstention from consumption on the part of the savers has begotten. In the farther course of the process they are again favored, now in their capacity as consumers, by the drop in prices that the increase in production tends to bring about.[10]

Economics describes the final outcome of this sequence of changes thus: An increase in capital invested results, with an unchanged number of people intent upon earning wages, in a rise of the marginal utility of labor and therefore of wage rates. What raises wage rates is an increase in capital exceeding the increase in population or, in other words, an increase in the per-head quota of capital invested. On the unhampered labor market, wage rates always tend toward the height at which they equal the marginal productivity of each kind of

10. See above, pp. 296–297.

labor, that is the height that equals the value added to or subtracted from the value of the product by the employment or discharge of a man. At this rate all those in search of employment find jobs, and all those eager to employ workers can hire as many as they want. If wages are raised above this market rate, unemployment of a part of the potential labor force inevitably results. It does not matter what kind of doctrine is advanced in order to justify the enforcement of wage rates that exceed the potential market rates.

Wage rates are ultimately determined by the value which the wage earner's fellow citizens attach to his services and achievements. Labor is appraised like a commodity, not because the entrepreneurs and capitalists are hardhearted and callous, but because they are unconditionally subject to the supremacy of the consumers of which today the earners of wages and salaries form the immense majority. The consumers are not prepared to satisfy anybody's pretensions, presumptions, and self-conceit. They want to be served in the cheapest way.

A Comparison Between the Historical Explanation of Wage Rates and the Regression Theorem

It may be useful to compare the doctrine of Marxism and the Prussian Historical School, according to which wage rates are a historical datum and not a catallactic phenomenon, with the regression theorem of money's purchasing power.[11]

The regression theorem establishes the fact that no good can be employed for the function of a medium of exchange which at the very beginning of its use for this purpose did not have exchange value on account of other employments. This fact does not substantially affect the daily determination of money's purchasing power as it is produced by the interplay of the supply of and the demand for money on the part of people intent upon keeping cash. The regression theorem does not assert that any actual exchange ratio between money on the one hand and commodities and services on the other hand is a historical datum not dependent on today's market situation. It merely explains how a new kind of media of exchange can come into use and remain in use. In this sense it says that there is a historical component in money's purchasing power.

It is quite different with the Marxian and Prussian theorem. As this doctrine sees it, the actual height of wage rates as it appears on the market is a historical datum. The valuations of the consumers who mediately are the buyers of labor and those of the wage earners, the sellers of labor, are of no avail. Wage rates are fixed by historical events of the past. They can neither rise above nor drop below this

11. See above, pp. 408–410.

height. The fact that wage rates are today higher in Switzerland than in India can be explained only by history, just as only history can explain why Napoleon I became a Frenchman and not an Italian, an emperor and not a Corsican lawyer. It is impossible, in the explanation of the discrepancy between the wage rates of shepherds or of bricklayers in these two countries, to resort to factors unconditionally in operation on every market. An explanation can only be provided by the history of these two nations.

7. The Supply of Labor as Affected by the Disutility of Labor

The fundamental facts affecting the supply of labor are:

1. Every individual can expend only a limited quantity of labor.

2. This definite quantity cannot be performed at any time desired. The interpolation of periods of rest and recreation is indispensable.

3. Not every individual is able to perform any kind of labor. There are innate as well as acquired diversities in the abilities to perform certain types of work. The innate faculties required for certain types of work cannot be acquired by any training and schooling.

4. The capacity of work must be dealt with appropriately if it is not to deteriorate or to vanish altogether. Special care is needed to preserve a man's abilities—both the innate and the acquired—for such a period as the unavoidable decline of his vital forces may permit.

5. As work approaches the point at which the total amount of work a man can perform at the time is exhausted and the interpolation of a period of recreation is indispensable, fatigue impairs the quantity and the quality of the performance.[12]

6. Men prefer the absence of labor, i.e., leisure, to labor, or as the economists put it: they attach disutility to labor.

The self-sufficient man who works in economic isolation for the direct satisfaction of his own needs only, stops working at the point at which he begins to value leisure, the absence of labor's disutility, more highly than the increment in satisfaction expected from working more. Having satisfied his most urgent needs, he considers the satisfaction of the still unsatisfied needs less desirable than the satisfaction of his striving after leisure.

The same is true for wage earners no less than for an isolated autarkic worker. They too are not prepared to work until they have

12. Other fluctuations in the quantity and quality of the performance per unit of time, e.g., the lower efficiency in the period immediately following the resumption of work interrupted by recreation, are hardly of any importance for the supply of labor on the market.

expended the total capacity of work they are capable of expending. They too are eager to stop working at the point at which the mediate gratification expected no longer outweighs the disutility involved in the performance of additional work.

Popular opinion, laboring under atavistic representations and blinded by Marxian slogans, was slow in grasping this fact. It clung and even today clings to the habit of looking at the wage earner as a bondsman, and at wages as the capitalist equivalent of the bare subsistence which the slave owner and the cattle owner must provide for their slaves and animals. In the eyes of this doctrine the wage earner is a man whom poverty has forced to submit to bondage. The vain formalism of the bourgeois lawyers, we are told, calls this subjection voluntary, and interprets the relation between employer and employee as a contract between two equal parties. In truth, however, the worker is not free; he acts under duress; he must submit to the yoke of virtual serfdom because no other choice is left to him, society's disinherited outcast. Even his apparent right to choose his master is spurious. The open or silent combination of the employers fixing the conditions of employment in a uniform way by and large makes this freedom illusory.

If one assumes that wages are merely the reimbursement of the expenses incurred by the worker in the preservation and reproduction of labor power or that their height is determined by tradition, it is quite consistent to consider every reduction in the obligations which the labor contract imposes on the worker as a unilateral gain for the worker. If the height of wage rates does not depend on the quantity and quality of the performance, if the employer does not pay to the worker the price the market assigns to his achievement, if the employer does not buy a definite quantity and quality of workmanship, but buys a bondsman, if wage rates are so low that for natural or "historical" reasons they cannot drop any further, one improves the wage earner's lot by forcibly shortening the length of the working day. Then it is permissible to look at the laws limiting the hours of work as tantamount to the decrees by means of which European governments of the seventeenth, eighteenth, and early nineteenth centuries step by step reduced and finally entirely abolished the amount of the unpaid statute labor (corvée) which the peasant bondsmen were liable to give to their lords, or to ordinances lightening the work to be done by convicts. Then the shortening of daily hours of work which the evolution of capitalist industrialism brought about is appraised as a victory of the exploited wage-slaves over the rugged selfishness of their tormentors. All laws imposing upon the employer the duty to make definite expenditures to the benefit of the employees are described as "social gains," i.e., as liberalities for the attainment of which the employees do not have to make any sacrifice.

It is generally assumed that the correctness of this doctrine is sufficiently demonstrated by the fact that the individual wage earner has only a negligible influence on the determination of the terms of the labor contract. The decisions concerning the length of the working day, work on Sundays and holidays, the time set for meals and many other things are made by the employers without asking the employees. The wage earner has no other choice than to yield to these orders or to starve.

The cardinal fallacy involved in this reasoning has already been pointed out in the preceding sections. The employers are not asking for labor in general, but for men who are fitted to perform the kind of labor they need. Just as an entrepreneur must choose for his plants the most suitable location, equipment, and raw materials, so he must hire the most efficient workers. He must arrange conditions of work in such a way as to make them appear attractive to those classes of workers he wants to employ. It is true that the individual worker has but little to say with regard to these arrangements. They are, like the height of wage rates itself, like commodity prices, and the shape of articles produced for mass consumption, the product of the interaction of innumerable people participating in the social process of the market. They are as such mass phenomena which are but little subject to modification on the part of a single individual. However, it is a distortion of truth to assert that the individual voter's ballot is without influence because many thousands or even millions of votes are required to decide the issue and that those of people not attached to any party virtually do not matter. Even if one were to admit this thesis for the sake of argument, it is a non sequitur to infer that the substitution of totalitarian principles for democratic procedures would make the officeholders more genuine representatives of the people's will than election campaigns. The counterparts of these totalitarian fables in the field of the market's economic democracy are the assertions that the individual consumer is powerless against the suppliers and the individual employee against the employers. It is, of course, not an individual's taste, different from that of the many, that determines the features of articles of mass production designed for mass consumption, but the wishes and likes of the majority. It is not the individual job-seeker, but the masses of job-seekers whose conduct determines the terms of the labor contracts prevailing in definite areas or branches of industry. If it is customary to have lunch between noon and one o'clock, an individual worker who prefers to have it between two and three p.m. has little chance of having his wishes satisfied. However, the social pressure to which this solitary individual is subject in this case is not exercised by the employer, but by his fellow employees.

Employers in their search for suitable workers are forced to accommodate themselves even to serious and costly inconveniences if they cannot find those needed on other terms. In many countries, some of them stigmatized as socially backward by the champions of anticapitalism, employers must yield to various wishes of workers motivated by considerations of religious ritual or caste and status. They must arrange hours of work, holidays, and many technical problems according to such opinions, however burdensome such an adjustment may be. Whenever an employer asks for special performances which appear irksome or repulsive to the employees, he must pay extra for the excess of disutility the worker must expend.

The terms of the labor contract refer to all working conditions, not merely to the height of wage rates. Teamwork in factories and the interdependence of various enterprises make it impossible to deviate from the arrangements customary in the country or in the branch concerned and thus result in a unification and standardization of these arrangements. But this fact neither weakens nor eliminates the employees' contribution in their setting up. For the individual workers they are, of course, an unalterable datum as the railroad's timetable is for the individual traveler. But nobody would contend that in determining the timetable the company does not bother about the wishes of the potential customers. Its intention is precisely to serve as many of them as possible.

The interpretation of the evolution of modern industrialism has been utterly vitiated by the anticapitalistic bias of governments and professedly prolabor writers and historians. The rise in real wage rates, the shortening of hours of work, the elimination of child labor, and the restriction of the labor of women, it is asserted, were the result of the interference of governments and labor unions and the pressure of public opinion aroused by humanitarian authors. But for this interference and pressure the entrepreneurs and capitalists would have retained for themselves all the advantages derived from the increase in capital investment and the consequent improvement in technological methods. The rise in the wage earners' standard of living was thus brought about at the expense of the "unearned" income of capitalists, entrepreneurs, and landowners. It is highly desirable to continue these policies, benefiting the many at the sole expense of a few selfish exploiters, and to reduce more and more the unfair take of the propertied classes.

The incorrectness of this interpretation is obvious. All measures restricting the supply of labor directly or indirectly burden the capitalists as far as they increase the marginal productivity of labor and reduce the marginal productivity of the material factors of production. As they restrict the supply of labor without reducing the supply of capital, they increase the portion allotted to the wage earners out of the total net product of the production effort. But this total net produce will drop too, and it depends on the specific data of each case whether the relatively greater quota of a smaller cake will be greater or smaller than the relatively smaller quota of a bigger cake. Profits and the rate of interest are not directly affected by the shortening of the total supply of labor. The prices of material factors of production drop and wage rates per unit of the individual worker's performance (not necessarily also per capita of the workers employed) rise. The prices of the products rise too. Whether all these changes result in an improvement or in a deterioration of the average wage earner's income is, as has been said, a question of fact in each instance.

But our assumption that such measures do not affect the supply of material factors of production is impermissible. The shortening of the hours of work, the restriction of night work and of the employment of certain classes of people impair the utilization of a part of the equipment available and are tantamount to a drop in the supply of capital. The resulting intensification of the scarcity of capital goods may entirely undo the potential rise in the marginal productivity of labor as against the marginal productivity of capital goods.

If concomitantly with the compulsory shortening of the hours of work the authorities or the unions forbid any corresponding reduction in wage rates which the state of the market would require or if previously prevailing institutions prevent such a reduction, the effects appear that every attempt to keep wage rates at a height above the potential market rate brings about: institutional unemployment.

The history of capitalism as it has operated in the last two hundred years in the realm of Western civilization is the record of a steady rise in the wage earners' standard of living. The inherent mark of capitalism is that it is mass production for mass consumption directed by the most energetic and far-sighted individuals, unflaggingly aiming at improvement. Its driving force is the profit-motive the instrumentality of which forces the businessman constantly to provide the consumers with more, better, and cheaper amenities. An excess of profits over losses can appear only in a progressing economy and only to the extent to which the masses' standard of living improves.[13] Thus capitalism is the system under which the keenest and most agile minds are driven to promote to the best of their abilities the welfare of the laggard many.

In the field of historical experience it is impossible to resort to measurement. As money is no yardstick of value and want-satisfaction, it cannot be applied for comparing the standard of living of people in various periods of time. However, all historians whose judgment is not muddled by romantic prepossessions agree that the evolution of capitalism has multiplied capital equipment on a scale which far exceeded the synchronous increase in population figures. Capital equipment both per capita of the total population and per capita of those able to work is immensely larger today than fifty, a hundred, or two hundred years ago. Concomitantly there has been a tremendous increase in the quota which the wage earners receive out of the total amount of commodities produced, an amount which in itself is much bigger than in the past. The ensuing rise in the masses' standard of living is miraculous when compared with the conditions of ages gone by. In those merry old days even the wealthiest people led an existence which must be called straitened when compared with the average standard of the American or Australian worker of our age. Capitalism, says Marx, unthinkingly repeating the fables of the eulogists of the Middle Ages, has an inevitable tendency to impoverish the workers more and more. The truth is that capitalism has poured a horn of plenty upon the masses of wage earners who frequently did all they could to sabotage the adoption of those innovations which render their life more agreeable. How uneasy an American worker would be if he were forced to live in the style of a medieval lord and to miss the plumbing facilities and the other gadgets he simply takes for granted!

The improvement in his material well-being has changed the worker's valuation of leisure. Better supplied with the amenities of life as he is, he sooner reaches the point at which he looks upon any further increment in the disutility of labor as an evil which is no longer outweighed by the expected further increment in labor's mediate gratification. He is eager to shorten the hours of daily work and to spare his wife and children the toil and trouble of gainful employment. It is not labor legislation and labor-union pressure that have shortened hours of work and withdrawn married women and children from the factories; it is capitalism, which has made the wage earner so prosperous that he is able to buy more leisure time for himself and

13. See above, pp. 294–300.

his dependents. The nineteenth century's labor legislation by and large achieved nothing more than to provide a legal ratification for changes which the interplay of market factors had brought about previously. As far as it sometimes went ahead of industrial evolution, the quick advance in wealth soon made things right again. As far as the allegedly prolabor laws decreed measures which were not merely the ratification of changes already effected or the anticipation of changes to be expected in the immediate future, they hurt the material interests of the workers.

The term "social gains" is utterly misleading. If the law forces workers who would prefer to work forty-eight hours a week not to give more than forty hours of work, or if it forces employers to incur certain expenses for the benefit of employees, it does not favor workers at the expense of employers. Whatever the provisions of a social security law may be, their incidence ultimately burdens the employee, not the employer. They affect the amount of take-home wages; if they raise the price the employer has to pay for a unit of performance above the potential market rate, they create institutional unemployment. Social security does not enjoin upon the employers the obligation to expend more in buying labor. It imposes upon the wage earners a restriction concerning the spending of their total income. It curtails the worker's freedom to arrange his household according to his own decisions.

Whether such a system of social security is a good or a bad policy is essentially a political problem. One may try to justify it by declaring that the wage earners lack the insight and the moral strength to provide spontaneously for their own future. But then it is not easy to silence the voices of those who ask whether it is not paradoxical to entrust the nation's welfare to the decisions of voters whom the law itself considers incapable of managing their own affairs; whether it is not absurd to make those people supreme in the conduct of government who are manifestly in need of a guardian to prevent them from spending their own income foolishly. Is it reasonable to assign to wards the right to elect their guardians? It is no accident that Germany, the country that inaugurated the social security system, was the cradle of both varieties of modern disparagement of democracy, the Marxian as well as the non-Marxian.

Remarks About the Popular Interpretation of the "Industrial Revolution"

It is generally asserted that the history of modern industrialism and especially the history of the British "Industrial Revolution" provide an empirical verification of the "realistic" or "institutional" doctrine and utterly explode the "abstract" dogmatism of the economists.[14]

The economists flatly deny that labor unions and government pro-labor legislation can and did lastingly benefit the whole class of wage earners and raise their standard of living. But the facts, say the anti-economists, have refuted these fallacies. The statesmen and legislators who enacted the factory acts displayed a better insight into reality than the economists. While laissez-faire philosophy, without pity and compassion, taught that the sufferings of the toiling masses are unavoidable, the common sense of laymen succeeded in quelling the worst excesses of profit-seeking business. The improvement in the conditions of the workers is entirely an achievement of governments and labor unions.

Such are the ideas permeating most of the historical studies dealing with the evolution of modern industrialism. The authors begin by sketching an idyllic image of conditions as they prevailed on the eve of the "Industrial Revolution." At that time, they tell us, things were, by and large, satisfactory. The peasants were happy. So also were the industrial workers under the domestic system. They worked in their own cottages and enjoyed a certain economic independence since they owned a garden plot and their tools. But then "the Industrial Revolution fell like a war or a plague" on these people.[15] The factory system reduced the free worker to virtual slavery; it lowered his standard of living to the level of bare subsistence; in cramming women and children into the mills it destroyed family life and sapped the very foundations of society, morality, and public health. A small minority of ruthless exploiters had cleverly succeeded in imposing their yoke upon the immense majority.

The truth is that economic conditions were highly unsatisfactory on the eve of the Industrial Revolution. The traditional social system was not elastic enough to provide for the needs of a rapidly increasing population. Neither farming nor the guilds had any use for the additional hands. Business was imbued with the inherited spirit of privilege and exclusive monopoly; its institutional foundations were licenses and the grant of a patent of monopoly; its philosophy was restriction and the prohibition of competition both domestic and foreign. The

14. The attribution of the phrase "the Industrial Revolution" to the reigns of the two last Hanoverian Georges was the outcome of deliberate attempts to melodramatize economic history in order to fit it into the Procrustean Marxian schemes. The transition from medieval methods of production to those of the free enterprise system was a long process that started centuries before 1760 and, even in England, was not finished in 1830. Yet, it is true that England's industrial development was considerably accelerated in the second half of the eighteenth century. It is therefore permissible to use the term "Industrial Revolution" in the examination of the emotional connotations with which Fabianism, Marxism, the Historical School, and Institutionalism have loaded it.

15. J. L. Hammond and Barbara Hammond, *The Skilled Labourer 1760–1832* (2d ed. London, 1920), p. 4.

number of people for whom there was no room left in the rigid system of paternalism and government tutelage of business grew rapidly. They were virtually outcasts. The apathetic majority of these wretched people lived from the crumbs that fell from the tables of the established castes. In the harvest season they earned a trifle by occasional help on farms; for the rest they depended upon private charity and communal poor relief. Thousands of the most vigorous youths of these strata were pressed into the service of the Royal Army and Navy; many of them were killed or maimed in action; many more perished ingloriously from the hardships of the barbarous discipline, from tropical diseases, or from syphilis.[16] Other thousands, the boldest and most ruthless of their class, infested the country as vagabonds, beggars, tramps, robbers, and prostitutes. The authorities did not know of any means to cope with these individuals other than the poorhouse and the workhouse. The support the government gave to the popular resentment against the introduction of new inventions and labor-saving devices made things quite hopeless.

The factory system developed in a continuous struggle against innumerable obstacles. It had to fight popular prejudice, old established customs, legally binding rules and regulations, the animosity of the authorities, the vested interests of privileged groups, the envy of the guilds. The capital equipment of the individual firms was insufficient, the provision of credit extremely difficult and costly. Technological and commercial experience was lacking. Most factory owners failed; comparatively few succeeded. Profits were sometimes considerable, but so were losses. It took many decades until the common practice of reinvesting the greater part of profits earned accumulated adequate capital for the conduct of affairs on a broader scale.

That the factories could thrive in spite of all these hindrances was due to two reasons. First there were the teachings of the new social philosophy expounded by the economists. They demolished the prestige of Mercantilism, paternalism, and restrictionism. They exploded the superstitious belief that labor-saving devices and processes cause unemployment and reduce all people to poverty and decay. The laissez-faire economists were the pioneers of the unprecedented technological achievements of the last two hundred years.

Then there was another factor that weakened the opposition to innovations. The factories freed the authorities and the ruling landed aristocracy from an embarrassing problem that had grown too large for them. They provided sustenance for the masses of paupers. They emptied the poor houses, the workhouses, and the prisons. They converted starving beggars into self-supporting breadwinners.

The factory owners did not have the power to compel anybody to

16. In the Seven Years' War 1,512 British seamen were killed in battle while 133,708 died of disease or were missing. Cf. W. L. Dorn, *Competition for Empire 1740–1763* (New York, 1940), p. 114.

take a factory job. They could only hire people who were ready to work for the wages offered to them. Low as these wage rates were, they were nonetheless much more than these paupers could earn in any other field open to them. It is a distortion of facts to say that the factories carried off the housewives from the nurseries and the kitchens and the children from their play. These women had nothing to cook with and to feed their children. These children were destitute and starving. Their only refuge was the factory. It saved them, in the strict sense of the term, from death by starvation.

It is deplorable that such conditions existed. But if one wants to blame those responsible, one must not blame the factory owners who —driven by selfishness, of course, and not by "altruism"—did all they could to eradicate the evils. What had caused these evils was the economic order of the precapitalistic era, the order of the "good old days."

In the first decades of the Industrial Revolution the standard of living of the factory workers was shockingly bad when compared with the contemporary conditions of the upper classes and with the present conditions of the industrial masses. Hours of work were long, the sanitary conditions in the workshops deplorable. The individual's capacity to work was used up rapidly. But the fact remains that for the surplus population which the enclosure movement had reduced to dire wretchedness and for which there was literally no room left in the frame of the prevailing system of production, work in the factories was salvation. These people thronged into the plants for no reason other than the urge to improve their standard of living.

The laissez-faire ideology and its offshoot, the "Industrial Revolution," blasted the ideological and institutional barriers to progress and welfare. They demolished the social order in which a constantly increasing number of people were doomed to abject need and destitution. The processing trades of earlier ages had almost exclusively catered to the wants of the well-to-do. Their expansion was limited by the amount of luxuries the wealthier strata of the population could afford. Those not engaged in the production of primary commodities could earn a living only as far as the upper classes were disposed to utilize their skill and services. But now a different principle came into operation. The factory system inaugurated a new mode of marketing as well as of production. Its characteristic feature was that the manufactures were not designed for the consumption of a few well-to-do only, but for the consumption of those who had hitherto played but a negligible role as consumers. Cheap things for the many, was the objective of the factory system. The classical factory of the early days of the Industrial Revolution was the cotton mill. Now, the cotton goods it turned out were not something the rich were asking for. These wealthy people clung to silk, linen, and cambric. Whenever the factory with its methods of mass production by means of power-driven machines invaded a new branch of production, it started with the production of cheap goods for the broad masses. The factories turned to the production of more refined and therefore more expensive goods only at a later stage, when the unprecedented improvement in the masses' standard of living which they caused made it profitable to apply the methods of mass production also to these better articles. Thus, for instance, the factory-made shoe was for many years bought only by the "proletarians" while the wealthier consumers continued to patronize the custom shoemakers. The much talked about sweatshops did not produce clothes for the rich, but for people in modest circumstances. The fashionable ladies and gentlemen preferred and still do prefer custom-made frocks and suits.

The outstanding fact about the Industrial Revolution is that it opened an age of mass production for the needs of the masses. The wage earners are no longer people toiling merely for other people's well-being. They themselves are the main consumers of the products the factories turn out. Big business depends upon mass consumption. There is, in present-day America, not a single branch of big business that would not cater to the needs of the masses. The very principle of capitalist entrepreneurship is to provide for the common man. In his capacity as consumer the common man is the sovereign whose buying or abstention from buying decides the fate of entrepreneurial activities. There is in the market economy no other means of acquiring and preserving wealth than by supplying the masses in the best and cheapest way with all the goods they ask for.

Blinded by their prejudices, many historians and writers have entirely failed to recognize this fundamental fact. As they see it, wage earners toil for the benefit of other people. They never raise the question who these "other" people are.

Mr. and Mrs. Hammond tell us that the workers were happier in 1760 than they were in 1830.[17] This is an arbitrary value judgment. There is no means of comparing and measuring the happiness of different people and of the same people at different times. We may agree for the sake of argument that an individual who was born in 1740 was happier in 1760 than in 1830. But let us not forget that in 1770 (according to the estimate of Arthur Young) England had 8.5 million inhabitants, while in 1831 (according to the census) the figure was 16 million.[18] This conspicuous increase was mainly conditioned by the Industrial Revolution. With regard to these additional Englishmen the assertion of the eminent historians can only be approved by those who endorse the melancholy verses of Sophocles: "Not to be born is, beyond all question, the best; but when a man has once seen the light of day, this is next best, that speedily he should return to that place whence he came."

17. J. L. Hammond and Barbara Hammond, *loc. cit.*

18. F. C. Dietz, *An Economic History of England* (New York, 1942), pp. 279 and 392.

The early industrialists were for the most part men who had their origin in the same social strata from which their workers came. They lived very modestly, spent only a fraction of their earnings for their households and put the rest back into the business. But as the entrepreneurs grew richer, the sons of successful businessmen began to intrude into the circles of the ruling class. The highborn gentlemen envied the wealth of the parvenus and resented their sympathies with the reform movement. They hit back by investigating the material and moral conditions of the factory hands and enacting factory legislation.

The history of capitalism in Great Britain as well as in all other capitalist countries is a record of an unceasing tendency toward the improvement in the wage earners' standard of living. This evolution coincided with the development of prolabor legislation and the spread of labor unionism on the one hand and with the increase in the marginal productivity of labor on the other hand. The economists assert that the improvement in the workers' material conditions is due to the increase in the per capita quota of capital invested and the technological achievements which the employment of this additional capital brought about. As far as labor legislation and union pressure did not exceed the limits of what the workers would have got without them as a necessary consequence of the acceleration of capital accumulation as compared with population, they were superfluous. As far as they exceeded these limits, they were harmful to the interests of the masses. They delayed the accumulation of capital thus slowing down the tendency toward a rise in the marginal productivity of labor and in wage rates. They conferred privileges on some groups of wage earners at the expense of other groups. They created mass unemployment and decreased the amount of products available for the workers in their capacity as consumers.

The apologists of government interference with business and of labor unionism ascribe all the improvements in the conditions of the workers to the actions of governments and unions. Except for them, they contend, the workers' standard of living would be no higher today than it was in the early years of the factory system.

It is obvious that this controversy cannot be settled by appeal to historical experience. With regard to the establishment of the facts there is no disagreement between the two groups. Their antagonism concerns the interpretation of events, and this interpretation must be guided by the theory chosen. The epistemological and logical considerations which determine the correctness or incorrectness of a theory are logically and temporally antecedent to the elucidation of the historical problem involved. The historical facts as such neither prove nor disprove any theory. They need to be interpreted in the light of theoretical insight.

Most of the authors who wrote the history of the conditions of labor under capitalism were ignorant of economics and boasted of this ignorance. However, this contempt for sound economic reasoning did not mean that they approached the topic of their studies without prepossession and without bias in favor of any theory. They were guided by the popular fallacies concerning governmental omnipotence and the alleged blessings of labor unionism. It is beyond question that the Webbs as well as Lujo Brentano and a host of minor authors were at the very start of their studies imbued with a fanatical dislike of the market economy and an enthusiastic endorsement of the doctrines of socialism and interventionism. They were certainly honest and sincere in their convictions and tried to do their best. Their candor and probity may exonerate them as individuals; it does not exonerate them as historians. However pure the intentions of a historian may be, there is no excuse for his recourse to fallacious doctrines. The first duty of a historian is to examine with the utmost care all the doctrines to which he resorts in dealing with the subject matter of his work. If he neglects to do this and naïvely espouses the garbled and confused ideas of popular opinion, he is not a historian but an apologist and propagandist.

The antagonism between the two opposite points of view is not merely a historical problem. It refers no less to the most burning problems of the present day. It is the matter of controversy in what is called in present-day America the problem of industrial relations.

Let us stress one aspect of the matter only. Vast areas—Eastern Asia, the East Indies, Southern and Southeastern Europe, Latin America—are only superficially affected by modern capitalism. Conditions in these countries by and large do not differ from those of England on the eve of the "Industrial Revolution." There are millions of people for whom there is no secure place left in the traditional economic setting. The fate of these wretched masses can be improved only by industrialization. What they need most is entrepreneurs and capitalists. As their own foolish policies have deprived these nations of the further enjoyment of the assistance imported foreign capital hitherto gave them, they must embark upon domestic capital accumulation. They must go through all the stages through which the evolution of Western industrialism had to pass. They must start with comparatively low wage rates and long hours of work. But, deluded by the doctrines prevailing in present-day Western Europe and North America, their statesmen think that they can proceed in a different way. They encourage labor-union pressure and alleged prolabor legislation. Their interventionist radicalism nips in the bud all attempts to create domestic industries. Their stubborn dogmatism spells the doom of the Indian and Chinese coolies, the Mexican peons, and millions of other peoples, desperately struggling on the verge of starvation.

8. Wage Rates as Affected by the Vicissitudes of the Market

Labor is a factor of production. The price which the seller of labor can obtain on the market depends on the data of the market.

The quantity and the quality of labor which an individual is fitted to deliver is determined by his innate and acquired characteristics. The innate abilities cannot be altered by any purposeful conduct. They are the individual's heritage with which his ancestors have endowed him on the day of his birth. He can bestow care upon these gifts and cultivate his talents, he can keep them from prematurely withering away; but he can never cross the boundaries which nature has drawn to his forces and abilities. He can display more or less skill in his endeavors to sell his capacity to work at the highest price which is obtainable on the market under prevailing conditions; but he cannot change his nature in order to adjust it better to the state of the market data. It is good luck for him if market conditions are such that a kind of labor which he is able to perform is lavishly remunerated; it is chance, not personal merit if his innate talents are highly appreciated by his fellow men. Miss Greta Garbo, if she had lived a hundred years earlier, would probably have earned much less than she did in this age of moving pictures. As far as her innate talents are concerned, she is in a position similar to that of a farmer whose farm can be sold at a high price because the expansion of a neighboring city converted it into urban soil.

Within the rigid limits drawn by his innate abilities, a man's capacity to work can be perfected by training for the accomplishment of definite tasks. The individual—or his parents—incurs expenses for a training the fruit of which consists in the acquisition of the ability to perform certain kinds of work. Such schooling and training intensify a man's one-sidedness; they make him a specialist. Every special training enhances the specific character of a man's capacity to work. The toil and trouble, the disutility of the efforts to which an individual must submit in order to acquire these special abilities, the loss of potential earnings during the training period, and the money expenditure required are laid out in the expectation that the later increment in earnings will compensate for them. These expenses are an investment and as such speculative. It depends on the future state of the market whether or not they will pay. In training himself the worker becomes a speculator and entrepreneur. The future state of the market will determine whether profit or loss results from his investment.

Thus the wage earner has vested interests in a twofold sense, as a man with definite innate qualities and as a man who has acquired definite special skills.

The wage earner sells his labor on the market at the price which the market allows for it today. In the imaginary construction of the evenly rotating economy the sum of the prices which the entrepreneur must expend for all the complementary factors of production together must equal—due consideration being made for time preference—the price of the product. In the changing economy changes in the market structure may bring about differences between these two magnitudes. The ensuing profits and losses do not affect the wage earner. Their incidence falls upon the employer alone. The uncertainty of the future affects the employee only as far as the following items are concerned:

1. The expenses incurred in time, disutility, and money for training.
2. The expenses incurred in moving to a definite place of work.
3. In case of a labor contract stipulated for a definite period of time, changes in the price of the specific type of labor occurring in the meantime and changes in the employer's solvency.

9. The Labor Market

Wages are the prices paid for the factor of production, human labor. As is the case with all the other prices of complementary factors of production their height is ultimately determined by the prices of the products as they are expected at the instant the labor is sold and bought. It does not matter whether he who performs the labor sells his services to an employer who combines them with the material factors of production and with the services of other people or whether he himself embarks upon his own account and peril upon these acts of combination. The final price of labor of the same quality is at any rate the same in the whole market system. Wage rates are always equal to the price of the full produce of labor. The popular slogan "the worker's right to the full produce of labor" was an absurd formulation of the claim that the consumers' goods should be distributed exclusively among the workers and nothing should be left to the entrepreneurs and the owners of the material factors of production. From no point of view whatever can artifacts be considered as the products of mere labor. They are the yield of a purposive combination of labor and of material factors of production.

In the changing economy there prevails a tendency for market wage rates to adjust themselves precisely to the state of the final wage rates. This adjustment is a time-absorbing process. The length of the period of adjustment depends on the time required for the training for new jobs and for the removal of workers to new places of residence. It depends furthermore on subjective factors, as for instance the workers' familiarity with the conditions and prospects of the labor market. The adjustment is a speculative venture as far as the training for new jobs and the change of residence involve costs which are expended only if one believes that the future state of the labor market will make them appear profitable.

With regard to all these things there is nothing that is peculiar to labor, wages, and the labor market. What gives a particular feature to the labor market is that the worker is not merely the purveyor of the factor of production labor, but also a human being and that it is impossible to sever the man from his performance. Reference to this fact has been mostly used for extravagant utterances and for a vain critique of the economic teachings concerning wage rates. However, these absurdities must not prevent economics from paying adequate attention to this primordial fact.

For the worker it is a matter of consequence what kind of labor he performs among the various kinds he is able to perform, where he performs it, and under what particular conditions and circumstances. An unaffected observer may consider empty or even ridiculous prejudices the ideas and feelings that actuate a worker to prefer certain jobs, certain places of work, and certain conditions of labor to others. However, such academic judgments of unaffected censors are of no avail. For an economic treatment of the problems involved there is nothing especially remarkable in the fact that the worker looks upon his toil and trouble not only from the point of view of the disutility of labor and its mediate gratification, but also takes into account whether the special conditions and circumstances of its performance interfere with his enjoyment of life and to what extent. The fact that a worker is ready to forego the chance to increase his money earnings by migrating to a place he considers less desirable and prefers to remain in his native place or country is not more remarkable than the fact that a wealthy gentleman of no occupation prefers the more expensive life in the capital to the cheaper life in a small town. The worker and the consumer are the same person; it is merely economic reasoning that integrates the social functions and splits up this unity into two schemes. Men cannot sever their decisions concerning the utilization of their working power from those concerning the enjoyment of their earnings.

Descent, language, education, religion, mentality, family bonds, and social environment tie the worker in such a way that he does not choose the place and the branch of his work merely with regard to the height of wage rates.

We may call that height of wage rates for definite types of labor which would prevail on the market if the workers did not discriminate between various places and, wage rates being equal, did not prefer one working place to another, standard wage rates (*S*). If, however, the wage earners, out of the above-mentioned considerations, value differently work in different places, the height of market wage rates (*M*) can permanently deviate from the standard rates. We may call the maximum difference between the market rate and the standard rate which does not yet result in the migration of workers from the places of lower market wage rates to those of higher market wage rates the attachment component (*A*). The attachment component of a definite geographical place or area is either positive or negative.

We must furthermore take into account that the various places and areas differ with regard to provision with consumers' goods as far as transportation costs (in the broadest sense of the term) are concerned. These costs are lower in some areas, higher in other areas. Then there are differences with regard to the physical input required for the attainment of the same amount of physical satisfaction. In some places a man must expend more in order to attain the same degree of want-satisfaction which, apart from the circumstances determining the amount of the attachment component, he could attain elsewhere more cheaply. On the other hand, a man can in some places avoid certain expenses without any impairment of his want-satisfaction while renunciation of these expenses would curtail his satisfaction in other places. We may call the expenses which a worker must incur in certain places in order to attain in this sense the same degree of want-satisfaction, or which he can spare without curtailing his want-satisfaction, the cost component (*C*). The cost component of a definite geographical place or area is either positive or negative.

If we assume that there are no institutional barriers preventing or penalizing the transfer of capital goods, workers, and commodities from one place or area to another and that the workers are indifferent with regard to their dwelling and working places, there prevails a tendency toward a distribution of population over the earth's surface in accordance with the physical productivity of the primary natural factors of production and the immobilization of inconvertible factors of production as effected in the past. There is, if we disregard the cost component, a tendency toward an equalization of wage rates for the same type of work all over the earth.

It would be permissible to call an area comparatively overpopulated if in it market wage rates plus the (positive or negative) cost component are lower than the standard rates, and comparatively underpopulated if in it market wage rates plus the (positive or negative) cost component are higher than the standard rates. But it is not expedient to resort to such a definition of the terms involved. It does not help us in explaining the real conditions of the formation of wage rates and the conduct of wage earners. It is more expedient to choose another definition. We may call an area comparatively overpopulated if in it market wage rates are lower than the standard rates plus both the (positive or negative) attachment component and the (positive or negative) cost component, that is where $M < (S + A + C)$. Accordingly an area is to be called comparatively underpopulated in which $M > (S + A + C)$. In the absence of institutional migration barriers workers move from the comparatively overpopulated areas to the comparatively underpopulated until everywhere $M = S + A + C$.

The same is true, mutatis mutandis, for the migration of individuals working on their own account and selling their labor in disposing of its products or in rendering personal services.

The concepts of the attachment component and the cost component apply in the same way to shifting from one branch of business or occupation to another.

It is hardly necessary to observe that the migrations which these theorems describe come to pass only in so far as there are no institutional barriers to the mobility of capital, labor, and commodities. In this age aiming at the disintegration of the international division of labor and at each sovereign nation's economic self-sufficiency, the tendencies they describe are fully operative only within each nation's boundaries.

The Work of Animals and of Slaves

For man, animals are a material factor of production. It may be that one day a change in moral sentiments will induce people to treat animals more gently. Yet, as far as men do not leave the animals alone and let them go their way, they will always deal with them as mere objects of their own acting. Social cooperation can exist only between human beings because only these are able to attain insight into the meaning and the advantages of the division of labor and of peaceful cooperation.

Man subdues the animal and integrates it into his scheme of action as a material thing. In taming, domesticating, and training animals man often displays appreciation for the creature's psychological peculiarities; he appeals, as it were, to its soul. But even then the gulf that separates man from animal remains unbridgeable. An animal can never get anything else than satisfaction of its appetites for food and sex and adequate protection against injury resulting from environmental factors. Animals are bestial and inhuman precisely because they are such as the iron law of wages imagined workers to be. As human civilization would never have emerged if men were exclusively dedicated to feeding and mating, so animals can neither consort in social bonds nor participate in human society.

People have tried to look upon fellow men as they look upon animals and to deal with them accordingly. They have used whips to compel galley slaves and barge haulers to work like capstan-horses. However, experience has shown that these methods of unbridled brutalization render very unsatisfactory results. Even the crudest and dullest people achieve more when working of their own accord than under the fear of the whip.

Primitive man makes no distinction between his property in women, children, and slaves on the one hand and his property in cattle and inanimate things on the other. But as soon as he begins to expect from his slaves services other than such as can also be rendered by draft and pack animals, he is forced to loosen their chains. He must try to substitute the incentive of self-interest for the incentive of mere fear; he must try to bind the slave to himself by human feelings. If the slave is no longer prevented from fleeing exclusively by being chained and watched and no longer forced to work exclusively under the threat of being whipped, the relation between master and slave is transformed into a social nexus. The slave may, especially if the memory of happier days of freedom is still fresh, bemoan his misfortune and hanker after liberation. But he puts up with what seems to be an inevitable state of affairs and accommodates himself to his fate in such a way as to make it as bearable as possible. The slave becomes intent upon satisfying his master through application and carrying out the tasks entrusted to him; the master becomes intent upon rousing the slave's zeal and loyalty through reasonable treatment. There develop between lord and drudge familiar relations which can properly be called friendship.

Perhaps the eulogists of slavery were not entirely wrong when they asserted that many slaves were satisfied with their station and did not aim at changing it. There are perhaps individuals, groups of individuals, and even whole peoples and races who enjoy the safety and security provided by bondage; who, insensible of humiliation and mortification, are glad to pay with a moderate amount of labor for the privilege of sharing in the amenities of a well-to-do household; and in whose eyes subjection to the whims and bad tempers of a master is only a minor evil or no evil at all.

Of course, the conditions under which the servile workers toiled in big farms and plantations, in mines, in workshops, and galleys were very different from the idyllically described gay life of domestic valets, chambermaids, cooks, and nurses and from the conditions of unfree laborers, dairymaids, herdsmen, and shepherds of small farming. No apologist of slavery was bold enough to glorify the lot of the Roman agricultural slaves, chained and crammed together in the *ergastulum,* or of the Negroes of the American cotton and sugar plantations.[19]

The abolition of slavery and serfdom is to be attributed neither to the teachings of theologians and moralists nor to weakness or generosity on the part of the masters. There were among the teachers of religion and ethics as many eloquent defenders of bondage as opponents.[20] Servile labor disappeared because it could not stand the competition of free labor; its unprofitability sealed its doom in the market economy.

The price paid for the purchase of a slave is determined by the net yield expected from his employment (both as a worker and as a progenitor of other slaves) just as the price paid for a cow is determined by the net yield expected from its utilization. The owner of a slave does not pocket a specific revenue. For him there is no "exploitation" boon derived from the fact that the slave's work is not remunerated and that the potential market price of the services he renders is possibly greater than the cost of feeding, sheltering, and guarding him. He who buys a slave must in the price paid make good for these economies as far as they may be expected; he pays for them in full, due allowance being made for time preference. Whether the proprietor employs the slave in his own household or enterprise or rents his services to other people, he does not enjoy any specific advantage from the existence of the institution of slavery. The specific boon goes totally to the slave-hunter, i.e., the man who deprives free men of their liberty and transforms them into slaves. But, of course, the profitability of the slave-hunter's business depends upon the height of the prices buyers are ready to pay for the acquisition of slaves. If these prices drop below the operation and transportation costs incurred in the business of slave-hunting, business no longer pays and must be discontinued.

Now, at no time and at no place was it possible for enterprises employing servile labor to compete on the market with enterprises employing free labor. Servile labor could always be utilized only where it did not have to meet the competition of free labor.

If one treats men like cattle, one cannot squeeze out of them more than cattle-like performances. But it then becomes significant that man is physically weaker than oxen and horses, and that feeding and guarding a slave is, in proportion to the performance to be reaped, more expensive than feeding and guarding cattle. When treated as a chattel, man

19. Margaret Mitchell, who in her popular novel *Gone With the Wind* (New York, 1936) eulogizes the South's slavery system, is cautious enough not to enter into particulars concerning the plantation hands, and prefers to dwell upon the conditions of domestic servants, who even in her account appear as an élite of their caste.

20. Cf. about the American proslavery doctrine Charles and Mary Beard. *The Rise of American Civilization* (1944), I, 703–710; and C. E. Merriam, *A History of American Political Theories* (New York, 1924), pp. 227–251.

renders a smaller yield per unit of cost expended for current sustenance and guarding than domestic animals. If one asks from an unfree laborer human performances, one must provide him with specifically human inducements. If the employer aims at obtaining products which in quality and quantity excel those whose production can be extorted by the whip, he must interest the toiler in the yield of his contribution. Instead of punishing laziness and sloth, he must reward diligence, skill, and eagerness. But whatever he may try in this respect, he will never obtain from a bonded worker, i.e., a worker who does not reap the full market price of his contribution, a performance equal to that rendered by a freeman, i.e., a man hired on the unhampered labor market. The upper limit beyond which it is impossible to lift the quality and quantity of the products and services rendered by slave and serf labor is far below the standards of free labor. In the production of articles of superior quality an enterprise employing the apparently cheap labor of unfree workers can never stand the competition of enterprises employing free labor. It is this fact that has made all systems of compulsory labor disappear.

Social institutions once made whole areas or branches of production reservations exclusively kept for the occupation of unfree labor and sheltered against any competition on the part of entrepreneurs employing free men. Slavery and serfdom thus became essential features of a rigid caste system that could be neither removed nor modified by the actions of individuals. Wherever conditions were different, the slave owners themselves resorted to measures which were bound to abolish, step by step, the whole system of unfree labor. It was not humanitarian feelings and clemency that induced the callous and pitiless slaveholders of ancient Rome to loosen the fetters of their slaves, but the urge to derive the best possible gain from their property. They abandoned the system of centralized big-scale management of their vast landholdings, the latifundia, and transformed the slaves into virtual tenants cultivating their tenements on their own account and owing to the landlord merely either a lease or a share of the yield. In the processing trades and in commerce the slaves became entrepreneurs and their funds, the *peculium,* their legal quasi-property. Slaves were manumitted in large numbers because the freedman rendered to the former owner, the *patronus,* services more valuable than those to be expected from a slave. For the manumission was not an act of grace and a gratuitous gift on the part of the owner. It was a credit operation, a purchase of freedom on the installment plan, as it were. The freedman was bound to render the former owner for many years or even for a lifetime definite payments and services. The patronus moreover had special rights of inheritance to the estate of the deceased freedman.[21]

21. Cf. Ciccotti, *Le Déclin de l'esclavage antique* (Paris, 1910), pp. 292 ff.; Salvioli, *Le Capitalisme dans le monde antique* (Paris, 1906), pp. 141 ff.; Cairnes, *The Slave Power* (London, 1862), p. 234.

With the disappearance of the plants and farms employing unfree laborers, bondage ceased to be a system of production and became a political privilege of an aristocratic caste. The overlords were entitled to definite tributes in kind or money and to definite services on the part of their subordinates; moreover their serfs' children were obliged to serve them as servants or military retinue for a definite length of time. But the underprivileged peasants and artisans operated their farms and shops on their own account and peril. Only when their processes of production were accomplished did the lord step in and claim a part of the proceeds.

Later, from the sixteenth century on, people again began to employ unfree workers in agricultural and even sometimes in industrial big-scale production. In the American colonies Negro slavery became the standard method of the plantations. In Eastern Europe—in Northeastern Germany, in Bohemia and its annexes Moravia and Silesia, in Poland, in the Baltic countries, in Russia, and also in Hungary and its annexes—big-scale farming was built upon the unpaid statute labor of serfs. Both these systems of unfree labor were sheltered by political institutions against the competition of enterprises employing free workers. In the plantation colonies the high costs of immigration and the lack of sufficient legal and judicial protection of the individual against the arbitrariness of government officers and the planter aristocracy prevented the emergence of a sufficient supply of free labor and the development of a class of independent farmers. In Eastern Europe the caste system made it impossible for outsiders to enter the field of agricultural production. Big-scale farming was reserved to members of the nobility. Small holdings were reserved to unfree bondsmen. Yet the fact that the enterprises employing unfree labor would not be able to stand the competition of enterprises employing free labor was not contested by anybody. On this point the eighteenth- and early nineteenth-century authors on agricultural management were no less unanimous than the writers of ancient Rome on farm problems. But the abolition of slavery and serfdom could not be effected by the free play of the market system, as political institutions had withdrawn the estates of the nobility and the plantations from the supremacy of the market. Slavery and serfdom were abolished by political action dictated by the spirit of the much-abused laissez faire, laissez passer ideology.

Today mankind is again faced with endeavors to substitute compulsory labor for the labor of the freeman selling his capacity to work as a "commodity" on the market. Of course, people believe that there is an essential difference between the tasks incumbent upon the comrades of the socialist commonwealth and those incumbent upon slaves or serfs. The slaves and serfs, they say, toiled for the benefit of an exploiting lord. But in a socialist system the produce of labor goes to society of which the toiler himself is a part; here the worker works for himself, as it were. What this reasoning overlooks is that the identification of the individual comrades and the totality of all comrades with the collective entity pocketing the produce of all work is merely fictitious. Whether the ends which the community's officeholders are aiming at agree or disagree with the wishes and desires of the various comrades, is of minor importance. The main thing is that the individual's contribution to the collective entity's wealth is not requited in the shape of wages determined by the market. A socialist commonwealth lacks any method of economic calculation; it cannot determine separately what quotas of the total amount of goods produced are to be assigned to the various complementary factors of production. As it cannot ascertain the magnitude of the contribution society owes to the various individuals' efforts, it cannot remunerate the workers according to the value of their performance.

In order to distinguish free labor from compulsory labor no metaphysical subtleties concerning the essence of freedom and compulsion are required. We may call free labor that kind of extroversive, not immediately gratifying labor that a man performs either for the direct satisfaction of his own wants or for their indirect satisfaction to be reaped by expending the price earned by its sale on the market. Compulsory labor is labor performed under the pressure of other incentives. If somebody were to take umbrage at this terminology because the employment of words like freedom and compulsion may arouse an association of ideas injurious to a dispassionate treatment of the problems involved, one could as well choose other terms. We may substitute the expression *F* labor for the term free labor and the term *C* labor for the term compulsory labor. The crucial problem cannot be affected by the choice of the terms. What alone matters is this: What kind of inducement can spur a man to submit to the disutility of labor if his own want-satisfaction neither directly nor—to any appreciable extent—indirectly depends on the quantity and quality of *his* performance?

Let us assume for the sake of argument that many workers, perhaps even most of them, will of their own accord dutifully take pains for the best possible fulfillment of the tasks assigned to them by their superiors. (We may disregard the fact that the determination of the task to be imposed upon the various individuals would confront a socialist commonwealth with insoluble problems.) But how to deal with those sluggish and careless in the discharge of the imposed duties? There is no other way left than to punish them. In their superiors must be vested the authority to establish the offense, to give judgment on its subjective reasons, and to mete out punishment accordingly. A hegemonic bond is substituted for the contractual bond. The worker becomes subject to the discretionary power of his superiors, he is personally subordinate to his chief's disciplinary power.

In the market economy the worker sells his services as other people sell their commodities. The employer is not the employee's lord. He is simply the buyer of services which he must purchase at their market price. Of course, like every other buyer an employer too can take liberties. But if he resorts to arbitrariness in hiring or discharging workers, he must foot the bill. An employer or an employee entrusted with the management of a department of an enterprise is free to discriminate in hiring workers, to fire them arbitrarily, or to cut down their wages below the market rate. But in indulging in such arbitrary acts he jeopardizes the profitability of his enterprise or his department and thereby impairs his own income and his position in the economic system. In the market economy such whims bring their own punishment. The only real and effective protection of the wage earner in the market economy is provided by the play of the factors determining the formation of prices. The market makes the worker independent of arbitrary discretion on the part of the employer and his aides. The workers are subject only to the supremacy of the consumers as their employers are too. In determining, by buying or abstention from buying, the prices of products and the employment of factors of production, consumers assign to each kind of labor its market price.

What makes the worker a free man is precisely the fact that the employer, under the pressure of the market's price structure, considers labor a commodity, an instrument of earning profits. The employee is in the eyes of the employer merely a man who for a consideration in money helps him to make money. The employer pays for services rendered and the employee performs in order to earn wages. There is in this relation between employer and employee no question of favor or disfavor. The hired man does not owe the employer gratitude; he owes him a definite quantity of work of a definite kind and quality.

That is why in the market economy the employer can do without the power to punish the employee. All nonmarket systems of production must give to those in control the power to spur on the slow worker to more zeal and application. As imprisonment withdraws the worker from his job or at least reduces considerably the value of his contribution, corporal punishment has always been the classical means of keeping slaves and serfs to their work. With the abolition of unfree labor one could dispense with the whip as a stimulus. Flogging was the symbol of bond labor. Members of a market society consider corporal punishment inhuman and humiliating to such a degree that it has been abolished also in the schools, in the penal code, and in military discipline.

He who believes that a socialist commonwealth could do without compulsion and coercion against slothful workers because everyone will spontaneously do his duty, falls prey to the illusions implied in the doctrine of anarchism.

XXII. THE NONHUMAN ORIGINAL FACTORS OF PRODUCTION

1. General Observations Concerning the Theory of Rent

IN the frame of Ricardian economics the idea of rent was an attempt at a treatment of those problems which modern economics approaches by means of marginal-utility analysis.[1] Ricardo's theory appears rather unsatisfactory when judged from the point of view of present-day insight; there is no doubt that the method of the subjective-value theory is far superior. Yet the renown of the rent theory is well deserved; the care bestowed upon its initiation and perfection brought forth fine fruits. There is no reason for the history of economic thought to feel ashamed of the rent theory.[2]

The fact that land of different quality and fertility, i.e., yielding different returns per unit of input, is valued differently does not pose any special problem to modern economics. As far as Ricardo's theory refers to the gradation in the valuation and appraisement of pieces of land, it is completely comprehended in the modern theory of the prices of factors of production. It is not the content of the rent theory that is objectionable, but the exceptional position assigned to it in the complex of the economic system. Differential rent is a general phenomenon and is not limited to the determination of the prices of land. The sophisticated distinction between "rents" and "quasi-rents" is spurious. Land and the services it renders are dealt with in the same way as other factors of production and their services. Control of a better tool yields "rent" when compared with the returns of less suitable tools which must be utilized on account of the insufficient supply of more suitable ones. The abler and more zealous worker earns a "rent" when compared with the wages earned by his less skillful and less industrious competitors.

The problems which the rent concept was designed to solve were for the most part generated by the employment of inappropriate

1. It was, says Fetter (*Encyclopaedia of the Social Sciences*, XIII, 291), "a garbled marginality theory."

2. Cf. Amonn, *Ricardo als Begründer der theoretischen Nationalökonomie* (Jena, 1924), pp. 54 ff.

terms. The general notions as used in everyday language and mundane thought were not formed with regard to the requirements of praxeological and economic investigation. The early economists were mistaken in adopting them without scruple and hesitation. Only if one clings naïvely to general terms such as *land* or *labor,* is one puzzled by the question why *land* and *labor* are differently valued and appraised. He who does not allow himself to be fooled by mere words, but looks at a factor's relevance for the satisfaction of human wants, considers it a matter of course that different services are valued and appraised differently.

The modern theory of value and prices is not based on the classification of the factors of production as land, capital, and labor. Its fundamental distinction is between goods of higher and of lower orders, between producers' goods and consumers' goods. When it distinguishes within the class of factors of production the original (nature-given) factors from the produced factors of production (the intermediary products) and furthermore within the class of original factors the nonhuman (external) factors from the human factors (labor), it does not break up the uniformity of its reasoning concerning the determination of the prices of the factors of production. The law controlling the determination of the prices of the factors of production is the same with all classes and specimens of these factors. The fact that different services rendered by such factors are valued, appraised, and dealt with in a different way can only amaze people who fail to notice these differences in serviceableness. He who is blind to the merits of a painting may consider it strange that collectors should pay more for a painting of Velasquez than for a painting of a less gifted artist; for the connoisseur it is self-evident. It does not astonish the farmer that buyers pay higher prices and tenants higher leases for more fertile land than for less fertile. The only reason why the old economists were puzzled by this fact was that they operated with a general term *land* that neglects differences in productivity.

The greatest merit of the Ricardian theory of rent is the cognizance of the fact that the marginal land does not yield any rent. From this knowledge there is but one step to the discovery of the principle of valuational subjectivism. Yet blinded by the *real cost* notion neither the classical economists nor their epigones took this step.

While the differential-rent idea, by and large, can be adopted by the subjective-value theory, the second rent concept derived from Ricardian economics, viz., the residual-rent concept, must be rejected altogether. This residual-claimant idea is based on the notion of *real* or *physical* costs that do not make any sense in the frame of the modern explanation of the prices of factors of production. The reason why the price of Burgundy is higher than that of Chianti is not the higher price of the vineyards of Burgundy as against those of Tuscany. The causation is the other way around. Because people are ready to pay higher prices for Burgundy than for Chianti, winegrowers are ready to pay higher prices for the vineyards of Burgundy than for those of Tuscany.

In the eyes of the accountant profits appear as a share left over when all costs of production have been paid. In the evenly rotating economy such a surplus of the prices of products over and above costs could never appear. In the changing economy differences between the prices of the products and the sum of the prices that the entrepreneur has expended for the purchase of the complementary factors of production plus interest on the capital invested can appear in either direction, i.e., either as profit or as loss. These differences are caused by changes which arise in the prices of the products in the time interval. He who succeeds better than others in anticipating these changes in time and acts accordingly, reaps profits. He who fails in his endeavors to adjust his entrepreneurial ventures to the future state of the market is penalized by losses.

The main deficiency of Ricardian economics was that it was a theory of the distribution of a total product of a nation's joint efforts. Like the other champions of classical economics Ricardo failed to free himself from the Mercantilist image of the Volkswirtschaft. In his thought the problem of the determination of prices was subordinated to the problem of the distribution of wealth. The customary characterization of his economic philosophy as "that of the manufacturing middle classes of contemporary England"[3] misses the point. These English businessmen of the early nineteenth century were not interested in the total product of industry and its distribution. They were guided by the urge to make profits and to avoid losses.

Classical economics erred when it assigned to land a distinct place in its theoretical scheme. Land is, in the economic sense, a factor of production, and the laws determining the formation of the prices of land are the same that determine the formation of the prices of other factors of production. All peculiarities of the economic teachings concerning land refer to some peculiarities of the data involved.

2. The Time Factor in Land Utilization

The starting point of the economic teachings concerning land is the distinction between two classes of original factors of production, viz., human and nonhuman factors. As the utilization of the non-

3. Cf., for example, Haney, *History of Economic Thought* (rev. ed. New York, 1927), p. 275.

human factors is as rule connected with the power to utilize a piece of the earth, we speak of land when referring to them.[4]

In dealing with the economic problems of land, i.e., the nonhuman original factors of production, one must neatly separate the praxeological point of view from the cosmological point of view. It may make good sense for cosmology in its study of cosmic events to speak of permanency and of the conservation of mass and energy. If one compares the orbit within which human action is able to affect the natural environmental conditions of human life with the operation of natural entities, it is permissible to call the natural powers indestructible and permanent or—more precisely—safe against destruction by human action. For the great periods of time to which cosmology refers, soil erosion (in the broadest sense of the term) of such an intensity as can be effected by human interference is of no importance. Nobody knows today whether or not cosmic changes will in millions of years transform deserts and barren soil into land that from the point of view of our present-day knowledge will have to be described as extremely fertile and the most luxuriant tropical gardens into sterile land. Precisely because nobody can anticipate such changes nor venture to influence the cosmic events which possibly could bring them about, it is supererogatory to speculate about them in dealing with the problems of human action.[5]

The natural sciences may assert that those powers of the soil that condition its serviceableness for forestry, cattle breeding, agriculture, and water utilization regenerate themselves periodically. It may be true that even human endeavors deliberately directed toward the utmost devastation of the productive capacity of the earth's crust could at best succeed only with regard to small parts of it. But these facts do not strictly count for human action. The periodical regeneration of the soil's productive powers is not a rigid datum that would face man with a uniquely determined situation. It is possible to use the soil in such a way that this regeneration is slowed down and postponed or the soil's productive power either vanishes altogether for a definite period of time or can be restored only by means of a considerable input of capital and labor. In dealing with the soil man has to choose between various methods different from one another with regard to the preservation and regeneration of its productive power. No less than in any other branch of production, the time factor enters also

4. Legal provisions concerning the separation of the right of hunting, fishing, and extracting mineral deposits from the other rights of the owner of a piece of land are of no interest for catallactics. The term land as used in catallactics includes also expanses of water.

5. Thus also the problem of entropy stands outside the sphere of praxeological meditation.

into the conduct of hunting, fishing, grazing, cattle breeding, plant growing, lumbering and water utilization. Here too man must choose between satisfaction in nearer and in more remote periods of the future. Here too the phenomenon of originary interest, entailed in every human action, plays its paramount role.

There are institutional conditions that cause the persons involved to prefer satisfaction in the nearer future and to disregard entirely or almost entirely satisfaction in the more distant future. If the soil is on the one hand not owned by individual proprietors and on the other hand all, or certain people favored by special privilege or by the actual state of affairs, are free to make use of it temporarily for their own benefit, no heed is paid to the future. The same is the case when the proprietor expects that he will be expropriated in a not too distant future. In both cases the actors are exclusively intent upon squeezing out as much as possible for their immediate advantage. They do not concern themselves about the temporally more remote consequences of their methods of exploitation. Tomorrow does not count for them. The history of lumbering, hunting, and fishing provides plenty of illustrative experience; but many examples can also be found in other branches of soil utilization.

From the point of view of the natural sciences, the maintenance of capital goods and the preservation of the powers of the soil belong to two entirely different categories. The produced factors of production perish sooner or later entirely in the pursuit of production processes, and piecemeal are transformed into consumers' goods which are eventually consumed. If one does not want to make the results of past saving and capital accumulation disappear, one must, apart from consumers' goods, also produce the amount of capital goods which is needed for the replacement of those worn out. If one were to neglect this, one would finally consume, as it were, the capital goods. One would sacrifice the future to the present; one would live in luxury today and be in want later.

But, it is often said, it is different with the powers of land. They cannot be *consumed*. Such a statement is meaningful, however, only from the point of view of geology. But from the geological point of view one could, or should, no less deny that factory equipment or a railroad can be "eaten up." The gravel and stones of a railroad's substructure and the iron and steel of the rails, bridges, cars, and engines do not perish in a cosmic sense. Only from the praxeological point of view is it permissible to speak of the consumption, the eating up, of a tool, a railroad, or a steel mill. In the same economic sense we speak of the consumption of the productive powers of the soil. In forestry, agriculture, and water utilization these powers are dealt with in the same way as other factors of production. With regard to the powers of the soil, too, the actors must choose between processes of production which render higher output at the expense of productivity in later periods and processes which do not impair future physical productivity. It is possible to extract so much from the soil that its later utilization will render smaller returns (per unit of the quantities of capital and labor employed) or practically no returns at all.

It is true that there are physical limits to the devastating powers of man. (These limits are sooner reached in lumbering, hunting, and fishing than in tilling the soil.) But this fact results only in a quantitative, not in a qualitative difference between capital decumulation and soil erosion.

Ricardo calls the powers of the soil "original and indestructible."[6] However, modern economics must stress the point that valuation and appraisement do not differentiate between original and produced factors of production and that the cosmological indestructibility of mass and energy, whatever it may mean, does not enjoin upon land utilization a character radically different from other branches of production.

3. The Submarginal Land

The services a definite piece of land can render in a definite period of time are limited. If they were unlimited, men would not consider land a factor of production and an economic good. However, the quantity of soil available is so vast, nature is so prodigal, that land is still abundant. Therefore, only the most productive pieces of land are utilized. There is land which people consider—either with regard to its physical productivity or with regard to its location—as too poor to be worth cultivating. Consequently the marginal soil, i.e., the poorest soil cultivated, yields no rent in the Ricardian sense.[7] Submarginal land would be considered entirely worthless if one were not to appraise it positively in anticipation of its being utilized in later days.[8]

The fact that the market economy does not have a more ample supply of agricultural products is caused by the scarcity of capital

6. Ricardo, *Principles of Political Economy and Taxation*, p. 34.

7. There are areas in which practically every corner is cultivated or otherwise utilized. But this is the outcome of institutional conditions barring the inhabitants of these regions from access to more fertile unused soil.

8. The appraisal of a piece of soil must not be confused with the appraisal of the improvements, i.e., the irremovable and inconvertible results of the investment of capital and labor that facilitate its utilization and raise future outputs per unit of current future inputs.

and labor, not by a scarcity of cultivable land. An increase in the surface of land available would—other things being equal—increase the supply of cereals and meat only if the additional land's fertility exceeded that of the marginal land already previously cultivated. On the other hand, the supply of agricultural products would be increased by any increase in the amount of labor and capital available, provided the consumers do not consider another employment of the additional amount of capital and labor more appropriate to fill their most urgent wants.[9]

The useful mineral substances contained in the soil are limited in quantity. It is true that some of them are the outgrowth of natural processes which are still going on and increasing the existing deposits. However, the slowness and length of these processes makes them insignificant for human action. Man must take into account that the available deposits of these minerals are limited. Every single mine or oil source is exhaustible; many of them are already exhausted. We may hope that new deposits will be discovered and that technological procedures will be invented which will make it possible to utilize deposits which today cannot be exploited at all or only at unreasonable costs. We may also assume that the further progress of technological knowledge will enable later generations to utilize substances which cannot be utilized today. But all these things do not matter for the present-day conduct of mining and oil drilling. The deposits of mineral substances and their exploitation are not characterized by features which would give a particular mark to human action dealing with them. For catallactics the distinction between soil used in agriculture and that used in mining is merely a distinction of data.

Although the available quantities of these mineral substances are limited, and although we may academically concern ourselves with the possibility that they will be entirely exhausted one day, acting men do not consider these deposits rigidly limited. Their activities take into account the fact that definite mines and wells will become exhausted, but they do not pay heed to the fact that at an unknown later date all the deposits of certain minerals may come to an end. For to present-day action the supply of these substances appears to be so abundant that one does not venture to exploit all their deposits to the full extent which the state of technological knowledge permits. The mines are utilized only as far as there is no more urgent employment available for the required quantities of capital and labor. There are therefore submarginal deposits that are not utilized at all.

9. These observations, of course, refer only to conditions in which there are no institutional barriers to the mobility of capital and labor.

In every mine operated the extent of the production is determined by the relation between the prices of the products and those of the required nonspecific factors of production.

4. The Land as Standing Room

The employment of land for the location of human residences, workshops, and means of transportation withdraws pieces of soil from other employments.

The particular place which older theories attributed to urban site rent need not here concern us. It is not especially noteworthy that people pay higher prices for land they value more for housing than for land which they value less. It is a matter of fact that for workshops, warehouses, and railroad yards people prefer locations which reduce costs of transportation, and that they are ready to pay higher prices for such land in accordance with the economies expected.

Land is also used for pleasure grounds and gardens, for parks and for the enjoyment of the grandeur and beauty of nature. With the development of the love of nature, this very characteristic feature of "bourgeois" mentality, the demand for such enjoyments increased enormously. The soil of the high mountain chains, once merely considered a barren dreariness of rocks and glaciers, is today highly appreciated as the source of the most lofty pleasures.

From time immemorial access to these spaces has been free to everybody. Even if the land is owned by private individuals, the owners as a rule have not the right to close it to tourists and mountain-climbers or to ask an entrance fee. Whoever has the opportunity to visit these areas, has the right to enjoy all their grandeur, and to consider them his own, as it were. The nominal owner does not derive any advantage from the satisfaction his property gives to the visitors. But this does not alter the fact that this land serves human well-being and is appreciated accordingly. The ground is subject to an easement that entitles everybody to pass along and to camp on it. As no other utilization of the area concerned is possible, this servitude completely exhausts all the advantages the proprietor could reap from his ownership. Since the particular services which these rocks and glaciers can render are practically inexhaustible, do not wear out, and do not require any input of capital and labor for their conservation, this arrangement does not bring about those consequences which appeared wherever it was applied to lumbering, hunting, and fishing grounds.

If, in the neighborhood of these mountain chains, the space available for the construction of shelters, hotels, and means of transportation (e.g., rack railroads) is limited, the owners of these scarce pieces of soil can sell or rent them on more propitious terms and thus divert to themselves a part of the advantages the tourists reap from the free accessibility of the peaks. If this is not the case, the tourists enjoy all these advantages gratuitously.

5. The Prices of Land

In the imaginary construction of the evenly rotating economy buying and selling of the services of definite pieces of land does not differ at all from buying and selling the services of other factors of production. All these factors are appraised according to the services they will render in various periods of the future, due allowance being made for time preference. For the marginal land (and, of course, for the submarginal land) no price is paid at all. Rent-bearing land (i.e., land that, compared with the marginal land, bears a higher output per unit of input of capital and labor) is appraised in accordance with the degree of its superiority. Its price is the sum of all its future rents, each of them discounted at the rate of originary interest.[10]

In the changing economy people buying and selling land take due account of expected changes in the market prices for the services rendered by the soil. Of course, they may err in their expectations; but this is another thing. They try to anticipate to the best of their abilities future events that may alter the market data and they act in accordance with these opinions. If they believe that the annual net yield of the piece of land concerned will rise, the price will be higher than it would have been in the absence of such expectations. This is, for instance, the case with suburban land in the neighborhood of cities growing in population or with forests and arable land in countries in which pressure groups are likely to succeed in raising, by means of tariffs, the prices of timber and cereals. On the other hand, fears concerning the total or partial confiscation of the net yield of land tend to lower the prices of land. In everyday business language people speak of the "capitalization" of the rent and observe that the rate of capitalization is different with different classes of land and varies even within the same class with different pieces of soil. This terminology

10. There is need to remember again that the imaginary construction of the evenly rotating economy cannot be carried consistently to its ultimate logical consequences (see above, p. 248). With regard to the problems of land one must stress two points: First, that in the frame of this imaginary construction, characterized by the absence of changes in the conduct of affairs, there is no room for the buying and selling of land. Second, that in order to integrate into this construction mining and oil drilling we must ascribe to the mines and oil wells a permanent character and must disregard the possibility that any of the operated mines and wells could be exhausted or even undergo a change in the quantity of output or of current input required.

is rather inexpedient as it misrepresents the nature of the process.

In the same way in which buyers and sellers of land take into account anticipated future events that will reduce the net return, they deal with taxes. Taxes levied upon land reduce its market price to the extent of the discounted amount of their future burden. The introduction of a new tax of this kind which is likely not to be abolished results in an immediate drop in the market price of the pieces of land concerned. This is the phenomenon that the theory of taxation calls *amortization* of taxes.

In many countries the owners of land or of certain estates enjoyed special political legal privileges or a great social prestige. Such institutions too can play a role in the determination of the prices of land.

The Myth of the Soil

Romanticists condemn the economic theories concerning land for their utilitarian narrow-mindedness. Economists, they say, look upon land from the point of view of the callous speculator who degrades all eternal values to terms of money and profit. Yet, the glebe is much more than a mere factor of production. It is the inexhaustible source of human energy and human life. Agriculture is not simply one branch of production among many other branches. It is the only natural and respectable activity of man, the only dignified condition of a really human existence. It is iniquitous to judge it merely with regard to the net returns to be squeezed out of the soil. The soil not only bears the fruits that nourish our body; it produces first of all the moral and spiritual forces of civilization. The cities, the processing industries, and commerce are phenomena of depravity and decay; their existence is parasitic; they destroy what the ploughman must create again and again.

Thousands of years ago, when fishing and hunting tribesmen began to cultivate the soil, romantic reverie was unknown. But if there had lived romanticists in those ages, they would have eulogized the lofty moral values of the hunt and would have stigmatized soil cultivation as a phenomenon of depravity. They would have reproached the ploughman for desecrating the soil that the gods had given to man as a hunting ground and for degrading it to a means of production.

In the preromantic ages in his actions no one considered the soil as anything other than a source of human well-being, a means to promote welfare. The magic rites and observances concerning the soil aimed at nothing else than improvement of the soil's fertility and increase in the quantity of fruits to be harvested. These people did not seek the unio mystica with the mysterious powers and forces hidden in the soil. All they aimed at was bigger and better crops. They resorted to magic rituals and adjurations because in their opinion this was the most efficient method of attaining the ends sought. Their sophisticated progeny erred when they interpreted these ceremonies from an "idealistic" point of view. A real peasant does not indulge in ecstatic babble about the soil and its mysterious powers. For him land is a factor of production, not an object of sentimental emotions. He covets more land because he desires to increase his income and to improve his standard of living. Farmers buy and sell land and mortgage it; they sell the produce of land and become very indignant if the prices are not as high as they want them to be.

Love of nature and appreciation of the beauties of the landscape were foreign to the rural population. The inhabitants of the cities brought them to the countryside. It was the city-dwellers who began to appreciate the land as *nature,* while the countrymen valued it only from the point of view of its productivity for hunting, lumbering, crop raising and cattle breeding. From time immemorial the rocks and glaciers of the Alps were merely waste land in the eyes of the mountaineers. Only when the townsfolk ventured to climb the peaks, and brought money into the valleys, did they change their minds. The pioneers of mountain-climbing and skiing were ridiculed by the indigenous population until they found out that they could derive gain from this eccentricity.

Not shepherds, but sophisticated aristocrats and city-dwellers were the authors of bucolic poetry. Daphnis and Chloë are creations of fancies far removed from earthy concerns. No less removed from the soil is the modern political myth of the soil. It did not blossom from the moss of the forests and the loam of the fields, but from the pavements of the cities and the carpets of the salons. The farmers make use of it because they find it a practical means of obtaining political privileges which raise the prices of their products and of their farms.

XXIII. THE DATA OF THE MARKET

1. The Theory and the Data

CATALLACTICS, the theory of the market economy, is not a system of theorems valid only under ideal and unrealizable conditions and applicable to reality merely with essential restrictions and modifications. All the theorems of catallactics are rigidly and without any exception valid for all phenomena of the market economy, provided the particular conditions which they presuppose are present. It is, for instance, a simple question of fact whether there is direct or indirect exchange. But where there is indirect exchange, all the general laws of the theory of indirect exchange are valid with regard to the acts of exchange and the media of exchange. As has been pointed out,[1] praxeological knowledge is precise or exact knowledge of reality. All references to the epistemological issues of the natural sciences and all analogies derived from comparing these two radically different realms of reality and cognition are misleading. There is, apart from formal logic, no such thing as a set of "methodological" rules applicable both to cognition by means of the category of causality and to that by means of the category of finality.

Praxeology deals with human action as such in a general and universal way. It deals neither with the particular conditions of the environment in which man acts nor with the concrete content of the valuations which direct his actions. For praxeology data are the bodily and psychological features of the acting men, their desires and value judgments, and the theories, doctrines, and ideologies they develop in order to adjust themselves purposively to the conditions of their environment and thus to attain the ends they are aiming at. These data, although permanent in their structure and strictly determined by the laws controlling the order of the universe, are perpetually fluctuating and varying; they change from instant to instant.[2]

The fullness of reality can be mentally mastered only by a mind resorting both to the conception of praxeology and to the under-

1. See above, p. 39.

2. Cf. Strigl, *Die ökonomischen Kategorien und die Organisation der Wirtschaft* (Jena, 1923), pp. 18 ff.

standing of history; and the latter requires command of the teachings of the natural sciences. Cognition and prediction are provided by the totality of knowledge. What the various single branches of science offer is always fragmentary; it must be complemented by the results of all the other branches. From the point of view of acting man the specialization of knowledge and its breaking up into the various sciences is merely a device of the division of labor. In the same way in which the consumer utilizes the products of various branches of production, the actor must base his decisions on knowledge brought about by various branches of thought and investigation.

It is not permissible to disregard any of these branches in dealing with reality. The Historical School and the Institutionalists want to outlaw the study of praxeology and economics and to occupy themselves merely with the registration of the data or, as they call them nowadays, the institutions. But no statement concerning these data can be made without reference to a definite set of economic theorems. When an institutionalist ascribes a definite event to a definite cause, e.g., mass unemployment to the alleged deficiencies of the capitalist mode of production, he resorts to an economic theorem. In objecting to the closer examination of the theorem tacitly implied in his conclusions, he merely wants to avoid the exposure of the fallacies of his argument. There is no such thing as a mere recording of unadulterated facts apart from any reference to theories. As soon as two events are recorded together or integrated into a class of events, a theory is operative. The question whether there is any connection between them can only be answered by a theory, i.e., in the case of human action by praxeology. It is vain to search for coefficients of correlation if one does not start from a theoretical insight acquired beforehand. The coefficient may have a high numerical value without indicating any significant and relevant connection between the two groups.[3]

2. The Role of Power

The Historical School and Institutionalism condemn economics for disregarding the role which power plays in real life. The basic notion of economics, viz., the choosing and acting individual, is, they say, an unrealistic concept. Real man is not free to choose and to act. He is subject to social pressure, to the sway of irresistible power. It is not the individuals' value judgments, but the interactions of the forces of power that determine the market phenomena.

3. Cf. Cohen and Nagel, *An Introduction to Logic and Scientific Method* (New York, 1939), pp. 316–322.

These objections are no less spurious than all other statements of the critics of economics.

Praxeology in general and economics and catallactics in particular do not contend or assume that man is free in any metaphysical sense attached to the term *freedom*. Man is unconditionally subject to the natural conditions of his environment. In acting he must adjust himself to the inexorable regularity of natural phenomena. It is precisely the scarcity of the nature-given conditions of his welfare that enjoins upon man the necessity to act.[4]

In acting man is directed by ideologies. He chooses ends and means under the influence of ideologies. The might of an ideology is either direct or indirect. It is direct when the actor is convinced that the content of the ideology is correct and that he serves his own interests directly in complying with it. It is indirect when the actor rejects the content of the ideology as false, but is under the necessity of adjusting his actions to the fact that this ideology is endorsed by other people. The mores of their social environment are a power which people are forced to consider. Those recognizing the spuriousness of the generally accepted opinions and habits must in each instance choose between the advantages to be derived from resorting to a more efficient mode of acting and the disadvantages resulting from the contempt of popular prejudices, superstitions, and folkways.

The same is true with regard to violence. In choosing man must take into account the fact that there is a factor ready to exercise violent compulsion upon him.

All the theorems of catallactics are valid also with regard to actions influenced by such social or physical pressure. The direct or indirect might of an ideology and the threat of physical compulsion are merely data of the market situation. It does not matter, for instance, what kind of considerations motivate a man not to offer a higher bid for the purchase of a commodity than the one he really makes without obtaining the good concerned. For the determination of the market price it is immaterial whether he spontaneously prefers to spend his money for other purposes or whether he is afraid of being looked upon by his fellow men as an upstart, or as a spendthrift, afraid of

4. Most social reformers, foremost among them Fourier and Marx, pass over in silence the fact that the nature-given means of removing human uneasiness are scarce. As they see it, the fact that there is not an abundance of all useful things is merely caused by the inadequacy of the capitalist mode of production and will therefore disappear in the "higher phase" of communism. An eminent Menshevik author who could not help referring to the nature-given barriers to human well-being, in genuinely Marxian style, calls Nature "the most relentless exploiter." Cf. Mania Gordon, *Workers Before and After Lenin* (New York, 1941), pp. 227, 458.

violating a government-decreed ceiling price or of defying a competitor ready to resort to violent revenge. In any case, his abstention from bidding a higher price contributes to the same extent to the emergence of the market price.[5]

It is customary nowadays to signify the position which the owners of property and the entrepreneurs occupy on the market as economic power or market power. This terminology is misleading when applied to the conditions of the market. All that happens in the unhampered market economy is controlled by the laws dealt with by catallactics. All market phenomena are ultimately determined by the choices of the consumers. If one wants to apply the notion of power to phenomena of the market, one ought to say: in the market all power is vested in the consumers. The entrepreneurs are forced, by the necessity of earning profits and avoiding losses, to consider in every regard—e.g. also in the conduct of the wrongly so-called "internal" affairs of their plants, especially personnel management—the best possible and cheapest satisfaction of the consumers as their supreme directive. It is very inexpedient to employ the same term "power" in dealing with a firm's ability to supply the consumers with automobiles, shoes, or margarine better than others do and in referring to the strength of a government's armed forces to crush any resistance.

Ownership of material factors of production as well as entrepreneurial or technological skill do not—in the market economy—bestow power in the coercive sense. All they grant is the privilege to serve the real masters of the market, the consumers, in a more exalted position than other people. Ownership of capital is a mandate entrusted to the owners, under the condition that it should be employed for the best possible satisfaction of the consumers. He who does not comply with this imposition forfeits his wealth and is relegated to a place in which his ineptitude no longer hurts people's well-being.

3. The Historical Role of War and Conquest

Many authors glorify war and revolution, bloodshed and conquest. Carlyle and Ruskin, Nietzsche, Georges Sorel, and Spengler were harbingers of the ideas which Lenin and Stalin, Hitler and Mussolini put into effect.

The course of history, say these philosophies, is not determined by the mean activities of materialistic peddlers and merchants, but by the heroic deeds of warriors and conquerors. The economists err in abstracting from the experience of the short-lived liberal

5. The economic consequences of the interference of external compulsion and coercion with the market phenomena are dealt with in the sixth part of this book.

episode a theory to which they ascribe universal validity. This epoch of liberalism, individualism, and capitalism; of democracy, tolerance, and freedom; of the disregard of all "true" and "eternal" values; and of the supremacy of the rabble is now vanishing and will never return. The dawning age of manliness requires a new theory of human action.

However, no economist ever ventured to deny that war and conquest were of utmost importance in the past and that Huns and Tartars, Vandals and Vikings, Normans and conquistadors played an enormous part in history. One of the determinants of the present state of mankind is the fact that there were thousands of years of armed conflicts. Yet, what remains and is the essence of human civilization, is not the legacy inherited from the warriors. Civilization is an achievement of the "bourgeois" spirit, not of the spirit of conquest. Those barbarian peoples who did not substitute working for plundering disappeared from the historical scene. If there is still any trace left of their existence, it is in the achievements they accomplished under the influence of the civilization of the subdued peoples. Latin civilization survived in Italy, France, and the Iberian peninsula in defiance of all barbarian invasions. If capitalist entrepreneurs had not succeeded Lord Clive and Warren Hastings, British rule in India might one day have become such an insignificant historical reminiscence as are the one hundred and fifty years of Turkish rule in Hungary.

It is not the task of economics to enter into an examination of the endeavors to revive the ideals of the Vikings. It has merely to refute the statements that the fact that there are armed conflicts reduces its teachings to nought. With regard to this problem there is need to emphasize again the following:

First: The teachings of catallactics do not refer to a definite epoch of history, but to all actions characterized by the two conditions *private ownership of the means of production* and *division of labor*. Whenever and wherever, in a society in which there is private ownership of the means of production, people not only produce for the direct satisfaction of their own wants but also consume goods produced by other people, the theorems of catallactics are strictly valid.

Second: If apart from the market and outside of the market there is robbing and plundering, these facts are a datum for the market. The actors must take into account the fact that they are threatened by murderers and robbers. If killing and robbing become so prevalent that any production appears useless, it may finally happen that productive work ceases and mankind plunges into a state of war of every man against every other man.

Third: In order to seize booty, something to be plundered must be available. The heroes can only live if there are enough "bourgeois" to be expropriated. The existence of producers is a condition for the survival of conquerors. But the producers could do without the plunderers.

Fourth: There are, of course, other imaginable systems of a society based on the division of labor besides the capitalist system of private ownership of the means of production. Champions of militarism are consistent in asking for the establishment of socialism. The whole nation should be organized as a community of warriors in which the noncombatants have no other task than that of supplying the fighting forces with all they need. (The problems of socialism are dealt with in the fifth part of this book.)

4. Real Man as a Datum

Economics deals with the real actions of real men. Its theorems refer neither to ideal nor to perfect men, neither to the phantom of a fabulous economic man (homo oeconomicus) nor to the statistical notion of an average man (homme moyen). Man with all his weaknesses and limitations, every man as he lives and acts, is the subject matter of catallactics. Every human action is a theme of praxeology.

The subject matter of praxeology is not only the study of society, societal relations, and mass phenomena, but the study of all human actions. The term "the social sciences" and all its connotations are in this regard misleading.

There is no yardstick that a scientific investigation can apply to human action other than that of the ultimate goals the acting individual wants to realize in embarking upon a definite action. The ultimate goals themselves are beyond and above any criticism. Nobody is called upon to establish what could make another man happy. What an unaffected observer can question is merely whether or not the means chosen for the attainment of these ultimate goals are fit to bring about the results sought by the actor. Only in answering this question is economics free to express an opinion about the actions of individuals and groups of individuals, or of the policies of parties, pressure groups, and governments.

It is customary to disguise the arbitrariness of the attacks launched against the value judgments of other people by converting them into a critique of the capitalist system or of the conduct of entrepreneurs. Economics is neutral with regard to all such statements.

To the arbitrary statement that "the balance between the production of different goods is admittedly faulty under capitalism,"[6] the economist does not oppose the statement that this balance is faultless.

6. Cf. Albert L. Meyers, *Modern Economics* (New York, 1946), p. 672.

What the economist asserts is that in the unhampered market economy this balance is in agreement with the conduct of the consumers as displayed in the spending of their incomes.[7] It is not the task of the economist to censure his fellow men and to call the result of their actions faulty.

The alternative to the system in which the individual's value judgments are paramount in the conduct of production processes is autocratic dictatorship. Then the value judgments of the dictators alone decide although they are no less arbitrary than those of other people.

Man is certainly not a perfect being. His human weakness taints all human institutions and thus also the market economy.

5. The Period of Adjustment

Every change in the market data has its definite effects upon the market. It takes a definite length of time before all these effects are consummated, i.e., before the market is completely adjusted to the new state of affairs.

Catallactics has to deal with all the various individuals' conscious and purposive reactions to the changes in the data and not, of course, merely with the final result brought about in the market structure by the interplay of these actions. It may happen that the effects of one change in the data are counteracted by the effects of another change occurring, by and large, at the same time and to the same extent. Then no considerable change in the market prices finally results. The statistician, exclusively preoccupied with the observation of mass phenomena and the outgrowth of the totality of market transactions as manifested in market prices, ignores the fact that the nonemergence of changes in the height of prices is merely accidental and not the outcome of a continuance in the data and the absence of specific adjustment activities. He fails to see any movement and the social consequences of such movements. Yet each change in the data has its own course, generates certain reactive responses on the part of the individuals affected and disturbs the relation between the various members of the market system even if eventually no considerable changes in the prices of the various goods and no changes at all in the figures concerning the total amount of capital in the whole market system result.[8]

Economic history can give vague information, after the fact, about

7. This is the general feature of democracy whether political or economic. Democratic elections do not provide the guarantee that the man elected is free from faults, but merely that the majority of the voters prefer him to other candidates.

8. With regard to changes in the elements determining the purchasing power of money see above, p. 416. With regard to the decumulation and accumulation of capital see above, pp. 516–517.

the length of adjustment periods. The method of attaining such information is, of course, not measurement, but historical understanding. The various adjustment processes are in reality not isolated. Synchronously an indefinite number of them take their course, their paths intersect, and they mutually influence one another. To disentangle this intricate tissue and to observe the chain of actions and reactions set into motion by a definite change in the data is a difficult task for the historian's understanding and the results are mostly meager and questionable.

The understanding of the length of adjustment periods is also the most difficult task incumbent upon those eager to understand the future, the entrepreneurs. Yet for success in entrepreneurial activities mere anticipation of the direction in which the market will react to a certain event is of little significance if it is not supplemented by an adequate anticipation of the length of the various adjustment periods involved. Most of the mistakes committed by entrepreneurs in the conduct of affairs and most of the blunders vitiating the prognoses of future business trends on the part of "expert" forecasters are caused by errors concerning the length of adjustment periods.

In dealing with effects brought about by changes in the data, it is customary to distinguish between the temporally nearer and the temporally remoter effects, viz., the short-run effects and the long-run effects. This distinction is much older than the terminology in which it is expressed nowadays.

In order to discover the immediate—the short-run—effects brought about by a change in a datum, there is as a rule no need to resort to a thorough investigation. The short-run effects are for the most part obvious and seldom escape the notice of a naïve observer unfamiliar with searching investigations. What started economic studies was precisely the fact that some men of genius began to suspect that the remoter consequences of an event may differ from the immediate effects visible even to the most simple-minded layman. The main achievement of economics was the disclosure of such long-run effects hitherto unnoticed by the unaffected observer and neglected by the statesman.

From their startling discoveries the classical economists derived a rule for political practice. Governments, statesmen, and political parties, they argued, in planning and acting should consider not only the short-run consequences but also the long-run consequences of their measures. The correctness of this inference is incontestable and indisputable. Action aims at the substitution of a more satisfactory state of affairs for a less satisfactory. Whether or not the outcome of a definite action will be considered more or less satisfactory depends on a correct anticipation of all its consequences, both short run and long run.

Some people criticize economics for alleged neglect of the short-run effects and for alleged preference given to the study of the long-run effects. The reproach is nonsensical. Economics has no means of scrutinizing the results of a change in the data other than to start with its immediate consequences and to analyze, step by step, proceeding from the first reaction to the remoter reactions, all the subsequent consequences, until it finally arrives at its ultimate consequences. The long-run analysis necessarily always fully includes the short-run analysis.

It is easy to understand why certain individuals, parties and pressure groups are eager to propagate the exclusive sway of the short-run principle. Politics, they say, should never be concerned about the long-run effects of a device and should never abstain from resorting to a measure from which benefits are expected in the short run merely because its long-run effects are detrimental. What counts is only the short-run effects; "in the long run we shall all be dead." All that economics has to answer to these passionate critics is that every decision should be based on a careful weighing of all its consequences, both those in the short run and those in the long run. There are certainly, both in the actions of individuals and in the conduct of public affairs, situations in which the actors may have good reasons to put up even with very undesirable long-run effects in order to avoid what they consider still more undesirable short-run conditions. It may sometimes be expedient for a man to heat the stove with his furniture. But if he does, he should know what the remoter effects will be. He should not delude himself by believing that he has discovered a wonderful new method of heating his premises.

That is all that economics opposes to the frenzy of the short-run apostles. History, one day, will have to say much more. It will have to establish the role that the recommendation of the short-run principle—this revival of Madame de Pompadour's notorious phrase *après nous le déluge*—played in the most serious crisis of Western civilization. It will have to show how welcome this slogan was to governments and parties whose policies aimed at the consumption of the spiritual and material capital inherited from earlier generations.

6. The Limits of Property Rights and the Problems of External Costs and External Economies

Property rights as they are circumscribed by laws and protected by courts and the police, are the outgrowth of an age-long evolution. The history of these ages is the record of struggles aiming at the abolition of private property. Again and again despots and popular movements have tried to restrict the rights of private property or to abolish it altogether. These endeavors, it is true, failed. But they have left traces in the ideas determining the legal form and definition of property. The legal concepts of property do not fully take account of the social function of private property. There are certain inadequacies and incongruities which are reflected in the determination of the market phenomena.

Carried through consistently, the right of property would entitle the proprietor to claim all the advantages which the good's employment may generate on the one hand and would burden him with all the disadvantages resulting from its employment on the other hand. Then the proprietor alone would be fully responsible for the outcome. In dealing with his property he would take into account all the expected results of his action, those considered favorable as well as those considered unfavorable. But if some of the consequences of his action are outside of the sphere of the benefits he is entitled to reap and of the drawbacks that are put to his debit, he will not bother in his planning about *all* the effects of his action. He will disregard those benefits which do not increase his own satisfaction and those costs which do not burden him. His conduct will deviate from the line which it would have followed if the laws were better adjusted to the economic objectives of private ownership. He will embark upon certain projects only because the laws release him from responsibility for some of the costs incurred. He will abstain from other projects merely because the laws prevent him from harvesting all the advantages derivable.

The laws concerning liability and indemnification for damages caused were and still are in some respects deficient. By and large the principle is accepted that everybody is liable to damages which his actions have inflicted upon other people. But there were loopholes left which the legislators were slow to fill. In some cases this tardiness was intentional because the imperfections agreed with the plans of the authorities. When in the past in many countries the owners of factories and railroads were not held liable for the damages which the conduct of their enterprises inflicted on the property and health of neighbors, patrons, employees, and other people through smoke, soot, noise, water pollution, and accidents caused by defective or inappropriate equipment, the idea was that one should not undermine the progress of industrialization and the development of transportation facilities. The same doctrines which prompted and still are prompting many governments to encourage investment in factories and railroads through subsidies, tax exemption, tariffs, and cheap credit were at work in the emergence of a legal state of affairs in which the liability of such enterprises was either formally or practically abated. Later again the opposite tendency began to prevail in many countries and the liability of manufacturers and railroads was increased as against that of other citizens and firms. Here again definite political objectives were operative. Legislators wished to protect the poor, the wage earners, and the peasants against the wealthy entrepreneurs and capitalists.

Whether the proprietor's relief from responsibility for some of the disadvantages resulting from his conduct of affairs is the outcome of a deliberate policy on the part of governments and legislators or whether it is an unintentional effect of the traditional wording of laws, it is at any rate a datum which the actors must take into account. They are faced with the problem of *external costs*. Then some people choose certain modes of want-satisfaction merely on account of the fact that a part of the costs incurred are debited not to them but to other people.

The extreme instance is provided by the case of no-man's property referred to above.[9] If land is not owned by anybody, although legal formalism may call it public property, it is utilized without any regard to the disadvantages resulting. Those who are in a position to appropriate to themselves the returns—lumber and game of the forests, fish of the water areas, and mineral deposits of the subsoil—do not bother about the later effects of their mode of exploitation. For them the erosion of the soil, the depletion of the exhaustible resources and other impairments of the future utilization are external costs not entering into their calculation of input and output. They cut down the trees without any regard for fresh shoots or reforestation. In hunting and fishing they do not shrink from methods preventing the repopulation of the hunting and fishing grounds. In the early days of human civilization, when soil of a quality not inferior to that of the utilized pieces was still abundant, people did not find any fault with such predatory methods. When their effects appeared in a decrease in the net returns, the ploughman abandoned his farm and moved to another place. It was only when a country was more densely settled and unoccupied first class land was no longer available for appropriation, that people began to consider such predatory methods wasteful. At that time they consolidated the institution of private property in land. They started with arable land and then, step by step, included pastures, forests, and fisheries. The newly settled

9. See above, p. 639.

colonial countries overseas, especially the vast spaces of the United States, whose marvelous agricultural potentialities were almost untouched when the first colonists from Europe arrived, passed through the same stages. Until the last decades of the nineteenth century there was always a geographic zone open to newcomers—the frontier. Neither the existence of the frontier nor its passing was peculiar to America. What characterizes American conditions is the fact that at the time the frontier disappeared ideological and institutional factors impeded the adjustment of the methods of land utilization to the change in the data.

In the central and western areas of continental Europe, where the institution of private property had been rigidly established for many centuries, things were different. There was no question of soil erosion of formerly cultivated land. There was no problem of forest devastation in spite of the fact that the domestic forests had been for ages the only source of lumber for construction and mining and of fuel for heating and for the foundries and furnaces, the potteries and the glass factories. The owners of the forests were impelled to conservation by their own selfish interests. In the most densely inhabited and industrialized areas up to a few years ago between a fifth and a third of the surface was still covered by first-class forests managed according to the methods of scientific forestry.[10]

It is not the task of catallactic theory to elaborate an account of the complex factors that produced modern American land-ownership conditions. Whatever these factors were, they brought about a state of affairs under which a great many farmers and lumber enterprises had reason to consider the disadvantages resulting from the neglect of soil and forest conservation as external costs.[11]

It is true that where a considerable part of the costs incurred are external costs from the point of view of the acting individuals or firms, the economic calculation established by them is manifestly

10. Late in the eighteenth century European governments began to enact laws aiming at forest conservation. However, it would be a serious blunder to ascribe to these laws any role in the conservation of the forests. Before the middle of the nineteenth century there was no administrative apparatus available for their enforcement. Besides the governments of Austria and Prussia, to say nothing of those of the smaller German states, virtually lacked the power to enforce such laws against the aristocratic lords. No civil servant before 1914 would have been bold enough to rouse the anger of a Bohemian or Silesian magnate or a German mediatized *Standesherr*. These princes and counts were spontaneously committed to forest conservation because they felt perfectly safe in the possession of their property and were eager to preserve unabated the source of their revenues and the market price of their estates.

11. One could as well say that they considered the advantages to be derived from giving care to soil and forest conservation external economies.

defective and their results deceptive. But this is not the outcome of alleged deficiencies inherent in the system of private ownership of the means of production. It is on the contrary a consequence of loopholes left in this system. It could be removed by a reform of the laws concerning liability for damages inflicted and by rescinding the institutional barriers preventing the full operation of private ownership.

The case of external economies is not simply the inversion of the case of external costs. It has its own domain and character.

If the results of an actor's action benefit not only himself, but also other people, two alternatives are possible:

1. The planning actor considers the advantages which he expects for himself so important that he is prepared to defray all the costs required. The fact that his project also benefits other people will not prevent him from accomplishing what promotes his own well-being. When a railroad company erects dikes to protect its tracks against snowslides and avalanches, it also protects the houses on adjacent grounds. But the benefits which its neighbors will derive will not hinder the company from embarking upon an expenditure that it deems expedient.

2. The costs incurred by a project are so great that none of those whom it will benefit is ready to expend them in full. The project can be realized only if a sufficient number of those interested in it share in the costs.

It would hardly be necessary to say more about external economies if it were not for the fact that this phenomenon is entirely misinterpreted in current pseudo-economic literature.

A project *P* is unprofitable when and because consumers prefer the satisfaction expected from the realization of some other projects to the satisfaction expected from the realization of *P*. The realization of *P* would withdraw capital and labor from the realization of some other projects for which the demand of the consumers is more urgent. The layman and the pseudo-economist fail to recognize this fact. They stubbornly refuse to notice the scarcity of the factors of production. As they see it, *P* could be realized without any cost at all, i.e., without foregoing any other satisfaction. It is merely the wantonness of the profit system that prevents the nation from enjoying gratuitously the pleasures expected from *P*.

Now, these short-sighted critics go on to say, the absurdity of the profit system becomes especially outrageous if the unprofitability of *P* is merely due to the fact that the entrepreneur's calculations neglect those advantages of *P* which for them are external economies. From the point of view of the whole of society such advantages are not external. They benefit at least some members of society and would increase "total welfare." The nonrealization of P is therefore a loss for society. As profit-seeking business, entirely committed to selfishness, declines to embark upon such unprofitable projects, it is the duty of government to fill the gap. Government should either run them as public enterprises or it should subsidize them in order to make them attractive for the private entrepreneur and investor. The subsidies may be granted either directly by money grants from public funds or indirectly by means of tariffs the incidence of which falls upon the buyers of the products.

However, the means which a government needs in order to run a plant at a loss or to subsidize an unprofitable project must be withdrawn either from the taxpayers' spending and investing power or from the loan market. The government has no more ability than individuals to create something out of nothing. What the government spends more, the public spends less. Public works are not accomplished by the miraculous power of a magic wand. They are paid for by funds taken away from the citizens. If the government had not interfered, the citizens would have employed them for the realization of profit-promising projects the realization of which they must omit because their means have been curtailed by the government. For every unprofitable project that is realized by the aid of the government there is a corresponding project the realization of which is neglected merely on account of the government's intervention. Yet this nonrealized project would have been profitable, i.e., it would have employed the scarce means of production in accordance with the most urgent needs of the consumers. From the point of view of the consumers the employment of these means of production for the realization of an unprofitable project is wasteful. It deprives them of satisfactions which they prefer to those which the government-sponsored project can furnish them.

The gullible masses who cannot see beyond the immediate range of their physical eyes are enraptured by the marvelous accomplishments of their rulers. They fail to see that they themselves foot the bill and must consequently renounce many satisfactions which they would have enjoyed if the government had spent less for unprofitable projects. They have not the imagination to think of the possibilities that the government has not allowed to come into existence.[12]

These enthusiasts are still more bewildered if the government's interference enables submarginal producers to continue producing

12. Cf. the brilliant analysis of public spending in Henry Hazlitt's book *Economics in One Lesson* (new ed. New York, 1962), pp. 21 ff.

and to stand the competition of more efficient plants, shops, or farms. Here, they say, it is obvious that total production is increased and something is added to the wealth that would not have been produced without the assistance of the authorities. What happens in fact is just the opposite; the magnitude of total production and of total wealth is curtailed. Outfits producing at higher costs are brought into existence or preserved while other outfits producing at lower costs are forced to curtail or to discontinue their production. The consumers are not getting more, but less.

There is, for instance, the very popular idea that it is a good thing for the government to promote the agricultural development of those parts of the country which nature has poorly endowed. Costs of production are higher in these districts than in other areas; it is precisely this fact that qualifies a large part of their soil as submarginal. When unaided by public funds, the farmers tilling these submarginal lands could not stand the competition of the more fertile farms. Agriculture would shrink or fail to develop and the whole area would become a backward part of the country. In full cognizance of this state of affairs profit-seeking business avoids investing in the construction of railroads connecting such inauspicious areas with the centers of consumption. The plight of the farmers is not caused by the fact that they lack transportation facilities. The causation is the other way round; because business realizes that the prospects for these farmers are not propitious, it abstains from investing in railroads which are likely to become unprofitable for lack of a sufficient amount of goods to be shipped. If the government, yielding to the demands of the interested pressure groups, builds the railroad and runs it at a deficit, it certainly benefits the owners of farm land in those poor districts of the country. As a part of the costs that the shipping of their products requires is borne by the treasury, they find it easier to compete with those tilling more fertile land to whom such aid is denied. But the boon of these privileged farmers is paid for by the taxpayers who must provide the funds required to defray the deficit. It affects neither the market price nor the total available supply of agricultural products. It merely makes profitable the operation of farms which hitherto were submarginal and makes other farms, the operation of which was hitherto profitable, submarginal. It shifts production from land requiring lower costs to land requiring higher costs. It does not increase total supply and wealth, it curtails them, as the additional amounts of capital and labor required for the cultivation of high-cost fields instead of low-cost fields are withheld from employments in which they would have made possible the production of some other consumers' goods. The government attains its end of benefiting some parts of the country with what they would have missed, but it produces somewhere else costs which exceed these gains of a privileged group.

The External Economies of Intellectual Creation

The extreme case of external economies is shown in the "production" of the intellectual groundwork of every kind of processing and constructing. The characteristic mark of formulas, i.e., the mental devices directing the technological procedures, is the inexhaustibility of the services they render. These services are consequently not scarce, and there is no need to economize their employment. Those considerations that resulted in the establishment of the institution of private ownership of economic goods did not refer to them. They remained outside the sphere of private property not because they are immaterial, intangible, and impalpable, but because their serviceableness cannot be exhausted.

People began to realize only later that this state of affairs has its drawbacks too. It places the producers of such formulas—especially the inventors of technological procedures and authors and composers—in a peculiar position. They are burdened with the cost of production, while the services of the product they have created can be gratuitously enjoyed by everybody. What they produce is for them entirely or almost entirely external economies.

If there are neither copyrights nor patents, the inventors and authors are in the position of an entrepreneur. They have a temporary advantage as against other people. As they start sooner in utilizing their invention or their manuscript themselves or in making it available for use to other people (manufacturers or publishers), they have the chance to earn profits in the time interval until everybody can likewise utilize it. As soon as the invention or the content of the book are publicly known, they become "free goods" and the inventor or author has only his glory.

The problem involved has nothing to do with the activities of the creative genius. These pioneers and originators of things unheard of do not produce and work in the sense in which these terms are employed in dealing with the affairs of other people. They do not let themselves be influenced by the response their work meets on the part of their contemporaries. They do not wait for encouragement.[13]

It is different with the broad class of professional intellectuals whose services society cannot do without. We may disregard the problem of second-rate authors of poems, fiction, and plays and second-rate composers and need not inquire whether it would be a serious disadvantage for mankind to lack the products of their efforts. But it is obvious that handing down knowledge to the rising generation and

13. See above, pp. 139–140.

familiarizing the acting individuals with the amount of knowledge they need for the realization of their plans require textbooks, manuals, handbooks, and other nonfiction works. It is unlikely that people would undertake the laborious task of writing such publications if everyone were free to reproduce them. This is still more manifest in the field of technological invention and discovery. The extensive experimentation necessary for such achievements is often very expensive. It is very probable that technological progress would be seriously retarded if, for the inventor and for those who defray the expenses incurred by his experimentation, the results obtained were nothing but external economies.

Patents and copyrights are results of the legal evolution of the last centuries. Their place in the traditional body of property rights is still controversial. People look askance at them and deem them irregular. They are considered privileges, a vestige of the rudimentary period of their evolution when legal protection was accorded to authors and inventors only by virtue of an exceptional privilege granted by the authorities. They are suspect, as they are lucrative only if they make it possible to sell at monopoly prices.[14] Moreover, the fairness of patent laws is contested on the ground that they reward only those who put the finishing touch leading to practical utilization of achievements of many predecessors. These precursors go empty-handed although their contribution to the final result was often much more weighty than that of the patentee.

It is beyond the scope of catallactics to enter into an examination of the arguments brought forward for and against the institution of copyrights and patents. It has merely to stress the point that this is a problem of the delimitation of property rights and that with the abolition of patents and copyrights authors and inventors would for the most part be producers of external economies.

Privileges and Quasi-privileges

The restrictions which laws and institutions impose upon the discretion to choose and to act are not always so insurmountable that they could not be overcome under certain conditions. To some favorites exemption from the obligation binding the rest of the people may be granted as an explicit privilege either by the laws themselves or by an administrative act of the authorities entrusted with the law's enforcement. Some may be ruthless enough to defy the laws in spite of the vigilance of the authorities; their daring insolence secures them a quasi-privilege.

A law that nobody observes is ineffectual. A law that is not valid for all or which not all obey, may grant to those who are exempt—whether by virtue of the law itself or by virtue of their own audacity—the opportunity to reap either differential rent or monopoly gains.

14. See above, pp. 364–365.

With regard to the determination of the market phenomena it does not matter whether the exemption is legally valid as a privilege or illegal as a quasi-privilege. Neither does it matter whether the costs, if any, incurred by the favored individual or firm for the acquisition of the privilege or quasi-privilege are legal (e.g., a tax levied on licensees) or illegal (e.g., bribes paid to corrupt officers). If an importation embargo is mitigated by the importation of a certain quantity, the prices are affected by the quantity imported and the specific costs incurred by the acquisition and the utilization of the privilege or quasi-privilege. But whether the importation was legal (e.g., a license granted under the system of quantitative trade control to some privileged people), or illegal contraband does not affect the price structure.

XXIV. HARMONY AND CONFLICT OF INTERESTS

1. The Ultimate Source of Profit and Loss on the Market

THE changes in the data whose reiterated emergence prevents the economic system from turning into an evenly rotating economy and produces again and again entrepreneurial profit and loss are favorable to some members of society and unfavorable to others. Hence, people concluded, *the gain of one man is the damage of another; no man profits but by the loss of others*. This dogma was already advanced by some ancient authors. Among modern writers Montaigne was the first to restate it; we may fairly call it the *Montaigne dogma*. It was the quintessence of the doctrines of Mercantilism, old and new. It is at the bottom of all modern doctrines teaching that there prevails, within the frame of the market economy, an irreconcilable conflict among the interests of various social classes within a nation and furthermore between the interests of any nation and those of all other nations.[1]

Now the Montaigne dogma is true with regard to the effects of cash-induced changes in the purchasing power of money on deferred payments. But it is entirely wrong with regard to any kind of entrepreneurial profit or loss, whether they emerge in a stationary economy in which the total amount of profits equals the total amount of losses or in a progressing or a retrogressing economy in which these two magnitudes are different.

What produces a man's profit in the course of affairs within an unhampered market society is not his fellow citizen's plight and distress, but the fact that he alleviates or entirely removes what causes his fellow citizen's feeling of uneasiness. What hurts the sick is the plague, not the physician who treats the disease. The doctor's gain is not an outcome of the epidemics, but of the aid he gives to those affected. The ultimate source of profits is always the foresight of future conditions. Those who succeeded better than others in antici-

1. Cf. Montaigne, *Essais*, ed. F. Strowski, Bk. I, chap. 22 (Bordeaux, 1906), I, 135–136; A. Oncken, *Geschichte der Nationalökonomie* (Leipzig, 1902), pp. 152–153; E. F. Heckscher, *Mercantilism*, transl. by M. Shapiro (London, 1935), II, 26–27.

pating future events and in adjusting their activities to the future state of the market, reap profits because they are in a position to satisfy the most urgent needs of the public. The profits of those who have produced goods and services for which the buyers scramble are not the source of the losses of those who have brought to the market commodities in the purchase of which the public is not prepared to pay the full amount of production costs expended. These losses are caused by the lack of insight displayed in anticipating the future state of the market and the demand of the consumers.

External events affecting demand and supply may sometimes come so suddenly and unexpectedly that people say that no reasonable man could have foreseen them. Then the envious may consider the profits of those who gain from the change as unjustified. Yet such arbitrary value judgments do not alter the real state of interests. It is certainly better for a sick man to be cured by a doctor for a high fee than to lack medical assistance. If it were otherwise, he would not consult the physician.

There are in the market economy no conflicts between the interests of the buyers and sellers. There are disadvantages caused by inadequate foresight. It would be a universal boon if every man and all the members of the market society would always foresee future conditions correctly and in time and act accordingly. If this were the case, retrospection would establish that no particle of capital and labor was wasted for the satisfaction of wants which now are considered as less urgent than some other unsatisfied wants. However, man is not omniscient.

It is wrong to look at these problems from the point of view of resentment and envy. It is no less faulty to restrict one's observation to the momentary position of various individuals. These are social problems and must be judged with regard to the operation of the whole market system. What secures the best possible satisfaction of the demands of each member of society is precisely the fact that those who succeeded better than other people in anticipating future conditions are earning profits. If profits were to be curtailed for the benefit of those whom a change in the data has injured, the adjustment of supply to demand would not be improved but impaired. If one were to prevent doctors from occasionally earning high fees, one would not increase but rather decrease the number of those choosing the medical profession.

The deal is always advantageous both for the buyer and the seller. Even a man who sells at a loss is still better off than he would be if he could not sell at all, or only at a still lower price. He loses on account of his lack of foresight; the sale limits his loss even if the price received is low. If both the buyer and the seller were not to consider the transaction as the most advantageous action they could choose under the prevailing conditions, they would not enter into the deal.

The statement that one man's boon is the other man's damage is valid with regard to robbery, war, and booty. The robber's plunder is the damage of the despoiled victim. But war and commerce are two different things. Voltaire erred when—in 1764—he wrote in the article "Patrie" of his *Dictionnaire philosophique:* "To be a good patriot is to wish that one's own community should enrich itself by trade and acquire power by arms; it is obvious that a country cannot profit but at the expense of another and that it cannot conquer without inflicting harm on other people." Voltaire, like so many other authors who preceded and followed him, deemed it superfluous to familiarize himself with economic thought. If he had read the essays of his contemporary David Hume, he would have learned how false it is to identify war and foreign trade. Voltaire, the great debunker of age-old superstitions and popular fallacies, fell prey unawares to the most disastrous fallacy.

When the baker provides the dentist with bread and the dentist relieves the baker's toothache, neither the baker nor the dentist is harmed. It is wrong to consider such an exchange of services and the pillage of the baker's shop by armed gangsters as two manifestations of the same thing. Foreign trade differs from domestic trade only in so far as goods and services are exchanged beyond the borderlines separating the territories of two sovereign nations. It is monstrous that Prince Louis Napoleon Bonaparte, the later Emperor Napoleon III, should have written many decades after Hume, Adam Smith, and Ricardo: "The quantity of merchandise which a country exports is always in direct proportion to the number of shells it can discharge upon its enemies whenever its honor and its dignity may require it."[2] All the teachings of economics concerning the effects of the international division of labor and of international trade have up to now failed to destroy the popularity of the Mercantilist fallacy, "that the object of foreign trade is to pauperize foreigners."[3] It is a task of historical investigation to disclose the sources of the popularity of this and other similar delusions and errors. For economics the matter is long since settled.

2. Cf. Louis Napoleon Bonaparte, *Extinction du pauperisme* (éd. populaire, Paris, 1848), p. 6.

3. With these words H. G. Wells (*The World of William Clissold,* Bk. IV, sec.10) characterizes the opinion of a typical representative of the British peerage.

2. The Limitation of Offspring

The natural scarcity of the means of sustenance forces every living being to look upon all other living beings as deadly foes in the struggle for survival, and generates pitiless biological competition. But with man these irreconcilable conflicts of interests disappear when, and as far as, the division of labor is substituted for economic autarky of individuals, families, tribes, and nations. Within the system of society there is no conflict of interests as long as the optimum size of population has not been reached. As long as the employment of additional hands results in a more than proportionate increase in the returns, harmony of interests is substituted for conflict. People are no longer rivals in the struggle for the allocation of portions out of a strictly limited supply. They become cooperators in striving after ends common to all of them. An increase in population figures does not curtail, but rather augments, the average shares of the individuals.

If men were to strive only after nourishment and sexual satisfaction, population would tend to increase beyond the optimum size to the limits drawn by the sustenance available. However, men want more than merely to live and to copulate; they want to live *humanly*. An improvement in conditions usually results, it is true, in an increase in population figures; but this increase lags behind the increase in bare sustenance. If it were otherwise, men would have never succeeded in the establishment of social bonds and in the development of civilization. As with rats, mice, and microbes, every increase in sustenance would have made population figures rise to the limits of bare sustenance; nothing would have been left for the seeking of other ends. The fundamental error implied in the iron law of wages was precisely the fact that it looked upon men—or at least upon the wage earners—as beings exclusively driven by animal impulses. Its champions failed to realize that man differs from the beasts as far as he aims also at specifically human ends, which one may call higher or more sublime ends.

The Malthusian law of population is one of the great achievements of thought. Together with the principle of the division of labor it provided the foundations for modern biology and for the theory of evolution; the importance of these two fundamental theorems for the sciences of human action is second only to the discovery of the regularity in the intertwinement and sequence of market phenomena and their inevitable determination by the market data. The objections raised against the Malthusian law as well as against the law of returns are vain and trivial. Both laws are indisputable. But the role to be assigned to them within the body of the sciences of human action is different from that which Malthus attributed to them.

Nonhuman beings are entirely subject to the operation of the biological law described by Malthus.[4] For them the statement that their numbers tend to encroach upon the means of subsistence and that the supernumerary specimens are weeded out by want of sustenance is valid without any exception. With reference to the nonhuman animals the notion of minimum sustenance has an unequivocal, uniquely determined sense. But the case is different with man. Man integrates the satisfaction of the purely zoological impulses, common to all animals, into a scale of values, in which a place is also assigned to specifically human ends. Acting man also rationalizes the satisfaction of his sexual appetites. Their satisfaction is the outcome of a weighing of pros and cons. Man does not blindly submit to a sexual stimulation like a bull; he refrains from copulation if he deems the costs—the anticipated disadvantages—too high. In this sense we may, without any valuation or ethical connotation, apply the term *moral restraint* employed by Malthus.[5]

Rationalization of sexual intercourse already involves the rationalization of proliferation. Then later further methods of rationalizing the increase of progeny were adopted which were independent of abstention from copulation. People resorted to the egregious and repulsive practices of exposing or killing infants and of abortion. Finally they learned to perform the sexual act in such a way that no pregnancy results. In the last hundred years the technique of contraceptive devices has been perfected and the frequency of their employment increased considerably. Yet the procedures had long been known and practiced.

The affluence that modern capitalism bestows upon the broad masses of the capitalist countries and the improvement in hygienic conditions and therapeutical and prophylactic methods brought about by capitalism have considerably reduced mortality, especially infant mortality, and prolonged the average duration of life. Today in these countries the restriction in generating offspring can succeed only if it is more drastic than in earlier ages. The transition to capitalism—

4. The Malthusian law is, of course, a biological and not a praxeological law. However, its cognizance is indispensable for praxeology in order to conceive by contrast the essential characteristic of human action. As the natural sciences failed to discover it, the economists had to fill the gap. The history of the law of population too explodes the popular myth about the backwardness of the sciences of human action and their need to borrow from the natural sciences.

5. Malthus too employed this term without any valuation or ethical implication. Cf. Bonar, *Malthus and His Work* (London, 1885), p. 53. One could as well substitute the term *praxeological restraint* for *moral restraint*.

i.e., the removal of the obstacles which in former days had fettered the functioning of private initiative and enterprise—has consequently deeply influenced sexual customs. It is not the practice of birth control that is new, but merely the fact that it is more frequently resorted to. Especially new is the fact that the practice is no longer limited to the upper strata of the population, but is common to the whole population. For it is one of the most important social effects of capitalism that it deproletarianizes all strata of society. It raises the standard of living of the masses of the manual workers to such a height that they too turn into "bourgeois" and think and act like well-to-do burghers. Eager to preserve their standard of living for themselves and for their children, they embark upon birth control. With the spread and progress of capitalism, birth control becomes a universal practice. The transition to capitalism is thus accompanied by two phenomena: a decline both in fertility rates and in mortality rates. The average duration of life is prolonged.

In the days of Malthus it was not yet possible to observe these demographical characteristics of capitalism. Today it is no longer permissible to question them. But, blinded by romantic prepossessions, many describe them as phenomena of decline and degeneration peculiar only to the white-skinned peoples of Western civilization, grown old and decrepit. These romantics are seriously alarmed by the fact that the Asiatics do not practice birth control to the same extent to which it is practiced in Western Europe, North America, and Australia. As modern methods of fighting and preventing disease have brought about a drop in mortality rates with these oriental peoples too, their population figures grow more rapidly than those of the Western nations. Will not the indigenes of India, Malaya, China, and Japan, who themselves did not contribute to the technological and therapeutical achievements of the West, but received them as an unexpected present, in the end by the sheer superiority of their numbers squeeze out the peoples of European descent?

These fears are groundless. Historical experience shows that all Caucasian peoples reacted to the drop in mortality figures brought about by capitalism with a drop in the birth rate. Of course, from such historical experience no general law may be deduced. But praxeological reflection demonstrates that there exists between these two phenomena a necessary concatenation. An improvement in the external conditions of well-being makes possible a corresponding increase in population figures. However, if the additional quantity of the means of sustenance is completely absorbed by rearing an additional number of people, nothing is left for a further improvement in the standard of living. The march of civilization is arrested; mankind reaches a state of stagnation.

The case becomes still more obvious if we assume that a prophylactic invention is made by a lucky chance and that its practical application requires neither a considerable investment of capital nor considerable current expenditure. Of course, modern medical research and still more its utilization absorb huge amounts of capital and labor. They are products of capitalism. They would never have come into existence in a noncapitalist environment. But there were, in earlier days, instances of a different character. The practice of smallpox inoculation did not originate from expensive laboratory research and, in its original crude form, could be applied at trifling costs. Now, what would the results of smallpox inoculation have been if its practice had become general in a precapitalist country not committed to birth control? It would have increased population figures without increasing sustenance, it would have impaired the average standard of living. It would not have been a blessing, but a curse.

Conditions in Asia and Africa are, by and large, the same. These backward peoples receive the devices for fighting and preventing disease ready-made from the West. It is true that in some of these countries imported foreign capital and the adoption of foreign technological methods by the comparatively small domestic capital synchronously tend to increase the per capita output of labor and thus to bring about a tendency toward an improvement in the average standard of living. However, this does not sufficiently counterbalance the opposite tendency resulting from the drop in mortality rates not accompanied by an adequate fall in fertility rates. The contact with the West has not yet benefited these peoples because it has not yet affected their minds; it has not freed them from age-old superstitions, prejudices, and misapprehensions; it has merely altered their technological and therapeutical knowledge.

The reformers of the oriental peoples want to secure for their fellow citizens the material well-being that the Western nations enjoy. Deluded by Marxian, nationalist, and militarist ideas they think that all that is needed for the attainment of this end is the introduction of European and American technology. Neither the Slavonic Bolsheviks and nationalists nor their sympathizers in the Indies, in China, and in Japan realize that what their peoples need most is not Western technology, but the social order which in addition to other achievements has generated this technological knowledge. They lack first of all economic freedom and private initiative, entrepreneurs and capitalism. But they look only for engineers and machines. What separates East and West is the social and economic system. The East is foreign to the Western spirit that has created capitalism. It is of no use to import the paraphernalia of capitalism without admitting capitalism as such. No achievement of capitalist civilization would have been accomplished in a noncapitalistic environment or can be preserved in a world without a market economy.

If the Asiatics and Africans really enter into the orbit of Western civilization, they will have to adopt the market economy without reservations. Then their masses will rise above their present proletarian wretchedness and practice birth control as it is practiced in every capitalistic country. No excessive growth of population will longer hinder the improvement in the standards of living. But if the oriental peoples in the future confine themselves to mechanical reception of the tangible achievements of the West without embracing its basic philosophy and social ideologies, they will forever remain in their present state of inferiority and destitution. Their populations may increase considerably, but they will not raise themselves above distress. These miserable masses of paupers will certainly not be a serious menace to the independence of the Western nations. As long as there is a need for weapons, the entrepreneurs of the market society will never stop producing more efficient weapons and thus securing to their countrymen a superiority of equipment over the merely imitative noncapitalistic Orientals. The military events of both World Wars have proved anew that the capitalistic countries are paramount also in armaments production. No foreign aggressor can destroy capitalist civilization if it does not destroy itself. Where capitalistic entrepreneurship is allowed to function freely, the fighting forces will always be so well equipped that the biggest armies of the backward peoples will be no match for them. There has even been great exaggeration of the danger of making the formulas for manufacturing "secret" weapons universally known. If war comes again, the searching mind of the capitalistic world will always have a head start on the peoples who merely copy and imitate clumsily.

The peoples who have developed the system of the market economy and cling to it are in every respect superior to all other peoples. The fact that they are eager to preserve peace is not a mark of their weakness and inability to wage war. They love peace because they know that armed conflicts are pernicious and disintegrate the social division of labor. But if war becomes unavoidable, they show their superior efficiency in military affairs too. They repel the barbarian aggressors whatever their numbers may be.

The purposive adjustment of the birth rate to the supply of the material potentialities of well-being is an indispensable condition of human life and action, of civilization, and of any improvement in wealth and welfare. Whether the only beneficial method of birth control is abstention from coitus is a question which must be decided from the point of view of bodily and mental hygiene. It is absurd to confuse the issue by referring to ethical precepts developed in ages which were faced with different conditions. However, praxeology is not interested in the theological aspects of the problem. It has merely to establish the fact that where there is no limitation of offspring there cannot be any question of civilization and improvement in the standard of living.

A socialist commonwealth would be under the necessity of regulating the fertility rate by authoritarian control. It would have to regiment the sexual life of its wards no less than all other spheres of their conduct. In the market economy every individual is spontaneously intent upon not begetting children whom he could not rear without considerably lowering his family's standard of life. Thus the growth of population beyond the optimum size as determined by the supply of capital available and the state of technological knowledge is checked. The interests of each individual coincide with those of all other individuals.

Those fighting birth control want to eliminate a device indispensable for the preservation of peaceful human cooperation and the social division of labor. Where the average standard of living is impaired by the excessive increase in population figures, irreconcilable conflicts of interests arise. Each individual is again a rival of all other individuals in the struggle for survival. The annihilation of rivals is the only means of increasing one's own well-being. The philosophers and theologians who assert that birth control is contrary to the laws of God and Nature refuse to see things as they really are. Nature straitens the material means required for the improvement of human well-being and survival. As natural conditions are, man has only the choice between the pitiless war of each against each or social cooperation. But social cooperation is impossible if people give rein to the natural impulse of proliferation. In restricting procreation man adjusts himself to the natural conditions of his existence. The rationalization of the sexual passions is an indispensable condition of civilization and societal bonds. Its abandonment would in the long run not increase but decrease the numbers of those surviving, and would render life for everyone as poor and miserable as it was many thousands of years ago for our ancestors.

3. The Harmony of the "Rightly Understood" Interests

From time immemorial men have prattled about the blissful conditions their ancestors enjoyed in the original "state of nature." From old myths, fables, and poems the image of this primitive happiness passed into many popular philosophies of the seventeenth and eighteenth centuries. In their language the term *natural* denoted what was good and beneficial in human affairs, while the term *civilization* had the connotation of opprobrium. The fall of man was seen in the deviation from the primitive conditions of ages in which there was but little difference between man and other animals. At that time, these romantic eulogists of the past asserted, there were no conflicts between men. Peace was undisturbed in the Garden of Eden.

Yet nature does not generate peace and good will. The characteristic mark of the "state of nature" is irreconcilable conflict. Each specimen is the rival of all other specimens. The means of subsistence are scarce and do not grant survival to all. The conflicts can never disappear. If a band of men, united with the object of defeating rival bands, succeeds in annihilating its foes, new antagonisms arise among the victors over the distribution of the booty. The source of the conflicts is always the fact that each man's portion curtails the portions of all other men.

What makes friendly relations between human beings possible is the higher productivity of the division of labor. It removes the natural conflict of interests. For where there is division of labor, there is no longer question of the distribution of a supply not capable of enlargement. Thanks to the higher productivity of labor performed under the division of tasks, the supply of goods multiplies. A preeminent common interest, the preservation and further intensification of social cooperation, becomes paramount and obliterates all essential collisions. Catallactic competition is substituted for biological competition. It makes for harmony of the interests of all members of society. The very condition from which the irreconcilable conflicts of biological competition arise—viz., the fact that all people by and large strive after the same things—is transformed into a factor making for harmony of interests. Because many people or even all people want bread, clothes, shoes, and cars, large-scale production of these goods becomes feasible and reduces the costs of production to such an extent that they are accessible at low prices. The fact that my fellow man wants to acquire shoes as I do, does not make it harder for me to get shoes, but easier. What enhances the price of shoes is the fact that nature does not provide a more ample supply of leather and other raw material required, and that one must submit to the disutility of labor in order to transform these raw materials into shoes. The catallactic competition of those who, like me, are eager to have shoes makes shoes cheaper, not more expensive.

This is the meaning of the theorem of the harmony of the rightly understood interests of all members of the market society.[6] When the classical economists made this statement, they were trying to stress two points: First, that everybody is interested in the preservation of the social division of labor, the system that multiplies the productivity of human efforts. Second, that in the market society consumers' demand ultimately directs all production activities. The fact that not all human wants can be satisfied is not due to inappropriate social institutions or to deficiencies of the system of the market economy. It is a natural condition of human life. The belief that nature bestows upon man inexhaustible riches and that misery is an outgrowth of man's failure to organize the good society is entirely fallacious. The "state of nature" which the reformers and utopians depicted as paradisiac was in fact a state of extreme poverty and distress. "Poverty," says Bentham, "is not the work of the laws, it is the primitive condition of the human race."[7] Even those at the base of the social pyramid are much better off than they would have been in the absence of social cooperation. They too are benefited by the operation of the market economy and participate in the advantages of civilized society.

The nineteenth-century reformers did not drop the cherished fable of the original earthly paradise. Frederick Engels incorporated it in the Marxian account of mankind's social evolution. However, they no longer set up the bliss of the *aurea aetas* as a pattern for social and economic reconstruction. They contrast the alleged depravity of capitalism with the ideal happiness man will enjoy in the socialist Elysium of the future. The socialist mode of production will abolish the fetters by means of which capitalism checks the development of the productive forces, and will increase the productivity of labor and wealth beyond all measure. The preservation of free enterprise and the private ownership of the means of production benefits exclusively the small minority of parasitic exploiters and harms the immense majority of working men. Hence there prevails within the frame of the market society an irreconcilable conflict between the interests of "capital" and those of "labor." This class struggle can disappear only when a fair system of social organization—either

6. For "rightly understood" interests we may as well say interests "in the long run."

7. Cf. Bentham, *Principles of the Civil Code*, in "Works," I, 309.

socialism or interventionism—is substituted for the manifestly unfair capitalist mode of production.

Such is the almost universally accepted social philosophy of our age. It was not created by Marx, although it owes its popularity mainly to the writings of Marx and the Marxians. It is today endorsed not only by the Marxians, but no less by most of those parties who emphatically declare their anti-Marxism and pay lip service to free enterprise. It is the official social philosophy of Roman Catholicism as well as of Anglo-Catholicism; it is supported by many eminent champions of the various Protestant denominations and of the Orthodox Oriental Church. It is an essential part of the teachings of Italian Fascism and of German Nazism and of all varieties of interventionist doctrines. It was the ideology of the Sozialpolitik of the Hohenzollerns in Germany and of the French royalists aiming at the restoration of the house of Bourbon-Orléans, of the New Deal of President Roosevelt, and of the nationalists of Asia and Latin America. The antagonisms between these parties and factions refer to accidental issues—such as religious dogma, constitutional institutions, foreign policy—and, first of all, to the characteristic features of the social system that is to be substituted for capitalism. But they all agree in the fundamental thesis that the very existence of the capitalist system harms the vital interests of the immense majority of workers, artisans, and small farmers, and they all ask in the name of social justice for the abolition of capitalism.[8]

All socialist and interventionist authors and politicians base their analysis and critique of the market economy on two fundamental

8. The official doctrine of the Roman Church is outlined in the encyclical *Quadragesimo anno* of Pope Pius XI (1931). The Anglo-Catholic doctrine is presented by the late William Temple, Archbishop of Canterbury, in the book *Christianity and the Social Order* (Penguin Special, 1942). Representative of the ideas of European continental Protestantism is the book of Emil Brunner, *Justice and the Social Order,* trans. by M. Hottinger (New York, 1945). A highly significant document is the section on "The Church and Disorder of Society" of the draft report which the World Council of Churches in September, 1948, recommended for appropriate action to the one hundred and fifty odd denominations whose delegates are members of the Council. For the ideas of Nicolas Berdyaew, the most eminent apologist of Russian Orthodoxy, cf. his book *The Origin of Russian Communism* (London, 1937), especially pp. 217–218 and 225. It is often asserted that an essential difference between the Marxians and the other socialist and interventionist parties is to be found in the fact that the Marxians stand for class struggle, while the latter parties look at the class struggle as upon a deplorable outgrowth of the irreconcilable conflict of class interests inherent in capitalism and want to overcome it by the realization of the reforms they recommend. However, the Marxians do not praise and kindle the class struggle for its own sake. In their eyes the class struggle is good only because it is the device by means of which the "productive forces," those mysterious forces directing the course of human evolution, are bound to bring about the "classless" society in which there will be neither classes nor class conflicts.

errors. First, they fail to recognize the speculative character inherent in all endeavors to provide for future want-satisfaction, i.e., in all human action. They naïvely assume that there cannot exist any doubt about the measures to be applied for the best possible provisioning of the consumers. In a socialist commonwealth there will be no need for the production tsar (or the central board of production management) to speculate. He will "simply" have to resort to those measures which are beneficial to his wards. The advocates of a planned economy have never conceived that the task is to provide for future wants which may differ from today's wants and to employ the various available factors of production in the most expedient way for the best possible satisfaction of these uncertain future wants. They have not conceived that the problem is to allocate scarce factors of production to the various branches of production in such a way that no wants considered more urgent should remain unsatisfied because the factors of production required for their satisfaction were employed, i.e., wasted, for the satisfaction of wants considered less urgent. This economic problem must not be confused with the technological problem. Technological knowledge can merely tell us what could be achieved under the present state of our scientific insight. It does not answer the questions as to what should be produced and in what quantities, and which of the multitude of technological processes available should be chosen. Deluded by their failure to grasp this essential matter, the advocates of a planned society believe that the production tsar will never err in his decisions. In the market economy the entrepreneurs and capitalists cannot avoid committing serious blunders because they know neither what the consumers want nor what their competitors are doing. The general manager of a socialist state will be infallible because he alone will have the power to determine what should be produced and how, and because no action of other people will cross his plans.[9]

The second fundamental error involved in the socialists' critique of the market economy stems from their faulty theory of wages. They have failed to realize that wages are the price paid for the wage earner's achievement, i.e., for the contribution of his efforts to the processing of the good concerned or, as people say, for the value which his services add to the value of the materials. No matter whether there are time wages or piecework wages, the employer always buys the worker's performance and services, not his time. It is therefore

9. The thorough exposure of this delusion is provided by the proof of the impossibility of economic calculation under socialism. See below the fifth part of this book.

not true that in the unhampered market economy the worker has no personal interest in the execution of his task. The socialists are badly mistaken in asserting that those paid a certain rate per hour, per day, per week, per month, or per year are not impelled by their own selfish interests when they work efficiently. It is not lofty ideals and the sense of duty that deter a worker paid according to the length of time worked from carelessness and loafing around the shop, but very substantial arguments. He who works more and better gets higher pay, and he who wants to earn more must increase the quantity and improve the quality of his performance. The hard-boiled employers are not so gullible as to let themselves be cheated by slothful employees; they are not so negligent as those governments who pay salaries to hosts of loafing bureaucrats. Neither are the wage earners so stupid as not to know that laziness and inefficiency are heavily penalized on the labor market.[10]

On the shaky ground of their misconception of the catallactic nature of wages, the socialist authors have advanced fantastic fables about the increase in the productivity of labor to be expected from the realization of their plans. Under capitalism, they say, the worker's zeal is seriously impaired because he is aware of the fact that he himself does not reap the fruits of his labor and that his toil and trouble enrich merely his employer, this parasitic and idle exploiter. But under socialism every worker will know that he works for the benefit of society, of which he himself is a part. This knowledge will provide him with the most powerful incentive to do his best. An enormous increase in the productivity of labor and thereby in wealth will result.

However, the identification of the interests of each worker and those of the socialist commonwealth is a purely legalistic and formalistic fiction which has nothing to do with the real state of affairs. While the sacrifices an individual worker makes in intensifying his own exertion burden him alone, only an infinitesimal fraction of the produce of his additional exertion benefits himself and improves his own well-being. While the individual worker enjoys completely the pleasures he may reap by yielding to the temptation to carelessness and laziness, the resulting impairment of the social dividend curtails his own share only infinitesimally. Under such a socialist mode of production all personal incentives which selfishness provides under capitalism are removed, and a premium is put upon laziness and negligence. Whereas in a capitalist society selfishness incites everyone to the utmost diligence, in a socialist society it makes for inertia and laxity. The socialists may still babble about the miraculous change in human nature that

10. Cf. above, pp. 601–603.

the advent of socialism will effect, and about the substitution of lofty altruism for mean egotism. But they must no longer indulge in fables about the marvelous effects the selfishness of each individual will bring about under socialism.[11]

No judicious man can fail to conclude from the evidence of these considerations that in the market economy the productivity of labor is incomparably higher than it would be under socialism. However, this cognition does not settle the question between the advocates of capitalism and those of socialism from a praxeological, i.e., scientific, point of view.

A bona fide advocate of socialism who is free from bigotry, prepossession, and malice could still contend: "It may be true that P, the total net income turned out in a market society, is larger than p, the total net income turned out in a socialist society. But if the socialist system assigns to each of its members an equal share of p (viz., $\frac{p}{z} = d$), all those whose income in the market society is smaller than d are favored by the substitution of socialism for capitalism. It may happen that this group of people includes the majority of men. At any rate it becomes evident that the doctrine of the harmony between the rightly understood interests of all members of the market society is untenable. There is a class of men whose interests are hurt by the very existence of the market economy and who would be better off under socialism." The advocates of the market economy contest the conclusiveness of this reasoning. They believe that p will lag so much behind P that d will be smaller than the income which even those earning the lowest wages get in the market society. There can be no doubt that this objection is well founded. However, it is not based on praxeological considerations and therefore lacks the apodictic and incontestable argumentative power inherent in a praxeological demonstration. It is based on a judgment of relevance, the quantitative appraisal of the difference between the two magnitudes P and p. In the field of human action such quantitative cognition is obtained by understanding, with regard to which full agreement between men cannot be reached. Praxeology, economics, and catallactics are of no use for the settlement of such dissensions concerning quantitative issues.

11. The doctrine refuted in the text found its most brilliant expositor in John Stuart Mill (*Principles of Political Economy* [People's ed. London, 1867], pp. 126 ff.). However, Mill resorted to this doctrine merely in order to refute an objection raised against socialism, viz., that, by eliminating the incentive provided by selfishness, it would impair the productivity of labor. He was not so blind as to assert that the productivity of labor would multiply under socialism. For an analysis and refutation of Mill's reasoning, cf. Mises, *Socialism*, pp. 173–181.

The advocates of socialism could even go farther and say: "Granted that each individual will be worse off under socialism than even the poorest under capitalism. Yet we spurn the market economy in spite of the fact that it supplies everybody with more goods than socialism. We disapprove of capitalism on ethical grounds as an unfair and amoral system. We prefer socialism on grounds commonly called non-economic and put up with the fact that it impairs everybody's material well-being."[12] It cannot be denied that this haughty indifference with regard to material well-being is a privilege reserved to ivory-tower intellectuals, secluded from reality, and to ascetic anchorites. What made socialism popular with the immense majority of its supporters was, on the contrary, the illusion that it would supply them with more amenities than capitalism. But however this may be, it is obvious that this type of prosocialist argumentation cannot be touched by the liberal reasoning concerning the productivity of labor.

If no other objections could be raised to the socialist plans than that socialism will lower the standard of living of all or at least of the immense majority, it would be impossible for praxeology to pronounce a final judgment. Men would have to decide the issue between capitalism and socialism on the ground of judgments of value and of judgments of relevance. They would have to choose between the two systems as they choose between many other things. No objective standard could be discovered which would make it possible to settle the dispute in a manner which allows no contradiction and must be accepted by every sane individual. The freedom of each man's choice and discretion would not be annihilated by inexorable necessity. However, the true state of affairs is entirely different. Man is not in a position to choose between these two systems. Human cooperation under the system of the social division of labor is possible only in the market economy. Socialism is not a realizable system of society's economic organization because it lacks any method of economic calculation. To deal with this fundamental problem is the task of the fifth part of this book.

The establishment of this truth does not amount to a depreciation of the conclusiveness and the convincing power of the antisocialist argument derived from the impairment of productivity to be expected

12. This mode of reasoning was mainly resorted to by some eminent champions of Christian socialism. The Marxians used to recommend socialism on the ground that it would multiply productivity and bring unprecedented material wealth to everybody. Only lately have they changed their tactics. They declare that the Russian worker is happier than the American worker in spite of the fact that his standard of living is much lower; the knowledge that he lives under a fair social system compensates by far for all his material hardships.

from socialism. The weight of this objection raised to the socialist plans is so overwhelming that no judicious man could hesitate to choose capitalism. Yet this would still be a choice between alternative systems of society's economic organization, preference given to one system as against another. However, such is not the alternative. Socialism cannot be realized because it is beyond human power to establish it as a social system. The choice is between capitalism and chaos. A man who chooses between drinking a glass of milk and a glass of a solution of potassium cyanide does not choose between two beverages; he chooses between life and death. A society that chooses between capitalism and socialism does not choose between two social systems; it chooses between social cooperation and the disintegration of society. Socialism is not an alternative to capitalism; it is an alternative to any system under which men can live as *human* beings. To stress this point is the task of economics as it is the task of biology and chemistry to teach that potassium cyanide is not a nutriment but a deadly poison.

The convincing power of the productivity argument is in fact so irresistible that the advocates of socialism were forced to abandon their old tactics and to resort to new methods. They are eager to divert attention from the productivity issue by throwing into relief the monopoly problem. All contemporary socialist manifestoes expatiate on monopoly power. Statesmen and professors try to outdo one another in depicting the evils of monopoly. Our age is called the age of monopoly capitalism. The foremost argument advanced today in favor of socialism is the reference to monopoly.

Now, it is true that the emergence of monopoly prices (not of monopoly as such without monopoly prices) creates a discrepancy between the interests of the monopolist and those of the consumers. The monopolist does not employ the monopolized good according to the wishes of the consumers. As far as there are monopoly prices, the interests of the monopolist take precedence over those of the public and the democracy of the market is restricted. With regard to monopoly prices there is not harmony, but conflict of interests.

It is possible to contest these statements with regard to the monopoly prices received in the sale of articles under patents and copyrights. One may argue that in the absence of patent and copyright legislation these books, compositions, and technological innovations would never have come into existence. The public pays monopoly prices for things it would not have enjoyed at all under competitive prices. However, we may fairly disregard this issue. It has little to do with the great monopoly controversy of our day. When people deal with the evils of monopoly, they imply that there prevails within the unhampered market economy a general and inevitable tendency toward the substitution of monopoly prices for competitive prices. This is, they say, a characteristic mark of "mature" or "late" capitalism. Whatever conditions may have been in the earlier stages of capitalist evolution and whatever one may think about the validity of the classical economists' statements concerning the harmony of the rightly understood interests, today there is no longer any question of such a harmony.

As has been pointed out already,[13] there is no such tendency toward monopolization. It is a fact that with many commodities in many countries monopoly prices prevail, and moreover, some articles are sold at monopoly prices on the world market. However, almost all of these instances of monopoly prices are the outgrowth of government interference with business. They were not created by the interplay of the factors operating on a free market. They are not products of capitalism, but precisely of the endeavors to counteract the forces determining the height of the market prices. It is a distortion of fact to speak of monopoly capitalism. It would be more appropriate to speak of monopoly interventionism or of monopoly statism.

Those instances of monopoly prices which would appear also on a market not hampered and sabotaged by the interference of the various national governments and by conspiracies between groups of governments are of minor importance. They concern some raw materials the deposits of which are few and geographically concentrated, and local limited-space monopolies. However, it is a fact that in these cases monopoly prices can be realized even in the absence of government policies aiming directly or indirectly at their establishment. It is necessary to realize that consumers' sovereignty is not perfect and that there are limits to the operation of the democratic process of the market. There is in some exceptional and rare cases of minor importance even on a market not hampered and sabotaged by government interference an antagonism between the interests of the owners of factors of production and those of the rest of the people. However, the existence of such antagonisms by no means impairs the concord of the interests of all people with regard to the preservation of the market economy. The market economy is the only system of society's economic organization that can function and really has been functioning. Socialism is unrealizable because of its inability to develop a method for economic calculation. Interventionism must result in a state of affairs which, from the point of view of its advo-

13. Cf. above, p. 366.

cates, is less desirable than the conditions of the unhampered market economy which it aims to alter. In addition, it liquidates itself as soon as it is pushed beyond a narrow field of application.[14] Such being the case, the only social order that can preserve and further intensify the social division of labor is the market economy. All those who do not wish to disintegrate social cooperation and to return to the conditions of primitive barbarism are interested in the perpetuation of the market economy.

The classical economists' teachings concerning the harmony of the rightly understood interests were defective in so far as they failed to recognize the fact that the democratic process of the market is not perfect, because in some instances of minor importance, even in the unhampered market economy, monopoly prices may appear. But much more conspicuous was their failure to recognize that and why no socialist system can be considered as a system of society's economic organization. They based the doctrine of the harmony of interests upon the erroneous assumption that there are no exceptions to the rule that the owners of the means of production are forced by the market process to employ their property according to the wishes of the consumers. Today this theorem must be based on the knowledge that no economic calculation is feasible under socialism.

4. Private Property

Private ownership of the means of production is the fundamental institution of the market economy. It is the institution the presence of which characterizes the market economy as such. Where it is absent, there is no question of a market economy.

Ownership means full control of the services that can be derived from a good. This catallactic notion of ownership and property rights is not to be confused with the legal definition of ownership and property rights as stated in the laws of various countries. It was the idea of legislators and courts to define the legal concept of property in such a way as to give to the proprietor full protection by the governmental apparatus of coercion and compulsion and to prevent anybody from encroaching upon his rights. As far as this purpose was adequately realized, the legal concept of property rights corresponded to the catallactic concept. However, nowadays there are tendencies to abolish the institution of private property by a change in the laws determining the scope of the actions which the proprietor is entitled to undertake with regard to the things which are his property. While retaining the term private property, these reforms aim at the

14. Cf. the sixth part of this book.

substitution of public ownership for private ownership. This tendency is the characteristic mark of the plans of various schools of Christian socialism and of nationalist socialism. But few of the champions of these schools have been so keen as the Nazi philosopher Othmar Spann, who explicitly declared that the realization of his plans would bring about a state of affairs in which the institution of private property will be preserved only in a "formal sense, while in fact there will be only public ownership."[15] There is need to mention these things in order to avoid popular fallacies and confusion. In dealing with private property, catallactics deals with control, not with legal terms, concepts and definitions. Private ownership means that the proprietors determine the employment of the factors of production, while public ownership means that the government controls their employment.

Private property is a human device. It is not sacred. It came into existence in early ages of history, when people with their own power and by their own authority appropriated to themselves what had previously not been anybody's property. Again and again proprietors were robbed of their property by expropriation. The history of private property can be traced back to a point at which it originated out of acts which were certainly not legal. Virtually every owner is the direct or indirect legal successor of people who acquired ownership either by arbitrary appropriation of ownerless things or by violent spoliation of their predecessor.

However, the fact that legal formalism can trace back every title either to arbitrary appropriation or to violent expropriation has no significance whatever for the conditions of a market society. Ownership in the market economy is no longer linked up with the remote origin of private property. Those events in a far-distant past, hidden in the darkness of primitive mankind's history, are no longer of any concern for our day. For in an unhampered market society the consumers daily decide anew who should own and how much he should own. The consumers allot control of the means of production to those who know how to use them best for the satisfaction of the most urgent wants of the consumers. Only in a legal and formalistic sense can the owners be considered the successors of appropriators and expropriators. In fact, they are mandataries of the consumers, bound by the operation of the market to serve the consumers best. Under capitalism, private property is the consummation of the self-determination of the consumers.

The meaning of private property in the market society is radically different from what it is under a system of each household's autarky.

15. Cf. Spann, *Der wahre Staat* (Leipzig, 1921), p. 249.

Where each household is economically self-sufficient, the privately owned means of production exclusively serve the proprietor. He alone reaps all the benefits derived from their employment. In the market society the proprietors of capital and land can enjoy their property only by employing it for the satisfaction of other people's wants. They must serve the consumers in order to have any advantage from what is their own. The very fact that they own means of production forces them to submit to the wishes of the public. Ownership is an asset only for those who know how to employ it in the best possible way for the benefit of the consumers. It is a social function.

5. The Conflicts of Our Age

Popular opinion sees the source of the conflicts which bring about the civil wars and international wars of our age in the collision of "economic" interests inherent in the market economy. Civil war is the rebellion of the "exploited" masses against the "exploiting" classes. Foreign war is the revolt of the "have-not" nations against those nations who have appropriated to themselves an unfair share of the earth's natural resources and, with insatiable greed, want to snatch even more of this wealth destined for the use of all. He who in face of these facts speaks of the harmony of the rightly understood interests, is either a moron or an infamous apologist of a manifestly unjust social order. No intelligent and honest man could fail to realize that there prevail today irreconcilable conflicts of material interests which can be settled only by recourse to arms.

It is certainly true that our age is full of conflicts which generate war. However, these conflicts do not spring from the operation of the unhampered market society. It may be permissible to call them economic conflicts because they concern that sphere of human life which is, in common speech, known as the sphere of economic activities. But it is a serious blunder to infer from this appellation that the source of these conflicts are conditions which develop within the frame of a market society. It is not capitalism that produces them, but precisely the anticapitalistic policies designed to check the functioning of capitalism. They are an outgrowth of the various governments' interference with business, of trade and migration barriers and discrimination against foreign labor, foreign products, and foreign capital.

None of these conflicts could have emerged in an unhampered market economy. Imagine a world in which everybody were free to live and work as entrepreneur or as employee where he wanted and how he chose, and ask which of these conflicts could still exist.

Imagine a world in which the principle of private ownership of the means of production is fully realized, in which there are no institutions hindering the mobility of capital, labor, and commodities, in which the laws, the courts, and the administrative officers do not discriminate against any individual or groups of individuals, whether native or alien. Imagine a state of affairs in which governments are devoted exclusively to the task of protecting the individual's life, health, and property against violent and fraudulent aggression. In such a world the frontiers are drawn on the maps, but they do not hinder anybody from the pursuit of what he thinks will make him more prosperous. No individual is interested in the expansion of the size of his nation's territory, as he cannot derive any gain from such an aggrandizement. Conquest does not pay and war becomes obsolete.

In the ages preceding the rise of liberalism and the evolution of modern capitalism, people for the most part consumed only what could be produced out of raw materials available in their own neighborhood. The development of the international division of labor has radically altered this state of affairs. Food and raw materials imported from distant countries are articles of mass consumption. The most advanced European nations could do without these imports only at the price of a very considerable lowering of their standard of living. They must pay for the badly needed purchase of minerals, lumber, oil, cereals, fat, coffee, tea, cocoa, fruit, wool, and cotton by exporting manufactures, most of them processed out of imported raw materials. Their vital interests are hurt by the protectionist trade policies of the countries producing these primary products.

Two hundred years ago it was of little concern to the Swedes or the Swiss whether or not a non-European country was efficient in utilizing its natural resources. But today economic backwardness in a foreign country, endowed by rich natural resources, hurts the interests of all those whose standard of living could be raised if a more appropriate mode of utilizing this natural wealth were adopted. The principle of each nation's unrestricted sovereignty is *in a world of government interference with business* a challenge to all other nations. The conflict between the have-nots and the haves is a real conflict. But it is present only in a world in which any sovereign government is free to hurt the interests of all peoples—its own included—by depriving the consumers of the advantages a better exploitation of this country's resources would give them. It is not sovereignty as such that makes for war, but sovereignty of governments not entirely committed to the principles of the market economy.

Liberalism did not and does not build its hopes upon abolition of the sovereignty of the various national governments, a venture which would result in endless wars. It aims at a general recognition of the idea of economic freedom. If all peoples become liberal and conceive that economic freedom best serves their own interests, national sovereignty will no longer engender conflict and war. What is needed to make peace durable is neither international treaties and covenants nor international tribunals and organizations like the defunct League of Nations or its successor, the United Nations. If the principle of the market economy is universally accepted, such makeshifts are unnecessary; if it is not accepted, they are futile. Durable peace can only be the outgrowth of a change in ideologies. As long as the peoples cling to the Montaigne dogma and think that they cannot prosper economically except at the expense of other nations, peace will never be anything other than a period of preparation for the next war.

Economic nationalism is incompatible with durable peace. Yet economic nationalism is unavoidable where there is government interference with business. Protectionism is indispensable where there is no domestic free trade. Where there is government interference with business, free trade even in the short run would frustrate the aims sought by the various interventionist measures.[16]

It is an illusion to believe that a nation would lastingly tolerate other nations' policies which harm the vital interest of its own citizens. Let us assume that the United Nations had been established in the year 1600 and that the Indian tribes of North America had been admitted as members of this organization. Then the sovereignty of these Indians would have been recognized as inviolable. They would have been given the right to exclude all aliens from entering their territory and from exploiting its rich natural resources which they themselves did not know how to utilize. Does anybody really believe that any international covenant or charter could have prevented the Europeans from invading these countries?

Many of the richest deposits of various mineral substances are located in areas whose inhabitants are too ignorant, too inert, or too dull to take advantage of the riches nature has bestowed upon them. If the governments of these countries prevent aliens from exploiting these deposits, or if their conduct of public affairs is so arbitrary that no foreign investments are safe, serious harm is inflicted upon all those foreign peoples whose material well-being could be improved by a more adequate utilization of the deposits concerned. It does not matter

16. Cf. above, pp. 366–368, and below, pp. 823–825.

whether the policies of these governments are the outcome of a general cultural backwardness or of the adoption of the now fashionable ideas of interventionism and economic nationalism. The result is the same in both cases.

There is no use in conjuring away these conflicts by wishful thinking. What is needed to make peace durable is a change in ideologies. What generates war is the economic philosophy almost universally espoused today by governments and political parties. As this philosophy sees it, there prevail within the unhampered market economy irreconcilable conflicts between the interests of various nations. Free trade harms a nation; it brings about impoverishment. It is the duty of government to prevent the evils of free trade by trade barriers. We may, for the sake of argument, disregard the fact that protectionism also hurts the interests of the nations which resort to it. But there can be no doubt that protectionism aims at damaging the interests of foreign peoples and really does damage them. It is an illusion to assume that those injured will tolerate other nations' protectionism if they believe that they are strong enough to brush it away by the use of arms. The philosophy of protectionism is a philosophy of war. The wars of our age are not at variance with popular economic doctrines; they are, on the contrary, the inescapable result of a consistent application of these doctrines.

The League of Nations did not fail because its organization was deficient. It failed because it lacked the spirit of genuine liberalism. It was a convention of governments imbued with the spirit of economic nationalism and entirely committed to the principles of economic warfare. While the delegates indulged in mere academic talk about good will among the nations, the governments whom they represented inflicted a good deal of evil upon all other nations. The two decades of the League's functioning were marked by each nation's adamant economic warfare against all other nations. The tariff protectionism of the years before 1914 was mild indeed when compared with what developed in the 'twenties and 'thirties—viz., embargoes, quantitative trade control, foreign exchange control, monetary devaluation, and so on.[17]

The prospects for the United Nations are not better, but rather worse. Every nation looks upon imports, especially upon imports of manufactured goods, as upon a disaster. It is the avowed goal of

17. For an appraisal of the abortive attempts of the League to do away with economic warfare, cf. Rappard, *Le Nationalisme économique et la Société des Nations* (Paris, 1938).

almost all countries to bar foreign manufactures as much as possible from access to their domestic markets. Almost all nations are fighting against the specter of an unfavorable balance of trade. They do not want to cooperate; they want to protect themselves against the alleged dangers of cooperation.

Part Five

Social Cooperation Without a Market

XXV. THE IMAGINARY CONSTRUCTION OF A SOCIALIST SOCIETY

1. The Historical Origin of the Socialist Idea

WHEN the social philosophers of the eighteenth century laid the foundations of praxeology and economics, they were confronted with an almost universally accepted and uncontested distinction between the petty selfish individuals and the state, the representative of the interests of the whole society. However, at that time the deification process which finally elevated the men managing the social apparatus of coercion and compulsion into the ranks of the gods was not yet completed. What people had in mind when speaking of government was not yet the quasi-theological notion of an omnipotent and omniscient deity, the perfect embodiment of all virtues; it was the concrete governments as they acted on the political scene. It was the various sovereign entities whose territorial size was the outcome of bloody wars, diplomatic intrigues, and dynastic intermarriage and succession. It was the princes whose private domain and revenue were in many countries not yet separated from the public treasury, and oligarchic republics, like Venice and some of the Swiss cantons, in which the ultimate objective of the conduct of public affairs was to enrich the ruling aristocracy. The interests of these rulers were in opposition to those of their "selfish" subjects exclusively committed to the pursuit of their own happiness on the one hand, and to those of foreign governments longing for booty and territorial aggrandizement on the other hand. In dealing with these antagonisms, the authors of books on public affairs were ready to espouse the cause of their own country's government. They assumed quite candidly that the rulers are the champions of the interests of the whole society, irreconcilably conflicting with those of the individuals. In checking the selfishness of their subjects, governments were promoting the welfare of the whole of society as against the mean concerns of individuals.

The liberal philosophy discarded these notions. From its point of view there are within the unhampered market society no conflicts of the rightly understood interests. The interests of the citizens are not opposed to those of the nation, the interests of each nation are not opposed to those of other nations.

Yet in demonstrating this thesis the liberal philosophers themselves contributed an essential element to the notion of the godlike state. They substituted in their inquiries the image of an ideal state for the real states of their age. They constructed the vague image of a government whose only objective is to make its citizens happy. This ideal had certainly no counterpart in the Europe of the *ancien régime*. In this Europe there were German princelings who sold their subjects like cattle to fight the wars of foreign nations; there were kings who seized every opportunity to rush upon the weaker neighbors; there was the shocking experience of the partitions of Poland; there was France successively governed by the century's most profligate men, the Regent Orléans and Louis XV; and there was Spain, ruled by the ill-bred paramour of an adulterous queen. However, the liberal philosophers deal only with a state which has nothing in common with these governments of corrupt courts and aristocracies. The state, as it appears in their writings, is governed by a perfect superhuman being, a king whose only aim is to promote the welfare of his subjects. Starting from this assumption, they raise the question of whether the actions of the individual citizens when left free from any authoritarian control would not develop along lines of which this good and wise king would disapprove. The liberal philosopher answers this question in the negative. It is true, he admits, that the entrepreneurs are selfish and seek their own profit. However, in the market economy they can earn profits only by satisfying in the best possible way the most urgent needs of the consumers. The objectives of entrepreneurship do not differ from those of the perfect king. For this benevolent king too aims at nothing else than such an employment of the means of production that the maximum of consumer satisfaction can be reached.

It is obvious that this reasoning introduces value judgments and political bias into the treatment of the problems. This paternal ruler is merely an alias for the economist who by means of this trick elevates his personal value judgments to the dignity of a universally valid standard of absolute eternal values. The author identifies himself with the perfect king and calls the ends he himself would choose if he were equipped with this king's power, welfare, commonweal, and *volkswirtschaftliche* productivity as distinct from the ends toward which the selfish individuals are striving. He is so naïve as not to see that this hypothetical chief of state is merely a hypostatization of his own arbitrary value judgments, and blithely assumes that he has discovered an incontestable standard of good and evil. Masked as the benevolent paternal autocrat, the author's own Ego is enshrined as the voice of the absolute moral law.

The essential characteristic of the imaginary construction of this king's ideal regime is that all its citizens are unconditionally subject to authoritarian control. The king issues orders and all obey. This is not a market economy; there is no longer private ownership of the means of production. The terminology of the market economy is retained, but in fact there is no longer any private ownership of the means of production, no real buying and selling, and no market prices. Production is not directed by the conduct of the consumers displayed on the market, but by authoritarian decrees. The authority assigns to everybody his station in the system of the social division of labor, determines what should be produced, and how and what each individual is allowed to consume. This is what nowadays can properly be called the German variety of socialist management.[1]

Now the economists compare this hypothetical system, which in their eyes embodies the moral law itself, with the market economy. The best they can say of the market economy is that it does not bring about a state of affairs different from that produced by the supremacy of the perfect autocrat. They approve of the market economy only because its operation, as they see it, ultimately attains the same results the perfect king would aim at. Thus the simple identification of what is morally good and economically expedient with the plans of the totalitarian dictator that characterizes all champions of planning and socialism was not contested by many of the old liberals. One must even assert that they originated this confusion when they substituted the ideal image of the perfect state for the wicked and unscrupulous despots and politicians of the real world. Of course, for the liberal thinker this perfect state was merely an auxiliary tool of reasoning, a model with which he compared the operation of the market economy. But it was not amazing that people finally raised the question as to why one should not transfer this ideal state from the realm of thought into the realm of reality.

All older social reformers wanted to realize the good society by a confiscation of all private property and its subsequent redistribution; each man's share should be equal to that of every other, and continuous vigilance by the authorities should safeguard the preservation of this equalitarian system. These plans became unrealizable when the large-scale enterprises in manufacturing, mining, and transportation appeared. There cannot be any question of splitting up large-scale business units and distributing the fragments in equal shares.[2] The

1. Cf. below, pp. 717–718.

2. There are, however, even today in the United States people who want to knock to pieces large-scale production and to do away with corporate business.

age-old program of redistribution was superseded by the idea of socialization. The means of production were to be expropriated, but no redistribution was to be resorted to. The state itself was to run all the plants and farms.

This inference became logically inescapable as soon as people began to ascribe to the *state* not only moral but also intellectual perfection. The liberal philosophers had described their imaginary state as an unselfish entity, exclusively committed to the best possible improvement of its subjects' welfare. They had discovered that in the frame of a market society the citizens' selfishness must bring about the same results that this unselfish state would seek to realize; it was precisely this fact that justified the preservation of the market economy in their eyes. But things became different as soon as people began to ascribe to the *state* not only the best intentions but also omniscience. Then one could not help concluding that the infallible state was in a position to succeed in the conduct of production activities better than erring individuals. It would avoid all those errors that often frustrate the actions of entrepreneurs and capitalists. There would no longer be malinvestment or squandering of scarce factors of production; wealth would multiply. The "anarchy" of production appears wasteful when contrasted with the planning of the *omniscient* state. The socialist mode of production then appears to be the only reasonable system, and the market economy seems the incarnation of unreason. In the eyes of the rationalist advocates of socialism, the market economy is simply an incomprehensible aberration of mankind. In the eyes of those influenced by historicism, the market economy is the social order of an inferior stage of human evolution which the inescapable process of progressive perfection will eliminate in order to establish the more adequate system of socialism. Both lines of thought agree that reason itself postulates the transition to socialism.

What the naïve mind calls reason is nothing but the absolutization of its own value judgments. The individual simply identifies the products of his own reasoning with the shaky notion of an absolute reason. No socialist author ever gave a thought to the possibility that the abstract entity which he wants to vest with unlimited power—whether it is called humanity, society, nation, state, or government—could act in a way of which he himself disapproves. A socialist advocates socialism because he is fully convinced that the supreme dictator of the socialist commonwealth will be reasonable from his—the individual socialist's—point of view, that he will aim at those ends of which he—the individual socialist—fully approves, and that he will try to attain these ends by choosing means which he—the individual socialist—

would also choose. Every socialist calls only that system a genuinely socialist system in which these conditions are completely fulfilled; all other brands claiming the name of socialism are counterfeit systems entirely different from true socialism. Every socialist is a disguised dictator. Woe to all dissenters! They have forfeited their right to live and must be "liquidated."

The market economy makes peaceful cooperation among people possible in spite of the fact that they disagree with regard to their value judgments. In the plans of the socialists there is no room left for dissenting views. Their principle is *Gleichschaltung,* perfect uniformity enforced by the police.

People frequently call socialism a religion. It is indeed the religion of self-deification. The State and Government of which the planners speak, the People of the nationalists, the Society of the Marxians and the Humanity of Comte's positivism are names for the God of the new religions. But all these idols are merely aliases for the individual reformer's own will. In ascribing to his idol all those attributes which the theologians ascribe to God, the inflated Ego glorifies itself. It is infinitely good, omnipotent, omnipresent, omniscient, eternal. It is the only perfect being in this imperfect world.

Economics is not called to examine blind faith and bigotry. The faithful are proof against every criticism. In their eyes criticism is scandalous, a blasphemous revolt of wicked men against the imperishable splendor of their idol. Economics deals merely with the socialist plans, not with the psychological factors that impel people to espouse the religion of statolatry.

2. The Socialist Doctrine

Karl Marx was not the originator of socialism. The ideal of socialism was fully elaborated when Marx adopted the socialist creed. Nothing could be added to the praxeological conception of the socialist system as developed by his predecessors, and Marx did not add anything. Neither did Marx refute the objections against the feasibility, desirability, and advantageousness of socialism raised by earlier authors and by his contemporaries. He never even embarked upon such a venture, fully aware as he was of his inability to succeed in it. All that he did to fight the criticisms of socialism was to hatch out the doctrine of polylogism.

However, the services that Marx rendered to the socialist propaganda were not confined to the invention of polylogism. Still more important was his doctrine of the inevitability of socialism.

Marx lived in an age in which the doctrine of evolutionary meliorism was almost generally accepted. The invisible hand of Providence leads men, independently of their wills, from lower and less perfect stages to higher and more perfect ones. There prevails in the course of human history an inevitable tendency toward progress and improvement. Each later stage of human affairs is, by virtue of its being a later stage, also a higher and better stage. Nothing is permanent in human conditions except this irresistible urge toward progress. Hegel, who died a few years before Marx entered the scene, had presented this doctrine in his fascinating philosophy of history, and Nietzsche, who entered the scene at the time when Marx withdrew, made it the focal point of his no less fascinating writings. It has been the myth of the last two hundred years.

What Marx did was to integrate the socialist creed into this meliorist doctrine. The coming of socialism is inevitable, and this by itself proves that socialism is a higher and more perfect state of human affairs than the preceding state of capitalism. It is vain to discuss the pros and cons of socialism. Socialism is bound to come "with the inexorability of a law of nature."[3] Only morons can be so stupid as to question whether what is bound to come is more beneficial than what preceded it. Only bribed apologists of the unjust claims of the exploiters can be so insolent as to find any fault with socialism.

If we attribute the epithet Marxian to all those who agree with this doctrine, we must call the immense majority of our contemporaries Marxians. These people agree that the coming of socialism is both absolutely inevitable and highly desirable. The "wave of the future" drives mankind toward socialism. Of course, they disagree with one another as to who is to be entrusted with the captaincy of the socialist ship of state. There are many candidates for this job.

Marx tried to prove his prophecy in a twofold way. The first is the method of Hegelian dialectics. Capitalist private property is the first negation of individual private property and must beget its own negation, viz., the establishment of public property in the means of production.[4] Things were as simple as that for the hosts of Hegelian writers who infested Germany in the days of Marx.

The second method is the demonstration of the unsatisfactory conditions brought about by capitalism. Marx's critique of the capitalist mode of production is entirely wrong. Even the most orthodox Marxians are not bold enough to support seriously its essential thesis, namely, that capitalism results in a progressive impoverishment of the wage earners. But if one admits for the sake of argument all the

3. Cf. Marx, *Das Kapital* (7th ed. Hamburg, 1914), I, 728.
4. *Ibid.*

absurdities of the Marxian analysis of capitalism, nothing is yet won for the demonstration of the two theses, viz., that socialism is bound to come and that it is not only a better system than capitalism, but even the most perfect system, the final realization of which will bring to man eternal bliss in his earthly life. All the sophisticated syllogisms of the ponderous volumes published by Marx, Engels, and hundreds of Marxian authors cannot conceal the fact that the only and ultimate source of Marx's prophecy is an alleged inspiration by virtue of which Marx claims to have guessed the plans of the mysterious powers determining the course of history. Like Hegel, Marx was a prophet communicating to the people the revelation that an inner voice had imparted to him.

The outstanding fact in the history of socialism between 1848 and 1920 was that the essential problems concerning its working were hardly ever touched upon. The Marxian taboo branded all attempts to examine the economic problems of a socialist commonwealth as "unscientific." Nobody was bold enough to defy this ban. It was tacitly assumed by both the friends and the foes of socialism that socialism is a realizable system of mankind's economic organization. The vast literature concerning socialism dealt with alleged shortcomings of capitalism and with the general cultural implications of socialism. It never dealt with the economics of socialism as such.

The socialist creed rests upon three dogmas:

First: Society is an omnipotent and ominiscient being, free from human frailty and weakness.

Second: The coming of socialism is inevitable.

Third: As history is a continuous progress from less perfect conditions to more perfect conditions, the coming of socialism is desirable.

For praxeology and economics the only problem to be discussed in regard to socialism is this: Can a socialist system operate as a system of the division of labor?

3. The Praxeological Character of Socialism

The essential mark of socialism is that *one will* alone acts. It is immaterial whose will it is. The director may be an anointed king or a dictator, ruling by virtue of his *charisma,* he may be a Führer or a board of Führers appointed by the vote of the people. The main thing is that the employment of all factors of production is directed by one agency only. One will alone chooses, decides, directs, acts, gives orders. All the rest simply obey orders and instructions. Organization and a planned order are substituted for the "anarchy" of production and for various people's initiative. Social cooperation under the division of labor is safeguarded by a system of hegemonic bonds in which a director peremptorily calls upon the obedience of all his wards.

In terming the director *society* (as the Marxians do), *state* (with a capital *S*), *government,* or *authority,* people tend to forget that the director is always a human being, not an abstract notion or a mythical collective entity. We may admit that the director or the board of directors are people of superior ability, wise and full of good intentions. But it would be nothing short of idiocy to assume that they are omniscient and infallible.

In a praxeological analysis of the problems of socialism, we are not concerned with the moral and ethical character of the director. Neither do we discuss his value judgments and his choice of ultimate ends. What we are dealing with is merely the question of whether any mortal man, equipped with the logical structure of the human mind, can be equal to the tasks incumbent upon a director of a socialist society.

We assume that the director has at his disposal all the technological knowledge of his age. Moreover, he has a complete inventory of all the material factors of production available and a roster enumerating all manpower employable. In these respects the crowd of experts and specialists which he assembles in his offices provide him with perfect information and answer correctly all questions he may ask them. Their voluminous reports accumulate in huge piles on his desk. But now he must act. He must choose among an infinite variety of projects in such a way that no want which he himself considers more urgent remains unsatisfied because the factors of production required for its satisfaction are employed for the satisfaction of wants which he considers less urgent.

It is important to realize that this problem has nothing at all to do with the valuation of the ultimate ends. It refers only to the means by the employment of which the ultimate ends chosen are to be attained. We assume that the director has made up his mind with regard to the valuation of ultimate ends. We do not question his decision. Neither do we raise the question of whether the people, the wards, approve or disapprove of their director's decisions. We may assume, for the sake of argument, that a mysterious power makes everyone agree with one another and with the director in the valuation of ultimate ends.

Our problem, the crucial and only problem of socialism, is a purely economic problem, and as such refers merely to means and not to ultimate ends.

XXVI. THE IMPOSSIBILITY OF ECONOMIC CALCULATION UNDER SOCIALISM

1. The Problem

THE director wants to build a house. Now, there are many methods that can be resorted to. Each of them offers, from the point of view of the director, certain advantages and disadvantages with regard to the utilization of the future building, and results in a different duration of the building's serviceableness; each of them requires other expenditures of building materials and labor and absorbs other periods of production. Which method should the director choose? He cannot reduce to a common denominator the items of various materials and various kinds of labor to be expended. Therefore he cannot compare them. He cannot attach either to the waiting time (period of production) or to the duration of serviceableness a definite numerical expression. In short, he cannot, in comparing costs to be expended and gains to be earned, resort to any arithmetical operation. The plans of his architects enumerate a vast multiplicity of various items in kind; they refer to the physical and chemical qualities of various materials and to the physical productivity of various machines, tools, and procedures. But all their statements remain unrelated to each other. There is no means of establishing any connection between them.

Imagine the plight of the director when faced with a project. What he needs to know is whether or not the execution of the project will increase well-being, that is, add something to the wealth available without impairing the satisfaction of wants which he considers more urgent. But none of the reports he receives give him any clue to the solution of this problem.

We may for the sake of argument at first disregard the dilemmas involved in the choice of consumers' goods to be produced. We may assume that this problem is settled. But there is the embarrassing multitude of producers' goods and the infinite variety of procedures that can be resorted to for manufacturing definite consumers' goods. The most advantageous location of each industry and the optimum size of each plant and of each piece of equipment must be determined.

One must determine what kind of mechanical power should be employed in each of them, and which of the various formulas for the production of this energy should be applied. All these problems are raised daily in thousands and thousands of cases. Each case offers special conditions and requires an individual solution appropriate to these special data. The number of elements with which the director's decision has to deal is much greater than would be indicated by a merely technological description of the available producers' goods in terms of physics and chemistry. The location of each of them must be taken into consideration as well as the serviceableness of the capital investments made in the past for their utilization. The director does not simply have to deal with coal as such, but with thousands and thousands of pits already in operation in various places, and with the possibilities for digging new pits, with the various methods of mining in each of them, with the different qualities of the coal in various deposits, with the various methods for utilizing the coal for the production of heat, power, and a great number of derivatives. It is permissible to say that the present state of technological knowledge makes it possible to produce almost anything out of almost everything. Our ancestors, for instance, knew only a limited number of employments for wood. Modern technology has added a multitude of possible new employments. Wood can be used for the production of paper, of various textile fibers, of foodstuffs, drugs, and many other synthetic products.

Today two methods are resorted to for providing a city with clean water. Either one brings the water over long distances in aqueducts, an ancient method long practiced, or one chemically purifies the water available in the city's neighborhood. Why does one not produce water synthetically in factories? Modern technology could easily solve the technological problems involved. The average man in his mental inertia is ready to ridicule such projects as sheer lunacy. However, the only reason why the synthetic production of drinking water today—perhaps not at a later day—is out of the question is that economic calculation in terms of money shows that it is a more expensive procedure than other methods. Eliminate economic calculation and you have no means of making a rational choice between the various alternatives.

The socialists, it is true, object that economic calculation is not infallible. They say that the capitalists sometimes make mistakes in their calculation. Of course, this happens and will always happen. For all human action points to the future and the future is always uncertain. The most carefully elaborated plans are frustrated if expectations concerning the future are dashed to the ground. However, this is quite a different problem. Today we calculate from the point of view of our present knowledge and of our present anticipation of future conditions. We do not deal with the problem of whether or not the director will be able to anticipate future conditions. What we have in mind is that the director cannot calculate from the point of view of his own present value judgments and his own present anticipations of future conditions, whatever they may be. If he invests today in the canning industry, it may happen that a change in consumers' tastes or in the hygienic opinions concerning the wholesomeness of canned food will one day turn his investment into a malinvestment. But how can he find out *today* how to build and equip a cannery most economically?

Some railroad lines constructed at the turn of the century would not have been built if people had at that time anticipated the impending advance of motoring and aviation. But those who at that time built railroads knew which of the various possible alternatives for the realization of their plans they had to choose from the point of view of their appraisements and anticipations and of the market prices of their day in which the valuations of the consumers were reflected. It is precisely this insight that the director will lack. He will be like a sailor on the high seas unfamiliar with the methods of navigation, or like a medieval scholar entrusted with the technical operation of a railroad engine.

We have assumed that the director has already made up his mind with regard to the construction of a definite plant or building. However, in order to make such a decision he already needs economic calculation. If a hydroelectric power station is to be built, one must know whether or not this is the most economical way to produce the energy needed. How can he know this if he cannot calculate costs and output?

We may admit that in its initial period a socialist regime could to some extent rely upon the experience of the preceding age of capitalism. But what is to be done later, as conditions change more and more? Of what use could the prices of 1900 be for the director in 1949? And what use can the director in 1980 derive from the knowledge of the prices of 1949?

The paradox of "planning" is that it cannot plan, because of the absence of economic calculation. What is called a planned economy is no economy at all. It is just a system of groping about in the dark. There is no question of a rational choice of means for the best possible attainment of the ultimate ends sought. What is called conscious planning is precisely the elimination of conscious purposive action.

2. Past Failures to Conceive the Problem

For more than a hundred years the substitution of socialist planning for private enterprise has been the main political issue. Thousands and thousands of books have been published for and against the communist plans. No other subject has been more eagerly discussed in private circles, in the press, in public gatherings, in the meetings of learned societies, in election campaigns, and in parliaments. Wars have been fought and rivers of blood have been shed for the cause of socialism. Yet in all these years the essential question has not been raised.

It is true that some eminent economists—Hermann Heinrich Gossen, Albert Schäffle, Vilfredo Pareto, Nikolaas G. Pierson, Enrico Barone—touched upon the problem. But, with the exception of Pierson, they did not penetrate to the core of the problem, and they all failed to recognize its primordial importance. Neither did they venture to integrate it into the system of the theory of human action. It was these failures which prevented people from paying attention to their observations. They were disregarded and soon fell into oblivion.

It would be a serious mistake to blame the Historical School and Institutionalism for this neglect of mankind's most vital problem. These two lines of thought fanatically disparage economics, the "dismal science," in the interests of their interventionist or socialist propaganda. However, they have not succeeded in suppressing the study of economics entirely. The puzzling thing is not why the detractors of economics failed to recognize the problem, but why the economists were guilty of the same fault.

It is the two fundamental errors of mathematical economics that must be indicted.

The mathematical economists are almost exclusively intent upon the study of what they call economic equilibrium and the static state. Recourse to the imaginary construction of an evenly rotating economy is, as has been pointed out,[1] an indispensable mental tool of economic reasoning. But it is a grave mistake to consider this auxiliary tool as anything else than an imaginary construction, and to overlook the fact that it has not only no counterpart in reality, but

1. Cf. above, pp. 246–250.

cannot even be thought through consistently to its ultimate logical consequences. The mathematical economist, blinded by the prepossession that economics must be constructed according to the pattern of Newtonian mechanics and is open to treatment by mathematical methods, misconstrues entirely the subject matter of his investigations. He no longer deals with human action but with a soulless mechanism mysteriously actuated by forces not open to further analysis. In the imaginary construction of the evenly rotating economy there is, of course, no room for the entrepreneurial function. Thus the mathematical economist eliminates the entrepreneur from his thought. He has no need for this mover and shaker whose never ceasing intervention prevents the imaginary system from reaching the state of perfect equilibrium and static conditions. He hates the entrepreneur as a disturbing element. The prices of the factors of production, as the mathematical economist sees it, are determined by the intersection of two curves, not by human action.

Moreover, in drawing his cherished curves of cost and price, the mathematical economist fails to see that the reduction of costs and prices to homogeneous magnitudes implies the use of a common medium of exchange. Thus he creates the illusion that calculation of costs and prices could be resorted to even in the absence of a common denominator of the exchange ratios of the factors of production.

The result is that from the writings of the mathematical economists the imaginary construction of a socialist commonwealth emerges as a realizable system of cooperation under the division of labor, as a full-fledged alternative to the economic system based on private control of the means of production. The director of the socialist community will be in a position to allocate the various factors of production in a rational way, i.e., on the ground of calculation. Men can have both socialist cooperation under the division of labor and rational employment of the factors of production. They are free to adopt socialism without abandoning economy in the choice of means. Socialism does not enjoin the renunciation of rationality in the employment of the factors of production. It is a variety of *rational* social action.

An apparent verification of these errors was seen in the experience of the socialist governments of Soviet Russia and Nazi Germany. People do not realize that these were not isolated socialist systems. They were operating in an environment in which the price system still worked. They could resort to economic calculation on the ground of the prices established abroad. Without the aid of these prices their actions would have been aimless and planless. Only because they were able to refer to these foreign prices were they able to calculate, to keep books, and to prepare their much talked about plans.

3. Recent Suggestions for Socialist Economic Calculation

The socialist tracts deal with everything except the essential and unique problem of socialism, viz., economic calculation. It is only in the last years that socialist writers have no longer been able to avoid paying attention to this primordial matter. They have begun to suspect that the Marxian technique of smearing "bourgeois" economics is not a sufficient method for the realization of the socialist utopia. They have tried to substitute a theory of socialism for the scurrilous Hegelian metaphysics of the Marxian doctrine. They have embarked upon designing schemes for socialist economic calculation. Of course, they have lamentably failed in this task. It would hardly be necessary to deal with their spurious suggestions were it not for the fact that such examination offers a good opportunity to bring into relief fundamental features both of the market society and of the imaginary construction of a nonmarket society.

The various schemes proposed can be classified in the following way:

1. Calculation in kind is to be substituted for calculation in terms of money. This method is worthless. One cannot add or subtract numbers of different kinds (heterogeneous quantities).[2]

2. Starting from the ideas of the labor theory of value, the labor-hour is recommended as the unit of calculation. This suggestion does not take into account the original material factors of production and ignores the different qualities of work accomplished in the various labor-hours worked by the same and by different people.

3. The unit is to be a "quantity" of utility. However, acting man does not measure utility. He arranges it in scales of gradation. Market prices are not expressive of equivalence, but of a divergence in the valuation of the two exchanging parties. It is impermissible to neglect the fundamental theorem of modern economics, namely, that the value attached to one unit of a supply of *n-1* units is greater than that attached to one unit of a supply of *n* units.

2. It would hardly be worth while even to mention this suggestion if it were not the solution that emanated from the very busy and obtrusive circle of the "logical positivists" who flagrantly advertise their program of the "unified science." Cf. the writings of the late chief organizer of this group, Otto Neurath, who in 1919 acted as the head of the socialization bureau of the short-lived Soviet republic of Munich, especially his *Durch die Kriegswirtschaft zur Naturalwirtschaft* (Munich, 1919), pp. 216 ff. Cf. also C. Landauer, *Planwirtschaft und Verkehrswirtschaft* (Munich and Leipzig, 1931), p. 122.

4. Calculation is to be made possible by the establishment of an artificial quasi-market. This scheme is dealt with in section 5 of this chapter.

5. Calculation is to be made with the aid of the differential equations of mathematical catallactics. This scheme is dealt with in section 6 of this chapter.

6. Calculation is to be made superfluous by resorting to the method of trial and error. This idea is dealt with in section 4 of this chapter.

4. Trial and Error

The entrepreneurs and capitalists do not have advance assurance about whether their plans are the most appropriate solution for the allocation of factors of production to the various branches of industry. It is only later experience that shows them after the event whether they were right or wrong in their enterprises and investments. The method they apply is the method of trial and error. Why, say some socialists, should not the socialist director resort to the same method?

The method of trial and error is applicable in all cases in which the correct solution is recognizable as such by unmistakable marks not dependent on the method of trial and error itself. If a man mislays his wallet, he may hunt for it in various places. If he finds it, he recognizes it as his property; there is no doubt about the success of the method of trial and error applied; he has solved his problem. When Ehrlich was looking for a remedy for syphilis, he tested hundreds of drugs until he found what he was searching for, a drug that killed the spirochetes without damaging the human body. The mark of the correct solution, the drug number 606, was that it combined these two qualities, as could be learned from laboratory experiment and from clinical experience.

Things are quite different if the only mark of the correct solution is that it has been reached by the application of a method considered appropriate for the solution of the problem. The correct result of a multiplication of two factors is recognizable only as the result of a correct application of the process indicated by arithmetic. One may try to guess the correct result by trial and error. But here the method of trial and error is no substitute for the arithmetical process. It would be quite futile if the arithmetical process did not provide a yardstick for discriminating what is incorrect from what is correct.

If one wants to call entrepreneurial action an application of the method of trial and error, one must not forget that the correct solution is easily recognizable as such; it is the emergence of a surplus of proceeds over costs. Profit tells the entrepreneur that the consumers approve of his ventures; loss, that they disapprove.

The problem of socialist economic calculation is precisely this: that in the absence of market prices for the factors of production, a computation of profit or loss is not feasible.

We may assume that in the socialist commonwealth there is a market for consumers' goods and that money prices for consumers' goods are determined on this market. We may assume that the director assigns periodically to every member a certain amount of money and sells the consumers' goods to those bidding the highest prices. Or we may as well assume that a certain portion of the various consumers' goods in kind is allotted to each member and that the members are free to exchange these goods against other goods on a market in which the transactions are effected through a common medium of exchange, a sort of money. But the characteristic mark of the socialist system is that the producers' goods are controlled by one agency only in whose name the director acts, that they are neither bought nor sold, and that there are no prices for them. Thus there cannot be any question of comparing input and output by the methods of arithmetic.

We do not assert that the capitalist mode of economic calculation guarantees the absolutely best solution of the allocation of factors of production. Such absolutely perfect solutions of any problem are out of reach of mortal men. What the operation of a market not sabotaged by the interference of compulsion and coercion can bring about is merely the best solution accessible to the human mind under the given state of technological knowledge and the intellectual abilities of the age's shrewdest men. As soon as any man discovers a discrepancy between the real state of production and a realizable better[3] state, the profit motive pushes him toward the utmost effort to realize his plans. The sale of his products will show whether he was right or wrong in his anticipations. The market daily tries the entrepreneurs anew and eliminates those who cannot stand the test. It tends to entrust the conduct of business affairs to those men who have succeeded in filling the most urgent wants of the consumers. This is the only important respect in which one can call the market economy a system of trial and error.

5. The Quasi-market

The distinctive mark of socialism is the oneness and indivisibility of the will directing all production activities within the whole social

3. "Better" means, of course, more satisfactory from the point of view of the consumers buying on the market.

system. When the socialists declare that "order" and "organization" are to be substituted for the "anarchy" of production, conscious action for the alleged planlessness of capitalism, true cooperation for competition, production for use for production for profit, what they have in mind is always the substitution of the exclusive and monopolistic power of only *one* agency for the infinite multitude of the plans of the individual consumers and those attending to the wishes of the consumers, the entrepreneurs and capitalists. The essence of socialism is the entire elimination of the market and of catallactic competition. The socialist system is a system without a market and market prices for the factors of production and without competition; it means the unrestricted centralization and unification of the conduct of all affairs in the hands of one authority. In the drafting of the unique plan that directs all economic activities the citizens cooperate, if at all, only by electing the director or the board of directors. For the rest they are only subordinates, bound to obey unconditionally the orders issued by the director, and wards of whose well-being the director takes care. All the excellences the socialists ascribe to socialism and all the blessings they expect from its realization are described as the necessary outcome of this absolute unification and centralization.

It is therefore nothing short of a full acknowledgment of the correctness and irrefutability of the economists' analysis and devastating critique of the socialists' plans that the intellectual leaders of socialism are now busy designing schemes for a socialist system in which the market, market prices for the factors of production, and catallactic competition are to be preserved. The overwhelmingly rapid triumph of the demonstration that no economic calculation is possible under a socialist system is without precedent indeed in the history of human thought. The socialists cannot help admitting their crushing final defeat. They no longer claim that socialism is matchlessly superior to capitalism because it brushes away markets, market prices, and competition. On the contrary. They are now eager to justify socialism by pointing out that it is possible to preserve these institutions even under socialism. They are drafting outlines for a socialism in which there are prices and competition.[4]

What these neosocialists suggest is really paradoxical. They want to abolish private control of the means of production, market exchange, market prices, and competition. But at the same time they want to organize the socialist utopia in such a way that people could

4. This refers, of course, only to those socialists or communists who, like professors H. D. Dickinson and Oskar Lange, are conversant with economic thought. The dull hosts of the "intellectuals" will not abandon their superstitious belief in the superiority of socialism. Superstitions die hard.

act *as if* these things were still present. They want people to play market as children play war, railroad, or school. They do not comprehend how such childish play differs from the real thing it tries to imitate.

It was, say these neosocialists, a serious mistake on the part of the older socialists (i.e., of all socialists before 1920) to believe that socialism necessarily requires the abolition of the market and of market exchange and even that this fact is both the essential element and the preeminent feature of a socialist economy. This idea is, as they reluctantly admit, preposterous and its realization would result in a chaotic muddle. But fortunately, they say, there is a better pattern for socialism available. It is possible to instruct the managers of the various production units to conduct the affairs of their unit in the same way they did under capitalism. The manager of a corporation operates in the market society not on his account and at his own peril, but for the benefit of the corporation, i.e., the shareholders. He will go on under socialism in the same way with the same care and attention. The only difference will consist in the fact that the fruits of his endeavors will enrich the whole society, not the shareholders. For the rest he will buy and sell, recruit and pay workers, and try to make profits in the same way he did before. The transition from the managerial system of mature capitalism to the managerial system of the planned socialist commonwealth will be smoothly effected. Nothing will change except the ownership of the capital invested. Society will be substituted for the shareholders, the people will henceforth pocket the dividends. That is all.

The cardinal fallacy implied in this and all kindred proposals is that they look at the economic problem from the perspective of the subaltern clerk whose intellectual horizon does not extend beyond subordinate tasks. They consider the structure of industrial production and the allocation of capital to the various branches and production aggregates as rigid, and do not take into account the necessity of altering this structure in order to adjust it to changes in conditions. What they have in mind is a world in which no further changes occur and economic history has reached its final stage. They fail to realize that the operations of the corporate officers consist merely in the loyal execution of the tasks entrusted to them by their bosses, the shareholders, and that in performing the orders received they are forced to adjust themselves to the structure of the market prices, ultimately determined by factors other than the various managerial operations. The operations of the managers, their buying and selling, are only a small segment of the totality of market operations. The market of the capitalist society also performs all those operations which allocate the capital goods to the various branches of industry. The entrepreneurs and capitalists establish corporations and other firms, enlarge or reduce their size, dissolve them or merge them with other enterprises; they buy and sell the shares and bonds of already existing and of new corporations; they grant, withdraw, and recover credits; in short they perform all those acts the totality of which is called the capital and money market. It is these financial transactions of promoters and speculators that direct production into those channels in which it satisfies the most urgent wants of the consumers in the best possible way. These transactions constitute the market as such. If one eliminates them, one does not preserve any part of the market. What remains is a fragment that cannot exist alone and cannot function as a market.

The role that the loyal corporation manager plays in the conduct of business is much more modest than the authors of these plans assume. His is only a managerial function, a subsidiary assistance granted to the entrepreneurs and capitalists, which refers only to subordinate tasks. It can never become a substitute for the entrepreneurial function.[5] The speculators, promoters, investors and moneylenders, in determining the structure of the stock and commodity exchanges and of the money market, circumscribe the orbit within which definite minor tasks can be entrusted to the manager's discretion. In attending to these tasks the manager must adjust his procedures to the structure of the market created by factors which go far beyond the managerial functions.

Our problem does not refer to the managerial activities; it concerns the allocation of capital to the various branches of industry. The question is: In which branches should production be increased or restricted, in which branches should the objective of production be altered, what new branches should be inaugurated? With regard to these issues it is vain to cite the honest corporation manager and his well-tried efficiency. Those who confuse entrepreneurship and management close their eyes to the economic problem. In labor disputes the parties are not management and labor, but entrepreneurship (or capital) and the salaried and wage-receiving employees. The capitalist system is not a managerial system; it is an entrepreneurial system. One does not detract from the merits of corporation managers if one establishes the fact that it is not their conduct that determines the allocation of the factors of production to the various lines of industry.

Nobody has ever suggested that the socialist commonwealth could

5. Cf. above, pp. 305–308.

invite the promoters and speculators to continue their speculations and then deliver their profits to the common chest. Those suggesting a quasi-market for the socialist system have never wanted to preserve the stock and commodity exchanges, the trading in futures, and the bankers and moneylenders as quasi-institutions. One cannot *play* speculation and investment. The speculators and investors expose their own wealth, their own destiny. This fact makes them responsible to the consumers, the ultimate bosses of the capitalist economy. If one relieves them of this responsibility, one deprives them of their very character. They are no longer businessmen, but just a group of men to whom the director has handed over his main task, the supreme direction of the conduct of affairs. Then they—and not the nominal director—become the true directors and have to face the same problem the nominal director could not solve: the problem of calculation.

In recognition of the fact that such an idea would be simply nonsensical, the advocates of the quasi-market plan sometimes vaguely recommend another way out. The director should act as a bank lending the available funds to the highest bidder. This again is an abortive idea. All those who can bid for these funds have, as is self-evident in a socialist order of society, no property of their own. In bidding they are not restrained by any financial dangers they themselves run in promising too high a rate of interest for the funds borrowed. They do not in the least alleviate the burden of responsibility incumbent upon the director. The insecurity of the funds lent to them is in no way restricted by the partial guarantee which the borrower's own means provide in credit transactions under capitalism. All the hazards of this insecurity fall only upon society, the exclusive owner of all resources available. If the director were without hesitation to allocate the funds available to those who bid most, he would simply put a premium upon audacity, carelessness, and unreasonable optimism. He would abdicate in favor of the least scrupulous visionaries or scoundrels. He must reserve to himself the decision on how society's funds should be utilized. But then we are back again where we started: the director, in his endeavors to direct production activities, is not aided by the division of intellectual labor which under capitalism provides a practicable method for economic calculation.[6]

The employment of the means of production can be controlled either by private owners or by the social apparatus of coercion and compulsion. In the first case there is a market, there are market prices

6. Cf. Mises, *Socialism,* pp. 137–142; Hayek, *Individualism and Economic Order* (Chicago, 1948), pp. 119–208; T. J. B. Hoff, *Economic Calculation in the Socialist Society* (London, 1949), pp. 129 ff.

for all factors of production, and economic calculation is possible. In the second case all these things are absent. It is vain to comfort oneself with the hope that the organs of the collective economy will be "omnipresent" and "omniscient."[7] We do not deal in praxeology with the acts of the omnipresent and omniscient Deity, but with the actions of men endowed with a human mind only. Such a mind cannot plan without economic calculation.

A socialist system with a market and market prices is as self-contradictory as is the notion of a triangular square. Production is directed either by profit-seeking businessmen or by the decisions of a director to whom supreme and exclusive power is entrusted. There are produced either those things from the sale of which the entrepreneurs expect the highest profits or those things which the director wants to be produced. The question is: Who should be master, the consumers or the director? With whom should the ultimate decision rest whether a concrete supply of factors of production should be employed for the production of the consumers' good *a* or the consumers' good *b?* Such a question does not allow of any evasive answer. It must be answered in a straightforward and unambiguous way.[8]

6. The Differential Equations of Mathematical Economics

In order to appraise adequately the idea that the differential equations of mathematical economics could be utilized for socialist economic calculation, we must remember what these equations really mean.

In devising the imaginary construction of an evenly rotating economy we assume that all the factors of production are employed in such a way that each of them renders the most highly valued services it can possibly render. No further change in the employment of any of these factors could improve the state of want-satisfaction under prevailing conditions. This situation, in which no further changes in the disposition of the factors of production are resorted to, is described by systems of differential equations. However, these equations do not provide any information about the human actions by means of which the hypothetical state of equilibrium has been reached. All they say is this: If, in this state of static equilibrium, *m* units of *a* are employed for the production of *p,* and *n* units of *a* for the production of *q,* no further change in the employment of the available units of *a* could result in an increment in want-satisfaction. (Even if we asume that *a* is perfectly divisible and take the unit of *a* as infinitesimal, it would

7. Cf. H. D. Dickinson, *Economics of Socialism* (Oxford, 1939), p. 191.
8. For an analysis of the scheme of a corporative state see below, pp. 816–820.

be a serious blunder to assert that the marginal utility of *a* is the same in both employments.)

This state of equilibrium is a purely imaginary construction. In a changing world it can never be realized. It differs from today's state as well as from any other realizable state of affairs.

In the market economy it is entrepreneurial action that again and again reshuffles exchange ratios and the allocation of the factors of production. An enterprising man discovers a discrepancy between the prices of the complementary factors of production and the future prices of the products as he anticipates them, and tries to take advantage of this discrepancy for his own profit. The future price which he has in mind is, to be sure, not the hypothetical equilibrium price. No actor has anything to do with equilibrium and equilibrium prices; these notions are foreign to real life and action; they are auxiliary tools of praxeological reasoning for which there is no mental means to conceive the ceaseless restlessness of action other than to contrast it with the notion of perfect quiet. For the theorists' reasoning every change is a step forward on a road which, provided no further new data appear, finally leads to a state of equilibrium. Neither the theorists, nor the capitalists and entrepreneurs, nor the consumers, are in a position to form, on the ground of their familiarity with present conditions, an opinion about the height of such an equilibrium price. There is no need for such an opinion. What impels a man toward change and innovation is not the vision of equilibrium prices, but the anticipation of the height of the prices of a limited number of articles as they will prevail on the market on the date at which he plans to sell. What the entrepreneur, in embarking upon a definite project, has in mind is only the first steps of a transformation which, provided no changes in the data occur other than those induced by his project, would result in establishing the state of equilibrium.

But for a utilization of the equations describing the state of equilibrium, a knowledge of the gradation of the values of consumers' goods in this state of equilibrium is required. This gradation is one of the elements of these equations assumed as known. Yet the director knows only his present valuations, not also his valuations under the hypothetical state of equilibrium. He believes that, with regard to his present valuations, the allocation of the factors of production is unsatisfactory and wants to change it. But he knows nothing about how he himself will value on the day the equilibrium will be reached. These valuations will reflect the conditions resulting from the successive changes in production he himself inaugurates.

We call the present day D_1 and the day the equilibrium will be established D_n. Accordingly we name the following magnitudes corresponding to these two days: the scale of valuation of the goods of the first order V_1 and V_n, the total supply[9] of all original factors of production O_1 and O_n, the total supply of all produced factors of production P_1 and P_n, and summarize $O_1 + P_1$ as M_1 and $O_n + P_n$ as M_n. Finally we call the state of technological knowledge, T_1 and T_n. For the solution of the equations a knowledge of V_n, $O_n + P_n = M_n$, and T_n is required. But what we know today is merely V_1, $O_1 + P_1 = M_1$, and T_1.

It would be impermissible to assume that these magnitudes for D_1 are equal to those for D_n because the state of equilibrium cannot be attained if further changes in the data occur. The absence of further changes in the data which is the condition required for the establishment of equilibrium refers only to such changes as could derange the adjustment of conditions to the operation of those elements which are already operating today. The system cannot attain the state of equilibrium if new elements, penetrating from without, divert it from those movements which tend toward the establishment of equilibrium.[10] But as long as the equilibrium is not yet attained, the system is in a continuous movement which changes the data. The tendency toward the establishment of equilibrium, not interrupted by the emergence of any changes in the data coming from without, is in itself a succession of changes in the data.

P_1 is a set of magnitudes that do not correspond to today's valuations. It is the outcome of actions which were guided by past valuations and faced a state of technological knowledge and of information about available resources of primary factors of production which was different from the present state. One of the reasons why the system is not in equilibrium is precisely the fact that P_1 is not adjusted to present conditions. There are plants, tools, and supplies of other factors of production which would not exist under equilibrium, and other plants, tools, and supplies must be produced in order to establish equilibrium. Equilibrium will emerge only when these disturbing parts of P_1, as far as they are still utilizable, will be worn out and replaced by items which correspond to the state of the other synchronous data, viz., V, O, and T. What acting man needs to know is not the state of affairs under equilibrium, but information about

9. Supply means a total inventory in which the whole supply available is specified in classes and quantities. Each class comprehends only such items as have in any regard (for instance, also in regard to their location) precisely the same importance for want-satisfaction.

10. Of course, we may assume that T_1 is equal to T_n if we are prepared to imply that technological knowledge has reached its final stage.

the most appropriate method of transforming, by successive steps, P_1 into P_n. With regard to this task the equations are useless.

One cannot master these problems by eliminating P and relying only upon O. It is true that the mode of utilizing the original factors of production uniquely determines the quality and quantity of the produced factors of production, the intermediary products. But the information that could be won in this way refers only to the conditions of equilibrium. It does not tell us anything about the methods and procedures to be resorted to for the realization of equilibrium. Today we are confronted with a supply of P_1 which differs from the state of equilibrium. We must take into account real conditions, i.e., P_1, and not the hypothetical conditions of P_n.

This hypothetical future state of equilibrium will appear when all methods of production have been adjusted to the valuations of the actors and to the state of technological knowledge. Then one will work in the most appropriate locations with the most adequate technological methods. Today's economy is different. It operates with other means which do not correspond to the equilibrium state and cannot be taken into account in a system of equations describing this state in mathematical symbols. The knowledge of conditions which will prevail under equilibrium is useless for the director whose task it is to act today under present conditions. What he must learn is how to proceed in the most economical way with the means available today which are the inheritance of an age with different valuations, a different technological knowledge, and different information about problems of location. He must know which step is the next he must make. In this dilemma the equations provide no help.

Let us assume that an isolated country whose economic conditions are those of Central Europe in the middle of the nineteenth century is ruled by a dictator who is perfectly familiar with the American technology of our day. This director knows by and large to what goal he should lead the economy of the country entrusted to his care. Yet even a full knowledge of today's American conditions could not be of use to him in regard to the problem of transforming by successive steps, in the most appropriate and expedient way, the given economic system into the system aimed at.

Even if, for the sake of argument, we assume that a miraculous inspiration has enabled the director without economic calculation to solve all problems concerning the most advantageous arrangement of all production activities and that the precise image of the final goal he must aim at is present to his mind, there remain essential problems which cannot be dealt with without economic calculation. For the director's task is not to begin from the very bottom of civilization and to start economic history from scratch. The elements with the aid of which he must operate are not only natural resources untouched by previous utilization. There are also the capital goods produced in the past and not convertible or not perfectly convertible for new projects. It is in precisely these artifacts, produced under a constellation in which valuations, technological knowledge and many other things were different from what they are today, that our wealth is embodied. Their structure, quality, quantity, and location is of primary importance in the choice of all further economic operations. Some of them may be absolutely useless for any further employment; they must remain "unused capacity." But the greater part of them must be utilized if we do not want to start anew from the extreme poverty and destitution of primitive man and want to survive the period which separates us from the day on which the reconstruction of the apparatus of production according to the new plans will be accomplished. The director cannot merely erect a new construction without bothering about his wards' fate in the waiting period. He must try to take advantage of every piece of the already available capital goods in the best possible way.

Not only the technocrats, but socialists of all shades of opinion, repeat again and again that what makes the achievement of their ambitious plans realizable is the enormous wealth hitherto accumulated. But in the same breath they disregard the fact that this wealth consists to a great extent in capital goods produced in the past and more or less antiquated from the point of view of our present valuations and technological knowledge. As they see it, the only aim of production is to transform the industrial apparatus in such a way as to make life more abundant for later generations. In their eyes contemporaries are simply a lost generation, people whose only purpose it must be to toil and trouble for the benefit of the unborn. However, real men are different. They want not only to create a better world for their grandsons to live in; they themselves also want to enjoy life. They want to utilize in the most efficient way those capital goods which are now available. They aim at a better future, but they want to attain this goal in the most economical way. For the realization of this desire too they cannot do without economic calculation.

It was a serious mistake to believe that the state of equilibrium could be computed, by means of mathematical operations, on the basis of the knowledge of conditions in a nonequilibrium state. It was no less erroneous to believe that such a knowledge of the conditions under a hypothetical state of equilibrium could be of any use for acting man in his search for the best possible solution of the problems with which he is faced in his daily choices and activities. There is therefore no need to stress the point that the fabulous number of equations which one would have to solve each day anew for a practical utilization of the method would make the whole idea absurd even if it were really a reasonable substitute for the market's economic calculation.[11]

11. With regard to this algebraic problem, cf. Pareto, *Manuel d'économie politique* (2d ed. Paris, 1927), pp. 233 f.; and Hayek, *Collectivist Economic Planning* (London, 1935), pp. 207–214.—Therefore the construction of electronic computers does not affect our problem.

Part Six

The Hampered Market Economy

XXVII. THE GOVERNMENT AND THE MARKET

1. The Idea of a Third System

PRIVATE ownership of the means of production (market economy or capitalism) and public ownership of the means of production (socialism or communism or "planning") can be neatly distinguished. Each of these two systems of society's economic organization is open to a precise and unambiguous description and definition. They can never be confounded with one another; they cannot be mixed or combined; no gradual transition leads from one of them to the other; they are mutually incompatible. With regard to the same factors of production there can only exist private control or public control. If in the frame of a system of social cooperation only some means of production are subject to public ownership while the rest are controlled by private individuals, this does not make for a mixed system combining socialism and private ownership. The system remains a market society, provided the socialized sector does not become entirely separated from the non-socialized sector and lead a strictly autarkic existence. (In this latter case there are two systems independently coexisting side by side—a capitalist and a socialist.) Publicly owned enterprises operating within a system in which there are privately owned enterprises and a market, and socialized countries, exchanging goods and services with nonsocialist countries, are integrated into a system of market economy. They are subject to the law of the market and have the opportunity of resorting to economic calculation.[1]

If one considers the idea of placing by the side of these two systems or between them a third system of human cooperation under the division of labor, one can always start only from the notion of the market economy, never from that of socialism. The notion of socialism with its rigid monism and centralism that vests the powers to choose and to act in *one* will exclusively does not allow of any compromise or concession; this construction is not amenable to any adjustment or alteration. But it is different with the scheme of the market economy. Here the dualism of the market and the government's power of coercion and compulsion suggests various ideas. Is it really peremptory

1. See above, pp. 258–259.

or expedient, people ask, that the government keep itself out of the market? Should it not be a task of government to interfere and to correct the operation of the market? Is it necessary to put up with the alternative of capitalism *or* socialism? Are there not perhaps still other realizable systems of social organization which are neither communism nor pure and unhampered market economy?

Thus people have contrived a variety of third solutions, of systems which, it is claimed, are as far from socialism as they are from capitalism. Their authors allege that these systems are nonsocialist because they aim to preserve private ownership of the means of production and that they are not capitalistic because they eliminate the "deficiencies" of the market economy. For a scientific treatment of the problems involved which by necessity is neutral with regard to all value judgments and therefore does not condemn any features of capitalism as faulty, detrimental, or unjust, this emotional recommendation of *interventionism* is of no avail. The task of economics is to analyze and to search for truth. It is not called upon to praise or to disapprove from any standard of preconceived postulates and prejudices. With regard to interventionism it has only one question to ask and to answer: How does it work?

2. The Intervention

There are two patterns for the realization of socialism.

The first pattern (we may call it the Lenin or the Russian pattern) is purely bureaucratic. All plants, shops, and farms are formally nationalized (*verstaatlicht*); they are departments of the government operated by civil servants. Every unit of the apparatus of production stands in the same relation to the superior central organization as does a local post office to the office of the postmaster general.

The second pattern (we may call it the Hindenburg or German pattern) nominally and seemingly preserves private ownership of the means of production and keeps the appearance of ordinary markets, prices, wages, and interest rates. There are, however, no longer entrepreneurs, but only shop managers (*Betriebsführer* in the terminology of the Nazi legislation). These shop managers are seemingly instrumental in the conduct of the enterprises entrusted to them; they buy and sell, hire and discharge workers and remunerate their services, contract debts and pay interest and amortization. But in all their activities they are bound to obey unconditionally the orders issued by the government's supreme office of production management. This office (the *Reichswirtschaftsministerium* in Nazi Germany) tells the shop managers what and how to produce, at what prices and from whom to buy, at what prices and to whom to sell. It assigns every worker to his job and fixes his wages. It decrees to whom and on what terms the capitalists must entrust their funds. Market exchange is merely a sham. All the wages, prices, and interest rates are fixed by the government; they are wages, prices, and interest rates in appearance only; in fact they are merely quantitative terms in the government's orders determining each citizen's job, income, consumption, and standard of living. The government directs all production activities. The shop managers are subject to the government, not to the consumers' demand and the market's price structure. This is socialism under the outward guise of the terminology of capitalism. Some labels of the capitalistic market economy are retained, but they signify something entirely different from what they mean in the market economy.

It is necessary to point out this fact in order to prevent a confusion of socialism and interventionism. The system of interventionism or of the hampered market economy differs from the German pattern of socialism by the very fact that it is still a market economy. The authority interferes with the operation of the market economy, but does not want to eliminate the market altogether. It wants production and consumption to develop along lines different from those prescribed by an unhampered market, and it wants to achieve its aim by injecting into the working of the market orders, commands, and prohibitions for whose enforcement the police power and its apparatus of violent compulsion and coercion stand ready. But these are *isolated* acts of intervention. It is not the aim of the government to combine them into an integrated system which determines all prices, wages and interest rates and thus places full control of production and consumption into the hands of the authorities.

The system of the hampered market economy or interventionism aims at preserving the dualism of the distinct spheres of government activities on the one hand and economic freedom under the market system on the other hand. What characterizes it as such is the fact that the government does not limit its activities to the preservation of private ownership of the means of production and its protection against violent or fraudulent encroachments. The government interferes with the operation of business by means of orders and prohibitions.

The intervention is a decree issued directly or indirectly, by the authority in charge of society's administrative apparatus of coercion and compulsion which forces the entrepreneurs and capitalists to employ some of the factors of production in a way different from what they would have resorted to if they were only obeying the dictates of the market. Such a decree can be either an order to do something or an order not to do something. It is not required that the decree be issued directly by the established and generally recognized authority itself. It may happen that some other agencies arrogate to themselves the power to issue such orders or prohibitions and to enforce them by an apparatus of violent coercion and oppression of their own. If the recognized government tolerates such procedures or even supports them by the employment of its governmental police apparatus, matters stand as if the government itself had acted. If the government is opposed to other agencies' violent action, but does not succeed in suppressing it by means of its own armed forces, although it would like to suppress it, anarchy results.

It is important to remember that government interference always means either violent action or the threat of such action. The funds that a government spends for whatever purposes are levied by taxation. And taxes are paid because the taxpayers are afraid of offering resistance to the tax gatherers. They know that any disobedience or resistance is hopeless. As long as this is the state of affairs, the government is able to collect the money that it wants to spend. Government is in the last resort the employment of armed men, of policemen, gendarmes, soldiers, prison guards, and hangmen. The essential feature of government is the enforcement of its decrees by beating, killing, and imprisoning. Those who are asking for more government interference are asking ultimately for more compulsion and less freedom.

To draw attention to this fact does not imply any reflection upon government activities. In stark reality, peaceful social cooperation is impossible if no provision is made for violent prevention and suppression of antisocial action on the part of refractory individuals and groups of individuals. One must take exception to the often-repeated phrase that government is an evil, although a necessary and indispensable evil. What is required for the attainment of an end is a means, the cost to be expended for its successful realization. It is an arbitrary value judgment to describe it as an evil in the moral connotation of the term. However, in face of the modern tendencies toward a deification of government and state, it is good to remind ourselves that the old Romans were more realistic in symbolizing the state by a bundle of rods with an ax in the middle than are our contemporaries in ascribing to the state all the attributes of God.

3. The Delimitation of Governmental Functions

Various schools of thought parading under the pompous names of philosophy of law and political science indulge in futile and empty brooding over the delimitation of the functions of government. Starting from purely arbitrary assumptions concerning allegedly eternal and absolute values and perennial justice, they arrogate to themselves the office of the supreme judge of earthly affairs. They misconstrue their own arbitrary value judgments derived from intuition as the voice of the Almighty or of the nature of things.

There is, however, no such thing as a perennial standard of what is just and what is unjust. Nature is alien to the idea of right and wrong. "Thou shalt not kill" is certainly not part of natural law. The characteristic feature of natural conditions is that one animal is intent upon killing other animals and that many species cannot preserve their own life except by killing others. The notion of right and wrong is a human device, a utilitarian precept designed to make social cooperation under the division of labor possible. All moral rules and human laws are means for the realization of definite ends. There is no method available for the appreciation of their goodness or badness other than to scrutinize their usefulness for the attainment of the ends chosen and aimed at.

From the notion of natural law some people deduce the justice of the institution of private property in the means of production. Other people resort to natural law for the justification of the abolition of private property in the means of production. As the idea of natural law is quite arbitrary, such discussions are not open to settlement.

State and government are not ends, but means. Inflicting evil upon other people is a source of direct pleasure only to sadists. Established authorities resort to coercion and compulsion in order to safeguard the smooth operation of a definite system of social organization. The sphere in which coercion and compulsion is applied and the content of the laws which are to be enforced by the police apparatus are conditioned by the social order adopted. As state and government are designed to make this social system operate safely, the delimitation of governmental functions must be adjusted to its requirements. The only standard for the appreciation of the laws and the methods for their enforcement is whether or not they are efficient in safeguarding the social order which it is desired to preserve.

The notion of justice makes sense only when referring to a definite system of norms which in itself is assumed to be uncontested and safe against any criticism. Many peoples have clung to the doctrine that what is right and what is wrong is established from the dawn of the remotest ages and for eternity. The task of legislators and courts was not to make laws, but to find out what is right by virtue of the unchanging idea of justice. This doctrine, which resulted in an adamant conservatism and a petrification of old customs and institutions, was challenged by the doctrine of natural right. To the positive laws of the country the notion of a "higher" law, the law of nature, was opposed. From the arbitrary standard of natural law the valid statutes and institutions were called just or unjust. To the good legislator was assigned the task of making the positive laws agree with the natural law.

The fundamental errors involved in these two doctrines have long since been unmasked. For those not deluded by them it is obvious that the appeal to justice in a debate concerning the drafting of new laws is an instance of circular reasoning. *De lege ferenda* there is no such a thing as justice. The notion of justice can logically only be resorted to *de lege lata*. It makes sense only when approving or disapproving concrete conduct from the point of view of the valid laws of the country. In considering changes in the nation's legal system, in rewriting or repealing existing laws and writing new laws, the issue is not justice, but social expediency and social welfare. There is no such thing as an absolute notion of justice not referring to a definite system of social organization. It is not justice that determines the decision in favor of a definite social system. It is, on the contrary, the social system which determines what should be deemed right and what wrong. There is neither right nor wrong outside the social nexus. For the hypothetical isolated and self-sufficient individual the notions of just and unjust are empty. Such an individual can merely distinguish between what is more expedient and what is less expedient for himself. The idea of justice refers always to social cooperation.

It is nonsensical to justify or to reject interventionism from the point of view of a fictitious and arbitrary idea of absolute justice. It is vain to ponder over the just delimitation of the tasks of government from any preconceived standard of perennial values. It is no less impermissible to deduce the proper tasks of government from the very notions of government, state, law and justice. It was precisely this that was absurd in the speculations of medieval scholasticism, of Fichte, Schelling, and Hegel, and the German *Bergriffsjurisprudenz*. Concepts are tools of reasoning. They must never be considered as regulative principles dictating modes of conduct.

It is a display of supererogatory mental gymnastics to emphasize that the notions of state and sovereignty logically imply absolute supremacy and thus preclude the idea of any limitations on the state's activities. Nobody questions the fact that a state has the power to establish totalitarianism within the territory in which it is sovereign. The problem is whether or not such a mode of government is expedient from the point of view of the preservation and functioning of social cooperation. With regard to this problem no sophisticated exegesis of concepts and notions can be of any use. It must be decided by praxeology, not by a spurious metaphysics of state and right.

The philosophy of law and political science are at a loss to discover any reason why government should not control prices and not punish those defying the price ceilings decreed, in the same way as it punishes murderers and thieves. As they see it, the institution of private property is merely a revocable favor graciously granted by the almighty sovereign to the wretched individuals. There cannot be any wrong in repealing totally or partially the laws that granted this favor; no reasonable objection can be raised against expropriation and confiscation. The legislator is free to substitute any social system for that of the private ownership of the means of production, just as he is free to substitute another national anthem for that adopted in the past. The formula *car tel est notre bon plaisir* is the only maxim of the sovereign lawgiver's conduct.

As against all this formalism and legal dogmatism, there is need to emphasize again that the only purpose of the laws and the social apparatus of coercion and compulsion is to safeguard the smooth functioning of social cooperation. It is obvious that the government has the power to decree maximum prices and to imprison or to execute those selling or buying at a higher price. But the question is whether such a policy can or cannot attain the ends which the government wants to attain by resorting to it. This is a purely praxeological and economic problem. Neither the philosophy of law nor political science can contribute anything to its solution.

The problem of interventionism is not a problem of the correct delimitation of the "natural," "just," and "proper" tasks of state and government. The issue is: How does a system of interventionism work? Can it realize those ends which people, in resorting to it, want to attain?

The confusion and lack of judgment displayed in dealing with the problems of interventionism are amazing indeed. There are, for instance, people who argue thus: It is obvious that traffic regulations on the public roads are necessary. Nobody objects to the government's interference with the car driver's conduct. The advocates of laissez faire contradict themselves in fighting government interference with market prices and yet not advocating the abolition of government traffic regulation.

The fallacy of this argument is manifest. The regulation of traffic on a road is one of the tasks incumbent upon the agency that operates the road. If this agency is the government or the municipality, it is bound to attend to this task. It is the task of a railroad's management to fix the timetable of the trains and it is the task of a hotel's managemen to decide whether or not there should be music in the dining room. If the government operates a railroad or a hotel, it is the government's task to regulate these things. With a state opera the government decides which operas should be produced and which should not; it would be a non sequitur, however, to deduce from this fact that it is also a task of the government to decide these things for a nongovernmental opera.

The interventionist doctrinaires repeat again and again that they do not plan the abolition of private ownership of the means of production, of entrepreneurial activities, and of market exchange. Also the supporters of the most recent variety of interventionism, the German "soziale Marktwirtschaft," stress that they consider the market economy to be the best possible and most desirable system of society's economic organization, and that they are opposed to the government omnipotence of socialism. But, of course, all these advocates of a middle-of-the-road policy emphasize with the same vigor that they reject Manchesterism and laissez-faire liberalism. It is necessary, they say, that the state interfere with the market phenomena whenever and wherever the "free play of the economic forces" results in conditions that appear as "socially" undesirable. In making this assertion they take it for granted that it is the government that is called upon to determine in every single case whether or not a definite economic fact is to be considered as reprehensible from the "social" point of view and, consequently whether or not the state of the market requires a special act of government interference.

All these champions of interventionism fail to realize that their program thus implies the establishment of full government supremacy in all economic matters and ultimately brings about a state of affairs that does not differ from what is called the German or the Hindenburg pattern of socialism. If it is in the jurisdiction of the government to decide whether or not definite conditions of the economy justify its intervention, no sphere of operation is left to the market. Then it is no longer the consumers who ultimately determine what should be produced, in what quantity, of what quality, by whom, where, and how—but it is the government. For as soon as the outcome brought about by the operation of the unhampered market differs from what the authorities consider "socially" desirable, the government interferes. That means the market is free as long as it does precisely what the government wants it to do. It is "free" to do what the authorities consider to be the "right" things, but not to do what they consider the "wrong" things; the decision concerning what is right and what is wrong rests with the government. Thus the doctrine and the practice of interventionism ultimately tend to abandon what originally distinguished them from outright socialism and to adopt entirely the principles of totalitarian all-round planning.

4. Righteousness as the Ultimate Standard of the Individual's Actions

According to a widespread opinion it is possible, even in the absence of government interference with business, to divert the operation of the market economy from those lines along which it would develop if left to exclusive control by the profit motive. Advocates of a social reform to be accomplished by compliance with the principles of Christianity or with the demands of "true" morality maintain that conscience should also guide well-intentioned people in their dealings on the market. If all people were prepared not only to concern themselves about profit, but no less about their religious and moral obligations, no government compulsion and coercion would be required in order to put things right. What is needed is not a reform of government and the laws of the country, but the moral purification of man, a return to the Lord's commandments and to the precepts of the moral code, a turning away from the vices of greed and selfishness. Then it will be easy to reconcile private ownership of the means of production with justice, righteousness, and fairness. The disastrous effects of capitalism will be eliminated without prejudice to the individual's freedom and initiative. People will dethrone the Moloch capitalism without enthroning the Moloch state.

The arbitrary value judgments which are at the bottom of these opinions need not concern us here. What these critics blame capitalism for is irrelevant; their errors and fallacies are beside the point. What does matter is the idea of erecting a social system on the twofold basis of private property and of moral principles restricting the utilization of private property. The system recommended, say its advocates, will be neither socialism nor capitalism nor interventionism. Not socialism, because it will preserve private ownership of the means of production; not capitalism, because conscience will be supreme and not the urge for profit; not interventionism, because there will be no need for government interference with the market.

In the market economy the individual is free to act within the orbit of private property and the market. His choices are final. For his fellow men his actions are data which they must take into account in their own acting. The coordination of the autonomous actions of all individuals is accomplished by the operation of the market. Society does not tell a man what to do and what not to do. There is no need to enforce cooperation by special orders or prohibitions. Noncooperation penalizes itself. Adjustment to the requirements of society's productive effort and the pursuit of the individual's own concerns are not in conflict. Consequently no agency is required to settle such conflicts. The system can work and accomplish its tasks without the interference of an authority issuing special orders and prohibitions and punishing those who do not comply.

Beyond the sphere of private property and the market lies the sphere of compulsion and coercion; here are the dams which organized society has built for the protection of private property and the market against violence, malice, and fraud. This is the realm of constraint as distinguished from the realm of freedom. Here are rules discriminating between what is legal and what is illegal, what is permitted and what is prohibited. And here is a grim machine of arms, prisons, and gallows and the men operating it, ready to crush those who dare to disobey.

Now, the reformers with whose plans we are concerned suggest that along with the norms designed for the protection and preservation of private property further ethical rules should be ordained. They want to realize in production and consumption things other than those realized under the social order in which the individuals are not checked by any obligation other than that of not infringing upon the persons of their fellow men and upon the right of private property. They want to ban those motives that direct the individual's action in the market economy (they call them selfishness, acquisitiveness, profit-seeking) and to replace them with other impulses (they call them conscientiousness, righteousness, altruism, fear of God, charity). They are convinced that such a moral reform would in itself be sufficient to safeguard a mode of operation of the economic system, more satisfactory from their point of view than that of unhampered capitalism, without any of those special governmental measures which interventionism and socialism require.

The supporters of these doctrines fail to recognize the role which those springs of action they condemn as vicious play in the operation of the market economy. The only reason why the market economy can operate without government orders telling everybody precisely what he should do and how he should do it is that it does not ask anybody to deviate from those lines of conduct which best serve his own interests. What integrates the individual's actions into the whole of the social system of production is the pursuit of his own purposes.

In indulging in his "acquisitiveness" each actor contributes his share to the best possible arrangement of production activities. Thus, within the sphere of private property and the laws protecting it against encroachments on the part of violent or fraudulent action, there is no antagonism between the interests of the individual and those of society.

The market economy becomes a chaotic muddle if this predominance of private property which the reformers disparage as selfishness is eliminated. In urging people to listen to the voice of their conscience and to substitute considerations of public welfare for those of private profit, one does not create a working and satisfactory social order. It is not enough to tell a man *not* to buy on the cheapest market and *not* to sell on the dearest market. It is not enough to tell him *not* to strive after profit and *not* to avoid losses. One must establish unambiguous rules for the guidance of conduct in each concrete situation.

Says the reformer: The entrepreneur is rugged and selfish when, taking advantage of his own superiority, he underbids the prices asked by a less efficient competitor and thus forces the man to go out of business. But how should the "altruistic" entrepreneur proceed? Should he under no circumstances sell at a price lower than any competitor? Or are there certain conditions which justify underbidding the competitor's prices?

Says the reformer on the other hand: The entrepreneur is rugged and selfish when, taking advantage of the state of the market, he asks a price so high that poor people are excluded from purchasing the merchandise. But what should the "good" entrepreneur do? Should he give away the merchandise free of charge? If he charges any price, however low, there will always be people who cannot buy at all or not so much as they would buy if the price were still lower. What group of those eager to buy is the entrepreneur free to exclude from getting the merchandise?

There is no need to deal at this point of our investigation with the consequences resulting from any deviation from the height of prices as determined on an unhampered market. If the seller avoids underbidding his less efficient competitor, a part at least of his supply remains unsold. If the seller offers the merchandise at a price lower than that determined on an unhampered market, the supply available is insufficient to enable all those ready to expend this lower price to get what they are asking for. We will analyze later these as well as other consequences of any deviation from the market prices.[2] What we must

2. See below, pp. 758–767.

recognize even at this point is that one cannot content oneself simply by telling the entrepreneur that he should *not* let himself be guided by the state of the market. It is imperative to tell him how far he must go in asking and paying prices. If it is no longer profit-seeking that directs the entrepreneurs' actions and determines what they produce and in what quantities, if the entrepreneurs are no longer bound by the instrumentality of the profit motive to serve the consumers to the best of their abilities, it is necessary to give them definite instructions. One cannot avoid guiding their conduct by specified orders and prohibitions, precisely such decrees as are the mark of government interference with business. Any attempt to render such interference superfluous by attributing primacy to the voice of conscience, to charity and brotherly love, is vain.

The advocates of a Christian social reform pretend that their ideal of greed and profit-seeking tamed and restrained by conscientiousness and compliance with the moral law worked rather well in the past. All the evils of our day are caused by defection from the precepts of the church. If people had not defied the commandments and had not coveted unjust profit, mankind would still enjoy the bliss experienced in the Middle Ages when at least the elite lived up to the principles of the Gospels. What is needed is to bring back those good old days and then to see that no new apostasy deprives men of their beneficent effects.

There is no need to enter into an analysis of the social and economic conditions of the thirteenth century which these reformers praise as the greatest of all periods of history. We are concerned merely with the notion of *just* prices and wage rates which was essential in the social teachings of the doctors of the church and which the reformers want to raise to the position of the ultimate standard of economic conduct.

It is obvious that with theorists this notion of just prices and wage rates always refers and always referred to a definite social order which they considered the best possible order. They recommend the adoption of their ideal scheme and its preservation forever. No further changes are to be tolerated. Any alteration of the best possible state of social affairs can only mean deterioration. The world view of these philosophers does not take into account man's ceaseless striving for improvement of the material conditions of well-being. Historical change and a rise in the general standard of living are notions foreign to them. They call "just" that mode of conduct that is compatible with the undisturbed preservation of their utopia, and everything else unjust.

However, the notion of just prices and wage rates as present to the mind of people other than philosophers is very different. When the nonphilosopher calls a price just, what he means is that the preservation of this price improves or at least does not impair his own revenues and station in society. He calls unjust any price that jeopardizes his own wealth and station. It is "just" that the prices of those goods and services which he sells rise more and more and that the prices of those goods and services he buys drop more and more. To the farmer no price of wheat, however high, appears unjust. To the wage earner no wage rates, however high, appear unfair. But the farmer is quick to denounce every drop in the price of wheat as a violation of divine and human laws, and the wage earners rise in rebellion when their wages drop. Yet the market society has no means of adjusting production to changing conditions other than the operation of the market. By means of price changes it forces people to restrict the production of articles less urgently asked for and to expand the production of those articles for which consumers' demand is more urgent. The absurdity of all endeavors to stabilize prices consists precisely in the fact that stabilization would prevent any further improvement and result in rigidity and stagnation. The flexibility of commodity prices and wage rates is the vehicle of adjustment, improvement, and progress. Those who condemn changes in prices and wage rates as unjust, and who ask for the preservation of what they call just, are in fact combating endeavors to make economic conditions more satisfactory.

It is not unjust that there has long prevailed a tendency toward such a determination of the prices of agricultural products that the greater part of the population abandoned farming and moved toward the processing industries. But for this tendency, 90 per cent or more of the population would still be occupied in agriculture and the processing industries would have been stunted in their growth. All strata of the population, including the farmers, would be worse off. If the scholastic doctrine of the just price had been put into practice, the thirteenth century's economic conditions would still prevail. Population figures would be much smaller than they are today and the standard of living much lower.

Both varieties of the just price doctrine, the philosophical and the popular, agree in their condemnation of the prices and wage rates as determined on the unhampered market. But this negativism does not in itself provide any answer to the question of what height the just prices and wage rates should attain. If righteousness is to be elevated to the position of the ultimate standard of economic action, one must unambiguously tell every actor what he should do, what prices he should ask, and what prices he should pay in each concrete case, and one must force—by recourse to an apparatus of violent compulsion and coercion—all those venturing disobedience to comply with these orders. One must establish a supreme authority issuing norms and regulating conduct in every respect, altering these norms if need be, interpreting them authentically, and enforcing them. Thus the substitution of social justice and righteousness for selfish profit-seeking requires for its realization precisely those policies of government interference with business which the advocates of the moral purification of mankind want to make superfluous. No deviation from the unhampered market economy is thinkable without authoritarian regimentation. Whether the authority in which these powers are vested is called lay government or theocratical priesthood makes no difference.

The reformers, in exhorting people to turn away from selfishness, address themselves to capitalists and entrepreneurs, and sometimes, although only timidly, to wage earners as well. However, the market economy is a system of consumers' supremacy. The sermonizers should appeal to consumers, not to producers. They should persuade the consumers to renounce preferring better and cheaper merchandise to poorer and dearer merchandise lest they hurt the less efficient producer. They should persuade them to restrict their own purchases in order to provide poorer people with the opportunity to buy more. If one wants the consumers to act in this way, one must tell them plainly what to buy, in what quantity, from whom, and at what prices; and one must provide for enforcing such orders by coercion and compulsion. But then one has adopted exactly that system of authoritarian control which moral reform wants to make unnecessary.

Whatever freedom individuals can enjoy within the framework of social cooperation is conditional upon the concord of private gain and public weal. Within the orbit in which the individual, in pursuing his own well-being, advances also—or at least does not impair—the well-being of his fellow men, people going their own ways jeopardize neither the preservation of society nor the concerns of other people. A realm of freedom and individual initiative emerges, a realm in which man is allowed to choose and to act of his own accord. This sphere of freedom, by the socialists and interventionists contemptuously dubbed "economic freedom," is alone what makes any of those conditions possible that are commonly called freedoms within a system of social cooperation under the division of labor. It is the market economy or capitalism with its political corollary (the Marxians would have to say: with its "superstructure"), representative government.

Those who contend that there is a conflict between the acquisitiveness of various individuals or between the acquisitiveness of individuals on the one hand and the commonweal on the other, cannot avoid advocating the suppression of the individuals' right to choose and to act. They must substitute the supremacy of a central board of production management for the discretion of the citizens. In their scheme of the good society there is no room left for private initiative. The authority issues orders and everybody is forced to obey.

5. The Meaning of Laissez Faire

In eighteenth-century France the saying *laissez faire, laissez passer* was the formula into which some of the champions of the cause of liberty compressed their program. Their aim was the establishment of the unhampered market society. In order to attain this end they advocated the abolition of all laws preventing more industrious and more efficient people from outdoing less industrious and less efficient competitors and restricting the mobility of commodities and of men. It was this that the famous maxim was designed to express.

In our age of passionate longing for government omnipotence the formula laissez faire is in disrepute. Public opinion now considers it a manifestation both of moral depravity and of the utmost ignorance.

As the interventionist sees things, the alternative is "automatic forces" or "conscious planning."[3] It is obvious, he implies, that to rely upon automatic processes is sheer stupidity. No reasonable man can seriously recommend doing nothing and letting things go as they do without interference on the part of purposive action. A plan, by the very fact that it is a display of conscious action, is incomparably superior to the absence of any planning. Laissez faire is said to mean: Let the evils last, do not try to improve the lot of mankind by reasonable action.

This is utterly fallacious talk. The argument advanced for planning is entirely derived from an impermissible interpretation of a metaphor. It has no foundation other than the connotations implied in the term "automatic" which it is customary to apply in a metaphorical sense for the description of the market process.[4] Automatic, says the *Concise Oxford Dictionary,*[5] means "unconscious, unintelligent, merely mechanical." Automatic, says *Webster's Collegiate Dictionary,*[6] means "not subject to the control of the will, . . . performed without active thought and without conscious intention or direction." What a triumph for the champion of planning to play this trump card!

3. Cf. A. H. Hansen, "Social Planning for Tomorrow," in *The United States after the War* (Cornell University Lectures, Ithaca, 1945), pp. 32-33.
4. See above, pp. 315–316.
5. (3d ed. Oxford, 1934), p. 74.
6. (5th ed. Springfield, 1946), p. 73.

The truth is that the alternative is not between a dead mechanism or a rigid automatism on one hand and conscious planning on the other hand. The alternative is not plan or no plan. The question is whose planning? Should each member of society plan for himself, or should a benevolent government alone plan for them all? The issue is not *automatism versus conscious action;* it is *autonomous action of each individual versus the exclusive action of the government.* It is *freedom versus government omnipotence.*

Laissez faire does not mean: Let soulless mechanical forces operate. It means: Let each individual choose how he wants to cooperate in the social division of labor; let the consumers determine what the entrepreneurs should produce. Planning means: Let the government alone choose and enforce its rulings by the apparatus of coercion and compulsion.

Under laissez faire, says the planner, it is not those goods which people "really" need that are produced, but those goods from the sale of which the highest returns are expected. It is the objective of planning to direct production toward the satisfaction of the "true" needs. But who is to decide what the "true" needs are?

Thus, for instance, Professor Harold Laski, the former chairman of the British Labor Party, would determine as the objective of the planned direction of investment "that the use of the investor's savings will be in housing rather than in cinemas."[7] It is beside the point whether or not one agrees with the professor's view that better houses are more important than moving pictures. It is a fact that the consumers, in spending part of their money for admission to the movies, have made another choice. If the masses of Great Britain, the same people whose votes swept the Labor Party into power, were to stop patronizing the moving pictures and to spend more for comfortable homes and apartments, profit-seeking business would be forced to invest more in building homes and apartment houses and less in the production of expensive pictures. It was Mr. Laski's desire to defy the wishes of the consumers and to substitute his own will for that of the consumers. He wanted to do away with the democracy of the market and to establish the absolute rule of the production tsar. Perhaps he believed that he was right from a higher point of view, and that as a superman he was called upon to impose his own valuations on the masses of inferior men. But then he ought to have been frank enough to say so plainly.

All this passionate praise of the supereminence of government action

7. Cf. Laski's broadcast, "Revolution by Consent," reprinted in *Talks,* X, no. 10 (October, 1945), 7.

is but a poor disguise for the individual interventionist's *self-deification*. The great god State is a great god only because it is expected to do exclusively what the individual advocate of interventionism wants to see achieved. Only that plan is genuine which the individual planner fully approves. All other plans are simply counterfeit. In saying "plan" what the author of a book on the benefits of planning has in mind is, of course, his own plan alone. He does not take into account the possibility that the plan which the government puts into practice may differ from his own plan. The various planners agree only with regard to their rejection of laissez faire, i.e., the individuals' discretion to choose and to act. They entirely disagree with regard to the choice of the unique plan to be adopted. To every exposure of the manifest and incontestable defects of interventionist policies the champions of interventionism react in the same way. These faults, they say, were the results of spurious interventionism; what we are advocating is good interventionism, not bad interventionism. And, of course, good interventionism is the professor's own brand.

Laissez faire means: Let the common man choose and act; do not force him to yield to a dictator.

6. Direct Government Interference with Consumption

In investigating the economic problems of interventionism we do not have to deal with those actions of the government whose aim it is to influence immediately the consumer's choice of consumers' goods. Every act of government interference with business must indirectly affect consumption. As the government's interference alters the market data, it must also alter the valuations and the conduct of the consumers. But if the aim of the government is merely to force the consumers directly to consume goods other than what they would have consumed in the absence of the government's decree, no special problems emerge to be scrutinized by economics. It is beyond doubt that a strong and ruthless police apparatus has the power to enforce such decrees.

In dealing with the choices of the consumers we do not ask what motives induced a man to buy *a* and not to buy *b*. We merely investigate what effects on the determination of market prices and thereby on production were brought about by the concrete conduct of the consumers. These effects do not depend on the considerations which led individuals to buy *a* and not to buy *b;* they depend only on the real acts of buying and abstention from buying. It is immaterial for the determination of the prices of gas masks whether people buy them of their own accord or because the government forces everybody to have a gas mask. What alone counts is the size of the demand.

Governments which are eager to keep up the outward appearance of freedom even when curtailing freedom disguise their direct interference with consumption under the cloak of interference with business. The aim of American prohibition was to prevent the individual residents of the country from drinking alcoholic beverages. But the law hypocritically did not make drinking as such illegal and did not penalize it. It merely prohibited the manufacture, the sale and the transportation of intoxicating liquors, the business transactions which precede the act of drinking. The idea was that people indulge in the vice of drinking only because unscrupulous businessmen prevail upon them. It was, however, manifest that the objective of prohibition was to encroach upon the individuals' freedom to spend their dollars and to enjoy their lives according to their own fashion. The restrictions imposed upon business were only subservient to this ultimate end.

The problems involved in direct government interference with consumption are not catallactic problems. They go far beyond the scope of catallactics and concern the fundamental issues of human life and social organization. If it is true that government derives its authority from God and is entrusted by Providence to act as the guardian of the ignorant and stupid populace, then it is certainly its task to regiment every aspect of the subject's conduct. The God-sent ruler knows better what is good for his wards than they do themselves. It is his duty to guard them against the harm they would inflict upon themselves if left alone.

Self-styled "realistic" people fail to recognize the immense importance of the principles implied. They contend that they do not want to deal with the matter from what, they say, is a philosophic and academic point of view. Their approach is, they argue, exclusively guided by practical considerations. It is a fact, they say, that some people harm themselves and their innocent families by consuming narcotic drugs. Only doctrinaires could be so dogmatic as to object to the government's regulation of the drug traffic. Its beneficent effects cannot be contested.

However, the case is not so simple as that. Opium and morphine are certainly dangerous, habit-forming drugs. But once the principle is admitted that it is the duty of government to protect the individual against his own foolishness, no serious objections can be advanced against further encroachments. A good case could be made out in favor of the prohibition of alcohol and nicotine. And why limit the government's benevolent providence to the protection of the individual's body only? Is not the harm a man can inflict on his mind and soul even more disastrous than any bodily evils? Why not prevent him from reading bad books and seeing bad plays, from looking at bad paintings and statues and from hearing bad music? The mischief done by bad ideologies, surely, is much more pernicious, both for the individual and for the whole society, than that done by narcotic drugs.

These fears are not merely imaginary specters terrifying secluded doctrinaires. It is a fact that no paternal government, whether ancient or modern, ever shrank from regimenting its subjects' minds, beliefs, and opinions. If one abolishes man's freedom to determine his own consumption, one takes all freedoms away. The naïve advocates of government interference with consumption delude themselves when they neglect what they disdainfully call the philosophical aspect of the problem. They unwittingly support the case of censorship, inquisition, religious intolerance, and the persecution of dissenters.

In dealing with the catallactics of interventionism we do not discuss these political consequences of direct government interference with the citizens' consumption. We are exclusively concerned with those acts of interference which aim at forcing the entrepreneurs and capitalists to employ the factors of production in a way different from what they would have done if they merely obeyed the dictates of the market. In doing this, we do not raise the question of whether such interference is good or bad from any preconceived point of view. We merely ask whether or not it can attain those ends which those advocating and resorting to it are trying to attain.

Corruption

An analysis of interventionism would be incomplete if it were not to refer to the phenomenon of corruption.

There are hardly any acts of government interference with the market process that, seen from the point of view of the citizens concerned, would not have to be qualified either as confiscations or as gifts. As a rule, one individual or a group of individuals is enriched at the expense of other individuals or groups of individuals. But in many cases, the harm done to some people does not correspond to any advantage for other people.

There is no such thing as a just and fair method of exercising the tremendous power that interventionism puts into the hands of the legislature and the executive. The advocates of interventionism pretend to substitute for the—as they assert, "socially" detrimental—effects of private property and vested interests the unlimited discretion of the perfectly wise and disinterested legislator and his conscientious and indefatigable servants, the bureaucrats. In their eyes the common man is a helpless infant, badly in need of a paternal guardian to protect him against the sly tricks of a band of rogues. They reject all traditional notions of law and legality in the name of a "higher and nobler" idea of justice. Whatever they themselves do is always right because it hurts those who selfishly want to retain for themselves what, from the point of view of this higher concept of justice, ought to belong to others.

The notions of selfishness and unselfishness as employed in such reasoning are self-contradictory and vain. As has been pointed out, every action aims at the attainment of a state of affairs that suits the actor better than the state that would prevail in the absence of this action. In this sense every action is to be qualified as selfish. The man who gives alms to hungry children does it, either because he values his own satisfaction expected from this gift higher than any other satisfaction he could buy by spending this amount of money, or because he hopes to be rewarded in the beyond. The politician is, in this sense, always selfish no matter whether he supports a popular program in order to get an office or whether he firmly clings to his own—unpopular—convictions and thus deprives himself of the benefits he could reap by betraying them.

In the terminology of anticapitalism the words *selfish* and *unselfish* are used to classify people from the point of view of a doctrine that considers equality of wealth and income as the only natural and fair state of social conditions, that brands those who own or earn more than the average as exploiters, and that condemns entrepreneurial activities as detrimental to the common weal. To be in business, to depend directly on the approval or disapproval of one's actions by the consumers, to woo the patronage of the buyers, and to earn profit if one succeeds in satisfying them better than one's competitors do is, from the point of view of officialdom's ideology, selfish and shameful. Only those on the government's payroll are rated as unselfish and noble.

Unfortunately the office-holders and their staffs are not angelic. They learn very soon that their decisions mean for the businessmen either considerable losses or—sometimes—considerable gains. Certainly there are also bureaucrats who do not take bribes; but there are others who are anxious to take advantage of any "safe" opportunity of "sharing" with those whom their decisions favor.

In many fields of the administration of interventionist measures, favoritism simply cannot be avoided. Take, for example, the case of export or import licenses. Such a license has for the licensee a definite cash value. To whom ought the government grant a license and to whom should it be denied? There is no neutral or objective yardstick available to make the decision free from bias and favoritism. Whether or not money changes hands in the affair does not matter. The scandal is the same when the license is given to people who have rendered or are expected to render other kinds of valuable services (e.g., in casting their votes) to the people upon whom the decision depends.

Corruption is a regular effect of interventionism. It may be left to the historians and to the lawyers to deal with the problems involved.[8]

8. It is usual today to plead the cause of communist revolutions by denouncing the attacked noncommunist government as corrupt. Thus one tried to justify the support that a part of the American press and some of the representatives of the American Administration gave first to the Chinese communists and then to those of Cuba by calling the regime of Chiang Kai-shek and later that of Batista corrupt. But from this point of view, every communist revolution against a government that is not fully committed to laissez faire appears as justified.

XXVIII. INTERFERENCE BY TAXATION

1. The Neutral Tax

To keep the social apparatus of coercion and compulsion running requires expenditure of labor and commodities. Under a liberal system of government these expenditures are small compared with the sum of the individuals' incomes. The more the government expands the sphere of its activities, the more its budget increases.

If the government itself owns and operates plants, farms, forests, and mines, it might consider covering a part or the whole of its financial needs from interest and profit earned. But government operation of business enterprises as a rule is so inefficient that it results in losses rather than in profits. Governments must resort to taxation, i.e., they must raise revenues by forcing the subjects to surrender a part of their wealth or income.

A neutral mode of taxation is conceivable that would not divert the operation of the market from the lines in which it would develop in the absence of any taxation. However, the vast literature on problems of taxation as well as the policies of governments have hardly ever given thought to the problem of the *neutral* tax. They have been more eager to find the *just* tax.

The neutral tax would affect the conditions of the citizens only to the extent required by the fact that a part of the labor and material goods available is absorbed by the government apparatus. In the imaginary construction of the evenly rotating economy the treasury continually levies taxes and spends the whole amount raised, neither more nor less, for defraying the costs incurred by the activities of the government's officers. A part of each citizen's income is spent for public expenditure. If we assume that in such an evenly rotating economy there prevails perfect income equality in such a way that every household's income is proportional to the number of its members, both a head tax and a proportional income tax would be neutral taxes. Under these assumptions there would be no difference between them. A part of each citizen's income would be absorbed by public expenditure, and no secondary effects of taxation would emerge.

The changing economy is entirely different from this imaginary construction of an evenly rotating economy with income equality. Continuous change and the inequality of wealth and income are essential and necessary features of the changing market economy, the only real and working system of the market economy. In the frame of such a system no tax can be neutral. The very idea of a neutral tax is as unrealizable as that of neutral money. But, of course, the reasons for this inescapable non-neutrality are different in the case of taxes from what they are in the case of money.

A head tax that taxes every citizen equally and uniformly without any regard to the size of his income and wealth, falls more heavily upon those with more moderate means than upon those with more ample means. It restricts the production of the articles consumed by the masses more sharply than that of the articles mainly consumed by the wealthier citizens. On the other hand, it tends to curtail saving and capital accumulation less than a more burdensome taxation of the wealthier citizens does. It does not slow down the tendency toward a drop in the marginal productivity of capital goods as against the marginal productivity of labor to the same extent as does taxation discriminating against those with higher income and wealth, and consequently it does not to the same extent retard the tendency toward a rise in wage rates.

The actual fiscal policies of all countries are today exclusively guided by the idea that taxes should be apportioned according to each citizen's "ability to pay." In the considerations which finally resulted in the general acceptance of the ability-to-pay principle there was some dim conception that taxing the well-to-do more heavily than those with moderate means renders a tax somewhat more neutral. However this may be, it is certain that any reference to tax neutrality was very soon entirely discarded. The ability-to-pay principle has been raised to the dignity of a postulate of social justice. As people see it today, the fiscal and budgetary objectives of taxation are of secondary importance only. The primary function of taxation is to reform social conditions according to justice. From this point of view, a tax appears as the more satisfactory the less neutral it is and the more it serves as a device for diverting production and consumption from those lines into which the unhampered market would have directed them.

2. The Total Tax

The idea of social justice implied in the ability-to-pay principle is that of perfect financial equality of all citizens. As long as any inequality of income of wealth remains it can as plausibly be argued that these larger incomes and fortunes, however small their absolute amount, indicate some excess of ability to be levied upon, as it can be argued that any existing inequalities of income and wealth indicate differences in ability. The only logical stopping place of the ability-to-pay doctrine is at the complete equalization of incomes and wealth by confiscation of all incomes and fortunes above the lowest amount in the hands of anyone.[1]

The notion of the total tax is the antithesis of the notion of the neutral tax. The total tax completely taxes away—confiscates—all incomes and estates. Then the government, out of the community chest thus filled, gives to everybody an allowance for defraying the costs of his sustenance. Or, what comes to the same thing, the government in taxing leaves free that amount which it considers everybody's fair share and completes the shares of those who have less up to the amount of their fair share.

The idea of the total tax cannot be thought out to its ultimate logical consequences. If the entrepreneurs and capitalists do not derive any personal benefit or damage from their utilization of the means of production, they become indifferent with regard to the choice between various modes of conduct. Their social function fades away, and they become disinterested irresponsible administrators of public property. They are no longer bound to adjust production to the wishes of the consumers. If only the income is taxed away while the captial stock itself is left free, an incentive is offered to the owners to consume parts of their wealth and thus to hurt the interests of everyone. A total income tax would be a very inept means for the transformation of capitalism into socialism. If the total tax affects wealth no less than income, it is no longer a tax, i.e., a device for collecting government revenue within a market economy. It becomes a measure for the transition to socialism. As soon as it is consummated, socialism has been substituted for capitalism.

Even when looked upon as a method for the realization of socialism, the total tax is disputable. Some socialists launched plans for a prosocialist tax reform. They recommended either a 100 per cent estate and gift tax or taxing away totally the rent of land or all unearned income—i.e., in the socialist terminology, all revenue not derived from manual labor performed. The examination of these projects is superfluous. It is enough to know that they are utterly incompatible with the preservation of the market economy.

1. Cf. Harley Lutz, *Guideposts to a Free Economy* (New York, 1945). p. 76.

3. Fiscal and Nonfiscal Objectives of Taxation

The fiscal and nonfiscal objectives of taxation do not agree with one another.

Consider, for instance, excise duties on liquor. If one considers them as a source of government revenue, the more they yield the better they appear. Of course, as the duty must enhance the price of the beverage, it restricts sales and consumption. It is necessary to find out by testing under what rate of duty the yield becomes highest. But if one looks at liquor taxes as a means of reducing the consumption of liquor as much as possible, the rate is better the higher it is. Pushed beyond a certain limit, the tax makes consumption drop considerably, and also the revenue concomitantly. If the tax fully attains its nonfiscal objective of weaning people entirely from drinking alcoholic beverages, the revenue is zero. It no longer serves any fiscal purpose; its effects are merely prohibitive. The same is valid not only with regard to all kinds of indirect taxation but no less for direct taxation. Discriminating taxes levied upon corporations and big business would, if raised above a certain limit, result in the total disappearance of corporations and big business. Capital levies, inheritance and estate taxes, and income taxes are similarly self-defeating if carried to extremes.

There is no solution for the irreconcilable conflict between the fiscal and the nonfiscal ends of taxation. The power to tax involves, as Chief Justice Marshall pertinently observed, the power to destroy. This power can be used for the destruction of the market economy, and it is the firm resolution of many governments and parties to use it for this purpose. With the substitution of socialism for capitalism, the dualism of the coexistence of two distinct spheres of action disappears. The government swallows the whole orbit of the individual's autonomous actions and becomes totalitarian. It no longer depends for its financial support on the means exacted from the citizens. There is no longer any such thing as a separation of public funds and private funds.

Taxation is a matter of the market economy. It is one of the characteristic features of the market economy that the government does not interfere with the market phenomena and that its technical apparatus is so small that its maintenance absorbs only a modest fraction of the total sum of the individual citizens' incomes. Then taxes are an appropriate vehicle for providing the funds needed by the government. They are appropriate because they are low and do not perceptibly disarrange production and consumption. If taxes grow beyond a moderate limit, they cease to be taxes and turn into devices for the destruction of the market economy.

This metamorphosis of taxes into weapons of destruction is the mark of present-day public finance. We do not deal with the quite arbitrary value judgments concerning the problems of whether heavy taxation is a curse or a benefit and whether the expenditures financed by the tax yield are or are not wise and beneficial.[2] What matters is that the heavier taxation becomes, the less compatible it is with the preservation of the market economy. There is no need to raise the question of whether or not it is true that "no country was ever yet ruined by large expenditures of money by the public and for the public."[3] It cannot be denied that the market economy can be ruined by large public expenditures and that it is the intention of many people to ruin it in this way.

Businessmen complain about the oppressiveness of heavy taxes. Statesmen are alarmed about the danger of "eating the seedcorn." Yet, the true crux of the taxation issue is to be seen in the paradox that the more taxes increase, the more they undermine the market economy and concomitantly the system of taxation itself. Thus the fact becomes manifest that ultimately the preservation of private property and confiscatory measures are incompatible. Every specific tax, as well as a nation's whole tax system, becomes self-defeating above a certain height of the rates.

4. The Three Classes of Tax Interventionism

The various methods of taxation which can be used for the regulation of the economy—i.e., as instruments of an interventionist policy—can be classified in three groups:

1. The tax aims at totally suppressing or at restricting the production of definite commodities. It thus indirectly interferes with consumption too. It does not matter whether this end is aimed at by the imposition of special taxes or by exempting certain products from a general tax imposed upon all other products or upon those products which the consumers would have preferred in the absence of fiscal discrimination. Tax exemption is employed as an instrument of interventionism in the case of customs duties. The domestic product is not burdened by the tariff which affects only the merchandise imported from abroad. Many countries resort to tax discrimination in regulating

2. This is the customary method of dealing with problems of public finance. Cf., e.g., Ely, Adams, Lorenz, and Young, *Outlines of Economics* (3d ed. New York, 1920), p. 702.

3. *Ibid.*

domestic production. They try, for instance, to encourage the production of wine, a product of small or medium-size grape growers, as against the production of beer, a product of big-size breweries, by submitting beer to a more burdensome excise tax than wine.

2. The tax expropriates a part of income or wealth.

3. The tax expropriates income and wealth entirely.

We do not have to deal with the third class, as it is merely a means for the realization of socialism and as such is outside the scope of interventionism.

The first class is in its effects not different from the restrictive measures dealt with in the following chapter.

The second class encompasses confiscatory measures dealt with in Chapter XXXII.

XXIX. RESTRICTION OF PRODUCTION

1. The Nature of Restriction

WE shall deal in this chapter with those measures which are directly and primarily intended to divert production (in the broadest meaning of the word, including commerce and transportation) from the ways it would take in the unhampered market economy. Each authoritarian interference with business diverts production, of course, from the lines it would take if it were only directed by the demand of the consumers as manifested on the market. The characteristic mark of restrictive interference with production is that the diversion of production is not merely an unavoidable and unintentional secondary effect, but precisely what the authority wants to bring about. Like any other act of intervention, such restrictive measures affect consumption also. But this again, in the case of the restrictive measures we are dealing with in this chapter, is not the primary end the authority aims at. The government wants to interfere with production. The fact that its measure influences the ways of consumption also is, from its point of view, either altogether contrary to its intentions or at least an unwelcome consequence with which it puts up because it is unavoidable and is considered as a minor evil when compared with the consequences of nonintervention.

Restriction of production means that the government either forbids or makes more difficult or more expensive the production, transportation, or distribution of definite articles, or the application of definite modes of production, transportation, or distribution. The authority thus eliminates some of the means available for the satisfaction of human wants. The effect of its interference is that people are prevented from using their knowledge and abilities, their labor and their material means of production in the way in which they would earn the highest returns and satisfy their needs as much as possible. Such interference makes people poorer and less satisfied.

This is the crux of the matter. All the subtlety and hair-splitting wasted in the effort to invalidate this fundamental thesis are vain. On the unhampered market there prevails an irresistible tendency to employ every factor of production for the best possible satisfaction of the most urgent needs of the consumers. If the government interferes with this process, it can only impair satisfaction; it can never improve it.

The correctness of this thesis has been proved in an excellent and irrefutable manner with regard to the historically most important class of government interference with production, the barriers to international trade. In this field the teaching of the classical economists, especially those of Ricardo, are final and settle the issue forever. All that a tariff can achieve is to divert production from those locations in which the output per unit of input is higher to locations in which it is lower. It does not increase production; it curtails it.

People expatiate on alleged government encouragement of production. However, government does not have the power to encourage one branch of production except by curtailing other branches. It withdraws the factors of production from those branches in which the unhampered market would employ them and directs them into other branches. It little matters what kind of administrative procedures the government resorts to for the realization of this effect. It may subsidize openly or disguise the subsidy in enacting tariffs and thus forcing its subjects to defray the costs. What alone counts is the fact that people are forced to forego some satisfactions which they value more highly and are compensated only by satisfactions which they value less. At the bottom of the interventionist argument there is always the idea that the government or the state is an entity outside and above the social process of production, that it owns something which is not derived from taxing its subjects, and that it can spend this mythical something for definite purposes. This is the Santa Claus fable raised by Lord Keynes to the dignity of an economic doctrine and enthusiastically endorsed by all those who expect personal advantage from government spending. As against these popular fallacies there is need to emphasize the truism that a government can spend or invest only what it takes away from its citizens and that its additional spending and investment curtails the citizens' spending and investment to the full extent of its quantity.

While government has no power to make people more prosperous by interference with business, it certainly does have the power to make them less satisfied by restriction of production.

2. The Price of Restriction

The fact that restricting production invariably involves a curtailment of the individual citizens' satisfaction does not mean that such restriction is necessarily to be regarded as a damage. A government does not wantonly resort to restrictive measures. It wants to attain certain ends and considers the restriction as the appropriate means for the realization of its plan. The appraisal of restrictive policies depends therefore on the answer to two questions: Is the means chosen by the government fitted to attain the end sought? Is the realization of this end a compensation for the individual citizens' privation? In raising these questions we look upon restriction of production as we look upon taxes. Payment of taxes also directly curtails the taxpayer's satisfaction. But it is the price he pays for the services which government renders to society and to each of its members. As far as the government fulfills its social functions and the taxes do not exceed the amount required for securing the smooth operation of the government apparatus, they are necessary costs and repay themselves.

The adequacy of this mode of dealing with restrictive measures is especially manifest in all those cases in which restriction is resorted to as a substitute for taxation. The bulk of expenditure for national defense is defrayed by the treasury out of the public revenue. But occasionally another procedure is chosen. It happens sometimes that the nation's preparedness to repel aggression depends on the existence of certain branches of industry which would be absent in the unhampered market. These industries must be subsidized, and the subsidies granted are to be considered as any other armaments expenditure. Their character remains the same if the government grants them indirectly by the imposition of an import duty for the products concerned. The difference is only that then the consumers are directly burdened with the costs incurred, while in the case of a government subsidy they defray these costs indirectly by paying higher taxes.

In enacting restrictive measures governments and parliaments have hardly ever been aware of the consequences of their meddling with business. Thus, they have blithely assumed that protective tariffs are capable of raising the nation's standard of living, and they have stubbornly refused to admit the correctness of the economic teachings concerning the effects of protectionism. The economists' condemnation of protectionism is irrefutable and free of any party bias. For the economists do not say that protection is bad from any preconceived point of view. They show that protection cannot attain those ends which the governments as a rule want to attain by resorting to it. They do not question the ultimate end of the government's action; they merely reject the means chosen as inappropriate to realize the ends aimed at.

Most popular among all restrictive measures are those styled pro-labor legislation. Here too the governments and public opinion badly misjudge the effects. They believe that restricting the hours of work and prohibiting child labor exclusively burdens the employers and is a "social gain" for the wage earners. However, this is true only to the extent that such laws reduce the supply of labor and thus raise the marginal productivity of labor as against the marginal productivity of capital. But the drop in the supply of labor results also in a decrease in the total amount of goods produced and thereby in the average per capita consumption. The total cake shrinks, but the portion of the smaller cake which goes to the wage earners is proportionately higher than what they received from the bigger cake; concomitantly the portion of the capitalists drops.[1] It depends on the concrete data of each case whether or not this outcome improves or impairs the real wage rates of the various groups of wage earners.

The popular appraisal of prolabor legislation was based on the error that wage rates have no causal relation whatever to the value that the workers' labor adds to the material. Wage rates, says the "iron law," are determined by the minimum amount of indispensable necessities of life; they can never rise above the subsistence level. The difference between the value produced by the worker and the wages paid to him goes to the exploiting employer. If this surplus is curtailed by restricting the working hours, the wage earner is relieved of a part of his toil and trouble, his wages remain unchanged, and the employer is deprived of a part of his unfair profit. The restriction of total output curtails only the income of the exploiting bourgeois.

It has been pointed out already that the role which prolabor legislation played in the evolution of Western capitalism was until a few years ago much less important than would be suggested by the vehemence with which the problems involved have been publicly discussed. Labor legislation, for the most part, merely provided a legal recognition of changes in conditions already consummated by the rapid evolution of business.[2] But in the countries which were slow in adopting capitalistic modes of production and are backward in developing modern methods of processing and manufacturing, the problem of labor legislation is crucial. Deluded by the spurious doctrines of interventionism, the politicians of these nations believe that they can improve the lot of the destitute masses by copying the labor legislation of the most advanced capitalistic countries. They look upon the problems involved as if they were merely to be treated from what

1. Entrepreneurial profits and losses are not affected by prolabor legislation as they entirely depend on the more or less successful adjustment of production to the changing conditions of the market. With regard to these, labor legislation counts only as a factor producing change.

2. Cf. above, pp. 614–617.

is erroneously called the "human angle" and fail to recognize the real issue.

It is a sad fact indeed that in Asia many millions of tender children are destitute and starving, that wages are extremely low when compared with American or Western European standards, that hours of work are long, and that sanitary conditions in the workshops are deplorable. But there is no means of eliminating these evils other than to work, to produce, and to save more and thus to accumulate more capital. This is indispensable for any lasting improvement. The restrictive measures advocated by self-styled philanthropists and humanitarians would be futile. They would not only fail to improve conditions, they would make things a good deal worse. If the parents are too poor to feed their children adequately, prohibition of child labor condemns the children to starvation. If the marginal productivity of labor is so low that a worker can earn in ten hours only wages which are substandard when compared with American wages, one does not benefit the laborer by decreeing the eight-hour day.

The problem under discussion is not the desirability of improving the wage earners' material well-being. The advocates of what are miscalled prolabor laws intentionally confuse the issue in repeating again and again that more leisure, higher real wages, and freeing children and married women from the necessity of seeking jobs would make the families of the workers happier. They resort to falsehood and mean calumny in calling those who oppose such laws as detrimental to the vital interests of the wage earners "labor-baiters" and "enemies of labor." The disagreement does not refer to the ends sought; it concerns solely the means to be applied for their realization. The question is not whether or not improvement of the masses' welfare is desirable. It is exclusively whether or not government decrees restricting the hours of work and the employment of women and children are the right means for raising the workers' standard of living. This is a purely catallactic problem to be solved by economics. Emotional talk is beside the point. It is a poor disguise for the fact that these self-righteous advocates of restriction are unable to advance any tenable objections to the economists' well-founded argumentation.

The fact that the standard of living of the average American worker is incomparably more satisfactory than that of the average Hindu worker, that in the United States hours of work are shorter and that the children are sent to school and not to the factories, is not an achievement of the government and of the laws of the country. It is the outcome of the fact that the capital invested per head of the employees is much greater than in India and that consequently the marginal productivity of labor is much higher. This is not the merit of "social policies"; it is the result of the laissez faire methods of the past which abstained from sabotaging the evolution of capitalism. It is this laissez faire that the Asiatics must adopt if they want to improve the lot of their peoples.

The poverty of Asia and other backward countries is due to the same causes which made conditions unsatisfactory in the early periods of Western capitalism. While population figures increased rapidly, restrictive policies delayed the adjustment of production methods to the needs of the growing number of mouths. It is to the imperishable credit of the laissez faire economists, whom the typical textbooks of our universities dismiss as pessimists and apologists of the unfair greed of exploiting bourgeois, that they paved the way for economic freedom which raised the average standard of living to an unprecedented height.

Economics is not dogmatic, as the self-styled "unorthodox" advocates of government omnipotence and totalitarian dictatorship contend. Economics neither approves nor disapproves of government measures restricting production and output. It merely considers it its duty to clarify the consequences of such measures. The choice of policies to be adopted devolves upon the people. But in choosing they must not disregard the teachings of economics if they want to attain the ends sought.

There are certainly cases in which people may consider definite restrictive measures as justified. Regulations concerning fire prevention are restrictive and raise the cost of production. But the curtailment of total output they bring about is the price to be paid for avoidance of greater disaster. The decision about each restrictive measure is to be made on the ground of a meticulous weighing of the costs to be incurred and the prize to be obtained. No reasonable man could possibly question this rule.

3. Restriction as a Privilege

Every disarrangement of the market data affects various individuals and groups of individuals in a different way. For some people it is a boon, for others a blow. Only after a while, when production is adjusted to the emergence of the new datum, are these effects exhausted. Thus a restrictive measure, while placing the immense majority at a disadvantage, may temporarily improve some people's position. For those favored the measure is tantamount to the acquisition of a privilege. They are asking for such measures because they want to be privileged.

Here again the most striking example is provided by protectionism. The imposition of a duty on the importation of a commodity burdens the consumers. But to the domestic producers it is a boon. From their point of view decreeing new tariffs and raising already existing tariffs is an excellent thing.

The same is valid with regard to many other restrictive measures. If the government restricts—either by direct restriction or by fiscal discrimination—big business and corporations, the competitive position of small-size enterprises is strengthened. If it restricts the operation of big stores and chain stores, the small shopkeepers rejoice.

It is important to realize that what those benefited by these measures consider an advantage for themselves lasts only for a limited time. In the long run the privilege accorded to a definite class of producers loses its power to create specific gains. The privileged branch attracts newcomers, and their competition tends to eliminate the specific gains derived from the privilege. Thus the eagerness of the law's pet children to acquire privileges is insatiable. They continue to ask for new privileges because the old ones lose their power.

On the other hand, the repeal of a restrictive measure to the existence of which the structure of production has already been adjusted means a new disarrangement of the market data, favors the short-run interests of some people and hurts the short-run interests of other people. Let us illustrate the issue by referring to a tariff item. Ruritania years ago, let us say in 1920, decreed a tariff on the importation of leather. This was a boon for the enterprises which at the moment happened to be engaged in the tanning industry. But then later the size of the industry expanded and the windfall gains which the tanners enjoyed in 1920 and in the following years petered out. What remains is merely the fact that a part of the world's leather production is shifted from locations in which the output per unit of input is higher, to locations in Ruritania in which production requires higher costs. The residents of Ruritania pay higher prices for leather than they would pay in the absence of the tariff. As a greater part of Ruritania's capital and labor is employed in the tanneries than would be the case under free trade for leather, some other domestic industries shrank or were at least prevented from growing. Less leather is imported from abroad and a smaller amount of Ruritanian products is exported as payment for leather imported. The volume of Ruritania's foreign trade is curtailed. Not a single soul in the whole world derives any advantage from the preservation of the old tariff. On the contrary, everyone is hurt by the drop in the total output of mankind's industrial effort. If the policy adopted by Ruritania with regard to leather were to be adopted by all nations and with regard to every kind of merchandise in the most rigid way so as to abolish international trade altogether and to make every nation perfectly autarkic, all people would have to forego entirely the advantages which the international division of labor gives them.

It is obvious that the repeal of the Ruritanian tariff on leather must in the long run benefit everybody, Ruritanians as well as foreigners. However, in the short run it would hurt the interests of the capitalists who have invested in Ruritanian tanneries. It would no less hurt the short-run interests of the Ruritanian workers specialized in tannery work. A part of them would have either to emigrate or to change their occupation. These capitalists and workers passionately fight all attempts to lower the leather tariff or to abolish it altogether.

This shows clearly why it is politically extremely difficult to brush away measures restricting production once the structure of business has been adjusted to their existence. Although their effects are pernicious to everybody, their disappearance is in the short run disadvantageous to special groups. These special groups interested in the preservation of the restrictive measures are, of course, only minorities. In Ruritania only the small fraction of the population engaged in the tanneries can suffer from the abolition of the tariff on leather. The immense majority are buyers of leather and leather goods and would be benefited by a drop in their prices. Outside the boundaries of Ruritania, only those people would be hurt who are engaged in those industries which will shrink because the leather industry will expand.

The last objection advanced by the opponents of free trade runs this way: Granted that only those Ruritanians engaged in tanning hides are immediately interested in the preservation of the tariff on leather. But every Ruritanian belongs to one of the many branches of production. If each domestic product is protected by the tariff, the transition to free trade hurts the interests of each industry and thereby those of all specialized groups of capital and labor the sum of which is the whole nation. It follows that repealing the tariff would in the short run be prejudicial to all citizens. And it is short-run interests only that count.

This argument involves a threefold error. First, it is not true that all branches of industry would be hurt by the transition to free trade. On the contrary. Those branches in which the comparative costs of production are lowest will expand under free trade. Their short-run interests would be favored by the abolition of the tariff. The tariff on those products they themselves turn out is of no advantage for them, as they could not only survive, but expand under free trade. The tariff on those products for which the comparative cost of production is higher in Ruritania than abroad hurts them by directing capital and labor, which otherwise would have fertilized them, into those other branches.

Second, the short-run principle is entirely fallacious. In the short run every change in the market data hurts those who did not anticipate it in time. A consistent champion of the short-run principle must advocate perfect ridigity and immutability of all data and oppose any change, including any therapeutical and technological improvement.[3] If in acting people were always to prefer the avoidance of an evil in the nearer future to the avoidance of an evil in the remoter future, they would come down to the animal level. It is the very essence of human action as distinct from animal behavior that it consciously renounces some temporally nearer satisfaction in order to reap some greater but temporally remoter satisfaction.[4]

Finally, if the problem of the abolition of Ruritania's comprehensive tariff system is under discussion, one must not forget the fact that the short-run interests of those engaged in tanning are hurt only by the abolition of one of the items of the tariff while they are favored by the abolition of the other items concerning the products of the industries in which comparative cost is high. It is true that wage rates of the tannery workers will drop for some time as against those in other branches and that some time will elapse until the appropriate long-run proportion between wage rates in the various branches of Ruritanian production will be established. But concomitantly with the merely temporary drop in their earnings, these workers will experience a drop in the prices of many articles they are buying. And this tendency toward an improvement in their conditions is not a phenomenon only of the period of transition. It is the consummation of the lasting blessings of free trade which, in shifting every branch of industry to the location in which comparative cost is lowest, increases the productivity of labor and the total quantity of goods produced. It is the lasting long-run boon which free trade secures to every member of the market society.

The opposition to the abolition of tariff protection would be reasonable from the personal point of view of those engaged in the leather industry if the tariff on leather were the only tariff. Then one could explain their attitude as dictated by status interests, the interests of a

3. This consistency was displayed by some Nazi philosophers. Cf. Sombart, *A New Social Philosophy*, pp. 242–245.

4. See above, pp. 479–488.

caste which would be temporarily hurt by the abolition of a privilege although its mere preservation no longer confers any benefit on them. But in this hypothetical case the opposition of the tanners would be hopeless. The majority of the nation would overrule it. What strengthens the ranks of the protectionists is the fact that the tariff on leather is no exception, that many branches of industry are in a similar position and are fighting the abolition of tariff items concerning their own branch. This is, of course, not an alliance based on each group's special group interests. If everybody is protected to the same extent, everybody not only loses as consumer as much as he gains as producer. Everybody, moreover, is harmed by the general drop in the productivity of labor which the shifting of industries from more favorable to less favorable locations brings about. Conversely the abolition of all tariff items would benefit everybody in the long run, while the short-run harm which the abolition of some special tariff item brings to the special interests of the group concerned is already in the short run at least partly compensated by the consequences of the abolition of the tariff on the products the members of this group are buying and consuming.

Many people look upon tariff protection as if it were a privilege accorded to their nation's wage earners, procuring them, for the full duration of its existence, a higher standard of living than they would enjoy under free trade. This argument is advanced not only in the United States, but in every country in the world in which average real wage rates are higher than in some other country.

Now, it is true that under perfect mobility of capital and labor there would prevail all over the world a tendency toward an equalization of the price paid for labor of the same kind and quality.[5] Yet, even if there were free trade for products, this tendency is absent in our real world of migration barriers and institutions hindering foreign investment of capital. The marginal productivity of labor is higher in the United States than it is in India because capital invested per head of the working population is greater, and because Indian workers are prevented from moving to America and competing on the American labor market. There is no need, in dealing with the explanation of this difference, to investigate whether natural resources are or are not more abundant in America than in India and whether or not the Indian worker is racially inferior to the American worker. However this may be, these facts, namely, the institutional checks upon the mobility of capital and labor, suffice to account for the absence of the equalization tendency. As the abolition of the American tariff could

5. For a detailed analysis, cf. above, p. 627.

not affect these two facts, it could not impair the standard of living of the American wage earner in an adverse sense.

On the contrary. Given a state of affairs in which the mobility of capital and labor is restricted, the transition to free trade for products must necessarily raise the American standard of life. Those industries in which American costs are higher (American productivity is lower) would shrink and those in which costs are lower (productivity is higher) would expand.

Under free trade the Swiss watchmakers would expand their sales on the American market and the sales of their American competitors would shrink. But this is only a part of the consequences of free trade. Selling and producing more, the Swiss would earn and buy more. It does not matter whether they themselves buy more of the products of other American industries or whether they increase their domestic purchases and those in other countries, for instance, in France. Whatever happens, the equivalent of the additional dollars they earned must finally go to the United States and increase the sales of some American industries. If the Swiss do not give away their products as a gift, they must spend these dollars in buying.

The popular opinion to the contrary is due to the illusory idea that America could expand its purchases of imported products by reducing the total sum of its citizens' cash holdings. This is the notorious fallacy according to which people buy without regard to the size of their cash holdings, and according to which the very existence of cash holdings is simply the outcome of the fact that something is left over because there is nothing more to buy. We have already shown why this Mercantilist doctrine is entirely wrong.[6]

What the tariff really brings about in the field of wage rates and the wage earners' standard of living is something quite different.

In a world in which there is free trade for commodities, while the migration of workers and foreign investment are restricted, there prevails a tendency toward an establishment of a definite relation between the wages paid for the same kind and quality of labor in various countries. There cannot prevail a tendency toward an equalization of wage rates. But the final price to be paid for labor in various countries is in a certain numerical relation. This final price is characterized by the fact that all those eager to earn wages get a job and all those eager to employ workers are able to hire as many hands as they want. There is "full employment."

Let us assume that there are two countries only—Ruritania and Laputania. In Ruritania the final wage rate is double what it is in

6. See above, pp. 448–452.

Laputania. Now the government of Ruritania resorts to one of those measures which are erroneously styled "prolabor." It burdens the employers with an additional expenditure the size of which is proportional to the number of workers employed. For example, it reduces the hours of work without permitting a corresponding drop in weekly wage rates. The result is a drop in the quantity of goods produced and a rise in the price of the unit of every good. The individual worker enjoys more leisure, but his standard of living is curtailed. What else could a general decrease in the quantity of goods available bring about?

This outcome is an internal event in Ruritania. It would emerge also in the absence of any foreign trade. The fact that Ruritania is not autarkic, but buys from and sells to Laputania, does not alter its essential features. But it implicates Laputania. As the Ruritanians produce and consume less, they will buy less from Laputania. In Laputania there will not be a general drop in production. But some industries which produced for export to Ruritania will henceforth have to produce for the domestic Laputanian market. Laputania will see the volume of its foreign trade drop; it will become, willy-nilly, more autarkic. This is a blessing in the eyes of the protectionists. In truth, it means deterioration in the standard of living; production at higher costs is substituted for that at lower costs. What Laputania experiences is the same thing that the residents of an autarkic country would experience if an act of God were to curtail the productivity of one of the country's industries. As far as there is division of labor, everybody is affected by a drop in the amount other people contribute to supplying the market.

However, these inexorable final international consequences of Ruritania's new pro-labor law will not affect the various branches of Laputania's industry in the same way. A sequence of steps is needed in both countries until at last a perfect adjustment of production to the new state of data is brought about. These short-run effects are different from the long-run effects. They are more spectacular than the long-run effects. While hardly anybody can fail to notice the short-run effects, the long-run effects are recognized only by economists. While it is not difficult to conceal the long-run effects from the public, something must be done about the easily recognizable short-run effects lest the enthusiasm for such allegedly pro-labor legislation fade away.

The first short-run effect to appear is the weakening of the competitive power of some Ruritanian branches of production as against those of Laputania. As prices rise in Ruritania, it becomes possible for some Laputanians to expand their sales in Ruritania. This is a temporary effect only; in the end the total sales of all Laputanian industries in Ruritania will drop. It is possible that in spite of this general drop in the amount of Laputanian exports to Ruritania, some of the Laputanian industries will expand their sales in the long run. (This depends on the new configuration of comparative costs.) But there is no necessary interconnection between these short-run and long-run effects. The adjustments of the period of transition create kaleidoscopically changing situations which may differ entirely from the final outcome. Yet the short-sighted public's attention is completely absorbed by these short-run effects. They hear the businessmen affected complain that the new Ruritanian law gives to Laputanians the opportunity to undersell both in Ruritania and in Laputania. They see that some Ruritanian businessmen are forced to restrict their production and to discharge workers. And they begin to suspect that something may be wrong with the teachings of the self-styled "unorthodox friends of labor."

But the picture is different if there is in Ruritania a tariff high enough to prevent Laputanians from even temporarily expanding their sales on the Ruritanian market. Then the most spectacular short-run effects of the new measure are masked in such a way that the public does not become aware of them. The long-run effects, of course, cannot be avoided. But they are brought about by another sequence of short-run effects which is less offensive because less visible. The talk about alleged "social gains" produced by the shortening of the hours of work is not exploded by the immediate emergence of effects which everyone, and most of all the discharged workers, consider undesirable.

The main function of tariffs and other protectionist devices today is to disguise the real effects of interventionist policies designed to raise the standard of living of the masses. Economic nationalism is the necessary complement of these popular policies which pretend to improve the wage earners' material well-being while they are in fact impairing it.[7]

4. Restriction as an Economic System

There are, as has been shown, cases in which a restrictive measure can attain the end sought by its application. If those resorting to such a measure think that the attainment of this goal is more important than the disadvantages brought about by the restriction—i.e., the curtailment in the quantity of material goods available for consump-

7. See also what has been said about the function of cartels on pp. 365–369.

tion—the recourse to restriction is justified from the point of view of their value judgments. They incur costs and pay a price in order to get something that they value more than what they had to expend or to forego. Nobody, and certainly not the theorist, is in a position to argue with them about the propriety of their value judgments.

The only adequate mode of dealing with measures restricting production is to look at them as sacrifices made for the attainment of a definite end. They are quasi-expenditures and quasi-consumption. They are an employment of things that could be produced and consumed in one way for the realization of certain other ends. These things are prevented from coming into existence, but this quasi-consumption is precisely what satisfies the authors of these measures better than the increase in goods available which the omission of the restriction would have produced.

With certain restrictive measures this point of view is universally adopted. If a government decrees that a piece of land should be kept in its natural state as a national park and should be withheld from any other utilization, nobody would classify such a venture as anything else than an expenditure. The government deprives the citizens of the increment in various products which the cultivation of this land could bring about, in order to provide them with another satisfaction.

It follows that restriction of production can never play any role other than that of an ancillary complement of a system of production. One cannot construct a system of economic action out of such restrictive measures alone. No complex of such measures can be linked together into an integrated economic system. They cannot form a system of production. They belong in the sphere of consumption, not in the sphere of production.

In scrutinizing the problems of interventionism we are intent upon examining the claims of the advocates of government interference with business that their system offers an alternative to other economic systems. No such claim can reasonably be raised with regard to measures restricting production. The best they can attain is curtailment of output and satisfaction. Wealth is produced by expending a certain quantity of factors of production. Curtailing this quantity does not increase, but decreases, the amount of goods produced. Even if the ends aimed at by shortening the hours of work could be attained by such a decree, it would not be a measure of production. It is invariably a way of cutting down output.

Capitalism is a system of social production. Socialism, say the socialists, is also a system of social production. But with regard to measures restricting production, even the interventionists cannot raise a similar claim. They can only say that under capitalism too much is produced and that they want to prevent the production of this surplus in order to realize other ends. They themselves must confess that there are limits to the application of restriction.

Economics does not contend that restriction is a bad system of production. It asserts that it is not at all a system of production but rather a system of quasi-consumption. Most of the ends the interventionists want to attain by restriction cannot be attained this way. But even where restrictive measures are fit to attain the ends sought, they are only restrictive.[8]

The enormous popularity which restriction enjoys in our day is due to the fact that people do not recognize its consequences. In dealing with the problem of shortening the hours of work by government decree, the public is not aware of the fact that total output must drop and that it is very probable that the wage earners' standard of living will be potentially lowered too. It is a dogma of present-day "unorthodoxy" that such a "prolabor" measure is a "social gain" for the workers and that the costs of these gains fall entirely upon the employers. Whoever questions this dogma is branded as a "sycophantic" apologist of the unfair pretensions of rugged exploiters, and pitilessly persecuted. It is insinuated that he wants to reduce the wage earners to the poverty and the long working hours of the early stages of modern industrialism.

As against all this slander it is important to emphasize again that what produces wealth and well-being is production and not restriction. That in the capitalist countries the average wage earner consumes more goods and can afford to enjoy more leisure than his ancestors, and that he can support his wife and children and need not send them to work, is not an achievement of governments and labor unions. It is the outcome of the fact that profit-seeking business has accumulated and invested more capital and thus increased the marginal productivity of labor.

8. As for the objections raised against this thesis from the point of view of the Ricardo effect, see below, pp. 773–776.

XXX. INTERFERENCE WITH THE STRUCTURE OF PRICES

1. The Government and the Autonomy of the Market

Interference with the structure of the market means that the authority aims at fixing prices for commodities and services and interest rates at a height different from what the unhampered market would have determined. It decrees, or empowers—either tacitly or expressly—definite groups of people to decree, prices and rates which are to be considered either as maxima or as minima, and it provides for the enforcement of such decrees by coercion and compulsion.

In resorting to such measures the government wants to favor either the buyer—as in the case of maximum prices—or the seller—as in the case of minimum prices. The maximum price is designed to make it possible for the buyer to procure what he wants at a price lower than that of the unhampered market. The minimum price is designed to make it possible for the seller to dispose of his merchandise or his services at a price higher than that of the unhampered market. It depends on the political balance of forces which groups the authority wants to favor. At times governments have resorted to maximum prices, at other times to minimum prices for various commodities. At times they have decreed maximum wages rates, at other times minimum wage rates. It is only with regard to interest that they have never had recourse to minimum rates; when they have interfered, they have always decreed maximum interest rates. They have always looked askance upon saving, investing, and moneylending.

If this interference with commodity prices, wage rates, and interest rates includes all prices, wage rates, and interest rates, it is tantamount to the full substitution of socialism (of the German pattern) for the market economy. Then the market, interpersonal exchange, private ownership of the means of production, entrepreneurship, and private initiative, virtually disappear altogether. No individual any longer has the opportunity to influence the process of production of his own accord; every individual is bound to obey the orders of the supreme board of production management. What in the complex of these orders are called prices, wage rates, and interest rates are no longer prices, wage rates, and interest rates in the catallactic sense of these terms. They are merely quantitative determinations fixed by the director without reference to a market process. If the governments resorting to price control and the reformers advocating price control were always intent upon the establishment of socialism of the German pattern, there would be no need for economics to deal with price control separately. All that has to be said with reference to such price control is already contained in the analysis of socialism.

Many advocates of government interference with prices have been and are very much confused with regard to this issue. They have failed to recognize the fundamental difference between a market economy and a nonmarket society. The haziness of their ideas has been reflected in vague and ambiguous language and in a bewildering terminology.

There were and are advocates of price control who have declared that they want to preserve the market economy. They are outspoken in their assertion that government fixing of prices, wage rates, and interest rates can attain the ends the government wants to attain by their promulgation without abolishing altogether the market and private ownership of the means of production. They even declare that price control is the best or the only means of preserving the system of private enterprise and of preventing the coming of socialism. They become very indignant if somebody questions the correctness of their doctrine and shows that price control, if it is not to make things worse from the point of view of the governments and the interventionist doctrinaires, must finally result in socialism. They protest that they are neither socialists nor communists, and that they aim at economic freedom and not at totalitarianism.

It is the tenets of these interventionists that we have to examine. The problem is whether it is possible for the police power to attain the ends it wants to attain by fixing prices, wage rates, and interest rates at a height different from what the unhampered market would have determined. It is beyond doubt that a strong and resolute government has the power to decree such maximum or minimum rates and to take revenge upon the disobedient. But the question is whether or not the authority can attain those ends which it wants to attain by resorting to such decrees.

History is a long record of price ceilings and anti-usury laws. Again and again emperors, kings, and revolutionary dictators have tried to meddle with the market phenomena. Severe punishment was inflicted on refractory dealers and farmers. Many people fell victim to persecutions which met with the enthusiastic approval of the masses. Nonetheless, all these endeavors failed. The explanation which the writings of lawyers, theologians and philosophers provided for the failure was in full agreement with the ideas held by the rulers and the masses. Man, they said, is intrinsically selfish and sinful, and the authorities were unfortunately too lax in enforcing the law. What was needed was more firmness and peremptoriness on the part of those in power.

Cognizance of the issue involved was first reached with regard to a special problem. Various governments long practiced currency debasement. They substituted baser and cheaper metals for a part of the gold or silver which the coins previously contained, or they reduced the weight and the size of the coins. But they retained for the debased coins the customary names of the old ones and they decreed that they should be given and received at the nominal par. Then later the governments tried to enjoin on their subjects analogous constraint with regard to the exchange ratio between gold and silver and that between metallic money and credit money or fiat money. In searching for the causes which made all such decrees abortive, the forerunners of economic thought had already discovered by the last centuries of the Middle Ages the regularity which was later called Gresham's Law. There was still a long way to go from this isolated insight to the point where the philosophers of the eighteenth century became aware of the interconnectedness of all market phenomena.

In describing the results of their reasoning the classical economists and their successors sometimes resorted to idiomatic expressions which could easily be misinterpreted by those who wanted to misinterpret them. They occasionally spoke of the "impossibility" of price control. What they really meant was not that such decrees are impossible, but that they cannot attain those ends which the governments are trying to attain and that they make things worse, not better, They concluded that such decrees are contrary to purpose and inexpedient.

It is necessary to see clearly that the problem of price control is not merely *one* of the problems to be dealt with by economics, not a problem with regard to which there can arise disagreement among various economists. The issue involved is rather: Is there any such thing as economics? Is there any regularity in the sequence and interconnectedness of the market phenomena? He who answers these two questions in the negative denies the very possibility, rationality and existence of economics as a branch of knowledge. He returns to the beliefs held in the ages which preceded the evolution of economics. He declares to be untrue the assertion that there is any economic law and that prices, wage rates, and interest rates are uniquely determined by the data of the market. He contends that the police have the power to determine these market phenomena ad libitum. An advocate of socialism need not necessarily negate economics; his postulates do not necessarily imply the indeterminateness of the market phenomena. But the interventionist, in advocating price control, cannot help nullifying the very existence of economics. Nothing is left of economics if one denies the law of the market.

The German Historical School was consistent in its radical condemnation of economics and in its endeavors to substitute *wirtschaftliche Staatswissenschaften* (the economic aspects of political science) for economics. So were many adepts of British Fabianism and American Institutionalism. But those authors who do not totally reject economics and yet assert that price control can attain the ends sought lamentably contradict themselves. It is logically impossible to reconcile the point of view of the economist and that of the interventionist. If prices are uniquely determined by the market data, they cannot be freely manipulated by government compulsion. The government's decree is just a new datum, and its effects are determined by the operation of the market. It need not necessarily produce those results which the government wants to realize in resorting to it. It may happen that the final outcome of the interference is, from the point of view of the government's intention, even more undesirable than the previous state of affairs which the government wanted to alter.

One does not invalidate these propositions by putting the term economic law in quotation marks and by finding fault with the notion of the law. In speaking of the laws of nature we have in mind the fact that there prevails an inexorable interconnectedness of physical and biological phenomena and that acting man must submit to this regularity if he wants to succeed. In speaking of the laws of human action we refer to the fact that such an inexorable interconnectedness of phenomena is present also in the field of human action as such and that acting man must recognize this regularity too if he wants to succeed. The reality of the laws of praxeology is revealed to man by the same signs that reveal the reality of natural law, namely, the fact that his power to attain chosen ends is restricted and conditioned. In the absence of laws man would either be omnipotent and would never feel any uneasiness which he could not remove instantly and totally, or he could not act at all.

These laws of the universe must not be confused with the man-made laws of the country and with man-made moral precepts. The laws of the universe about which physics, biology, and praxeology provide knowledge are independent of the human will, they are primary ontological facts rigidly restricting man's power to act. The moral precepts and the laws of the country are means by which men seek to attain certain ends. Whether or not these ends can really be attained this way depends on the laws of the universe. The man-made laws are suitable if they are fit to attain these ends and contrary to purpose if they are not. They are open to examination from the point of view of their suitableness or unsuitableness. With regard to the laws of the universe any doubt of their suitableness is supererogatory and vain. They are what they are and take care of themselves. Their violation penalizes itself. But the man-made laws need to be enforced by special sanctions.

Only the insane venture to disregard physical and biological laws. But it is quite common to disdain praxeological laws. Rulers do not like to admit that their power is restricted by any laws other than those of physics and biology. They never ascribe their failures and frustrations to the violation of economic law.

Foremost in the repudiation of economic knowledge was the German Historical School. It was an unbearable idea to those professors that their lofty idols, the Hohenzollern Electors of Brandenburg and Kings of Prussia, should have lacked omnipotence. To refute the teachings of the economists, they buried themselves in old documents and compiled numerous volumes dealing with the history of the administration of these glorious princes. This, they wrote, is a realistic approach to the problems of state and government. Here you find unadulterated facts and real life, not the bloodless abstractions and faulty generalizations of the British doctrinaires. In truth, all that these ponderous tomes report is a long record of policies and measures which failed precisely because of their neglect of economic law. No more instructive case history could ever be written than these *Acta Borussica*.

However, economics cannot acquiesce in such exemplification. It must enter into a precise scrutiny of the mode in which the market reacts to government interference with the price structure.

2. The Market's Reaction to Government Interference

The characteristic feature of the market price is that it tends to equalize supply and demand. The size of the demand coincides with the size of supply not only in the imaginary construction of the evenly rotating economy. The notion of the plain state of rest as developed by the elementary theory of prices is a faithful description of what comes to pass in the market at every instant. Any deviation of a market price from the height at which supply and demand are equal is—in the unhampered market—self-liquidating.

But if the government fixes prices at a height different from what the market would have fixed if left alone, this equilibrium of demand and supply is disturbed. Then there are—with maximum prices—

potential buyers who cannot buy although they are ready to pay the price fixed by the authority, or even a higher price. Then there are—with minimum prices—potential sellers who cannot sell although they are ready to sell at the price fixed by the authority, or even at a lower price. The price can no longer segregate those potential buyers and sellers who can buy or sell from those who cannot. A different principle for the allocation of the goods and services concerned and for the selection of those who are to receive portions of the supply available necessarily comes into operation. It may be that only those are in a position to buy who come first, or only those to whom particular circumstances (such as personal connections) assign a privileged position, or only those ruthless fellows who chase away their rivals by resorting to intimidation or violence. If the authority does not want chance or violence to determine the allocation of the supply available and conditions to become chaotic, it must itself regulate the amount which each individual is permitted to buy. It must resort to rationing.[1]

But rationing does not affect the core of the issue. The allocation of portions of the supply already produced and available to the various individuals eager to obtain a quantity of the goods concerned is only a secondary function of the market. Its primary function is the direction of production. It directs the employment of the factors of production into those channels in which they satisfy the most urgent needs of the consumers. If the government's price ceiling refers only to one consumers' good or to a limited amount of consumers' goods while the prices of the complementary factors of production are left free, production of the consumers' goods concerned will drop. The marginal producers will discontinue producing them lest they suffer losses. The not absolutely specific factors of production will be employed to a greater extent for the production of other goods not subject to price ceilings. A greater part of the absolutely specific factors of production will remain unused than would have remained in the absence of price ceilings. There emerges a tendency to shift production activities from the production of the goods affected by the maximum prices into the production of other goods. This outcome is, however, manifestly contrary to the intentions of the government. In resorting to price ceilings the authority wanted to make the commodities concerned more easily accessible to the consumers. It considered precisely those commodities so vital that it singled them

1. For the sake of simplicity we deal in the further disquisitions of this section only with maximum prices for commodities and in the next section only with minimum wage rates. However, our statements are, mutatis mutandis, equally valid for minimum prices for commodities and maximum wage rates.

out for a special measure in order to make it possible even for poor people to be amply supplied with them. But the result of the government's interference is that production of these commodities drops or stops altogether. It is a complete failure.

It would be vain for the government to try to remove these undesired consequences by decreeing maximum prices likewise for the factors of production needed for the production of the consumers' goods the prices of which it has fixed. Such a measure would be successful only if all factors of production required were absolutely specific. As this can never be the case, the government must add to its first measure, fixing the price of only one consumers' good below the potential market price, more and more price ceilings, not only for all other consumers' goods and for all material factors of production, but no less for labor. It must compel every entrepreneur, capitalist, and employee to continue producing at the prices, wage rates, and interest rates which the government has fixed, to produce those quantities which the government orders them to produce, and to sell the products to those people—producers or consumers—whom the government determines. If one branch of production were to be exempt from this regimentation, capital and labor would flow into it; production would be restricted precisely in those other—regimented—branches which the government considered so important that it interfered with the conduct of their affairs.

Economics does not say that isolated government interference with the prices of only one commodity or a few commodities is unfair, bad, or unfeasible. It says that such interference produces results contrary to its purpose, that it makes conditions worse, not better, *from the point of view of the government and those backing its interference*. Before the government interfered, the goods concerned were, in the eyes of the government, too dear. As a result of the maximum price their supply dwindles or disappears altogether. The government interfered because it considered these commodities especially vital, necessary, indispensable. But its action curtailed the supply available. It is therefore, from the point of view of the government, absurd and nonsensical.

If the government is unwilling to acquiesce in this undesired and undesirable outcome and goes further and further, if it fixes the prices of all goods and services of all orders and obliges all people to continue producing and working at these prices and wage rates, it eliminates the market altogether. Then the planned economy, socialism of the German *Zwangswirtschaft* pattern, is substituted for the market economy. The consumers no longer direct production by their buying and abstention from buying; the government alone directs it.

There are only two exceptions to the rule that maximum prices restrict supply and thus bring about a state of affairs which is contrary to the aims sought by their imposition. One refers to absolute rent, the other to monopoly prices.

The maximum price results in a restriction of supply because the marginal producers suffer losses and must discontinue production. The nonspecific factors of production are employed for the production of other products not subject to price ceilings. The utilization of the absolutely specific factors of production shrinks. Under unhampered market conditions they would have been utilized up to the limit determined by the absence of an opportunity to use the nonspecific among the complementary factors for the satisfaction of more urgent wants. Now only a smaller part of the available supply of these absolutely specific factors can be utilized; concomitantly that part of the supply that remains unused increases. But if the supply of these absolutely specific factors is so scanty that under the prices of the unhampered market their total supply was utilized, a margin is given within which the government's interference does not curtail the supply of the product. The maximum price does not restrict production as long as it has not entirely absorbed the absolute rent of the marginal supplier of the absolutely specific factor. But at any rate it results in a discrepancy between the demand for and the supply of the product.

Thus the amount by which the urban rent of a piece of land exceeds the agricultural rent provides a margin in which rent control can operate without restricting the supply of rental space. If the maximum rents are graduated in such a way as never to take away from any proprietor so much that he prefers to use the land for agriculture rather than for the construction of buildings, they do not affect the supply of apartments and business premises. However, they increase the demand for such apartments and premises and thus create the very shortage that the governments pretend to fight by their rent ceilings. Whether or not the authorities resort to rationing the space available is catallactically of minor importance. At any rate, their price ceilings do not abolish the catallactic phenomenon of the urban rent. They merely transfer the rent from the landlord's income into the tenant's income.

In practice, of course, governments resorting to rent restriction never adjust their ceilings to these considerations. They either rigidly freeze gross rents as they prevailed on the eve of their interference or allow only a limited addition to these gross rents. As the proportion between the two items included in the gross rent, urban rent proper and price paid for the utilization of the superstructure, varies according to the special circumstances of each dwelling, the effect of rent ceilings is also very different. In some cases the expropriation of the owner to the benefit of the lessee involves only a fraction of the difference between the urban rent and the agricultural rent; in other cases it far exceeds this difference. But however this may be, the rent restriction creates a housing shortage. It increases demand without increasing supply.

If maximum rents are decreed not only for already available rental space, but also for buildings still to be constructed, the construction of new buildings is no longer remunerative. It either stops altogether or slumps to a low level; the shortage is perpetuated. But even if rents in new buildings are left free, construction of new buildings drops. Prospective investors are deterred because they take into account the danger that the government will at a later date declare a new emergency and expropriate a part of their revenues in the same way as it did with the old buildings.

The second exception refers to monopoly prices. The difference between a monopoly price and the competitive price of the commodity in question provides a margin in which maximum prices could be enforced without defeating the ends sought by the government. If the competitive price is p and the lowest among the possible monopoly prices m, a ceiling price of c, c being higher than p and lower than m, would make it disadvantageous for the seller to raise the price above p. The maximum price could reestablish the competitive price and increase demand, production, and the supply offered for sale. A dim cognizance of this concatenation is at the bottom of some suggestions asking for government interference in order to preserve competition and to make it operate as beneficially as possible.

We may for the sake of argument pass over the fact that all such measures would appear as paradoxical with regard to all those instances of monopoly prices which are the outcome of government interference. If the government objects to monopoly prices for new inventions, it should stop granting patents. It would be absurd to grant patents and then to deprive them of any value by forcing the patentee to sell at the competitive price. If the government does not approve of cartels, it should rather abstain from all measures (such as import duties) which provide business with the opportunity to erect combines.

Things are different in those rare instances in which monopoly prices come into existence without assistance from the governments. Here governmental maximum prices could reestablish competitive conditions if it were possible to find out by academic computation at which height a nonexisting competitive market would have determined the price. That all endeavors to construct nonmarket prices are vain has been shown.[2] The unsatisfactory results of all attempts to determine what the fair or correct price for the services of public utilities should be are well known to all experts.

Reference to these two exceptions explains why in some very rare cases maximum prices, when applied with very great caution within a narrow margin, do not restrict the supply of the commodity or the service concerned. It does not affect the correctness of the general rule that maximum prices bring about a state of affairs which, from the point of view of the government decreeing them, is more undesirable than conditions as they would have been in the absence of price control.

Observations on the Causes of the Decline of Ancient Civilization

Knowledge of the effects of government interference with market prices makes us comprehend the economic causes of a momentous historical event, the decline of ancient civilization.

It may be left undecided whether or not it is correct to call the economic organization of the Roman Empire capitalism. At any rate it is certain that the Roman Empire in the second century, the age of the Antonines, the "good" emperors, had reached a high stage of the social division of labor and of interregional commerce. Several metropolitan centers, a considerable number of middle-sized towns, and many small towns were the seats of a refined civilization. The inhabitants of these urban agglomerations were supplied with food and raw materials not only from the neighboring rural districts, but also from distant provinces. A part of these provisions flowed into the cities as revenue of their wealthy residents who owned landed property. But a considerable part was bought in exchange for the rural population's purchases of the products of the city-dwellers' processing activities. There was an extensive trade between the various regions of the vast empire. Not only in the processing industries, but also in agriculture there was a tendency toward further specialization. The various parts of the empire were no longer economically self-sufficient. They were interdependent.

What brought about the decline of the empire and the decay of its civilization was the disintegration of this economic interconnectedness, not the barbarian invasions. The alien aggressors merely took advantage of an opportunity which the internal weakness of the empire offered to them. From a military point of view the tribes which invaded the empire in the fourth and fifth centuries were not more formidable than the armies which the legions had easily defeated

2. Cf. above, pp. 395–397.

in earlier times. But the empire had changed. Its economic and social structure was already medieval.

The freedom that Rome granted to commerce and trade had always been restricted. With regard to the marketing of cereals and other vital necessities it was even more restricted than with regard to other commodities. It was deemed unfair and immoral to ask for grain, oil, and wine, the staples of these ages, more than the customary prices, and the municipal authorities were quick to check what they considered profiteering. Thus the evolution of an efficient wholesale trade in these commodities was prevented. The policy of the *annona,* which was tantamount to a nationalization or municipalization of the grain trade, aimed at filling the gaps. But its effects were rather unsatisfactory. Grain was scarce in the urban agglomerations, and the agriculturists complained about the unremunerativeness of grain growing.[3] The interference of the authorities upset the adjustment of supply to the rising demand.

The showdown came when in the political troubles of the third and fourth centuries the emperors resorted to currency debasement. With the system of maximum prices the practice of debasement completely paralyzed both the production and the marketing of the vital foodstuffs and disintegrated society's economic organization. The more eagerness the authorities displayed in enforcing the maximum prices, the more desperate became the conditions of the urban masses dependent on the purchase of food. Commerce in grain and other necessities vanished altogether. To avoid starving, people deserted the cities, settled on the countryside, and tried to grow grain, oil, wine, and other necessities for themselves. On the other hand, the owners of the big estates restricted their excess production of cereals and began to produce in their farmhouses—the villae—the products of handicraft which they needed. For their big-scale farming, which was already seriously jeopardized because of the inefficiency of slave labor, lost its rationality completely when the opportunity to sell at remunerative prices disappeared. As the owner of the estate could no longer sell in the cities, he could no longer patronize the urban artisans either. He was forced to look for a substitute to meet his needs by employing handicraftsmen on his own account in his *villa.* He discontinued big-scale farming and became a landlord receiving rents from tenants or sharecroppers. These *coloni* were either freed slaves or urban proletarians who settled in the villages and turned to tilling the soil. A tendency toward the establishment of autarky of each landlord's estate emerged. The economic function of the cities, of commerce, trade, and urban handicrafts, shrank. Italy and the provinces of the empire returned to a less advanced state of the social

3. Cf. Rostovtzeff, *The Social and Economic History of the Roman Empire* (Oxford, 1926), p. 187.

division of labor. The highly developed economic structure of ancient civilization retrograded to what is now known as the manorial organization of the Middle Ages.

The emperors were alarmed with that outcome which undermined the financial and military power of their government. But their counteraction was futile as it did not affect the root of the evil. The compulsion and coercion to which they resorted could not reverse the trend toward social disintegration which, on the contrary, was caused precisely by too much compulsion and coercion. No Roman was aware of the fact that the process was induced by the government's interference with prices and by currency debasement. It was vain for the emperors to promulgate laws against the city-dweller who "relicta civitate rus habitare maluerit."[4] The system of the *leiturgia*, the public services to be rendered by the wealthy citizens, only accelerated the retrogression of the division of labor. The laws concerning the special obligations of the shipowners, the *navicularii*, were no more successful in checking the decline of navigation than the laws concerning grain dealing in checking the shrinkage in the cities' supply of agricultural products.

The marvelous civilization of antiquity perished because it did not adjust its moral code and its legal system to the requirements of the market economy. A social order is doomed if the actions which its normal functioning requires are rejected by the standards of morality, are declared illegal by the laws of the country, and are prosecuted as criminal by the courts and the police. The Roman Empire crumbled to dust because it lacked the spirit of liberalism and free enterprise. The policy of interventionism and its political corollary, the Führer principle, decomposed the mighty empire as they will by necessity always disintegrate and destroy any social entity.

3. Minimum Wage Rates

The very essence of the interventionist politicians' wisdom is to raise the price of labor either by government decree or by violent action or the threat of such action on the part of labor unions. To raise wage rates above the height at which the unhampered market would determine them is considered a postulate of the eternal laws of morality as well as indispensable from the economic point of view. Whoever dares to challenge this ethical and economic dogma is scorned both as depraved and ignorant. Many of our contemporaries look upon people who are foolhardy enough "to cross a picket line" as primitive tribesmen looked upon those who violated the precepts of taboo conceptions. Millions are jubilant if such *scabs* receive their well-deserved punishment from the hands of the strikers while the

4. *Corpus Juris Civilis*, l. un. C. X. 37.

police, the public attorneys, and the penal courts preserve a lofty neutrality or openly side with the strikers.

The market wage rate tends toward a height at which all those eager to earn wages get jobs and all those eager to employ workers can hire as many as they want. It tends toward the establishment of what is nowadays called full employment. Where there is neither government nor union interference with the labor market, there is only voluntary or catallactic unemployment. But as soon as external pressure and compulsion, be it on the part of the government or on the part of the unions, tries to fix wage rates *at a higher point,* institutional unemployment emerges. While there prevails on the unhampered labor market a tendency for catallactic unemployment to disappear, institutional unemployment cannot disappear as long as the government or the unions are successful in the enforcement of their fiat. If the minimum wage rate refers only to a part of the various occupations while other sectors of the labor market are left free, those losing their jobs on its account enter the free branches of business and increase the supply of labor in them. When unionism was restricted to skilled labor mainly, the wage rise achieved by the unions did not lead to institutional unemployment. It merely lowered the height of wage rates in those branches in which there were no efficient unions or no unions at all. The corollary of the rise in wages for organized workers was a drop in wages for unorganized workers. But with the spread of government interference with wages and with government support of unionism, conditions have changed. Institutional unemployment has become a chronic or permanent mass phenomenon.

Writing in 1930, Lord Beveridge, later an advocate of government and union meddling with the labor market, pointed out that the potential effect of "a high-wages policy" in causing unemployment is "not denied by any competent authority."[5] In fact, to deny this effect is tantamount to a complete disavowal of any regularity in the sequence and interconnectedness of market phenomena. Those earlier economists who sympathized with the unions were fully aware of the fact that unionization can achieve its ends only when restricted to a minority of workers. They approved of unionism as a device beneficial to the group interests of a privileged labor aristocracy, and did not concern themselves about its consequences for the rest of the wage earners.[6] No one has ever succeeded in the effort

5. Cf. W. H. Beveridge, *Full Employment in a Free Society* (London, 1944), pp. 92 f.

6. Cf. Hutt, *The Theory of Collective Bargaining,* pp. 10–21.

to demonstrate that unionism could improve the conditions and raise the standard of living of *all* those eager to earn wages.

It is important to remember also that Karl Marx did not contend that unions could raise the average standard of wages. As he saw it, "the general tendency of capitalistic production is not to raise, but to sink the average standard of wages." Such being the tendency of things, all that unionism can achieve with regard to wages is "making the best of the occasional chances for their temporary improvement."[7] The unions counted for Marx only as far as they attacked "the very system of wage slavery and present-day methods of production."[8] They should understand that "instead of the *conservative* motto, *A fair day's wages for a fair day's work!* they ought to inscribe on their banner the *revolutionary* watchword, *Abolition of the wages system.*"[9] Consistent Marxians always opposed attempts to impose minimum wage rates as detrimental to the interests of the whole labor class. From the beginning of the modern labor movement there was always an antagonism between the unions and the revolutionary socialists. The older British and American unions were exclusively dedicated to the enforcement of higher wage rates. They looked askance upon socialism, "utopian" as well as "scientific." In Germany there was a rivalry between the adepts of the Marxian creed and the union leaders. Finally, in the last decades preceding the outbreak of the first World War, the unions triumphed. They virtually converted the Social Democratic Party to the principles of interventionism and unionism. In France, Georges Sorel aimed at imbuing the unions with that spirit of ruthless aggression and revolutionary bellicosity which Marx wanted to impart to them. There is today in every nonsocialist country a manifest conflict between two irreconcilable factions within the unions. One group considers unionism a device for the improvement of the workers' conditions within the frame of capitalism. The other group wants to drive the unions into the ranks of militant communism and approves of them only as far as they are the pioneers of a violent overthrow of the capitalistic system.

The problems of labor unionism have been obfuscated and utterly confused by pseudo-humanitarian blather. The advocates of minimum wage rates, whether decreed and enforced by the government or by violent union action, contend that they are fighting for the improvement of the conditions of the working masses. They do not permit

7. Cf. Marx, *Value, Price and Profit,* ed. E. Marx Aveling (Chicago, Charles H. Kerr & Company), p. 125.

8. Cf. A. Lozovsky, *Marx and the Trade Unions* (New York, 1935), p. 17.

9. Cf. Marx, *op. cit.,* pp. 126–127.

anyone to question their dogma that minimum wage rates are the only appropriate means of raising wage rates permanently and for all those eager to earn wages. They pride themselves on being the only true friends of "labor," of the "common man," of "progress," and of the eternal principles of "social justice."

However, the problem is precisely whether there is any means for raising the standard of living of all those eager to work other than raising the marginal productivity of labor by accelerating the increase of capital as compared with population. The union doctrinaires are intent upon obscuring this primary issue. They never refer to the only point that matters, viz., the relation between the number of workers and the quantity of capital goods available. But certain policies of the unions involve a tacit acknowledgment of the correctness of the catallactic theorems concerning the determination of wage rates. Unions are anxious to cut down the supply of labor by anti-immigration laws and by preventing outsiders and newcomers from competing in the unionized sectors of the labor market. They are opposed to the export of capital. These policies would be nonsensical if it were true that the per capita quota of capital available is of no importance for the determination of wage rates.

The essence of the union doctrine is implied in the slogan *exploitation.* According to the union variety of the exploitation doctrine, which differs from the Marxian creed, labor is the only source of wealth, and expenditure of labor the only real costs. By rights, all proceeds from the sale of products should belong to the workers. The manual worker has a fair claim to the "whole produce of labor." The wrong that the capitalistic mode of production does to the worker is seen in the fact that it permits landowners, capitalists, and entrepreneurs to withhold a part of the workers' portion. The share which goes to these parasites is called unearned income. The workers are right in their endeavors to raise wage rates step by step to such a height that finally nothing will be left for the support of a class of idle and socially useless exploiters. In aiming at this end, the unions pretend to continue the battle which earlier generations fought for the emancipation of slaves and serfs and for the abolition of the imposts, tributes, tithes, and unpaid statute labor with which the peasantry was burdened for the benefit of aristocratic landlords. The labor movement is a struggle for freedom and equality, and for the vindication of the inalienable rights of man. Its ultimate victory is beyond doubt, for it is the inevitable trend of historical evolution to wipe out all class privileges and to establish firmly the realm of freedom and equality. The attempts of reactionary employers to halt progress are doomed.

Such are the tenets of present-day social doctrine. It is true that some people, although in perfect agreement with its philosophical ideas, support the practical conclusions derived by the radicals only with certain reservations and qualifications. These moderates do not propose to abolish "management's" share altogether; they would be satisfied with cutting it down to a "fair" amount. As the opinions concerning the fairness of the revenues of the entrepreneurs and capitalists vary widely, the difference between the point of view of the radicals and that of the moderates is of little moment. The moderates also endorse the principle that real wage rates should always rise and never drop. In both world wars few voices in the United States disputed the claim of the unions that the wage earners' take-home pay, even in a national emergency, should go up faster than the cost of living.

As the union doctrine sees it, there is no harm in confiscating the specific revenue of the capitalists and entrepreneurs partially or altogether. In dealing with this issue they speak of profits in the sense in which the classical economists applied this term. They do not distinguish between entrepreneurial profit, interest on the capital employed, and compensation for the technical services rendered by the entrepreneur. We will deal later with the consequences resulting from the confiscation of interest and profits and with the syndicalist elements involved in the "ability to pay" principle and in profit-sharing schemes.[10] We have examined the purchasing power argument as advanced in favor of a policy of raising wage rates above the potential market rates.[11] What remains is to scrutinize the purport of the alleged Ricardo effect.

Ricardo is the author of the proposition that a rise in wages will encourage capitalists to substitute machinery for labor and vice versa.[12] Hence, conclude the union apologists, a policy of raising wage rates, irrespective of what they would have been on the unhampered labor market, is always beneficial. It generates technological improvement and raises the productivity of labor. Higher wages always pay for themselves. In forcing the reluctant employers to raise wage rates, the unions become the pioneers of progress and prosperity.

Many economists approve of the Ricardian proposition although few of them are consistent enough to endorse the inference the union apologists draw from it. The Ricardo effect is by and large a stock-

10. Cf. below, pp. 804–820.

11. Cf. above, pp. 301–303.

12. Cf. Ricardo, *Principles of Political Economy and Taxation,* chap. i, sec. v. The term, "Ricardo effect" is used by Hayek, *Profits, Interest and Investment* (London, 1939), p. 8.

in-trade of popular economics. Nonetheless, the theorem involved is one of the worst economic fallacies.

The confusion starts with the misinterpretation of the statement that machinery is "substituted" for labor. What happens is that labor is rendered more efficient by the aid of machinery. The same input of labor leads to a greater quantity or a better quality of products. The employment of machinery itself does not *directly* result in a reduction of the number of hands employed in the production of the article *A* concerned. What brings about this secondary effect is the fact that—other things being equal—an increase in the available supply of *A* lowers the marginal utility of a unit of *A* as against that of the units of other articles and that therefore labor is withdrawn from the production of *A* and employed in the turning out of other articles. The technological improvement in the production of *A* makes it possible to realize certain projects which could not be executed before because the workers required were employed for the production of *A* for which consumers' demand was more urgent. The reduction of the number of workers in the *A* industry is caused by the increased demand of these other branches to which the opportunity to expand is offered. Incidentally, this insight explodes all talk about "technological unemployment."

Tools and machinery are primarily not labor-saving devices, but means to increase output per unit of input. They appear as labor-saving devices if looked upon exclusively from the point of view of the individual branch of business concerned. Seen from the point of view of the consumers and the whole of society, they appear as instruments that raise the productivity of human effort. They increase supply and make it possible to consume more material goods and to enjoy more leisure. Which goods will be consumed in greater quantity and to what extent people will prefer to enjoy more leisure depends on people's value judgments.

The employment of more and better tools is feasible only to the extent that the capital required is available. Saving—that is, a surplus of production over consumption—is the indispensable condition of every further step toward technological improvement. Mere technological knowledge is of no use if the capital needed is lacking. Indian businessmen are familiar with American ways of production. What prevents them from adopting the American methods is not the lowness of Indian wages, but lack of capital.

On the other hand, capitalist saving necessarily causes employment of additional tools and machinery. The role that plain saving, i.e., the piling up of stocks of consumers' goods as a reserve for rainy days, plays in the market economy is negligible. Under capitalism saving is as a rule capitalist saving. The excess of production over consumption is invested either directly in the saver's own business or farm or indirectly in other peoples' enterprises through the instrumentality of savings deposits, common and preferred stock, bonds, debentures, and mortgages.[13] To the extent to which people keep their consumption below their net income, additional capital is created and at the same time employed for the expansion of the capital equipment of the apparatus of production. As has been pointed out, this outcome cannot be affected by any synchronous tendency toward an increase in cash holdings.[14] On the one hand, what is unconditionally needed for the employment of more and better tools is additional accumulation of capital. On the other hand, there is no employment available for additional capital other than that provided by the application of more and better tools.

Ricardo's proposition and the union doctrine derived from it turn things upside down. A tendency toward higher wage rates is not the cause, but the effect, of technological improvement. Profit-seeking business is compelled to employ the most efficient methods of production. What checks a businessman's endeavors to improve the equipment of his firm is only lack of capital. If the capital required is not available, no meddling with wage rates can provide it.

All that minimum wage rates can accomplish with regard to the employment of machinery is to shift additional investment from one branch into another. Let us assume that in an economically backward country, Ruritania, the stevedores' union succeeds in forcing the entrepreneurs to pay wage rates which are comparatively much higher than those paid in the rest of the country's industries. Then it may result that the most profitable employment for additional capital is to utilize mechanical devices in the loading and unloading of ships. But the capital thus employed is withheld from other branches of Ruritania's business in which, in the absence of the union's policy, it would have been employed in a more profitable way. The effect of the high wages of the stevedores is not an increase, but a drop in Ruritania's total production.[15]

Real wage rates can rise only to the extent that, other things being equal, capital becomes more plentiful. If the government or the

13. As we are dealing here with the conditions of the unhampered market economy, we may disregard the capital-consuming effects of government borrowing.

14. See above, pp. 522–523.

15. The example is merely hypothetical. Such a powerful union would probably prohibit the employment of mechanical devices in the loading and unloading of ships in order to "create more jobs."

unions succeed in enforcing wage rates which are higher than those the unhampered labor market would have determined, the supply of labor exceeds the demand for labor. Institutional unemployment emerges.

Firmly committed to the principles of interventionism, governments try to check this undesired result of their interference by resorting to those measures which are nowadays called full-employment policy: unemployment doles, arbitration of labor disputes, public works by means of lavish public spending, inflation, and credit expansion. All these remedies are worse than the evil they are designed to remove.

Assistance granted to the unemployed does not dispose of unemployment. It makes it easier for the unemployed to remain idle. The nearer the allowance comes to the height at which the unhampered market would have fixed the wage rate, the less incentive it offers to the beneficiary to look for a new job. It is a means of making unemployment last rather than of making it disappear. The disastrous financial implications of unemployment benefits are manifest.

Arbitration is not an appropriate method for the settlement of disputes concerning the height of wage rates. If the arbitrators' award fixes wage rates exactly at the potential market rate or below that rate, it is supererogatory. If it fixes wage rates above the potential market rate, the consequences are the same that any other mode of fixing minimum wage rates above the market height brings about, viz., institutional unemployment. It does not matter to what pretext the arbitrator resorts in order to justify his decision. What matters is not whether wages are "fair" or "unfair" by some artitrary standard, but whether they do or do not bring about an excess of supply of labor over demand for labor. It may seem fair to some people to fix wage rates at such a height that a great part of the potential labor force is doomed to lasting unemployment. But nobody can assert that it is expedient and beneficial to society.

If government spending for public works is financed by taxing the citizens or borrowing from them, the citizens' power to spend and invest is curtailed to the same extent as that of the public treasury expands. No additional jobs are created.

But if the government finances its spending program by inflation—by an increase in the quantity of money and by credit expansion—it causes a general cash-induced rise in the prices of all commodities and services. If in the course of such an inflation the rise in wage rates sufficiently lags behind the rise in the prices of commodities, institutional unemployment may shrink or disappear altogether. But what makes it shrink or disappear is precisely the fact that such an outcome is tantamount to a drop in *real* wage rates. Lord Keynes considered credit expansion an efficient method for the abolition of unemployment; he believed that "gradual and automatic lowering of real wages as a result of rising prices" would not be so strongly resisted by labor as any attempt to lower money wage rates.[16] However, the success of such a cunning plan would require an unlikely degree of ignorance and stupidity on the part of the wage earners. As long as workers believe that minimum wage rates benefit them, they will not let themselves be cheated by such clever tricks.

In practice all these devices of an alleged full employment policy finally lead to the establishment of socialism of the German pattern. As the members of an arbitration court whom the employers have appointed and those whom the unions have appointed never agree with regard to the fairness of a definite rate, the decision virtually devolves upon the members appointed by the government. The power to determine the height of wage rates is thus vested in the government.

The more public works expand and the more the government undertakes in order to fill the gap left by the alleged "private enterprise's inability to provide jobs for all," the more the realm of private enterprise shrinks. Thus we are again faced with the alternative of capitalism or socialism. There cannot be any question of a lasting policy of minimum wage rates.

The Catallactic Aspects of Labor Unionism

The only catallactic problem with regard to labor unions is the question of whether or not it is possible to raise by pressure and compulsion the wage rates of all those eager to earn wages above the height the unhampered market would have determined.

In all countries the labor unions have actually acquired the privilege of violent action. The governments have abandoned in their favor the essential attribute of government, the exclusive power and right to resort to violent coercion and compulsion. Of course, the laws which make it a criminal offense for any citizen to resort—except in case of self-defense—to violent action have not been formally repealed or amended. However, actually labor union violence is tolerated within broad limits. The labor unions are practically free to prevent by force anybody from defying their orders concerning wage rates

16. Cf. Keynes, *The General Theory of Employment, Interest and Money* (London, 1936), p. 264. For a critical examination of this idea see Albert Hahn, *Deficit Spending and Private Enterprise,* Postwar Readjustments Bulletin No. 8, U.S. Chamber of Commerce, pp. 28–29; Henry Hazlitt, *The Failure of the "New Economics"* (Princeton, 1959), pp. 263–295. About the success of the Keynesian stratagem in the 'thirties, cf. below, pp. 792–793.

and other labor conditions. They are free to inflict with impunity bodily evils upon strikebreakers and upon entrepreneurs and mandataries of entrepreneurs who employ strikebreakers. They are free to destroy property of such employers and even to injure customers patronizing their shops. The authorities, with the approval of public opinion, condone such acts. The police do not stop such offenders, the state attorneys do not arraign them, and no opportunity is offered to the penal courts to pass judgment on their actions. In excessive cases, if the deeds of violence go too far, some lame and timid attempts at repression and prevention are ventured. But as a rule they fail. Their failure is sometimes due to bureaucratic inefficiency or to the insufficiency of the means at the disposal of the authorities, but more often to the unwillingness of the whole governmental apparatus to interfere successfully.[17]

Such has been the state of affairs for a long time in all nonsocialist countries. The economist in establishing these facts neither blames nor accuses. He merely explains what conditions have given to the unions the power to enforce their minimum wage rates and what the real meaning of the term collective bargaining is.

As union advocates explain the term collective bargaining, it merely means the substitution of a union's bargaining for the individual bargaining of the individual workers. In the fully developed market economy bargaining concerning those commodities and services of which homogeneous items are frequently bought and sold in great quantities is not effected by the manner in which nonfungible commodities and services are traded. The buyer or seller of fungible consumers' goods or of fungible services fixes a price tentatively and adjusts it later according to the response his offer meets from those interested until he is in a position to buy or to sell as much as he plans. Technically no other procedure is feasible. The department store cannot haggle with its patrons. It fixes the price of an article and waits. If the public does not buy sufficient quantities, it lowers the price. A factory that needs five hundred welders fixes a wage rate which, as it expects, will enable it to hire five hundred men. If only a minor number turns up, it is forced to allow a higher rate. Every employer must raise the wages he offers up to the point at which no competitor lures the workers away by overbidding. What makes the enforcement of minimum wage rates futile is precisely the fact that with wages raised above this point competitors do not turn up with a demand for labor big enough to absorb the whole supply.

If the unions were really bargaining agencies, their collective bargaining could not raise the height of wage rates above the point of

17. Cf. Sylvester Petro, *The Labor Policy of the Free Society* (New York, 1957); Roscoe Pound, *Legal Immunities of Labor Unions* (Washington, D.C., American Enterprise Association, 1957).

the unhampered market. As long as there still are unemployed workers available, there is no reason for an employer to raise his offer. Real collective bargaining would not differ catallactically from the individual bargaining. It would, like individual bargaining, give a virtual voice to those job-seekers who have not yet found the jobs they are looking for.

However, what is euphemistically called collective bargaining by union leaders and "pro-labor" legislation is of a quite different character. It is bargaining at the point of a gun. It is bargaining between an armed party, ready to use its weapons, and an unarmed party under duress. It is not a market transaction. It is a dictate forced upon the employer. And its effects do not differ from those of a government decree for the enforcement of which the police power and the penal courts are used. It produces institutional unemployment.

The treatment of the problems involved by public opinion and the vast number of pseudo-economic writings is utterly misleading. The issue is not the right to form associations. It is whether or not any association of private citizens should be granted the privilege of resorting with impunity to violent action. It is the same problem that relates to the activities of the Ku Klux Klan.

Neither is it correct to look upon the matter from the point of view of a "right to strike." The problem is not the right to strike, but the right—by intimidation or violence—to force other people to strike, and the further right to prevent anybody from working in a shop in which a union has called a strike. When the unions invoke the right to strike in justification of such intimidation and deeds of violence, they are on no better ground than a religious group would be in invoking the right of freedom of conscience as a justification of persecuting dissenters.

When in the past the laws of some countries denied to employees the right to form unions, they were guided by the idea that such unions have no objective other than to resort to violent action and intimidation. When the authorities in the past sometimes directed their armed forces to protect the employers, their mandataries, and their property against the onslaught of strikers, they were not guilty of acts hostile to "labor." They simply did what every government considers its main duty. They tried to preserve their exclusive right to resort to violent action.

There is no need for economics to enter into an examination of the problems of jurisdictional strikes and of various laws, especially of the American New Deal, which were admittedly loaded against the employers and assigned a privileged position to the unions. There is only one point that matters. If a government decree or labor union pressure and compulsion fix wage rates above the height of the potential market rates, institutional unemployment results.

XXXI. CURRENCY AND CREDIT MANIPULATION

1. The Government and the Currency

MEDIA of exchange and money are market phenomena. What makes a thing a medium of exchange or money is the conduct of parties to market transactions. An occasion for dealing with monetary problems appears to the authorities in the same way in which they concern themselves with all other objects exchanged, namely, when they are called upon to decide whether or not the failure of one of the parties to an act of exchange to comply with his contractual obligations justifies compulsion on the part of the government apparatus of violent oppression. If both parties discharge their mutual obligations instantly and synchronously, as a rule no conflicts arise which would induce one of the parties to apply to the judiciary. But if one or both parties' obligations are temporally deferred, it may happen that the courts are called to decide how the terms of the contract are to be complied with. If payment of a sum of money is involved, this implies the task of determining what meaning is to be attached to the monetary terms used in the contract.

Thus it devolves upon the laws of the country and upon the courts to define what the parties to the contract had in mind when speaking of a sum of money and to establish how the obligation to pay such a sum is to be settled in accordance with the terms agreed upon. They have to determine what is and what is not legal tender. In attending to this task the laws and the courts do not *create* money. A thing becomes money only by virtue of the fact that those exchanging commodities and services commonly use it as a medium of exchange. In the unhampered market economy the laws and the judges in attributing legal tender quality to a certain thing merely establish what, according to the usages of trade, was intended by the parties when they referred in their deal to a definite kind of money. They interpret the customs of the trade in the same way in which they proceed when called to determine what is the meaning of any other terms used in contracts.

Mintage has long been a prerogative of the rulers of the country. However, this government activity had originally no objective other than the stamping and certifying of weights and measures. The authority's stamp placed upon a piece of metal was supposed to certify its weight and fineness. When later princes resorted to substituting baser and cheaper metals for a part of the precious metals while retaining the customary face and name of the coins, they did it furtively and in full awareness of the fact that they were engaged in a fraudulent attempt to cheat the public. As soon as people found out these artifices, the debased coins were dealt with at a discount as against the old better ones. The governments reacted by resorting to compulsion and coercion. They made it illegal to discriminate in trade and in the settlement of deferred payments between "good" money and "bad" money and decreed maximum prices in terms of "bad" money. However, the result obtained was not that which the governments aimed at. Their decrees failed to stop the process which adjusted commodity prices (in terms of the debased currency) to the actual state of the money relation. Moreover, the effects appeared which Gresham's Law describes.

The history of government interference with currency is, however, not merely a record of debasement practices and of abortive attempts to avoid their inescapable catallactic consequences. There were governments that did not look upon their mintage prerogative as a means of cheating that part of the public who placed confidence in their rulers' integrity and who, out of ignorance, were ready to accept the debased coins at their face value. These governments considered the manufacturing of coins not as a source of surreptitious fiscal lucre but as a public service designed to safeguard a smooth functioning of the market. But even these governments—out of ignorance and dilettantism—often resorted to measures which were tantamount to interference with the price structure, although they were not deliberately planned as such. As two precious metals were used side by side as money, authorities naïvely believed that it was their task to unify the currency system by decreeing a rigid exchange ratio between gold and silver. The bimetallic system proved a complete failure. It did not bring about bimetallism, but an alternating standard. That metal which, compared with the instantaneous state of the fluctuating market exchange rate between gold and silver, was overvalued in the legally fixed ratio, predominated in domestic circulation, while the other metal disappeared. Finally the governments abandoned their vain attempts and acquiesced in monometallism. The silver purchase policy that the United States practiced for many decades was virtually no longer a device of monetary policy. It was merely a scheme for raising the price of silver for the benefit of the owners of silver mines, their employees, and the states within the boundaries of which the mines were located. It was a poorly disguised subsidy. Its monetary significance consisted merely in the fact that it was financed by issuing additional dollar bills whose legal tender quality does not differ essentially from that of the Federal Reserve notes, although they bear the practically meaningless imprint "Silver Certificate."

Yet economic history also provides instances of well-designed and successful monetary policies on the part of governments whose only intention was to equip their countries with a smoothly working currency system. Laissez-faire liberalism did not abolish the traditional government prerogative of mintage. But in the hands of liberal goverments the character of this state monopoly was completely altered. The ideas which considered it an instrument of interventionist policies were discarded. No longer was it used for fiscal purposes or for favoring some groups of the people at the expense of other groups. The government's monetary activities aimed at one objective only: to facilitate and to simplify the use of the medium of exchange which the conduct of the people had made money. A nation's currency system, it was agreed, should be sound. The principle of soundness meant that the standard coins—i.e., those to which unlimited legal tender power was assigned by the laws—should be properly assayed and stamped bars of bullion coined in such a way as to make the detection of clipping, abrasion, and counterfeiting easy. To the government's stamp no function was attributed other than to certify the weight and the fineness of the metal contained. Pieces worn by usage or in any other way reduced in weight beyond the very narrow limits of tolerated allowance lost their legal tender quality; the authorities themselves withdrew such pieces from circulation and reminted them. For the receiver of an undefaced coin there was no need to resort to the scales and to the acid test in order to know its weight and content. On the other hand, individuals were entitled to bring bullion to the mint and to have it transformed into standard coins either free of charge or against payments of a seigniorage generally not surpassing the actual expenses of the process. Thus the various national currencies became genuine gold currencies. Stability in the exchange ratio between the domestic legal tender and that of all other countries which had adopted the same principles of sound money was brought about. The international gold standard came into being without intergovernmental treaties and institutions.

In many countries the emergence of the gold standard was effected by the operation of Gresham's Law. The role that government policies played in this process in Great Britain consisted merely in ratifying the results brought about by the operation of Gresham's Law; it transformed a de facto state of affairs into a legal state. In other countries governments deliberately abandoned bimetallism just at the moment when the change in the market ratio between gold and silver would have brought about a substitution of a de facto silver currency for the then prevailing de facto gold currency. With all these nations the formal adoption of the gold standard required no other contribution on the part of the administration and the legislature than the enactment of laws.

It was different in those countries which wanted to substitute the gold standard for a—de facto or de jure—silver or paper currency. When the German Reich in the 'seventies of the nineteenth century wanted to adopt the gold standard, the nation's currency was silver. It could not realize its plan by simply imitating the procedure of those countries in which the enactment of the gold standard was merely a ratification of the actual state of affairs. It had to replace the standard silver coins in the hands of the public with gold coins. This was a time-absorbing and complicated financial operation involving vast government purchases of gold and sales of silver. Conditions were similar in those countries which aimed at the substitution of gold for credit money or fiat money.

It is important to realize these facts because they illustrate the differerence between conditions as they prevailed in the liberal age and those prevailing today in the age of interventionism.

2. The Interventionist Aspect of Legal Tender Legislation

The simplest and oldest variety of monetary interventionism is debasement of coins or diminution of their weight or size for the sake of debt abatement. The authority assigns to the cheaper currency units the full legal tender power previously granted to the better units. All deferred payments can be legally discharged by payment of the amount due in the meaner coins according to their face value. Debtors are favored at the expense of creditors. But at the same time future credit transactions are made more onerous for debtors. A tendency for gross market rates of interest to rise ensues as the parties take into account the chances for a repetition of such measures of debt abatement. While debt abatement improves the conditions of those who were already indebted at the moment, it impairs the position of those eager or obliged to contract new debts.

The antitype of debt abatement—debt aggravation through monetary measures—has also been practiced, though rarely. However, it has never deliberately been planned as a device to favor the creditors at the expense of the debtors. Whenever it came to pass, it was the unintentional effect of monetary changes considered as peremptory from other points of view. In resorting to such monetary changes governments put up with their effects upon deferred payments either because they considered the measures unavoidable or because they assumed that creditors and debtors, in determining the terms of the contract, had already foreseen these changes and duly taken them into account. The best examples are provided by British events after the Napoleonic wars and again after the first World War. In both instances Great Britain some time after the end of hostilities returned, by means of a deflationary policy, to the prewar gold parity of the pound sterling. The idea of engineering the substitution of the gold standard for the war-time credit-money standard by acquiescing in the change in the market exchange ratio between the pound and gold, which had already taken place, and of adopting this ratio as the new legal parity, was rejected. This second alternative was scorned as a kind of national bankruptcy, as a partial repudiation of the public debt, and as a malicious infringement upon the rights of all those whose claims had originated in the period preceding the suspension of the unconditional convertibility of the banknotes of the Bank of England. People labored under the delusion that the evils caused by inflation could be cured by a subsequent deflation. Yet the return to the prewar gold parity could not indemnify the creditors for the damage they had suffered as far as the debtors had repaid their old debts during the period of money depreciation. Moreover, it was a boon to all those who had lent during this period and a blow to all those who had borrowed. But the statesmen who were responsible for the deflationary policy were not aware of the import of their action. They failed to see consequences which were, even in their eyes, undesirable, and if they had recognized them in time, they would not have known how to avoid them. Their conduct of affairs really favored the creditors at the expense of the debtors, especially the holders of the government bonds at the expense of the taxpayers. In the 'twenties of the nineteenth century it aggravated seriously the distress of British agriculture and a hundred years later the plight of British export trade. Nonetheless, it would be a mistake to call these two British monetary reforms the consummation of an interventionism intentionally aiming at debt aggravation. Debt aggravation was merely the unintentional outcome of a policy aiming at other ends.

Whenever debt abatement is resorted to, its authors protest that the measure will never be repeated. They emphasize that extraordinary conditions which will never again present themselves have created an emergency which makes indispensable recourse to noxious devices, absolutely reprehensible under any other circumstances. Once and never again, they declare. It is easy to conceive why the authors and supporters of debt abatement are compelled to make such promises. If total or partial nullification of the creditors' claims becomes a regular policy, lending of money will stop altogether. The stipulation of deferred payments depends on the expectation that no such nullification will be decreed.

It is therefore not permissible to look upon debt abatement as a device of a system of economic policies which could be considered as an alternative to any other system of society's permanent economic organization. It is by no means a tool of constructive action. It is a bomb that destroys and can do nothing but destroy. If it is applied only once, a reconstruction of the shattered credit system is still possible. But if the blows are repeated, total destruction results.

It is not correct to look upon inflation and deflation exclusively from the point of view of their effects upon deferred payments. It has been shown that cash-induced changes in purchasing power do not affect the prices of the various commodities and services at the same time and to the same extent, and what role this unevenness plays in the market.[1] But if one regards inflation and deflation as means of rearranging the relations between creditors and debtors, one cannot fail to realize that the ends sought by the government resorting to them are attained only in a very imperfect degree and that, besides, consequences appear which, from the government's point of view, are highly unsatisfactory. As is the case with every other variety of government interference with the price structure, the results obtained not only are contrary to the intentions of the government but produce a state of affairs which, in the opinion of the government, is more undesirable than conditions on the unhampered market.

As far as a government resorts to inflation in order to favor the debtors at the expense of the creditors, it succeeds only with regard to those deferred payments which were stipulated before. Inflation does not make it cheaper to contract new loans; it makes it, on the contrary, more expensive by the appearance of a positive price premium. If inflation is pushed to its ultimate consequences, it makes any stipulation of deferred payments in terms of the inflated currency cease altogether.

1. See above, pp. 411–413.

3. The Evolution of Modern Methods of Currency Manipulation

A metallic currency is not subject to government manipulation. Of course, the government has the power to enact legal tender laws. But then the operation of Gresham's Law brings about results which may frustrate the aims sought by the government. Seen from this point of view, a metallic standard appears as an obstacle to all attempts to interfere with the market phenomena by monetary policies.

In examining the evolution which gave governments the power to manipulate their national currency systems, we must begin by mentioning one of the most serious shortcomings of the classical economists. Both Adam Smith and David Ricardo looked upon the costs involved in the preservation of a metallic currency as a waste. As they saw it, the substitution of paper money for metallic money would make it possible to employ capital and labor, required for the production of the quantity of gold and silver needed for monetary purposes, for the production of goods which could directly satisfy human wants. Starting from this assumption, Ricardo elaborated his famous *Proposals for an Economical and Secure Currency,* first published in 1816. Ricardo's plan fell into oblivion. It was not until many decades after his death that several countries adopted its basic principles under the label *gold exchange standard* in order to reduce the alleged waste involved in the operation of the gold standard nowadays decried as "classical" or "orthodox."

Under the classical gold standard a part of the cash holdings of individuals consists in gold coins. Under the gold exchange standard the cash holdings of individuals consist entirely in money-substitutes. These money-substitutes are redeemable at the legal par in gold or foreign exchange of countries under the gold standard or the gold exchange standard. But the arrangement of monetary and banking institutions aims at preventing the public from withdrawing gold from the Central Bank for domestic cash holdings. The first objective of redemption is to secure the stability of foreign exchange rates.

In dealing with problems of the gold exchange standard all economists—including the author of this book—failed to realize the fact that it places in the hands of governments the power to manipulate their nations' currency easily. Economists blithely assumed that no government of a civilized nation would use the gold exchange standard intentionally as an instrument of inflationary policy. Of course, one must not exaggerate the role that the gold exchange standard played in the inflationary ventures of the last decades. The main factor was the proinflationary ideology. The gold exchange standard was merely a convenient vehicle for the realization of the inflationary plans. Its absence did not hinder the adoption of inflationary measures. The United States was in 1933 by and large still under the classical gold standard. This fact did not stop the New Deal's inflationism. The United States at one stroke—by confiscating its citizens' gold holdings—abolished the classical gold standard and devalued the dollar against gold.

The new variety of the gold exchange standard as it developed in the years between the first and the second World Wars may be called the flexible gold exchange standard or, for the sake of simplicity, the *flexible standard.* Under this system the Central Bank or the Foreign Exchange Equalization Account (or whatever the name of the equivalent governmental institution may be) freely exchanges the money-substitutes which are the country's national legal tender either against gold or against foreign exchange, and vice versa. The ratio at which these exchange deals are transacted is not invariably fixed, but subject to changes. The parity is flexible, as people say. This flexibility, however, is almost always a downward flexibility. The authorities used their power to lower the equivalence of the national currency in terms of gold and of those foreign currencies whose equivalence against gold did not drop; they never ventured to raise it. If the parity against another nation's currency was raised, the change was only the consummation of a drop that had occurred in that other currency's equivalence (in terms of gold or of other nations' currencies which had remained unchanged). Its aim was to bring the appraisal of this definite foreign currency into agreement with the appraisal of gold and the currencies of other foreign nations.

If the downward jump of the parity is very conspicuous, it is called a devaluation. If the alteration of the parity is not so great, editors of financial reports describe it as a weakening in the international appraisal of the currency concerned.[2] In both cases it is usual to refer to the event by declaring that the country concerned has raised the price of gold.

The characterization of the flexible standard from the catallactic point of view must not be confused with its description from the legal point of view. The catallactic aspects of the issue are not affected by the constitutional problems involved. It is immaterial whether the power to alter the parity is vested in the legislative or in the administrative branch of the government. It is immaterial whether the au-

2. See above, p. 461.

thorization given to the administration is unlimited or, as was the case in the United States under New Deal legislation, limited by a terminal point beyond which the officers are not free to devalue further. What counts alone for the economic treatment of the matter is that the principle of flexible parities has been substituted for the principle of the rigid parity. Whatever the constitutional state of affairs may be, no government could embark upon "raising the price of gold" if public opinion were opposed to such a manipulation. If, on the other hand, public opinion favors such a step, no legal technicalities could check it altogether or even delay it for a short time. What happened in Great Britain in 1931, in the United States in 1933, and in France and Switzerland in 1936 clearly shows that the apparatus of representative government is able to work with the utmost speed if public opinion endorses the so-called experts' opinion concerning the expediency and necessity of a currency's devaluation.

One of the main objectives of currency devaluation—whether large-scale or small-scale—is, as will be shown in the next section, to rearrange foreign trade conditions. These effects upon foreign trade make it impossible for a small nation to take its own course in currency manipulation irrespective of what those countries are doing with whom its trade relations are closest. Such nations are forced to follow in the wake of a foreign country's monetary policies. As far as monetary policy is concerned they voluntarily become satellites of a foreign power. By keeping their own country's currency rigidly at par against the currency of a monetary "suzerain-country," they follow all the alterations which the "suzerain" brings about in its own currency's parity against gold and the other nations' currencies. They join a monetary *bloc* and integrate their country into a monetary *area*. The most talked about bloc or area is the sterling bloc or area.

The flexible standard must not be confused with conditions in those countries in which the government has merely proclaimed an official parity of its domestic currency against gold and foreign exchange without making this parity effective. The characteristic feature of the flexible standard is that any amount of domestic money-substitutes can in fact be exchanged at the parity chosen against gold or foreign exchange, and vice versa. At this parity the Central Bank (or whatever the name of the government agency entrusted with the task may be) buys and sells any amount of domestic currency and of foreign currency of at least one of those countries which themselves are either under the gold standard or under the flexible standard. The domestic banknotes are really redeemable.

In the absence of this essential feature of the flexible standard, decrees proclaiming a definite parity have a quite different meaning and bring about quite different effects.[3]

4. The Objectives of Currency Devaluation

The flexible standard is an instrument for the engineering of inflation. The only reason for its acceptance was to make reiterated inflationary moves technically as simple as possible for the authorities.

In the boom period that ended in 1929 labor unions had succeeded in almost all countries in enforcing wage rates higher than those which the market, if manipulated only by migration barriers, would have determined. These wage rates already produced in many countries institutional unemployment of a considerable amount while credit expansion was still going on at an accelerated pace. When finally the inescapable depression came and commodity prices began to drop, the labor unions, firmly supported by the governments, even by those disparaged as anti-labor, clung stubbornly to their high-wages policy. They either flatly denied permission for any cut in nominal wage rates or conceded only insufficient cuts. The result was a tremendous increase in institutional unemployment. (On the other hand, those workers who retained their jobs improved their standard of living as their hourly real wages went up.) The burden of unemployment doles became unbearable. The millions of unemployed were a serious menace to domestic peace. The industrial countries were haunted by the specter of revolution. But union leaders were intractable, and no statesman had the courage to challenge them openly.

In this plight the frightened rulers bethought themselves of a makeshift long since recommended by inflationist doctrinaires. As unions objected to an adjustment of wages to the state of the money relation and commodity prices, they chose to adjust the money relation and commodity prices to the height of wage rates. As they saw it, it was not wage rates that were too high; their own nation's monetary unit was overvalued in terms of gold and foreign exchange and had to be readjusted. Devaluation was the panacea.

The objectives of devaluation were:

1. To preserve the height of nominal wage rates or even to create the conditions required for their further increase, while real wage rates should rather sink.

2. To make commodity prices, especially the prices of farm products, rise in terms of domestic money or, at least, to check their further drop.

3. To favor the debtors at the expense of the creditors.

3. See below, section 6 of this chapter.

4. To encourage exports and to reduce imports.

5. To attract more foreign tourists and to make it more expensive (in terms of domestic money) for the country's own citizens to visit foreign countries.

However, neither the governments nor the literary champions of their policy were frank enough to admit openly that one of the main purposes of devaluation was a reduction in the height of real wage rates. They preferred for the most part to describe the objective of devaluation as the removal of an alleged "fundamental disequilibrium" between the domestic and the international "level" of prices. They spoke of the necessity of lowering domestic costs of production. But they were anxious not to mention that one of the two cost items they expected to lower by devaluation was real wage rates, the other being interest stipulated on long-term business debts and the principal of such debts.

It is impossible to take seriously the arguments advanced in favor of devaluation. They were utterly confused and contradictory. For devaluation was not a policy that originated from a cool weighing of the pros and cons. It was a capitulation of governments to union leaders who did not want to lose face by admitting that their wage policy had failed and had produced institutional unemployment on an unprecedented scale. It was a desperate makeshift of weak and inept statesmen who were motivated by their wish to prolong their tenure of office. In justifying their policy, these demagogues did not bother about contradictions. They promised the processing industries and the farmers that devaluation would make prices rise. But at the same time they promised the consumers that rigid price control would prevent any increase in the cost of living.

After all, the governments could still excuse their conduct by referring to the fact that under the given state of public opinion, entirely under the sway of the doctrinal fallacies of labor unionism, no other policy could be resorted to. No such excuse can be advanced for those authors who hailed the flexibility of foreign exchange rates as the perfect and most desirable monetary system. While governments were still anxious to emphasize that devaluation was an emergency measure not to be repeated again, these authors proclaimed the flexible standard as the most appropriate monetary system and were eager to demonstrate the alleged evils inherent in stability of foreign exchange rates. In their blind zeal to please the governments and the powerful pressure groups of unionized labor and farming, they overstated tremendously the case of flexible parities. But the drawbacks of standard flexibility became manifest very soon. The enthusiasm for devaluation vanished quickly. In the years of the second World War, hardly more than a decade after the day when Great Britain had set the pattern for the flexible standard, even Lord Keynes and his adepts discovered that stability of foreign exchange rates has its merits. One of the avowed objectives of the International Monetary Fund is to stabilize foreign exchange rates.

If one looks at devaluation not with the eyes of an apologist of government and union policies, but with the eyes of an economist, one must first of all stress the point that all its alleged blessings are temporary only. Moreover, they depend on the condition that only one country devalues while the other countries abstain from devaluing their own currencies. If the other countries devalue in the same proportion, no changes in foreign trade appear. If they devalue to a greater extent, all these transitory blessings, whatever they may be, favor them exclusively. A general acceptance of the principles of the flexible standard must therefore result in a race between the nations to outbid one another. At the end of this competition is the complete destruction of all nations' monetary systems.

The much talked about advantages which devaluation secures in foreign trade and tourism, are entirely due to the fact that the adjustment of domestic prices and wage rates to the state of affairs created by devaluation requires some time. As long as this adjustment process is not yet completed, exporting is encouraged and importing is discouraged. However, this merely means that in this interval the citizens of the devaluating country are getting less for what they are selling abroad and paying more for what they are buying abroad; concomitantly they must restrict their consumption. This effect may appear as a boon in the opinion of those for whom the balance of trade is the yardstick of a nation's welfare. In plain language it is to be described in this way: The British citizen must export more British goods in order to buy that quantity of tea which he received before the devaluation for a smaller quantity of exported British goods.

The devaluation, say its champions, reduces the burden of debts. This is certainly true. It favors debtors at the expense of creditors. In the eyes of those who still have not learned that under modern conditions the creditors must not be identified with the rich nor the debtors with the poor, this is beneficial. The actual effect is that the indebted owners of real estate and farm land and the shareholders of indebted corporations reap gains at the expense of the majority of people whose savings are invested in bonds, debentures, savings-bank deposits, and insurance policies.

There are also foreign loans to be considered. When Great Britain, the United States, France, Switzerland and some other European creditor countries devalued their currencies, they made a gift to their foreign debtors.

One of the main arguments advanced in favor of the flexible standard is that it lowers the rate of interest on the domestic money market. Under the classical gold standard and the rigid gold exchange standard, it is said, a country must adjust the domestic rate of interest to conditions on the international money market. Under the flexible standard it is free to follow in the determination of interest rates a policy exclusively guided by considerations of its own domestic welfare.

The argument is obviously untenable with regard to those countries in which the total amount of debts to foreign countries exceeds the total amount of loans granted to foreign countries. When in the course of the nineteenth century some of these debtor nations adopted a sound money policy, their firms and citizens could contract foreign debts in terms of their national currency. This opportunity disappeared altogether with the change in these countries' monetary policies. No foreign banker would contract a loan in Italian lire or try to float an issue of lire bonds. As far as foreign credits are concerned, no change in a debtor country's domestic currency conditions can be of any avail. As far as domestic credits are concerned, devaluation abates only the already previously contracted debts. It enhances the gross market rate of interest of new debts as it makes a positive price premium appear.

This is valid also with regard to interest rate conditions in the creditor nations. There is no need to add anything to the demonstration that interest is not a monetary phenomenon and cannot in the long run be affected by monetary measures.

It is true that the devaluations which were resorted to by various governments between 1931 and 1938 made real wage rates drop in some countries and thus reduced the amount of institutional unemployment. The historian in dealing with these devaluations may therefore say that they were a success as they prevented a revolutionary upheaval of the daily increasing masses of unemployed and as, under the prevailing ideological conditions, no other means could be resorted to in this critical situation. But the historian will no less have to add that the remedy did not affect the root causes of institutional unemployment, the faulty tenets of labor unionism. Devaluation was a cunning device to elude the sway of the union doctrine. It worked because it did not impair the prestige of unionism. But precisely because it left the popularity of unionism untouched, it could work only for a short time. Union leaders learned to distinguish between nominal wage rates and real wage rates. Today their policy aims at raising real wage rates. They can no longer be cheated by a drop in the monetary unit's purchasing power. Devaluation has worn out its usefulness as a device for reducing institutional unemployment.

Cognizance of these facts provides a key for a correct appraisal of the role which Lord Keynes's doctrines played in the years between the first and second World Wars. Keynes did not add any new idea to the body of inflationist fallacies, a thousand times refuted by economists. His teachings were even more contradictory and inconsistent than those of his predecessors who, like Silvio Gesell, were dismissed as monetary cranks. He merely knew how to cloak the plea for inflation and credit expansion in the sophisticated terminology of mathematical economics. The interventionist writers were at a loss to advance plausible arguments in favor of the policy of reckless spending; they simply could not find a case against the economic theorem concerning institutional unemployment. In this juncture they greeted the "Keynesian Revolution" with the verses of Wordsworth: "Bliss was it in that dawn to be alive, but to be young was very heaven."[4] It was, however, a short-run heaven only. We may admit that for the British and American governments in the 'thirties no way was left other than that of currency devaluation, inflation and credit expansion, unbalanced budgets, and deficit spending. Governments cannot free themselves from the pressure of public opinion. They cannot rebel against the preponderance of generally accepted ideologies, however fallacious. But this does not excuse the office-holders who could resign rather than carry out policies disastrous for the country. Still less does it excuse authors who tried to provide a would-be scientific justification for the crudest of all popular fallacies, viz., inflationism.

5. Credit Expansion

It has been pointed out that it would be an error to look upon credit expansion exclusively as a mode of government interference with the market. The fiduciary media did not come into existence as instruments of government policies deliberately aiming at high prices and high nominal wage rates, at lowering the market rate of interest and at debt abatement. They evolved out of the regular business of banking. When the bankers, whose receipts for call money deposited were

4. Cf. P. A. Samuelson, "Lord Keynes and the *General Theory*," *Econometrica*, 14 (1946), 187; reprinted in *The New Economics*, ed. S. E. Harris (New York, 1947), p. 145.

dealt with by the public as money-substitutes, began to lend a part of the funds deposited with them, they had nothing else in view than their own business. They considered it harmless not to keep the whole equivalent of the receipts issued as a cash reserve in their vaults. They were confident that they would always be in a position to comply with their obligations and, without delay, redeem the notes issued even if they were to lend a part of the deposits. Banknotes became fiduciary media within the operation of the unhampered market economy. The begetter of credit expansion was the banker, not the authority.

But today credit expansion is exclusively a government practice. As far as private banks and bankers are instrumental in issuing fiduciary media, their role is merely ancillary and concerns only technicalities. The governments alone direct the course of affairs. They have attained full supremacy in all matters concerning the size of circulation credit. While the size of the credit expansion that private banks and bankers are able to engineer on an unhampered market is strictly limited, the governments aim at the greatest possible amount of credit expansion. Credit expansion is the governments' foremost tool in their struggle against the market economy. In their hands it is the magic wand designed to conjure away the scarcity of capital goods, to lower the rate of interest or to abolish it altogether, to finance lavish government spending, to expropriate the capitalists, to contrive everlasting booms, and to make everybody prosperous.

The inescapable consequences of credit expansion are shown by the theory of the trade cycle. Even those economists who still refuse to acknowledge the correctness of the monetary or circulation credit theory of the cyclical fluctuations of business have never dared to question the conclusiveness and irrefutability of what this theory asserts with regard to the necessary effects of credit expansion. These economists too must admit and do admit that the upswing is invariably conditioned by credit expansion, that it could not come into being and continue without credit expansion, and that it turns into depression when the further progress of credit expansion stops. Their explanation of the trade cycle in fact boils down to the assertion that what first generates the upswing is not credit expansion, but other factors. The credit expansion which even in their opinion is an indispensable requisite of the general boom, is, they say, not the outcome of a policy deliberately aiming at low interest rates and at encouraging additional investment for which the capital goods needed are lacking. It is something which, without active interference on the part of the authorities, in a miraculous way always appears whenever these other factors begin their operation.

It is obvious that these economists contradict themselves in opposing plans to eliminate the fluctuations of business by abstention from credit expansion. The supporters of the naïve inflationist view of history are consistent when they infer from their—of course, utterly fallacious and contradictory—tenets that credit expansion is the economic panacea. But those who do not deny that credit expansion brings about the boom that is the indispensable condition of the depression disagree with their own doctrine in fighting the proposals to curb credit expansion. Both the spokesmen of the governments and the powerful pressure groups and the champions of the dogmatic "unorthodoxy" that dominates the university departments of economics agree that one should try to avert the recurrence of depressions and that the realization of this end requires the prevention of booms. They cannot advance tenable arguments against the proposals to abstain from policies encouraging credit expansion. But they stubbornly refuse to listen to any such idea.They passionately disparage the plans to prevent credit expansion as devices which would perpetuate depressions. Their attitude clearly demonstrates the correctness of the statement that the trade cycle is the product of policies intentionally aimed at lowering the rate of interest and engendering artificial booms.

It is a fact that today measures aimed at lowering the rate of interest are generally considered highly desirable and that credit expansion is viewed as the efficacious means for the attainment of this end. It is this prepossession that impels all governments to fight the gold standard. All political parties and all pressure groups are firmly committed to an easy money policy.[5]

The objective of credit expansion is to favor the interests of some groups of the population at the expense of others. This is, of course, the best that interventionism can attain when it does not hurt the interests of all groups. But while making the whole community poorer, it may still enrich some strata. Which groups belong to the latter class depends on the special data of each case.

The idea which generated what is called *qualitative credit control*

5. If a bank does not expand circulation credit by issuing additional fiduciary media (either in the form of banknotes or in the form of deposit currency), it cannot generate a boom even if it lowers the amount of interest charged below the rate of the unhampered market. It merely makes a gift to the debtors. The inference to be drawn from the monetary cycle theory by those who want to prevent the recurrence of booms and of the subsequent depressions is not that the banks should not lower the rate of interest, but that they should abstain from credit expansion. Of course, credit expansion necessarily entails a temporary downward movement of market interest rates. Professor Haberler (*Prosperity and Depression,* pp. 65–66) has completely failed to grasp this primary point, and thus his critical remarks are vain.

is to channel the additional credit in such a way as to concentrate the alleged blessings of credit expansion upon certain groups and to withhold them from other groups. The credits should not go to the stock exchange, it is argued, and should not make stock prices soar. They should rather benefit the "legitimate productive activity" of the processing industries, of mining, of "legitimate commerce," and, first of all, of farming. Other advocates of qualitative credit control want to prevent the additional credits from being used for investment in fixed capital and thus immobilized. They are to be used, instead, for the production of liquid goods. According to these plans the authorities give the banks concrete directions concerning the types of loans they should grant or are forbidden to grant.

However, all such schemes are vain. Discrimination in lending is no substitute for checks placed on credit expansion, the only means that could really prevent a rise in stock exchange quotations and an expansion of investment in fixed capital. The mode in which the additional amount of credit finds its way into the loan market is only of secondary importance. What matters is that there is an inflow of newly created credit. If the banks grant more credits to the farmers, the farmers are in a position to repay loans received from other sources and to pay cash for their purchases. If they grant more credits to business as circulating capital, they free funds which were previously tied up for this use. In any case they create an abundance of disposable money for which its owners try to find the most profitable investment. Very promptly these funds find outlets in the stock exchange or in fixed investment. The notion that it is possible to pursue a credit expansion without making stock prices rise and fixed investment expand is absurd.[6]

The typical course of events under credit expansion was until a few decades ago determined by two facts: that it was credit expansion under the gold standard, and that it was not the outcome of concerted action on the part of the various national governments and the central banks whose conduct these governments directed. The first of these facts meant that governments were not prepared to abandon the convertibility of their country's banknotes according to the rigidly fixed parity. The second fact resulted in a lack of quantitative uniformity in the size of credit expansion. Some countries got ahead of other countries and their banks were faced with the danger of a serious external drain upon their reserves in gold and foreign exchange. In order to preserve their own solvency, these banks were forced to take recourse to drastic credit restriction. Thus they

6. Cf. Machlup, *The Stock Market, Credit and Capital Formation,* pp. 256–261.

created the panic and inaugurated the depression on the domestic market. The panic very soon spread to other countries. Businessmen in these other countries became frightened and increased their borrowing in order to strengthen their liquid funds for all possible contingencies. It was precisely this increased demand for new credits which impelled the monetary authorities of their own countries, already alarmed by the crisis in the first country, also to resort to contraction. Thus within a few days or weeks the depression became an international phenomenon.

The policy of devaluation has to some extent altered this typical sequence of events. Menaced by an external drain, the monetary authorities do not always resort to credit restriction and to raising the rate of interest charged by the central banking system. They devalue. Yet devaluation does not solve the problem. If the government does not care how far foreign exchange rates may rise, it can for some time continue to cling to credit expansion. But one day the crack-up boom will annihilate its monetary system. On the other hand, if the authority wants to avoid the necessity of devaluing again and again at an accelerated pace, it must arrange its domestic credit policy in such a way as not to outrun in credit expansion the other countries against which it wants to keep its domestic currency at par.

Many economists take it for granted that the attempts of the authorities to expand credit will always bring about the same almost regular alternation between periods of booming trade and of subsequent depression. They assume that the effects of credit expansion will in the future not differ from those that have been observed since the end of the eighteenth century in Great Britain and since the middle of the nineteenth century in Western and Central Europe and in North America. But we may wonder whether conditions have not changed. The teachings of the monetary theory of the trade cycle are today so well known even outside of the circle of economists, that the naïve optimism which inspired the entrepreneurs in the boom periods of the past has given way to a certain skepticism. It may be that businessmen will in the future react to credit expansion in a manner other than they have in the past. It may be that they will avoid using for an expansion of their operations the easy money available because they will keep in mind the inevitable end of the boom. Some signs forebode such a change. But it is too early to make a definite statement.

In another direction the monetary theory of the trade cycle has certainly affected the course of events. Although no official —whether he works in the bureaus of a government's financial services or of a central bank, or whether he teaches at a neo-orthodox university—is prepared to admit it, public opinion by and large no longer denies the two main theses of the circulation credit theory: viz., that the cause of the depression is the preceding boom and that this boom is engendered by credit expansion. The awareness of these facts alarms the financial press as soon as the first signs of the boom appear. Then even the authorities begin to talk about the necessity of preventing a further rise in prices and profits, and they really begin to restrict credit. The boom comes to an early end; a recession starts. The result has been that in the last decade the length of the cycle was considerably cut down. There was still an alternation of boom and slump, but the phases lasted a shorter time and succeeded one another more frequently. This is a far cry from the "classical" period of the ten and a half years of William Stanley Jevon's crop cycle. And, most important, as the boom comes to an earlier end, the amount of malinvestment is smaller and in consequence the following depression is milder too.

The Chimera of Contracyclical Policies

An essential element of the "unorthodox" doctrines, advanced both by all socialists and by all interventionists, is that the recurrence of depressions is a phenomenon inherent in the very operation of the market economy. But while the socialists contend that only the substitution of socialism for capitalism can eradicate the evil, the interventionists ascribe to the government the power to correct the operation of the market economy in such a way as to bring about what they call "economic stability." These interventionists would be right if their antidepression plans were to aim at a radical abandonment of credit expansion policies. However, they reject this idea in advance. What they want is to expand credit more and more and to prevent depressions by the adoption of special "contracyclical" measures.

In the context of these plans the government appears as a deity that stands and works outside the orbit of human affairs, that is independent of the actions of its subjects, and has the power to interfere with these actions from without. It has at its disposal means and funds that are not provided by the people and can be freely used for whatever purposes the rulers are prepared to employ them for. What is needed to make the most beneficent use of this power is merely to follow the advice given by the experts.

The most advertised among these suggested remedies is contracyclical timing of public works and expenditure on public enterprises. The idea is not so new as its champions would have us believe. When depression came in the past, public opinion always asked the government to embark upon public works in order to create jobs and to stop the drop in prices. But the problem is how to finance these public works. If the government taxes the citizens or borrows from them, it does not add anything to what the Keynesians call the aggregate amount of spending. It restricts the private citizen's power to consume or to invest to the same extent that it increases its own. If, however, the government resorts to the cherished inflationary methods of financing, it makes things worse, not better. It may thus delay for a short time the outbreak of the slump. But when the unavoidable payoff does come, the crisis is the heavier the longer the government has postponed it.

The interventionist experts are at a loss to grasp the real problems involved. As they see it, the main thing is "to plan public capital expenditure well in advance and to accumulate a shelf of fully worked out capital projects which can be put into operation at short notice." This, they say, "is the right policy and one which we recommend all countries should adopt."[7] However, the problem is not to elaborate projects, but to provide the material means for their execution. The interventionists believe that this could be easily achieved by holding back government expenditure in the boom and increasing it when the depression comes.

Now, restriction of government expenditure may certainly be a good thing. But it does not provide the funds a government needs for a later expansion of its expenditure. An individual may conduct his affairs in this way. He may accumulate savings when his income is high and spend them later when his income drops. But it is different with a nation or all nations together. The treasury may hoard a considerable part of the lavish revenue from taxes which flows into the public exchequer as a result of the boom. As far and as long as it withholds these funds from circulation, its policy is really deflationary and contracyclical and may to this extent weaken the boom created by credit expansion. But when these funds are spent again, they alter the money relation and create a cash-induced tendency toward a drop in the monetary unit's purchasing power. By no means can these funds provide the capital goods required for the execution of the shelved public works.

The fundamental error of these projects consists in the fact that they ignore the shortage of capital goods. In their eyes the depression is merely caused by a mysterious lack of the people's propensity both to consume and to invest. While the only real problem is to produce more and to consume less in order to increase the stock of capital goods available, the interventionists want to increase both consumption and investment. They want the government to embark upon projects which are unprofitable precisely because the factors of pro-

7. Cf. League of Nations, *Economic Stability in the Post-War World,* Report of the Delegation on Economic Depressions, Pt. II (Geneva, 1945), p. 173.

duction needed for their execution must be withdrawn from other lines of employment in which they would fulfill wants the satisfaction of which the consumers consider more urgent. They do not realize that such public works must considerably intensify the real evil, the shortage of capital goods.

One could, of course, think of another mode for the employment of the savings the government makes in the boom period. The treasury could invest its surplus in buying large stocks of all those materials which it will later, when the depression comes, need for the execution of the public works planned and of the consumers' goods which those occupied in these public works will ask for. But if the authorities were to act in this way, they would considerably intensify the boom, accelerate the outbreak of the crisis, and make its consequences more serious.[8]

All this talk about contracyclical government activities aims at one goal only, namely, to divert the public's attention from cognizance of the real cause of the cyclical fluctuations of business. All governments are firmly committed to the policy of low interest rates, credit expansion, and inflation. When the unavoidable aftermath of these short-term policies appears, they know only of one remedy—to go on in inflationary ventures.

6. Foreign Exchange Control and Bilateral Exchange Agreements

If a government fixes the parity of its domestic credit or fiat money against gold or foreign exchange at a higher point than the market—that is, if it fixes maximum prices for gold and foreign exchange below the potential market price—the effects appear which Gresham's Law describes. A state of affairs results which—very inadequately—is called a scarcity of foreign exchange.

It is the characteristic mark of an economic good that the supply

8. In dealing with the contracyclical policies the interventionists always refer to the alleged success of these policies in Sweden. It is true that public capital expenditure in Sweden was actually doubled between 1932 and 1939. But this was not the cause, but an effect, of Sweden's prosperity in the 'thirties. This prosperity was entirely due to the rearmament of Germany. This Nazi policy increased the German demand for Swedish products on the one hand and restricted, on the other hand, German competition on the world market for those products which Sweden could supply. Thus Swedish exports increased from 1932 to 1938 (in thousands of tons): iron ore from 2,219 to 12,485; pig iron from 31,047 to 92,980; ferro-alloys from 15,453 to 28,605; other kinds of iron and steel from 134,237 to 256,146; machinery from 46,230 to 70,605. The number of unemployed applying for relief was 114,00 in 1932 and 165,000 in 1933. It dropped, as soon as German rearmament came into full swing, to 115,000 in 1934, to 62,000 in 1935, and was 16,000 in 1938. The author of this "miracle" was not Keynes, but Hitler.

available is not so plentiful as to make any intended utilization of it possible. An object that is not in short supply is not an economic good; no prices are asked or paid for it. As money must necessarily be an economic good, the notion of a money that would not be scarce is absurd. What those governments who complain about a scarcity of foreign exchange have in mind is, however, something different. It is the unavoidable outcome of their policy of price fixing. It means that at the price arbitrarily fixed by the government demand exceeds supply. If the government, having by means of inflation reduced the purchasing power of the domestic monetary unit against gold, foreign exchange, and commodities and services, abstains from any attempt at controlling foreign exchange rates, there cannot be any question of a scarcity in the sense in which the government uses this term. He who is ready to pay the market price would be in a position to buy as much foreign exchange as he wants.

But the government is resolved not to tolerate any rise in foreign exchange rates (in terms of the inflated domestic currency). Relying upon its magistrates and constables, it prohibits any dealings in foreign exchange on terms different from the ordained maximum price.

As the government and its satellites see it, the rise in foreign exchange rates was caused by an unfavorable balance of payments and by the purchases of speculators. In order to remove the evil, the government resorts to measures restricting the demand for foreign exchange. Only those people should henceforth have the right to buy foreign exchange who need it for transactions of which the government approves. Commodities the importation of which is superfluous in the opinion of the government should no longer be imported. Payment of interest and principal on debts due to foreigners is prohibited. Citizens must no longer travel abroad. The government does not realize that such measures can never "improve" the balance of payments. If imports drop, exports drop concomitantly. The citizens who are prevented from buying foreign goods, from paying back foreign debts, and from traveling abroad, will not keep the amount of domestic money thus left to them in their cash holdings. They will increase their buying either of consumers' or of producers' goods and thus bring about a further tendency for domestic prices to rise. But the more prices rise, the more will exports be checked.

Now the government goes a step further. It nationalizes foreign exchange transactions. Every citizen who acquires—through exporting, for example—an amount of foreign exchange, is bound to sell it at the official rate to the office of foreign exchange control. If this provision, which is tantamount to an export duty, were to be effectively enforced, export trade would shrink greatly or cease altogether. The government certainly does not like this result. But neither does it want to admit that its interference has utterly failed to achieve the ends sought and has produced a state of affairs which is, from the government's own point of view, much worse even than the previous state of affairs. So the government resorts to a makeshift. It subsidizes the export trade to such an extent that the losses which its policy inflicts upon the exporters are compensated.

On the other hand, the government bureau of foreign exchange control, stubbornly clinging to the fiction that foreign exchange rates have not "really" risen and that the official rate is an effective rate, sells foreign exchange to importers at this official rate. If this policy were to be really followed, it would be equivalent to paying bonuses to the merchants concerned. They would reap windfall profits in selling the imported commodity on the domestic market. Thus the authority resorts to further makeshifts. It either raises import duties or levies special taxes on the importers or burdens their purchases of foreign exchange in some other way.

Then, of course, foreign exchange control works. But it works only because it virtually acknowledges the market rate of foreign exchange. The exporter gets for his proceeds in foreign exchange the official rate plus the subsidy, which together equal the market rate. The importer pays for foreign exchange the official rate plus a special premium, tax, or duty, which together equal the market rate. The only people who are too dull to grasp what is really going on and let themselves be fooled by the bureaucratic terminology, are the authors of books and articles on new methods of monetary management and on new monetary experience.

The monopolization of buying and selling of foreign exchange by the government vests the control of foreign trade in the authorities. It does not affect the determination of foreign exchange rates. It does not matter whether or not the government makes it illegal for the press to publish the real and effective rates of foreign exchange. As far as foreign trade is still carried on, only these real and effective rates are in force.

In order to conceal better the true state of affairs, governments are intent upon eliminating all reference to the real foreign exchange rate. Foreign trade, they think, should no longer be transacted by the intermediary of money. It should be barter. They enter into barter and clearing agreements with foreign governments. Each of the two contracting countries should sell to the other country a quantity of goods and services and receive in exchange a quantity of other goods and services. In the text of these treaties any reference to the real market rates of foreign exchange is carefully avoided. However, both parties calculate their sales and their purchases in terms of the world market prices expressed in gold. These clearing and barter agreements substitute bilateral trade between two countries for the triangular or multilateral trade of the liberal age. But they in no way affect the fact that a country's national currency has lost a part of its purchasing power against gold, foreign exchange, and commodities.

As a policy of foreign trade nationalization, foreign exchange control is a step on the way toward a substitution of socialism for the market economy. From any other point of view it is abortive. It can certainly neither in the short run nor in the long run affect the determination of the rate of foreign exchange.

XXXII. CONFISCATION AND REDISTRIBUTION

1. The Philosophy of Confiscation

INTERVENTIONISM is guided by the idea that interfering with property rights does not affect the size of production. The most naïve manifestation of this fallacy is presented by confiscatory interventionism. The yield of production activities is considered a given magnitude independent of the merely accidental arrangements of society's social order. The task of the government is seen as the "fair" distribution of this national income among the various members of society.

The interventionists and the socialists contend that all commodities are turned out by a social process of production. When this process comes to an end and its fruits ripen, a second social process, that of distribution of the yield, follows and allots a share to each. The characteristic feature of the capitalist order is that the shares allotted are unequal. Some people—the entrepreneurs, the capitalists, and the landowners—appropriate to themselves more than they should. Accordingly, the portions of other people are curtailed. Government should by rights expropriate the surplus of the privileged and distribute it among the underprivileged.

Now in the market economy this alleged dualism of two independent processes, that of production and that of distribution, does not exist. There is only one process going on. Goods are not first produced and then distributed. There is no such thing as an appropriation of portions out of a stock of ownerless goods. The products come into existence as somebody's property. If one wants to distribute them, one must first confiscate them. It is certainly very easy for the governmental apparatus of compulsion and coercion to embark upon confiscation and expropriation. But this does not prove that a durable system of economic affairs can be built upon such confiscation and expropriation.

When the Vikings turned their backs upon a community of autarkic peasants whom they had plundered, the surviving victims began to work, to till the soil, and to build again. When the pirates returned after some years, they again found things to seize. But capitalism cannot stand such reiterated predatory raids. Its capital accumulation and investments are founded upon the expectation that no such expropriation will occur. If this expectation is absent, people will prefer to consume their capital instead of safeguarding it for the expropriators. This is the inherent error of all plans that aim at combining private ownership and reiterated expropriation.

2. Land Reform

The social reformers of older days aimed at the establishment of a community of autarkic farmers only. The shares of land allotted to each member were to be equal. In the imagination of these utopians there is no room for division of labor and specialization in processing trades. It is a serious mistake to call such a social order *agrarian socialism.* It is merely a juxtaposition of economically self-sufficient households.

In the market economy the soil is a means of production like any other material factor of production. Plans aiming at a more or less equal distribution of the soil among the farming population are, under the conditions of the market economy, merely plans for granting privileges to a group of less efficient producers at the expense of the immense majority of consumers. The operation of the market tends to eliminate all those farmers whose cost of production is higher than the marginal costs needed for the production of that amount of farm products the consumers are ready to buy. It determines the size of the farms as well as the methods of production applied. If the government interferes in order to make a different arrangement of the conditions of farming prevail, it raises the average price of farm products. If under competitive conditions m farmers, each of them operating a 1,000-acre farm, produce all those farm products the consumers are ready to acquire, and the government interferes in order to substitute $5m$ farmers, each of them operating a 200-acre farm, for m, the previous numbers of farmers, the consumers foot the bill.

It is vain to justify such land reforms by referring to natural law and other metaphysical ideas. The simple truth is that they enhance the price of agricultural products and that they also impair nonagricultural production. As more manpower is needed to turn out a unit of farm produce, more people are employed in farming and less are left for the processing industries. The total amount of commodities available for consumption drops and a certain group of people is favored at the expense of the majority.

3. Confiscatory Taxation

Today the main instrument of confiscatory interventionism is taxation. It does not matter whether the objective of estate and income taxation is the allegedly social motive of equalizing wealth and income or whether the primary motive is that of revenue. What alone counts is the resulting effect.

The average man looks at the problems involved with unveiled envy. Why should anybody be richer than he himself is? The lofty moralist conceals his resentment in philosophical disquisitions. He argues that a man who owns ten millions cannot be made happier by an increment of ninety millions more. Inversely, a man who owns a hundred millions does not feel any impairment of happiness if his wealth is reduced to a bare ten millions only. The same reasoning holds good for excessive incomes.

To judge in this way means to judge from an individualistic point of view. The yardstick applied is the supposed sentiments of individuals. Yet the problems involved are social problems; they must be appraised with regard to their social consequences. What matters is neither the happiness of any Croesus nor his personal merits or demerits; it is society and the productivity of human effort.

A law that prohibits any individual from accumulating more than ten millions or from making more than one million a year restricts the activities of precisely those entrepreneurs who are most successful in filling the wants of consumers. If such a law had been enacted in the United States fifty years ago, many who are multimillionaires today would live in more modest circumstances. But all those new branches of industry which supply the masses with articles unheard of before would operate, if at all, on a much smaller scale, and their products would be beyond the reach of the common man. It is manifestly contrary to the interest of the consumers to prevent the most efficient entrepreneurs from expanding the sphere of their activities up to the limit to which the public approves of their conduct of business by buying their products. Here again the issue is who should be supreme, the consumers or the government? In the unhampered market the behavior of consumers, their buying or abstention from buying, ultimately determines each individual's income and wealth. Should one vest in the government the power to overrule the consumers' choices?

The incorrigible statolatrist objects. In his opinion what motivates the activities of the great entrepreneur is not the lust for wealth, but the lust for power. Such a "royal merchant" would not restrict his activities if he had to deliver all the surplus earned to the tax collector. His lust for power cannot be weakened by any considerations of mere money making. Let us, for the sake of argument, accept this psychology. But on what else is the power of a businessman founded than on his wealth? How would Rockefeller and Ford have been in a position to acquire "power" if they had been prevented from acquiring wealth? After all, those statolatrists are on comparatively better grounds who want to prohibit the accumulation of wealth precisely because it gives a man economic power.[1]

Taxes are necessary. But the system of discriminatory taxation universally accepted under the misleading name of progressive taxation of income and inheritance is not a mode of taxation. It is rather a mode of disguised expropriation of the successful capitalists and entrepreneurs. Whatever the governments' satellites may advance in its favor, it is incompatible with the preservation of the market economy. It can at best be considered a means of bringing about socialism. Looking backward on the evolution of income tax rates from the beginning of the Federal income tax in 1913 until the present day, one can hardly believe that the tax will not soon absorb 100 per cent of all the surplus above the average height of the common man's wages.

Economics is not concerned with the spurious metaphysical doctrines advanced in favor of tax progression, but with its repercussions on the operation of the market economy. The interventionist authors and politicians look at the problems involved from the angle of their arbitrary notions of what is "socially desirable." As they see it, "the purpose of taxation is never to raise money," since the government "can raise all the money it needs by printing it." The true purpose of taxation is "to leave less in the hands of the taxpayer."[2]

Economists approach the issue from a different angle. They ask first: what are the effects of confiscatory taxation on capital accumulation? The greater part of that portion of the higher incomes which is taxed away would have been used for the accumulation of additional capital. If the treasury employs the proceeds for current expenditure, the result is a drop in the amount of capital accumulation. The same is valid, even to a greater extent, for death taxes. They force the heirs to sell a considerable part of the testator's estate. This capital

1. There is no need to emphasize again that the use of the terminology of political rule is entirely inadequate in the treatment of economic problems. See above, pp. 272–273.

2. Cf. A. B. Lerner, *The Economics of Control, Principles of Welfare Economics* (New York, 1944), pp. 307–308.

is, of course, not destroyed; it merely changes ownership. But the savings of the purchasers, which are spent for the acquisition of the capital sold by the heirs, would have constituted a net increment in capital available. Thus the accumulation of new capital is slowed down. The realization of technological improvement is impaired; the quota of capital invested per worker employed is reduced; a check is placed upon the rise in the marginal productivity of labor and upon the concomitant rise in real wage rates. It is obvious that the popular belief that this mode of confiscatory taxation harms only the immediate victims, the rich, is false.

If capitalists are faced with the likelihood that the income tax or the estate tax will rise to 100 per cent, they will prefer to consume their capital funds rather than to preserve them for the tax collector.

Confiscatory taxation results in checking economic progress and improvement not only by its effect upon capital accumulation. It brings about a general trend toward stagnation and the preservation of business practices which could not last under the competitive conditions of the unhampered market economy.

It is an inherent feature of capitalism that it is no respecter of vested interests and forces every capitalist and entrepreneur to adjust his conduct of business anew each day to the changing structure of the market. Capitalists and entrepreneurs are never free to relax. As long as they remain in business they are never granted the privilege of quietly enjoying the fruits of their ancestors' and their own achievements and of lapsing into a routine. If they forget that their task is to serve the consumers to the best of their abilities, they will very soon forfeit their eminent position and will be thrown back into the ranks of the common man. Their leadership and their funds are continually challenged by newcomers.

Every ingenious man is free to start new business projects. He may be poor, his funds may be modest and most of them may be borrowed. But if he fills the wants of consumers in the best and cheapest way, he will succeed by means of "excessive" profits. He ploughs back the greater part of his profits into his business, thus making it grow rapidly. It is the activity of such enterprising parvenus that provides the market economy with its "dynamism." These nouveaux riches are the harbingers of economic improvement. Their threatening competition forces the old firms and big corporations either to adjust their conduct to the best possible service of the public or to go out of business.

But today taxes often absorb the greater part of the newcomer's "excessive" profits. He cannot accumulate capital; he cannot expand his own business; he will never become big business and a match for the vested interests. The old firms do not need to fear his competition; they are sheltered by the tax collector. They may with impunity indulge in routine, they may defy the wishes of the public and become conservative. It is true, the income tax prevents them, too, from accumulating new capital. But what is more important for them is that it prevents the dangerous newcomer from accumulating any capital. They are virtually privileged by the tax system. In this sense progressive taxation checks economic progress and makes for rigidity. While under unhampered capitalism the ownership of capital is a liability forcing the owner to serve the consumers, modern methods of taxation transform it into a privilege.

The interventionists complain that big business is getting rigid and bureaucratic and that it is no longer possible for competent newcomers to challenge the vested interests of the old rich families. However, as far as their complaints are justified, they complain about things which are merely the result of their own policies.

Profits are the driving force of the market economy. The greater the profits, the better the needs of the consumers are supplied. For profits can only be reaped by removing discrepancies between the demands of the consumers and the previous state of production activities. He who serves the public best, makes the highest profits. In fighting profits governments deliberately sabotage the operation of the market economy.

Confiscatory Taxation and Risk-Taking

A popular fallacy considers entrepreneurial profit a reward for risk-taking. It looks upon the entrepreneur as a gambler who invests in a lottery after having weighed the favorable chances of winning a prize against the unfavorable chances of losing his stake. This opinion manifests itself most clearly in the description of stock-exchange transactions as a sort of gambling. From the point of view of this widespread fable, the evil caused by confiscatory taxation is that it disarranges the ratio between the favorable and the unfavorable chances in the lottery. The prizes are cut down, while the unfavorable hazards remain unchanged. Thus capitalists and entrepreneurs are discouraged from embarking upon risky ventures.

Every word in this reasoning is false. The owner of capital does not choose between more risky, less risky, and safe investments. He is forced, by the very operation of the market economy, to invest his funds in such a way as to supply the most urgent needs of the consumers to the best possible extent. If the methods of taxation resorted to by the government bring about capital consumption or restrict the accumulation of new capital, the capital required for marginal employments is lacking and an expansion of investment which would have been effected in the absence of these taxes is prevented. The wants of the consumers are satisfied to a lesser extent only. But this outcome is not caused by a reluctance of capitalists to take risks; it is caused by a drop in capital supply.

There is no such thing as a safe investment. If capitalists were to behave in the way the risk fable describes and were to strive after what they consider to be the safest investment, their conduct would render this line of investment unsafe and they would certainly lose their input. For the capitalist there is no means of evading the law of the market that makes it imperative for the investor to comply with the wishes of the consumers and to produce all that can be produced under the given state of capital supply, technological knowledge, and the valuations of the consumers. A capitalist never chooses that investment in which, according to his understanding of the future, the danger of losing his input in smallest. He chooses that investment in which he expects to make the highest possible profit.

Those capitalists who are aware of their own lack of ability to judge correctly for themselves the trend of the market do not invest in equity capital, but lend their funds to the owners of such venture capital. They thus enter into a sort of partnership with those on whose better ability to appraise the conditions of the market they rely. It is customary to call venture capital *risk* capital. However, as has been pointed out, the success or failure of the investment in preferred stock, bonds, debentures, mortgages, and other loans depends ultimately also on the same factors that determine success or failure of the venture capital invested.[3] There is no such thing as independence of the vicissitudes of the market.

If taxation were to strengthen the supply of loan capital at the expense of the supply of venture capital, it would make the gross market rate of interest drop and at the same time, by increasing the share of borrowed capital as against the share of equity capital in the capital structure of the firms and corporations, render the investment in loans more uncertain. The process would therefore be self-liquidating.

The fact that a capitalist as a rule does not concentrate his investments, both in common stock and in loans, in one enterprise or one branch of business, but prefers to spread out his funds among various classes of investment, does not suggest that he wants to reduce his "gambling risk." He wants to improve his chances of earning profits.

Nobody embarks upon any investment if he does not expect to make a good investment. Nobody deliberately chooses a malinvestment. It is only the emergence of conditions not properly anticipated by the investor that turns an investment into a malinvestment.

3. Cf. above, pp. 539–540.

As has been pointed out, there cannot be such a thing as noninvested capital.[4] The capitalist is not free to choose between investment and noninvestment. Neither is he free to deviate in the choice of his investments in capital goods from the lines determined by the most urgent among the still-unsatisfied wants of the consumers. He must try to anticipate these future wants correctly. Taxes may reduce the amount of capital goods available by bringing about consumption of capital. But they do not restrict the employment of all capital goods available.[5]

With an excessive height of the income and estate tax rates for the very rich, a capitalist may consider it the most advisable thing to keep all his funds in cash or in bank balances not bearing any interest. He consumes part of his capital, pays no income tax and reduces the inheritance tax which his heirs will have to pay. But even if people really behave this way, their conduct does not affect the employment of the capital available. It affects prices. But no capital good remains uninvested on account of it. And the operation of the market pushes investment into those lines in which it is expected to satisfy the most urgent not yet satisfied demand of the buying public.

4. Cf. above, pp. 521–523.

5. In using the term "capital goods available," due consideration should be given to the problem of convertibility.

XXXIII. SYNDICALISM AND CORPORATIVISM

1. The Syndicalist Idea

THE term *syndicalism* is used to signify two entirely different things.

Syndicalism, as used by the partisans of Georges Sorel, means special revolutionary tactics to be resorted to for the realization of socialism. Labor unions, it implies, should not waste their strength in the task of improving the conditions of wage earners within the frame of capitalism. They should adopt *action directe,* unflinching violence to destroy all the institutions of capitalism. They should never cease to fight—in the genuine sense of the term—for their ultimate goal, socialism. The proletarians must not let themselves be fooled by the catchwords of the bourgeoisie, such as liberty, democracy, representative government. They must seek their salvation in the class struggle, in bloody revolutionary upheavals and in the pitiless annihilation of the bourgeois.

This doctrine played and still plays an enormous role in modern politics. It has provided essential ideas to Russian Bolshevism, Italian Fascism, and German Nazism. But it is a purely political issue and may be disregarded in a catallactic analysis.

The second meaning of the term syndicalism refers to a program of society's economic organization. While socialism aims at the substitution of government ownership of the means of production for private ownership, syndicalism wants to give the ownership of the plants to the workers employed in them. Such slogans as "The railroads to the railroadmen" or "The mines to the miners" best indicate the ultimate goals of syndicalism.

The ideas of socialism and those of syndicalism in the sense of *action directe* were developed by intellectuals whom consistent adepts of all Marxian sects cannot help describing as bourgeois. But the idea of syndicalism as a system of social organization is a genuine product of the "proletarian mind." It is precisely what the naïve employee considers a fair and expedient means for improving his own material well-being. Eliminate the idle parasites, the entrepreneurs and capitalists, and give their "unearned incomes" to the workers! Nothing could be simpler.

If one were to take these plans seriously, one would not have to deal with them in a discussion of the problems of interventionism. One would have to realize that syndicalism is neither socialism, nor capitalism, nor interventionism, but a system of its own different from these three schemes. However, one cannot take the syndicalist program seriously, and nobody ever has. Nobody has been so confused and injudicious as to advocate syndicalism openly as a social system. Syndicalism has played a role in the discussion of economic issues only as far as certain programs unwittingly contained syndicalist features. There are elements of syndicalism in certain objectives of government and labor-union interference with market phenomena. There are, moreover, guild socialism and corporativism, which pretended to avoid the government omnipotence inherent in all socialist and interventionist ventures by adulterating them with a syndicalist admixture.

2. The Fallacies of Syndicalism

The root of the syndicalist idea is to be seen in the belief that entrepreneurs and capitalists are irresponsible autocrats who are free to conduct their affairs arbitrarily. Such a dictatorship must not be tolerated. The liberal movement, which has substituted representative government for the despotism of hereditary kings and aristocrats, must crown its achievements by substituting "industrial democracy" for the tyranny of hereditary capitalists and entrepreneurs. The economic revolution must bring to a climax the liberation of the people which the political revolution has inaugurated.

The fundamental error of this argument is obvious. The entrepreneurs and capitalists are not irresponsible autocrats. They are unconditionally subject to the sovereignty of the consumers. The market is a consumers' democracy. The syndicalists want to transform it into a producers' democracy. This idea is fallacious, for the sole end and purpose of production is consumption.

What the syndicalist considers the most serious defect of the capitalist system and disparages as the brutality and callousness of autocratic profit-seekers is precisely the outcome of the supremacy of the consumers. Under the competitive conditions of the unhampered market economy the entrepreneurs are forced to improve technological methods of production without regard to the vested interests of the workers. The employer is forced never to pay workers more than corresponds to the consumers' appraisal of their achievements. If an employee asks for a raise because his wife has borne him a new baby and the employer refuses on the ground that the infant does not contribute to the factory's effort, the employer acts as the mandatary of the consumers. These consumers are not prepared to pay more for any commodity merely because the worker has a large family. The naïveté of the syndicalists manifests itself in the fact that they would never concede to those producing the articles which they themselves are using the same privileges which they claim for themselves.

The syndicalist principle requires that the shares of every corporation should be taken away from "absentee ownership" and be equally distributed among the employees; payment of interest and principal of debts is to be discontinued. "Management" will then be placed in the hands of a board elected by the workers who are now also the shareholders. This mode of confiscation and redistribution will not bring about equality within the nation or the world. It would give more to the employees of those enterprises in which the quota of capital invested per worker is greater and less to those in which it is smaller.

It is a characteristic fact that the syndicalists in dealing with these issues always refer to management and never mention entrepreneurial activities. As the average subordinate employee sees things, all that is to be done in the conduct of business is to accomplish those ancillary tasks which are entrusted to the managerial hierarchy within the frame of the entrepreneurial plans. In his eyes the individual plant or workshop as it exists and operates today is a permanent establishment. It will never change. It will always turn out the same products. He ignores completely the fact that conditions are in a ceaseless flux, and that the industrial structure must be daily adjusted to the solution of new problems. His world view is stationary. It does not allow for new branches of business, new products, and new and better methods for manufacturing the old products. Thus the syndicalist ignores the essential problems of entrepreneurship: providing the capital for new industries and the expansion of already existing industries, restricting outfits for the products of which demand drops, technological improvement. It is not unfair to call syndicalism the economic philosophy of short-sighted people, of those adamant conservatives who look askance upon any innovation and are so blinded by envy that they call down curses upon those who provide them with more, better, and cheaper products. They are like patients who grudge the doctor his success in curing them of a malady.

3. Syndicalist Elements in Popular Policies

The popularity of syndicalism manifests itself in various postulates of contemporary economic policies. The essence of these policies is always to grant privileges to a minority group at the expense of the immense majority. They invariably result in impairing the wealth and income of the majority.

Many labor unions are intent upon restricting the number of workers employed in their field. While the public wants more and cheaper books, periodicals and newspapers, and would get them under the conditions of an unhampered labor market, the typographical unions prevent many newcomers from working in printing offices. The effect is, of course, an increase in the wages earned by the union members. But the corollary is a drop of wage rates for those not admitted and an enhancement in the price of printed matter. The same effect is brought about by union opposition to the utilization of technological improvements and by all sorts of featherbedding practices.

Radical syndicalism aims at entirely eliminating payment of dividends to shareholders and of interest to creditors. The interventionists in their enthusiasm for middle-of-the-road solutions want to appease the syndicalists by giving the employees a part of the profits. Profit-sharing is a very popular slogan. There is no need to enter anew into an examination of the fallacies implied in the underlying philosophy. It suffices to show the absurd consequences to which such a system must lead.

It may sometimes be good policy for a small shop or for an enterprise employing highly skilled workers, to grant an extra bonus to employees if business is prosperous. But it is a non sequitur to assume that what under special conditions may be wise for an individual firm could work satisfactorily as a general system. There is no reason why one welder should make more money because his employer earns high profits and another welder less because his employer earns lower profits or no profits at all. The workers themselves would rebel against such a method of remuneration. It could not be preserved even for a short time.

A caricature of the profit-sharing scheme is the *ability-to-pay* principle as recently introduced into the program of American labor unionism. While the profit-sharing scheme aims at an allocation to the employees of a part of profits already earned, the ability-to-pay scheme aims at a distribution of profits which some external observers believe the employer may earn in the future. The issue has been obfuscated by the fact that the Truman Administration, after having accepted the new union doctrine, announced that it was appointing a "fact-finding" board which would have the authority to examine the books of the employers in order to determine their ability to pay an increase in wages. However, the books can provide information only about past costs and proceeds and past profits and losses. Estimates of future volume of production, future sales, future costs, or future profits or losses are not facts, but speculative anticipations. There are no facts about future profits.[1]

There cannot be any question of realizing the syndicalist ideal according to which the proceeds of an enterprise should completely go to the employees and nothing should be left for interest on the capital invested and profits. If one wants to abolish what is called "unearned income," one must adopt socialism.

4. Guild Socialism and Corporativism

The ideas of guild socialism and corporativism originated from two different lines of thought.

The eulogists of medieval institutions long praised the eminence of the guilds. What was needed to wash away the alleged evils of the market economy was simply to return to the well-tried methods of the past. However, all these diatribes remained sterile. The critics never attempted to particularize their suggestions or to elaborate definite plans for an economic reconstruction of the social order. The most they did was to point out the alleged superiority of the old quasi-representative assemblies of the type of the French *États-Généraux* and the German *Ständische Landtage* as against the modern parliamentary bodies. But even with regard to this constitutional issue their ideas were rather vague.

The second source of guild socialism is to be found in specific political conditions of Great Britain. When the conflict with Germany became aggravated and finally in 1914 led to war, the younger British socialists began to feel uneasy about their program. The state idolatry of the Fabians and their glorification of German and Prussian institutions was paradoxical indeed at a time when their own country was involved in a pitiless struggle against Germany. What was the use of fighting the Germans when the most "progressive" intellectuals of the country longed for the adoption of German social policies? Was it possible to praise British liberty as against Prussian bondage and at the same time to recommend the methods of Bismarck and his

1. Cf. F. R. Fairchild, *Profits and the Ability to Pay Wages* (Irvington-on-Hudson, 1946), p. 47.

successors? British socialists yearned for a specifically British brand of socialism as different as possible from the Teutonic brand. The problem was to construct a socialist scheme without totalitarian state supremacy and omnipotence, an individualistic variety of collectivism.

The solution of this problem is no less impossible than that of the construction of a triangular square. Yet the young men of Oxford confidently tried to solve it. They borrowed for their program the name *guild socialism* from the little known group of the eulogists of the Middle Ages. They characterized their scheme as industrial self-government, an economic corollary of the most renowned principle of English political rule, local government. In their plans they assigned the leading role to the most powerful British pressure group, the trade unions. Thus they did everything to make their device palatable to their countrymen.

However, neither these captivating adornments nor the obtrusive and noisy propaganda could mislead intelligent people. The plan was contradictory and blatantly impracticable. After only a few years it fell into complete oblivion in the country of its origin.

But then came a resurrection. The Italian Fascists badly needed an economic program of their own. After having seceded from the international parties of Marxian socialism, they could no longer pose as socialists. Neither were they, the proud scions of the invincible Roman legionaries, prepared to make concessions to Western capitalism or to Prussian interventionism, the counterfeit ideologies of the barbarians who had destroyed their glorious empire. They were in search of a social philosophy, purely and exclusively Italian. Whether or not they knew that their gospel was merely a replica of British guild socialism is immaterial. At any rate, the *stato corporativo* was nothing but a rebaptized edition of guild socialism. The differences concerned only unimportant details.

Corporativism was flamboyantly advertised by the bombastic propaganda of the Fascists, and the success of their campaign was overwhelming. Many foreign authors exuberantly praised the miraculous achievements of the new system. The governments of Austria and Portugal emphasized that they were firmly committed to the noble ideas of corporativism. The Pope's encyclical *Quadragesimo anno* (1931) contained passages which could—but need not—be interpreted as an endorsement of corporativism. In any case it is a fact that Catholic authors supported this interpretation in books which were published with the imprimatur of the Church authorities.

Yet neither the Italian Fascists nor the Austrian and Portuguese governments ever made any serious attempt to realize the corporativist utopia. The Italians attached to various institutions the label *corporativist* and transformed the university chairs of political economy into chairs of *economia politica e corporativa*. But never was there any question of the much talked about essential feature of corporativism, self-government of the various branches of trade and industry. The Fascist Government clung first to the same principles of economic policies which all not outright socialist governments have adopted in our day, interventionism. Then later it turned step by step toward the German system of socialism, i.e., all-round state control of economic activities.

The fundamental idea both of guild socialism and of corporativism is that every branch of business forms a monopolistic body, the guild or *corporazione*.[2] This entity enjoys full autonomy; it is free to settle all its internal affairs without interference of external factors and of people who are not themselves members of the guild. The mutual relations between the various guilds are settled by direct bargaining from guild to guild or by the decisions of a general assembly of the delegates of all guilds. In the regular course of affairs the government does not interfere at all. Only in exceptional cases, when an agreement between the various guilds cannot be attained, is the state called in.[3]

In drafting this scheme the guild socialists had in mind the conditions of British local government and the relation between the various local authorities and the central government of the United Kingdom. They aimed at self-government of each branch of industry; they wanted, as the Webbs put it, "the right of self-determination for each vocation."[4] In the same way in which each municipality takes care of its local community affairs and the national government handles only those affairs which concern the interests of the whole nation, the guild alone should have jurisdiction over its internal affairs and the government should restrict its interference to those things which the guilds themselves cannot settle.

However, within a system of social cooperation under the division of labor there are no such things as matters of concern only to those

2. The most elaborate description of guild socialism is provided by Sidney and Beatrice Webb, *A Constitution for the Socialist Commonwealth of Great Britain* (London, 1920); the best book on corporativism is Ugo Papi, *Lezioni di Economia Generale e Corporativa*, Vol. III (Padova, 1934).

3. Mussolini declared on January 13, 1934, in the Senate: "Solo in un secondo tempo, quando le categorie non abbiano trovato la via dell' accordo e dell' equilibrio, lo Stato potrà intervenire." (Quoted by Papi, *op. cit.*, p. 225).

4. Sidney and Beatrice Webb, *op, cit.*, pp. 227 ff.

engaged in a special plant, enterprise, or branch of industry and of no concern to outsiders. There are no internal affairs of any guild or *corporazione* the arrangement of which does not affect the whole nation. A branch of business does not serve only those who are occupied in it; it serves everybody. If within any branch of business there is inefficiency, a squandering of scarce factors of production, or a reluctance to adopt the most appropriate methods of production, everybody's material interests are hurt. One cannot leave decisions concerning the choice of technological methods, the quantity and quality of products, the hours of work, and a thousand other things to the members of the guild, because they concern outsiders no less than members. In the market economy the entrepreneur in making such decisions is unconditionally subject to the law of the market. He is responsible to the consumers. If he were to defy the orders of the consumers, he would suffer losses and would very soon forfeit his entrepreneurial position. But the monopolistic guild does not need to fear competition. It enjoys the inalienable right of exclusively covering its field of production. It is, if left alone and autonomous, not the servant of the consumers, but their master. It is free to resort to practices which favor its members at the expense of the rest of the people.

It is of no importance whether within the guild the workers alone rule or whether and to what extent the capitalists and the former entrepreneurs cooperate in the management of affairs. It is likewise without importance whether or not some seats in the guild's governing board are assigned to representatives of the consumers. What counts is that the guild, if autonomous, is not subject to pressure that would force it to adjust its operations to the best possible satisfaction of the consumers. It is free to give the interests of its members precedence over the interests of consumers. There is in the scheme of guild socialism and corporativism nothing that would take into account the fact that the only purpose of production is consumption. Things are turned upside down. Production becomes an end in itself.

When the American New Deal embarked upon the National Recovery Administration scheme, the government and its brain trust were fully aware of the fact that what they planned was merely the establishment of an administrative apparatus for full government control of business. The short-sightedness of the guild socialists and corporativists is to be seen in the fact that they believed that the autonomous guild or corporazione could be considered a device for a working system of social cooperation.

It is very easy indeed for each guild to arrange its allegedly internal affairs in such a way as to satisfy its members fully. Short hours of work, high wage rates, no further improvements in technological methods or in the quality of the products which could inconvenience the members—very well. But what will the result be if all guilds resort to the same policies?

Under the guild system there is no longer any question of a market. There are no longer any prices in the catallactic sense of the term. There are neither competitive prices nor monopoly prices. Those guilds which monopolize the supply of vital necessities attain a dictatorial position. The producers of indispensable foodstuffs and fuel and the suppliers of electric current and of transportation can with impunity squeeze the whole people. Does anybody expect that the majority will tolerate such a state of affairs? There is no doubt that any attempt to realize the corporativist utopia would in a very short time lead to violent conflicts, if the government did not interfere when the vital industries abused their privileged position. What the doctrinaires envisage only as an exceptional measure—the interference of the government—will become the rule. Guild socialism and corporativism will turn into full government control of all production activities. They will develop into that system of Prussian Zwangswirtschaft which they were designed to avoid.

There is no need to deal with the other fundamental shortcomings of the guild scheme. It is as deficient as any other syndicalist project. It does not take into account the necessity of shifting capital and labor from one branch to another and of establishing new branches of production. It entirely neglects the problem of saving and capital accumulation. In short, it is nonsense.

XXXIV. THE ECONOMICS OF WAR

1. Total War

THE market economy involves peaceful cooperation. It bursts asunder when the citizens turn into warriors and, instead of exchanging commodities and services, fight one another.

The wars fought by primitive tribes did not affect cooperation under the division of labor. Such cooperation by and large did not exist between the warring parties before the outbreak of hostilities. These wars were unlimited or total wars. They aimed at total victory and total defeat. The defeated were either exterminated or expelled from their dwelling places or enslaved. The idea that a treaty could settle the conflict and make it possible for both parties to live in peaceful neighborly conditions was not present in the minds of the fighters.

The spirit of conquest does not acknowledge restraints other than those imposed by a power which resists successfully. The principle of empire building is to expand the sphere of supremacy as far as possible. The great Asiatic conquerors and the Roman Imperators stopped only when they could not march farther. Then they postponed aggression for later days. They did not abandon their ambitious plans and did not consider independent foreign states as anything else than targets for later onslaughts.

This philosophy of boundless conquest also animated the rulers of medieval Europe. They too aimed first of all at the utmost expansion of the size of their realms. But the institutions of feudalism provided them with only scanty means for warfare. Vassals were not obliged to fight for their lord more than a limited time. The selfishness of the vassals who insisted on their rights checked the king's aggressiveness. Thus the peaceful coexistence of a number of sovereign states originated. In the sixteenth century a Frenchman, Bodin, developed the theory of national sovereignty. In the seventeenth century a Dutchman, Grotius, added to it a theory of international relations in war and peace.

With the disintegration of feudalism, sovereigns could no longer rely upon summoned vassals. They "nationalized" the country's armed forces. Henceforth, the warriors were the king's mercenaries.

The organization, equipment, and support of such troops were rather costly and a heavy burden on the ruler's revenues. The ambitions of the princes were unbounded, but financial considerations forced them to moderate their designs. They no longer planned to conquer a whole country. All they aimed at was the conquest of a few cities or of a province. To attain more would also have been unwise politically. For the European powers were anxious not to let any one of them become too powerful and a menace to their own safety. A too impetuous conqueror must always fear a coalition of all those whom his bigness has frightened.

The combined effect of military, financial, and political circumstances produced the limited warfare which prevailed in Europe in the three hundred years preceding the French Revolution. Wars were fought by comparatively small armies of professional soldiers. War was not an affair of the peoples; it concerned the rulers only. The citizens detested war which brought mischief to them and burdened them with taxes and contributions. But they considered themselves victims of events in which they did not participate actively. Even the belligerent armies respected the "neutrality" of the civilians. As they saw it, they were fighting the supreme warlord of the hostile forces, but not the noncombatant subjects of the enemy. In the wars fought on the European continent the property of civilians was considered inviolable. In 1856 the Congress of Paris made an attempt to extend this principle to naval warfare. More and more, eminent minds began to discuss the possibility of abolishing war altogether.

Looking at conditions as they had developed under the system of limited warfare, philosophers found wars useless. Men are killed or maimed, wealth is destroyed, countries are devastated for the sole benefit of kings and ruling oligarchies. The peoples themselves do not derive any gain from victory. The individual citizens are not enriched if their rulers expand the size of their realm by annexing a province. For the people wars do not pay. The only cause of armed conflict is the greed of autocrats. The substitution of representative government for royal despotism will abolish war altogether. Democracies are peaceful. It is no concern of theirs whether their nation's sovereignty stretches over a larger or smaller territory. They will treat territorial problems without bias and passion. They will settle them peacefully. What is needed to make peace durable is to dethrone the despots. This, of course, cannot be achieved peacefully. It is necessary to crush the mercenaries of the kings. But this revolutionary war of the people against the tyrants will be the last war, the war to abolish war forever.

This idea was already dimly present in the minds of the French revolutionary leaders when, after having repelled the invading armies of Prussia and Austria, they embarked upon a campaign of aggression. Of course, under the leadership of Napoleon they themselves very soon adopted the most ruthless methods of boundless expansion and annexation until a coalition of all European powers frustrated their ambitions. But the idea of durable peace was soon resurrected. It was one of the main points in the body of nineteenth-century liberalism as consistently elaborated in the much abused principles of the Manchester School.

These British liberals and their continental friends were keen enough to realize that what can safeguard durable peace is not simply government by the people, but government by the people under unlimited laissez faire. In their eyes free trade, both in domestic affairs and in international relations, was the necessary prerequisite of the preservation of peace. In such a world without trade and migration barriers no incentives for war and conquest are left. Fully convinced of the irrefutable persuasiveness of the liberal ideas, they dropped the notion of the last war to abolish all wars. All peoples will of their own accord recognize the blessings of free trade and peace and will curb their domestic despots without any aid from abroad.

Most historians entirely fail to recognize the factors which replaced the "limited" war of the ancien régime by the "unlimited" war of our age. As they see it, the change came with the shift from the dynastic to the national form of state and was a consequence of the French Revolution. They look only upon attending phenomena and confuse causes and effects. They speak of the composition of the armies, of strategical and tactical principles, of weapons and transportation facilities, and of many other matters of military art and administrative technicalities.[1] However, all these things do not explain why modern nations prefer aggression to peace.

There is perfect agreement with regard to the fact that total war is an offshoot of aggressive nationalism. But this is merely circular reasoning. We call aggressive nationalism that ideology which makes for modern total war. Aggressive nationalism is the necessary derivative of the policies of interventionism and national planning. While laissez faire eliminates the causes of international conflict, government interference with business and socialism creates conflicts for

1. The best presentation of the traditional interpretation is provided by the book, *Makers of Modern Strategy, Military Thought from Machiavelli to Hitler*, ed. E. M. Earle (Princeton University Press, 1944); cf. especially the contribution of R. R. Palmer, pp. 49–53.

which no peaceful solution can be found. While under free trade and freedom of migration no individual is concerned about the territorial size of his country, under the protective measures of economic nationalism nearly every citizen has a substantial interest in these territorial issues. The enlargement of the territory subject to the sovereignty of his own government means material improvement for him or at least relief from restrictions which a foreign government has imposed upon his well-being. What has transformed the limited war between royal armies into total war, the clash between peoples, is not technicalities of military art, but the substitution of the welfare state for the laissez-faire state.

If Napoleon I had reached his goal, the French Empire would have stretched far beyond the limits of 1815. Spain and Naples would have been ruled by kings of the house of Bonaparte-Murat instead of kings of another French family, the Bourbons. The palace of Kassel would have been occupied by a French playboy instead of one of the egregious Electors of the Hesse family. All these things would not have made the citizens of France more prosperous. Neither did the citizens of Prussia win anything from the fact that their king in 1866 evicted his cousins of Hanover, Hesse-Kassel and Nassau from their luxurious residences. But if Hitler had realized his plans, the Germans expected to enjoy a higher standard of living. They were confident that the annihilation of the French, the Poles, and the Czechs would make every member of their own race richer. The struggle for more Lebensraum was their own war.

Under laissez faire peaceful coexistence of a multitude of sovereign nations is possible. Under government control of business it is impossible. The tragic error of President Wilson was that he ignored this essential point. Modern total war has nothing in common with the limited war of the old dynasties. It is a war against trade and migration barriers, a war of the comparatively overpopulated countries against the comparatively underpopulated. It is a war to abolish those institutions which prevent the emergence of a tendency toward an equalization of wage rates all over the world. It is a war of the farmers tilling poor soil against those governments which bar them from access to much more fertile soil lying fallow. It is, in short, a war of wage earners and farmers who describe themselves as underprivileged "have-nots" against the wage earners and farmers of other nations whom they consider privileged "haves."

The acknowledgment of this fact does not suggest that victorious wars would really do away with those evils about which the aggressors complain. These conflicts of vital interests can be eliminated only by a general and unconditional substitution of a philosophy of mutual cooperation for the prevailing ideas of allegedly irreconcilable antagonisms between the various social, political, religious, linguistic, and racial subdivisions of mankind.

It is futile to place confidence in treaties, conferences, and such bureaucratic outfits as the League of Nations and the United Nations. Plenipotentiaries, office clerks and experts make a poor show in fighting ideologies. The spirit of conquest cannot be smothered by red tape. What is needed is a radical change in ideologies and economic policies.

2. War and the Market Economy

The market economy, say the socialists and the interventionists, is at best a system that may be tolerated in peacetime. But when war comes, such indulgence is impermissible. It would jeopardize the vital interests of the nation for the sole benefit of the selfish concerns of capitalists and entrepreneurs. War, and in any case modern total war, peremptorily requires government control of business.

Hardly anybody has been bold enough to challenge this dogma. It served in both World Wars as a convenient pretext for innumerable measures of government interference with business which in many countries step by step led to full "war socialism." When the hostilities ceased, a new slogan was launched. The period of transition from war to peace and of "reconversion," people contended, requires even more government control than the period of war. Besides, why should one ever return to a social system which can work, if at all, only in the interval between two wars? The most appropriate thing would be to cling permanently to government control in order to be duly prepared for any possible emergency.

An examination of the problems which the United States had to face in the second World War will clearly show how fallacious this reasoning is.

What America needed in order to win the war was a radical conversion of all its production activities. All not absolutely indispensable civilian consumption was to be eliminated. The plants and farms were henceforth to turn out only a minimum of goods for nonmilitary use. For the rest, they were to devote themselves completely to the task of supplying the armed forces.

The realization of this program did not require the establishment of controls and priorities. If the government had raised all the funds needed for the conduct of war by taxing the citizens and by borrowing from them, everybody would have been forced to cut down his consumption drastically. The entrepreneurs and farmers would have turned toward production for the government because the sale of goods to private citizens would have dropped. The government, now by virtue of the inflow of taxes and borrowed money the biggest buyer on the market, would have been in a position to obtain all it wanted. Even the fact that the government chose to finance a considerable part of the war expenditure by increasing the quantity of money in circulation and by borrowing from the commercial banks would not have altered this state of affairs. The inflation must, of course, bring about a marked tendency toward a rise in the prices of all goods and services. The government would have had to pay higher nominal prices. But it would still have been the most solvent buyer on the market. It would have been possible for it to outbid the citizens who on the one hand had not the right of manufacturing the money they needed and on the other hand would have been squeezed by enormous taxes.

But the government deliberately adopted a policy which was bound to make it impossible for it to rely upon the operation of the unhampered market. It resorted to price control and made it illegal to raise commodity prices. Furthermore it was very slow in taxing the incomes swollen by the inflation. It surrendered to the claim of the unions that the workers' real take-home wages should be kept at a height which would enable them to preserve in the war their prewar standard of living. In fact, the most numerous class of the nation, the class which in peacetime consumed the greatest part of the total amount of goods consumed, had so much more money in their pockets that their power to buy and to consume was greater than in peacetime. The wage earners—and to some extent also the farmers and the owners of plants producing for the government—would have frustrated the government's endeavors to direct industries toward the production of war materials. They would have induced business to produce more, not less, of those goods which in wartime are considered superfluous luxuries. It was this circumstance that forced the Administration to resort to the systems of priorities and of rationing. The shortcomings of the methods adopted for financing war expenditure made government control of business necessary. If no inflation had been made and if taxation had cut down the income (after taxes) of all citizens, not only of those enjoying higher incomes, to a fraction of their peacetime revenues, these controls would have been supererogatory. The endorsement of the doctrine that the wage earners' real income must in wartime be even higher than in peacetime made them unavoidable.

Not government decrees and the paper work of hosts of people on the government's payroll, but the efforts of private enterprise produced those goods which enabled the American armed forces to win the war and to provide all the material equipment its allies needed for their cooperation. The economist does not infer anything from these historical facts. But it is expedient to mention them as the interventionists would have us believe that a decree prohibiting the employment of steel for the construction of apartment houses automatically produces airplanes and battleships.

The adjustment of production activities to a change in the demand of consumers is the source of profits. The greater the discrepancy between the previous state of production activities and that agreeing with the new structure of demand, the greater adjustments are required and the greater profits are earned by those who succeed best in accomplishing these adjustments. The sudden transition from peace to war revolutionizes the structure of the market, makes radical readjustments indispensable and thus becomes for many a source of high profits. The planners and interventionists regard such profits as a scandal. As they see it, the first duty of government in time of war is to prevent the emergence of new millionaires. It is, they say, unfair to let some people become richer while other people are killed or maimed.

Nothing is fair in war. It is not just that God is for the big battalions and that those who are better equipped defeat poorly equipped adversaries. It is not just that those in the front line shed their life-blood in obscurity, while the commanders, comfortably located in headquarters hundreds of miles behind the trenches, gain glory and fame. It is not just that John is killed and Mark crippled for the rest of his life, while Paul returns home safe and sound and enjoys all the privileges accorded to veterans.

It may be admitted that it is not "fair" that war enhances the profits of those entrepreneurs who contribute best to the equipment of the fighting forces. But it would be foolish to deny that the profit system produces the best weapons. It was not socialist Russia that aided capitalist America with lend-lease; the Russians were lamentably defeated before American-made bombs fell on Germany and before they got the arms manufactured by American big business. The most important thing in war is not to avoid the emergence of high profits, but to give the best equipment to one's own country's soldiers and sailors. The worst enemies of a nation are those malicious demagogues who would give their envy precedence over the vital interests of their nation's cause.

Of course, in the long run war and the preservation of the market economy are incompatible. Capitalism is essentially a scheme for peaceful nations. But this does not mean that a nation which is forced to repel foreign aggressors must substitute government control for private enterprise. If it were to do this, it would deprive itself of the most efficient means of defense. There is no record of a socialist nation which defeated a capitalist nation. In spite of their much glorified war socialism, the Germans were defeated in both World Wars.

What the incompatibility of war and capitalism really means is that war and high civilization are incompatible. If the efficiency of capitalism is directed by governments toward the output of instruments of destruction, the ingenuity of private business turns out weapons which are powerful enough to destroy everything. What makes war and capitalism incompatible with one another is precisely the unparalleled efficiency of the capitalist mode of production.

The market economy, subject to the sovereignty of the individual consumers, turns out products which make the individual's life more agreeable. It caters to the individual's demand for more comfort. It is this that made capitalism despicable in the eyes of the apostles of violence. They worshiped the "hero," the destroyer and killer, and despised the bourgeois and his "peddler mentality" (Sombart). Now mankind is reaping the fruits which ripened from the seeds sown by these men.

3. War and Autarky

If an economically self-sufficient man starts a feud against another autarkic man, no specific problems of "war-economy" arise. But if the tailor goes to war against the baker, he must henceforth produce his bread for himself. If he neglects to do this, he will be in distress sooner than his adversary, the baker. For the baker can wait longer for a new suit than the tailor can for fresh bread. The economic problem of making war is therefore different for the baker and for the tailor.

The international division of labor was developed under the assumption that there would no longer be wars. In the philosophy of the Manchester School free trade and peace were seen as mutually conditioning one another. The businessmen who made trade international did not consider the possibility of new wars.

Nor did general staffs and students of the art of warfare pay any attention to the change in conditions which international division of labor brought about. The method of military science consists in examining the experience of wars fought in the past and in abstracting general rules from it. Even the most scrupulous occupation with the campaigns of Turenne and Napoleon I could not suggest the existence of a problem which was not present in ages in which there was practically no international division of labor.

The European military experts slighted the study of the American Civil War. In their eyes this war was not instructive. It was fought by armies of irregulars led by nonprofessional commanders. Civilians like Lincoln interfered with the conduct of the operations. Little, they believed, could be learned from this experience. But it was in the Civil War that, for the first time, problems of the interregional division of labor played the decisive role. The South was predominantly agricultural; its processing industries were negligible. The Confederates depended on the supply of manufactures from Europe. As the naval forces of the Union were strong enough to blockade their coast, they soon began to lack needed equipment.

The Germans in both World Wars had to face the same situation. They depended on the supply of foodstuffs and raw materials from overseas. But they could not run the British blockade. In both wars the outcome was decided by the battles of the Atlantic. The Germans lost because they failed in their efforts to cut off the British Isles from access to the world market and could not themselves safeguard their own maritime supply lines. The strategical problem was determined by the conditions of the international division of labor.

The German warmongers were intent upon adopting policies which, as they hoped, could make it possible for Germany to wage a war in spite of the handicap of the foreign trade situation. Their panacea was *Ersatz,* the substitute.

A substitute is a good which is either less suitable or more expensive or both less suitable and more expensive than the proper good which it is designed to replace. Whenever technology succeeds in manufacturing or discovering something which is either more suitable or cheaper than the thing previously used, this new thing represents a technological innovation; it is improvement and not Ersatz. The essential feature of Ersatz, as this term is employed in the economico-military doctrine, is inferior quality or higher costs or both together.[2]

The *Wehrwirtschaftslehre,* the German doctrine of the economics of war, contends that neither cost of production nor quality are important in matters of warfare. Profit-seeking business is concerned with costs of production and with the quality of the products. But

2. In this sense wheat produced, under the protection of an import duty, within the Reich's territory is *Ersatz* too: it is produced at higher costs than foreign wheat. The notion of *Ersatz* is a catallactic notion, and must not be defined with regard to technological and physical properties of the articles.

the heroic spirit of a superior race does not care about such specters of the acquisitive mind. What counts alone is war preparedness. A warlike nation must aim at autarky in order to be independent of foreign trade. It must foster the production of substitutes irrespective of mammonist considerations. It cannot do without full government control of production because the selfishness of the individual citizens would thwart the plans of the leader. Even in peacetime the commander-in-chief must be entrusted with economic dictatorship.

Both theorems of the Ersatz doctrine are fallacious.

First, it is not true that the quality and suitability of the substitute are of no importance. If soldiers are sent into battle badly nourished and equipped with weapons made of inferior material, the chances for victory are impaired. Their action will be less successful, and they will suffer heavier casualties. The awareness of their technical inferiority will weigh on their minds. Ersatz jeopardizes both the material strength and the morale of an army.

No less incorrect is the theorem that the higher costs of production of the substitutes do not count. Higher costs of production mean that more labor and more material factors of production must be expended in order to achieve the same effect which the adversary, producing the proper product, attains with a lower expenditure. It is tantamount to squandering scarce factors of production, material and manpower. Such waste under conditions of peace results in lowering the standard of living, and under conditions of war in cutting down the supply of goods needed for the conduct of operations. In the present state of technological knowledge it is only a slight exaggeration to say that everything can be produced out of anything. But what matters is to pick out from the great multitude of possible methods those with which output is highest per unit of input. Any deviation from this principle penalizes itself. The consequences in war are as bad as they are in peace.

In a country like the United States, which depends only to a comparatively negligible extent on the importation of raw materials from abroad, it is possible to improve the state of war preparedness by resorting to the production of substitutes such as synthetic rubber. The disadvantageous effects would be small when weighed against the beneficial effects. But a country like Germany was badly mistaken in the assumption that it could conquer with synthetic gasoline, synthetic rubber, Ersatz textiles and Ersatz fats. In both World Wars Germany was in the position of the tailor fighting against the man who supplies him with bread. With all their brutality the Nazis could not alter this fact.

4. The Futility of War

What distinguishes man from animals is the insight into the advantages that can be derived from cooperation under the division of labor. Man curbs his innate instinct of aggression in order to cooperate with other human beings. The more he wants to improve his material well-being, the more he must expand the system of the division of labor. Concomitantly he must more and more restrict the sphere in which he resorts to military action. The emergence of the international division of labor requires the total abolition of war. Such is the essence of the laissez-faire philosophy of Manchester.

This philosophy is, of course, incompatible with statolatry. In its context the state, the social apparatus of violent oppression, is entrusted with the protection of the smooth operation of the market economy against the onslaughts of antisocial individuals and gangs. Its function is indispensable and beneficial, but it is an ancillary function only. There is no reason to idolize the police power and ascribe to it omnipotence and omniscience. There are things which it can certainly not accomplish. It cannot conjure away the scarcity of the factors of production, it cannot make people more prosperous, it cannot raise the productivity of labor. All it can achieve is to prevent gangsters from frustrating the efforts of those people who are intent upon promoting material well-being.

The liberal philosophy of Bentham and Bastiat had not yet completed its work of removing trade barriers and government meddling with business when the counterfeit theology of the divine state began to take effect. Endeavors to improve the conditions of wage earners and small farmers by government decree made it necessary to loosen more and more the ties which connected each country's domestic economy with those of other countries. Economic nationalism, the necessary complement of domestic interventionism, hurts the interests of foreign peoples and thus creates international conflict. It suggests the idea of amending this unsatisfactory state of affairs by war. Why should a powerful nation tolerate the challenge of a less powerful nation? Is it not insolence on the part of small Laputania to injure the citizens of big Ruritania by customs, migration barriers, foreign exchange control, quantitative trade restrictions, and expropriation of Ruritanian investments in Laputania? Would it not be easy for the army of Ruritania to crush Laputania's contemptible forces?

Such was the ideology of the German, Italian, and Japanese warmongers. It must be admitted that they were consistent from the point of view of the new "unorthodox" teachings. Interventionism generates economic nationalism, and economic nationalism generates bellicosity. If men and commodities are prevented from crossing the borderlines, why should not the armies try to pave the way for them?

From the day when Italy, in 1911, fell upon Turkey, fighting was continual. There was almost always shooting somewhere in the world. The peace treaties concluded were virtually merely armistice agreements. Moreover they had to do only with the armies of the great powers. Some of the smaller nations were always at war. In addition there were no less pernicious civil wars and revolutions.

How far we are today from the rules of international law developed in the age of limited warfare! Modern war is merciless, it does not spare pregnant women or infants; it is indiscriminate killing and destroying. It does not respect the rights of neutrals. Millions are killed, enslaved, or expelled from the dwelling places in which their ancestors lived for centuries. Nobody can foretell what will happen in the next chapter of this endless struggle.

This has little to do with the atomic bomb. The root of the evil is not the construction of new, more dreadful weapons. It is the spirit of conquest. It is probable that scientists will discover some methods of defense against the atomic bomb. But this will not alter things, it will merely prolong for a short time the process of the complete destruction of civilization.

Modern civilization is a product of the philosophy of laissez faire. It cannot be preserved under the ideology of government omnipotence. Statolatry owes much to the doctrines of Hegel. However, one may pass over many of Hegel's inexcusable faults, for Hegel also coined the phrase "the futility of victory" (*die Ohnmacht des Sieges*).[3] To defeat the aggressors is not enough to make peace durable. The main thing is to discard the ideology that generates war.

3. Cf. Hegel *Vorlesungen über die Philosophie der Weltgeschichte,* ed Lasson (Leipzig, 1920), IV, 930–931.

XXXV. THE WELFARE PRINCIPLE VERSUS THE MARKET PRINCIPLE

1. The Case Against the Market Economy

THE objections which the various schools of Sozialpolitik raise against the market economy are based on very bad economics. They repeat again and again all the errors that the economists long ago exploded. They blame the market economy for the consequences of the very anticapitalistic policies which they themselves advocate as necessary and beneficial reforms. They fix on the market economy the responsibility for the inevitable failure and frustration of interventionism.

These propagandists must finally admit that the market economy is after all not so bad as their "unorthodox" doctrines paint it. It delivers the goods. From day to day it increases the quantity and improves the quality of products. It has brought about unprecedented wealth. But, objects the champion of interventionism, it is deficient from what he calls the social point of view. It has not wiped out poverty and destitution. It is a system that grants privileges to a minority, an upper class of rich people, at the expense of the immense majority. It is an unfair system. The principle of *welfare* must be substituted for that of profits.

We may try, for the sake of argument, to interpret the concept of welfare in such a way that its acceptance by the immense majority of nonascetic people would be probable. The better we succeed in these endeavors, the more we deprive the idea of welfare of any concrete meaning and content. It turns into a colorless paraphrase of the fundamental category of human action, viz., the urge to remove uneasiness as far as possible. As it is universally recognized that this goal can be more readily, and even exclusively, attained by social division of labor, men cooperate within the framework of societal bonds. Social man as differentiated from autarkic man must necessarily modify his original biological indifference to the well-being of people beyond his own family. He must adjust his conduct to the requirements of social cooperation and look upon his fellow men's success as an indispensable condition of his own. From this point of view one may describe the objective of social cooperation as the realization of the greatest happiness of the greatest number. Hardly anybody would venture to object to this definition of the most desirable state of affairs and to contend that it is *not* a good thing to see as many people as possible as happy as possible. All the attacks directed against the Bentham formula have centered around ambiguities or misunderstandings concerning the notion of happiness; they have not affected the postulate that the good, whatever it may be, should be imparted to the greatest number.

However, if we interpret *welfare* in this manner, the concept is void of any specific significance. It can be invoked for the justification of every variety of social organization. It is a fact that some of the defenders of Negro slavery contended that slavery is the best means of making the Negroes happy and that today in the South many Whites sincerely believe that rigid segregation is beneficial no less to the colored man than it allegedly is to the white man. The main thesis of racism of the Gobineau and Nazi variety is that the hegemony of the superior races is salutary to the true interests even of the inferior races. A principle that is broad enough to cover all doctrines, however conflicting with one another, is of no use at all.

But in the mouths of the welfare propagandists the notion of welfare has a definite meaning. They intentionally employ a term the generally accepted connotation of which precludes any opposition. No decent man likes to be so rash as to raise objections against the realization of welfare. In arrogating to themselves the exclusive right to call their own program the program of welfare, the welfare propagandists want to triumph by means of a cheap logical trick. They want to render their ideas safe against criticism by attributing to them an appellation which is cherished by everybody. Their terminology already implies that all opponents are ill-intentioned scoundrels eager to foster their selfish interests to the prejudice of the majority of good people.

The plight of Western civilization consists precisely in the fact that serious people can resort to such syllogistic artifices without encountering sharp rebuke. There are only two explanations open. Either these self-styled welfare economists are themselves not aware of the logical inadmissibility of their procedure, in which case they lack the indispensable power of reasoning; or they have chosen this mode of arguing purposely in order to find shelter for their fallacies behind a word which is intended beforehand to disarm all opponents. In each case their own acts condemn them.

There is no need to add anything to the disquisitions of the preceding chapters concerning the effects of all varieties of interventionism. The ponderous volumes of welfare economics have not brought forth any arguments that could invalidate our conclusions. The only task that remains is to examine the critical part of the welfare propagandists' work, their indictment of the market economy.

All this passionate talk of the welfare school ultimately boils down to three points. Capitalism is bad, they say, because there is poverty, inequality of incomes and wealth, and insecurity.

2. Poverty

We may depict conditions of a society of agriculturists in which every member tills a piece of land large enough to provide himself and his family with the indispensable necessities of life. We may include in such a picture the existence of a few specialists, artisans like smiths and professional men like doctors. We may even go further and assume that some men do not own a farm, but work as laborers on other people's farms. The employer remunerates them for their help and takes care of them when sickness or old age disables them.

This scheme of an ideal society was at the bottom of many utopian plans. It was by and large realized for some time in some communities. The nearest approach to its realization was probably the commonwealth which the Jesuit padres established in the country which is today Paraguay. There is, however, no need to examine the merits of such a system of social organization. Historical evolution burst it asunder. Its frame was too narrow for the number of people who are living today on the earth's surface.

The inherent weakness of such a society is that the increase in population must result in progressive poverty. If the estate of a deceased farmer is divided among his children, the holdings finally become so small that they can no longer provide sufficient sustenance for a family. Everybody is a landowner, but everybody is extremely poor. Conditions as they prevailed in large areas of China provide a sad illustration of the misery of the tillers of small parcels. The alternative to this outcome is the emergence of a huge mass of landless proletarians. Then a wide gap separates the disinherited paupers from the fortunate farmers. They are a class of pariahs whose very existence presents society with an insoluble problem. They search in vain for a livelihood. Society has no use for them. They are destitute.

When in the ages preceding the rise of modern capitalism statesmen, philosophers, and lawyers referred to the poor and to the problems of poverty, they meant these supernumerary wretches. Laissez faire and its off-shoot, industrialism, converted the employable poor into wage earners. In the unhampered market society there are people with higher and people with lower incomes. There are no longer men, who, although able and ready to work, cannot find regular jobs because there is no room left for them in the social system of production. But liberalism and capitalism were even in their heyday limited to comparatively small areas of Western and Central Europe, North America, and Australia. In the rest of the world hundreds of millions still vegetate on the verge of starvation. They are poor or paupers in the old sense of the term, supernumerary and superfluous, a burden to themselves and a latent threat to the minority of their more lucky fellow citizens.

The penury of these miserable masses of—in the main colored—people is not caused by capitalism, but by the absence of capitalism. But for the triumph of laissez faire, the lot of the peoples of Western Europe would have been even worse than that of the coolies. What is wrong with Asia is that the per capita quota of capital invested is extremely low when compared with the capital equipment of the West. The prevailing ideology and the social system which is its off-shoot check the evolution of profit-seeking entrepreneurship. There is very little domestic capital accumulation, and manifest hostility to foreign investors. In many of these countries the increase in population figures even outruns the increase in capital available.

It is false to blame the European powers for the poverty of the masses in their former colonial empires. In investing capital the foreign rulers did all they could do for an improvement in material well-being. It is not the fault of the Whites that the Oriental peoples are reluctant to abandon their traditional tenets and abhor capitalism as an alien ideology.

As far as there is unhampered capitalism, there is no longer any question of poverty in the sense in which this term is applied to the conditions of a noncapitalistic society. The increase in population figures does not create supernumerary mouths, but additional hands whose employment produces additional wealth. There are no able-bodied paupers. Seen from the point of view of the economically backward nations, the conflicts between "capital" and "labor" in the capitalist countries appear as conflicts within a privileged upper class. In the eyes of the Asiatics, the American automobile worker is an "aristocrat." He is a man who belongs to the 2 per cent of the earth's population whose income is highest. Not only the colored races, but also the Slavs, the Arabs, and some other peoples look upon the average income of the citizens of the capitalistic countries—about 12 or 15 per cent of the total of mankind—as a curtailment of their own material well-being. They fail to realize that the prosperity of these allegedly privileged groups is, apart from the effects of migration barriers, not paid for by their own poverty, and that the main obstacle to the improvement of their own conditions is their abhorrence of capitalism.

Within the frame of capitalism the notion of poverty refers only to those people who are unable to take care of themselves. Even if we disregard the case of children, we must realize that there will always be such unemployables. Capitalism, in improving the masses' standard of living, hygienic conditions, and methods of prophylactics and therapeutics, does not remove bodily incapacity. It is true that today many people who in the past would have been doomed to life-long disability are restored to full vigor. But on the other hand many whom innate defects, sickness, or accidents would have extinguished sooner in earlier days survive as permanently incapacitated people. Moreover, the prolongation of the average length of life tends toward an increase in the number of the aged who are no longer able to earn a living.

The problem of the incapacitated is a specific problem of human civilization and of society. Disabled animals must perish quickly. They either die of starvation or fall prey to the foes of their species. Savage man had no pity on those who were substandard. With regard to them many tribes practiced those barbaric methods of ruthless extirpation to which the Nazis resorted in our time. The very existence of a comparatively great number of invalids is, however paradoxical, a characteristic mark of civilization and material well-being.

Provision for those invalids who lack means of sustenance and are not taken care of by their next of kin has long been considered a work of charity. The funds needed have sometimes been provided by governments, more often by voluntary contributions. The Catholic orders and congregations and some Protestant institutions have accomplished marvels in collecting such contributions and in using them properly. Today there are also many nondenominational establishments vying with them in noble rivalry.

The charity system is criticized for two defects. One is the paucity of the means available. However, the more capitalism progresses and increases wealth, the more sufficient become the charity funds. On the one hand, people are more ready to donate in proportion to the improvement in their own well-being. On the other hand, the number of the needy drops concomitantly. Even for those with moderate incomes the opportunity is offered, by saving and insurance policies, to provide for accidents, sickness, old age, the education of their children, and the support of widows and orphans. It is highly probable that the funds of the charitable institutions would be sufficient in the capitalist countries if interventionism were not to sabotage the essential institutions of the market economy. Credit expansion and inflationary increase of the quantity of money frustrate the "common man's" attempts to save and to accumulate reserves for less propitious days. But the other procedures of interventionism are hardly less injurious to the vital interests of the wage earners and salaried employees, the professions, and the owners of small-size business. The greater part of those assisted by charitable institutions are needy only because interventionism has made them so. At the same time inflation and the endeavors to lower the rate of interest below the potential market rates virtually expropriate the endowments of hospitals, asylums, orphanages, and similar establishments. As far as the welfare propagandists lament the insufficiency of the funds available for assistance, they lament one of the results of the policies that they themselves are advocating.

The second defect charged to the charity system is that it is charity and compassion only. The indigent has no legal claim to the kindness shown to him. He depends on the mercy of benevolent people, on the feelings of tenderness which his distress arouses. What he receives is a voluntary gift for which he must be grateful. To be an almsman is shameful and humiliating. It is an unbearable condition for a self-respecting man.

These complaints are justified. Such shortcomings do indeed inhere in all kinds of charity. It is a system that corrupts both givers and receivers. It makes the former self-righteous and the latter submissive and cringing. However, it is only the mentality of a capitalistic environment that makes people feel the indignity of giving and receiving alms. Outside of the field of the cash nexus and of deals transacted between buyers and sellers in a purely businesslike manner, all interhuman relations are tainted by the same failing. It is precisely the absence of this personal element in market transactions that all those deplore who blame capitalism for hard-heartedness and callousness. In the eyes of such critics cooperation under the *do ut des* principle dehumanizes all societal bonds. It substitutes contracts for brotherly love and readiness to help one another. These critics indict the legal order of capitalism for its neglect of the "human side." They are inconsistent when they blame the charity system for its reliance upon feelings of mercy.

Feudal society was founded on acts of grace and on the gratitude of those favored. The mighty overlord bestowed a benefit upon the vassal and the latter owed him personal fidelity. Conditions were human in so far as the subordinates had to kiss their superiors' hands and to show allegiance to them. In a feudal environment the element of grace inherent in charitable acts did not give offense. It agreed with the generally accepted ideology and practice. It is only in the setting of a society based entirely upon contractual bonds that the idea emerged of giving to the indigent a legal claim, an actionable title to sustenance against society.

The metaphysical arguments advanced in favor of such a right to sustenance are based on the doctrine of natural right. Before God or nature all men are equal and endowed with an inalienable right to live. However, the reference to inborn equality is certainly out of place in dealing with the effects of inborn inequality. It is a sad fact that physical disability prevents many people from playing an active role in social cooperation. It is the operation of the laws of nature that makes these people outcasts. They are stepchildren of God or nature. We may fully endorse the religious and ethical precepts that declare it to be man's duty to assist his unlucky brethren whom nature has doomed. But the recognition of this duty does not answer the question concerning what methods should be resorted to for its performance. It does not enjoin the choice of methods which would endanger society and curtail the productivity of human effort. Neither the able-bodied nor the incapacitated would derive any benefit from a drop in the quantity of goods available.

The problems involved are not of a praxeological character, and economics is not called upon to provide the best possible solution for them. They concern pathology and psychology. They refer to the biological fact that the fear of penury and of the degrading consequences of being supported by charity are important factors in the preservation of man's physiological equilibrium. They impel a man to keep fit, to avoid sickness and accidents, and to recover as soon as possible from injuries suffered. The experience of the social security system, especially that of the oldest and most complete scheme, the German, has clearly shown the undesirable effects resulting from the elimination of these incentives.[1] No civilized community has callously allowed the incapacitated to perish. But the substitution of a legally enforceable claim to support or sustenance for charitable relief does not seem to agree with human nature as it is. Not metaphysical prepossessions, but considerations of practical expediency make it inadvisable to promulgate an actionable right to sustenance.

1. Cf. Sulzbach, *German Experience with Social Insurance* (New York, 1947), pp. 22–32.

It is, moreover, an illusion to believe that the enactment of such laws could free the indigent from the degrading features inherent in receiving alms. The more openhanded these laws are, the more punctilious must their application become. The discretion of bureaucrats is substituted for the discretion of people whom an inner voice drives to acts of charity. Whether this change renders the lot of those incapacitated any easier, is hard to say.

3. Inequality

The inequality of incomes and wealth is an inherent feature of the market economy. Its elimination would entirely destroy the market economy.[2]

What those people who ask for equality have in mind is always an increase in their own power to consume. In endorsing the principle of equality as a political postulate nobody wants to share his own income with those who have less. When the American wage earner refers to equality, he means that the dividends of the stockholders should be given to him. He does not suggest a curtailment of his own income for the benefit of those 95 per cent of the earth's population whose income is lower than his.

The role that income inequality plays in the market society must not be confused with the role it plays in a feudal society or in other types of noncapitalistic societies.[3] Yet in the course of historical evolution this precapitalistic inequality was of momentous importance.

Let us compare the history of China with that of England. China has developed a very high civilization. Two thousand years ago it was far ahead of England. But at the end of the nineteenth century England was a rich and civilized country while China was poor. Its civilization did not differ much from the stage it had already reached ages before. It was an arrested civilization.

China had tried to realize the principle of income equality to a greater extent than did England. Land holdings were divided and subdivided. There was no numerous class of landless proletarians. But in eighteenth-century England this class was very numerous. For a very long time the restrictive practices of nonagricultural business, sanctified by traditional ideologies, delayed the emergence of modern entrepreneurship. But when the laissez-faire philosophy had opened the way for capitalism by utterly destroying the fallacies of restrictionism, the evolution of industrialism could proceed at an accelerated pace because the labor force needed was already available.

2. Cf. above, pp. 288–289 and pp. 806–808.
3. Cf. above, p. 312.

What generated the "machine age" was not, as Sombart imagined, a specific mentality of acquisitiveness which one day mysteriously got hold of the minds of some people and turned them into "capitalistic men." There have always been people ready to profit from better adjusting production to the satisfaction of the needs of the public. But they were paralyzed by the ideology that branded acquisitiveness as immoral and erected institutional barriers to check it. The substitution of the laissez-faire philosophy for the doctrines that approved of the traditional system of restrictions removed these obstacles to material improvement and thus inaugurated the new age.

The liberal philosophy attacked the traditional caste system because its preservation was incompatible with the operation of the market economy. It advocated the abolition of privileges because it wanted to give a free hand to those men who had the ingenuity to produce in the cheapest way the greatest quantity of products of the best quality. In this negative aspect of their program the utilitarians and economists agreed with the ideas of those who attacked the status privileges from the point of view of an alleged right of nature and the doctrine of the equality of all men. Both these groups were unanimous in the support of the principle of the equality of all men under the law. But this unanimity did not eradicate the fundamental opposition between the two lines of thought.

In the opinion of the natural law school all men are biologically equal and therefore have the inalienable right to an equal share in all things. The first theorem is manifestly contrary to fact. The second theorem leads, when consistently interpreted, to such absurdities that its supporters abandon logical consistency altogether and ultimately come to consider every institution, however discriminating and iniquitous, as compatible with the inalienable equality of all men. The eminent Virginians whose ideas animated the American Revolution acquiesced in the preservation of Negro slavery. The most despotic system of government that history has ever known, Bolshevism, parades as the very incarnation of the principle of equality and liberty of all men.

The liberal champions of equality under the law were fully aware of the fact that men are born unequal and that it is precisely their inequality that generates social cooperation and civilization. Equality under the law was in their opinion not designed to correct the inexorable facts of the universe and to make natural inequality disappear. It was, on the contrary, the device to secure for the whole of mankind the maximum of benefits it can derive from it. Henceforth no man-made institutions should prevent a man from attaining that station in which he can best serve his fellow citizens. The liberals approached the problem not from the point of view of alleged inalienable rights of the individuals, but from the social and utilitarian angle. Equality under the law is in their eyes good because it best serves the interests of all. It leaves it to the voters to decide who should hold public office and to the consumers to decide who should direct production activities. It thus eliminates the causes of violent conflict and secures a steady progress toward a more satisfactory state of human affairs.

The triumph of this liberal philosophy produced all those phenomena which in their totality are called modern Western civilization. However, this new ideology could triumph only within an environment in which the ideal of income equality was very weak. If the Englishmen of the eighteenth century had been preoccupied with the chimera of income equality, laissez-faire philosophy would not have appealed to them, just as it does not appeal today to the Chinese or the Mohammedans. In this sense the historian must acknowledge that the ideological heritage of feudalism and the manorial system contributed to the rise of our modern civilization, however different it is.

Those eighteenth-century philosophers who were foreign to the ideas of the new utilitarian theory could still speak of a superiority of conditions in China and in the Mohammedan countries. They knew, it is true, very little about the social structure of the oriental world. What they found praiseworthy in the dim reports they had obtained was the absence of a hereditary aristocracy and of big land holdings. As they fancied it, these nations had succeeded better in establishing equality than their own nations.

Then later in the nineteenth century these claims were renewed by the nationalists of the nations concerned. The cavalcade was headed by Panslavism, whose champions exalted the eminence of communal cooperation as realized in the Russian *mir* and *artel* and in the *zadruga* of the Yugoslavs. With the progress of the semantic confusion which has converted the meaning of political terms into their very opposite, the epithet "democratic" is now lavishly spent. The Moslem peoples, which never knew any form of government other than unlimited absolutism, are called democratic. Indian nationalists take pleasure in speaking of traditional Hindu democracy!

Economists and historians are indifferent with regard to all such emotional effusions. In describing the civilizations of the Asiatics as inferior civilizations they do not express any value judgments. They merely establish the fact that these peoples did not bring forth those ideological and institutional conditions which in the West produced that capitalist civilization the superiority of which the Asiatics today implicitly accept in clamoring at least for its technological and therapeutical implements and paraphernalia. It is precisely when one recognizes the fact that in the past the culture of many Asiatic peoples was far ahead of that of their Western contemporaries, that the question is raised as to what causes stopped progress in the East. In the case of the Hindu civilization the answer is obvious. Here the iron grip of the inflexible caste system stunted individual initiative and nipped in the bud every attempt to deviate from traditional standards. But China and the Mohammedan countries were, apart from the slavery of a comparatively small number of people, free from caste rigidity. They were ruled by autocrats. But the individual subjects were equal under the autocrat. Even slaves and eunuchs were not barred from access to the highest dignities. It is this equality before the ruler to which people refer today in speaking of the supposed democratic customs of these Orientals.

The notion of the economic equality of the subjects to which these peoples and their rulers were committed was not well defined but vague. But it was very distinct in one respect, namely, in utterly condemning the accumulation of a large fortune by any private individual. The rulers considered wealthy subjects a threat to their political supremacy. All people, the rulers as well as the ruled, were convinced that no man can amass abundant means otherwise than by depriving others of what by rights should belong to them, and that the riches of the wealthy few are the cause of the poverty of the many. The position of wealthy businessmen was in all oriental countries extremely precarious. They were at the mercy of the officeholders. Even lavish bribes failed to protect them against confiscation. The whole people rejoiced whenever a prosperous businessman fell victim to the envy and hatred of the administrators.

This antichrematistic spirit arrested the progress of civilization in the East and kept the masses on the verge of starvation. As capital accumulation was checked, there could be no question of technological improvement. Capitalism came to the East as an imported alien ideology, imposed by foreign armies and navies in the shape either of colonial domination or of extraterritorial jurisdiction. These violent methods were certainly not the appropriate means to change the traditionalist mentality of the Orientals. But acknowledgment of this fact does not invalidate the statement that it was the abhorrence of capital accumulation that doomed many hundreds of millions of Asiatics to poverty and starvation.

The notion of equality which our contemporary welfare propagandists have in mind is the replica of the Asiatic idea of equality. While vague in every other respect, it is very clear in its abomination of large fortunes. It objects to big business and great riches. It advocates various measures to stunt the growth of individual enterprises and to bring about more equality by confiscatory taxation of incomes and estates. And it appeals to the envy of the injudicious masses.

The immediate economic consequences of confiscatory policies have been dealt with already.[4] It is obvious that in the long run such policies must result not only in slowing down or totally checking the further accumulation of capital, but also in the consumption of capital accumulated in previous days. They would not only arrest further progress toward more material prosperity, but even reverse the trend and bring about a tendency toward progressing poverty. The ideals of Asia would triumph; and finally East and West would meet on an equal level of distress.

The welfare school pretends not only to stand for the interests of the whole of society as against the selfish interests of profit-seeking business; it contends moreover that it takes into account the lasting secular interests of the nation as against the short-term concerns of speculators, promoters, and capitalists who are exclusively committed to profiteering and do not bother about the future of the whole of society. This second claim is, of course, irreconcilable with the emphasis laid by the school upon short-run policies as against long-run concerns. However, consistency is not one of the virtues of the welfare doctrinaires. Let us for the sake of argument disregard this contradiction in their statements and examine them without reference to their inconsistency.

Saving, capital accumulation, and investment withhold the amount concerned from current consumption and dedicate it to the improvement of future conditions. The saver foregoes the increase in present satisfaction in order to improve his own well-being and that of his family in the more distant future. His intentions are certainly selfish in the popular connotation of the term. But the effects of his selfish conduct are beneficial to the lasting secular interests of the whole of society as well as of all its members. His conduct produces all those phenomena to which even the most bigoted welfare propagandist attributes the epithets *economic improvement* and *progress*.

The policies advocated by the welfare school remove the incentive to saving on the part of private citizens. On one hand, the measures directed toward a curtailment of big incomes and fortunes seriously

4. Cf. above, pp. 804–809.

reduce or destroy entirely the wealthier people's power to save. On the other hand, the sums which people with moderate incomes previously contributed to capital accumulation are manipulated in such a way as to channel them into the lines of consumption. When in the past a man saved by entrusting money to a savings bank or by taking out an insurance policy, the bank or the insurance company invested the equivalent. Even if the saver at a later date consumed the sums saved, no disinvestment and capital consumption resulted. The total investments of the savings banks and the insurance companies steadily increased in spite of these withdrawals.

Today there prevails a tendency to push banks and insurance companies more and more toward investment in government bonds. The funds of the social security institutions completely consist in titles to the public debt. As far as public indebtedness was incurred by spending for current expenditure, the saving of the individual does not result in capital accumulation. While in the unhampered market economy saving, capital accumulation, and investment coincide, in the interventionist economy the individual citizens' savings can be dissipated by the government. The individual citizen restricts his current consumption in order to provide for his own future; in doing this he contributes his share to the further economic advancement of society and to an improvement of his fellow men's standard of living. But the government steps in and removes the socially beneficial effects of the individuals' conduct. Nothing explodes better than this example the welfare cliché that contrasts the selfish and narrow-minded individual, exclusively committed to the enjoyment of the pleasures of the moment and having no regard for the well-being of his fellow men and for the perennial concerns of society, and the far-sighted benevolent government, unflaggingly devoted to the promotion of the lasting welfare of the whole of society.

The welfare propagandist, it is true, raises two objections. First, that the individual's motive is selfishness, while the government is imbued with good intentions. Let us admit for the sake of argument that individuals are devilish and rulers angelic. But what counts in life and reality is—in spite of what Kant said to the contrary—not good intentions, but accomplishments. What makes the existence and the evolution of society possible is precisely the fact that peaceful cooperation under the social division of labor in the long run best serves the selfish concerns of all individuals. The eminence of the market society is that its whole functioning and operation is the consummation of this principle.

The second objection points out that under the welfare system capital accumulation by the government and public investment are to be substituted for private accumulation and investment. It refers to the fact that not all the funds which governments borrowed in the past were spent for current expenditure. A considerable part was invested in the construction of roads, railroads, harbors, airports, power stations, and other public works. Another no less conspicuous part was spent for waging wars of defense which admittedly could not be financed by other methods. The objection, however, misses the point. What matters is that a part of the individual's saving is employed by the government for current consumption, and that nothing hinders the government from so increasing this part that it in fact absorbs the whole.

It is obvious that if governments make it impossible for their subjects to accumulate and to invest additional capital, responsibility for the formation of new capital, if there is to be any, devolves upon government. The welfare propagandist, in whose opinion government control is a synonym for God's providential care that wisely and imperceptibly leads mankind to higher and more perfect stages of an inescapable evolutionary progress, fails to see the intricacy of the problem and its ramifications.

Not only further saving and accumulation of additional capital, but no less the maintenance of capital at its present level, require curtailing today's consumption in order to be more amply supplied later. It is abstinence, a refraining from satisfactions which could be reaped instantly.[5] The market economy brings about an environment in which such abstinence is practiced to a certain extent, and in which its product, the accumulated capital, is invested in those lines in which it best satisfies the most urgent needs of the consumers. The questions arise whether government accumulation of capital can be substituted for private accumulation, and in what way a government would invest additional capital accumulated. These problems do not refer only to a socialist commonwealth. They are no less urgent in an interventionist scheme that has either totally or almost totally removed the conditions making for private capital formation. Even the United States is manifestly more and more approaching such a state of affairs.

5. To establish this fact is, to be sure, not an endorsement of the theories which tried to describe interest as the "reward" of abstinence. There is in the world of reality no mythical agency that rewards or punishes. What originary interest really is has been shown above in Chapter XIX. But as against the would-be ironies of Lassalle (*Herr Bastiat-Schulze von Delitzsch* in *Gesammelte Reden und Schriften,* ed. Bernstein, V, 167), reiterated by innumerable textbooks, it is good to emphasize that saving is privation (*Entbehrung*) in so far as it deprives the saver of an instantaneous enjoyment.

Let us consider the case of a government that has got control of the employment of a considerable part of the citizens' savings. The investments of the social security system, of the private insurance companies, of savings banks, and of commercial banks are to a great extent determined by the authorities and channeled into the public debt. The private citizens are still savers. But whether or not their savings bring about capital accumulation and thus increase the quantity of capital goods available for an improvement of the apparatus of production depends on the employment of the funds borrowed by the government. If the government squanders these sums either by spending them for current expenditure or by malinvestment, the process of capital accumulation as inaugurated by the saving of individuals and continued by the investment operations of the banks and insurance enterprises is cut off. A contrast between the two ways may clarify the matter:

In the process of the unhampered market economy Bill saves one hundred dollars and deposits it with a savings bank. If he is wise in choosing a bank which is wise in its lending and investing business, an increment in capital results, and brings about a rise in the marginal productivity of labor. Out of the surplus thus produced a part goes to Bill in the shape of interest. If Bill blunders in the choice of his bank and entrusts his hundred dollars to a bank that fails, he goes emptyhanded.

In the process of government interference with saving and investment, Paul in the year 1940 saves by paying one hundred dollars to the national social security institution.[6] He receives in exchange a claim which is virtually an unconditional government IOU. If the government spends the hundred dollars for current expenditure, no additional capital comes into existence, and no increase in the productivity of labor results. The government's IOU is a check drawn upon the future taxpayers. In 1970 a certain Peter may have to fulfill the government's promise although he himself does not derive any benefit from the fact that Paul in 1940 saved one hundred dollars.

Thus it becomes obvious that there is no need to look at Soviet Russia in order to comprehend the role that public finance plays in our day. The trumpery argument that the public debt is no burden because "we owe it to ourselves" is delusive. The Pauls of 1940 do not owe it to themselves. It is the Peters of 1970 who owe it to the Pauls of 1940. The whole system is the acme of the short-run principle. The statesmen of 1940 solve their problems by shifting them to the statesmen of 1970. On that date the statesmen of 1940 will be either

6. It makes no difference whether Paul himself pays these hundred dollars or whether the law obliges his employer to pay it. Cf. above, p. 602.

dead or elder statesmen glorying in their wonderful achievement, social security.

The Santa Claus fables of the welfare school are characterized by their complete failure to grasp the problems of capital. It is precisely this defect that makes it imperative to deny them the appellation *welfare economics* with which they describe their doctrines. He who does not take into consideration the scarcity of capital goods available is not an economist, but a fabulist. He does not deal with reality but with a fabulous world of plenty. All the effusions of the contemporary welfare school are, like those of the socialist authors, based on the implicit assumption that there is an abundant supply of capital goods. Then, of course, it seems easy to find a remedy for all ills, to give to everybody "according to his needs" and to make everyone perfectly happy.

It is true that some of the champions of the welfare school feel troubled by a dim notion of the problems involved. They realize that capital must be maintained intact if the future productivity of labor is not to be impaired.[7] However, these authors too fail to comprehend that even the mere maintenance of capital depends on the skillful handling of the problems of investment, that it is always the fruit of successful speculation, and that endeavors to maintain capital intact presuppose economic calculation and thereby the operation of the market economy. The other welfare propagandists ignore the issue completely. It does not matter whether or not they endorse in this respect the Marxian scheme or resort to the invention of new chimerical notions such as "the self-perpetuating character" of useful things.[8] In any event their teachings are designed to provide a justification for the doctrine which blames oversaving and underconsumption for all that is unsatisfactory and recommends spending as a panacea.

When pushed hard by economists, some welfare propagandists and socialists admit that impairment of the average standard of living can only be avoided by the maintenance of capital already accumulated and that economic improvement depends on accumulation of additional capital. Maintenance of capital and accumulation of new capital, they say, will henceforth be a task of government. They will no longer be left to the selfishness of individuals, exclusively concerned with their own enrichment and that of their families; the authorities will deal with them from the point of view of the common weal.

7. This refers especially to the writings of Professor A. C. Pigou, the various editions of his book *The Economics of Welfare* and miscellaneous articles. For a critique of Professor Pigou's ideas, cf. Hayek, *Profits, Interest and Investment* (London, 1939), pp. 83–134.

8. Cf. F. H. Knight, "Professor Mises and the Theory of Capital," *Economica*, VIII (1941), 409–427.

The crux of the issue lies precisely in the operation of selfishness. Under the system of inequality this selfishness impels a man to save and always to invest his savings in such a way as to fill best the most urgent needs of the consumers. Under the system of equality this motive fades. The curtailment of consumption in the immediate future is a perceptible privation, a blow to the individuals' selfish aims. The increment in the supply available in more distant periods of the future which is expected from this immediate privation is less recognizable for the average intellect. Moreover, its beneficial effects are, under a system of public accumulation, so thinly spread out that they hardly appear to a man as an appropriate compensation for what he foregoes today. The welfare school blithely assumes that the expectation that the fruits of today's saving will be reaped equally by the whole of the future generation will turn everybody's selfishness toward more saving. Thus they fall prey to a corollary of Plato's illusion that preventing people from knowing which children's parents they are will inspire them with parental feelings toward all younger people. It would have been wise if the welfare school had been mindful of Aristotle's observation that the result will rather be that all parents will be equally indifferent to all children.[9]

The problem of maintaining and increasing capital is insoluble for a socialist system which cannot resort to economic calculation. Such a socialist commonwealth lacks any method of ascertaining whether its capital equipment is decreasing or increasing. But under interventionism and under a socialist system which is still in a position to resort to economic calculation on the basis of prices established abroad, things are not so bad. Here it is at least possible to comprehend what is going on.

If such a country is under a democratic government, the problems of capital preservation and accumulation of additional capital become the main issue of political antagonisms. There will be demagogues to contend that more could be dedicated to current consumption than those who happen to be in power or the other parties are disposed to allow. They will always be ready to declare that "in the present emergency" there cannot be any question of piling up capital for later days and that, on the contrary, consumption of a part of the capital already available is fully justified. The various parties will outbid one another in promising the voters more government spending and at the same time a reduction of all taxes which do not exclusively burden the rich. In the days of laissez faire people looked

9. Cf. Aristotle, *Politics,* Bk. II, chap. iii in *The Basic Works of Aristotle*, ed. R. McKeon (New York, 1945), pp. 1148 f.

upon government as an institution whose operation required an expenditure of money which must be defrayed by taxes paid by the citizens. In the individual citizens' budgets the state was an item of expenditure. Today the majority of the citizens look upon government as an agency dispensing benefits. The wage earners and the farmers expect to receive from the treasury more than they contribute to its revenues. The state is in their eyes a spender, not a taker. These popular tenets were rationalized and elevated to the rank of a quasi-economic doctrine by Lord Keynes and his disciples. Spending and unbalanced budgets are merely synonyms for capital consumption. If current expenditure, however beneficial it may be considered, is financed by taking away by inheritance taxes those parts of higher incomes which would have been employed for investment, or by borowing, the government becomes a factor making for capital consumption. The fact that in present-day America there is probably[10] still a surplus of annual capital accumulation over annual capital consumption does not invalidate the statement that the total complex of the financial policies of the Federal Government, the States, and the municipalities tends toward capital consumption.

Many who are aware of the undesirable consequences of capital consumption are prone to believe that popular government is incompatible with sound financial policies. They fail to realize that not democracy as such is to be indicted, but the doctrines which aim at substituting the Santa Claus conception of government for the night watchman conception derided by Lassalle. What determines the course of a nation's economic policies is always the economic ideas held by public opinion. No government, whether democratic or dictatorial, can free itself from the sway of the generally accepted ideology.

Those advocating a restriction of the parliament's prerogatives in budgeting and taxation issues or even a complete substitution of authoritarian government for representative government are blinded by the chimerical image of a perfect chief of state. This man, no less benevolent than wise, would be sincerely dedicated to the promotion of his subjects' lasting welfare. The real Führer, however, turns out to be a mortal man who first of all aims at the perpetuation of his own supremacy and that of his kin, his friends, and his party. As far as he may resort to unpopular measures, he does so for the sake of these objectives. He does not invest and accumulate capital. He constructs fortresses and equips armies.

10. The attempts to answer this question by statistics are futile in this age of inflation and credit expansion.

The much talked about plans of the Soviet and Nazi dictators involved restriction of current consumption for the sake of "investment." The Nazis never tried to suppress the truth that all these investments were designed as a preparation for the wars of aggression that they planned. The Soviets were less outspoken at the beginning. But later they proudly declared that all their planning was directed by considerations of war preparedness. History does not provide any example of capital accumulation brought about by a government. As far as governments invested in the construction of roads, railroads, and other useful public works, the capital needed was provided by the savings of individual citizens and borrowed by the government. But the greater part of the funds collected by the public debts was spent for current expenditure. What individuals had saved was dissipated by the government.

Even those who look upon the inequality of wealth and incomes as a deplorable thing, cannot deny that it makes for progressing capital accumulation. And it is additional capital accumulation alone that brings about technological improvement, rising wage rates, and a higher standard of living.

4. Insecurity

The vague notion of security which the welfare doctrinaires have in mind when complaining about insecurity refers to something like a warrant by means of which society guarantees to everybody, irrespective of his achievements, a standard of living which he considers satisfactory.

Security in this sense, contend the eulogists of times gone by, was provided under the social regime of the Middle Ages. There is, however, no need to enter into an examination of these claims. Real conditions even in the much-glorified thirteenth century were different from the ideal picture painted by scholastic philosophy; these schemes were meant as a description of conditions not as they were but as they ought to be. But even these utopias of the philosophers and theologians allow for the existence of a numerous class of destitute beggars, entirely dependent on alms given by the wealthy. This is not precisely the idea of security which the modern usage of the term suggests.

The concept of security is the wage earners' and small farmers' pendant to the concept of stability held by the capitalists.[11] In the same way in which capitalists want to enjoy permanently an income which is not subject to the vicissitudes of changing human conditions,

11. Cf. above, pp. 225–227

wage earners and small farmers want to make their revenues independent of the market. Both groups are eager to withdraw from the flux of historical events. No further occurrence should impair their own position; on the other hand, of course, they do not expressly object to an improvement of their material well-being. That structure of the market to which they have in the past adjusted their activities should never be altered in such a way as to force them to a new adjustment. The farmer in a European mountain valley waxes indignant upon encountering the competition of Canadian farmers producing at lower cost. The house painter boils over with rage when the introduction of a new appliance affects conditions in his sector of the labor market. It is obvious that the wishes of these people could be fulfilled only in a perfectly stagnant world.

A characteristic feature of the unhampered market society is that it is no respecter of vested interests. Past achievements do not count if they are obstacles to further improvement. The advocates of security are therefore quite correct in blaming capitalism for insecurity. But they distort the facts in implying that the selfish interests of capitalists and entrepreneurs are responsible. What harms the vested interests is the urge of the consumers for the best possible satisfaction of their needs. Not the greed of the wealthy few, but the propensity of everyone to take advantage of any opportunity offered for an improvement of his own well-being makes for producer insecurity. What makes the house painter indignant is the fact that his fellow citizens prefer cheaper houses to more expensive ones. And the house painter himself, in preferring cheaper commodities to dearer ones, contributes his share to the emergence of insecurity in other sectors of the labor market.

It is certainly true that the necessity of adjusting oneself again and again to changing conditions is onerous. But change is the essence of life. In an unhampered market economy the absence of security, i.e., the absence of protection for vested interests, is the principle that makes for a steady improvement in material well-being. There is no need to argue with the bucolic dreams of Virgil and of eighteenth-century poets and painters. There is no need to examine the kind of security which the real shepherds enjoyed. No one really wishes to change places with them.

The longing for security became especially intense in the great depression that started in 1929. It met with an enthusiastic response from the millions of unemployed. That is capitalism for you, shouted the leaders of the pressure groups of the farmers and the wage earners. Yet the evils were not created by capitalism, but, on the contrary, by the endeavors to "reform" and to "improve" the operation of the market economy by interventionism. The crash was the necessary outcome of the attempts to lower the rate of interest by credit expansion. Institutional unemployment was the inevitable result of the policy of fixing wage rates above the potential market height.

5. Social Justice

In one respect at least present-day welfare propagandists are superior to most of the older schools of socialists and reformers. They no longer stress a concept of social justice with whose arbitrary precepts men should comply however disastrous the consequences may be. They endorse the utilitarian point of view. They do not oppose the principle that the only standard for appreciating social systems is judging them with regard to their ability to realize the ends sought by acting men.

However, as soon as they embark upon an examination of the operation of the market economy, they forget their sound intentions. They invoke a set of metaphysical principles and condemn the market economy beforehand because it does not conform to them. They smuggle in through a back door the idea of an absolute standard of morality which they had barred from the main entrance. In searching for remedies against poverty, inequality, and insecurity, they come step by step to endorse all the fallacies of the older schools of socialism and interventionism. They become more and more entangled in contradictions and absurdities. Finally they cannot help catching at the straw at which all earlier "unorthodox" reformers tried to grasp—the superior wisdom of perfect rulers. Their last word is always state, government, society, or other cleverly designed synonyms for the superhuman dictator.

The welfare school, foremost among them the German *Kathedersozialisten* and their adepts, the American Institutionalists, have published many thousands of volumes stuffed with punctiliously documented information about unsatisfactory conditions. In their opinion the collected materials clearly illustrate the shortcomings of capitalism. In truth they merely illustrate the fact that human wants are practically unlimited and that there is an immense field open for further improvements. They certainly do not prove any of the statements of the welfare doctrine.

There is no need to tell us that an ampler supply of various commodities would be welcome to all people. The question is whether there is any means of achieving a greater supply other than by increasing the productivity of human effort by the investment of additional capital. All the babble of the welfare propagandists aims only at one end, namely, obscuring this point, the point that alone matters. While the accumulation of additional capital is the indispensable means for any further economic progress, these people speak of "oversaving" and "overinvestment," of the necessity of spending more and of restricting output. Thus they are the harbingers of economic retrogression, preaching a philosophy of decay and social disintegration. A society arranged according to their precepts may appear to some people as fair from the point of view of an arbitrary standard of social justice. But it will certainly be a society of progressing poverty for all its members.

For more than a century public opinion in Western countries has been deluded by the idea that there is such a thing as "the social question" or "the labor problem." The meaning implied was that the very existence of capitalism hurts the vital interests of the masses, especially those of the wage earners and the small farmers. The preservation of this manifestly unfair system cannot be tolerated; radical reforms are indispensable.

The truth is that capitalism has not only multiplied population figures but at the same time improved the people's standard of living in an unprecedented way. Neither economic thinking nor historical experience suggest that any other social system could be as beneficial to the masses as capitalism. The results speak for themselves. The market economy needs no apologists and propagandists. It can apply to itself the words of Sir Christopher Wren's epitaph in St. Paul's: *Si monumentum requiris, circumspice.*[12]

12. If you seek his monument, look around.

XXXVI. THE CRISIS OF INTERVENTIONISM

1. The Harvest of Interventionism

THE interventionist policies as practiced for many decades by all governments of the capitalistic West have brought about all those effects which the economists predicted. There are wars and civil wars, ruthless oppression of the masses by clusters of self-appointed dictators, economic depressions, mass unemployment, capital consumption, famines.

However, it is not these catastrophic events which have led to the crisis of interventionism. The interventionist doctrinaires and their followers explain all these undesired consequences as the unavoidable features of capitalism. As they see it, it is precisely these disasters that clearly demonstrate the necessity of intensifying interventionism. The failures of the interventionist policies do not in the least impair the popularity of the implied doctrine. They are so interpreted as to strengthen, not to lessen, the prestige of these teachings. As a vicious economic theory cannot be simply refuted by historical experience, the interventionist propagandists have been able to go on in spite of all the havoc they have spread.

Yet the age of interventionism is reaching its end. Interventionism has exhausted all its potentialities and must disappear.

2. The Exhaustion of the Reserve Fund

The idea underlying all interventionist policies is that the higher income and wealth of the more affluent part of the population is a fund which can be freely used for the improvement of the conditions of the less prosperous. The essence of the interventionist policy is to take from one group to give to another. It is confiscation and distribution. Every measure is ultimately justified by declaring that it is fair to curb the rich for the benefit of the poor.

In the field of public finance progressive taxation of incomes and estates is the most characteristic manifestation of this doctrine. Tax the rich and spend the revenue for the improvement of the condition of the poor, is the principle of contemporary budgets. In the field of industrial relations shortening the hours of work, raising wages, and a thousand other measures are recommended under the assumption that they favor the employee and burden the employer. Every issue of government and community affairs is dealt with exclusively from the point of view of this principle.

An illustrative example is provided by the methods applied in the operation of nationalized and municipalized enterprises. These enterprises very often result in financial failure; their accounts regularly show losses burdening the state or the city treasury. It is of no use to investigate whether the deficits are due to the notorious inefficiency of the public conduct of business enterprises or, at least partly, to the inadequacy of the prices at which the commodities or services are sold to the customers. What matters is the fact that the taxpayers must cover these deficits. The interventionists fully approve of this arrangement. They passionately reject the two other possible solutions: selling the enterprises to private entrepreneurs or raising the prices charged to the customers to such a height that no further deficit remains. The first of these proposals is in their eyes manifestly reactionary because they believe that the inevitable trend of history is toward more and more socialization. The second is deemed "antisocial" because it places a heavier load upon the consuming masses. It is fairer to make the taxpayers, i.e., the wealthy citizens, bear the burden. Their ability to pay is greater than that of the average people riding the nationalized railroads and the municipalized subways, trolleys, and busses. To ask that such public utilities should be self-supporting, is, say the interventionists, a relic of the old-fashioned ideas of orthodox finance. One might as well aim at making the roads and the public schools self-supporting.

It is not necessary to argue with the advocates of this deficit policy. It is obvious that recourse to this ability-to-pay principle depends on the existence of such incomes and fortunes as can still be taxed away. It can no longer be resorted to once these extra funds have been exhausted by taxes and other interventionist measures.

This is precisely the present state of affairs in most of the European countries. The United States has not yet gone so far; but if the actual trend of its economic policies is not radically altered very soon, it will be in the same condition in a few years.

For the sake of argument we may disregard all the other consequences which the full triumph of the ability-to-pay principle must bring about and concentrate upon its financial aspects.

The interventionist in advocating additional public expenditure is not aware of the fact that the funds available are limited. He does not realize that increasing expenditure in one department enjoins restricting it in other departments. In his opinion there is plenty of money available. The income and wealth of the rich can be freely tapped. In recommending a greater allowance for the schools he simply stresses the point that it would be a good thing to spend more for education. He does not venture to prove that to raise the budgetary allowance for schools is more expedient than to raise that of another department, e.g., that of health. It never occurs to him that grave arguments could be advanced in favor of restricting public spending and lowering the burden of taxation. The champions of cuts in the budget are in his eyes merely the defenders of the manifestly unfair class interests of the rich.

With the present height of income and inheritance tax rates, this reserve fund out of which the interventionists seek to cover all public expenditure is rapidly shrinking. It has practically disappeared altogether in most European countries. In the United States the recent advances in tax rates produced only negligible revenue results beyond what would be produced by a progression which stopped at much lower rates. High surtax rates for the rich are very popular with interventionist dilettantes and demagogues, but they secure only modest additions to the revenue.[1] From day to day it becomes more obvious that large-scale additions to the amount of public expenditure cannot be financed by "soaking the rich," but that the burden must be carried by the masses. The traditional tax policy of the age of interventionism, its glorified devices of progressive taxation and lavish spending have been carried to a point at which their absurdity can no longer be concealed. The notorious principle that, whereas private expenditures depend on the size of income available, public revenues must be regulated according to expenditures, refutes itself. Henceforth, governments will have to realize that one dollar cannot be spent twice, and that the various items of government expenditure are in conflict with one another. Every penny of additional government spending will have to be collected from precisely those people who hitherto have been intent upon shifting the main burden to other groups. Those anxious to get subsidies will themselves have to foot the bill. The deficits of publicly owned and operated enterprises will be charged to the bulk of the population.

1. In the United States the surtax rate under the 1942 Act was 52 per cent on the taxable income bracket $22,000–26,000. If the surtax had stopped at this level, the loss of revenue on 1942 income would have been about $249 million or 2.8 per cent of the total individual income tax for that year. In the same year the total net incomes in the income classes of $10,000 and above was $8,912 million. Complete confiscation of these incomes would not have produced as much revenue as was obtained in this year from all taxable incomes, namely, $9,046 million. Cf. *A Tax Program for a Solvent America,* Committee on Postwar Tax Policy (New York, 1945), pp. 116–117, 120.

The situation in the employer-employee nexus will be analogous. The popular doctrine contends that wage earners are reaping "social gains" at the expense of the unearned income of the exploiting classes. The strikers, it is said, do not strike against the consumers but against "management." There is no reason to raise the prices of products when labor costs are increased; the difference must be borne by employers. But when more and more of the share of the entrepreneurs and capitalists is absorbed by taxes, higher wage rates, and other "social gains" of employees, and by price ceilings, nothing remains for such a buffer function. Then it becomes evident that every wage raise, with its whole momentum, must affect the prices of the products and that the social gains of each group fully correspond to the social losses of the other groups. Every strike becomes, even in the short run and not only in the long run, a strike against the rest of the people.

An essential point in the social philosophy of interventionism is the existence of an inexhaustible fund which can be squeezed forever. The whole system of interventionism collapses when this fountain is drained off: The Santa Claus principle liquidates itself.

3. The End of Interventionism

The interventionist interlude must come to an end because interventionism cannot lead to a permanent system of social organization. The reasons are threefold.

First: Restrictive measures always restrict output and the amount of goods available for consumption. Whatever arguments may be advanced in favor of definite restrictions and prohibitions, such measures in themselves can never constitute a system of social production.

Second: All varieties of interference with the market phenomena not only fail to achieve the ends aimed at by their authors and supporters, but bring about a state of affairs which—from the point of view of their authors' and advocates' valuations—is less desirable than the previous state of affairs which they were designed to alter. If one wants to correct their manifest unsuitableness and preposterousness by supplementing the first acts of intervention with more and more of such acts, one must go farther and farther until the market economy has been entirely destroyed and socialism has been substituted for it.

Third: Interventionism aims at confiscating the "surplus" of one part of the population and at giving it to the other part. Once this surplus is exhausted by total confiscation, a further continuation of this policy is impossible.

Marching ever further along the path of interventionism, all those countries that have not adopted full socialism of the Russian pattern are more and more approaching what is called a planned economy, i.e., socialism of the German or Hindenburg pattern. In regard to economic policies, there is nowadays little difference among the various nations and, within each nation, among the various political parties and pressure groups. The historical party names have lost their significance. There are, as far as economic policy is concerned, practically only two factions left: the advocates of the Lenin method of all-round nationalization and the interventionists. The advocates of the free market economy have little influence upon the course of events. What economic freedom still exists is the outcome of the failure of the measures resorted to by the governments, rather than of an intentional policy.

It is difficult to find out how many of the supporters of interventionism are conscious of the fact that the policies they recommend directly lead toward socialism, and how many hold fast to the illusion that what they are aiming at is a middle-of-the-road system that can last as a permanent system—a "third solution" of the problem of society's economic organization. At any rate, it is certain that all interventionists believe that the government, and the government alone, is called upon to decide in every single case whether one has to let things go as the market determines them or whether an act of intervention is needed. This means that they are prepared to tolerate the supremacy of the consumers only as far as it brings about a result of which they themselves approve. As soon as something happens in the economy that any of the various bureaucratic institutions does not like or that arouses the anger of a pressure group, people clamor for new interventions, controls, and restrictions. But for the inefficiency of the law-givers and the laxity, carelessness, and corruption of many of the functionaries, the last vestiges of the market economy would have long since disappeared.

The unsurpassed efficiency of capitalism never before manifested itself in a more beneficial way than in this age of heinous anticapitalism. While governments, political parties, and labor unions are sabotaging all business operations, the spirit of enterprise still succeeds in increasing the quantity and improving the quality of products and in rendering them more easily accessible to the consumers. In the countries that have not yet entirely abandoned the capitalistic system the common man enjoys today a standard of living for which the princes and nabobs of ages gone by would have envied him. A short time ago the demagogues blamed capitalism for the poverty of the masses. Today they rather blame capitalism for the "affluence" that it bestows upon the common man.

It has been shown that the managerial system, i.e., the assignment of ancillary tasks in the conduct of business to responsible helpers to whom a certain amount of discretion can be granted, is possible only within the frame of the profit system.[2] What characterizes the manager as such and imparts to him a condition different from that of the mere technician is that, within the sphere of his assignment, he himself determines the methods by which his actions should conform to the profit principle. In a socialist system in which there is neither economic calculation nor capital accounting nor profit computation, there is no room left for managerial activities either. But as long as a socialist commonwealth is still in a position to calculate on the ground of prices determined on foreign markets, it can also utilize a quasi-managerial hierarchy to some extent.

It is a poor makeshift to call any age an age of transition. In the living world there is always change. Every age is an age of transition. We may distinguish between social systems that can last and such as are inevitably transitory because they are self-destructive. It has already been pointed out in what sense interventionism liquidates itself and must lead to socialism of the German pattern. Some European countries have already reached this phase, and nobody knows whether or not the United States will follow suit. But as long as the United States clings to the market economy and does not adopt the system of full government control of business, the socialist economies of Western Europe will still be in a position to calculate. Their conduct of business still lacks the most characteristic feature of socialist conduct; it is still based on economic calculation. It is therefore in every respect very different from what it would become if all the world were to turn toward socialism.

It is often said that one half of the world cannot remain committed to the market economy when the other half is socialist, and vice versa. However, there is no reason to assume that such a partition of the earth and the coexistence of the two systems is impossible. If this is really the case, then the present economic system of the countries that have discarded capitalism may go on for an indefinite period of time. Its operation may result in social disintegration, chaos, and misery for the peoples. But neither a low standard of living nor progressive impoverishment automatically liquidates an economic system. It gives way to a more efficient system only if people themselves are intelligent enough to comprehend the advantages such a change might bring them. Or it may be destroyed by foreign invaders provided with better military equipment by the greater efficiency of their own economic system.

2. Cf. above, pp. 305–308.

Optimists hope that at least those nations which have in the past developed the capitalist market economy and its civilization will cling to this system in the future too. There are certainly as many signs to confirm as to disprove such an expectation. It is vain to speculate about the outcome of the great ideological conflict between the principles of private ownership and public ownership, of individualism and totalitarianism, of freedom and authoritarian regimentation. All that we can know beforehand about the result of this struggle can be condensed in the following three statements:

1. We have no knowledge whatever about the existence and operation of agencies which would bestow final victory in this clash on those ideologies whose application will secure the preservation and further intensification of societal bonds and the improvement of mankind's material well-being. Nothing suggests the belief that progress toward more satisfactory conditions is inevitable or a relapse into very unsatisfactory conditions impossible.

2. Men must choose between the market economy and socialism. They cannot evade deciding between these alternatives by adopting a "middle-of-the-road" position, whatever name they may give to it.

3. In abolishing economic calculation the general adoption of socialism would result in complete chaos and the disintegration of social cooperation under the division of labor.

Part Seven

The Place of Economics in Society

XXXVII. THE NONDESCRIPT CHARACTER OF ECONOMICS

1. The Singularity of Economics

WHAT assigns economics its peculiar and unique position in the orbit both of pure knowledge and of the practical utilization of knowledge is the fact that its particular theorems are not open to any verification or falsification on the ground of experience. Of course, a measure suggested by sound economic reasoning results in producing the effects aimed at, and a measure suggested by faulty economic reasoning fails to produce the ends sought. But such experience is always still historical experience, i.e., the experience of complex phenomena. It can never, as has been pointed out, prove or disprove any particular theorem.[1] The application of spurious economic theorems results in undesired consequences. But these effects never have that undisputable power of conviction which the *experimental facts* in the field of the natural sciences provide. The ultimate yardstick of an economic theorem's correctness or incorrectness is solely reason unaided by experience.

The ominous import of this state of affairs is that it prevents the naïve mind from recognizing the reality of the things economics deals with. "Real" is, in the eyes of man, all that he cannot alter and to whose existence he must adjust his actions if he wants to attain his ends. The cognizance of reality is a sad experience. It teaches the limits on the satisfaction of one's wishes. Only reluctantly does man resign himself to the insight that there are things, viz., the whole complex of all causal relations between events, which wishful thinking cannot alter. Yet sense experience speaks an easily perceptible language. There is no use arguing about experiments. The reality of experimentally established facts cannot be contested.

But in the field of praxeological knowledge neither success nor failure speaks a distinct language audible to everybody. The experience derived exclusively from complex phenomena does not bar escape into interpretations based on wishful thinking. The naïve man's propensity to ascribe omnipotence to his thoughts, however confused

1. Cf. above, pp. 31–32.

and contradictory, is never manifestly and unambiguously falsified by experience. The economist can never refute the economic cranks and quacks in the way in which the doctor refutes the medicine man and the charlatan. History speaks only to those people who know how to interpret it on the ground of correct theories.

2. Economics and Public Opinion

The significance of this fundamental epistemological difference becomes clear if we realize that the practical utilization of the teachings of economics presupposes their endorsement by public opinion. In the market economy the realization of technological innovations does not require anything more than the cognizance of their reasonableness by one or a few enlightened spirits. No dullness and clumsiness on the part of the masses can stop the pioneers of improvement. There is no need for them to win the approval of inert people beforehand. They are free to embark upon their projects even if everyone else laughs at them. Later, when the new, better and cheaper products appear on the market, these scoffers will scramble for them. However dull a man may be, he knows how to tell the difference between a cheaper shoe and a more expensive one, and to appreciate the usefulness of new products.

But it is different in the field of social organization and economic policies. Here the best theories are useless if not supported by public opinion. They cannot work if not accepted by a majority of the people. Whatever the system of government may be, there cannot be any question of ruling a nation lastingly on the ground of doctrines at variance with public opinion. In the end the philosophy of the majority prevails. In the long run there cannot be any such thing as an unpopular system of government. The difference between democracy and despotism does not affect the final outcome. It refers only to the method by which the adjustment of the system of government to the ideology held by public opinion is brought about. Unpopular autocrats can only be dethroned by revolutionary upheavals, while unpopular democratic rulers are peacefully ousted in the next election.

The supremacy of public opinion determines not only the singular role that economics occupies in the complex of thought and knowledge. It determines the whole process of human history.

The customary discussions concerning the role the individual plays in history miss the point. Everything that is thought, done and accomplished is a performance of individuals. New ideas and innovations are always an achievement of uncommon men. But these great men cannot succeed in adjusting social conditions to their plans if they do not convince public opinion.

The flowering of human society depends on two factors: the intellectual power of outstanding men to conceive sound social and economic theories, and the ability of these or other men to make these ideologies palatable to the majority.

3. The Illusion of the Old Liberals

The masses, the hosts of common men, do not conceive any ideas, sound or unsound. They only choose between the ideologies developed by the intellectual leaders of mankind. But their choice is final and determines the course of events. If they prefer bad doctrines, nothing can prevent disaster.

The social philosophy of the Enlightenment failed to see the dangers that the prevalence of unsound ideas could engender. The objections customarily raised against the rationalism of the classical economists and the utilitarian thinkers are vain. But there was one deficiency in their doctrines. They blithely assumed that what is reasonable will carry on merely on account of its reasonableness. They never gave a thought to the possibility that public opinion could favor spurious ideologies whose realization would harm welfare and well-being and disintegrate social cooperation.

It is fashionable today to disparage those thinkers who criticized the liberal philosophers' faith in the common man. Yet, Burke and Haller, Bonald and de Maistre paid attention to an essential problem which the liberals had neglected. They were more realistic in the appraisal of the masses than their adversaries.

Of course, the conservative thinkers labored under the illusion that the traditional system of paternal government and the rigidity of economic institutions could be preserved. They were full of praise for the ancient régime which had made people prosperous and had even humanized war. But they did not see that it was precisely these achievements that had increased population figures and thus created an excess population for which there was no room left in the old system of economic restrictionism. They shut their eyes to the growth of a class of people which stood outside the pale of the social order they wanted to perpetuate. They failed to suggest any solution to the most burning problem with which mankind had to cope on the eve of the "Industrial Revolution."

Capitalism gave the world what it needed, a higher standard of living for a steadily increasing number of people. But the liberals, the pioneers and supporters of capitalism, overlooked one essential point.

A social system, however beneficial, cannot work if it is not supported by public opinion. They did not anticipate the success of the anticapitalistic propaganda. After having nullified the fable of the divine mission of anointed kings, the liberals fell prey to no less illusory doctrines, to the irresistible power of reason, to the infallibility of the *volonté générale* and to the divine inspiration of majorities. In the long run, they thought, nothing can stop the progressive improvement of social conditions. In unmasking age-old superstitions the philosophy of the Enlightenment has once and for all established the supremacy of reason. The accomplishments of the policies of freedom will provide such an overwhelming demonstration of the blessings of the new ideology that no intelligent man will venture to question it. And, implied the philosophers, the immense majority of people are intelligent and able to think correctly.

It never occurred to the old liberals that the majority could interpret historical experience on the ground of other philosophies. They did not anticipate the popularity which ideas that they would have called reactionary, superstitious, and unreasonable acquired in the nineteenth and twentieth centuries. They were so fully imbued with the assumption that all men are endowed with the faculty of correct reasoning that they entirely misconstrued the meaning of the portents. As they saw it, all these unpleasant events were temporary relapses, accidental episodes to which no importance could be attached by the philosopher looking upon mankind's history sub specie aeternitatis. Whatever the reactionaries might say, there was one fact which they would not be able to deny; namely, that capitalism provided for a rapidly increasing population a steadily improving standard of living.

It was precisely this fact that the immense majority did contest. The essential point in the teachings of all socialist authors, and especially in the teachings of Marx, is the doctrine that capitalism results in a progressive pauperization of the working masses. With regard to the capitalistic countries the fallacy of this theorem can hardly be ignored. With regard to the backward countries, which were only superficially affected by capitalism, the unprecedented increase in population figures does not suggest the interpretation that the masses sink deeper and deeper. These countries are poor when compared with the more advanced countries. Their poverty is the outcome of the rapid growth of population. These peoples have preferred to rear more progeny instead of raising the standard of living to a higher level. That is their own affair. But the fact remains that they had the wealth to prolong the average length of life. It would have been impossible for them to bring up more children if the means of sustenance had not been increased.

Nonetheless not only the Marxians but many allegedly "bourgeois" authors assert that Marx's anticipation of capitalist evolution has been by and large verified by the history of the last hundred years.

XXXVIII. THE PLACE OF ECONOMICS IN LEARNING

1. The Study of Economics

THE natural sciences are ultimately based on the facts as established by laboratory experiment. Physical and biological theories are confronted with these facts, and are rejected when in conflict with them. The perfection of these theories no less than the improvement of technological and therapeutical procedures requires more and better laboratory research. These experimental ventures absorb time, painstaking effort of specialists, and costly expenditure of material. Research can no longer be conducted by isolated and penniless scientists, however ingenious. The seat of experimentation today is in the huge laboratories supported by governments, universities, endowments, and big business. Work in these institutions has developed into professional routine. The majority of those employed in it are technicians recording those facts which the pioneers, of whom some are themselves experimenters, will one day use as building stones for their theories. As far as the progress of scientific theories is concerned, the achievements of the rank-and-file researcher are only ancillary. But very often his discoveries have immediate practical results in improving the methods of therapeutics and of business.

Ignoring the radical epistemological difference between the natural sciences and the sciences of human action, people believe that what is needed to further economic knowledge is to organize economic research according to the well-tried methods of the institutes for medical, physical, and chemical research. Considerable sums of money have been spent for what is labeled economic research. In fact the subject matter of the work of all these institutes is recent economic history.

It is certainly a laudable thing to encourage the study of economic history. However instructive the result of such studies may be, one must not confuse them with the study of economics. They do not produce facts in the sense in which this term is applied with regard to the events tested in laboratory experiments. They do not deliver bricks for the construction of a posteriori hypotheses and theorems. On the contrary, they are without meaning if not interpreted in the light of theories developed without reference to them. There is no need to add anything to what has been said in this respect in the preceding chapters. No controversy concerning the causes of a historical event can be solved on the ground of an examination of the facts which is not guided by definite praxeological theories.[1]

The foundation of institutes for cancer research can possibly contribute to the discovery of methods for fighting and preventing this pernicious disease. But a business cycle research institute is of no help in endeavors to avoid the recurrence of depressions. The most exact and reliable assemblage of all the data concerning economic depressions of the past is of little use for our knowledge in this field. Scholars do not disagree with regard to these data; they disagree wth regard to the theorems to be resorted to in their interpretation.

Still more important is the fact that it is impossible to collect the data concerning a concrete event without reference to the theories held by the historian at the very outset of his work. The historian does not report all facts, but only those which he considers as relevant on the ground of his theories; he omits data considered irrelevant for the interpretation of the events. If he is misled by faulty theories, his report becomes clumsy and may be almost worthless.

Even the most faithful examination of a chapter of economic history, though it be the history of the most recent period of the past, is no substitute for economic thinking. Economics, like logic and mathematics, is a display of abstract reasoning. Economics can never be experimental and empirical. The economist does not need an expensive apparatus for the conduct of his studies. What he needs is the power to think clearly and to discern in the wilderness of events what is essential from what is merely accidental.

There is no conflict between economic history and economics. Every branch of knowledge has its own merits and its own rights. Economists have never tried to belittle or deny the significance of economic history. Neither do real historians object to the study of economics. The antagonism was intentionally called into being by the socialists and interventionists who could not refute the objections raised against their doctrines by the economists. The Historical School and the Institutionalists tried to displace economics and to substitute "empirical" studies for it precisely because they wanted to silence the economists. Economic history, as they planned it, was a means

1. Cf., about the essential epistemological problems involved, pp. 31–41, about the problem of "quantitative" economics, pp. 55–57 and 350–352, and about the antagonistic interpretation of labor conditions under capitalism, pp. 617–623.

of destroying the prestige of economics and of propagandizing for interventionism.

2. Economics as a Profession

The early economists devoted themselves to the study of the problems of economics. In lecturing and writing books they were eager to communicate to their fellow citizens the results of their thinking. They tried to influence public opinion in order to make sound policies prevail in the conduct of civic affairs. They never conceived of economics as a profession.

The development of a profession of economists is an offshoot of interventionism. The professional economist is the specialist who is instrumental in designing various measures of government interference with business. He is an expert in the field of economic legislation, which today invariably aims at hindering the operation of the market economy.

There are thousands and thousands of such professional experts busy in the bureaus of the governments and of the various political parties and pressure groups and in the editorial offices of party newspapers and pressure-group periodicals. Others are employed as advisers by business or run independent agencies. Some of them have nation-wide or even world-wide reputations; many are among the most influential men of their country. It often happens that such experts are called to direct the affairs of big banks and corporations, are elected into the legislature, and are appointed as cabinet ministers. They rival the legal profession in the supreme conduct of political affairs. The eminent role they play is one of the most characteristic features of our age of interventionism.

There can be no doubt that a class of men who are so preponderant includes extremely talented individuals, even the most eminent men of our age. But the philosophy that guides their activities narrows their horizon. By virtue of their connection with definite parties and pressure groups, eager to acquire special privileges, they become one-sided. They shut their eyes to the remoter consequences of the policies they are advocating. With them nothing counts but the short-run concerns of the group they are serving. The ultimate aim of their efforts is to make their clients prosper at the expense of other people. They are intent upon convincing themselves that the fate of mankind coincides with the short-run interests of their group. They try to sell this idea to the public. In fighting for a higher price of silver, of wheat, or of sugar, for higher wages for the members of their union, or for a tariff on cheaper foreign products, they claim to be fighting for the supreme good, for liberty and justice, for their nation's flowering, and for civilization.

The public looks askance upon the lobbyists and blames them for the dismal features of interventionist legislation. However, the seat of the evil is much deeper. The philosophy of the various pressure groups has penetrated the legislative bodies. There are in the present-day parliaments representatives of wheat growers, of cattle breeders, of farmers' cooperatives, of silver, of the various labor unions, of industries which cannot stand foreign competition without tariffs, and of many other pressure groups. There are few for whom the nation counts more than their pressure group. The same holds true for the departments of the administration. The cabinet minister of agriculture considers himself the champion of the interests of farming; his main objective is to make food prices soar. The minister of labor considers himself the advocate of labor unions; his foremost aim is to make the unions as formidable as possible. Each department follows its own course and works against the endeavors of the other departments.

Many people complain today about the lack of creative statesmanship. However, under the predominance of interventionist ideas, a political career is open only to men who identify themselves with the interests of a pressure group. The mentality of a union leader or of a secretary of farmers' associations is not what is required for a far-sighted statesman. Service to the short-run interests of a pressure group is not conducive to the development of those qualities which make a great statesman. Statesmanship is invariably long-run policy; but pressure groups do not bother about the long run. The lamentable failure of the German Weimar system and of the Third Republic in France was primarily due to the fact that their politicians were merely experts in pressure group interests.

3. Forecasting as a Profession

When the businessmen finally learned that the boom created by credit expansion cannot last and must necesarily lead to a slump, they realized that it was important for them to know in time the date of the break. They turned to the economists for advice.

The economist knows that such a boom must result in a depression. But he does not and cannot know when the crisis will appear. This depends on the special conditions of each case. Many political events can influence the outcome. There are no rules according to which the duration of the boom or of the following depression can be computed. And even if such rules were available, they would be of no use to businessmen. What the individual businessman needs in order to avoid losses is knowledge about the date of the turning point at a time when other businessmen still believe that the crash is farther away than is really the case. Then his superior knowledge will give him the opportunity to arrange his own operations in such a way as to come out unharmed. But if the end of the boom could be calculated according to a formula, all businessmen would learn the date at the same time. Their endeavors to adjust their conduct of affairs to this information would immediately result in the appearance of all the phenomena of the depression. It would be too late for any of them to avoid being victimized.

If it were possible to calculate the future state of the market, the future would not be uncertain. There would be neither entrepreneurial loss nor profit. What people expect from the economists is beyond the power of any mortal man.

The very idea that the future is predictable, that some formulas could be substituted for the specific understanding which is the essence of entrepreneurial activity, and that familiarity with these formulas could make it possible for anybody to take over the conduct of business is, of course, an outgrowth of the whole complex of fallacies and misconceptions which are at the bottom of present-day anticapitalistic policies. There is in the whole body of what is called the Marxian philosophy not the slightest reference to the fact that the main task of action is to provide for the events of an *uncertain* future. The fact that the term speculator is today used only with an opprobrious connotation clearly shows that our contemporaries do not even suspect in what the fundamental problem of action consists.

Entrepreneurial judgment cannot be bought on the market. The entrepreneurial idea that carries on and brings profit is precisely that idea which did not occur to the majority. It is not correct foresight as such that yields profits, but foresight better than that of the rest. The prize goes only to the dissenters, who do not let themselves be misled by the errors accepted by the multitude. What makes profits emerge is the provision for future needs for which others have neglected to make adequate provision.

Entrepreneurs and capitalists expose their own material well-being if they are fully convinced of the soundness of their plans. They would never venture to take their economic life into their hands because an expert advised them to do so. Those ignorant people who operate on the stock and commodity exchanges according to tips are destined to lose their money, from whatever source they may have got their inspiration and "inside" information.

In fact reasonable businessmen are fully aware of the uncertainty of the future. They realize that the economists do not dispense any reliable information about things to come and that all that they provide is interpretation of statistical data referring to the past. For the capitalists and entrepreneurs the economists' opinions about the future count only as questionable conjectures. They are skeptical and not easily fooled. But as they quite correctly believe that it is useful to know all the data which could possibly have any relevance for their affairs, they subscribe to the newspapers and periodicals publishing the forecasts. Anxious not to neglect any source of information available, big business employs staffs of economists and statisticians.

Business forecasting fails in the vain attempts to make the uncertainty of the future disappear and to deprive entrepreneurship of its inherent speculative character. But it renders some services in assembling and interpreting the available data about economic trends and developments of the recent past.

4. Economics and the Universities

Tax-supported universities are under the sway of the party in power. The authorities try to appoint only professors who are ready to advance ideas of which they themselves approve. As all nonsocialist governments are today firmly committed to interventionism, they appoint only interventionists. In their opinion, the first duty of the university is to sell the official social philosophy to the rising generation.[2] They have no use for economists.

However, interventionism prevails also at many of the independent universities.

According to an age-old tradition the objective of the universities is not only teaching, but also the promotion of knowledge and science. The duty of the university teacher is not merely to hand down to the students the complex of knowledge developed by other men. He is supposed to contribute to the enlargement of this treasure by his own work. It is assumed that he is a full-fledged member of the world-embracing republic of scholarship, an innovator and a pioneer on the road toward more and better knowledge. No university would

2. G. Santayana, in speaking of a professor of philosophy of the—then Royal Prussian—University of Berlin, observed that it seemed to this man "that a professor's business was to trudge along the governmental towpath with a legal cargo." (*Persons and Places* [New York, 1945], II, 7.)

admit that the members of its faculty are inferior to anybody in their respective fields. Every university professor considers himself equal to all other masters of his science. Like the greatest of them, he too contributes his share to the advancement of learning.

This idea of the equality of all professors is, of course, fictitious. There is an enormous difference between the creative work of the genius and the monograph of a specialist. Yet in the field of empirical research it is possible to cling to this fiction. The great innovator and the simple routinist resort in their investigations to the same technical methods of research. They arrange laboratory experiments or collect historical documents. The outward appearance of their work is the same. Their publications refer to the same subjects and problems. They are commensurable.

It is quite otherwise in theoretical sciences like philosophy and economics. Here there is nothing that the routinist can achieve according to a more or less stereotyped pattern. There are no tasks which require the conscientious and painstaking effort of sedulous monographers. There is no empirical research; all must be achieved by the power to reflect, to meditate, and to reason. There is no specialization, as all problems are linked with one another. In dealing with any part of the body of knowledge one deals actually with the whole. An eminent historian once described the psychological and educational significance of the doctoral thesis by declaring that it gives the author the proud assurance that there is a little corner, although small, in the field of learning in the knowledge of which he is second to none. It is obvious that this effect cannot be realized by a thesis on a subject of economic analysis. There are no such isolated corners in the complex of economic thought.

There never lived at the same time more than a score of men whose work contributed anything essential to economics. The number of creative men is as small in economics as it is in other fields of learning. Besides, many of the creative economists do not belong to the teaching profession. But there is a demand for thousands of university and college teachers of economics. Scholastic tradition requires that each of them should attest his worth by the publication of original contributions, not merely by compiling textbooks and manuals. An academic teacher's reputation and salary depend more on his literary work than on his didactic abilities. A professor cannot help publishing books. If he does not feel the vocation to write on economics, he turns to economic history or descriptive economics. But then, in order not to lose face, he must insist on the claim that the problems he treats are economics proper, not economic history.

He must even pretend that his writings cover the only legitimate field of economic studies, that they alone are empirical, inductive, and scientific, while the merely deductive outpourings of the "armchair" theorists are idle speculations. If he were to neglect this, he would admit that there are among the teachers of economics two classes—those who themselves have contributed to the advancement of economic thought and those who have not, although they may have done a fine job in other disciplines such as recent economic history. Thus the academic atmosphere becomes unpropitious for the teaching of economics. Many professors—happily not all of them—are intent upon disparaging "mere theory." They try to substitute an unsystematically assembled collection of historical and statistical information for economic analysis. They dissolve economics into a number of integrated branches. They specialize in agriculture, in labor, in Latin American conditions, and in many other similar subdivisions.

It is certainly one of the tasks of university training to make students familiar with economic history in general and no less with recent economic developments. But all such endeavors are doomed to failure if not firmly grounded upon a thorough acquaintance with economics. Economics does not allow of any breaking up into special branches. It invariably deals with the interconnectedness of all the phenomena of action. The catallactic problems cannot become visible if one deals with each branch of production separately. It is impossible to study labor and wages without studying implicitly commodity prices, interest rates, profit and loss, money and credit, and all the other major problems. The real problems of the determination of wage rates cannot even be touched in a course on labor. There are no such things as "economics of labor" or "economics of agriculture." There is only one coherent body of economics.

What these specialists deal with in their lectures and publications is not economics, but the doctrines of the various pressure groups. Ignoring economics, they cannot help falling prey to the ideologies of those aiming at special privileges for their group. Even those specialists who do not openly side with a definite pressure group and who claim to maintain a lofty neutrality unwittingly endorse the essential creeds of the interventionist doctrine. Dealing exclusively with the innumerable varieties of government interference with business, they do not want to cling to what they call mere negativism. If they criticize the measures resorted to, they do it only in order to recommend their own brand of interventionism as a substitute for other people's interventionism. Without a qualm they endorse the fundamental thesis of both interventionism and socialism that the unhampered market economy unfairly harms the vital interests of the immense majority for the sole benefit of callous exploiters. As they see it, an economist who demonstrates the futility of interventionism is a bribed champion of the unjust claims of big business. It is imperative to bar such scoundrels from access to the universities and their articles from being printed in the periodicals of the associations of university teachers.

The students are bewildered. In the courses of the mathematical economists they are fed formulas describing hypothetical states of equilibrium in which there is no longer any action. They easily conclude that these equations are of no use whatever for the comprehension of economic activities. In the lectures of the specialists they hear a mass of detail concerning interventionist measures. They must infer that conditions are paradoxical indeed, because there is never equilibrium, and wage rates and the prices of farm products are not so high as the unions or the farmers want them to be. It is obvious, they conclude, that a radical reform is indispensable. But what kind of reform?

The majority of the students espouse without any inhibitions the interventionist panaceas recommended by their professors. Social conditions will be perfectly satisfactory when the government enforces minimum wage rates and provides everybody with adequate food and housing, or when the sale of margarine and the importation of foreign sugar are prohibited. They do not see the contradictions in the words of their teachers, who one day lament the madness of competition and the next day the evils of monopoly, who one day complain about falling prices and the next day about rising living costs. They take their degrees and try as soon as possible to get a job with the government or a powerful pressure group.

But there are many young men who are keen enough to see through the fallacies of interventionism. They accept their teachers' rejection of the unhampered market economy. But they do not believe that the isolated measures of interventionism could succeed in attaining the ends sought. They consistently carry their preceptors' thoughts to their ultimate logical consequences. They turn toward socialism. They hail the Soviet system as the dawn of a new and better civilization.

However, what has made many of the present-day universities by and large nurseries of socialism is not so much the conditions prevailing in the departments of economics as the teachings handed down in other departments. In the departments of economics there can still be found some economists, and even the other teachers may be familiar with some of the objections raised against the practicability of socialism. The case is different with many of the teachers of philosophy, history, literature, sociology, and political science. They interpret history on the ground of a garbled vulgarization of dialectical materialism. Even many of those who passionately attack Marxism on account of its materialism and atheism are under the sway of the ideas developed in the *Communist Manifesto* and in the program of the Communist International. They explain depressions, mass unemployment, inflation, war and poverty as evils necessarily inherent in capitalism and intimate that these phenomena can disappear only with the passing of capitalism.

5. General Education and Economics

In countries which are not harassed by struggles between various linguistic groups public education can work if it is limited to reading, writing, and arithmetic. With bright children it is even possible to add elementary notions of geometry, the natural sciences, and the valid laws of the country. But as soon as one wants to go farther, serious difficulties appear. Teaching at the elementary level necessarily turns into indoctrination. It is not feasible to represent to adolescents all the aspects of a problem and to let them choose between dissenting views. It is no less impossible to find teachers who could hand down opinions of which they themselves disapprove in such a way as to satisfy those who hold these opinions. The party that operates the schools is in a position to propagandize its tenets and to disparage those of other parties.

In the field of religious education the nineteenth-century liberals solved this problem by the separation of state and church. In liberal countries religion is no longer taught in public schools. But the parents are free to send their children into denominational schools supported by religious communities.

However, the problem does not refer only to the teaching of religion and of certain theories of the natural sciences at variance with the Bible. It concerns even more the teaching of history and economics.

The public is aware of the matter only with regard to the international aspects of the teaching of history. There is some talk today about the necessity of freeing the teaching of history from the impact of nationalism and chauvinism. But few people realize that the problem of impartiality and objectivity is no less present in dealing with the domestic aspects of history. The teacher's or the textbook author's own social philosophy colors the narrative. The more the treatment must be simplified and condensed in order to be comprehensible to the immature minds of children and adolescents, the worse are the effects.

As the Marxians and the interventionists see it, the teaching of history in the schools is tainted by the endorsement of the ideas of classical liberalism. They want to substitute their own interpretation of history for the "bourgeois" interpretation. In Marxian opinion the English Revolution of 1688, the American Revolution, the great French Revolution, and the nineteenth-century revolutionary movements in continental Europe were bourgeois movements. They resulted in the defeat of feudalism and in the establishment of bourgeois supremacy. The proletarian masses were not emancipated; they merely passed from the class rule of the aristocracy to the class rule of the capitalist exploiters. To free the working man, the abolition of the capitalist mode of production is required. This, contend the interventionists, should be brought about by Sozialpolitik or the New Deal. The orthodox Marxians, on the other hand, assert that only the violent overthrow of the bourgeois system of government could effectively emancipate the proletarians.

It is impossible to deal with any chapter of history without taking a definite stand on these controversial issues and the implied economic doctrines. The textbooks and the teachers cannot adopt a lofty neutrality with regard to the postulate that the "unfinished revolution" needs to be completed by the communist revolution. Every statement concerning events of the last three hundred years involves a definite judgment on these controversies. One cannot avoid choosing between the philosophy of the Declaration of Independence and the Gettysburg Address and that of the *Communist Manifesto*. The challenge is there, and it is useless to bury one's head in the sand.

On the high school level and even on the college level the handing down of historical and economic knowledge is virtually indoctrination. The greater part of the students are certainly not mature enough to form their own opinion on the ground of a critical examination of their teachers' representation of the subject.

If public education were more efficient than it really is, the political parties would urgently aim at the domination of the school system in order to determine the mode in which these subjects are to be taught. However, general education plays only a minor role in the formation of the political, social, and economic ideas of the rising generation. The impact of the press, the radio, and environmental conditions is much more powerful than that of teachers and textbooks. The propaganda of the churches, the political parties, and the pressure groups outstrips the influence of the schools, whatever they may teach. What is learned in school is often very soon forgotten and cannot carry on against the continuous hammering of the social milieu in which a man moves.

6. Economics and the Citizen

Economics must not be relegated to classrooms and statistical offices and must not be left to esoteric circles. It is the philosophy of human life and action and concerns everybody and everything. It is the pith of civilization and of man's human existence.

To mention this fact is not to indulge in the often derided weakness of specialists who overrate the importance of their own branch of knowledge. Not the economists, but all the people today assign this eminent place to economics.

All present-day political issues concern problems commonly called economic. All arguments advanced in contemporary discussion of social and public affairs deal with fundamental matters of praxeology and economics. Everybody's mind is preoccupied with economic doctrines. Philosophers and theologians seem to be more interested in economic problems than in those problems which earlier generations considered the subject matter of philosophy and theology. Novels and plays today treat all things human—including sex relations—from the angle of economic doctrines. Everybody thinks of economics whether he is aware of it or not. In joining a political party and in casting his ballot, the citizen implicitly takes a stand upon essential economic theories.

In the sixteenth and seventeenth centuries religion was the main issue in European political controversies. In the eighteenth and nineteenth centuries in Europe as well as in America the paramount question was representative government versus royal absolutism. Today it is the market economy versus socialism. This is, of course, a problem the solution of which depends entirely on economic analysis. Recourse to empty slogans or to the mysticism of dialectical materialism is of no avail.

There is no means by which anyone can evade his personal responsibility. Whoever neglects to examine to the best of his abilities all the problems involved voluntarily surrenders his birthright to a self-appointed elite of supermen. In such vital matters blind reliance upon "experts" and uncritical acceptance of popular catchwords and prejudices is tantamount to the abandonment of self-determination and to yielding to other people's domination. As conditions are today, nothing can be more important to every intelligent man than economics. His own fate and that of his progeny is at stake.

Very few are capable of contributing any consequential idea to the body of economic thought. But all reasonable men are called upon to familiarize themselves with the teachings of economics. This is, in our age, the primary civic duty.

Whether we like it or not, it is a fact that economics cannot remain an esoteric branch of knowledge accessible only to small groups of scholars and specialists. Economics deals with society's fundamental problems; it concerns everyone and belongs to all. It is the main and proper study of every citizen.

7. Economics and Freedom

The paramount role that economic ideas play in the determination of civic affairs explains why governments, political parties, and pressure groups are intent upon restricting the freedom of economic thought. They are anxious to propagandize the "good" doctrine and to silence the voice of the "bad" doctrines. As they see it, truth has no inherent power which could make it ultimately prevail solely by virtue of its being true. In order to carry on, truth needs to be backed by violent action on the part of the police or other armed troops. In this view, the criterion of a doctrine's truth is the fact that its supporters succeeded in defeating by force of arms the champions of dissenting views. It is implied that God or some mythical agency directing the course of human affairs always bestows victory upon those fighting for the good cause. Government is from God and has the sacred duty of exterminating the heretic.

It is useless to dwell upon the contradictions and inconsistencies of this doctrine of intolerance and persecution of dissenters. Never before has the world known such a cleverly contrived system of propaganda and oppression as that instituted by contemporary governments, parties, and pressure groups. However, all these edifices will crumble like houses of cards as soon as a great ideology attacks them.

Not only in the countries ruled by barbarian and neobarbarian despots, but no less in the so-called Western democracies, the study of economics is practically outlawed today. The public discussion of economic problems ignores almost entirely all that has been said by economists in the last two hundred years. Prices, wage rates, interest rates, and profits are dealt with as if their determination were not subject to any law. Governments try to decree and to enforce maximum commodity prices and minimum wage rates. Statesmen exhort businessmen to cut down profits, to lower prices, and to raise wage rates as if these matters were dependent on the laudible intentions of individuals. In the treatment of international economic relations people blithely resort to the most naïve fallacies of Mercantilism. Few are aware of the shortcomings of all these popular doctrines, or realize why the policies based upon them invariably spread disaster.

These are sad facts. However, there is only one way in which a man can respond to them: by never relaxing in the search for truth.

XXXIX. ECONOMICS AND THE ESSENTIAL PROBLEMS OF HUMAN EXISTENCE

1. Science and Life

It is customary to find fault with modern science because it abstains from expressing judgments of value. Living and acting man, we are told, has no use for *Wertfreiheit;* he needs to know what he should aim at. If science does not answer this question, it is sterile. However, the objection is unfounded. Science does not value, but it provides acting man with all the information he may need with regard to his valuations. It keeps silence only when the question is raised whether life itself is worth living.

This question, of course, has been raised too and will always be raised. What is the meaning of all these human endeavors and activities if in the end nobody can escape death and decomposition? Man lives in the shadow of death. Whatever he may have achieved in the course of his pilgrimage, he must one day pass away and abandon all that he has built. Each instant can become his last. There is only one thing that is certain about the individual's future—death. Seen from the point of view of this ultimate and inescapable outcome, all human striving appears vain and futile.

Moreover, human action must be called inane even when judged merely with regard to its immediate goals. It can never bring full satisfaction; it merely gives for an evanescent instant a partial removal of uneasiness. As soon as one want is satisfied, new wants spring up and ask for satisfaction. Civilization, it is said, makes people poorer, because it multiplies their wishes and does not soothe, but kindles, desires. All the busy doings and dealings of hard-working men, their hurrying, pushing, and bustling are nonsensical, for they provide neither happiness nor quiet. Peace of mind and serenity cannot be won by action and secular ambition, but only by renunciation and resignation. The only kind of conduct proper to the sage is escape into the inactivity of a purely contemplative existence.

Yet all such qualms, doubts, and scruples are subdued by the irresistible force of man's vital energy. True, man cannot escape death. But for the present he is alive; and life, not death, takes hold of him. Whatever the future may have in store for him, he cannot withdraw from the necessities of the actual hour. As long as a man lives, he cannot help obeying the cardinal impulse, the *élan vital.* It is man's innate nature that he seeks to preserve and to strengthen his life, that he is discontented and aims at removing uneasiness, that he is in search of what may be called happiness. In every living being there works an inexplicable and nonanalyzable *Id.* This *Id* is the impulsion of all impulses, the force that drives man into life and action, the original and ineradicable craving for a fuller and happier existence. It works as long as man lives and stops only with the extinction of life.

Human reason serves this vital impulse. Reason's biological function is to preserve and to promote life and to postpone its extinction as long as possible. Thinking and acting are not contrary to nature; they are, rather, the foremost features of man's nature. The most appropriate description of man as differentiated from nonhuman beings is: a being *purposively* struggling against the forces adverse to his life.

Hence all talk about the primacy of irrational elements is vain. Within the universe the existence of which our reason cannot explain, analyze, or conceive, there is a narrow field left within which man is capable of removing uneasiness to some extent. This is the realm of reason and rationality, of science and purposive action. Neither its narrowness nor the scantiness of the results man can obtain within it suggest the idea of radical resignation and lethargy. No philosophical subtleties can ever restrain a healthy individual from resorting to actions which—as he thinks—can satisfy his needs. It may be true that in the deepest recesses of man's soul there is a longing for the undisturbed peace and inactivity of a merely vegetative existence. But in living man these desires, whatever they may be, are outweighed by the urge to act and to improve his own condition. Once the forces of resignation get the upper hand, man dies; he does not turn into a plant.

It is true, praxeology and economics do not tell a man whether he should preserve or abandon life. Life itself and all the unknown forces that originate it and keep it burning are an ultimate given, and as such beyond the pale of human science. The subject matter of praxeology is merely the essential manifestation of *human* life, viz., action.

2. Economics and Judgments of Value

While many people blame economics for its neutrality with regard to value judgments, other people blame it for its alleged indulgence in them. Some contend that economics must necessarily express judgments of value and is therefore not really scientific, as the criterion of science is its valuational indifference. Others maintain that good economics should be and could be impartial, and that only bad economists sin against this postulate.

The semantic confusion in the discussion of the problems concerned is due to an inaccurate use of terms on the part of many economists. An economist investigates whether a measure *a* can bring about the result *p* for the attainment of which it is recommended, and finds that *a* does not result in *p* but in *g*, an effect which even the supporters of the measure *a* consider undesirable. If this economist states the outcome of his investigation by saying that *a* is a bad measure, he does not pronounce a judgment of value. He merely says that from the point of view of those aiming at the goal *p*, the measure *a* is inappropriate. In this sense the free-trade economists attacked protection. They demonstrated that protection does not, as its champions believe, increase but, on the contrary, decreases the total amount of products, and is therefore bad from the point of view of those who prefer an ampler supply of products to a smaller. It is in this sense that economists criticize policies from the point of view of the ends aimed at. If an economist calls minimum wage rates a bad policy, what he means is that its effects are contrary to the purpose of those who recommend their application.

From the same point of view praxeology and economics look upon the fundamental principle of human existence and social evolution, viz., that cooperation under the social division of labor is a more efficient way of acting than is the autarkic isolation of individuals. Praxeology and economics do not say that men should peacefully cooperate within the frame of societal bonds; they merely say that men must act this way *if* they want to make their actions more successful than otherwise. Compliance with the moral rules which the establishment, preservation, and intensification of social cooperation require is not seen as a sacrifice to a mythical entity, but as the recourse to the most efficient methods of action, as a price expended for the attainment of more highly valued returns.

It is against this substitution of an autonomous, rationalistic and voluntaristic ethics for the heteronomous doctrines both of intuitionism and of revealed commandments that the united forces of all antiliberal schools and dogmatisms direct the most furious attacks. They all blame the utilitarian philosophy for the pitiless austerity of its description and analysis of human nature and of the ultimate springs of human action. It is not necessary to add anything more to the refutation of these criticisms which every page of this book provides. Only one point should be mentioned again, because on the one hand it is the acme of the doctrine of all contemporary pied pipers and on the other hand it offers to the average intellectual a welcome excuse to shun the painstaking discipline of economic studies.

Economics, it is said, in its rationalistic prepossessions assumes that men aim only or first of all at material well-being. But in reality men prefer irrational objectives to rational ones. They are guided more by the urge to realize myths and ideals than by the urge to enjoy a higher standard of living.

What economics has to answer is this:

1. Economics does not assume or postulate that men aim only or first of all at what is called material well-being. Economics, as a branch of the more general theory of human action, deals with all human action, i.e., with man's purposive aiming at the attainment of ends chosen, whatever these ends may be. To apply the concept *rational* or *irrational* to the ultimate ends chosen is nonsensical. We may call irrational the ultimate given, viz., those things that our thinking can neither analyze nor reduce to other ultimately given things. Then every ultimate end chosen by any man is irrational. It is neither more nor less rational to aim at riches like Croesus than to aim at poverty like a Buddhist monk.

2. What these critics have in mind when employing the term *rational ends* is the desire for material well-being and a higher standard of living. It is a question of fact whether or not their statement is true that men in general and our contemporaries especially are driven more by the wish to realize myths and dreams than by the wish to improve their material well-being. Although no intelligent being could fail to give the correct answer, we may disregard the issue. For economics does not say anything either in favor of or against myths. It is perfectly neutral with regard to the labor-union doctrine, the credit-expansion doctrine and all such doctrines as far as these may present themselves as myths and are supported as myths by their partisans. It deals with these doctrines only as far as they are considered doctrines about the means fit for the attainment of definite ends. Economics does not say labor unionism is a bad myth. It merely says it is an inappropriate means of raising wage rates for all those eager to earn wages. It leaves it to every man to decide whether the realization of the labor-union myth is more important than the avoidance of the inevitable consequences of labor-union policies.

In this sense we may say that economics is apolitical or non-political, although it is the foundation of politics and of every kind of political action. We may furthermore say that it is perfectly neutral with regard to all judgments of value, as it refers always to means and never to the choice of ultimate ends.

3. Economic Cognition and Human Action

Man's freedom to choose and to act is restricted in a threefold way. There are first the physical laws to whose unfeeling absoluteness man must adjust his conduct if he wants to live. There are second the individual's innate constitutional characteristics and dispositions and the operation of environmental factors; we know that they influence both the choice of the ends and that of the means, although our cognizance of the mode of their operation is rather vague. There is finally the regularity of phenomena with regard to the interconnectedness of means and ends, viz., the praxeological law as distinct from the physical and from the physiological law.

The elucidation and the categorial and formal examination of this third class of the laws of the universe is the subject matter of praxeology and its hitherto best-developed branch, economics. The body of economic knowledge is an essential element in the structure of human civilization; it is the foundation upon which modern industrialism and all the moral, intellectual, technological, and therapeutical achievements of the last centuries have been built. It rests with men whether they will make the proper use of the rich treasure with which this knowldge provides them or whether they will leave it unused. But if they fail to take the best advantage of it and disregard its teachings and warnings, they will not annul economics; they will stamp out society and the human race.

INDEX

Prepared by Vernelia A. Crawford

NOTE: This index includes the titles of parts, chapters, and sections, each listed under appropriate subject classifications. With the exception of these specific page references, which are hyphenated, the numbers in each instance refer to the *first* page of a discussion.